Human Rights Commissions and Ombudsman Offices

National Experiences throughout the World

Editors

Dr. Kamal Hossain

Senior Advocate, Supreme Court of Bangladesh; Chairman, International Committee on Legal Aspects of Sustainable Development, International Law Association; Chairman, Commonwealth Human Rights Initiative Advisory Commission

Dr. Leonard F. M. Besselink

Executive Editor

Associate Professor of Constitutional Law, Utrecht University

Dr. Haile Selassie Gebre Selassie

Project Co-ordinator, Law Faculty, University of Amsterdam; lecturer, Faculty of Law, Erasmus University Rotterdam

Dr. Edmond Völker

Institute of International Legal Research, Law Faculty, University of Amsterdam

KLUWER LAW INTERNATIONAL

THE HAGUE / LONDON / BOSTON

Published by:
Kluwer Law International
P.O. Box 85889, 2508 CN The Hague, The Netherlands
sales@kli.wkap.nl
http://www.kluwerlaw.com

Sold and Distributed in North, Central and South America by:
Kluwer Law International
101 Philip Drive, Norwell, MA 02061, USA
kluwerlaw@wkap.com

Sold and Distributed in all other countries by:
Kluwer Law International
Distribution Centre, P.O. Box 322, 3300 AH Dordrecht, The Netherlands

Library of Congress Cataloging-in-Publication Data is available

Printed on acid-free paper.

ISBN 90-411-1586-2

Kluwer Law International incorporates the publishing programmes
of Graham & Trotman Ltd, Kluwer Law and Taxation Publishers
and Martinus Nijhoff Publishers

Printed and bound in Great Britain by Antony Rowe Limited.

Acknowledgements

The conference and publication of this book have been made possible by the generous financial support of:

The European Commission
The United Nations Development Program
The International Labour Organisation
The Netherlands
Austria
Ireland
Spain
Finland
Sweden
Vatican
Canada

Table of Contents

Kamal Hossain
Introduction 1

Dr Haile Selassie Gebre Selassie and Dr Edmond Völker
Contextualizing the Establishment of the Institutions of Human Rights Protection in Ethiopia 7
Introduction 7
Historical and Socio-Political Setting 10
Change of Regime, Human Rights and Law Enforcement Bodies Post-1991 18
Implementation Mechanisms and the Forthcoming National Commission 23
Concluding Remarks 33

Part One:
Background Papers and Special Topics

Chapter I. Background Papers

Yash Ghai
The Structure of Human Rights in Federations 41
Human Rights in Federations 44
The scope of rights protected in federations 44
Accommodating Bills of Rights to 'ethnic' federation 48
Economic rights in a federation 50
International human rights and the structure of rights 50
General assessment of human rights record of federations 51
Conclusion: The Case of Ethiopia 51

Kamal Hossain
Human Rights and Development 55
Evolving Human Rights Norms and Development 55
National Constitutions, Human Rights and Development 57
Human Rights and Development: An Integrated Approach 58
Role Judiciary and National Institutions 61

Patricia Hyndman
The Role of International Organizations and NGOs in the Protection of Human Rights 63
Introduction 63
The Development of the Protection of Rights 64
The development of the protection of rights at the international level 66

The development of the protection of human rights within domestic arrangements 68
The Role of International Organizations in the Protection of Human Rights 68
The protection of rights by international intergovernmental organizations 68
The protection of rights by regional intergovernmental organizations 70
(I) Europe 71
(II) The Americas 72
(III) Africa 72
(IV) Asia and the Pacific 73
The protection of rights by different types of intergovernmental organizations 73
(I) The Organization of the Islamic Conference 73
(II) The Commonwealth 74
The Role of Non-governmental Organizations (NGOs) in the Protection of Human Rights 74
Conclusion 78

Chapter II. Special Topics

Dealing with Human Rights Violations Committed under a Previous Regime

Luc Huyse
To Punish or to Pardon – A Devil's Choice: Dealing with Human Rights Violations Committed under a Previous Regime 83
I. Policies 83
II. Dilemmas 84
The case for prosecution and/or lustration 84
The case against punishment 85
Meeting ethical requirements and political constraints 86
III. Constraints 87
IV. Conclusion 88

Alex Boraine
The Truth and Reconciliation Commission in South Africa 89
Past Injustice, Future Reconciliation 90
Unique Features of the South African Model 91
Amnesty 93
The Need to Know 93
A Commitment to Truth 94
Conclusion 95

Rodolfo Mattarollo
The Importance of the Ethiopian Trials in Reinforcing Human Rights Protection in Ethiopia 97

Bernard A. Muna
Safeguarding the Rights of the Accused in the Prosecution Process at the International Criminal Tribunal for (of) **Rwanda** 101
Introduction 101
I. The Role of Legal Professionals At the Various Stages of the Process 102
The Judiciary 102
The Prosecutor 103
Defence Counsel 105
II. Guarantee of the Rights of the Accused At the Pretrial Stage 107
Investigation 107
Indictment 108

Initial appearance 109
Further questioning of the accused by the prosecutor 109
Disclosure obligations 110
III. The Trial Stage 111
IV. At the Conclusion of Trial 112
The right to life 112
V. The Post-Trial Stage 112
Conclusion 113

Craig Etcheson
Dilemmas of Accountability in Cambodia 115
The Trials and Tribulations of a Democratizing Regime Change in Cambodia 115
The Failure of Past Efforts to Achieve Accountability in Cambodia 117
The Cambodian Genocide Program 123
Chaos and Accountability in Cambodian Politics 124
Conclusion 128

Human Rights and the Child

Peter Newell
The Place of Child Rights in a Human Rights and Ombudsman System 133
Children are the future 135
Children are individuals 136
Children are more affected by the actions – or inaction – of government than any other group 136
Children have no vote, play no part in the political process 137
Children – and especially young children – have particular difficulty in finding and using legal remedies when their rights are breached 137
ANNEX 142
Children's Commissioners and Ombudspeople Around the World 142
The Norwegian Act establishing the Commissioner for Children (Barneombudet) 143
Evaluating the world's first children's ombudsperson – the Norwegian Barneombudet. 144
The Swedish Act to establish the Office of the Children's Ombudsman 145
Bibliography 145

Elisa Pozza Tasca
From the New York Convention to the Institution of the Ombudsman 147
Introduction 147
Human rights and children: from the first international charters to the United Nations Convention 147
An Ombudsman for children: a new voice to defend children 149
Crimes against children are crimes against humanity 151

Part Two:
National Institutions for the Protection of Fundamental Rights

Introduction

Leonard F. M. Besselink
Types of National Institutions for the Protection of Human Rights: An Overview of Organizational and Legal Issues 157
Single, dual and multi-organ systems 157
Relation to courts 158

Relations between ombudman and human rights commission 159
Competence 159
Investigations on complaint or motu proprio; investigative powers 160
Institutional and functional independence 161
Remedies 162
ANNEX 163
Questionnaire on National Human Rights Commission 163
A. Tasks and Competences 163
B. Organization 163
Questionnaire on Ombudsman Institutions 164

Chapter III. Single Organ Systems

National Human Rights Commissions

Cameroon

S. Nfor Gwei
The Cameroon Experience in Creating and Running a National Commission for the Promotion and Protection of Human Rights 169
1. The Creation and Organization of the Commission 169
a. Creating the National Commission 170
b. The Organization 171
I) The General Assembly 171
II) The Bureau 171
III) The Specialised Committees 172
IV) External Branches 172
c. The Technical and Administrative Staff 172
2. The Mandate of the Commission 172
3. The Resources and Administrative Management of the Commission 173
4. Work Programme of the Commission in Promoting *and Protecting Human Rights and Freedoms* 174
A. The Promotion of Human Rights and Freedoms 174
I) Contact tours 174
II) Campaign sensitisation and information 175
III) Education and training in human rights and freedoms 175
IV) Working with NGOs 176
V) Briefing the international human rights community 176
VI) Working with researchers 176
VII) International activities 177
VIII) Celebrating Human Rights Day 177
B. Protecting Human Right and Fundamental Freedoms 178
I) Investigating incidents and complaints 178
II) Visits to detention cells and prisons 180
III) Observing elections 180
IV) Refuge problems 180
V) Other areas of the work of the commission 180
5. Some Lessons from the Cameroon Experience 181
A. Authority and powers of the Commission 181
B. Selection of members 181
C. The credibility of the Commission 181
D. Understanding, cohesion and teamwork 182
E. Incentives or remuneration for members 182
F. Administrative and technical staff 182

G. Adequate material and financial resources 182
H. Advantages as government-created institutions 182
6. Recommendations 182

Legislation 183
Decree No. 90–1459 of 8 November 1990 to set up the National Commission on Human Rights and Freedoms. 183

Ghana

Emile Short
The Development and Growth of Human Rights Commissions in Africa – the Ghanaian Experience 187
The Establishment of the Ghana Human Rights Commission 188
Independence 189
Accessibility 190
Constitutional and Statutory Mandate 191
Powers 192
Competence 192
Enforcement Power 193
Functioning of the Commission 194
Investigation of complaints 194
(a) Administrative justice complaints 194
(b) Human rights complaints 195
Proactive investigations 195
Promotion of human rights 196
Inspection of prison and police cell 196
Campaign to eliminate dehumanizing cultural practices 197
Economic and Political Accountability Jurisdiction 197
Collaboration with Non-governmental Organizations 198
Problems and Prospects 199
Concluding Remarks 199

Legislation 200
Constitution 1992 200
Chapter Eighteen 200
The Commission on Human Rights and Administrative Justice Act 1993 (Act 456) 201
Part I – Establishment of Commission on Human Rights And Administrative Justice 202
Part II – Functions of The Commission 202
Part III – Provisions Relating to Complaints And Investigations 204
Part IV – Procedure After Investigation by the Commission 206
Part V – Miscellaneous Provisions 206
Commission on Human Rights and Administrative Justice (Complaints Procedure) Regulations 1994 (Constitutional Instrument No. 7) 208

India

Justice V.S. Malimath
Report on the National Human Rights Commission of India 211
A. Tasks and Competences 211
B. Organization 214
C. Procedure 217
D. Rulings 218
E. Review of Experience of the Human Rights Commission. 219

Legislation 219
The Protection of Human Rights Act, 1993 [No 10 of 1994 (8 January 1994)] 219
Chapter I Preliminary 219
Chapter II The National Human Rights Commission 220
Chapter III Functions and Powers of the Commission 222
Chapter IV Procedure 224
Chapter V State Human Rights Commissions 225
Chapter VI Human Rights Courts 228
Chapter VII Finance, Accounts and Audit 228
Chapter VIII Miscellaneous 229

Ombudsman Institutions

Argentina

Louis Maiorano
The Ombudsman Institution in Argentina 233
A. Legal or constitutional basis 233
B. Independence and impartiality 234
C. Complaints regarding acts of government 235
D. Investigations, report and recommendation 235

Legislation 236
National Constitution of Argentina 236
Defensor Del Pueblo of the Argentine Nation Act 24, 284 237
Title I Establishment, Appointment, Removal, Terms and Conditions 237
Chapter I – Capacity and Appointment 237
Chapter II – Limitations, Removal, Vacancies, Privileges 238
Chapter III – Deputies 239
Title II Proceedings 239
Chapter I – Jurisdiction. Commencement and content of the investigation 239
Chapter II – Handling of the complaint 240
Chapter III – Collaboration, Responsibility 241
Title III Decisions 242
Single Chapter – Scope of decisions, Notifications, Reports 242
Title IV Human and material resources 243
Single Chapter – Staff, Financial Resources, Terms 243
Regulation for the Organization and Functional Structure of the Office of the Defensor Del Pueblo 243
I. General Provisions 243
II. The Defensor Del Pueblo 244
III. Deputies 245
IV. Economic and Financial Organization 245
V. Administrative Board 245
VI. Handling of Complaints 245
VII. Staff of the Office of the Defensor Del Pueblo 246
VIII. Publication 246

Austria

Nikolaus Schwärzler
The Ombudsman Institutions in Austria 247
1. The norms for the ombudsman institutions 247

a) The statutory basis of the Ombudsman Board (Volksanwaltschaft) in Vienna 247
b) The statutory basis for the state ombudsmen 248
c) Comparative survey of characteristics of the three Ombudsman Institutions in Austria 248
2. History and Background 249
3. Access to the Ombudsman 251
4. The competences of the Ombudsman 252
5. The procedure before the ombudsman 255
6. Organization of Ombudsman offices 256
7. Appointment and relative position of the Ombudsmen 256
8. Statistics of interest regarding ombudsman offices in Austria 257
9. A glance into the past and into the future 258

Legislation 259
Austrian Federal Constitution 259
Chapter VII Ombudsmen Council 259
Federal Law on the Austrian Ombudsman Board [Volksanwaltschaftsgesetz/ Ombudsman Board Act 1982] 261
Chapter I. Organization of the Ombudsman Board 261
Chapter II. Proceedings before the Ombudsman Board 262
Chapter III. Final provision 262
State Constitutional Act of 21 September 1988 on the Constitution of the State of Tyrol (Tyrolean State Order 1989) [Tiroler Landesordnung] 262
Law on the Constitution of *Land* (State) Vorarlberg 263
Law on the *Landesvolksanwalt* [Vorarlberg] 264

Belgium

Pierre-Yves Monnette
The Parliamentary Ombudsman in Belgium: Strengthening Democracy 269
Introduction 269
The different roles of the parliamentary ombudsman in Belgium 270
1. Mediation role between citizens and public authorities. 271
Who may call upon the parliamentary ombudsman in Belgium? 272
Which are the authorities concerned by claims examined by the parliamentary ombudsman of Belgium? 272
Which acts can be concerned by claims before the Belgian parliamentary ombudsman? What sort of activities can be targeted by the complaints filed with him? 274
Which conditions have to be complied with in order to make a valid request to the parliamentary ombudsman in Belgium? 274
What are the grievances that can be formulated on the occasion of a complaint laid before the parliamentary ombudsman? Which activities can he examine? 275
2. The exercise of external control by the parliamentary ombudsman. 276
3. The reporting function of the parliamentary ombudsman. 276
4. The moral role of the parliamentary ombudsman. 277
The means allocated to the parliamentary ombudsman in Belgium for the accomplishment of his above missions. 277
1. The powers of investigation 278
2. The powers of injunction 278
3. The powers of recommendation 278
The Independence of the Belgian parliamentary ombudsman 279
1. Statutory independence. 279

2. Organic independence. 280
3. Financial independence. 280
4. Functional independence. 281
5. Political independence. 281
6. Intellectual independence. 282
7. Organizational independence. 282
Conclusion. 282

Legislation 283
The Constitution of the Kingdom of Belgium (excerpts) 283
The Federal Ombudsman Act, Kingdom of Belgium, March 22, 1995. 284
Chapter I. The Federal Ombudsmen 284
Chapter II. Complaints 285
Chapter III. Reports by the ombudsmen 286
Chapter IV. Various provisions 286

Colombia

Jose F. Castro Caycedo
The Defender of the Public of the Republic of Colombia 289
A. Legal and Constitutional Bases 289
B. Independence and Impartiality 289
C. Complaints Regarding Acts of Government 291
D. Research, Reports and Recommendations 291

Legislation 292
Constitution of Colombia 292
Law 24 of 1992 (December 15) 294
Title I. Legal Nature 294
Title II. Regulation of the office of the Public Defender 295
Chapter I. Law of the Defender 295
Chapter II. Powers 296

Costa Rica

Rodrigo Alberto Carazo
The Ombudsman of Costa Rica 299
Tasks and Competence 300
Organization 306
Procedure 310
Rulings 312
Review of experience 314

Mauritius

Veda Bhadain
The Institution of the Ombudsman in Mauritius 315
Constitutional Basis 315
Independence and Impartiality 316
Complaints regarding acts of Governments 317
Jurisdiction of the Ombudsman 317
Investigations, Report and Recommendation 318
Investigation upon the Ombudsman's own motion 318
Investigation upon receiving a complaint 318
Proceedings 318

Power to call and examine witnesses 318
Power of the Ombudsman and the doctrine of Crown Privilege 319
Privilege of communication 319
Remedy after investigation 319
The Human Rights Commission 320

Legislation 320
Constitution of Mauritius 320
Chapter IX – The Ombudsman 320
96 Office of Ombudsman 320
97 Investigations by Ombudsman 320
98 Procedure in respect of investigations 322
99 Disclosure of information 322
100 Proceedings after investigation 323
101 Discharge of functions of Ombudsman 323
102 Supplementary and ancillary provision 324
102A Allegation of fraud or corruption 324
The Protection of Human Rights Act 1998 (Entry into force 23 February 1998) 325
1. Short title 325
2. Interpretation 325
3. Establishment and appointment of the Commission 326
4. Functions of the Commission 326
5. Staff of the Commission 327
6. Powers and duties of the Commission 327
7. Investigation 328
8. Protection of witnesses 328
9. Persons likely to be prejudicially affected 328
10. Protection of action taken in good faith 328
11. Reports of the Commission 328
12. Finance 329
13. Offences 329
14. Jurisdiction 329
15. Regulations 329
16. Consequential amendment 329
17. Commencement 329

Namibia

J. Malan
The Office of the Ombudsman in Namibia 331
Independence of the Ombudsman 331
Appointment of the Ombudsman 332
Duties and Functions of the Ombudsman 333
Complaints and Confidentiality 334
Refusal to accept Matters 335
Powers of the Ombudsman 335
Procedures following an inquiry or investigation 336
Reports of Ombudsman 337
Compliance with the provisions of the Act 338
Conclusion 339

Legislation 339
The Namibian Constitution (February 1990) 339

The Netherlands

Ric de Rooij
National Ombudsman of the Netherlands 343
Constitution and the National Ombudsman Act 343
Appointment 343
Independence 344
(Impartiality and) Competence 345
Acts of government 346
Complaints 347
Petition 347
Own initiative 348
Investigation, report and recommendation 349
Intervention method 349
Investigation leading to a report 349
Procedure 349
Powers of investigation 350
Report of findings 350
The report 351
Drafting of the judgement 351
Status of the judgement 351
Criteria for assessment and their use 352
Annual Report 353
Functions of the National Ombudsman and the impact of the work of the National Ombudsman 354
Functions of the National Ombudsman 354
Impact of the work 354

Legislation 355
Constitution of the Kingdom of the Netherlands (as most recently amended, 25 March 1999) 355
National Ombudsman Act [Act of February 4, 1981; Staatsblad 1981, 53, most recently amended by Act of Parliament of April 26, 1995 (Staatsblad 1995, 250)] 355
Definitions 356
Chapter I. The National Ombudsman 356
Chapter II. The Investigation 359
Chapter III. Transitional and Final Provisions 363

Norway

Arne Fliflet
Legal Institution of the Ombudsman 365
Legal or constitutional basis 365
Independence and impartiality 365
Complaints regarding acts of government 366
Investigation, report and recommendation 366

Legislation 367
The Constitution of the Kingdom of Norway of 17 May, § 75, 1) 367
Act concerning the Storting's Ombudsman for Public Administration (22 June 1962, amended by 367
Acts of 22 March 1968, 8 February 1980, 6 September 1991, 11 June 1993 and 15 March 1996) 367
§ 1. Election of Ombudsman 367
§ 2. Directive 368

§ 3. Purpose 368
§ 4. Scope of powers 368
§ 5. Basis for work 368
§ 6. Details regardign complaints and time limit for complaints 368
§ 7. Right to obtain information 369
§ 8. Access to offices in the public administration 369
§ 9. Pledge of secrecy 369
§ 10. Termination of a complaints case 369
§ 11. Notification 369
§ 12. Report to the Storting 370
§ 13. Pay, pension, other business 370
§ 14. Staff 370
§ 15. [Entry into force] 370
Directive to the Storting's Ombudsman for Public Administration (Laid down by the Storting 19 February 1980 in pursuance of § 2 of the Ombudsman Act. 370
§ 1. Purpose 370
§ 2. Scope of Powers 370
§ 3. The form and basis of a complaint 371
§ 4. Exceeding the time limit for complaints 371
§ 5. Terms and conditions for complaints proceedings 371
§ 6. Investigation of complaints 371
§ 7. Notification to the compalinant if a case is not proceeded with 371
§ 8. Cases taken up on own initiative 372
§ 9. Termination of the Ombudsman's proceedings 372
§ 10. Instructions for the staff 372
§ 11. Pledge of secrecy in reports to the public 372
§ 12. Annual report to the Storting 372
§ 13. Entry into force 372

Slovenia

Ivan Bizjak
The Human Rights Ombudsman of Slovenia 373
Legal and constitutional basis 373
Independence and impartiality 374
Complaints regarding acts of government 375
Investigation, report and recommendation 376

Legislation 377
Constitution of the Republic of Slovenia 377
Human Rights Ombudsman Act 377
I. General provisions 377
II. Election and position of the Ombudsman and his deputies 378
III. Jurisdiction of the Ombudsman 380
IV. Proceedings 380
V. The rights of the Ombudsman 383
VI. The bureau of the Ombudsman 384
VII. Penalties 384
VIII. Interim and final provisions 384
Human Rights Ombudsman Rules of Procedure 385
I. General provisions 385
II. The organization and the system of work 385
III. The proceedings 387
IV. Other provisions 390

V. Temporary and final provisions 390
Act on the Constitutional court (Uradni list Republike Slovenije, Official Gazette RS, No. 15/94) 390

Spain

Prof. Juan Vintó Castells
The Ombudsman and the Parliamentary Committees on Human Rights in Spain 393
I. Introduction 393
II. The Spanish Ombudsman 393
1. The normative framework 393
2. Juridical nature: the Ombudsman is a body of constitutional relevance with full functional independence. 394
3. Elements which guarantee the independence of the Ombudsman 396
A. Parliamentary election 396
a) Importance 396
b) Term 396
c) Proposal for candidate or candidates 396
d) Requirements for the candidates 397
e) Secret vote and majority of three fifths in each House of Parliament 397
f) Re-election 398
B. Functional autonomy and the system of incompatibilities and prerogatives 398
a) Functional autonomy 398
b) Incompatibilities 399
c) Prerogatives 399
C. Causes and effects of the dismissal 399
a) Causes 399
b) Effects 400
D. Final consideration 401
4. Organization and personal and material resources 401
A. Organic dependence of Parliament 401
B. Organization and personal resources 401
a) The Ombudsman as a unipersonal body 401
b) The Deputy Ombudsmen 402
c) Staff in the service of the Ombudsman 402
d) Material means 403
5. Functions: defence of the constitutional rights and supervision of the activities of the Administration 403
6. Scope of action: the Administration in a broad sense 404
A. General Layout 404
B. Special cases 404
a) The administration of justice 404
b) Military administration 405
c) Administration of the Autonomous Communities 405
d) Parliamentary administration 406
7. Proceedings 406
A. Ex officio action 406
B. Intervention at the petition of a party 406
a) The complaints brought by citizens or legal entities 406
b) Petitions of Membership or Parliament or of the parliamentary committees 407
C. Admissibility of the complaints. 407
a) Acknowledgement of receipt and admission of the transaction 407

b) Investigation and resolution 407
c) Time limit 408
D. Permanent functioning 408
8. Powers 408
A. Investigation 408
B. Powers to ensure the collaboration of the Administration during the investigations 408
a) The public statement of lack of collaboration 408
b) Transfer of record to the Public Prosecutor for the institution of criminal proceedings for the offence of disobedience 408
C. Resolutions on the investigations 409
a) Lack of coercive power 409
b) Power of direction: warnings, recommendations, reminders and suggestions 409
D. Dissemination of the actions and resolutions: identification and publicity of the noncompliance of the Administration 410
E. Legitimation in judicial procedures 410
a) Habeas corpus 410
b) Appeal of unconstitutionality 411
c) Appeal for protection 411
9. Relationships with the Parliament 412
A. The Parliamentary Joint Committee 412
B. The Annual Report 412
III. The parliamentary Committees on Human Rights 413
Basic Bibliography 413

Legislation 414
Constitution of Spain 414
Organic Act Regarding the Ombudsman 414
Part I Appointment Functions and Term of Office 414
Chapter I Nature and Appointment 414
Chapter II Dismissal, Resignation and Replacement 415
Chapter III Prerogatives Immunities and Incompatibilities 415
Chapter IV The Deputy Ombudsmen 416
Part II Procedure 416
Chapter I Initiation and Scope of Investigations 416
Chapter II Scope of Competence 417
Chapter III Complaints procedure 417
Chapter IV Obligatory Co-operation of Bodies Requested to do so 418
Chapter V Confidential Documents 419
Chapter VI Responsibilities of Authorities and Civil Servants 419
Chapter VII Reimbursement of Expense to Individuals 420
Part III Decisions 420
Chapter I Content of Decisions 420
Chapter II Notifications and Communications 421
Chapter III Reports to Parliament 421
Part IV Human and Financial Resources 422
Chapter I Staff 422
Chapter II Financial Resources 422

Sweden

Claes Eklundh
The Swedish Parliamentary Ombudsman System 423
Introduction 423

Historical Background 423
The Parliamentary Ombudsmen and the Constitution 424
The Duties of the Ombudsmen 425
The Jurisdiction of the Ombudsmen 425
The Investigatory power of the Ombudsmen 426
The Weapons of the Ombudsmen 426
The Organization 427
The Handling of Complaint Cases 427
Cases initiated by the Ombudsmen 429
Inspections 430
Annual Reports 430
The Impact of the Ombudsmen 430

Legislation 431
Act with Instructions for the Parliamentary Ombudsmen (issued 13 November 1986, consolidated 1 April 1999) 431
Tasks 431
Organization 433
Complaints 434
General regulations about the treatment of cases 434
Miscellaneous regulations 436

Zambia

J.K. Kampekete
The Investigator-General (Ombudsman) of Zambia 437
Introduction 437
Constitutional and Legal Basis 437
Details 438
Power of Appointment in the Office of Ombudsman 438
Independence and Impartiality 438
Impartiality 439
Separation of His Field of Competence From The Courts and Human Rights Commission 439
Separation 440
Complaints Regarding Acts of Government 440
Complaint Handling 440
Investigation, Report and Recommendation 440
Reporting and Recommendation 441

Legislation 441
Constitution of Zambia 441
Part V 441
Part XII Human Rights Commission (As amended by Act No. 18 of 1996) 442
Commission for Investigations Act 1991. 443
Part I Preliminary 443
Part II Establishment of Commission and Appointments 444
Part III Power and Procedure 444
Part IV Reports and Enforcement, Submission of reports to the President 447
Part V Immunities of the Commission 448

Chapter IV. Dual Systems

Canada

Michelle Falardeau Ramsy
Canadian Human Rights Commission 453

Tasks and Competences 453
Organization 454
Procedure 455
Rulings 456
Review of the experience of existing Human Rights Commissions 457

Gerard Savard, Director General, Canadian Human Rights Commission
Complaint Handling at the Canadian Human Rights Commission 459
The Canadian Human Rights Act 460
Dealing with Complaints 460
Systemic Discrimination 461
Challenges 463

Legislation 464
Canadian Human Rights Act 464
Chapter H-6 (An Act to extend the laws in Canada that proscribe discrimination) 464
Part I Proscribed Discrimination 464
General 464
Discriminatory Practices 464
Part II Canadian Human Rights Commission 471
Remuneration 473
Officers and Staff 473
Part III Discriminatory Practices and General Provisions 475
Investigation 475
Conciliator 479
Canadian Human Rights Tribunal 480
Inquiries into Complaints 484
Offences and Punishment 488
Reports 488
Minister Responsible 489
Application 489
Part IV 490
Application 490
Related Provisions 490
Employment Equity Act 491
Part I Employment Equity 493
Employer Obligations 493
Records and Reports 497
Part II Compliance 500
Undertakings and Directions 501
Employment Equity Review Tribunals 503
Limitations respecting Directions and Order 505
Privileged Information 505
Part III Assessment of Monetary Penalties 506
Violations 506
Options 506
Enforcement of Monetary Penalties 507
Part IV General 508
Transitional Provision 509
Consequential Amendments 510
Repeal 510
Coming into Force 510
Related Provisions 510

Roberta L. Jamieson
The Ombudsman of Ontario, Canada 511
The Legal Foundation for the Ombudsman 511
Selection of the Ombudsman 511
Independence and Impartiality 512
The Impartiality of the Ombudsman 512
Complaints Regarding Acts of Government 512
Investigation, Reports and Recommendation 513
Investigative Powers 514
Access and Equity 514
The Ombudsman As Advocate 514
Accountability 515

Legislation 515
Ontario Ombudsman Act 515
Revised Statutes of Ontario, 1990, Chapter 0.6 515
Regulation Under Ombudsman Act 523
General Rules R.R.O. 1990, Reg. 865 (No Amendments, This Regulation is made in English only.) 523

Malawi

Justice E.M. Singini
Malawi's Human Rights Commission 527
Tasks, competences and organizational structure 527
Organization 530
Procedure 531
Rulings 531
Review of experience of Malawi's HCR 532

Hon. James Makoza Chirwa
A General Overview on the Set-up of the Malawi Office of the Ombudsman 533
Background 533
Duties, Functioning and Powers of the Malawi Office of the Ombudsman 533
Independence and Privileges of the Ombudsman 535
Investigations, report and recommendation. 536
Conclusion 537

Legislation 537
Constitution of the Republic of Malawi 537
Chapter X The Ombudsman 538
Chapter XI Human Rights Commission 539
Human Rights Commission Act 1998 540
Part II – Membership of the Commission 541
Part III – Competence and Responsibilities of the Commission 542
Part IV – Hearings, Investigations and Remedies 544
Part V – Meetings 546
Part VI – Administrations 547
Part VII – Finance 548
Part VIII – Miscellaneous 548
Schedule s.36 549
Organizations 549

Nigeria

Dr Muhammed Tabiu
National Human Rights Commission of Nigeria 553

Introduction 553
Mandate and Competence of the Commission 553
Scope of Competence 554
Role of NGO's 555
Organizational Structure 555
Governing Council 555
The Secretariat 556
Zonal Offices 556
Complaint Procedure 556
Manner of lodging complaints 556
Treatment of complaints 557
Redress 557
Representation 557
Provisional measures 557
Funding 558
Conclusion: Review of Experience 558
Prioritising its work 558
Power to obtain information 558
Assertion of independence 558
Effective working relations 559
Delegation of functions and powers 559
Accessibility 559

Chief J.I. Edokpa
The Ombudsman Institution 561
Introduction 561
Historical Background 561
Organizational Structure 562
Activities of the Public Complaints Commission 563
Operational Procedure 564
Publicity 565
Limitations of Commissioners' Powers 566
Impact of the Public Complaints Commission on Good Governance in Nigeria 566

Legislation 567
National Human Rights Commission Decree 1995 (Supplement to Official Gazette Extraordinary No. 28, Vol. 82, 6th October 1995 Part A) 567
Decree No. 22 567
Part I – Establishment of the Human Rights Commission, etc. 568
Part II – Functions and Powers 568
Part III – Staff 569
Part IV – Financial Provisions 570
Part V – Miscellaneous Provisions 571
Schedule Section 2 (4) (Supplementary Provisions Relating to the Council, etc. 571
Proceedings of the Council 571
Committees 572
Public Complaints Commission Act (Laws of Nigeria 1990, Chapter 377) 572

Uganda

Edmond R.B. Nkalubo
Uganda Human Rights Commission including the Office of the Inspectorate of Government (Ombudsman) 579
The Uganda Human Rights Commission 579

Background to the UHRC 579
Staff and activities 584
Inadequate funds for the programmes 584
Investigations carried out 584
Civic education, training and research in human rights in the Constitution 585
Civic education for the public 585
Research on human rights and freedoms 586
Publication of civic educational material 586
Civic education for schools 586
Education on the Constitution 586
Co-ordination and overseeing of civic education programmes 586
Monitoring bovernment's compliance with international instruments on human rights 587
The Inspectorate of the Government 588
Background 588
The current status of the Inspectorate of government 589
Functions 589
Structure 590
Jurisdiction of Inspectorate 590
Independence of the Inspector General of Government 590
Financial resources 591
Special powers of Inspectorate 591
Reports of Inspectorate 591
Methodology 591
Recommendations 591

Legislation 593
The Uganda Human Rights Commission Act 1997. 597
Inspector-General of Government Statute 1987 601
Part I Preliminary Provisions. 601
Part II Establishment of Office and Appointments. 602
Part III Functions Powers 603
Part IV Procedure for Investigations 605
Part V Investigations 606
Part VI Reports. 608
Schedules 608
First Schedule 608
Part A 608
A. Oath of the Inspector-General of Government 608
B. Official Oath 609
Part B 609
Column 1, Person to take Oath 609
Column 2, Nature of Oath (omitted) 609
Column 3, Authority to Administer Oath (omitted) 609
Second Schedule 609
Search Warrant. Form 1. 609
Witness Oath. Form 2. 610
Witness Summons. Form 3. 610
Warrant of Arrest. Form 4. 610

Chapter V. Multi Organ Systems

South Africa

David McQuoid-Mason
The Role of Human Rights Institutions in South Africa 617

Introduction 617
The Public Protector 617
Role 617
Achievements 618
Budget 618
The Human Rights Commission 618
Role 618
Achievements 619
Budget 619
The Commission for Gender Equality 619
Role 619
Achievements 619
Budget 619
The Youth Commission 620
Role 620
Achievements 620
Budget 620
Commission for the Restitution of Land Rights 620
Role 621
Achievements 621
Budget 621
The Truth and Reconciliation Commission 621
Role 621
Achievements 622
Budget 622
Other Commissions Supporting Human Rights and Democracy 622
Commissions for the Promotion and Protection of the Rights of Cultural, Religious and Linguistic Communities 622
The Auditor-General 623
The Electoral Commission 623
Independent Broadcasting Authority 624
The Pan South African Language Board 624
Conclusion 624

N. Barney Pityana
The South African Human Rights Commission 627
Establishment and Operations 628
Relations with the Executive 629
Independence of the Commission 630
Programmes 631
Complaints Handling 632
Human Rights Education and Public Awareness 633
Other Programmes 634
Accountability 635
Challenges 636

Adv. S.A.M. Baqwa
South Africa's Ombudsman 639
The Ombudsman 640
The Public Protector 640
Conclusion 642

Legislation 643
Constitution of South Africa 1996 643

Chapter 9 State Institutions Supporting Constitutional Democracy 643
Public Protector Act, 1994 (No. 23 of 1994) 647
Act 647
Preamble 647
Definitions 647
Deputy Public Protector and staff of Public Protector 648
Finances and accountability 650
Reporting matters to and additional powers of Public Protector 650
Investigation by Public Protector 651
Publication of findings 652
Contempt of Public Protector 652
Compensations for expenses 652
Offences and Penalties 652
Guideline for Provincial public protectors 653
Application of Act 653
Repeal of laws 653
Short title 653
Human Rights Commission Act 1994 (No. 54 of 1994) 653
Act 653
Preamble 653
Definitions 654
Seat of Commission 654
Term of office of members of Commission 654
Independence and Impartiality 655
Committees of Commission 655
Commission may approach President or Parliament 655
Powers, duties and functions of Commission 655
Mediation, conciliation or negotiation by Commission 656
Investigations by Commission 656
Entering and search of premises and attachment and removal of articles 657
Vacancies in Commission 659
Meetings of Commission 659
Remuneration and allowances of members of Commission 660
Compensation for certain expenses and damage 660
Reports by Commission 660
Staff, finances and accountability 660
Legal proceedings against Commission 661
Offences and Penalties 661
Regulations 662

United Kingdom

Stephen C. Neff and Eric Avebury
Human Rights Mechanisms in the United Kingdom 667
Introduction: The UK Legal System 667
Ombudsmen And Similar Entities 668
Central government 668
Local government 669
Legal services 670
Data protection 670
Health services 671
Prisons 671
Private-sector housing 672
Press and Broadcasting standards 673

Police 673
Trade unions 674
Northern Ireland (general) 675
II. Human Rights Commission and Related Bodies 675
Commission for Racial Equality 675
Equal Opportunities Commissions 676
Criminal Cases Review Commissions 676
Fair Employment Commission for Northern Ireland 677
Standing Advisory Commissions on Human Rights (for Northern Ireland) 677
III. Other Human Rights Safeguards in UK Law 678
Civil actions against public officials for violations of law 678
Judicial review of official acts 678
Challenges to forms of detention 678
Unlawfully obtaining evidence in criminal trials 679
Recourse to the European Commission and Court of Human Rights 679
Actions of members of Parliament 680
Activities of human rights NGOs 680

Legislation 680
Parliamentary Commissioner Act 1967 (1967 c 13) 680
The Parliamentary Commissioner for Administration 680
1. Appointment and tenure of office 680
2. Salary and pension 680
3. Administrative provisions 681
3a. Appointment of acting Commissioner 681
4. Investigation by the Commissioner 681
5. Matters subject to investigation 682
6. Provisions relating to complaints 683
7. Procedure in respect of investigations 684
8. Evidence 684
9. Obstruction and contempt 685
10. Reports by Commissioner 685
11. Provision for secrecy of information 686
11A. Consultations between Parliamentary Commissioner and Health Service Commissioners 686
12. Interpretation 686
13. Application to Northern Ireland 687
14. Short title and commencement 687
Schedule 4 (section 5(8)) 689

Christopher Boothman
The Commission of Racial Equality 691
Tasks and Competencies 691
Codes of Practice 692
Rights 692
Specified Unlawful Acts or Behaviours 692
Direct discrimination 692
Indirect discrimination 693
Victimisation 693
Aiding unlawful acts 693
Commission named proceedings 693
Discriminatory advertisements 693
Instructions to discriminate 694
Pressure to discriminate 694

Discriminatory practices 694
Persistent discrimination 694
Judicial Review 694
Specified Fields 694
Limitation Period 695
Organization 695
Geographical Remit 696
Organizational Structure 696
Procedures 696
Applications for assistance 696
Such inquiries as it thinks fit 697
Remedies 697
Formal investigation 697
Power to obtain information 698
Disclosure of information 698
Non-discrimination notices 699
Recommendations and public reports of investigations 700

Legislation 700
The Race Relations Act 1976 700
Part I – Discrimination to Which Act Applies 700
Part II – Discrimination in The Employment Field 701
Part III – Discrimination in Other Fields 706
Part IV – Other Unlawful Acts 710
Part V – Charities 711
Part VI – General Exceptions From Parts II to IV 712
Part VII – The Commission For Racial Equality 714
General 714
Establishment and duties of the Commission 714
Assistence to organizations 715
Research and education 715
Annual reports 715
Codes of practice 715
Investigations 716
Power to conduct formal investigations 716
Terms of reference 716
Power to obtain information 717
Recommendations and reports of formal investigations 718
Restriction on disclosure of information 718
Part VIII – Enforcement 719
General 719
Part IX – Enforcement of Part III 720
Non-discrimination notices 721
Other enforcement by Commission 722
Period within which proceedings to be brought 725
Evidence 726
Part X – Supplemental 727
Schedules Section 43 727
Schedule I – The Commission For Racial Equality 727
Incorporation and status 727
Tenure of office of Commissioners 727
State 727
Tenure of office of chairman and deputy chairmen 727
Remuneration of Commissioners 727

Additional Commissioners 728
Staff 728
Advisory committees 729
Proceedings and business 729
Finance 729
Disqualification Acts 729

Chapter VI. National Human Rights Institutions in Africa

Richard Carver and Paul Hunt
National Human Rights Institutions in Africa 733
Introduction 733
Historical Review 735
Key Features 737
Mandate 737
Appointment and accountability 739
Investigations 741
Case Studies 744
Tanzania 744
Togo 745
Uganda 747
Zaire 749
The Gambia 750
Observations and Suggestions 751
Independence and impartiality 751
Human rights institutions and the judiciary 755
Compulsory powers and enforcement 756
Governmental and non-governmental human rights bodies 757
The importance of promotion 758

Alex de Waal
Human Rights in Africa; Values, Institutions, Opportunities 759
Overview 759
Human Rights Traditions in Western Europe and North America 760
Primary mobilization 760
Legal aid and ublic interest litigation 761
Philanthropy 762
The laws of war 763
Second Generation Human Rights Organizations 763
What are second generation human rights organizations? 765
Successes of second generation human rights organizations 768
Possible failures of second generation human rights organizations 769
Human rights organizations as an exportable commodity 770
Human Rights as a Foreign Policy Tool for Western Governments 772
Aid conditionalities 772
Free enterprise as a fundamental right 774
Have Human Rights Instruments become “Over-Inflated”? 775
The Genocide in Rwanda and the Routinisation of Human Rights 777
A Human Rights Agenda for Africa 780

Part Three:
Principles and Guidelines for Establishing Human Rights Institutions

Harley Johnson
Ombudsman – Essential Elements 785

Essential Elements 786
Independence 786
Impartiality 786
Investigator 787
Powers of Recommendation 787
Jurisdiction 787
Confidentiality 787
Delegation 787
Communications 787
Referrals 788
Discretion 788
Fees 788
Prisons and Mental Hospitals 788
Government files 788
Public reporting 788
Review 789
Concrete Models 789
Malta 789
USSR 789
Thailand, Cambodia, Vietnam 789
Yukon Territory 789

Tom Hadden
The Role of a National Commission in the Protection of Human Rights 791
Introduction 791
National and International Protection of Human Rights 792
Monitoring and Enforcement 793
Human Rights Commissions 793
International standards for national commissions 793
Human rights and anti-discrimination commissions in common law jurisdictions 794
A Human Rights Commission for Ethiopia 795
Human Rights And Constitutional Courts 796
The Creation of A Human Rights Culture 797

Brian Burdekin
Human Rights Commissions 801
Introduction and definition 801
The office of ombudsman and human rights commissions 801
Scope of the paper 802
Domestic and international scope 803
Participation in international meetings 809
Participation in the drafting of legislation 811
Review of human rights legislation 811
Drafting or review of other legislation (existing or proposed) 811
Recommending legislative action 812
Quasi-judicial powers 812
Power to compel production of documents and giving of evidence and powers to prevent interference with activities 813
Power to make determinations 814
Activities For Promotion And Protection of Human Rights 816
Effective and accessible remedies 816
Involvement in legal proceedings 818
Community education, awareness of human rights and participation 818

Public inquiry powers 819
Relations with Non-governmental Organizations (NGOs) 820
Specific issues of general human rights jurisdiction 822
Relations with individuals 824
Individual complaints 824
"Class Actions" and representative complaints 825
Complaints by third parties or NGOs 825
Can the Commission initiate investigations itself? 826
Relations with the State 826
Advisory Or Binding Jurisdiction 827
Conflicts of jurisdiction 828
National commissions and the courts 828
Human rights commissions, ombudsmen and other agencies 829
Federal – state conflicts 829
Conclusion and Recommendations 829
Appendix A (Structure And Functions of Australian Human Rights and Equal Opportunity Commission) 831
Human Rights and Equal Opportunities Act 831
Appendix B (Public Inquiries on Human Rights in Australia) 832
The Toomelah Inquiry 832
The Homeless Children Inquiry 832
The Racist Violence Inquiry 833
The Cooktown Inquiry 834
The Mental Illness Inquiry 834

APPENDIX

Ethiopian Legislation Establishing the Institution of the Ombudsman and the Human Rights Commission 835

Introductory Note 837

Ethiopian Human Rights Commission Establishment Proclamation No. 210/2000 839
Part One General Provisions 839
Part Two Powers and Duties of Appointees 843
Part Three Rules of Procedure of the Commission 844
Part Four Administration of the Council of Commissioners and Staff of the Commission 845
Part Five Miscellaneous Provisions 846

Institution of the Ombudsman Establishment Proclamation No. 211/2000 849
Part One General Provisions 849
Part Two Powers and Duties of Appointees 853
Part Three Rules of Procedure of the Institution 854
Part Four The Council Ombudsmen and Administration of the Staff of the Institution 855
Part Five Miscellaneous Provisions 856

Index 859

Introduction

Kamal Hossain*

The International Conference on the Establishment of the Ethiopian Human Rights Commission and the Institution of Ombudsman hosted by the Ethiopian legislators was an extraordinary global consultation, on the experiences of national human rights institutions and the institution of ombudsman. The Ethiopian legislators in their wisdom had invited participation from all over the world, not only of leading jurists to share specialised knowledge about human rights and their implementation but also of members of national human rights commissions, "ombudsmen" and activists from human rights organisations to share their insights and practical experience. This was part of the preparation for formulating national legislation to establish effective institutions for promotion and protection of human rights and to prevent and combat corruption.

It was a uniquely productive conference since the global sharing of ideas and experience provided a wealth of material for designing and establishing effective national institutions for promoting human rights and integrity in public life. The link between human rights, integrity in public life, democracy and good governance was widely recognised. A common frame of reference was provided by the Universal Declaration of Human Rights. The Declaration had set a standard of achievement. All nations committed themselves to strive to secure universal and effective recognition and observance of human rights so that men and women could live in freedom and with dignity. This was done at a time when war-ravaged societies bore scare of the unspeakable horrors inflicted by some sections of humanity on others, and when colonialism and apartheid still continued to defy claims of the majority of the world's people to freedom and equality. It had required enormous faith in the human spirit to make a commitment to transform that reality.

Implementation of human rights at root involved bringing about fundamental change, through strengthening the capacity to initiate and sustain change in the face of formidable obstacles. It involved an orchestration of efforts at the international, regional and national levels.

International efforts had involved the elaboration of human rights covenants and conventions and the establishment of machinery of supervision. Regional efforts produced regional conventions and regional machinery. It is at the national level, however, that the real challenge was to be faced since here

---

*Senior Advocate, Supreme Court of Bangladesh; Chairman, International Committee on Legal Aspects of Sustainable Development, International Law Association; Chairman, Commonwealth Human Rights Initiative Advisory Commission

K. Hossain et al. (eds), Human Rights Commissions and Ombudsman Offices, 1–5.

implementation on the ground required transforming present reality, often a legacy from an authoritarian past, but buttressed by powerful interests which felt threatened by the advance of human rights.

Efforts at the national level began with bills of rights being incorporated in national constitutions by newly-independent states. In most of these, a dichotomy was maintained between civil and political rights. ("first generation rights"), which were enforceable by courts, and economic, civil and cultural rights ("second generation rights") which were not judicially enforceable but which parliaments and governments were urged to make their best efforts to implement, subject to availability of resources.

This problem was described by one of the architects of the new South African Constitution, Justice Albie Sachs, in the following terms:

> "The fundamental constitutional problem, however, is not to set one generation of rights against another, but to harmonise all three. The web of rights is unbroken in fabric, simultaneous in operation, and all-extensive in character ...
>
> ... the achievement of first generation rights is fundamental to the establishment of democracy and the overcoming of national oppression. But for the vote to have meaning, for the Rule ofLaw to have content, the vote must be the instrument for the achievement of second and third generation rights. It would be a sad victory if the people had the right every five or so years to emerge from their forced-removal hovels and second-rate Group Area homesteads to go to the polls, only thereafter to return to their inferior houses, inferior education, and inferior jobs."[1]

The need for concrete measures of implementation was emphasized. The transformation of economic, social and cultural rights into positive law, whether in constitutions or in statutory law, was, however, not enough. The rights had to be realized in fact, which required comprehensive administrative measures and social action. The success of the transformation depended on the evolution of a human rights culture where individuals enjoying their rights and recognisedtheir duties to the community which made the enjoyment of rights possible.

The relevance of civil and political rights in the realisation of economic and social rights has been well explained by the Nobel laureate, Professor Amartya Sen, thus:

> "Civil and political rights give people the opportunity not only to do things for themselves, but also to draw attention forcefully to general needs, and to demand appropriate public action. Whether and how a government responds to needs and sufferings may well depend on how much pressure is put on it, and the exercise of political rights (such as voting, criticizing, protesting, and so on) can make a real difference. For example, one of the remarkable facts in the terrible history of famines in the world is that no substantial famine has ever occurred in any country with a democratic form of government and a relatively free press."[2]

Societies engaged in transition from an authoritarian to a democratic political order face a formidable challenge. The institutions, values and mind-sets which are the legacies of the past persist. Traditions of arbitrariness, secrecy, decision-making without consultation or open debate, and lack of accountability impede

---

[1] Albie Sachs, *Promoting Human Rights in a New South Africa*, Oxford University Press, Cape Town, 1990. pp. 8–9.

[2] A. Sen "Human Rights and Economic Achievements", in J. Bauer and D. Bell, eds, *The East Asian Challenge for Human Rights*, 1999, p. 92.

the building of a framework of good governance in which democratic institutions and human rights can be nurtured under the rule of law.

Indeed there are few societies that have not faced these difficulties. There has been a widely shared realisation that injecting a bill of rights into a constitution with conventional modes of judicial enforcement for only some of the rights is simply not enough. The need was felt to fill these glaring gaps acquired as a result of the experience of gross human rights violations which went unredressed in different societies. These included cases of torture and rape in police custody, custodial deaths and disappearances, ethnic and communal violence, trafficking in women and bonded labour, pervasive gender discrimination and sexual harassment.

This encouraged new modes of judicial activism in the sphere of human rights through resort to public interest and social action litigation. It also provided the impetus for the establishment of new national institutions, such as human rights commissions, women's commissions, the office of ombudsman and a variety ofcommissions for investigation of public complaints and for protection against discrimination.

The experience of the working of national human rights commissions and the office of ombudsmen presented at the Conference enable us to identify the best practices which merit emulation, noting both the positive features which have contributed to effectiveness and the negative ones which have detracted from it. The features that may be singled out include:

- *Mode of Establishment:* The mode of establishment is relevant. Institutions gain in prestige and effectiveness if they are established by the Constitution itself or at least by legislation, and not by an executive order.

- *Mandate:* The mandate of a commission is important. The mandate must be proportionate to the challenges that are to be faced. In the case of human rights commissions, social and economic rights (second generation rights) must get equal importance with first generation civil and political rights, and indeed a third generation of rights, the right to development and to a healthy environment, should be given due attention. In the case of ombudsmen, a mandate which would not be limited to abuse of authority by civil servants but would also include abuse by holders of public office (ministers including head of government) would give a greater degree of credibility and effectiveness to the office.

- *Independence:* Independence of a commission or the office of ombudsman is essential to its effectiveness. It must be manned by persons who enjoy public confidence and are known for their integrity and impartiality of judgement. The appointment should be through afair and transparent selection process involving effective consultations between the government and the opposition, and others such as head of the judiciary. They should have security of tenure and enjoy safeguards against removal from office similar to those enjoyed by a judge of the highest court.

- *Availability of Financial and Human Resources:* It is selfevident that a commission which is expected to monitor and redress violations of human rights and abuse of authority would be seriously impaired if it did not have adequate financial resources assured to it and not have to depend upon those whose abuses are to be checked by it. It should also have the capacity to employ staff having professional competence and other qualities necessary for carrying out the commission's tasks

- *Scope of Powers:* The scope of powers of the national institution is equally important. Its effectiveness would normally be impaired if it did not have power to compel production of evidence and the attendance of witnesses, or if it did not have the capacity in appropriate case to initiate investigations and prosecutions. Having only a power to make recommendations and not binding decisions would normally detract from its effectiveness though this is an aspect which would depend on the political culture of a society. It should have power to adopt innovative techniques to monitor implementation of economic and social rights, to commission studies and to evaluate reports with regard to progress in implementation. Most important it should have the power to promote human rights education and awareness of human rights in all sections of society, in particular the police and security forces.

Principles and standards laying down guidelines relating to the statue and functioning of national human rights institutions have been formulated. The Paris Principles on this subject were adopted by the United Nations commission on Human Rights in 1992, and guidelines were issued by Amnesty International in 1993. Further improvements have been suggested by a number of regional meetings.

The institution of ombudsman, since its early origins in the Nordic countries, has been the forerunner of a variety of independent bodies, including the office of the Public Protectors, of inspector-general, and independent anti-corruption commissions, which have been set up in different countries. While some constitutions have expressly provided for their establishment, typically they are set up by statute, and are aimed to promote integrity in public life. The survey of the experience of different countries shows a wide variety in the structure of these bodies and the scope of their powers. In Subsaharan Africa, the prevailing model is that of an "executive" ombudsman reporting to the head of government rather than to the legislature. These often lack the independence necessary for a true ombudsman. The office of Public Protector established by the Constitution in South Africa, however, presents a model of an effective "ombudsman". He is empowered to investigate any conduct in state affairs or in the public administration in any sphere of government that is alleged or suspected to be improper or to result in any impropriety or prejudice. He reports to legislature and has the power take appropriate remedial action. As in the case of South African Human Rights Commission, the office of the Public Protector is declared by the Constitution to be an institution which is independent and subject only to Constitution and the law. The Constitution also provides for them to be accountable to the National Assembly, to which they are to submit their report. It is further provided that the report of the Public Protector must be open to the public, and only in exceptional circumstances, to be determined national legislation, may the report be kept confidential. The South African model may be taken to represent the best practice. Such bodies for providing integrity in public life can be effective if they are truly independent of the executive and are seen to be operating independently and impartially and not as an instrument of partisan politics.

The strength of such institutions would depend upon public confidence and therefore, it is important that there should be easy access to them. In a large country the presence of regional offices where public complaints may be received is, therefore, important. The power as well as capacity to undertake effective investigation and to make public reports to the legislature as well as to take remedial action, are important to ensure the effectiveness of such bodies.

The re-affirmation by the universality of human rights and of the commitment to their effective implementation expressed in the conference was an acknowledgement of the history made in Africa and Asia by Nelson Mandela and Mahatama Gandhi and the millions they inspired - who struggled, suffered and made enormous sacrifices to vindicate the rights of all men and women to human dignity and to equality, regardless of race, creed, colour and political belief.

That history should continue to be a source of inspiration for all those who are committed to promote and protect human rights. Inspiring words from another Asian Nobel Laureate Aung San Suu Kyi, reflect the spirit of those who participated in the Conference, thus:

"The quintessential revolution is that of the spirit, born of an intellectual conviction of the need for change in those mental attitudes and values which shape the course of a nation's development. A revolution which aims merely at changing official policies and institutions with a view to an improvement in material conditions has little chance of genuine success. Without a revolution of the spirit, the forces which produced the iniquities of the old order would continue to be operative, posing a constant threat to the process of reform and regeneration. It is not enough merely to call for freedom, democracy and human rights. There has to be a united determination to persevere in the struggle, to make sacrifices in the name of enduring truths, to resist the corrupting influences of desire, ill will, ignorance and fear.

Saints, it has been said, are the sinners who go on trying. So free men are the oppressed who go on trying and who in the process make themselves fit to bear the responsibilities and to uphold the disciplines which will maintain a free society."[3]

---

[3] Aung San Suu Kyi, *Freedom from Fear*, 1995, p. 183.

Contextualizing the Establishment of the Institution of Human Rights Protection in Ethiopia

Haile Selassie Gebreselassie and Edmund Völker*

I. Introduction

Several years have elapsed since human rights in Ethiopia became a significant issue and a central concern on the political agenda of organizations of all spectrums, including the ruling party and the opposition. Given the poor human rights record and abuse of political authority in the past and the resulting sensitivities that surfaced in the wake of the downfall of the military regime in 1991, the issue of human rights began to pervade public, academic and political debates among Ethiopians in the country and abroad. Newly created human rights NGOs filed several cases openly accusing the government of violating human rights, but often without having any serious consequences on the latter's activities. It should be recalled that accusations against and open criticisms of the public authorities were not tolerated during the previous regime, when the rights of individuals and groups were grossly violated, and abuse of authority on ideological pretexts was practised on a wide scale. One could perhaps contend that, in the past, concerns for the protection of human rights were expressed domestically, such as in national legal documents, depending on the limits of political power and authority at different times. Even the first written Ethiopian constitution of 1931 contained some provisions on human rights (see articles 18–29). Likewise, the Revised Constitution of 1955 did incorporate certain rights under the title of "Rights and Duties of the People" (see articles 37–65). Similarly, articles 35–58 of the constitution introduced in 1987 by the defunct socialist military regime contained provisions on the fundamental freedoms, rights and duties of the people. It is further claimed that the UN Charter on Human Rights was believed to have been used as an important source of reference in the making of the Ethiopian Civil and Criminal Codes. However, generally speaking, the structures and institutions of the previous regimes hardly accommodated any form of protection against human rights abuses, and this only consisted of words and rhetorics usually incorporated in speeches.

The new government that replaced the military regime in 1991 has consistently carried out reforms aimed at building a democratic frame of governance with a degree of commitment to the respect of human rights. From the outset, the Transitional Charter of 1991 imposed following the takeover of power by the

* Law Faculty, University of Amsterdam.

K. Hossain et al. (eds), Human Rights Commissions and Ombudsman Offices, 7–35.

EPRDF guaranteed that the Universal Declaration of Human Rights will be incorporated into Ethiopian law (see article 1 of the Charter). Later, the International Bill of Rights was declared to be incorporated into the Ethiopian constitution of 1994.

Cognizant of the fact that it can only attain legitimacy domestically and recognition abroad primarily on the basis of its performance on the democratic and human rights fronts, the new government introduced a constitution which enshrines more than the provisions of human rights based on the International Bill of Rights. In fact, chapter 15 of the Constitution calls for the establishment of institutions of human rights protection, which is the main focus of this introduction.

Institutions for human rights protection as we understand them today are a novelty in the Ethiopian political and legal environment. Not only were such institutions previously unknown in Ethiopia in their modern functional and institutional sense, but attempts at their creation were usually met with a multitude of challenges, largely engendered by socio-cultural, institutional and political difficulties, most of which were bequeathed from the past. Authoritarian value sytems deeply ingrained even in the social institutions (families, schools, religious institutions) and government institutions such as the police, the public prosecutor, prison administration, etc. are likely to still produce obstacles. This is complicated by the lack of adequate public awareness of the values and practices of the rule of law, democracy and human rights.

Hierarchically structured, culturally and ethnically diverse, the Ethiopian polity and its concomitant institutions have committed grave violations of the fundamental rights of people throughout their existence, most of which had taken place in the course of the expansion and consolidation of the empire. Its successive iron-fisted rulers, including the Emperors of different ages, had often employed unitary nationalism as a vehicle to hold onto power, fomented wars, and inflicted atrocities against the people. Abuse of power and violations of rights were the expensive cost levied to keep the Ethiopian Empire together, which was originally a conglomerate of forcefully incorporated peoples and ethnic groups; ethnic and religious tensions and bloodshed characterized the transformation to an empire ruled by the Christian Abyssinian elite. In this regard, it is pertinent to describe the cultural superposition and socio-political domination conducted by the Abyssinian Christian elite against the southern people in the 19th century, in the course of which violations of human rights and dismantling of traditional mechanisms for the protection of fundamental rights became commonplace.

One could argue that the legitimation of the notion of fundamental human rights on a global scale as the basis of modern international human rights law dates from the San Francisco Charter of 1945. Then, the newly conceived UN affirmed its belief in fundamental human rights by declaring that discrimination based on sex, religion and race was repugnant. Later in 1948, it proclaimed not only the traditional rights and freedoms, but also economic and cultural rights. There is no doubt that the 1945 San Francisco Charter and the Universal Declaration on Human Rights (adopted on Dec. 10, 1949) have in this respect ushered in a new chapter in the movement for respect of human rights. However, it should also be noted that the foundation of the notion of human rights and the dignity of the human person are related to "natural" law and "right" conduct, which were often entrenched in religious doctrines. It is also claimed that the rights defined by the UN Universal Declaration of Human Rights "had been foreshadowed in the American Declaration of Independence and in the French Declaration of the Rights of Man" (Furley, 1995: 279). Hence, the notion of the Universal Declaration of Human Rights anchored its basic tenets on the recognition of the dignity and rights of the human person. It should also be added that the identification of the need for respect of fundamental human rights goes back to the 17th century. Despite the lack of attention by the international community and the absence of any form of international regime (international law) governing human rights standards, the practice of abuse and deprivation of rights to life, liberty, and property of people by powerful entities, like that of the pervasive power of the state, stretches back to time immemorial. States and institutions were free to exercise absolute power and authority in the treatment of their citizens in any way that served their purpose. No mechanisms were in place to check and monitor the abuse and deprivation of human rights. It is against this historical background that the practice which characterized the structural nexus between state and society in Ethiopia will be presented to contextualize the study of the establishment of institutions of human rights protection.

Theoretically, such institutions are believed to have a legal competence to retain a large degree of independence viz-à-viz the unconstrained power of the state authorities. What is at stake revolves around the following issues:

- in political circumstances where there are diametrically opposed views regarding the facts and reports about human rights violations,
- in a culture where political discourse is not mainly aimed at coming up with a feasible basis for a workable condition, instead going for a zero-sum loyalty to one's position: to the winner,
- where denigratory and destructive propaganda is the distinctive feature of the political culture.

How are institutions of human rights protection expected to cut across such complications and function objectively and independently? Given the resource constraints to maintain their independence, will the institutions be capable of generating sufficient income? How are they going to handle delicate human rights issues and investigate the implementation of international covenants which are ratified in government documents, but not realizable for capacity-related and other reasons? In the absence of the minimum structural, institutional and political conditions to enforce human rights respect at all levels (local, regional and federal) of the new federal arrangement, what will be the added value of the institutions under review? Where impunity and not impeachment has virtually been the rule of the game for abuse of authority and violation of rights by local leaders, what challenges lie ahead? The purpose of this introductory note is to outline the historical and political setting of Ethiopian society and to describe the legal and socio-cultural matrix on which the institutions under review are to take shape and commence functioning towards the fulfillment of their mandated tasks free of interference. We shall attempt to place the new constitutional provisions in their proper historical and socio-political perspective by examining not only existing law enforcement bodies and implementation mechanisms provided by the national law but also by exploring prospects and challenges awaiting the new institutions.

It should be stressed from the outset that the central issue at stake here is not whether the present government in Ethiopia is adhering to the international declarations. We want rather to highlight some pertinent points so as to assist in determining the kind of commission of human rights protection that would function effectively.

II. Historical and Socio-Political Setting

Ethiopia is a multi- ethnic cultural society which hosts approximately 70 different ethnic and linguistic groups, many of whom had been forcefully incorporated into the Abyssinian core during the conquests of the last quarter of the 19th century to become subjects of the highland Christian minority. Ever since the conquests, the relationship between the inhabitants of these newly incorporated territories and the rulers has been characterized by violations of the most fundamental human rights and freedom. During and following the conquests, people in the newly acquired territories were forced to abandon their own languages and religions in favour of those of the conquerors. Such a politico-cultural preponderance extended vertically from the dominant centre of the Christian highlands and was perpetuated by the subsequent regimes in charge of the unitary state of Ethiopia for over a century. This type of socio-cultural profile and the imbalance inherent in the structural relations provided the rulers of the Ethiopian polity with an environment conducive to their violent behaviour.

In a bold attempt to redress the past, the EPRDF (Ethiopian Poeople's Revolutionay Front), which formed the new government after having overthrown the Mengistu regime in 1991 introduced a constitution in 1994 which confers democracy and human rights on the nations, nationalities and peoples of Ethiopia up to and including the right of secession. In order to enhance the implementation of the stated guarantees, the constitution puts substantive limits on the power of the state organs.

In fact, a remarkable distinction between the 1994 constitution and the previous ones (in 1931, 1955, 1987) lies in the structure and content of the Bills of Rights. The 1994 Constitution significantly accords a constitutional status to the fully-fledged Bill of Rights as detailed in the three generations of the human rights system. In this regard, it can be stated that the constitution has created an environment conducive to human rights and enforceable by making it part of the domestic legal system.

Article 39 of the Constitution unambiguously guarantees the decentralization of power and administrative reorganization of the regions. The move towards this form of governance was deemed necessary in view of the diversity of the ethnic composition of the country, the nature of the organization of the resistance movements against the previous regimes over the past few decades, and the feelings and strained relationships between the dominant and the dominated groups. It must also be uemphasised that at a time when ethnicity and ethnic nationalism have once again become salient rather than fading away, the introduction of constitutional guarantees respecting ethnic and nationality rights certainly meets current requirements. It also reflects the shifts in attitudes towards nationalism and self-determination as an effective strategic approach to enhancing the fundamental rights of previously oppressed people. To that effect, the current regime has restructured the country into a federation of ethnic regions as a solution to the problems engendered by the character of state society relations in an ethnically diverse setting.

Before delving into the assessment of the execution of these rights, it is proper to provide a brief description of the state-society nexus in the Ethiopian political culture in which the implementation mechanisms will be placed to exercise their mandates.

State-Society Nexus in Ethiopia's Past

States in theory have a principal responsibility and duty to promote and protect human rights for their citizens regardless of gender, ethnicity, religion, race or socio-economic status. In practice, however, the behaviour of state entities has varied from place to place and from time to time. Today's world is known to host governments ranging from ones committed to securing the rights of human beings to those at the opposite side of the spectrum. We need to highlight briefly the character exhibited by the consecutive regimes and the political culture of Ethiopian society.

Abuses and the violation of fundamental freedoms of peoples in Ethiopia took various forms under different regimes. The violent behaviour of consecutive political regimes in Ethiopia was predominantly reflected in the prominent features of the social structures of the Ethiopian polity: political, economic, cultural and religious organizations.

The most obvious of these violations took place during the last quarter of the 19th century and early 20th century when conquest and territorial expansion to the south, southeast and southwest of Ethiopia intensified. These conquests were accompanied by state centralization. In the absence of a professional military establishment, no payment of salaries, and a lack of effective state bureaucracy to coordinate systematic extraction of tribute and revenue, the old regimes resorted to plunder and predatory appropriation of the belongings of the common people during conquests. This devastating practice is said to have continued until the early 20th century. The state of the imperial regime, in this respect, can be characterized as the central machinery of the violation of human rights. Furthermore, the constantly mobile nature of the monarchs in those days, with their wandering capitals in search of loot, often worsened the practice of plunder. However, it was in times of armed confrontation among the nobles feuding for power and territory that such practices found their worst expression. One 17th-century eyewitness wrote:

> Large companies of men, soldiers and lords bringing many servants come daily to quarter themselves in small villages. Each one goes to the house he likes best and turns the owner into the street or occupies it with him. Sometimes it is a widow or a married women whose husband is away, and then by force he gets at not only food and her property, but her honour. (Cited in Beckingham and Huntingford eds. 1967: 80).

Apparently, the practice of plunder continued until the Italian occupation of Ethiopia in 1936, although Emperor Haile Selassie was reported to have passed strict warnings to the fighters that "all who ravage the country or steal from the peasant will be shot".

With further centralization and territorial expansion, the predatory and violent practice of the state of the imperial regime was systematized with manifold ramifications. Emperor Menelik's expansion projects to the south in the last quarter of the 19th century were accompanied by confiscation of land and imposition of the highland Abyssinian culture, which included forced conversion of the local inhabitants to the Coptic religion. The magnitude and form of repression and subjugation depended on the level of resistance offered by the conquered people. In localities where, for instance, the inhabitants submitted peacefully, Menelik's rule was effected via existing indigenous institutions. Nevertheless, the local nobles, who upon conquest became servants of the conquerors, were obliged to be baptized and were required to abandon the use of their own languages for public affairs. Where fierce resistance was offered (Arsi, Wolaita, Kaffa and Harrar), "pacification" and subjugation methods involved an all-out violation of fundamental human rights through military means until total submission was obtained.

In order to sustain rule and domination in the newly conquered regions, an institutional order called "Neftegna" was put in place, which would become instrumental in perpetuating control and preponderance through systematic violation of human rights for nearly a century. Neftegna literally translated means "gunman", denoting that the communication between the Neftegnas and the local inhabitants was regulated and expressed by guns. Most of the Neftegna army that took part during the campaigns to subjugate the inhabitants of the conquered areas settled in the newly established garrison towns known as "Ketemas" under the leadership of the Neftegnas. Eventually, a classic feudal socio economic order was imposed, whose effective functioning involved the continuity of military, social, religious, political and other coercive methods of subjugation. With the establishment of this feudal edifice and the concomitant institutions of domination in the newly conquered territories, abuse of rights became a common practice.

Gebru Tarekegn, a prominent Ethiopian historian, describes the structural relations imposed by the Abyssinian highland Neftegnas and the way the conquerors treated the indigenous inhabitants in the following words:

> "… . Abyssinians looked upon and treated the indigenous people as backward, heathen, filthy, deceitful, lazy, and even stupid – stereotypes that European colonialists commonly ascribed to the African subjects. Both literally and symbolically, southerners became the object of scorn and ridicule." (1990:71)

In addition, the Neftegnas, representing the newly occupying force, were engaged in an open practice of dispossessing the arable land of the local population under the pretext of "empty land" inhabited by the "idle, lazy, local inhabitants" not working on the land they possessed. The local population, having been deprived of their basic rights of access to land, were instantly relegated into a position of a tenant rendering services to the Neftegna order. Consequently, as a result of expropriation following the conquests and continued alienation of the inhabitants, a large part of the land was owned by the Neftegna landlords, leading to the appearance of a vast social stratum of landless peasants.

This form of violation and dispossession fits into the traditional practice which attributed unlimited powers to the Emperor over the disposition of land in his domain. Ethiopian Emperors have traditionally acted on the premise stated by 14th-century Emperor Seife Ared (1344–1372) who declared, "God gave all the land to me." (Cited in Tamirat, 1972:.98.) In the last decades of the 19th century, the actions of Emperor Menelik and his institutional regime of the Neftegnas with regard to land in the conquered provinces of the south were in accordance with the tradition of imperial control over land (Markakis, 1974: 82).

Subsequently, the Gabbar system was established, which was based on an extensive confiscation of land from the native people and the major redistribution of land including the allotment of the Gabbars to the new settlers protected by the Neftegna regime. As the newly acquired territories offered rich resources to the captors, more people from central and northern Ethiopia were attracted and began to immigrate to the south to become members of the Neftegna order, thereby consolidating the social hierarchy.

For the individual Northerner, immigration provided an opportunity to relieve pressures on the northern household unit, insuring more land for those left behind, as well as to gain power, status and wealth in the south. Attraction was strongest for the young who had the last opportunity in the north. Life would be hard, but the chances for both economic and social mobility were better. (IJHAS,17,4,1984:660)

The deprivation of the fundamental rights of the peoples of the newly conquered territories was most evident in the sphere of language and religion. Coptic Christianity is a dominant element in the Ethiopian culture, pervading all aspects of the social and political life. It also determined the positions of other religions in society, including the other Monotheistic Semitic religions in the region. In the Ethiopian tradition, Christianity has been seen as a natural partner of the political establishment, its role ranging from ordaining monarchs and endorsing their violent practices to sharing the resources of the country, which it obtained, as quid pro quo, for providing a spiritual service to the establishment in order to gain legitimacy and acceptance in society. While the monarchy, the most important institution in the country's political life, needed blessing and recognition by the church, the latter endorsed and justified the absolutist behaviour of the monarchical order and its manifold ramifications.

In this respect, the often quoted "cuius regio eius religio" (the one who rules, his religion) medieval principle which was applied as a general rule to European dependencies during the colonial expansion was applied to the conquered territories during the Abyssinian expansion in the late 19th century.

Being a partner in the extraction of resources and the largest landowning institution next to the state, the church was used as a tool by the political system for the concentration of power and other privileges in a narrow centre controlled by a few aristocrats. In this regard, the role of the church was nowhere more evident than in the southern regions, where it became instrumental to the regime in depriving the non-Christian natives of their rights of participation and representation. During the reign of Haile Selassie, the people of the conquered areas, particularly the non-Christian section which constituted about half the country's population, lacked any sort of representation in the central government (Clapham, 1969:65)

At the official level, Christianity was pronounced the state religion of Ethiopia in a country where Muslims were equally numerous. To varying degrees, Muslims have often been treated as unequal to Christians in their own communities. At times, forced baptizing of Muslims into the Christian faith by Ethiopian emperors was not uncommon. Emperor Tewodros (1855–1868), on one occasion, was believed to have ordered the conversion of the largely Muslim Oromos, Falashas and Agow communities (Mondon-Vidailhet, 1905). The Emperor issued a decree in 1864 outlawing Islam and declaring those who dared to resist as rebels. Subsequently, Emperor Yohannes (1872–1889), perhaps alarmed by the changing contours of the international politics of the region, took stiffer steps against the religion of Islam. In his decree of 1878, he ordered all men in the Empire to join the Orthodox Christian Church, which was accompanied by special orders forcing all Muslim communities to build churches in their localities and pay tribute to the Christian clergy, making it the culmination of the religious discrimination practised by the highland Christian ruling elites. Although done with rather less fanatical zeal, the forceful conversion of Muslims and followers of other religions into Orthodox Christianity continued to be the official policy of the Emperors that followed Yohannes.

This act of deprivation of fundamental rights committed through conquest and expropriation of the local population was institutionalized with the help of spiritual documents forged by the church. The Kibre Negest (The Glory of Kings), an apocalyptic work containing the Solomonic legend compiled by one Yishak in Ethiopia in the 14th century, not only served as a legitimizing ideology for the dominant position of the Christian ruling aristocratic elite led by the monarchs in the highlands but also as a justification of the wars, conquests and expansions to subdue the people of the South. The Kibre Negest provided spiritual justification to the king's claims and command of absolute authority, the exercise of dictatorial power and violence over the territories he ruled. In addition, all non-Christians who did not speak Amharic were excluded from positions of political power, including Muslims who were the hardest hit by this structural practice. Commenting on such discrimination, one scholar has this to say:

It was easier for a non Christian who also did not speak Amharigna to pass through the eye of the needle than to enter the charmed circle of power and privilege (Markakis, 1987:274).

Until the revolution of 1974, which officially declared all religions equal, the nearly symbiotic relationship between the state and the church had continued for several centuries as reflected in the arenas of socio-political and economic life.

This brings us to the other element of discrimination: language. Without even considering dialects, the Ethiopian Empire is believed to have housed as many as over 70 different languages. Amharic, the language of the dominant group, gained political prominence and was eventually to become the lingua franca of the country. The development and further advance of Amharic were assisted by the communication media, the state administration and the educational system. The other languages were suppressed by not being taught at schools nor appearing in print. In this way, the Amharic language, which came to serve as one of the instruments of assimilation, was employed as a principal medium of imposing Abyssinian culture in the conquered territories. This practice of unifocal language policy meant systematic deprivation of the developments of the cultures and languages of native nationalities. Describing the extent of the cultural imposition and denial of rights to the others, one American sociologist wrote:

It was not permissible to publish, preach, teach or broadcast in Oromo. In court or before an official, an Oromo had to speak Amharic or use an interpreter. Even a case between two Oromos before an Oromo magistrate had to be heard in Amharic. I sat through a mission church service in which the preacher and all the congregation were

Oromo but the sermon as well as the service was given in Amharic which only few of the congregation understood at all, then translated into Oromo. To have preached in Oromo would have resulted in the preacher being fired or imprisoned (Baxter, 1983:137).

The consolidation of the Empire and centralization of the unitary state by the imperial regime of Haile Selassie in the last century was to leave no legal or cultural space for the protection of the cultural, socio-economic and political rights of the people. The institution of the monarchy became unequivocally and systematically absolutist in such a way that any group or individual daring to question or deviate from it faced the death sentence.

It should be recalled that, as a member of the UN and thereby a party to the UN Charter, Ethiopia was, in theory, obliged in accordance with Article 55 and 56 of the Charter to promote and encourage the "universal respect for and observance of human rights and fundamental freedom for all without distinction as to race, language or religion". In practice, the provision of human rights was never seriously deliberated in the domestic law of the country despite some tepid acknowledgements of the fundamental human rights, which were accompanied by a series of clarifications and conditions that relegated the provisions into a marginal position where they could hardly be realized. True, some references were made to the respect of human rights in the first ever written constitution of Ethiopia (1931). Articles 18–29 declared the right of free movement, freedom from sentence or imprisonment except in pursuance of the law, the right not to be denied justice in a legally established court, the right of owning property and possessions, etc. Later, these rights were broadened in scope by the revised constitution of 1955. Article 37–65 of the Revised Constitution under the heading "Rights and Duties of the People" contained provisions for fundamental rights and freedoms. Similarly, the 1987 constitution also incorporated rights in Articles 35–58 under the title of fundamental freedom, rights and duties of the citizens. However, there were no mechanisms nor judicial or quasi-judicial safeguards to put them into effect.

More importantly, before the introduction of the 1994 constitution, Ethiopia was never a party to many of the most critical international instruments in the area of human rights, such as the International Covenant on Civil and Political Rights, the Convention against Torture and other Cruel, Inhuman or Degrading Treatment or Punishment, which gave its consecutive authoritarian rulers a free hand to practice violence.

Gradually, highhandedness and despotic rule of such magnitude began to produce its opposite: persistent resistance. Furthermore, this phenomenon of resistance to the old practice of rule was aided by exposure of the educated segment of society to political and social theories following the introduction of modern educational institutions. It should be noted that originally the imperial regime had encouraged the introduction of modern education with defined objectives to serve its purposes. Nevertheless, as one writer remarked:

The educational system itself was in many respects, given the realities of ancien regime Ethiopia, subversive: secular discourse in the form of systematized academic disciplines taught and thought out as intra-mural exercise while its expression as extra-mural was ostracized. The regime never cogitated the contradictions that inhered in the educational system it imported nuts and bolts from outside; it saw only one side of the janus – the bureaucratizing, instrumental aspect and not its provisionally subversive dynamic, however bourgeois, even because of its bourgeois character (Addishiwot:23).

Modern education in many respects brought about rather unintended results. The introduction of modern education up to the tertiary level in the post-World War II years meant subsequent exposure by a generation of students to new intellectual traditions containing a variety of political philosophies and social theories of emancipation in which the notion of civil and political rights were ingrained. Beginning from the 1950s, demonstrations by students and strikes by the fledgling workers' unions against the monarchy began to surface. The late 1960s and the early 1970s were marked by a wave of unrest and accelerated momentum in the movement for democracy and fundamental freedoms.

Continued deprivation of fundamental human rights generated manifold conflicts eventually leading to the emergence of armed opposition in various corners of the country. Gradually, the legitimacy of the old order began to be seriously challenged. The state and the monarchy personified by the Emperor, which had dominated Ethiopia without even a party apparatus to defend its ideological stance, was now faced with political opposition, with serious consequences leading to its ultimate collapse. As a result, these factors (violation of basic civil and political rights narrowing all resources to a unifocal political arena and allowing access only to a small number of the elite originating from the dominant centre, the absence of lower and broader levels of participation, the deprivation of cultural, religious and economic rights for the overwhelming majority of the people, the terror and violence by the consecutive regimes against ethnic nationalities demanding basic rights and political freedom) accounted for the crisis that led to the collapse of the ancien regime.

While movements for democracy, greater participation, cultural and religious equality and regional autonomy for ethnic nationalities played a key role in the articulation of the revolution, further domestic socio-economic and political conditions aided by international developments in the early 1970s compounded to shake the age-old feudal establishment. Opposition to the manifold abuses and violations of human rights committed by the imperial regime and its institutional layers over the decades were then to find an outlet, at least temporarily. Imbued by the revolutionary situation of the days, the educated elite became instrumental in the organization of mass protests and student movements which were later to be joined by the army and other groups in society that brought the final collapse of the government and the overthrow of the autocrat in 1974. Thus, ended a 3000-year-old monarchy and its ideological mainstay: the Solomonic myth and its 16 centuries of Christian theocracy that provided it with the spiritual justification to endorse coercion and violence.

Now that the old order was abolished and a revolutionary ideology adopted to guide the revolution, new political and economic reforms were enacted by the new incumbents. What is at stake here pertains to whether any significant changes occurred in the system of human rights and respect for fundamental freedoms following the adoption of the revolutionary ideology.

In the course of the revolution, it became evident that abolition of the old order was no guarantee of bringing about a new social order committed to the respect of fundamental human rights. The cure was worse than the disease; the new revolutionary regime which claimed to be the champion of respect for basic rights and equality of people, adapting a newly imported emancipatory ideology, began to consolidate power and continued to rule in essentially the same manner as its predecessors. The military regime unambiguously exhibited the continuity of the past by employing a new social myth to justify the practice of the old coercion (Haileselassie, 1994:287). The ideological parallel between the Christianity-based Solomonic myth of the past and the socialism of the present is even more striking when examining the socialist ideology which was employed to institutionalize a system of centralist rule under a new ruling elite with a different social origin (ibid).

It was indeed the case that in the early days of the revolution, the military regime's programme emphasised respect for fundamental freedoms and emancipation of the oppressed people. Civil and political rights, freedom of press, and freedom of speech were declared. The regime had explicitly pledged to break with the past by ending atrocities and violence against forces fighting for their democratic and political rights. On the social, cultural and economic fronts, packages of reforms were introduced that primarily intended to redress past mistakes. The regime declared the equality of all religions including Islam and Christianity by separating the church from the state, which required the former to relinquish its traditional role. A land reform destroyed the economic basis of the ruling landed aristocracy, thereby returning the economic rights to the rural population. By declaring all nationalities and languages equal, the people of the south were made publicly visible.

The question that arises at this juncture is why did a regime with such an authoritarian behaviour introduce these economic and social reforms? Behind these short-lived and deceptive reforms was the fact that the soldiers in power had neither the political know-how to run the state nor a cohesive ideology to unite political tendencies and oppositions. Therefore, to win the support of and temporary alliance with the civilian groups who were actively engaged in the movements for democracy and fundamental rights, they chose to introduce these reforms. However, the soldiers' regime began eventually to design alternative mechanisms by which they could consolidate the power of the state and deal with the civilian movements through cooptation and/or elimination (ibid: 297).

The beginning of the implementation of this strategy marked the end of the civil and political rights introduced. The legal and political landscape of the country was quickly to be transformed into a dictatorial one-party regime under Colonel Mengistu Haile Mariam. This abrupt move was accompanied by gross violations of fundamental human rights. Shortly afterwards, the regime began a campaign of assassination and systematic elimination of members of the civilian opposition, labelling them with different tags: "white terrorists", "right-wingers", "5th Columnists", "Trotskites", etc. Despite the series of radical reforms enacted to abolish the old social order, no significant changes were brought about, particularly in the human rights protection system. On the contrary, horrifying terror and systematic atrocities became the order of the day. The civic institutions that were established by the regime became ironically instrumental in its campaign of terror, when all rights and freedoms were violated in the name of the defense of socialism and the regime. Arbitrary detentions, systematic elimination of opponents, brutal suppression of dissidents were the political hallmarks of the regime. The preamble of the Constitution of 1987, introduced by the same military regime, explicitly subordinated all rights to the socialist party.

As it resorted to violations and violent practices, the regime's legitimacy began to be seriously challenged. Opposition emerged from various corners of urban and rural Ethiopia. The most serious challenge came from the regionally and ethnically based nationalist armed movements, which had their roots in poverty, inequality and lack of access to material and political resources. Diverse ethnic groups and regions that were denied access to the state allocation of resources, which as a result had already begun to challenge the imperial rule in the early 1960s, now intensified their resistance movements against the new regime following the revolution of 1974. As outlined earlier, the origins of the conflicts could be traced, to a large extent, to the forceful expansion and unification process undertaken by the Ethiopian state, which culminated in the cultural and political alienation of diverse groups.

Thus, originally, the Abyssinian order determined the institutional and political development of the state in which the Abyssinian culture and Coptic Christianity were promoted to the denigration of other cultures and religions. Access to power, prestige and material wealth for the non-Abyssinian elite and masses required them to undergo a certain degree of acculturation. This practice generated a deep-seated hatred against the dominant culture and the unitary state among diverse ethnic groups. This was later transformed into an ethnic/regional consciousness, and hence politicization and intensification of the struggle for fundamental rights became a reality in many parts of the country, which eventually led to the collapse of the military regime.

A detailed discussion of these developments requires more research. What has been attempted so far is to skim through the political struggle for democracy and human rights over the last two and half decades. The next section will highlight the major items related to the human rights system vis-à-vis the political regime and the law enforcement bodies following the change of regime in 1991.

III. Change of Regime, Human Rights and Law Enforcement Bodies Post-1991

The end of the Cold War and the subsequent demise of the Soviet power and its respective allies in the late 1980s gave way to the emergence of new regimes in Africa and elsewhere with democratic stances and respect for human rights. The change of regime that took place in Ethiopia in 1991 and the subsequent political reforms and movements for human rights could be seen as part of this shifting global situation.

The protection of human rights in a society characterized by historical imbalance and gross violation of fundamental human rights is a subject of profound concern. The Ethiopian people, having struggled persistently for decades to do away with despotic rule and authoritarian regimes, have now embarked upon a democratic transition and economic reconstruction. The issue of human rights was to become the new regime's preoccupation and a prime focus of attention. With the weak economic infrastructure and non-participatory political culture inherited from the past, compounded by a lack of adequate resources and trained manpower, the new leadership's preoccupation has been to overcome poverty and disease and to introduce basic political freedoms for its citizens, all of which, no doubt, require minimum stability. Well aware of the unfortunate experience of the past characterized by injustices perpetrated against people by its predecessors, the new leadership could have hardly contemplated any other alternative but to depart from it in favour of respect for human rights and democracy. This can also be seen as part of the wider political movement in contemporary Africa and elsewhere in the world, where democratic transition and the adoption of new constitutions enshrining a fully fledged bill of rights has become commonplace (South Africa, Namibia, Malawi, Zambia, Mozambique, etc.).

The seriousness of the new regime's stand against human rights abuses and the violation of fundamental freedoms was clearly expressed in article 1 of the Transitional Charter of 1991 and subsequently in Chapter 3 of the 1994 Constitution which exclusively caters for fundamental rights and freedoms as detailed in articles 14–28 of Part One and articles 29–44 of Part Two. Close scrutiny of the content of these provisions reflects the extent to which the Federal Constitution has incorporated the International Bill of Rights. It is emphasized in Chapter 3 of the Constitution that the provisions dealing with human rights are to be interpreted in a manner conforming to the principles of the Universal Declaration of Human Rights and international instruments adopted by Ethiopia (Article 9/4). These profound steps did not surprise many people, as the new government had inherited a system under which hundreds of thousands of lives had perished in a systematic and massive perpetration of violations. In principle, the rights enshrined in the constitution need not be regarded as privileges granted by a leadership in charge of the state. As they are directly derived from the Universal Declaration, these are fundamental entitlements of the individual against the all-powerful state.

The entrenchment of all three generations of human rights and the further provisional prescription to establish the quasi-legal enforcement bodies (Human Rights Commission) in the national constitution demonstrate a clear departure from the past by the state; and the supremacy provided to human rights in the constitution is evidence of the fact that the issue is considered pivotal, and an essential aspect of democracy in the new political process which the federal arrangement seeks to strengthen. The Federal Constitution proclaims a new human rights system anchored on the principles of the International Bill of Rights, which has resulted in open controversy between the government and opposition groups in Ethiopia today on human rights issues. More so, the government is fully aware of the central role its human rights record plays in obtaining legitimacy. Undoubtedly, decentralization of authority and devolution of power to the regions as the right of ethnic nationalities to self-rule, land ownership as a right of the rural population to the basic economic resources, both essentially human rights issues, provide the government already with a certain basis of legitimacy. Indeed, government sensitivities on its human rights record and attempts to gain a positive reputation from the public and the international community are reflected in a series of pronouncements.

Ever since its takeover of power, the new government has been monitored by national and international observers alike, which have made serious efforts to present the human rights issue among the central concerns on both the domestic and international fronts.

Internally, respect for human rights and political freedom are considered to be the litmus test of political pluralism to which the new government professes adherence.

Externally, the effective implementation of government policies that would, as a matter of necessity, require international input is, to a large extent, contingent upon the regime's respect for human rights in accordance with the Universal

Declaration of Human Rights, democratic governance and fair distribution of resources in line with the federal option which Ethiopia has adopted. In a nutshell, the government's fundamental policies (federalism based on a democratic structure of government and a free market economy) are to be, in principle, founded on respect for human rights and a democratic frame of governance. The major reforms and the changes in the political landscape that the country has been undergoing over the last decade have been accompanied by marked changes in the constitution. Consequently, a new constitution was drawn up to reflect these changed political realities and the democratic transition underway since 1991. It goes without saying that the building of a new political culture can only succeed if solidly based on the conception and implementation of human rights. It should also be added that the new state rising from the ashes of the autocratic rule of the ancien regime, and later from the military regime, needed a general reorientation aimed at crafting a participatory constitution that ought to include commitment to the recognition and protection of individual human rights based on the International Bill of Rights.

There is also a significant political aspect in the sense that any violation of human rights by the government would be used by its opponents to erode its position, not necessarily to redress the human rights situation.

In view of these circumstances, the government is fully aware that it can only attain legitimacy domestically and abroad on the basis of its performance on the democratic and human rights fronts. There is no doubt that its policy of decentralization to the regions is very much in line and duly intended to address the rights of ethnic groups, which in the past had been incorporated forcefully into an unitary state.

The Regime's Human Rights Policy and the Opposition

In the Transitional Charter drafted in 1991 following the takeover of power by the EPRDF, the Universal Declaration of Human Rights was declared part of Ethiopian law. In order to deal with the human rights abuses of the officials of the previous regime, the Special Prosecutor's Office was established to investigate in a War Crime Tribunal the cases of about 3000 government officials, party cadres and military officers who were jailed on allegations of abuse. The International Bill of Rights and all international conventions dealing with basic rights were incorporated into the new Ethiopian Constitution of 1994. The various UN conventions which target particular human rights abuses such as torture, extra-judicial killings, ill-treatment of prisoners and prolonged detentions were declared valid. Having extricated the country from an authoritarian regime, the current government strongly believes that it is defending the path towards respect for human rights and democracy.

At the practical level, the government has embarked upon a decentralization of authority and devolution of power to the ethnically delineated regions. This form of power devolution is important for a country composed of heterogeneous groups, most of which were forcefully brought under the rule of the hierarchically structured political and cultural order of the Abyssinian highlanders.

Undoubtedly, compared with that of its predecessors, the record of the present regime on human rights has substantially improved. In addition to the major constitutional rights of decentralization of authority to the regions and enactment of lower levels of participation, the rural communities in Ethiopia feel relieved of government interference in their economic and productive affairs. The former military regime, despite the land distribution of 1974, had continued to interfere and control the lives of the farmers by fixing prices, planning production, and restricting their movements to better markets through a government-controlled body called the Agricultural Marketing Corporation, which was solely established for this purpose.

Theoretically and substantively, the content of the present provisions cannot be subjected to any serious attack. Nevertheless, accusations and counter-accusations have become common where the government and government sympathizers on the one side and national and international human rights advocates on the other are engaged in controversies about violations and abuses. Reports of such accusations were constantly voiced by the Addis Ababa-based Ethiopian Human Rights Council (better known by its acronym, EHRCO), Amnesty International, the New York-based American Association of the International Committee of Jurists, and organs of the private press. The government has been severely criticized by the political opposition based in the capital Addis Ababa and abroad, and international human rights NGOs. In particular, EHRCO headed by the retired Professor Mesfin Woldemariam severely criticized the government for its human rights abuses in its 170-page report from 1995 entitled "Democracy, Rule of Law and Human Rights in Ethiopia: Rhetoric and Practice". The report included, among many other things, 184 cases of extra-judicial killings, 98 forced disappearances, 36 cases of torture, 16,801 cases of violations of the right to work and 4,357 violations of pension rights (EHRCO, 1995:6–7). On a number of occasions, EHRCO claimed that democracy and human rights were not in reality respected in Ethiopia; and that they were depicted as a smoke-screen by the regime to win support from the international community. The opposition has accused the government of restrictions on political participation during elections, and the political freedom of opinion and organization guaranteed by the constitution are limited in practice. Both opposition and human rights NGOs have openly accused the government of imposing serious restrictions on the exercise of the right of participation in elections. Complaints concerning freedom of press and associations and participation during elections have been reported by various organizations; Amnesty International, AAICJ and the US Department of State claim that the government has arbitrarily arrested and detained journalists and political activists (US Department of State, 1996:2). There have also been reports by national and international human rights organizations expressing concern about the violation and restriction of rights guaranteed in the constitution. The decertification of the Confederation of the Ethiopian Labor Union in 1994 by the government following its failure to resolve internal disputes and being accused by the government of acting in a political manner, the alleged restriction of academic freedom at the University of Addis Ababa which led to the dismissal of 41 teaching staff of various faculties in 1995, the ban against university students to engage in political associations or activities on campus, and the alleged killing of one student during student demonstrations against Eritrea's independence when former UN Secretary General Boutros Ghali visited Ethiopia in 1994 have all been cases in point stressed by human rights organizations. Similar incidents of abuses by the government have been reported in the field of civil rights.

For example, extra-judicial executions had been commonly practised in the past, often upon government orders. Even after the constitution of 1994, cases of extra-judicial killings by government forces were reported to have taken place, though not necessarily under government orders. In one case in 1995, six Oromo youths were found dead during detention by the government, which reportedly admitted that this was indeed a case of abuse (cited in Pausewang, 1995:222).

Similarly, the UN Working Group on Enforced or Involuntary Disappearances expressed concern about the disappearances of suspected opponents by the new government on various occasions by pointing to the failure of the police and security forces to reply to inquiries by relatives of missing persons (UNDOCS.E/CN4/1995/36, December 30, 1994).

A series of reports and concerns by national and international human rights groups have been published on the alleged violation of civil rights involving torture, ill-treatment of prisoners, arbitrary and harsh conditions of detention, prolonged pre-trial detentions including the well-known delay of the trial of high-level officials of the previous regime who have been detained since 1991.

While each of the views arising from the various parts of the spectrum on the facts of human rights violations may contain some element of truth, their interpretations must be placed in the broader context of the political culture and the polarized nature of the discourse that characterized the mid-1990s when the government on one side and the political opposition on the other were engaged in confrontational debates and acrimonious exchanges.

In the first place, the political opposition and human rights NGOs (both national and international) have tended to confuse human rights issues with political agendas, thus transforming the former automatically into a political issue. Such confusion raises a serious concern and reduces the credibility of human rights NGOs to a questionable level, which makes them unable to establish the facts objectively. This has even further implications on the validity of the work of the international human rights NGOs, which very likely base their reports and findings on facts gathered from their counterpart domestic organizations. Of course, opposition forces may face a potential threat of arrest and execution in an environment where human rights are commonly abused and in which their members and candidates could be subjected to harassment and arrest. Also, it would be dishonest to deny the fact that human rights abuses do exist, although the incidents are not comparable in scale and motives to those perpetrated by the previous regime. Despite the lack of objectivity in the facts contained in the reports, there is little doubt about some human rights abuses being sporadically committed in the capital city and the regions. In the absence of strong judicial and quasi-judicial mechanisms to enforce human rights in various parts of the country and lower levels of the central administration, it is not difficult to comprehend that human rights abuses could easily take place. What is more, it is indeed the case that a mutual presupposition exists between modern democratic governance and human rights; the two are closely intertwined, and the significance of human rights protection in a constitutional democracy can hardly be overlooked. We want to allude that the two should not be perceived as synonymous, and that the parties involved in the discourse need to make a clear conceptual distinction. It is not our intention here to address the issue of the conceptual and practical nexus between democracy and human rights.

Another item worth mentioning at this juncture relates to the continued abuse of rights in the regions and lower levels of the central administration which may not have necessarily resulted from an intentionally perpetrated act of violence but rather from the lack of effective enforcement mechanisms. Given the institutional and structural difficulties in the regions, violation of personal freedom and democratic rights are likely to happen frequently, for which the government naturally cannot be absolved.

Another aspect of the human rights abuse issue relates to the role played by non-state actors in the violation of human rights. Liberation fronts, opposition forces, etc. have been allegedly engaged in the plundering of communities and killing of individuals in the achievement of their political motives. The OLF, the Oromo Liberation Front, a former partner in the ruling coalition until 1994, for instance, was believed to have carried out mass killings in Eastern Ethiopia in 1995 following its withdrawal from the government and Parliament. Several other instances can be cited where opposition forces were openly engaged in the violation of human rights. In areas where a confrontation between government forces and opposition armed units of resistance took place, harsh violations of human rights were reported against suspected opponents among the civilian population. Accusations and counter-accusations, dismissal and counter-dismissals of human rights performances characterized by heated polemics have continued to dominate the political profile in the relations between the government and opposition forces.

The point that needs to be highlighted in this context relates to problems of an institutional and structural nature that have produced a serious challenge to the realization of the human rights reforms and implementation procedures. They coincide with an extremely weak local administration composed of ill-trained manpower relying on top down communication channels, an authoritarian tradition, and a tendency to protect personal position and authority.

IV. Implementation Mechanisms and the Forthcoming National Commission

Generally speaking, Ethiopia's current human rights policy focusses on:

- the adoption of and incorporation into laws of various International Conventions and Treaties that pertain to human rights,
- public education in the field of human rights by various means with a view to raising public legal awareness,
- the protection, excercise and enforcement of human rights as guaranteed in the laws.

An important provision enshrined in the 1994 Ethiopian Constitution refers to the Universal Declaration of Human Rights and the International Conventions adopted thereafter. The inclusion of the Bill of Rights in the constitution and the need to establish the law-enforcing machinery to guarantee their legal protection implies the commitment of the government to promote the civil liberties detailed in the provisions.

Of particular relevance is the declaration of the establishment of the Human Rights Commission in the constitution with a defined legal mandate to protect and promote human rights activities. Considerations arising from violations of human rights in the past provided the driving force and also the acknowledgement that such institutions are instrumental in the protection and promotion of human rights.

The protection of human rights and the effective functioning of the institutions under review will certainly need a legal infrastructure and a system of enforcement mechanisms essential to meet the basic requirements. There is a need for a rule of law where a constitutional framework explicitly delimits the authority of the executive, the legislative and the judicial branches of government, where the government in power exercises its mandates as provided by law. These are the central institutional mechanisms to ensure the protection of human rights. The establishment of an independent judicial system with full constitutional rights to monitor and follow up the exercise of executive and administrative powers as well as an effective opposition in parliament to check and control injustice are among the vital institutions that need to be in place. It must also be stressed that constitutional guarantees for the protection and promotion of fundamental rights are only one part of the developing democratization process. The constitution also contains further provisions of legal competence and authority entrusted to the judicial and semi-judicial institutions in order to protect and safeguard the individual and collective rights expressed in the social, economic and cultural spheres. These institutions include the organization of the judiciary, the constitutional courts, the Council of Constitutional Enquiry as well as the semi-judiciary institutions.

The institutions of human rights promotion and protection in Ethiopia are bodies entrusted to ensure compliance by government organs with the rights and freedoms guaranteed by the new constitution. Ideally, these semi-judicial safeguards (human rights and ombudsman) should not replace the mechanisms inherent in the legal structures. Instead, their activities must go hand in hand to complement the work of existing legal and other institutions in order to make them more effective institutions of human rights protection. Given the current lack of an effective court system and representatives of the judiciary in many parts of the regional administrations, the new institutions of human rights protection can be duly utilized in gathering complaints and facts, in reporting findings to the relevant authorities, and in actively taking part in promotional activities to raise the public's legal awareness. This is particularly so in cultures where the rights and position of vulnerable groups in society (women and children) are at risk.

The idea of establishing human rights institutions in Ethiopia has been around since the promulgation of the 1994 Constitution, with subsequent effects. In 1996, the House of People's Representatives of the Federal Republic of Ethiopia approved a bill to launch a preparatory project to create a Human Rights Commission and the Office of the Ombudsman. In order to expedite the process, the House of Representatives in collaboration with various multilateral (EU, UNDP) and bilateral donors organized a five-day conference at the UN conference centre in the Ethiopian capital Addis Ababa, on May 18–22, 1998, where over 80 country and expert reports on the variety of legislative and functioning aspects of institutions of human rights protection were delivered. A wide range of legislative and functional practices of national institutions was presented in the conference working groups. The main objective of this conference was to prepare the ground and to assist in the drafting of the national legislation and subsequent formation of a viable institutional mechanism for Ethiopia. The exercise in the exchange of experiences has undoubtedly helped the Ethiopian legislators draw lessons from existing institutions elsewhere which are engaged in similar duties.

Based on the proceedings from the conference, a concept paper containing issues to be included in the legislation was developed and examined during the follow-up Civil Society Consultations held on May 10–12, 1999, in Addis Ababa in which various civil society groups (NGOs, professional associations, unions), the media and other representatives of segments of the public participated. Follow-up consultations are envisaged both at the regional and central levels. The feedback gained from the specialists, stakeholders, the public and civil society at large during these consultations is highly valued in terms of the contribution to the production of a well-informed legislation and the eventual creation of effective institutions to protect civil and human rights in Ethiopia. There is little doubt about the contribution made by the substantial input from the conference that will eventually assist in the choice, determination, mandate, working methods and type of institutions of human rights protection to be established in Ethiopia.

Moreover, the practical diversity and the similarities in the set of standards derived from the legislative framework of other systems of government (depending of course on whether the state has a unitary or federal structure) can be regarded as a lesson to be emulated in the course of the drafting of the national legislation and the eventual establishment of the institutions. In particular, the reports delivered by the national commissions functioning in multi-ethnic settings where multi-commission systems of human rights protection operate effectively will be valued as highly relevant to the Ethiopian setting due to their contextual similarities. All this has offered the Ethiopian legislative body a great opportunity to acquire relevant lessons in synthesizing an appropriate legal document. It is also true that the establishment of the commission is an important step to sustain the momentum of the human rights movement in Ethiopia. Most importantly, the creation of national institutions will not only enhance human rights protection, but also help forge links between the international standards and national constitutional guarantees derived from the universal norms.

Nevertheless, despite the relatively smooth process of integration of the provisions derived from the Universal Declaration of of Human Rights into the written constitution of 1994, their practical application is likely to be faced by a set of limitations mainly emanating from the conditions outlined below.

Limitations

A variety of constraints (socio-political, economic and cultural) are likely to limit the full realization of the tasks mandated to the institutions under review. For the purpose of this discussion, we, nevertheless, assume that the national commission will have a legal mandate to perform a number of important tasks in the field of human rights, the main ones being the promotional and protective activities. While the promotional activities will focus on raising the awareness of the public and of members of relevant institutions and civil society organizations by way of education and publicity, the protective aspect will concentrate on the investigation of complaints of human rights abuses. What factors then limit the national commission in the realization of its mandated tasks?

There is a serious concern related to the potential ineffectiveness of the institutions in the fulfilment of the minimum standards prescribed in the "Paris Principles" (Principles Relating to the Status of National Institutions, UNGA Resolution 48/134, December 20).

One potential setback involves the obvious limitation of human and financial resources with possible serious implications for the commission's work. Given the likely large number of complaints on the one hand and the limited financial and human resources available on the other, there is serious doubt about the commission's capability to discharge its responsibilities, especially in the early stage of its establishment. It is quite natural to suspect that the integrity and independence of the commission might be compromised. This is particularly so as its leaders may be busy supplementing their livelihood through various activities that may not be compatible with the responsibilities and tasks entrusted to them.

Availability of sufficient funding and a large degree of independence for drafting and proposing its own budget are important preconditions for sustaining the credibility of the commission. That will indeed give the commission a measure of independence from any possible rules and pressures of government institutions dealing with the financial regime.

Another structural setback relates to the obvious lack of public awareness about the exercise of human rights and the absence of commitment by government institutions supposedly engaged in the protection of fundamental rights. Noteworthy is the negative role played by the military, police and security establishments in the past in the gross violation of the collective and individual rights of people in Ethiopia in defense of the authoritarian regimes. Extra-judicial executions were commonly carried out by these institutions, often upon government orders. Members of the revolutionary councils, police and security forces were responsible for untold human rights abuses in the late 1970s and 1980s, including indiscriminate killings and throwing away the dead bodies of thousands of young schoolboys and girls on the streets of the capital and other major towns. These practices were openly perpetrated by the state and para-statal armed institutions.

The violent character of the communication between state institutions and society calls for the promotion of human rights among these state and para-statal institutions as a fundamental prerequisite for the respect and recognition of the rights guaranteed in the constitution. The institutions which are directly involved with the enforcement of human rights include the military, the police, security forces, courts, prosecution and prison administration. Any attempt to enforce and safeguard human rights without securing their support and direct involvement despite their former negative role would be a futile exercise. Thus, such institutions must be equipped with a basic knowledge of human and democratic rights. They need to have a clear, correct and accurate comprehension and interpretation of the various provisions of the working documents which have a direct relationship with human rights. They need to be constantly updated on international laws, conventions, agreements, etc. related to human rights.

The national commission of human rights protection in Ethiopia has the important task of promoting the awareness and education of human rights among the public, civil society and the sectors most responsible for violating human rights. It is important that the public and various strategic groups (NGOs, the police, associations, public authorities) become aware of the broader constitutional guarantees adopted, in addition to the basic human rights principles limited to the conventional civil and political rights. The fact that these broad guarantees are protected by the constitution [economic rights in Article 41 (1–10), the right of children in Article 36 (1–9), the rights of women in Article 35 (1–8), the right to development in Article 43 (1–4)] and are contained in the 1994 constitution makes it legitimate to place the stated provisions in the Ethiopian human rights agenda in particular and the agenda of the legal system in general.

Notwithstanding the tremendous limitations in the availability of resources, social and economic rights are guaranteed in a prescriptive way in Articles 40 and 41 of the Constitution. This could generate a debate as to which of the two sets of rights (civil and political rights, and economic, social and cultural rights) should have priority in the Ethiopian socio-economic context. This point could be examined on the basis of the braoder human rights paradigms that gave rise to the African Charter of Human and People's Rights. Although apparently giving priority to economic, social and cultural rights, the African Charter contains a text which links the two sets of rights together in its preamble.

> "…. that it is henceforth essential to pay particular attention to the right of development and that civil and political rights cannot be dissociated from economic, social and cultural rights in their conception as well as universality and that the satisfaction of economic, social and cultural rights is a guarantee for the enjoyment of civil and political rights.
> In order to attain these rights, equal access to public resources, improved living conditions, access to farm land, health and education are all listed in the constitution." (cited in Eze, 1984:254)

It must be reiterated while all three generations of human rights are significant to the protection of human rights, the second and third generations are even more relevant to the Ethiopian setting, given the long history of the economic, cultural and other forms of imbalances which many groups of people have had to suffer and still endure. In the final analysis, these rights need to be effectively implemented, for which the necessary infrastructural and material resources must be available. However, scarcity of resources and more so the macro-economic policy and the structural adjustment programs will make the execution of such rights no easy task.

It must also be noted that there are also important guarantees pertaining to the protection of fundamental rights including the independence of the judiciary. If properly utilized, the 1994 Constitution provides Ethiopian courts with an opportunity to develop a constitutional jurisprudence in which a human rights regime will play a major role. The proper comprehension of such a human rights jurisprudence is a precondition for the development of a human rights culture and ultimately to a viable system of human rights protection within the domestic legal environment. In this respect, the independence of the judiciary is indeed an important strategic right. The application of the specific and broader human rights guarantees enshrined in the constitution into the existing Criminal Procedure Law and the Penal Code in dealing with accused or arrested persons will certainly require the judges at every level of the judiciary to possess the skills and sufficient knowledge to be able to interpret the existing legal codes on the basis of the human rights provisions. The judges need to be conversant with the relevance of the new human rights provisions in the judicial decision making under the new constitutional dispensation of Ethiopia. One important promotional task will therefore be to train the judges in the interpretation and effect of all binding human rights on the existing legal body; the commission could play a key role in this respect.

Another relevant item pertains to the necessary link between human rights and development. The full realization of respect for human rights as prescribed in the constitution primarily requires the development and the fair distribution of resources in society (schools, health, resource availability). In fact, the actual realization of human rights should not focus attention on losses and/or gains of competing elite groups for political power, as tends to be the case. Often the positions of politically marginalized elite groups is at risk and therefore their rights violated in a squabble for power with the members of the ruling establishment to the extent that several members and opposition groups end up in prison, tortured or subjected to prolonged detention without trial. Human rights NGOs have often focussed their activities on filing cases of prisoners. It is, nevertheless, unfortunate that more structural violations of human rights take place in the broader range of economic, social, and cultural reality which are often neglected by human rights NGOs. This negligence makes human rights NGOs elite-oriented. This is not to dismiss or overlook the rights of expression and dissent by members of political opposition to the ruling establishment. What we are alluding to is the not infrequent lack of balance in the focus and reporting by human rights NGOs of such abuses. This calls for a new pattern of awareness and method of working to deal with structural deprivation of the rights of groups in society: children, women, the disabled, minorities, etc. No human rights organization has made efforts to report on the need to research the situation at the local level, to identify groups or persons at risk of violation and abuse. For instance, in government and non-government organs or periodicals produced in Ethiopia, one rarely finds any explicit reference to the structural deprivation or socio-cultural abuse of groups in society.

As discussed earlier, the constitution of 1994 recognizes the independence of the judiciary in Article 78 of Chapter 9, where the structures and powers of the courts are determined. Article 79(2) declares: “The courts of any level shall be free from interference or influence of any government body, official of government or from any other source.” To realise this independence, competence and accountability of judges, adequate training and skills are needed in addition to laying down the rules that govern their appointment and removal. The level of education, in particular, of the state prosecutors and judges vis-à-vis the standard of performance expected of them towards human rights demands further training. One serious constraint resulting from the decentralization of authority to the regions and the exercise of lower levels of participation relates to the lack of sufficient trained personnel to build the multi-structural administration and judiciary.

In addition, procedural guarantees including legal aid, an appeal system, fair trial, and equality before the law are given in principle in the constitution. Nevertheless, the weak and developing court system with a severe shortage of trained staff but inexperienced personnel lacking the confidence to function independently of the regional bosses and the traditional perception by the public that the court is an extension of state power rather than a law enforcement body will make the full realization of the constitutionally guaranteed rights uncertain. There are provisions for procedures and institutions to ensure the execution of the constitutionally guaranteed rights. This provides the context to examine the need to create national commissions as quasi-judicial institutional safeguards that complement and provide a considerable amount of legal and paralegal assistance to the judiciary and the persons involved, who would otherwise probably be denied justice as a result of serious delays. In particular, the lack of the regular judicial safeguards at the regional and local levels highlights the dire need for the establishment of complementary institutions of human rights protection such as the commissions under review. In circumstances where the judges' political independence in the regional judiciary could be potentially threatened, the work of the commissions becomes all the more indispensable for the independence of the very institution of the judiciary and the judges.

"In 1994 an incident was reported in the Southern region, one of the regional constituents of the Ethiopian federation, about a judge in the high court of the Shaketcho who was threatened for issuing an arrest of the Head of the Economic Section of the Shaketcho zone, for alleged homicide. The accused reacted by writing a letter to suspend the judge from his duties. While the judge was travelling to the regional capital and later to Addis Ababa, to seek support which he failed to receive, the police arrested and tortured the wife of the judge now at large" (Pausewang, 1996:226). Reports of such incidents are not uncommon in the regions.

Another potential constraint to the effective functioning of the institutions of human rights protection relates to the autochthonous practices and religious institutions which have continued to function at a limited level with substantial influence in society. Article 91(2) of the 1994 constitution declares the "government shall have the duty to support on the basis of equality the growth and enrichment of cultures and traditions that are compatible with the fundamental rights, human dignity, democratic norms and ideals, and the provisions of the constitution". The constitution also guarantees freedom of religion and specifically authorizes Islam and the institution of Sharia courts if the disputants agree, to hear cases arising from religious and family conflicts. The continuity of this practice brings the long-standing debate on universalism versus relativism in human rights into the picture, which will certainly have some relevance to the existing judicial practice in Ethiopia as reflected in the multiplicity of the courts in the country. This debate is beyond the intended scope of this essay but will have a persistent impact on the function of human rights institutions as long as cultural practices continue to be accorded status in the municipal law. The fact that religious institutions remain active in the practice of customary law in certain spheres of social life (family) does not mean that the institutions of human rights protection will be compromised in their activities. As far as the functioning of the commission is concerned, we feel that both human rights traditions can be promoted within the same system, although conditions for their implementation may need to take account of contextual differences. The fact that the new constitution of Ethiopia includes both traditions testifies to the approach it has adopted.

One significant point regarding the 1994 constitution relates to the international conventions ratified by the government. The incorporation of these provisions in the municipal law will create a compatible regime for the implementation of the conventions domestically. However, problems related to the realizability of certain conventions declared in the constitution produces another challenge to the effective functioning of the constitution.

For example, obligatory basic child education is contained in the 1994 convention which Ethiopia has signed. The implementation of this convention in rural Ethiopia where 85% of the people live is limited due to social, cultural and economic factors. Children of both sexes are among the vulnerable groups in society subjected to a variety of harmful cultural and social practices, abuse and exploitation. It is a common practice in rural Ethiopia to assign duties to children from the age of 5 which could have serious implications for their physical and mental growth. Exploitative labor practices including engagement of underage children in activities like fetching water, collecting firewood from distant locations, watching livestock, gathering crops without caring for their physical safety, let alone giving them access to basic education, are predominant practices in rural Ethiopia. One would contend that in the Ethiopian rural community, helping the family on the farmland, caring for younger siblings and taking part in other family activities should not be considered as exploitation. It is in fact part of the education and socialization process of the child. However, in many cases heavy tasks are assigned to the child at such an early age that it could endanger his/her physical and mental development. Article 32 of the UN convention on the right of children declares that child work becomes exploitative when it is hazardous, harmful to a child's health and normal development, or interferes with the child's education. It is also the case that very many children are forced to work as early as the age of 6 as a result of poverty: many are engaged in hawking newspapers, cigarettes, or shining shoes as the main breadwinners of their families at the age when they should be obtaining a basic education.

There are also customary practices and expressions that are harmful to the development of the child. Among the most serious and pervasive of female abuses is the practice of genital mutilation and underage marriage common all over Ethiopia. Verbal abuse through proverbs and expressions that hurt the feelings of the child and have long-term psychological implications is not uncommon in many cultures of the Ethiopian society: "Children and dogs are supposed to eat whatever is provided to them" (Oromigna proverb); "Do not play with a child, he will prick your body with something sharp" (Amharic proverb). These examples of cultural expressions reflect the perception of and the way children are treated in society. Similar abusive expressions which entail material and psychological effect on the life of the child exist in other cultures in the country as well.

In 1994, Ethiopia ratified the UN convention on child rights. The question is in a culture where a "threefold" violation of child rights is usual (family, school, society), how are the international conventions to which Ethiopia has committed itself and the national provisions guaranteed in the constitution of 1994 to be implemented? While the practical application is likely to be inhibited due to the scarcity of resources and the continuity of well-entrenched traditional practices, it is hoped that promotional efforts using various means of communication and awareness-raising programmes will be more fruitful. In the absence of courts and effective legal mechanisms to implement these conventions, the institutions of human rights protection should carry out promotional tasks and protection of children from exploitative and abusive practices.

Implementing the provisions for the rights of the child as the constitution dictates and tackling the problem of child abuse in such a socio-cultural profile are indubitably challenging tasks. A great deal of effort is indeed needed to raise the awareness of the community to encourage attitudinal changes through which harmful traditional practices and values could be molded into a better child-raising regime. To this end, the Commission could play a positive role by helping design training and awareness-raising programs for the community.

Schools in Ethiopia are among the institutional environments where the child's rights are violated through, among others, corporal punishment. By the same token, the school system could provide an ideal opportunity for undertaking promotional activities on child rights to effect changes in the attitude of the school communities and the society at large. In this respect, one of the Commission's primary targets will be to enhance the development of programs aimed at schoolchildren and teachers.

While multiple court structures are likely to interpret the child rights issues according to the respective cultural and religious beliefs, the institution of the Ombudsman and the Human Rights Commission could cut across these cultural and religious values in terms of raising their awareness and in looking for alternative means regarding the implementation of the conventions. Furthermore, in situations where national legal specifications do not exist to be used by the courts as reference documents, one could imagine the service the human rights institutions could render. Exploitation of child labor, forced conscription of children into military service and exposure to danger, forced early marriage, mistreatment and domestic violence resulting in walk outs ending up on the street, and verbal violence are among the most serious child abuse practices besetting the Ethiopian society today which should be targetted.

It might take a long time before appropriate legal mechanisms are in place with a mandate to investigate cases of such practices as constitutional prescriptions per se are not sufficient to implement the provisions. However, the promotional activities of the commissions could be targeted towards attitudinal change. In addition, the Human Rights Commission will certainly be of immense assistance to the regular judicial bodies by gathering and verifying facts. The complementary role of the commissions will be invaluable.

The result of the work of the Commission, although not enforceable in strictly legal terms, could be enhanced by involving and utilizing positive values of traditional institutions in certain cases. However, the quality of the work will be determined by its objectivity and method of operation.

Another setback that could possibly limit the institutions relates to political constraints. The continuity of elements inherited from the old authoritarian political culture and possible restrictions put on the democratization process by those who would prefer to maintain the status quo could become hindrances. These limitations undermine further the credibility of the institutions under discussion. It is also possible that some appointed members of the Commission may at the same time be affiliated to the government or the ruling party, or even still hold government positions, which is a potential source of conflictual interests, thereby compromising their ability to function as independent members of the Commission. In this respect, some basic conditions must be promulgated from the outset in relation to the nomination of commissioners: the nominee may not be a member of the executive branch of the government, the nominee should not be hand-picked but chosen by a wide consensus for personal integrity, and the nominee may not be associated directly or indirectly with any state institution.

In the Ethiopian context, where society has been polarized along ideological, ethnic and to some extent religious lines, it is no easy task to identify such persons. It is at this critical juncture that initiatives should be accompanied by a determined government policy aimed at upholding the independence of the Commission with sufficient power to effectively fulfill its functions. Efforts must be made to avoid all forms of subordination of the Commission to any political influence, which would only undermine its effectiveness. In addition, the Commission's authority to publish measures taken should not be subjected to government control. Only this level of competence and authority can ensure the credibility and legitimacy of the Commission.

The issue of status is another area to be examined in this regard. The fact that the investigation and decision produced by the Commission on certain cases of violation filed by individuals or groups are not legally enforceable and indeed its lack of formal power would mean that the institution will make no significant impression on public perception. In a culture where authority and respect for office holders are derived less from the quality of their work than from the legal competence and authority given to them to enforce it in a coercive manner, the institutions will have great difficulty in being taken seriously by the public.

Communication and infrastructural problems are other areas that need to be assessed with respect to the functioning of the commission. In principle, in order to fulfill their tasks, the national commissions must be visible and accessible to the public, which must develop confidence in their impartiality and method of operation. However, given the disparity between the urban and rural communities, they are likely to focus on promotional and protectional activities in urban areas, hence limiting their accessibility to the larger public in the rural areas where the masses of the populace are concentrated. It should also be noted that the illiteracy rate in rural Ethiopia is much higher than that in urban centres, resulting in a low level of awareness of their rights in the former. This is not to suggest that the new human rights institutions need to reach out directly to all rural communities as doing so would incur insurmountable resource costs. Alternatively, the commission must cooperate with strategic groups that could complement part of its activities. Grassroots NGOs and other groups, provided the groundwork is prepared, could play a considerable role in the promotion of human rights by publicizing and disseminating relevant information to the public throughout the country.

Civil society and existing human rights organizations could make a considerable contribution. Societies with a relatively strongly organized civil society can minimize possible human rights abuses by their own states. In addition, they can serve as an important line of defense against gross violations of fundamental freedoms. They can appraise cases and complaints that need to be addressed under the judicial or quasi-judicial safeguards. As the infrastructural and communication limitations are expected to produce a serious challenge to the work of the human rights commissions, the active participation of civil society organisations and NGOs in the protection and promotion of human rights becomes indispensable.

The service of NGOs and civil society organizations may range from expert and consultancy services to monitoring human rights abuses and submission of complaints on behalf of the individuals or groups from locations that for some reason are inaccessible to the commissions. In view of this, a rule of procedure may have to be included in the establishment of the commission regarding cooperation between NGOs and the national commission in the performance of human rights protection and promotional activities. In the absence of coordinated efforts between the national commissions on the one hand and NGOs and civil society organizations on the other, no significant breakthrough can be expected in the implementation of the provisions.

What role do existing human rights NGOs in Ethiopia play in the protection and promotion of human rights? The Ethiopian Human Rights Council (EHRCO), established in 1991 following the downfall of the Mengistu regime, has been actively involved in the collection of allegations and reports of human rights violations in Ethiopia. Although not an officially registered human rights organization, allegedly seen by government authorities as politically motivated, EHRCO has regularly published reports of alleged violations of human rights including extra-judicial killings, disappearances, tortures, violations of the right to work, etc. (EHRCO Report 1995) without serious consequences for its operation. Its founder, a former Professor of Geography at Addis Ababa University, is an outspoken critic of the government on its politics of decentralization and human rights. The government in turn has consistently refused to register EHRCO on the grounds of its affiliation to the political opposition.

The Ethiopian Human Rights and Peace Center (EHRPC), another human rights organization, was established in 1991 at the Law Faculty of the University of Addis Ababa, with the stated task to promote human rights through research and dissemination of information on human rights. EHRPC, being a research-oriented institution, has refrained from active involvement in reporting human rights violations.

The Human Rights Department in the Office of the Attorney General is a government institution basically set up to investigate allegations of human rights violations.

An important step taken by the government towards the establishment of human rights institutions involved preparing the conference on the establishment of the HRC and the Ombudsman in May 1998, followed by the public consultative seminars in 1999. Currently, the drafting of the legislation for the establishment of the commission is under way, a significant step in the institutionalization of a new human rights system in the country.

V. Concluding Remarks

All of the above show the extent of the impact the fundamental Bill of Rights enumerated in the constitution will have on society. From the vantage point of the Constitution which has given the law enforcement bodies an explicit role in the implementation process, it can be stated that one of the principles upon which the present government of Ethiopia was founded is the commitment to the respect of human rights based on the UN Declaration. It can also be added that this lays the basis for Ethiopia's accession to the various international human rights conventions.

No particular model of human rights commission has been proposed in the foregoing discussion. Nevertheless, it should be emphasised that the legislation and functioning of the forthcoming institutions of human rights protection in Ethiopia must reflect the objective realities of the society for which they have been designed. In this regard, the socio-economic, cultural, political and ideological elements briefly presented above are important foundations for the institutions. The structure and content of human rights should reflect the principles governing the relationship between individuals, society and the state.

The establishment of national institutions of human rights protection is important for strengthening human rights protection. It must be noted, however, that the functioning of such institutions can only become effective if the safeguards inherent in the legal structures are properly implemented by an independent and accessible judiciary. It is also vital that government policy guidelines are in place so that the Commission can play a key role in promoting and protecting human rights, including the mandate to investigate human rights violations by armed, paramilitary and police forces deployed in various parts of the country.

It must also be reiterated that these institutions should not be seen as an extension of the central state to the community. In principle, they derive their legal existence and human and financial resources apart from the state. The promotion of the Human Rights Commission as an independent institution for enhancing human rights needs to be vigorously encouraged.

What has been highlighted in the aforementioned discussion ought not to be interpreted as suggesting the postponement of the establishment of the Commission until the most essential prerequisites are fulfilled. This discussion is rather meant to illuminate the main concerns and issues surrounding the proposed institutions so that they can be carefully scrutinized prior to their creation. The authors of this piece are convinced that the creation of the institutions in Ethiopia, in spite of potential setbacks, will usher in a new phase of the promotion and protection of human rights. It is certainly true that the shortcomings outlined above will act as a brake upon the effectiveness of the activities of the Commission for years to come. Nevertheless, the constitutionally guaranteed rights are likely to provide the Commission with the legal mechanisms to enhance its protective and promotional activities, and thus, gradually but surely, the Commission will effectively realize its mandated tasks.

References

The Ethiopian Constitution of 1931.
The Revised Ethiopian Constitution of 1955.
The Ethiopian Constitution of 1987.
The Ethiopian Constitution of 1994.
The Charter of The Transitional Government of Ethiopia, 1991.
Markakis, John. *Ethiopia: Anatomy of a Traditional Polity*, Oxford: Clarendon Press. 1974.
McClellan, Charles. State Transformation and Social Reconstruction in Ethiopia: The Allure of the South. *International Journal of African Historical Studies*, 17, No.4 (1984): 657–675.

Almedia, Manoel de. The History of High Ethiopia or Abassia. In C.F. Beckingham and G.W.B. Huntingford (eds.), *Some Records of Ethiopia 1593–1646*. Kraus reprint Limited, 1967.

Gebru Tareke. *Ethiopia: Power and Protest: Peasant revolts in the Twentieth Century*. Cambridge, etc.: Cambridge University Press,1991.

Baxter, Paul T.W. Ethiopia's Unacknowledged Problem: the Oromo. In Lewis, I.M. (ed), *Nationalism and Self Determination in the Horn of Africa*. London: Ethaca Press, 1978.

Addis Hiwet. *A Critical Political Vocation: Reflections on the Ethiopian Intelligentsia*. Studies in Ethiopian Politics: Social Science Monograph Series, Discussion Paper 3. London.

Eze, Ostia C. *Human Rights in Africa*. Nigeria: Macmillan. 1984.

Furley, Oliver. *Conflict in Africa*. London: I.B. Tauris Publishers.1995.

Taddesse Tamirat. *Church and State in Ethiopia, 1270–1527*. Oxford: Clarendon Press, 1972.

Chronique de Theodros II, Trans. into French by C. Mondon- Vidailhet, Paris, 1905.

Clapham, Christopher. *Haile Selassie's Government*. Praeger: New York, 1969.

The Ethiopian Human Rights Council Report of 1995. Addis Ababa.

The Paris Principles: Principles Related to the Status of National Institutions.

UNGA Resolution 48/134.

United Nations. United Nations Economic and Social Council, Commission on Human Rights, *Involuntary Disappearances*, UNDoc.E/CN4/1995/36.30 December 1994.

H. Gebreselassie. *The Role of the Foreign Element in the Making and Unmaking of Local Polities in the Horn of Africa*, PhD Thesis, University of Amsterdam, 1994.

US Department of State. *Ethiopia, Human Rights Practices*, 1995, US Department of State. Washington, March 1996.

Pausewang, Siegfried. Ethiopia. In: *Yearbook of Human Rights in Developing Countries 1996*.

Part One

Chapter I

Background Papers

The Structure of Human Rights in Federations

Yash Ghai*

I propose in this paper to discuss some aspects of the protection of human rights in federations or autonomy systems. The issues I want to discuss are: (a) whether federations are better than other political systems in protecting rights; (b) whether the national constitutional norms for human rights bind "states" (using here the terminology of the Ethiopian Constitution to refer to sub-national units); (c) the effect of international human rights instruments on federal jurisdiction and the consequences for the protection of human rights; (d) the modification of Bills of Rights to suit ethnically based federations; (e) the consequences of the national economic system on rights. In the conclusion, I attempt briefly to relate these issues to the Ethiopian Constitution adopted in 1995.

It is difficult to generalize about these issues across federations. The reason is that the structure of rights in a federation depends on a number of factors which vary from one federation to another. I mention these factors now before discussing them later. The importance of the constitutional protection of rights has altered over time. Although it is now standard practice to include Bills of Rights in constitutions (whether of federal or unitary states), this was not always the case. Secondly, legal or political traditions place different values on the constitutional protection of rights, the English tradition for a long time being to avoid guarantees of rights in constitutions. Thirdly, the structure of rights frequently depends on whether the federation is achieved by aggregation or disaggregation. By aggregation I mean the situation whereby a federation is formed by the coming together of several independent states to form one union (as in the US, Switzerland, Australia and to some extent Canada).[1] Federations by disaggregation are those that result from the decentralisation of power in what were previously unitary states (as in India, Spain, Bosnia, Kenya for a short while after independence, and Ethiopia). States which come together to form a federation have their own constitutions which may provide for protection of rights, so that either it is considered appropriate that rights continue to be protected at that level and no specific arrangements are made at the federal level (as happened at first with the US Constitution) or to limit protection at the federal level in

*Department of Law, University of Hong Kong. I am grateful to Ms Swati Singh for research assistance.

[1]Canada is an interesting case because it represents elements of both aggregation and disaggregation. Quebec and Ontario were one territorial unit before they were divided into different provinces, while what are now other provinces were separate colonies before the establishment of the Canadian federation. Currently plans to give autonomy to "reserves" of the first nations (or aboriginal peoples) would represent disaggregation.

K. Hossain et al. (eds), Human Rights Commissions and Ombudsman Offices, 41–53.

relation to matters under the jurisdiction of the federal authorities (as in the second phase of the US Constitution). In federations by disaggregation, the general practice is to have national norms which apply throughout the federation, dispensing with separate state protection.

A fourth factor is the purpose for which the federation is formed. To simplify, one can divide federations into two broad categories. First, there are federations which are formed for purpose of defence, or to decentralize decision-making due to vastness of territory, or to increase economic strength. Such federations are formed on the basis of equal rights of citizens regardless of which state they live in; they cut across race, religion and other distinctions, to devolve power to territorial units. The second kind are those which choose federal arrangements to recognize religious or ethnicity diversity. (The distinction is not always easy to make, for the formation of the Canadian federation owes itself to both motives – and this is reflected in the differences in constitutional arrangements for the province of Quebec from those for other provinces). The first type places a high value on common national standards of rights and responsibilities, and consequently seek a uniform set of human rights. The second kind values or least recognizes different cultural practices, which makes it difficult to have one common set of human rights.

Before I examine how these issues are reflected in law or practice in different federations. I would like to review briefly two major developments of the last half of this century which have had a profound effect on constitution making and the design of states. The first is the emergence of an internationally accepted regime of rights. The first was the struggle for decolonisation which was based primarily on the right to self-determination and civil and political rights. Most constitutions which accompanied the grant of independence contained bills of rights. The second reason was the mandate of the UN to promote the development and protection of rights as a response to the atrocities committed by the Nazis and the Fascists. Under this mandate a large number of international covenants and treaties were negotiated, starting with the Universal Declaration of Human Rights fifty years ago. Consequently we have, more or less, international agreement on certain norms as constituting minimum guarantees of rights. By ratifying international conventions, states undertake to promote rights guaranteed in them. It is then natural to give effect to these obligations through constitutions or other organic laws. The United Nations support for such an approach is manifest from instances when national constitutions have been drafted under its auspices, as in Cambodia or, indirectly, Bosnia. It is hard to conceive of a constitution being drafted today without an extensive bill of rights. The emergence of a strong regime of rights has been parallelled by another development, the emergence of ethnic groups seeking constitutional recognition, which in some respects seems to run counter to it. The rise of ethnic groups in contemporary times can be traced to the end of colonial empires. In most cases imperial powers had brought disparate peoples under common boundaries, and in some cases had divided an ethnic group between two or more states. As independence became a possibility, ethnic groups, especially if they were a minority, became conscious of their separateness from other groups. They demanded either a separate state for themselves or a substantial degree of autonomy. These demands were resisted by other groups, although the colonial powers were often sympathetic. Thus Britain divided India into two parts, one of which (Pakistan) was to be the "homeland" of Muslims (and recommended partition plans for Palestine and Eritrea, among others). In other places autonomy systems were established, as in Eritrea vis-a-vis Ethiopia, regionalism in Kenya, federation in Indonesia, etc. However, these federal or autonomy systems did not survive for long, for the majority were driven by desire to create a "nation-state" out of the new state. The dominant ideology of the time was modernisation, which emphasized the centralisation of political power and the enhanced capacity of the state. It was frequently argued that bills of rights which aimed to protect rights of all individuals were sufficient protection for minorities. Minority ethnic groups continued their fight for separate statehood or autonomy, but failed to secure external support. There were exceptions to this, of which the best known case is Indian support for the secession of Bangladesh. The Soviet Union, inspired by Lenin, had a different concept of the place of "nationalities" in the constitutional system from that in liberal systems. It provided for considerable autonomy for "nationalities", defined largely in terms of language, even permitting them to secede from the Union. In reality, however, the dominance of the Communist Party negated the constitutional autonomy of these groups.

It was with the collapse of the Soviet Union that attitudes towards the claims of ethnic groups changed. For the collapse of the Soviet Union meant the end of the Cold War, which resulted in the support by big powers for clientelist states, which now had to make their peace with dissident groups. Second, successors to the Soviet Union and other East European states had to come to terms with their minorities. Numerous conflicts erupted throughout the region on the basis of ethnic differences, most horrendously in former Yugoslavia. The settlement of these conflicts resulted in a changed political landscape, influenced to a significant extent by the constitutional recognition of ethnicity. This provided the impetus for the renewal of ethnic claims in other parts of the world, and some settlement of disputes by recognising them (as in the Philippines in relation to Muslims in Mindanao, Bangladesh in relation to the Chittagong Hills tract and the intensification of efforts for a settlement for East Timor). The new Ethiopian Constitution is an outstanding example of a state which seeks to root itself in the recognition of its wide ethnic diversity.

As far as rights are concerned, the political recognition of ethnicity has at least two consequences. First it compels the acceptance of group rights. This is reflected in the new convention on indigenous peoples, the General Assembly Declaration on the Rights of Minorities, and in various instruments of the Council of Europe and the Organization of Security and Co-operation in Europe. This recognition goes against a strong tradition in international human rights ideology which regards only individuals as bearers of rights. The second consequence is that there may be a conflict between individual rights and group rights. This problem is illustrated most clearly in the position of the women of the group concerned. Among many aboriginal groups in Canada there is a rule that a woman of the group who marries an outsider forfeits her rights to land or other resources of the community. The same rule does not apply to men who marry outside the community. The rule applying to women not only (effectively) violates her right to marry a person of her choice, but also discriminates against her. Another example comes from India where the law provided that the maintenance rights of divorced Muslim women are to be determined by the Sharia, not the statutory law of India which provides a better remedy for divorced women. It then seems that a choice must be made between a woman's right to equality or the autonomy or the right of the group.

Ethnically based federations therefore raise the issue of the extent to which there should be norms and standards applying nationally. Not all human rights norms may be compatible with the customs or rules of an ethnic group, as the above illustrations show. (There may also be problems of compatibility as regards modes of trials or forms of punishments). It is possible to confer group autonomy without compromising human rights standards, as for example where the group is interested primarily in exercising significant decision making powers in the geographical area where it lives. To some extent this has been achieved in India where the federation can be described as linguistically based. There are not necessarily any great cultural differences between these linguistic groups, so that the adoption of common standards does not pose a problem. However, the problems of compatibility arise in an acute form where the ethnic groups are religious or culturally based. (It is partly for this reason that India has resisted accepting religion as the basis of territorial organizations). When cultural differences are great, or when a community is still tightly organized around its ancient cultural values and traditions (as in many parts of Ethiopia), there can arise major problems of compatibility. There are various options to deal with this difficulty. One is to provide the universal application of national norms in relation to the areas covered by federal jurisdiction (which was the US position after the first amendments), leaving diverse standards to apply in the states. Another is to subordinate all laws and policies to national standards. A compromise between these positions is to allow some limited exemptions from the national standards for the purpose of enforcing customary group rules. On the other hand, it could be said that the more the federal arrangements provide for the recognition of diversity, the stronger the need for uniform national standards as cohesion and identity for the country.

Human Rights in Federations

The scope of rights protected in federations

The scope of rights protected in federations vary as between one federation and another. They also vary over time, as new rights may be introduced as the need for them arises or is recognized. The salient level of government at which rights are protected may also change, due both to constitutional amendments or the energy with which a particular government protects rights. These propositions may be illustrated by an examination of provisions in some federations. I start with that of the US.

Although the Constitution of the United States binds both federal and state authorities, many of its provisions relate only to the federal authorities. Each of the fifty states of the United States of America has its own constitution. Thus, the altogether novel principle of modern federalism which emerged at the Federal Convention contained two distinctive features: it preserved for the states a significant constituent power by involving them in the workings of the national government, principally through the election of federal officials; and it required that the Constitution recognize and protect the division of powers between the federal government and the states so as to insure individual liberty and self-government.

The US Constitution, as originally enacted in 1787, was adopted to ensure adequate protection for rights but did not have a Bill of Rights. Express constitutional protection of rights made their first appearance in the bill of rights of states as independent entities, prior to the federation. These declarations of rights were important in the creation of federal Bill of Rights. At first the US Constitution did not contain a bill of rights on the grounds that the federal authority was rather limited. This did not satisfy many states, who ratified the Constitution only on the undertaking that there would be a federal bill of rights. Consequently a Bill of Rights was added by the first nine Amendments (1791). The first amendment was the most extensive, guaranteeing the freedom of religion and prohibiting laws which provide for the establishment of religion, the abridgement of the freedom of speech, or the press, the right to assemble peaceably and to petition the government for the redress of grievances. Most amendments deal with rights in relation to the legal process.

The addition of a Bill of Rights binding on the federal authorities did not help in the protection of rights in states which practised slavery or in other ways denied rights to coloured people. Following the Civil War and the recognition that not all states could be trusted to safeguard the rights of the newly freed black citizens, the Thirteenth, Fourteenth and Fifteenth Amendments were adopted respectively in 1865, 1868 and 1870. The Thirteenth Amendment abolished slavery and involuntary servitude throughout the US. In retrospect the Fourteenth Amendment was the most important. It prohibits states from making any law which abridges the privileges and immunities of US citizens and prohibits states from depriving any person of life, liberty, or property, without due process of law, or denying to any person within its jurisdiction the equal protection of the law. The Fifteenth Amendment guarantees the right of all US citizens to vote regardless of race, colour or previous condition of servitude. All the three amendments empower the Federal Legislature (Congress) to enforce these rights through appropriate legislation. The attempt on the part of the federal government to enforce these amendments, particularly Fourteenth Amendment, were frustrated by the US Supreme Court in the *Slaughterhouse Cases*, 83 US 36 (1873) and *The Civil Rights Cases*, 109 US 3 (1883). Other rulings limited their immediate impact. Consequently the responsibility to protect rights reverted to state governments in the latter part of the 19th century.

Nonetheless, doubts about the states' commitment to protecting individual rights led to intermittent national action to secure rights. An example of this was the Nineteenth Amendment which abolished gender as a criterion for the right to vote. Consciousness of human rights changed drastically after the two world wars. Yet the major innovation in protecting rights during the 20th century has been the expansion in the role played by federal courts – and particularly the US Supreme Court – through the process of constitutional litigation. The Court has adopted the selective incorporation doctrine, under which provisions of the Bill of Rights become fully applicable to state governmental action. In addition, some important rulings have given broader scope to federal constitutional provisions and have imposed new and often detailed requirements on the states. In effect these rulings encouraged litigants to base their claims on federal constitutional guarantees and precedents and to ignore state law. The Court started giving a wider interpretation to the due process clause in the Fourteenth Amendment according to which gradually all the rights included in the first nine amendments were incorporated in the Fourteenth Amendment. Similarly, the right to equality in the Fourteenth Amendment was included in the due process clause of the Fifth Amendment.

States are free to provide a greater protection of rights than under the national constitution. The US federal system of dual constitutionalism requires that a balance be struck as to who is to protect, and to what extent, particular rights. In *City of Mesquite* v. *Aladdin's Castle* 455 US 283 (1982), the Court stated that a state court is entirely free to read its own state's constitution more broadly than this Court reads the federal Constitution, or to reject the mode of analysis used by this Court in favour of a different analysis of its corresponding constitutional guarantee. If there is a question of jurisdiction to be decided, the Supreme Court held in *Sterling* v. *Cupp*, 466 US 736 (1984) that the proper sequence is to analyse the state's law, including its constitutional law, before reaching a federal constitutional claim. This is required, not for the sake either of parochialism or of style, but because the state does not deny any right claimed under the federal constitution when the claim before the court in fact is fully met by state law. As to jurisdiction, the federal government may make laws binding individual citizens but only on matters within its jurisdiction such as war, peace, negotiations, foreign trade, etc. The Constitution has reserved residuary and sovereign powers on the states.

The Canadian federation similarly shows progressive changes in the structure of rights. The British North America Act of 1867, which brought the federation into existence, did not contain a bill of rights, influenced by the English notion that rights are best protected through the political process reflecting the supremacy of an elected legislature. However, since one reason for federating was the co-existence of Anglophones and Francophones, there is some protection for the two linguistic groups. Section 133 provides for bilingualism in the federal and Quebec legislatures and courts. Additionally, laws of Canada and Quebec have to be published in both languages. Section 93 protects the right to establish denominational schools. In 1951 the federal Parliament was given the power to provide old age pension, without prejudice to any provincial scheme for similar purpose.

Unlike the situations in the US, the constitutions of units which formed the federation or joined it subsequently, did not contain any bill of rights either. It was therefore held that neither the federal nor the provincial governments had exclusive jurisdiction over matters relating to human rights (*Saumar* v. *City of Quebec and AG of Quebec* (1953) 4 LR 641). Despite the absence of the constitutional protection of rights at either level, courts did play some role in protecting rights. This was done principally by invalidating legislation which prejudiced rights on the basis that the subject matter of the legislation was beyond the competence of the enacting body. Therefore the jurisprudence of rights became closely connected with questions of the division of legislative powers between the federation and provinces. This was hardly a satisfactory basis for the protection of rights, an issue which assumed increasing importance after the second world war with the mandate of the UN and the recognition of the failure of the Canadian legal system to protect minorities.

It was in order to overcome this lacuna that the federal Parliament adopted the Canadian Bill of Rights in 1958. The Bill covered the standard civil and political rights, but its impact was very limited. For one, its status was that of ordinary legislation (although one distinguished judge tried to establish a quasi-constitutional status for it). Secondly, it applied only to federal legislation. Thirdly, even subsequent federal legislation could be immunized from its effect by a declaration to that effect.

These defects could only be overcome through a bill of rights which was incorporated into the Constitution and was made applicable throughout the federation. That step was taken with the enactment of the Canadian Charter of Rights and Freedoms in 1982. The Charter applies to both the federal and provincial government in respect of all matters within the authority of their legislature. It has a more extensive set of rights than in the Bill of Rights. However, it suffers from one defect in common with the Bill of Rights – the "notwithstanding clause" whereby either the federal or provincial legislatures may opt out of a provision of the Charter in respect of a particular law (Article 33). But the article is more tightly drafted than the parallel provision in the Bill. Certain rights may not be suspended by this device (these include mobility and language rights). Secondly, the exclusion of a right is valid only for a maximum of five years, although this does not prevent the continuation of the exclusion for similar periods by fresh enactment's.

The Canadian Charter was enacted in order to strengthen a Canadian identity by providing for national values and standards which cut across linguistic or ethnic divisions, which were seen to threaten the unity of the country. For that reason it was resisted by a sizeable section of the Quebec francophones. But the Charter goes to considerable lengths to make concessions to the diversity of languages and cultures of the Canadian people perhaps more than any other bill of rights. I deal with this issue later.

I turn finally to India which provides an example of the structure of rights in federations of more recent vintage. The Indian Constitution was adopted on 26th November 1949 and was brought into force on 26th January 1950. Unlike many other federal constitutions, the constitution of India covers not only the powers and structure of the federal government but also that of states, which do not have their own separate constitutions. The Constitution has a chapter on Fundamental Rights (Part III) and a chapter on Directive Principles of State Policy (Part IV). These bind both the federal and state authorities.

While the chapter on fundamental rights generally protects the civil and political rights, the chapter on directive principles generally protects the social and economic rights. The difference between the fundamental rights and directive principles is that while fundamental rights are enforceable in the courts, directive principles are not. However, it does not mean that the directive principles are less important for the simple reason that they are not judicially enforceable. Through judicial interpretation several directive principles have been converted into fundamental rights and have become judicially enforceable. Similarly a directive principle enforced through legislation also becomes judicially enforceable. In *Bandhua Muktl Morcha* v. *Union of India*, AIR 1984 SC 802 it was held that once legislation in pursuance of a directive principle has been passed, the courts can order a state to enforce the law, particularly when non-enforcement of law leads to denial of a fundamental right. Article 37 of the Constitution emphatically states that directive principles are nevertheless fundamental in the governance of the country and it shall be the duty of the State to apply these principles in making laws either through executive or legislative action. The courts have held that since the judiciary is a part of the State the courts are also under an obligation to enforce the directive principles. Therefore, if in a dispute before the courts a question of enforcement of a directive principle arises the courts do not hesitate to enforce them.

The Indian Constitution also guarantees certain rights in other parts, such as the right to franchising (Article 325), the rights of the minorities (Part XVI), and the freedom of trade, commerce and intercourse (Article 301).

The Indian Constitution provides for a complex scheme for the division of legislative and executive powers between the federal and state authorities. However unlike the Canadian pre-Charter or the present Australian situation, such division has no significance for human rights since the constitutional provisions for rights bind both federal and state authorities. However, some kinds of limitations on rights, as of affirmative action, can only be made by the federal Parliament.

Accommodating Bills of Rights to "Ethnic" Federation

I have already identified problems arising from an overriding Bill of Rights in an "ethnic" federation. Similar problems arise when a religious or ethnic community is recognized as a corporate entity for the purpose of religious or personal law. I discuss here briefly some responses in federations to deal with this difficulty. Federations which avoid an ethnic orientation normally provide for the federal bill of rights to apply throughout the country. We have seen how the US steadily extended the range of protected rights over state laws and acts. The rights guaranteed in the German Basic Law cover laws and policies of both federation and Länder (states). Even in India, which recognizes culture in some sense in its federal scheme, rights are binding on all public authorities. However, the jurisprudence of the US Supreme Court has recognized different moral standards in states by a selective incorporation of "due process" in the states, and has accepted higher protection in state than provided in the national constitution.

In general, it must be said that even ethnic federations do not provide for modifications of bills of rights. A striking modern example comes from the Bosnian Constitution adopted as part of the Dayton Accord. It is hard to imagine a more ethnically based constitution. It provides for separate electorates for different communities (principally Bosnians, Croats and Serbs), joint presidency of a member from each community, mutual vetoes, and federalism. Nevertheless, all authorities are bound by the bill of rights which allegedly draws its inspiration form the Universal Declaration of Human Rights and the two international covenants as well as the Declaration of Rights of Persons Belonging to National or Ethnic, Religious and Linguistic Minorities (Article II.6) The Constitution provides emphatically that both the federal and state ("Entity") authorities "shall ensure the highest level of internationally recognized human rights and fundamental freedoms" (Article II.1). Nevertheless it could be argued that the general scheme of the Constitution and some of its specific provisions (restricting presidency to specified groups) is against the tenor as well as the substance of rights.

In some states (whether federal or not) whose constitution makes a concession to ethnic diversity, a standard provision in bills of rights (deriving from British legacy) is the exemption of personal or religious laws from the some or all provisions of the bill (some have an unnecessarily broad exemption). India provides an example of an uneasy compromise. At the time of the drafting of the constitution, there was a strong move to abolish communal personal laws in favour of a national civil code. This was resisted by the leaders of the Muslim community, who wanted their personal and family relations to continue to be governed by the Sharia. The compromise was to preserve the personal laws of Muslims but to impose some obligation on the state to take steps towards the unification of laws. Thus one the Directive Principles provides, "The State shall endeavour to secure for the citizens a uniform civil code throughout the territory of India" (Article 44).

In recent years the most interesting debates on this issue have taken place in Canada and South Africa. Space allows me to deal only with the Canadian experience. As I have mentioned above, a sizeable number of francophones in Canada resented the adoption of the Charter of Rights and Freedoms. Pierre Trudeau, then Prime Minister, had introduced the Charter explicitly to promote a Canadian identity, around universal liberal values inherent in it. Francophones had made heavy investment in cultivating their own (largely but not solely, linguistically based) identity on the basis of which they claimed special treatment under the Constitution. So their first anxiety was the erosion of their identity or its submergence in a wider Canadian identity. The second concern was that a Charter of Rights universally applicable would make it illegal for Quebec to discriminate against others or to provide for special privileges in regard to the use of French.

Francophones were not the only group who were anxious about the implications of the Charter. The first nations were fearful that the rights and protection they enjoyed under treaties with the British Crown would be affected, and that universal norms derived from western values would undermine their own cultural traditions. Also worried were newer immigrants (who collectively outnumbered the francophones) that the concern with the interests of the francophones and the first nations would eclipse their own cultural practices. So they lobbied for the recognition of the multi-cultural nature of Canadian society. In addition there were groups with more specialized identities, feminists and gays who wanted a recognition of their concerns.

The final shape of the Charter was influenced by the need to accommodate these concerns. The major concession to the francophones was the "notwithstanding" clause which I have already discussed. The recognition of French, a minority language, as an official language of Canada and the province of Brunswick is another" (Articles 16–22). The concerns of the aboriginal peoples are taken care of through a provision which says that the Charter does not abrogate or derogate from their previous rights (or those which may be acquired under future land claim agreements) (Article 25). Finally the concession to the supporters of multi-culturalism is contained in Article 27 which requires the Charter to be interpreted consistently with the "preservation and enhancement of the multicultural heritage of Canadians". The primary responsibility for this lies with the courts, which have already grappled with this difficult concept.

Economic Rights in a Federation

There is a special category of rights in a federation which is connected with the organization and operation of the market economy. This category exists less for the protection of the rights of individuals as for the efficiency of the market. Thus in the US the power to impose import and export duties is vested in the federal authorities, but they are enjoined to ensure that they "shall be uniform throughout the United States" (Article 1, sec. 8). States cannot impose duties on trade within the US (except with the approval of the US Congress for the purpose only of inspection and the resulting revenue must be turned over to the federal exchequer). No duties may be imposed on trade within the US (Article 1, sec. 8). The power to regulate "commerce among the states" is vested in the US Congress, which enables it to overrule local grants of monopolies or other restrictions by states, and to enforce civil rights when connected with inter-state commerce activities. These provisions are intended to ensure equal rights to participate in the national economy. For the same but also broader reasons, it is provided that "citizens of each state shall be entitled to all Privileges and Immunities of Citizens in the several states" (Article IV, sec. 2). The rights of mobility within the federation have been protected by the courts, principally under the principle of the equal protection of laws, although some short period of residence in a state before claiming certain rights (as of pension or free education) has been allowed under stringent conditions.

This pattern of economic laws has been followed in most federations which have a market economy, usually with clearer specification in the constitution than in the US where some doctrines are the result of the jurisprudence of the courts (such as India, Australia and Germany).

International Human Rights and the Structure of Rights

It is customary to provide foreign affairs powers in the federal authorities. In recent decades this power has become the basis of both federal responsibility for and authority over human rights. This development has followed from the adoption of a growing member of international conventions on human rights. Once a state has ratified a convention, it becomes bound under international law to enforce its terms. These obligations then fall under foreign affairs. As a general rule under most federal constitutions, the federal authorities may take whatever legislative or executive steps are necessary to implement these obligations throughout the country, regardless of the legislative division of powers in the constitution. Courts may (or perhaps must) also take international obligations into account in the interpretation of laws. Thus the government or the courts in Australia have been able to protect environmental rights, the rights of refugees, the rights of indigenous peoples and the rights of gays.

The exception to the general rule that federal authorities may enforce international obligations regardless of the constitutional allocation of subject matter as between them and state authorities, is Canada. Canadian courts have held that while the federal authorities may make or sign treaties on any subject, they cannot implement them when the subject matter is within the competence of provinces without the consent of provinces (following a landmark Privy Council decision which held that the federal Parliament could not implement international labour standards on its own; *Attorney-General for Canada* v. *Attorney-General for Ontario* [1937] AC 3260). This does not prevent courts from referring to international treaties or foreign case law on rights in interpreting Canadian law. In fact the courts have referred to foreign materials increasingly since the adoption of the Charter.

General Assessment of Human Rights Record of Federations

The record of federations in protecting rights is so varied that it is hard to generalize. However, there are several theoretical reasons why federations should provide better protection of rights than other forms of state. First, there is the division of powers between the centre and states, which means that no one unit of government has a monopoly of state power. Such a division also serves as a kind of checks and balances. Second, in some federations there is protection of rights at both federal and state level. If government at one level is not supportive of rights, citizens can go to the other level for protection. We have seen how the oppression of blacks in the US was overcome by the initiatives of the federal authorities. Australia has had similar experiences, with the federation being more protective of indigenous people than some states, and also more protective of the environment or minority sexual preferences. It is also noticeable than in the US, when under Nixon and Reagan the federal authorities abandoned their support of rights, some states at least, began to fill in the gap. Thirdly, federalism often generates a culture of dialogue and compromise, and a spirit of tolerance. These qualities are conducive to the enjoyment of rights. Fourthly, federalism may help to solve some difficult political problems that might otherwise lead to the violation of rights. In modern terms one of the principal causes of the violation of rights has been ethnic or religious conflicts. Federalism permits the accommodation of ethnic and other forms of diversity which can help to diffuse ethnic violence.

When one turns from this theoretical position to actual practice, the picture is somewhat varied. On the one hand, some of the countries with notably good record of the respect and protection of rights are federations: the US, Canada, Australia, Germany and Switzerland are obvious examples. India has a somewhat mixed record, but it is arguable that its record would have been worse but for the moderating influence of federalism. But federalism can also generate its own tensions, as in Pakistan–Bangladesh or in the former Yugoslavia, which can lead to wide scale violation of rights. The communist federations did not have a good record but they were perhaps not true federations since power was centralized through the mechanism of the communist party. While it would be simplistic to say that rights are always better protected in federations than other systems, there is some justification for the view that federalism provided better prospects for the protection of rights.

Conclusion: The Case of Ethiopia

In this brief conclusion, I try to relate the preceding analysis of the relationship between the nature of federations and the structure of rights in Ethiopia. Ethiopia can be described as an ethnically based federation. It is federation of "Nations, Nationalities and Peoples" of Ethiopia. A "Nations, Nationality or People" is defined as "a group of people who have or share a large measure of a common culture or similar customs, mutual intelligibility of language, belief in a common or related identities, a common psychological make-up, and who inhabit an identifiable, predominantly contiguous territory (Article 39(5)). The chapter dealing with Fundamental Rights and Freedoms also contains a provision on "Rights of Nations, Nationalities, and Peoples" (Article 39). They are given "an unconditional right to self-determination, including the right to secession" (Article 39(1)). In addition each group has the "right to speak, to write and to develop its own language; the express, to develop and to promote its culture; and to preserve its history" (Article 39(2)). Each group has the right to "a full measure of self-government which includes the right to establish institutions of government in the territory that it inhabits and to equitable representation in state and Federal governments" (Article 39(3)). The states of the Federation "shall be delimited on the basis of the settlement patterns, language, identity and consent of the people concerned" (Article 46). Seven states are established by the Constitution, based presumably on ethnic criteria laid down in Article 46 (Article 47). It is also provided that nations, nationalities and peoples within these states have the right to establish, at any time, their own States (Article 47(2)).

Although the federation is established by "disaggregation", the constitutions of states are not specified in the national Constitution. The adoption of the constitution of a state, consistently with the national Constitution (Article 50(4)), is the responsibility of the state Council (described as the highest organ of state authority). State constitutions therefore have to be consistent with the Bill of Rights, as I show below. A further requirement of state constitutions is that "Adequate power shall be granted to the lowest units of government to enable the People to participate directly in the administration of such units." (Article 50(4)). Presumably a state constitution must be consistent with a state's obligation to "establish a State administration that best advances self-government, a democratic order based on the rule of law, to protect and defend the Federal Constitution" (Article 52(2)(a)). The powers of states are of course those which are prescribed in the national Constitution (Article 52 is the principal source of state powers).

The federal Constitution has extensive provisions for human rights, contained in chapter 3. Article 13 states:

> "1. All Federal and State legislative, executive and judicial organs at all levels shall have the responsibility and duty to respect and enforce the provisions of this Chapter.
> 2. The fundamental rights and freedoms specified in this Chapter shall be interpreted in a manner conforming to the principles of the Universal Declaration of Human Rights, International Covenants on Human Rights and international instruments adopted by Ethiopia."

It is therefore clear that states are bound by the human rights provisions and that they share in the responsibility for the protection of rights. It is also provided that all international agreements ratified by Ethiopia are an integral part of the law of the land (Article 9.4). Since foreign affairs are also vested in the Federation (Article 51.8), it follows that any international human rights agreement ratified by the federal authorities are binding on states.

It is likely that there will be some tensions between the obligations to respect a very extensive set of individual rights, in conformity with the Universal

Declaration and the two Covenants, and the pursuit of group rights. To some extent this tension may be minimized if it is accepted that groups may only pursue their cultural and economic rights within the framework of other rights. This approach is already implicit in Chapter 3, where scope and manner of the rights of children and women are probably inconsistent with customary and cultural practices of many "nations, nationalities and peoples" of Ethiopia. The tension is also likely to be minimized due to the extensive legislative powers of the Federation and particularly its control over land and economic issues, and its ability to establish standards for health, education etc. Until such time as states begin to establish their governments and policies it is difficult to say what the conflicts might be. It is sufficient now to state that the potential is there and deliberate and concerned attempts should be made to ensure that rights and freedoms of all citizens are respected and that cultural practices that are inconsistent with them are gradually eliminated. Similarly it is important that group rights are not asserted in a manner that threatens the rights of dignity of members of other groups. A further problem that may arise is that the ethnic criteria for the establishment of new states may lead some "leaders" to "manufacture" differences between their and the neighbouring communities and to create hostility between them. This could lead to serious conflicts in which rights of individuals would be trampled upon. Again the way to overcome this danger would be to emphasize rights and the commonalities that unite the different communities of Ethiopia rather than to manipulate differences to divide them.

Human Rights and Development

Kamal Hossain*

Evolving Human Rights Norms and Development

The integral link between human rights and development is today recognized beyond dispute. The Agenda for Development adopted by the United Nations General Assembly ("UNGA") in June 1997 records as follows:

"A consensus has emerged, inter alia, that economic development, social development and environmental protection are interdependent and mutually reinforcing components of sustainable development, which is the framework of our efforts to achieve a higher quality of life for all people. In this context, we reaffirm that democracy, development and respect for human rights and fundamental freedoms, including the right to development, are interdependent and mutually reinforcing ..."

"Respect for all human rights and fundamental freedoms, democratic and effective institution's, combatting corruption, transparent, representative and accountable governance, popular participation, an independent judiciary, the rule of law and civil peace are among the indispensable foundations for development. At the same time, we reaffirm that the right to development is a universal and inalienable right and an integral part of human rights."[1]

This evolution spans a period of more than five decades. Major milestones which mark the evolution include the following:

- The UN Charter (1945), which imposed an obligation on all member states to promote the development and recognition of human rights everywhere (Articles 55 and 56);
- The Universal Declaration of Human Rights (1948), which enumerated the universal rights which were to be developed and set forth "a common standard of achievement for all peoples as well as all nations". This declaration was accepted and repeatedly affirmed in a wide variety of international instruments – in Africa, member states of the Organization of African Unity ("OAU") reaffirmed allegiance to the Universal Declaration, when they adopted the OAU Charter;
- The International Covenants on Civil and Political Rights and on Economic, Social and Cultural Rights (1966), which elaborated the rights set out in the Universal Declaration in the form of explicit treaty obligations;

---

*Senior Advocate, Supreme Court of Bangladesh; Chairman, International Committee on Legal Aspects of Sustainable Development, International Law Association; Chairman, Commonwealth Human Rights Initiative Advisory Commission.

[1] Agenda for Development, United Nations New York 1997, pp. 12–13.

K. Hossain et al. (eds), Human Rights Commissions and Ombudsman Offices, 55–62.

- The African Charter on Human and Peoples' Rights and other regional covenants, which re-affirmed commitment to the international human rights instruments;
- Instruments adopted by the UNGA such as the Convention on Elimination of All Forms of Discrimination Against Women (1979) and the Convention against Torture (1984);
- Declarations adopted at UN sponsored world congresses and conferences;
- ILO sponsored World Employment Conference (1976) which formulated the basic needs approach to development, an approach which proclaimed the primacy of rights to food, health, education and development planing and the role of participation in the realisation of basic needs;
- The FAO sponsored World Conference on Agrarian Reform and Rural Development (1979) which reaffirmed the central importance of the basic right of participation in rural development processes and the right to form their own organization as a vehicle to exercise those rights;
- The UN-sponsored Brundtland Commission (1987) which underlined the link between human rights and sustainable development.

The United Nations Declaration on the Right to Development (1986) asserted that international human rights are indispensable, inter-dependent ends and means of development and that international development agencies are bound to promote them. In its preamble the concept of development was elucidated in the following terms:

"Development is a comprehensive economic, social, cultural and political process, which aims at the constant improvement and the well-being of the entire population and of all individuals on the basis of their active, free and meaningful participation in development and in the fair distribution of benefits resulting therefrom",[2]

and the inter-relatedness of development and human rights was emphasized thus:

"all human rights and fundamental freedoms are indivisible and interdependent"

and that

"states shall take steps to eliminate obstacles to development resulting from failure to observe civil and political rights as well as economic, social and cultural rights".[3]

Article 8 of the Declaration identified as important elements, which ought to be embraced by the concept of development: first, equal opportunity for all in their access to basic resources, education, health services, food, housing, employment and fair distribution of income, ensuring an active role for women in the development process; second, the adoption of economic and social reforms to remove social injustices and third, the encouragement of popular participation in all spheres relating to development.

The Declaration of the UN Conference on Environment and Development (1992) held in Rio de Janeiro proclaimed as its first principle that human beings are at the centre of concerns for sustainable development. The Rio Declaration included as one of its principles the right to development.

The Vienna Declaration (1993) of the World Conference on Human Rights

---

[2]UNGA Resolution 41/128 adopted on 4 December, 1986.
[3]Ibid.

recognized that civil and political rights and social and economic rights are indivisible, interdependent and interrelated and affirmed as follows:

"Democracy, development and respect for human rights and fundamental freedoms are interdependent and mutually reinforcing. Democracy is based on the freely expressed will of the people to determine their own political, economic, social and cultural systems and their full participation in all aspects of their lives."[4]

National Constitutions, Human Rights and Development

National constitutions of newly independent states and of societies in transition from an authoritarian to a democratic order invariably declare their commitment to bring about social and economic development.

This is particularly true in societies which have inherited poverty and social and economic inequalities as a part of the legacy of their colonial or authoritarian past. An early example is the Indian Constitution (1949).While introducing the constitution, its architect emphasized the imperative of using political freedom to bring about economic and social change, that is, to use civil and political rights to achieve economic and social rights, thus:

"We are going to enter into a life of contradictions; in politics we shall have equality and in social and economic life, we shall have inequality. We must remove this contradictions at the earliest possible moment."[5]

In the Indian Constitution, a dichotomy was maintained between civil and political rights (the first generation rights) which were enforceable by courts and economic, social and cultural rights (the second generation rights) which were not judicially enforceable, but which parliaments and governments were urged to make their best efforts to implement, subject to availability of resources. Third generation rights, such as the right to development and the right to a healthy environment, had not emerged when the constitution was adopted in 1949 but a directive principle was inserted into the constitution by the 42nd amendment in 1976 providing that "the State shall endeavour to protect and improve the environment" (Article 48A).

This problem was described by one of the architects of the new South African Constitution, Justice Albie Sachs, in the following terms:

"The fundamental constitutional problem, however, is not to set one generation of rights against another, but to harmonize all three. The web of rights is unbroken in fabric, simultaneous in operation, and all-extensive in character [...] The achievement of first generation rights is fundamental to the establishment of democracy and the overcoming of national oppression. But for the vote to have meaning, for the Rule of Law to have content, the vote must be the instrument for the achievement of second and third generation rights. It would be a sad victory if the people had the right every five or so years to emerge from their forced removal hovels and second-rate Group Area homesteads to go to the polls, only thereafter to return to their inferior houses, inferior education, and inferior jobs."[6]

---

[4]World Conference on Human Rights: The Vienna Declaration and Programme of Action, June 1993, pp. 30–31.
[5]G. Omvedt, Reinventing Revolution, New York, 1993 p. xi.
[6]A. Sachs, Promoting Human Rights in a New South Africa, Cape Town, 1990, pp. 8–9.

The South African Constitution, reflecting the evolution which envisages an integrated approach to the implementation of civil and political rights and economic and social rights, has eliminated the dichotomy which was a feature of some of the earlier constitutions. Civil and political rights as well as social and economic rights are given the same status as constitutionally recognized rights. The state's obligation with regard to the right to health care, food, water and social security is expressed in terms which provide that "the state must take reasonable legislative and other measures, within its available resources, to achieve the progressive realisation of each of these rights." (Article 27)

Human Rights and Development: An Integrated Approach

Today there is a consensus on the need to adopt an integrated approach to the implementation of human rights; civil and political on the one hand, and economic, social and cultural rights, on the other. Parallel to this, the development "paradigm" has also shifted, so that development is no longer measured in terms of an exclusively economic yardstick such as per capita GDP but instead is viewed in terms of its wider social impact. There is increasing recognition that sustainable development must be "human-focussed" or centred around the realisation of human rights – indeed we speak today of "sustainable human development".

In designing development programmes and projects, feasibility studies instead of being confined to narrow economic appraisals of cost and benefit, have begun to include assessments of their environmental impact. A significant step forward is the recognition of the need to include assessments of social and human rights impacts. How will the benefits and costs of a project or programme be distributed among the different sections of a community. A sensitive assessment will need to be made of the impact of a development project or programme not only on the environment but of its 'social impact' – which would involve taking into account such matters as: How will it affect different sections of a community, in particular, women and children, the poor and the vulnerable? Is it likely to favour the privileged and the powerful? Will the implementation involve procedures which would enable the more powerful to pre-empt the benefits, or lead to corruption? How will it impact on human rights?[7]

In the same vein a report, reviewing development experience in Africa, outlined the following approach:

"Measurement of project impact can start with easy questions that become gradually more difficult: how many children (boys and girls) are in school and how many not? How do operations in agriculture, forestry, irrigation, affect access to and control of land? What about resettlement (whether voluntary or not!) and impacts on income distribution? Who are the gainers and who the losers? How effective is the popular participation in setting the objectives and defining the tasks of a given project? In part, these questions are difficult because of their overlap with and roots in economic, social, and cultural rights. Education is a basic (and universal) human right, as is food, shelter, and adequate

---

[7] K. Hossain "Evolving Principles of Sustainable Development and Good Governance" in K. Ginther et al., Sustainable Development and Good Governance, Dordrecht, 1995, pp. 21–22; also, N.H. Moller, "The World Bank: Human Rights, Democracy and Governance", Netherlands Quarterly of Human Rights, March 1997, pp. 33–35.

health care. So is having the means to secure an ... "adequate standard of living." At what point does the rather dry measurement of how many kids are in school become a measure of our contribution to (or our failure to) contribute to meeting basic, universally recognized (even when poorly specified) economic, social and cultural rights?"[8]

Concrete measures of implementation are needed. The transformation of economic, social and cultural rights into positive law, whether in constitutions or in statutory law, is, however, not enough. The rights must be realized in fact, which may require comprehensive administrative measures and social action. The success of the transformation depends on the evolution of a human rights culture where individuals accept both their own rights and their duties to the community which make the enjoyment of rights possible.[9]

The relevance of civil and political rights in the realisation of economic and social rights has been explained, thus:

"Civil and political rights give people the opportunity not only to do things for themselves, but also to draw attention forcefully to general needs, and to demand appropriate public action. Whether and how a government responds to needs and sufferings may well depend on how much pressure is put on it, and the exercise of political rights (such as voting, criticizing, protesting, and so on) can make a real difference. For example, one of the remarkable facts in the terrible history of famines in the world is that no substantial famine has ever occurred in any country with a democratic form of government and a relatively free press."[10]

The new human rights-centred approach to development calls for greater popular participation in the designing of development programmes and policies and in their implementation. It calls for a re-definition and re-orientation of the role of governments. The exercise of arbitrary discretion of centralized bureaucracies, taking decisions behind closed doors, and making policies without consulting those affected by the policies, must be replaced by a new mode of participatory governance which would seek to involve citizens through dissemination of information, consultation and participation. This was well expressed in the resolution of the 1976 World Conference on Agrarian Reform and Rural Development, thus:

"Participation of the people in the institutions and systems which govern their lives is a basic human right and also essential for realignment of political power in favour of disadvantaged groups and for social and economic development. [...] Rural development strategies can realize their full potential only through the motivation, active involvement and organization at the grassroots level of rural people with special emphasis on the least advantaged strata, in conceptualizing and designing policies and programs and in creating administrative, social and economic institutions, including cooperative and other voluntary forms of organization for implementing and evaluating them."[11]

A useful enumeration of a broad array of rights which should be enjoyed in

---

[8]"The Interface between Human Rights, Development, and the Role of the Bank" Report of Symposium on Governance in Africa, October 1, 1992 p. 6.

[9]A. Eide et al., Economic, Social and Cultural Rights, Dordrecht, 1995, p. 30.

[10]Amartya Sen, "Human Rights and Economic Achievements", Paper presented at a Conference on The Growth of East Asia and Its Impact on Human Rights, June 23–25, 1995, Japan Institute of International Affairs, Tokyo, p. 16.

[11]James C.N. Paul, "International Development Agencies, Human Rights, and Humane Development Projects", in I. Becher et al, Human Rights, Development and Foreign Policy: Canadian Perspectives, 1989, p. 284.

relation to rural development projects (and mutatis mutandis to other development projects) and the negative practices which frustrate these rights has been presented in the following terms:[12]

- Timely notification of the project proposal and access to information about it: rights which are frustrated by rules and policies of both development agencies and governments that regularly treat development plans, decisions, reports, and operating rules as "state secrets".
- Access to legal resources: rights which are frustrated by failure to provide rural people with knowledge of their legal rights and capacities to exercise them.
- Power to form their own self-managed associations and engage in organized activities: rights which are regularly frustrated by national regimes of law and practice regulating formation of associations, by practices of local officials that deter formation of "unauthorized" groups and collective action, and by deliberate efforts of development agencies to coopt and manipulate grassroots collective activities.
- Freedom of communication: rights which are regularly suppressed by oppressive enforcement of laws dealing with public demonstrations and protest which are often the only means of expression available to poor people.
- Access to the media: rights regularly frustrated by government monopolization of the media, or by social gaps which separate the independent press from rural communities, notably the concerns of the rural poor.
- Access to officials and agencies: rights which are frustrated by the absence of regimes of law requiring public hearings on measures proposed and due process for people who claim to be harmed by official actions.
- Access to institutions (courts or other agencies) which can redress legal harms and impose accountability: rights regularly frustrated by the absence of legal resources for project-affected people, by the insensitivity of courts to the interests of project-affected people, and by legal doctrines such as "immunity," "standing," and "justiciability" that can be used to insulate agencies and officials.

A national strategy for an integrated approach to the promotion of human rights and development needs to be adopted if results are to be achieved on the ground. The core elements of the strategy should include:[13]

- Education and Awareness
- Information and Communication
- Effective Participation
- Accountability and Transparency

1. Education and Awareness: Basic education for all is essential for creating the conditions under which people can be effectively involved in the planning and implementation of development goals, in democratic decision-making and in being aware of and exercising their fundamental human rights.

---

[12] Ibid, pp. 283–284.

[13] P. O'Brien and S. Bastian, Towards an Integrated Agenda, Government and Civil Society Working Together to Promote Development, Human Rights and Democracy, An Overview Paper, Commonwealth Secretariat, London, June 1995, pp. 9–10. 1

2. Information and Communication: Information exchange and effective communication are critically important from several perspectives. For example, to function effectively both government and civil society need access to accurate and timely information and must have the means both to disseminate and receive information. Open channels of communication are essential not just between government and civil society but within each sector.
3. Effective Participation: The active involvement of the people is central to the success of any activities in the area of development, human rights and democracy. This applies as much to socio-economic development projects as it does to the preparations for and conduct of democratic elections and to the observance of human rights.
4. Accountability and Transparency: Accountability and transparency are deemed to be fundamental to the practice of good governance in successful democracies. This derives from the basic principle that those governing should be fully accountable to the governed, and in doing so be fully transparent in their actions. This means more than the right to elect or dismiss political leaders and parliamentarians at regular elections. Strong democracies also need effective mechanisms to ensure that civil servants are answerable at all times, and indeed that representatives of civil society are answerable for their actions.

Role of Judiciary and National Institutions

It is a widely shared experience that simply injecting a bill of rights into a constitution with conventional modes of judicial enforcement for some of the rights is not enough. In many jurisdictions throughout the world there has been a felt need to fill these gaps as a result of many human rights violations remaining unredressed.

The advocacy of human rights organizations and the growth of citizens' activism, promoted by professional associations and NGOs, brought home the need for new approaches and new institutions. These have encouraged new modes of judicial activism in the sphere of human rights through resort to public interest and social action litigation and provided the impetus for the establishment of new national institutions: human rights commissions, women's commissions, and the office of ombudsman.

The working of national institutions (human rights commissions and the office of ombudsman) has now generated enough experience for us to begin to identify the best practices which merit emulation, noting both the positive features which have contributed to effectiveness and the negative ones which have detracted from it. The features that may be singled out include:

- Mode of Establishment: The mode of establishment is relevant. Institutions gain in prestige and effectiveness if they are established by the Constitution itself.
- Mandate: The mandate of a commission is important. The mandate must be proportionate to the challenges that are to be faced. Social and economic rights (second generation rights) must get equal importance with first generation civil and political rights, and indeed a third generation of rights, the right to development and to a healthy environment, should be given due attention.

- Independence: Independence of a commission or the office of ombudsman is essential to its effectiveness. It must be manned by persons who enjoy public confidence and are known for their integrity and impartiality of judgement. The appointment should be through a fair and transparent selection process involving effective consultations between the government and the opposition and others such as head of the judiciary. They should have security of tenure and enjoy safeguards against removal from office similar to those enjoyed by a judge of the highest court.
- Availability of Financial and Human Resources: It is self-evident that a commission which is expected to monitor and redress violations of human rights and abuse of authority would be seriously impaired if it did not have adequate financial resources assured to it and had to depend upon those whose abuses are to be checked by it. It should also have the capacity to employ staff having professional competence and other qualities necessary for carrying out its tasks.
- Scope of powers: The scope of powers of the national institution is equally important. Its effectiveness would normally be impaired if it did not have power in appropriate cases to initiate investigations and prosecutions. It should have power to adopt innovative techniques to monitor implementation of economic and social rights, to commission studies and to evaluate reports with regard to progress in their implementation. Most important it should have the power to promote human rights education and awareness of human rights in all sections of society, in particular the police and security forces.

Principles and standards laying down guidelines relating to the status and functioning of national human rights institutions have been formulated. The Paris Principles on this subject were adopted by the United Nations Commission on Human Rights in 1992 and approved by the UNGA in 1993. Further improvements have been suggested by a number of regional meetings held during the last year.

An important lesson is that effective human rights implementation must be able to strengthen the constituencies for change and development in a society and to overcome, in as peaceful and orderly a manner as possible, the opposition and the barriers to change. This calls for consensus-building and imaginative coalition-building among all the protagonists of human rights and development within a society – among state and non-state actors, within government and parliament, within professional associations and women's organizations, and NGOs. These would provide essential sustenance for the institutions engaged in implementation of human rights with the aim of promoting development.

The Role of International Organizations and NGOs in the Protection of Human Rights

Patricia Hyndman*

Introduction

have been asked to speak on the topic of the role of international organizations nd the NGOs in the protection of human rights. For the purposes of this paper have taken "international organizations" to mean "intergovernmental organizaions" and, under the heading NGOs (non-governmental organizations), I have ncluded both domestic and international NGOs.

As you will all no doubt be well aware, international organizations played he pivotal role in bringing to fruition the structure of the international system or the protection of human rights as it exists today, and both international rganizations and NGOs have been, and remain, vital to the endeavour to nsure both that the system continues to develop and that it is effectively nplemented. As well, both types of organization have had major influence on he development of human rights protection in the domestic laws and practices f many countries.

The approach I have taken has been to look at the protection afforded to uman rights in universal, in regional, and in national systems and, in that ontext, to consider the role played by international organizations and by NGOs n bringing about the development, modification and implementation of these urrent arrangements.

Some of the contributions of major intergovernmental organizations are escribed in the sections in which the role of those organizations is explained, ut there is no attempt to list NGOs or to describe the contribution each has nade to the current system of protection, they are too various and too numerous o cover in this way. This account seeks, not to study particular organizations nd their achievements, but rather to describe the contribution these organizaions, as a whole, have made to the protection of human rights. Thus, where pecific NGOs are mentioned it is as an illustration of a particular kind of ctivity. In almost all cases other, different, unnamed, organizations have also een involved in the same work, and may have been doing it equally, or even nore, effectively. No judgement is implied. The aim is simply to give an account, vith illustrations, of some of the many ways in which international organizations nd NGOs have acted to protect human rights.

Fellow of Wolfson College, Cambridge, UK.

. Hossain et al. (eds), *Human Rights Commissions and Ombudsman Offices*, 63–79.

They have done this work by a variety of means – for example: by painstaking work on the drafting of texts of new, internationally agreed, instruments which establish human rights standards; by encouraging governments to ratify those instruments and thus to accept their terms as obligations which they must observe; by the establishment of a variety of structures to adjudicate upon supervise or monitor, compliance with human rights standards; by careful documentation of human rights breaches; by increasing public awareness and by agitating to bring about change; by putting pressure on governments, legislators and others who are in a position to affect law and policy to persuade them that compliance with human rights standards is essential; by working persistently towards securing a means for the redress of breaches of human rights standards and by the provision of direct assistance to the victims of such breaches.

In order to set in context the contributions made in these spheres by international organizations and by NGOs, the way in which the current international system for the protection of human rights has developed is first briefly outlined and then, also briefly, the provision for the protection of rights under the domestic law and practice of different countries is surveyed. In these early sections some contributions made by international organizations and NGOs will be flagged, and more detailed consideration of the kinds of work they have undertaken will be made in the sections which follow.

The Development of the Protection of Rights

The Development of the Protection of Rights at the International Level

The first thing to note is that international human rights law and the development of the major international human rights instruments is of comparatively recent origin. Although before 1945 there had been some sporadic international actions to protect interests which today would be classified as involving the human rights of the individuals in question, these actions had been specific rather than general.

The first international texts dealing with what in modern terms would be classified as a human rights issue were those dealing with the abolition of slavery in the early 19th century. Then in the mid-19th century rules to protect the victims of war were developed. The protection afforded by the initial treaties adopted to deal with these issues continues to expand, as efforts are constantly being made to combat different forms of slavery and different modes of warfare. In the process of the development of both these protections outstanding individuals (for example Lord William Wilberforce in the case of the abolition of slavery, Henri Dunant in the case of the rules of international humanitarian law), intergovernmental cooperation and, in the case of the laws of warfare, one NGO in particular – the International Red Cross, were all active from the very beginning.[1]

[1] In the case of the laws of armed conflict Henri Dunant, a Swiss businessman, was so appalled by the suffering of those involved affected by warfare that he wrote a book about it in 1862, A Memory of Solferino. A society of active individuals was then organized in Geneva and decided to hold an international conference to formulate a plan for organizing national relief societies. Thirty-six delegates from 14 European states attended (the first conference was held in 1863) and, at the second conference in 1864, in which 15 European states were represented, the First Geneva Convention was

There were other instances too where international law afforded protection to the interests of individuals prior to the development of a more general system of protection, for example treaties concerning certain minority groups. After World War I, a number of governments accepted treaty obligations to guarantee protection for minorities within their boundaries. In addition, from the early 20th century onwards other international agreements between states conferred protection on particular groups of refugees. As well, interests of a rather different kind received protection under ILO treaties directed, for example, against oppressive labour conditions – in this case the agreements were tripartite: involving governments, unions of employers and employees, a unique combination of governmental and non-governmental representation in an intergovernmental organization.

It was not, however, until after the Second World War that there was any real impetus to protect the fundamental rights of all individuals – whoever and wherever they may happen to be. Legal rules are the reflection of social standards in international, as well as in national communities, and the development of international human rights law came about as a reflection of a new consciousness.

After the atrocities perpetrated during the Second World War there was an increased awareness and concern about the treatment being accorded in different parts of the world to other human beings, a growing conviction that all people should be accorded a minimum standard of observance of fundamental rights, no matter what their race, culture, nationality, language or religion, and a widespread determination that a system be established to ensure that similar atrocities could not occur again.

In terms of traditional international law, the current international system for the protection of individuals against violations of their rights by their own state is a wholly new phenomenon. The classical doctrine of international law is based on a premise of national sovereignty, hence breaches of rights of individuals were long regarded as a matter for the domestic jurisdiction in which those violations occurred. Indeed, on occasion, governments still refer to national sovereignty as an answer to criticisms of their human rights practices towards their own citizens, or towards others present in their territory.

The change from this traditional approach came about primarily through the development of international human rights norms drafted into universal and regional human rights instruments and agreed to by governments. International organizations (most obviously the United Nations Organization) and human rights NGOs have played a significant role in the identification of rights in need of this protection, in the drafting of the treaties, in the encouragement of states to ratify and implement them and in the establishment, and utilization, of mechanisms to monitor their implementation. The initial and most influential of these instruments are the Universal Declaration of Human Rights of 1948, and the International Covenant of Civil and Political Rights and the International Covenant of Economic, Social and Cultural Rights, both of 1966.

Ratification by states of these and other international human rights instruments carries with it an acknowledgement of the standards contained within

---

drafted – to accord humane treatment to the sick and wounded of armies in time of war and all those who care for them. By 1870 every major power and most of the smaller states in Europe had ratified it. Since then the International Red Cross has been responsible for the drafting and adoption of a variety of international instruments all with the aim of attenuating the suffering attached to armed conflict.

them, standards which may then be used as a measure against which their domestic laws, and the actions of their government in the exercise of its internal jurisdiction, may be assessed. The significance of this change of approach given that, as noted above, the underlying premise of the system was the sovereignty of states, and the immunity from question of actions committed by a government within its own borders, has to be appreciated before the magnitude of the effort required to bring about this change can be fully understood.

Under the circumstances it is not hard to see why developing, and then making effective, this new system has taken time and persistent effort and patience – and it is to the persistence, persuasion, and sheer hard work of both international organizations and NGOs that the credit must go for the developments achieved thus far.

The Development of the Protection of Human Rights Within Domestic Arrangements

Although international law did not afford protection to individuals until fairly recently, in some countries domestic legislation has recognized and protected the fundamental rights and liberties of citizens for a considerable time. For example, Bills of Rights have been a feature of national legal systems for over two hundred years – France adopted the Declaration of the Rights of Man in 1789, and the United States its Bill of Rights in 1791.

Many of the Bills of Rights drafted in recent years owe much to the texts of the two major UN international covenants of 1966 mentioned above – the International Covenant on Civil and Political Rights and the International Covenant on Economic, Social and Cultural Rights, and also to the European Human Rights Convention. This means that the work of international organizations towards the drafting and adoption of those treaties has not only served to increase the protection of human rights at the international level, but has also assisted with the incorporation of the protection of rights within the domestic laws of numbers of states.

Though Constitutions and Bills of Rights are an obvious starting point to any enquiry into the protection of rights afforded within states, there are many other types of mechanisms currently existing in the domestic arrangements of different countries which provide, or have the potential to provide, some protection for citizens' human rights, and NGOs frequently have had significant input into the creation, as well as the subsequent utilization, of these mechanisms.

The account which follows is drawn from examples to be found in common law countries. My field of expertise does not allow me to stray into other arenas, but no doubt many comparative measures could be found in countries whose legal systems are of a different kind.

Of particular interest in this context are domestic Human Rights Commissions and the Office of the Ombudsman. Their establishment often, although not always, follows concern about particular human rights situations, a concern not infrequently highlighted by NGOs. Human Rights Commissions, typically, are endowed with a variety of powers – usually including the power to examine government legislation and practice for compatibility with existing international human rights obligations. Ombudsmen generally conduct investigations in relation to charges of maladministration in government departments, in some instances they look also into defects in laws and administrative practices.

Of course, the mere establishment of a Human Rights Commission or the Office of Ombudsman does not, of itself and without more, automatically ensure the observance of human rights standards by the establishing government though it is likely to assist. To be effective such bodies must be given both real power and real independence. Here domestic NGOs, through activities such as the lobbying of parliamentarians at the time of the drafting of the relevant legislation, can have the effect of ensuring that the body concerned is accorded real power and an adequate structural base.

Other examples of mechanisms which serve to protect human rights in a number of countries include a wide variety of complaint structures which allow individuals to appeal against adverse bureaucratic decisions and actions and include, also, judicial remedies developed by the courts to provide review for people affected by the ever increasing reach of officialdom. Protection for human rights may be provided as well by ordinary legislation dealing with particular issues – for example freedom of information legislation – issues which may well have been brought to the forefront of public attention by the activities of concerned NGOs.

In addition, it may be possible to persuade judges to take into account international human rights norms when they consider cases before them, and this may be so even though the country in question does not have a Bill of Rights – for example Australia. Some NGOs have been particularly active in this regard, holding seminars for judges to alert them to this possibility – for example: the Aspen Institute (New York); Interights (London), and the International Commission of Jurists (Geneva) have all held workshops highlighting the opportunities which exist for judges to do this. Such teaching has not been the province of NGOs alone, the Commonwealth Secretariat (an intergovernmental organization) has also been actively involved in programmes of education for the judiciary, as well as for foreign ministry officials and other government officers, and the United Nations concerns itself with running a wide variety of human rights education programmes within different countries at all levels of society.

Some governments have set up citizens' advice bureaus. Many finance free or subsidized legal services to people otherwise unable to afford them, or give advice to particular categories of people in need of assistance. NGOs are involved in this kind of work as well, an instance is the advice given to asylum-seekers by NGO refugee organizations in many countries. Some governments, and some NGOs, make available programmes through which people can learn both about their basic rights and how best to enforce them. As well, both governments and NGOs have developed new forms of training to better equip para-legal personnel many of whom will assist in the protection of basic rights.

To take just one illustration of training to increase the observance of human rights standards, numbers of NGOs in India have been involved in programmes to educate parents, employers and children about the hazards to child labourers: what the rights of these children are; how to begin to deal with the social and economic consequences of not relying on children to be breadwinners; how to change social standards and mores about exploiting children in the labour force; and how to draft, enact and (most importantly) enforce standards of protection for children who work.

In addition, specific mechanisms have been established to deal with complaints of particular kinds – for example anti-discrimination tribunals and equal opportunity bodies. As well, recourse to the media, to politicians, local government members or parliamentarians often can be of assistance in obtaining redress for breaches or in achieving better protection for human rights.

Governments establish these mechanisms, and parliaments enact the laws, but NGOs are frequently the catalysts.

Societies do not have to be wealthy in order to take these measures – examples of almost all the mechanisms and approaches described above can be found in use today in small Pacific island states, bearing testimony to the enterprise both of the governments there and of NGOs.

The Role of International Organizations in The Protection of Human Rights

International organizations have played, and continue to play, crucial roles in the protection of human rights. As noted already, it was due to the determination to bring about change after the Second World War, that the current system of universal human rights standards initially came into being – created primarily by the drafting, and the adoption by governments, of international human rights instruments, and the establishment of mechanisms for their implementation.

In this section intergovernmental organizations have been subdivided into the following categories: 1. international (meaning in this context open to all governments to join should they so choose); 2. regional (meaning available only to governments in a particular geographical region e.g. Africa), and 3. those organized on some other basis.

The Protection of Rights by International Intergovernmental Organizations

The major intergovernmental organization involved in the protection of human rights is, of course, the Organization of the United Nations which was established in 1945 in response to the horrors perpetrated during the Second World War. In the statement of its aims (in the Preamble to the United Nations Charter) respect for human rights is ranked second only to the need to save later generations from the scourge of war. On joining the United Nations and signing the Charter, Member States "pledge themselves to take joint and separate action" for " the achievement of the United Nations" goal of the promotion of respect for human rights and fundamental freedoms "for all without distinction as to race, sex, language or religion".[2]

It has thus been clear from the outset that the United Nations has a strong commitment to protect human rights, and that all member states agree not only to honour this commitment but also to take action to bring it into reality. Consequently, activity to further the protection of human rights is to be expected both from the United Nations as a body, and from governments and intergovernmental groupings.

The nature of the human rights and fundamental freedoms which states undertake to promote when joining the United Nations receives no elaboration in the Charter, but the UN has been very active in the formulation and definition

[2] UN Charter, Articles 55 and 56.

of international norms of behaviour regarding human rights and this particular omission was remedied when, on December 10th, 1948, the United Nations General Assembly (by 48 votes to none with 8 abstentions) adopted the Universal Declaration of Human Rights. This instrument contains an extensive list of civil, political, economic, social and cultural rights. The Declaration did not purport to be a statement of law, and contains no provisions for enforcement. In its Preamble it is proclaimed as "a common standard of achievement for all peoples and all nations."

Today the rights referred to in the Universal Declaration are for the most part incorporated in the two major international covenants on human rights: the International Covenant on Civil and Political Rights and the International Covenant on Economic, Social and Cultural Rights, which. were adopted by the UN General Assembly in 1966. These two instruments are legally binding on the states which are parties to them.

Many other United Nations instruments for the protection of human rights have now been drafted and adopted as a result of the hard work and cooperation, often over long periods of time, by member governments (with, it must be remembered, significant input from NGOs). Many of these instruments have been ratified, or acceded to, by member states and thus are legally binding on them. Indeed, some of the provisions of these instruments may also, as a result of the acceptance of governments of their principles, have become incorporated into international customary law. Where this is so those principles are now binding on all states – whether or not governments have ratified them. An example would be the principle of the *non-refoulement* of refugees contained in Article 33 of the 1951 *Convention Relating to the Status of Refugees.*

United Nations human rights instruments include: conventions for the abolition of slavery; for the elimination of racial discrimination and for the suppression and punishment of the crime of apartheid; conventions for the prevention and punishment of the crime of genocide; conventions against torture, and other cruel, inhuman or degrading treatment and punishments; conventions on the reduction and problem of statelessness; on the status of refugees; on the rights of women and on the rights of children.

Added to these are treaties drafted and promoted by specific United Nations agencies – such as the UNESCO conventions on educational rights, and instruments brought into being by other United Nations affiliated bodies – for example the ILO conventions on particular economic and social rights and on the fair regulation of labour.

The ILO (International Labour Organization) was established in 1919 by the *Treaty of Versailles.* After the Second World War it became a specialized UN agency. Its structure is unique among intergovernmental organizations, being composed of: (1) member states; (2) employers, and (3) workers. The non-governmental members attend meetings and have voting powers. It has established a highly developed reporting system and mechanism for dealing with breaches of the standards it has promulgated.

The ILO focuses on issues such as rights to form trade unions; to safe and healthy working conditions; to social security and to protection from compulsory labour and child labour. It has formulated and adopted, and encouraged governments to ratify, conventions on, inter alia: collective bargaining; freedom of association; the right to organize; the abolition of forced labour; migrant workers;

the employment of women; occupational safety and health; social security and indigenous peoples. Here, clearly here is an instance of both governments and NGOs working together to formulate and then implement international human rights standards.

In terms of implementation, the United Nations has designed and created a number of mechanisms and procedures. Many human rights treaties are monitored by Committees especially established for the purpose, for example the Committee established under the *Convention for the Elimination of All Forms of Discrimination Against Women*. The UN treaty bodies examine the reports on national implementation which ratifying States undertake to provide to the UN. Independently of these reports the UN Human Rights Commission and other Sub-Commissions and Working Groups meet each year to consider human rights issues. Further, states ratifying the Protocol to the *International Covenant on Civil and Political Rights* allow individuals to take complaints against that state to the Human Rights Committee if violations of the covenant by it are alleged.

More recently, the United Nations has sought to enforce compliance with international standards in a rather different way. Pending a determination on whether or not a general International Criminal Court should be established, the Security Council has set up two ad hoc international tribunals for the purpose of prosecuting persons for grave violations of international humanitarian law committed in former Yugoslavia and in Rwanda.

Although there are serious shortcomings in the international human rights implementation machinery, nonetheless, both its adoption and the adoption of international human rights instruments, have been a significant step forward.

The process of bringing into existence an international instrument is time consuming, and the difficulties in reaching agreement on the text are at times exasperating – it took from 1948 until 1966 to reach agreement on the text of the two 1966 Covenants, and it was another ten years before either instrument entered into force. However, once treaty texts are adopted, and states become parties to them then those treaties can provide an internationally recognized standard against which state behaviour may be examined and measured by others, and violations of those provisions now amount to a breach by the government in power in the state in question, of its obligations under international law. Because this is so, great importance is attributed by bodies such as the United Nations, other intergovernmental organizations, (and NGOs) to the drafting and adoption of international treaties which set down standards of behaviour.

The Protection of Rights by Regional Intergovernmental Organizations

While these developments were taking place at the wider international (universal) level, some regional intergovernmental organizations developed regional systems for the protection of human rights. First European States and then the American States drafted and adopted regional human rights conventions. As well, these organizations have established regional commissions and courts of human rights. More recently, the Organization of African Unity developed a regional charter of human and peoples' rights and, in 1987, established a commission on human rights. The Arab world, which has had a commission on human rights since 1968,[3] has a draft regional charter of human rights.

The regional settlement of disputes threatening international peace and security is specifically envisaged in Articles 33 and 52 of the United Nations Charter and can extend to disputes concerning human rights violations, as Article 44 of the International Covenant on Civil and Political Rights expressly recognizes.

(i) *Europe*

The European system of human rights protection was developed primarily by the Council of Europe which was set up by a group of ten states in 1949 to promote greater unity, democracy and the rule of law within Europe. It now has forty state members.

The *European Convention for the Protection of Human Rights and Fundamental Freedoms* was adopted under the Council's auspices. It was signed in 1950 and came into force in 1953. The Convention was pioneering in that it was the first comprehensive human rights treaty. It established the first international complaints procedure and set up the first international court for the adjudication of human rights issues. Today the European system has the most extensive jurisprudence and is the most developed of the regional systems for human rights protection.

Other European instruments on human rights adopted by the Council of Europe include: the *European Social Charter* (which is concerned with economic and social rights), and the *European Convention for the Prevention of Torture.* European institutions for dealing with human rights issues include, besides the European Court of Human Rights, the European Commission of Human Rights and the Committee of Experts on the European Social Charter. Recently Protocol 11 to the European Human Rights Convention was ratified. It establishes a single permanent Court of Human Rights in Strasbourg which will replace the present system of two part-time bodies: the Court and Commission.

The OSCE (formerly the CSCE) which is also mainly European, is a somewhat different intergovernmental organization. Initially there were thirty-five participating states, including all European states except Albania and including also two states outside the region: Canada and the United States. Its membership has since extended to over fifty states. In contrast to the European Council's main focus on protection through judicial and quasi-judicial structures, the OSCE is concerned with conflict within and between states. The standards it promulgates (which include human rights standards, for example the Helsinki Agreement)[4] are "solemn undertakings" but are not in treaty form and thus not formally binding. NGOs had considerable input into many of the CSCE's earlier successes, and a good deal has been achieved in the area of standard-setting for the protection of minorities. Since 1991 additional institutions have been established including an Office for Democratic Institutions and Human Rights, an Office for Free Elections, and a High Commissioner on National Minorities.

---

[3]The Council of the League decided to establish a Permanent Arab Regional Commission on Human Rights in September 1968 (Arab League Council Resolution 2443, Sept 3 1968). The creation of the Commission was reported to the UNHRC at its 25th Session (UN doc. E/CN.4/6.1042 Feb 18, 1969).

[4]The Final Act of the Conference on Security and Cooperation in Europe, Helsinki, August 1975.

(*ii*) *The Americas*

The Organization of American States was set up in 1948 to, *inter alia*, strengthen peace, security and democracy and encourage the pacific settlement of any disputes arising among its members. It now has over thirty member states.

The American Declaration of the Rights and Duties of Man was adopted in 1948, some months prior to the adoption by the United Nations of the Universal Declaration, and two years prior to the adoption of the European Human Rights Convention. The development of a treaty based system with supervisory machinery was to take somewhat longer, and in 1969 the American Convention on Human Rights was adopted. It entered into force in 1978.

Despite the fact that the issues with which the system has had to deal (states of emergency, wide-spread instances of torture and disappearances, military and authoritarian governments) have been very different to those existing in Europe, the standards in the Conventions and the structure of human rights machinery established under both the American and European systems are very similar.

There is an Inter-American Commission on Human Rights and an Inter-American Court on Human Rights. The resources of the American system have been smaller than those of the European system, nonetheless the Commission and the Court have been able to make a considerable contribution to the protection of human rights in the region. The Court has built up a body of jurisprudence, and the Commission's work in visiting countries and reporting on the human rights situation it finds in them has, in particular, been widely praised.

There is also an Inter-American Council for Education, Science and Culture, and an Economic and Social Council, but these two bodies have yet to achieve a great deal in the protection of economic and social rights.

(*iii*) *Africa*

The Organization of African Unity is the regional body for Africa. Its Charter was adopted in 1963 by a Conference of Heads of State and Government.

In 1981 the OAU adopted the *African Charter on Human and Peoples' Rights* and this has been ratified by fifty of the fifty-three African states. It emphasizes cooperation and the peaceful settlement of disputes between members, seeks to promote unity and solidarity, and defend members' sovereignty, territorial integrity and independence. The Charter is in some respects very different to other regional and universal human rights instruments. For example, one of its main themes is cultural and regional distinctiveness, another difference is the inclusion of several collective or peoples' rights, and yet another its enumeration of the duties of individuals.

The African Commission on Human and Peoples Rights is the machinery established to implement the Charter. Because the Commission is comparatively recent in origin and because it has operated under resource and procedural constraints, and has received very little publicity for its activities, it has, as yet, not achieved anything near the impact of the regional mechanisms discussed above. Recently, however, several international NGOs the International Commission of Jurists and Interights, and many African NGOs – RADDHO (Rencontre Africain pour la Defense des Droits de L'Homme) and the Constitutional Rights Project in Nigeria, to take just a few examples – have become much more active before and with the Commission, and its activities and decisions are both increasing and becoming more widely known.

The main functions in the mandate of the Commission are the promotion, the protection and the interpretation of human rights. In relation to promotion the Commission has passed resolutions to the effect that states should include the teaching of human rights at all stages of the national educational curriculums, should establish committees on human rights and integrate the provisions of the Charter into national laws. Regarding protection there are provisions under which communications may be made to the Commission regarding breaches of human rights, and victims of violations have come before the Commission to establish their complaints. Procedures for periodic reporting by states on the human rights situations in their countries have been developed, and there is provision for observations to be made by the Commission after the study of these reports. As yet the system requires more development, but the fact that it exists is an important step towards the protection of human rights in Africa. As well, it should be noted that experts representing member states of the OAU have been working for some time on a revised *Protocol for the Establishment of an African Court on Human and Peoples' Rights.*

(*iv*) *Asia and the Pacific*

Notably absent from concrete regional human rights promotion and protection arrangements is the Asia–Pacific region. Significantly, there is no regional intergovernmental structure for the whole region, although some intergovernmental structures operate in parts of it: ASEAN and SAARC. So far, these regional organizations have not played a notably useful role in the protection of human rights, and perhaps the major reason for there being no arrangement for human rights protection in this part of the world is the lack of a committed intergovernmental organization to take up and run with the idea.

NGOs have attempted to fill the vacuum. Over the last decade and a half a number of non-governmental organizations have taken steps to bring about the establishment of a regional protection mechanism. Particular effort has been made by LAWASIA (the Law Association for Asia and the Pacific). In a series of meetings and activities LAWASIA has sought to encourage wide-ranging discussion of possible sub-regional arrangements, and a Pacific regional charter has been drafted for circulation to, and consultation with, Pacific island governments.

The Protection of Rights by Different Types of Intergovernmental Organizations

(*i*) *The Organization of the Islamic Conference*

Another instrument of interest is the *Universal Islamic Declaration* of 1981, brought into being by the Organization of the Islamic Conference. The signatories here share the common factor of religion, rather than region, and the instrument has more in common with the *Universal Declaration on Human Rights*, and the *American Declaration of the Rights and Duties of Man*, than with the regional or universal human rights conventions. Nonetheless, as was the case with the *Universal Declaration of Human Rights*, it is a beginning and could ultimately lay the foundations for a binding instrument to protect human rights within these states. It is interesting to note that there is considerable similarity between many of its provisions and those of the other major human rights instruments.

(ii) The Commonwealth

In addition to the intergovernmental organizations mentioned above, there is one large organization which is neither universal in its remit as is the UN, nor regional, nor based on a common religion, as was the case with those outlined earlier. The Commonwealth of Nations is an interesting form of intergovernmental organization which has had some successes in the protection of human rights. It is an association of member states, which until very recently contemplated as members only countries which were at one time a part of the former British Empire.

Now comprising more than fifty states and one quarter of the world's population the Commonwealth has evolved over the last forty years from a colonial past into a free association of sovereign and independent countries embracing both the developed and developing world. "The modern Commonwealth is rooted in the movement to end colonialism and the divisive notion of superior and inferior human racial groups; its raison d'être is the pursuit of equality and cooperation among all races."[5]

As a consequence there is a Commonwealth focus on issues of self-determination and anti-racism and, since the membership includes both the developing states of the South and the industrialized states of the North, there has been emphasis on economic development. More recently, reflecting the common heritage of the common law, emphasis has been placed also on the rule of law and on the formation and strengthening of democratic institutions in different Commonwealth countries.

Although the general record of the Commonwealth in the field of human rights is not very good, the organization has had some success in its work for human rights protection, and it undoubtedly played a leading role both in decolonisation and in the fight against apartheid.

The Role of Non-governmental Organizations (NGOs) in the Protection of Human Rights

NGOS, as well as governments, have played a major role in the protection and promotion of human rights and, as has been mentioned from time to time in previous sections, are involved in many of the activities already described. These contributions of NGOS are assumed here and so are not mentioned again.

There are, of course, NGOS of many different kinds: anti-corruption pressure groups; consumer unions and all kinds of associations of citizens to name but a few. For the purposes of this paper when NGOS are referred to, the reference is to those involved with human rights issues (a definition that even then has boundaries which are none too clear).

One form of classification of these bodies is into: local NGOs – those limiting

[5] *Racism in South Africa: The Commonwealth Stand*, Commonwealth Secretariat, 1985.

their activities to human rights breaches in their own country, for example the Civil Rights Movement in Sri Lanka or CODEHUTAB (Comite de Derechos Humanos de Tabasco) in Mexico; regional NGOs for example AFRONET (the Inter-African Network for Human Rights and Development) or AHRINET (the Arab Human Rights Information Network) whose activities are confined to a particular geographical region; or international NGOs, meaning here NGOs which act on issues in a number of countries not necessarily from the same region, for example the Minority Rights Group based in the UK.

Another form of classification can be made according to structure. Broadly speaking human rights NGOs fall into three types of organizational structure: some, like the International Committee of the Red Cross, have been created by a group of individuals who then continue to control the organization; secondly there are organizations into which a number of bodies have combined in order more effectively to pursue their work, for example the Fédération International des Droits de l'Homme; and, thirdly, Amnesty International being the main example, some have a decentralized democratic structure with the constituent parts both doing work and having an input into the management.

Some NGOs have good funding, large offices and staff, some have minimal staff and operate on a shoe-string budget.

Further classifications could be made according to mandate – the issue or issues covered. Examples of NGOs involved in different kinds of human rights issues include: civil liberties organizations; organizations concerned with the rights of women; organizations concerned with education, both formal and non-formal; with torture and disappearances; with prison conditions; with the rights of indigenous peoples; with the rights of minorities; with refugee and asylum issues; with issues of freedom of expression, association or freedom of religion; with the protection and enhancement of culture; with social and economic rights, and organizations concerned with children's rights.

A further distinct category of human rights NGOs is that of professional organizations whose membership transcends state boundaries and who work to support colleagues in other countries who are exposed to danger for speaking out under repressive governments – for example PEN provides support for writers silenced by oppressive regimes, and Physicians for Human Rights supports dissident scientists.

The diversity of NGOs in itself has meant that they have brought a range of view-points and approaches to human rights work, have successfully challenged assumptions, thrown new light onto discussions, and have galvanised the movement for the protection and promotion of human rights with a dynamism and inventiveness that would not have existed without them. Article 71 of the UN Charter acknowledges the important role played by NGOs.

NGOs have been crucial in making effective the mechanisms established by governments. To take as an example the UN treaty reporting requirements whereby governments must submit information to the appropriate treaty body, on their national implementation of international standards – here some NGOs assist the government in the country in which they are based to compile this information. They may provide useful insights and knowledge, and their assistance can be of great value to governments operating with few resources.

At the other end of the reporting process the UN treaty bodies themselves, when considering the government reports, rely heavily on NGOs to provide them with additional and alternative information to that put forward by governments. Generally speaking, for reasons such as trade interests and regional security, governments have been reluctant to protect human rights through international institutions, and are also reluctant to admit to deficiencies in the protection of human rights themselves. NGOs have worked to fill the gap, and have become essential in monitoring the work of governments and intergovernmental organizations, and issuing critical reports documenting human rights breaches or inadequate protective practices. The various UN implementation mechanisms have come to depend on this work of NGOs.

NGOs have an input at UN meetings in a variety of ways, for example: those with consultative status with ECOSOC (the UN Economic and Social Council) and hundreds do have this status, may intervene directly at both the UN Commission on Human Rights and at the UN Sub-Commission on Prevention of Discrimination and Protection of Minorities. Interventions by NGOs at meetings such as those of the Commission on Human Rights are significant because the government delegates are then directly faced with current issues of real concern. Without NGO input, UN consideration of human rights matters would be likely to be both less immediate and less relevant to the major issues of the moment.

In another facet of implementation work the United Nations relies on NGOs to bring pressure to bear on governments when they are in breach of human rights standards. NGOs do this by the collection and dissemination of information on particular human rights breaches and analysis as to how these violations contravene international norms, by the mobilizeation of public opinion to insist on compliance with international obligations, and by the persuasion of other governments to pressure offending governments.

Whatever the particular emphasis of the activities of NGOs most spend a great deal of their time on the preparation and dissemination of information such as that described above. Clearly, if the NGO contributions are to have an impact – before UN, regional or other bodies, or in increasing public awareness and affecting opinion – careful research, accuracy and impartiality are essential. As a consequence, the documentation process takes a great deal of NGO time. It is carried out on the assumption that if people know of the breaches of human rights which are taking place, they will take action and the breach will be stopped.[6]

Whatever the area of enquiry, NGO reports are generally distributed and publicised, media attention is sought and the information contained in the reports is frequently used in the task of lobbying officials, governments, international organizations, etc. It should be noted, however, that not all NGOs seek publicity for their findings. The International Red Cross addresses its reports to the government concerned, and operates under the principle of confidentiality. As well, many NGOs show the reports to, and seek the comments of, the government in question prior to publication.

Of course, not all NGOs are successful in obtaining the coverage they desire for their reports, that task in itself requires skill, and staff to carry it out. It is

---

[6]An assumption which is not always borne out, see S. Cohen, Denial and Acknowledgement: The Impact of Information about Human Rights Violations, Centre for Human Rights, The University of Jerusalem, 1995.

in fact crucial since without the follow-through required to secure publicity the reports, however excellent, are in danger of gathering dust on shelves instead of achieving their intended aim of increasing awareness of the situation they seek to expose.

Government involvement in standard-setting was described earlier, NGOs, as well as governments, have played a significant role here. Examples of NGO action towards the development of regional instruments are: the work of the International Commission of Jurists towards the drafting and adoption of the African Charter, and the attempts (so far not successful) of the LAWASIA Human Rights Committee to encourage the drafting and adoption of a regional Charter of Human Rights for the Pacific. As well, NGOs have been major contributors to standard-setting activity in the UN context where, as mentioned above, many have consultative status with the United Nations and, as a consequence, are able to participate, although not to vote, in the drafting discussions. To give just two examples, some NGO groups had considerable input into the drafting of the *Convention on The Rights of The Child,* and also in the drafting of the *Convention against Torture and other Cruel, Inhuman or Degrading Treatment or Punishment.*

A striking contribution to have been made to standard-setting is that of the International Red Cross – in its case to the international conventions on the laws of war. There are an impressive number of these conventions,[7] and the International Red Cross has been behind them all. This is an area of the law known as international humanitarian law. It has as its object the regulation of hostilities, and the attenuation of the accompanying hardships to individuals so far as military necessity permits. International humanitarian law is distinguished from the law of human rights in a number of ways, hence these activities have not been elaborated here in any detail.

The International Red Cross is a unique organization. It remained practically the only large international organization not to be absorbed into the United Nations when the major re-organization of international institutions was carried out in 1945, and has retained its characteristics as a private body. This independence has enabled it to intervene where political considerations would hamper government bodies, and it has brought relief to countless numbers of victims of war, internal conflict or other forms of disaster, when otherwise they would have been left without help.

To mention just a few of its other activities, the International Red Cross has done a great deal to assist refugees, in receiving and housing them as well as in assisting in their emigration to other countries. It has developed a Tracing Agency, to trace missing persons dispersed as a result of hostilities and re-unite them with their families. It has been involved in the training of nurses and the safeguarding of public health, and national Red Cross Societies have played a pioneering role in the organization of social services.

In addition to the NGO activities mentioned thus far, NGOs involve them-

[7]E.g. the Geneva Convention for the Amelioration of the Condition of the Wounded and Sick in Armed Forces in the Field; Geneva Convention for the Amelioration of the Condition of the Wounded, Sick and Shipwrecked Members of Armed Forces at Sea; Geneva Convention relative to the Treatment of Prisoners of War; Geneva Convention relative to the Protection of Civilian Persons in Time of War; and the two Additional Protocols.

selves in a variety of other modes of protecting human rights. Some of them – for instance PIL (Public Interest Litigation) based in India, initiate litigation on human rights issues, or seek to join it as an amicus curiae. Others, concerned about the importance of free and fair elections, have involved themselves in election monitoring (intergovernmental organizations are involved in this activity as well).

NGOs also concern themselves in human rights education, in letter-writing campaigns, in the organization of demonstrations, conferences and other modes of bringing public attention to human rights issues. They frequently lobby their own governments. Some will do this in relation to breaches of human rights standards occurring on the domestic front, others lobby their own governments in relation to breaches of human rights by other states in this case urging their government to put pressure on another government to observe human rights standards.

Although the executive arm of government is generally the chief focus of NGO lobbying, attention may also be turned to legislative bodies – for instance in an attempt to ensure that the drafting of particular legislation pays due regard to international human rights standards. A recent example here is the activity of Amnesty International UK in seeking to ensure due recognition of the rights of refugees and asylum-seekers in proposed asylum legislation in Britain.

It is well known that individual staff members of local NGOs which operate under autocratic and ruthless regimes can be faced with considerable danger, whereas those operating on the same issues elsewhere are in a very different situation. Hence another NGO activity is the provision of support, by those operating in countries under more liberal regimes, to human rights organizations and activists operating under repressive systems. To take just a few examples concerning support for organizations and individuals within the former USSR: the World Psychiatric Association investigated, challenged and censured Soviet psychiatrists for their involvement in brutal treatment for dissidents; the International League for Human Rights established a formal bond with the Soviet Human Rights Committee founded in 1970 in Moscow and worked with it to support activists there; meanwhile, Human Rights Internet compiled and disseminated information on Soviet human rights issues. More recently, numbers of NGOs have assisted in the establishment of human rights organizations, training, and the provision of expertise and information on international standards to Eastern European organizations (e.g. to the Hungarian Bar Association and the Bulgarian Civic Forum for Free Speech) as those countries have emerged from the former Soviet bloc.

The number of effective NGOs and the number of their varied activities has been far too numerous to more than indicate here. With their myriad mandates, activities, focus and variety, NGOs have been a significant and crucial catalyst for the promotion and protection of human rights world-wide.

Conclusion

"Since 1945, human rights have become one of the central pillars of the international political and legal orders, together with the outlawing of aggressive war, and the equal rights and self-determination of peoples ... the time is [now] ...

over when nations were legitimately entitled to claim that how they treated their citizens was entirely their own business, and that any criticism of this was an illegitimate interference in the domestic affairs of a sovereign state."[8]

As we have seen, human rights today receive much more protection in domestic legal systems as well. Some of the ways in which these changes have occurred have been documented in this paper. The credit for the transformation which has been wrought – for making "human rights one of the central pillars of the international political and legal orders," and for giving them increased protection in domestic systems – must go to governments, intergovernmental and non-governmental organizations, and to the many dedicated individuals within them whose work, determination and vision have brought about this greatly increased protection of rights.

---

[8] P. Sieghart, An Introduction to the International Covenants on Human Rights, Commonwealth Secretariat Human Rights Unit Occasional Paper, London, March 1988, pp. 18,19.

Chapter II

Special Topics

Dealing with human rights violations committed under a previous regime

To Punish or to Pardon: a Devil's Choice Dealing with Human Rights Violations Committed Under a Previous Regime

Luc Huyse*

I. Policies

Coping with the past during the transition from a repressive regime to democracy has taken a wide variety of forms. Strategies have ranged from massive criminal prosecution of the supporters of the previous order to unconditionally closing the book. All policy choices involve answers to two key questions: whether to remember or forget the abuses and whether to impose sanctions on the individuals who are responsible for these abuses.

1. The granting of absolute amnesty is at one end of the spectrum. In some cases the unrestricted pardon is the result of the self amnesty that the outgoing elites unilaterally award themselves before the transition gets underway. In other instances impunity is the outcome of negotiations between old and new leaders. In Uruguay, for instance, the government that succeeded the military dictatorship enacted, under pressure from the military, an amnesty law (1986). Post-Franco Spain is an example of a third route toward impunity: almost all democratic forces agreed to confer immunity to individuals who committed crimes defending or opposing the Franco regime.

2. Forgiving, but not forgetting is the substance of a second major policy choice. Its usual format is the national or international *Truth Commission.* The first goal of such a commission is to investigate the fates, under the preceding regime, of individuals and of the nation as a whole. Its aim is not to prosecute and punish, A truth telling operation, including full disclosure of all human rights abuses, must ensure that 'the facts' are not forgotten, but remain alive in the memory of the collectivity. Well-known examples are the Chilean National Commission on Truth and Reconciliation (1990), the South African Truth and Reconciliation Commission (1995–1998) and the UN-sponsored Truth Commission in El Salvador (1991). Sometimes, as in the case of the South African Truth and Reconciliation Commission, amnesty is given to individuals who give full disclosure of their role in human rights violations.

3. *Lustration* or disqualification of the agents of the secret police and their informers, of judges and teachers, of civil servants and military personnel is a

*Law and Society Institute, Law Department, University of Leuven, Belgium.

K. Hossain et al. (eds), Human Rights Commissions and Ombudsman Offices, 83–88.

third way to address the question of reckoning for past wrongs. It sometimes includes the loss of political and civil rights. In some of the post-communist countries of East and Central Europe the screening of officials has been the only policy step.

4. By far the most radical interpretation of acknowledgement and accountability is to be found in the outright *criminal prosecution* of the perpetrators. This task can be taken up by an international body, as in the case of the International Criminal Tribunal for the Former Yugoslavia. National courts also perform this function. A prominent example is Ethiopia where some 5000 officials of the fallen Mengistu regime have been named for trial. By contrast, as a strategy for dealing with the past criminal prosecution has encountered almost no support in post-1989 Eastern and Central Europe and in the post-authoritarian regimes of Latin America.

5. Prosecution and/or general knowledge of the truth might be seen as an incomplete dealing with the crimes of the previous regime. Additional steps may include compensation by the state (monetary reparation, free medical and psychological treatment, reduced interests on loans for education and home building) and the establishment of permanent reminders of the legacy of the past, such as monuments, museums, public holidays and ceremonies. In South Africa such measures are seen to provide channels for the non-violent expression of pain and anger.

Some of these policies are offender-oriented (amnesty, prosecution and lustration), others are victim-oriented (compensation and symbolic measures). Truth commissions are directed towards both offenders and victims.

II. Dilemmas

In the ongoing public debate over post-transition justice political leaders, academics and journalists are divided on numerous points. But by far the most divisive question is how to balance the demands of justice against the many, mainly political, factors that make prosecution a major risk to the new regime.

The Case for Prosecution and/or Lustration

Those who emphasize the beneficial effects of prosecution bring forward two crucial reasons. Firstly, punishing the perpetrators of the old regime advances the cause of building or reconstructing a morally just order. The second reason has to do with establishing and upholding the young democracy that succeeds the authoritarian system.

1. Putting back in place the moral order that has broken down requires that 'justice be done', the proponents of prosecutions argue. They believe that the successor government owes it, first of all, as a moral obligation to the victims of the repressive system. Post-authoritarian justice serves to heal the wounds and to repair the private and public damage the antecedent regime provoked. It also, as a sort of ritual cleansing process, paves the way for a moral and political renaissance.

2. A second argument in favour of a judicial operation against the advocates of the old regime is that it strengthens fragile democracies. In the first months after the transition, it is said, the survival of the successor regime depends on swift and firm action against pro-authoritarian officials and their following. Such action is seen as a necessary protection against sabotage 'from within'. Moreover, if the prosecution issue remains untouched, other forms of social and political disturbance may be triggered, with perhaps a risk of vigilante justice with summary executions. What a new or reinstated democracy needs most, however, is legitimacy. Failure to prosecute and lustrate may generate in the population feelings of cynicism and distrust towards the political system. This is precisely what happened in some of the Latin American countries.

Some analysts believe that prosecutions also advance long-term democratic consolidation. Opponents of impunity argue that amnesty endangers the inculcation of codes of conduct based on the rule of law. They claim that a discriminatory application of the criminal law, privileging certain defendants (such as military leaders) will breed cynicism toward the rule of law. With impunity there is no implanting of a human rights culture in the society at large.

Prosecutions, finally, are seen as the most potent deterrence against future abuses of human rights.

The Case Against Punishment

Other participants in the debate have argued that prosecuting those alleged to bear responsibility for the crimes of the past is not without considerable ambivalence. There is no guarantee, they say, that its effects will be merely beneficial for democracy. They argue chiefly that partisan justice always lurks from behind the corner and, secondly, that prosecutions can have highly destabilising effects on an immature democracy.

1. Young democracies affirm that they highly value the rule of law and human rights. But post-transition justice involves a number of decisions that may trespass on those very legal principles. Dealing with the past by prosecutions, some analysts argue, therefore holds a sizeable risk. It may force the successor elites to violate rule of law principles today while judging the undemocratic behaviour of yesterday. This can, as a consequence, considerably weaken the legitimacy of the new regime.

The principles of the separation of powers and of judicial impartiality are at stake when answering the question of who will be the judges of the authoritarian regime. Political pressure, time constraints and the unavailability of sufficient judicial personnel may incite the post-transition elites to create special tribunals in which lay-judges play a prominent role. This, the opponents of prosecutions argue, makes lapses from important legal norms almost unavoidable. Such special courts can, indeed, become instruments of partisan vengeance since non-professional judges are easier targets for pressure by the executive, the media and public opinion.

Justice after transition must take place within a temporal frame. This frame consists of answers to two questions. The first one is: do we accept ex post facto criminal legislation? It is *the nullum crimen sine lege, nulla poena sine lege* principle which is at stake here. This principle means that no conduct may be held punishable unless it is precisely described in a penal law, and no penal sanction may be imposed except in pursuance of a law that describes it prior to the commission of the offense. The second question involves the problem of eventually lifting or upholding the existing statute of limitation. This question is particularly acute in the post-communist countries. Atrocities against the life and property of men and women took place mostly in the late 1940's and during the 1950's. In most cases, as in Hungary where a 30-year statute of limitations exists, criminal proceedings for the most reprehensible human rights abuses are thus precluded by reason of lapse of time. Those who disapprove of prosecutions assert that post-transition trials ultimately will result in changing the rules of the game after the fact, either by applying retroactive legislation or by recommencing the statute of limitation once it has run out.

Another argument of those who disapprove of prosecutions is that post-transition justice tends to be emergency justice – particularly if it comes in the early phases of the transition. The climate is then seldom well suited for a scrupulous sorting out of all the gradations in responsibility for the abuses of the past.

2. A new or reinstated democracy is a frail construct. For that reason impunity or, at least, tolerance in the handling of past abuses might be a prerequisite for the survival of the democratic process.

There is, first, the risk of a destabilising backlash. Military leaders who feel threatened by projected prosecution may try to reverse the course of events by a coup or a rebellion. This problem especially haunts the young democracies of Latin America.

A prolonged physical and social expulsion, based on criminal court decisions, of certain sections of the population may obstruct democratic consolidation in yet another way. It could drive the supporters of the previous regime into social and political isolation. This in turn could result in the creation of subcultures and networks, which in the long run will become hostile to democracy. Criminal prosecutions may also preclude the reconciliation required for a democracy to function. The need for closing the ranks is one of the main arguments of advocates of amnesty laws.

The viability of a young democracy depends too on its efficacy. A far-reaching purge of administrative and managerial manpower can be counterproductive as it endangers the badly needed political and economic development of the country. Prudent considerations of the problematic consequences of dismissals from civil service and high industrial jobs are been heard regularly in post-communist East and Central Europe.

Meeting Ethical Requirements and Political Constraints

Dealing with the past is an inescapable task for new democratic regimes. Successor elites may be put off by the many delicate and explosive aspects of such assignment. But there is no way out. Choices must be made. One of Samuel Huntington's guidelines to democratizers reads: "Recognize that on the issue of 'prosecute and punish vs. forgive and forget', each alternative presents grave problems, and that the least unsatisfactory course may well be: do not prosecute, do not punish, do not forgive, and, above all, do not forget."

A major problem is that some of the arguments in the debate on pardon vs. punish are quite contradictory. Most political leaders, journalists and academics seem to agree that the crucial challenge is to strike a balance between the demands of justice and political prudence or, in other words, to reconcile ethical imperatives and political constraints. This is no easy enterprise. It entails a difficult and, on occasion, torturous cost-benefit analysis. All costs and gains, political and moral, of pardoning and punishing, must be balanced against each other.

III. Constraints

In their confrontation with the many questions and dilemmas which dealing with the past poses, political and judicial elites have limited freedom of action. Several factors restrict the number of accessible politico-legal strategies: earlier experiences with post-transitional justice, the international context at the time of the regime change, the presence or absence of organizational resources, the state of the judiciary.

But the determining factor is the balance of power between the forces of the old and the new order during and shortly after the transition. A first case involves the violent overthrow or the collapsing of the repressive regime, as in Ethiopia. There is then a clear victory of the new forces over the old order. Democracy can arrive, second, at the initiative of reformers inside the forces of the past. That is what happened in the Soviet Union. South Africa belongs to a third category: democratization resulted from joint action by and the negotiated settlement between governing and opposition groups.

The most important consequence of the mode of transition is the density of the political constraints it generates. The widest scope for prosecutions and punishment arises in the case of an overthrow. Almost no political limits exist. Full priority can be given to the thirst for justice and retribution. A totally different situation comes up if the transition is based on reform or compromise. In that case the forces of the previous order have not lost all power and control. They are to a certain degree able to dictate the terms of the transition. The new elites have only limited options. They may be forced to grant the outgoing authorities a safe passage in return for their total or partial abdication. The need to avoid confrontation becomes the rationale for exchanging criminal prosecution and severe lustration for a policy of forgiveness.

IV. Conclusion

Many of the policy suggestions, mentioned in part I, depart from the premise that post-authoritarian elites can actually make choices. However, the first lesson of the study of past examples is that the actions of such elites is a function of the circumstances of the journey to democracy. The second conclusion is that there are no miracle solutions to the question of how to deal with a repressive past. In almost all cases the passage of time has not fully exorcized the ghosts of this past. Too much forgiveness undermines the respect for the law, induces the anger of those who suffered, is an impediment to an authentic reconciliation and an invitation to recidivism. That is why most analysts argue that if the balance of forces at the time of the transition makes a negotiated mildness inevitable, a truth-telling operation with full exposure of the crimes of the former regime is the least unsatisfactory solution. Memory, it is said, is the ultimate form of justice. The truth is both retribution and deterrence, and undermines the mental foundation of future human rights abuses.

Further Reading

Much of the recent literature can be found in these readers and special issues of journals:

Kritz, N.J. (ed.), *Transitional Justice. How Emerging Democracies Reckon With Former Regimes*, Volume I: General Considerations, Volume II: Country Studies, Volume III: Laws, Rulings, Reports, Washington D.C.: United Institute of Peace, 1995.

Jongman, A.J. (ed.), *Contemporary Genocide's: Causes, Cases, Consequences*, Leiden: PIOOM, 1996.

Law and Lustration: Righting the Wrongs of the Past, special issue of *Law and Social Inquiry*, Journal of the American Bar Foundation, 1995.

Accountability for International Crimes, special issue of *Law and Contemporary Problems*, Duke University, 1998.

Huntington, S.P., *The Third Wave. Democratisation in the Late Twentieth Century*, University of Oklahoma Press, 1991.

O'Donnell, G., Schmitter, P. (eds), *Transitions from Authoritarian Rule: Prospects for Democracy*, Baltimore: The Johns Hopkins University Press, 1986.

The Truth and Reconciliation Commission in South Africa

Alex Boraine*

South Africa, like many other countries coming out of a period of totalitarianism or military dictatorship, has tried to address the question of historic human rights violations committed during the period of oppression and conflict. Bearing in mind the historical, political and social circumstances and the nature of the transition, there were only three genuine options open to South Africa.

Firstly, a blanket of general amnesty. There was a strong demand for this, particularly from the former government, i.e. the National Party, as well as the security forces.

Secondly, criminal justice through the normal working of courts where anyone proven guilty would be sentenced. This was an option which for a long time was strongly motivated by the African National Congress. As Thabo Mbeki, Deputy President of South Africa, put it,

> "Within the ANC the cry was to 'catch the bastards and hang them', but we realized you could not simultaneously prepare for a peaceful transition while saying we want to catch and hang people, so we paid a price for the peaceful transition. If we had not taken this route, I don't know where the country would be today. Had there been a threat of Nuremberg-style trials over members of the apartheid security establishment, we would never have undergone the peaceful change".

There were many who, at the time of transition, demanded and called for prosecutions.

A third choice was that of a Truth and Reconciliation Commission which would offer amnesty to perpetrators under very clearly defined criteria; the restoration of dignity to victims and survivors, and a search for truth which would exorcize the fantasy of denial. Our view is that the third option, which we chose, has avoided the extremes of amnesia on the one hand, and a protracted series of trials and prosecutions on the other.

In a very real sense amnesty is a price we are paying for a relatively peaceful shift from totalitarianism to democracy. It is a very heavy price, and one that is still opposed by many victims. Our view, however, is that the benefits arising from this process outweigh the denial of full justice. There can be little doubt that if we had gone the route of pure criminal justice, the resistance from the former security forces would have made a peaceful transition impossible, would have heightened the conflict and cost many lives, and destroyed any possibility of peace and prosperity for our country.

---

*Deputy Chairperson, Truth and Reconciliation Commission, South Africa.

K. Hossain et al. (eds), Human Rights Commissions and Ombudsman Offices, 89–95.

Justice Richard Goldstone puts it this way:

"The decision to opt for a Truth and Reconciliation Commission was an important compromise. If the ANC had insisted on Nuremburg-style trials for the leaders of the former apartheid government, there would have been no peaceful transition to democracy, and if the former government had insisted on a blanket amnesty, then similarly the negotiations would have broken down. A bloody revolution, sooner rather than later, would have been inevitable. The Truth and Reconciliation Commission is therefore a bridge from the old to the new."

Past Injustice, Future Reconciliation

The transition from oppression to democracy came not as a result of a victory on the battle field nor through the resignation of the government of the day but through the process of negotiation. In negotiation politics the search for consensus and if a win-win situation is to flourish then compromises are inevitable. This was certainly true of the South African transition and remains true today.

The cost of these compromises is very high, but the cost of not accepting them would have been higher, with continued conflict, disruption and serious loss of life.

One such compromise was the introduction of amnesty provisions for those who were involved in gross human rights violations during the period 1960 to 1994.

The title of the founding Act speaks volumes for the fundamental intent of the Truth and Reconciliation Commission, i.e. The Promotion of National Unity and Reconciliation Act. The long title of the Act develops this theme:

- to establish the truth in relation to past events as well as the motives for and circumstances in which gross violations of human rights have occurred, and to make the findings known in order to prevent a repetition of such acts in future;
- the pursuit of national unity, the well-being of all South African citizens and peace require reconciliation between the people of South Africa and the reconstruction of society;
- a need for understanding but not for vengeance, a need for ubuntu but not for victimisation;
- in order to advance such reconciliation and reconstruction, amnesty shall be granted in respect of acts, omissions and offences associated with political objectives committed in the course of the conflicts of the past.

Whilst South Africa's Commission has been shaped very much by its own history and the circumstances and the nature of its particular and peculiar transition, there are many similarities to the experiences in eastern Europe and South America which impinge on the Commission in South Africa.

Briefly, these are:

- a shift from totalitarianism to a form of democracy;
- a negotiated settlement, not a revolutionary process;
- a legacy of oppression and serious violations of human rights;
- a fragile democracy and precarious unity;

- a commitment to the attainment of a culture of human rights and a respect for the rule of law;
- a determination that the work of the Commission will help to make it impossible for the gross violations of human rights of the past to happen again.

South Africa, in company with many other countries, has had to face up to three critical questions: Firstly, how do emerging democracies deal with past violations of human rights? Secondly, how do new democratic governments deal with leaders and individuals who were responsible for disappearances, death squads, psychological and physical torture and other violations of human rights? Thirdly, how does a new democracy deal with the fact that some of the perpetrators remain part of the new government and/or security forces or hold important positions in public life?

Priscilla B. Hayner reminds us that there have been some 19 truth commissions in 16 countries over the last 20 years, including those now in formation. We have, in the work leading up to the appointment of the Truth and Reconciliation Commission, been greatly influenced and assisted in studying many of these commissions and particularly in Chile and Argentina.

There are, however, some unique features to the South African model which may be of some relevance and assistance to this conference.

Unique Features of the South African Model

The process by which South Africa arrived at its Commission is quite different from any other that I know of. It was essentially democratic and gave as many people as possible an opportunity to participate in the formation of the Commission.

From the very outset the process leading to the actual promulgation of the Act as well as the appointment of the Commissioners has been as open and as transparent and democratic as possible. I think this will contribute in no small measure to any success which the Commission may achieve.

It was an Act of Parliament which brought the Truth and Reconciliation Commission into being. This, too, is very different from any other commission that I know of. In most instances the commission is appointed by the President or Prime Minister of the country concerned and they have to work out their procedures, objectives, methodologies, etc. The benefit of a commission being based in an Act of Parliament is that you have democratically elected legislators participating in the debate and finalising the objectives, procedures and powers of the commission.

Objectives are clearly set out, restraints are laid down and the Commissioners have to abide by the Act.

In the Act provision is made for 17 Commissioners who serve full time. The Commission has to complete its work by 31 July 1998. The Act also provides for three separate committees:

- The *Human Rights Violations Committee* which conducts public hearings for victims/survivors;
- The *Reparation and Rehabilitation Committee* which works on policies and recommendations arising from those hearings; and

– The *Amnesty Committee* which hears applications for amnesty.

In addition to the 17 Commissioners a number of Committee Members are allowed for, plus a professional and administrative staff and an Investigative Unit. Provisions is also made for a Witness Protection Programme.

A critical decision was made relating to the hearings of the Committees, both in terms of human rights violations and the stories of victims, as well as the amnesty hearings. Despite the risk and the additional complications, it was decided that those hearings should be open to the media and to the general public. This has placed an enormous burden on the Commissioners who travel throughout South Africa conducting hearings, because they do not have the benefit of working quietly and in private, but are constantly under the scrutiny of the media and of the public. On the other hand, there is the advantage of the nation participating in the hearings and the work of the Commission from the very beginning through radio, television and the print media and the rights of anyone to attend any of the hearings. This encourages transparency and provides a strong educative opportunity so that knowledge, healing and reconciliation is not confined to a small group, but is a possibility for all South Africans.

A further departure from the norm was the decision to publish the names not only of the victims and some details of the human rights violation suffered by them, but also the publication of the names of perpetrators. A major problem was the need to ensure due process and a fairly elaborate system has been worked out so that people who are going to be named by victims are alerted ahead of time and are invited to make either written representation or, if desired, they may appear at a subsequent public hearing.

These names are not only mentioned during the process of the hearing, but once the Investigative Unit has had an opportunity to recommend its findings to the Commission, the Commission will publish the names on the balance of probability in its Final Report and in the Government Gazette.

A further difference from most commissions is the powers which are vested in the Commission. The Commission has powers of subpoena and of search and seizure. This enables the Commission firstly to invite alleged perpetrators or those who may have critical information to come to the Commission and share that information with the Commission. If that invitation is spurned, it can proceed to subpoena those concerned.

It also means that the Commission can secure files and documents which have been secreted away by the previous government and its agents. This has resulted in agreements made by political parties and military and security institutions to make public submissions to the Commission.

We have also widened the mandate to include public hearings of major institutions such as the media, the legal sector, business and labour, the armed forces, the health sector and political parties.

The provision of amnesty to perpetrators of gross human rights violations has been and is a source of heated debate and controversy. South Africa has not escaped this debate. However, there is a major difference in the approach of South Africa's Commission to amnesty than is the case in most other countries.

Amnesty

General amnesty has created considerable problems in the whole quest for reconciliation and justice. There is a widespread debate, particularly in South Africa, which continues to focus on this dilemma. The following quotes exquisitely sum up the contradiction inherent in "blanket amnesty":

"How can I ever have peace when every day I risk meeting my unpunished tortures in the neighbourhood?" (tortured ex political prisoner, Argentina)

"How is reconciliation possible when lies and denials are institutionalized by the responsible authorities?" (human rights activist, Chile)

and

"No government can forgive – they don't know my pain – only I can forgive and I must know before I can forgive." (widow testifying at a TRC hearing in South Africa)

South Africa has attempted to avoid the problem of a general amnesty in the following way:

- Firstly, amnesty has to be applied for on an individual basis – there is no blanket amnesty;
- Secondly, applicants for amnesty must complete a prescribed form which is published in the Government Gazette and which calls for very detailed information relating to specific human rights violations;
- Thirdly, applicants must make 'full disclosure' of their human rights violations in order to qualify for amnesty;
- Fourthly, there is a time limit set in terms of the Act. Only those gross human rights violations committed in the period of 1960 to May 1994 will be considered for amnesty. Secondly, there is a specific time period during which amnesty applications may be made, from the time of the promulgation of the Act – which was December 1995 – to the cut-off point on 14 May 1994. – Fifthly, there is a list of criteria laid down in the Act which will determine whether or not the applicant for amnesty will be successful.

The need to know

South Africa's experience is very similar to many other countries, in that witness after witness at the Human Rights Violations Committee hearings have emphasized their deep fundamental need to know the truth surrounding the loss of their loved one. Over and over again people have pleaded to know what happened to the father, or the mother, the sister, the brother, son or the daughter. Where is he or she buried? Why did they do this? This is a common refrain at almost every public hearing. In other words, knowing the details and circumstances of the human rights violation in itself is part of the healing process.

But how will we know the truth if perpetrators do not come forward? The fact of the matter is that repression has been with us for generations in South Africa and there is very little likelihood of new evidence coming to light or even of witnesses being prepared to testify. The only way we are going to know some of the truth is for perpetrators to come and tell their story of what they did, to whom and how. But they will only come forward if amnesty is offered.

This may be a denial of full justice, but in terms of the pleas of victims it is of some consolation tot them as they try to reconstruct their lives.

A Commitment to Truth

Essentially the Truth and Reconciliation Commission is committed to the development of a human rights culture and to respect for the rule of law in South Africa. In attempting to do this, I believe that there is an irreducible minimum and that is commitment to truth. As President Aylwin of Chile said when he assumed office:

> "This leaves the excruciating problem of human rights violations and other violent crimes which have caused so many victims and so much suffering in the past. They are an open wound in our national soul that cannot be ignored. Nor can it heal through mere forgetfulness. To close our eyes and pretend none of this ever happened would be to maintain at the core of our society a source of pain, division, hatred and violence. Only the disclosure of the truth and the search for justice can create the moral climate in which reconciliation and peace will flourish".

More recently, Switzerland has been confronted by its past, especially in relation to its treatment of Jews during the Second World War and its cosy relationship with the Nazi regime.

Thomas Borer, who has been entrusted with the investigation, stated, "Jews are not our enemies. Our history is not our enemy. But the way we deal with or not deal with our own history – that would be our enemy."

Switzerland's Foreign Minister Cotti echoes this approach: "I have spent ten years in the government and until last year no one, I mean no one, spoke of the fundamental necessity of re-examining Swiss history. Now I realize this must be done because a country that has not really faced its past cannot decide its history."

I believe that we cannot achieve reconciliation without the truth. However costly the search for truth and knowing the truth might be, its is of fundamental importance to base peace and unity on truth.

In South Africa we have come out for a period where our society was based on lies and deceit. Radio and television was little more than a giant propaganda factory producing a packaged product to reinforce oppression and exclusivity. The search for truth, the recording of that truth can exorcize the fantasy of denial which makes transformation impossible.

In a book entitled, "The Healing of a Nation?" which I published two years ago I stated as follows:

> "It is when South Africa begins to take its past seriously that there will be new possibilities for all; for some to say sorry and for many more to be ready to forgive."

South Africans desperately need to create a common memory that can be acknowledged by those who created and implemented the apartheid system, by those who fought against it and the many more who were in the middle and claimed not to know what was happening in their country.

H Richard Niebuhr put it succinctly in his book, "The Story of Life":

> "Where common memory is lacking, where men do not share in the same past, there can be no real community and where community is to be formed common memory must be

created. The measure of our distance from each other in our nations and our groups can be taken by noting the divergence, the separateness and the lack of sympathy in our social memories. Conversely, the measure of our unity is the extent of our common memory."

One of the overarching problems we face is the unwillingness of some political leaders to accept accountability for the past. As in so many other parts of the world it is the foot soldiers, the middle management of the security forces and even the generals who are blamed for implementing the policies and laws devised by political parties and political leaders. The moral order can only be restored when it begins where people make the laws, i.e. in Parliament. It can only flourish when judges and magistrates interpret those laws for the benefit of the disadvantaged, the oppressed and the poor. Reconciliation begins when new laws and their interpretation are implemented. Without political will and courage they remain words and phrases with no life.

This is beginning to emerge in South Africa. In the Truth and Reconciliation Commission, in government, in civil society and in the professions there is a determination that what we have experienced in the past must never happen again.

Conclusion

South Africa remains a deeply divided society and no single limited-life commission can on its own achieve reconciliation. It can only lay down foundations stones on which both government and civil society must build. These stones include at least truth-telling, accountability and acknowledgement.

In our search for genuine reconciliation, which is always costly, there must always be a commitment to economic justice. The restoration of the moral order and the transformation of the social order must go hand in hand.

The Importance of the Ethiopian Trials in Reinforcing Human Rights Protection in Ethiopia

Rodolfo Mattarollo*

1. When the organization of the conference proposed as a subject for one panel the issue of dealing with human rights abuses committed under a previous regime, they were entirely conscious of the link between the question of reining in impunity of these abuses and building the new institutions created by the Constitution, namely the Human Rights Commission and Office of Ombudsman.
2. The World Conference on Human Rights took a very strong position on the question of fighting impunity. According to the Vienna Declaration (June 1993) paragraphs 60 and 62: "States should abrogate legislation leading to impunity for those responsible for grave violations of human rights such as torture, and prosecute such violations, thereby providing a firm basis for the rule of law. [...] The World Conference on Human Rights reaffirms that it is the duty of all States, under any circumstances, to make investigations whenever there is reason to believe that an enforced disappearance has taken place on a territory under their jurisdiction and, if allegations are confirmed, to prosecute its perpetrators."
3. Probably not everybody, perhaps particularly non-Ethiopian colleagues, is aware of the great efforts made in Ethiopia to abide by these principles. I have no time to give here the background of the Ethiopian trials. Let me say that former Dergue members, including Mengistu Haile Mariam, have been charged with genocide and other related offences, and as an alternative with aggravated homicide (in 1994). Objections to these charges by defence counsels were responded to by the Special Prosecutor in 1995. These charges were filed on the basis of the Ethiopian Penal Code of 1957, which remains a part of the law of the country. The Code provides for the punishment of the crime of genocide and – unusually – includes political organizations amongst protected groups.
4. In December 1996 fifty percent of the charges (excluding those related to Dergue members' trials referred to above) were submitted to the Federal High Court in Addis Ababa. In February 1997 the remainder of the charges were submitted to the Federal High Court in Addis Ababa, and to the Regional State Supreme Courts. The actual trial of these cases started in

*Deputy Executive Director, International Civilian Mission in Haiti. I make this statement in my personal capacity and as a former adviser to the Special Prosecutor's Office (SPO) of the Government of Ethiopia (from December 1993 to June 1995).

K. Hossain et al. (eds), Human Rights Commissions and Ombudsman Offices, 97–99.

October/November 1997. The charges in question concern 5000 individuals, either tried in person (3000) or in absentia (2000). The Harari National Regional State Supreme Court fixed a date in January 1998 for its first hearing; in Oromia National Regional State the court session started in April 1998; the Amhara Court has fixed a date for the first hearing in June 1998. However, in Tigray and the Southern Ethiopian Peoples' National Regional States hearings have not yet been scheduled.

5. The SPO has now 22 public prosecutors and 172 case files. These files related to the 5000 persons who have been charged, grouped according to alleged crimes. As a result, each prosecutor is in charge of around 8 files. Eighty percent of defence counsels are appointed by the courts. In the Dergue members' trial, only five or six defendants have private lawyers.
6. During the conference several participants raised the question of linking the creation of new institutions like the Ombudsman and the Human Rights Commission to the reinforcement of the Judiciary and the Parliament. I would stress that the new institutions are not contradictory but complementary with others like the Judiciary and the Parliament.
7. In the experience of countries that abide by the obligation of the state under domestic and international law to prosecute past human rights violations, prosecutions and reinforcement of the judiciary, as well as the creation of the Ombudsman, are related. This is the case in Argentina, to give an example.
8. In Ethiopia there is a dire need to continue the support from the international community in the field of institution building. According to the information received there are two aspects which deserve priority attention of all those who are sensitive to the question of human rights in this country. First the budget and training of the courts; and second the organization of the defence of the accused.
9. I should like to express my concern regarding three factors which may be argued to weaken the significance of these trials, within the context of human rights law and principles. First, the fact that the death penalty is still in force in Ethiopia. Second, the excessive delay of the procedures. Third, weaknesses in the organization of the defence.
10. The European Court of Human Rights stated that the right to be tried within a reasonable period should be assessed in accordance with the three following elements: (a) the complexity of the case; (b) the behaviour of the defendants; and (c) the behaviour of the State authorities.
11. Even those who believe that Ethiopia could have done better – and I personally would ask them to provide examples of how this could have been the case in this particular context – are not easily able to argue that the prolonged nature of these proceedings is sufficient ground to regard them as flawed. To be consistent with the obligations vested in the States by domestic and international law, more effort should be made to help our Ethiopian colleagues to fulfil this task.
12. The continuation and completion of these proceedings in a timely and satisfactory manner, according to international standards of a fair trial and due process of law, is essential not only in terms of reining in impunity, but also in terms of building the capacity of the Ethiopian judiciary necessary to ensure the respect of rule of law in this country. It is only if the capacity

of the judiciary as a whole is built in this way, that the new institutions of the Human Rights Commission and Ombudsman will be able to fulfil their mandate.

13. In conclusion therefore, as a former legal adviser to the SPO, I would like to appeal to participants and observers of, and donors to this conference, to keep in mind the heavy burden of the material and human resources required for the continuation and completion of this essential judicial undertaking.

Safeguarding the Rights of the Accused in the Prosecution Process at the International Criminal Tribunal of Rwanda

Bernard A. Muna*

Introduction

One major cause of respect for human rights in any society is how its justice system treats those it accuses of committing crimes. The essence of this treatment translates into a simple ideal expressed in the concept of fairness to the accused. This ideal as simply as it is, must be rigorously and consciously pursued through a regime of certain minimum guarantees without which a justice system is that much the poorer.

The key notion in this regard is the concept of presumption of innocence. Everyone is presumed innocent until (s)he is proved guilty on an appropriate standard of proof. This is the mother of all those other rules of fairness for an accused person. The idea is simple. A citizen is charged with a crime. That is a state of affairs that essentially entails a plethora of legal circumstances. There is a lowering of the esteem in the eyes of the community. There is restriction of freedom, not only in terms of possible detention during the trial, but also the rather mundane, but patent, restriction that comes with having the obligation to attend proceedings at a given place and time. There is the obligation to answer questions from lawyers and judges – some of which are quite intrusive to the privacy and the dignity of the person. There is the expenditure of funds in legal fees (barring the availability of legal aid). And so forth. In view of all of this, the best that the system can do is guarantee a fair trial to this person who is in the inconsistent position of suffering all these legal and social encumbrances, while at the same time enjoying the presumption of innocence.

At the International Criminal Tribunal for Rwanda (ICTR) some safeguards prevail to guarantee fair trial to the accused. These safeguards range from measures to be found at the various stages of the criminal prosecution process. The stages include the following:

(i) the role of legal professionals at the various stages of the process,
(ii) the pre-trial stage,
(iii) the trial stage,
(iv) the conclusion of trial, and
(v) the post-trial stage.

---

*Deputy Prosecutor, International Criminal Tribunal for Rwanda.

K. Hossain et al. (eds), Human Rights Commissions and Ombudsman Offices, 101–113.

I. The Role of Legal Professionals At the Various Stages of the Process

Before reviewing some of these guarantees, it is perhaps wise to begin first with a few thoughts on those entrusted with the task of bringing the law to bear on the trial of accused persons.

The Judiciary

The chief guarantee of all rights of the accused rests in the idea of an independent judiciary of a high moral fibre, integrity and competence. At the ICTR, the fountain of such an idea of the judiciary will be found in Articles 11 and 12. They provide as follows:

Article 11. Composition of the Chambers
The Chambers shall be composed of fourteen independent judges, no two of whom may be nationals of the same State, who shall serve as follows:
(a) Three judges shall serve in each of the Trial Chambers;
(b) Five judges shall serve in the Appeals Chamber.

Article 12: Qualification and election of judges
1. The judges shall be persons of high moral character, impartiality and integrity who possess the qualifications required in their respective countries for appointment to the highest judicial offices. In the overall composition of the Chambers due account shall be taken of the experience of the judges in criminal law, international law, including international humanitarian law and human rights law. [...]

These provisions bear out the accepted trends in international law embodied in a number of international conventions and such evidence of customary international law as most clearly expressed in the United Nations Basic Principles on the Independence of the Judiciary (1985) which provides as follows in relevant parts:

Independence of the judiciary
1. The independence of the judiciary shall be guaranteed by the State and enshrined in the Constitution or the law of the country. It is the duty of all governmental and other institutions to respect and observe the independence of the judiciary.
2. The judiciary shall decide matters before them impartially, on the basis of facts and in accordance with the law, without any restrictions, improper influences, inducements, pressures, threats or interferences, direct or indirect, from any quarter or for any reason.
3. The judiciary shall have jurisdiction over all issues of a judicial nature and shall have exclusive authority to decide whether an issue submitted for its decision is within its competence as defined by law.
4. There shall not be any inappropriate or unwarranted interference with the judicial process, nor shall judicial decisions by the courts be subject to revision. This principle is without prejudice to judicial review or to mitigation or commutation by competent authorities of sentences imposed by the judiciary, in accordance with the law.
5. Everyone shall have the right to be tried by ordinary courts or tribunals using established legal procedures. Tribunals that do not use the duly established procedures of the legal process shall not be created to displace the jurisdiction belonging to the ordinary courts or judicial tribunals.
6. The principle of the independence of the judiciary entitles and requires the judiciary to ensure that judicial proceedings are conducted fairly and that the rights of the parties are respected.
7. It is the duty of each Member State to provide adequate resources to enable the judiciary to properly perform its functions.

Qualifications, selection and training

10. Persons selected for judicial office shall be individuals of integrity and ability with appropriate training or qualifications in law. Any method of judicial selection shall safeguard against judicial appointments for improper motives. In the selection of judges, there shall be no discrimination against a person on the grounds of race, colour, sex, religion, political or other opinion, national or social origin, property, birth or status, except that a requirement, that a candidate for judicial office must be a national of the country concerned, shall not be considered discriminatory.

Without a judiciary imbued with such internal quality, it will much harder to guarantee to the accused the rights which everyone agrees must be put down on paper.

The Prosecutor

Although the Prosecutor is a representative of the public whose interest in law and order is the raison d'être of public prosecutions, the Prosecutor and (his) her battery of lawyers must, like the judges be independent of political influences, and must be highly qualified people of integrity and honour, who must remain sensitive to the rights of the accused. These ideals are given expression in Article 15(2) of the ICTR Statute which provides as follows:

2. The Prosecutor shall act independently as a separate organ of the International Tribunal for Rwanda. He or she shall not seek or receive instructions from any Government or from any other source.

Again, this is quite consonant with the state of general international law, which is given the clearest expression in the United Nations Guidelines on the Role of Prosecutors (1990). In relevant part, it provides as follows:

Qualifications, selection and training

1. Persons selected as prosecutors shall be individuals of integrity and ability, with appropriate training and qualifications.
2. States shall ensure that:
   (a) Selection criteria for prosecutors embody safeguards against appointments based on partiality or prejudice, excluding any discrimination against a person on the grounds of race, colour, sex, language, religion, political or other opinion, national, social or ethnic origin, property, birth, economic or other status, except that it shall not be considered discriminatory to require a candidate for prosecutorial office to be a national of the country concerned;
   (b) Prosecutors have appropriate education and training and should be made aware of the ideals and ethical duties of their office, of the constitutional and statutory protections for the rights of the suspect and the victim, and of human rights and fundamental freedoms recognized by national and international law.

Status and conditions of service

3. Prosecutors, as essential agents of the administration of justice, shall at all times maintain the honour and dignity of their profession.
4. States shall ensure that prosecutors are able to perform their professional functions without intimidation, hindrance, harassment, improper interference or unjustified exposure to civil, penal or other liability.
5. Prosecutors and their families shall be physically protected by the authorities when their personal safety is threatened as a result of the discharge of prosecutorial functions.
6. Reasonable conditions of service of prosecutors, adequate remuneration and, where

applicable, tenure, pension and age of retirement shall be set out by law or published rules or regulations.

7. Promotion of prosecutors, wherever such a system exists, shall be based on objective factors, in particular professional qualifications, ability, integrity and experience, and decided upon in accordance with fair and impartial procedures.

Freedom of expression and association

8. Prosecutors like other citizens are entitled to freedom of expression, belief, association and assembly. In particular, they shall have the right to take part in public discussion of matters concerning the law, the administration of justice and the promotion and protection of human rights and to join or form local, national or international organizations and attend their meetings, without suffering professional disadvantage by reason of their lawful action or their membership in a lawful organization. In exercising these rights, prosecutors shall always conduct themselves in accordance with the law and the recognized standards and ethics of their profession.
9. Prosecutors shall be free to form and join professional associations or other organizations to represent their interests, to promote their professional training and to protect their status. Role in criminal proceedings 10. The office of prosecutors shall be strictly separated from judicial functions.
11. Prosecutors shall perform an active role in criminal proceedings, including institution of prosecution and, where authorized by law or consistent with local practice, in the investigation of crime, supervision over the legality of these investigations, supervision of the execution of court decisions and the exercise of other functions as representatives of the public interest.
12. Prosecutors shall, in accordance with the law, perform their duties fairly, consistently and expeditiously, and respect and protect human dignity and uphold human rights, thus contributing to ensuring due process and the smooth functioning of the criminal justice system.
13. In the performance of their duties, prosecutors shall:
    (a) Carry out their functions impartially and avoid all political, social, religious, racial, cultural, sexual or any other kind of discrimination;
    (b) Protect the public interest, act with objectivity, take proper account of the position of the suspect and the victim, and pay attention to all relevant circumstances, irrespective of whether they are to the advantage or disadvantage of the suspect;
    (c) Keep matters in their possession confidential, unless the performance of duty or the needs of justice require otherwise;
    (d) Consider the views and concerns of victims when their personal interests are affected and ensure that victims are informed of their rights in accordance with the Declaration of Basic Principles of Justice for Victims of Crime and Abuse of Power.
14. Prosecutors shall not initiate or continue prosecution, or shall make every effort to stay proceedings, when an impartial investigation shows the charge to be unfounded.
15. Prosecutors shall give due attention to the prosecution of crimes committed by public officials, particularly corruption, abuse of power, grave violations of human rights and other crimes recognized by international law and, where authorized by law or consistent with local practice, the investigation of such offences.
16. When prosecutors come into possession of evidence against suspects that they know or believe on reasonable grounds was obtained through recourse to unlawful methods, which constitute a grave violation of the suspect's human rights, especially involving torture or cruel, inhuman or degrading treatment or punishment, or other abuses of human rights, they shall refuse to use such evidence against anyone other than those who used such methods, or inform the Court accordingly, and shall take all necessary steps to ensure that those responsible for using such methods are brought to justice.

Discretionary functions

17. In countries where prosecutors are vested with discretionary functions, the law or

published rules or regulations shall provide guidelines to enhance fairness and consistency of approach in taking decisions in the prosecution process, including institution or waiver of prosecution.

Alternatives to prosecution

18. In accordance with national law, prosecutors shall give due consideration to waiving prosecution, discontinuing proceedings conditionally or unconditionally, or diverting criminal cases from the formal justice system, with full respect for the rights of suspect(s) and the victim(s). For this purpose, States should fully explore the possibility of adopting diversion schemes not only to alleviate excessive court loads, but also to avoid the stigmatisation of pre-trial detention, indictment and conviction, as well as the possible adverse effects of imprisonment.
19. In countries where prosecutors are vested with discretionary functions as to the decision whether or not to prosecute a juvenile, special considerations shall be given to the nature and gravity of the offence, protection of society and the personality and background of the juvenile. In making that decision, prosecutors shall particularly consider available alternatives to prosecution under the relevant juvenile justice laws and procedures. Prosecutors shall use their best efforts to take prosecutory action against juveniles only to the extent strictly necessary.

Relations with other government agencies or institutions

20. In order to ensure the fairness and effectiveness of prosecution, prosecutors shall strive to co-operate with the police, the courts, the legal profession, public defenders and other government agencies or institutions.

Defence Counsel

Apart from judges and prosecutors that are independent, fair, competent and honourable, perhaps the most fundamental player in the protection of the rights of an accused is defence counsel who is also independent, competent, honourable and fearless. The right to such counsel is the cornerstone of a fair criminal trial. At the ICTR, the right to counsel is very much a guarantee at every stage of the process in. which an accused is recognized as a proper party. Where the accused is unable to afford one, (s)he will be assigned one (see Rules 44 and 45 of the Rules of Procedure and Evidence; see also Articles 2 and 3 of the Directive on Assignment of Defence Counsel (1996).) At all times, the ICTR's processes in relation to defence counsel strive to respect the following principles of international law which one may find most clearly expressed in the United Nations Basic Principles on the Role of Lawyers (1990):

Access to lawyers and legal services

1. All persons are entitled to call upon the assistance of a lawyer of their choice to protect and establish their rights and to defend them in all stages of criminal proceedings.
2. Government shall ensure that efficient procedures and responsive mechanisms for effective and equal access to lawyers are provided for all persons within their territory and subject to their jurisdiction, without distinction of any kind, such as discrimination based on race, colour, ethnic origin, sex, language, religion, political or other opinion, national or social origin, property, birth, economic or other status.
3. Governments shall ensure the provision of sufficient funding and other resources for legal services to the poor and, as necessary, to other disadvantaged persons. Professional associations of lawyers shall co-operate in the organization and provision of services, facilities and other resources.
4. Governments and professional associations of lawyers shall promote programmes to

inform the public about their rights and duties under the law and the important role of lawyers in protecting their fundamental freedoms. Special attention should be given to assisting the poor and other disadvantaged persons so as to enable them to assert their rights and where necessary call upon the assistance of lawyers.

Special safeguards in criminal justice matters

5. Governments shall ensure that all persons are immediately informed by the competent authority of their right to be assisted by a lawyer of their own choice upon arrest or detention or when charged with a criminal offence.
6. Any such persons who do not have a lawyer shall, in all cases in which the interests of justice so require, be entitled to have a lawyer of experience and competence commensurate with the nature of the offence assigned to them in order to provide effective legal assistance, without payment by them if they lack sufficient means to pay for such services.
7. Governments shall further ensure that all persons arrested or detained, with or without criminal charge, shall have prompt access to a lawyer, and in any case not later than forty-eight hours from the time of arrest or detention.
8. All arrested, detained or imprisoned persons shall be provided with adequate opportunities, time and facilities to be visited by and to communicate and consult with a lawyer, without delay, interception or censorship and in full confidentiality. Such consultations may be within sight, but not within the hearing, of law enforcement officials.

Qualifications and training

9. Governments, professional associations of lawyers and educational institutions shall ensure that lawyers have appropriate education and training and be made aware of the ideals and ethical duties of the lawyer and of human rights and fundamental freedoms recognized by national and international law.
10. Governments, professional associations of lawyers and educational institutions shall ensure that there is no discrimination against a person with respect to entry into or continued practice within the legal profession on the grounds of race, colour, sex, ethnic origin, religion, political or other opinion, national or social origin, property, birth, economic or other status, except that a requirement, that a lawyer must be a national of the country concerned, shall not be considered discriminatory.
11. In countries where there exist groups, communities or regions whose needs for legal services are not met, particularly where such groups have distinct cultures, traditions or languages or have been the victims of past discrimination Governments, professional associations of lawyers and educational institutions should take special measures to provide opportunities for candidates from these groups to enter the legal profession and should ensure that they receive training appropriate to the needs of their groups.

Duties and responsibilities

12. Lawyers shall at all times maintain the honour and dignity of their profession as essential agents of the administration of justice.
13. The duties of lawyers towards their clients shall include:
    (a) Advising clients as to their legal rights and obligations, and as to the working of the legal system in so far as it is relevant to the legal rights and obligations of the clients;
    (b) Assisting clients in every appropriate way, and taking legal action to protect their interests;
    (c) Assisting clients before courts, tribunals or administrative authorities, where appropriate.
14. Lawyers, in protecting the rights of their clients and in promoting the cause of justice, shall seek to uphold human rights and fundamental freedoms recognized by national

and international law and shall at all times act freely and diligently in accordance with the law and recognized standards and ethics of the legal profession.
15. Lawyers shall always loyally respect the interests of their clients.

Guarantees for the functioning of lawyers
16. Governments shall ensure that lawyers (a) are able to perform all of their professional functions without intimidation, hindrance, harassment or improper interference; (b) are able to travel and to consult with their clients freely both within their own country and abroad; and (c) shall not suffer, or be threatened with, prosecution or administrative, economic or other sanctions for any action taken in accordance with recognized professional duties, standards and ethics.
17. Where the security of lawyers is threatened as a result of discharging their functions, they shall be adequately safeguarded by the authorities.
18. Lawyers shall not be identified with their clients or their clients' causes as a result of discharging their functions.
19. No court or administrative authority before whom the right to counsel is recognized shall refuse to recognize the right of a lawyer to appear before it for his or her client unless that lawyer has been disqualified in accordance with national law and practice and in conformity with these principles.
20. Lawyers shall enjoy civil and penal immunity for relevant statements made in good faith in written or oral pleadings or in their professional appearances before a court, tribunal or other legal or administrative authority.
21. It is the duty of the competent authorities to ensure lawyers access to appropriate information, files and documents in their possession or control in sufficient time to enable lawyers to provide effective legal assistance to their clients. Such access should be provided at the earliest appropriate time.
22. Governments shall recognize and respect that all communications and consultations between lawyers and their clients within their professional relationship are confidential.

Having now reviewed the places and roles of the various categories of legal practitioners charged with ensuring that justice is treated fairly in the course of a criminal trial, we must now examine some of the other substantive guarantees of the rights of the accused in the processes of the ICTR.

II. Guarantee of the Rights of the Accused at the Pre-trial Stage

At the ICTR, some of the main guarantees of protection of the rights of the accused at the pre-trial stage include the following.

Investigation

It may be necessary for the Prosecutor to make contact with the potential accused during the investigation stage. At this stage, the target is not yet an accused. (S)he is merely a suspect. Even then, the target is not without rights. These rights are most clearly articulated in Article 42 and 43 of the Rules of Procedure and Evidence. It provides as follows:

Rule 42 Rights of Suspects during Investigation
(A) A suspect who is to be questioned by the Prosecutor shall have the following rights, of which he shall be informed by the Prosecutor prior to questioning, in a language he speaks and understands:
(i) the right to be assisted by counsel of his choice or to have legal assistance

assigned to him without payment if he does not have sufficient means to pay for it;

(ii) the right to have the free assistance of an interpreter if he cannot understand or speak the language to be used for questioning; and

(iii) the right to remain silent, and to be cautioned that any statement he makes shall be recorded and may be used in evidence.

(B) Questioning of a suspect shall not proceed without the presence of counsel unless the suspect has voluntarily waived his right to counsel. In case of waiver, if the suspect subsequently expresses a desire to have counsel, questioning shall thereupon cease, and shall only resume when the suspect has obtained or has been assigned counsel.

Rule 43
Recording Questioning of Suspects Whenever the Prosecutor questions a suspect, the questioning shall be audio-recorded or video-recorded, in accordance with the following procedure:

(i) the suspect shall be informed in a language he speaks and understands that the questioning is being audio-recorded or video-recorded;

(ii) in the event of a break in the course of the questioning, the fact and the time of the break shall be recorded before audio-recording or video-recording ends and the time of resumption of the questioning shall also be recorded;

(iii) at the conclusion of the questioning the suspect shall be offered the opportunity to clarify anything he has said, and to add anything he may wish, and the time of conclusion shall be recorded;

(iv) the tape shall then be transcribed as soon as practicable after the conclusion of questioning and a copy of the transcript supplied to the suspect, together with a copy of the recorded tape or, if multiple recording apparatus was used, one of the original recorded tapes; and

(v) after a copy has been made, if necessary, of the recorded tape for purposes of transcription, the original recorded tape or one of the original tapes shall be sealed in the presence of the suspect under the signature of the Prosecutor and the suspect.

Indictment

At the ICTR, no one may be brought to trial without a formal indictment reviewed and confirmed by an independent judge. Such an indictment shall be dismissed if the reviewing judge is left unsatisfied that the Prosecutor has made out a prima facie case to warrant confirmation: Art 18(1) of the ICTR Statute.

Where indictment is confirmed, then the reviewing judge may issue "such orders and warrants for the arrest, detention, surrender or transfer of persons, and any other orders as may be required for the conduct of the trial" (Article 18(2) of the ICTR Statute).

Ideally, indictment confirmation ought to precede any act of arrest and detention of the accused and the search and seizure of things. But things are not always ideal. There may be urgent cases, where it is not practical to go through the foregoing steps. In those circumstances, the Prosecutor may request any State (i) to arrest a suspect provisionally, (ii) to seize physical evidence, or (iii) to take all necessary measures to prevent the escape of a suspect or an accused, injury to or intimidation of a victim or witness, or the destruction of evidence (Rule 40 of the Rules of Procedure and Evidence). This, of course, is the exception rather than the rule.

Initial Appearance

Accused persons brought before the Tribunal must be promptly arraigned before a Trial Chamber in an initial appearance, where they are charged formally. The process essentially contains guarantees to ensure a fair trial for the accused. This will be seen in the provisions of art 19 of the Statute and of Rule 62 of the Rules, which provide as follows:

Article 19
Commencement and conduct of trial proceedings

1. The Trial Chambers shall ensure that a trial is fair and expeditious and that proceedings are conducted in accordance with the rules of procedure and evidence, with full respect for the rights of the accused with due regard for the protection of victims and witnesses.
2. A person against whom an indictment has been confirmed shall, pursuant to an order or an arrest warrant of the International Tribunal for Rwanda, be taken into custody, immediately informed of the charges against him or her and transferred to the International Tribunal for Rwanda.
3. The Trial Chamber shall read the indictment, satisfy itself that the rights of the accused are respected, confirm that the accused understands the indictment, and instruct the accused to enter a plea. The Trial Chamber shall then set the date for trial.
4. The hearings shall be public unless the Trial Chamber decides to close the proceedings in accordance with its rules of procedure and evidence.

Rule 62
Initial Appearance of Accused Upon his transfer to the Tribunal, the accused shall be brought before a Trial Chamber without delay, and shall be formally charged. The Trial Chamber shall:

(i) satisfy itself that the right of the accused to counsel is respected;
(ii) read or have the indictment read to the accused in a language he speaks and understands, and satisfy itself that the accused understands the indictment;
(iii) call upon the accused to enter a plea of guilty or not guilty on each count; should the accused fail to do so, enter a plea of not guilty on his behalf;
(iv) in case of a plea of not guilty, instruct the Registrar to set a date for trial;
(v) in case of a plea of guilty, instruct the Registrar to set a date for the pre-sentencing hearing;
(vi) instruct the Registrar to set such other dates as appropriate.

This process of initial appearance or arraignment signals the formal joinder of issues between the Prosecutor and the person who used to be a mere “suspect”. (S)he is now to be known formally as an “accused”. The adversarial process has now been moved into a higher gear.

Further Questioning of the Accused by the Prosecutor

Now that the issues are joined between the Prosecutor and the Accused the prosecutor may not question the accused in the absence of his counsel. Rule 63 provides:

Questioning of Accused
After the initial appearance of the accused the Prosecutor shall not question him unless his counsel is present and the questioning is audio-recorded or video-recorded in accordance with the procedure provided for in Rule 43. The Prosecutor shall at the beginning of the questioning caution the accused that he is not obliged to say anything unless he wishes to do so but that whatever he says may be given in evidence.

Disclosure Obligations

At the centre of the right of the accused to a fair trial is the right to make full answer and defence to the charges against him/her, it is fundamental that the Prosecutor disclose to the defence the material upon which the Prosecutor's case rests. The ICTR Rules of Procedure and Evidence regulate strictly how and when disclosure may be done, who has the obligation, as well as what is to be disclosed and what is exempt from disclosure. The relevant provisions are as follows:

Rule 66
Disclosure by the Prosecutor

(A) Subject to the provisions of Rules 53 and 69, the Prosecutor shall make available to the Defence:
  (i) within 30 days of the initial appearance of the accused copies of the supporting material which accompanied the indictment when confirmation was sought as well as all prior statements obtained by the prosecutor from the accused, and
  (ii) no later than 60 days before the date set for trial, copies of the statements of all witnesses whom the Prosecutor intends to call to testify at trial.

(B) The Prosecutor shall on request, subject to Sub-rule (C), permit the defence to inspect any books, documents, photographs and tangible objects in his custody or control, which are material to the preparation of the defence, or are intended for use by the Prosecutor as evidence at trial or were obtained from or belonged to the accused.

(C) Where information is in the possession of the Prosecutor, the disclosure of which may prejudice further or ongoing investigations, or for any other reasons may be contrary to the public interest or affect the security interests of any State, the Prosecutor may apply to the Trial Chamber sitting in camera to be relieved from the obligation to disclose pursuant to Sub-rule (B). When making such application the Prosecutor shall provide the Trial Chamber (but only the Trial Chamber) with the information that is sought to be kept confidential.

Rule 67
Reciprocal Disclosure

(A) As early as reasonably practicable and in any event prior to the commencement of the trial:
  (i) the Prosecutor shall notify the defence of the names of the witnesses that he intends to call in proof of the guilt of the accused and in rebuttal of any defence plea of which the Prosecutor has received notice in accordance with Sub-rule (ii) below;
  (ii) the defence shall notify the Prosecutor of its intent to offer:
    (a) the defence of alibi; in which case the notification shall specify- the place or places at which the accused claims to have been present at the time of the alleged crime and the names and addresses of witnesses and any other evidence upon which the accused intends to rely to establish the alibi;
    (b) any special defence, including that of diminished or lack of mental responsibility; in which case the notification shall specify the names and addresses of witnesses and any other evidence upon which the accused intends to rely to establish the special defence.

(B) Failure of the defence to provide notice under this Rule shall not limit the right of the accused to rely on the above defences.

(C) If the defence makes a request pursuant to Rule 66(B), the Prosecutor shall be entitled to inspect any books, documents, photographs and tangible objects, which are within the custody or control of the defence and which it intends to use as evidence at the trial.

(D) If either party discovers additional evidence or material which should have been produced earlier pursuant to the Rules, that party shall promptly notify the other party and the Trial Chamber of the existence of the additional evidence or material.

Rule 68
Disclosure of Exculpatory evidence
The Prosecutor shall, as soon as practicable, disclose to the defence the existence of evidence known to the Prosecutor which in any way tends to suggest the innocence or mitigate the guilt of the accused or may affect the credibility of prosecution evidence.

Rule 69
Protection of Victims and Witnesses
(A) In exceptional circumstances, the Prosecutor may apply to a Trial Chamber to order the non-disclosure of the identity of a victim or witness who may be in danger or at risk until such person is brought under the protection of the Tribunal.
(B) In the determination of protective measures for victims and witnesses, the Trial Chamber may consult the Victims and Witnesses Unit.
(C) Subject to Rule 75, the identity of the victim or witness shall be disclosed in sufficient time prior to the trial to allow adequate time for preparation of the defence.

Rule 70
Matters not Subject to Disclosure
(A) Notwithstanding the provisions of Rules 66 and 67 reports, memoranda, or other internal documents prepared by a party. its assistants or representatives in connection with the investigation or preparation of the case, are not subject to disclosure or notification under those Rules.
(B) If the Prosecutor is in possession of information which has been provided to him on a confidential basis and which has been used solely for the purpose of generating new evidence, that initial information and its origin shall not be disclosed by the Prosecutor without the consent of the person or entity providing the initial information and shall in any event not be given in evidence without prior disclosure to the accused.
(C) If, after obtaining the consent of the person or entity providing information under this Rule, the Prosecutor elects to present as evidence any testimony, document or other material so provided, the Trial Chamber, notwithstanding Rule 98, may not order either party to produce additional evidence received from the person or entity providing the initial information, nor may the Trial Chamber for the purpose of obtaining such additional evidence itself summon that person or a representative of that entity as a witness or order their attendance.

The foregoing is just a brief overview of how the rights of the accused persons are protected in the processes of the ICTR, at the pre-trial stage of the proceedings.

III. The Trial Stage

At the trial stage, the Statute of the ICTR continues to guarantee certain rights to the accused. These rights will be found mostly in Article 20, which provides as follows:

Article 20
Rights of the Accused
1. All persons shall be equal before the International Tribunal for Rwanda.
2. In the determination of charges against him or her, the accused shall be entitled to a fair and public hearing, subject to article 21 of the Statute.

3. The accused shall be presumed innocent until proven guilty according to the provisions of the present Statute.
4. In determination of any charge against the accused pursuant to the present Statute, the accused shall be entitled to the following minimum guarantees, in full equality:
   (a) To be informed promptly and in detail in a language which he or she understands of the nature and cause of the charge against him or her;
   (b) To have adequate time and facilities for the preparation of his or her defence and to communicate with counsel of his or her own choosing;
   (c) To be tried without undue delay;
   (d) To be tried in his or her presence, and to defend himself or herself in person or through legal assistance of his or her own choosing; to be informed, if he or she does not have legal assistance, of this right; and to have legal assistance assigned to him or her, in any case where the interest of justice so require, and without payment by him or her in any such case if he or she does not have sufficient means to pay for it;
   (e) To examine, or have examined, the witnesses against him or her and to obtain the attendance and examination of witnesses on his or her behalf under the same conditions as witnesses against him or her;
   (f) To have the free assistance of an interpreter if he or she cannot understand or speak the language used in the International Tribunal for Rwanda;
   (g) Not to be compelled to testify against himself or herself or to confess guilt.

IV. At The Conclusion of Trial

The ICTR system does not stop guaranteeing the rights of the accused upon the conclusion of trial. At the conclusion of trial, the rights of the accused continue to be safeguarded in the process of judgement and sentencing. In this connection, art 22(2) of the Statute provides as follows:

The judgement shall be rendered by a majority of the judges of the Trial Chamber, and shall be delivered by the Trial Chamber in public, It shall be accompanied by a reasoned opinion in writing, to which separate or dissenting opinions may he appended. [Emphasis added.]

The Right to Life

Perhaps the must fundamental guarantee of the rights allowed the accused in the ICTR process is the right to life – regardless of the magnitude of the crime of which (s)he may be convicted or the degree of (his)her culpability in it. This is expressed in terms of art 23(1) which provides that "the penalty to be imposed by the Trial Chamber shall be limited to imprisonment."

V. The Post-Trial Stage

Beyond the trial and judgement and sentencing, the accused remains vested with fundamental rights. This time it is the right of appeal and review. They are expressed respectively in Articles 24 and 25 as follows:

Article 24 Appellate Proceedings

1. The Appeals Chamber shall hear appeals from persons convicted by the Trial Chambers or from the Prosecutor on the following grounds:

(a) An error on a question of law invalidating the decision; or
(b) An error of fact which has occasioned a miscarriage of justice.

2. The Appeals Chamber may affirm, reverse or revise the decisions taken by the Trial Chambers.

Article 25
Review Proceedings
Where a new fact has been discovered which was not known at the time of the proceedings before the Trial Chambers or the Appeals Chamber and which could have been a decisive factor in reaching the decision, the convicted person or the Prosecutor may submit to the International Tribunal for Rwanda an application for review of the judgement.

Conclusion

These are but a brief review of the rights guaranteed accused persons who are tried before the ICTR. They are by no means the most comprehensive statements of such rights. In addition to other provisions in the Statute and the Rules that may translate into protection of rights of the accused, there are many international legal instruments and general principles that are animated by the need to protect the rights of accused persons. We at the ICTR do our work, in full awareness of those rules of law. It is hoped that they too will find full expression and actuation in this new ethos of human rights, which the people of Ethiopia have now resolved to guide them.

Dealing with Human Rights Violations from a Previous Regime: Dilemmas of Accountability in Cambodia

Craig Etcheson*

This paper examines the performance of the Kingdom of Cambodia in reckoning with criminality under the Khmer Rouge regime of 1975 to 1979, and in rectifying the still festering injustices following a democratizing regime change in 1993. The ruling elites of the regime(s) in power since 1993 have repeatedly called for the establishment of an international tribunal to judge the Khmer Rouge leadership for these crimes. Yet, the Royal Government of Cambodia has been slow to transform these sentiments into official action. Events such as the 1996 royal amnesty for Ieng Sary (the number three Khmer Rouge leader) have fed cynicism in the international human rights community about the seriousness of Cambodia's verbal commitment to retributive justice. It is commonplace among scholars who study the impact of genocide and war crimes on societies that successor regimes must reiterate principles of accountability in order to reestablish themselves as moral authorities that can claim to represent entire communities. In light of this thesis, there remain serious questions about the depth of legitimacy which can be claimed by the Cambodian government. Cambodia still faces a serious struggle to end the Khmer Rouge insurgency, achieve national reconciliation, and forge respect for democratic accountability and the rule of law. Nonetheless, recent developments regarding the question of accountability in Cambodia, and a changing role by the international community in encouraging observance of international norms with respect to gross violations of human rights, suggest that despite nearly twenty years of impunity in Cambodia, it is possible that the near future may finally see the international community assist Cambodia in dealing with human rights violations committed by the Khmer Rouge regime.

The Trials and Tribulations of a Democratizing Regime Change in Cambodia

On April 17, 1975, Cambodia's Khmer Rouge guerilla movement came to power after a vicious five year civil war against General Lon Nol's Khmer Republic. The resulting State of Democratic Kampuchea (DK) proceeded to implement

*Independent Consultant, formerly International Monitor Institute, New Haven, USA.

K. Hossain et al. (eds), Human Rights Commissions and Ombudsman Offices, 115–129.

what was arguably the most radical experiment in social engineering ever witnessed.[1] It was also one of the most violent regimes of the twentieth century. Some twenty to twenty-five percent of the Cambodian people perished during the three years, eight months and twenty days of the Khmer Rouge regime. The violence perpetrated against the Cambodian people by the Khmer Rouge was also reflected in the foreign relations of DK, as the regime launched military attacks against all three of its neighbors, Vietnam, Laos and Thailand. The military attacks against Vietnam were particularly sharp, and eventually the Vietnamese leadership determined that drastic action was required to end the raids.

On Christmas day, 1978, a dissident faction of the Khmer Rouge which had fled to Vietnam rode back into Cambodia among the advance echalons of a Vietnamese invasion force. Within two weeks, the invading forces had captured the Cambodian capitol, Phnom Penh, and thereby brought an end to the terror of the Khmer Rouge regime. With the help of Vietnam, the dissident Khmer Rouge faction subsequently established a socialist regime, the People's Republic of Kampuchea (PRK). But this did not end the conflict. Faced with Vietnamese troops approaching their border, the Thais decided to host a Khmer Rouge resistance against Thailand's traditional Vietnamese rivals. Soon this resistance was augmented with other Cambodian forces drawn from the two regimes preceeding the Khmer Rouge. Republican militias remaining from the Lon Nol regime, and a royalist force representing former King Norodom Sihanouk's partisans from the 1950s and 1960s joined with the Khmer Rouge in an exile regime, the Coalition Government of Democratic Kampuchea (CGDK).[2] With support from most Southeast Asian nations, China and the United States, the CGDK fought the PRK and its Vietnamese patrons to a standstill over the course of another twelve years of war.[3]

The collapse of the Soviet Union and the end of Soviet assistance to its third world clients set the stage for a United Nations peace process in Cambodia. With the loss of Soviet aid, Vietnam increasingly found itself unable to maintain its occupation of Cambodia and its war against the Khmer Rouge and their allies. In turn, faced with a decline in Vietnamese support, the *de facto* Cambodian government (which had renamed itself the State of Cambodia in 1989) elected to sue for peace. In October 1991, the Paris Peace Accords were signed. This agreement created a quadripartite transitional ruling council, bringing together representatives of the State of Cambodia, the Khmer Rouge, republicans and royalists under the auspices of a United Nations peacekeeping operation.[4]

The Cambodian peacekeeping operation was the largest ever mounted by the United Nations, and it had both successes and failures. Perhaps the greatest success of this peacekeeping operation was the conduct of a free and fair election

---

[1] See, for example, Craig Etcheson, *The Rise and Demise of Democratic Kampuchea* (Boulder, CO and London: Westview Press and Pinter Publishers, 1984); Karl Jackson, ed., *Cambodia 1975–1978: Rendezvous with Death* (Princeton: Princeton University Press, 1989); and Ben Kiernan, *The Pol Pot Regime* (New Haven: Yale University Press, 1996).

[2] See Craig Etcheson, Civil War and the Coalition Government of Democratic Kampuchea, *Third World Quarterly* 9(1): 187–202, January 1987.

[3] Craig Etcheson, The Khmer Way of Exile: Lessons from Three Indochinese Wars, pp. 92–116 in Yossi Shain, ed., *Governments in Exile in Contemporary World Politics*. London: Routledge, 1991.

[4] Craig Etcheson, Cambodia's Hot Peace, Current History, pp. 413–417, December 1992.

in May 1993, resulting in the promulgation of the Royal Cambodian Government in September of that year. Perhaps the greatest shortcoming of the peacekeeping operation was its failure to disarm and demobilize the four competing armies aligned with the principal Cambodian political factions, resulting in the effective dissolution of the Royal Government four years later. The Khmer Rouge had decided to boycott the UN-sponsored election, and immediately resumed combat operations against the newly established regime, the Royal Cambodian Government.[5] Eventually, the struggle for power and patronage among factions of the new coalition government, disagreements about how to deal with the question of accountability for the Khmer Rouge, competition for the loyalty of defecting Khmer Rouge units, and friction among military units loyal to various factions of the Royal Government resulted in combat beginning in July 1997, and a major realignment of factional forces within Cambodian politics. One constant amid this chaos has been that through-out the 18 years since the Khmer Rouge regime was ousted from power, Khmer Rouge leaders have continued to enjoy impunity for the gross violations of human rights perpetrated during their years in power.

The Failure of Past Efforts to Achieve Accountability in Cambodia

The case of Cambodia's Khmer Rouge is most instructive for the analysis of obstacles to accountability for *jus cogens* crimes and the persistence of impunity.[6] Repeated efforts to achieve accountability for massive violations of internationally protected human rights in Cambodia between 1975 and 1979 have foundered due to a wide range of factors. Cambodia has seen an international criminal tribunal, domestic criminal prosecutions, two proposed lawsuits before the International Court of Justice, efforts to impose financial penalties on the Khmer Rouge, an international investigative commission, a civil action prepared under the U.S. Alien Tort Claims Act, a national lustration law, and renewed efforts to establish an ad hoc international criminal tribunal. All of these have been attempted in efforts to achieve accountability for crimes during the Khmer Rouge regime. Yet despite these efforts spanning nearly two decades, impunity continues to reign in Cambodia. Why? The range of reasons for the failure of these efforts constitutes a rich catalogue of obstacles to accountability.

The persistence of impunity in Cambodia has been extraordinary. Virtually every legal scholar who has examined the matter of Cambodia's Khmer Rouge has found a *prima facie* case against the leaders of the Khmer Rouge for war crimes, genocide and other crimes against humanity. Most recently, this has been found by Stephen Ratner and Jason Abrams, in their recently published

---

[5]See Craig Etcheson, Cambodia, the UN and the Aftermath, paper presented to the Center for Southeast Asian Studies, Free University of Berlin, February 7, 1994; and Craig Etcheson, Anarchy in Cambodia: A Persistent Historical Pattern, paper for the American Bar Association Standing Committee on Law and National Security, Conference on Anarchy in the Third World, June 3–4, 1994, Washington, DC.

[6]Craig Etcheson, The Persistence of Impunity in Cambodia, Paper for the proceedings of the International Conference on Reining in Impunity for International Crimes and Serious Violations of Fundamental Human Rights, September 17–21, 1997, Siracusa, Italy.

book from Oxford University Press.[7] Despite this consistent record of scholarly and legal opinion, impunity has persisted in Cambodia in the face of repeated attempts to achieve some form of accountability over the last 18 years. Several examples illustrate this persistence of impunity in Cambodia.

From August 15 to 19, 1979, an international criminal tribunal called the People's Revolutionary Tribunal (PRT) sat in Phnom Penh to judge Pol Pot and Ieng Sary on charges of genocide. The PRT heard evidence, and then rendered *in absentia* convictions and death sentences against the two defendants. The legitimacy of this proceeding has been questioned, since the regime under which the proceedings were conducted was not recognized by the UN as the *de jure* government of Cambodia. The PRT was also hampered by certain legal irregularities, which can perhaps summed up by the pleading of the counsel assigned to defend Pol Pot, US attorney Hope Stevens. Stevens began her arguments by saying, "I have not come from halfway around the world to give approval to monstrous crimes nor to ask for mercy for the criminals. No! A thousand times no!"[8] The findings of guilt were unsurprising.

From 1980 to 1982 and again from 1995 through 1997, there were a variety of domestic criminal prosecutions on charges relating to membership in Khmer Rouge organizations and/or the commission of criminal acts in the furtherance of Khmer Rouge aims. This little known area of accountability for the Cambodian genocide theoretically targeted certain low level perpetrators of the Cambodian genocide. However, in the case of the 1980–1982 prosecutions, the precise numbers of defendants involved in such proceedings, and the exact nature of the juridical process, remain in some doubt. In the case of prosecutions by the Royal Cambodian Government in 1995–1997, human rights workers have shown that in numerous cases, persons charged with Khmer Rouge involvement in fact had nothing to do with the Khmer Rouge. There is substantial evidence of improper prosecutions. In all these cases, no ranking perpetrators have been brought to account in domestic prosecutions. For some of those who have been charged, there have been elements of caprice and arbitrariness in the selection of persons so prosecuted.

In the mid-1980s, an advocacy organization called the Cambodian Genocide Project sought to prepare a draft memorial to the International Court of Justice (ICJ), outlining the case that the exile Coalition Government of Democratic Kampuchea (CGDK) was in violation of its obligations under the Convention on the Prevention and Punishment of the Crime of Genocide. The leading role of Pol Pot and his chief lieutenants in the CGDK rendered that government-in-exile vulnerable to charges of harboring genocidists. The Cambodian Genocide Project dispatched human rights lawyer Gregory Stanton to work with the Commonwealth of Australia in an effort to persuade that government to challenge the CGDK on these grounds. In the end, nothing came of the exercise because such an action was contrary to the agenda of ASEAN states, the PRC and the United States, who were determined to back the CGDK.[9]

---

[7] Steven R. Ratner and Jason S. Abrams, *Accounting for Human Rights Atrocities in International Law: Beyond the Nuremburg Legacy*, Oxford University Press, 1997.

[8] Pleading on Behalf of the Accused by Hope Stevens, p. 265 in *People's Revolutionary Tribunal Held in Phnom Penh for the Trial of the Genocide Crime of the Pol Pot-Ieng Sary Clique, August 1979 – Documents*, Phnom Penh: Foreign Languages Publishing House, 1990.

[9] See Greg Stanton, The Khmer Rouge Genocide and International Law, pp. 141–162 in Ben Kiernan, ed., *Genocide and Democracy in Cambodia*, New Haven: Yale University Southeast Asia Studies, 1993.

By September of 1986, another effort to bring a case before the ICJ was launched by a group known as the Cambodia Documentation Commission. Hurst Hannum and David Hawk prepared a brief titled The Case Against the Standing Committee of the Communist Party of Kampuchea, and sought to induce a Scandinavian country to bring the complaint before the ICJ. Again, the effort was frustrated by the exigencies of international politics, in the guise of superpower and regional power interests.[10]

In 1992, an attempt was made to impose immigration and travel restrictions on the Khmer Rouge under the proposed US Khmer Rouge Prosecution and Exclusion Act.[11] This legislation would have made it the policy of the United States to support efforts to establish and international tribunal to judge those accused of crimes against humanity in Cambodia. The legislation was defeated through the intervention of the Bush administration, on the argument that it would interfere with the peace process. Similar legislation was introduced again in 1993, and defeated again on the same argument, this time by the Clinton administration.

In 1993, there was an effort to impose financial penalties on the Khmer Rouge under the Cambodian commercial code.[12] Three activists operating under the auspices of the Campaign to Oppose the Return of the Khmer Rouge suggested to King Norodom Sihanouk that he recommend to the Royal Government of Cambodia that it establish a system of "certificates of origin" to regulate trade in tropical hardwood and gemstones. A massive but illicit trade in these commodities funded the Khmer Rouge war against the Royal Government, and thus the system was quickly adopted, aiming to rein in Khmer Rouge illegal revenues. The Khmer Rouge were able to defeat this strategem by arranging to purchase legitimate certificates of origin for their natural resource products from officials of the Royal Government.

In the autumn of 1993, it was expected that Khieu Samphan would represent the Khmer Rouge in New York at the opening session of the United Nations General Assembly. Khieu had performed this function in numerous preceding years, and there was reason to believe that he might attend the 1993 session in his capacity as a member of the Supreme National Council of Cambodia, the transitional governing body established pursuant to the Paris Peace Accords of 1991. A U.S. law known as the Alien Tort Claims Act (ATCA) allows plaintiffs to bring civil actions to seek remedy for damages suffered in jurisdictions other than the United States. A Californian named Karl Deeds decided to sue Khieu Samphan under ATCA for the wrongful death of his brother, Michael Scott Deeds, who was one of four Americans known to have been tortured and executed by the Khmer Rouge at the heinous Tuol Sleng prison.[13] Khieu Samphan was the President and Head of State of Democratic Kampuchea from 1976 through the fall of the regime in January 1979, and thus he might in theory

---

[10]See Hurst Hannum, International Law and the Cambodian Genocide: The Sounds of Silence, *Human Rights Quarterly*, 11 (1989) 82–138.

[11]See S.2622, 102nd Congress, 2d Session, April 10, 1992, the Khmer Rouge Prosecution and Exclusion Act. Compare with HR.5708, 102nd Congress, 2nd Session, July 28, 1992, the Khmer Rouge Prosecution Act.

[12]Global Witness, Forests, Famine and War: The Key to Cambodia's Future, London: Global Witness, 1995, p. 7.

[13]Personal communication from Karl Deeds, November 4, 1997.

bear responsibility for such damages. Bringing such a civil action against a representative of the regime required, in the first place, that such representative be physically present within the jurisdiction of the United States in order to be served with court papers detailing the complaint. In the event, Khieu elected not to attend the United Nations General Assembly opening session in 1993. Thus, he avoided the lawsuit, any proceedings, and any possible liability for damages which may subsequently have been awarded.

Early 1993 and 1994 saw a continuing series of attempts to impose financial penalties on the Khmer Rouge, this time under the US Foreign Operations Act.[14] Congress adopted legislation terminating some categories of US military assistance to the Kingdom of Thailand and threatening to cut all US assistance to Thailand if that country failed to end its role as a supplier of military equipment to the Khmer Rouge and curb the highly profitable trade in gemstones and tropical hardwoods with the Khmer Rouge.[15] While this pressure eventually resulted in an end to Thai military resupply of the Khmer Rouge, the trade relationship has continued to flourish.[16]

In May of 1994, U.S. President Bill Clinton signed into law the Cambodian Genocide Justice Act.[17] This legislation directed the U.S. Department of State to contract with private individuals and organizations for an expert investigation into violations of international criminal and humanitarian law during the Democratic Kampuchea regime between April 17, 1975 and January 7, 1979. Attorneys Jason Abrams and Stephen Ratner were commissioned by the State Department to prepare an analysis of the potential culpability of members of the Khmer Rouge on charges of war crimes, genocide, and other crimes against humanity. Their study concluded, in part, with respect to charges of genocide: "We find *prima facie* culpability for acts against religious and ethnic groups, such as the Cham, Vietnamese and Chinese communities, and the Buddhist monkhood."[18] Similarly, they found *prima facie* culpability for war crimes and other crimes against humanity.

Also under the authority of the Cambodian Genocide Justice Act, the US State Department concluded a cooperative agreement with Yale University's Cambodian Genocide Program (CGP), providing funds for Yale University to carry out documentation, research and training related to the prospective establishment of an accountability mechanism to deal with Khmer Rouge crimes. In the course of three years of research, the CGP has assembled a remarkable

---

[14]See, for example, H.R. 4426, 103rd Congress, 2nd Session, July 15, 1994; especially Title III – Military Assistance, p. 34, ll. 9–18, describing restrictions on the International Military Assistance Training program for Thailand.

[15]See Craig Etcheson, Avoiding a New War in Cambodia, Testimony of Craig Etcheson before the Subcommittee on Foreign Operations, Export Financing and Related Programs, Committee on Appropriations, United States House of Representatives, United States Congress, March 1, 1993, pp. 575–587 in *Foreign Operations, Export Financing, and Related Programs Appropriations for 1994*, Hearings before a Subcommittee of the Committee on Appropriations, House of Representatives, 103rd Congress, 1st Session, Washington: U.S. Government Printing Office, 1993.

[16]Craig Etcheson, Punish Thai Military Over Khmer Rouge Aid, *The Asian Wall Street Journal Weekly*, June 27, 1994, p. 16.

[17]PL 103–236, April 30, 1994, 108 Stat. 486; 22 USC 2656, The Cambodian Genocide Justice Act.

[18]Page 275 in Jason Abrams and Stephen Ratner, Striving for Justice: Accountability and the Crimes of the Khmer Rouge, typescript, 1995, a study for the United States Department of State under the Cambodian Genocide Justice Act. This is the draft manuscript which was to become *Beyond the Nuremburg Legacy* (see *infra*, note 7).

collection of evidentiary materials which clearly implicates the entire top leadership of the Communist Party of Kampuchea in directing the mass terror.[19] While these efforts have greatly advanced the quality of legal opinion and the evidentiary basis upon which accountability mechanisms could be mounted, these efforts alone have no force of law.

Again in 1994, there was another effort, this time by the Cambodians. On July 7, 1994, the Royal Government of Cambodia adopted a lustration law, the Law on the Outlawing of the Democratic Kampuchea Group. Following a spirited debate and a number of important amendments to the draft text, the Law on the Outlawing of the Democratic Kampuchea Group was approved by the National Assembly of the Kingdom of Cambodia.[20] Commonly known as the Anti-Khmer Rouge Law, this statute formally declares members of the Khmer Rouge political and military organizations to be outlaws, placing them outside of civil society and prescribing penalties for membership in these organizations. The law defines persons covered under the statute, and distinguishes behaviors to be treated under existing law (rape, murder, robbery, etc.) from special criminal acts to be punished under a new set of penalties (including succession, destruction of the organs of state authority, incitement to take up arms, etc.). The law also provided for a six month amnesty period, during which members of the Khmer Rouge could surrender to the government without penalty, and reaffirmed the constitutional authority of the King to grant royal amnesty at any time. The specified six month amnesty period did not apply to Khmer Rouge "leaders," although the law neglected to define what constitutes a leader.

In essence, the Anti-Khmer Rouge Law codified in Cambodian legal code a policy which had been in force since 1979: rally to the government, and you will likely be forgiven for any crimes committed while having served the Khmer Rouge. Over the previous 15 years, this policy had been successful in convincing tens of thousands of Khmer Rouge cadre and soldiers to abandon their struggle and return to the national fold. The new law not only gave this policy the force of law, but it also specified a date certain – January 7, 1995 – after which this leniency would no longer be available. A small rush of cadre and soldiers were thus induced to defect from the Khmer Rouge during the six month amnesty period. At the same time, the law explicitly recognized that responsibility for genocidal acts during the Khmer Rouge regime 1975–1979 "cannot be annulled by the passage of time." Both the six month termination date on amnesty for "members" as well as the ban on amnesty for "leaders" has been ignored in practice. We will return to this topic below, in the context of the case of Khmer Rouge leader Ieng Sary.

The year 1996 and early 1997 saw a rash of efforts to establish a truth commission to deal with issues of crimes against humanity during the Khmer Rouge regime. Prominent in these efforts was Thomas Hammarberg, the Special Representative of the Secretary-General of the United Nations for Human Rights

---

[19] For an overview of the Cambodian Genocide Program's work, see Craig Etcheson, From Theory to Facts in the Cambodian Genocide, *International Network on Holocaust and Genocide*, 12: 1–2 (1997) 4–7.

[20] The full text of the law is reprinted in the *Phnom Penh Post*, July 15–28, 1994, p. 16.

in Cambodia.[21] Hammarberg successfully argued before the Commission that, "In relation to the problem of impunity, it was important that there be a serious discussion in Cambodia about how to handle the cases of gross violations in the past and how to investigate them."[22] The idea of a truth commission was not, however, well received in Cambodia, in part because Cambodians generally believe that they already know the truth about the Khmer Rouge genocide.[23] Nothing came of these initiatives beyond a heightened interest on the part of SRSG Hammarberg as regards the matter of impunity and accountability in Cambodia.[24]

None of these efforts to achieve accountability for the crimes of the Democratic Kampuchea regime over the last eighteen years has had an appreciable impact on the persistence of impunity for the Khmer Rouge leadership. There are various reasons for the failure of these efforts to end Khmer Rouge impunity, including but not limited to:

1. Disputes over the legitimacy of various Cambodian regimes;
2. Irregularities in the various legal proceedings;
3. Lack of institutionalized accountability mechanisms;
4. Failure to obtain custody of the accused;
5. Failure to obtain jurisdiction over the accused;
6. Capricious selection of persons to be prosecuted;
7. Considerations of "national reconciliation";
8. Financial corruption;
9. Superpower politics;
10. Regional politics;
11. Domestic politics; and last, but not least,
12. A general lack of political will.

Thus, we have in Cambodia a virtual encyclopedia of attempts to achieve accountability, and similarly, an encyclopedia of causes of the persistence of impunity.

---

[21] Commission on Human Rights, Fifty-third session, Item 18 of the provisional agenda, *Situation of Human Rights in Cambodia: Report of the Special Representative of the Secretary-General for Human Rights in Cambodia, Mr. Thomas Hammarberg, submitted in accordance with Commission Resolution 1996/54*, United Nations Economic and Social Council, E/CN.4/1997/85, January 31, 1997.

[22] Summary of Thomas Hammarberg's remarks upon presentation of the Report, E/CN.4/1997/85.

[23] In a series of structured interviews carried out in a collaboration of the Cambodian Genocide Program, the Orville H. Schell, Jr., Center for International Human Rights at Yale Law School, and the Documentation Center of Cambodia, twenty-two Cambodian political leaders representing all major Cambodian parties except the Khmer Rouge were questioned. The investigators found these leaders virtually unanimous in favoring an international criminal tribunal for the Khmer Rouge over the options of a domestic tribunal or a truth commission. See Jaya Ramji and Christine Barton, Accounting for the Crimes of the Khmer Rouge: Interviews with Cambodians, Phnom Penh: Documentation Center of Cambodia, Summer 1997.

[24] See Tricia Fitzgerald, Truth Body urged for Khmer Rouge genocide, South China Morning Post, February 3, 1997; and Leo Dobbs, U.N. Official calls for Cambodian truth commission, Reuters News, February 6, 1997.

The Cambodian Genocide Program

Partially in response to this litany of impunity, in 1994, Yale University established the Cambodian Genocide Program.[25] In work supported by the United States, Australia, the Netherlands, Sweden, Norway and the Royal Cambodian Government, as well as by a group of foundations and nongovernmental organizations, the Cambodian Genocide Program set out to implement a three-part mandate:

- A Research Project, aiming to commission original research on a variety of specific topics pertaining to Khmer Rouge behavior where gaps were perceived to exist in the scholarly literature;
- A Training Project, aiming to undertake the training of Cambodian judges, lawyers, police and human rights activists on the legal, technical and procedural knowledge required to participate effectively in an accountability exercise for the Khmer Rouge; and
- A Documentation Project, aiming to comprehensively document Khmer Rouge violations pertaining to war crimes, genocide and other crimes against humanity.

This third and most important element of the Cambodian Genocide Program mandate, documenting Khmer Rouge crimes, deserves a more extensive description. The CGP has assembled databases of bibliographic, biographic, photographic and geographic information about Khmer Rouge crimes.

For the bibliographic database, the CGP set out to catalogue all known primary and secondary documents pertaining to Khmer Rouge violations of international humanitarian law, international criminal law, and Cambodian domestic law. This would have been easy, except that during fieldwork in Cambodia, the CGP discovered several large, previously unknown archives of primary documents from within the Khmer Rouge bureaucracy – amounting to some 500,000 pages of material – much of it from the Khmer Rouge secret police, detailing the operations of the nationwide network of extermination centers.

For the biographical database, the CGP set out to create individual personal histories for all significant members of Khmer Rouge political and military organizations. To date, the effort has assembled dossiers on some 18,000 members of the Khmer Rouge, at the central, zone, region, district, commune and village levels of the organization.

For the photographic database, the CGP has digitally scanned more than 10,000 photographs and images dating to the Khmer Rouge regime of 1975–1979. These include such items as mug shots of prisoners before and after execution, personnel file photos of Khmer Rouge security cadre, views of forced labor gangs, mass grave site pictures, and so on.

Finally, for the geographic database, the CGP set out to create a comprehensive inventory of Khmer Rouge extermination centers and mass grave sites. This project turned out to be far more extensive than originally envisioned. The

---

[25] See Craig Etcheson, Digging in the Killing Fields: New Evidence About the Internal Security Apparatus of Democratic Kampuchea, paper presented to the International Conference on Khmer Studies, Phnom Penh University, Kingdom of Cambodia, August 27, 1996.

Documentation Center of Cambodia has just begun a fourth year of fieldwork on this project, and so far has carefully surveyed less than 40% of Cambodia's national territory. To date, this project has identified 9,138 mass graves dating from the Khmer Rouge regime, containing an estimated 500,000 victims.[26]

Chaos and Accountability in Cambodian Politics

Massive defections from the Khmer Rouge to the Cambodian government in August 1996 caused tremendous reverberations in Pol Pot's camp at Anlong Veng in northern Cambodia. The 1996 defections entailed the loss of the Khmer Rouge's principal economic base, consisting of gem mines and logging deals in western Cambodia, as well as the loss of the bulk of their military manpower. The proximate cause of the schism seems to have been unhappiness on the part of the western Khmer Rouge with an order from Pol Pot to confiscate their private property and to execute a purge of zone leaders, all as part of a drive to reimpose discipline among the troops and population. But rather than recognize that his own extremist directives caused the revolt, Pol Pot blamed his military aides Son Sen and Mok, who had been in nominal command of the military forces which went over to Ieng Sary. Heads would have to roll for this strategic disaster.

By turns, the unrest in Pol Pot's camp came to a head in early June 1997, as Pol Pot attempted to purge his longtime military chief of staff, Son Sen, and his senior military commander, Ta Mok. Sen Sen, his wife and fellow Central Committee member, Yun Yat, and thirteen of their family members, were executed on June 10. Panic gripped Khmer Rouge headquarters. In the ensuing chaos, Pol Pot found himself purged, instead. Ta Mok managed to overthrow Pol Pot and seize the top leadership role in the Khmer Rouge for himself. Mok selected Pol Pot's favorite diplomat, Khieu Samphan, to become the new public face of the Khmer Rouge.[27] The rest of the surviving Khmer Rouge Central Committee members remained in place. After Pol Pot's ouster, the Khmer Rouge declared that "we are not the Khmer Rouge," and moved to cement the incipient alliance with Prince Ranariddh's royalist party.[28]

At the same time the Khmer Rouge camp was falling into turmoil, the Royal Cambodian Government was also coming unglued. Relations between coalition leaders Norodom Ranariddh and Hun Sen had reached a crisis point by the beginning of June. Ranariddh was facing serious dissent inside his royalist party over the issue of power sharing with the People's Party. He was leaning towards the counsel of those who argued he could redress the power imbalance with their People's Party rivals by forming a united front with the Khmer Rouge

[26] Summaries of CGP findings to date can be found in Craig Etcheson, Centralized Terror in Democratic Kampuchea: Scope and Span of Control, Paper presented to the 49th Annual Meeting of the Association for Asian Studies, Chicago, Illinois, March 14–16, 1997; and by the same author, Terror in the East: Phases of Repression in Region 23 of Democratic Kampuchea, Paper presented to the Annual Meeting of the Society for Historians of American Foreign Relations, Washington, DC, June 19–22, 1997.

[27] See Craig Etcheson, The new Khmer Rouge emperor is still naked, Phnom Penh Post, August 15, 1997.

[28] William Branigin, Pol Pot is Past, but Khmer Rouge's Future May Be Much the Same, *Washington Post*, July 30, 1997.

forces based in Anlong Veng. Ranariddh began calling for amnesty to be given to the Anlong Veng Khmer Rouge, in exchange for their surrender of the now ousted Pol Pot. On May 19, Ranariddh offered Khmer Rouge leader Khieu Samphan a "very great welcome" to the "National United Front."[29] Ranariddh's co-premier became increasingly incensed and combative about his colleague's efforts to form a political alliance with a formally outlawed genocidal organization. On June 18, Hun Sen said of Ranariddh, "I don't understand why my partner in the coalition government went to negotiate with the Khmer Rouge ... Now I give you only a few days to decide whether to carry on to work in the coalition government or go to work with the government of Democratic Kampchea led by Khieu Samphan. This is the betrayal which cannot be accepted."[30] At this juncture, many analysts of Cambodian politics were predicting war.

Meanwhile, the Special Representative of the Secretary General, Thomas Hammarberg, had been focused on trying to establish an international criminal tribunal for the Khmer Rouge. Acting on Hammarberg's recommendation, the United Nations Commission on Human Rights had passed a resolution early in 1997 requesting that, among other things:[31]

> "the Secretary-General, through his Special Representative for human rights in Cambodia, in collaboration with the Centre for Human Rights, [...] examine any request by Cambodia for assistance in responding to past serious violations of Cambodian and international law as a means of bringing about national reconciliation, strengthening democracy and addressing the issue of individual accountability."

Armed with this resolution, Special Representative Hammarberg travelled to Cambodia in June and sought to find common ground between the co-premiers on the issue of accountability. He felt this was an issue which could bring them together, for both First Prime Minister Norodom Ranariddh and Second Prime Minister Hun Sen had a long record of rhetorical support for an international tribunal to judge the Khmer Rouge leadership for genocide and other crimes against humanity. For example, at the International Conference on Striving for Justice hosted by Yale University in 1995, Ranariddh said "the high leaders of the Khmer Rouge responsible for the atrocities must be caught, brought before the law and punished accordingly, if necessary, under the war tribunals act in the framework of an International Criminal Court."[32] At the same conference, in reference to a vote in the National Assembly on the issue of an international tribunal for the Khmer Rouge, Second Prime Minister Hun Sen said "We will have a good decision, because the Royal Government has achieved consensus. In the National Assembly, I cannot say 100%, but I can say 98%."[33] His Majesty the King, Norodom Sihanouk, was also on record supporting the creation of an

---

[29] Cambodia PM says Khmer Rouge leaders forms new party, Reuter, May 19, 1997.
[30] Katya Robinson, Tension rises in Cambodia as Hun Sen gives warning, Reuter, June 18, 1997.
[31] United Nations High Commissioner for Human Rights, Situation of Human Rights in Cambodia, Commission on Human Rights resolution 1997/49, paragraph 12.
[32] Speech by Samdech Krom Preah Norodom Ranariddh made in conjunction with the International Conference on Striving for Justice: International Criminal Law in the Cambodian Context, Sofitel Cambodiana Hotel, Phnom Penh, August 21, 1995.
[33] Author's notes from the International Conference on Striving for Justice: International Criminal Law in the Cambodian Context, Sofitel Cambodiana Hotel, Phnom Penh, August 21, 1995.

international tribunal for the Khmer Rouge.[34] Hammarberg believed that all the principals needed was a little encouragement.

On June 21, 1997, Hammarberg obtained a letter from the Co-Prime Ministers of Cambodia, Prince Norodom Ranariddh and Hun Sen, requesting "the assistance of the United Nations and the international community in bringing to justice those persons responsible for the genocide and crimes against humanity during the rule of the Khmer Rouge from 1975 to 1979."[35] The letter was presented to Secretary-General Kofi Annan, and transmitted to the Security Council and the General Assembly. Conscious of the fact that the Chinese had strongly hinted they would veto any such proposal in the Security Council, the Secretary-General directed his chief legal officer, Hans Corell, to issue the unprecedented ruling that either the Security Council *or* the General Assembly could establish an *ad hoc* tribunal.[36] The two existing tribunals, for the Former Yugoslavia and Rwanda, were established by Security Council resolutions.

With this clear signal from the Co-Prime Ministers of Cambodia, and claims by Prince Ranariddh that he would soon deliver Pol Pot to international justice, the United States government leapt into action. The day after the Cambodian appeal to the Secretary-General for international assistance in establishing a tribunal for "those accused of crimes against humanity," U.S. Secretary of State Madeleine Albright told reporters the United States was committed to bringing Pol Pot to justice: "We will be seeking to make sure that there is international justice carried out against this major war criminal."[37] From the travelling White House in Denver, US Presidential spokesman Mike McCurry added, "We clearly have taken the position that those responsible for heinous crimes ought to be brought to justice and that would be true in the case of Cambodia and Pol Pot as well."[38]

As there are no institutionalized international justice mechanisms with the jurisdiction to prosecute Pol Pot, creative alternatives were immediately brought to the fore. Secretary Albright's team began to canvass U.S. allies, seeking a country willing and legally able under their domestic law to hold and possibly even prosecute Pol Pot. Canada was approached, but after a quick policy review it was indicated that "Canada's involvement would be difficult because the legal structure is not in place."[39] Discussions also took place with Australia, but an Australian Foreign Ministry spokesman called a Pol Pot trial in Australia "unlikely."[40] The Pol Pot hot potato was passed from capital to capital across the globe, and in Cambodia trouble was brewing.

On Friday, July 4, Prince Ranariddh's top political and military strategist, General Nhek Bun Chhay, flew to the Khmer Rouge stronghold at Anlong Veng to finalize the agreement establishing a united front alliance between the royalists

[34]See, for example, Sihanouk Backs International Court for Pol Pot, Reuter, June 26, 1997.

[35]Letter from Co-Prime Ministers to SG Kofi Annan, June 21, 1997; distributed on the Internet via Camnews news group on June 23.

[36]Robert H. Reid, Try Pol Pot? U.N. and other member-states say not in my backyard, Associated Press, June 25, 1997.

[37]US urges international trial for Pol Pot, Reuter, June 22, 1997.

[38]U.S./Pol Pot, Kyodo, June 22, 1997.

[39]Canadian Foreign Ministry spokeswoman Jennifer Ledwidge as cited in Craig Turner, U.N. Examines How to Bring Pol Pot to Trial, Los Angeles Times, June 24, 1997.

[40]Robert H. Reid, Try Pol Pot? *op. cit.*

and the Khmer Rouge.[41] It was not entirely a coincidence that within twenty-four hours, there were tanks on the streets of Phnom Penh. Fierce battles raged at key points all over the capital. Having failed to heed the warning from his coalition partner, Hun Sen, that a united front between the royalists and the Khmer Rouge would mean civil war between the royalists and the People's Party, Ranariddh's gambit exploded the coalition government and ignited a new conflagration in Cambodia.

Royalist forces were rapidly routed from Phnom Penh and the provincial cities. Prince Ranariddh's military organization then split, with part of it fleeing into the jungle to join forces with the Khmer Rouge, and part of it remaining under the auspices of the Royal Government. Ranariddh's alliance with the Khmer Rouge quickly took on the character of the exile military and political organization of the 1980s, the Coalition Government of Democratic Kampuchea. On August 13th, Khmer Rouge radio announced the formation of a "joint general staff" under Ranariddh's General Nhek Bun Chhay to command combat operations of the unified royalist and Khmer Rouge forces.[42] Ranariddh immediately denied the report, insisting "There is no alliance with the Khmer Rouge, either political or military ... Nhek Bun Chhay could not do anything without my approval."[43] He was soon contradicted by his top general, who told reporters three days later that his forces had indeed joined together with the Khmer Rouge to battle the government.[44] The royalist-Khmer Rouge military alliance had already been reported by independent media in the field with the armies.[45] The big difference was that in the 1990s, in the wake of the Cold War, the international community was not willing to support a royalist alliance with the Khmer Rouge as it had during the 1980s.

During and following the fighting in Phnom Penh, a number of Nhek Bun Chhay's associates were captured and executed by forces loyal to Hun Sen. These extrajudicial executions sowed terror in the Cambodian population and drew the condemnation of the international community. The shock of the putsch and subsequent terror was enough to derail the momentum which had been generated for an international tribunal.

At the end of July, 1997, the world was treated to a unique spectacle when Pol Pot was subjected to a "people's tribunal" in the Cambodian jungle.[46] His former associates forced him to endure a public vilification, which was filmed and shown on television around the world. "Crush, crush, crush! Pol Pot and his clique" was chanted by the crowd assembled to denounce their fallen leader. The "tribunal" declared that Pol Pot was guilty of "rebelliousness" against the leadership of the Khmer Rouge, and of murder for the killing of Son Sen, Yun Yat and their family. The charges and specifications against Pol Pot made no mention of his two million ordinary victims. He was sentenced to life imprisonment under house arrest. The surviving Khmer Rouge leaders then pressed

---

41 Nate Thayer, The Deal That Died, *Far Eastern Economic Review*, pp. 14–17, August 21, 1997.
42 Cambodia Khmer Rouge set alliance to fight Hun Sen, Reuters, August 15, 1997.
43 Katya Robinson, Cambodia's Ranariddh denies Khmer Rouge alliance, Reuter, August 15, 1997.
44 Gary Thomas, Cambodia Fighting, Voice of America, August 18, 1997.
45 See, for example, Ian Stewart, In Trenches With Cambodia's Rebels, Associated Press, August 11, 1997.
46 See, especially, Nate Thayer, Brother Number Zero, *Far Eastern Economic Review*, pp. 14–18, August 7, 1997, for Thayer's extraordinary account of the July 25 event.

forward with their historic objective of overthrowing the Cambodian government and resuming their interrupted utopian revolution.

It is useful to note that the Khmer Rouge "jungle trial" bore no relationship to civilized notions of justice. No evidence was presented; none is necessary at a Khmer Rouge sentencing. No lawyers or judges were available; the Khmer Rouge have systematically killed every lawyer that has ever fallen into their hands. No laws were cited; the Khmer Rouge believe only in the policies of their leaders. Evidence, laws and lawyers are superfluous to the Khmer Rouge brand of justice.

Early in 1998, another round of massive defections from the Khmer Rouge rocked the final bastion of Khmer Rouge power, their jungle redoubt at Anlong Veng near the border with Thailand in remote northern Cambodia. After a large portion of the last hardline Khmer Rouge forces made a deal to defect to the government, the remaining loyal Khmer Rouge leaders and troops were forced out of their base, retreating into the surrounding mountains. The Khmer Rouge leadership appeared to have decided to turn Pol Pot over to the international community, perhaps in exchange for rice and medicine.[47] But just as this offer from the Khmer Rouge became known to governments and journalists, Pol Pot died of a heart attack.

The death of Khmer Rouge leader Pol Pot has energized international efforts to establish a tribunal to judge the crimes of the Khmer Rouge regime. Immediately after news of the death, UN Special Representative Thomas Hammarberg announced that efforts to try the remaining leadership of the Khmer Rouge should move forward.[48] President Bill Clinton declared that the United States intended to pursue the remaining Khmer Rouge leaders, saying "We must not permit the death of the most notorious of the Khmer Rouge leaders to deter us from the equally important task of bringing these others to justice."[49] Negotiations at the UN Security Council and among interested governments took on a new urgency, one never before seen in the twenty years since the genocidal Khmer Rouge regime was driven from power. Nonetheless, given the long history of impunity in Cambodia, it would be imprudent to expect quick results from these on-going efforts.

Conclusion

The years 1997 and 1998 have seen dramatic developments in the long history of efforts to achieve accountability for Khmer Rouge violations of international criminal and humanitarian law. A growing international interest has been catalyzed by a variety of factors, including publicity surrounding findings by Yale University's Cambodian Genocide Program, a new determination to seek accountability for war crimes introduced into US policy by Secretary of State Madeleine Albright, original initiatives undertaken by the UN Secretary-General's Special Representative for Human Rights in Cambodia, internal splits in the Khmer Rouge movement, a growing realization among observers that the

---

[47] See report by Nate Thayer in the April 23, 1998, issue of the *Far Eastern Economic Review*.
[48] See Robert Birsel, Pol Pot's Men Should Be Tried, U.N. Official Says, Reuters, April 17, 1998.
[49] Elizabeth Becker, Pol Pot's Death Won't End U.S. Pursuit of His Associates, *New York Times*, April 17, 1998.

Khmer Rouge problem lies at the heart of political instability and the failure to achieve national reconciliation in Cambodia, and, surprisingly, by the death of Pol Pot. But trumping all of these factors militating towards accountability in the Cambodian genocide has been the chaotic nature of Cambodia's fundamentally feudal political culture, and the deeply engrained factionalism of Cambodia's political elites. Bringing the Khmer Rouge leadership to justice remains a deeply held aspiration among the Cambodian people and much of the international community, but the dilemmas of accountability in Cambodia continue to stymie efforts toward this goal.

Human Rights and the Child

The Place of Child Rights in a Human Rights and Ombudsman System

Peter Newell*

The purpose of this paper is to highlight the importance of ensuring that the constitutionally mandated National Commission for the Protection of Human Rights and the Ombudsman should include powers and functions designed to ensure effective protection and promotion of the human rights of Ethiopia's children.

The last thing one wants to do is to seek to divide up human rights. Human rights are universal and the promotion and protection of children's human rights needs to be fully integrated with the promotion and protection of adults' human rights. But integration must not mean invisibility. The current low status of children and of their rights in most countries world wide, the low political priority accorded to them, and the particular, dependent state of children requires a special focus and distinct powers and activities.

Over a short period, Ethiopia has already taken important steps towards respecting the human rights of its 30 million children under the age of 18. It has – along with 190 other countries worldwide – ratified the Convention on the Rights of the Child. It has fulfilled its first reporting obligations under the Convention. It has adopted an innovative and detailed Constitution which requires that all international agreements ratified by Ethiopia become an integral part of the laws of the country (Article 9(4)). And it has included within the Constitution a special section – Article 36 – upholding the rights of the child (one of the first countries in the world to do so). It has started the process of ensuring that its domestic laws are consistent with the Convention on the Rights of the Child, and begun to develop special coordinating structures to try to ensure that Government at all levels works effectively for children. The Convention on the Rights of the Child has introduced for the first time a system of international accountability for the way States treat their children. While the condition of Ethiopia's children is grave indeed, Ethiopia should know that no country can be complacent about the state of its children. If this Government of goodwill towards children pursues the goal of developing institutions, administrative structures and laws which give real recognition to the human rights of its children, it will be in the vanguard of progress world wide.

One of the welcome clauses in the Constitution states that "the conduct of the affairs of government shall be public and transparent" (Article 12(1)). Most

*Co-author, UNICEF's Implementation Handbook for the Convention on the Rights of the Child; Chair, Council of the Children's Rights Development Unit, UK.

K. Hossain et al. (eds), Human Rights Commissions and Ombudsman Offices, 133–146.

Ethiopians must know that the state of the human rights of their children is in many, many cases desperate. Acknowledging the true state of children's lives, as measured against internationally accepted principles and standards, is a first, essential step towards action. The Government's own 1994 report under the Convention on the Rights of the Child is, in comparison with many such Government reports, quite open in describing the terrible impact on children of years of war and recurrent drought, the "untold suffering", the grave, desperate state of children, and acknowledging "the lack of adequate and effective implementation mechanisms". Reports from UNICEF, from other UN agencies and from the non-governmental organizations concerned with children add further detail.

That most basic of human rights, the right to life, is upheld for "everyone" in the International Bill of Human Rights and expanded for children in Article 6 of the Convention on the Rights of the Child to cover the right to survival and development to the maximum extent possible. For literally millions of Ethiopian children, the right to survival and development is limited by the daily reality of poverty and despair.

The infant mortality rate is among the highest in the world, with according to Government reports, about 154 out of every 1,000 Ethiopian children not living beyond the age of five; at least two thirds of under five's are severely wasted or stunted; desperate poverty affects millions; access to adequate food and shelter is denied to a majority of children; only 18 per cent have access to clean water. It appears only about a third of the age groups are in primary education; 10 per cent or less in any form of secondary education. Basic health services are available to only a small proportion of children; immunisation coverage is improving steadily but remains very low.

People – especially in international conferences – very quickly become immune to statistics. There is little purpose in reciting such statistics unless they help to sharpen the focus on the actual day-to-day suffering of the individual small human beings which make up the numbers. Once visible, these breaches of the fundamental human rights of individual children are surely intolerable.

It is the task of independent human rights institutions to ensure first that such breaches of human rights are visible and then that the energies of all those with any power to change things are focussed effectively on the task of remedying them. While it is government that takes on obligations under international law, other groups must be mobilized to work with government in support of human rights: civil society including non-governmental organizations, religious groups, and advocates for children – particularly their families, other carers and teachers. In addition, the active participation of children and young people themselves must be engaged.

And of course limitations of human rights on the scale of those affecting Ethiopia's children must be on the conscience not only of people including politicians within Ethiopia, but on the conscience of the international community too. The Convention on the Rights of the Child requires that international cooperation should be called on when needed. This conference is an example of international cooperation in action; let us hope that the considerable resources we represent will prove to be an investment which truly benefits the absent millions of Ethiopia's children.

Human rights institutions cannot solve children's problems, here or anywhere else. In a democracy such bodies cannot overrule the decisions of democratically elected representatives, cannot fix budgets or provide more money or basic services. They cannot directly alleviate hunger or illness or get children clean water or into schools. But they can, if given appropriate independence, powers and duties and adequate resources, make a big difference. They can force populations and politicians to accept the reality of children's lives; they can make proposals for change and they can encourage, cajole and, when required, embarrass governments and others into shifting priorities, into necessary action.

In Ethiopia the case for setting up national human rights institutions is already accepted and part of the Constitution. My concern is to make the case for some special arrangements for children, a case already advocated to the Government by the Committee on the Rights of the Child in its comments on the first report from Ethiopia and by the NGO community. Making that case does not deny that government must be responsive to the human rights of all its citizens, and that other large and small groups within society may need special forms of representation too.

The constitutions of many countries tend to uphold the basic human rights of "everyone", reflecting the most basic international human rights instruments, the International Bill of Human Rights comprising the Universal Declaration and the two International Covenants on Civil and Political Rights and on Economic, Social and Cultural Rights. But this has proved inadequate to protect children's human rights, because traditional attitudes within the family and institutions tend to confirm a lesser status for children who are seldom regarded as holders of rights, more often as possessions, or objects of concern. The drafting and adoption in 1989 of the Convention on the Rights of the Child and the commitments made by world leaders at the World Summit for Children were a recognition by the international community that children's human rights demand special, priority attention, re-affirmed at the 1993 World Conference on Human Rights (Vienna). This recognition has to be reflected in arrangements for respecting their rights at the national level, including within national human rights institutions.

The following section provides a series of general justifications, which apply in any society, for a special focus on children and for designing distinct components within the proposed national institutions to promote and protect the human rights of children. In setting out these justifications, I shall try to illustrate them where possible by reference to the state of Ethiopia's children (and please accept that what I know comes from Government and other reports and from briefings). In speaking of children I take the definition in the Convention on the Rights of the Child – every human being below the age of 18.

First, we must recognize that in Ethiopia children aged 0 to 18 account for more than half, of the population.

Children are the Future

Children's survival, healthy development and active participation are uniquely crucial to the healthy future of any society. In Ethiopia we all know that children's survival remains threatened in many preventable ways. Of those who survive, millions lack an adequate standard of living, social security, education and basic health services. If these issues are not tackled effectively, the hopes and aspirations of this nation cannot, will not, be fulfilled. We know – governments know – the huge costs of failing children. What happens to children in the early years and even before birth, in the womb, significantly determines their positive, or negative, growth and development. This, in turn, determines their cost or contribution to society spread over the rest of their lives.

Children are Individuals

Children have equal status to adults as members of the human race. They are not possessions of parents, products of the State, not people-in-the-making. Yet traditional attitudes and practices challenge this status and the enjoyment by children of their rights. Children start by being totally dependent. They grow towards independence only with the help of adults. Of course poverty and homelessness and hunger affect all human beings, all family members. But children's dependence and developmental state make them particularly vulnerable; they are more affected than adults by the conditions under which they live. The state of children is a very sensitive barometer by which to measure the effects of social and economic conditions and changes.

Families, and parents in particular, are vital to children's development. The Convention on the Rights of the Child acknowledges the family as "the fundamental group of society and the natural environment for the growth and well-being of all its members and particularly children" (Preamble). The Convention requires states to assure support to the family; to accept that parents have the primary responsibility for the upbringing and development of the child; to respect parents' responsibilities, rights and duties; only to separate children from their parents when it is in the best interests of children; and to ensure that education promotes respect for the child's parents (Articles 5, 9, 18, 29).

Human rights do not stop at the door of the family home for any family member. For most children, parents are normally the first and most vigorous defenders of their human rights. But parents can and do abuse children's rights. Violence to children within the family is regrettably common in most societies, and limited evidence suggests it is common in Ethiopian families. Traditional practices frequently violate children's rights and are only now becoming visible and open to challenge. Traditional attitudes can prevent or delay respect for the child's own views and feelings, for their civil rights – vital to their development as active, participating citizens. In seeking to safeguard the human rights of children, the actions and inaction of parents, families and other carers have to be reviewed as well as those of governments. This is a distinct and controversial, but inescapable role for any office charged with promoting and protecting the human rights of children. And increasingly private bodies take on services to children and their activities must be open to scrutiny too.

Children are more affected by the actions – or inaction – of government than any other group

The basic decisions that governments make about priorities, the proportion of the national budget devoted to the social sector in comparison to that devoted to defence for example, affects children's development more fundamentally than adults'. Education policies can mould and limit or expand their future lives;

public health policies target children's developing bodies and life styles. Almost every area of government policy affects children to some degree, either directly or indirectly, positively or negatively.

Thus children's need for an independent watchdog to monitor their relationship with government is particular and very strong. There must be adequate data collection, disaggregated to reveal discrimination against particular groups of children, and indicators and targets must be set and monitored.

Children have no vote, play no part in the political process

While, reflecting the Convention's participation principle, there may be the beginnings of laws and policies to promote the involvement of children in decision-making, to encourage us to listen to children, in the family, schools, health services, and local communities, these initiatives are everywhere still in their infancy. In most countries the views of children play no part in the forming of governments, or in the forming of governments' policies. This provides another overwhelming justification for seeking to give children a powerful, independent voice, both to speak for them and to promote growing respect for children's own views, as Article 12 of the Convention requires.

Children – and especially young children – have particular difficulty in finding and using legal remedies when their rights are breached

Children need independent advocates, advocates who can lobby both for children as a group and for individual children, and when necessary initiate legal action on their behalf it is not enough, for the reasons set out above, that Ethiopian children should be able to lodge complaints through parents or legal guardians.

So those, briefly, are some of the justifications for a special focus on children. In seeking to ensure this special focus within the Ethiopian Human Rights Commission and Office of Ombudsman, what should we have in mind? I will first look at the aims, and then at how these aims might be achieved, in legislation and in the form of the offices, and finally briefly describe the development of independent offices for children's human rights in other countries, and their proliferation in the context of the Convention.

These are some of the aims I would suggest a Children's Rights Unit or Children's Ombudsman within the national institutions should have:

- to promote full implementation of the Convention on the Rights of the Child, which is to promote the recognition and enjoyment of the rights upheld by the Convention for all children in Ethiopia;
- to promote a higher priority for children and a greater visibility of children, in central, regional or local government and in civil society, and to improve public attitudes to children;
- to influence law, policy and practice which wilt affect the human rights of children, both by responding to government and other proposals and by actively proposing changes;
- to promote proper coordination of government for children at all levels and ensure that the impact on children of policy proposals is assessed and given proper consideration;

- to promote effective use of scarce resources – money and other resources – for children;
- to provide a channel for children's views (which implies being accessible to children and making contact with children who are as far as possible representative of the whole population), and to encourage government and the public to give proper respect to children's views;
- to collect and publish data on the recognition and enjoyment of children's human rights and/or encourage the government to collect and publish adequate data;
- to promote awareness of the human rights of children among children themselves and adults;
- to conduct investigations and undertake or encourage research;
- to review children's access to, and the effectiveness of, all forms of advocacy and complaints systems, for example in detention, other institutions and schools and in relation to violence within the family, and including a review of children's access to the courts;
- to respond to individual problems or complaints from children or those representing children, and where appropriate to initiate or support legal action on behalf of children.

This last function raises some special issues. It is clear from the experiences of many other countries that advocates for the interests of children will only use complaints procedures if these institutions are well publicised and readily accessible, particularly at the local level. Of course, it is not realistic to think of an Ombudsman in Addis Ababa being able to receive, let alone respond effectively to, complaints about breaches of the rights of children throughout the country. Unless a local network of ombudsman offices can be contemplated, it is more realistic to see the national institutions' role as that of seeking to ensure that children's interests are effectively represented in advocacy systems and complaints procedures wherever they are located. Perhaps the ombudsman's role should be to provide a "last resort" place of appeal when complaints or conflicts cannot be sorted out at other levels. In considering how to design a complaints procedure and a children's rights advocacy service, it is essential to start from children's real situation. We must consider not only where complaints concerning the violation of the rights of children can be registered, but also how to ensure that people have the confidence and support necessary to effectively defend the interests and rights of children:

- in the family (and one has to think of ways of ensuring independent monitoring of and advocacy for very young children – babies)? ... in alternative forms of non-institutional care?
- in any other sort of care (pre-school)?
- in school?
- in any form of detention (in the penal system, mental health institutions and welfare system)?
- in other institutions?
- in the health system?
- living and/or working on the street?

And particular groups of children – disabled children, children of minorities – will require special arrangements. In developing advocacy and complaints procedures for all children, it will be essential to engage representative children themselves in the planning and evaluation.

Many of the aims I have just listed for a Children's Rights Unit or Children's Ombudsman are parallel to the aims of institutions for the protection and promotion of all human rights. Much invaluable and detailed advice on the necessary independent status, responsibilities and methods of operation of national human rights institutions already exists and is entirely relevant to those components of national institutions which focus on the human rights of children, in particular, the "Principles Relating to the Status of National Institutions" adopted by the UN General Assembly in 1993, and the advice in the Handbook on National Human Rights Institutions published in 1995 by the Centre for Human Rights in Geneva.

But the general necessity to make children, and the state of their human rights, more visible in government and in society can best be met by ensuring:

- that the legislative framework for the national human rights institutions includes provisions setting out specific functions, rights and duties relating to children, linked to the Convention and to the Constitution (for example, the duty to pay particular regard to the views and feelings of children and to take active steps to maintain direct contact with children; the right to have access to children in all forms of alternative care and all institutions which include children);
- that there is an identifiable individual "ombudsman" or representative for children (ideally someone who will bring status and public and political respect to the task, have a high public profile and so enhance the status and visibility of children);
- that this individual has appropriate staffing and a "ring-fenced" minimum budget. In a number of countries, such an individual or unit has been able to attract funding, notably from UNICEF.

Finally, how have special independent offices to promote and protect the human rights of children developed in other countries and continents?

As with many positive developments for children, the idea of a children's ombudsman was first developed by NGOs. Rädda Barnen, Swedish Save the Children, established an Ombudsman for Children in the 1970s and promoted the idea internationally during International Year of the Child (1979). "Ombudsman" is of course a Scandinavian word, and Sweden had established the first such office, an Ombudsman for Justice, in 1809.

It was neighbouring Norway whose Government was the first to use legislation to set up an independent ombudsman for children. An Act establishing the Barneombud was passed by the Norwegian Parliament in 1981 (see annex). In 1975 the Ministry of Justice had established a committee to look at legislation on parents and children and to consider whether there was a need for some special public body for children. The unanimous proposal of the Committee in its 1977 report was that a public, national office of Ombudsman for Children should be established. The proposal was examined by an inter-departmental Committee representing the six departments with major responsibilities for children. The Act establishing the office as an autonomous body is short; the statutory duty of the *Barneombud* is to "promote the interests of children vis-à-vis public and private authorities." In 1987, Costa Rica established a "Defender for Children," very much modelled on the Norwegian model. Also in the 1980s one of the states of Australia, South Australia, established the Children's Interests

Bureau through child welfare legislation. And in the Canadian state of British Columbia the position of Deputy Ombudsman for Children and Youth was created within the general Ombudsman's office. "Ombudsman" is a popular concept, but by no means all the independent offices established for children fit the common perception of an ombudsman as a person or agency taking up and investigating individual complaints.

The Convention on the Rights of the Child was adopted in 1989; in September 1990 the largest meeting of leaders of nations at the World Summit for Children stated, "The well-being of children requires political action at the highest level. We make a solemn commitment to give high priority to the rights of children." It is in this new context – the coming of age of children's rights – that independent offices to protect and promote children's human rights have proliferated. During the 1990s, a decade in which almost every country in the world has ratified the Convention, the number of NGOs actively working for children's rights has also expanded with NGO coalitions for children established in many states. NGOs play a key role as independent advocates for children, or for particular groups of children. NGOs' role is not diminished – although it may be changed – by the existence of an independent office for children established by parliament with legislative powers. Where such an office exists, it is likely to develop a close and mutually supportive relationship with NGOs.

The Convention requires "States Parties" – the 191 states which have ratified it – to report regularly to the Committee on the Rights of the Child. The Committee, established by the Convention, consists of ten experts, elected by States Parties to monitor progress towards implementation. As States go through the process of gathering information for these reports on how their laws, policies and practice affect children, and on the situation of children themselves, they find not just that they need new laws and new policies. They also need new mechanisms, structures and activities to promote a new priority for children.

The Committee on the Rights of the Child has consistently encouraged all the States whose reports it examines to establish special mechanisms, structures and activities for children (terming them "general measures of implementation"). Examples include developing a comprehensive national agenda for children, based on the Convention; ensuring that all legislation is fully compatible with the Convention, and that there is effective coordination of children's policies across federal government departments, between federal and regional, and regional and local government, and between government and public and private bodies, including NGOs; developing permanent governmental bodies for coordination, monitoring and evaluation, again using the Convention as the framework; ensuring sufficient data collection on the state of children and carrying out adequate budget analysis to determine the proportion spent on children and making children visible when budget decisions are being made; ensuring awareness of children's rights among adults and children, and providing or supporting training concerning the Convention for all those involved in government for children, and those who work with or for children.

In addition, the Committee has encouraged the development of independent offices to promote the human rights of children, to act as watchdogs for children and the recognition and enjoyment of their rights. In its examination of reports from states, it has commended countries which have appointed ombudspersons for children or similar offices, and recommended that several countries consider establishing such an office. The Committee's January 1997 response on Ethiopia's implementation of the Convention "recommends that the setting up of an independent mechanism, such as an Ombudsperson on the Rights of the Child ... to ensure observance of children's rights, be considered." The Committee's very detailed guidelines to states about the preparation of periodic reports under the Convention – and Ethiopia's next report is due to be submitted in 1998 – asks whether an independent office has been established. The Committee does not advocate a particular model, but it does emphasise the importance of independence from government, and in more than one case where a national institution to promote and protect human rights in general has been established, it has proposed the creation of a specific post for children.

In Europe in 1993 Sweden established the first children's ombudsman with legislation which links the office to implementation of the Convention (see annex). Other countries, in particular in Europe and in Latin America, have followed. In many, including Spain, Portugal, Guatemala and Colombia, representatives or units for children have been established within national human rights institutions. Other countries have followed the Norwegian model of a separate office with its own Act of Parliament. New Zealand has a Commissioner for Children. Austria has a children's ombudsman in each of its nine regions; they form a conference of ombudsmen in order to comment collectively on federal issues – new federal laws, for example – that will affect children in all regions. And there is now a European Network of Ombudsmen for Children (ENOC) established with UNICEF as its secretariat to provide a new voice for children in Europe, to share information, approaches and strategies for the benefit of children and to support new independent offices.

In several countries in Eastern Europe, where children are generally acknowledged to have suffered hugely during periods of dramatic social and economic change, there are current moves to develop independent offices for children in the Russian Federation and in other smaller countries. In Ukraine, for example, with a population of 55 million, similar to Ethiopia's, a Parliamentary Delegate for Human Rights was appointed in May 1998 with a model act setting out appropriate powers and duties. The woman appointed is well known and respected, including for her advocacy of children's rights. She has announced that a Parliamentary Decree will be used to establish a Representative within her Office for the promotion and protection of children's rights, with similar special representation for children within each of the regional offices.

No one could seriously question that the situation of Ethiopia's children demands strong, independent advocacy. The Ethiopian Parliament has already shown it has the courage to test its commitment to human rights by requiring in the Constitution the establishment of independent national human rights institutions. It is a small but vital further step to ensure that these institutions include the necessary focus on children and the powers to effectively advocate their human rights. Ethiopian legislators should be reassured to learn that where independent offices for children have been established for a period, and have been evaluated, they have been found to be highly popular, not just with children but with the population at large (annex). And while the case for special arrangements is made by reference to the status and condition of children, its purpose is to benefit the whole society.

As Gabriela Mistral, the Nobel prize-winning Chilean poet wrote:

> *Many things we need can wait, The child cannot ...*
> *To him we cannot say tomorrow. His name is today.*

ANNEX

Children's Commissioners and Ombudspeople Around the World

Successful and popular working models of independent offices to promote the human rights of children exist in various countries world-wide, among them:

Australia: in South Australia the Children's Interests Bureau opened in 1984, established under the Community Welfare Amendment Act. But in 1995 it suffered some curb on its independence, when it was amalgamated with the Office for Families and the Domestic Violence Unit, to create the Office for Families and Children; in Queensland a Children's Commissioner with particular child protection functions was established in 1997 by statute.

Austria: the Youth Welfare Act 1989 promoted the establishment of a system of local ombudspeople in each region for children under the age of 18; additionally a federal children's ombudsperson was introduced in 1991 (Kinder und Jugendanwaltin des Bundes) in the Ministry of Environment, Youth and the Family.

Belgium: the Council of the French Community established a Commissioner for Children's Rights in 1991; in Flemish-speaking Belgium, a children's ombudsman is currently (1998) being appointed.

Canada: in British Columbia the Ombudsman Services created a new post of Deputy Ombudsman for Children and Youth in 1987, but the specific role for children ceased to exist in 1990 and was absorbed into the general remit.

Costa Rica: the Ombudsman Office for Children was established under the jurisdiction of the Ministry of Justice in 1987; in 1993 the various specialised ombudsman offices were incorporated into a national independent Ombudsman Office (Defensor de los Habitantes de la Republica) which includes a children's unit.

Denmark: a National Council for Children's Rights was set up in 1995 for a three year trial period as an independent body based on the Ministry of Social Affairs; after evaluation it has now become a permanent body. Three members including the Chair are appointed by the Minister; the remaining four by the coalition of children's NGOs.

Finland: the Child Ombudsman Office is staffed and run by an NGO, the Mannerheim League for Child Welfare, and has no official constitutional status. The Ombudsman aims to provide independent legal information and counsel to children, young people and adults, with the primary aim of safeguarding the interests of the child.

Germany: the Kinderkommission (Children's Commission) is an all-party parliamentary body with a small secretariat; proposals for a federal children's commissioner are also under consideration, and children's ombudsmen exist in certain cities and one region.

Guatemala: the children's ombudsperson, Defensor de los Derechos de la Niñez, was set up as a special unit of a new government office established to investigate human rights under the constitution of 1986.

Hungary: In the Office of the Parliamentary Commissioner for Human Rights, the Deputy Commissioner covers children's issues and there is a small specialist staff.

Iceland: a children's ombudsperson office was set up by statute in 1995, linked to implementation of the Convention.

Israel: the Ministry for Education has created an ombudsman to provide pupils with a telephone information and advice line.

New Zealand: a statutory Commissioner for Children was created in 1989.

Norway: appointed the world's first children's ombudsman in 1981.

Peru: Defensoria Municipal del Nino y Adolescente. Established under the provisions of the new Child and Adolescent Code. The Defence Offices provide individual casework – but not legal advocacy – on a local level of daily life where the judicial and law enforcement systems either do not or cannot act.

Portugal: The Portuguese Ombudsman for Justice (Provedoria de Justica) has specific staff covering children's issues and to respond to children's inquiries and complaints (there is a telephone "hotline" for children).

Russian Federation: current (1997/8) plans to appoint children's ombudspeople in five regions including St Petersburg.

Spain: the national human rights institution includes an office for children's rights; in addition an Ombudsman for Children has been established by legislation in Madrid (Defensor del Menor en la Comunidad de Madrid), Seville and Catalonia.

Sweden: established a children's ombudsman, with statutory powers linked to the UN Convention, in 1993.

Ukraine: a Parliamentary Delegate for Human Rights was appointed in April 1998 and plans to appoint a Representative for Children's Rights through a Parliamentary Decree.

* * *

Some examples of legislation establishing offices of ombudsman for children:

The Norwegian Act establishing the Commissioner for Children (Barneombudet) (Act No. 5 of March 1981)

1. Purpose
   The purpose of this Act is to contribute to promoting the interests of children in society.

2. Commissioner for Children
   The King shall appoint a Commissioner for Children for a period of four years. The King shall appoint a Panel which shall act as an advisory body to the Commissioner for Children.
3. Duties of the Commissioner
   The duties of the Commissioner are to promote the interests of children vis-à-vis public and private authorities and to follow up the development of conditions under which children grow up. In particular the Commissioner shall:
   (a) on own initiative or at a hearing instance protect the interests of children in connection with planning and study-reports in all fields
   (b) ensure that legislation relating to the protection of children's interests is observed
   (c) propose measures which can strengthen children's safety under the law
   (d) put forward proposals for measures which can solve or prevent conflicts between children and society
   (e) ensure that sufficient information is given to the public and private sectors concerning children's rights and measures required for children.

The Commissioner may act on his own initiative or at the request of other people. The Commissioner for Children himself decides whether an application offers sufficient grounds for action.

4. Access to institutions and duty to provide information, etc.
   "The Commissioner shall have free access to all public and private institutions for children. Government authorities and public and private institutions for children shall, notwithstanding the pledge of secrecy, give the Commissioner the information needed to carry out the duties of the Commissioner pursuant to this Act. Information which is needed for the accomplishment of the Commissioner's tasks pursuant to section 3 ... may also, notwithstanding the pledge of secrecy, be demanded from others. When information can be demanded pursuant to this item, it may also be required that records and other documents be produced ..."

Evaluating the world's first children's ombudsperson – the Norwegian Barneombudet

In 1993 the Norwegian Parliament asked the Ministry of Children and Family Affairs to set up an evaluation of the Ombudsman for Children; the institution had been in place for 12 years without any studies of its objectives or impact. The Ministry appointed a committee to evaluate the office, and also organizational structures concerning children and adolescents in Norway. Its report was published in 1995, and circulated for comment to about 650 advisory bodies. Amongst the Committee's findings were:

- the Ombudsman for Children has helped to throw the political spotlight on children and their situation, thereby putting children on the political agenda;
- Norwegian children appear to be well acquainted with the office and its functions;
- the office has been instrumental in developing a greater general acceptance that children are entitled to be heard and have their own rights;
- work on disseminating information about children's rights has helped to make the rule of law more effective, and improved the position of the child in law;
- internationally, the office has been important "as an export item and as a practical model for other countries ... Furthermore, the Ombudsman for Children has helped to put children on the international agenda".

For the future, the Committee believes that the Ombudsman "could have an important function as coordinator and initiator of professional and political processes and could help to form more holistic policies related to children and adolescents". The Committee also proposed that in general the Ombudsman should concentrate his or her efforts on general cases and questions of principle, and work to a lesser extent on individual cases (The Ombudsman for Children and Childhood in Norway, Norwegian Official Report (NOU) 1995:26, A summary of the Committee's conclusions (Ministry of Children and Family Affairs, Oslo, 1996).

The Swedish Act to Establish the Office of the Children's Ombudsman

(a very short – two section – Act):

"Section 1: The Children's Ombudsman has the task of observing matters relating to the rights and interests of children and young persons. In particular the Ombudsman shall observe the compliance of Acts of the Riksdag, other statutory instruments and implementation of the same with Sweden's commitments under the United Nations Convention on the Rights of the Child.

"Section 2: The Children's Ombudsman is assisted by a special Council. The Ombudsman is Chairman of the Council and directs its activities. The Ombudsman and other members of the Council are appointed by the Government for a specified period.
"The Act enters into force on 1 July 1993".

Standing instructions expand on the Ombudsman's duties: "Within the scope of its responsibilities, the Office of the Children's Ombudsman shall:

1. initiate measures fur asserting the rights and interests of children and young persons;
2. represent and support children and young persons in public debate;
3. propose to the Government the legislative changes or other measures needed in order for the rights and interests of children and young people to be provided for; and
4. initiate the coordination of public measures of prevention in the context of child safety.

"The Office of Children's Ombudsman shall devote special attention to questions relating to children and young people at risk.

"The Office of the Children's Ombudsman shall in the course of its activities maintain contacts with children and young persons and with voluntary organizations, public authorities etc., and shall actively observe research and development work relating to children and young persons. "The Office of the Children's Ombudsman shall, not later than 1 October every year, present to the Government a report on its activities between 1 July of the preceding year and 30 June of the current year ..."

Bibliography

Children's Ombudsmen and the Promotion of Children's Rights, Rädda Barnen, Swedish Save the Children, Stockholm, Sweden, 1996 (an overview of what ombudsman institutions for children do and how they are established, with two case studies – Peru and Costa Rica).

Concluding Observations of the Committee on the Rights of the Child: Ethiopia, CRC/C/15/Add.67, 24 January 1997, par. 25: recommendation for an Ombudsman on the Rights of the Child.

Implementation Handbook for the Convention on the Rights of the Child, prepared by Rachel Hodgkin and Peter Newell, UNICEF, 1998 (article-by-article analysis of the implications of the Convention that includes, under Article 4, an analysis of the Committee on the Rights of the Child's comments on general measures for implementation, including development of independent offices for children – page 51 *et seq*).

National Human Rights Institutions, a Handbook on the Establishment and Strengthening or National Institutions for the Promotion and Protection of Human Rights, Professional Training Series No. 4, Centre for Human Rights, Geneva. 1995 (provides detailed guidance and UN principles for development of national institutions).

NGOs Complementary Report on the Implementation of the UN Convention on the Rights of the Child, Ethiopia, March 1996, para. 106: recommendation for a children's ombudsman.

The Ombudsman for Children and Childhood in Norway, Norwegian Official Report, Ministry of Children and Family Affairs, Oslo, 1996 (a summary in English of the conclusions of a Committee established to evaluate the office of the children's ombudsman after its first 12 years).

Ombudswork for Children, Innocenti Digest No. 1, UNICEF International Child Development Centre, Florence, Italy, 1997 (a summary of the development, legal status and functions of independent offices for children; includes lengthy bibliography on ombudswork; individual copies available free from: International Child Development Centre, Piazza SS Annunziata 12, 50122 Florence, Italy; fax 39 55 244 817).

Taking Children Seriously – a Proposal for a Children's Rights Commissioner, Martin Rosenbaum and Peter Newell, Calouste Gulbenkian Foundation, London, 1991 (makes the case for establishing an independent office to promote children's rights in the UK, including detailed discussion of functions).

A voice for Children: Speaking out as Their Ombudsman, Malfrid Grude Flekkøy, Jessica Kingsley, London, 1991 (a detailed account of the establishment and activities of Norway's and the world's first children's ombudsman).

Human Rights and the Child: From the New York Convention to the Institution of the Ombudsman

Elisa Pozza Tasca*

Introduction

It is a very emotional experience for me to be addressing you today, in this country. A very special emotion because of my origins: I was born in Africa and I am a daughter of Italians who had spent many years of their lives in this fascinating part of the world.

And the emotion is all the stronger because Addis Ababa is hosting an historic event at the present time: Africa is crying out to promote and defend human rights. It is warning to the world, and coming as it does from Africa it acquires even greater value when one recalls the words of Willy Brandt: "What does justice, freedom and human dignity mean to a person who goes to bed on an empty stomach and does not know whether he will have anything to eat tomorrow?" I would therefore like to pay a warm tribute to Ethiopia's institutions for having convened this international conference.

I am here in a dual capacity, as the Chairperson of the bilateral Italian–Ethiopian Friendship Committee of the Inter-Parliamentary Union, and as the Deputy Chair of the Subcommittee on Children of the Council of Europe. And I am proud to be here, representing both these bodies because the leitmotif that has constantly inspired everything these institutions do is the promotion of human rights, world-wide.

It is precisely because of my specific interest in protecting and promoting the rights of the child that I should like to focus my address on the need to institute a Ombudsman specifically for children. By doing this, Ethiopia would blaze the trail in Africa for the real, practical and effective promotion of the rights of the child.

Human Rights and Children: from the first international charters to the United Nations Convention

The importance of children as persons in their own right is something that has only been recognized recently: for thousands of yeas, children were not viewed as having a value of their own or a specific personality, because they were

*President of the Italo–Ehiopian Parliamentary Friendship Group, Chamber of Deputies, Rome, Italy.

K. Hossain et al. (eds), Human Rights Commissions and Ombudsman Offices, 147–151.

considered only in terms of their future adulthood. One only has to recall the way in which deformed babies used to be left to die of exposure, or the right the Roman *pater familias* had over the life and death of his own children.

The Declarations and Constitutions of the 18th and 19th centuries totally ignored the status of children and were only concerned with adult citizens, who were vested with rights by virtue of their capacity to perform duties. It was only Rousseau who acknowledged the absolute value of the personality of a child, who was recognized as having the right to develop at his own pace, and his own specific needs.

The whole issue of children's rights was only placed on the agenda in the wake of the Great War, when the Geneva Declaration (1924) was formulated on behalf of the League of Nations. It was based upon the new approach to education, but was also dictated by the sufferings inflicted by the war on young innocent victims, and was essentially designed to provide them with assistance. In 1942, the Children's Charter was drafted in London, partly managing to supersede the assistance-oriented approach.

It was on the basis of these two documents that the 1959 Declaration of the Rights of the Child came into being, drawing on the universal spirit running throughout the 1948 Universal Declaration of Human Rights. Recognising that children are persons, the Declaration substantially changed the approach previously adopted towards children, making them "subjects" rather than "objects" of rights.

On the twentieth anniversary of the Declaration, the United Nations General Assembly declared 1979 as the international year of the Child. That same year the Assembly decided to install an ad hoc working group in Geneva to draft an International Convention on the Rights of the Child, taking up a proposal tabled by the Polish delegation.

On 20 November 1989 the United Nations General Assembly adopted the Convention on the Rights of the Child. And I have proposed that this same date should be adopted as Europe's Children's Day. From today onwards, Africa could also begin to have its own day dedicated to children. Since that date, the Convention has been ratified by every country in the world, except Somalia. No other human rights treaty has ever attracted such broad endorsement. The Convention obliges the ratifying countries to adopt every necessary measure to assist parents and institutions in the performance of their obligations toward children, as stipulated in the Convention.

But even though the duty of mobilizeation demanded by the Convention is incumbent on every civilised country concerned about the problems of those who are weak by definition, it has not always been sufficient. It is certainly the minimum common denominator of the various national cultures regarding the protection of children, and must therefore be understood as a minimum starting point based on certainty (the certainty of international law). The United Nations Convention has probably been more rhetorically extolled than actually interpreted in terms of all its aspects, particularly the positive and policy-oriented aspects. Collective responsibility has been piecemeal and uncoordinated. No serious attempt has been made to translate the principles of the convention into practice in all the various areas to which the provisions refer.

An Ombudsman for Children: a new voice to defend children

To guarantee real, and not only virtual, citizenship to the United Nations Convention and put into practice what is sanctioned on paper alone; the Committee for the Rights of the Child is bringing pressure to bear to ensure that the largest number of signatory States to the Convention institute a Children's Ombudsman. The Committee believes that unless adequate structures are put into place that are able to oversee, in total independence, the implementation of the Convention in different countries, the rights of children will not be given the priority and attention that they must have.

Other international organizations have already spoken out in the same vein: one only has to think of the Council of Europe's recommendation 1286 (1996) on a European Strategy for Children, which recommended that the Committee of Ministers set up a permanent intergovernmental structure to deal with all issues relating to children (paragraph 10(1)). Or resolution A3 – 314/91 adopted by the European Union on the problems of children in the EEC, inviting all the Member States to institute a children's ombudsman (paragraph 22).

At the present time 16 countries (Australia, Austria, Belgium, Canada, Costa Rica, Denmark, Finland, Germany, Guatemala, Iceland, Israel, Luxembourg, New Zealand, Norway, Peru and Sweden) have set up the Office of the Children's Ombudsman.

The functions of the Ombudsman are to safeguard the needs, rights and interests of children. In the various forms they have taken, they ensure that the New York Convention on the Rights of the Child is fully implemented, encourage its dissemination, and represent the interests of children independently of the legal representatives of parents for children in every civil or criminal case in which children are directly or indirectly involved. In some countries the Ombudsman is also required to make appraisals, such as the Child Impact Statement, in order to assess the possible impacts on children of all draft legislation or regulations or any other measures being proposed.

There is no doubt that in order to perform these functions the Ombudsman must above all be independent, and not subject to any form of control by governments or political parties. The Ombudsman must effectively implement Article 12 of the New York Convention on the Rights of the Child, which recognizes that children have the right to express their own opinions freely on every issue of relevance to them, and the possibility of being heard in any judicial or administrative proceeding relating to them. This means that there no bureaucratic barriers must be placed between children and the Ombudsman, but that they must be able to discuss directly, without intermediaries. The main purpose of introducing the Ombudsman must therefore be to provide someone who can speak out, representing the interests of all children, whatever their age and ethnic origin. In order to collect all the input which children submit to the Ombudsman, the latter must be guaranteed the right to gain access to all children's institutions, with powers to carry out inspections and investigations in cases in which children are involved. The possibility of bringing influence to bear on every act relating to children must be guaranteed by giving the Ombudsman consultative powers, and, in some countries, binding powers, as in the case of Costa Rica's "Defensoría de la Infancia".

The institution has been created in some countries through a specific act of Parliament (Sweden, Norway, Belgium, Guatemala, Costa Rica, Peru, Colombia and Luxembourg); in others, as a result of specific legislation on children, making provision for the law to be monitored through Parliament by a "tutor" (New Zealand, Australia, Austria and Canada); in other countries the Ombudsman may be appointed directly by the government (Israel, Denmark and Germany). There are also cases in which the Ombudsman has been instituted and is being financed by NGOs, which provide assistance to give children legal protection (in Finland, for example, the Mannerheim League for Child Welfare set up the Ombudsman for Children in 1981 to provide free legal aid to any children requesting it).

Analysing the legislation in different countries and the data on security for children in the countries which have an Ombudsman already, one may say that the institution guarantees greater protection for children. One emblematic case is New Zealand, where the Ombudsman trains the police to identify situations of deprivation involving children, so that they can recognize and provide immediate help for abused children, or girls subject to genital mutilation. In Norway, the Ombudsman has promoted legislation to protect children from every form of ill-treatment by the family or society, and has drawn up a Charter to protect children in hospital. In Costa Rica a child welfare agency has been instituted, and very stringent legislation adopted to protect minors from violence in the media. In Austria, the Federal Ombudsman has distributed to every school a booklet containing the Convention on the Rights of the Child. In Guatemala the "Defensoria de los derechos de la Niñez" has been promoting courses for children on the New York Convention in every school, and afternoon courses for families are being run on the same subject.

Recently, eleven European countries set up the "European Network of Ombudspersons for Children" – ENOC. The representatives of Austria, Belgium, the Czech Republic, Denmark, Finland, Germany, Hungary, Norway, the Russian Federation, Spain and Sweden have concluded an agreement so that all the members of this new organization will work together to improve the lives of European children, encouraging the full implementation of the United Nations Convention and the Council of Europe's European Strategy for the Child; exchanging information, approaches and working strategies; offering opportunities for the national Ombudsmen to meet in order to exchange ideas and conduct promotional campaigns; supporting all organizations and individuals throughout Europe working for the rights of children within the framework of the European Union, the Council of Europe, the Committee on Children's Rights; promoting the establishment and supporting the work of independent centres to protect the rights of the child; encouraging national policies in favour of children, monitoring the situation of children and the impact of political and economic changes on children. The Norwegian representative, Trond Waage, has been elected the first President of ENOC. The new network will certainly make a response to the urgent need for closer cooperation between individuals and organizations responsible for protecting children. The increasingly dramatic information we are hearing about child labour and the sexual exploitation of children makes it essential for international coordination without further ado. I believe that Ethiopia could really play a locomotive role in its own continent to promote the rights of children by setting up ad hoc Ombudsmen, and could begin establishing agreements with other States so that Africa has its place in this network as well.

Crimes against children are crimes against humanity

I would like, at this point, to conclude with an appeal. This year, we are celebrating the fiftieth anniversary of the signing of the Declaration of Human Rights. Like many other conferences held this year, this one has also recalled that date, with one eye looking towards the future. Because human rights, even after fifty years, still run the risk of not being properly safeguarded. But I believe that the greatest tribute we can pay to all those who placed their signature on the Universal Declaration fifty years ago is to continue what they began, with a new role of control and authority. Celebrations remain sterile unless they lay the foundations for a future construction. And I would like to appeal here to all the participants to sign the Lausanne Appeal for Children which demands that "Organized Crime Against Children be considered Crimes against Humanity".

From Addis Ababa a bridge is being built toward Rome where the Conference for the Institution of the Permanent Criminal Court will be convened in June. And we must all speak out here, to ensure that the statute of the Court makes specific mention of the fact that in order to ensure universal recognition of its exceptional gravity, organized crime against children must be prosecuted and judged as a crime against humanity.

Children are not citizens of only one particular state but of a global village, and they are members of the human community which has the obligation to protect and defend them. The children whose throats are being slit in Algeria, the child soldiers in Rwanda, the child slaves in Pakistan, the children being mutilated by landmines in Angola and Mozambique, the Albanian baby prostitutes ... all these are symbolically Italian babies, American babies, German babies. And we all have the moral duty to help children. If not, what is the point of holding trials for crimes against humanity if equally barbaric crimes are being perpetrated, even today, and every day, amid the apathy of international public opinion?

Part Two

National Institutions for the Protection of Fundamental Rights

Introduction

Types of National Institutions for the Protection of Human Rights and Ombudsman Institutions: An Overview of Legal and Institutional Issues[1]

Leonard F.M. Besselink*

This introduction briefly presents a number of the central issues concerning national institutions for the protection of human rights and ombudsman institutions as they are discussed more in detail for each country in the reports reproduced in this part of the book.

Single, Dual and Multi-organ Systems

The country reports have been organized along the lines of "single organ systems", "dual systems" and "multi-organ systems". A single system for the purpose of this book is a system in which either there is only a human rights commission which can deal with complaints concerning the infringement of human rights, or an ombudsman institute with a general competence to investigate claims from citizens. A dual system for the purpose of this book, is a system in which there is both a national human rights commission and an ombudsman institution. A multiple organ system is a legal system in which there are various human rights institutions and ombudsman institutions, each having limited competence.

As is usually the case with a typological division of legal systems, we occasionally have had to refrain from historical exactitude. Thus we have included under the single organ systems also a few countries which in reality have not only either a national human rights commission or an ombudsman organization, but apart from one such general institution also a more specialized institution with a quite restricted task. This is for instance the case with the Netherlands. In the Netherlands there is a National Ombudman with broad powers, but there is also a Commission for Equal Treatment (*Commissie gelijke behandeling*), which can investigate certain claims of discrimination only, and hence has a comparatively limited competence. Also, local and provincial authorities in the Netherlands sometimes have their own ombudsman (or ombudsman-like) institution, while other have opted for making the national ombudsman competent. Yet, we have refrained from classifying the Netherlands as a dual or multi-organ system, due to the predominance of the ombudsman institution. Also the Swedish

1 This introduction should be read in conjunction with the contributions of Carver and Hunt, below Part Two, chapter vi, and the essays contained in Part Three.

* Associate Professor of Constitutional Law, University of Utrecht, Netherlands.

K. Hossain et al. (eds), *Human Rights Commissions and Ombudsman Offices*, 157–165.

ombudsman system, although at the origin of the very concept of the ombuds man, is actually based on several ombudsman institutions each having a fairl restricted scope of competence. However, we can say that together they constitut a single ombudsman system. Also reasons of purely practical convenience hav led to similar simplifications. Thus we have no report on the Zambian Huma Rights Commission, although recently such a Commission came into existenc (see the provisions of the Zambian Constitution appended to the report o Zambia). In order to keep the materials manageable, we have decided to tak these inexactitudes – much as they are regretted from the perspective of scholarl preciseness – for granted.

The reports have been based on a set of questionnaires, which are append to this introduction. These questions try to elicite responses from the experienc from countries in various parts of the world concerning key issues of the protec tion of human rights and good governance. A number of these issues ar discussed in this introduction.

Relation to Courts

One crucial issue in all three types of systems is the mutual relationship betwee the ombudsman, human rights commission and normal or specialized courts.

In single systems with an ombudsman, the distinction between ombudsman' competence and that of courts, is that the grounds for assessing a complain brought to the ombudsman, is broader than that of law in a strict sense. Usuall grounds of administrative propriety are used. This includes legal norms an principles but also extra-legal norms of propriety and good governance. In s far as legal norms are involved in an ombudsman institution's investigation and judgements, there is the issue of the formal relationship with courts. I many systems there is no need first to have addressed oneself to a court of la or otherwise to have exhausted legal remedies; but in some there is such necessity (e.g. the Netherlands). In cases where the ombudsman is not competen as long as a court is competent, a duty to refer citizens to the competent cou of law and actually assisting him in doing so, prevents citizens from falling victi to the complexities of formal requirements for the redress of grievances.

As to exhaustion of judicial remedies, the same can be said of human right commissions. In case exhaustion of judicial remedies is not necessary, th ombudsman or human rights institution provides a powerful alternative t judicial protection with all its attendant barriers, because usually the access t the ombudsman and human rights institutions has a very low threshold. Ther are few formalities and very low financial costs for pursuing complaints.

Another aspect of the relationship with courts concerns the fact that in mos cases the ombudsman institution and/or human rights commission does no have competence with regard to cases pending or decided by courts. In tha sense, the ombudsman or human rights commission are not an instance of appe against court decisions. On the other hand, in some countries the decisions c an ombudsman institution or human rights commission – though most ofte not legally binding in themselves – can be enforced in or be referred to court (e.g Ghana, India, Canada). In other countries the ombudsman or human right commission may ask for a ruling on incidental legal questions (see e.g. th

Austrian report). Sometimes this power to ask for a court ruling extends (or is restricted) to constitutional issues (Slovenia, Spain).

Although usually no court cases can be investigated, in a number of countries it has been established (though not without controversy, see e.g. Costa Rica) that procedural complaints unrelated to the substance of court cases can be investigated. These may be questions of undue delay in court proceedings, misbehaviour of court clerks, or cases of corruption of judges or clerks. It should be remembered that in some of the countries where also these cases are outside the competence of an ombudsman or human rights institution, there may exist other mechanisms for dealing with complaints concerning the judiciary. This also goes for certain other excluded public entities.

Relations Between Ombudsman and Human Rights Commission

In dual and multi-organ systems, the relationship between ombudsman institutions and human rights commissions is a separate issue. The substantive grounds for review of actions and omissions of public authorities usually are different, but overlap in as much as human rights are often grounds for review for more than one of the existent institutions. Especially in dual systems, moreover, there tends to be a possible overlap in the competence to review actions and omissions by executive authorities. Various solutions have been tried to avoid some of the negative consequences of such overlap. These range from lack of competence as long as the other institution is investigating a particular claim to the membership *ex officio* of the ombudsman in the human rights commission (see Malawi report). Also with regard to the type of cases investigated by the respective institutions, by law or by mutual agreement some division of labour is usually made. The division of labour in dual systems is often made on the basis of practical working arrangements, which may be tacit. In multi-organ systems, the division of labour is a consequence of the legal attribution of competence being restricted to certain types of complaints only. At the background of the formal or informal division of labour are practical considerations. These include avoiding confusion among citizens. But also the efficient use of scarce resources is a prime consideration (see e.g. the reports on South Africa).

A difference in competence of ombudsman and human rights commission is often found in the important additional task of human rights commissions to promote the respect of human rights by education and publicity. This task of promoting human rights, to educate and sensitize public officials and the public at large on human rights issues, is nearly always a separate but no less important task of human rights commissions. This is not an explicit task of most ombudsman institutions (see however Colombia). It must be noted, however, that this task is sometimes considered to interfere with the neutral and objective investigation of individual complaints, especially when it concerns cases of infringement of certain human rights by private parties (e.g. employers in discrimination cases, see the Canadian reports).

Competence

With regard to individual ombudsman institutions and human rights commissions a set of questions arise. We already mentioned the issue of the competence of these respective bodies in terms of the grounds for review, and also the exclusion of some aspects of the judicial function from being the object of investigations.

In many countries the ombudsman institution has no power to investigate complaints concerning legislative acts, acts of parliament or even of members of parliament. But there are some important exceptions. Nevertheless, the perceived function of ombudsman institutions is usually to exert powers of investigation and scrutiny of administrative and other acts and omissions of the executive. Human rights commissions, however, usually have as one of their primary tasks to give advisory opinions to the legislature. This will include the power to express its opinion on specific legislation or bills and their compatibility with human rights.

The competence of national ombudsman institutions and human rights commissions at the central state level covers the relevant branches of the executive at the national level. As states can be unitary or federal states, the question arises whether these institutions may also investigate complaints or cases at the level of decentralized, regional or sub-federal public authorities. This matter, as will be evident from the various reports, is very differently addressed in different countries. Not only in federal states, but also in some centralized states competence is (though not without exception) limited to national (in federal states federal) authorities. Both ombudsman and human rights institutions sometimes have the possibility of opening regional offices or branches (eg Ghana); sometimes with ombudsman institutions, there are local (or in federations: state) ombudsman offices independent from the national (or in federations: federal) ombudsman institution; sometimes the national institution functions as a form of appeal from local or state institutions (see Belgium). Also there exist systems in which an optional arrangement has been made. In this case decentralized, regional, local or state legislatures may opt to make the national institution competent in decentralized or non-federal matters (see e.g. Austria and the Netherlands).

Sometimes also private entities, such as private companies, can be the object of investigations by an ombudsman or human rights institution (e.g. Costa Rica, Colombia), although this is not the case in most countries. In most countries private entities are subject to the scrutiny of ombudsman or human rights bodies at most only in as far as they carry out governmental tasks in an official capacity (see e.g. Argentina, Sweden). In as far as private entities can be the object of a complaint for infringing human rights, and hence human rights can be enforced by the state as against private entities, these rights actually apply as between private citizens *inter se*. There is reason to assume that this is justified in cases of gross violations of the most fundamental human rights and in cases in which private entities exert power which is comparable in scale and impact to that of public authorities.

Investigations of Complaints or *motu proprio*; Investigative Powers

The initiative to investigate an alleged case of incorrect behaviour of public authorities lie with the complainant or lie with the ombudsman institution or human rights commission itself.

Usually very few formal requirements exist for making a complaint admissible. Access to the institutions does not have to live up to very strict requirements

However, in a few countries there is a special privileged procedural role attributed to members of parliament. In the UK it is thus necessary that a member of parliament forwards a complaint to the parliamentary ombudsman. A special right of members of parliament to petition the ombudsman exists in Spain. Otherwise requirements are restricted to being not anonymous, in writing (but not where illiteracy exists), sometimes a personal interest of the complainant must exist, but usually a third person may bring forward a complaint on behalf of an interested party.

The investigations at the initiative of the investigating body may involve individual cases, but may often also concern structural problems concerning (infringement of) citizens' rights which cannot or do not need to be reduced to individual cases.

The actual powers of investigation vary to a great extent, but are often far-reaching in not by law, at least in fact. Thus the investigative bodies may have powers to summon witnesses, to hear them under oath, to make on the spot investigations, to seize documents or other evidence. If such formal powers are lacking, still public authorities may have far-reaching general duties to cooperate in the investigation of complaints by ombudsman institutions or human rights commissions. Sometimes it is the very informal character of the investigative powers which may contribute to the effectiveness of investigations conducted (see e.g. the report on Costa Rica). Much depends on the legitimacy which the investigating institution has been able to muster not only in the eyes of citizens, but also with the public authorities subject to scrutiny.

Institutional and Functional Independence

The legitimacy of ombudsman and human rights institutions is contributed to by the institutional setup of these bodies.

Ombudsman institutions have traditionally had an institutional connection with parliaments. In the United Kingdom this is most evident both from the name of the institution and by the fact that he can only be accessed through the intermediary of a member of parliament. Ombudsmen are usually appointed by parliament (exceptionally the ombudsman in Zambia is institutionally dependent on the president). In Spain, parliament even determines the rules of procedure, while in Sweden the ombudsman requires the confidence of parliament and loss of confidence leads to dismissal. Also ombudsman institutions report to parliament, either in the form of yearly general reports, or by formally transmitting all reports and individual decisions.

This institutional connection with parliament also explains why the ombudsman institutions are considered not only as a less formal alternative for (or complement to) the judicial protection of citizens' rights against administrative failures, but also as a help to parliament in its supervisory powers over executive policies and of much assistance to parliament's scrutiny of the administration. Obviously, this function is mainly of importance in parliamentary (non-presidential) systems of government. Nevertheless, this 'political' function tends to be nonpartisan and in principle tends only to regard fundamental issues of procedural or substantive propriety of policies towards citizens and their fundamental rights. This function can only be carried out if there is a certain aloofness from party politics on the part of the ombudsman. Functional independence outweigh institutional ties.

As concerns human rights commissions, the links with parliament are not by tradition so strong. In many countries the members are appointed by the president (or head of state), often on the proposal of certain persons such as the Speaker of Parliament, presidents of Supreme Court, Council of State or by a special procedure on recommendation by parliament, which may be required to hear representatives of civil society, etc. Also here, functional independence outweighs (or at any rate should outweigh) institutional ties.

This is not to say that no guarantees are sought by institutional measures Thus financial and budgetary independence is of importance. A financially dependent institution is liable to pressures from whatever branch of government determines the budget. Also autonomy with regard to the appointment of staff the determination of rules of procedure, housing, etc., can contribute to independence.

External factors are of importance. Thus factual access to the human rights or ombudsman institutions is dependent on the knowledge of members of the public of their existence, and knowledge as to how they can be approached Publicity is important for these institutions, which may be greatly fostered by access of these institutions to the mass media. Success may mean a heavy caseload; and if not met with an increase in capacity to cope with increased workloads, ombudsman and human rights institutions may fall victim to their own success. Such problems in third world countries are often very great due to lack of financial resources, but not only there.

Non-governmental organizations may have an important supplementary role to play with regard both to ombudsman and human rights institutions Sometimes there is a formal possibility for such organizations to bring forward cases for investigation. But also resources in terms of expertise and support form non-governmental organizations may be important.

This is also valid for international governmental organizations. There is a counterpart to this role: national human rights commissions in many countries have a role to play in preparing state reports to international supervisory bodies in the sphere of human rights.

Remedies

Usually the direct remedies are limited. Often the ombudsman and human rights institution can only deliver advisory opinions and give non-binding judgements. This includes the power to recommend specific forms of redress, including the award of financial compensation. In some countries the judgements can be followed up in court, administrative of human rights tribunals. In some countries a relevant finding may by law lead to the introduction of criminal proceedings against officials involved. In some countries the judgements of the ombudsman or the human rights commission are legally binding.

All this should not detract from the fact that often the beneficiaries of a finding that citizens' rights have been infringed upon, are not only the citizens only. The power of recommendation may often greatly benefit the relevant public authorities as well. It is therefore important that the authority of the ombudsman nstitution and human rights commission creates trust not only among citizens out in the government apparatus as well.

ANNEX

The country reports which form the substance of the next chapters, are – as has been mentioned – based on uniform questionnaires. Obviously, not all questions are equally relevant to all countries on which reports have been written. Nevertheless, they constitute a uniform basis which facilitates the consultation and comparison of the reports. The questionnaires are reproduced below.

Questionnaire on National Human Rights Commissions

A. Tasks and Competences

1. Who determines the tasks, competence and organizational structure of the Human Rights Commission, and where are the relevant provisions to be found?
2. What is/are the task or tasks of Human Rights Commission?
3. Which fundamental rights fall within the sphere of competence of the Human Rights Commission?
4. Is there any limitation on bringing a claim with regard to the time lapsed since the alleged violations were committed?
5. Is the Human Rights Commission allowed to investigate on the spot the alleged violations?
6. In addition to national or federal authorities, do regional authorities fall within the sphere of competence of the Human Rights Commission?
7. Does the Human Rights Commission judge only the acts of the executive authorities or also acts of members of the legislature and judiciary? Can it entertain complaints against non-state actors?
8. If acts of the legislature fall within the jurisdiction of the Human Rights Commission, can it pronounce on such acts previous to them coming into force or only in cases of actual application?
9. Who have access to or can complain to the Human Rights Commission? Can e.g. family members bring claims on behalf of a possible victim?
10. Can the Human Rights Commission entertain general complaints by international organizations regarding specific legislation?
11. Can non-governmental organizations bring claims regarding violations? If so, do such NGO's have to be established within the jurisdiction of the Human Rights Commission?

B. Organization

12. How many members does the Human Rights Commission have, by whom are they selected and by whom appointed, and for how long? To whom are they accountable and by whom can they be dismissed and by what procedure (e.g. consultation with – members of – the parliamentary opposition)?
13. How is the independence of the Human Rights Commission as a body, and that of the individual members, secured?
14. Are the members of the Human Rights Commission remunerated for their work, and from what source is the payment, if any, made?
15. How are the financial resources of the Human Rights Commission made available to it, and who determines the size of its budget? Can the budget be spent as it sees fit, e.g., on travelling, or reports or studies by foreign experts?

16. Is there a Human Rights Commission for the country as a whole or are there separate Commissions or departments for the various States?
17. How is the organization of the Human Rights Commission structured? Does it have a permanent Secretary? If so, who has the right of appointment and how is the payment of the salary provided for?
18. How does the Human Rights Commission obtain staff, by direct appointment under its own powers, or by secondment from other government bodies or otherwise? Can the Human Rights Commission increase its number of staff if the need arises?
19. Which requirements need to be fulfilled before a complaint can be accepted by the Human Rights Commission (e.g. costs, dead-lines, exhaustion of other remedies like a complaint to the authority involved)? Is there any form of free legal aid available or compensation for the costs involved?
20. Are there any requirements with regard to the language to be used for complaints, the language used in the procedure and the language used for the findings of the Human Rights Commission?
21. What is the procedure followed by the Human Rights Commission when it is seized of a complaint with respect to e.g. public hearings, written procedure, hearing of the plaintiffs, witnesses and government representatives?
22. Can the Human Rights Commission give rulings or is it dependent on e.g. Parliament or the Supreme court?
23. What is the legal status of rulings of the Human Rights Commission? Are they binding with respect to the authorities or do they have the status of opinion/advice only? Who decides on publication of its rulings?
24. Can the Human Rights Commission award compensation to the plaintiffs to be paid by the government?
25. Are the rulings of the Human Rights Commission published and if so, where?
26. Is the Human Rights Commission's ruling in last instance or is there an appeals body?
27. How many complaints are received per month and how many cases result in a ruling?
28. Are there particular difficulties which have been experienced in the present functioning of the Human Rights Commission? If so, what could be a possible solution?

Questionnaire on Ombudsman Institutions

1. Where are the provisions to be found defining the tasks and organizational structure of the Ombudsman Institution? In the Constitution or in regular acts of parliament or other forms of statute law? Is this perceived as a (dis-)advantage (e.g. with respect to independence)? Should the constitution or legislation go into details?
2. Who has the power of appointment of the Ombudsman Institution? Where is this power to be found, and what is the procedure laid down? If appointment is not by the Parliament, is that a disadvantage? If the Ombudsman Institution does not report to the Parliament, is that seen as a disadvantage or weakness in the system?
3. In what way is the independence of the Ombudsman Institution secured? Are these guarantees found to be sufficient? What are the minimum requirements to guarantee impartiality? (e.g. finance, independent staff among other things).
4. How is the impartiality of the Ombudsman Institution in fact secured? How is his field of competence separated from those of other organs of control of government power like e.g. the courts and the Human Rights Commission?
5. If complaints to the Ombudsman Institution concern acts of government, does that also include inaction of government organs and also acts or actions of government personnel or civil servants? Is any (category of) government act(s) the possible object of complaint or are there exceptions? (e.g. judiciary, ministry of defence, police, the army, semi-government organs)? Similar questions pertain to acts of the federal government vs. state authorities.

6. Are there any restrictions because of the requirements? If so, are these found to be inhibiting or in another way restrictive? Can complaints be lodged directly with the Ombudsman Institution or not, and can the Ombudsman Institution decide independently to entertain complaints?
7. Is the Ombudsman Institution in any way restricted as to the grounds on which government action is to be judged? Are there legal grounds or grounds of effectivity or good government? When is a complaint considered well founded? If the Ombudsman Institution has full powers of investigation, are these then supplemented by right of access to all government documents and the duty on the side of government authorities and civil servants of full co-operation?
8. To whom does the Ombudsman Institution report?

Chapter III

Single Organ Systems

National Human Rights Commissions

The Cameroon Experience in Creating and Running a National Commission for the Promotion and Protection of Human Rights

Solomon Nfor Gwei**

We are here to share the various experiences from our national institutions or other human rights organizations so that the Ethiopian Parliament may benefit from them in drafting the legislation setting up Ethiopia's National Commission and Ombudsman. I am glad to share in this exercise by contributing what Cameroon's National Commission on Human Rights and Freedoms (NCHRF) has gathered in the form of experience in its six years of existence. I will make my presentation in about six parts, namely:

- the creation and organization of the Commission;
- its mandate;
- the resources of the Commission and its administrative or management work;
- its work in promoting and protecting human rights in Cameroon;
- some lessons from the experience, and
- some conclusions and recommendations.

1. The Creation and Organization of the Commission

The wind of the human rights revolution blowing throughout the world, beginning in the late 1980s, was felt very strongly in Cameroon. It was so, especially, because Cameroon was struggling to emerge from a situation of governance characterized by dictatorial rule which for decades stifled the respect of human rights, democratic practices and the rule of law and justice.

When Mr. Paul Biya became President in 1992, he clearly declared his views on democracy and human rights and proceeded to put in place the necessary machinery to ensure the promotion, protection and encouragement of respect for human rights. In his book titled *Communal Liberalism*, he stated:

"... because of its high moral and ethical value, democracy has an indisputable superiority over other forms of government. Government of the people by the people and for the people, government of all by all and for all, democracy is indeed a socio-political system in which relations among men are regulated in accordance with the principle of respect for their liberty and equality. In this respect, it is the only form of government which really endeavours to base social order on the requirements of social justice.

**Chairman National Commission on Human Rights and Freedoms, Yaounde.

K. Hossain et al. (eds), Human Rights Commissions and Ombudsman Offices, 169–185.

"No matter what type of interpretation is given to the concepts of liberty an equality, there is no doubt that their combined interpretation is an essentia condition for the smooth running of democratic governments as long as th welfare of the governed is the prime concern of governments. In this contex liberty embodies a two fold dimension: freedom and autonomy. It requires tha every citizen should be provided with a guarantee against any kind of arbitrar constraint.

"As for the principle of equality, its goal is that all citizens should enjoy th same rights and obligations ...

"Now I declare without mincing words that real democracy should not b jeopardised by any form of oppression, tyranny or dictatorship from civilian o military authoritarian regimes which, even when they claim to be serving th aspirations of the governed, sacrifice the liberty and equality of citizen on th alter of order.

"Cameroon can and must embark on this tract. It can and must be adapte to the positive evolution of the world and, while developing into a nation, i must resolutely undertake to build a real democracy".[1]

In June 1990 the President, who is also head of the ruling party – the Cameroo People's Democratic Movement (CPDM) – declared at his party's ordinar congress, that he was soon going to set in motion the democratic process i Cameroon. A few months later, he submitted to the National Assembl (Parliament) a series of bills which were debated, approved and which h promulgated into law. They came to be referred to as the "Liberty Laws". The covered a whole range of democratic and human rights standards such a freedom to travel within and outside the country, freedoms of association, speech the press and mass communications, regulations governing public meetings processions, political parties, etc. Ordinances on repression of subversive activi ties were repealed.

In addition to these "Liberty Laws" two Presidential Decrees were issue creating the Higher Counsel for Communications, and the National Commissio on Human Rights and Freedoms.

The importance of these laws and decrees lay in the fact that they reflected fo the first time and in a concrete way the determination of the Cameroonia Government to engage resolutely in the course of democratising and bringin about respect for human rights in the Cameroonian society. They also mad possible the creation of a human rights machinery in the country. To demonstrat its seriousness, the government took a decisive step in creating the Nationa Commission on Human Rights and Freedoms, thereby showing its favourabl response to the United Nations' call to Member States to create nationa institutions for the promotion and protection of human rights.

a. *Creating the National Commission*

Legal Basis

The National Commission on Human rights and Freedoms (NCHRF) o Cameroon was created by Presidential Decree N° 90/1459 of 8 November, 1990 Its members were appointed a year later by another Presidential Decree N°

[1] Paul Biya (President of Cameroon). Communal Liberalism (Macmillan Publishers Ltd.; London 1987), pp. 39 and 40.

91/478 of 27 November, 1991. The Commission became operational on 6 February, 1992 when it was installed by the Prime Minister.

Composition

Made up of substantive and alternate members, the composition of the Commission reflects the pluralistic representation recommended by the "Paris Principles" for National Institutions. The Chairman is an independent personality and the members are drawn from the government, the supreme court, the university, religious denominations, local administrative authorities (councils), the public and private press, the economic and social council and women's organizations. Besides the composition of the Commission and the neutrality of its Chairman, its autonomy is further guaranteed by the fact that it is legally and financially autonomous, per article 1(2) of its Decree of Creation. Chapter V of the Internal Regulations of the Commission deals with the "Identification and Protection of Members". Article 11(1) in this Chapter stipulates that "The Commission shall issue a special identity card to each of its members. It shall clearly bear the inscription "National Commission on Human Rights and Freedoms", the full name of the member, date and place of birth, occupation and status (substantive or alternate member). Paragraph 2 of the article further states that each member shall be bound to be in possession of his special identity card when performing his official duties. In addition, the Commission and its members carry special "laissez-passer" stickers on their vehicles. The identification cards and laissez-passer afford the Commission and its members safe passage and access into such places as detention centres and prisons without any problems from Government authorities.

b. *The Organization*

As soon as the Commission became functional in 1992, it set up its organizational structure and drew up its internal regulations. As provided in the Internal Regulations, the organs of the Commission comprise the General Assembly, the Bureau, Four Specialised Committees and External Branches.

(i) *The General Assembly*

It is made up of all the substantive members of the Commission and is the "supreme decision-making body of the Commission." It functions as a deliberative body and sits at least once a year in January in an ordinary session. As the supreme decision-making organ, it:

- provides guidelines for the Commission's activities;
- adopts and amends the Internal Regulations;
- approves the organization of the administrative and operational structures of the Commission;
- elects members of the Bureau other than the Ex-officio ones;
- approves the annual "progress report" of the Commission as well as the "situation report" on the human rights in the country.

(ii) *The Bureau*

The Bureau is composed of 10 members, five of them elected for a one-year term. Four are ex-officio who are in the Bureau by virtue of their being the chairmen of the Specialised Committees. The Chairman of the Commission, who is the chief executive officer, is appointed by presidential decree for a five-year term. The other officers of the Commission are the Vice Chairman, the Secretary General, the Treasurer General and their assistants.

The Bureau follows up and implements the decisions of the Commission. It also has wide powers in the administrative and financial management of the Commission.

(iii) *The Specialised Committees*

There are four Standing Specialised Committees of the Commission created to implement projects and programmes of the Commission in their areas of expertise. They are:

- the Committee for Petitions, Inquiries and Investigations;
- the Committee for Information, Education and Promotion;
- the Committee for Relations with National and International Human Rights Organizations; and – the Committee for Studies, Research and Publications.

The functions of these Committees are delimited as indicated by the titles. The Commission also uses ad hoc Committees from time to time in carrying out some projects as need arises.

(iv) *External Branches*

Due to lack of funding, the Commission has not been able to decentralise and establish branches outside of the capital city of Yaounde. This means that all the work of the Commission so far is being done from its headquarters.

From the inception of the Commission, careful thought was given to the issue of accessibility of the Commission to the population and it was then decided that at least three Branches would be established in different zones of the country beginning with the ones in Bamenda, Douala and Garoua. The budget for these branches will be presented to Parliament in 1998.

c. *The Technical and Administrative Staff*

The Internal Regulations of the Commission provide for the employment of permanent administrative and technical support staff composed of senior, middle and junior level employees.

The day-to-day management of the affairs of the Commission is the joint business of the executive members of the Bureau and the staff. In principle, the Secretary General, functioning under the authority of the Chairman, ensures the administration and management of the Commission. He manages the administrative and technical staff of the Commission.

2. The Mandate of the Commission

Like most human rights national institutions, the NCHRF was vested with the competence to promote and protect human rights throughout the country and given a broad mandate spelt out in the decree of creation. Its responsibilities include the following:

- receive all denunciations relating to violations of human rights and freedoms;
- conduct all inquiries and carry out all necessary investigations of violations of human rights and freedoms and report thereon to the President of the Republic;
- refer cases of violations of human rights and freedoms to competent authorities;
- as and when necessary, inspect all types of penitentiaries, police stations and gendarmerie brigades in the presence of the State Counsel with jurisdiction or his representative. Such inspections may lead to the drafting of a report submitted to competent authorities;
- study all matters relating to the protection and promotion of human rights and freedoms;
- propose to public authorities measures to be taken in the area of human rights and freedoms;
- publicize by all possible means instruments relating to human rights;
- collect and disseminate international documentation relating to human rights;
- co-ordinate where necessary, the activities of non-governmental organizations wishing to participate in its tasks and whose stated objective is to work in Cameroon for the defence and promotion of human rights and freedoms;
- maintain where necessary, relations with the United Nations Organizations, international organizations, and foreign committees or associations pursuing humanitarian objectives, and inform the Minister in charge of External Relations thereon.

In conformity with the provision authorizing the Commission to propose to public authorities measures to be taken in the area of human rights, it does act in advisory capacity not only to the Executive but also the other Branches of Government. It makes observations on human rights related bills before they are passed into law. It participated in the revision of the Penal Code, and is regularly invited by the Government to participate in drawing up periodic reports for human rights treaty bodies.

The Commission works in close collaboration with human rights NGOs in keeping with its mandate. The NGOs do forward or lay complaints before the Commission, especially when they encounter difficulties with Government authorities in carrying out investigations.

The Commission prepares and submits two annual reports to the President of the Republic, one on the state of human rights and freedoms in the country and the other a progress report of its activities.

3. The Resources and Administrative Management of the Commission

Per its decree of creation, the NCHRF is legally and financially autonomous and is authorized to acquire its resources from state grants, gifts and legacies from various sources and proceeds from its studies. This provision is meant to provide it with "adequate funding" which should enable it "to have its own staff and premises, in order to be independent of the Government and not be subject to financial control which might affect its independence," as stipulated in the "Principles Relating to the Status and Functioning of National Institutions for the Protection and Promotion of Human Rights," commonly referred to as the "Paris Principles".

The economic and financial crisis ravaging Cameroon made it impossible for the State to provide regular adequate funding to the Commission.

The negative impact of the lack of adequate funding for the Commission has affected the administrative and programme activities of the Commission in no small way. It has submitted proposals for funding to organizations and international bodies. The international assistance donor community, especially the diplomatic missions and international organizations in Cameroon, have responded quite favourably, showing their interest and concern for the Commission and its work. The assistance has come in the form of materials, equipment and cash grants for projects including seminars and posters.

4. Work Programme of the Commission in Promoting and Protecting Human Rights and Freedoms

The work programme of the NCHRF consists of activities which it carries out in the discharge of its twin mandate of promoting and protecting human rights and freedoms. This work is carried out in two main components, namely: Promotion and Protection. The promotion work involves enlightening the people about their human rights and freedoms through sensitisation, information, education and training. Protection entails efforts to prevent violations, stop any abuses in progress and seek redress for victims. Ultimately, the NCHRF is striving to ensure the respect of human rights and to create in Cameroon a human rights culture which should provide a solid foundation for democracy, the rule of law and justice, peaceful coexistence, development and the pursuit of happiness.

The work of the Commission is guided, among other things by the decree which created it, the "Paris Principles" and the Vienna Declaration and Programme of Action stemming from the 1993 Vienna World Conference on Human Rights. In the absence of a national human rights charter, the Commission works to ensure the implementation and respect of national laws protecting human rights and international human rights instruments.

A. *The Promotion of Human Rights and Freedoms*

Upon its creation, the NCHRF went to work with the firm belief that ensuring the respect of human rights and creating a human rights culture would be achieved through enlightening the public on human rights and fundamental freedoms. Consequently, it has placed much emphasis on the promotion aspect of its work.

(i) *Contact Tours*

The NCHRF kicked off its work of promoting human rights and freedoms by touring the country to make its existence and mandate known to the public and to seek the collaboration of relevant groups in society, such as members of government, administrative officers, the forces of law and order, political, religious and traditional leaders, etc.. All the people contacted in this exercise were sensitised about the respect for human rights and fundamental freedoms.

(ii) *Campaign of Sensitisation and Information*

The Commission carries on a continuous campaign of sensitisation and information of the general public through national and foreign press and broadcast media. It has designed, and produced 76,000 posters in English and French on human rights principles including basic human rights and freedoms, the dignity of the human being, the rule of law and justice, equality before the law and the participation of citizens in their governance. These posters are being distributed and displayed in public places in towns throughout the country. The Commission has also produced and distributed a brochure on free and fair elections and is preparing to publish another one on human rights in Cameroon for general distribution.

(iii) *Education and Training in Human Rights and Freedoms*

So far, the Commission has been conducting education and training in human rights through lectures, seminars and curriculum design for formal education. It has seized every opportunity to give lectures on human rights to classes and at seminars organized by NGOs and social, cultural, religious and development associations.

The Commission started its seminar series with one for its own members in order to render them more functional in the discharge of their responsibilities.

The Commission conducts two types of seminars: general educational seminars for the general public and training seminars for targeted professional groups. The groups targeted for training include administrative and law enforcement officers, jurists, political leaders, parliamentarians, mayors, government delegates and councillors, customs officers, trade union leaders, taxi men, women and children's organizations, traditional rulers, farmers co-operatives and cultural and development associations.

The purpose of the training seminars for targeted professional groups is to train high-level individuals as trainers in those aspects of human rights that are most relevant to their work. The objective is that individuals so trained would, in turn, help train their colleagues and subordinates. The Commission has so far conducted five seminars for administrative and law enforcement officers and one for jurists. The themes treated by experts include:

- Basic Principles and characteristics of Human rights;
- National Instruments Protecting Human rights;
- International Human Rights Instruments;
- National Institutions for the Promotion and Protection of Human Rights;
- Human Rights and Acts of States in the Context of the Rule of Law;
- Human rights and the Forces of Law and Order;
- Arbitrary Arrests and Detention;
- Abuse of Power and Authority;
- Administrative Detention and Administrative Acts Involving Human Rights;
- Torture: A Human Rights Abuse;
- Freedom of the Press and Administrative Censorship;
- The Forces of Law and Order and the Protection of Women Rights;
- The Protection of Children's Rights;
- The Forces of Law and Order and the Protection of the Rights of the Vulnerable Groups;

– Code of Conduct for the Forces of Law and Order.

The seminar for jurists covered topics and issues including the protection of human rights by these groups, the rule of law and justice, etc..

In the Vienna Declaration and Programme of Action, the 1993 World Conference on Human rights called on "all States and institutions to include human rights, humanitarian law, democracy and the rule of law as subjects in the curricula of all learning institutions in the formal and informal setting." The educational authorities of Cameroon have decided to heed this call, and the Commission has been assisting in the design of curricula for the school system and human rights courses for some professional schools.

(iv) *Working with NGOs*

Article 2 of the Decree creating the Commission mandates it to "co-ordinate, where necessary, the activities of (human rights) Non-Governmental Organizations (NGOs) wishing to participate in its task and whose stated objectives are to work in Cameroon for the defence and promotion of human rights and freedoms." In order to ensure the implementation of this part of its mandate, the Commission sought and reached a formal agreement in 1992 with the NGOs to hold at least three joint meetings per year as forums for co-ordinating their activities in promoting and protecting human rights.

Besides the meetings with the NGOs, the Commission has developed a very strong tradition of working directly with individual NGOs and facilitating their work in anyway possible. The Commission not only participates in seminars organized by NGOs when invited but also provides documents and resource persons to lecture or conduct workshops upon request. As a matter of policy, the Commission avails human rights NGOs the use of its conference room and other facilities gratis as its own support and encouragement for their work.

(v) *Briefing the International Human Rights Community*

Ever since the Commission became functional, both resident and visiting members of international human rights organizations have sought and received briefings on the human rights situation in the country and the work of the Commission. Receiving and briefing resident diplomats and the staff of international organizations is an ongoing event at the Commission and heads of most diplomatic missions, including the European Union in Yaounde have visited the offices of the Commission.

(vi) *Working with Researchers*

Ever since the Commission started operating, it has served as a source of information for researchers. Individuals working on papers, theses, dissertations and preparing for examinations on subjects related to human rights have visited the Commission in search of relevant information. The Commission not only provides them the information which they need but also briefs and counsels them on the treatment of the topics in question.

People seeking information include students and scholars from universities abroad, including students from the University of Paris I, Pantheon-Sorbonne in France and some American Universities. Some have requested on-the-job training and experience with the Commission.

(vii) *International Activities*

The Commission's activities have not been limited to only the national scene. At the international level, the Commission has initiated action and also got actively involved in the activities of international human rights organizations. One of the very first actions which the commission took in conformity with Article 2(10) of the Decree of its Creation, was to write to human rights organizations, especially the national institutions of other countries, to inform them about its creation and to seek their collaboration as well as assistance in the form of advice, literature, information, etc. It made contacts with the national human rights institutions in Benin, Senegal, Morocco, Tunisia, Brazil, Canada, France, Mexico, etc.

Since then, the Commission has been participating actively in international human rights fora, notably the preparatory sessions in Geneva, Tunis and Sydney for the 1993 World Conference on Human Rights held in Vienna, the Vienna Conference itself, the annual sessions of the UN Human Rights Commission with the attendant meetings of the International Co-ordinating Committee of national human rights institutions in Geneva, Regional National Institution Meetings in Algiers, Lome, Accra, Cairo, Pretoria; the Biennial Conference or Workshops of National Human Rights Institutions in Tunis, Manila, and Mérida in Mexico. It has also participated in the Conferences of the African Commission on Human and People's Rights in Mauritius and Banjul as well as international seminars in Abuja, Maiduguri and Kampala. The Chairman was invited to present the keynote address at the first ever National Human Rights Conference organized by the South African Human Rights Commission. He participated and presented a paper in London on the Co-ordination of African National Human Rights Institutions. He also paid a working visit to China on the invitation of the Chinese Government interested in the functioning of the Commission.

The effective participation of the Commission in the international fora did not go unnoticed. It has been rewarded to the honour of Cameroon. First, the Chairman of the Commission was elected a member of the International Co-ordinating Committee of National Institutions and placed in charge of the Sub-region of Africa South of the Sahara. Second, the Commission was entrusted with the organization of the first-ever Conference of African Human Rights Institutions which took place in Yaounde in February 1996 and brought together participants not only from Africa but also from Canada, France and the United Nations Centre for Human rights in Geneva. This conference honoured Cameroon by electing the Chairman of its Commission as the first Chairman of the Co-ordinating Committee of African National Human Rights Institutions for a two-year term. France's National Institution awarded the Commission a medal for its outstanding performance in the field of human rights.

(viii) *Celebrating Human Rights Day*

Ever since its creation, the Commission has celebrated Human Rights Day, December 10, in collaboration with the United Nations Sub-Regional Information Centre and the Ministry of External Relations. It is actively preparing to celebrate the 50th Anniversary of the UDHR come the 10th of December

1998. In 1992, the Commission visited certain prisons, with token gifts, to demonstrate its concern for the rights of prisoners. The gifts included medicines and copies of the Universal Declaration of Human Rights (UDHR) which were read in French and English to all prisoners and prison-workers.

In 1994, the Commission prepared a program for recording and broadcast over the Cameroon Radio Television (CRTV) in English and French on the Vienna Declaration and Programme of Action.

B. *Protecting Human Rights and Fundamental Freedoms*

Protection activities constitute the second major component of the programme activities of the Commission. The mandate of the Commission on the protection of human rights was described above in paragraph 2 of this paper.

The protection of human rights and freedoms is the most difficult aspect of the Commission's work for a number of reasons. One, violations of human rights which are committed by both individuals, groups and the agents of the State, especially administrative and law enforcement officers, are most visible to the public and draw much emotional reaction, usually calling for action or criticism for the lack of it. Two, the public seems to think that protecting human rights and freedoms is the sole responsibility of the Commission, and as a result, the Commission is often subjected to serious erroneous criticism for allegedly not doing one thing or another when violations occur.

In discharging its mandate of protecting human rights and freedoms, the Commission carries out, among other activities:

- field investigations of incidents which appear to involve violations of human rights and freedoms;
- treating complaints submitted to it either in writing or verbally;
- carries out impromptu inspection visits to detention centres, especially police and gendarmerie cells, prisons and to hospitals;
- counselling, mediation, conciliation and reconciliation of the parties, especially private individuals involved;
- dialoguing with Government authorities on human rights situations and abuses;
- preparing two annual reports for submission to the President of the Republic, one on the progress of its activities and the other on the state of human rights in the country.

(i) *Investigating Incidents and Complaints*

The procedures for treating incidents and investigating complaints of violations are laid down in the decree creating the Commission and the Internal Regulations. The Internal Regulations state that "The Commission shall inquire into cases of violations of human rights and freedoms on its own initiative. Cases may also be referred to it by any natural person or corporate body or any group of individuals resident in Cameroon claiming to be victims of violations of fundamental human rights and freedoms recognized by international legal instruments in force in Cameroon as well as by Cameroonian legislation."

"A case shall be brought before the Commission by a written petition addressed to its Chairman by post, through a Branch or a member of the Commission or by directly depositing such petition at the headquarters of the Commission."

"The Commission shall not examine anonymous petitions."

The Commission entertains complaints/petitions from national and international sources against anybody or any institutions including those of the state. It is to be noted that there is no limitation as to when a complaint may be submitted to the Commission from the time the alleged violation took place. The Commission has received complaints about cases pending before the courts for many years. Indeed, per the decree creating the Commission none of the Branches of Government is exempted from the action of the Commission. There is no requirement about exhausting other remedies before submitting a complaint to the Commission.

Nevertheless it avoids entertaining matters pending before the courts, except where there appears to be undue delay resulting in the denial of justice. The Commission provides free legal counselling but due to lack of funds it is unable to provide lawyers to handle cases in courts for the poor victims who cannot afford a lawyer's charges. It is to be noted that the submission of complaints to the Commission does not involve any fees.

The investigative work of the Commission is the responsibility of its Specialised Committee for Petitions, Inquiry and Investigations, working together with the technical staff in the area of protection.

It is in conformity with the laid down procedures that the Commission carries out investigations of alleged human rights violations either on its own initiative or based on written or verbal complaints. When a serious incident, with the potential of involving human rights violations, comes to its attention, the Commission immediately dispatches members of the Commission to the scene to investigate and determine whether or not violations have occurred.

Verbal or written complaints, in English or French or any local language, are received and assigned for investigation to those members who are professionally most competent to treat the matter.

Upon the completion of any investigation, a report is written. In cases where the problem involves the Government, an extract of the findings and recommendations for redress are addressed, with a covering letter, to the competent Government authority for action. If the situation involves only private citizens, the Commission uses mediation and conciliation methods to try to solve the problem. The mediation approach is proving quite effective because it does not lead to confrontation of the parties concerned neither does it results in the bitterness which often occurs in cases of arbitration and adjudication. It is to be noted that the decree creating the Commission has not given it the power to bring final solutions to any cases. The Commission is not in a position to take any further action if a Government official ignores its recommendation and when individuals refuse to honour its mediation and conciliation efforts. It neither issues rulings nor awards compensation to the plaintiffs or victims of violations.

In its operations over the years, the Commission deals with an average of 500 complaints and incidents of violations yearly. Based upon the findings of the Commission, and in summary, the violations which are recurrent relate to:

- arbitrary arrest and detention;
- torture, cruel, inhuman and degrading treatment or punishment;
- extra-judicial killing;

- interference with privacy of the family and correspondence;
- lack of fair hearing, delayed and denied justice, long periods of awaiting trial;
- discrimination based on tribalism;
- interfering with freedom of the press;
- tampering with freedom of peaceful assembly and association;
- problems of the right to work;
- family problems with women and children as victims;
- bribery and corruption.

(ii) *Visits to Detention Cells and Prisons*

In conformity with its mandate, the Commission has paid impromptu visits of inspection to most of the major prisons throughout the country and most of the gendarmerie and police detention cells in the capital city of Yaounde. Whenever the Commission visits the prisons in the Provinces, it also seizes the opportunity to inspect some of the police and gendarmerie cells in the towns visited. These visits are conducted to check if the conditions under which the detainees are held are humane and to ensure that torture and other cruel, inhuman, and degrading treatment or punishment are not practised in the institutions.

The prevailing conditions in most of the prisons, which leave much to be desired, include poor health, inadequate rations, overcrowding and insufficient medicines. Each time the Commission visits any of the prisons, it draws the attention of the relevant government authorities to its findings and makes recommendations for the improvement of the situation. The Commission itself has not only distributed copies of the UDHR to prison officials and the prisoners, but also donated some token quantities of medicines to the worst cases.

(iii) *Observing Elections*

The Commission has observed all five general elections which have taken place in the country since it came into existence in 1992. It has submitted a report and recommendations in each case to the appropriate quarters.

(iv) *Refugee Problems*

The Commission has also found itself being pulled more and into dealing with refugee problems. It has been receiving an increasing number of refugees who encounter difficulties in obtaining refugee status and assistance for one reason or another, from the Office of the UN High Commissioner for Refugees (UNHCR) in Yaounde. Consequently, the Commission is being obliged to spend much time dealing with those problems as it works with the UNHCR Office, the Ministry of External Relations and humanitarian organizations in search of solutions.

(v) *Other Areas of the Work of the Commission*

There are other areas of the work of the Commission in the protection of human rights and fundamental freedoms which have not yet been effectively taken up due to the lack of expertise, human and financial resources. They include conducting studies on human rights issues and the making of proposals to public authorities.

5. Some Lessons from the Cameroon Experience

As the first national institution for the promotion and protection of human rights in Cameroon, the NCHRF had no past experience to draw from in its work. Having been on the job now for about six years, it can look back and draw some lessons stemming from the experience.

A. *Authority and Powers of the Commission*

This stems from its statute of creation. The inability of the Commission to ensure the final solution of cases which it investigates is a function of the lack of legal and coercive power to enforce its decisions. The Commission does investigate incidents and complaints and makes findings but it must turn to a public official for a final solution and if the official ignores the recommendations, the Commission has no recourse. Also, if individuals reject its mediation effort, it cannot do anything. The Commission has no standing before the courts and lacks the financial means to assist a human rights abuse victim in any legal undertaking.

B. *Selection of Members*

According to the "Paris Principles" the composition of the national human rights institutions should aim at guaranteeing the independence of institution. The appointment of Cameroon's NCHRF took this principle into consideration. Members, appointed by a Presidential decree, were drawn from various sectors of the Cameroonian society.

As a result of its experience, the NCHRF is working with the Government to include in its composition representative(s) of the media organization, trade unions and the Ministry of External Relations omitted in the initial composition. The expertise of these groups is needed in the work of the Commission.

C. *The Credibility of the Commission*

Because national institutions are created by governments, most of whom are seen by the public as the main violators of human rights, the problem of gaining credibility from the various groups which judge its performance is considerable. Such groups include the government itself, especially if it expects the Commission to toe its policy line; the general public; opposition parties which may perceive the Commission as taking government's line; the press and the international community.

This was the case with the NCHRF. The general public and the press questioned how the Government could create an organization which would criticize it. Some saw the Commission as Government's umbrella to cover its human rights violations. The international community watched and waited to see how the Commission would perform. This was a challenge to the Commission and it had to work hard to establish its objectivity and credibility by the way it handled violations especially those committed by government agents. It can be concluded that foreign assistance donors came to the aid of the Commission only after judging that it was not just the government's window dressing.

D. *Understanding, Cohesion and Teamwork*

For a human rights Commission to be effective in its performance, there must be a good measure of understanding and unity of purpose among its members and teamwork involving the staff. Understanding holds the members and staff together, and it is through teamwork that the institution can plan and effectively carry out its activities.

E. *Incentives or Remuneration for Members*

There should be a clear policy on financial rewards or remuneration for members, who are called upon from time to time to leave their daily occupations to carry out missions for the Commission. Members are often reluctant to leave their jobs to do work for the Commission gratis.

F. *Administrative and Technical Staff*

Without a good and adequate administrative and technical staff, the Commission cannot expect to achieve great things. Also, any attempt to down-play the role of the staff would certainly limit the performance capability of the Commission. The NCHRF has suffered greatly from lack of staff.

G. *Adequate Material and Financial Resources*

The Paris Principles recommend that "the national institution shall have an infrastructure which is suited to the smooth conduct of its activities, in particular adequate funding. The purpose of this funding is to enable it to have its own staff and premises, in order to be independent of the Government and not be subject to financial control which might affect its independence." The NCHRF has had a bitter experience in acquiring funding and knows just too well the difficulties of trying to exist without the necessary finances. Its work would have advanced much further if it had adequate funds to acquire staff, remunerate members and carry out its programme of activities.

H. *Advantages as Government-created Institutions*

As a government-created human rights national institution, the Commission has certain advantages which it must exploit in its work. First of all, it is entitled to a state subvention, but may have to fight for it continuously as is the case with the NCHRF. It has access to sources and locations of information not readily available to the NGOs.

6. Recommendations

In the light of the experience of the NCHRF, the following recommendations, among others, can be made:

(a) The "Paris Principles" should be scrupulously respected in general in creating a national human rights institution.
(b) The national human rights institution should be given adequate material,

human and financial resources to enable it to function independently and effectively.

(c) The national human rights institution should be created with enough authority and power to enable it to carry its responsibilities to their logical conclusion. That is, it should be able to bring about a final solution in cases which it treats.

(d) Both the members of the Commission and the public must be kept educated at all times on human rights issues and trends and the need to promote and encourage the respect of human rights at all times. A culture of human rights, democracy and the rule of law and justice can only be successfully created in a society that is enlightened and has internalised human rights values.

(e) Members of the Commission must be seen at all times to be living examples of those who respect human rights and freedoms, and the Commission must be objective and credible in handling cases of violations of human rights and freedoms.

(f) The organization of the Commission should be decentralised with offices or branches established throughout the national territory to provide the citizens easy access to it.

(g) Provision should be made for both written and non-written complaints to be submitted or received. This will enable both the literate and illiterate to benefit from the Commission.

(h) The Commission must prepare and publish its annual reports for public information.

(i) Challenges to Parliamentarians and Government of Ethiopia:
Permit me to use the strong words "must" and "should" in addressing you. You must first believe in what you are to create. You must have a clear view of what you want to achieve.
You must see your institution as a means to an end.
You should create what you believe can work to achieve your aims and objectives.
You should see that the Ethiopian person, the Ethiopian communities and the Ethiopian Nation fully enjoys human rights and freedoms when you put your instrument into operation.
You have mobilized the international community to help you create a Human Rights Commission and an Ombudsman. By so doing you have raised the hopes and expectations of all Ethiopians.
Some of our experience may help you, others may not.
The future of the enjoyment of human rights in Ethiopian rests in your hands.

LEGISLATION

Decree No. 90-1459 of 8 November 1990 to set up the National Commission on Human Rights and Freedoms

Official Gazette of the Republic of Cameroon 1 January 1991.

The President of the Republic,

Mindful of the Constitution:
Mindful of the Universal Declaration of Human Rights:

Mindful of the African Charter on Human and People's Rights.

Hereby decrees as follows:

1. (1) A National Commission on Human Rights and Freedoms hereinafter referred to as the "Commission" is hereby set up.
   (2) The Commission shall have legal status and financial autonomy.
   (3) Its headquarters shall be in Yaounde.
   (4) It may have branches in other towns.
2. The Commission shall be charged with the defence and promotion of human rights and freedom. In this capacity, it shall:
   - receive all denunciations relating to violations of human rights and freedoms;
   - conduct all enquiries and carry out all the necessary investigations; on violation of human rights and freedoms and report thereon to the President of the Republic;
   - refer cases of violation, of human rights and freedoms to the competent authorities;
   - as and when necessary, inspect all types of penitentiaries, police stations and gendarmerie brigades in the presence of the State Counsel with jurisdiction or his representative. Such inspections may lead to the drafting of a report submitted to the competent authorities;
   - study all matters relating to the defence and promotion of human rights and freedoms – propose to public authorities measures to be taken in the area of human rights and freedoms;
   - popularise by all possible means instruments relating to human rights and freedoms;
   - collect and disseminate international documentation relating to human rights and freedoms;
   - co-ordinate, where necessary, the activities of non-governmental organizations wishing to participate in its tasks and whose stated objective is to work in Cameroon for the defence and promotion of human rights and freedoms;
   - maintain, where necessary, relations with the United Nations Organization, international organizations, and foreign committees or associations pursuing humanitarian objectives, and inform the Minister in charge of external relations thereon.
3. The resources of the Commission shall be derived from State grants, gifts and legacies from various sources, and proceeds from its studies.
4. (1) The Commission shall comprise the following: Chairman: a neutral person; Members: 3 representatives of the government, one of whom shall come from the Ministry of Justice, Keeper of the Seals;
      - 2 representatives of the Supreme Court who shall he members of the bench;
      - 1 representative of each political party represented in the National Assembly;
      - 2 representatives of the Bar;
      - 2 lecturers in Law;
      - 4 representatives of religious denominations;
      - 1 representative of local authorities;
      - 2 journalists of the public and private press;
      - 1 representative of the Economic and Social Council;
      - 2 representatives of women's organizations.
   (2) The Chairman and members of the Commission shall be appointed by decree of the President of the Republic for a five-year term.
   (3) An alternate member shall he appointed for every member following the same criteria.
5. The Commission shall elect from among its members a Vice-president, a Secretary, an Assistant Secretary, a Treasurer and Assistant Treasurer.
6. The Commission shall draw up internal regulation to govern its functioning.
7. The Commission may set up working groups whose duties shall he determined by the internal regulations.
8. (1) The Commission shall forward an annual report to the President of the Republic on the state of human rights and freedoms.

(2) It shall prepare an annual progress report of its activities to the President of the Republic.

9. This decree shall be registered, published according to the procedure of urgency and inserted in the Official Gazette in English and French.

Yaounde, 8 November 1990.

Paul Biya
President of the Republic

The Development and Growth of Human Rights Commissions in Africa – the Ghanian Experience

Emile Francis Short*

The nineties witnessed in many sub-Saharan African states a transition from autocratic civilian rule and military regimes to constitutional rule and democracy. This new move was manifested in part by the promulgation in some countries of constitutions, which incorporated a Bill of Rights. In 1989 the World Bank observed that the crisis in Africa was primarily a result of the lack of good governance. The demand for good governance meant political pluralism, an end to corruption, more respect for human rights, accountability, transparency, and a free market economy etc. Although all organs of state and indeed all sectors of society have important roles and responsibilities in relation to human rights, it has long been recognized that the effective realisation and enjoyment of human rights can only be achieved by the establishment of national institutions whose functions are specifically defined in terms of the promotion and protection of human rights. These national institutions are generally referred to as Human Rights Commissions. The importance of national institutions in the promotion and protection of human rights rests on the fact that it is primarily at the national level that human rights can be translated into a reality in the lives of men, women and children.

The United Nations has consistently encouraged member states to establish national human rights institutions to ensure the effective realisation of human rights. The World Conference on Human Rights in Vienna Conference also emphasised the important role that national institutions could play in the promotion and protection of human rights. While recognising that each state has the right to choose a model that meets the needs and aspirations of its people having regard to its economic, social and political conditions, the World Conference encouraged the establishment and strengthening of human rights institutions based on certain principles called the Paris Principles which were formulated at the First International meeting of national institutions in Paris and later adopted by the General Assembly of the United Nations.

The Paris Principles stated that, in addition to the promotion and protection of human rights at the national level, national human rights institutions should have the following responsibilities:

(a) To submit to the Government, Parliament and any other competent bodies, opinions, recommendations, proposals and reports on any matter concerning

---

*The Commission on Human Rights and Administrative Justice.

K. Hossain et al. (eds), Human Rights Commissions and Ombudsman Offices, 187–210.

the promotion and protection of human rights;
(b) To promote and ensure the harmonisation of national legislation, regulations and practices with international human rights instruments and their effective implementation of such instruments;
(c) To encourage ratification of international human rights instruments and their implementation;
(d) To contribute to reports which states are required to submit to United Nations bodies and committees, and where necessary, to express an opinion on the subject, with due respect for their independence;
(e) To assist in the formulation of programmes for the teaching of, research into human rights and to take part in their execution in schools, universities and professional circles.

The Paris Principles also stressed the importance of maintaining the independence of national human rights institutions in the promotion and protection of human rights. This independence was to be achieved in the following ways:

(i) Independence through legal and operational autonomy;
(ii) Independence through financial autonomy;
(iii) Independence through transparent appointment and dismissal procedures and
(iv) Independence through composition.

As at 1990 there were only a few Human Rights Commissions in Africa. At the Second African National Human Rights Conference held in Durban South Africa in July 1998, it was disclosed that the figure has risen to 20. Traditionally, human rights commissions in Africa have been viewed by many analytical observers with mistrust and suspicion, being regarded as appendages of the Government. Their independence from control and manipulation by the executive was considered to be doubtful, so much so that the success story of a truly independent African Human Rights Institution was received with some amount of scepticism. The purpose of this presentation, therefore, is to show that the Ghana Human Rights Commission falls within this rare category and to postulate that independent human rights institutions in Africa have a crucial role to play in promoting and consolidating democracy and good governance. The Commission also represents a model that consolidates various functions in one institution, those of an ombudsman and a Human Rights Commission with additional responsibility for investigating allegations and complaints of corruption.

I shall now proceed to consider the role and functioning of the Ghana Human Rights Commission

The Establishment of the Ghana Human Rights Commission

Article 216 of the 1992 Constitution provides for the setting up of the Commission on Human Rights and Administrative Justice. The Commission on Human Rights and Administrative Justice Act 1993, (Act 456) was passed to spell out the structure, functions and special powers of the Commission. The Commission was vested with the functions of an Ombudsman and a Human Rights

Commission as well as a mandate to investigate allegations and complaints of corruption.

The Ghana Commission represents the model of a national institution that has adopted a holistic approach by combining various responsibilities in one institution. This approach may be contrasted with the South African model where you have a Public Protector (equivalent of an Ombudsman), a Human Rights Commission, a Commission For Gender Equality and other complaints handling institutions.

One of the disadvantages of having several national institutions with jurisdiction to handle different types of complaints is the likelihood of their functions overlapping with the result that many an aggrieved complainant will be in doubt as to which body to approach. Another important consideration, especially in a developing country, is the obvious economic burden of adequately financing several national institutions with similar mandates. In the case of Ghana, it was this latter factor that tilted the scales in favour of a fused institution when the Consultative Assembly, which drafted the Constitution, debated the issue. It must, however be conceded that a national institution that has a multiplicity of functions is likely to be saddled with an inordinate number of petitions that could stretch its financial and human resources to the limit. It must, therefore, be provided with adequate resources.

Independence

It is fair to say that most African governments do not like independent national institutions. They tend to look on them with suspicion and resent their independence. This is unfortunate. It is submitted that African Governments must do everything to ensure the independence and credibility of their autonomous constitutional bodies. The existence of such institutions is integral to success of the democratic process and they enhance the image of their governments. They must also be prepared to accept constructive criticism from such institutions.

The framers of the 1992 Constitution appreciated the importance of safeguarding the independence of the Commission. Article 225 of the Constitution provides that the Commission shall not be subject to the control of any person or authority. The Commission functions independently inasmuch as it does not fall under any Ministry or government department. It makes its own regulations governing its procedure and appoints its own staff in consultation with the Public Services Commission. It is empowered by its enabling Act to enforce its decisions. Its obligation is to submit an annual report to Parliament. Parliament may debate the report and pass resolutions but it cannot change any of the decisions of the Commission. The Commission consists of a Commissioner and two Deputy Commissioners (Article 216, 1992 Ghana Constitution). The President in consultation with the Council of State appoints them (ibid, art. 217). The Council, which is a non-partisan body comprising elder statesmen and women, acts as an advisory body to the President. The Commissioner and Deputy Commissioners must qualify to be a Justice of the Court of Appeal and High Court respectively (ibid, art. 221). They hold office until they reach retiring age. However once appointed they cannot be removed at the President's pleasure except for stated misbehaviour or incompetence or on ground of inability to perform the functions of their office arising from infirmity of body or mind Where such an allegation is made to the President, he shall refer it to the Chie Justice who shall determine whether there is a prima facie case.

Where the Chief Justice decides there is a prima facie case, he shall set up a Committee consisting of 5 persons to investigate the complaint and make it recommendations to the President (ibid, art. 146).

With regard to financial autonomy, Article 227 of the Constitution provide that the administrative expenses of the Commission including salaries, allowance and pensions payable to, or in respect of, persons serving with the Commissio shall be charged on the Consolidated Fund. The Commission's budget is no linked to any government department, ministry or other body.

The Commission prepares its own budget but unfortunately it has to go through a lengthy vetting process before the Ministry of Finance which may cu the proposed budget. Moreover, there is no guarantee that all the funds vote and approved by Parliament for the Commission will be disbursed by th Ministry of Finance if projected revenue estimates are not met in the course o the year. The Commission has recommended to Parliament that it should b permitted to submit its budget directly to Parliament to make its independenc guaranteed in the Constitution more meaningful (see Annual Report 1995 page 3).

The Commission's core funding is therefore provided by the Government However, the Commission has over the years received financial and logistic support from the donor community including the foreign embassies, internationa non-governmental institutions, the European Union etc.

Accessibility

An effective national institution must be readily accessible to the widest possibl number of the people it is intended to serve. In recognition of the fact that abou seventy percent of the Ghanaian population lives in the rural areas the enablin Act made express provision for the decentralisation of the Commission. It state that the Commission may open offices in all the Regions and Districts (Section 10 of the Commission On Human Rights And Administrative Justice 1993 (Ac 456)).

Presently, the Commission has 10 Regional Offices and 39 District Office with a total staff strength of 450. Parliament recently approved a Budget, whic will enable the Commission to open 25 more District Offices within the nex twelve months bringing the total number of District Offices to 64. It is hope that in two years time the full complement of 110 District Offices will have bee established. The objective is to make the services of the Commission accessibl to the majority of the Ghanaian public.

A complaint may be made by any individual or a body of persons whethe corporate or unincorporated (ibid, Section 12(5)). This would include NGOs o an international organization. Where a person entitled to bring an action ha died or for some reason or is for any sufficient reason unable to act for himsel the complaint may be made by his personal representative or by a member o his family or other individual suitable to represent him (ibid, Section 12(b)).

Constitutional and Statutory Mandate

The Commission has a broad mandate. The functions of the Commission are set out in Article 218 of the Constitution and Section 7 of Act 456 and they include the duty:

(a) To investigate complaints of violations of fundamental human rights and freedoms, injustice, corruption, abuse of power and unfair treatment of any person by a public officer in the exercise of his official duties;
(b) To investigate complaints concerning the functioning of the Public Services Commission, administrative organs of State, offices of the Regional Co-ordinating Council and the District Assembly, the Armed Forces, the Police Service and the Prison Service insofar as the complaints relate to a failure to achieve a balanced structuring of those services or equal access by all to recruitment of those services or fair administration in relation to those services;
(c) To investigate complaints concerning practices and actions by persons, private enterprises and other institutions where those complaints allege violations of fundamental rights and freedoms under the Constitution;
(d) To take appropriate action to call for the remedying, correction and reversal of instances specified in paragraphs (a), (b) and (c) of this clause through such means as are fair, proper and effective, including:
   (i) Negotiation and compromise between the parties concerned;
   (ii) Causing the complaint and its finding on it to be reported to the superior of an offending person;
   (iii) Bringing proceedings in a competent Court for a remedy to secure the termination of the offending action or conduct, or the abandonment or alteration of the offending procedures;
   (iv) Bringing proceedings to restrain the enforcement of such legislation or regulation by challenging its validity if the offending action or conduct is sought to be justified by subordinate legislation or regulation which is unreasonable or otherwise ultra vires;
   (v) To investigate an allegation that a public officer has contravened or has not complied with a provision of Chapter 24 of the Constitution, which deals with the Code of Conduct for Public Officers;
   (vi) To investigate all instances of alleged or suspected corruption and the misappropriation of public moneys by officials and to take appropriate steps, including reports to the Attorney-General and Auditor General resulting from such investigations;
   (vii) To educate the public on human rights and freedoms by such means as the Commissioner may decide, including publications, lectures and symposia; and
   (viii) To report to Parliament annually on the performance of its functions.

By virtue of Article 35(2) of the Transitional Provisions of the 1992 Constitution, the Commissioner is also empowered to restore to any person any property confiscated by or under the authority of the Armed Forces Revolutionary Council and the Provisional National Defence Council under certain specified conditions stated in the said Article.

In broad terms the functions of the Commission can be categorized under three main headings, namely, receiving and investigating complaints of human rights violations and other acts of administrative injustice, investigating all instances of alleged or suspected corruption or embezzlement of moneys by officials, and public education on human rights issues.

It can be seen from the above functions that no institution is excluded from the jurisdiction of the Commission. However, it cannot investigate a matter pending before a court or judicial tribunal, a matter involving the relations or dealings between the Government and any other Government or an international organization or a matter relating to the exercise of the prerogative of mercy (Section 8(2)).

Powers

To enable the Commission perform the above functions effectively, Section 8 of Act 456 has given the following special powers to the Commission:

(a) The power of subpoena to compel the attendance of witnesses and the production of documents.
(b) To cite a person before a court of competent jurisdiction for contempt for failure to obey a subpoena and
(c) The right to request for any information relevant to a matter before the commission.

The Commission may enter any premises occupied by a department, authority or a person to inspect the premises or to carry out on the premises any investigation within its jurisdiction (Section 23).

Competence

The Commission is empowered by Section 18(1) of Act 456 to determine that a decision, recommendation, act or omission that was the subject matter of an investigation:

(a) Amounts to a breach of any of the fundamental rights and freedoms under the Constitution; or
(b) Appears to have been contrary to law; or
(c) Was unreasonable, unjust, oppressive, discriminatory or was in accordance with a rule of law or provision of any Act or a practice that is unreasonable unjust, oppressive, or discriminatory; or
(d) Was based on irrelevant grounds or made for an improper purpose or
(e) Was made in the exercise of a discretionary power and reasons should have been given for the decision.

It can be seen from the above section that the Commission may look beyond the legalities of a case and make a determination, which is in accord with the dictates of justice.

The Commission may refuse to investigate a matter or cease its investigation if it appears to the Commission:

(a) that under the law or existing administrative practice there is adequate remedy for the complaint, whether or not the complainant has availed himself of it; or

b) that having regard to all the circumstances of the case, any further investigation is unnecessary (Section 13(1)).

The Commission may also refuse to investigate a complaint if it relates to a decision, recommendation, act or omission of which the complainant has had knowledge for more than twelve months before the complaint is received by the Commission. The Commission has exercised this discretion liberally (Section 13(2)(a)) bearing in mind that many citizens do not know their rights and in view of the fact that the eleven years preceding the establishment of the Commission witnessed a period of military rule.

The Supreme Court of Ghana has held that the Statutes of Limitation which regulate the time within which actions may be brought to court does not apply to the Commission (Attorney General v Commissioner for Human Rights & Administrative Justice (Suit No. 17/96)).

Enforcement Powers

One unique power given to the Commission is the power to go to any Court for the enforcement of its decisions and recommendations if they are not complied with within three months from the submission of the decision. Such a power was deemed necessary to give some clout to the Commission and to give recognition to the higher qualification necessary for membership of the Commission. The exact wording of the provision is as follows:

> 'If within three months after the report is made no action is taken which seems to the Commission to be adequate and appropriate, the Commissioner, may after considering the comments, if any, made by or on behalf of the department, authority or persons against whom the complaint was made bring an action before any court and seek such remedy as may be appropriate for the enforcement of the recommendations of the Commission."

The experience of the former Ombudsman, who had no enforcement powers, was that many of his recommendations were disregarded to the frustration of the petitioners and the embarrassment of the Ombudsman himself.

Much debate has raged in Ghana over the appropriateness of granting the Commission such enforcement powers. The opponents of this provision argue that the dignity of the Commission will be undermined whenever the Courts refused to enforce the decision of the Commission by rejecting its findings and recommendations. It is further argued that the Commission occupies an unenviable position in that it already exercises various functions, a situation, which has the potential of compromising its neutrality in some cases. In other words, it receives and investigates complaints, attempts mediation and where that fails assumes an adjudicative role. It is argued that it would be inappropriate to add to these various functions, the role of enforcement of its own decision by court action.

Notwithstanding the force of these arguments, the experience of the Commission so far justifies the retention of its enforcement powers. Firstly, it is a power that is rarely invoked. Out of the 8775 cases disposed of from October

1993 – December 1996, it is only in thirteen cases that the Commission has bee compelled to institute court action to enforce its recommendations. Forty t fifty per cent of the cases handled by the Commission are resolved by mediatio to the satisfaction of both parties. In the vast majority of the remaining case the recommendations of the Commission are accepted and implemented by th respondents. The enforcement powers of the Commission, therefore, serve as back-up power, which may be invoked, as and when necessary.

The Commission releases for publication significant decisions or those that i considers to be in the public interest.

Functioning of the Commission

Investigation of Complaints

(a) *Administrative Justice Complaints*

Under its administrative justice jurisdiction the Commission seeks to promot efficient and fair public administration by investigating complaints by citizen against public officers alleging abuse of office, acts of injustice, improper o arbitrary exercise of power or discretion and the unfair treatment of any perso by a public officer in the discharge of his duties. By this process the Commissio holds public officers accountable for their actions and helps to promote transpar ency and accountability in the affairs of public administration.

By the end of December 1996 (barely thirty-eight months after it starte operating) the Commission had received a total of 12,409 complaints out o which 8775 had been disposed of. The vast majority of the cases dealt with b the Commission involve complaints by individuals who allege they have suffere injustice as a result of the wilful abuse of power, unfairness or arbitrariness o the part of public officials. Examples of such cases are wrongful dismissal an termination of employment, acts of victimization such as punitive transfers, dela in promotion, delay or refusal in the payment of end-of service benefits an other entitlements or wrongful computation of such benefits etc. Others includ complaints alleging wrongful cancellation of examination results, cancellation o mining licenses, refusal by the Central Bank to grant a license to operate a Foreign Exchange Bureau, etc. A significant number of the cases submitted to the Commission are labour-related complaints. Most of them are made agains public officials, Government Ministries and institutions. This is to be expected since the government is the single largest employer. However, with the on-going process of the divestiture of most of the State-owned enterprises and the liberali- sation of the economy, the private sector is becoming an active player in the economy of Ghana. As a result, the number of complaints lodged against private employers has been growing over the years.

Statistics from the Commission's 1996 Annual Report indicate for example that, out of a total of 5200 petitions received during that year, 2209 of them were labour-related. Allegations of wrongful dismissals were highest among the labour-related cases, accounting for 517 of the total number. Claims for Severance Awards, Salary arrears, Salary withholding, Salary discrimination together followed with the total of 440 whilst Termination of appointments followed third with a total of 339 cases. Other cases totalling 913 such as

Resignation, Redundancy/Redeployment, Retirement, Pension/Gratuity, End-Of-Service Benefit, Suspension/Interdiction, Promotion and other labour discriminations accounted for the rest of the labour-related cases.

b) *Human Rights Complaints*

The Commission has the duty to investigate all complaints of violation of fundamental human rights and freedoms. This jurisdiction applies to complaints against public officials and institutions, individuals and private enterprises. However, in the case of the private sector, it is restricted to human rights and freedoms under the Constitution.

The 1992 Constitution contains a comprehensive list of human rights and freedoms embracing civil and political rights as well as economic, social and cultural rights. Civil and political rights include the right to life, personal liberty, fair and speedy trial, human dignity, protection from slavery and forced labour freedom of speech and expression, freedom of association, freedom of assembly and movement, freedom from discrimination etc. (Sections 13–21, 1992 Ghana Constitution). Economic and social rights recognized under the Constitution include the right to work under satisfactory, safe and healthy conditions, the property right of spouses, the right to property, the right to equal educational opportunities, women and children's rights, the rights of the disabled and the rights of the sick. Cultural rights include the right to practice, profess and maintain any culture, language tradition, or religion (ibid, Sections 22–30).

Typical human rights complaints lodged with the Commission include wrongful detention and assault by the security agencies, delay in the trial of suspects remanded into custody, gender discrimination and sexual harassment at the work place, domestic violence etc. The Commission has intervened in a number of cases where children were being denied medical treatment, such as blood transfusion or open-heart surgery, because of the beliefs of their parents.

Litigants whose cases have been unreasonably delayed in the courts have sought the Commission's assistance and the Commission's intervention has resulted in the speedy disposal of some cases. Although the Commission has no jurisdiction to investigate a matter pending in court, it has intervened to ensure speedy disposal of cases in criminal cases.

Proactive Investigations

The Commission has adopted a proactive stance by investigating cases on its own initiative. For example, it has intervened on a number of occasions to secure the release on bail or arraignment before Court of suspects who have been arrested and detained by the Police and other law enforcement agencies beyond the permissible constitutional period. It has taken action in response to reports in the media about human rights violations.

Of late, the Commission has on its own initiative intervened in cases where children were being denied medical treatment, such as blood transfusion or open-heart surgery, because of the religious beliefs of their parents. In a few cases where children have died as a result of their parents refusal to give their consent for a doctor to administer blood transfusion, the Commission, after thorough investigation, has recommended to the Attorney-General prosecution of such parents.

Promotion of Human Rights

Democracy and good governance requires upholding the rule of law and promoting respect and observance of human rights. The creation and maintenance of a human rights culture is integral to human development. One of the primary functions of the Commission as stated earlier is to educate the general public on their human rights and civic responsibilities by means of workshops, seminars, lectures, symposia etc. Education plays a very important role in the promotion of human rights. The elaborate human rights provisions in the Constitution would be mere abstract guarantees if people do not know about or understand them.

Education on human rights, it has been observed, involves informing people about their rights and duties and the mechanism available to enforce them, creating awareness and provoking discussion on human rights issues; shaping values and attitudes; and encouraging people to stand up for and defend their rights. Accordingly, we have organized seminars and workshops for the Police Service, District Chief Executives, Presiding Members and members of the District Assemblies, women organizations, religious bodies, chiefs, the youth, panel members and chairman of the community and circuit tribunals as well as the general public. The Commission has been instrumental in the establishment of human rights clubs in some secondary schools and one of the Universities.

On the 11th February 1997 the Commission launched a human rights education pilot program, which aims at educating people in rural communities on their human rights and the mechanisms available for their enforcement. This pilot project, which was a success, has recently been extended to the other Districts. The educational programme of the Commission for the rest of the year will focus on the community and regional tribunals as well as rural human rights education with particular emphasis on women empowerment.

Inspection of Prison and Police Cell

The Commission has the responsibility of monitoring the observance and respect of human rights in Ghana. In 1995 we carried out a nation-wide inspection of Police Cells and Prisons to ensure that the conditions therein meet minimum international standards. This exercise was also intended among other things, to find out the details and particulars of suspects who have been remanded into custody pending trial for an unreasonable period of time.

Our main findings from this inspection include overcrowding and congestion in many prisons, poor sanitation in most Police Cells, inadequate feeding allowance, the conviction and sentence to prison of pregnant women who invariably give birth in prison. Other findings are the conviction and sentence to adult prisons of juveniles, the indefinite holding of about 300 condemned prisoners under mentally torturous conditions and the continued detention of remand prisoners for periods ranging from a year to eight years without trial. The Commission issued a report outlining its findings and made certain recommendations to the appropriate authorities.

As a result of the wide publicity given to the report in the press and electronic media, the Government has introduced significant reforms. The feeding allowance has been increased by 300 percent (which is still inadequate). All the young hildren in adult prisons have been transferred to Borstal institutions and the Ainistry of Health is considering the possibility of exempting prisoners from payment for prescribed drugs. The Government has also undertaken a review of the sentence of some selected inmates releasing some on grounds of ill health nd old age. Annual follow-up inspections of most prisons and police cells are arried out and the results published in the media.

Campaign to Eliminate Dehumanizing Cultural Practices

The Commission has undertaken the task of examining social and customary practices in society, which it considers dehumanising and a violation of the human rights provisions of the Constitution. Such customary practices include the "Trokosi" system which is a form of servitude and forced labour whereby women and children mostly in the Volta Region of Ghana are sent to shrines to serve the fetish priests as atonement for transgressions allegedly committed by members of their family. Through dialogue and interaction with the practitioners of this system, the Commission in collaboration with International Needs Ghana, a local NGO, has succeeded in securing the release of some of these women and children.

Recent media reports have disclosed practices in parts of the Northern Region where women, especially old women between the ages of 60–85, suspected of being witches have been banished from their communities and are being kept in witches homes. In some cases, they have been lynched to death. The Commission has conducted a thorough investigation into the practice, and is in the process of starting an educational program in the affected communities to have informed discussions on the phenomenon of witchcraft and on the rights of people suspected to be witches. It is hoped that eventually these suspected witches would be released from the camps, rehabilitated and integrated into society.

Economic and Political Accountability Jurisdiction

The Commission is mandated by the Constitution to ensure compliance by public officers with the Code of Conduct for Public Officers as contained in Chapter 24 of the Constitution. The Code requires that a public officer shall not put himself/herself in a position where his/her personal interest conflicts or is likely to conflict with the performance of the functions of his/her office. Another provision in the Code of Conduct is that certain top public officers, including the President, Vice President, Speaker, Ministers, Heads of Departments, Members of Parliament etc, should submit to the Auditor-General written declaration of all property or assets owned by, or liabilities owed by them, whether directly or indirectly,

(a) Within three months after coming into force of the Constitution or before taking office, as the case may be;
(b) At the end of every four years; and
(c) At the end of their term of office. (Article 286 (1) of the 1992 Ghana Constitution)

Article 287 of the Constitution provides that allegations that a public officer has not complied with the Code of conduct shall be made to the Commissioner of CHRAJ, and he shall in the absence of a written admission cause investigation to be made and shall take any appropriate action based on such investigations. The Commission's duty to enforce the Leadership Code of Conduct goes a long way to promote ethics in the public service and to minimise illegal acquisition of wealth by public officers.

Equally important in promoting transparency and accountability is the Commission's duty to investigate all instances of alleged or suspected corruption and embezzlement of public funds by public officers.

During 1995 and 1996 the Commission investigated some Ministers of State and top government officials who were alleged by sections of the media to have acquired assets illegally. The Commission's reports on three Ministers of State and a Presidential Staffer were released in October 1996. Adverse findings were made against two of the Ministers and a Presidential Staffer in the office of the President all of whom have since tendered their resignation. Investigations are still pending in respect of one former and one serving Minister who are also alleged by the media of having amassed wealth illegally.

Almost six months after the Commission released its reports on four of the Ministers investigated the Government issued a White Paper in which it accepted some of the recommendations but sought to exonerate some of the officers against whom the Commission had made adverse findings. The White Paper provoked such a huge public outcry that the Government moved to stem the tide of public opposition by assuring the public that the White Paper was not intended to give any direction or instruction to the Commission and that the Commission was at liberty to take whatever steps it considers appropriate to enforce its recommendations.

However, it must be admitted that the fact that the Commission can investigate serving Ministers of State is evidence of the healthy political environment in Ghana and the effectiveness of the Commission. Some of the positive results from this exercise include the President's acceptance of our recommendation that the category of public officers required by law to declare their assets should be expanded to include certain public officers holding high and sensitive positions but who presently are not required by the Constitution to do so. Parliament has recently passed a law, which enlarges the category of public officers required to declare their assets. The Law regulating waiver of customs and import duties on fish imported into the country is also been reviewed to address the deficiencies in the law unearthed during our investigation.

Collaboration with Non-governmental Organizations

The Commission appreciates the importance of establishing and maintaining close co-operation with non-governmental organizations that are directly or indirectly involved in the promotion and protection of human rights. Consequently, the Commission has held a workshop for all human rights NGOs with a view to exploring ways in which both the Commission and the NGOs can work together to advance the cause of human rights in Ghana. In 1995 the Commission undertook a joint project with a local NGO called International Needs for the abolition of the Trokosi practice mentioned above. We have also ecently received a grant to undertake with another NGO WILDAF an educaional programme aimed at educating and empowering women in the Northern arts of Ghana.

Problems and Prospects

nsufficient funding from Central Government has been one of the reasons for he inability of the Commission to make its service delivery more efficient and ffective. However, the Commission receives substantial funding from other ources such as the Western embassies, European Union, international NGOs tc. Our experience has been that the donor community and other agencies are villing to give financial and technical assistance to human rights institutions vhich have proved to be independent and credible.

One of the challenges facing the Commission's Headquarters Office is the eavy workload of cases it has to handle. The inordinate number of petitions eceived by the Commission is due mainly to its extensive functions, functions hat in other jurisdictions would be shared among three or more different nstitutions. The fact that the Commission's services, which are provided by rofessional lawyers and investigators, are delivered free coupled with its informal rocedure has made it a more attractive forum than the traditional Courts for lispute resolution.

Low salaries and unattractive conditions of service for staff of the Commission as resulted in the exodus of competent and trained personnel from the Commission for other institutions.

Concluding Remarks

From the experience of Ghana's Human Rights Commission it is my view that he establishment of Human Rights Commissions/Ombudsmen should be ncouraged throughout Africa. Ombudsman and/or national human rights instiutions can play an important role in promoting democracy and good governance f they are established under the right legal framework, granted broad functions nd powers and are independent from the control and influence of any person r authority. In this regard, it is not sufficient that their independence is guaraneed under the Constitution or a statute. Their independence from control or nfluence by any person or authority must be respected. The members of the Commission must themselves prove their independence and impartiality.. However, it is important to stress that independence does not mean confrontation with the executive or any other arm of government. Co-operation is essential without compromising independence. There must, of course, be a certain mininum amount of political will to ensure the survival and smooth functioning of hese democratic institutions.

LEGISLATION

Constitution 1992

Chapter Eighteen
Commission on Human Rights and Administrative Justice

216. There shall be established by Act of Parliament within six months after Parliamer first meets after the coming into force of this Constitution, a Commission on Huma Rights and Administrative Justice which shall consist of:
    (a) a Commissioner for Human Rights and Administrative Justice; and
    (b) two Deputy Commissioners for Human Rights and Administrative Justice.
217. The President shall appoint the members of the Commission under Article 70 c this Constitution.
218. The functions of the Commission shall be defined and prescribed by Act c Parliament and shall include the duty:
    (a) to investigate complaints of violations of fundamental rights and freedom injustice, corruption, abuse of power and unfair treatment of any person by public officer in the exercise of his official duties;
    (b) to investigate complaints concerning the functioning of the Public Servic Commission, the administrative organs of the State, the Armed Forces, th Police Service and the Prisons Service in so far as the complaints relate to th failure to achieve a balanced structuring of those services or equal access by a to the recruitment of those services or fair administration in relation to thes services;
    (c) to investigate complaints concerning practices and actions by persons; privat enterprises and other institutions where those complaints allege violations c fundamental rights and freedoms under this Constitution;
    (d) to take appropriate action to call for the remedying; correction and reversal c instances specified in paragraphs (a), (b), and (c) of this clause through suc means as are fair, proper and effective, including
        (i) negotiation and compromise between the parties concerned;
        (ii) causing the complaint and its findings on it to be reported to the superio of an offending person;
        (iii) bringing proceedings in a competent Court for a remedy to secure th termination of the offending action or conducting or the abandonment o alteration of the offending procedures; and
        (iv) bringing proceedings to restrain the enforcement of such legislation o regulation by challenging its validity if the offending action or conduct i sought to be justified by subordinate legislation or regulation which i unreasonable or otherwise ultra vires;
    (e) to investigate all instances of alleged suspected corruption and the misappropria tion of public moneys by officials and to take appropriate steps, including report to the Attorney-General and the Auditor-General, resulting from suc investigations;
    (f) to educate the public as to human rights and freedoms by such means as th Commissioner may decide, including publications, lectures and symposia; and
    (g) to report annually to Parliament on the performance of its functions.
219. (1) The powers of the Commission shall be defined by Act of Parliament and sha include the power
        (a) to issue subpoenas requiring the attendance of any person before th Commission and the production of any record relevant to any investigatio by the Commission;
        (b) to cause any person contemptuous of any such subpoena to be prosecute

before a competent Court;
(c) to question any person in respect of any subject matter under investigation before the Commission;
(d) to require any person to disclose truthfully and an frankly any information within his knowledge relevant to any investigation by the Commissioner.

(2) The Commissioner shall not investigate
(a) a matter which is pending before a court or judicial tribunal; or
(b) a matter involving the relations or dealings between the Government and any other Government or an international organization; or
(c) a matter relating to the exercise of the prerogative of mercy.

20. An Act of Parliament enacted under Articles 216 of this Constitution shall provide for the creation of regional and district branches of the Commission.
21. A person shall not be qualified for appointment as a Commissioner or a Deputy Commissioner for Human Rights and Administrative Justice, unless he is
(a) in the case of Commissioner, qualified for appointment as a Justice of the Court of Appeal: and
(b) in the case of a Deputy Commissioner; qualified for appointment as a Justice of the High Court.
22. The Commissioner and Deputy Commissioners shall not hold any other public office.
23. (1) The Commissioner and Deputy Commissioners shall enjoy the terms and conditions of service of a Justice of the Court of Appeal and High Court respectively.
(2) The Commissioner and Deputy Commissioners shall cease to hold office upon attaining the ages of seventy and sixty-five years respectively.
24. Where the Commissioner dies, resigns or is removed from office or is for any other reason unable to perform the functions of his office, the President shall, acting in consultation with the Council of State, appoint a person qualified to be appointed Commissioner to perform those functions until the appointment of a new Commissioner.
25. Except as provided by this Constitution or by any other law not inconsistent with this Constitution, the Commission and the Commissioners shall in the performance of their functions, not be subject to the direction or control of any person or authority.
26. The appointment of officers and other employees of the Commission shall be made by the Commission acting in consultation with the Public Services Commission.
27. The administrative expenses of the Commission including salaries, allowances and pensions payable to, or in respect of, persons serving with the Commission, shall be charged on the Consolidated Fund.
28. The procedure for the removal of the Commissioner and Deputy Commissioners shall be the same as that provided for the removal of a Justice of the Court of Appeal and a Justice of the High Court respectively under this Constitution.
29. For the purpose of performing his functions under this Constitution and any other law, the Commissioner may bring an action before any court in Ghana and may seek remedy which may be available from that court.
30. Subject to the provisions of this Constitution and to any Act of Parliament made under this Chapter, the Commission shall make, by constitutional instrument, regulations regarding the manner and procedure for bringing complaints before it and the investigation of such complaints.

The Commission on Human Rights and Administrative Justice Act 1993

Act 456

An Act to establish a Commission on Human Rights and Administrative Justice to investigate complaints of violations of fundamental human rights and freedoms, injustices and corruption; abuse of power and unfair treatment of persons by public officers in the exercise of their duties, with power to seek remedy in respect of such acts or omissions and to provide for other related purposes.

Date of Assent: 6th July, 1993

Be It Enacted by Parliament as follows:

Part I Establishment of Commission on Human Rights And Administrative Justice

1. There is established by this Act a body to be known as the Commission on Human Rights and Administrative Justice, in this Act referred to as "the Commission."
2. (1) The Commission shall consist of:
   (a) a Commissioner for Human Rights and Administrative Justice, in this Act referred to as "The Commissioner"; and
   (b) two Deputy Commissioners for Human Rights and Administrative Justice in this Act referred to as "the Deputy Commissioners."
   (2) The President shall, acting in consultation with the Council of State appoint the Commissioner and the Deputy Commissioners.
3. (1) A person shall not be qualified for appointment as Commissioner or a Deputy Commissioner for Human Rights and Administrative Justice, unless he is:
   (a) in the case of the Commissioner, qualified for appointment as a Justice of the Court of Appeal; and
   (b) in the case of a Deputy Commissioner, qualified for appointment as a justice of the High Court.
   (2) The Commissioner and Deputy Commissioners shall not while holding office as Commissioners hold any other public office.
4. (1) The Commissioner and Deputy Commissioners shall enjoy the terms and conditions of service of a Justice of the Court of Appeal and High Court respectively.
   (2) The Commissioner and Deputy Commissioners shall cease to hold office upon attaining the ages of seventy and sixty-five years respectively.
   (3) Where the Commissioner or a Deputy Commissioner dies, resigns or is removed from office, the President shall, in consultation with the Council of State, appoint a person qualified to be appointed Commissioner or Deputy Commissioner to perform those functions until the appointment of a new Commissioner or Deputy Commissioner.
5. The procedure for the removal of the Commissioner and Deputy Commissioner shall be the same as that provided for the removal of Justice of the Court of Appeal and a Justice of the High Court respectively under Article 146 of the Constitution.
6. Except as provided by the Constitution or by any other law not inconsistent with the Constitution, the Commission and the Commissioners shall, in the performance of their functions not be subject to the direction or control of any person or authority.

Part II
Functions of The Commission

7. (1) The functions of the Commission are:
   (a) to investigate complaints of violations of fundamental rights and freedoms, injustice, corruption, abuse of power and unfair treatment of any person by a public officer in the exercise of his official duties;
   (b) to investigate complaints concerning the functioning of the Public Service Commission, the administrative organs of the State, the Armed Forces, the Police Service and the Prisons Service in so far as the complaints relate to the failure to achieve a balanced structuring of those services or equal access by all to the recruitment of those services or fair administration in relation to these services;

(c) to investigate complaints concerning practices and actions by persons, private enterprises and other institutions where those complaints allege violations of fundamental rights and freedoms under this Constitution;

(d) to take appropriate action to call for the remedying, correction and reversal of instances specified in paragraphs (a), (b), and (c) of this clause through such means as are fair, proper and effective, including:

(i) negotiation and compromise between the parties concerned;

(ii) causing the complaint and its findings on it to be reported to the superior of an offending person;

(iii) bringing proceedings in a competent Court for a remedy to secure the termination of the offending action or conduct, or the abandonment or alteration of the offending procedures; and

(iv) bringing proceedings to restrain the enforcement of such legislation or regulation by challenging its validity if the offending action or conduct is sought to be justified by subordinate legislation or regulation which is unreasonable or otherwise ultra vires;

(e) to investigate allegations that a public officer has contravened or has not complied with a provision of Chapter Twenty-four (Code of Conduct for Public Officers) of the Constitution;

(f) to investigate all instances of alleged suspected corruption and the misappropriation of public moneys by officials and to take appropriate steps, including reports to the Attorney-General and the Auditor-General, resulting from such investigations;

(g) to educate the public as to human rights and freedoms by such means as the Commissioner may decide; including publications. lectures and symposia; and

(h) to report annually to Parliament on the performance of its functions.

(2) All costs and expenses related to investigations conducted by the Commission into a complaint shall be borne by the Commission.

8. (1) The Commission shall for the purpose of performing its functions under this Act, have power

(a) to issue subpoenas requiring the attendance of any person before the Commission and the production of any record relevant to any investigation by the Commission;

(b) to cause any person contemptuous of any such subpoena to be prosecuted before a competent Court;

(c) to question any person in respect of any subject matter under investigation before the Commission;

(d) to require any person to disclose truthfully and frankly any information within his knowledge relevant to any investigation by the Commissioner.

(2) The Commissioner shall not investigate

(a) a matter which is pending before a court or,judicial tribunal; or

(b) a matter involving the relations or dealings between the Government and any other Government or an international organization; or

(c) a matter relating to the exercise of the prerogative of mercy.

9. For the purpose of performing his functions under the Constitution, this Act and other law, the Commissioner may bring an action before any court in Ghana and may seek any remedy which may be available from that court.

10. (1) There shall be established in each Region and District of Ghana Regional and District branches respectively of the Commission.

(2) There shall be appointed by the Commission an officer who shall be the head of a Regional or District branch of the Commission.

(3) The Commission may create such other lower structures as would facilitate its operations.

11. (1) A representative of the Commission in a Regional or District office of the Commission shall:
   (a) receive complaints from the public in the Region or District;
   (b) make such on-the-spot investigations as may be necessary; and
   (c) discharge any other duties relating to the functions of the Commission that may be assigned to him by the Commissioner.

Part III
Provisions Relating to Complaints And Investigations

12. (1) A complaint to the Commission shall be made in writing or orally to the national offices of the Commission or to a representative of the Commission in the Regional or District branch.
   (2) Where a complaint is made in writing, it shall be signed by the complainant or his agent.
   (3) Where a complaint is made orally, the person to whom the complaint is made shall reduce the complaint into writing and shall append his signature and the signature or thumbprint of the complainant.
   (4) Notwithstanding any law to the contrary where a letter written by
   (a) a person in custody; or
   (b) a patient in a hospital;
   is addressed to the Commission, it shall be immediately forwarded unopened and unaltered to the Commission by the person for the time being in charge of the place or institution where the writer of the letter is detained or of which he is a patient.
   (5) A complaint under this Act may be made by any individual or a body of persons whether corporate or unincorporated.
   (6) Where a person by whom a complaint might have been made under this Act has died or is for any sufficient reason unable to act for himself, the complaint may be made by his personal representative or by a member of his family or other individual suitable to represent him.

13. (1) Where in the course of the investigation of any complaint it appears to the Commission
   (a) that under the law or existing administrative practice there is adequate remedy for the complaint, whether or not the complainant has availed himself of it; or
   (b) that having regard to all the circumstances of the case, any further investigation in unnecessary, it may refuse to investigate the matter further.
   (2) The Commission may refuse to investigate or cease to investigate any complaint
   (a) if the complaint relates to a decision, recommendation, act or omission of which the complainant has had knowledge for more than twelve months before the complaint is received by the Commission; or
   (b) if the Commission considers that
      (i) the subject matter of the complaint is trivial;
      (ii) the complaint is frivolous or vexatious or is not made in good faith; or
      (iii) the complainant does not have sufficient personal interest in the subject matter of the complaint.
   (3) Notwithstanding subsection (2) of this section, if within six months after the Commission's refusal or ceasing to investigate any complaint under this section, fresh evidence in favour of the complainant becomes available, the Commissioner shall, at the request of the complainant; re-open the case.
   (4) Where the Commission decides not to investigate or to cease to investigate a complaint, it shall within 30 days of the decision inform the complainant of its decision and the reasons for so refusing.

14. (1) Where the Commission decides to conduct an investigation under this Act, it shall give the authority or person concerned and to any other person who is alleged in the complaint to have taken or authorized the act or omission complained of, an opportunity to comment on any allegations contained in the complaint and the representative of the authority or person concerned shall submit his comments within such time as the Commission may specify.

(2) The public may be excluded from investigations conducted by the Commission.

(3) Without prejudice to the generality of the provisions of this section, the Commission may obtain information from such persons and in such manner and make such inquiries as it considers necessary.

(4) The Commission may pay to a person by whom a complaint is made and to any other person who attends and furnishes information for the purposes of an investigation under this Act

(a) sums in respect of expenses properly incurred by them; and

(b) allowances by way of compensation for the loss of their time, in accordance with such scales and subject to such conditions as may be determined by the Commission having regard to the rates for the time being applicable to the courts.

15. (1) Subject to this section the Commission may require any person who, in its opinion, is able to give any information relating to a matter being investigated by the Commission

(a) to furnish the information to it;

(b) to produce any document, paper or thing that in its opinion relates to the matter being investigated and which may be in the possession or control of that person.

(2) The Commission may summon before it and examine on oath or affirmation

(a) a person required to give information or produce anything under subsection (1) of this section;

(b) a complainant;

(c) any other person who the Commission considers will be able to give information required under subsection (1) of this Section.

(3) Subject to subsection (4) of this section, a person who is bound by law to maintain secrecy in relation to, or not to disclose, any matter may not

(a) supply information to or answer a question put by the Commission in relation to that matter; or

(b) produce to the Commission a document, paper or thing relating to it, if compliance with that requirement would be in breach of the obligation of secrecy or non-disclosure.

(4) A person to whom subsection (3) of this section applies may be required by the Commission to supply information or answer a question or produce a document, paper or thing that relates to a matter under investigation; and subject to section 16 of this Act; it shall be the duty of that person to comply with the requirement.

(5) A witness before the Commission shall be entitled to the same privileges to which he would have been entitled if he were a witness before the High Court.

(6) No person shall be liable to prosecution for an offence under any enactment by reason of his compliance with a requirement of the Commission under this section.

16. Article 135 of the Constitution which relates to production of official documents in court shall apply to proceedings before the Commission as it applies to proceedings before a court.

17. (1) The Commissioner or a Deputy Commissioner and every person holding an office or appointment under the Commission shall maintain secrecy in respect of all matters that come to their knowledge in the exercise of their functions.

(2) Every person holding office or appointment under the Commission who is likely

to have access to confidential information of the Commission shall before proceeding to carry out his functions under this Act, take and subscribe to the Oath of Secrecy set out in the Second Schedule to the Constitution.

(3) The Commission shall determine the category of persons to whom subsection (2) of this section shall apply.

Part IV
Procedure After Investigation by the Commission

18. (1) Where after making an investigation under this Act, the Commission is of the view that the decision, recommendation, act or omission that was the subject matter of the investigation
(a) amounts to a breach of any of the fundamental rights and freedoms provided in the Constitution; or
(b) appears to have been contrary to law; or
(c) was unreasonable, unjust, oppressive, discriminatory or was in accordance with a rule of law or a provision of any Act or a practice that is unreasonable, unjust; oppressive, or discriminatory; or
(d) was based wholly or partly on an mistake of law or fact; or
(e) was based on irrelevant grounds or made for an improper purpose; or
(f) was made in the exercise of a discretionary power and reasons should have been given for the decision; the Commission shall report its decision and the reasons for it to the appropriate person, Minister, department or authority concerned and shall make such recommendations as it thinks fit and the Commission shall submit a copy of its report and recommendations to the complainant.

(2) If within three months after the report is made no action is taken which seems to the Commission to be adequate and appropriate, the Commissioner, may after considering the comments, if any made by or on behalf of the department, authority or persons against whom the complaint was made, bring an action before any court and seek such remedy as maybe appropriate for the enforcement of the recommendations of the Commission.

19. (1) The Commissioner shall annually submit a report to Parliament which shall include a summary of the matters investigated, and the action on them by the Commission during the preceding year.

(2) Parliament may debate the report of the Commission and may pass such resolution as it considers fit.

(3) A resolution of Parliament shall not alter a decision made by a court on a matter instituted before the court by the Commissioner.

(4) The Commissioner may in the public interest or in the interest of any person or department or any other authority, publish reports relating
(a) generally to the exercise of the functions of the Commission under this Act; or
(b) to any particular case investigated by the Commission whether or not the matters in the report have been the subject of a report to Parliament.

Part V
Miscellaneous Provisions

20. The appointment of officers and other employees of the Commission shall be made by the Commission acting in consultation with the Public Services Commission.

21. The administrative expenses of the Commission including all salaries, allowances and pensions payable to or in respect of, persons serving with the Commission are charged on the Consolidated Fund.

22. (1) Subject to the supervisory jurisdiction of the Supreme Court, no proceedings

shall lie against the Commission or against any person holding an office or appointment under the Commission for anything done, reported of his functions under this Act, unless it is shown that he acted in bad faith.

(2) Anything said, any information supplied, or any document, paper or thing produced by any person in the course of an inquiry by or proceedings before the Commission under this Act is privileged in the same manner as if the inquiry or proceedings were proceedings in a court.

(3) For the purpose of the rules of law relating to defamation any report made by the Commission under this Act shall be privileged and a fair and accurate report on it in a newspaper or a broadcast shall also be privileged.

23. For the purposes of this Act, the Commissioner or any public officer authorized by him, may at any time enter any premises occupied by a department, authority or a person to whose act or omission this Act applies and inspect the premises and, subject to sections 16 and 17 of this Act carry out on the premises any investigation that is within the jurisdiction of the Commission.

24. A person who

(a) without lawful justification or excuse, willfully obstructs, hinders or resists a member of the Commission or an officer authorized by the Commission in the exercise of any powers under this Act; or

(b) without lawful justification or excuse, refuses or willfully fails to comply with any lawful request of the Commissioner or a Deputy Commissioner or any other person under this Act; or

(c) willfully makes any false statement to or misleads or attempts to mislead the Commissioner or any other person in the exercise of his functions under this Act, commits an offence and is liable on summary conviction to a fine not exceeding ¢500,000.00 and in default of payment to imprisonment for a term not exceeding six months or to both.

25. The provisions of this Act are in addition to the provisions of any other Act or any rule of law under which

(a) a remedy or right of appeal or objection is provided for any person; or

(b) any procedure is provided for the inquiry into or investigation of any matter, and nothing in this Act shall be taken to limit or affect a remedy or right of appeal or objection or procedure.

26. (1) Subject to the provisions of the Constitution and to any Act of Parliament made under the Constitution, the Commission shall make. by constitutional instrument, regulations regarding the manner and procedure for bringing complaints before it and the investigation of such complaints.

(2) The exercise of the power to make regulations may be signified under the hand of the Commissioner or in his absence, a Deputy Commissioner.

27. In this Act a reference to a member of a complainant's family means

(a) in the case of a person belonging to a family based on the paternal system – mother, father, wife, son, daughter, brother, sister, father's brother, father's father, father's brother's son, and brother's son;

(b) in the case of a person belonging to a family based on the maternal system – mother, father, wife, son, daughter, brother, sister, mother's mother; mother's brother, mother's sister, sister's son, sister's daughter, mother's sister's son and mother's sister's daughter.

28. (1) The Ombudsman Act 1980 (Act 400) is repealed. (2) Notwithstanding the repeal of the Ombudsman Act, 1980 (Act 400)

(a) any regulation made under it and in force on the coming into force of this Act shall until altered, amended or revoked, continue in force and shall be applied with such modifications as may be necessary for giving effect to the provisions of this Act; and

(b) Any complaint pending before the Ombudsman immediately before the coming into force of this Act may be proceeded with under, and shall be subject to the provisions of, this Act.

Commission on Human Rights and Administrative Justice (Complaints Procedure) Regulations 1994

Constitutional Instrument No. 7

In exercise of the powers conferred on the Commission on Human Rights and Administrative Justice under Section 26 of the Commission on Human Rights and Administrative Justice Act 1993 (Act 456) these Regulations are made this lst day of September, 1994.

1. (1) A complaint to the Commission shall be made in writing or orally to the national office of the Commission or to a representative of the Commission at the regional or district branch of the Commission.
 (2) Where the complaint is in writing, it shall be addressed to the Commissioner or to his regional or district representative and shall be signed or thumbprinted by the complainant or his agent.
 (3) Where the complaint is made orally or the complainant cannot read and write, the complaint shall be reproduced into writing by the officer at the registry of the Commission or its branch to whom the complaint is made or by any other person chosen by the complainant.
 (4) A person who reduces into writing the oral complaint of any person shall:
 (a) read over and explain the contents to the complainant;
 (b) declare on the document that the complainant has fully understood or appeared to understand and appreciate the contents of the complaint;
 (c) cause the complainant to append his signature to the written complaint.
2. (1) A complaint lodged with the Commission shall contain:
 (a) the full name and contact address of the complainant;
 (b) the body, organization or person against whom the complaint is made;
 (c) particulars of the nature of the complaint together with copies of any document in support of the complaint;
 (d) the nature of the injustice or harm that the complainant has suffered as a result of the action, inaction or omission of the body or organization or person against whom the complaint is made; and
 (e) the relief sought by the complainant.
 (2) A person who lodges a complaint with the Commission on behalf of another person shall state in writing the capacity in which he does so and the reason for so doing.
 (3) A complainant shall be given a reasonable time (depending on the circumstances of the case) within which to check on his complaint.
 (4) Where a complaint lodged with the Commission is not pursued for three months from the date it is lodged, the complaint shall lapse thereafter.
3. (1) Where the Commissioner considers that a complaint lodged with the Commission is a matter within the function of the Commission, he shall cause a copy of the complaint to be transmitted to the head of the body or organization or the person against whom the complaint is made with a request for comment and response.
 (2) The head of the body or organization or person against whom the complaint is made shall within ten days from the date of receipt of the complaint or such further period as the Commissioner may specify submit his comment or response to the Commissioner.
 (3) The Commissioner or his representative may assign an investigator or officer of

the Commission to make a preliminary investigation into any complaint lodged with the Commission.

(4) The Commission may for the purposes of performing its functions require the services of a member of the Police Force or any public institution with expert knowledge relevant for redressing any particular complaint.

4. (1) Upon receipt of the comments or response the Commissioner, where he considers that in view of the response, the complaint could be mediated upon and settled, may invite the parties concerned and attempt a settlement of the issue between the parties.

(2) No provision of these regulations shall preclude the Commission on receipt of a complaint from inviting the parties concerned and attempting a settlement of the issue between the parties.

5. (1) Where the Commission decides to institute a full investigation into a complaint, the Commission shall in writing invite

(a) the complainant;

(b) a representative of the body, organization or person against whom the complaint is made; and

(c) such other persons as are considered by the Commission to be concerned in the investigation to attend to be interviewed by the Commission at a date, time and place specified in the notice.

(2) The date for attendance shall not be less than seven days from the date of notice.

(3) A person appearing before the Commission in answer to a complaint shall:

(a) be informed again of the particulars of the complaint and the relief sought;

(b) be afforded full opportunity to answer the complaint and to question any witness.

(4) Any person who appears before the Commission in any investigation shall be given a fair hearing.

(5) Persons appearing before the Commission to be investigated shall appear in person and may be represented by counsel.

(6) Records of the investigation shall be kept in writing.

6. (1) For the purposes of regulation 5, the Commission may on the recommendation of any other member of the Commission, an investigator of the Commission or any other officer of the Commission, constitute a panel to investigate any complaint and report to the Commission.

(2) The panel shall be composed of a Chairman who shall be a member of the Commission or any legal officer in the employment of the Commission and not less than two other officers of the Commission.

(3) Notwithstanding sub-regulation (2) of this regulation there maybe coopted on any such panel such person as the Commissioner may approve.

(4) A person appearing before a panel under these regulations may raise an objection to the membership of the panel to the Commissioner who shall determine the issue.

7. (1) A panel composed under these regulations shall make a full report in any matter before it with its recommendations to the Commission.

(2) The Commission shall consider every report submitted under sub-regulation (1) and may accept or reject the recommendations or ask for further investigations.

8. An officer appointed as the regional or district head of the branch of the Commission shall ensure the prompt investigation by officers in the regional or district of all complaints and may refer complaints to the national office where he considers it necessary or where directed by the Commissioner.

9. (1) The head of a district office of the Commission shall within five days of the end of every month submit to the head of the regional branch of the Commission, a report of all complaints investigated by the district office in the preceding month and recommendation of the office on the complaints.

(2) The designated head of a regional branch of the Commission shall submit a monthly report on all complaints investigated by the district offices and the regional office together with the recommendations to the national office.

10. The final decision in any complaint lodged with the Commission shall be taken by the Commission.
11. For the purpose of sections 9 and 18 (2) of the Act, the Commissioner may by writing, authorize any public officer to bring an action in any court in the name of the Commissioner.
12. In these Regulations: "Act" means the Commission on Human Rights and Administrative Justice Act, 1993 (Act 456).

Dated at Accra this 1st day of September, 1994.

Report of the National Human Rights Commission of India

Justice V.S. Malimath*

A. Tasks and Competences

1. The National Human Rights Commission of India (for short "the Commission") is a statutory body constituted on 12th October 1993, under the Human Rights Ordinance (Ordinance 30 of 1993) promulgated by the President of India on 28.9.1993 in exercise of the powers conferred on him by Article 123(1) of the Constitution of India. The President exercises this legislative power only when both Houses of Parliament are not in session and he is satisfied that circumstances exist which render it necessary for him to take immediate action. The ordinance was later substituted by the Parliament enacting the Protection of Human Rights Act, 1993 (for short, "the Act") which came into force on the 8th January 1994. Section 3(1) of the Act confers power on the Central Government to constitute the Commission. Sub-section (2) of Section 3 provides that the Commission shall consist of:

(a) a Chairperson who has been a Chief Justice of the Supreme Court of India;
(b) one Member who is, or has been, a Judge of the Supreme Court;
(c) one Member who is, or has been, the Chief Justice of a High Court;
(d) two Members to be appointed from amongst persons having knowledge of, or practical experience in, matters relating to human rights.

In addition to the five permanent Members contemplated by Sub-section (2) of Section 3, there are three ex-officio Members as provided in Sub-section (3) of Section 3 viz.,

(i) Chairperson of the National Commission for Minorities;
(ii) Chairperson of the National Commission for Scheduled Castes and Scheduled Tribes; and
(iii) Chairperson of the National Commission for Women.

The functions of these three ex-officio Members are limited to the discharge of functions specified in Clauses (b) to (j) of Section 12 only.

The functions of the Commission are enumerated in Section 12, the powers relating to holding of enquiries are prescribed by Section 13 and the powers relating to investigation are contained in Section 14. The procedure for enquiring into general complaints is prescribed by Section 17 and Section 18 deals with

*Member of the National Human Rights Commission of India.

K. Hossain et al. (eds), Human Rights Commissions and Ombudsman Offices, 211–230.

action or steps that may be taken after the completion of the inquiry. As far as the armed forces are concerned, Section 19 prescribes a slightly different procedure.

2. The tasks/functions of the Commission have been listed in Section 12 of the Act. They are the following:

(a) inquire, suo motu or on a petition presented to it by a victim or any person on his behalf, into complaint of
  (i) violation of human rights or abetment thereof or
  (ii) negligence in the prevention of such violation;
  by a public servant
(b) intervene in any proceeding involving any allegation of violation of human rights pending before a court with the approval of such court;
(c) visit, under intimation to the State Government, any jail or any other institution under the control of the State Government, where persons are detained or lodged for purposes of treatment, reformation or protection to study the living conditions of the inmates and make recommendations thereon;
(d) review the safeguards provided by or under the Constitution or any law for the time being in force for the protection of human rights and recommend measures for their effective implementation;
(e) review the factors, including acts of terrorism that inhibit the enjoyment of human rights and recommend appropriate remedial measures;
(f) study treaties and other international instruments on human rights and make recommendations for their effective implementation;
(g) undertake and promote research in the field of human rights;
(h) spread human rights literacy among various sections of society and promote awareness of the safeguards available for the protection of these rights through publications, the media, seminars and other available means;
(i) encourage the efforts of non-governmental organizations and institutions working in the field of human rights;
(j) such other functions as it may consider necessary for the promotion of human rights.

3. The preamble to the Act says that the National Human Rights Commission is constituted for better protection of human rights and for matters connected therewith or incidental thereto. Human rights that fall within the sphere of competence of the National Human Rights Commission are defined in Section 2(d) to mean the rights relating to life, liberty, equality and dignity of the individual guaranteed by the Constitution or embodied in the international covenants and enforceable by courts in India. Part III of the Constitution of India enumerates the Fundamental Rights or Human Rights guaranteed to the citizens of India. Articles 14 to 18 guarantee the right to equality. Article 19 guarantees

(a) the right to freedom of speech and expression;
(b) the right to assemble peacefully and without arms;
(c) the right to form associations or unions;
(d) the right to move freely throughout the territory of India;
(e) the right to settle in any part of the territory of India;

(f) the right to practise any profession or to carry on any occupation, trade or business.

The right to freedom of religion is contained in Articles 25 to 28. Cultural and educational rights are found in Articles 29 and 30 of the Constitution. The right to protection of personal life and liberty is guaranteed by Articles 20, 21 and 22. Article 23 prohibits traffic in human beings and forced labour, and Article 24 prohibits employment of children in factories, mines or in any other hazardous job.

The International Covenants referred to in Section 2(d) and (f) of the Act are the International Covenant on Civil and Political Rights and the International Covenant on Economic, Social and Cultural Rights adopted by the General Assembly of the United Nations on the 16th December 1966.

4. Section 36(2) of the Act prescribes a period of limitation of one year from the date on which the act constituting violation of human rights is alleged to have been committed. There is no provision to enable the National Human Rights Commission to entertain a complaint which is barred by limitation.

5. The power to investigate conferred by Section 14 can, in the absence of any express provision to the contrary, be exercised by the National Human Rights Commission to investigate on the spot, the alleged violations.

6. In addition to national or federal authorities, the regional authorities fall within the sphere of competence of the National Human Rights Commission, except the State of Jammu & Kashmir for which there are special provisions contained in the proviso to Section 1(2) and the proviso to Sub-section (5) of Section 21.

7. Section 12(a) provides that the Commission can inquire suo motu or on a petition presented to it by a victim or any person on his behalf into complaint on (i) violation of human rights or abetment thereof, or (ii) negligence in the prevention of such violation by a public servant. The expression "public servant" has been defined in Section 2(iii) which says that it shall have the meaning assigned to it in Section 21 of the Indian Penal Code. Section 21 says that a public servant includes Commissioned Officers of Armed Forces, Judges, officers of Court of Justice, jurors, etc. assisting courts or public servant, arbitrators, every person empowered to place a person in confinement, officers of Government empowered to prevent offences etc., every officer empowered to keep property of Government etc., every officer empowered to levy tax, etc. for secular, common purposes, etc., every officer empowered to prepare electoral roll, etc., and to conduct elections and every one paid by Government or local authority to perform public duty, etc.

National Human Rights Commission cannot entertain complaints of violation of human rights against non-State actors. The decisions of the legislatures and the verdicts of the judiciary rendered under their respective jurisdictions, do not appear to fall within the ambit of the Commission's power to entertain complaints under Section 12(a) of the Act. However, it may be pointed out that the National Human Rights Commission has the power to recommend, repeal or amendment of the laws in view of the functions conferred by Clauses (d) and (e) of Section 12 of the Act which read as follows:

"(d) review the safeguards provided by or under the Constitution or any law for the time being in force for the protection of human rights and recommend measures for their effective implementation;

(e) review the factors, including acts of terrorism that inhibit the enjoyment of human rights and recommend appropriate remedial measures."

8. Further, Section 12(b) enables the National Human Rights Commission to intervene in any judicial proceedings involving any allegation of violation of human rights pending before a Court with the approval of such Court. Section 18(2) of the Act enables the National Human Rights Commission to approach the Supreme Court or the High Court concerned for such directions, orders or writs as the Court may deem necessary. If the National Human Rights Commission finds that any law infringes the fundamental rights, it can (a) approach the High Court or the Supreme Court for a declaration that such law is void, or (b) move the Parliament to suitably amend the law.

9. Any person can make a complaint to the National Human Rights Commission about a violation of human rights. Besides, the National Human Rights Commission also has suo motu power to take action when a violation of human rights comes to its notice. The family members of a victim can also bring their grievances before the Commission. The National Human Rights Commission can entertain petitions from anyone including international organizations complaining that particular legislation abridges the fundamental rights guaranteed to the citizens by the Constitution of India. The Commission can look into such grievances in the exercise of its functions under Clauses (d) and (e) and if satisfied, make appropriate recommendations. Such a petition cannot be entertained as a complaint under Section 12(a) of the Act as that provision can be invoked only in cases of violation of human rights by a public servant. Non-governmental organizations can bring complaints of violation of human rights to the Commission. It is not necessary that such NGO's should have been established within the jurisdiction of the National Human Rights Commission.

B. Organization

10. The National Human Rights Commission consists of 5 full-fledged Members and 3 ex-officio Members. At present, there are only 3 full-fledged Members, including the Chairman. Two vacancies are yet to be filled.

The Chairman and four full-fledged Members of the National Human Rights Commission are appointed by the President of India by warrant under his hand and seal on the recommendation of a Committee consisting of:

(a) the Prime Minister (Chairperson)
(b) Speaker of the House of he People (Member)
(c) Minister in-charge of Ministry of Home Affairs in he Government of India (Member)
(d) Leader of the Opposition in the House of the People (Member)
(e) Leader of the Opposition in the Council of States (Member)
(f) Deputy Chairman of the Council of States (Member) provided that no sitting Judge of the Supreme Court or sitting Chief Justice of a High Court shall be appointed except after consultation with the Chief Justice of India – vide Section 4.

Section 6 provides that on being appointed, the Chairperson/Members shall hold office for a term of five years or until he attains the age of 70 years, whichever is earlier. A Member is eligible for re-appointment for another term of five years.

The Chairman and Members are not accountable to any one with regard to the discharge of their functions.

The Chairperson or Member can be removed from his office by order of the President on the ground of proved misbehaviour or incapacity after the Supreme Court, on reference being made to it by the President, has, on inquiry held in accordance with the procedure prescribed in that regard by the Supreme Court, reported that the Chairman or Member ought on any such ground to be removed – vide Section 5(1).

The President can also remove from office the Chairman or Member if he:

(a) is adjudged an insolvent; or
(b) engages during his term of office in any paid employment outside the duties of his office; or
(c) is unfit to continue in office by reason of infirmity of mind or body; or
(d) is of unsound mind and stands so declared by a competent court; or
(e) is convicted and sentenced to imprisonment for an offence which in the opinion of the President involves moral turpitude, vide Section 5(2).

The National Human Rights Commission is an independent and autonomous body. The Members enjoy complete independence. This is ensured by the incorporation of appropriate provisions in the Act.

The power of selecting the Chairman or Members vests with the Committee, which consists of not only government functionaries but also leaders of the Opposition in both the Houses of Parliament. This is to ensure that the appointees enjoy not only the confidence of the government in power but also of the leaders of the Opposition. Three of the five full-fledged Members have to be persons who have held the highest positions in the Supreme Court and the High Courts. As judges of the superior courts in India enjoy great reputation as persons of highest integrity, character and fearless independence, their induction inspires confidence in the people.

There are two other matters of importance in this regard. On ceasing to hold office, the Chairman or Member is ineligible for further employment under the Government of India or under the Government of any State – vide Section 6(3).

The salary and allowances and other terms and conditions of service of the Chairman or Member cannot be varied to his disadvantage after his appointment – vide proviso to Section 8. These provisions are intended to ensure the independence of the Chairman and Members.

Unlike government servants, the Chairman or Members do not hold their office at the pleasure of the President of India. They can be removed only on grounds of proved misbehaviour or incapacity on an inquiry being held by a Judge of the Supreme Court of India. The removal is possible only on the basis of objective criteria prescribed by law and not on the basis of any subjective satisfaction. The stringent procedure for removal has been prescribed to ensure the independence of the National Human Rights Commission as a body as well as that of the individual Members.

11. The Commission enjoys financial autonomy and it can spend such sums as it thinks fit for the performance of its functions. [Vide Section 32(2)].

The five full-fledged Members of the National Human Rights Commission are full-time employees and are duly remunerated for the work. The three ex-officio Members receive emoluments from their respective organizations. The rules framed regulating the conditions of service of the Chairman and the four Members, provide that it is prescribed that they shall be paid the same emoluments as are payable to the Chief Justice of India and the Judges of the Supreme Court, respectively. The remuneration is paid from the funds given to the Commission by way of grant after due appropriation is made by Parliament by law in this behalf – vide Section 32.

The National Human Rights Commission prepares its budget and forwards it to the Central Government. The Central Government, after considering the same, formulates proposals for grants and places the same before Parliament. The Parliament passes the law providing for due appropriation of grants to the National Human Rights Commission – Vide Section 32(1). The Commission is entitled to spend the amount as it deems fit for performing its functions – vide Section 32(2).

12. The National Human Rights Commission is for the country as a whole. The Act, however, contains enabling provisions for constituting State Human Rights Commissions – vide Section 21. The Commission can, under Section 3(5), establish its offices in different parts of the country with the previous approval of the Central Government.

13. The Administration of the National Human Rights Commission is headed by the Secretary-General who holds the rank of Secretary to the Government of India. There is an Investigation Wing which is headed by an officer of the rank of Director General of Police. There is a Law Division which is headed by the Registrar of the rank of an Additional Secretary. In addition, there exists an Administrative Division, Research Division, Information & Public Relations Division, Accounts Section, Library Section and a Computer Section. Each Division or Section is manned by the requisite number of subordinate staff.

Section 11(1) requires the Central Government to make available to the Commission an officer of the rank of Secretary to the Government of India to be the Secretary-General of the Commission and such police investigative staff under an officer not below the rank of a Director General of Police and such other officers and staff as may be necessary for the efficient performance of the functions of the Commission. Section 11(2) provides that subject to such rules as may be made by the Central Government, the Commission may appoint such other administrative, technical and scientific staff as it may consider necessary. Under the rules framed by the Central Government under Section 40 of the Act in this regard, the Commission can appoint the other members of the administrative staff.

The salaries, allowances and conditions of service of the officers and staff appointed under sub-section (2), are prescribed by the rules. The payment of salary to all the members of the staff is made by the Commission out of the funds made available to it in accordance with the appropriation law made by Parliament.

The National Human Rights Commission can obtain its subordinate staff by direct recruitment or on deputation from Government. As far as the increase in the number of staff is concerned, it needs the concurrence of the Central Government.

C. Procedure

Section 12(a) of the Act has conferred on the Commission the power to inquire suo motu or on a petition presented to it by a victim or any person on his behalf, into the complaint of violation of human rights or abetment thereof, or negligence in the prevention of such violation, by a public servant. No form or fee is prescribed for the complaint. There is no specific bar against entertaining complaints before the other available remedies are exhausted. The complainant is not required to pay any compensation or costs. Legal aid is available to litigants under the Legal Services Act. This is normally given to indigent persons for conduct of litigation in the courts of law.

There is no requirement with regard to the use of any particular language for presenting complaints to the Commisssion. The complainant is free to use any language of his choice. If the Members are not familiar with the language of the complaint, the same would be translated at the cost of the Commission. The Commission normally records its findings in English.

For inquiring into the complaints, the Commission is conferred the powers of a civil court under Section 13 in respect of:

(a) summoning and enforcing the attendance of witnesses and examining them on oath;
(b) discovery and production of any document;
(c) receiving evidence on affidavits;
(d) requisitioning any public record or copy thereof from any court or office;
(e) issuing commissions for the examination of witnesses or documents;
(f) any other mater which may be prescribed.

The Commission has the power under Section 13(2) to require any person, subject to any claim of privilege, to furnish information on relevant matters. It also has power to seize documents – vide Section 13(3).

If, upon examination of the complaint, the Commission is of the opinion that there is a prima facie case of violation of human rights, it can call upon the concerned Government or authority to furnish the required information or report in regard to the complaint, within the specified time. If there is no response, the Commission is entitled to proceed to inquire into the complaint on its own – vide Section 17. If, on receipt of the information or report, the Commission is satisfied that no further inquiry is required or that the required action has been taken, it may not proceed with the complaint. If the Commission on consideration of all aspects, is of the opinion that further probe is necessary, it may initiate an inquiry – vide Section 17. The Commission can hold public hearings, including examination of witnesses. The parties are given full opportunity to adduce evidence and submit oral arguments. The parties may be permitted to be represented by lawyers.

If, after the inquiry, the Commission finds that there is violation of human rights or negligence in prevention of the same by a public servant, it can recommend to the concerned Government or authority, initiation of proceedings for prosecution or such other action as may be deemed fit – vide Section 18(1).

The Commission can also approach the Supreme Court or the High Court concerned if it considers it necessary to obtain the orders or directions of the Court – vide Section 18(2).

If at any stage of inquiry, the Commission considers it necessary to inquire into the conduct of any person, or is of the opinion that the reputation of any person is likely to be prejudiced or affected by the inquiry, a reasonable opportunity of being heard and of producing evidence must be given to such a person – vide Section 16.

Copies of the inquiry report and the recommendations have to be furnished to the complainant and the concerned Government or authority – vide Section 18(4) & (5).

D. Rulings

The National Human Rights Commission can give rulings with regard to matters in controversy. In doing so, it would follow the law laid down by the Supreme Court, which is binding on every one. The Commission is independent of the Parliament in this regard. The findings recorded and the orders made by the National Human Rights Commission are recommendatory in nature. On receipt of the recommendations of the Commission, the Government or the authority concerned should within a period of one month or such further time as may be allowed by the Court, forward its comments on the report, including the action taken or proposed to be taken thereon, to the Commission.

If the recommendation of the Commission is not accepted, it is open to the Commission to approach the Supreme Court or the High Court concerned and to request it to make the recommendation of the Commission a binding order of the Court. On the request being granted, the order of the Commission can be enforced as an order of the Court in accordance with law. It is the Commission that decides on the publication of its rulings. The summaries of important rulings/recommendations are published in its monthly Newsletter. Some of the important decisions are also extracted in the Annual Report of the Commission which is submitted to the Central Government under Section 20(1) of the Act.

The report received from the Commission must be placed by the Government before each House of Parliament along with a memorandum of action taken or proposed to be taken on the recommendations of the Commission and the reasons for non-acceptance of the recommendations, if any. Vide Section 20(2). This gives Parliament an opportunity to debate on all the matters. The Human Rights Commission can award interim relief, including interim compensation, to the complainant to be paid by the Government – vide Section 18(3). Every decision of the Commission rendered on the complaint is required to be published along with the comments of the concerned Government or authority and the action taken or proposed to be taken. Vide Section 18(6). Such statutory publication is done on the notice-board of the Commission.

There is no appeal against the decision of the National Human Rights Commission. The High Court and the Supreme Court have a prerogative right under the Constitution to issue writs or orders or directions against the State or any authority, including the Commission. The Commission registered 20,589 complaints during the year 1996–97. Out of these, 7,388 were dismissed in limine. 3,718 cases were disposed of with directions or recommendations. The exact figures for the year 1997–98 are awaited.

E. Review of Experience of the Human Rights Commission

One of the major problems the Commission is facing is the enormous increase in the receipt of complaints. The Commission has framed procedural regulations which, inter alia, provide that complaints can be entertained and disposed of by a single Member. The inflow of complaints being quite high, the Commission is exploring the possible remedies for the purpose of disposing of the complaints within a reasonable time. One possible solution is to create a Judicial Wing at an intermediary level, comprising officers of the rank of Senior District Judges and to entrust to them the task of dealing with the complaints, reserving only matters of importance or complexity to be dealt with by the Members of the Commission.

LEGISLATION

The Protection of Human Rights Act, 1993

No. 10 of 1994 (8 January 1994)

An Act to provide for the constitution of a National Human Rights Commission. State Human Rights Commission in States and Human Rights Courts for better protection of Human Rights and for matters connected therewith or incidental thereto.

Be it enacted by the parliament in the forty-fourth year of the Republic of India as follows

Chapter I
Preliminary

1. Short title, extent and commencement
   (1) This Act may be called the Protection of Human Rights Act, 1993.
   (2) It extends to the whole of India.
   Provided that it shall apply to the State of Jammu and Kashmir only in so far as it pertains to the matters relatable to any of the entries enumerated in List I or List III in the Seventh Schedule to the Constitution as applicable to that State.
   (3) It shall be deemed to have come into force on the 28th day of September, 1993.
2. Definitions
   (1) In this Act, unless the context otherwise requires:
      (a) "armed forces" means the naval, military and air forces and includes any other armed forces of the Union;
      (b) "Chairperson" means the Chairperson of the Commission or of the State Commission, as the case may be;
      (c) "Commission" means the National Human Rights Commission con ed under section 3;
      (d) "human rights" means the rights relating to life, liberty, equality and dignity of the individual guaranteed by the Constitution or embodied in the International Covenants and enforceable by courts in India;

(e) "Human Rights Court" means the Human Rights Court specified under section 30;
(f) "International Covenants" means the International Covenant on Civil and Political Rights and the International Covenant on Economic, Social and Cultural Rights adopted by the General Assembly of the United Nations on the 16th December, 1966;
(g) "Member" means a Member of the Commission or of the State Commission as the case may be, and includes the Chairperson;
(h) "National Commission for Minorities" means the National Commission for Minorities constituted under section 3 of the National Commission for Minorities Act, 1992;
(i) "National Commission for the Scheduled Castes and Scheduled Tribes" means the National Commission for the Scheduled Castes and Scheduled Tribes referred to in article 338 of the Constitution;
(j) "National Commission for Women" means the National Commission for Women constituted under section 3 of the National Commission for Women Act, 1990;
(k) "Notification" means a notification published in the official Gazette;
(l) "Prescribed" means prescribed by rules made under this Act;
(m) "Public servant" shall have the meaning assigned to it in section 21 of the Indian Penal Code;
(n) "State Commission" means a State Human Rights Commission constituted under section 21.

(2) Any reference in this Act to a law, which is not in force in the State of Jammu and Kashmir, shall, in relation to that State, be construed as a reference to a corresponding law, if any, in force in that State.

Chapter II
The National Human Rights Commission

3. Constitution of a National Human Rights Commission
(1) The Central Government shall constitute a body to be known as the National Human Rights Commission to exercise the powers conferred upon, and to perform the functions assigned to it, under this Act.
(2) The Commission shall consist of
(a) A Chairperson who has been a Chief Justice of the Supreme Court;
(b) One Member who is or has been, a Judge of the Supreme Court;
(c) One Member who is, or has been, the Chief Justice of a High Court;
(d) Two Members to be appointed from amongst persons having knowledge of, or practical experience in, matters relating to human rights.
(3) The Chairpersons of the National Commission for Minorities, the National Commission for the Scheduled Castes and Scheduled Tribes and the National Commission for Women shall be deemed to be Members of the Commission for the discharge of functions specified in clauses (b) to (j) of section 12.
(4) There shall be a Secretary-General who shall be the Chief Executive Officer of the Commission and shall exercise such powers and discharge such functions of the Commission as it may delegate to him.
(5) The headquarters of the Commission shall be at Delhi and the Commission may, with the previous approval of the Central Government, establish offices at other places in India.

4. Appointment of Chairperson and other Members
(1) The Chairperson and other Members shall be appointed by the President by warrant under his hand and seal. Provided that every appointment under this sub-section shall be made after obtaining the recommendations of a Committee consisting of:

(a) The Prime Minister – Chairperson
(b) Speaker of the House of the People – Member
(c) Minister in-charge of the Ministry of Home Affairs in the Government of India – Member
(d) Leader of the Opposition in the House of the People – Member
(e) Leader of the Opposition in the Council of States – Member
(f) Deputy Chairman of the Council of States – Member Provided further that no sitting Judge of the Supreme Court or sitting Chief Justice of a High Court shall be appointed except after consultation with the Chief Justice of India.

(2) No appointment of a Chairperson or a Member shall be invalid merely by reason of any vacancy in the Committee.

5. Removal of a Member of the Commission

(1) Subject to the provisions of sub-section (2), the Chairperson or any other Member of the Commission shall only be removed from his office by order of the President on the ground of proved misbehaviour or incapacity after the Supreme Court, on reference being made to it by the President, has, on inquiry held in accordance with the procedure prescribed in that behalf by the Supreme Court, reported that the Chairperson or such other Member, as the case may be, ought on any such ground to be removed.

(2) Notwithstanding anything in sub-section (1), the President may by order remove from office the Chairperson or any other Member if the Chairperson or such other Member, as the case may be:
(a) is adjudged an insolvent; or
(b) engages during his term of office in any paid employment out side the duties of his office: or (c)is unfit to continue in office by reason of infirmity of mind or body; or
(d) is of unsound mind and stands so declared by a competent court; or
(e) is convicted and sentenced to imprisonment for an offence which in the opinion of the President involves moral turpitude.

6. Term of office of Members

(1) A person appointed as Chairperson shall hold office for a term of five years from the date on which he enters upon his office or until he attains the age of seventy years, whichever is earlier.

(2) A person appointed as a Member shall hold office for a term of five years from the date on which he enters upon his office and shall be eligible for re-appointment for another term of five years. Provided that no Member shall hold office after he has attained the age of seventy years.

(3) On ceasing to hold office, a Chairperson or a Member shall be ineligible for further employment under the Government of India or under the Government of any State.

7. Member to act as Chairperson or to discharge his functions in certain circumstances

(1) In the event of the occurrence of any vacancy in the office of the Chairperson by reason of his death, resignation or otherwise, the President may, by notification, authorize one of the Members to act as the Chairperson until the appointment of a new Chairperson to fill such vacancy.

(2) When the Chairperson is unable to discharge his functions owing to absence on leave or otherwise, such one of the Members as the President may, by notification, authorize in this behalf, shall discharge the functions of the Chairperson until the date on which the Chairperson resumes his duties.

8. Terms and conditions of service of Members

The salaries and allowances payable to, and other terms and conditions of service of, the Members shall be such as may be prescribed. Provided that neither the salary and allowances nor the other terms and conditions of service of a Member shall be varied to his disadvantage after his appointment.

9. Vacancies, etc., not to invalidate the proceedings of the Commission.
   No act or proceedings of the Commission shall be questioned or shall be invalidated merely on the ground of existence of any vacancy or defect in the constitution of the Commission.
10. Procedure to be regulated by the Commission
    (1) The Commission shall meet at such time and place as the Chair son may think fit.
    (2) The Commission shall regulate its own procedure.
    (3) All orders and decisions of the Commission shall be audited by the Secretary General or any other officer of the Commission duly authorized by the Chairperson in this behalf.
11. Officers and other staff of the Commission
    (1) The Central Government shall make available to the Commission:
        (a) an officer of the rank of the Secretary to the Government of India who shall be the Secretary-General of the Commission; and
        (b) such police and investigative staff under an officer not below the rank of a Director General of Police and such other officers and staff as may be necessary for the efficient performance of the functions of the Commission.
    (2) Subject to such rules as may be made by the Central Government in this behalf the Commission may appoint such other administrative, technical and scientifi staff as it may consider necessary.
    (3) The salaries, allowances and conditions of service of the officers and other staff appointed under sub-section (2) shall be such as may be prescribed.

Chapter III

Functions and Powers of the Commission

12. Functions of the Commission
    The Commission shall perform all or any of the following functions, namely:
    (a) inquire, suo motu or on a petition presented to it by a victim or any person on his behalf, into complaint of:
        (i) violation of human rights or abetment thereof or
        (ii) negligence in the prevention of such violation, by a public servant;
    (b) intervene in any proceeding involving any allegation of violation of human right pending before a court with the approval of such court;
    (c) visit, under intimation to the State Government, any jail or any other institution under the control of the State Government, where persons are detained or lodged for purposes of treatment, reformation or protection to study the living condition of the inmates and make recommendations thereon;
    (d) review the safeguards provided by or under the Constitution or any law for the time being in force for the protection of human rights and recommend measure for their effective implementation;
    (e) review the factors, including acts of terrorism that inhibit the enjoyment of human rights and recommend appropriate remedial measures;
    (f) study treaties and other international instruments on human rights and make recommendations for their effective implementation;
    (g) undertake and promote research in the field of human rights;
    (h) spread human rights literacy among various sections of society and promote awareness of the safeguards available for the protection of these rights through publications, the media, seminars and other available means;
    (i) encourage the efforts of non-governmental organizations and institutions working in the field of human rights;
    (j) such other functions as it may consider necessary for the protection of human rights.
13. Powers relating to inquiries

(1) The Commission shall, while inquiring into complaints under this Act, have all the powers of a civil court trying a suit under the Code of Civil Procedure, 1908, and in particular in respect of the following matters, namely:
   (a) summoning and enforcing the attendance of witnesses and examining them on oath;
   (b) discovery and production of any document;
   (c) receiving evidence on affidavits;
   (d) requisitioning any public record or copy thereof from any court or office;
   (e) issuing commissions for the examination of witnesses or documents;
   (f) any other matter which may be prescribed.

(2) The Commission shall have power to require any person, subject to any privilege which may be claimed by that person under any law for the time being in force, to furnish information on such points or matters as, in the opinion of the Commission, may be useful for, or relevant to, the subject matter of the inquiry and any person so required shall be deemed to be legally bound to furnish such information within the meaning of section 176 and section 177 of the Indian Penal Code.

(3) The Commission or any other officer, not below the rank of a Gazetted Officer, specially authorized in this behalf by the Commission may enter any building or place where the Commission has reason to believe that any document relating to the subject matter of the inquiry may be found, and may seize any such document or take extracts or copies therefrom subject to the provisions of section 100 of the Code of Criminal Procedure, 1973, in so far as it may be applicable.

(4) The Commission shall be deemed to be a civil court and when any offence as is described in section 175, section 178, section 179, section 180 or section 228 of the Indian Penal Code is committed in the view or presence of the Commission, the Commission may, after recording the facts constituting the offence and the statement of the accused as provided for in the Code of Criminal Procedure, 1973, forward the case to a Magistrate having jurisdiction to try the same and the Magistrate to whom any such case is forwarded shall proceed to hear the complaint against the accused as if the case has been forwarded to him under section 346 of the Code of Criminal Procedure, 1973.

(5) Every proceeding before the Commission shall be deemed to be a judicial proceeding within the meaning of sections 193 and 228, and for the purposes of section 196, of the Indian Penal Code, and the Commission shall be deemed to be a civil court for all the purposes of section 195 and Chapter XXVI of the Code of Criminal Procedure, 1973.

4. Investigation

(1) The Commission may, for the purpose of conducting any investigation pertaining to the inquiry, utilize the services of any officer or investigation agency of the Central Government or any State Government with the concurrence of the Central Government or the State Government, as the case may be.

(2) For the purpose of investigating into any matter pertaining to the inquiry, any officer or agency whose services are utilized under sub-section (1) may, subject to the direction and control of the Commission:
   (a) summon and enforce the attendance of any person and examine him;
   (b) require the discovery and production of any document; and
   (c) requisition any public record or copy thereof from any office.

(3) The provisions of section 15 shall apply in relation to any statement made by a person before any officer or agency whose services are utilized under sub-section (1) as they apply in relation to any statement made by a person in the course of giving evidence before the Commission.

(4) The officer or agency whose services are utilized under sub-section (1) shall

investigate into any matter pertaining to the inquiry and submit a report thereo to the Commission within such period as may be specified by the Commissio in this behalf.

(5) The Commission shall satisfy itself about the correctness of the facts stated an the conclusion, if any, arrived at in the report submitted to it under sub-sectio (4) and for this purpose the Commission may make such inquiry (including th examination of the person or persons who conducted or assisted in the investiga tion) as it thinks fit.

15. Statement made by persons to the Commission
No statement made by a person in the course of giving evidence before th Commission shall subject him to, or be used against him in, any civil or crimina proceeding except a prosecution for giving false evidence by such statement: Provide that the statement:
(a) is made in reply to the question which he is required by the Commission t answer; or
(b) is relevant to the subject matter of the inquiry.

16. Persons likely to be prejudicially affected to be heard
If, at any stage of the inquiry, the Commission:
(a) considers it necessary to inquire into the conduct of any person; or
(b) is of the opinion that the reputation of any person is likely to be prejudiciall affected by the inquiry; it shall give to that person a reasonable opportunity c being heard in the inquiry and to produce evidence in his defence: Provided tha nothing in this section shall apply where the credit of a witness is being impeachec

Chapter IV
Procedure

17. Inquiry into complaints The Commission while inquiring into the complaints c violations of human rights may:
(i) call for information or report from the Central Government or any Stat Government or any other authority or organization subordinate thereto withi such time as may be specified by it; Provided that:
(a) if the information or report is not received within the time stipulated by th Commission, it may proceed to inquire re into the complaint on its own;
(b) if, on receipt of information or report, the Commission is satisfied either tha no further inquiry is required or that the required action has been initiate or taken by the concerned Government or authority, it may not procee with the complaint and inform the complainant accordingly;
(ii) without prejudice to anything contained in clause (i), if it considers necessary having regard to the nature of the complaint, initiate an inquiry.

18. Steps after inquiry
The Commission may take any of the following steps upon the completion of a inquiry held under this Act namely:
(1) where the inquiry discloses, the commission of violation of human rights o negligence in the prevention of violation of human rights by a public servant, i may recommend to the concerned Government or authority the initiation c proceedings for prosecution or such other action as the Commission may deen fit against the concerned person or persons;
(2) approach the Supreme Court or the High Court concerned for such directions orders or writs as that Court may deem necessary;
(3) recommend to the concerned Government or authority for the grant of suc immediate interim relief to the victim or the members of his family as th Commission may consider necessary;
(4) subject to the provisions of clause (5), provide a copy of the inquiry report t the petitioner or his representative;

(5) the Commission shall send a copy of its inquiry report together with its recommendations to the concerned Government or authority and the concerned Government or authority shall, within a period of one month, or such further time as the Commission may allow, forward its comments on the report, including the action taken or proposed to be taken thereon, to the Commission;
(6) the Commission shall publish its inquiry report together with the comments of the concerned Government or authority, if any, and the action taken or proposed to be taken by the concerned Government or authority on the recommendations of the Commission.

9. Procedure with respect to armed forces
(1) Notwithstanding anything contained in this Act, while dealing with complaints of violation of human rights by members of the armed forces, the Commission shall adopt the following procedure, namely:
(a) it may, either on its own motion or on receipt of a petition, seek a report from the Central Government;
(b) after the receipt of the report, it may, either not proceed with the complaint or, as the case may be, make its recommendations to that Government.
(2) The Central Government shall inform the Commission of the action taken on the recommendations within three months or such further time as the Commission may allow.
(3) The Commission shall publish its report together with its recommendations made to the Central Government and the action taken by that Government on such recommendations.
(4) The Commission shall provide a copy of the report published under sub-section (3) to the petitioner or his representative.

0. Annual and special reports of the Commission
(1) The Commission shall submit an annual report to the Central Government and to the State Government concerned and may at any time submit special reports on any matter which, in its opinion, is of such urgency or importance that it should not be deferred till submission of the annual report.
(2) The Central Government and the State Government, as the case may be, shall cause the annual and special reports of the Commission to be laid before each House of Parliament or the State Legislature respectively, as the case may be, along with a memorandum of action taken or proposed to be taken on the recommendations of the Commission and the reasons for non-acceptance of the recommendations, if any.

hapter V
tate Human Rights Commissions

1. Constitution of State Human Rights Commissions
(1) A State Government may constitute a body to be known as the .... (name of the State) Human Rights Commission to exercise the powers conferred upon, and to perform the functions assigned to, a State Commission under this chapter.
(2) The State Commission shall consist of:
(a) a Chairperson who has been a Chief Justice of a High Court;
(b) one Member who is, or has been, a Judge of a High Court;
(c) one Member who is, or has been, a district judge in that State;
(d) two Members to be appointed from amongst persons having knowledge of, or practical experience in, matters relating to human rights.
(3) There shall be a Secretary who shall be the Chief Executive Of er of the State Commission and shall exercise such powers and discharge such functions of the State Commission as it may delegate to him.
(4) The headquarters of the State Commission shall be at such place as the State Government may, by notification, specify.

(5) A State Commission may inquire into violation of human rights only in respe of matters relatable to any of the entries enumerated in List II and List III i the Seventh Schedule to the Constitution: Provided that if any such matter already being inquired into by the Commission or any other Commission du constituted under any law for the time being in force, the State Commission sha not inquire into the said matter: Provided further that in relation to the Jamm and Kashmir Human Rights Commission, this sub-section shall have effect as for the words and figures "List ll and List III in the Seventh Schedule to th Constitution", the words and figures "List III in the Seventh Schedule to th Constitution as applicable to the State of Jammu and Kashmir and in respect matters in relation to which the Legislature of that State has power to mak laws" had been substituted.

22. Appointment of Chairperson and other Members of State Commission

(1) The Chairperson and other Members shall be appointed by the Governor b warrant under his hand and seal: Provided that every appointment under th sub-section shall be made after obtaining the recommendation of a Committe consisting of:

(a) the Chief Minister – Chairperson

(b) Speaker of the Legislative – Member Assembly

(c) Minister in-charge of the Department – Member of Home, in that State

(d) Leader of the Opposition in the – Member Legislative Assembly Provide further that where there is a Legislative Council in a State, the Chairman c that Council and the Leader of the Opposition in that Council shall also b members of the Committee. Provided also that no sitting Judge of a Hig Court or a sitting District Judge shall be appointed except after consultatio with the Chief Justice of the High Court of the concerned State.

(2) No appointment of a Chairperson or a Member of the State Commission sha be invalid merely by reason of any vacancy in the Committee.

23. Removal of a Member of the State Commission

(1) Subject to the provisions of sub-section (2), the Chairperson or any other membe of the State Commission shall only be removed from his office by order of th President on the ground of proved misbehaviour or incapacity after the Suprem Court, on a reference being made to it by the President, has, on inquiry held i accordance with the procedure prescribed in that behalf by the Supreme Cour reported that the Chairperson or such other Member, as the case may be, ough on any such ground to be removed.

(2) Notwithstanding anything in sub-section (1), the President may by order remov from office the Chairperson or any other Member if the Chairperson or suc other Member, as the case may be:

(a) is adjudged an insolvent; or

(b) engages during his term of office in any paid employment outside the dutie of his office; or

(c) is unfit to continue in office by reason of infirmity of mind or body;

(d) is of unsound mind and stands so declared by a competent court; or

(e) is convicted and sentenced to imprisonment for an offence which in th opinion of the President involves moral turpitude.

24. Term of office of Members of the State Commission

(1) A person appointed as Chairperson shall hold office for a term of five years fron the date on which he enters upon his office or until he attains the age of sevent years, whichever is earlier.

(2) A person appointed as a Member shall hold office for a term of five years fron the date on which he enters upon his office and shall be eligible for re-appointmen for another term of five years; Provided that no Member shall hold office afte he has attained the age of seventy years.

(3) On ceasing to hold office, a Chairperson or a Member shall be ineligible for further employment under the Government of a State or under the Government of India.

25. Member to act as Chairperson or to discharge his functions in certain circumstances

(1) In the event of the occurrence of any vacancy in the office of the Chairperson by reason of his death, resignation or otherwise, the Governor may, by notification, authorize one of the Members to act as the Chairperson until the appointment of a new Chairperson to fill such vacancy.

(2) When the Chairperson is unable to discharge his functions owing to absence on leave or otherwise, such one of the Members as the Governor may, by notification, authorize in this behalf, shall discharge the functions of the Chairperson until the date on which the Chairperson resumes his duties.

26. Terms and conditions of service of Members of the State Commission

The salaries and allowances payable to, and other terms and conditions of service of, the Members shall be such as may be prescribed by the State Government. Provided that neither the salary and allowances nor the other terms and conditions of service of a Member shall be varied to his disadvantage after his appointment.

27. Officers and other staff of the State Commission

(1) The State Government shall make available to the Commission

(a) an officer not below the rank of a Secretary to the State Government who shall be the Secretary of the State Commission; and

(b) such police and investigative staff under an officer not below the rank of an Inspector General of Police and such other officers and staff as may be necessary for the efficient performance of the functions of the State Commission.

(2) Subject to such rules as may be made by the State Government in this behalf, the State Commission may appoint such other administrative, technical and scientific staff as it may consider necessary.

(3) The salaries, allowances and conditions of service of the officers and other staff appointed under sub-section (2) shall be such as may be prescribed by the State Government.

28. Annual and special reports of State Commission

(1) The State Commission shall submit an annual report to the State Government and may at any time submit special reports on any matter which, in its opinion, is of such urgency or importance that it should not be deferred till submission of the annual report.

(2) The State Government shall cause the annual and special reports of the State Commission to be laid before each House of State Legislature where it consists of two Houses, or where such Legislature consists of one House, before that House along with a memorandum of action taken or proposed to be taken on the recommendations of the State Commission and the reasons for non-acceptance of the recommendations, if any.

29. Application of certain provisions relating to National Human Rights Commission to State Commissions The provisions of sections 9, 10, 12, 13, 14, 15, 16, 17 and 18 shall apply to a State Commission and shall have effect, subject to the following modifications, namely:

(a) references to "Commission" shall be construed as references to "State Commission";

(b) in section 10, in sub-section (3), for the word "Secretary General", the word "Secretary" shall be substituted;

(c) in section 12, clause (f) shall be omitted;

(d) in section 17, in clause (i), the words "Central Government or any" shall be omitted.

Chapter VI
Human Rights Courts

30. For the purpose of providing speedy trial of offences arising out of violation of huma rights, the State Government may, with the concurrence of the Chief Justice of th High Court, by notification, specify for each district a Court of Session to be Human Rights Court to try the said offences. Provided that nothing in this sectio shall apply if:
    (a) a Court of Session is already specified as a special court; or
    (b) a special court is already constituted, for such offences under any other law fc the time being in force.
31. Special Public Prosecutor
    For every Human Rights Court, the State Government shall, by notification, specif a Public Prosecutor or appoint an advocate who has been in practice as an advocat for not less than seven years, as a Special Public Prosecutor for the purpose c conducting cases in that Court.

Chapter VII
Finance, Accounts and Audit

32. Grants by the Central Government
    (1) The Central Government shall after due appropriation made by Parliament b law in this behalf, pay to the Commission by way of grants such sums of mone as the Central Government may think fit for being utilized for the purposes c this Act.
    (2) The Commission may spend such sums as it thinks fit for performing the function under this Act, and such sums shall be treated as expenditure payable out of th grants referred to in sub-section (1).
33. Grants by the State Government
    (1) The State Government shall, after due appropriation made by Legislature b law in this behalf, pay to the State Commission by way of grants such sums c money as the State Government may think fit for being utilized for the purpose of this Act.
    (2) The State Commission may spend such sums as it thinks fit for performing th functions under Chapter V, and such sums shall be treated as expenditure payabl out of the grants referred to in sub-section (1).
34. Accounts and Audit
    (1) The Commission shall maintain proper accounts and other relevant records an prepare an annual statement of accounts in such form as may be prescribed b the Central Government in consultation with the Comptroller and Auditor General of India.
    (2) The Accounts of the Commission shall be audited by the Comptroller an Auditor-General at such intervals as may be specified by him and any expenditur incurred in connection with such audit shall be payable by the Commission t the Comptroller and Auditor-General.
    (3) The Comptroller and Auditor-General or any person ap ed by him in connectio with the audit of the accounts of the Commission under this Act shall have th same rights and privileges and the authority in connection with such audit a the Comptroller and Auditor-General generally has in connection with the audi of Government ac counts and, in particular, shall have the right to demand th production of books, accounts, connected vouchers and other documents an papers and to inspect any of the offices of the Commission.
    (4) The accounts of the Commission as certified by the Comptroller and Auditor General or any other person appointed by him in this behalf, together with th audit report thereon shall be forwarded only to the Central Government by th

Commission and the Central Government shall cause the audit report to be laid as soon as may be after it is received before each House of Parliament.

35. Accounts and Audit of State Commission
   (1) The State Commission shall maintain proper accounts and other relevant records and prepare an annual statement of accounts in such form as may be prescribed by the State Government in consultation with the Comptroller and Auditor-General of India.
   (2) The accounts of the State Commission shall be audited by the Comptroller and Auditor-General at such intervals as may be specified by him and any expenditure incurred in connection with such audit shall be payable by the State Commission to the Comptroller and Auditor-General.
   (3) The Comptroller and Auditor-General or any person ap ed by him in connection with the audit of the accounts of the State Commission under this Act shall have the same rights and privileges and the authority in connection with such audit as the Comptroller and Auditor-General generally has in connection with the audit of Government accounts and, in particular, shall have the right to demand the production of books, accounts, connected vouchers and other documents and papers and to inspect any of the offices of the State Commission
   (4) The accounts of the State Commission, as certified by the Comptroller and Auditor-General or any other person appointed by him in this behalf, together with the audit report thereon, shall be forwarded annually to the State Government by the State Commission and the State Government shall cause the audit report to be laid, as soon as may be after it is received, before the State Legislature.

Chapter VIII
Miscellaneous

36. Matters not subject to jurisdiction of the Commission
   (1) The Commission shall not inquire into any matter which is pending before a State Commission or any other Commission duly constituted under any law for the time being in force.
   (2) The Commission or the State Commission shall not inquire into any matter after the expiry of one year from the date on which the act constituting violation of human rights is alleged to have been committed.

37. Constitution of special investigation teams
Notwithstanding anything contained in any other law for the time being in force, where the Government considers it necessary so to do, it may constitute one or more special investigation teams, consisting of such police officers as it thinks necessary for purposes of investigation and prosecution of offences arising out of violations of human rights.

38. Protection of action taken in good faith
No suit or other legal proceeding shall lie against the Central Government, State Government, Commission, the State Commission or any Member thereof or any person acting under the direction either of the Central Government, State Government, Commission or the State Commission in respect of anything which is in good faith done or intended to be done in pursuance of this Act or of any rules or any order made thereunder or in respect of the publication by or under the authority of the Central Government, State Government, Commission or the State Commission of any report paper or proceedings.

39. Members and officers to be public servants
Every Member of the Commission, State Commission and every officer appointed or authorized by the Commission or the State Commission to exercise functions under this Act shall be deemed to be a public servant within the meaning of section 21 of the Indian Penal Code.

40. Power of Central Government to make rules
   (1) The Central Government may, by notification, make rules to carry out th provisions of this Act.
   (2) In particular and without prejudice to the generality of the foregoing power, such rules may provide for all or any of the following matters namely:
      (a) the salaries and allowances and other terms and conditions of serv ice of th Members under section 8;
      (b) the conditions subject to which other administrative, technical and scientifi staff may be appointed by the Commission and the salaries and allowance of officers and other staff under sub-section (3) of section 11;
      (c) any other power of a civil court required to be prescribed under clause (f of sub-section (1) of section 13;
      (d) the form in which the annual statement of accounts is to be pre pared by th Commission under sub-section (1) of section 34; and
      (e) any other matter which has to be, or may be, prescribed.
   (3) Every rule made under this Act shall be laid, as soon as may be after it is made before each House of Parliament, while it is in session, for a total period of thirty days which may be comprised in one session or in two or more successive sessions, and if, before the expiry of the session immediately following the session or the successive sessions aforesaid, both Houses agree in making any modification in the rule or both Houses agree that the rule should not be made, the rule shall thereafter have effect only in such modified form or be of no effect, as the case may be; so however, that any such modification or annulment shall be without prejudice to the validity of anything previously done under that rule.
41. Power of State Government to make rules
   (1) The State Government may, by notification, make rules to carry out the provis ions of this Act.
   (2) In particular and without prejudice to the generality of the foregoing power, such rules may provide for all or any of the following matters, namely:
      (a) the salaries and allowances and other terms and conditions of serv ice of the members under section 26;
      (b) the conditions subject to which other administrative, technical and scientific staff may be appointed by the State Commission and the salaries and allow ances of officers and other staff under sub-section (3) of section 27;
      (c) the form in which the annual statement of accounts is to be prepared under sub-section (1) of section 35.
   (3) Every rule made by the State Government under this section shall be laid, as soon as may be after it is made, before each House of the State Legislature where it consists of two Houses, or where such Legislature consists of one House, before that House.
42. Power to remove difficulties
   (1) If any difficulty arises in giving effect to the provisions of this Act, the Central Government, may by order published in the Official Gazette, make such provis ions, not inconsistent with the provisions of this Act as appear to it to be necessary or expedient for removing the difficulty. Provided that no such order shall be made after the ex ry of the period of two years from the date of commencement of this Act.
   (2) Every order made under this section shall, as soon as may be after it is made be laid before each house of Parliament.
43. Repeal and Savings
   (1) The Protection of Human Rights Ordinance, 1993 is hereby repealed.
   (2) Notwithstanding such repeal, anything done or any action taken under the said Ordinance, shall be deemed to have been done or taken under the corresponding provisions of this Act.

Ombudsman Institutions

The Ombudsman Institution in Argentina

Jorge Louis Maiorano*

A. Legal or Constitutional Basis

. The provisions dealing with the Defensor del Pueblo de la Nación Argentina nd his organizational structure are found in the National Constitution (Sections 6 and 43) and in Act N° 24,284, modified text by Act N° 24,379, copies of which are attached hereto.

In this respect, Section 86 of the National Constitution provides:

> The Defensor del Pueblo is an independent organ, created within the jurisdiction of the National Congress. The Defensor del Pueblo shall function with full autonomy, receiving o instruction from any authority whatsoever. The aims of the office are the defence and rotection of human rights and any other rights, guarantees and interests protected in his Constitution and the laws, against the acts, actions and omissions of the administration; and the control of public administrative functions ..."

Moreover, Section 1 of Act N° 24,284 provides that the Institution's aim is to lefend the rights and interests of individuals and of the community against acts, acts and omissions of the National Public Administration. Section 14 of the forementioned Act states:

> The *Defensor del Pueblo* shall, either at his own initiative or after the presentation of a omplaint by the aggrieved party, institute an investigation in order to clarify those acts, ctions or omissions of the National Public Administration or its agents which may be eemed illegitimate, defective, irregular, abusive, arbitrary, discriminatory, negligent, seriusly inconvenient or untimely, including those which may affect diffuse or collective ights ..."

Undoubtedly, the fact that the Defensor del Pueblo de la Nación Argentina is n Institution with constitutional rank is a great advantage because as it is ituated on the highest legal rank it is a fundamental state Institution and also . real protective shield because it prevents that by means of a simple Act its ndependence or faculties may be limited.

As regards the advantage or disadvantage of establishing the details referring o the Defensor del Pueblo de la Nación in the National Constitution or in an Act, it is important to mention that the Supreme Act of a State can only set orth programmatic rules and fundamental characteristics of each of the State nstitutions. It cannot stipulate the details regarding the organization and

---

Defensor del Pueblo de la Nación, Argentina.

. Hossain et al. (eds), Human Rights Commissions and Ombudsman Offices, 233–246.

internal functioning of each of the Institutions. These items must be included in those legal texts approved to that effect.

2. Section 2 of Act 24,284 states that the Defensor del Pueblo de la Nación Argentina shall be appointed by the National Congress according to th following procedure: both Houses of Congress shall appoint a permanent bicam eral Commission, which shall consist of seven (7) senators and seven (7) represen tatives. The composition of this committee shall be apportioned among it members; Within thirty (30) days as from the enactment of this Act, th Commission, presided over by the President of the Senate, shall propose one t three candidates for the office of the Defensor del Pueblo before both House of Congress.

Within thirty (30) days after the submission of the proposal above mentioned both Houses of Congress shall choose one of the candidates by a vote of tw thirds of the members present. Should no candidate obtain the majority require in the first ballot, another vote shall be cast until the required majority i obtained. Should three candidates be nominated and should none obtain th majority required under subsection (d), a new ballot shall be conducted amon the two candidates who have obtained the greatest number of votes.

The Ombudsman Institution developed and increased taking into account th parliamentary concept and, occasionally, the executive concept. As the Institutio is created to control the Public Administration, it may be considered that a Ombudsman of executive origin, due to the fact that he is directly appointed b the head of the Executive, may have less independence than an Ombudsman o parliamentary origin because he is appointed by a joint body which he doe not control.

The Defensor del Pueblo de la Nación must submit a report on his work t the Congress every year before May 31st, without prejudice to the forwardin of a special report in case of urgency or serious acts. Publicity is an essentia requirement of every act carried out by State organs. Thus, said acts must b communicated to the public opinion so that the citizens know about them. Th fact of submitting a report to the National Congress composed of the people' representatives is much more than complying with a duty and exercising a right it is an advantage to undergo the society's careful and transparent examinatio to deepen the confidence of those whom he is appointed to serve.

B. Independence and Impartiality

3. Pursuant to Section 86 of the National Constitution the Defensor del Pueblo' independence is guaranteed because he is an independent institution, create within the jurisdiction of the National Congress. He shall function with ful autonomy, receiving no instructions from any authority whatsoever.

Likewise, Section 36 of Act 24,284 stipulates that the Defensor del Pueblo d la Nación appoints his personnel and has his own administrative and financia service. Additionally, he must have an absolute personal conviction to fulfil hi high function with full independence.

4. The Defensor del Pueblo's independence is guaranteed, in practice, by th due fulfilment of the legal provisions in force which determine his effectiv

unctional independence and, as aforementioned, by the personal conviction of he person who exercises the persuasion method.

The National Constitution of Argentina allocates the different public functions o the different state bodies which are independent of each other. The scope of he different fields in which they have competence is indicated by the legal rovision which determines the powers which correspond to each of them in a articular and exclusive way.

The National Constitution and the Act N° 24, 284 clearly delimit the Defensor lel Pueblo de la Nación's competence in respect to other control organs of Government; such as courts. In this regard, it should be taken into account that ection 16 of the aforementioned Act provides that the Judiciary is excluded rom the Defensor del Pueblo de la Nación's competence, in relation to the xercise of the jurisdictional function, but not with respect to the exercise of the dministrative functions of the Judiciary.

In Argentina there is no Commission of Human Rights because the protection of human rights is within the competence of the Defensor del Pueblo de la Nación as set forth in Section 86 of the National Constitution.

C. Complaints Regarding Acts of Government

5. The State's power as the expression of the public's will is exercised by the nen that act in it. The State has no will of its own, independent of the will of he people (public agents) that carry out acts which are assigned to the state as legal person. The acts, facts or omissions of these public agents are within the Defensor del Pueblo's competence.

The Legislature and Judiciary are excluded from his competence, with regard only to legislative and jurisdictional acts, respectively.

6. As regards the restrictions, we can conclude that there are some restrictions as regards the Ombudsman's performance. Traditionally, the Ombudsman or Defensor del Pueblo of parliamentary origin does not control the organ which appoints him. He cannot control the jurisdictional activity of the judicial power lue to the principle of division of powers.

Any natural or legal person can lodge a complaint without the help of a awyer. Likewise provincial or national legislators may accept the complaints rom the interested party and send them immediately to the Defensor del Pueblo le la Nación.

As the Defensor is an independent organ who exercises his functions without eceiving orders from any authority, he decides to accept the complaints or not pursuant to the competence established in the National Constitution and Act N° 24, 284.

D. Investigations, Report and recommendation

7. A governmental or political function exists in the execution of the direct constitutional authority due to opportunity, merit or convenience, which is different from the administrative function. If the government acts are not included n the latter function, they are out of the Defensor del Pueblo's competence.

The legal framework which establishes the guidelines which administrative organization must comply with in the exercise of state duties, constitutes the legal basis for effective and good government.

The complaint must be submitted in writing, signed by the interested party with his/her name, surname and address within the calendar year in which the act, fact or omission which is the subject matter of the complaint, takes place and must be within the Defensor del Pueblo de la Nación's competence.

As set forth in Section 24 of Act 24, 284 the National Public Administration, centralized and decentralised administration, all autonomous entities, State companies, State corporations, public-private corporations, corporations in which the State holds the majority of shares and any other organ within the National State whatever its legal nature, name, special act ruling it or place where it may render its services, as well as non-state legal persons in exercise of public functions and those private companies rendering public services and their agents, shall co-operate with the Defensor del Pueblo in the investigations and inspections carried out.

The Defensor del Pueblo or his deputies shall be entitled to request the production of records, reports, documents, antecedents and any other documentation they may deem useful to the investigation, according to the conditions established. The information so requested shall not be denied on the grounds of its confidential nature. Refusal to give information shall only be justified if related to the protection of the national security.

Moreover, the Defensor del Pueblo is entitled to conduct inspections, verifications and any other fact-finding procedure necessary for the clarification of the matter under investigation.

The Defensor del Pueblo de la Nación must submit a report on his work to the Congress every year before May 31st, without prejudice to the forwarding of a special report in case of urgency or serious acts.

The Judiciary, the Legislature, the Municipality of the City of Buenos Aires as well as defence and security organs shall be excluded from the jurisdiction of the Defensor del Pueblo.

LEGISLATION

National Constitution of Argentina

Section 86. The Defensor del Pueblo is an independent organ, created within the jurisdiction of the National Congress. The Defensor del Pueblo shall function with full autonomy, receiving no instruction from any authority whatsoever. The aims of the office are the defence and protection of human rights and any other rights, guarantees and interests protected in this Constitution and the laws, against the acts, actions and omissions of the Administration; and the control of public administrative functions.

The Defensor del Pueblo has legal standing. The office holder is appointed and dismissed by Congress with the vote of two thirds of the present members of both Houses. The Defensor del Pueblo enjoys the immunities and privileges of legislators. The office holder is appointed for a term of five years and may be reappointed for one more period.

The organization and functions of this institution shall be ruled according to a special act.

Section 43. Should there be no other available legal remedy, all individuals may bring an action for the protection of their constitutional rights (acción de amparo) against any act or omission on the part of any authority or individual which, actually or potentially might damage, restrict, alter or threaten the rights and guarantees protected by this Constitution, a treaty or an act. In such event, the judge may render the rule on which the act or omission is based unconstitutional.

The interested party, the Defensor del Pueblo or any association registered according to law, may file this remedy against any form of discrimination, in relation with the rights which safeguard the environment, competitiveness, the rights of service users and consumers as well as any collective right. The law shall determine the requirements and organization rules necessary to fulfil this procedure.

Any individual may file this action in order to get access to personal data kept in records or databases, either public or private, intended to be disclosed and, in case of falsity or discrimination, the interested party shall be entitled to request their elimination, rectification, confidentiality or updating. The secrecy of journal information sources shall not be affected.

Should the physical freedom of any individual be damaged, restricted, altered or threatened or in the case of serious irregularities in the conditions and procedures of an arrest or illegitimate detention or the forceful disappearance of persons, a writ for habeas corpus shall be filed by the aggrieved party or any person on his behalf and the competent judge shall issue his judgement forthwith, even under state of siege.

Section 41. All inhabitants are entitled to a healthy and well-balanced environment, fit for human development and for productive activities to satisfy all actual needs without affecting the activities of future generations. Inhabitants must protect their environment. Any damage inflicted upon the environment shall be repaired, as prescribed by law.

The authorities shall provide for the protection of this right, the rational use of natural resources, the preservation of the natural and cultural patrimony and the biological diversity as well as the provision of environmental education and information.

The Nation shall enact rules assigning minimum protection funds and the provinces shall enact the necessary rules to complement them, without prejudice to the local jurisdictions. The entrance of radioactive waste and dangerous or potentially dangerous residues to the national territory is forbidden.

Defensor Del Pueblo of the Argentine Nation Act 24, 284

Organic and Functional Regulation of the Office of the Defensor del Pueblo

The Senate and the House of Representatives of Argentina Assembled At the National Congress Sanction the Following Act

Title I
Establishment, Appointment, Removal, Terms and Conditions

Chapter I
Capacity and Appointment

Section 1. Establishment
The office of the Defensor del Pueblo is hereby established within the scope of the National Congress. This institution shall exercise the functions provided for in this Act and shall not receive instructions from any authority whatsoever.

The aim of this institution shall be the protection of the rights and interests of the individual and the community against the acts, actions and omissions on the part of the National Public Administration as described in Section 14.

Section 2. Incumbent. Appointment
An officer called the "Defensor del Pueblo" shall preside this institution. The Defensor del Pueblo shall be appointed by the National Congress according to the following procedure:

(a) Both Houses of Congress shall appoint a permanent Bicameral Commission (Comisión Bicameral), which shall consist of seven (7) senators and seven (7) representatives. The composition of this committee shall be apportioned among its members.
(b) Within thirty (30) days as from the enactment of this Act, the Commission, presided over by the President of the Senate, shall propose one to three candidates for the office of the Defensor del Pueblo before both Houses of Congress. The decisions of the Commission shall be adopted by simple majority of votes.
(c) Within thirty (30) days after the submission of the proposal above mentioned, both Houses of Congress shall choose one of the candidates with the vote of two thirds of their present members.
(d) Should no candidate obtain the majority required in the first ballot, another vote shall be cast until the required majority is obtained.
(e) Should three candidates be nominated and should none obtain the majority required under subsection (d), a new ballot shall be conducted among the two candidates who have obtained the greatest number of votes.

Section 3. Tenure
The Defensor del Pueblo shall hold office for a term of five years. The Defensor del Pueblo may only be reappointed for another term.

Section 4. Qualifications
The Defensor del Pueblo shall fulfil the following requirements:
(a) he shall have the Argentine citizenship by birth or option;
(b) he shall have attained the age of 30.

Section 5. Appointment
The Defensor del Pueblo shall be appointed by the joint decision of the Presidents of both Houses of Congress. The decision reached shall be published in the Official Bulletin and in the Session Journal of both Houses of Congress.

Before entering into the execution of the office, the Defensor del Pueblo shall take an oath before the Presidents of both Houses.

Section 6. Salary
The Defensor del Pueblo shall receive a salary to be determined by the National Congress on a joint decision of the Presidents of both Houses. The Defensor del Pueblo shall enjoy the exemptions established in Section 20, subsection (q) of the National Income Tax Act and its amendments.

Chapter II
Limitations, Removal, Vacancies, Privileges

Section 7. Limitations
The Defensor del Pueblo shall not perform any other public, commercial or professional activity outside his official function, with the exception of a professorship. He shall not be engaged in politics.

The rules on recusation provided for in the Civil and Commercial Code of Procedure shall apply to the Defensor del Pueblo.

Section 8. Activity
The activity of the Office of the Defensor del Pueblo shall not be interrupted during the legislative recess.

Section 9. Limitation. Termination
Within ten (10) days after the appointment is made and before entering into the execution of his office, the Defensor del Pueblo shall cease to perform any activity deemed to be inconsistent with the exercise of his official duties. Non compliance with such provision shall be deemed as a refusal to hold the office.

Section 10. Removal from office
The Defensor del Pueblo shall cease to perform his official functions in the following cases:
a) upon his resignation;
b) upon the termination of his mandate;
c) overcoming disability;
d) on conviction for a serious offence;
e) misbehaviour in office or in the cases defined under section 9.

Section 11. Removal from office
Procedure. In the cases described in Section 10, subsections (a), (c) and (d), the Defensor del Pueblo shall be removed from office by the Presidents of both Houses of Congress. In the case described in subsection (c) the overcoming disability shall be duly certified.

In the case described in subsection (e), the Defensor del Pueblo shall be removed from office by both Houses of Congress with the vote of two thirds of their present members, after considering the issue and hearing the interested party.

In case of death of the Defensor del Pueblo, the office shall become vacant and such vacancy shall be promptly filled according to the rules established in Section 13. The new incumbent shall be appointed according to the procedure described in Section 2.

Section 12. Privileges
The Defensor del Pueblo shall enjoy all privileges granted by the National Constitution to the members of Congress. He shall not be arrested from the date of his designation until his removal or suspension from office, except in the event he is convicted for an offence, in which case a summary report shall be submitted to both Houses of Congress.

In the case a court decision is entered against the Defensor del Pueblo for a serious offence, both Houses shall suspend him from office until his final acquittal.

Chapter III
Deputies

Section 13. Deputies
On the Defensor del Pueblo's recommendation, the Commission mentioned in Section 2, subsection (a) shall appoint two deputies who shall assist the Defensor in the discharge of his official function. Deputies to the Defensor del Pueblo may replace him in the event of removal, death, suspension or temporary inability, following such order of precedence as the Commission shall establish.

Without limiting the requisites established under Section 4, the Deputies to the Defensor del Pueblo shall meet the following requirements:

- To be a lawyer with an experience of at least eight years in the legal profession or have served for an equal term in the Judiciary, the Legislature, public administration or have hold a professorship;
- To evidence renowned experience in public law.

The provisions of sections 3, 5, 7, 10, 11 and 12 of this Act shall be applied to deputies. They shall receive the salary fixed by the National Congress according to the decision taken by the Presidents of both Houses.

Title II
Proceedings

Chapter I
Jurisdiction, Commencement and content of the investigation

Section 14. Complaint. Form and scope
The Defensor del Pueblo shall, either at his own initiative or after the presentation of a complaint by the aggrieved party, institute an investigation in order to clarify those acts, actions or omissions of the National Public Administration or its agents which may be

deemed illegitimate, defective, irregular, abusive, arbitrary, discriminatory, negligent, seriously inconvenient or untimely, including those which may affect diffuse or collective rights.

National and provincial legislators shall be entitled to receive complaints from the aggrieved parties and they shall immediately submit them to the Defensor del Pueblo for his consideration.

Section 15. Recurring and general dysfunctions
Notwithstanding the powers granted under section 14, the Defensor del Pueblo shall pay special attention to those situations causing recurring and general dysfunctions in the Public Administration. He shall try to recommend mechanisms to eliminate or diminish the effects of such irregularities.

Section 16. Jurisdiction
To the purposes of this act, the National Public Administration shall comprise the centralised and decentralised administration, all autonomous entities; State companies; State corporations; public-private corporations, corporations in which the State holds the majority of shares and any other organ within the National State whatever its legal nature, name, special act ruling it or place where it may render its services.

The Judiciary, the Legislature, the Municipality of the City of Buenos Aires as well as defence and security organs shall be excluded from the jurisdiction of the Defensor del Pueblo.

Section 17. Sphere of action
The jurisdiction of the Defensor del Pueblo shall also include all non-state legal persons in exercise of public functions and those private companies rendering public services. In the latter case, and with no prejudice to other powers granted by this Act, the Defensor del Pueblo may request the competent administrative authorities to exercise the powers granted by law.

Section 18. Legal standing
Any individual or legal person who feels damaged by the acts, actions or omissions included in section 14 may resort to the Defensor del Pueblo irrespective of their nationality, residence, confinement in a penitentiary and, in general, any employment relationship with the State.

Chapter II
Handling of the complaint

Section 19. Complaint. Form
All complaints must be lodged in writing and shall be signed by the complainant, including his or her full name and address. Complaints shall be lodged within a year as from the date in which the act, action or omission complained against took place.

No other requirement shall be met in order to submit a complaint.

All presentations made to the Defensor del Pueblo shall be free of charge and the complainant shall not be compelled to seek legal advice.

Section 20. Reference. Powers
In the event the matter that has given rise to the complaint is outside the jurisdiction of the office of the Defensor del Pueblo, or the time limit set in Section 19 has expired, the Defensor del Pueblo shall be entitled to refer the complaint to the competent authority, giving notice of this decision to the complainant.

Section 21. Dismissal of the complaint
The Defensor del Pueblo shall refuse to investigate complaints in the following cases:

– when the complaint was lodged in bad faith, is unfounded or the complainant has not got sufficient interest in the issue or the subject is trivial or vexatious;

- when the subject of the complaint is pending administrative review or court decision

He may also dismiss a complaint when, in his opinion, it might affect the rights of a third party.

If, once the investigation is started, the complainant files an administrative remedy or a legal action, the Defensor del Pueblo shall suspend his intervention.

Notwithstanding the above mentioned, the Defensor del Pueblo is entitled to investigate those general problems raised in the complaint. In all cases, he shall give notice to the interested party of the decision made.

Section 22. Decisions may not be appealed
Decisions on the admissibility of complaints submitted shall not be appealed.

The filing of a complaint shall not interrupt the terms for the filing of administrative remedies or a lawsuit provided for in the legal order.

Section 23. Procedure
Once the complaint has been accepted, the Defensor del Pueblo shall institute a summary investigation in the manner set in the regulation for the clarification of the issues raised. In all cases, the Defensor del Pueblo shall inform its content to the organ or body involved and said organ or body shall, within a period not exceeding thirty (30) days, submit a written report. The term may be extended if the Defensor del Pueblo deems it necessary.

Once the report is submitted, and if the reasons given by the informant are considered reasonable, the Defensor del Pueblo shall terminate the proceedings and inform the complainant accordingly.

Chapter III
Collaboration, Responsibility

Section 24. Duty to co-operate
All organs and bodies described in Section 16, all persons mentioned in Section 17 and their agents, shall co-operate with the Defensor del Pueblo in the investigations and inspections carried out.

To this end, the Defensor del Pueblo or his deputies shall be entitled to the following:

- To request the production of records, reports, documents, antecedents and any other documentation they may deem useful to the investigation, according to the conditions established. The information so requested shall not be denied on the grounds of its confidential nature. Refusal to give information shall only be justified if related to the protection of the national security.
- To conduct inspections, verifications and any other fact-finding procedure necessary for the clarification of the matter under investigation.

Section 25. Obstruction
Hindrance. Any person who wilfully obstructs the filing of a complaint before the Defensor del Pueblo or hinders the investigation carried out by refusing to submit the documentation required or hinders the access to records or documents necessary to the investigation, shall incur in disobedience as set in section 239 of the Criminal Code. The Defensor del Pueblo shall inform this situation to the Public Prosecutor to take the necessary actions.

The persistence of a hindering attitude on the part of any organ or administrative authority in the investigations carried out by the office of the Defensor del Pueblo shall be included in a special section of the Annual Report described in Section 31. In the case the organizations and bodies defined under Section 16, or the individuals mentioned in Section 17 or their agents fail to produce the documentation requested by the Defensor del Pueblo, the Defensor del Pueblo shall be entitled to seek judicial intervention.

Section 26. Offences
Whenever the Defensor del Pueblo, in the exercise of his duties, has knowledge of facts

evidencing crimes committed by any public officer, he shall immediately inform the situation to the Public Prosecutor. The National General Prosecutor shall, from time to time or at his request, inform the Defensor del Pueblo on the state of the actions taken through his intervention.

Title III
Decisions

Single Chapter
Scope of decisions, Notifications, Reports

Section 27. Restrictions to jurisdiction
The Defensor del Pueblo shall not be entitled to modify, substitute or repeal administrative decisions. Without prejudice to this provision, he may recommend the modification of the criteria on which such decisions are based.
If, as a consequence of an investigation, the Defensor del Pueblo is of the opinion that the strict fulfilment of a certain rule may give rise to an unfair or damaging situation to the administered individuals, he may recommend the Legislative Power or the public administration to modify it.

Section 28. Warnings and recommendations. Procedure
Once the investigation is finished, the Defensor del Pueblo may issue warnings, recommendations and reminders of the legal and official duties and submit recommendations for the adoption of new rules. In all cases, the authorities involved shall submit a written answer within a term of thirty (30) days.
If, within a reasonable time and after the recommendation is submitted to the administrative body involved, no action is taken by the administrative authority or the grounds for the non compliance with the recommendation are not given, the Defensor del Pueblo shall inform the competent Minister or the highest authority and submit a copy of the recommendation made. If the answer given is not deemed justified, the Defensor del Pueblo shall include the matter in the annual report or in a special report disclosing the names of the officers involved.

Section 29. Notifications on the investigation
The Defensor del Pueblo shall communicate the complainant the outcome of the investigation and the proceedings as well as the answer given by the organ or body involved, provided such information is not considered of confidential nature.

The Defensor del Pueblo will also inform the General Auditor's Office, whenever convenient, on the outcome of the investigations of organs under its control.

Section 30. Relations with Congress
The Commission established in subsection (a), Section 2 of this Act, shall be in permanent contact with the Defensor del Pueblo and shall inform both Houses of Congress whenever requested to do so.

Section 31. Reports
The Defensor del Pueblo shall give account of the activities carried out by the Office in an yearly report which shall be submitted before May 31st each year.

Whenever the seriousness or urgency of facts make it necessary, the Defensor del Pueblo may submit a special report on the issue.

Annual reports and special reports, whenever submitted, shall be published in the Official Bulletin and in the Sessions Journal of both Houses of Congress.

A copy of these reports shall be sent to the National Executive Power for their consideration.

Section 32. Content of the report
In the Annual Report, the Defensor del Pueblo shall give account of the number and

type of complaints received, those which were rejected and the reasons thereof and the complaints investigated and their outcome.

The report shall not include any personal information which may identify the complainant notwithstanding the provisions of Section 26.

The report shall include an annex, addressed to both Houses, on the expenses incurred in by the institution during the period under review.

In the annual report, the Defensor del Pueblo may include any modification of this Act which may improve the conduction of the activities carried out by the Office.

Title IV
Human and material resources

Single Chapter
Staff, Financial Resources, Terms

Section 33. Structure. Staff. Appointments
The Defensor del Pueblo shall provide for the functional and administrative structure of the office which shall be accepted by the Commission mentioned in Section 2, subsection (a).

The staff of the office shall be appointed by the Defensor del Pueblo according to the Office regulation and within budget possibilities.

The Defensor del Pueblo may propose the Presidents of both Houses of Congress a list of candidates rendering services in any of those Houses whom the Defensor del Pueblo may wish to be assigned to his Office.

Section 34. Office regulation
The Defensor del Pueblo shall provide for the internal functioning of the office. The regulation so made shall be approved by the Commission mentioned in Section 2, subsection (a) of this Act.

Section 35. Terms
Except as otherwise provided for, the terms fixed in this Act shall be calculated on the basis of working administrative days.

Section 36. Budget
The expenses incurred in the administration of this Act shall be payable out of the budget appropriated by the Budget Act to the National Legislature.

To all operative effects, the Office of the Defensor del Pueblo shall have its own administrative and financial system.

Section 37. Be it communicated to the Executive

IN THE SESSION ROOM OF THE ARGENTINE CONGRESS, IN BUENOS AIRES, ON DECEMBER 1, 1993.

NUMBER 24284.

Regulation for the Organization and Functional Structure of the Office of the Defensor Del Pueblo

I. GENERAL PROVISIONS

Section 1. The office of the Defensor del Pueblo is a constitutional institution, with full functional, administration and financial autonomy. The office is not subject to any mandatory disposition and receives no instructions from any authority whatsoever. The Defensor del Pueblo acts at his own discretion.

The mission of the office of the Defensor del Pueblo is the defence and protection of human rights and all other rights, guaranties and interests protected in the National Constitution and the laws against the acts, actions and omissions on the part of the Administration. The Defensor del Pueblo shall also supervise the exercise of public administrative functions.

In order to fulfil these aims, the Defensor del Pueblo shall monitor the activities carried out by the Public Administration as well as by the organs, bodies and persons mentioned in sections 16 and 17 of Act No 24,284, amended by Act No 24,379.

Section 2. The Defensor del Pueblo enjoys the immunities and privileges granted by the National Constitution, Act No 24,284 and the Amendment No 24,379.

These rules shall be applied to the Defensor del Pueblo's Deputies in the exercise of their duties.

Section 3. The Defensor del Pueblo shall only be accountable for his activities to the National Congress.

The Deputies, in their capacity as assistants to the Defensor del Pueblo, are accountable of their actions to the Defensor, in virtue of the individual nature of this office.

Section 4. Ruling and administrative functions of the office are only exercised by the Defensor del Pueblo.

Section 5. In the fulfilment of his duties, the Defensor del Pueblo shall be assisted by an Administrative Board.

II. THE DEFENSOR DEL PUEBLO

Section 6. In exercise of the powers assigned to the Defensor del Pueblo by the National Constitution, Act No 24,284 and its Amendment No 24,379, the Defensor del Pueblo shall:

- represent the institution, grant general or special powers and establish legal domicile to the effects set forth in the National Constitution (section 86 and consequential ones) and the legislation in force;
- propose Deputies to be appointed by the Bicameral Commission, established in section 2, subsection (a) of Act No 24,284;
- propose the Commission the removal of Deputies and, in this case, submit possible candidates to fill the vacancies as provided for in Section 13 of Act No 24,284.
- maintain a regular contact with the National Congress through the Permanent Bicameral Commission above mentioned;
- establish the sphere of action of both Deputies;
- enter into inter-institutional agreements and contracts with natural or legal persons, national or foreign institutions or organs and international organizations;
- suggest the modification of those rules which he may consider unfair or detrimental and recommend mechanisms which may avoid or minimise those behaviours which may give rise to recurring or general mistakes in the Public Administration;
- call and establish the agenda for the Administrative Board meetings and preside over said meetings;
- appoint and remove the members of the Institution staff and establish the salary to be perceived;
- provide for the organization and functional structure of the office;
- evaluate budgetary needs;
- administer the budget assigned to the Office according to the Institution's organic and functional needs;
- authorize the acquisition of goods and the hiring of services pursuant to the procedure established in Decree No 2662/92 or any other act which may replace it;
- take any necessary step, enter into any contract to fulfil the duties assigned, within budgetary possibilities;
- introduce modifications into the organization structure and accept the creation of lower units, if this does not imply expenses beyond budgetary possibilities.

III. DEPUTIES

Section 7. The duties to the Defensor del Pueblo's Deputies shall be the following:
- fulfil the duties assigned to the Defensor del Pueblo in case of delegation of powers or substitution of the incumbent established in Act No 24,284;
- intervene, pursuant to the delegation made by the Defensor del Pueblo, in the attention of complaints started on the Defensor's own motion or at the complainant's request, suggesting the office holder the acceptance or rejection of complaints and the adequate resolutions, as the case may be.

IV. ECONOMIC AND FINANCIAL ORGANIZATION

Section 8. The activities carried out by the Defensor del Pueblo shall be paid as follows:
- out of the office Budget, included within the Budget assigned to the Honourable Congress of the Nation;
- subsidies, contributions, grants and gifts accepted by the Defensor del Pueblo and informed to the National Congress in the annual reports;
- the money received from the sale of publications made by the Institution;
- any other source the special laws and rules may provide for.

Section 9. The Defensor del Pueblo shall receive the assistance of the Office's own administrative and financial service to manage the budget assigned, according to the provisions of Section 36, Act No 24,284 amended by Act No 24,379.

V. ADMINISTRATIVE BOARD

Section 10. The Defensor del Pueblo, the Deputies and the Secretary General, who will be acting as Secretary, shall make up the Administration Board.

Section 11. In fulfilling its duties, the Administration Board shall enjoy the following powers:
- to inform and assist the Defensor del Pueblo on those issues related to the institution staff;
- to discuss the proposals for the rendering of services and the provision of works and material;
- to assist the Defensor del Pueblo in the co-ordination of the activities of the diverse units and the best organization of services;
- to assist the Defensor del Pueblo on those issues submitted for their consideration.

Section 12. Any person, whose presence may be deemed convenient in order to supply information, may participate in the Administration Board meetings, which shall be duly called by the Defensor del Pueblo.

All issues discussed shall be included in the agenda of the meeting and all agreements adopted by the Board shall be notified to all its members.

VI. HANDLING OF COMPLAINTS

Section 13. The Defensor del Pueblo, in the exercise of his powers, shall intervene on his own motion or at the complainant's request. Complaints shall be handled according to the provisions of Act No 24,284 modified by Act No 24,379 and this regulation.

Section 14. Complaints filed with the Defensor del Pueblo must be lodged in writing and shall be signed by the complainant including his or her full name and address. In case the complainant is not able to sign, for his or her illiteracy or disability, a member of the staff will meet this requirement on his or her behalf if so requested.

The filing of complaints in the office of the Defensor del Pueblo is free of charge and the complainant shall not be compelled to seek legal advice.

The filing and attention of complaints shall be the Defensor del Pueblo's sole responsibility.

Section 15. Those documents deemed secret or reserved shall only be known to the Defensor, and if convenient, to the Deputies and the Secretary General.

As regards internal information, the Defensor del Pueblo shall determine which documents shall be deemed classified.

In no case shall reference be made to the content of secret documents in the reports submitted by the Defensor del Pueblo or in the notifications sent to the complainant or the person requesting the intervention of this office.

The reference made to reserved documents in the reports submitted to Congress shall be decided by the Defensor del Pueblo.

VI. STAFF OF THE OFFICE OF THE DEFENSOR DEL PUEBLO

Section 16. The Defensor del Pueblo shall make the selection of those staff members who will work under his orders and shall establish the rules and corresponding hierarchy, within budgetary possibilities and pursuant to the provisions of section 33 of Act No 24,284, amended by Act No 24,379.

Section 17. All members of the staff shall fulfil their duties on a full or part time basis, as the Defensor del Pueblo shall establish according to service requirements.

Section 18. The staff of the Defensor del Pueblo shall maintain secrecy of all matters attended in the institution.

VII. PUBLICATION

Section 19. The present regulation shall be published in the Sessions Journal of both Houses of Congress and in the Official Bulletin. It shall enter into force on the day following its publication.

The Ombudsman Institution in Austria

Dr. Nikolaus Schwäzler*

1. The Norms for the Ombudsman Institutions

(a) *The Statutory Basis of the Ombudsman Board (Volksanwaltschaft) in Vienna*

The Federal Law of 24 February 1977, Federal Law Gazette (Bundesgesetzblatt) 121, legally created the Ombudsman Board for the Republic of Austria. The legislators expressed their initial doubts by establishing the institution for a limited period from 1 July 1977 to 30 June 1983. However, in 1981 the Law on the Ombudsman Board (Gesetz über die Volksanwaltschaft) was already being incorporated as the Seventh Chapter of the Austrian Federal Constitution in the version of 1 July, Federal Law Gazette 350. In 1986 and 1988 certain provisions were amended.

The statute which implements the basic provisions now contained in the Federal Constitution, is the Federal Law on the Ombudsman Board (Bundesgesetz über die Volksanwaltschaft) of 1982, Federal Law Gazette 433. This law is the repromulgation of the provisions regulating the organization of the Ombudsman Board and the procedure before the Ombudsman in the law of 1977 which were not adopted in the Constitution itself. The Ombudsman Board decides on its own internal rules and the internal allocation of duties. The current versions are published in the Federal Law Gazette 1996/96 and 1996/272 respectively.

Austria is organized as a Federal State in compliance with the federal principles of the Constitution. This principle is extended into the ombudsman system of legal protection by empowering the States (Länder) either to create their own ombudsmen for their own administrative authorities, or to declare the Ombudsman Board in Vienna to be competent for those authorities. There is no legal obligation to opt for either alternative. The States also have the choice of doing nothing. However, this option would not be viable for political reasons. In the discussion below, the term "Ombudsman Board" always refers to the Vienna office in its capacity as a Federal Ombudsman and in its capacity as a state ombudsman of the States (Länder) summed up in the following paragraph.

The Federated States (Bundesländer) Burgenland, Carinthia, Lower Austria, Upper Austria, Salzburg, Styria and Vienna have all availed themselves of the option to declare the Ombudsman Board in Vienna competent for the state

*Former Ombudsman of the State of Vorarlberg; President of the European Ombudsman Institute; Member of the Independent Federal Asylum Commission.

K. Hossain et al. (eds), Human Rights Commissions and Ombudsman Offices, 247–267.

administrative authorities of the respective states. Vorarlberg and Tyrol, by contrast, have opted to appoint their own ombudsmen to oversee their state administration.

Tyrol and Vorarlberg are the two States with the greatest distance from Vienna, the capital of the Federation.

(b) *The Statutory Basis for the State Ombudsmen*

The legal basis for the Ombudsman (Landesvolksanwalt) of Vorarlberg can be found in Art. 57 to 59 of the Vorarlberg Constitution (Landesverfassung), Vorarlberg Law Gazette (Landesgesetzblatt, LGBI) 1984130, and the Law on the Landesvolksanwalt (Gesetz über den Landesvolksanwalt), Vorarlberg Law Gazette (Landesgesetzblatt, LGBI) 1985/29. The legal basis for the State Ombudsman of Tyrol is Art. 59 of the Tyrolean State Order (Landesordnung: equivalent to a state constitution), Tyrol Law Gazette 1988/61. In Tyrol the State Ombudsman is also responsible for indirect federal administrative authorities (the part of the administration of the Federation which is provided by authorities of the State (Land). Several States (Länder) have declared the Ombudsman Board in Vienna to be responsible for a limited time for the domain of their own state administration (just as the Federation itself has done). When the regulations setting up the Tyrolean State Ombudsman became effective on 1 March 1989, the authority of the Austrian Ombudsman Board was extended over the entire administration of the Federal Government and the States (Länder).

(c) *Comparative Survey of Characteristics of the Three Ombudsman Institutions in Austria*

Theme	Federation	Tyrol	Vorarlberg
Required qualification	Eligible to be elected to the Lower House (Nationalrat), i.e. at least 19 years old	Personal and professional qualification	Eligible to be elected to the State Parliament (Landtag)
Public announcement of the function	No	No	In the Law Gazette of the State and in the daily newspapers with place of publication in Voralberg
Interview with candidates	No	No	Before the election in the Volksanwalt Committee
Incompatibilities	Member of the Government of the Federation or of the Government of a State or a representative body; any other profession	Member of the Government of the Federation or of the Government of the State of Tyrol or a representative body	Member of the Government of the Federation or of the Government of a State or a representative body; any other profession; Mayor

Theme	Federation	Tyrol	Vorarlberg
Appointment	By the Parliament with a majority of 50% of votes cast	On proposal of the President of the Parliament by the Parliament with a majority of 50% of votes cast	By the Parliament with a majority of 75% of votes cast
Removal	Not provided for in the statutory basis	On proposal of the President of the Parliament if the Ombudsman loses the qualification for his appointment	Not provided for in the statutory basis
Term of office	Six years; re-election only possible for a second term	Six years; unlimited re-election is admissible	Six years; re-election only possible for a second term
Budget	No budgetary competence of his own	No budgetary competence of his own	Budgetary competence of his own
Relationship with other (judicial) organs of last resort	With the Constitutional Court – to investigate the legality of a decree and – to decide a dispute with the government as to the competencies of the ombudsman	No	With the Constitutional Court – to investigate the legality of a decree and – to decide a dispute with the government as to the competencies of the ombudsman
Limitations of the powers of investigation as to subject matter/time	None	None	None

2. History and Background

The Austrian legal term "Volksanwalt",[1] which was mentioned earlier as the German language designation for ombudsman, is too sweeping given the actual powers of the institution. Its similarity to the German word for lawyer (Rechtsanwalt) implies that the "Volksanwalt", too, is empowered with virtually universal competence in legal matters. As a result of this misleading designation, the "Volksanwälte" are very often approached about matters of civil or penal law for which they have no competence (except to file a reprimand concerning the duration of a proceeding).

[1] E.g. "Der Volksanwalt", a magazine published in Leipzig in 1927 – "A publication fighting on behalf of the working people, merchants and traders. Serves no party! Free advice for everyone!"

Known under a wide variety of different designations, ombudsman-like institutions in numerous countries do share similar objectives. However, though comparable in many essential aspects, these institutions also differ in some major respects that should not be overlooked. For instance, the Austrian Ombudsman is not competent in a case until the person affected by the case has exhausted all legal remedies open to him/her. By contrast, the Italian equivalent of the ombudsman in the autonomous province of Bolzano (South Tyrol) was, until 1997, competent only until a final judgement was handed down in the case. According to one model adopted in the United Kingdom, the ombudsman receives the complaints from the Parliamentary Committee on Petitions, in another model he reviews them and then forwards them to the same Committee.

The Ombudsman Board (Volksanwaltschaft) established in Vienna for the Federal Republic of Austria was the eighth institution of its kind to be set up in Europe, not counting special ombudsmen (e.g. responsible for the military, health institutions or for municipalities). Austria followed the lead of Sweden, Finland, Norway, Denmark, Great Britain, France, Rhineland-Palatinate and Portugal, and was subsequently to be followed by Italy (at the regional level), Ireland, Netherlands, Spain, Poland and Hungary.

The available literature on the ombudsman system cites several parallels and roots. They extend historically to the organization of the state in ancient Greece; geographically to Arabia; and intellectually to the philosophers Althusius and Fichte.

In Austria the institution of the ombudsman is associated most closely with the names Hans Kelsen, Rene Marcic and the journalist Karl Steinhauser. It was a report published in 1960 on the Danish Ombudsman (established in 1955) and a lecture given in 1963 by the ombudsman then in office, Stephan Hurwitz, that helped to intensify public discussion on the issue. Mr. Schnherr has written extensively on this subject. Former Austrian Federal Chancellor Bruno Kreisky, in his government policy statement of 1970, refers specifically to the idea of the Federal Government establishing a collegial body in which each of the parties would be represented.

Citing the various sources, Schnherr summarises why the cry for an ombudsman had become so urgent in Austria as well. The ultimate reason for establishing ombudsmen was the people's increasing uneasiness about their "bureaucratised lives". As governmental spending increased, so too did the intricacy and with it the bureaucratisation of the administrative structure; everything had become more complicated and less understandable. This in turn had created a growing distrust in the general populace with regard to enforcement and legislation. Standardised down to the last detail, the administrative state and its "legal justice" had become all too far removed from the average citizen's natural sense of justice.

Others who shared the view that Austria, too, could no longer do without an ombudsman noted that the adage "a rule is a rule" had begun to distort the idea of abiding by the law. They argued that formal justice was vying with substantive justice; that the many regulations only served to obscure, even suppress, the law, and in any case dulled our legal sensibilities. According to them, the machinery of state frequently operated in a heartless and thoughtless manner, people were often treated as nothing more than numbers and would no longer be willing to put up with it. And finally, it was not the people's responsibility to adjust to the state; the state had to change and adjust to the people, it had to be humanised. It was to be the ombudsman's task to prevent these fears from becoming reality.

3. Access to the Ombudsman

All three ombudsman models[2] in Austria have one feature in common: the right to appeal to an ombudsman is not limited to Austrian citizens or to natural persons. The word "anyone" is to be interpreted in the broadest possible sense. Along with physical, adult, individual persons the word also includes loosely connected bodies of persons, elective parties, special interest associations, citizens' political action groups as well as minors and prisoners. Klecatsky and Pickl view this right of everyone to file complaints as a right that is directly guaranteed by constitutional law, an "individual's public right", comparable to the right to complain before the public law courts. As a result, there is virtually no limit in Austria as to who has access to the ombudsman.

Objectively, the following criteria must be met before an ombudsman can be appealed to:

(a) There must be a grievance.
(b) The complainant must be directly affected by the grievance.
(c) The person appealing to the ombudsman must have exhausted all remedies open to him/her or not have been entitled to any remedies in the first place.

The concept of "grievance" is broadly defined by all ombudsmen and can mean anything from a public official treating a person impolitely to that official engaging in conduct punishable under criminal law; from an agency failing to act to that same agency committing qualified malfeasance. However, a line is drawn for a matter to be considered a grievance, that is when the authorities or the institution dealing with the public are granted a real measure of discretion or power to shape policy. It is not considered a grievance, for example, when a municipality avails itself of its right to reformulate or alter its local planning and zoning objectives. Administrations of public subsidies, too, are granted broad discretion in their activities. For the ombudsmen it is the factual content of the rule and/or the action that is the standard for evaluation. In the end, the major determinant of the admissibility of the appeal is that the person appealing to the ombudsman asserts that a grievance does exist.

Also the standard to determine "direct effect of the measure" (i.e. whether a measure directly affects the compalainant), should be applied broadly, because the ombudsmen's purpose is to act as a safety net to catch all cases that would otherwise slip through the cracks of the traditional (classic) legal protection system. There is no great importance in asking whether the complainant is entitled to the status of party as defined in the rules of administrative procedure; more important is whether the effects of the depicted action influence his life, whether he could in some way or another be burdened by them. If a person not

[2](1) The Ombudsman Board in Vienna acting as the Ombudsman of the Federal Government and for the administration of the Federated States (Länder) of Burgenland, Carinthia, Upper Austria, Lower Austria, Salzburg, Styria and Vienna. (2) The State Ombudsman of Tyrol. (3) The State Ombudsman of Vorarlberg.

directly affected by a matter appeals to an ombudsman, that person has no right himself/herself to have "his/her" case dealt with; at the same time, however, the ombudsman is not prevented from investigating the matter ex officio. Direct effect and representation are separate issues. Needless to say, the complainant can be represented by other persons and only the person represented need be affected by the matter, not the person representing him/her.

In cases of complaints against administrative authorities, a person is also required to have exhausted all legal remedies before he/she may legitimately turn to an ombudsman. In other words, he/she must have gone through all possible stages of appeal, including an appeal to a supervisory authority. The right to file a complaint with an ombudsman is, therefore, subordinate to the right of appeal. The ombudsmen were not set up as an appeal authority per se. If a person addressed by an administrative decree (Bescheid) fails to avail himself/herself of the right of appeal, the Ombudsman Board becomes competent; the latter may not reproach the complainant on the grounds that he/she failed to act – regardless of the reason for the said failure. During the period in which a petition can still be filed with the Administrative Court (Verwaltungsgerichtshof) or with the Constitutional Court (Verfassungsgerichtshof), the ombudsman does not consider himself competent. The reason an ombudsman is not made legally competent so long as another remedy (in the broadest sense of the word) exists, is to prevent redundant and parallel actions. The Tyrolean State Ombudsman is not bound by this requirement. He can become active even while a proceeding is in progress. The Ombudsman Board and the State Ombudsman of Vorarlberg make two important exceptions to the principle of incompetence as long as a right of appeal to a Court has not yet been exercised. These exceptions are surely in keeping with the intent of the Constitution and the law. The exceptions are when an authority either fails to act or is dilatory in its duties. If there is a delay in the proceedings, all ombudsmen consider themselves competent to investigate the alleged or assumed grievance of delayed proceedings. At that point, the party to the proceeding can still file an application to have the duty to decide that his case be transferred to a higher authority competent for the subject or to lodge a complaint of dilatoriness with the Administrative Court (Verwaltungsgerichtshof); however, neither of these rights hinders him from appealing to the ombudsman according to generally held legal opinion.

4. The Competencies of the Ombudsman

The ombudsmen are consulting and controlling bodies, The primary statutory mandate of the Ombudsman Board is to investigate complaints. The ombudsman provisions in the State Constitutions of Tyrol and Vorarlberg place the investigation of complaints on an equal footing with the granting of advice. If one reads the reports of the Ombudsman Board to the Lower House of Parliament and the respective State Parliaments carefully, it becomes obvious that the ombudsmen in Vienna settle many cases simply by advising the complainant – even though they have no actual statutory mandate to do so. The difference is that people are not allowed to turn to the Ombudsman Board in Vienna from the outset for information or concrete advice, as they may with the State Ombudsmen of Tyrol and Vorarlberg. However, a very large number of complaint proceedings ended not only with the ruling “alleged grievance unfounded”, but at the same time with the ruling “information clarified the case”.

The Vorarlberg State Constitution describes the task of the State Ombudsman (Volksanwalt) as follows: “The Parliament of Vorarlberg (Landtag) will appoint a Landesvolksanwalt to advise its citizens and to investigate their complaints.” The corresponding provision in the Tyrolean State Order lays down that the State Ombudsman “must counsel any person or hear complaints ...”. Both provisions are further extensions of the basic provisions in Art. 148a of the Federal Constitution (Bundesverfassungsgesetz) which, however, makes no mention of advising the citizens. It reads: “Anyone is entitled to file a complaint on the grounds of an alleged grievance of federal administration including those cases where the Federation is a holder of private rights, to the extent that the said person has been affected directly by these grievances and he/she does not have, or no longer has, a right of appeal with regard to them.” The ombudsmen's right of examination extends not only to the authority's activity, the sovereign action, but also to its activity as a holder of private rights; in Vorarlberg this right also exists regardless of whether this activity was carried out by the State (Land) itself or by another legal entity at the State's bidding. The ombudsmen investigate upon request in order to protect the affected persons; however, they also have the right (except for the State Ombudsman of Tyrol) to investigate an action by the administrative authorities at their own discretion (ex officio). This ex officio intervention preserves the rule of law per se and is not dependent on a given individual being directly affected. At the close of a requested grievance investigation, the result of the investigation is announced along with any directions of the intervener. All organs of the Federal Government and the States (Länder) are obliged to provide the ombudsman with information and assistance; they may not appeal to their duty to maintain secrecy.

A closer look at the statutorily defined scope of authority reveals formal though essential differences among the three sets of provisions on ombudsmen. However, their significance is often relativized in practice, as the earlier example of advising and informing showed. The chart below presents a synoptic summary of the scope of authority for each type of ombudsman.

	Statutory basis		
Competencies/ Authorized to	Federal Constitution/ Ombudsman Law	Tyrolean State Order	Vorarlberg State Constitution/Law on State Ombudsman
Provide information and advice	–	Art. 59(2)	Art. 57(2)/§ 2(1)
Propose legislation	–	–	Art. 57(2)/§ 2(4)
Propose administrative action	–	–	Art. 57(2)/§ 2(4)
Examine a grievance on request	Art. 148a(1)	Art. 59(2)	Art. 57(4)/§ 1(2)
Examine a grievance ex officio	Art. 148a(2)	–	Art. 57(4)/§ 1(3)

Competencies/ authorized to	Statutory basis		
	Federal Constitution/ Ombudsman Law	Tyrolean State Order	Vorarlberg State Constitution/Law o[f] State Ombudsman
Have a role in handling petitions	Art. 148a(3)	–	–
Offer advice to the general public	–	–	Art. 57(4)/§ 2(1)
Make a recommendation to the highest body authorized to issue directions	Art. 148c /§6	–	Art. 58(1)/§ 3(2)
Make a recommendation to the highest body within a self-governed entity*	Art. 148c /§ 6	-	Art. 58(1)/§ 3(2)
File an application with the Constitutional Court for a review of the legality of a decree (Verordnung)	Art. 148e	–	Art. 58(2)
File an application with the Constitutional Court to decide a dispute with the Federal (State) Government	Art. 148f	–	Art. 58(3)

* The Vorarlberg provision is narrower because it relates only to the local government and not t[o] self-governed/managed bodies in general.

Each year the ombudsmen must submit to Parliament a report, the standard[s] of which they themselves determine. Whereas the Vorarlberg State Ombudsma[n] is mandated by separate legal provisions to submit proposals to the legislatur[e] and to the administrative authorities enabling him to make these proposal[s] independent of the annual report, the Ombudsman Board and in Tyrol the Stat[e] Ombudsman achieve the same effect – with a slight delay – by presenting th[e] problem in a report to the Parliament.

Two functions which the other two institutions do not have, are the role i[n] handling petitions granted to the Ombudsman Board and the authority to advis[e] the general public granted to the Vorarlberg State Ombudsman. The only wa[y] practicably to carry out the latter is through the use of the mass media. Wit[h] regard to its role in handling petitions, the Ombudsman Board has this responsi-bility or right in relation to the Lower House of Parliament (Nationalrat) only not to the State Parliaments when the Ombudsman Board is also called upo[n] to act as the State Ombudsman. For cases in which the Ombudsman Board i[s] declared by state constitutional law to be competent for the administration o[f] the respective State (Land), the Federal Constitution mandates that the provis-ions of Art. 148e and 148f of the Federal Constitution be applied mutati[s] mutandis, but not those of Art. 148a, § 3 of the Federal Constitution.

It has been noted quite accurately that the ombudsmen are not vested with the legal power to decide cases or to impose sanctions. The effectiveness of their control is based on personal authority; they bring about changes in administrative actions through "gentle application of the law", that is through "soft law". But this is not all. For instance, within 8 weeks of an ombudsman submitting his recommendations, they must either be complied with or a written statement must be submitted explaining why they have not been complied with. If the public authority fails to comply with the recommendations, three factors combine to exert greater pressure on them than the personal authority of the ombudsman alone would have:

- their obligation to submit a written statement of reasons,
- the publicising of their behaviour or the problems of the case in the annual report, and
- the possible handling of the case in public.

The two possibilities to appeal to the Constitutional Court provided for in the Federal Constitution are very effective weapons that extend far beyond the ombudsman's personal authority. As of the end of 1990, this competence to appeal to the Constitutional Court to decide a dispute was utilized only once and it was the Ombudsman Board which availed itself of that competence. A judgement for the petitioning ombudsman leaves the administrative authorities no latitude; the sentence of the Constitutional Court must be complied with and resistance can be broken by means of execution. The authority to appeal to the Constitutional Court to examine a decree (Verordnung) is similarly powerful. If the petition of the ombudsman is allowed and the decree is repealed, the administrative authority – in contract to the case of a recommendation – has no latitude whatsoever; it must comply with the ombudsman's opinion. This authority, which is granted only to the Ombudsman Board in Vienna and the Vorarlberg State Ombudsman, was utilized by the former six times and by the latter twenty nine times up until the end of 1997.

5. The Procedure Before the Ombudsman

There are no formal rules of procedure for dealings with ombudsmen. Anyone who wishes to turn to an ombudsman for assistance may do so orally, in writing, by telegram, by telefax, by telex, in person or through an agent. If a person opts for the written approach, the usual fees for petitions and enclosures do not apply. Whereas the Law on the Ombudsman Board and the Law on the Vorarlberg State Ombudsman declare a series of provisions from the General Law on Administrative Procedure (Allgemeines Verwaltungsverfahrensgesetz) to be applicable mutatis mutandis, the laws for the Tyrolean State Ombudsman make no provisions whatsoever for procedures. The Vorarlberg provisions stipulate in general that the procedure should be kept as simple as possible for the complainant. Due to the mutatis mutandis application of the procedural provisions in general procedural law, the ombudsmen do have a certain amount of latitude in creating procedures that really are as simple as possible.

However, though the mutatis mutandis application of procedural provisions does allow for the questioning of witnesses to be accepted as evidence, the ombudsmen themselves are not granted a right to summon witnesses – mutati mutandis or otherwise. This is probably in keeping with the basic attitude o the legislature s that the ombudsmen should receive no official authority. Th ombudsmen must – and as experience shows can – live with this state of actua powerlessness.

6. Organization of Ombudsman Offices

Vienna has been established as the official location of the Ombudsman Boar in the Federation. If the States (Länder) declare this Ombudsman Board to b competent for their state administration, the seat for this function is also Vienna Innsbruck has been designated as the official seat of the Tyrolean Stat Ombudsman appointed to deal with state administration and the indirect federa administration in the State (Land) of Tyrol. Since Vorarlberg has three cities o equal size and importance, the Vorarlberg State Ombudsman may choose an one of the three as the seat for his office; the State Ombudsman's office i currently located in Bregenz. All ombudsmen are obligated to set aside date for appointments at places other than their official locations, if required. Fron 1985 to 1988, the Ombudsman Board set aside an average of 68 days a year fo appointments outside Vienna; this number increased up until 1997 to abou 100 days.

Whereas the Ombudsman Board in Vienna is a collegial body made up o three members, the State Ombudsmen of Tyrol and Vorarlberg were set up a monocratic bodies.

The allocation of duties and/or the rules of procedure establish which matter the Ombudsman Board decides on collectively and which ones are ruled on b individual members of the body. These two norms, in turn, can only be estab lished and changed on the basis of a unanimous resolution by the entire body This type of resolution is also required for the annual report to Parliament an for the appeal to the Constitutional Court; otherwise all that is usually require is a simple majority vote. The members can represent each other but may no abstain from voting if they are present. Each ombudsman is entitled to entrus a legally well-versed staff member with the conducting of the ombudsman' business. All three ombudsmen decide as a body on the assignment of a give staff member to a given sphere of business; a unanimous vote is required. A director, who is directly subordinate to the instructions of the Chairman, i charged with managing the Ombudsman Board.

The chair of the Ombudsman Board rotates each year, changing in the orde of the relative strength (number of parliamentary seats) of the three majo political parties, each of whom names one of the members. The chairman mus call a meeting of the body at least twelve times a year. The members, too, ar entitled to request that meetings be convened.

7. Appointment and Relative Position of the Ombudsmen

The executive committee of the Lower House of Parliament (Nationalrat) draw up a nomination list of three members, the political parties with the larges number of seats in the Lower House of Parliament each being given the righ o name one member. The Lower House of Parliament then elects the three mbudsmen on the basis of this list of nominees. If a member retires before is/her six-year term of office has expired, the party which nominated him/her s entitled to name a new member to serve the rest of the term. Members can e re-elected for a six-year term once. A member is elected by simple majority ote. To be eligible for selection as a member of the Ombudsman Board, a erson must be eligible to serve in the Lower House of Parliament. While in ffice, the ombudsmen are not permitted to be members of the Federal Government or a State Government or a general representative body. Nor may hey practise any other profession. The personal and professional requirements or serving as the State Ombudsman of Tyrol are also standardised. He/she is lected on the proposal of the President of the State Parliament by majority ote for a term of six years, whereby re-election is not limited to one six-year erm. He/she, too, is subject to the same incompatibility restrictions, as is the State Ombudsman of Vorarlberg who is also barred from filling the position of Mayor. However, the provisions regulating the Tyrolean State Ombudsman do not prohibit the practice of another profession as do those for the State Ombudsman of Vorarlberg.

Prior to the election of the State Ombudsman of Vorarlberg – which requires hree-quarters of the votes cast – the position must be advertised and a hearing or the applicants suggested to fill it must be conducted before the Ombudsman Committee. No provisions have been made for the removal from office of mbudsmen elected by the Lower House of Parliament and the Vorarlberg State Ombudsman. On the basis of this absolute irremovability, these ombudsmen ave the strongest position of all the constitutionally established organs, the State Ombudsman of Tyrol can be removed from office if he/she no longer meets he personal and professional requirements for the position.

The respective Constitutions grant ombudsmen unlimited autonomy in the erformance of their duties of office; they cannot be given directions or mandates. This provision is also in keeping with the fact that their legal position with egard to earnings is not determined by the Salary Law for Civil Servants (Gehaltsgesetz der Beamten), but by the Remuneration Law (Bezügegesetz).

The State Ombudsman of Vorarlberg is also entitled to budgetary sovereignty. The government has no means of influencing his/her budget; it must allocate he budget amount submitted in the State Draft Budget.

The ombudsmen are entitled to speak while the reports are being discussed n Parliament (with the exception of Tyrol). The members of the Ombudsman Board have this right in committees consulting on matters within their jurisdic-ion, as does the State Ombudsman of Vorarlberg in the Ombudsman Committee. This committee is appointed in accordance with the State Constitution and is upposed to meet three times a year. The State Ombudsman is obligated to articipate in its meetings in order to present his/her report. This committee has 14 members, 7 appointed by the parties with the majority in Papliament and 7 ppointed by the opposition parties. The Chairman has until now always elonged to the opposition.

8. Statistics of Interest Regarding Ombudsman Offices in Austria

The figures above that the workload of an ombudsman office is significantly igher in regions which have their own ombudsman office. Whereas the average case load per year for states who made the Vienna Ombudman competer ranged between 83 (Carintia) to 257 (Vienna), the average case load for th Tyrol Ombudsman was 1304 and for the Vorarlberg Ombudsman 466. Th average number of cases per year for the federal government was 3643.

The total staff size for the Ombudsman Board in Vienna (including th Ombudsmen) is 47, whereas the staff size for the Tyrol Ombudsman is 4 an for the Vorarlberg Ombudsman is 3 1/2.

9. A Glance Into the Past and Into the Future

From their initial introduction in Austria in 1977 until the year 1990, th ombudsmen handled nearly 65,000 cases submitted by their fellow Austrian The State Ombudsmen of Tyrol and Vorarlberg have each dealt with some 2,50 cases from their establishment up until 1990.

Of course, being an ombudsman means acting in two directions at onc although only one direction is evident from the statistics. As a general rule thos who come to the ombudsman do so because they do not agree with the pas conduct of a public authority; in the 14-year period cited there were over 70,00 such people. The ombudsman institutions were actually able to help the com plainant in an average of one quarter to one third of the cases, an impressiv number. However, that is only a fraction of what the ombudsmen do and th effect that they have. It is impossible to measure the future effect of their action the number of cases that will not even arise because of them. One representativ of Parliament declared in a debate that the ombudsmen would be justified eve if they had nothing to do, but by their very existence caused the governmen administration to function better by binding it more closely to the true inten of the law. The importance of this preventive aspect of the ombudsmen's wor is clearly illustrated by the numerous stories citizens tell about how their men tioning a possible appeal to the ombudsman has caused the administrativ authorities to reconsider their handling of a case.

By contrast, other officials sometimes appear to be almost disconcertingl offended when a citizen asks the ombudsman to review a case. In general, th higher up in the administrative hierarchy, the greater the co-operation. Th municipalities, which are responsible for by far the largest share of the complaint in the domain of the state administration, often display an uncanny inertia whe it comes to altering illegal conduct.

The earlier statement about the ombudsmen making do with the virtua powerlessness they have been granted, should not be construed as an invitatior to resign oneself to the current legal status quo. The Ombudsman Board wa incorporated into the Austrian legal system like an erratic boulder into a wal of uniformly sized bricks and many suggestions eminently worthy of discussior have been brought up on ways to improve the interaction between the tor control authorities as they respond to the action or inaction of the government in whatever from it appears. The ombudsmen, who themselves are not ever required to be legal practitioners, cannot now request clarification of a point o ordinary law from the Administrative Court (Verwaltungsgerichtshof), which is normally authorized to do so and which adjudicates in Administrative Tribunals

Verwaltungssenate); they cannot even do so when a concrete statement regarding the legality of a ruling (Bescheid) is crucial to their work. There is no reason why a relationship could not be established between these two high-level bodies, the Ombudsman Board and the Administrative Court.

There is a broad spectrum of ideas on how the legal protection afforded by the ombudsmen should develop in the future; they range from granting the ombudsmen the power to initiate a resumption of proceedings, to allowing the ombudsmen to reverse particularly crass misjudgements themselves. The amendment to the Federal Constitution of 1988 regarding the independent Administrative Tribunals (unabhängige Verwaltungssenate) granted the latter the authority to appeal to the Constitutional Court (Verfassungsgerichtshof) to examine a statute. This amendment made it all the more obvious that the ombudsmen lack the same authority. In the hands of the ombudsmen, it would be an inestimably powerful means of implementing the legality principle, for even the abstract contestation of a law is a means of controlling the administration and is not aimed against the legislators. Armed with these powers, the ombudsmen could compel the administrative authorities to abandon positions that appear constitutionally untenable on the grounds that the statute on which the relevant authority relies, would itself be unconstitutional. However, if the ombudsmen could offer an interpretation that is in accordance with the Constitution, the norms would not be rescinded.

In its proceedings of judicial review of the statutes, the Constitutional Court could come to the conclusion that the public authority held the correct position (contrary to the presumption of the ombudsmen) or that even though the authority's interpretation would result in the unconstitutionality of the norm, a constitutional interpretation did exist (that offered by the ombudsman) and the norm should, therefore, not be rescinded.

Members of the Ombudsman Board until 1991 appeared every Sunday evening on a prime time Austrian television show, making the public aware of them far beyond the borders of Austria, and to an extent that was unimaginable in other countries that have such an institution. All in all, the show – "A Case for the Ombudsman?" ("Ein Fall fur den Volksanwalt?") – was a resounding success, occasional criticisms notwithstanding. The show's effect was further reinforced by the presence of ombudsmen on the radio (during the days the ombudsmen set aside for consultation in the States (Länder) for example). It is a pity that a serious disagreement between the presenter of the show and an ombudsman arose right in the middle of a public transmission one Sunday evening. That scandal heralded the end of the show and was also the end of a period of very important and successful activity in the field of public relations. In the following years the workload of the Vienna Ombudsman Institution significantly declined, because the ombudsman (Volksanwalt) was no longer as present in the consciousness of the people as he used to be.

LEGISLATION

Austrian Federal Constitution

Chapter VII – Ombudsmen Council

Article 148a [Standing, Investigation, Independence]

(1) Everyone can lodge complaint with the Ombudsmen Council against alleged maladministration by the Federation, including its activity as a holder of private rights,

provided that they are affected by such maladministration and in so far as they d not or no longer have recourse to legal remedy. All such complaints must be invest gated by the Ombudsmen Council. The complainant shall be informed of the investiga tion's outcome and what action, if necessary, has been taken.

(2) The Ombudsmen Council is ex officio entitled to investigate its suspicions of malac ministration by the Federation including its activity as a holder of private rights.

(3) The Ombudsmen Council is independent in the exercise of its authority.

Article 148b [State Support, Secrecy]

(1) All Federal, State, and County authorities shall support the Ombudsmen Council i the performance of its tasks, allow it inspection of its records, and upon reques furnish the information required. Official secrecy is inoperative in the case of th Ombudsmen Council.

(2) The Ombudsmen Council must observe official secrecy to the same degree as th authority whom it has approached in the fulfilment of its tasks. The Ombudsme Council is however bound by the observation of official secrecy in its reports to th House of Representatives only in so far as this is requisite on behalf of the interes of the parties concerned or of national security.

Article 148c [Recommendations]

The Ombudsmen Council can issue to the authorities entrusted with the Federation' highest administrative business recommendations on measures to be taken in or by reaso of a particular case. The authority concerned must within a deadline to be settled b Federal law either conform to these recommendations and inform the Ombudsme Council accordingly or state in writing why the recommendations have not been com plied with.

Article 148d [Annual Report]

The Ombudsmen Council shall annually submit to the House of Representatives a repor on its activities.

Article 148e [Court Application]

On application by the Ombudsmen Council, the Constitutional Court pronounces o the illegality or otherwise of ordinances by a Federal authority.

Article 148f [Ruling on Interpretation]

If differences of opinion arise between the Ombudsmen Council and the Federa Government or a Federal Minister on the interpretation of legal provisions, th Constitutional Court, on application by the Federal Government or the Ombudsme Council, decides the matter in closed proceedings.

Article 148g [Establishment]

(1) The Ombudsmen Council has its seat in Vienna and consists of three members, on of whom acts in turn as chairman. The term of office lasts six years. Reelection o the Ombudsmen Council's members more than once is inadmissible.

(2) Ombudsmen Council members are elected by the House of Representatives on th basis of a joint recommendation drawn up by the Main Committee in the presenc of at least half its members. Each of the three parties with the largest number of vote in the House of Representatives is entitled to nominate one member for this recom mendation. The members of the Ombudsmen Council render an affirmation to th Federal President before their assumption of office.

(3) The Ombudsmen Council chairmanship rotates annually between the members ir the sequence of the voting strength possessed by the parties who have nominatec them. This sequence remains unchanged during the Ombudsmen Council's term of office.

(4) Should a Ombudsmen Council member retire prematurely, the party represented in the House of Representatives who nominated this member shall nominate a new

member. The new election shall pursuant to Paragraph (2) be operative for the remaining term of office.

(5) Ombudsmen Council members must be eligible for the House of Representatives; during their service in office, they may belong neither to the Federal Government nor to a State government nor to any popular representative body and they may not practice any other profession.

Article 148h [Appointment]

(1) Ombudsmen Council officials are appointed by the Federal President on the recommendation and with the countersignature of the Ombudsmen Council chairman. The Federal President can however authorize him to appoint officials in certain categories. Auxiliary personnel is appointed by the chairman who is to this extent the highest administrative authority and exercises these powers in his own right.

(2) The Federation's service prerogative with regard to Ombudsmen Council employees is exercised by the Ombudsmen Council chairman.

(3) The Ombudsmen Council determines its Standing Orders and an allocation of business that regulates which tasks shall be autonomously performed by its members. The adoption of the Standing Orders and the allocation of business requires the unanimous vote of the Ombudsmen Council's members.

Article 148i [State Matters]

(1) The States can by State constitutional law declare the Ombudsmen Council competent also in the sphere of the particular State's administration. In such case Articles 148e and 148f shall apply analogously.

(2) If States create agencies in the sphere of State administration with tasks similar to the Ombudsmen Council, State constitutional law can prescribe a provision corresponding to Articles 148e and 148f.

Article 148j [Ombudsmen Law]

Detailed provisions relating to the implementation of this chapter shall be made by Federal constitutional law.

Federal Law on the Austrian Ombudsman Board

[Volksanwaltschaftsgesetz/Ombudsman Board Act 1982]

Chapter I

Organization of the Ombudsman Board

Section 1

(1) Collective decisions by the Ombudsman Board require the presence of all members of the Board. Provisions in the Rules of Procedure regarding the representation of members of the Ombudsman Board in matters requiring a collective decision are admissible. Unless provided otherwise by the Constitution, decisions are taken by majority vote; abstentions are not admissible.

(2) Collective decisions by the Ombudsman Board are required for all matters reserved for collective decision-making in accordance with the Rules of Procedure or Rules of Business Allocation, including the Rules of Procedure and the Rules of Business Allocation as well as decisions on Reports to the Nationalrat (lower chamber of parliament) and appeals to the Constitutional Court pursuant to Art. 148e and 148f of the Federal Constitution (B-VG).

(3) Mutual representation of members of the Ombudsman Board in the fulfilment of matters to be handled by them independently in cases of temporary absence or on a permanent basis is regulated by the Rules of Procedure of the Ombudsman Board.

Section 2
If a member of the Ombudsman Board resigns from office before the end of his or he term, the chairperson shall immediately inform the President of the Nationalrat.

Section 3
Members of the Ombudsman Board whose opinion on the content of a Report to th Nationalrat is not shared by the majority may submit a Minority Report along wit that Report.

Section 4
(1) The Rules of Procedure may provide for regularly recurring tasks designed to facilitat the preparation of forthcoming measures to be fulfilled by the Secretariat on behal of the Board.
(2) The Rules of Procedure and the Rules of Business Allocation of the Ombudsma Board shall be published in the Federal Gazette.

Chapter II
Proceedings before the Ombudsman Board

Section 5
Proceedings before the Ombudsman Board are governed, mutatis mutandis, by section 6, 7, 10, 13, 14, 16, 18 paras. 1 and 4, 21 through 31, 45 paras. 1 and 2 as well as section 46 through 55 of the General Administrative Procedures Act (Allgemeine Verwaltungsverfahrensgestz) of 1950, Federal Gazette No. 172.

Section 6
Organs performing supreme administrative tasks of the Federal Government are oblige to follow the recommendations given to them by the Ombudsman Board within a time limit of eight weeks and to inform the Ombudsman Board accordingly or to submit a statement in writing as to why the recommendation was not followed. Upon justifie request, extensions of the above time-limit may be granted by the Ombudsman Board Appellants shall be informed of such communications.

Section 7
To the extent that applications to public authorities or agencies may be submitted in a language other than German, complaints to the Ombudsman Board are also admissibl in that language.

Section 8
If investigations are deemed necessary by the Ombudsman Board for the establishmen of facts underlying a complaint, any costs associated with them shall be borne by the Federal Government.

Section 9
Submissions to the Ombudsman Board and all other documents issued for use in proceedings before the Ombudsman Board shall be exempt from stamp duty.

Chapter III
Final provision

Section 10
The execution of this Federal law is incumbent on the Federal Chancellor and, in matters relating to section 9, the Federal Minister of Finance.

State Constitutional Act of 21 September 1988 on the Constitution of the State of Tyrol (Tyrolean State Order 1989)

Tiroler Landesordnung

Article 59 The State Ombudsman (Landesvolksanwalt)
(1) The State Ombudsman is competent to perform the functions enumerated in paragraph 2.

(2) The State Ombudsman must counsel any person or hear complaints in matters relating to the administration of the State, the intermediate administration of federal matters by the State an din matters of federal assets of which the administration has been delegated to the Governor of the State. The State Ombudsman must examine each complaint immediately and in so far as he is not able to resolve the case on the basis of the information provided by the complainant, he must ask the competent authority to provide an explanation or remedy and communicate the result of these efforts as soon as possible to the complainant. The State Ombudsman must submit an annual report of his activities to the State Diet (Landtag).

(3) The State Ombudsman is an organ of the State Diet. He reports directly to the State Diet and is only accountable to it and is independent of the State government.

(4) The State Ombudsman's office is located in Innsbruck. In so far as it is appropriate for fulfilling his functions, the State Ombudsman nay have office hours outside the State capital Innsbruck.

(5) The State Ombudsman is elected by the State Diet on the proposal of the President of the State diet for a six year term of office. Only a person possessing the necessary personal and professional skills may be appointed to the office of State Ombudsman. The State Ombudsman just not be a member of a the Federal Government, the State Government or a member of a general representative assembly.

(6) On the proposal of the President of the State Diet, the State Diet must remove the State Ombudsman from office before the end of the term pursuant to paragraph 5, first sentence, if he does not meet the requirements any more laid down in paragraph 5, second and third sentence.

(7) The State Government, after hearing the President of the State Diet, must provide the necessary non-monetary and monetary means which the State Ombudsman needs to perform his functions and must put the necessary number of state employees according to the State roster at the State Ombudsman's disposal.

(8) The State Ombudsman is the superior of the state employees in his office. He is competent to instruct them.

(9) All organs of the State and of the municipalities must support the State Ombudsman in his functions, allow him to inspect files and inform him at his request. Official secrecy cannot be invoked as against the State Ombudsman. The State Ombudsman is bound to official secrecy to the same degree as the organ which he has addressed in performing his functions.

Law on the Constitution of *Land* (State) Vorarlberg[3]

Published in the *Land* Vorarlberg Law Gazette on 31 May 1984

Article 57
Appointment and Functions of a *Landesvolksanwalt* (*Land* Commissioner for Complaints from the Public)

(1) The *Landtag* (*Land* legislature) will appoint a *Landesvolksanwalt* to advise its citizens and to investigate their complaints. The *Landesvolksanwalt* shall be independent in the exercise of his office.

(2) Anyone can seek information from the *Landesvolksanwalt* respecting the Land's administration and present proposals relating to the Land's legislation and administration.

(3) Anyone can lodge complaint with the *Landesvolksanwalt* against alleged maladminis-

[3]Translated by Charles Kessler. Terminological explanation: *Bezirkshauptmannschaft* = District Commissioner's Office; *Bund* = Federal (Government); *Bürgermeister* = Mayor; *Gemeinde* = municipality; *Land* = state; *Landesvolksanwalt* = *Land* Commissioner for Complaints from the Public; *Landtag* = *Land* Legislature; *Volksanwalt* = Commissioner for Complaints from the Public.

tration by the *Land* provided that they are affected by such maladministration and in so far as they do not or no longer have recourse to legal remedy. All such complaints must be investigated by the *Landesvolksanwalt*. The complainant shall be informed of the investigation's outcome.

(4) The *Landesvolksanwalt* is ex officio entitled to investigate suspicions on his part of maladministration by the Land.

(5) The *Landesvolksanwalt* will pass to the appropriate authorities the proposals put to him and those complaints whose investigation lies outside his competence. He may annex his observations to this communication.

(6) The *Landesvolksanwalt* will render the Landtag annually a report on his activities.

Article 58

Recommendations by the Landesvolksanwalt, Support for His Activities, Appeal to the Constitutional Court

(1) The *Landesvolksanwalt* can make recommendations to the highest authority entitled to issue instructions within the branch of the Land administration investigated by reason of a particular case. This authority must within two months meet the recommendations or show cause why they have not, or have not punctually, been fulfilled.

(2) The Constitutional court will on application by the *Landesvolksanwalt* decide on the illegality of ordinances promulgated within the Land administration

(3) If differences arise between the *Landesvolksanwalt* and the *Land* Government on the competence of the *Landesvolksanwalt* the Constitutional Court will on application by the Land Government or the *Landesvolksanwalt* decide the matter in closed proceedings.

(4) All *Bund* (Federal), land, and *Gemeinde* (municipality) authorities shall support the *Landesvolksanwalt* within the scope of their obligation to render official aid, afford him access to records, and on request give him the requisite information. The duty to observe official secrecy is inoperative in the case of the *Landesvolksanwalt*. The maintenance of official secrecy is incumbent on the *Landesvolksanwalt* to the same extent as it is on the authority whom he has approached.

Article 59

Election and Term of office of the *Landesvolksanwalt*, Incompatibilities, Place and Conduct of Business

(1) The *Landesvolksanwalt* is elected by the Landtag with a majority of three quarters of the votes cast. The term of office lasts six years. Reelection is admissible once only.

(2) If the *Landesvolksanwalt* is impeded longer than one month from the discharge of his responsibilities, the Landtag elects for the period of his impediment a deputy. If the impediment lasts longer than three months or if the appointment is continuously in abeyance, a new election will take place without delay.

(3) The *Landesvolksanwalt* must be eligible for the Landtag. During his term of office the *Landesvolksanwalt* may belong neither to the Federal Government nor to a *Land* Government nor to any popular representative body nor may he act as Burgermeister (mayor). He may likewise not practise any other profession.

(4) The *Land* will furnish the *Landesvolksanwalt* with the means requisite for his activities as well as for the necessary staff and material outlay.

Law on the *Landesvolksanwalt*

Published in the *Land* Vorarlberg Law Gazette on 31 May 1985

Article 1 – General

(1) The Landtag will appoint a *Landesvolksanwalt* to advise its citizens and to investigate their complaints. The *Landesvolksanwalt* shall be independent in the exercise of his office.

Article 2 – Tasks of the *Landesvolksanwalt*

(1) The *Landesvolksanwalt* shall advise and inform each and every inquirer on matters relating to the Land administration. He can likewise extend advice to the community at large on matters relating to the Land administration.

(2) The *Landesvolksanwalt* shall investigate complaints about alleged maladministration by the *Land* if the complainant is affected by the alleged maladministration and in so far as he does not or no longer has recourse to legal remedy.

(3) The *Landesvolksanwalt* may ex officio investigate suspicions on his part of maladministration by the Land.

(4) The *Landesvolksanwalt* shall receive proposals relating to the Land's legislation and administration.

(5) Within the meaning of this provision the Land's administration includes

(a) all administrative matters within the Land's autonomous sphere of competence inclusive of the Land's activities as holder of civil rights exercised by Land authorities or other legal persons on the Land's behalf,

(b) matters relating to Gemeinde's own sphere of competence in so far as this comprises matters pertaining to the Land's sphere of execution and Gemeinde's activities as holders of civil rights.

Article 3 – Procedure

(1) Procedure before the *Landesvolksanwalt* shall be as simple as possible for the individuals seeking advice and for complainants.

(2) On the grounds of a procedure to investigate maladministration the *Landesvolksanwalt* can make recommendations to the highest authority entitled to issue instructions within the branch of the Land's administration investigated as to how the established maladministration can as far as possible be now and in future obviated. This authority must meet the recommendations of the *Landesvolksanwalt* as quickly as possible, at the most however within two months, and inform the *Landesvolksanwalt* accordingly or state in writing why they have not, or not within this deadline, been met. The *Land* Government shall be notified of recommendations made to Gemeinde authorities.

(3) In the procedure for the investigation of maladministration initiated on account of complaints the *Landesvolksanwalt* shall, in so far as preponderant objections of public or private interest do not stand in the way, inform the complainants of the investigatory procedure's result and the measures taken to meet the particular case.

(4) The *Landesvolksanwalt* shall refer complaints whose investigation is not within his competence to the competent analogous Federal or other *Land* agency.

(5) The *Landesvolksanwalt* shall refer to the Landtag the proposals relating to *Land* legislation put to him. Proposals relating to the administration in cases falling under Art. 2 para. 5 (a) shall be transmitted to the *Land* Government, in cases falling under Art. 2 para. 5(b) to the *Gemeinde* head concerned.

(6) Arts. 7, 10, 13, 14, 16, 18 paras. 1 and 4, 21, 22, 45 paras. 1 and 2, as well as Arts. 46 to 55 of the General Administrative Procedure Law shall be analogously applied in the procedure before the *Landesvolksanwalt*.

Article 4 – Office Days

The *Landesvolksanwalt* is bound in case of need to hold office days also outside his official place of business. In this connection he shall as far as possible have regard for an impartial treatment for all regions of the Land.

Article 5 – Imposts and Fees Immunity

Official acts by the *Landesvolksanwalt* are free of land administrative imposts. Applications to the *Landesvolksanwalt* and all other documents issued for use in proceedings before the *Landesvolksanwalt* are freed from stamp duties.

Article 6 – Reports by the *Landesvolksanwalt*

(1) The *Landesvolksanwalt* shall render the Landtag annually a report on his activities The annual report shall be transmitted to the *Land* Government simultaneously wit its presentation to the Landtag.

(2) The *Landesvolksanwalt* shall at four-monthly intervals report in writing or orally t the Volksanwalt Committee of the Landtag on the complaints submitted to him an on the results of the investigatory procedure implemented by him.

(3) The *Landesvolksanwalt* is entitled to, and on demand must, attend in an advisor capacity sessions of the Landtag and of the Volksanwalt committee whe *Landesvolksanwalt* reports are under discussion. He shall on request furnish th Landtag and the Volksanwalt Committee with all the information requisite to dealin with his reports.

(4) Whoever publishes the annual report of the *Landesvolksanwalt* or parts thereof prio to the report having undergone a reading by the Landtag commits an offence. An this notwithstanding that he has acted in another Federal *Land* or abroad. He sha be sentenced by the Bezirkshauptmannschaft (District Commissioner's Office) to fine of up to 30.000 schillings.

Article 6a – Public Announcement, Interview With Candidates

[Amendment to the Law on the *Landesvolksanwalt*, published in the *Land* Vorarlber Law Gazette 10 March 1987.]

The election of the *Landesvolksanwalt* shall be preceded by a public announcement i the Land Vorarlberg Law Gazette and in the dailies whose place of publication is situate in Vorarlberg. An interview with the candidates proposed for election to the office o *Landesvolksanwalt* shall moreover be held before the election in the Volksanwal Committee.

Article 7 – Office of the *Landesvolksanwalt*

(1) The *Landesvolksanwalt* shall establish an office at his official place of business. H shall appoint the staff necessary for the fulfilment of his duties and shall see to th appropriate equipment of the office.

(2) The *Landesvolksanwalt* has authority to make rules for, and to issue instructions to the office staff.

(3) The office staff shall perform the preliminary tasks and other forms of assistanc allotted to them by the *Landesvolksanwalt*. The performance in his name of officia acts of minor importance can be entrusted by the *Landesvolksanwalt* to staff members Such committal must be put in writing. The head of the office shall in case of bia deputize for the *Landesvolksanwalt*.

Article 8 – Budget Matters

(1) The expenditure on staff and equipment incurred by the work of the *Landesvolksanwal* shall be borne by the Land.

(2) The *Landesvolksanwalt* shall draw up annually a budget estimate confined to hi sphere of activity and shall transmit this to the Land Government for it to be take into account in the preparation of the Land budget estimate. Similarly th *Landesvolksanwalt* shall submit to the Land Government for inclusion in its fina budget account a statement on the actual expenditure.

(3) The *Landesvolksanwalt* is empowered to dispose over the incoming and outgoin earmarked for his sphere of activity by the *Land* budget estimate. Excepted therefron are the matters prescribed in Article 9.

Article 9 – Emoluments

The *Landesvolksanwalt* has claim to emoluments, miscellaneous fees, and retiremen allowances. His surviving dependants have claim to pension benefits. The claims ar determined by analogous application of Chapters II and III of the *Land* Emolument Law with

a) emoluments to the *Landesvolksanwalt* being based on a rate of one hundred and twenty per cent of the current salary of a Land civil servant in service grade IX, salary bracket 2, plus any special allowances and cost of living bonuses (Art. 18, para. 2 of the *Land* Emoluments Law),
b) the provision of Art. 22 of the *Land* Emoluments Law, also inclusive of employees (recipients of a retirement and pension benefit) of a public law corporation and such endowment, insti tution or fund whose employment regulations as regards legislation fall within *Land* competence, being applied,
c) the retirement allowance being due only after a service of six years (Art. 24, para. 1, Arts. 25 and 26 or the *Land* Emoluments Law) and – apart from instances of an earlier occurrence of service or professional incapacity – at the earliest becoming payable at the age of sixty (Art. 28 of the *Land* Emoluments Law).

The Parliamentry Ombudsman in Belgium: Strengthening Democracy

Pierre-Yves Monette*

Introduction

How could we fail to rejoice to see the federal and democratic Republic of Ethiopia, a country that has chosen the path of democracy, willing to establish an institution for the protection of human rights and an office of ombudsman by taking advantage of the lessons learned.

I salute the wisdom of those who have been at the origin of the international conference on international experiences in the matter of institutions for the protection of human rights and the office of ombudsman, which I hope will permit Ethiopia in the future to avoid the mistakes that are sometimes made during the setting up of an effective, independent office of ombudsman.

When it comes to the concept of ombudsman, it is difficult not to repeat what has already been said or not to say what will be said by others. Nonetheless, as the youngest national parliamentary ombudsman in the world, let me share with you my approach, enthusiastic but also without concession as to what must be the role, the means of action and the independence of a parliamentary ombudsman.[1] Let us take note of three preliminary remarks.

First of all, the recent development of the function of ombudsman and the 'ombudsmania' that followed has in fact shown the confusion that often exists between the function of ombudsman and that of a complaint department within the Civil Service, a marketing department meant for consumers or other information departments in touch with the customers of public utilities. The role of the parliamentary ombudsman is indeed unique in a democratic State and it would be a pity to confuse it with others and to change its nature.[2]

Secondly, it is fortunately a long time since the countries in Europe have tried

---

* Federal Ombudsman of Belgium; Honorary Private Assistant to H.M. the King of the Belgians.

1 The generic name "parliamentary ombudsman" is only used in parliamentary regimes (Belgium, Scandinavian countries, Spain, Netherlands, New Zealand, etc.), where the Parliament controls the Government. In the presidential democracies (France, Russia, United States, many African democracies, etc.), the ombudsman is not a parliamentary institution. One then refers to the "(national) ombudsman".

2 On the definition of mediation and the distinctions between the various types of ombudsman, see Pierre-Yves Monette, *Mediation, considered as a dispute resolution process, and its various applications (in French: De la médiation, comme mode de règlement des conflits, et de ses différentes applications)*, Brussels, to be published, 1999.

K. Hossain et al. (eds), Human Rights Commissions and Ombudsman Offices, 269–287.

to impose their concept of democracy. The Office of the Federal Ombudsmen of Belgium cannot be simply transferred from Belgium to Ethiopia. Moreover one ombudsman is not the same as another. Nonetheless, all the ombudsmen must fulfil certain specific criteria.

Without any doubt, I admit that the ideal ombudsman does not exist, or at least not yet, and I would not dare to think that the Office of the federal ombudsmen of Belgium is a perfect model. It will thus be with a humble heart that I shall illustrate both its strengths and its weaknesses.

Finally, this paper relates to the office of the ombudsman and not the institution for the protection of human rights. Indeed, although there is a tendency in some countries to distinguish the office of ombudsman from that of protector of human rights, such a distinction is not made in Western European countries since the parliamentary ombudsman is not only a tool for seeking conciliation between citizens and public authorities and controlling proper administration but also a tool for controlling proper compliance with human rights by these authorities.

Ethiopia's constitution[4] has provided for the separate creation of a human rights commission and of an office of ombudsman. By so doing, Ethiopia has chosen to distinguish these two institutions although this distinction is not really indispensable. The single creation of an office of ombudsman which would be competent in the matters of both conciliation/proper administration and human rights protection, is perfectly conceivable.[5] In Europe, we consider that such an office is even more effective: chopping up and dividing an institution for the protection of citizens always entails the weakening of such institution rather than its strengthening.

The Different Roles of the Parliamentary Ombudsman in Belgium

In Belgium as in other democracies, one cannot speak of a single role, but rather of the roles of the parliamentary ombudsman.[6] There are indeed four of them a mediation role; a role as external controller; a reporting role; a moral role.

[3] Official name of the parliamentary ombudsman in Belgium, at federal level, as created by "the Federal Ombudsmen Act" of March 22, 1995, attached to the present article. Two of the five State members of Belgium also have their parliamentary ombudsman: the Walloon Region (since 1994 and the Flemish Region/Community (since 1998). The Brussels Region, the French Community and the German Community do not.

[4] Ethiopian Constitution, Article 55, paragraphs 14 and 15.

[5] On the role of the parliamentary ombudsman in the matters of human rights protection, see Fernando Alvarez de Miranda y Torres, parliamentary ombudsman of Spain, Human rights and their function in the institutional strengthening of the ombudsman, in: The International Ombudsman Yearbook, Volume 2–1998, Kluwer Law International, The Hague/Boston/London, 1999 pp. 146–158. See also Daniel Jacoby, parliamentary ombudsman of Quebec, The world-wide development of the 'ombudsmediator' (in French: Le développement de 'l'ombudsmédiateur' à l'échelle mondiale), Symposium "What future for ombudsmanship", organized for the 25th anniversary of the national ombudsman of France, Paris, February 5–6, 1998, in: Le médiateur de la République Paris, 1998, pp. 64–67. See finally Jacob Söderman, parliamentary ombudsman of the European Union, The European ombudsman and Human Rights, Symposium "European Union and Human Rights: towards an agenda for the year 2000", European University Institute on the occasion of the 50th anniversary of the adoption of the universal declaration of Human Rights, October 9–10 Vienna 1998, Office the ombudsman of the European Union, Strasbourg, 1998.

[6] The parliamentary ombudsman of Belgium referred to in this paper is the one at the federal level.

1. *Mediation Role Between Citizens and Public Authorities*

[T]he role played by the Belgian ombudsman in mediation,[7] as is the case with [a]ll his colleagues around the world, is the best known. His role is to try to [r]econcile the points of view of a citizen and an administration who are on [o]pposite sides of a dispute. Like the French word indicates, the "médiateur" [(]mediator) tries to mediate. Hence, he is not a judge or referee who settles [a] dispute.

To make things clear, the task of the parliamentary ombudsman in Belgium [h]as to be distinguished from that of a judge:

- the filing process with the parliamentary ombudsman is not formalist, whilst submitting a case to a judge is much more so;[8]
- the mediation process of the parliamentary ombudsman is completely free of charge, whilst proceedings before a judge can turn out to be very costly;
- the mediation process is a non-legal process, whilst proceedings before a judge are legal proceedings;[9]
- the parliamentary ombudsman can only make a recommendation to the administration, whilst a decision by a judge is enforceable and binding for the parties;
- there are three criteria on which the Belgian parliamentary ombudsman bases his recommendation in Belgium: the respect for legality, the respect for principles of proper administration (or principles of good governance) and finally, in some extreme situations, the respect for the principle of equity. The criterion on which the judge makes his decision or his decree is only the criterion of legality: "has the law been respected or not?";
- a mediation process is swift whilst many countries like Belgium often suffer from a large judicial backlog;
- finally, the parliamentary ombudsman in Belgium, as its name indicates, operates within the framework of the legislative Power, whilst the judge by nature comes under the Judiciary.

[O]ne important question is whether the intervention of the parliamentary [o]mbudsman and that of the judge are or not exclusive of one another. Belgium [c]hose to exclude the intervention of the ombudsman when judicial proceedings [a]re pending. France, as many other countries, made a different choice. The latter [s]eems to be a better one because it is not rare to see how opportune a mediation

---

[7] The concept of mediation is frequently used to describe the conciliation role of the parliamentary [o]mbudsman, reason why in many French speaking countries (Algeria, Belgium, Burkina Faso, [F]rance, Guinea, Mauritania, Senegal, etc.) the ombudsman is referred to as "le médiateur" or the [m]ediator, although this name unfortunately gives a false idea of the different functions of the [p]arliamentary ombudsman by reducing them to that of conciliation only. Regarding this point, see [O]ffice of the federal ombudsmen, *Annual Report*, Brussels, 1997, pp. 12 and 61.

[8] About the importance of the general flexibility which characterizes the framework and working [m]ethods of parliamentary ombudsman institutions and distinguishes them from the courts and other [q]uasi-judicial bodies, see Hans Gammeltoft-hansen, parliamentary ombudsman of Denmark, *The [O]mbudsman as a non-traditional tool for citizen participation*, in "The International Ombudsman [Y]earbook/Volume 2 – 1998", op. cit., pp. 189–197.

[9] The semantic difference between "process" (as far as the ombudsman is concerned) and "proceed[i]ngs" (as far as the judge is concerned) is particularly relevant.

process turns out to be for a citizen and a Civil Service department who are already in court.[10]

After these distinctions between the parliamentary ombudsman and the judge and in order to create a better understanding of the mediation role of the parliamentary ombudsman in Belgium, the five following questions will be approached: who may call upon the Belgian parliamentary ombudsman? Which are the authorities concerned by the claims he examines? Which acts can be concerned by claims laid before him? Which conditions have to be complied with in order to make a valid request to him? And finally, what are the grievances that can be formulated on the occasion of a complaint laid before him?

Who may call upon the parliamentary ombudsman in Belgium?

In Belgium, the parliamentary ombudsman may be approached as well by a natural person as by a legal entity (company, association, etc.), both national or foreign, whether living – or having his registered office – in the Kingdom of Belgium or not.[11]

In most countries, but not yet in Belgium, the ombudsman can deal with a matter on his own initiative and thus analyse the malfunction without any formal complaint being made. On the other hand, few countries, and here Belgium is the exception, have empowered their parliamentary ombudsman to be competent regarding a complaint by a civil servant against his own administration.[12]

Which are the authorities concerned by claims examined by the parliamentary ombudsman of Belgium?

Here one sees many differences between the various parliamentary ombudsmen. In federal States,[13] the national ombudsman – also called federal ombudsman – can only be competent with regard to claims concerning the federal State and not the federated authorities (State members).

Often, the national ombudsman is also competent, even in a federal State, to handle complaints elated to local authorities (provinces, municipalities, local bodies, etc.), but this is not the case in Belgium.[14]

---

[10] On the impossibility in Belgium to launch a mediation process when legal proceedings are pending, see Office of the federal ombudsmen, Annual Report, Brussels, 1997, pp. 21–23 and 62.

[11] The interest requested in order to be allowed to put a matter before the parliamentary ombudsman in Belgium has been deliberately widened by the Parliament: unlike the interest requested in legal proceedings, there is no need for a legal interest to refer a complaint to the parliamentary ombudsman. As one can see, here is another major difference between the rules of the mediation process and those of legal proceedings.

[12] In his answer to the standing Committee of the Senate for home Affairs and Civil Services on the reasons for this quite unique characteristic of the Belgian Parliamentary Ombudsman Act, the Vice Prime minister and minister for Home Affairs explained that the small number of possibilities of appeal existing for the Belgian civil servants confronted with problems with their hierarchy compared with those in the neighbouring countries was one element that justified the right for them to lay a complaint before the parliamentary ombudsman (see Belgian Senate, *preparatory works*, session 1994–1995, 1284–2, pp. 7–8). So far, 5% of the complaints referred to the parliamentary ombudsman originate from civil servants.

[13] Like Ethiopia, Belgium is a federal State since the adoption in 1993 of Article 1 of the new Constitution of the Kingdom of Belgium, attached to the present article.

[14] The parliamentary ombudsman has recommended to the Parliament to adopt the Dutch system. There, the municipalities have indeed the choice between organizing their own local parliamentary

In Belgium, the parliamentary ombudsman is competent to deal with complaints concerning the 'federal administrative authorities'. Those are: the members of the federal Government,[15] the federal Ministries,[16] federal governmental agencies,[17] Belgian diplomatic and consular posts, scientific and cultural federal institutions and certain State Bodies (inter alia the armed Forces, the national Police, the civil and military information agencies). Belgium has, however, provided for two exceptions: there are indeed federal administrative authorities with regard to which the parliamentary ombudsman is not competent.

On the one hand, these are the appellate bodies of the executive Power (administrative appeals tribunals). On the other hand, there are various federal administrative authorities which have their own (non parliamentary) ombudsman.[18] In this latter case, it is to be noted that, as inspired by the examples of Portugal and South Africa for instance, Belgium considers making the parliamentary ombudsman competent on a second (appeal) level in the event that a company or other administrative ombudsman – i.e. not a parliamentary one – intervenes initially without solving the problem satisfactorily.[19]

Besides the Executive Power, the parliamentary ombudsmen are sometimes competent to handle claims concerning the activities of the Judicial Power.[20] Due to the principle of the separation of Powers in a democracy, it should be underlined at this stage that the parliamentary ombudsman is never competent to hear complaints regarding judgments or judicial decrees, but only the claims

---

ombudsman (where the size of the municipality allows it), extending voluntarily the competence of the parliamentary national ombudsman for complaints concerning local governments or not organizing any right of parliamentary mediation for their people at local level: see Office of the federal ombudsmen, *Annual Report*, Brussels, 1997, pp. 26–28 and 67 and 1998, pp. 12 and 50.

[15] There are a maximum of 15 ministers, the Prime minister included, and possibly an undefined number of secretaries of State (2 in the current Government) according to the Belgian constitution, Article 99.

[16] The twelve federal Ministries in Belgium are the Chancellery of the Prime minister (in other words his administration, not his office), the Ministry for civil servants' matters, the Ministry of Justice, the Ministry for Home Affairs, the Ministry for Foreign Affairs, Foreign trade and Co-operation, the Ministry of Defence, the Ministry for Employment, the Ministry for Social Affairs, Public Health and Environment, the Ministry for Middle Classes and Agriculture, the Ministry for Economic Affairs and the Ministry of Communications and Infrastructure.

[17] There are more than 100 governmental agencies on the federal level in Belgium. The most important are the ones dealing with social security.

[18] There are three federal administrative authorities having developed their own company ombudsman: The Railways, the postal Service and the Public Telecommunications company. About the differences between such a company ombudsman and a parliamentary ombudsman, see Pierre-Yves Monette, op. cit.; See also Herman Wuyts, the other federal parliamentary ombudsman of Belgium, *The Ombudsman in prospect (in Dutch, De Ombudsman in perspectief)*, Tijdschrift voor Bestuurswetenschappen en publiekrecht, Brussels, June 1999; See finally Sir Brian Elwood, Chief parliamentary ombudsman of New Zealand, *How to harmonise general ombudsman activities with those related to specialised ombudsmen*, in "The International Ombudsman Yearbook/Volume 2 – 1998", op. cit., pp. 198–206.

[19] On this issue, see Office of the federal ombudsmen, *Annual Report*, Brussels, 1997, pp. 16–17 and 61 and 1998, pp. 11–12 and 48.

[20] On the competence of the parliamentary ombudsman to examine administrative decisions of the Judicial Power, see Claes Eklundh, Chief parliamentary ombudsman of Sweden, *The ombudsman specialised in judicial matters*, in "The International Ombudsman Yearbook/Volume 2 – 1998", op. cit., pp. 180–188; See also Jacob Söderman, The Ombudsman and the Judiciary, on the occasion of the symposium "The 10th anniversary of the parliamentary ombudsman of the Netherlands", organized on January 29th, 1992, in The Hague, Ed. Office of the Parliamentary Ombudsman, Helsinki (Mr. Söderman was at that time parliamentary ombudsman of Finland), 1992.

concerning the way in which justice was carried out (judicial backlog, denial of justice, partiality of the judge, behaviour of the judge at the hearing, etc.). In Belgium however, unlike Finland, Sweden or Spain for instance, the parliamentary ombudsman is not competent with regard to such administrative decisions of the courts.[21]

Which acts can be concerned by claims laid before the Belgian parliamentary ombudsman? What sort of activities can be targeted by the complaints filed with him?

The acts regarding which a complaint can be lodged with the parliamentary ombudsman are administrative acts. We have just seen that in Belgium, the parliamentary ombudsman is not competent to hear complaints concerning judicial decisions, be these in administrative (i.e. relating to the executive Power) or in civil and criminal cases. Likewise, the parliamentary ombudsman must always declare himself incompetent when the complaint concerns a political decision of the Executive Power. In fact, the parliamentary ombudsman is the protector or the guarantor of proper administration and proper application of the law by the administration. He is in no way the judge of the opportunities of one political choice over another. This is exclusively the role of the House of Representatives, amongst the essential tasks of which, is that of exercising political control on the Government.[22]

One sees very quickly that distinctions between an administrative act and an act of a political nature are not always well understood by the citizens who turn to the parliamentary ombudsman and this is why it is his duty to explain those to them.

Should the parliamentary ombudsman handle complaints concerning political acts, he would commit himself on a political level and would lose his neutrality, his impartiality and his independence which are absolutely essential to the correct exercise of the function of the parliamentary ombudsman, in Belgium as in all true democracies.

Which conditions have to be complied with in order to make a valid request to the parliamentary ombudsman in Belgium?

In order to avoid submerging his office with work and also to make the citizens aware of their responsibilities, complaints to the parliamentary ombudsman can be declared admissible provided that:

- the claimant has previously approached the administration concerned with a view to settling the dispute. However, unlike in many countries, in Belgium it is not required that the claimant must have applied all available administrative or judicial means in order to be allowed to file a claim with the parliamentary ombudsman.
- the claim concerns events that occurred within the last twelve month period. Claims regarding events that occurred earlier than this may be dealt with,

[21] In 1998, article 151 of the Belgian Constitution has been modified in order to create the High Council of Justice, a half external controlling organ with a mediation competence that will be authorized to receive complaints concerning administrative decisions of the Belgian judicial courts.
[22] Belgian Constitution, Article 46.

however, provided that the claimant has continually made efforts to satisfy the claim on his/her own with the administration concerned.

What are the grievances that can be formulated on the occasion of a complaint laid before the parliamentary ombudsman? Which activities can he examine?

As mentioned above, the Belgian parliamentary ombudsman is competent to analyse whether the law, the constitution or the treaties have been correctly complied with (control of legality). It follows that the parliamentary ombudsman is also competent to verify the application of the European and international agreements on human rights.[23]

Moreover, the Belgian ombudsman is competent to verify whether the criteria of proper administration have been complied with (control of proper administration).

There are several criteria of proper administration. Let us examine six of them:

- did the administration duly justify its decisions?
- did the administration not abuse its power by using it for purposes other that those for which it was granted?
- did the administration not infringe the principle of legal certainty, indispensable in a State founded on the rule of law or, in other words, did it not deceive the legitimate confidence that each citizen is entitled to have in the Civil Service?
- was the administration impartial and did it treat the citizen as equal to the other citizens?
- was the administration reasonable in the application of the law or, in other words, was the advantage gained by the Civil Service by its application of the law commensurate to the possible disadvantage caused to the citizen concerned by the decision?
- finally, did the administration handle the case in a conscientious manner (proper reception, reasonable delay in answering, respect of the right of defence, etc.)?

Besides his competence to control legality and proper administration, the parliamentary ombudsman in Belgium is also competent to allow the Civil Service department to take equity into consideration in its decisions. The principle of equity goes further than the principle of reasonableness.[24]

Although the principle of equity is known in the countries that are based on Equity Law, it is rather new for the countries that have a judicial system inspired by continental law and more precisely by the Napoleonic code. In these countries, equity hardly occurs except with regard to the function of the parliamentary ombudsman.

By nature, the parliamentary ombudsman is empowered to advise the administration, even when the latter has perfectly respected both the legality and the

---

[23] See note 6.

[24] On the use of the principle of equity by the parliamentary ombudsman, see Pierre-Yves Monette, *The intervention in equity of the parliamentary ombudsman (in French: L'intervention de l'ombudsman parlementaire en équité)*, on the occasion of the symposium "The mediation and the rule of law", organized on October 2nd, 1998, in Sofia, Ed. de l'Agence de la Francophonie, Paris, to be published; See also Paul Legatte, national ombudsman of France, *The principle of equity (in French: Le principe d'équité)*, Presses de la Renaissance, Paris, 1992.

principles of proper administration, to modify its decision to attain a more equitable result, and if need be to apply the law in a more flexible manner in order to take into consideration the particular interests of an individual. However, to avoid an arbitrary decision, only the parliamentary ombudsman can make "recommendations based on equity" to the Civil Service, to the exclusion of all other State institutions. In addition, the ombudsman exercises the utmost restraint in making such recommendations.[25]

2. *The Exercise of External Control by the Parliamentary Ombudsman*

As explained, the parliamentary ombudsman is not only competent to control the legality of the Civil Service's acts. He also ensures that the criteria of proper administration are complied with. However, he is not part of the administration as such, quite the contrary. This is why the parliamentary ombudsman is a control body external to the Civil Service. The parliamentary ombudsman is thus a valuable tool for analysing malfunctions within the Executive Power and possibly within the Judiciary.

If this role of external controller sometimes makes him feared by the Civil Service departments, it is important to underline that the parliamentary ombudsman is not a censor who makes use of the carrot and the stick vis-aÁ-vis the administration. In many cases, he is in fact an objective ally of the administration which is extremely interested in receiving constructive criticism from an external body. On the basis of observations he has made, he is able to advise it on different ways to improve its functioning. This is how the parliamentary ombudsman and the administration often collaborate for the purpose of improving public services.

So, if the first task of the parliamentary ombudsman – the mediation function – allows him to play the role of a privileged intermediary between the citizen and the apparatus of the State by guaranteeing better harmony and good mutual understanding, his second task – the performance of external control – allows him, within the State apparatus, to bring together the Civil Service departments and the political power, as well inside the Government as inside the Parliament. Indeed, it is not unusual for the parliamentary ombudsman to reveal to the political power the needs of the Civil Service which the latter had already tried to put forward to them, but in vain. This is how the parliamentary ombudsman can be as much a defender of the citizen as a defender of the administration, which he can actually help to become more efficient.

Moreover, it is vital to make this aspect of things well understood by the civil servants as well as by the staff of the parliamentary ombudsman itself, in order to avoid any harmful confrontation.

3. *The reporting function of the parliamentary ombudsman*

If the parliamentary ombudsman has been created in Belgium to assist the citizens (mediation function) and to help the administration to improve itself (external control function), its function is also to assist the federal Parliament in

[25] On the very strict criteria to be respected by the parliamentary ombudsman to call for equity, see Office of the federal ombudsmen, The office of the federal ombudsmen and equity, in: Annual report, Brussels, 1998, pp. 13–21.

performing its two essential missions: the legislative mission and the mission of political control of the federal Government.[26]

According to the Scandinavian tradition, the Belgian parliamentary ombudsman is thus a collateral body of the Parliament in the sense that he assists the latter in better carrying out its control on the federal Government by informing the Chamber of Representatives of malfunctions within the Civil Service. Thanks to this kind of information, the federal Parliament can then put a question to the federal Government or sanction the ministers or those in charge of the Civil Service departments or federal government agencies whose failures have been reported.

The parliamentary ombudsman also helps the federal Parliament to perform its legislative mission by suggesting to it the legislative measures or amendments to the law that he feels appropriate in order to correct the reported malfunctions. This does not mean that the parliamentary ombudsman is empowered to draw up bills, but that he does have the power to advise Parliament to take legislative initiatives in the direction he recommends. The Parliament remains of course totally free to follow these recommendations or not. In this respect it is interesting to note that in Finland, in order to reinforce the parliamentary status of the ombudsman, the latter even has a special seat in Parliament which allows him to take the floor and to comment his recommendations directly in front of the MPs.[27]

4. *The Moral Cole of the Parliamentary Ombudsman*

From these first three roles of the parliamentary ombudsman in the functioning of the State, a fourth one emerges: a moral role. In each country where there is a parliamentary ombudsman, the latter ought to fulfil what one calls a "high magistrate's office of influence".[28] It is indeed so that he has no decision-making power, but only a power of recommendation and of persuasion which are directly dependent on his credibility. This credibility is itself dependent on both his absolute political neutrality[29] and on his complete impartiality. In many countries around the world, these different elements often make the parliamentary ombudsman a genuine moral authority, a valuable defender of the best possible functioning of democracy.

The means allocated to the parliamentary ombudsman in Belgium for the accomplishment of his above missions

The powers of the parliamentary ombudsman in Belgium are threefold: he has powers of investigation, powers of injunction and powers of recommendation.

[26] The Ethiopian Parliament has the two same missions: see the Ethiopian constitution, Article 55, paragraphs 1 (legislative mission), 10, 17 and 18 (mission of political control).

[27] As all other parliamentary ombudsmen, he only has a power of recommendation and not of decision-making, the reason why he is only authorized to advise, not to vote on laws.

[28] The expression is of André Molitor, Honorary Private Secretary to H.M. King Baudouin I of the Belgians, *The royal function in Belgium (in French: La fonction royale en Belgique)*, Ed. CRISP, Brussels, 1994.

[29] The neutrality of the parliamentary ombudsman makes it impossible for him to have any elective mandate at the same time. Let us note the unique situation of the French national ombudsman who can at the same time be national ombudsman and elected mayor, although he is competent to receive complaint against his own local administration and that a political election does not of course guarantee his total neutrality.

Like any parliamentary ombudsman in the world – this is essential to understand his function and the philosophy of his intervention – he has no power of sanction, reason why one says that the parliamentary ombudsman can bark but not bite.[30]

1. *The Powers of Investigation*

The Belgian parliamentary ombudsman has the right to receive any and all documents, even those classified State secret. He has the right to enter the premises of all Civil Services departments (Ministries, Embassies, Prisons, etc.). He also has the right to call before him any civil servant, to require the assistance of experts and to be delivered any information he thinks fit within the context of his investigation and, last but not least, to release anyone (civil servant, medical doctor, lawyer etc.) of his obligation of professional secrecy.[31]

2. *The Powers of Injunction*

In Belgium, the parliamentary ombudsman may impose on civil servants deadlines for answering, within which they must deliver the information requested by him within the framework of his investigation.

Although the parliamentary ombudsman is not authorized to start disciplinary proceedings against a civil servant who does not co-operate, he does nevertheless have the authority to suggest to the hierarchy of the civil servant concerned that disciplinary proceedings should be started against him.

3. *The powers of recommendation*

The power of recommendation of the Belgian parliamentary ombudsman is crucial. He effectively has the authority to make recommendations to the Parliament, to the Government or to the administration.

- To the Parliament: as explained, it is part of the parliamentary ombudsman's task to report to the federal Parliament. It should be pointed out that in Belgium, the ombudsman also has the right to be heard at his own request by the federal Parliament.
- With regard to the Government: the parliamentary ombudsman is authorized to recommend to the federal Government or one of its members to take measures in order to improve the functioning of the Civil Service and/or to develop proper administration.
- Finally, with regard to the Administration: the parliamentary ombudsman is empowered to recommend to the federal Civil Service departments to review their decisions when he considers these as not conforming to the law, the principles of proper administration or the principle of equity.

Besides these powers of investigation, injunction and recommendation, the parliamentary ombudsman has another fundamental power: he may contact the press when he considers that making his recommendations public would increase their impact.

---

[30] Dr Donald C. Rowat, *The Ombudsman. Citizen's Defender*, University of Toronto Press, 1965, p. 7.
[31] The Federal Ombudsmen Act, Article 11, paragraph 3.

In true democracies, along with the Legislative, Executive and Judicial Powers, a free and independent press constitutes what one calls the "fourth power". The link between the parliamentary ombudsman and this fourth power is therefore very natural in Belgium, as it is around the world.[32]

The Independence of the Belgian Parliamentary Ombudsman

An ombudsman cannot exist without true independence. This word is often overused and one must understand the term here in its broadest meaning. As such, the independence of the parliamentary ombudsman must also be viewed as statutory, organic, financial, functional, political, intellectual and organizational.

1. *Statutory Independence*

To protect the function of the parliamentary ombudsman and even guarantee the permanency of this institution, it is indispensable to recognize this in the Constitution.[33] That is, to lay down in the constitution – and not only in a law – what his mission and means of action are, or even what financial means are allocated to him for the accomplishment of his missions.

This is not yet the case in Belgium but the parliamentary ombudsman has recommended to the federal Parliament to recognize in the Belgian constitution both the right to parliamentary mediation on federal level and the Office of the Federal Ombudsmen.[34] In the current situation, this Office is created by law.[35] Besides Belgium, among the 22 out of 41 members States of the Council of Europe that have an office of ombudsman on national level and a written constitution, only Cyprus, France, Iceland and Ireland have not included such recognition in the constitution.[36,37]

The place of the ombudsman within the structure of a democratic state can vary. Either the ombudsman does not come under any of the three Powers (Legislative, Executive or Judicial) and is located just outside or beyond them,[38] or – and this is the case in Belgium – the ombudsman comes under the Legislative Power and is thus called parliamentary ombudsman.[39] In any case, the ombudsman cannot come under the Executive Power. Indeed, he would then effectively

---

[32]On this issue, see Miguel Madilla, *The ombudsman and the Mass Media*, in "The International Ombudsman Yearbook – 1995", Kluwer Law International, The Hague/Boston/London, 1996.

[33]Ethiopian constitution, Article 55, paragraph 15.

[34]On this issue, see Office of the Federal Ombudsmen, *Annual Report*, Brussels, 1997, pp. 14–15 and 61 and 1998, p. 10 and 48.

[35]See note 4.

[36]*Legal and comparative note concerning the inclusion of the Office of the Federal Ombudsmen in the constitution (in French: Note juridique et comparative concernant la constitutionnalisation du Collège des médiateurs fédéraux)*, Ed. Office of the Federal Ombudsmen, Brussels, 1997.

[37]As in Belgium, the idea of recognising 'Le médiateur de la République' in the constitution is also officially pursued in France, specially since the symposium of February 1998 organized for the 25th anniversary of this institution; On this issue, see Jacques Pelletier, national ombudsman of France, "What future for ombudsmanship", op cit.

[38]This is the case in France for example.

[39]See note 2.

be 'judge in his own case', as he would be depending on the power that he is deemed to control, and his independence would therefore not be effective.

2. *Organic Independence*

Although the parliamentary ombudsman falls within the sphere of the Legislative Power, he does however not depend on the Parliament. The organic independence of the parliamentary ombudsman, indeed, requires that he depends on no one.[40] He does report however – but in a completely independent manner – to the Parliament, the Government, the people[41] and the press.[42]

Let us be quite clear about this: the parliamentary ombudsman does not have to justify his activities to the Parliament or to the Government, as this would be contrary to his independence; he informs and if necessary makes recommendations to the Parliament,[43] to the Government and/or its Civil Service departments.[44] That is very different.

The most appropriate ways to do so are the drafting of his annual and quarterly reports and when appropriate his hearings by the House.

This complete organic independence obviously raises the question of possible abuse by the parliamentary ombudsman of his independence and of the sanctions that should be applied in such a case. Indeed, the parliamentary ombudsman is not above the law and his independence does not allow him to do everything. Therefore, one must be allowed to take possible impeachment proceedings against him in case of serious infringements. These proceedings must however be very detailed and organized by law to avoid all arbitrary actions. However, such a statute has not yet been adopted in Belgium.[45]

Let us note that an effective punishment of a parliamentary ombudsman abusing his independence would consist in the non-following of his recommendations and, of course, the non-renewal of his term of office.

3. *Financial Independence*

Without financial autonomy, the parliamentary ombudsman would not be really independent. This is why in Belgium, his budget[46] is not drawn either from the parliamentary budget or from that of the Government, but is totally independent of them.[47] Likewise, his budget is not endorsed, neither a priori or a posteriori by the State Audit office. In addition, and even if this is not the case in Belgium, the financial autonomy of the parliamentary ombudsman should be guaranteed by the mention of the allocated and index-linked amount in the constitution.

---

[40]The Federal Ombudsman Act, Article 7, paragraph 1.

[41]On this issue, see Kevin Murphy, Parliamentary ombudsman of Ireland, Accountability to the citizen, in The International Ombudsman Yearbook/Volume 2 – 1998, op cit., pp. 98–111.

[42]See note 33.

[43]The Federal Ombudsman Act, Articles 1, 3° and 15, paragraph 1.

[44]The Federal Ombudsman Act, Article 14, paragraph 3.

[45]Although the parliamentary ombudsman cannot be relieved of his duties due to activities conducted within the framework of his functions (The Federal Ombudsmen Act, Article 7, paragraph 2), Article 6 of same Act stipulates that the House of Representatives can remove him from office for serious reasons, but does not define such a serious reason nor the proceedings to be respected by the House to implement such a removal of office.

[46]Approximately 100 millions Belgian Francs or 2.478.900 Euros.

[47]The Federal Ombudsman Act, Article 18.

4. *Functional Independence*

To guarantee the independence of the parliamentary ombudsman, it is important:

- to allow him to be covered by professional secrecy;[48]
- to grant him immunity for everything he may say in the framework of the performance of his tasks;[49]
- to make his appointment irrevocable, with the exception of the impeachment procedure in the event of serious infraction as explained above.[50]

5. *Political Independence*

Whether he is appointed by the Parliament[51] or by the Head of State, it is fundamental that the nomination of the ombudsman is free of political considerations.

There are various ways to make sure of this:

- by requesting a qualified vote (of two thirds or three quarters) in Parliament, in order to go beyond the majority/opposition division at the time of the appointment of the parliamentary ombudsman (example: Quebec);
- by granting to a neutral committee the authority to recommend two or three candidates to Parliament. This is the system used in the Netherlands where the Vice President of the State Council, the President of the Court of Auditors and the President of the Supreme Court propose three names to the Parliament;
- by organizing an objective examination procedure for his appointment, as it is done in Belgium. Such examinations take place under the supervision of a jury on which no MP or member of the Government sit, but only professors of various universities,[52] the Parliament appointing the person who achieves the highest score.

Besides these different appointment procedures, one also has to provide for certain restrictions in order to guarantee the independence of the parliamentary ombudsman. This is the reason why in Belgium the parliamentary ombudsman cannot be at the same time a civil servant, a lawyer, a magistrate, a manager of a publicly owned company, a member of the federal Government or of the Government of any State member, a mayor, a province governor, a MP or another elected official.[53] In certain countries, to avoid that the office of parliamentary ombudsman be entrusted to a former politician for good and loyal services, the parliamentary ombudsman cannot have held a public office within a five year period preceding his appointment.

---

48 The Federal Ombudsman Act, Article 16.

49 The Federal Ombudsman Act, Article 7.

50 See note 46.

51 According to the Federal Ombudsman Act, Article 2, the parliamentary ombudsman is appointed by the House of Representatives for a renewable six-year period. The appointment procedure as described above has been adopted by the board of the House in 1996. It would however be in the best interest of the permanency of the independence of the parliamentary ombudsman that it also be incorporated in the Federal Ombudsman Act itself.

52 The presence of civil servants in the jury would be contradictory, since they would be 'judges in their own case', which is not the case with university professors who are not civil servants.

53 The Federal Ombudsman Act, Article 5.

Finally, a parliamentary ombudsman must offer the best guarantees of morality.

6. *Intellectual Independence*

By definition, a parliamentary ombudsman must be independent vis-aÁ-vis the citizen who has filed the complaint he handles as well as the Civil Service departments concerned by such complaint. This need for intellectual independence is crucial for the good performance of the mission of the parliamentary ombudsman.

For example, the credibility – and thus the efficiency – of the ombudsman would be affected if, prior to his appointment as ombudsman, he had been a civil servant within an administrative authority susceptible to be investigated by him as ombudsman.

The same intellectual independence of the parliamentary ombudsman would furthermore be fully guaranteed if there would be no possibility for him to be appointed shortly after his term of office to one of the administrative services he has been investigating. Even if a former civil servant who has become a parliamentary ombudsman would certainly act with intellectual independence, a doubt would still subsist in the public mind which would affect his credibility and moral authority, and thus harm his efficiency.

7. *Organizational Independence*

It is essential that the parliamentary ombudsman himself appoints, manages and dismisses his staff.[54] Moreover, the staff of the parliamentary ombudsman must be recruited specifically and should not be seconded from the Parliament, nor from the Executive Power nor from the Judicial Power. In addition, the parliamentary ombudsman must himself have the choice of his staff,[55] even though it is important to make the appointment of such staff objective through selective contests, as is the case in Belgium.[56]

Conclusion

Much could be said about the parliamentary ombudsman. To cut a long story short, let us conclude with two words which describe this function perfectly: service and independence.

The role of the parliamentary ombudsman is to serve the people so that an administrative decision can be corrected if the law or a principle of proper administration have been violated, and also to make a recommendation in equity in the event that the parliamentary ombudsman deems it appropriate. He also helps the Civil Service to function better and if need be to obtain improved

---

[54]The Federal Ombudsman Act, Article 19, paragraph 1.

[55]In Belgium, the staff of the parliamentary ombudsman includes 40 people.

[56]These examinations evaluate the knowledge of French and Dutch – the two most used official languages in the country – the personality, the motivation, the analytic and synthetic mental abilities and the academic background of the candidates. These selection contests are organized through the official and neutral State recruitment agency.

egal, human or technical tools to fulfil its missions. He finally assists the Parliament in its constitutional control of the Government and its own legislaive action.

The independence that the parliamentary ombudsman must be granted is nultifaceted: constitutional recognition, immunity, sovereign autonomy of ction, non-political appointment, freedom of contact with free and independent nedia, principle of not being 'judge in his own case', guarantee of financial neans, quality staff, etc. Of course, this independence cannot be conceived utside a truly democratic state. Consequently, it is not exaggerated to say that ne can measure the degree of democracy of a given state by the effective ndependence of its parliamentary ombudsman.

LEGISLATION

The Constitution of the Kingdom of Belgium (excerpts)

Article 1
Belgium is a Federal State made up of communities and regions.

Article 46
The King has only the right to dissolve the Chamber of Representatives if the latter, with he absolute majority of its members:

1°) either rejects a motion of confidence in the Federal Government and does not propose to the King, within three days from the day of the rejection of the motion, the nomination of a successor to the Prime Minister;
2°) or adopts a motion of disapproval with regard to the Federal Government and does not simultaneously propose to the King the nomination of a successor to the Prime Minister;

The motions of confidence and disapproval can only be voted on after a delay of fortyight hours after the introduction of the motion.

Moreover, the King may, in the event of the resignation of the Federal Government, lissolve the Chamber of Representatives after having received its agreement expressed y the absolute majority of its members.

The dissolution of the Chamber of Representatives entails the dissolution of the Senate.

The act of dissolution involves the convoking of the electorate within forty days and of the Chambers within two months.

Article 99
The Council of Ministers (the Cabinet) includes fifteen members at most.

With the possible exception of the Prime Minister, the Council of Ministers includes as many French-speaking members as Dutch-speaking members.

Article 151 (excerpt)
1. (...)
2. There is a High Council of Justice for all of Belgium.(...)
3. The High Council of Justice is competent for the following matters:
(...)
6°) to formulate advice and proposals concerning the general functioning and the organization of the Judicial Power;
...)
8°) to receive and handle complaints concerning the functioning of the Judicial power ...) but has no disciplinary and criminal authority.
...)

The Federal Ombudsmen Act

Kingdom of Belgium, March 22, 1995

CHAPTER 1. The Federal Ombudsmen

Article 1

There are two Federal Ombudsmen, one French-speaking, the other Dutch-speaking whose mission it is:

(1°) to examine the claims relating to the operation of the federal administrative authorities;

(2°) at the request of the House of Representatives, to lead any investigation on the functioning of the federal administrative services that it designates;

(3°) to make recommendations and submit a report on the operation of the administrative authorities, in compliance with Article 14, paragraph 3, and Article 15, paragraph 1, based on the observations made while implementing the duties referred to in 1 and 2, above.

The ombudsmen carry out their duties with regard to the federal administrative authorities referred to in Article 14 of the coordinated laws on the Council of State, except for those administrative authorities endowed with their own ombudsman by an specific legal provision.

When the ombudsman's office is assumed by a woman, she is designated by the French term "médiatrice" or the Dutch term "ombudsvrouw" (in English: ombudswoman).

The ombudsmen act collectively.

Article 2

The ombudsmen and the staff who assist them are subject to the provisions of the laws on the language used in administrative matters, coordinated on July 18, 1966. They are regarded as services which are extended to the entire country.

Article 3

The ombudsmen are appointed by the House of Representatives for a renewable six year period. To be appointed ombudsman, it is necessary:

(1°) to be Belgian;

(2°) to be of irreproachable conduct and to enjoy the civil and political rights;

(3°) to hold a degree, giving access to the functions of level 1 of the Civil Service departments of the State;

(4°) to demonstrate sufficient knowledge of the other national languages, according to the standards laid down by the House of Representatives;

(5°) to have had relevant professional experience of at least five years, either in the legal, administrative or social spheres, or in another field relevant to carrying out this function.

Article 4

Before taking up duty, the ombudsmen take the following oath before the Speaker of the House of Representatives: "I swear fidelity to the King, obedience to the constitution and to the laws of the Belgian people".

Article 5

During their period in office, the ombudsmen may not carry out the following duties or hold any of the following positions or offices:

(1°) magistrate, notary public or bailiff;

(2°) lawyer;

(3°) minister of a recognized religion or delegate of an organization recognized by the law which gives moral assistance according to a non-religious philosophy;

(4°) a public office conferred by election;

(5°) employment remunerated in the public services referred to in Article 1, paragraph 2.

The ombudsmen cannot hold an office, public or otherwise, which could compromise the dignity or the performance of their duties.

For the application of this article, the following are treated as a public office conferred by election: a position as mayor appointed separately from the communal council; director of a public interest organization and a position as a Government commissioner, including that of Governor of province, Deputy Governor or Vice-Governor.

The holder of a public office conferred by election who accepts a nomination for the office of ombudsman is legally excluded from his elective mandate.

Articles 1, 6, 7, 10, 11 and 12 of the Act of 18 September 1986 instituting political leave for the members of staff of the public service are applicable to the ombudsmen, if they are entitled to such leave, and the necessary adaptations are made.

Article 6

The House of Representatives can terminate the ombudsmen's functions:

(1°) at their request;

(2°) when they reach the age of 65;

(3°) when their health seriously compromises the exercise of their duties.

The House of Representatives can remove the ombudsmen from office:

(1°) if they carry out the duties or hold one of the positions or offices referred to in Article 5, paragraph 1 and paragraph 3;

(2°) for serious reasons.

Article 7

Within the limits of their mission, the ombudsmen do not receive instructions from any authority.

They cannot be relieved of their duties due to activities conducted within the framework of their functions.

CHAPTER II. Complaints

Article 8

Any interested person can lodge a complaint with the ombudsmen, in writing or verbally, regarding the activities or functioning of the administrative authorities.

As a preliminary matter, the interested party must contact these authorities in order to obtain satisfaction.

Article 9

The ombudsmen can refuse to investigate a complaint when:

(1°) the complainant's identity is unknown;

(2°) the complaint refers to facts which occurred more than one year before the lodgement of the complaint.

The ombudsmen will refuse to investigate a complaint when:

(1°) the complaint is obviously unfounded;

(2°) the complainant obviously took no steps to approach the administrative authority concerned to obtain satisfaction;

(3°) the complaint is primarily the same as a complaint dismissed by the ombudsmen, if it contains no new facts.

When the complaint refers to a federal, regional, community and other administrative authority which has its own ombudsman by virtue of legal regulation, the ombudsmen will pass it on to the latter without delay.

Article 10

The ombudsmen will inform the complainant without delay of their decision of whether or not the complaint will be handled, or whether it will be passed on to another ombudsman. Any refusal to handle a complaint will be substantiated.

The ombudsmen will inform the administrative authority of their intention to investigate a complaint.

Article 11
The ombudsmen can impose binding deadlines for response on the agents or services to which they address questions in the course of their duties.

They can similarly make any observation, acquire all the documents and information that they consider necessary and hear all persons concerned on the spot.

Persons who are entrusted with privileged information by virtue of their status or profession, are relieved of their obligation to maintain confidentiality within the framework of the enquiry carried out by the ombudsmen.

The ombudsmen may seek assistance by experts.

Article 12
If, in the performance of their duties, the ombudsmen notice a fact which could constitute a crime or an offence, they must inform the Public Prosecutor in compliance with Article 29 of the Code of Criminal Procedure.

If, in the performance of their duties, they notice a fact which could constitute a disciplinary offence, they must inform the competent administrative authority.

Article 13
The examination of a complaint is suspended when the facts are subject of judicial appeal or of organized administrative appeal. The administrative authority will inform the ombudsmen of legal proceedings.

In this event, the ombudsmen will report to the complainant of the suspension of the examination of his or her complaint without delay.

The lodgement and the examination of a complaint neither suspend nor stop time limits for judicial or organized administrative appeal.

Article 14
The complainant is kept periodically informed of the progress of his or her complaint.

The ombudsmen will endeavour to reconcile the complainant's point of view and those of the services concerned.

They can send any recommendation to the administrative authority that they consider useful. In this case, they will inform the minister responsible.

CHAPTER III
Reports by the ombudsmen

Article 15
Every year, during the month of October, the ombudsmen send a report on their activities to the House of Representatives. They can, in addition, submit intermediate quarterly reports if they consider it useful. These reports contain the recommendations that the ombudsmen consider useful and expose possible difficulties that they encounter in the performance of their duties.

The identity of the complainants and of members of staff in the administrative authorities may not be divulged in these reports.

The reports are made public by the House of Representatives.

The ombudsmen may be heard by the House at any time, either at their request, or at the request of the House.

CHAPTER IV. Various provisions

Article 16
Article 458 of the Penal Code applies to the ombudsmen and their staff (professional secrecy).

Article 17
The Ombudsmen adopt house rules determining the methods of handling of the complaints. It is approved by the House of Representatives and is published in the Moniteur belge.

Article 18

The appropriations necessary for the functioning of the ombudsmen's office are budgeted as special allocations (distinct from the budgets of the House and the Government). Correspondence sent as part of the ombudsmen's office is sent free of postage.

Article 19

Without prejudice to the assignments agreed upon by collegial decision, the ombudsmen appoint, dismiss and direct the members of staff who will assist them in the performance of their duties.

The staffing and the members status are decided by the House of Representatives at the suggestion of the ombudsmen.

Article 20

The ombudsmen enjoy a status identical to that of the counsellors of the Court of Auditors. The rules governing the financial status of the counsellors of the Court of Auditors, in the Act of 21 March 1964 on the salaries of the members of the Court of Auditors, as amended by the acts of 14 March 1975 and 5 August 1992, are applicable to the ombudsmen.

The ombudsmen's pension on retirement is calculated on the basis of the average salary for the last five years, determined in accordance with the applicable arrangement for retirement pensions to be paid by the State, at a rate of one thirtieth per year of service as an ombudsman, providing he or she has carried out his or her functions in the aforementioned capacity for at least twelve years.

Services by the ombudsmen which are not governed by the previous paragraph and which are acceptable for the calculation of a pension on retirement to be paid by the State, are calculated according to the laws fixing retirement pensions pertaining to these services.

If an ombudsman is not considered fit to carry out his or her functions due to illness or infirmity, but has not reached the age of 65, he or she may draw a pension irrespective of age.

The ombudsmen's pension on retirement shall not be higher than nine tenths of the average salary for the last five years.

The Defender of the Public of the Republic of Colombia

José F. Castro Caycedo*

'he Office of Ombudsman in Colombia is called the Office of the Defender of ıe Public and the person holding the office, the Defender of the Public, will be ɛferred to as such throughout this document.

A. Legal and Constitutional Bases

. Colombia's Political Constitution and the Law 24 of 1992 establish all the ıemes that are related to the Defender of the Public. The Constitution in its .rticle 118 indicates the position and mission of the Office of the Defender of ıe Public.

Article 281 of the Constitution determines who must supervise the)mbudsman work and who must elect the holder of this office and the period f functions of the person who is elected.

Law 24 applies these constitutional regulations and determines the organiza-on and functioning of the Office of the Defender of the Public.

The functions and powers of the Defender of the Public are defined in Article 82 of the Constitution and in Article 9 of Law 24. This must not be taken to e a disadvantage for its autonomy, because it is the application of one of the rinciples that supports the entire concept of a State of Law, that is, subjection ɔ the rule of law, to which all public servants are subject. Possible disadvantages ıay be found within the specific content of each regulation.

. The Defender of the Public is elected by one of the houses of Congress – the 'hamber of Representatives – from a trio presented by the President of the tepublic, for a period of four years.

The Defender of the Public must submit an annual report to Congress on the ılfilment of his/her functions.

B. Independence and Impartiality

'he autonomy of our Defender of the Public, just as that of any Ombudsman, ; linked to the way in which he/she is appointed, his/her hierarchical, functional, dministrative and budgetary autonomy, as well as to the way his/her functions nd powers are formulated, to the attitude assumed with respect to the branches

National Ombudsman.

. Hossain et al. (eds), *Human Rights Commissions and Ombudsman Offices*, 289–297.

of public power and to the authority of the Defender him/herself, that is, his/h moral prestige.

Constitutional and/or legal regulations do not establish either a hierarchic or a functional dependency on the executive, legislative and judicial branche The law indicates that the Defender will exercise his/her functions with admi istrative and budgetary autonomy, under the supreme direction of the Prosecut General of the Nation, who is the representative of the Public Ministry.

In this respect, the law establishes that the Defender has the following power

- To direct and coordinate the various offices making up the institution.
- To enter into contracts and issue administrative acts required for the functio ing of the agency.
- To appoint Delegate Defenders.
- To order expenditure inherent to the office itself, subject to the stipulations the Organic Law of the General Budget of the nation and rulings dealing wit appropriation, addition, expense and transfer.
- To present the budget proposal for the agency to the National Government
- To administer the goods and resources allocated to the operation of the Offic of the Defender of the Public and to answer for their correct allocation an utilization.
- To appoint and remove the public servants of the Office and define the administrative situation.
- To hand down the necessary regulations for efficient and effective functionin of the Office of the Defender of the Public, those dealing with the intern organization and functions and the regulation of administrative processes n specified by law.
- To develop the structure of the Institution, inasmuch as it is not stipulate by law.
- To assign personnel to each office and establish a manual of functions an requirements for each public servant.

In spite of the administrative and budget autonomy, the budget of the Offic of the Defender of the Public depends on the National Budget, which create functional problems every time the Government wants to make a reduction c it. Therefore, it is important to declare the budget of the Office of the Defende of the Public a national interest to avoid its reduction.

4. In order to guarantee the impartiality of the Office of the Defender of th Public the Colombian regulations establish:

- The functions and powers of the Office of the Defender of the Public.
- The qualifications required of an Office of the Defender of the Public.
- The prohibitions regarding the Office of the Defender of the Public.
- The rules on disqualifications and incompatibilities of the Office of th Defender of the Public.

The opinions, reports and recommendations of the Defender of the Public hav the strength awarded them by the National Constitution, the law, society, it autonomy, his/her moral qualities and high position within the State.

The Office of the Defender of the Public forms part of the Public Ministry with the task of the safeguarding and promotion of human rights, the protectio f the public interest and surveillance of the official conduct of all those individ-als performing public duties within the national territory.

The Defender of the Public receives a constitutional mandate to oversee the romotion, exercise and publicizing of human rights. He/She does not exercise ither judicial nor disciplinary functions, but does exercise the power of criticism y means of opinion, reports and recommendations.

C. Complaints Regarding Acts of Government

. The complaints received by the Office of the Defender of the Public do not efer only to actions or omissions that threaten or violate human rights on the art of members of government, but rather it also receives and processes com-laints when those involved are public authorities of any branch of the public ower, other State institutions or private parties – for example, when they have een assigned or perform public functions or when mediation is needed between he users of public services and the private enterprises that render the services, etc.

The Office of the Defender of the Public may resort to judicial means: invoking he right of habeas corpus; placing a tutelage claim or popular suits; suing, efuting or defending before the Constitutional Court – at government initiative r at the request of any person – the regulations dealing with human rights, pplying writs of performance and filing public suits in defence of the National Constitution, the Law, the general welfare and that of individuals. This last unction can be carried out before any jurisdiction, public servant or authority.

The only restriction of the Office of the Defender of the Public to intervene xists with respect to the Government acts is in the area of National Security.

. The Defender of the Public is the titleholder of each one of the forms of udicial recourse indicated above and can decide independently whether to file ny of these actions on the basis of an examination of each of the specific cases. Ie/she may also directly counsel persons affected in the filing of each of these udicial actions.

In the practice of the defence of the human rights in general and in the rights f individuals in particular, when the Office of the Defender of the Public ndertakes action, it has to comply with the requirements established. These ormalities are not restrictive for the Office or for any individual involved.

D. Research, Reports and Recommendations

. The jurisdiction of the Defender of the Public is nationwide and he/she can arry out his/her duties in any part of the territory. The Office of the Defender f the Public may make visits to any public or private agency or resort to any neans of proof and request information from public authorities and private ersons when so required in order to verify the truth of a complaint or in order o prevent the violation of human rights.

The Constitution indicates that with the exceptions noted in the Constitution tself and the law, the Defender of the Public may require authorities to provide nformation needed for the exercise of his/her functions, without any reservations vhich would obstruct such requests.

The law establishes, firstly that public authorities and private parties to whor the rendering of a public service has been assigned or granted must furnis information needed for the exercise of the Defender's office, without any reserva tion whatsoever, except for stipulations made in the Constitution.

The law also specifies that in the case that information is needed from a authority or a private party in order to certify the veracity of complaints or t prevent the violation of human rights, no reservation whatsoever may be mad as an obstruction thereof.

The public authorities and private parties to whom the rendering of a publi service has been assigned or granted must collaborate with the Defender of th Public in a diligent and timely manner in support of the fulfilment of his/he functions and supply the necessary information for its effective exercise.

Any authority that hinders or hampers the exercise of public defence function shall be sanctioned with dismissal from the respective position. This fact consti tutes bad conduct without prejudice to penal sanctions. If a private party shoul demonstrate such conduct, the Defender will communicate this fact to the agenc in charge of the assignment or grant and the name of the individual will b included as an unwilling collaborator in the report to Congress and in thos reports that the Defender periodically submits.

In the case of a complaint, the Defender will remit the complaint to th respective agency so that it can inform the person filing the complaint of th steps taken and the result – with a copy to the Office of the Defender of th Public. Denial or negligence in responding to such a request constitutes a grav fault and will be sanctioned with removal from position and will be considere as hampering the duty of the Defender. In these cases, the Defender can includ the name of the unwilling party in the Report presented to Congress or mak it known to public opinion.

8. The Office of Defender of the Public is required to present annual reports o the activities of the Office to the Congress of the Republic. In furtherance o his/her duties the Defender in addition to the recommendations and observation made to the authorities, must make facts and conduct that may constitute violation of penal law and disciplinary stipulations known to judicial authoritie and those that undertake disciplinary investigation so that the correspondin investigation be undertaken.

9. In addition to the above mentioned duties, the Defender of the Public mus direct and organize the public defence service in order to guarantee access t justice by those who are economically or socially unable to provide for thei own defence.

He/she also enjoys legislative initiative, that is, the Defender of the Publi may present legislative bills on human rights.

LEGISLATION

Constitution of Colombia

Article 118

The Public Ministry will be exercised by the Prosecutor General of the Nation, the Publi Defender, delegate prosecutors and agents of the Public Ministry before jurisdictiona uthorities, by municipal representatives and by other officials as stipulated by the law. It is the Public Ministry's duty to safeguard and promote human rights, protection of public welfare and to oversee the official conduct of individuals holding public office.

Article 275
The Prosecutor General of the Nation is the Supreme Director of the Public Ministry.

Article 276
The Prosecutor General of the Nation shall be elected by the Senate for a period of four ears from among a trio of candidates proposed by the President of the Republic, the Supreme Court of Justice and the Council of State

Article 277
The Prosecutor General of the Nation shall fulfil the following duties either on his own ccount or through his delegates and agents:

1. To oversee observance of the Constitution, laws judicial decisions and administrative acts;
2. To protect human rights and ensure the effectiveness thereof, with the aid of the public defender;
3. To defend the interests of society;
4. To defend collective interests, particularly the environment;
5. To oversee the diligent and efficient exercise of administrative functions;
6. To exercise supervision over the official conduct of those who hold public office, even those awarded by popular election; to exercise in particular disciplinary power; to undertake the corresponding investigations and to impose the respective sanctions according to the law;
7. To intervene in judicial actions and before judicial or administrative authorities when necessary in defence of the legal order, public property, or fundamental rights and guarantees;
8. To present an annual report on administration to Congress;
9. To require public officials and private parties to provide the information considered necessary;
10. Any other functions determined by law.

In order to fulfil its duties the Prosecutor's Office shall have the powers of judicial police and may file suits as considered necessary.

Article 278
The Prosecutor General of the Nation will directly exercise the following functions:

1. To remove from office, following a hearing and by means of resolution, any public employee who commits one of the following faults: deliberate violation of the Constitution or law; to derive evident and undue material benefit from his/her functions during his/her term of office; to seriously hinder investigations undertaken by the Prosecutor General or an administrative or jurisdictional authority; to act with obvious negligence in the investigation and sanctioning of disciplinary faults committed by employees of his/her office, or in the denouncement of punishable acts of which he/she has knowledge within the exercise of his/her functions.
2. To issue concepts in disciplinary cases being heard against employees with special exemptions;
3. To present legislative bills on matters related to his/her area of competence;
4. To exhort Congress to issue laws that will ensure the promotion, exercise and protection of human rights and to demand fulfilment thereof by competent authorities;
5. To issue an opinion in the suits dealing with control of constitutionality;
6. To appoint and remove from office those officials and employees according to law.

Article 279
The law will determine the structure and functioning of the Office of the Prosecutor General of the Nation. It will regulate admission and determination of merits, as well as

retirement from service; disqualifications, incompatibilities, posts, qualifications, remune ation and disciplinary code of all officials and employees of said agency.

Article 280
The agents of the Public Ministry will have the same qualifications, categories, remunera tion, rights and benefits as the magistrates and judges of highest rank before whom the exercise their duties.

Article 281
The Public Defender shall be part of the Public Ministry and will exercise the function under the maximum supervision of the Prosecutor General of the Nation. He/she will b elected by the Chamber of Representatives for a period of four years from within a tri prepared by the President of the Republic.

Article 282
The Public Defender will safeguard the promotion, exercise and public dissemination c human rights, for which it will exercise the following functions:

1. Orient and instruct the residents of the national territory and Colombians abroad i the exercise and defence of their rights before competent authorities or entities of private nature.
2. To disseminate human rights and recommend policies for the teaching thereof.
3. To invoke the right of habeas corpus and to instigate tutelage actions, without impai ment of the right to aid interested parties.
4. To organize and direct the Office of the Public Defender in the terms indicated by law
5. To instigate popular actions in matters related to its area of competence.
6. To present legislative bills on matters related to the area of its competence.
7. To present reports to Congress on the fulfilment of its functions and duties.
8. Any other functions or duties determined by law.

Article 283
The law will determine the organization and functioning of the Office of the Publi Defender.

Article 284
The Prosecutor General of the Nation and the Office of the Public Defender may requir authorities to provide information needed for the exercise of their functions, except i contrary cases provided for in the Constitution and the law, without the opposition c any reservations.

Law 24 of 1992 (December 15)

By means of which the organization and functioning of the Office of the Public Defende is established and other measures are defined in furtherance of article 283 of the Politica Constitution of Colombia.

The Congress of Colombia,

DECREES:

Title I – Legal Nature

Article 1
The Office of the Public Defender is a body that forms part of the Public Ministry. I exercises its functions under the maximum direction of the Prosecutor General of the Nation and it is basically charged with overseeing the promotion, exercise and dissemina tion of Human Rights.

The Office of the Public Defender has administrative and budget autonomy.

Article 2
The Public Defender is elected by the Chamber of Representatives from among a trio proposed by the President of the Republic, for a period of four years, initiating on September 1, 1992.

The trio will be presented within the first fifteen days following the inauguration of sessions in the four year legislative period.

The election shall take place during the first month of sessions.

Title II – Regulation of the Office of the Public Defender

Chapter I
Law of the Defender

Article 3
The Public Defender must present the same qualifications required to be a Magistrate of the Supreme Court of Justice, of the Constitutional Court or the Council of State. He/she will be sworn into office before the President of the Republic or before the person fulfilling said duties on the date of initiation of the period.

The following do not qualify for Public Defender:

1. Any person who has been condemned to a judicial sentence and denied his liberty, except for political crime or misdemeanour.
2. Any person who has been sanctioned by a competent authority and sentenced to removal or suspension from office in a disciplinary proceeding.
3. Any person excluded from the exercise of a profession by means of legal decision.
4. Any person under judicial restraint.
5. Any person subject to an accusatory resolution, duly executed, until such time as his/her legal situation is defined, except if it was issued based on political crimes or misdemeanours.
6. Any person who is related within the fourth degree of consanguinity, first degree affinity or first degree civil or who are associated through marriage or permanent union with the Representatives of the Chamber who take place in the election, with the Prosecutor General of the Nation and with the President of the Republic or the person representing said office and taking part in the nomination.
7. In all cases the regulation on disqualification and incompatibilities established by law for the Prosecutor General of the Nation will be applicable to the Public Defender.

Article 4
The investiture of Public Defender is incompatible with the exercise of any other public or private office or any professional activity or employment, except for university teaching.

Article 5
In the case of a temporary absence by the Defender, his functions will be exercised by the Secretary General of the Office of Public Defence. In the case of resignation accepted by the Chamber of Representatives or permanent absence, the President of the Republic will proceed to appoint a Defender who will exercise the respective duties until such time as the Chamber elects one, in accordance with the procedure established in the National Constitution.

Article 6
The Public Defender will provide orientation and support as needed to the Municipal Representatives, either directly or through the Regional Defenders, in their work as Public Defenders and citizen overseers.

Article 7
The Public Defender may not exercise judicial or disciplinary functions, except those

assigned to his Office. His opinions, reports and recommendations shall have the strengt lent to them by the National Constitution, the law, society, their autonomy, mor characteristics and esteemed position within the State.

Article 8
Any private person or legal entity may present plans, proposals or projects for the defenc and promotion of Human Rights. The Public Defender will assess the objectives, nee and transcendence of said programmes, their feasibility and the way to put them int practice.

Chapter II
Powers

Article 9
In addition to the powers indicated in the Constitution, the Public Defender shall hav the following:

1. Design and adopt policies for promoting and disseminating Human Rights in th country with the Prosecutor General of the Nation, in order to demand and defen them.
2. Direct and coordinate the work of the various divisions making up the Office c Public Defence.
3. Make recommendations and observations to authorities and private parties in th case of a threat against or violation of Human Rights and to oversee the promotio and exercise thereof. The Defender may make such recommendations public an report to Congress on the response received.
4. Perform diagnoses of a general nature on the economic, social, cultural, legal an political situations in which individuals may find themselves with respect to the Stat
5. Pressure private organizations so that they abstain from neglecting a right.
6. Disseminate knowledge of the Political Constitution of Colombia, especially th fundamental social, economic, cultural, collective and environmental rights.
7. Present an annual report to Congress on its activities in which will be included listing of the type and number of complaints received, the measures taken to dea with it and results, express mention of officials refusing to cooperate or of individual implicated and the recommendations of an administrative and legal nature considere necessary.
8. Assist the Prosecutor General in the drafting of reports on the situation of Huma Rights in the country.
9. Demand, refute or defend any rules related to Human Rights by own initiative or a the request of any person when indicated. Instate public action in defence of th National Constitution, law, general welfare or of individuals before any jurisdiction public servant or authority.
10. Design the mechanisms needed to establish permanent communication and shar information with governmental and non-governmental organizations on a nationa and international basis for the protection and defence of Human Rights.
11. Enter into agreements with national and international educational and researc institutions for the dissemination and promotion of Human Rights.
12. Enter into contracts and issue administrative acts as required for the functioning o the Office, as well as to perform the legal and judicial representation of the institution using the powers or mandates granted to it for this purpose as necessary.
13. Appoint Delegate Defenders by subject area for the study and defence of particula rights.
14. Exercise expenditure inherent to the Office as such, subject to the measures establishe in the Organic Law of the General Budget of the Nation and regulatory standard with respect to appropriations, additions, transfers, expenditure agreements, pro gramme for cash, payments and formation of payment reserves.

5. Present the Budget Proposal for the Office of Public Defence to the consideration of the National Government.
6. Administer the goods and resources allocated to the operation of the Office of Public Defence and assume responsibility for its correct assignment and use.
7. Appoint and remove employees from the Office, as well as define their administrative status.
8. Establish regulations needed for the efficient and effective functioning of the Office of Public Defence, all of that related to its organization and internal functions and the regulation of administrative processes not provided for by law.
9. Be mediator for the collective petitions put forth by civic or popular organizations directed at public administration, when they require it.
0. Oversee the rights of ethnic minorities and consumers.
1. Participate in the monthly meetings held by the Commission on Human Rights and Congressional Hearings, and at the holding of Special Hearings in order to establish joint policies in a coordinated fashion in defence of Human Rights according to the provisions of articles 56 and 57 of the Regulation of Congress (Law OS of June 17, 1992).
2. Present periodic reports to public opinion on the results of investigations, publicly denouncing the failure to acknowledge Human Rights.
3. To serve as mediator between users and public or private companies that render public services when they so request in the defence of their presumably violated rights.
4. Any others indicated in other legal measures.

rticle 10
he Public Defender may delegate his/her functions to the Secretary General, National irectors, Delegate Defenders, Regional Defenders, Municipal Representatives and other fficials of his/her Office, except the obligation to present annual reports to Congress.

rticle 11
hen considered necessary the Public Defender may directly assume or through a special elegate, the functions assigned by law to other officials of his/her Office.

rticle 12
he Public Defender may delegate the ordering of expenditure to the Secretary General nd the Regional Public Defenders in accordance with the stipulations of the law.

rticle 13
he Public Defender may establish the number and the sites of the Regional Offices of ublic Defence, in accordance with the needs for service.

The Regional Public Defenders will perform the duties assigned to them by the Public efender.

The Ombudsman of Costa Rica

Rodrigo Alberto Carazo*

In October 1996, five months before the tenure of Costa Rica's first elected Ombudsman was to finish, the leading national newspaper published the results of a survey, done within a series that measured the population's allegiance to the system and its institutions. In that survey, the Ombudsman institution, which had begun functioning three years before, scored highest both in perception of efficacy and in trustworthiness, scoring in both counts above 66 positive percentage points and surpassing longstanding institutions such as the Catholic Church (previously leader in both counts), the communication media, private enterprise and all other public entities.

For those of us who had been involved in the institution since its creation, the results came as a great reward for our intense work, and much as a surprise. Although not functioning in pursuit of high standing in polls, we had set ourselves a goal of becoming acknowledged by 1% of the country's population monthly, hoping thus that by the end of our term some 40–42% of the country's inhabitants would have an idea of the existence of the institution and of its general purpose.

We could thus not believe another survey, which came out several months later, and in which more than 92% of those surveyed (an a national basis) rated the work of the Ombudsman institution as having been good, very good or excellent.

The following paragraphs, written along the lines of the general questionnaire provided by the organizers of the conference, attempt to portray the legal and social background that stood behind the institution that the author had the honour to lead for four exciting and plentiful years. If the account seems to be very personal, I must say at this moment that it only reflects some of the moments that I was privileged to experience throughout this most meaningful period of my life. Although it has been a year since my term expired, many of the following comments are written in the first person plural form. Yes, I still feel very strongly what I lived through, and somehow, in writing these reflections, I could not abandon my identification with the institution (though I have made it a point, since I finished, not to interfere in any way whatsoever with my successor. She has, I know for sure, a most demanding job and she should not be hearing comments from a person that did already have the opportunity to do as he felt. Now it is her turn and I would, at anytime, give the discreet advice she could request).

---

*Former Ombudsman (1993–1997).

K. Hossain et al. (eds), Human Rights Commissions and Ombudsman Offices, 299–314.

In Costa Rica the Ombudsman institution, aptly called la "Defensorþa de los Habitantes de la Republica" (the Defender of the Republic's Inhabitants) was created by a law enacted in December 1992, after being more than eight years before the Parliament. Meanwhile, some Ombudsman-type offices functioned within the executive power, though with very low profile and limited success. In 1990, a law enacted in favour of women's rights established the Women's Ombudsman institution (Defensorþa de la Mujer), which was to function as a body of the Ministry of Justice until it merged, through working agreements with the national Ombudsman institution mid-1993.

Tasks and Competence

1. It is an ordinary law, passed by Congress in 1992 which determines the tasks and competence of the Ombudsman (Law number 7319 of November 17, 1992). The law provides that the institution would have the organizational structure defined in a decree that would be issued by the executive power within three months after the election of the first Ombudsman.

Once the Ombudsman was elected, the Ministry of Justice entrusted him with the writing of a draft decree which, once prepared, was duly issued and decreed by the President and the Minister of Justice in June 1993.

Most other Ombudsman institutions are created through a constitutional provision. As a matter of fact, those who presented draft legislation for an Ombudsman institution in 1985, presented also a constitutional amendment that would provide for the institution. It happened that the draft legislation was finally approved, but the constitutional amendment did not get to be voted.

When sworn in, the legislator that led both initiatives offered to follow up on the constitutional amendment. At that time, I figured, it would lead to some type of dispute that could affect the institution itself. I declined the proposition and rather told him that then we needed to wait until the institution had proved its worth in reality.

By the end of the term, we thought that such proof existed. Furthermore, we proved that the institution could operate even if only existing on the basis of an ordinary law, but that it had gained a position high in the country's organizational system. We spoke personally with all 57 members of Congress, of which 55 concurred with the proposal and some offered to advance it. Nothing happened.

2. The Ombudsman institution is the public "body in charge of protecting the rights and the interests of the inhabitants." (Art. 1). It must see to it that the whole public sector adheres to the moral principles of justice, to the Constitution, to the laws of the country, to the international treaties to which the country is a party, and to the general principles of law. It should also promote and disseminate the rights of the inhabitants (ibid.). Further on, however, the law states that the competence of the Ombudsman should be deemed as being that of control of legality (and hence, some will say, not of morality or of justice).

A first issue that had to be analysed by the Ombudsman was this relation to the concepts of morality and of justice. We adopted a definition of morality used by the country's Constitutional Court which stated recently that "morality is the set of conducts socially deemed to concur with the people's standards". But rather than become "a judge of morality", we decided, first, to limit our morality issue exclusively to the exercise of public functions, and second, to link it to some objective principles already present in legislation (such as standards for checking illicit enrichment while in office, the principles of state contracts, the principles of equality in rendering public services) and the Ombudsman, in its actions, followed the more general attribution that entitled the institution to analyse issues in terms of morality and of justice, and not only in terms of mere legality. Not all laws are just (and if a law is unjust, it must be changed), and not all official acts that stay within the boundaries of legality are necessarily moral. We thus denounced as unjust the general tax structure of the country, which did not tax wealth and income in a manner proportional to the possibilities of recipients and that rather relied on indirect taxation (which account far more than 87% of public income). We publicly denounced as immoral an act by the Board of Directors of a state corporation which, though following the principles of valid legislation, hurriedly approved and disbursed some one-time-only enticements to persons holding high positions in the institution.

The Ombudsman has not accepted that its prerogatives are limited only to control of the *legality* of acts an has acted accordingly.

3. As mentioned, it is the task of the Ombudsman to protect all rights of the individuals from illegal, unjust, immoral or arbitrary acts (and omissions) by public sector agents.

4. The law (Art 17.1) states that the Ombudsman may act on any alleged violation having occurred within the past twelve months. However, it gives large discretion to accept claims for alleged violations having occurred even before, if the Ombudsman would consider his/her intervention as necessary.

This issue is important, precisely when an Ombudsman institution is first established. It is the experience of all that the claims received during the first months generally surpass the institution's capability to deal with them (since all in the office are "learning the trade"). Furthermore, the opening of the Ombudsman's institution may be perceived by some as the possibility of righting past wrongs. It is my advice that the institution should refrain from reviewing history, and rather begin dealing with current violations (which surely will be abundant). Going back would hamper efforts to the rights of the people at that moment, create a backlog of cases which will be hard to cope with and which may even damage the good reputation of the institution at very crucial moments. This is not to say that wrongs of the past should be forgotten; they must be dealt with if still possible, but by some other means (including international tribunals if necessary). The advice is not to begin by opening old – and frequently badly healed – wounds.

5. The Ombudsman is allowed to investigate alleged violations on the spot, and by any means possible. Being alert and responsive is a most needed qualification of the Ombudsman institution. We once followed a citizen who complained of having been asked for a bribe, and were able to photograph and record a repeated violation just within minutes of hearing of it. On another occasion, a couple of officers working late answered a phone call denouncing that an official vehicle was stationed in front of a bar and that its occupants were having a big feast inside. Our workers were there within minutes and found all the incriminating evidence. Many other cases may be cited.

6. All public authorities, be they national or regional, fall within the sphere c competence of the Ombudsman institution. Moreover, it was established throug practice that any individual acting on behalf of the public sector (a Publi Notary, or a Chartered Public Accountant, for example) would fall within tha sphere of competence in as much as they would perform, or omit, public dutie

7. The Ombudsman institution does not "judge" acts of anyone. Its competenc is not such, but rather one of protecting the rights of the individuals (singl individuals, groups of them, entire communities and even the population as whole). "Judging" would require some type of "evidentiary presentations", an the Ombudsman would better deal with solving issues that affect people throug the voluntary actions of those obliged to act accordingly and which, for on reason or another, have gone astray or have refrained from acting.

The Ombudsman institution may receive complaints of alleged violation incurred by executive authorities (including servants of any decentralized govern ment agency), as well as by members of the legislature or the judiciary. Som further explanation regarding these two groups follow.

Members of the legislature, as individuals, would not hamper rights of other As members of Congress they could only do so acting as a deliberative body and such actions, being of political nature, are of course beyond the sphere o competence of the Ombudsman. Legislative bodies may however impinge upo the rights of the individuals as happened in the case of an investigative commis sion that after hearing a witness who did not receive any warning about th possible incriminate nature of his testimony, was "politically condemned" by th Commission and by the Congress in its entirety, which recommended that th citizen should not ever be employed by the public sector. In the aftermath procedures before such investigative commissions were modified such as t assure the basic rights of defence for any person called before it, and th Ombudsman pleaded repeatedly – and vainly, with no reasons for the absenc of remedial action – for a rehearing of the individual.

It is clearly stated that the Ombudsman institution should not receive claim on issues for which judgment in courts is pending, and that it should suspen its procedure if the claimant were to file a judiciary action on the issue. Th Ombudsman may however continue investigating the general problems presente in the claims. (Art. 19.2)

In Costa Rica the judiciary has been frankly opposed to the Ombudsman' intervention in what it claims to be "its affairs". The principle of division o powers and the constitutional autonomy of the judiciary are invoked in repeate rulings by the governing body of the judiciary. Yet, as Ombudsman I found tha nothing precluded our institution from receiving and investigating a claim tha dealt with acts or omissions of the judiciary, as long as the claims did not involv any consideration of the judicial aspects of the acts of the judiciary. That is, th Ombudsman should never entertain issues questioning the validity, soundnes or legality of a ruling by the judiciary. But it is, of course, allowed by law (Art 12.4) to analyse any administrative act of the judiciary deemed a violation o any individual's rights. The judiciary stills refrains from accepting such a intervention. Our first case was that of a landlord who rented a house for us by the judiciary, who alleged that it was being damaged without compensation We investigated and recommended that the rights of the landlord be respecte and that the house, when vacated, be given back in the condition in which it was when it was received.

A much debated issue has been that of the denial of access to justice, or that of denial to prompt justice. Justice, and access to a fair and prompt one is, no doubt, a fundamental right of everyone. It is the judiciary that must assure it but, if it fails, it needs to be the task of the Ombudsman institution to protect that right. Who else would do it ? This is simply said, but hardly accepted by the judiciary, which in Costa Rica maintains that it is through its own disciplinary entities that justice, prompt and fair, would be assured to anyone.

We did not give up on this issue. Despite denials and even reprimands from the judiciary's governing body, the Ombudsman institution has continued to receive claims regarding the non-judicial actions of the judiciary and has done its best to protect the rights and interests of claimants, sometimes through informal means such as a telephone conversation with a judge who is delaying, maybe unknowingly, a ruling that would declare justice.

The issue will remain an object of discussion. The Ombudsman should not cede. It is his task to protect the rights of the individuals and nothing precludes the institution from doing so in non-judicial acts of the judiciary. In a democracy, no power or institution should go uncontrolled, has been stated. The state is *one*, created by the individuals who form it. It is the tasks which are "divided" among different organs.

The manner in which the Ombudsman may – or may not – intervene in non-judicial acts of the judiciary must be very carefully considered in the legislation creating the Ombudsman institution. In Costa Rica the judiciary was careful enough, through the years in which the draft legislation was in Congress, to introduce amendments that would somehow "protect" it from the competence of the Ombudsman (but who "protects" the people is of course the question). In Panama, where the Ombudsman law was passed in 1997, the issue was taken to Court – which was thus deciding on matter of its own interest – and it declared that the Ombudsman could not, by any means, investigate any action of the judiciary, despite the fact that the law – declared unconstitutional – allowed it to review non-judicial acts. Protection of the people's rights should be foremost in the minds of legislators drafting Ombudsman's laws, rather than "protection" of turf.

One more comment on the matter. In Costa Rica, the investigative police is part of the judiciary. The Ombudsman's law provides (Art. 19.3) that the institution should act with regard to actions performed by the investigative police in matters relating to the "human rights" of the inhabitants. In its nearly absurd argumentation of its independence and constitutional autonomy, the judiciary currently denies even this competence of the Ombudsman institution. One example of our findings in this field is that of a claim received alleging torture on the part of the investigative police. Our actions led to a "cloth mask" which the claimant indicated was put over his head and face while being hit by interrogators. Forensic analysis of the mask showed evidence of hair belonging to the claimant adhered to the mask, and indicated also that it contained hair belonging to at least 18 different persons.

The Ombudsman institution may entertain claims involving (and not necessarily "against") non-state actors. A particular procedure needs to be put into effect in such cases. The law was amended in 1997, providing expressly for such type of intervention and details on the procedure, but was vetoed partially and is now pending.

In any case, and despite the proposed amendment, the decree on the Ombudsman institution provided, from the beginning, the possibility to investigate claims involving non-state actors that exercise a public function (public notary, for example), or that have been granted a concession to provide a public service, or that operate using public funds.

It is necessary to determine the manner through which such competence is to be exercised. We found that those non-state actors would always be subject to the authority of some formal public entity and that it was through this public authority that we could address our comments and recommendations regarding the manner in which such non-state actors comply with their obligations and thus with the rights of the people. Only in those cases in which the non-state actor exercises a public function has the Ombudsman incorporated the non-states actor in its proceedings. The part of the amendment that has been vetoed calls for the Ombudsman to notify of its proceedings not only non-state actors acting in the capacities cited but also any other non-state actors that may have any interest in the result of the investigation. The example would be that of a factory that is polluting the environment in some way, which generates a claim by some individual. So far, and according to legislation and practice, the Ombudsman institution calls upon the public authority in charge of applying the law that should prevent such pollution, and would eventually ask this authority to do as it is required in respect of the people's rights and interests. The factory, in this case, would not be part of the proceedings, since it is considered to have no right to protect. It is the public authority which should decide, with due procedures if necessary, if there is a breach of the regulations and should therefore act upon the infringer and restore the people's rights. Of course, there is always, or almost always, a forceful presence of the alleged violators, many times reflected in writings to the Ombudsman, which of course are incorporated into the investigation and the decision.

8. In regard to the acts of the legislature, the Ombudsman institution in Costa Rica has a particular prerogative that no other entity has. The Law creating the Constitutional Court allows the Ombudsman, on its own decision, to suspend legislative procedures on draft legislation approved on the first of two mandatory votes, and to request that such draft legislation be examined in terms of its constitutionality by the Constitutional Court.

This competence is rarely found in other legal systems, and entails that the Ombudsman has the capability of exercising something similar to a "popular action". On several occasions, parties interested in stopping legislation for some reason have asked the Ombudsman to exercise the prerogative. Only once it has been done, and on his own initiative, concurrently with the Constitutional Court doing an obligatory review of draft legislation which purported some drastic change in some Constitutional principles (having to do with state expenditure and placing a ceiling on public deficits). The ruling of the Court, though concurring in substance with the Ombudsman, did not fully address the legitimacy of the Ombudsman to act in the manner it did, thus not developing case law yet.

9. Any person including those of a legal nature such as corporations, foundations and similar entities, without any exception, may address himself or herself to the Ombudsman institution. (Art. 16)

The decree on the Ombudsman institution states that related parties, such as family members, may bring claims on behalf of a possible victim and also provides that such claims, if possible, must be ratified by the person directly affected, or that they may be cancelled by such a person.

The purpose has been that of making access to the Ombudsman institution as easy and pleasant as possible. Any one, without exception, may come. Minors, of course, are no exception, even if unaccompanied, nor are foreigners even if just visiting or, as has been the case many times over, if they happen to be foreigners attempting to enter the country in an irregular manner (they are also entitled to some fundamental rights which the Country in which they attempt to enter must respect).

We decided early on that we would discourage third-party patronizing of claimants. In one particular case, which was brought by a lawyer practising his trade, we did not begin proceedings until the claimant himself visited us and was advised that the institution would receive his claim directly and he should not incur any cost whatsoever to do so.

We have tried to facilitate access to the institution. As long normal working hours as possible; open doors at all times possible; access to the institution by telephone (we were the first ones in the country to use telephone line with charges on us, which could be dialled from anywhere in the country); access through fax, which we also facilitated by covering charges upon receipt from any post office in the land. After the second year we began a program of "mobile" units – cars fully equipped that travelled throughout the country, especially in the most remote areas, visiting periodically on fixed schedules and receiving in parks, open offices, and easily accessible places.

10. The Ombudsman institution can entertain requests (rather than complaints) by international organizations regarding specific legislation. With UNICEF, for example, we entered a process of promotion of new child legislation that would adhere to the principles of the Convention on the Rights of the Child. We chaired a working group that prepared the draft legislation and lobbied, together with UNICEF and all non-governmental organizations in the field of children's rights, for its approval.

We have had working relationships with the High Commissioner for Refugees and with the Committee for International Migrations regarding migrants' rights, and with International Labour Organization regarding child labour, and have worked with them in proposing legislation.

11. It being so that "any person, even entities" can bring claims regarding violations, the non- governmental organizations may of course bring such claims. It is not necessary that they be established within Costa Rica's territory.

Costa Rica's Ombudsman institution works closely with several non-governmental organizations, both domestic and international (Amnesty International, Defence of Children International, for example, and with their local chapters). Not only do we receive their claims if presented but also establish partnerships with them to advance legislation or to promote human rights in general or particular rights being violated for some specific groups.

Organization

12. The Ombudsman is elected by Congress, by simple majority of members voting, for a four year term. He may be re-elected just for one additional term. The Ombudsman, who in doctrine is held to be a "parliamentary commissioner" is not accountable to any other authority, but must present an Annual Report to Congress about the manner in which he has fulfilled his functions (Art. 15). The Annual Report, presented in the first week of June, is to be defended personally by the Ombudsman before a plenary session of Congress three weeks later, which "evaluates" the manner in which the institution has functioned. (Art. 2).

The Ombudsman may only be dismissed by Congress, provided that he has either incurred in any of the incompatibilities stated in the law (political participation or performing any other position, public or private), or that he has been condemned in a criminal court. The law does not provide a process for dismissal in either two cases, stating only that Congress would declare the vacancy (Art. 6 and 7.1). Another cause of dismissal is that of "notorious negligence or serious violations of the legal framework in fulfilling his duties" (Art. 6c). In this case, the President of Congress would name a Special Commission that within 15 working days would hear the Ombudsman and inform the Plenary of the results of its investigation (Art. 7.2).

Within the first month after being sworn-in, the Ombudsman must submit to Congress a list of three persons from which an Adjunct Ombudsman is to be elected also for four years. The Adjunct Ombudsman, functionally, is to be a "direct assistant" to the Ombudsman and will fulfil the tasks assigned by the Ombudsman. In the case of a temporary absence of the Ombudsman, the Adjunct Ombudsman will substitute, with all the prerogatives of the incumbent. The Adjunct Ombudsman has a rank only second to the Ombudsman, must fill the same personal requirements and can only be dismissed by Congress for the same reasons that the Ombudsman.(Art. 10)

Costa Rica's legislation provides a unique procedure for the selection and election of the Ombudsman (Art. 3 and 4). Any Costa Rican older than 30 may submit his or her name for consideration. A Special Commission of Representatives, selected by the Plenary, receives and analyses all "proposals, or applications". Practice has established that the Commission holds public sessions in which the candidates are interviewed by Representatives and anyone in the public may also ask particular questions (through a Member). In the first election the Commission sent a questionnaire to each candidate, asking for his or her views in particular areas dealing with the respect and protection of the rights of people. An examination of the essentials, the written answers and the interview itself allow the Commission to grade the candidates on a scale previously agreed upon and propose the plenary a list of all those qualified for the position, followed by a short-list of the ten candidates which scored best, and an even shorter list of the four candidates best qualified according to the Commission. In the two elections that have taken place so far, the candidates ranked third and fourth respectively have been elected by significant majorities encompassing Representatives from different political parties.

A most delicate issue is the definition of the role and the tasks belonging to the Adjunct Ombudsman (or the Adjuncts, for there are two or more in some countries), and more so when the Adjunct is elected by Congress, as is the case in Costa Rica (even if nominated by the Ombudsman himself in a list of three persons). If the Congress makes the election, there is no doubt that the Adjunct has a very special – and strong – position, with "full powers" if acting in substitution. Functionally, however, the Adjunct should not be a "second head" in the organization but must work under the guidance and authority of the Ombudsman, ultimate responsible for the institution and its acts. The balance is difficult. It was difficult for myself and for my dear colleague Ms. Zurcher, whom I proposed and Congress elected to the position. Similar difficulties have been encountered in most countries establishing an adjunct in legislation. With the benefit of hindsight, however, I would agree now that, with clearly stated legislation about the organizational role of the Adjunct – in presence of the Ombudsman – it is convenient to have one adjunct elected by Congress. The Adjunct would always do only what the Ombudsman delegates on him or her, except in the absence of the Ombudsman.

When I had to propose a list of three persons among whom Congress would select the Adjunct Ombudsman, I decided that they should have characteristics that were complementary to my own conditions rather than the persons who would be very much like myself. Therefore, the persons presented were all female (recognizing the rights of women to occupy such position), and had different professions and work experience than what I had. Congress would not choose "the wrong one, I figured, while proposing a list of three very able persons.

13. The Ombudsman institution, which is inscribed within the legislative power (as is the Comptroller General), exercises its activities with functional and administrative independence (Art. 2). According to some other legislation, the Ombudsman takes no directions from any authority whatsoever.

The first weeks and months are crucial to affirm such independence. We had to make clear, from the beginning, that being "ascribed" to the Legislative power did not mean any "adscription" to the Legislative Assembly, though recognizing the Assembly as the foremost organ of the legislative, but one from which we had full independence and decided to exert it. Independence is to be gained, as well, from other official organs, from civil servants involved in a case, from claimants, from special interests, and from everyone interested in influencing the Ombudsman. Step by step we had to do it. Diplomacy, dialogue, negotiation, argumentation, impartiality, firmness – all of these had to be employed. Second-echelon officers of the treasury department, for example, determined that the budget of the Ombudsman institution should be a section of the budget of the Legislative Assembly. We appealed to the President of the Republic who stood on our side; others argued that we must follow budgetary restrictions set to be complied with by the executive and its agencies, and we were able to convince that they should not apply to us. Even such a minor matter as the "rank of precedence" in official functions, and the fact itself that the Ombudsman and the Adjunct Ombudsman, both elected by Congress, were to be considered as "High Officers of the State", needed to be slowly established for all purposes.

Independence of the Ombudsman institution, and of the Ombudsman himself, is established by law. It had to be established in the field. Many of our initial actions went in this direction, and we succeeded.

14. The Ombudsman and the Adjunct Ombudsman are full-time officers of the institution. In fact, they can not hold any other position, public or private, and are therefore remunerated for their work. Their regular monthly payment comes from the budget of the institution, and it was at all times public and subject to public scrutiny.

Remuneration of high public officers is frequently object of controversy in the media and projected to the population. Although at level lower than those obtainable in the private sector or in liberal professions, public renunciation of some of the benefits available in the public sector was done by the Ombudsman, who set a voluntary ceiling on his total remuneration, which was not to be, at any time, more than ten times as large as the minimum salary for non-skilled workers.

15. The budget of the Ombudsman institution is an integral part of the national budget, prepared and itemized by the Treasury Ministry and analysed and approved by Congress. It is through this combined manner that the size of the institution's budget is determined. According to legislation and practices, and due to its administrative independence, the Ombudsman institution may transfer amounts among items approved, except in remunerations and personal services, which are set and unchangeable. Budget execution is reviewed yearly by the Comptroller General, and the Ombudsman decided on his own volition that monthly reports of such execution were to be sent to the President of Congress. The Annual Report of the institution, submitted to Congress but also available in print and through Internet, contains full disclosure of budget appropriations, modifications and execution.

International cooperation has found in Ombudsman institutions entities which, due to their tasks in protecting, promoting and advancing human rights, are worthy beneficiaries of Official Development Assistance. In fact, some of the other Central American Ombudsman institutions derived, in the first half of the 1990's, a sizable amount of their budget from international cooperation, both from countries (noticeably the Scandinavian nations), from groups of countries – the European Union – and from international organizations, such as the United Nations Development Program.

Having adequate resources from the national budget, the Costa Rican institution did not rely as heavily on international cooperation. We did however receive sizeable donations from the Democratization and Human Rights Program of the European Union and decided that, in order to make all resources "public", such donations were to be incorporated into the public budget and be fully administered as public resources.

It is thus important for any new Ombudsman institution to search for available programs from international organizations that may add to the always limited resources available in developing nations.

In Costa Rica, negotiations for the first budget allocation were crucial. We found a very cooperative and conscientious President and Finance Ministry, who allotted sufficient resources to launch the institution. In the following years we, as well as all other public institutions, were subject to necessary limitations and thus our total budget barely increased at the rate of inflation.

It should be noted that budget allocation is the soft part of an Ombudsman institution, especially at the beginning. By cutting funds, a government unsatisfied with the institution – especially when it begins doing its tasks of protecting people's rights from government actions – may suffocate the fledgling organization. Once established firmly, it is more difficult for a government to cut funds, since there would be a special affection of the constituents – the people – for the institution, and they would stand up for it in case of such action occurring.

16. In Costa Rica, there is only one Ombudsman institution, with competence over the entire territory. Ours is a centralized system (not federal).

17. The Ombudsman institution is organized in the manner that best serves the public needs. I must note that, without prior experience, nor even an estimation of the volume of work that would come to us, we had to carry out continuous modifications of the organizational structure during the first four years, and even an in-depth restructuring after the second year.

Currently the institution has the following divisions:

(a) The Ombudsman's Officer, where primary decisions are taken.
(b) An Admissions Department, where people are met and interviewed. It also handles written complaints and phone inquiries.
(c) Four specialized areas of investigation (defence): women's issues; children and other vulnerable groups; environmental and quality of life issues, including social services; economic, financial and administrative issues and public services other than those of social content.
(d) An area analysing issues of general interests (rather then individual complaints).
(e) A division of rights' promotion and dissemination.
(f) A division of technological services (computing system, mail handling, etc.)
(g) A division for general administration
(h) A special office of seven mobile units that travel continuously through the country, visiting more than 240 different sites monthly.

All salaries are paid from the institutional budget. The salaries of 16 persons in mobile units are paid with funds provided by the European Union and incorporated in the institutional budget.

18. At the end of the tenure of its first incumbent, the Ombudsman institution in Costa Rica employed 100 persons, all of them selected (with support of the personnel office) by the Ombudsman himself and appointed by him. (Art. 11). Upon completing a six-month trial period, the employee acquires the position for an indefinite period of time. They are accountable to the Ombudsman and can only be dismissed due to specified causes for termination of a working relationship, following a procedure that assures full defence possibilities and of course, having the possibility of bringing the case to Courts who may even rule that the dismissed employee be reinstalled in the position he or she occupied. This has happened once in our tenure.

Staff can only be increased on a permanent basis through budget allocations which are very difficult to obtain. Special contracts for short periods are somewhat easier to achieve, though in very limited numbers. They are employed for very specific short term purposes.

Procedure

19. A complaint is accepted with only one requirement: that it falls within the sphere of competence of the institution. We attempt to avoid formalities and rigidities, and even intruding into the complainant's individuality (why should we ask his or her age, marital status, occupation, for example). It is necessary that we get an address to communicate with him or her and, if the complaint involves accusations against someone, we must make sure of the identity of the complainant (if done by phone it must be ratified in person, somehow). We can, however, preserve as confidential the identity of the complainant if he or she so requests and we determine that disclosure may bring reprisals or dangers. We may also file confidential dossiers, which would be revealed only with a court order.

There should not be any cost involved in requiring the Ombudsman's intervention, and no special formalities need to be complied with (Art. 17.1).

A complainant does not need to have exhausted other remedies. We do however advise "first hand" complainants to file a petition first in the office involved, and help him or her in doing so, often referring them to special officers in each institution, with whom we have developed working relationships. We advise the complainant that if no response is obtained within a short (specified) period of time, we would welcome him or her back and begin proceedings.

Actually, we do our best in order to give everyone who looks for our services the best attention possible, including initial legal or psychological aid and referral to better equipped public entities that would follow up on our request. It is a principle of action that no one coming to us should leave empty handed. Often, just listening attentively to an individual's plight and making some comment or giving some advice helps in healing the wound that led the person to our office.

The Ombudsman's office does not compensate individuals for any cost, nor are its actions at any moment oriented towards monetary rewards or compensation to complainants, but rather to have their rights respected by those who have to respect them.

20. There are no requirements with regard to the language used for complaints. Spanish is the only official language of the country, but we have received complaints written or expressed in languages known by someone on the staff. Language used in the procedure and for the findings is Spanish.

Referring to another conception of the term "language", it must be said that despite in-bred tendencies to use legal parlance and even legal terminology on the part of some of the staff, we attempt to use more easily understandable terminology, avoiding legalisms of any type.

Only 1% of Costa Rica's population is aboriginal, and more than one half of it speaks only Spanish. The other half, some 15,000 individuals, speak one of seven native languages and about two-thirds of those 15,000 speak Spanish as well. I do not recall any occasion in which we dealt with a person speaking only a native language (none on the staff knows any of them). If the case were to occur, we would be in difficulties, and would have to assure that person full recognition and understanding of his cultural traits, including the language.

21. Once seized of a complaint, the Ombudsman institution first attempts, very rapidly, informal ways to find satisfaction for the complainant's rights. Very

often, in his own presence, a phone call is made to the relevant administrative office and a dialogue searching for solutions is held with people "on the other side of the line". It is very pleasant when we can tell a complainant to go back where he came from and be entirely assured that satisfactory attention will be granted this time; but then we ask ourselves why this could not be solved right at the first moment and thus avoid inconveniences, time lost and many other things. As the Ombudsman institution gains ever more credit in the public's favour (remember that public servants are also inhabitants, as are also their friends and relatives) we get more and more solutions through this informal – and rapid – approach.

If we find no solution by informal means, we must start formal procedures, which begin by clearly stating, on paper, the nature of the claim and the request of the claimant. In order to do so, we often have to articulate the content of the claim ourselves. The claimant is unsatisfied, and he or she knows it, but does not know precisely how he or she can express such dissatisfaction. It is our work to "translate".

We then serve notice of the complaint, by the fastest possible channel, to the administration and, if there is one or more, to the public officers concerned, requesting them to refer to the complaint within the following five working days.

As mentioned before, we attempt to avoid legal terminology in the language we use in the performance of our tasks. The model forms prepared for the different steps of the procedure follow this pattern, though they have had to be modified several times in order to achieve the greatest precision possible. In our forms we also attempt to avoid giving the impression that there is a contention, or that there are sides or parties. We encourage alternative solutions to a conflict without even labelling it as a conflict.

During the first year of our work, not only were our forms a bit harsh – or rude, or menacing – but also the attitude of the recipients in the public sector was more of annoyance and rejection and even fear, than of cooperation. This meant delays in responding, which back-logged our proceedings. It took time, modifications in the forms, and increased good will from the addressees of our requests (and public relations with them, who also began to identify themselves with what we did for the population elsewhere) to begin shortening the time of their response.

The worst case was when our request fell on a lawyer's desk. We lawyers somehow learn – or are taught – that if we cannot win a case, we must make it a complicated one, so that the other party doesn't win either, or wins with great delay. This culture reflected in many of the responses written by lawyers of the public institutions, which have also learnt better with time about the Ombudsman institution.

Once we get the response, we must begin our investigation of the case. The law provides that we should end cases within sixty days of receipt. Impossible in many instances, but a valid aim in most cases.

Investigation is done, without formalities, in the best ways available. We have found that the most convenient, usually, is an on site visit, where we can see for ourselves what others have conveyed to us, speak with people who are knowledgeable of the issue, and basically get a "feel" of it. Frequently we learn about issues by asking friends or authorities in the field (always eager to cooperate with our investigations). Less used are the more formal ways of legal proceedings, such as witness depositions or formally recorded hearings.

The institution's prerogatives for investigation are very ample. The Ombudsman, or his delegates, may inspect any public facility, at any time. The institution may request from public entities any documentation or information relevant to its duties, may ask any civil servants or public officer (except those protected by immunity) to make a declaration at any time, at the Ombudsman institution. All the rest of the public sector must give the Ombudsman preferential assistance of any type required for the conduct of its tasks: all have, of course, to reply to any official request of the Ombudsman. Only the documents declared secret by law may be shielded from the regard of the Ombudsman.

We are always available to receive anyone's comments on the issue being investigated and file it in the document, even if the commentator is not a "party" to the issue.

Rulings

22. Being independent from any authority, the Ombudsman institution can make decisions – or resolutions – on its own, without consideration to any other authority, and after having followed all procedures that would comply with the rights of individuals which are the object of the complaint.

23. Resolutions of the Ombudsman are distinct from other frequently used administrative or jurisdictional acts. They are not rulings, nor decisions of jurisdictional content, nor are they administrative acts that entail their own thrust for enforcement. They are simply "the Ombudsman's resolutions", and are not binding on any one, and have the status of "recommendations" of the Ombudsman. In Costa Rica, the law goes one step further than in other countries when it states that the recommendations of the Ombudsman should be complied with, unless there is a justification (any, I would say) not to do so (Art. 14.3).

It is said that the Ombudsman does not have authority, but that the institution develops "auctoritas" or respect for its decisions. All acts and resolutions of the Ombudsman and of the institution should have such a circumstance in view. Resolutions should be phrased as recommendations, but based on objective formulation of the facts, the allegations of the claimant and of the administration, and the interpretation given by the Ombudsman from the viewpoint of the rights of the individuals and of the people.

This "auctoritas" is developed through a particular contact and identification with the people, with the individual inhabitants. Communication media, for many reasons, are very prone to report on the activities of the Ombudsman institution and in doing so helps the institution to gain identification and respect from the people and from the administration itself.

It is not common that resolutions of the Ombudsman be published as such. What is common is that resolutions of the Ombudsman are reported by the press, radio and television stations.

As a matter of fact, the Ombudsman must be keen in regard to this type of coverage and even plan to develop into a really familiar and respected champion of right causes, who speaks up on behalf of those who are not given any attention.

24. The Ombudsman institution does not award anything in its resolutions, much less compensation to be paid by government. After attempting a rapid

resolution of any dispute involving a person and the government, the Ombudsman would begin its procedure, which is oriented towards the enjoyment of the right having been denied by the government, and the resolution would basically recommend the restoration of the right, rather than payment of compensation. If the right is to receive a compensation, we would orient our recommendations towards the realization of the right of receiving compensation, and would ask that it be made, without necessarily indicating amounts. Sometimes, because of the great length of time during which the right to receive compensation has been denied, we would recommend that interest be paid together with the compensation, or that in some way the purchasing power of the compensation is made to reflect what it would have been if it had been in time.

25. In our experience, many of the cases we handled attracted media attention either when they were first presented – or began, as the Ombudsman may open cases of its own volition – or became known while being investigated, or somehow the authority involved made it public. In all of these cases, plus may others for which the Ombudsman felt that making them public would benefit future respect for the rights infringed, the institution has made them public. Several ways were used. Sometimes a special statement of the Ombudsman was prepared and distributed to the media; on other occasions the issue was mentioned in a special press release – sent to some 60 correspondents – and in very important cases, a press conference was called. In particular cases, perhaps those initiated after a publication in a particular media channel, or having been previously covered by it, we called journalists from that media and further explained the resolution taken.

The Ombudsman Institution Annual Report is not meant to contain a listing of all cases handled (an abridged list is submitted to each Congressperson, together with the Annual Report), nor of course the contents of the resolutions taken. It does, however, contain details of some salient cases in each of the areas of defence, as well as profiles of the issues most frequently brought to the attention of the Ombudsman Institution. The Report contains, for these cases, a presentation of the way in which the issue is decided, and some observations in regard to the need to ensure full protection of the right being analysed, so that many more persons are made aware of the issue, and so that public servants know about their obligations.

In this way, the series of Annual Reports of the Ombudsman institution becomes a most valuable source for research, be it academic or practical, on human rights in the country. Of course, the institution keeps records – increasingly electronic – of all the thousands of issues brought to its attention.

26. The resolution of the Ombudsman – again, it is not a ruling – is done in last instance. There is not an appeals body. Any interested party may, within eight days of receiving notification, ask the Ombudsman for reconsideration of the resolution (Art. 22).

The possibility to ask reconsideration is one frequently used by lawyers, when they are the ones, on their own or on behalf of their superior, receive the resolution. Other "addressees" do not use it as often. The request must be duly explained and sustained, and the Ombudsman institution would only address the issues subject to objection.

All the resolutions are subscribed, and signed by the Ombudsman himself, or by the Adjunct Ombudsman in the areas delegated to her, or if she is acting in the absence of the Ombudsman, in which case she would be Acting Ombudsman. In case the resolution has been subscribed by the Adjunct Ombudsman, the Ombudsman would pursue the reconsideration request, in the way he deems fit. If the request regards a resolution of the Ombudsman himself, what is done is to select a person in the staff different from the one who made the original investigation to review the case and advise the Ombudsman on the new resolution. A custom was established early on to give credit, in the resolution itself, to the staff member who had done the investigation and to the Director who had guided it.

27. Some statistics:

Year	Submissions	Cases resolved
1993–94	6,201	3,797
1994–95	11,242	2,721
1995–96	19,916	5,629
1996–97	25,064	8,820

During these 43 months, the institution opened 8217 formal investigations and reached conclusions and resolutions in 6851 of them.

Review of Experience

Personally, I must say that the experience of leading an Ombudsman institution has been most rewarding. It is, no doubt, a highly exacting position; one which demands attention and many, many hours a day, six-and-a-half days a week. It gets you in contact with thousands of people you meet continuously, and with many more thousands you always keep in your mind, and who give you continuous strength to keep up your efforts. You cannot fail them. They trust in what you do and see their "defender" as someone who cares, and who has to care. They expect it.

As with any organization deeply involved with society, there are many difficulties experienced. It is the task of the Ombudsman to deal with them. The office, as time goes by, becomes ever stronger and better equipped to face difficulties. After all, it takes time, and much effort, to build up "auctoritas". The delicate task of doing it, being always in the spot-light, makes facing each difficulty a new adventure and brings forth the need to keep the balance that has led you so far, and you must do it keeping in mind those who trust you. It is worth it.

The Institution of the Ombudsman in Mauritius

Veda Bhadain*

Constitutional Basis

The provisions defining the tasks and organizational structure of the Office of the Ombudsman (as it is referred to in Mauritius) are contained in the Constitution, where the whole of chapter IX describes the mode of appointment and functioning of the institution. A further piece of legislation, the Ombudsman Act 1969, lays down in some further details the procedures for making complaints to the Ombudsman.

This Constitutional status brings in an element of reinforced independence of the institution as this status is designed to protect it from Executive control so that it can perform its functions with independence and impartiality. Had the basis of the institution been in an ordinary law as opposed to the Constitution, any amendment as to its role and scope could have been possible by the ordinary process of legislation. In fact the required majority for amendments to the law is a simple majority while generally, amendments to Constitutional provisions require a three-quarter majority of votes. In the case of the institution of the Ombudsman, further safeguards have been brought in by making Chapter IX an entrenched part of the Constitution which can only be amended by strictly complying with section 47 of the Constitution.

The Mauritian Constitution in fact goes into detailed provisions as to the functioning of that office, namely, detailed provisions describe the investigations that may be carried out by the Ombudsman, the procedure in respect of the investigations, the disclosure of information, the proceedings after investigations, etcetera.

The fact that such detailed provisions are contained within the Constitution itself may sometimes be seen as a handicap in so far as it may sometimes be necessary to amend certain provisions with time so as to render the machinery more effective and this may be difficult in practice. However, giving Constitutional status to the procedure by which it operates gives more certainty to an efficient functioning of the institution.

There is no risk that once the institution is set up, the mechanisms through which it operates become so loose and permeable that the very objectivity with which it is supposed to operate is threatened.

---

* Barrister-at-Law.

K. Hossain et al. (eds), Human Rights Commissions and Ombudsman Offices, 315–329.

Section 96 of the Constitution lays down the mode of appointment of the Ombudsman. It states that the Ombudsman shall be appointed by the President of the Republic, acting after consultation with the Prime Minister, the Leader of the Opposition and any such other persons as appear to the President to be leaders of parties in the legislative Assembly.

Section 97(3) of the Constitution specifically provides that the Ombudsman cannot be a member of or a candidate for election to the Legislative Assembly any local Authority nor can he be holder of a public office nor be a Local Government Officer. The above provisions are aimed, on the one hand, at reinforcing the independence of the office and, on the other, at ensuring that the choice of the Ombudsman is a generally accepted one and not contested from different quarters.

By laying down that the power of appointment of the Ombudsman rests with the President of the Republic as opposed to the Parliament, is seen as an advantage as it is aimed at ensuring the political impartiality of the holder of the position of Ombudsman. It should be highlighted here that the President does not hold an elected position but is nominated and he does not have executive powers except for certain residual executive powers as expressly stated in the Constitution. In fact the President of the Republic has the same prerogatives as the Governor General prior to Mauritius acquiring the status of Republic.

The history of Mauritian institutions has shown that the President of the Republic acts with political impartiality despite the fact that his nomination must be effected by the Prime Minister.

Independence and Impartiality

Section 101 lays the foundation for independence and impartiality by stating that in the discharge of his functions, the Ombudsman shall not be subject to the direction and control of any other person or authority and that proceedings of the Ombudsman (except in cases of allegations of fraud and corruption) shall not be called in question in any court of law.

Further protection of his independence is afforded by the provisions regarding the tenure of office of the holder of the position of the Ombudsman. In fact he holds office during good behaviour and may be removed only by reason of inability (infirmity of body or mind) or misbehaviour. The procedure is that the President of the Republic, acting in his own deliberate judgement, appoints a tribunal composed of a Chairman and two members, who are usually Judges, to conduct the case. The Ombudsman may only be removed if his unfitness is established and the Tribunal makes a recommendation in that sense to the President of the Republic. This procedure is a safeguard against any possibility of the removal of the Ombudsman at the pleasure of the President.

Another aspect of the high degree of protection is the salary attached to the office. Section 108 of the Constitution provides that the salary of the Ombudsman is charged on the Consolidated Fund just like the salaries of Judges. Thus the authority for payment is permanent and does not have to be renewed in Parliament every year.

The Staffing of the Office is also given particular attention. Section 96(3) of he Constitution makes provision for a special status of the officers who are public officers but subject to the direction and control of the Ombudsman.

The relationship between the office of the Ombudsman and the legislature is one of responsibility to the Parliament. There is no doubt that the role of the Ombudsman is designed as a means of exercising control on government business.

The Ombudsman has the Constitutional duty to investigate complaints of maladministration addressed to him by the public and to make a report every year to the President of the Republic which is laid before the Parliament.

At the conclusion of the investigation, the Ombudsman reports his opinion to the department concerned and he may make appropriate recommendations to remedy the grievance. Where within reasonable time no action is taken he may make a report to the Parliament. This is used as a means of pressure which he Ombudsman can put on the administration.

Complaints Regarding Acts of Governments

Complaints can be made to the Ombudsman for any act of maladministration. For the purpose of the Ombudsman's casework, the term has been interpreted with great flexibility and has been described as any kind of administrative shortcoming. It includes such defects as delay or neglect in dealing with a citizen's case, failure to take action or to reply to a letter, failure to ensure a power, disparity of treatment between individuals, inefficiency and unfairness.

Jurisdiction of the Ombudsman

The Ombudsman may investigate any action taken by the following officers and authorities:

(a) any department of the Government
(b) the Police Force or any member thereof
(c) the Mauritius Prison Service or any other service maintained and controlled by the Government or any authority for such services
(d) any authority empowered to determine the person with whom any contract or class of contracts is to be entered into or on behalf of the Government or any such officer or authority
(e) such other authorities or officers as may be prescribed by the Parliament.

There are provisions in the Constitution to amend the list to include other public officers and authorities. This can be done by act of Parliament.

On the other hand, the Ombudsman has no jurisdiction over the following officers and authorities:

(a) the president of the Republic and his personal staff
(b) the Chief Justice
(c) any Commission established by the Constitution or his staff
(d) the Director of Public Prosecutions or any person acting in accordance with his instructions.

It should also be pointed out that not all actions taken by public officers and authorities are subject to the Ombudsman's jurisdiction. Section 97(1) of the

Constitution authorizes him to investigate only actions taken in an administrative function. The Ombudsman has no jurisdiction to investigate complaints against legislation and against judicial functions of public authorities. These would be matters to be dealt with by the courts of law and tribunals.

Investigations, Report and Recommendation

Investigation Upon the Ombudsman's Own Motion

Besides complaints made to the Ombudsman on the basis of which he can act, the Ombudsman can act on his own motion by virtue of section 97 (1) of the Constitution. This procedure would normally be triggered if the Ombudsman finds that there is a prima facie case of maladministration which requires an investigation.

Investigation Upon Receiving a Complaint

In cases when complaints are made, the Ombudsman has the power to determine whether the complaint was duly made. This gives him a wide measure of discretion in deciding whether the procedural requirements prescribing the manner in which complaints are to be referred to him have been followed.

Upon receiving a complaint, the Ombudsman has to decide whether the matter is within his jurisdiction. This is done taking into consideration the areas where his jurisdiction is ousted as pointed out above. Then in deciding whether the complaint has been duly made, he takes into account such questions as the time limit for making a complaint, whether the complainant has sufficient interest in the matter and any other such issue which he judges relevant according to the circumstances of the case. The decision to investigate or not is a discretionary one according to section 101(2) of the Constitution. The exercise of this discretionary power is not subject to the control of any court or authority. Furthermore when investigation is under way, the Ombudsman may in his discretion decide to continue or discontinue with the case.

Proceedings

In so far as the proceedings are concerned, section 98(2) of the Constitution gives the Ombudsman the power to determine the procedure for conducting his investigations. There are therefore no set rules of procedure for investigation. Each time there is a complaint of maladministration, the Ombudsman decides whether to investigate or not and at the same time decides on the procedure most appropriate for the case. This brings in an element of procedural flexibility which has shown to be very productive.

Power to Call and Examine Witnesses

For the purpose of an investigation, the Ombudsman has wide powers of compelling any person, including public officers, who in his opinion is able to produce documents and furnish information. In this respect the Ombudsman has the same powers as the Supreme Court. This means that the Ombudsman exercises the powers which the law relating to contempt of court has developed to prevent or punish conduct which tends to obstruct or prejudice the due administration of justice.

Similarly, in respect of witnesses, the Ombudsman has the same powers as the Supreme Court to summon any person to appear before him to give evidence or to answer questions in respect of the matter under investigation. Failure to attend or refusal to give evidence or to answer questions may render him liable for contempt.

Power of the Ombudsman and the Doctrine of Crown Privilege

In law, certain documents are protected from production as evidence in legal proceedings by a rule which authorizes non-disclosure of such documents which it would be injurious to the public interest to disclose. This rule does not apply to the investigations of the Ombudsman in the same manner. Section 99(3) of the Constitution provides:

> "The Crown shall not be entitled in relation to any such investigation to any such privilege in respect of the production of documents or the giving of evidence as is allowed by law in legal proceedings ..."

The Ombudsman can therefore, for the purpose of investigation, require and have access to files, documents and information which are privileged in the legal sense. However, this does not mean that the power to require information and documents is unrestricted. Section 99(4) of the Constitution provides that information and documents relating to Cabinet proceedings are privileged on production of a certificate by the Secretary to the Cabinet with the approval of the Prime Minister to the effect that these information or documents relate to proceedings of the Cabinet or a committee of the Cabinet.

Privilege of Communication

Proceedings before the Ombudsman, just like judicial proceedings, are privileged. Section 5 of the Ombudsman Act provides that a report or communication relating to an investigation made by or to the Ombudsman is absolutely privileged in the law of defamation. Consequently, no person may be liable in the courts for words spoken or any statements made in the course of proceedings before the Ombudsman. This is to encourage any person to have a complete right of free speech without any fear that his motives or intentions will be held against him thereafter. On the other hand, contents of reports and communications relating to an investigation cannot be used as evidence in an action for defamation.

Remedy After Investigation

If after investigation it is found that the complaint is justified, the Ombudsman's office cannot take sanctions. This is a major drawback of the system. In fact, the Ombudsman cannot quash a decision nor declare it to be of no effect. The Ombudsman can do no more than express his opinion on the matter and recommend that steps be taken to remedy the grievance. The department concerned is under no obligation to give effect to the recommendation made.

Any remedial action will depend on the willingness of the administration to cooperate in the process of investigation. There is however the course of action whereby the Ombudsman reports the non-observance of his recommendation in the report submitted to the President of the Republic which is laid before the Parliament. This will constitute a source of pressure on the Minister concerned and thus on the administration. But it is to be noted that recommendations of the Ombudsman are not binding as would have been a decision of a court of justice.

The Human Rights Commission

The Mauritian system used not to comprise of a specific body referred to as a Human Rights Commission. Matters pertaining to the guarantee and protection of fundamental rights were within the jurisdiction of the Supreme Court, which is the highest level of jurisdiction available locally, the final court of appeal being the Judicial Committee of the Privy Council in England.

The basic human rights are embodied in Chapter II of the Constitution entitled "Protection of Fundamental Rights and Freedoms of the Individual". The Supreme Court, being the guardian of the Constitution, is the body to which any issue relating to Human Rights are referred to.

There has been a recent evolution in the legislative framework concerning Human Rights in Mauritius since this paper was first written. In fact the Mauritian Parliament has enacted "The Protection of Human Rights Act 1998" in December 1998. This Act provides for the setting up of a National Human Rights Commission for the better protection of human rights, for the better investigation of complaints against members of the police force and other incidental matters. The Act provided for the entry into force of this legislation by proclamation. Such Proclamation was effected in February 1999.

LEGISLATION

Constitution of Mauritius

Chapter IX – The Ombudsman

96. Office of Ombudsman

(1) There shall be an Ombudsman, whose office shall be a public office.

(2) The Ombudsman shall be appointed by the President, acting after consultation with the Prime Minister, the Leader of the Opposition and such other persons, if any, as appear to the President, acting in his own deliberate judgment to be leaders of parties in the Assembly.

(3) No person shall be qualified for appointment as Ombudsman if he is a member of, or a candidate for election to, the Assembly or any local authority or is a local government officer, and no person holding the office of Ombudsman shall perform the functions of any other public office.

(4) The offices of the staff of the Ombudsman shall be public offices and shall consist of that of a Senior Investigations Officer and such other offices as may be prescribed by the President, acting after consultation with the Prime Minister. [Amended 48/91]

97. Investigations by Ombudsman

(1) Subject to this section, the Ombudsman may investigate any action taken by any officer or authority to which this section applies in the exercise of administrative

functions of that officer or authority, in any case in which a member of the public claims, or appears to the Ombudsman, to have sustained injustice in consequence of maladministration in connection with the action so taken and in which

(a) a complaint under this section is made;
(b) he is invited to do so by any Minister or other member of the Assembly; or
(c) he considers it desirable to do so of his own motion.

(2) This section applies to the following officers and authorities:

(a) any department of the Government;
(b) the Police Force or any member thereof;
(c) the Mauritius Prison Service or any other service maintained and controlled by the Government or any officer or authority of any such service;
(d) any authority empowered to determine the person with whom any contract or class of contracts is to be entered into by or on behalf of the Government or any such officer or authority;
(e) such other officers or authorities as may be prescribed by Parliament:
Provided that it shall not apply in relation to any of the following officers and authorities -
(i) the President or his personal staff;
(ii) the Chief Justice;
(iii) any Commission established by this Constitution or its staff;
(iv) the Director of Public Prosecutions or any person acting in accordance with his instructions;
(v) any person exercising powers delegated to him by the Public Service Commission or the Police Service Commission, being powers the exercise of which is subject to review or confirmation by the Commission by which they were delegated.

(3) A complaint under this section may be made by an individual, or by any body of persons whether incorporated or not, not being:

(a) an authority of the Government or a local authority or other authority or body constituted for purposes of the public service or local government; or
(b) any other authority or body whose members are appointed by the President or by a Minister or whose revenues consist wholly or mainly of money provided from public funds.

(4) Where any person by whom a complaint might have been made under subsection (3) has died or is for any reason unable to act for himself, the complaint may be made by his personal representative or by a member of his family or other individual suitable to represent him; but except as specified in this subsection, a complaint shall not be entertained unless made by the person aggrieved himself.

(5) The Ombudsman shall not conduct an investigation in respect of any complaint under this section unless the person aggrieved is resident in Mauritius (or, if he is dead, was so resident at the time of his death) or the complaint relates to action taken in relation to him while he was present in Mauritius or in relation to rights or obligations that accrued or arose in Mauritius.

(6) The Ombudsman shall not conduct an investigation under this section in respect of any complaint under this section in so far as it relates to

(a) any action in respect of which the person aggrieved has or had a right of appeal, reference or review to or before a tribunal constituted by or under any law in force in Mauritius; or
(b) any action in respect of which the person aggrieved has or had a remedy by way of proceedings in any court of law:
Provided that
(i) the Ombudsman may conduct such an investigation notwithstanding that the person aggrieved has or had such a right or remedy if satisfied that in the particular circumstances it is not reasonable to expect him to avail

himself or to have availed himself of that right or remedy; and
(ii) nothing in this subsection shall preclude the Ombudsman from conductin any investigation as to whether any of the provisions of Chapter II ha been contravened.

(7) The Ombudsman shall not conduct an investigation in respect of any complai made under this section in respect of any action if he is given notice in writing b the Prime Minister that the action was taken by a Minister in person in the exercis of his own deliberate judgment.

(8) The Ombudsman shall not conduct an investigation in respect of any complai made under this section where it appears to him:
(a) that the complaint is merely frivolous or vexatious;
(b) that the subject-matter of the complaint is trivial;
(c) that the person aggrieved has no sufficient interest in the subject-matter of th complaint; or
(d) that the making of the complaint has, without reasonable cause, been delaye for more than 12 months.

(9) The Ombudsman shall not conduct an investigation under this section in respect c any matter where he is given notice by the Prime Minister that the. investigation c that matter would not be in the interests of the security of Mauritius.

(10) In this section, "action" includes failure to act.
[Amended 2/82; 48/91)

98. Procedure in respect of investigations

(1) Where the Ombudsman proposes to conduct an investigation under section 97, h shall afford to the principal officer of any department or authority concerned, and t any other person who is alleged to have taken o authorized the action in questio an opportunity to comment on any allegations made to the Ombudsman in respec of it.

(2) Every such investigation shall be conducted in private but, except as provided in thi Constitution or as prescribed under section 102, the procedure for conducting a investigation shall be such as the Ombudsman considers appropriate in the circum stances of the case; and without prejudice to subsection (1), the Ombudsman ma obtain information from such persons and in such manner, and make such enquirie as he thinks fit, and may determine whether any person may be represented, b counsel or attorney or otherwise, in the investigation.

99. Disclosure of information

(1) For the purposes of an investigation under section 97, the Ombudsman may requir any Minister, officer or member of any department or authority concerned or an other person who in his opinion is able to furnish information or produce document relevant to the investigation to furnish any such information or produce any suc document.

(2) For the purposes of any such investigation, the Ombudsman shall have the sam powers as the Supreme Court in respect of the attendance and examination o witnesses (including the administration of oaths and the examination of witnesse abroad) and in respect of the production of documents.

(3) No obligation to maintain secrecy or other restriction upon the disclosure of informa tion obtained by or furnished to persons in the public service imposed by any law i force in Mauritius or any rule of law shall apply to the disclosure of information fo the purposes of any such investigation, and the State shall not be entitled in relatio to any such investigation to any such privilege in respect of the production o documents or the giving of evidence as is allowed by law in legal proceedings.

(4) No person shall be required or authorized by virtue of this section to furnish an information or answer any question or produce any document relating to proceeding of the Cabinet or any committee of Cabinet, and for the purposes of this subsection

a certificate issued by the Secretary to the Cabinet with the approval of the Prime Minister and certifying that any information, question or document so relates shall be conclusive.

(5) The Attorney-General may give notice to the Ombudsman, with respect to any document or information specified in the notice, or any class of documents or information so specified, that in his opinion the disclosure of that document or information, or of documents or information of that class, would be contrary to the public interest in relation to defence, external relations or internal security; and where such a notice is given nothing in this section shall be construed as authorizing or requiring the Ombudsman or any member of his staff to communicate to any person for any purpose any document or information specified in the notice, or any document or information of a class so specified.

(6) Subject to subsection (3), no person shall be compelled for the purposes of an investigation under section 97 to give any evidence or produce any document which he could not be compelled to give or produce in proceedings before the Supreme Court.

[Amended 48/91]

100. Proceedings after investigation

(1) This section shall apply in every case where, after making an investigation, the Ombudsman is of opinion that te action that was the subject-macer of investigation was

(a) contrary to law;
(b) based wholly or partly on a mistake of law or fact;
(c) unreasonably delayed; or
(d) otherwise unjust or manifestly unreasonable.

(2) Where in any case to which this section applies the Ombudsman is of opinion

(a) that the matter should be given further consideration;
(b) that an omission should be rectified;
(c) that a decision should be cancelled, reversed or varied;
(d) that any practice on which the act, omission, decision or recommendation was based should be altered;
(e) that any law on which the act, omission, decision or recommendation was based should be reconsidered;
(f) that reasons should have been given for the decision; or
(g) that any other steps should be taken,

the Ombudsman shall report his opinion, and his reasons, to the principal officer of any department or authority concerned, and may make such recommendations as he thinks fit; he may request that officer to notify him, within a specified time, of any steps that it is proposed to take to give effect to his recommendations; and he shall also send a copy of his report and recommendations to the Prime Minister and to any Minister concerned.

(3) Where within a reasonable time after the report is made no action is taken which seems to the Ombudsman to be adequate and appropriate, the Ombudsman, if he thinks fit, after considering any comments made by or on behalf of any department, authority, body or person affected, may send a copy of the report and recommendations to the Prime Minister and to any Minister concerned, and may thereafter make such further report to the Assembly on the matter as he thinks fit.

101. Discharge of functions of Ombudsman

(1) In the discharge of his functions, the Ombudsman shall not be subject to the direction or control of any other person or authority and no proceedings of the Ombudsman other than proceedings under section 102A, shall be called in question in any court of law.

(2) In determining whether to initiate, to continue or discontinue an investigation under section 97, the Ombudsman shall act in accordance with his own discretion; and any

question whether a complaint is duly made for the purposes of that section shall b determined by the Ombudsman.

(3) The Ombudsman shall make an annual report to the President concerning th discharge of his functions, which shall be laid before the Assembly.
(Amended 48/91]

102. Supplementary and ancillary provision

There shall be such provision as may be prescribed for such supplementary and ancillar matters as may appear necessary or expedient in consequence of any of the provisior of this Chapter, including (without prejudice to the generality of the foregoing powe provision

(a) for the procedure to be observed by the Ombudsman in performing his functions;
(b) for the manner in which complaints under section 97 may be made (including requirement that such complaints should be transmitted to the Ombudsman throug the intermediary of a member of the Assembly);
(c) for the payment of fees in respect of any complaint or investigation;
(d) for the powers, protection and privileges of the Ombudsman and his staff or of othe persons or authorities with respect to any investigation or report by the Ombudsma including the privilege of communications to and from the Ombudsman and hi staff; and
(e) the definition and trial of offences connected with the functions of the Ombudsma and his staff and the imposition of penalties for such offences.

102A. Allegation of fraud or corruption

(1) (a) Notwithstanding the other provisions of this Chapter and subject to subsectio (2), the Ombudsman may investigate any allegation of fraud or corruptio against a person, other than a Judge of the Supreme Court, who holds or ha held an office specified in the Fourth Schedule, concerning an act or omissio related to the exercise of the, duties of that person.
(b) The Ombudsman may investigate any allegation of fraud or corruption unde paragraph (a)
(i) on a complaint made to him in writing;
(ii) of his own motion.
(c) In paragraph (a), "allegation of fraud or corruption" means an allegation tha the person concerned has by an act or omission rendered himself liable to b prosecuted for an offence involving fraud or corruption which is punishabl under the Criminal Code or such other enactment as may be prescribed.

(2) The Ombudsman shall not conduct an investigation in respect of an allegation mad under subsection (1) where it appears to him that
(a) the allegation is merely frivolous or vexatious;
(b) the subject-matter of the allegation is trivial;
(c) the making of the allegation has, without reasonable cause, been delayed fo more than twelve months.

(3) Where the Ombudsman proposes to conduct an investigation under this section, he shall afford to the person against whom the allegation is made an opportunity to comment thereon.

(4) Where after hearing the person concerned and after making such preliminary investigation as he may deem fit, the Ombudsman is of the opinion that the allegation is groundless, he shall
(a) put an end to the investigation;
(b) inform the maker of the allegation as well as the person against whom the allegation was made accordingly;
(c) make a report to the President accordingly.

(5) The Ombudsman may obtain information from such person and an such manner and make such enquiries, as he thinks fit.

(6) Where after making a preliminary investigation, the Ombudsman is of the opinion that a full enquiry is necessary, he shall inform the maker of the allegation as well as the person against whom the allegation was made accordingly.

(7) (a) The Ombudsman shall, when making a full enquiry under this section, be assisted by two assessors appointed on such terms and conditions as the President may deem fit.
   (b) Any assessor appointed under this subsection shall take such oath as may be prescribed.

(8) The procedure for conducting a preliminary investigation or a full enquiry shall be such as the Ombudsman considers appropriate in the circumstances of the case.

(9) Section 99 shall apply to a full enquiry under this section.

(10) Subject to the other provisions of this section, the Ombudsman shall be bound by the law of evidence as is applicable in proceedings before the Supreme Court.

(11) Any complaint made in writing to the Ombudsman or any evidence given before the Ombudsman shall not, where made or given in good faith, give rise to any civil or criminal proceedings.

(12) On the completion of an enquiry under this section, the Ombudsman shall make a report to the President.

(13) (a) On receipt of a report under subsection (12), the President shall submit a copy thereof to the Prime Minister.
   (b) The Prime Minister shall, within 3 months of the receipt of a copy of the report, lay it before the Assembly.
   [Added 48/91]

The Protection of Human Rights Act 1998

Entry into force 23 February 1999

An Act
To provide for the setting up of a National Human, Rights Commission, for the better protection of human rights, for the better investigation of complaints against members of the police force, and for matters connected therewith or incidental thereto

ENACTED by the Parliament of Mauritius, as follows -

1. Short title
   This Act may be cited as the Protection of Human Rights Act 1998.

2. Interpretation
   In this Act:
   "Commission" means the National Human Rights Commission established under section 3;
   "human rights" means any right or freedom referred to in Chapter II of the Constitution;
   "member"
   (a) means a member of the Commission;
   (b) includes the Chairman;
   "Minister" means the Minister to whom responsibility for the subject of human rights is assigned; '
   "public body" means
   (a) a Ministry or Government department;
   (b) a local authority;
   (c) a statutory corporation;
   (d) any other company, partnership or other entity of which the Government or an

agency of the Government is, by the holding of shares or some other financi input or in any other manner, in a position to influence the policy or decisions;

3. Establishment and appointment of the Commission
   (1) There is established, for the purposes of this Act, a National Human Right Commission, which shall be a body corporate and which shall consist of Chairman and 3 other members.
   (2) The Chairman shall be a person who has been a Judge.
   (3) The other members of the Commission shall be
      (a) a person who has been a Judge or is a barrister of more than 10 year standing; and
      (b) 2 other persons having knowledge of, or practical experience in, matter relating to human rights.
   (4) The Chairman and other members shall be appointed by the President, actin on the advice of the Prime Minister, on such terms and conditions as he thinks fi
   (5) Every member shall hold office for a term of 4 years or until he attains the ag of 70, whichever occurs earlier.
   (6) Subject to subsection (6), every member shall be eligible for reappointment for second term of 4 years.
   (7) The President may, on the advice of the Prime Minister, remove any membe from office for inability to perform the functions of his office. whether arisin from infirmity of body or mind, or for misbehaviour.
   (8) Where any vacancy occurs in the office of the Chairman by reason of deat resignation or any other cause, the President may authorize another member t act as Chairman until the vacancy is filled.
   (9) Where the Chairman is absent or on leave, the President may authorize anothe member to discharge the functions of the Chairman until the date on which th Chairman resumes his office.
   (10) A member shall not enter upon the duties of his office unless he has taken an subscribed before the President the oath set out in the Schedule.

4. Functions of the Commission
   (1) Subject to subsection (2), the Commission may, without prejudice to the jurisdic tion of the Courts or the powers conferred on the Director of Public Prosecution or the appropriate Service Commission:
      (a) enquire into any written complaint from any person alleging that any if hi human rights has been, is being or is likely to be violated by the act o omission of any other person acting in the performance of any public functio conferred by any law or otherwise in the performance of the functions of an public office or any public body;
      (b) enquire into any other written complaint from any person against an act o omission of a member of the police force in relation to him, other than a act or omission which is the subject of an investigation by the Ombudsman
      (c) where it has reason to believe that an act or omission such as is referred t in paragraph (a) or (b) has occurred, is occurring or is likely to occur, of it own motion enquire into the matter;
      (d) visit any police station, prison or other place of detention under the contro of the State to study the living conditions of the inmates and the treatmen afforded to them;
      (e) review the safeguards provided by or under any enactment for the protectio of human rights;
      (f) review the factors or difficulties that inhibit the enjoyment of human rights;
      (g) exercise such other functions as it may consider to be conducive to th promotion and protection of human rights.
      (a) The Commission shall not enquire into any matter after the expiry of 2 year

from the date on which the act or omission which is the subject of a complaint is alleged to have occurred.

(b) The Commission shall not exercise its functions and powers in relation to any of the officers and authorities specified in the proviso to section 97(2) of the Constitution.

(3) The Commission shall, in the first place, attempt to resolve any complaint, or any matter which is the subject of an enquiry pursuant to subsection (1) (c), by a conciliatory procedure.

(4) Where the Commission has not been able to resolve a matter through conciliation, it shall, on the completion of its enquiry -

(a) where the enquiry discloses a violation of human rights or negligence in the prevention of such violation, refer the matter to:

(i) the Director of Public Prosecutions where it appears that an offence may have been committed;

(ii) the appropriate Service Commission where it appears that disciplinary procedures may be warranted;

(iii) to the chief executive officer of the appropriate public body where it appears that disciplinary action is warranted against an employee of a public body who is not within the jurisdiction of a Service Commission;

(b) recommend the grant of such relief to the complainant or to such other person as the Commission thinks fit;

(c) inform the complainant, if any, of any action taken under this subsection.

(5) The Commission shall, on the completion of its enquiry, send a written communication setting out its conclusion and any recommendation to the Minister who shall, as soon as practicable, report to the Commission the action taken or proposed to be taken.

(6) (a) Where any person makes a written complaint to a police officer against an act or omission of another police officer in relation to him, the Commissioner of Police shall, as soon as is reasonably practicable:

(i) forward to the Secretary of the Commission a copy of the complaint; and

(ii) inform the Commission of any criminal or disciplinary proceedings taken or to be taken as a result of the complaint.

(b) The Commission may require the Commissioner of Police to provide it with such further information as it thinks fit in relation to any matter referred to in paragraph (a).

(c) Where, in relation to any matter referred to in paragraph (a), the Commission is informed that no criminal or disciplinary proceedings are to be taken, it may enquire into the matter and exercise in relation thereto any of the powers conferred upon it under this Act.

5. Staff of the Commission

(1) The Secretary to the Cabinet shall make available to the Commission an officer of the rank of Principal Assistant Secretary who shall be the Secretary of the Commission and such other administrative and other staff as the Commission may require.

(2) The Secretary of the Commission shall be the Chief Executive Officer of the Commission and shall exercise such powers and discharge such administrative functions as the Commission may delegate to him.

6. Powers and duties of the Commission

(1) The Commission may, for the purposes of this Act -

(a) summon witnesses and examine them on oath;

(b) call for the production of any document or other exhibit;

(c) obtain such information, file or other record, if necessary by an order from the Judge in Chambers, as may be necessary for the exercise of its functions.

(2) Any officer of the Commission specially authorization in that behalf by th Chairman may, on a warrant issued by the Commission, enter any building o place where the Commission has reason to believe that any document or oth exhibit relating to the subject matter of an enquiry may be found and may sei any such document or other exhibit or take extracts or copies therefrom.

(3) Every order, authorization, warrant or decision of the Commission shall be authe ticated by the Secretary of the Commission or any other officer of the Commissio duly authorized by the Chairman in that behalf.

(4) The Commission shall regulate its meetings and proceedings in such manner as thinks fit, and three members shall constitute a quorum.

7. Investigation

(1) The Commission may, for the purposes or conducting any investigation pertainin to an enquiry, utilize the services of any police officer or other Public offic designated for the purpose by the Commissioner of Police or the Secretary to th Cabinet, as the case may be.

(2) The officer whose services are utilized under subsection (1) shall investigate an matter pertaining to an enquiry held by the Commission and submit a repo thereon to the Commission within such time as may be specified by th Commission.

8. Protection of witnesses

Notwithstanding any enactment but subject to section 13, no statement made by an person in the course of giving evidence before the Commission or made by or to an person whose services are utilized under section 7(I) shall, where it is:

(a) made in reply to a question which he is required by the Commission to answer; c

(b) relevant to the subject-matter of the inquiry,

subject the maker of the statement to, or be used against him in, any civil o criminal proceedings, unless he has given false evidence in the statement.

9. Persons likely to be prejudicially affected

(1) Subject to subsection (2), where at any stage of an enquiry, the Commission

(a) considers it necessary to enquire into the conduct of any person;

(b) is, of the opinion that the reputation of any such person is likely to be prejudicial affected lay the enquiry, it shall give to that person a reasonable opportunity o being heard in the enquiry and of producing such relevant evidence as that perso deems appropriate.

(2) Subsection (1) shall not apply where only the credibility of a witness is bein impeached.

10. Protection of action taken in good faith

No suit or other legal proceeding shall lie against the Commission or any membe or any person acting under the direction of the Commission in respect of anythin which is done or purported to be done in good faith in pursuance of this Act or i respect of the publication by or under the authority of the Commission or of an report, proceedings or other matter under this Act.

11. Reports of the Commission

(1) The Commission shall, not later than 31 March in each year, submit a report o its activities during the preceding year to the President and may, at any othe time, submit a special report on any matter which, in its opinion, is of suc urgency or importance that it should not be deferred until submission of th annual report..

(2) The President shall cause every report of the Commission to be laid before th Assembly within one month of its submission.

2. Finance

(1) The Commission shall, not less than 3 months before the commencement of every financial year, submit to the Minister an estimate of its expenditure.

(2) The accounts of the Commission shall be audited by the Director of Audit and any expenditure incurred in connection with such audit shall be payable by the Commission to the Director of Audit.

(3) The accounts of the Commission, as certified by the Director of Audit, together with the audit report thereon shall be forwarded annually to the Minister by the Commission and the Minister shall cause the audit report to be laid, as soon as may be after it is received, on the table of the Assembly.

3. Offences

ny person who:

(a) fails to attend the Commission after having been required to do so;

(b) refuses to take an oath before the Commission or to answer fully and satisfactorily to the best of his knowledge and belief any question lawfully put to him in any proceedings before the Commission or to produce any document or other exhibit when required so to do by the Commission;

(c) knowingly gives false evidence, or evidence which he knows to be misleading, before the Commission;

(d) at any sitting of the Commission:

(i) insults a member;

(ii) interrupts the proceedings; or

(iii) commits a contempt of the Commission,

shall commit an offence and shall, on conviction, be liable to a fine not exceeding 10,000 rupees and to imprisonment for a term not exceeding one year.

4. Jurisdiction

otwithstanding:

(a) section 114 of the Courts Act; and

(b) section 72 of the District and Intermediate Courts (Criminal Jurisdiction) Act,

a Magistrate shall have jurisdiction to try any offence against this Act and may impose any penalty provided by this Act.

5. Regulations

(1) The Minister may make such regulations as he thinks fit for the purposes of this Act.

(2) Any regulations made under subsection (1) may provide that any person who contravenes them shall commit an offence, and shall on conviction be liable to a fine not exceeding 10,000 rupees and to imprisonment for a term not exceeding one year.

6. Consequential amendment

he Statutory Bodies (Accounts and Audit) Act is amended in Part II of the Schedule y adding in its appropriate alphabetical order the following

ational Human Rights Commission

7. Commencement

his Act shall come into operation on a day to be fixed by Proclamation.

assed by the National Assembly on the eighth day of December one thousand nine undred and ninety-eight.

ndre Pompon
lerk of the National Assembly

The Office of the Ombudsman in Namibia

J. Malan*

The institution of the Office of the Ombudsman is one of the mechanisms developed and created, in addition to resorting to the judicial system, to check the exercise of administrative power. In order to have an effective institution, it is important that the Office of the Ombudsman be seen and regarded by the people as impartial and independent, and an effective way to address their problems.

The Namibian Constitution provides for the establishment of the Office of the Ombudsman. The provisions of the Constitution are amplified by the Ombudsman Act, Act No 7 of 1990.

Independence of the Ombudsman

The independence of the Office of the Ombudsman is guaranteed by the Constitution, which states that the Ombudsman shall be independent and subject only to the Constitution and the law.[1] Interference by members of the Cabinet or the Legislature or any other person with the Ombudsman in the exercise of his or her functions is prohibited, and all organs of the State are enjoined to accord such assistance as may be needed for the protection of the independence, dignity and effectiveness of the Ombudsman.[2]

While the independence of the Office is guaranteed by the Constitution, it is submitted that the efficiency and proper functioning of the Office depend on the political will of officials. It is the political maturity of officials that will guarantee that the Office of the Ombudsman is to achieve the purposes for which it was created. It is imperative that the institution of Ombudsman should be seen in its proper context. As was stated by the Ombudsman in her report:

> 'The impression created of the Office is that it is a witch-hunt institution and we would like to take this opportunity to dispel any such impression. The Office of the Ombudsman is an indispensable organ in the search for good governance and the promotion and protection of the rights of people. It is not an advocate on behalf of anybody but rather an advocate for good administration. It does not replace the courts but rather act complimentary to the courts in its pursuit of justice."[3]

---

* Legal Assistance Centre, Windhoek, Republic of Namibia.

[1] Article 89(2). Henceforth, "Articles" (or "Art") will refer to constitutional provisions.

[2] Art. 89(3).

[3] Annual Report: 1 January – 31 December 1997, Office of the Ombudsman, Republic of Namibia, p. 8.

K. Hossain et al. (eds), Human Rights Commissions and Ombudsman Offices, 331–342.

Other mechanisms to ensure the impartiality of the Office are that the Ombudsman and her/his staff members are not competent and cannot be compelled to give evidence in a court of law or before any body or institution or commission established by law regarding information obtained in the investigation of a complaint, or to produce any book or other documentation obtained as a result of such an investigation,[4] and the Ombudsman and the deputy are also not allowed to perform or commit her- or himself to perform remunerative work outside official duties without the permission of the President.[5]

The Office of the Ombudsman resorts under the Ministry of Justice for its budgetary and institutional arrangments. Budgetary constraints upon the Ministry of Justice will have an effect on the Office of the Ombudsman, as in the case of under-staffing, and the efficiency of the Office may also be negatively influenced by this relationship. It is envisaged by the Ombudsman that "(I)t may be necessary to develop a long term strategy for the Office, with a view to de-link in future ..."[6] however, it would appear that the Office thus far has operated completely freely and autonomously in its functions.[7]

Appointment of the Ombudsman

The Ombudsman is appointed by proclamation by the President on the recommendation of the Judicial Service Commission,[8] a provision that was expanded to a certain extent by the provisions of the Act, which state that the appointment of the Ombudsman pursuant to Article 90 of the Constitution shall be on such terms and conditions as the President may determine.[9]

In 1996, the controversial appointment of the acting Ombudsman as Ombudsman by the President was withdrawn following a public outcry, resulting in the appointment of the current Ombudsman. The President appointed the Ombudsman unilaterally, not in accordance with the provisions of the Constitution and not on the recommendation of the Judicial Service Commission.

The Ombudsman must either be a judge of Namibia or must possess the legal qualifications which will allow her/him to practise in all the courts of Namibia.[10] Provision is made for the appointment of a fit and proper person as deputy Ombudsman[11] and acting Ombudsman.[12]

The Ombudsman holds office until the age of 65, but the retiring age of the Ombudsman may be extended by the President to 70.[13]

---

[4] Section 4(4), Ombudsman Act, Act No '7 of 1990. "Section" or "Sec" will refer to the provisions of the Ombudsman act.
[5] Sec. 2(4).
[6] Annual Report, supra, page 7.
[7] Ibid, p. 7.
[8] Art. 90(1). In terms of Article 85 of the Constitution, the Judicial Service Commission consists of the Chief Justice, a Judge appointed by the President, the Attorney-General and two members of the legal profession nominated in accordance with an Act of Parliament by the professional organization or organizations representing the interests of the legal profession in Namibia.
[9] Sec. 2(1).
[10] Art 89(4).
[11] Sec. 2(2).
[12] Sec. 2(3).
[13] Art. 90(2).

The Ombudsman may be removed from office before the expiry of his/her term of office by the President acting on the recommendation of the Judicial Service Commission,[14] only on the ground of mental incapacity or for gross misconduct[15] and in accordance with the procedures laid down in the Constitution.[16] The President, on the recommendation of the Judicial Service Commission, may suspend the Ombudsman pending the investigations by the Judicial Service Commission into the removal of the Ombudsman.[17]

Duties and Functions of the Ombudsman

The functions of the Ombudsman are set out in the Constitution[18] with the provision that they should be defined and prescribed by an Act of Parliament, which was done in the Ombudsman Act, Act No. 7 of 1990.

The Ombudsman must investigate complaints regarding:

i) alleged or apparent or threatened instances or matters of violations of infringements of fundamental rights and freedoms, abuse of power, unfair, harsh, insensitive or discourteous treatment of an inhabitant of Namibia by an official[19] in the employ of any organ of Government (whether national or local), manifest injustice, or corruption or conduct by such official which would properly be regarded as unlawful, oppressive or unfair in a democratic society;[20]

ii) the functioning of the Public Service Commission, administrative organs of the State, the defence force, the police force and the prison service insofar as such complaints relate to the failure to achieve a balanced structuring of such services or equal access by all to the recruitment of such services or fair administration in relation to such services;[21]

iii) the over-utilization of living natural resources, the irrational exploitation of non-renewable resources, the degradation and destruction of ecosystems and failure to protect the beauty and character of Namibia;[22]

iv) practices and actions by persons, enterprises and other private institutions where such complaints allege that violations of fundamental rights and freedoms have taken place;[23] and

---

[14] Art. 94(1).

[15] Art. 94(2).

[16] Art. 94(3) provides for the investigation by the Judicial Service Commission into the removal from office of the Ombudsman, and to inform the President of its decision where it is found that the Ombudsman must be removed.

[17] Art. 94(4).

[18] Art. 91.

[19] Art. 93 defines "official" as including "any elected or appointed official or employee of any organ of the central or local government, any official of a para-statal enterprise owned or managed and controlled by the State or in which the State or the Government has substantial interest, or any officer of the defence force, the police force or the prison service, but shall not include a Judge of the Supreme Court or the High Court or, insofar as a complaint concerns the performance of a judicial function, any other judicial officer."

[20] Sec. 3(1)(a).

[21] Sec. 3(1)(b).

[22] Sec. 3(1)(c).

[23] Sec. 3(1)(d).

(v) all instances or matters of alleged or suspected corruption and the misappropriation of public moneys or other public property by officials.[24]

Complaints may include any instance or matter in respect of which the Ombudsman has reason to suspect that any decision, recommendation or act taken or performed or about to be taken or performed by the State abolishes, diminishes or derogates from the fundamental rights and freedoms or will abolish, diminish or derogate from any such rights and freedoms,[25] is or will be in conflict with any provision of any law or the common law,[26] is or will be unreasonable, unjust, unfair, irregular, unlawful or discriminatory or is based on any practice which may be deemed to be as such,[27] or is based on a wrong interpretation of the law or the relevant facts.[28]

Furthermore, complaints may also include situations where the Ombudsman has reason to suspect that the provisions of any law or any other matter is administered by or under the authority of the State in a manner which is not in the public interest,[29] that the powers, duties or functions which vest in the State are exercised or performed in an incompetent, dishonest or irregular manner or are not exercised or performed,[30] that moneys forming part of the funds of the State or received or held by or on behalf of the State or its other property are being or have been dealt with in a dishonest, irregular or improper manner,[31] that any person either directly or indirectly has been or is being enriched, or has received or is receiving any advantage, in an unlawful or improper manner through or as a result of any act or omission in connection with the administration of the affairs of the State, or has so received or is so receiving any advantage at the expense of the State.[32]

Any matter of which the administration vests in the State may be referred by the State, when it deems it necessary or expedient in the public interest, to the Ombudsman for inquiry or investigation. The Ombudsman has to inquire into the matter and report thereon, or take such other steps as may be prescribed by the Act.[33]

The functions of the Ombudsman do not relate to private individuals or enterprises, except where the complainants allege violations of fundamental rights and freedoms.[34]

Complaints and Confidentiality

Complaints are made in a manner determined or allowed by the Ombudsman.[35] At present, complaints are received if made in person, in writing or telephonically. In the case of prisoners or other people detained, the complaint can be made in

[24] Sec. 3(1)(e).
[25] Sec. 3(2)(a)(i).
[26] Sec. 3(2)(a)(ii).
[27] Sec. 3(2)(a)(iii).
[28] Sec. 3(2)(a)(iv).
[29] Sec. 3(2)(b).
[30] Sec. 3(2)(c).
[31] Sec. 3(2)(d).
[32] Sec. 3(2)(e).
[33] Sec. 3(4).
[34] Sec. 3(1)(d).
[35] Sec. 3(3)(a).

writing, and should be transmitted in a sealed envelope to the Ombudsman by the person in charge of the place where such person is detained.[36]

The Ombudsman and staff have to preserve and aid in preserving secrecy in respect of the instances or matters that may come to his or her knowledge in the exercise of his or her powers or the performance or his or her duties and functions, and may not communicate the contents to any person or permit a person to have access to any documents in his or her possession or custody, except insofar as any such communication is required to or may be made in terms of this Act or any other law.[37] The reason for confidentiality is that it protects the identity of complainants who fear retribution and punishment, but it also facilitates solutions because culprits are not exposed to scrutiny by the media, thereby also protecting the identity of officials who have made a mistake and are willing to redress the situation.[38]

A contravention of this section is an offence and punishable with a fine not exceeding N$2000.00 or imprisonment not exceeding 12 months or both such fine and imprisonment.[39]

Refusal to Accept Matters

The Ombudsman can refuse to investigate matters, or to continue with the investigation, where the grounds on which the investigation are required are, in the opinion of the Ombudsman, of a vexatious or trivial nature,[40] and also where the complaint relates to a decision taken in or in connection with any civil or criminal case[41] by a court of law. Obviously, where the complaint does not fall within the jurisdiction of the Office of the Ombudsman as envisaged in the Act, the matter cannot be dealt with by the Ombudsman. The complainant will be referred to an organization or institution that can address the issue at hand.

Where the complaint falls within the jurisdiction of the Office of the Ombudsman, the staff at the Office interviewing the complainant will inquire whether other remedies have been exhausted, and, if not, the complainant will usually be encouraged to exhaust them. Not having exhausted other alternatives does not mean that the complainants will be barred from approaching the Ombudsman as a matter of first instance.[42]

Powers of the Ombudsman

The powers of the Ombudsman with regard to the investigation of complaints are prescribed in the Act. The Ombudsman, in his or her discretion, may determine the nature and extent of any inquiry or investigation,[43] and shall have

[36] Sec. 3(3)(b).
[37] Sec. 8.
[38] Gottehrer, D M, Confidentiality and Accountability of an Ombudsman, as reported in Annual Report: 1 January–31 December 1966 Office of the Ombudsman, Republic of Namibia, p. 23.
[39] Sec. 10(d).
[40] Sec. 3(5).
[41] 1Sec. 3(6).
[42] 1997 Annual Report, supra, page 12.
[43] Sec. 4(1)(a).

the right, subject to any laws regulating the privileges or immunities of the President, members of the Cabinet or Parliament or any other persons provided for in any other law, to enter any building or premises and to make inquiries and to question any person employed there with regard to the matter in question,[44] to access all books, documentation, equipment and stores,[45] the right to request particulars and information from any person which the Ombudsman may deem necessary in connection with that inquiry or investigation,[46] the right to make copies and extracts from documentation without the payment of fees[47] and the right to seize anything which is deemed necessary in connection with the inquiry of investigation, and to retain any such thing in safe custody for as long as it is necessary for purposes of the inquiry or investigation.[48] Premises or buildings used as private homes may not be entered,[49] and private correspondence and goods may not be accessed.[50]

The Ombudsman may in writing subpoena any person to appear before her of him at a particular time and place in relation to an inquiry or investigation, and to bring documentation or other things in that person's possession, relating to the inquiry or investigation, along.[51] The Ombudsman may administer an oath or take an affirmation from any person so subpoenaed and question such person under oath or affirmation in connection with any matter which the Ombudsman may deem necessary in connection with that inquiry or investigation.[52] Witnesses are required to co-operate with the Ombudsman and to disclose truthfully and frankly any information within his or her knowledge relevant to any inquiry or investigation[53] of the Ombudsman, and are compelled to produce any book, voucher or other document or thing which the Ombudsman may deem necessary in connection with that inquiry or investigation.[54] Persons whose presence is not desirable may be excluded from any proceedings of the inquiry or investigation.[55] Witness fees are payable to people who are not in the public service.[56]

Procedures Following an Inquiry or Investigation

After holding an inquiry, the Ombudsman must notify the complainant of the outcome of the inquiry or investigation and to such extent as the Ombudsman may deem necessary in the public interest. If the Ombudsman decided not to inquire into or investigate the matter on the grounds of its trivial or vexatious nature, the complainant should be informed accordingly.[57]

---

[44] Sec. 4(1)(b)(i).
[45] Sec. 4(1)(b)(ii).
[46] Sec. 4(1)(b)(iii).
[47] Sec. 4(1)(b)(iv).
[48] Sec. 4(1)(b)(v).
[49] Sec. 4(1)(b)(i).
[50] Sec. 4(1)(b)(ii).
[51] Sec. 4(1)(c).
[52] Sec. 4(1)(d).
[53] Sec. 4(3)(a).
[54] Sec. 4(3)(b).
[55] Sec. 4(1)(e).
[56] Sec. 4(2).
[57] Sec. 5(1)(a)(i).

The Ombudsman must take appropriate action to remedy, correct or reverse the matter or instance complained about through such means as are fair, proper and effective. This action can include negotiation and compromise,[58] reporting the complaint and the Ombudsman's finding thereon to the offending person's superior[59] and referring the matter to the Prosecutor-General or the Auditor-General or both, as the case may be.[60]

Proceedings can be brought in a Court of competent jurisdiction for an interdict or some other suitable remedy to secure the termination of the offending action or conduct or the abandonment or alteration of the offending procedures,[61] or to prohibit its enforcement by challenging the validity of such legislation or regulation if the offending action or conduct is sought to be justified by subordinate legislation or regulation which is grossly unreasonable or otherwise ultra vires.[62] Laws in operation before the time of the independence of Namibia can be reviewed in order to ascertain whether they violate the letter or the spirit of the Namibian Constitution and consequential recommendations can be made to the President, the Cabinet or the Attorney-General for appropriate action.[63]

Regrettably, no legal proceedings have been instituted to date in a court of law in Namibia by the Office of the Ombudsman in terms of section 5 to secure the termination of offending action or conduct or to forbid the enforcement of offending legislation, an omission which can create the impression that the Office of the Ombudsman is not to be taken seriously.

The Ombudsman may also, if she or he is of the opinion that any instance or matter inquired into or investigated by her or him, can be rectified or remedied in any lawful manner, notify the State or relevant authority of her or his findings and the manner in which the matter can, in her or his opinion, the rectified or remedied.[64] The State or authority, or any person acting under its authority, may rectify or remedy the matter accordingly and must notify the Ombudsman, if, pursuant to the notification of the Ombudsman, it is found that the matter ought to rectified or remedied in the manner recommended by the Ombudsman.[65]

Reports of Ombudsman

The Ombudsman has to submit an annual report not later than 31 March to the Speaker of the National Assembly in connection with all the Office's activities during the period ending on 31 December of the previous year.[66] The Speaker must table the annual and special reports[67] in the National Assembly within 14 days of their submission. Transparency of the work of the Office is enhanced by

[58] Sec. 5(1)(a)(ii)(aa).
[59] Sec. 5(1)(a)(ii)(bb).
[60] Sec. 5(1)(a)(ii)(cc).
[61] Sec. 5(1)(a)(ii)(dd).
[62] Sec. 5(1)(a)(ii)(ee).
[63] Sec. 5(1)(a)(ii)(ff).
[64] Sec. 5(1)(b).
[65] Sec. 5(2).
[66] Sec. 6(2).
[67] See footnote 69 infra.

the publication of the annual report, and it also serves as a means to inform the public of the functions of the Office and how the Office can be utilized to address grievances.

Where the Ombudsman investigated a matter which had not been rectified, corrected or remedied to the satisfaction of the Ombudsman, the latter must forthwith come with a full report on the matter and submit such report as soon as possible to the Speaker of the National Assembly, the Cabinet and the body concerned.[68] The report must include, inter alia, details concerning the nature of the instance or matter inquired into,[69] the facts found to be proved,[70] the nature and extent of the inquiry,[71] the findings made by the Ombudsman in the course of he inquiry or investigation and such other matters which in his or her opinion should be brought to the attention of the National Assembly,[72] the opportunities afforded to a person, with regard to whom an adverse finding was made to contradict allegations or facts on which that finding is based or to reply thereto and what such person has adduced in contradicting it or replying thereto.[73] The action or steps taken to remedy, rectify, correct or reverse the instance or matter in question[74] and the outcome of the action or steps so taken must be reported.[75] The Ombudsman may make such recommendations in the report as he or she may deem necessary or expedient, including whether such report should be laid upon the table of the National Assembly as a confidential paper.[76] Confidential reports relate to the protection of sensitive information and are dealt with by select committees of the National Assembly.[77]

Compliance with the Provisions of the Act

In order to ensure compliance with the Act, various offenses have created penalizing noncompliance or interference with the exercise of the duties of the Ombudsman. These include failure to hand over to the Ombudsman a written complaint by a person in detention,[78] failure to comply with a subpoena by the Ombudsman or to take the oath or affirmation and willfully providing false answers or refusing to provide information,[79] insulting and belittling the Ombudsman,[80] willfully hindering and obstructing the Ombudsman or staff in the exercise of their duties,[81] the commission of anything calculated to improperly influence the Ombudsman or his or her deputy in respect of any matter being investigated,[82] threatening complainants or their next of kin, or people who have

---

[68] Sec. 6(1).
[70] Sec. 6(4)(a).
[71] Sec. 6 (4) (b).
[71] Sec. 6(4)(c).
[72] Sec. 6(4)(e).
[73] Sec. 6(3)(f).
[74] Sec. 6(4)(g).
[75] Sec. (4)(h).
[76] Sec. 6(4)(i).
[77] Sec. 6(5).
[78] Sec. 10(a).
[79] Sec. 10(b).
[80] Sec. 10(e).
[81] Sec. 10(f).
[82] Sec. 10(i).

furnished information or documentary proof with regard to any investigation by the Ombudsman.[83]

Persons convicted can be sentenced to a fine not exceeding N$2 000 or to imprisonment for a period not exceeding 12 months or to both such fine and such imprisonment.[84]

Conclusion

Administrative bodies and officials must act fairly and reasonably in the exercise of their powers and functions, and, in scrutinizing the exercise of such powers, the Office of the Ombudsman ensures that the principles of transparency and accountability with regard to the functioning of a democratic government are given effect to.

The effectiveness of the institution of Ombudsman depends on the independence and impartiality of the office, the character of the Ombudsman and the attitude of administrative officials and their adherence to the principles of democracy, which require accountability and transparency in order to effect good government.

LEGISLATION

The Namibian Constitution

February 1990

Article 25 [Enforcement of Fundamental Rights and Freedoms]

(1) Save in so far as it may be authorized to do so by this Constitution, Parliament or any subordinate legislative authority shall not make any law, and the Executive and the agencies of Government shall not take any action which abolishes or abridges the fundamental rights and freedoms conferred by this chapter, and any law or action in contravention thereof shall to the extent of the contravention be invalid; provided that:
   (a) a competent Court, instead of declaring such law or action to be invalid, shall have the power and the discretion in an appropriate case to allow Parliament, any subordinate legislative authority, or the Executive and the agencies of Government, as the case may be, to correct any defect in the impugned law or action within a specified period, subject to such conditions as may be specified by it. In such event and until such correction, or until the expiry of the time limit set by the Court, whichever be the shorter, such impugned law or action shall be deemed to be valid;
   (b) any law which was in force immediately before the date of Independence shall remain in force until amended, repealed or declared unconstitutional, it may either set aside the law, or allow Parliament to correct any defect in such law, in which event the provisions of Paragraph (a) shall apply.

(2) Aggrieved persons who claim that a fundamental right or freedom guaranteed by this Constitution has been infringed or threatened shall be entitled to approach a competent Court to enforce or protect such a right or freedom, and may approach the Ombudsman to provide them with such legal assistance or advice as they require,

[83] Sec. 10(j).
[84] Sec. 10.

and the Ombudsman shall have the discretion in response thereto to provide such legal or other assistance as he or she may consider expedient.

(3) Subject to the provisions of this Constitution, the Court referred to in Paragraph (2) shall have the power to make all such orders as shall be necessary and appropriate to secure such applicants the enjoyment of the rights of freedoms conferred on them under the provisions of this Constitution, should the Court come to the conclusion that such rights or freedoms have been unlawfully denied or violated, or that grounds exist for the protection of such rights or freedoms by interdict.

(4) The power of the Court shall include the power to award monetary compensation in respect of any damage suffered by the aggrieved persons in consequence of such unlawful denial or violation of their fundamental rights and freedoms, where it considers such an award to be appropriate in the circumstances of particular cases.

Chapter V – The President

Article 32 [Functions, Powers and Duties]

[...]

(4) The President shall also have the power, subject to this Constitution, to appoint:
  (a) on the recommendation of the Judicial Service Commission:
    (aa) the Chief Justice, the Judge-President of the High Court and other Judges of the Supreme Court and the High Court;
    (bb) the Ombudsman;
    (cc) the Prosecutor-General;
    [...]

Chapter X – The Ombudsman

Article 89 [Establishment and Independence]

(1) There shall be an Ombudsman, who shall have the powers and functions set out in this Constitution.

(2) The Ombudsman shall be independent and subject only to this Constitution and the law.

(3) No member of the Cabinet or the Legislature or any other person shall interfere with the Ombudsman in the exercise of his or her functions and all organs of the State shall accord such assistance as may be needed for the protection of the independence, dignity and effectiveness of the Ombudsman.

(4) The Ombudsman shall either be a Judge of Namibia, or a person possessing the legal qualifications which would entitle him or her to practice in all the Courts of Namibia.

Article 90 [Appointment and Term of Office]

(1) The Ombudsman shall be appointed by Proclamation by the President on the recommendation of the Judicial Service Commission.

(2) The Ombudsman shall hold office until the age of sixty-five (65) but the President may extend the retiring age of any Ombudsman to seventy (70).

Article 91 [Functions]

The functions of the Ombudsman shall be defined and prescribed by an Act of Parliament and shall include the following:

(a) the duty to investigate complaints concerning alleged or apparent instances of violations of fundamental rights and freedoms, abuse of power, unfair, harsh, insensitive or discourteous treatment of an inhabitant of Namibia by an official in the employ of any organ of Government (whether central or local), manifest injustice, or corruption or conduct by such official which would properly be regarded as unlawful, oppressive or unfair in a democratic society;

(b) the duty to investigate complaints concerning the functioning of the Public Service Commission, administrative organs of the State, the defence force, the police force and the prison service in so far as such complaints relate to the failure to achieve a balanced structuring of such services or equal access by all to the recruitment of such services or fair administration in relation to such services;

(c) the duty to investigate complaints concerning the over-utilization of living natural resources, the irrational exploitation of non-renewable resources, the degradation and destruction of ecosystems and failure to protect the beauty and character of Namibia;

(d) the duty to investigate complaints concerning practices and actions by persons, enterprises and other private institutions where such complaints allege that violations of fundamental rights and freedoms under this Constitution have taken place;

(e) the duty and power to take appropriate action to call for the remedying, correction and reversal of instances specified in the preceding Paragraphs through such means as are fair, proper and effective, including:
   (aa) negotiation and compromise between the parties concerned;
   (bb) causing the complaint and his or her finding thereon to be reported to the superior of an offending person;
   (cc) referring the matter to the Prosecutor-General;
   (dd) bringing proceedings in a competent Court for an interdict or some other suitable remedy to secure the termination of the offending action or conduct, or the abandonment or alteration of the offending procedures;
   (ee) bringing proceedings to interdict the enforcement of such legislation or regulation by challenging its validity if the offending action or conduct is sought to be justified by subordinate legislation or regulation which is grossly unreasonable or otherwise ultra vires;
   (ff) reviewing such laws as were in operation before the date of Independence in order to ascertain whether they violate the letter or the spirit of this Constitution and to make consequential recommendations to the President, the Cabinet or the Attorney-General for appropriate action following thereupon;

(f) the duty to investigate vigorously all instances or alleged or suspected corruption and the misappropriation of public monies by officials and to take appropriate steps, including reports to the Prosecutor-General and the Auditor-General pursuant thereto;

(g) the duty to report annually to the National Assembly on the exercise of his or her powers and functions.

Article 92 [Powers of Investigation]

The powers of the Ombudsman shall be defined by Act of Parliament and shall include the power:

(a) to issue subpoenas requiring the attendance of any person before the Ombudsman and the production of any document or record relevant to any investigation by the Ombudsman;

(b) to cause any person contemptuous of any such subpoena to be prosecuted before a competent Court;

(c) to question any person;

(d) to require any person to co-operate with the Ombudsman and to disclose truthfully and frankly any information within his or her knowledge relevant to any investigation of the Ombudsman.

Article 93 [Meaning of "Official"]

For the purposes of this chapter the word "official" shall, unless the context otherwise indicate, include any elected or appointed official or employee of any organ of the central or local Government, any official of a para-statal enterprise owned or managed or controlled by the State, or in which the State or the Government has substantial interest, or any officer of the defence force, the police force or the prison service, but shall not include a Judge of the Supreme Court or the High Court or, in so far as a complaint concerns the performance of a judicial function, any other judicial officer.

Article 94 [Removal from Office]

(1) The Ombudsman may be removed from office before the expiry of his or her term of office by the President acting on the recommendation of the Judicial Service Commission.

(2) The Ombudsman may only be removed from office on the ground of mental incapacity or for gross misconduct, and in accordance with the provisions of Paragraph (3).

(3) The Judicial Service Commission shall investigate whether or not the Ombudsman shall be removed from office on the grounds referred to in Paragraph (2) and, if it decides that the Ombudsman shall be removed, it shall inform the President of its recommendation.

(4) While investigations are being carried out into the necessity of the removal of the Ombudsman in terms of this article, the President may, on the recommendation of the Judicial Service Commission and, pending the outcome of such investigations and recommendation, suspend the Ombudsman from office.

National Ombudsman of the Netherlands

Ric de Rooij*

Constitution and the National Ombudsman Act

The provisions defining the tasks and organizational structure of the National Ombudsman of the Netherlands are found in the National Ombudsman Act. This law regulates sufficiently and in some detail the appointment of the National Ombudsman, his powers and his method of working.

The National Ombudsman was until recently not directly mentioned in the Constitution. Article 108, paragraph 1 of the Constitution read as follows:

"The establishment, powers and procedures of any general independent bodies for investigating complaints relating to actions of the authorities shall be regulated by an Act of Parliament."

In 1996, however, the government decided to set in motion the procedure to include the National Ombudsman in the formal Constitution, side by side with the other High Councils of State. This has resulted in the insertion of a new Article 78 a:

1. The National ombudsman investigates, if so requested or at his own initiative, the behaviour of public authorities of the central government and of other public authorities indicated by or pursuant to an act of parliament.
2. The National ombudsman and a deputy ombudsman shall be appointed by the Lower House of the States General for a term specified by act of parliament. At his own request and for the attainment of a certain age determined by act of parliament, they shall be dismissed. In cases laid down by act of parliament they may be suspended or dismissed by the Lower House. An act of parliament shall determine their legal status in all other respects.
3. The powers of and procedure followed by the National ombudsman shall be regulated by act of parliament.
4. The National ombudsman can be attributed with other tasks by or pursuant to an act of parliament.

Appointment

In the Netherlands, the National Ombudsman is one of the High Councils of State (Hoge Colleges van Staat), as are both Houses of Parliament, the Council of State (Raad van State), and the Netherlands Court of Audit (Algemene

*Vice-Director of the Bureau of the National Ombudsman of the Netherlands.

K. Hossain et al. (eds), Human Rights Commissions and Ombudsman Offices, 343–363.

Rekenkamer). The High Councils of State – like the judiciary – are characterized by formal independence from the government. Another mark of the National Ombudsman's independence from the executive is that – exceptionally under Netherlands constitutional law – he is appointed by the Lower House, not by the Crown (Art. 78a, paragraph 2 of the Constitution; see also section 2, subsection 2 of the National Ombudsman Act.) Appointment of the Ombudsman by Parliament is also common in many other countries, hence the term "parliamentary Ombudsman".

The appointment of the National Ombudsman by the Lower House follows a recommendation by a committee comprising the Vice President of the Council of State (this Council is presided by Her Majesty the Queen), the President of the Supreme Court of the Netherlands (Hoge Raad der Nederlanden), and the President of the Netherlands Court of Audit (section 2, subsection 2 National Ombudsman Act). The National Ombudsman's appointment is for a term of six years (section 2, subsection 3), and re-appointment is possible.

The Act recognizes a number of incompatibilities, especially holding certain other public offices or holding any position "which is incompatible with the correct performance of his official duties or with his impartiality and independence or with public confidence therein" (section 5, subsection 2). The Act does not lay down any formal qualifications for the post; legal expertise and a knowledge of public administration are, however, obvious selection criteria.

The National Ombudsman can only be dismissed on the grounds laid down in the Act, which are similar to those applying to members of the judiciary. One of the grounds for dismissal is that the National Ombudsman "in the opinion of the Lower House, as a result of his acts or omissions, seriously undermines the confidence placed in him " (section 3). The legal status of the National Ombudsman is established by law and is the same as that of holders of political office (section 6). His salary is laid down in a separate act, and is the same as that of Ministers.

The National Ombudsman Act provides for the possibility to appoint one or more Deputy Ombudsmen. The appointment of a Deputy Ombudsman is also made by the Lower House, following a recommendation by the National Ombudsman, and is for the duration of the latter's term of office (section 9).

Independence

The independence of the National Ombudsman is secured by the way he is appointed by the Lower House of Parliament. It is the task of the Lower House of Parliament to see that an *impartial* National Ombudsman with the right qualifications is appointed (section 5, subsection 2 of the National Ombudsman Act).

The National Ombudsman's budget is allocated under item II of the National Budget (High Councils of State and the Queen's Secretariat). In this way the influence of Parliament is sufficiently secured.

The National Ombudsman has an independent Staff, that is not related to any government body. In addition to the National Ombudsman and Deputy Ombudsman, some 98 staff members are employed at the National Ombudsman

Bureau. Almost all staff involved in the National Ombudsman's investigations have a law degree.

Day to day management of the Bureau is in the hands of a Director, who is appointed and dismissed by the Crown, on the recommendation of the National Ombudsman; all other staff are appointed and dismissed by the National Ombudsman. The Bureau has three investigation departments: Department I is mainly responsible for assessing petitions on the grounds of competence and admissibility, before the National Ombudsman decides whether to investigate a case or not. Staff in Department I also deal with the many enquiries (often by telephone) from the public.

Two other departments are charged with the actual investigation of acts of public bodies and officials which fall within the competence of the National Ombudsman. Department II deals with the Police, and the General Affairs, Foreign Affairs, and Justice ministries, as well as some independent government agencies/bodies. Department III covers the other ministries, the district water boards and most of the independent government agencies/bodies; a large proportion of its work concerns complaints regarding employment and income (e.g. taxes, social security, and manpower services).

In addition to the three investigation departments, there are among others public relations and information systems departments, and also a library.

Competence

Not all acts of administrative bodies fall within the jurisdiction of the National Ombudsman. An explanation of the definition of acts committed by an administrative body also gives some insight into how the office of National Ombudsman fits into the relationship between the executive and the legislature or the judiciary. The National Ombudsman has jurisdiction to review the manner in which the government carries out its tasks. This is apparent from section 1a of the Act, and is also a consequence of various definitions in section 16.

In the first place, section 16 lays down that general government policy and generally binding statutory regulations are outside the jurisdiction of the National Ombudsman (section 16(a) and (b)). This refers to acts of administrative bodies committed in their legislative capacity, a sphere in which they cooperate with and are accountable to Parliament. Similar arrangements exist for political accountability with respect to general government policy. It would clearly not be right for the National Ombudsman to intervene in matters such as those between an administrative body and Parliament. There is nothing in the law, however, to stop the National Ombudsman from recommending, as a result of his investigation of an actual act performed in the execution of government policy, that a piece of legislation or a policy should be amended.

In the second place, section 16 sets out the National Ombudsman's relationship with the executive and the judiciary, especially with regard to the system of administrative courts and tribunals as it exists in the Netherlands. For instance, the National Ombudsman is prevented from acting – temporarily at least – as long as there remains recourse to an appeal under administrative law; rather short periods of appeal normally apply in these cases. However, if a statutory remedy is available under administrative law in respect of a failure of an administrative body to make an order in good time, the National Ombudsman remains entitled to institute an investigation.

Likewise, such a – temporary – limitation of the competence of the National Ombudsman does not apply when the complaint is about an act in respect of which a petition may be lodged with the civil courts. As long as proceedings are pending before an administrative or other court or tribunal, the National Ombudsman is, however, incompetent to investigate. Finally, the National Ombudsman cannot investigate where an administrative tribunal has already pronounced on the matter in question. The National Ombudsman should therefore refrain, sometimes temporarily, from investigating certain cases concerning the relationship between administrative bodies and the judiciary (see section 16 (c), (d), (e) and (f)).

A situation can arise where someone goes to the National Ombudsman when he or she still has recourse to a statutory remedy under administrative law; in practice, however, this happens rarely. In a case like this, the National Ombudsman is bound to forward the petition to the appropriate judicial body (section 13). As a rule, this is first discussed with the petitioner.

The limitation of the National Ombudsman's authority in relation to the jurisdiction of the administrative courts has consequences for the kind of acts that the National Ombudsman investigates. Where government takes action affecting private individuals in the specific form of dispositions, jurisdiction in the Netherlands lies, with only rare exceptions, with the administrative courts. This means that the area of competence of the National Ombudsman comprises principally the area of the administrative practice of government bodies.

Acts of Government

The task of the National Ombudsman is to investigate the acts of administrative bodies. For this purpose, *any* act of an official carried out in the exercise of his duty is deemed to be an act of the administrative body which employs him (section 1a, subsection 3). By administrative bodies, the National Ombudsman Act means Ministers and – in so far as concerns their statutory duties in relation to the Police (section 1a, subsection 1 (c)) – Queen's Commissioners (*Commissarissen der Koningin*) and burgomasters (mayors). Any other body entrusted with public authority in the Netherlands can be designated as falling within the competence of the National Ombudsman by order in council. The intention of this provision was that the law would cover both the administrative bodies of lower statutory authorities (municipalities, provinces and district water boards), and the 'independent' administrative bodies (those government agencies/bodies at the national level which are so independent that ministerial responsibility does not extend to the practical exercise of their activities).

It was decided to introduce the office of the National Ombudsman in stages, giving him at first jurisdiction over national government (department of defence and the intelligence and Security services included) and the police. Several orders in council were made establishing the National Ombudsman's competence with respect to some specific independent administrative bodies.

As of November 1, 1993, the competence of the National Ombudsman is extended to all independent government agencies/bodies, of which there are several hundreds. At the request of the Union of district water boards, the district water boards were brought under the competence of the National Ombudsman as of January 1, 1994.

With a letter to the Lower House of Parliament, dated May 30, 1995, the State Secretary for Home Affairs presented a note about the competence of the National Ombudsman with regard to local and regional authorities (municipalities, provinces). This letter was in part a reaction on the request from the Association of the Provinces of the Netherlands, made to the legislature in February 1995, to bring the twelve provinces within the jurisdiction of the National Ombudsman. In the State Secretary's letter, the request was based on good grounds. Furthermore, the State Secretary stated that the local and provincial authorities have a responsibility of their own to make arrangements for the institution of an Ombudsman. The national government wished not to impose such an institution, but to leave the decision to the local and provincial authorities whether to create their own institution, or to opt for making the National Ombudsman competent. The costs of the institution would have to be borne by the local and provincial authorities themselves.

In their meeting of June 15, 1995, a large majority of the Lower House backed the views of the State Secretary. A number of municipalities showed interest in making the National Ombudsman competent with regard to themselves. As of January 1, 1998, the competence of the National Ombudsman was extended to all the provinces and eleven municipalities.

Outside the National Ombudsman's competence are the legislature, the other High Councils of State and the judiciary, as well as bodies whose acts are supervised by the judiciary (section 1a, subsection 2). The Judiciary (Organization) Act and the Council of State Act have their own provisions for dealing with complaints against judges and State Councillors..

Complaints

The National Ombudsman's main task is to investigate and issue judgements on the acts of administrative bodies. There are two avenues that can lead to an investigation: when petitioned to do so and at the own initiative of the Ombudsman.

Petition

"Any person has the right to petition the Ombudsman in writing to investigate the way in which an administrative body has acted towards a natural person or legal entity in a particular matter, unless more than a year has elapsed since the conduct in question" (section 12, subsection 1 National Ombudsman Act). Before submitting the petition, the petitioner must inform the appropriate administrative body or the civil servant about his complaint regarding the way in which that body or public servant has acted. The administrative body or civil servant is hereby given the opportunity to give an explanation and/or a rectification (section 12, subsection 2). In addition to the requirements of this provision, a petition must also contain:

- the name and address of the petitioner;
- a description of the act involved in the complaint and the identity of the person who committed it;
- the reasons why the petitioner believes the complaint to be justified (section 12, subsection (3).

Once the petition has been tested against the various provisions on jurisdiction (in section 1 and section 16), it also has to be examined for admissibility. On this point, the National Ombudsman has a discretionary power (section 14) allowing him to decide against pursuing the investigation requested.

Several major stipulations are laid down in this connection:

- the requirement that a complaint should be made known beforehand to the appropriate administrative body or civil servant (section 14(h));
- the requirements which a petition must meet (section 14(a)); in practice the requirements relating to description and supporting evidence for the complaint are applied fairly flexibly;
- the one year deadline (section 14(a)); this is fairly strictly applied;
- whether the petition is manifestly unfounded (section 14(b)). If it is immediately clear from information provided by the petitioner that the complaint is unfounded, for example because a request has been dealt with in full accordance with the appropriate procedure, the National Ombudsman will not start an investigation;
- whether the interest of the petitioner or the seriousness of the act is manifestly insufficient (section 14(c)). The latter ground will only rarely lead to the petition being refused; the first ground might more readily lead to a refusal, for instance if another body has found the complaint entirely well founded but the petitioner seeks the National Ombudsman's judgement as well;
- whether the petitioner is in fact the person affected by the act (section 14(d)); if not, the consent of the person directly affected is usually sought before proceeding;
- whether resort has also been had to the parliamentary committee of one of the two Houses of Parliament empowered to deal with petitions, and whether the petition has been handled there.

Working agreements have been made with the committees in order to prevent duplication of proceedings; the choice in this respect lies with the petitioner:

- whether a statutory remedy under administrative law was available, but has not been used; in principle, in such cases investigations are not pursued, to prevent the statutory right to appeal from being eroded.

There is no charge for submitting a petition.

Own Initiative

The National Ombudsman has the power "to institute an investigation on his own initiative into the way in which an administrative body has acted in a particular matter" (section 15). This option provides among other things the opportunity – whether or not as an extension of the research resulting from petitions – to focus on problems of a more structural kind in the administrative practice of government bodies.

Investigation, Report and Recommendation

There are two ways in which the National Ombudsman conducts an investigation. The principal avenue, as designed in the National Ombudsman Act, is the investigation which leads to establishing the facts regarding an action of the government. As a rule this investigation results in a report (section 27, subsection 1) in which the National Ombudsman determines whether or not the investigated action is 'proper' (section 26, subsection 1).

This type of investigation takes time. In the first place, the National Ombudsman has to meet the requirement that both sides of the argument should be heard. And furthermore, he first has to lay down the results of the investigation of the facts (section 25). After that, the judgement as to whether the action investigated is proper or not, can be pronounced.

Intervention Method

The other type of investigation is called the 'intervention method'. This method is frequently used in cases where before anything else a prompt interference of the National Ombudsman to solve a case is in the interest of the complainant. These are frequently cases in which the complainant has been waiting for some length of time for a response on the part of the authorities or that the authorities had until then proved unwilling to reach a compromise. In these cases the National Ombudsman can decide to inform the administrative body concerned about the complaint, and ask whether there is a prospect of the complaint being solved. If the reply is satisfactory, the complainant will be informed and the investigation will not be continued, since the continuation of the investigation will not be of particular interest to the complainant (section 14(c)); furthermore it does not serve any general purpose to issue a report in such cases.

After a successful intervention, the National Ombudsman will inform all parties involved about his decision not to continue the investigation in writing (section 17, subsection 1). However when, in the opinion of the National Ombudsman, there is reason for further investigation, he may decide to continue the investigation as described above under the principal avenue.

In the middle of 1994, the National Ombudsman decided to make more use of the intervention method in suitable cases.

In other cases the investigation was broken off on the initiative of the complainant, mainly because the government was still willing to compromise.

Investigation Leading to a Report

Procedure

The investigation of a case as described above as the principal avenue, usually begins with a summary of the complaint. The petitioner receives notification that, in response to his petition, it has been decided to institute an investigation. He then has an opportunity to comment on the summary. The administrative body receives the summary of the complaint and the petition, sometimes supplemented by specific questions, with the request to comment on these. Four weeks is generally allowed for this. If possible, copies are sent, simultaneously, directly to the department concerned as well as to the official about whose behaviour the complaint has been made, if his identity is known. In straightforward cases the investigation starts with a telephone call, in which case the report on the findings (see below) is the first actual documentation.

In principle, the administration's response is made known to the petitioner who may comment on it. In appropriate, the petitioner's response is in turn forwarded to the administrative body. This ensures that justice is done to the principle that both sides of the argument are heard (section 18, subsection 1), a basic prerequisite for any proper process of investigation. The National Ombudsman plays an active role during the investigation, taking initiatives, asking questions, and deciding when in his view those involved have had adequate opportunities to comment back and forth and that the report of findings can be drawn up. In some cases, it is not possible to establish the facts beyond question, because of contradictions between the parties' statements or lack of conclusive information. In those cases, no judgement can be given on the act in question.

Powers of Investigation

The National Ombudsman possesses a number of far-reaching statutory powers of investigation (sections 19 through 24), such as the power of site inspection, and the power to summon the administrative body, the petitioner, witnesses and experts. Summonses can, if necessary, be enforced by the forces of law and order – a power which so far has not had to be used.

Witnesses may be heard under oath, but this has happened in only a few cases. The administrative body has the duty to supply information requested and to allow the National Ombudsman access to all places where it carries out its duties. Staff from the National Ombudsman's office frequently visit administrative bodies to take evidence on site.

The duty to supply information extends to papers and information classified as confidential, as in the cases of the intelligence and security services, and some judicial and fiscal data. The National Ombudsman himself is bound by a statutory duty of confidentiality (section 27, subsection 5).

Information is provided in many cases in writing or, especially in simple cases, often by telephone. This is supplemented where necessary by information given directly in the presence of an investigator.

Report of Findings

Except when the intervention method has been followed, the investigation of the facts concludes with a report of findings (section 25), drawn up under the responsibility of the Deputy Ombudsman. This is sent to the administrative body, commonly to the official whose act has been the object of investigation, and to the petitioner. They have two weeks in which to comment, resulting occasionally in some last minute modification. This procedure ensures that the facts in relation to the act under investigation are established as firmly as possible. Absence of dispute as to the facts of the case is a cornerstone for the authority of the judgement to be given on the act under investigation.

The investigation sometimes reveals that the administrative body has responded to notification of the complaint by (at last) taking measures to satisfy the petitioner. This may cause the petitioner subsequently to withdraw his complaint. The National Ombudsman then decides in each individual case whether to terminate the investigation without issuing a report, the most frequent outcome.

The Report

The National Ombudsman Act decrees (section 27, subsection 1) that: "When an investigation has been closed, the Ombudsman shall draw up a report of his findings and his judgement." On the basis of his findings, the judgement is made: "The Ombudsman shall determine whether or not the administrative body concerned has acted properly in the matter under investigation" (section 26, subsection 1). This judgement is discussed separately below with particular reference to the standard of proper behaviour as the criterion provided by statute for the judgement of the National Ombudsman. The judgement may be accompanied by a recommendation (section 27, subsection 3).

The report is sent to the administrative body concerned, usually to the official concerned, and to the petitioner. A version of the report not revealing the identity of individuals is made public and sent to the Lower House and other interested recipients. Publication of the report closes the investigation.

Drafting of the Judgement

On the basis of the report of findings, the National Ombudsman formulates his judgement on the act under investigation. The judgement can take two forms, specified in section 26 of the Act: the behaviour investigated was proper or not proper. This is reached via the grounds, establishing definitively: the facts on which the judgement is based and the specific standards relevant to the decision. The combination of standards and facts leads to the judgement whether the act under investigation is proper or not. After that, the report ends with the conclusion in which, in relation to the judgement, the answer is given to the question, whether the complaint was well founded or not.

In the judgement and in the formulation of the conclusion, prominence is given to the act under investigation. A judgement is given on this act, together with the mention in the conclusion, of the administrative body responsible for the act. Where a complex act is concerned (an act consisting of various different elements) this is reflected in the judgement, where each element is the object of separate assessment. Frequently, the administrative body will have taken steps in the course of the National Ombudsman's investigation which go at least some way towards meeting the complaint. In these cases, a postscript is always added to the report, following the formulation of the conclusion, that the National Ombudsman appreciates the steps taken. If there is reason to suggest that the authority should consider taking steps, that suggestion is made at the end of the report, under the heading Recommendation.

Status of the Judgement

The National Ombudsman's judgement is not legally enforceable: it is up to the administrative body to decide what action, if any, should be taken consequent to the report and, in particular, to the judgement. That is the difference between the judgement of the National Ombudsman and the verdict of a court.

The fact that the National Ombudsman's judgement is not legally enforceable means that the quality of his work is all the more important. This quality is an essential basis for the authority of the National Ombudsman, and hence for the effectiveness of his work. Important aspects which account for this quality include the following:

- the investigation of facts must be carried out conscientiously, and produce conclusions which are not open to future dispute;
- the judgement and any recommendation must be persuasive. This sets particular standards for the reason given in the judgement.

These requirements are particularly important since there is no right of appeal to the judgement of the National Ombudsman. Moreover, great interest is often attached to the judgement.

Criteria for Assessment and Their Use

When is behaviour proper or not proper? To answer this question, the relationship between government and the citizen can be approached from two angles. The first is the 'legal relationship': the law underpins and regulates countless forms of action by the authorities, while the 'products' of that action often take a legal shape. Seen from this angle, the executive function of government involves the application of the law.

However, not all government dealings with citizens are governed by the law or have legal consequences: the relationship between citizen and government is not confined to their roles determined by the law. This second type of interaction could be qualified as a 'social relationship'. Approached from this angle, action by the authorities is a matter of how government treats its citizens, and of the management of government bodies.

On the basis of this duality, the standard of proper conduct referred to in section 26, subsection 1, has been elaborated in practice into a system of criteria for the assessment of government actions. This is important in several respects and for several reasons: for the reasoning on which the judgement is based, as well as for the conclusion based thereupon (i.e. the conclusion whether conduct investigated was 'proper' or 'not proper', whether the complaint was well founded or not, respectively). Other reasons are the importance to impart uniformity to the way the National Ombudsman arrives at his decisions, and the educative function of the National Ombudsman's work.

The criteria for assessment used by the National Ombudsman fall into two groups.

The first group embodies the notion of the rule of law. This covers the requirement that government acts in conformity with provisions in international law and with the regulations of written statutes, which express the will of Parliament, and also with unwritten legal principles. If a particular government act conflicts with these regulations and principles, and does not appear to be justified on other grounds, it cannot in principle be regarded as proper conduct. Accordingly, the National Ombudsman reviews the act under investigation in the light of the regulations of written law on the one hand, such as human rights, constitutional rights, definitions of competence, prescriptions of form, procedure and substance.

On the other hand, the National Ombudsman reviews the act under investigation in the light of unwritten legal principles, developed in case law and legal doctrine, and contributing to the judgement on the lawfulness of government conduct. Examples of the (partly) unwritten standards, which can contribute to judgements of the National Ombudsman of the lawfulness of government conduct, are the principles of equal treatment for equal cases, of reasonableness, of proportionality between means and end, of legal certainty (no arbitrary action by the authorities), the requirement to provide reasons for decisions, and certain duties of care.

There is another group of criteria for assessment. This second group is important because not every government act which conforms to requirements of legality or – broader – lawfulness, is proper in every other respect. In this context, the National Ombudsman uses standards which can be seen as guidelines for good government. They are the starting points for executive action by the authorities, which contribute to the propriety of the way action is undertaken. These standards, on which the judgement of the National Ombudsman can be based, can be summed up in the idea of a duty of care, which manifests itself in certain accepted standards for the administrative process and the conduct of civil servants in relation to the citizen.

These include the requirements to act without undue delay, to supply the individual with relevant information and listen to his point of view, the requirements to treat people fairly, to respect human dignity, and to be unbiased and helpful. Finally it sets standards for the government organization – standards of coordination, monitoring of progress, protection of the individual's privacy, accessibility of the authorities and adequate accommodation (e.g. in police cells).

The National Ombudsman applies these criteria in the deliberations leading up to this final judgement on the propriety of the conduct investigated. For all reports, and for the cases dealt with by the intervention method, a record is made of which criteria were used, so that these data can be fed into a case law database.

The computer provides print-outs for the annual report. The extent to which different criteria were used gives an impression of the kinds of complaints that lead to investigation in particular years. Breaking down the judgements (proper/not proper) by criterion may highlight common areas where problems arise in those acts investigated, such as a violation of a certain statutory provision, or a breach of the requirement that undue delays be avoided. Finally, the statistics can form the basis for comparisons between different administrative bodies, and to make visible whether their conduct has changed compared to a previous period. The criteria for assessment, then, are important analytical tools in the National Ombudsman's annual review of the subjects he has investigated.

Annual Report

The National Ombudsman is required to report annually to both Houses of Parliament and to the Ministers (section 28, subsection 1). The annual report is a public document given wide distribution. It contains an overview of the results of investigations in the various policy fields as well as statistical material and, as an appendix, brief summaries of all reports issued. The introduction to th report always provides a summing up of the problems have been most frequentl encountered in investigations of government action, their causes and any oth relevant developments.

Functions of the National Ombudsman and the Impact of the Work of the National Ombudsman

There are two more issues that can be raised in this context, namely: functio of the National Ombudsman and the impact of the work of the Nation Ombudsman.

Functions of the National Ombudsman

The institution of National Ombudsman has been established in order to giv individual citizens an opportunity – in addition to existing provisions, such a petitioning Parliament, judicial proceedings, and internal complaints procedur – to bring complaints about the administrative practices of government befo an independent and expert body. Doing so may result in (immediate) steps bein taken in their particular cases, and, more broadly, help to restore public conf dence. With a view to this function in relation to the individual citizen, th National Ombudsman Act has deliberately chosen to make a single person, th National Ombudsman, represent the institution to the outside world, as counterbalance to an often faceless bureaucracy.

The National Ombudsman can also contribute to the quality of governmen by providing feedback as to how the administration is performing its tasks. Thi is important for government organizations which want to do their work in client friendly way and place an appropriately high value on high quality polic implementation. Complaints are signals, constituting valuable information for policy of quality. This feedback can be of particular value to government organ izations, because they generally have a monopoly in their own field. The criteri of proper conduct mentioned before, in short, contribute to the rationality an legitimacy of public administration.

For the National Ombudsman to fulfil his role, he must be visible to th public, which must have confidence in his impartiality and procedures. Wher the government is concerned, it has been remarked already above that judge ments made by the National Ombudsman are not legally enforceable. Wher formal power is lacking, respect for the authority of the National Ombudsma and his judgements is of particular importance, if they are to have any impac at all. That authority is determined in the first place by the quality of the wor itself: a brisk and careful investigation, well reasoned judgements, and readabl reports. Good quality work is a sine qua non, but not enough in itself. It is th mainstay viewed from within the organization; but also it is of vital importanc externally: political support for the National Ombudsman and public awarenes of his work, particularly via the news media.

Impact of the Work

The work of the National Ombudsman can have effects in different ways. Th fact that the National Ombudsman has decided to investigate a case in itsel brings a matter to the attention of top officials and politicians, or both. Thi regularly results in steps being taken even before the National Ombudsman has published his report. From the point of view of speed and instructiveness for the organization, this is an extremely important effect and one which must be positively valued. Furthermore, the intervention of the National Ombudsman results in the solution of the complaint in many hundreds of cases a year. There are other cases however where a report is published, with the judgement 'not proper' and where no steps have yet been taken by the government body responsible, even though these might be expected. In such cases, usually a recommendation is given. Experience shows that over 95% of the recommendations are followed.

Different sorts of impact can be distinguished in the work of the National Ombudsman. Steps are sometimes taken by the administrative body in favour of a person submitting a complaint found by the National Ombudsman to be justified, e.g. paying compensation. This sort of impact in individual cases aside, there are also more structural effects: administrative practice or existing rules may be altered in response to a problem or problems signalled via individual reports or in the annual report, with the aim of preventing complaints in the future. In this way, the work of the National Ombudsman can have a preventive effect. In a wider sense, moreover, the very existence of the National Ombudsman can be said to have had an impact in any case where administrative bodies decide on their own initiative to improve administrative practice, in order to give as little reason as possible for the lodging of complaints with the National Ombudsman; this also takes place as a result of the implementation of internal procedures to deal with complaints, by the administrative bodies themselves. It is also true that the public find it useful for their contact with government bodies to be able to threaten to petition the National Ombudsman.

LEGISLATION

Constitution of the Kingdom of the Netherlands

(as most recently amended, 25 March 1999)

Article 78a

1. The National ombudsman investigates, if so requested or at his own initiative, the behaviour of public authorities of the central government and of other public authorities indicated by or pursuant to an act of parliament.
2. The National ombudsman and a deputy ombudsman shall be appointed by the Lower House of the States General for a term specified by act of parliament. At his own request and for the attainment of a certain age determined by act of parliament, they shall be dismissed. In cases laid down by act of parliament they may be suspended or dismissed by the Lower House. An act of parliament shall determine their legal status in all other respects.
3. The powers of and procedure followed by the National ombudsman shall be regulated by act of parliament.
4. The National ombudsman can be attributed with other tasks by or pursuant to an act of parliament.

National Ombudsman Act

Act of February 4, 1981; *Staatsblad* 1981, 35, most recently amended by Act of Parliament of April 26, 1995 (*Staatsblad* 1995, 250).

We Beatrix, by the grace of God, Queen of the Netherlands, Princess of Orange Nassa etc ... .

Considering that the need exists for a special provision for investigating the way in whic government has acted in a particular matter towards the individual citizen and that it desirable in this connection to proceed to the establishment of the office of Nation Ombudsman ... ;
So be it, etc ...

DEFINITIONS
Section 1

In this Act:

(a) Ombudsman means: the National Ombudsman referred to in section 2;
(b) public servant means: a public servant, a former public servant, a person employe by an administrative body under a contract of employment governed by civil law, person formerly so employed, or a conscript either before or after termination of th period of a compulsory military service.

Section 1a
1. This Act is applicable to acts of the following administrative bodies:
(a) Our Ministers;
(b) the administrative bodies working within the area of responsibility of Our Minister
(c) the King's Commissioners and burgomasters, in so far as they are charged by la with any duties regarding the police;
(d) other administrative bodies designated by order in council.
2. Contrary to the first subsection, this Act is not applicable to acts which are supervise by the judiciary, nor to acts of the Equal Treatment Commission referred to in th Equal Treatment Act.
3. An act of a public servant in the exercise of his duties shall be deemed to be an act c the administrative body which employs him.

CHAPTER 1. THE NATIONAL OMBUDSMAN

Section 21. There shall be a National Ombudsman.
2. The National Ombudsman will be appointed by the Lower House of Parliament. T that purpose the vice president of the Council of State, the president of the Suprem Court and the president of the General Chamber of Audit jointly draw up a recommen dation containing the names of at least three persons.
3. The appointment shall be for a term of six years.
4. If the Lower House wishes to re-appoint the current Ombudsman, it may stipulat that subsection 2 shall not apply.
5. If it proves to be impossible for the Lower House to appoint a new Nationa Ombudsman in time, the Lower House shall provide for the temporary occupation c the office of Ombudsman. Section 10, fifth to seventh subsection is applicable.

Section 3
1. The Lower House shall terminate the employment of the National Ombudsman a the commencement of the first month following that in which he reaches the age o sixty five.
2. The Lower House shall also terminate the employment of the National Ombudsman
(a) at his request;
(b) if he is permanently unable to carry out his duties because of illness or disability;
(c) if he accepts an office or post declared by this Act to be incompatible with the offic of Ombudsman;

d) if he loses Netherlands' citizenship;
e) if he is convicted of a crime, or is deprived of his liberty by a final and irrevocable sentence of a court;
f) if he has been made the subject of a guardianship order, has been declared bankrupt, has obtained a moratorium for the payment of his debts or has been imprisoned for debts by final and irrevocable sentence of a court;
g) if, in the opinion of the Lower House of Parliament, he seriously undermines the confidence placed in him as a result of his acts or omissions.

Section 4
1. The Lower House shall suspend the Ombudsman if:
a) he is remanded in custody;
b) he is convicted of a crime or deprived of his liberty by sentence of a court of justice which is not yet final and irrevocable;
c) he is made the subject of a guardianship order, or is declared bankrupt, or obtains a moratorium for the payment of his debts, or is imprisoned for non-payment of debts by sentence of a court of justice which is not yet final and irrevocable.
2. The Lower House may suspend the Ombudsman if he is the subject of a preliminary judicial examination instituted in respect of a crime, or if there is a strong suspicion of the existence of facts or circumstances which could lead to dismissal, other than those referred to under section 3, subsection 2 (b).
3. In the case referred to in subsection 2 of this section the suspension shall end after three months. The Lower House may however extend the suspension for periods of three months at a time.
4. The Lower House shall lift the suspension as soon as the reasons for suspension cease to exist.
5. The Lower House may order, when suspending the Ombudsman, that he will receive no salary, or only a specified part of his salary, during his suspension.
6. If the suspension ends otherwise than by dismissal, the Lower House may decree that all or a specified part of the salary the Ombudsman has not received, shall be paid to him.

Section 5
1. The Ombudsman may not:
(a) be a member of a public body for which elections are prescribed by law;
(b) hold public office for which he receives a fixed salary or remuneration;
(c) be a member of a permanent government advisory body;
(d) act as an advocate, solicitor, or notary.
2. The Ombudsman shall not hold any position which is incompatible with the correct performance of his official duties or with his impartiality and independence or with public confidence therein.

Section 6
The provisions of the General Pensions (Holders of Political Office) Act (Act of 10 December 1969, Staatsblad 1969,594) shall apply to the Ombudsman, in such a way that he is treated as a member of the Lower House of Parliament, but that his income is settled according to section 9 of the said Act.

Section 7
We shall lay down rules by order in council governing claims in case of illness, and the other rights and duties of the Ombudsman which pertain to his legal status, in so far as the same are not prescribed by law.

Section 8
Before accepting office the Ombudsman shall swear on oath or solemnly affirm in the presence of the Speaker of the Lower House of Parliament:

(a) that he has not given a promised anything on any pretext whatsoever to any person either directly or indirectly and either in his own name or that of any other person to obtain his appointment, and that he has not accepted and will not accept any present or any promise from any person, either directly or indirectly, to do or to refrain from doing anything in the exercise of his function;
(b) to observe faithfully the Constitution.

Section 9

1. At the request of the Ombudsman the Lower House shall if necessary appoint one or more persons as Deputy Ombudsman. To that purpose the Ombudsman draws up a recommendation containing the names of at least three persons.
2. Any Deputy Ombudsman shall be appointed for the term of office of the Ombudsman requesting his appointment. On the recommendation of the new Ombudsman the Lower House can extend the term of office of the Deputy Ombudsman by a period not exceeding six months.
3. If the Lower House wishes to re-appoint a Deputy Ombudsman, it may stipulate that the second sentence of subsection 1 shall not apply.
4. Sections 3 to 8, 18 to 24 and 27, subsection 5 shall apply mutatis mutandis to a Deputy Ombudsman.
5. The Ombudsman shall determine the activities of the Deputy Ombudsman.
6. The Ombudsman can delegate the powers mentioned in the sections 25, 26, 27,subsection 1 to 4, and 28, subsection 3, to a Deputy Ombudsman.

The Ombudsman can draw up directions for the exercise of those powers.

Section 10

1. The Ombudsman shall make arrangements for his replacement by a Deputy Ombudsman, in case he is temporarily not able to exercise his duties.
2. If no Deputy Ombudsman is present or available, the Lower House shall provide for the replacement of the Ombudsman as soon as possible. In that case the replacement will end as soon as the Ombudsman is able to resume his duties, or, if the Ombudsman has been suspended, the moment the suspension is lifted.
3. If the Ombudsman dies or is removed from his office under section 3, the Deputy Ombudsman will stay on, contrary to the rule stated in section 9, subsection 2, first sentence, until the moment on which a new Ombudsman takes up his duties. In that case the Lower House shall provide for the temporary occupation of the office of Ombudsman.
4. If no Deputy Ombudsman is present or available, the Lower House shall provide for the temporary occupation of the office of Ombudsman as soon as possible.
5. The replacement will ipso jure end at the moment on which a new Ombudsman takes up his duties.
6. Section 2, subsection 2, second sentence and subsections 3 and 4, section 3, subsection 1, and sections 6 and 9 of this Act, as well as section F2, subsection 4(e) of the General Civil Pensions Act (Staatsblad 1986,540) are not applicable on the person who replaces the Ombudsman or temporarily holds his office.
7. If the person who replaces the Ombudsman or temporarily holds his office as referred to in the sixth subsection accepts or is going to accept an office or membership as indicated in section 5, subsection one, under b and c, he shall ipso jure be suspended for the time he holds that office or the duration of that membership.

Section 11

1. The Ombudsman shall be provided with a secretariat.
2. The personnel of the secretariat shall be appointed, promoted, suspended and dismissed by Us on the recommendation of the Ombudsman.
3. We shall decide in which cases members of the secretariat's personnel are appointed, promoted, suspended and dismissed by the Ombudsman.

CHAPTER II. THE INVESTIGATION

Section 12

1. Any person has the right to petition the Ombudsman in writing to investigate the way in which an administrative body has acted towards a natural person or legal entity in a particular matter, unless more than a year has elapsed since the conduct in question. If the act in question has been submitted to the judgement of a judicial body or has been referred for judgement to another body pursuant to a statutory provision of administrative law within one year of the date on which the act took place, the term of one year shall end one year after the date on which the court gives a judgement against which no appeal is open, or after the proceedings have ended in some other way.
2. Before submitting the petition referred to in subsection 1, the petitioner shall inform the appropriate administrative body, agency or department or the appropriate company operating under the aegis of that body, or the public servant, as to his complaint regarding the way in which that body or public servant has acted, and give that body or public servant an opportunity to explain its or his point of view.
   If the body or public servant has been so informed within one year of the date on which the act took place, the term of one year referred to in subsection 1 shall end one year after the date on which it or he was so informed.
3. The petition should contain:
a) the name and address of the petitioner;
b) as clear as possible a description of the act concerned and the name of the person whose actions are complained of and the name and address of the person against whom the act was directed;
c) the reasons why the petitioner believes the complaint to be justified;
d) the name of the person who was informed as described in subsection 2 and the manner in which that person was informed and, if that person has explained his point of view on the matter, a statement of that point of view.
4. Unless section 16 applies, the Ombudsman shall be entitled, and, unless section 14 applies, shall also be obliged to grant a petition as referred to in subsection 1.

Section 13

If some other statutory remedy is available to the petitioner under administrative law regarding the act complained of in the petition, the Ombudsman shall refer the petitioner forthwith to the competent authority and shall submit the petition to such body after the date of receipt has been noted on it. For the purposes of the rules governing the remedy available, the petition shall be deemed to satisfy the provisions of such rules governing the way in which the petition should be lodged and completed. Moreover, the date of receipt of the petition by the Ombudsman shall be deemed to be the date on which proceedings are initiated before the body referred to in such rules. The said body shall allow the petitioner thirty days (from the date of notification), to complete or amend the petition in accordance with the relevant rules and to pay such fees as may be owed for the case to be heard.

Section 14

The Ombudsman shall not be obliged to institute or to continue an investigation as referred to in section 12, subsection 1, if:
a) the petition is filed too late or does not meet the requirements listed in section 12, subsection 3;
b) the petition is manifestly unfounded;
c) the interest of the petitioner or the seriousness of the act is manifestly insufficient;
d) the petitioner is not the person affected by the act in question;
e) a petition concerning the same act is either being considered by himself or by a parliamentary committee empowered to deal with petitions, or – unless a new fact or a new circumstance has come to light which might justify a different evaluation

of the said act – has been dealt with by him or has led to a proposal to the Upper or Lower House of Parliament or to a joint session of either House of Parliament by the parliamentary committee;

(f) a statutory remedy under administrative law was available to the petitioner but was not used;

(g) judgement has been passed by a judicial body other than pursuant to a statutory provision of administrative law;

(h) the administrative body, agency or department or the appropriate company operating under the aegis of that body, or the public servant, was not informed of the complaint against the act by the petitioner or the person against whom the act was directed and was not given an opportunity to explain its or his point of view;

(i) if a case is pending before a court or tribunal concerning an act by an administrative body, which act is closely related to the substance of the petition, or if such a case is pending before any other body invested with judicial authority under statutory administrative provisions.

Section 15

Unless section 16 applies, the Ombudsman shall be entitled to institute an investigation on his own initiative into the way in which an administrative body has acted in a particular matter.

Section 16

The Ombudsman shall not be entitled to institute an investigation as referred to in sections 12, subsection 1, or 15:

(a) concerning matters of general government policy, including general policy on the maintenance of law or matters which fall within the ambit of the general policy of the administrative body concerned;

(b) concerning binding regulations of a general scope;

(c) if a statutory remedy is available under administrative law in respect of the act in question, unless section 6:12 of the General Administrative Law Act is applicable, or proceedings have been instituted to obtain such a remedy;

(d) if proceedings concerning the act in question have been instituted before a judicial body other than pursuant to a statutory provision of administrative law, or if appeal is available against a judgement given in such proceedings;

(e) if a judgement has been given by a judicial body in respect of the act in question pursuant to a statutory provision of administrative law;

(f) in matters relating to taxes and other impositions if a remedy has been available under administrative law in respect of the act in question.

Section 17

1. If the Ombudsman decides not to grant a petition to institute an investigation on the grounds referred to in sections 14 or 16 or not to continue an investigation he shall inform the petitioner as soon as possible in writing, giving his reasons. In the event that he does not continue an investigation, he shall also inform the administrative body and, where appropriate, the public servant in question. With a view to the provisions of subsection 3, he shall take into account the last sentence of section 19, subsection 4, of this Act and section 10 of the Government Information (Public Access) Act.
2. If, pursuant to the provisions of section 14, subsection 1 (h), the Ombudsman decides not to institute an investigation or does not continue an investigation, he shall make known to the petitioner the possibility of informing the administrative body, agency or department or the company operating under the aegis of that body, or the public servant, as to his complaint regarding the way in which that body or public servant has acted, giving that body or public servant an opportunity to explain its or his point of view.

. The Ombudsman shall agree to a request by any person for a copy of or excerpt from the written statement referred to in subsection 1. With regard to the fees for providing such information or the provisions free of charge of such information, the provisions of or pursuant to the Civil Cases (Fees) Act (Staatsblad 1960, 541) shall apply mutatis mutandis.

The Ombudsman shall also make the statement available for public inspection in a lace to be designated by him.

ection 18

. The Ombudsman shall give the administrative body, the person responsible for the act in question, and in the case referred to in section 12, subsection 1, the petitioner, the opportunity to explain their point of view either in writing or verbally and, at the discretion of the Ombudsman, either in each other's presence or not.

. The parties concerned may be represented or assisted by counsel. The Ombudsman may refuse to hear as representative certain persons who make it their business to give legal assistance, but who are not advocates or solicitors.

ection 19

. The Ombudsman shall be entitled to order the attendance of the administrative body and the person responsible for the act in question, witnesses and, in the case referred to in section 12, subsection 1, the petitioner. The person whose attendance is ordered must provide the Ombudsman with the information needed by him for his investigation, and must for that purpose appear in person before him. The same duties rest on any official body, provided always that the body decides which member is to discharge its obligations, unless the summons designates one or more members. Save for witnesses, persons whose attendance is required may be assisted by counsel.

. The obligation to appear before the Ombudsman shall not apply to Our Ministers. If a Minister does not appear in person, he shall appoint a representative.

. The Ombudsman may obtain information concerning acts committed on the responsibility of a Minister or an administrative body from the public servants concerned only through the Minister or the administrative body in question.

. The persons whose attendance is required under subsection 1 may refuse to give information on the grounds that they are under a duty of secrecy by virtue of their office or profession, but only regarding matters which have been disclosed to them in such capacity. Public servants may refuse to give information on the ground of the duty of secrecy imposed by the Public Service Personnel Act, the Military Personnel Act 1931 or the Police Act only if the provision of the information required would be contrary to any other statutory provision concerning secrecy or to the interests of the State.

. The Ombudsman may request the body from which information may be sought under subsection 3 to submit a special written confirmation to substantiate the claim of secrecy. The body may decide that the duty of secrecy will be waived in respect of information to the Ombudsman only on condition that the information remains secret.

. The body from which information is sought may be represented when the public servants are interviewed.

ection 20

. The Ombudsman shall be entitled to entrust certain work to experts. He shall also be entitled to obtain the assistance of experts and interpreters to further his investigations. Persons summoned as experts or interpreters shall be obliged to appear before the Ombudsman and render their services.

. Subsections 3, 4 and 5 of section 19 shall apply mutatis mutandis to experts who are also public servants.

. Experts and interpreters shall be under a duty of secrecy in respect of matters that have become known to them in the course of their duties.

Section 21
1. Summonses to attend under sections 19 and 20 shall be sent by registered letter.
2. The Ombudsman may order that persons who fail to appear despite an officia summons to attend, shall be brought before him by the police to discharge thei obligations.

Section 22
1. The Ombudsman may order that witnesses shall not be heard and that interpreter shall not be permitted to carry out their duties until they have taken an oath or mad a solemn affirmation.
2. In such cases, they shall take the oath, or make the solemn affirmation, in the presenc of the Ombudsman; if they are heard as a witness they shall swear to speak the whol truth and nothing but the truth; the interpreters shall swear to carry out their dutie meticulously.
3. The experts shall be obliged to perform their task impartially, and to the best o their ability.

Section 23
1. Persons summoned to attend under this Act shall receive, on request, payment of thei travelling and accommodation expenses and compensation for lost working hour from government funds in accordance with the provisions of the Fees in Civil Cases Ac
2. Unless provided otherwise by order in council, persons referred to in subsection 1 wh are public servants shall not receive any payment as referred to in section 1 if they ar summoned to give evidence in their capacity as public servant.
3. The Ombudsman shall determine the compensation to be paid in accordance wit this section.

Section 24
1. On the written request of the Ombudsman, documents or papers or copies of docu ments or papers drawn up in performance of the government's task in the matte concerned, shall be submitted to him for the purposes of the investigation. Section 19 subsections 3 and 4, shall apply mutatis muntandis.
2. If he considers it necessary in the interests of the investigation the Ombudsman ma enter without consent any place other than a dwelling where the administrative bod responsible for the act under investigation carries out its duties. He may enter residence only with consent of the occupier.
3. Our Ministers may deny entry to certain places to the Ombudsman if in their opinio entry would endanger the safety of the state.

Section 25
1. Before closing the investigation, the Ombudsman shall communicate his findings t the administrative body concerned in writing and, in appropriate cases, to the publi servant whose actions have been the subject of the investigation, and in the cas referred to in section 12, subsection 1, to the petitioner.
2. The Ombudsman shall give the administrative body, the public servant and th petitioner the opportunity to comment on his findings within a period fixed by him.

Section 26
1. The Ombudsman shall determine whether or not the administrative body concerne has acted properly in the matter under investigation.
2. If a judicial body has passed judgement, other than pursuant to a provision o administrative law, in respect of the act to which the Ombudsman's investigatio relates, the Ombudsman shall take into account the legal grounds on which th judgement was based either in whole or in part.

Section 27
1. When an investigation has been closed the Ombudsman shall draw up a report of hi

findings and his judgement. With a view to the provisions of subsection 4, he shall take into account the last sentence of section 19, subsection 4, of this Act and section 10 of the Government Information (Public Access) Act.

2. The Ombudsman shall send his report to the administrative body concerned and, where appropriate, to the public servant whose actions have been investigated. If the investigation was carried out in response to a petition as referred to in section 12 he shall also send his report to the petitioner.
3. If he deems fit, the Ombudsman may notify the body concerned of any measures which he considers should be taken.
4. The Ombudsman shall provide anyone who asks for it a with a copy of or an extract of a report as referred to in subsection 1. The provisions of the Fees in Civil Cases Act and provisions made pursuant to it shall apply mutatis mutandis to the assessment of costs or exemption from the payment of costs. He shall also deposit a copy of the report for public inspection at a place to be designated by him.
5. In all other respects, the Ombudsman shall be under a duty not to disclose matters that have become known to him in the exercise of his duties, in so far as the nature of such matters makes this necessary.

Section 28
1. The Ombudsman shall submit yearly a report of his activities to either House of Parliament and to Our Ministers. Section 10 of the Government Information (Public Access) Act shall apply mutatis mutandis, provided always that the Ombudsman may add items to be communicated confidentially to the members of Parliament and Our Ministers
2. He shall publish the report and make it generally available.
3. The Ombudsman may also notify either House of Parliament of his findings and judgement immediately after closing an investigation, whenever he deems earlier communication necessary or whenever one of the chambers requests such information.

CHAPTER III. TRANSITIONAL AND FINAL PROVISIONS

Section 29
Proposals for decrees implementing this Act shall be submitted to Us by Our Minister for Home Affairs.

Section 30
Section 12 shall not apply with regard to acts performed by bodies designated by order in council as referred to in section 1a, subsection 1 (d) prior to the date on which the said order in council came into force.

Section 31
This Act may be cited as: National Ombudsman Act.

Legal Institution of Ombudsman

Arne Fliflet*

Legal or Constitutional Basis

1. The basic provision for the Ombudsman is found in the Norwegian Constitution. The Norwegian written Constitution, which dates from 1814, had originally no provision about the Ombudsman The Norwegian Ombudsman was established by law in 1962. The constitutional provision of the Norwegian Ombudsman dates from 1995. The inclusion in the Constitution did not take place as a result of any conflict, but it was felt that it was natural to give the ombudsman a constitutional foothold. The tasks and scope of powers of the ombudsman are mentioned in the Act, whereas details about procedure etcetera are dealt with in a Directive given by the Parliament, the Storting. In accordance with Norwegian legal custom, the Constitution (Basic law) does not go into details. However, it would hardly be coherent with the Constitution if Parliament (or other bodies) were given authority to intervene in the decisions of the ombudsman in particular cases.

2. The ombudsman is elected (or appointed) by the Parliament in its plenary session. The nomination process has by tradition and custom been based on the idea that the ombudsman should be a person who can be accepted and ultimately elected (appointed) unanimously by the Parliament. Accordingly, the formally appointment or election will take place as a result of complex talks and negotiations, in a process based on both formal and informal procedures. These rules have been followed by tradition or custom but are not laid down in the Constitution, in law or any formal binding legal rule. No political debate takes place in Parliament concerning the ombudsman election. All elections (appointments) have since 1963 been unanimous (there have been 4 ombudsmen including the current office holder). It is stated in the Ombudsman Act that the Ombudsman should not be a member of Parliament, and this implies, too, that he is not a representative of any political party. The ombudsman reports annually to the Parliament.

Independence and Impartiality

3. The *independence* of the ombudsman is secured by the fact that he is appointed by the Parliament and his budget and finances are exclusively dealt with by the

* Parliamentary Ombudsman in Norway.

K. Hossain et al. (eds), *Human Rights Commissions and Ombudsman Offices*, 365–372.

Parliament and accordingly are not dependent upon any body outside th
Parliament. His staff can only be instructed by himself.

4. The ombudsman is barred from holding any public or private office, positio
or commission. The *impartiality* of the ombudsman is further secured by the fac
that he is elected (appointed) by the Parliament on his own merits as a lawye
He has to meet the qualifications required for a Supreme Court judge, and h
is not to be elected as a representative of any political party. The ombudsma
cannot deal with cases which have been brought before a court of law.

Complaints Regarding Acts of Government

5. The ombudsman may take under consideration not only decisions or acts o
government, but also omissions or inaction. Quite a few of the cases brough
before the ombudsman concern lack of reply to the citizenry.

The ombudsman may not assess decisions done by the King in Council, i.e
the body of ministers meeting in plenary session together with the King. Th
ombudsman may neither look into decisions by the courts of law, nor certai
acts of municipal bodies (local government councils). The ombudsman may no
consider decisions made by the Parliament, or certain other bodies deriving thei
authority directly from the Parliament.

However, the main rule is that the ombudsman may oversee any action b
the state or by municipal authorities. The latter were not originally under th
auspices of the ombudsman in Norway, but were included as from 1969. Th
ombudsman can also look into the departments of defence and the police
However, the ombudsman will exercise some restraint when scrutinizing matter
concerning the discretionary decisions of the authorities. That includes th
discretionary powers which the prosecuting authorities have concerning whethe
to institute criminal proceedings, to prosecute or to drop charges.

6. It is held that the ombudsman should not go into every detail in discretionar
matters, and this seems on the whole to be satisfactory. Complaints can an
should be lodged directly with the ombudsman, but he can also decide t
investigate a case even if there is no complaint lodged, or the matter is no
suitable for deciding on the basis of individual complaints. Each year, th
ombudsman chooses certain areas to look further into on his own account.

Investigation, Report and Recommendation

7. The ombudsman can assess approximately the same parts of governmen
actions as the courts, but his competence will be slightly broader in certai
aspects, e.g. concerning the reasonableness of the decision scrutinized. However
the ombudsman cannot deal with questions concerning discretionary matters o
questions requiring non-judicial skill, e.g. whether a person would be the bette
candidate for a post in government offices, whether a certain technical solutio
is the better etcetera. However, the ombudsman will also look into procedura
matters concerning questions of *sound* administrative practice. In such question
the ombudsman will state his opinion, although the questions will be of discretionary nature. The ombudsman investigations are made in writing and he i

naking his decisions and stating his opinions on the basis of written documenta-ion. Thus, he does not assess the evidence or hear witnesses, as would often iappen in a court of law.

The ombudsman has a right to see most government documents, and the government and the civil servants are obliged to be fully cooperative. If the uthorities fail to comply, the ombudsman may demand that the facts of the ase are assessed in a court hearing. This has never been necessary, as he authorities have always complied. However, a few times it has been necessary o remind the authorities of this option in order to get a voluntary answer. 'ailure to comply may also result in criticism from the Parliament.

A complaint is considered well founded if there has not been a fair handling of the case according to the act on handling administrative affairs or general principles of good government, or if government has acted outside the scope of he law (the principle of legality).

3. In the cases investigated the ombudsman will report the outcome of the nvestigations to the administrative agency concerned. These reports will form part of the annual reports to the Parliament. Regarding the activities of the ombudsman in general the ombudsman reports to the Parliament. This is done egularly on a once-a-year-basis. The ombudsman may also give special reports o the Parliament – or to the administrative agencies concerned – on certain natters of importance. For instance, the ombudsman has recently given a special eport to the Parliament on the handling of the Act on Public Access to Government Files in one of the ministries.

LEGISLATION

The Constitution of the Kingdom of Norway of 17 May 1814, § 75, 1

The Constitution, as laid down on 17 May 1814 by the Constituent Assembly at Eidsvoll with subsequent amendments, the most recent being of 23 July 1995).

Section 75
t devolves upon the Storting:
[...]
1. to appoint a person, not a member of the Storting, in a manner prescribed by a law, to supervise the public administration and all who work in its service, to assure that no injustice is done against the individual citizen.

Act Concerning the Storting's Ombudsman for Public Administration

22 June 1962, amended by Acts of 22 March 1968, 8 February 1980, 6 September 1991, 11 June 1993 and 15 March 1996

Section 1. Election of Ombudsman
After each General Election the Storting shall elect an Ombudsman for Public Administration, the Civil Ombudsman. The Election is for a period of four years reckoned rom 1 January of the year following the General Election.

The Ombudsman must satisfy the qualifications prescribed for a Supreme Court Justice. He must not be a member of the Storting.

If the Ombudsman dies or becomes unable to discharge his duties, the Storting shall elect a new Ombudsman for the remaining period of office. The same applies if the Ombudsman relinquishes his office, or if the Storting decides by a majority of at least two thirds of the votes cast to deprive him of his office.

If the Ombudsman is temporarily prevented by illness or for other reasons from discharging his duties, the Storting may elect an acting Ombudsman to serve during the period of absence. In the event of absence up to 3 months the Ombudsman may empower the Head of Division to act in his place.

If the Presidium of the Storting should deem the acting Ombudsman to be disqualified to deal with a particular matter, it shall appoint a substitute Ombudsman to deal with the said matter.

Section 2. Directive
The Storting shall issue a general directive for the functions of the Ombudsman. Apart from this the Ombudsman shall discharge his duties autonomously and independently of the Storting.

Section 3. Purpose
The task of the Ombudsman is, as the Storting's representative and in the manner prescribed in this Act and in the Directive to him, to endeavour to ensure that injustice is not committed against the individual citizen by the public administration.

Section 4. Scope of Powers
The scope of the Ombudsman's powers embraces the public administration and all engaged in its service. Nevertheless, his powers do not include:
(a) matters on which the Storting or Odelsting has adopted a standpoint,
(b) decisions adopted by the King in Council of State,
(c) the functions of the Courts of Law,
(d) the activities of the Auditor General,
(e) matters which, as prescribed by the Storting, come under the Ombudsman's Board or the Ombudsman for National Defence and the Ombudsman's Board or the Ombudsman for Civilian Conscripts,
(f) decisions which, as provided by law, may only be adopted by the municipal council or the county council itself, unless the decision is adopted by the municipal board of aldermen, county board of aldermen, standing committees, the municipal executive board or the county executive board in accordance with § 13 of Act no. 107 of 25 September 1992 concerning Municipalities and County Municipalities. A decision such as referred to here may nevertheless be investigated by the Ombudsman on his own initiative if he considers that regard for the rule of law or other special reasons so indicate.

The Storting may stipulate in its Directive to the Ombudsman:
(a) whether a particular public institution or enterprise shall be regarded as public administration or a part of the state's, the municipalities' or the county municipalities' service according to this Act,
(b) that certain parts of the activity of a public agency or a public institution shall fall outside the scope of the Ombudsman's powers.

Section 5. Basis for the work
The Ombudsman may deal with matters either following a complaint or on his own initiative.

Section 6. Details regarding complaints and time limit for complaints
Any person who believes he has sustained an injustice form the public administration may bring a complaint to the Ombudsman.

Any person who is deprived of his personal freedom is entitled to complain to the Ombudsman in a closed letter.

The complaint shall mention the name of the complainant and must be submitted not later than one year after the administrative action or circumstance which is complained of was committed or ceased. If the complainant has brought the matter before a higher administrative agency, the time limit shall be reckoned from the date on which this authority renders its decision.

The Ombudsman shall decide whether there are sufficient grounds for dealing with a complaint.

Section 7. Right to obtain information
The Ombudsman may demand from public officials and from all others who serve in the public administration such information as he requires to discharge his duties. To the same extent he may demand that minutes/records and other documents be produced.

The rules in §§ 204–209 of the Civil Disputes Act shall apply correspondingly to the Ombudsman's right to demand information.

The Ombudsman may request the taking of evidence by the Courts of Law, in accordance with § 43 second paragraph of the Courts of Justice Act. The court hearings shall not be open to the public.

Section 8. Access to offices in the public administration
The Ombudsman shall have access to places of work, offices and other premises of any administrative agency and any enterprise which come under the scope of his powers.

Section 9. Pledge of secrecy
Unless otherwise provided with respect to his duties under this Act, the Ombudsman is subject to pledge of secrecy as regards information which comes to his knowledge in the course of his duties regarding circumstances which are not generally known. Information on industrial or trade secrets shall under no circumstances be made public. The pledge of secrecy shall also remain in effect after the Ombudsman's retirement from office. The same pledge of secrecy is incumbent upon his staff.

The Storting may prescribe specific rules in the Directive to the Ombudsman regarding the extent to which the Ombudsman's case documents shall be made public.

Section 10. Termination of a complaints case
The Ombudsman is entitled to express his opinion on matters which come under the scope of his powers.

The Ombudsman may point out that an error has been committed or that negligence has been shown in the public administration. If he finds sufficient reason for so doing, he may inform the prosecuting authority or appointments authority what action he believes should be taken in the particular case against the official concerned. If the Ombudsman concludes that a decision rendered must be considered invalid or clearly unreasonable, or that it clearly conflicts with good administrative practice, he may say so. If the Ombudsman believes that there is justifiable doubt regarding factors of importance in the case, he may draw the attention of the appropriate administrative agency thereto.

If the Ombudsman finds that there are circumstances which may lead to liability for damages, he may, depending on the situation, suggest that damages should be paid.

The Ombudsman may let the matter rest when the error has been rectified or the explanation has been given.

The Ombudsman shall notify the complainant and others involved in the case of the outcome of his handling of the case. He may also notify the superior administrative agency concerned.

The Ombudsman himself shall decide whether, and if so in what manner, he shall inform the public of his handling of a case.

Section 11. Notification of shortcomings in statutory law and in administrative practice.

If the Ombudsman becomes aware of shortcomings in statutory law, administrative regulations or administrative practice, he may notify the Ministry concerned to this effect.

Section 12. Report to the Storting
The Ombudsman shall submit an annual report on his activities to the Storting. The report shall be printed and published.

If the Ombudsman becomes aware of negligence or errors of major significance or scope he may make a special report to the Storting and to the appropriate administrative agency.

Section 13. Pay, pension, other business
The Ombudsman's pay and pension shall be determined by the Storting. The same applies to remuneration for the acting Ombudsman appointed in accordance with § 1 fourth paragraph first sentence. The remuneration for an acting Ombudsman appointed according to the fourth paragraph second sentence may be determined by the Storting's Presidium.

The Ombudsman must not hold any public or private appointment or office without the consent of the Storting.

Section 14. Staff
The staff of the Ombudsman's office shall be appointed by the Storting's Presidium upon the recommendation of the Ombudsman or, in pursuance of a decision of the Presidium, by an appointments board. Temporary appointments of up to 6 months shall be made by the Ombudsman.

The Presidium shall lay down specific rules regarding the appointments procedure and regarding the composition of the board. The pay of the staff shall be fixed in the same manner as for the staff of the Storting.

Section 15
1. This Act shall enter into force:

In Chap. IV of the amending Act of 8 February 1980 it is provided that:
"The amendments shall enter into force on the date decided by the Storting."

On 19 February 1980 the Storting set 1 March 1980 as the date of entry into force of the amending Act.

Directive to the Storting's Ombudsman for Public Administration

Laid down by the Storting 19 February 1980 in pursuance of § 2 of the Ombudsman Act

Section 1. Purpose
(Re § 3 of the Ombudsman Act.)
The Storting's Ombudsman for Public Administration – the Civil Ombudsman – shall endeavour to ensure that injustice is not committed against the individual citizen by the public administration and that civil servants and other persons employed or involved in public administration service do not commit errors or fail to carry out their duties.

Section 2. Scope of Powers
(Re § 3 of the Ombudsman Act.)
The scope of the Ombudsman's powers embraces the public administration and all engaged in its service with the exceptions prescribed in § 4 of the Act.

The Select Committee of the Storting for the Scrutiny of the Intelligence Services shall not be regarded as part of the public administration pursuant to the Ombudsman Act. The Ombudsman shall not investigate complaints concerning the Intelligence Services which has been examined by the Select Committee of the Storting for the Scrutiny of the Intelligence Services.

The exception laid down for the functions of the Courts of Law in accordance with the first paragraph litra (c) of § 4 of the Act also embraces decisions which may be brought before a court by means of a complaint, an appeal or some other legal remedy.

Section 3. The form and basis of a complaint
(Re § 6 of the Ombudsman Act.)
A complaint may be brought directly before the Ombudsman. It should be made in writing and be signed by the complainant or someone acting on his behalf. If the complaint is made orally to the Ombudsman, he shall ensure that it is immediately set up in writing and signed by the complainant.

The complainant should as far as possible give the grounds on which the complaint is based and submit evidence and other documents relating to the case.

Section 4. Exceeding the time limit for complaints
(Re § 6 of the Ombudsman Act.)
If the time limit pursuant to § 6 of the Act – one year – is exceeded, this should represent no hindrance to the Ombudsman taking the matter up on his own initiative.

Section 5. Terms and conditions for complaints proceedings
If a complaint is made against a decision which the complainant has a right to submit for review before a superior agency of the public administration, the Ombudsman shall not deal with the complaint unless he finds special grounds for taking the matter up immediately. The Ombudsman shall advise the complainant of the right he has to have the decision reviewed through administrative channels. If the complainant cannot have the decision reviewed because he has exceeded the time limit for complaints, the Ombudsman shall decide whether he, in view of the circumstances, shall nevertheless deal with the complaint.

If the complaint concerns other matters which can be brought before a higher authority of the public administration or before a special supervisory agency, the Ombudsman should advise the complainant to take the matter up with the authority concerned or himself submit the case to such authority unless the Ombudsman finds special reason for taking the matter up himself immediately.

The provisions in the first and second paragraphs are not applicable if the King is the only complaints instance open to the complainant.

Section 6. Investigation of complaints
(Re §§ 7 and 8 of the Ombudsman Act.)
A complaint which the Ombudsman takes up for closer investigation shall usually be brought before the administrative agency or the public official involved in the complaint. The same applies to subsequent statements and information from the complainant. The relevant administrative agency or public official shall always be given the opportunity to make a statement before the Ombudsman expresses his opinion as mentioned in the second and third paragraphs of § 10 of the Ombudsman Act.

The Ombudsman decides what steps should be taken to clarify the facts of the case. He may obtain such information as he deems necessary in accordance with the provisions of § 7 of the Ombudsman Act and may set a time limit for complying with an injunction to provide information or submit documentation etc. He may also undertake specific investigations at the administrative agency or enterprise to which the complaint relates, cf. § 8 of the Ombudsman Act.

The complainant has a right to acquaint himself with statements and information given in the complaints case, unless he is not entitled thereto under the applicable rules for the administrative agency concerned.

If the Ombudsman deems it necessary on special grounds, he may obtain statements from experts.

Section 7. Notification to the complainant if a case is not proceeded upon
(Re § 6 fourth paragraph of the Ombudsman Act.)

If the Ombudsman finds that there are no grounds for proceeding upon a complaint, the complainant shall immediately be notified to this effect. As far as possible the Ombudsman should advise him of any other channel of complaint which may exist or himself refer the case to the correct authority.

Section 8 Cases taken up on own initiative
(Re § 5 of the Ombudsman Act.)
If the Ombudsman finds reason to do so, he may undertake a closer investigation on his own initiative concerning administrative proceedings, decisions or other matters. The provisions in the first, second and fourth paragraphs of § 6 shall apply correspondingly to such investigations.

Section 9. Termination of the Ombudsman's proceedings
(Re § 10 of the Ombudsman Act.)
The Ombudsman shall personally express his views in all incoming cases which follow a complaint or which he takes up on his own initiative. He may nevertheless authorize the Head of Division to terminate cases which must obviously be rejected.

The Ombudsman expresses his views in a statement where he gives his opinion on the questions relating to the case and coming under the scope of his powers, cf. § 10 of the Ombudsman Act.

Section 10. Instructions for the staff
(Re § 2 of the Ombudsman Act.)
The Ombudsman shall issue specific instructions for his staff. He may authorize his office staff to undertake the necessary preparations of cases to be dealt with.

Section 11. Pledge of secrecy in reports to the public
Restrictions on the right to give information pursuant to § 12 third paragraph, shall apply correspondingly in reports to the public under § 10 sixth paragraph of the Ombudsman Act.

Section 12. Annual report to the Storting
(Re § 12 of the Ombudsman Act.)
The annual report of the Ombudsman to the Storting shall be submitted by 1 April each year and shall cover the Ombudsman's activities during the period 1 January-31 December of the previous year.

The report shall contain a survey of the proceedings in the individual case which the Ombudsman feels is of general interest and shall mention those cases where he has drawn attention to shortcomings in statutory law, administrative regulations or administrative practice or has made a special report in accordance with § 12 second paragraph of the Ombudsman Act.

If the Ombudsman has found that the complaint is without foundation, neither the complainant's nor the public official's name shall be mentioned in the report. If the Ombudsman finds reason to do so, he may also in other cases omit names. The report must not contain information on industrial or trade secrets. The Ombudsman shall also ensure that information subject to the pledge of secrecy does not appear in the report.

Any description of cases where the Ombudsman has expressed his opinion as mentioned in § 10 second, third and fourth paragraphs of the Ombudsman Act, shall contain an account of what the administrative agency or public official has stated in respect of the complaint, cf. § 6 first paragraph third sentence.

Section 13. Entry into force
This Directive shall enter into force 1 March 1980. From the same date the Storting's Directive for the Ombudsman of 8 June 1968 is repealed.

The Human Rights Ombudsman of Slovenia

Ivan Bizjak*

Legal and Constitutional Basis

1. After the gaining of independence, the Slovenian Parliament adopted the first Constitution of the Republic of Slovenia in December 1991. It is based on the principles of a state governed by the rule of law, parliamentary democracy, and the respect for human rights and fundamental freedoms. The Constitution grants protection to the human rights and fundamental freedoms of all persons on the territory of the Republic of Slovenia.

In the Slovenian legal system, the Ombudsman is an entirely new institution for the protection of constitutionality and legality, and is designated as a constitutional institution. The founding texts are the Constitution of the Republic of Slovenia, the Human Rights Ombudsman Act and the Rules of Procedure of the Human Rights Ombudsman. According to Article 159 of the Slovenian Constitution, "the Human Rights Ombudsman shall be established by law to protect human rights and fundamental freedoms against the state bodies, local self-government bodies, and bodies entrusted with public authorities". According to the same article, special ombudsmen may be appointed for individual fields of citizens' rights. The Slovenian Parliament has so far decided to establish only one national parliamentary Ombudsman of general jurisdiction.

The Law on the Ombudsman (Human Rights Ombudsman) was passed in December 1993 following the regular three parliamentary readings. The law was proposed directly by a deputy, not through the government. The law modelled the duties and authorities of the ombudsman on a classical Scandinavian type of ombudsman, combining it with some provisions of the legislation in those European countries, which recently established such institutions (e.g. Netherlands, Spain).

The Human Rights Ombudsman Institution was established and began to work on January 1, 1995, although the first Slovenian Human Rights Ombudsman, Mr. Ivan Bizjak, was elected already on September 29, 1994. The Human Rights Ombudsman is a single-headed institution.

The Human Rights Ombudsman Act does not require any specific qualifications for the Ombudsman. The only condition which has to be fulfilled is that a candidate for Ombudsman must be a citizen of the Republic of Slovenia.

It should be stressed that the fact that the institution of the Ombudsman is constitutionally based constitutes an important advantage for the work and

* Human Rights Ombudsman.

K. Hossain et al. (eds), Human Rights Commissions and Ombudsman Offices, 373–392.

position of the Ombudsman. It is not necessary for the constitution to go into details, on the other hand it is important that the jurisdiction and the competencies of the Ombudsman are well described and determined in the law.

2. The Ombudsman, according to the Human Rights Ombudsman Law, is elected by the Parliament by a two-thirds majority of MPs upon nomination by the President of the Republic, for the term of six years and may be re-elected only once. The appointment by the Parliament is important and it is also good if quite a large majority is needed for appointment. The possibility to report to the Parliament is to be seen as an advantage.

Independence and Impartiality

3. According to Article 4 of the Human Rights Ombudsman Act in Slovenia, the Ombudsman shall be autonomous and perform his functions independently. The Office of the Ombudsman is an independent state body funded from the national budget. The level of funding is set by the National Assembly on the proposal of the ombudsman and not by the government as is the case with other budget recipients. This is an important aspect of independence.

The other important aspect of independence is the question of possible dismissal of the Ombudsman. The Ombudsman in Slovenia may be dismissed from his/her office on his own request or if he/she has been convicted of a criminal act and sentenced to imprisonment, or due to his/her permanent loss of ability to perform the duties of his/her office. The procedure for removing the Ombudsman shall be started upon a motion made by one third of MPs. The Parliament shall remove the Ombudsman from his office if two thirds of the present MPs. have voted for the removal.

Also very important is the immunity of the Ombudsman. According to Article 20 of the Human Rights Ombudsman Act, the Ombudsman shall not be held responsible for an opinion or recommendation given while performing his function. The Ombudsman shall not be held in custody in criminal proceedings instituted against him for having performed his function, without the prior consent of the Parliament.

4. The Office of the Ombudsman is completely autonomous. The organization, size of staff and all the other organizational questions are defined by the Ombudsman himself (Rules of procedure and other acts). The ombudsman shall have an expert service and he shall appoint and dismiss, when necessary, his counsels, advisers and other employees in his office. He shall appoint the secretary general, who shall manage the office.

The Ombudsman may appoint advisers and other experts in his service for a fixed period, from among employees of governmental bodies, who shall retain the right to return to their former posts or employment after the expiry of that period.

In Slovenia there is no Human Rights Commission. The ombudsman mainly cooperates with the Petition Committee of the Parliament and with the Office of the President of the Republic.

Complaints Regarding Acts of Government

5. The Ombudsman shall protect human rights and fundamental freedoms in matters involving state bodies, local self-government bodies and bodies entrusted with public authority. He may also investigate cases of maladministration of the above mentioned bodies. From the competence of the Ombudsman no body is specifically excluded. If complaints to the Ombudsman concern acts of government, this also includes inaction of government organs and also acts or actions of government persons or civil servants. The Ombudsman shall have the right to obtain any information from state bodies, bodies of local self-government or bodies entrusted with public authority, irrespective of the level of secrecy and the respective bodies have to enable him to carry out the investigation.

6. According to Article 24 of the Human Rights Ombudsman Act the Ombudsman in principle shall not interfere in the cases before a court or in any other legal proceedings which are being conducted, except in case of undue delay in the proceedings or evident abuse of authority.

The Ombudsman shall not begin proceedings if more than one year has elapsed from the last decision of a body, or the act in question, except where he assesses that the petitioner could not meet the deadline for justifiable reasons or that the matter is of such importance that he should start proceedings despite the delay.

The restrictions mentioned are not found to be inhibiting or in another way restrictive because there are always possible exceptions. According to Article 25 of the Human Rights Ombudsman Act the Ombudsman may communicate to each body his opinion, from the aspect of protection of human rights and fundamental freedoms, on the case he is investigating, irrespective of the type or stage of procedures which are being followed by the respective body.

Any person, who believes that their human rights or fundamental freedoms have been violated by an act or deed of a state body, a body of local self-government or a body entrusted with public authority, may directly lodge a petition with the Ombudsman to start proceedings. The procedure is confidential. The Ombudsman may also institute the proceedings on his own initiative or the initiative of a third party but with the consent of the affected person. He may make suggestions and recommendations, give opinions and critiques to these bodies, which are bound to consider them and respond within the deadline specified by the Ombudsman. All officials of the above mentioned bodies are bound to respond to the ombudsman's call, to cooperate in an investigation and to provide explanations. The Ombudsman may summon any witness or expert to talk about the matter he is dealing with and the summoned person must respond to the summons.

The Ombudsman may enter any official premises of the abovementioned bodies; he may inspect prisons and other places of detention or other institutions with restricted freedom and he shall be entitled to talk in private with persons in these institutions.

The Ombudsman may submit to the Parliament and Government initiatives for amending laws or other legal acts within their competence. He may also make suggestions to state bodies, institutions and organizations entrusted with public authority, for improving their work and conduct with clients. He may also lodge a request with the Constitutional Court for the assessment of the constitutionality and legality of acts or other enactments. Besides, the Ombudsman may also lodge a constitutional appeal relating to an individual matter he is dealing with.

Investigation, Report and Recommendation

7. The Ombudsman shall have power over the state bodies, local self-government bodies and bodies entrusted with public authorities. There is no restriction concerning the question on which grounds government action is to be judged. The law primarily gives the ombudsman the authority to obtain information from the state and other bodies that it monitors, irrespective of the level of secrecy, to carry out inquiries, and to invite witnesses to hearings as part there of. He may inspect any state body, facilities for people with restricted personal freedom, and psychiatric and similar institutions at any time.

An important power of the ombudsman is that he can lodge a constitutional complaint against violations of human rights, in agreement with the affected party. He may also address a proposal to the Constitutional Court to assess the constitutionality of regulations without the Constitutional Court having to establish his legal standing as is the case for other proposers.

The complaint is considered well founded when there is a violation of human rights or fundamental freedoms, a violation of the constitution, legal acts or binding international documents, if there is undue delay in the court or some other legal proceedings and in the case of some other maladministration.

The Ombudsman has full powers of investigation including the right of access to all government documents. According to Article 34 of the Human Rights Ombudsman Act all state bodies are obliged to help the Ombudsman in conducting an investigation and render him adequate assistance upon his request. All officials and other employees of the state bodies, local self-government bodies, and bodies entrusted with public authority must respond to the Ombudsman·s call to co-operate in an investigation and provide explanations. The president of the Parliament, the Prime Minister, and every minister shall be bound to grant personal audience to the Ombudsman within 48 hours of his request.

8. After the investigation has been concluded, the Ombudsman drafts a report on his findings and communicates it to both parties concerned. They are both entitled to make their comments on the findings about the actual situation, or give proposals for completing the findings in the report. In his final report, the Ombudsman states his assessment of facts and circumstances of each individual case and establishes whether or not the human rights or fundamental freedoms have been violated in that particular investigated matter, and how they have been violated; or, whether or not some other wrongs have been committed.

Concurrently, the Ombudsman shall propose a way to redress the wrong established. Provided that the respective procedural regulations so allow, the Ombudsman may propose that the particular procedure in which a violation has occurred or maladministration has taken place, should be repeated.

If this is not possible, the Ombudsman may propose that the respective body should compensate that particular individual for the damage that he/she has suffered due to the violation or maladministration. The Ombudsman may also propose that the respective body make apologies to the aggrieved person for the maladministration. In his final report the Ombudsman may propose the instituting of disciplinary proceedings against the responsible official of the respective body.

The decisions of the Ombudsman are not legally binding.

In accordance with Article 43 of Human Rights Ombudsman Act, the Ombudsman shall lay before the Parliament his annual and special reports on his work. An annual report includes findings about respecting human rights and fundamental freedoms, and on the legal security of the citizens in the Republic of Slovenia. The Ombudsman has to submit the annual report for the previous year not later than September 30 of the current year. He may also submit special reports to competent parliamentary bodies (committees) or directly to the Parliament.

During the debate on the annual report at the session of the Parliament, the Ombudsman may himself present a summary of the report and ensuing conclusions. The general annual report of the Ombudsman shall be published. It is published as a separate publication but also in the Parliamentary Gazette. In both forms it is widely distributed among the bodies and officials concerned and the general public. An abbreviated English version is published as well and distributed to the respective representatives of other countries, international institutions and related institutions in other countries.

LEGISLATION

CONSTITUTION OF THE REPUBLIC OF SLOVENIA

Article 159
The Office of the Ombudsman
An Ombudsman, responsible for the protection of human rights and fundamental freedoms in matters involving State bodies, local government bodies and statutory authorities, shall be appointed pursuant to an Act of Parliament. Special ombudsmen may be empowered by statute to make determinations on particular subjects.

HUMAN RIGHTS OMBUDSMAN ACT

I. GENERAL PROVISIONS

Article 1
To protect human rights and fundamental freedoms against the state bodies, local self-government bodies, and bodies entrusted with public authorities the Human Rights Ombudsman and his/her jurisdiction and powers shall be established by this act.

Article 2
The Human Rights Ombudsman (hereinafter: Ombudsman; he – his) shall be elected by the Parliament upon the nomination made by the President of the Republic.

Article 3
In performing his function he shall act according to the provisions of the Constitution and international legal acts on human rights and fundamental freedoms. While intervening he may invoke the principles of equity and good administration.

Article 4
The Ombudsman shall be autonomous and perform his function independently.

Article 5
The Ombudsman shall lay before the Parliament general annual reports and special reports on his work.

The funds for the Ombudsman's work shall be allocated by the Parliament from the state budget.

Article 6
State bodies, local self-government bodies, and bodies entrusted with public authorities (hereinafter: bodies) shall furnish the Ombudsman, upon his requirement, all the information and data within their competence, irrespective of the level of secrecy, and shall enable him to carry out the investigation.

Article 7
The Ombudsman may make suggestions and give recommendations, opinions and critiques to the bodies which are bound to consider them and respond within the deadline specified by the Ombudsman.

Article 8
Proceedings before the Ombudsman shall be confidential.

The Ombudsman shall inform the public and the Parliament about his finding of the facts and steps that have been taken.

Article 9
Any person who believes that his/her human rights or fundamental freedoms have been violated by an act or an action of a body may lodge a petition with the Ombudsman to start the proceedings. The Ombudsman may also institute the proceedings on his own initiative.

The Ombudsman may also deal with more general issues relevant to the protection of human rights and fundamental freedoms and legal security of the citizens of the Republic of Slovenia.

The proceedings before the Ombudsman shall be informal and free of charge for the petitioners.

The Ombudsman shall conduct impartial and independent investigation and shall obtain the opinions in each case by all the parties concerned.

Article 10
The seat of the Ombudsman shall be in Ljubljana.

The Ombudsman shall specify the organizational scheme and work of his bureau in the Rules of Procedure and other general acts.

II. ELECTION AND POSITION OF THE OMBUDSMAN AND HIS DEPUTIES

Article 11
Only a citizen of the Republic of Slovenia may be elected as the Ombudsman.

Article 12
The Ombudsman shall be elected by the Parliament with the two-third majority of all MP votes for the term of six years, and after the expiration of this term of office, he may be re-elected only once.

Article 13
The election procedure for the Ombudsman shall start not later than six months prior to the expiration of the term of office of the actual Ombudsman.

The Parliament shall decide on the nomination made by the President of the Republic within forty five (45) days after it has been submitted.

Article 14
The provisions of the Law on the Constitutional Court, regulating the candidature of the constitutional judges, shall apply, respectively, to the candidature of the Ombudsman.

Article 15
The Ombudsman shall have not less than two but no more than four deputies. Deputies shall be appointed by the Parliament upon the nominations made by the Ombudsman.

The Ombudsman shall submit nomination for his deputy to the Parliament not later than six months prior to the expiration of the term of office of the actual deputy.

The Parliament shall decide on the nomination of the Deputy Ombudsman within forty-five (45) days after its submission.

Article 16
The term of office of a Deputy Ombudsman shall be six years. After the expiration of this term of office, he/she may be re-appointed.

Article 17
In the case of absence, death, expiration of the term of office, permanent or temporary incapacity of performing the duties of his office, the Ombudsman shall be replaced by a Deputy Ombudsman.

The Ombudsman shall specify the sequence of his deputies to replace him.

Article 18
The Ombudsman and his deputies shall assume their offices after having taken the oath before the Parliament. The oath shall be:
"I swear that I will perform my duties in accordance with the Constitution and the laws, I will protect human rights and fundamental freedoms, I will perform these duties thoroughly and impartially, and in doing so I will adhere to the principles of equity and good administration."

Article 19
The holding of the office of the Ombudsman shall be incompatible with the holding of any office in the state bodies, local self-government bodies, political parties and trade unions, or the performing of other functions and activities which are incompatible by law with the holding of a public office.

An office, incompatible with the holding of the function of the Ombudsman, shall cease to the Ombudsman or it shall be suspended, if so regulated by the law.

If the Ombudsman does not discontinue a profitable activity incompatible by law with the performing of the function of the Ombudsman within 30 days of the day when the competent committee at the Parliament has established this incompatibility, his office of the Ombudsman shall be terminated.

Article 20
The Ombudsman shall not be held responsible for the opinion or recommendation given while performing his function.

The Ombudsman shall not be held in custody in the criminal proceedings instituted against him for having performed his function, without the prior consent of the Parliament.

Article 21
The Ombudsman may be untimely relieved of his office only on his own request, or may be removed from office if he has been convicted of a criminal act and sentenced to imprisonment, or due to his permanent loss of ability for performing the duties of his office.

The procedure for removing the Ombudsman from his office shall be started upon the motion made by one third of MPs.

The Parliament shall remove the Ombudsman from his office if two thirds of the present MPs have voted for it.

Article 22
Provisions of the Article 19, Article 20, and Article 21 shall also apply to a Deputy Ombudsman.

III. JURISDICTION OF THE OMBUDSMAN

Article 23
The Ombudsman shall have the powers, specified by this Act, over the state bodies, local self-government bodies, and bodies entrusted with public authorities.

Article 24
The Ombudsman shall not interfere in the cases in which court or some other legal proceedings are being conducted, except in case of undue delay in the proceedings or evident abuse of authority.

Article 25
The Ombudsman may communicate to each body his opinion, from the aspect of protection of human rights and fundamental freedoms, about the case he is investigating, irrespective of the type or stage of proceedings which are being conducted by the respective body.

IV. PROCEEDINGS

Article 26
Any person who believes that his/her human rights or fundamental freedoms have been violated by an act, an action or maladministration of a state body, local self-government body, or body entrusted with public authority may lodge a petition with the Ombudsman to start the proceedings.

The Ombudsman may also institute the proceedings on his own initiative.

If the Ombudsman is to institute the proceedings, either on his own initiative, or upon a petition which has been lodged on behalf of the aggrieved person by a third party, the consent by the aggrieved person shall be required to start the proceedings.

Article 27
Each petition lodged with the Ombudsman shall be signed and have all personal data of the petitioner, as well as comprise all circumstances, facts, and evidence on which the petition is based. The petitioner must also state whether or not legal remedies have already been applied, and if they have been, which of them.

Each petition to start the proceedings (hereinafter: petition) shall be, as a rule, lodged in writing. Neither the form nor the assistance by a counsellor shall be required for lodging a petition.

Persons deprived of liberty shall have the right to lodge a petition with the Ombudsman in a sealed envelope.

Article 28
Having received a petition, the Ombudsman shall screen it and decide on this basis either

(1) to give a 'fast-track' treatment to the case; or
(2) to launch a full investigation; or
(3) to reject the petition; or
(4) to decline the petition because it is either anonymous or too late or insulting, thus abusing the right of petition.

The Ombudsman having decided to reject a petition or decline it due to the reasons stated under the items (3) and (4) of the above paragraph, shall inform the petitioner in the shortest possible time about his decision, and explain him the reasons for it and point out, if possible, another adequate way of settling the case.

Article 29
The Ombudsman shall decide on giving the 'fast-track' treatment (item (1) of the Article 28) particularly in the case when the actual situation and the standpoints of all parties concerned are already evident from the petition itself and the attached documents.

Article 30
The Ombudsman shall reject a petition (item (3) of the Article 28) particularly due to the following reasons:
- when it is obvious from the available data and circumstances that human rights or fundamental freedoms have not been violated nor other maladministration done;
- when the petition is incomplete and has not been completed on the Ombudsman's requirement;
- when proceedings are being conducted in the case before the judicial bodies, except for the cases specified in this act;
- when the case falls within the competence of investigating commissions at the Parliament, related to public officials;
- when all regular and extraordinary legal remedies have not been exhausted, except if he assesses that it would be useless for the petitioner to start or continue such proceedings, or if he assesses that individuals would suffer great or irreparable damage in the meantime;
- when the petition clearly reveals a case of lesser importance in which, even after a conducted investigation, no adequate results could be expected.

Article 31
The decision by the Ombudsman to decline or reject a petition shall be final.

Article 32
The Ombudsman shall not institute the proceedings if more than one year has elapsed from the wrong-doing or the last decision of a body, except when he assesses that the petitioner has been late for justifiable reasons, or the case is so relevant that he should launch an investigation notwithstanding the time lag.

Article 33
When the Ombudsman decides to launch an investigation (item (2) of Article 28) he shall communicate his decision to the petitioner and the body or bodies against which the petition has been lodged, and require all the necessary explanations and additional information.

The Ombudsman shall specify a deadline by which the body must furnish all the explanations and information stated in the previous paragraph. The deadline may not be shorter than 8 days. A body having failed to furnish the required information or explanations to the Ombudsman by the deadline must immediately communicate to the Ombudsman the reasons of not having fulfilled his requirement.

The Ombudsman may directly inform its superior body about the delay from the previous paragraph.

The rejection or ignoring of the Ombudsman's requirements shall be deemed an obstruction to the Ombudsman's work.

The Ombudsman may report about this in a special report to a competent working group at the Parliament or to the Parliament itself, or he may publicize these facts.

Article 34
All state bodies shall be obliged to help the Ombudsman in conducting an investigation and render him adequate assistance upon his requirement.

Article 35
Within the scope of his work, the Ombudsman shall have unrestricted access to all the data and documents within the competence of the state bodies.

Regulations on observing the secrecy of data shall be binding to the Ombudsman, his deputies, and his staff.

Article 36
All officials and other employees of the bodies stated in the Article 6 of this Act must

respond to the Ombudsman's call to co-operate in an investigation and provide explanations.

The Ombudsman may summon any witness or expert to an interview about the case he is dealing with. The summoned must respond to the summon.

Article 37
The Ombudsman may discontinue the investigation if he has established that the case has already been settled in some other way, or, if the petitioner does not cooperate in the investigation with any justifiable excuse, or, if it has become obvious from the petitioner's actions that he/she is no more interested in the continuation of the investigation.

Article 38
The investigation having been completed, the Ombudsman shall draft a report on his finding of the facts and forward it to the parties concerned. Within the deadline set by the Ombudsman, they may communicate their comments or proposals to complete the finding of the facts stated in the draft report.

In urgent cases, or when the Ombudsman assesses on the basis of available documents that the facts are indisputable, he may decide on the basis of his finding of the facts and give recommendations without previous verifying from the preceding paragraph.

Article 39
In his final report the Ombudsman shall state his assessment of the facts and circumstances of that individual case, and establish whether or not human rights or fundamental freedoms have been violated, or some other maladministration has been done in the investigated case.

At the same time, the Ombudsman shall recommend the way how to remedy the established wrong-doing. In this, he may recommend that the body should repeat a certain procedure in accordance with the law, recommend the compensation for the damage, or recommend some other way how to remedy the wrong-doing that has affected the individual. In this, he shall not interfere in civil legal rights of the individual to the compensation for the damage.

The Ombudsman may propose the initiation of disciplinary proceedings against the officials of the bodies who did the established maladministration that led to an injustice.

Article 40
The bodies stated in the Article 39 must inform the Ombudsman within 30 days about the steps taken in accordance with his proposals, opinions, critiques, or recommendations.

If the body does not submit a report on adhering to the Ombudsman's recommendations, or these are adhered to only partially, the Ombudsman may directly inform about it its superior body or respective ministry, or submit a special report to the Parliament or publicize these facts.

The Ombudsman may publish his report and his proposals in mass media at the expense of the body if the latter, after a repeated requirement, has not adequately responded to his proposals or recommendations.

Article 41
In dealing with the acts and maladministration of local self-governments the Ombudsman shall be bound to take into account the special character of their position, and their way of taking decisions in particular.

Article 42
The Ombudsman or his authorized representative may enter any official premises of each state body, local self-government body, or body entrusted with public authority.

The Ombudsman may inspect prisons or other places where people are kept detained and other institutions with restricted freedom of movement.

The Ombudsman shall have the right to talk in private with persons from the institutions of the preceding paragraph.

Article 43
The Ombudsman shall lay before the Parliament his general and special reports on his work, his findings about respecting human rights and fundamental freedoms, and on legal security of the citizens in the Republic of Slovenia.

He shall submit the annual report for the previous year not later than September 30 of the current year.

The Ombudsman may submit special reports to competent working groups at the Parliament or directly to the Parliament.

Article 44
During the debate on the general annual report at the session of the Parliament, the Ombudsman may himself present a summary of the report and ensuing conclusions.

The general annual report of the Ombudsman shall be promulgated.

Article 45
The Ombudsman may submit to the Parliament and Government initiatives for amending laws or other legal acts within their competence.

The Ombudsman may make suggestions to the state bodies, institutions, and organizations performing the functions of public authorization, for improving their work and conduct with clients.

Article 46
The President of the Parliament, the Prime Minister, and the ministers shall be bound to grant personal audience to the Ombudsman within 48 hours after his request.

V. THE RIGHTS OF THE OMBUDSMAN

Article 47
The Ombudsman shall be granted a salary equal to the salary of the President of the Constitutional Court.

A Deputy Ombudsman shall be granted a salary equal to the salary of a judge of the Constitutional Court.

Article 48
After the expiration of his term of office the Ombudsman who had been a judge or had held another permanent office in a state body until he was elected the Ombudsman, shall have the right to re-assume his former function if he notifies the competent body, within three months after the expiration of his term of office, that he wishes to re-assume his former function.

The Ombudsman who had occupied a certain job until he was elected the Ombudsman, shall have the right to return to his former job within three months after the expiration of his term of office, or to get some other job which must be adequate to his education and professional skill.

Article 49
The Ombudsman whose term of office has expired and can, for justified reasons, neither continue his former job nor get another adequate job, nor has he fulfilled the conditions for retirement by general regulations, shall be entitled to receive a substitute salary in the amount he would receive if he did that job, until he gets employed or fulfills the conditions for retirement under general regulations, but no longer than one year after the expiration of his term of office.

Article 50
The provisions of Article 48 and Article 49 shall also apply to a Deputy Ombudsman.

VI. THE BUREAU OF THE OMBUDSMAN

Article 51
Having previously obtained the opinion by the competent working group at the Parliament, the Ombudsman shall pass the Rules of Procedure which specify the division of fields of work, the organization of work, and the method of dealing with petitions. The Rules of Procedure shall be published in the Uradni list Republike Slovenije [Official Gazette of the Republic of Slovenia].

Article 52
The Ombudsman shall have an expert service. The Ombudsman shall appoint and dismiss, when necessary, his counsels and other employees.

The Ombudsman shall appoint the secretary general who shall manage the Bureau of the Ombudsman.

Article 53
The Ombudsman may appoint advisers and other experts for a fixed time to the service of the Ombudsman from among the employees of the state bodies. They have the right to re-assume their former functions or jobs after their terms have expired.

Article 54
As regards the salary, remuneration, and other personal incomes, allowances and rights the provisions of the State Officials Act shall respectively apply to the secretary general and the provisions of the act on the employees in the state bodies shall respectively apply to other employees.

Article 55
The funds for the work of the Ombudsman shall be granted within the state budget of the Republic of Slovenia. The amount shall be allocated by the Parliament upon the proposal made by the Ombudsman.

VII. PENALTIES

Article 56
The following persons shall be fined for a minor offence with at least 10,000 SIT fine:
- the responsible person of a body that has failed to produce the required materials to the Ombudsman upon his requirement (Article 6);
- a person who has failed to respond to the Ombudsman's summons to an interview (Article 36).

VIII. INTERIM AND FINAL PROVISIONS

Article 57
The Ombudsman shall begin his work after the required expert staff has been appointed and premises and other material conditions provided.

On the day the Ombudsman begins his work, the Council of Human Rights and Fundamental Freedoms shall cease to operate under this Act.

The Ombudsman shall take over the files, unsettled cases and assets of the Council of Human Rights and Fundamental Freedoms.

Article 58
On the day, the Ombudsman begins his work, the Act on the Council of Human Rights and Fundamental Freedoms (Uradni list Republike Slovenije – Official Gazette of the Republic of Slovenia, no 14/90) shall cease to be effective.

Article 59
This Act shall take effect on the fifteenth (15th) day after having been published in the Uradni list Republike Slovenije [Official Gazette of the Republic of Slovenia].

HUMAN RIGHTS OMBUDSMAN

RULES OF PROCEDURE

. GENERAL PROVISIONS

rticle 1
'hese Rules of Procedure shall regulate the organization and the system of work of the Iuman Rights Ombudsman (hereinafter: the Ombudsman; he, his), specify the division f fields and the proceeding of dealing with petitions.

rticle 2
lovenian shall be the official language of the Ombudsman. Whoever does not master lovenian, he/she may lodge a petition with the Ombudsman in his/her mother tongue.

rticle 3
'he seal of the Ombudsman shall be round, bearing the Republic of Slovenia's coat of rms in the centre, encircled with the inscription "Republika Slovenija Varuh ... lovekovih ravic" (which says: "The Republic of Slovenia, Human Rights Ombudsman").

rticle 4
'he questions concerning the organization of the Bureau and the system of work of the)mbudsman which are not regulated with the Human Rights Ombudsman Act or the urrent Rules of Procedure shall be regulated with other Ombudsman acts of general pecific.

rticle 5
'he Ombudsman shall cooperate with related institutions and their associations in foreign ountries and with the corresponding international organizations.

rticle 6
'he Ombudsman shall inform the public on his work through regular annual or special eports, through the presentation of his work at press conferences, press releases, by ublishing his reports and proposals in mass media and in special publications.

In doing so, the Ombudsman shall observe the regulations on ensuring the secrecy of lata and confidentiality of the proceedings in accordance with the Ombudsman Act.

rticle 7
The Ombudsman shall inform the public directly or through his Cabinet.

rticle 8
The proceedings before the Ombudsman shall be confidential.

The proceedings having been completed, the Ombudsman shall issue a final report to nform the petitioner and the body to which the petition refers about his finding of the facts.

The Ombudsman shall not be obliged to show the file to any of the parties concerned.

I. THE ORGANIZATION AND THE SYSTEM OF WORK

rticle 9
The service of the Ombudsman shall be organized in the Bureau of the Human Rights)mbudsman (hereinafter: the Ombudsman Bureau).

The Ombudsman Bureau shall consist of:
1) The Cabinet of the Ombudsman;
2) The Secretary General Office;
3) The Expert Service of the Ombudsman.

The Cabinet of the Ombudsman shall provide for the proceeding of handling petitions, erform the administrative-technical tasks, furnish information, and perform other tasks vhich are required for carrying out the tasks within the jurisdiction of the Ombudsman nd the Deputy Ombudsmen.

The work of the Cabinet of the Ombudsman shall be organized and managed by th Head of the Cabinet following the instructions by the Ombudsman.

The Secretary General Office shall perform, independently or in cooperation with th associate performers, all tasks in the fields of organization, legal matters, administratio material- and financial matters, and matters related to the staff, which are necessary fo the functioning of the Ombudsman Bureau.

The Expert Service of the Ombudsman shall perform expert tasks for the Ombudsma and the Deputy Ombudsmen.

The Expert Service shall be managed by the Head of the Expert Service.

The Ombudsman Bureau shall be managed by the Secretary General.

Article 10

In the managing of work in the Bureau and handling labour relations, the Secretar General shall have the powers and duties of a Head of administration in accordance wit the State Administration Act, except when such powers are explicitly entrusted to th Ombudsman by the Ombudsman Act or other general acts.

The Secretary General shall decide on the use of funds for the work of th Ombudsman Bureau.

The Secretary General shall be responsible for her/his work to the Ombudsman.

During her/his absence the Secretary General shall be substituted by the Head of th Cabinet or some other official appointed by the Ombudsman.

Article 11

The matters falling within the jurisdiction of the Ombudsman are divided into th following fields:

- constitutional rights;
- restrictions of personal freedom (habeas corpus);
- social security;
- employment;
- administrative matters;
- law court proceedings;
- environment and planning;
- public services;
- housing.

Each field shall fall within the competence of one of the Deputy Ombudsmen.

The matters that can not be ranked into one of these fields shall be treated by th Cabinet of the Ombudsman.

A more detailed division of individual fields shall be specified by the Ombudsma taking into account the following:

- subject related problems;
- organizations and types of procedures before the state bodies and other bodies, fo which he is empowered; and
- the consistency of expert fields.

Article 12

In connection with his/her work, a Deputy Ombudsman shall have, in the field falling within his/her competence, all the powers that are granted to the Ombudsman by the Act

The Ombudsman may grant general or special authorizations to the officials and employees of the Ombudsman Bureau for the investigation or other activities they must perform.

Article 13

The Ombudsman, the Deputy Ombudsmen, the officials and the authorized employees of the Ombudsman Bureau shall carry official identification cards with their photographs identity data, and quotation of powers.

The form of identification card and the procedure for its issuing shall be specified by he Ombudsman.

The Secretary General to the Ombudsman shall be responsible for issuing identification ards and keeping records on the issued cards.

rticle 14

'he working time of the Ombudsman Bureau shall be determined by the Ombudsman o that it is coordinated with the working time of the state administration.

rticle 15

'he Ombudsman may also perform his work away from his seat.

rticle 16

'he Ombudsman and the Deputy Ombudsmen shall have talks with petitioners at the reviously agreed times.

Has the time of a talk not been previously agreed upon, yet a petitioner wishes to have talk, he/she shall have it with an expert employee or adviser who shall be appointed y the Secretary General.

rticle 17

'etitions to start the proceedings before the Ombudsman and other complaints and etters shall be received by the Main Office.

II. THE PROCEEDINGS

rticle 18

'he proceedings for establishing violations of human rights or fundamental freedoms hall be started upon a petition.

A petition to start the proceedings may be lodged by any person who believes that is/her human rights or fundamental freedoms have been violated by an act or an action f a state body, a body of local self-government or a body entrusted with public authority.

The Ombudsman may also start the proceedings on his own initiative.

He shall start the proceedings on his own initiative when an exceptionally important ase occurs of the violation of human rights or fundamental freedoms, or some other naladministration has been done.

If the Ombudsman is to start the proceedings on his own initiative in an individual ase, the consent by the aggrieved person shall be required to start the proceedings.

rticle 19

petition to start the proceedings shall be lodged in writing, as a rule.

On the claim by a petitioner, a petition may be lodged orally and put on records by n expert employee or adviser who shall be appointed by the Secretary General.

In urgent cases, the Ombudsman may receive a petition also by telephone.

Such a petition must be later lodged in writing by the petitioner. Be it not lodged vithin a month, the proceedings may be terminated.

rticle 20

petition to start the proceedings must be signed by the petitioner and contain his/her ersonal data. It must contain the following facts and items of evidence:

- a state body, or a body of local self-government, or a body entrusted with public authority (hereinafter: body) to which the petition refers;
- the description of human rights or fundamental freedoms which have been violated, or the maladministration done by the body;
- the facts and items of evidence on which the petition is founded;
- the description of legal remedies which have already been applied in the case.

hould a petition be lodged by someone else on behalf of the aggrieved person, the onsent and authorization by the latter must be attached to the petition.

Article 21
Petitions and other letters without the character of a petition to start the proceedings shall be answered by the Secretary General or the Head of the Cabinet.

Article 22
Should a petition be incomplete or incomprehensible, the petitioner shall be given reasonable time to complete or correct the petition.

Article 23
Should expertise be required for the establishing, clarification or judgement of a certain fact which is important for solving the case, and this expertise cannot be obtained from the Ombudsman Bureau, an expert may be engaged in the proceedings.

The engagement of an expert shall be decided upon by the Ombudsman.

Article 24
As regards elimination, records, summons, services, specifying deadlines, and finding of the facts, the provisions of the General Administration Procedure Act shall be reasonably applied, observing the non-formal character of the proceedings before the Ombudsman.

Article 25
Before deciding on the way of processing a petition, the Ombudsman may perform the necessary preliminary inquiries. For this purpose he shall obtain by the specified deadline from the respective bodies the explanations, all the necessary items of information and other data.

Article 26
When possible, the Ombudsman shall strive, throughout the entire course of proceedings, to establish the mediating approach and settle the case by mutual agreement on a friendly settlement.

When the friendly settlement is reached the proceedings started upon the petition shall be terminated.

The achieved friendly settlement of the case shall not mean that the Ombudsman does not come to his own findings and make proposals or recommend a remedy in accordance with the law.

Article 27
Following the established relevant facts, the Ombudsman may communicate to each body his opinion, from the aspect of protection of human rights and fundamental freedoms about the case he is investigating, irrespective of the type or stage of proceedings which are being conducted by the respective body.

Article 28
The Ombudsman shall make his decision on the petition by applying a 'fast-track' treatment, especially when the relevant facts and standpoints of the parties concerned are clearly evident from the documentation attached to the petition to start the proceedings.

The decision shall comprise the established relevant facts, the judgement on the violation of human rights or fundamental freedoms or maladministration, and the means of redressing the violation or wrong-doing.

Article 29
The Ombudsman shall launch an investigation by taking the decision on the investigation first.

Article 30
The decision on the investigation shall particularly include the following clues:

- a summary of the petition and the statement of a body to which the petition refers;
- the statement of the fact which supposedly stands for the violation of human rights or fundamental freedoms or other wrong-doing;
- the persons who are going to carry out the investigation.

Article 31
The Ombudsman may discontinue the investigation has he established that the case was already settled in some other way, if the petitioner does not cooperate in the investigation for unjustified reasons, or if it is evident from the petitioner's actions that he/she shows no interest for the continuation of the investigation.

The discontinuation of the investigation shall terminate the proceeding of handling the petition.

The petitioner and the body to which the petition refers shall be notified about the discontinuation.

Article 32
After the completed investigation the Ombudsman shall make a draft report on his finding of the facts and send it to the parties concerned. These may, by the deadline set by the Ombudsman, send their comments or proposals for completing the finding of the facts in the report.

In urgent cases, or when the Ombudsman assesses on the basis of available documentation that the facts are indisputable, he may decide on the basis of his finding of the facts and give recommendations without previous verifying from the preceding paragraph.

Article 33
In his final report, the Ombudsman shall state his assessment of the facts and circumstances of that individual case, and establish whether or not human rights or fundamental freedoms have been violated or some other maladministration has been done in the investigated case.

At the same time, the Ombudsman shall recommend the way how to remedy the established wrong-doing. In this, he may recommend that the body repeat a certain procedure in accordance with the law, recommend the compensation for the damage, or recommend some other means of redressing the wrong-doing that has affected the individual. In this, he shall not interfere with the civil-legal rights of the individual to the compensation for the damage.

In his final report, the Ombudsman shall also specify his views on the comments, if any, on his draft report, made by the parties concerned, which have not been taken into account.

The Ombudsman may propose the initiation of disciplinary proceedings against the officials of the bodies who did the established maladministration that led to an injustice.

Article 34
The Ombudsman or a person empowered by the Ombudsman may enter the official premises of any state body, body of local self-government, or body entrusted with public authority.

Related to his/her work, the Ombudsman or a person empowered by the Ombudsman shall have unrestricted access to the data and documents within the competence of the state bodies.

Article 35
The Ombudsman may inspect prisons or other places where people are kept detained, and other institutions with restricted freedom of movement.

The Ombudsman shall have the right to talk in private with persons from the institutions of the preceding paragraph.

Inspections may be carried out without a previous notification.

Persons to talk with may be adequately chosen at random.

Article 36
In dealing with more general issues which are important for the protection of human

rights and fundamental freedoms and legal security of citizens, the Ombudsman shall obtain information and standpoints on the handled case from the competent bodies.

After having investigated the case, the Ombudsman may state his opinion with proposals and recommendations.

He shall send his opinion to the competent body, and he may also send it to the Parliament and the Government of the Republic of Slovenia.

IV. OTHER PROVISIONS

Article 37
In connection with an individual case he is dealing with the Ombudsman may lodge an appeal for the assessment of constitutionality and legality of Regulations and other Acts of general nature, issued for the purpose of implementing public authority.

Article 38
Under conditions provided by the law, the Ombudsman may lodge a constitutional complaint with the Constitutional Court in relation to an individual case he is dealing with.

The constitutional complaint shall be lodged after the previous consent of the person whose human right or fundamental freedom the Ombudsman is protecting in that particular case.

Article 39
Statistical records shall be kept on the received petitions and their processing.

Article 40
The annual report shall include the findings on the level of respecting human rights and fundamental freedoms and legal security of the citizens of the Republic of Slovenia, the description of essential problems, statistical survey of received, handled and processed petitions, the description of individual typical cases of violations or maladministration, and the report on other activities of the Ombudsman.

V. TEMPORARY AND FINAL PROVISIONS

Article 41
The processing of petitions lodged before these Rules of Procedure take effect shall proceed and conclude in accordance with the provisions of these Rules of Procedure.

Article 42
These Rules of Procedure shall take effect the day after being published in Uradni list Republike Slovenije (Official Gazette of the Republic of Slovenia).

ACT ON THE CONSTITUTIONAL COURT

(*Uradni list Republike Slovenije*, Official Gazette RS, No. 15/94)

Article 1
(1) The Constitutional Court is the highest body of judicial authority for the protection of legality, human rights and basic freedoms.
(2) In relation to other state bodies, the Constitutional Court is an autonomous and independent state body.
(3) Decisions of the Constitutional Court are legally binding.
[...]

Article 9
Any citizen of the Republic of Slovenia who is a legal expert and has reached at least 40 years of age may be elected judge of the Constitutional Court.

[...]

Article 12

(1) The President of the Republic shall within 30 days publish an invitation for proposals for candidates for the post of Constitutional Court judge in the Official Gazette of the Republic of Slovenia.

(2) Proposals must be submitted within a determined period which may not be shorter than 30 days, or in the case of premature expiry of the term of office not shorter than 15 days. Proposals must be substantiated and the written consent of the candidate, stating his agreement to stand as a candidate, must be enclosed.

Article 13

(1) The President of the Republic shall propose candidates for the vacant position of judge of the Constitutional Court from among the candidates proposed in the manner described in the first paragraph of the preceding article, or he may propose others.

(2) The President of the Republic may propose more candidates than there are vacant positions for judges of the Constitutional Court. Each candidacy proposal must be substantiated and the consent of the candidate enclosed.

Article 14

(1) Judges of the Constitutional Court shall be elected by the National Assembly in a secret ballot by a majority of all deputies.

(2) If no Constitutional Court judge is elected, new elections shall be held with new candidates.

(3) If the President of the Republic proposes more candidates than there are judges of the Constitutional Court to be elected, the order of candidates on the voting list shall be determined by lot. If none of the candidates succeeds in obtaining the required majority or if an insufficient number of judges are elected, the elections shall be repeated with those candidates who succeeded in obtaining the largest number of votes. As many candidates shall be voted upon as the number of judges required to be elected to the Constitutional Court. If, even after repeat elections, an insufficient number of candidates are elected as judges to the Constitutional Court, new elections on the basis of new candidacies shall be held.

(4) A candidate may withdraw his candidacy at any time before voting begins.

[...]

Article 22

(1) The procedure for the assessment of the constitutionality and legality of regulations and general acts issued for the exercise of public authority shall begin with the submitting of a written request by the proposer or with a resolution of the Constitutional Court on the acceptance of an initiative for initiating procedures.

(2) The assessment of the constitutionality and legality of regulations and general acts issued for the exercise of public authority shall also consist of an assessment of the conformity of laws and other regulations with ratified international treaties and the general principles of international law.

Article 23

(1) A request may be submitted by:

the National Assembly,

at least one third of the deputies of the National Assembly,

the National Council,

the government,

a court of law, the state prosecutor, the Bank of Slovenia, court of accounts if a question relating to constitutionality or legality arises during procedures they are conducting,

human rights ombudsman in association with individual cases he is discussing, representative bodies of local communities, if the rights of a local community have been violated,

representatives of trade unions for the regions of the state, if the rights of workers have been violated,

(2) Bodies from the preceding paragraph may not submit a request to begin the procedure for assessment of regulations and general acts issued for the execution of public authorizations which they themselves adopted.

[...]

Article 50

(1) Any person may, under the conditions determined by this Law, lodge a constitutional appeal with the Constitutional Court if he believes that his human rights and basic freedoms have been violated by a particular act of a state body, local community body or statutory authority.

(2) The human rights ombudsman can, under the conditions defined by law, lodge a constitutional appeal with the Constitutional Court concerning a particular issue which it is discussing.

[...]

Article 52

(1) A constitutional appeal shall be lodged within 60 days after the day of the acceptance of a particular act against which a constitutional appeal is permitted.

(2) A human rights ombudsman shall submit a constitutional appeal with the agreement of the person whose human rights or basic freedoms are being protected during a particular matter.

(3) In specially founded cases the Constitutional Court may exceptionally decide on the constitutional appeal which has been lodged after the time-limit defined in the first paragraph of this article.

The Ombudsman and the Parliamentary Committees on Human Rights in Spain

Juan Vintró Castells*

Introduction

The present report will deal with the Ombudsman institution in Spain and the parliamentary committees on human rights. It must be pointed out from the start that at the State level only one of the above mentioned institutions exists, that of the Ombudsman. However, Spain is, since the development of the 1978 Constitution, a politically decentralized State and within the Autonomous Communities we find several institutional solutions for the protection of the human rights. In some Autonomous Communities the State model of Ombudsman is reproduced, in others there is no autonomous Ombudsman and we have a parliamentary committee on human rights or on petitions, and yet in others both the Ombudsman and the parliamentary committee on human rights are present. It is for this reason that we shall divide this report into two main parts. In the first, we shall examine the institution of the State Ombudsman, the institution which has jurisdiction to defend human rights within the whole Spanish territory. In the second, we shall make a brief reference to parliamentary committees on human rights within the sphere of the Autonomous Communities.

The Spanish Ombudsman

1. *The Normative Framework*

The Ombudsman institution is provided for by Article 54 of the Spanish Constitution of 1978. According to that constitutional precept, the institution in Spain is called "Defensor del Pueblo" (Defender of the People). The Spanish constitutional text makes five main remarks on the nature and functions of the Ombudsman:

- He/she is commissioned by the Parliament.
- He/she is elected by the Parliament.
- His/her mission is to defend the rights acknowledged in the Constitution.
- In the exercise of his/her functions he/she may supervise the activity of the Administration.
- He/she must inform Parliament of his/her actions.

*Professor of Constitutional Law, University of Barcelona, Spain.

K. Hossain et al. (eds), Human Rights Commissions and Ombudsman Offices, 393–422.

The above mentioned constitutional provision has been legally developed by means of the Organic Law 3/1981, April 6, on the Ombudsman. This law regulates four main issues:

- The appointment and dismissal of the Ombudsman.
- The way of acting of the Ombudsman.
- The nature and contents of the Ombudsman's resolutions and the reports to the Parliament.
- The personal and material means in the service of the Ombudsman.

That law has been modified by the Organic Law 2/1992 in order to establish a new channel in the relationship between the Ombudsman and the Parliament.

To complete the constitutional and legal normative framework, on April 6, 1983 the Regulations on the Organization and Functioning of the Defensor del Pueblo were passed, modified on April 21, 1992.

Finally, in this section of normative references we must mention the law 36/1985, on the relationships between the Defensor del Pueblo and similar institutions of the Autonomous Communities.

2. *Juridical Nature: The Ombudsman is a Body of Constitutional Relevance with Full Functional Independence*

The constitutional definition of the Spanish Ombudsman as a parliamentary commissioned person for the defence of rights and his/her election by Parliament make it necessary to state clearly the predominantly juridical nature of this institution.

There is no doubt that when the Constitution refers to the "Institution of the Defensor del Pueblo", it is placing it among the State bodies. But the fact that at the same time it confers on it the nature of "parliamentary commissioned person" demands, in the first place, a clarification of the unanswered question of whether the Spanish Ombudsman is an internal body of Parliament. The answer has to be "no" for three fundamental reasons:

- The powers of the Parliament (to legislate and to control the Government according to Article 66.2 of the Spanish Constitution) and those of the Ombudsman (the defence of rights in accordance with Article 54 of the Spanish Constitution) are different.
- The Spanish Ombudsman is not subject to an imperative mandate and does not receive directions from any kind of authority (Article 6 of the law that regulates it, the Ley Organica de Defensor del Pueblo, the Organic Act regarding the Ombudsman; henceforth LODP).
- The Ombudsman can act against decisions of the Spanish Parliament, since Article 162.1.a of the Spanish Constitution allows him/her to lodge an appeal of unconstitutionality against laws passed by the legislative power.

It is clear, then, that the decisions of the Spanish Ombudsman cannot be attributed to the Parliament, but only to himself/herself, since he/she acts in his/her own name and according to his/her discernment.

Once it is established that the Spanish Ombudsman is not an internal body of Parliament, another aspect of its juridical nature has to be clarified. It is the question of whether it can be considered an auxiliary body of Parliament. In this connection there is no doubt that the definition of the Spanish Ombudsman as a "parliamentary commissioned person" is unfortunate and may lead to confusion. Indeed, the term "commissioned person" seems to indicate that the Ombudsman has to act in the fulfilment of an assignment of Parliament and is strictly dependent on it. However, if one examines the constitutional and legal configuration of the Ombudsman as a whole, one arrives at a totally different conclusion. In this sense we have already pointed out that the functions of the Ombudsman are specific and different from parliamentary functions, they are exercised with full independence and can be projected against decisions of the Parliament itself. Several legal provisions contribute to reinforce this functional independence of the Spanish Ombudsman with respect to Parliament, in particular the following three:

- The Ombudsman is elected by the Parliament but, once he/she has received the confidence of Parliament, he/she no longer requires it to continue in office (Article 5.1 LODP). There is no motion of censure provided for against the Ombudsman.
- The provision referred to previously (Article 6 LODP) excludes the possibility of a parliamentary group or of an organ of Parliament giving directions to the Ombudsman.
- The duration of the Ombudsman's mandate is longer than the Parliament's (five and four years respectively, according to Articles 2.1 LODP and 68.4 CE) and is not affected by the anticipated dissolution of Parliament.

Next to this undeniable functional independence of the Spanish Ombudsman, one can also observe an organic dependence of this institution with respect to the Parliament. The said link already appears in the constitutional text when it establishes the parliamentary election of the Ombudsman and his/her obligation to inform the legislative power about his/her actions. Other elements that illustrate the aforementioned organic dependence are the integration of the economic funds of the Ombudsman within the Parliamentary Budget and the parliamentary approval of the Regulations on the Organization and Functioning of the Ombudsman. This organic dependence by no means alters the functional independence so often underlined. It is merely an instrumental dependence that reflects above all the will to separate the Ombudsman from the Government and from the executive power as a whole, since these are the addressees of the control that the Ombudsman has to exercise.

Up to now it has been pointed out that the Spanish Ombudsman is a State body but is neither an internal nor a simple auxiliary body of Parliament. In accordance with the functions that the Constitution assigns to this institution, it cannot be included within the category of constitutional bodies. In fact, constitutional bodies are those are that fundamentally characterized by the exercise of functions indispensable to the State life and with direct repercussions on the structure of State. Without prejudice to the relevance of the function of defence of rights that the Ombudsman fulfils, this function does not have the same character as those carried out by constitutional bodies like the Parliament, the Government or the Judiciary. In other words, the existence of the Ombudsman is neither indispensable to the life of the State nor does it characterize the State's structure in Spain.

At this point the most suitable option is to include the Spanish Ombudsman within the category of organs of constitutional relevance. These are organs which the Constitution places in a pre-eminent position for, although they do not carry out vital or indispensable functions to the State, they are entrusted with tasks of control, of consultation, of vigilance of the observance of the Constitution and of the law, and have full functional independence to do so. The constitutional and legal design of the Spanish Ombudsman as an institution entrusted with the defence of rights and with full independence for the fulfilment of its functions allows one, thus, to characterize it as an organ of constitutional relevance.

3. *Elements Which Guarantee the Independence of the Ombudsman*

A. *Parliamentary Election*

(a) Importance

Previously we have noted that the function of the Spanish Ombudsman is the protection of rights and that in order to do so he/she can supervise the activities of the Administration. Since the executive power is the addressee of the control that the Ombudsman has to carry out, parliamentary election is a guarantee to prevent the controlled from being the one that appoints the controller. In that sense, one can say that if the Ombudsman is not elected by the legislative power the said institution is partially distorted. In the Spanish case, parliamentary election is required by Article 54 of the Constitution. The regulation of the designation procedure corresponds to the LODP and to the Rules of Procedure of each of the two Houses that form the Spanish Parliament (The Congress of Deputies and the Senate).

(b) Term

Each time the post of Ombudsman is vacant, a procedure has to be initiated to appoint a new Ombudsman within a period that must not exceed one month (Article 5.3 LODP). This is a reasonable period: on the one hand, it leaves sufficient time so that the parliamentary groups can agree on a candidate, and, on the other, it tries to prevent the temporary situation from lasting too long. In practice, however, this term is not always respected as political parties find it hard to find a quick consensus about a name enabling it to obtain the qualified majority necessary to be elected as Ombudsman. Such a situation occurred, for instance, between 1993 and 1994 and then the Spanish Ombudsman was in a temporary situation that lasted nineteen months. Below we examine how Spanish legislation regulates the temporary situation, but in any case it is clear that it cannot last for such a long time. To achieve that goal there are neither magical nor fully satisfactory juridical solutions as we shall see later on in another section of this report. The solution has to be found elsewhere: the political responsibility and the institutional sense of the parliamentary groups have to prevent the repetition of episodes like the one in 1993–1994 in future, because they damage the prestige of the Ombudsman institution by making it appear an object of covetousness and of dispute among parties.

(c) Proposal of candidate or candidates

The formal proposal of candidates for Ombudsman is the task of a parliamentary committee: the Joint Committee of Congress and Senate in charge of relations with the Ombudsman. In practice that means to leave in the hands of the parliamentary groups the power to propose names to occupy the post of Ombudsman. The different proposals of the groups go to the Committee and those that obtain a favourable vote by a simple majority of the said committee are the ones that will go to the plenary assembly of each House for the final election (Articles 2.2 and 2.3 LODP). It has to be noted that the Joint Committee does not need a qualified majority to approve the proposal of one or more candidates for Ombudsman. In the first stage of the election procedure the rule is more flexible because one simply wants a first position of the political forces.

As a last reference on this point it has to be pointed out that some Spanish authors have suggested the desirability of reforming the present system of proposal of candidates for Ombudsman. It would consist of granting the faculty of proposal to bodies other than Parliament (i.e., universities or other State institutions.)

d) Requirements for the candidates

To be eligible, the requirements according to Article 3 of the LODP are Spanish citizenship, legal age and full possession of civil and political rights. The aforementioned requirements are common to the regulations of other countries and they do not necessitate further comment. It can be pointed out, however, that concerning legal age, Spanish legislation does not contemplate a higher limit to be elected or reelected Ombudsman.

It deserves reflection, though, that Spanish law does not require particular training or particular qualities of the candidates for Ombudsman. In Scandinavia the Ombudsman has to have juridical training.

When preparing the LODP, the inclusion of the said requirement was subject to discussion, but finally it was eliminated since it reduced the number of eligible persons considerably. However, in practice all the Spanish Ombudsmen -three in total- up to now have been important jurists. That shows that the Spanish Parliament, despite not formalizing it in the law, has considered that jurists are the suitable persons to occupy the post of Ombudsman. There is no doubt that to fulfil the task of defence of rights and of supervision of the Administration, juridical training is highly valuable to the Ombudsman and, to a great degree, is a guarantee to the citizen.

Spanish legislation does not establish the need for the candidates for Ombudsman to have special integrity or ethics. The legislation of other countries, on the contrary, has provisions in that regard (Sweden, for instance.)

Beyond the specific legal stipulations, it seems necessary that when the Parliament elects the Ombudsman, it has all the data concerning the training and qualities of the candidates. To that purpose, given the absence of parliamentary procedures on the matter, some authors in Spanish literature have suggested the possibility that the candidates for Ombudsman be examined by a parliamentary committee. The said committee would study their curricula and could summon them to complete the information on their suitability for the post of Ombudsman.

e) Secret vote and majority of three fifths in each House of Parliament

The LODP does not refer to the type of voting required to elect the Ombudsman. From the provisions in the Rules of Procedure of each House one can infer that the election of the Ombudsman has to be by means of a secret vote in both the

Congress and the Senate. In practice it has been that way in the three elections that have taken place in Spain up to now. That solution seems the most adequate to reinforce the authority and legitimacy of the Ombudsman, since the result of an election by secret vote is the unequivocal expression of the free will of the Members of Parliament and party discipline does not conclusively interfere with it.

As to the parliamentary majority needed to be elected Ombudsman, the LODP (Article 2.4) requires a favourable vote of a three fifths majority of the Congress and of a three fifths majority of the Senate. Insofar as in Spain it is almost inconceivable that a political force by itself can have that majority in either House, this requirement is a fundamental element to guarantee the Ombudsman's independence. This rules out the possibility that a party, while having an absolute majority in a House, can impose a candidate for Ombudsman. Thus, it is essential that the different parliamentary groups – or at least the most important in each House – reach a consensus in order for a candidate to achieve the established majority to be elected.

The difficulty in finding a candidate for Ombudsman that rallies the support of such a qualified parliamentary majority accounts for the fact that sometimes the election procedure lasts longer than the law provides. To prevent that and the consequent interim discharge of the office of Ombudsman the simplest solution is to reduce the required majority for election. Such a formula is provided for in some Spanish Autonomous Communities so that if, in a period of three months, the corresponding Parliament has not elected the Ombudsman by a three fifths majority, the next vote will only require an absolute majority. This does not seem a desirable situation since as a result thereof the Ombudsman's independence can be called into question. Take for instance the parliamentary situation – already existing in Spain and in many other countries – in which only one party has the absolute majority and holds office. If we reduce the majority required, we could de facto arrive at the point where the executive power appoints the Ombudsman and, thus, perverts that institution dangerously.

(f) Re-election

Spanish legislation does not prevent the re-election of an Ombudsman once his/her mandate has ended. In practice, though, the holder of the institution has never been re-elected. The future will tell if the practice of non-re-election becomes a consolidated usage or is abandoned.

In favour of the re-election of the Ombudsman, two reasons may be advanced: in the first place, the use of the experience acquired during the exercise of the mandate; in the second place, the prestige earned for the institution thanks to the effective fulfilment of his/her functions.

Against the re-election we can also advance two reasons: on the one hand, the danger of lack of inspiration or stimulus due to holding office for a long period of time; on the other, the risk that the prospect of and the desire for a re-election can compromise the functional independence of the Ombudsman.

B. *Functional Autonomy and the System of Incompatibilities and Prerogatives*

(a) Functional autonomy

At this point it is necessary to repeat the significance of Article 6.1 of the LODP, according to which the Spanish Ombudsman cannot receive instructions from

.ny authority and has full functional independence in the fulfilment of the duties ›f his/her post.

b) Incompatibilities

n order to ensure the independence and the impartiality of the Ombudsman, Article 7 of the LODP establishes a rigorous juridical system of incompatibilities or the holder of the position. In that sense, the Spanish Ombudsman cannot carry out any activity, whether public or private. He/she cannot, thus, hold a epresentative mandate, hold political or administrative posts, belong to political parties or unions, act as a judge or public prosecutor or pursue professional ıctivities.

As to the incompatibility of the Ombudsman in relation to his/her belonging o a political party or union and to activities in the service of a political or ocial group, we have to point out that Spanish legislation does not prevent the lection as Ombudsman of a person who is a member or a leader of a political party. Spanish law does not seek it as its aim that the appointment of the Ombudsman necessarily falls to a person who is politically neutral. However, if ı member of a political party is elected Ombudsman, he/she has to withdraw rom the party before taking possession of the post. In short, the incompatibility of political activism aims to prevent that, once in office, the Ombudsman may be subject to the party's discipline.

c) Prerogatives

The juridical acknowledgement of the prerogatives of parliamentary immunity and of exemption (Articles 6.2 and 6.3 LODP) also contribute to reinforce the ndependence of the Ombudsman.

The prerogative of parliamentary immunity establishes that the Spanish Ombudsman is not juridically responsible for any actions performed in the exercise of his/her office. Therefore, he/she can be neither fined nor arrested nor udged for the activities carried out in the fulfilment of his/her duties as Ombudsman.

Note that the protection given by means of this prerogative affects the activities of the Ombudsman only in the fulfilment of his/her institutional mission; it does not affect his/her other actions.

The prerogative of exemption, on the other hand, gives the Ombudsman pecial guarantees in case he/she may be prosecuted or judged for a presumed crime. Therefore, the Ombudsman, while holding office, cannot be arrested unless caught in the act and the decisions concerning his/her indictment, imprisonment, prosecution and trial will have to be adopted exclusively by the Penal Chamber of the Supreme Court.

C. Causes and Effects of the Dismissal

a) Causes

The LODP (Article 5) regulates in detail the causes for dismissal of the Spanish Ombudsman. There are six grounds: resignation, expiry of the mandate, death, ınexpected incapacity, notoriously negligent action in the fulfilment of his/her unctions, final sentence for fraudulent crime. Although this series of norms has the clear aim of detail and in some aspects reinforces the independence of the Ombudsman, some of the causes taken into account and their procedures can give rise to several objections. Next we shall make brief reference to each of these causes for dismissal.

The voluntary resignation, the expiry of the mandate and the demise of the Ombudsman are causes for dismissal that do not require further comment because, logically, we find them in the regulations of all countries. We have only to take into account that the advent of an incompatibility is equivalent to resignation if in the period provided by law the said situation has not been eliminated. On the other hand, as to the duration of the mandate of the Ombudsman, it has to be remembered that Spanish legislation establishes a period of five years. That way, the mandate of the Ombudsman and the duration of the legislative term (four years) do not coincide and this gives more independence to the institution in relation to Parliament.

Incapacity as a cause for dismissal of the Ombudsman refers to situations of serious and prolonged illness that prevent the normal fulfilment of the functions of the post. The said incapacity must be decided by a majority of three fifths of each House of Parliament by means of a debate and with the prior hearing of the interested person. If the prior hearing of the interested person is not possible due to the health of the Ombudsman, it may be replaced by a written statement.

Notoriously negligent action – the following cause for dismissal – demands, however, a more detailed examination. From the start it has to be noted that it also has to be appraised by a majority of three fifths of each House of Parliament by means of a debate and with the prior hearing of the interested person. It is necessary to clarify that this is not a similar mechanism to the motion of censure. In other words, the Parliament cannot dismiss the Spanish Ombudsman alleging generically that it has lost its confidence in him/her or that it disagrees with a particular action. On the contrary, it has to base its decision of dismissal on particular actions of the holder of the institution that deviate manifestly from the fulfilment of the obligations and duties of the post of Ombudsman.

Finally, the final sentence for fraudulent crime as a cause for dismissal does not give rise to objections in itself. What is amazing is that this alone is not enough to provoke the automatic removal from office of the Ombudsman; to do so a majority of three fifths of each House of the Parliament by means of a debate and with the prior hearing of the interested person is required. Nevertheless, in practice, the Parliament, in view of a final sentence for fraudulent crime, cannot do anything but dismiss the Ombudsman. If Parliament did not do it, it would make a doubly dangerous operation: it would deprive the Judiciary of authority – a job that does not correspond to Parliament; and on the other hand, it would called into question the prestige of the Ombudsman institution by maintaining at the head of it a person sentenced for a fraudulent crime.

(b) Effects

According to the LODP (Article 5.4) and the Rules of Procedure of 1983 (Article 9.2) in all cases of dismissal of the Spanish Ombudsman the Deputy Ombudsmen are the ones that in turn occupy his/her post. In other words, in no case does the Ombudsman hold office as an interim measure. The temporary situation is ensured by the Deputy Ombudsmen, which we shall deal with later on. This solution has given rise to several doctrinal criticisms, especially in the most common case of dismissal: the expiry of the mandate. Indeed, there is no justification in this case for the preference of some Deputy Ombudsmen who do not have the same parliamentary legitimacy as the Ombudsman, as we shall see further on. We should not forget, on the other hand, that this situation already occurred and lasted nineteen months in the years 1993–1994. It seems that the best solution, thus, is that at the end of the mandate, the Ombudsman himself/herself is the one who occupies the post temporarily until the new Ombudsman is elected.

D. *Final Consideration*

In this section we have examined the different provisions of the Spanish legislation that aim to ensure the independence of the Ombudsman and his/her withdrawal from political influences. In general terms, the legal solutions can be considered satisfactory for the end they pursue. However, we should never lose sight of the fact that the force of the Ombudsman lies in the moral authority of his/her decisions and that the latter is fundamentally derived from the human qualities of the holder of the post.

4. *Organization and Personal and Material Resources*

A. *Organic Dependence of Parliament*

The regulation of the internal and organizational aspects of the Spanish Ombudsman is found in the LODP, and specifically in the Rules of Procedure on the Organization and Functioning of the Defensor del Pueblo of April 6, 1983 (henceforth: ROFDP). This latter norm was passed, on a proposal of the Ombudsman, by the Presiding Boards of both the Congress and the Senate in a joint meeting. The LODP did not say anything about the body that ought to pass the aforementioned Rules of Procedure. Practice has decided that it should be Parliament. This fact has been criticized in the Spanish literature, which defends the full power of the Ombudsman to regulate itself in order to respect and ensure to the maximum the independence and autonomy of this institution. Without prejudice to the basis of this criticism, we shall bear in mind that organic dependence does not imply functional dependence, as we have stated earlier.

B. *Organization and Personal Resources*

(a) The Ombudsman as a uni-personal body

Spanish legislation shapes the Ombudsman as a uni-personal body. This is so although it may appear to have a more or less complex internal organization and although the existence of the Deputy Ombudsmen to whom he/she may delegate functions is mandatory. The determining element for the Ombudsman to be considered a uni-personal body is the concentration of the responsibility for the decisions in the holder of the institution and in the fact that he/she alone is the one that has to give account before Parliament. The option for the uni-personal character of the institution has the advantage of preventing situations of conflict and blockade that may arise in a collegiate system.

(b) The Deputy Ombudsmen

The existence of Deputy Ombudsmen is not provided for in the Constitution. The LODP (Article 8) introduces them with a mandatory character and establishes that the Ombudsman will be assisted by a First Deputy and a Second Deputy. This precept was later developed in the ROFDP (Articles 12 to 16).

The Deputy Ombudsmen are proposed by the Ombudsman; the Joint Committee Congress – Senate in charge of the relationships with this institution has to pass judgement on the proposal. A simple majority of this parliamentary committee is needed to have its approval. In the practice followed in Spain up to now, this regulation has resulted in the procedure that the two main parties in Parliament come to an agreement as to the names of the Deputy Ombudsmen. That way, one of the Deputy Ombudsmen is usually close to the majority party and the other usually has a political inclination close to the first party in the opposition.

As regards the causes for dismissal of the Deputy Ombudsmen, it is necessary to point out that they are the same that of the Ombudsman. It stands out that the Ombudsman cannot freely dismiss the Deputy Ombudsmen, not even for notorious neglect. If this be the case, the Ombudsman can propose the dismissal but it will have to be passed by the Joint Committee with the prior hearing of the interested person. In any case, Deputy Ombudsmen are dismissed automatically when a new Ombudsman takes office (Article 36 LODP).

The norms described on the election and dismissal of the Deputy Ombudsmen emphasize three important elements: the clear limit of the power of self-organization of the Ombudsman since he/she can neither appoint nor freely dismiss his Deputy Ombudsmen; the minor parliamentary legitimacy of the Deputy Ombudsmen in comparison to that of the Ombudsman; and the major politicization of the appointment of the Deputy Ombudsmen. Nevertheless, in order to qualify the last consideration, one has to bear in mind that the Deputy Ombudsmen have a juridical status of functional autonomy, incompatibilities and prerogatives equivalent to that of the Ombudsman and that this contributes without doubt to reinforce their independent action.

As to their functions, they are mainly three: to assist the Ombudsman, to take on the jurisdiction that the Ombudsman delegates to them and to replace the Ombudsman in turn in the case of dismissal. Among the ordinary tasks that correspond to the Deputy Ombudsmen stand out the management of the procedures, the study of the matters that come before the Ombudsman and the formulation of the decision proposals. The Ombudsman has to delimit the scope of functions of each Deputy.

(c) Staff in the service of the Ombudsman

The regulation of the staff in the service of the Ombudsman is provided for in the LODP (Articles 34 to 36) and in the ROFDP (Articles 27 to 31). The staff is made up of advisors responsible of an area, technical advisors, administrators, Deputy Ombudsmen and subordinates. At present that totals one hundred and twenty civil servants, a figure which is higher than that of other countries – like France or Great Britain – with a larger number of inhabitants.

The appointment of this staff is to be done in accordance with the constitutional principles of merit and ability, but it depends on the free decision of the

Ombudsman. The LODP provides that in appointment, an attempt should be made to give priority to people who are already civil servants. The system of provision of services will be that of exclusive dedication.

The Ombudsman is also free to dismiss people in his/her service when considered necessary. This complete freedom of the Ombudsman to freely appoint and dismiss his/her staff has been partially criticized in the literature. On the other hand, nobody questions that the advisors are posts in the confidence of the Ombudsman, because they are the immediate associates in the juridical and technical preparation of his/her actions. In this sense the LODP establishes that the advisors will quit when another Ombudsman holds the office.

To manage and co-ordinate the staff and the departments of the institution, there is a Secretary General appointed by the Ombudsman and a Co-ordinating and Internal Rules Board composed of the Ombudsman, the Deputy Ombudsmen and the Secretary General.

(d) Material means

The economic budget of the Spanish Ombudsman is an item within the Budget of the Parliament (Article 37 of the LODP). This is another example of the Ombudsman's organic dependence in relation to Parliament. As a consequence, the system of bookkeeping and auditing will be the one applicable to the legislative power; the Audit and Accounts Department of Parliament will exercise the function of supervision.

At present the budget of the Spanish Ombudsman is over one thousand million pesetas a year (around six million dollars). To balance properly the scope of this economic allowance, one has to bear in mind that Spain has about forty million inhabitants, a territory of five hundred and five thousand square kilometres and one hundred and twenty people are in the service of the Ombudsman.

5. *Functions: Defence of the Constitutional Rights and Supervision of the Activities of the Administration*

Historically the original function of the Ombudsman has been to supervise the action of the Administration and as such is incorporated in the regulations of some countries. Later on, the object of the activity of the Ombudsman was extended and modified in certain respects. In this sense, Article 54 of the Spanish Constitution refers to the defence of rights as the basic mission of the Ombudsman and seems to give a purely instrumental character to the task of supervision of the Administration. This constitutional regulation puts forward three main questions: Which are the rights that enter the sphere of protection of the Spanish Ombudsman? Can the task of supervision of the Administration that corresponds to the Ombudsman be extended to cases not directly related to the defence of constitutional rights? Can the mission of the Ombudsman in the defence of constitutional rights be projected to cases derived from the relationships among individuals?

The answer to the first question is in the very Article 54 of the constitutional text. Indeed, the said precept points out clearly that the rights which are the objects of protection of the task of the Spanish Ombudsman are the ones included in Title I of the Constitution. That means that the action of the Ombudsman as a guarantor of rights must not only be projected to the individual rights but also to the economic, social and cultural rights. In practice an important part of the matters that arrive at the Ombudsman refer precisely to these latter rights.

As to the other two questions, the solution is found in Article 9 of the LODP. This provision, on the one hand, clearly establishes that the object of the Ombudsman's control has to be the Administration, not individuals and, on the other, that the supervision of the Administration may take place even if there is no direct violation of a constitutional right. It is enough to have an administrative action presumably ineffective or contrary to the legality principle. This has also been the pattern followed by the Ombudsman in practice. Regarding this matter it can also be observed that the number of rights in Title I of the Spanish Constitution easily allows the Ombudsman to connect any disfunction or administrative irregularity with a violation of rights.

Finally, defence of constitutional rights and supervision of the Administration are two functions of the Ombudsman that in practice are often inseparable.

6. *Scope of Action: The Administration in a Broad Sense*

A. *General Layout*

The term "Administration", present both in the Constitution and in the LODP in order to identify the object of supervision of the Spanish Ombudsman, has been interpreted by the literature and used in a broad sense. In the said sense, the Ombudsman can control the central Administration of the State, those of the Autonomous Communities, those of the provinces, those of the municipalities, those of the corporations and those that affect certain public services conceded to private enterprises. Therefore, in order to determine the extent of the Ombudsman's jurisdiction, one has to follow a functional approach, not an organic one. Because of this, one can consider that the Administration is present when there is an entity which – its legal status and juridical regime aside – depends on the former because it follows its directives or uses public funds. According to this approach, one must include autonomous organizations, public companies and corporate entities in the wide sense of Administration. In the latter case (for instance, professional associations) this only applies in relation to the exercise of functions of general interest by the aforementioned corporations. As to the possibility of inspecting the public services provided by individuals, the key element to legitimate the intervention of the Ombudsman is the effective existence of a public service activity, regardless of who provides it: the Administration itself or a private individual that offers it by virtue of a concession or an administrative authorization.

On the other hand, in relation to the bodies subject to the Ombudsman's control, the LODP (Article 9.2) states that the authority of this institution extends to the activities of the ministers, administrative authorities, civil servants and any other person who acts in the service of the Public Administration.

B. *Special Cases*

(a) The Administration of Justice

In order to guarantee the principle of judicial independence established in the Constitution, the LODP (Article 17) states that the Ombudsman cannot examine the matters awaiting resolution by the Courts of Justice. This means that in the judicial field the Ombudsman cannot interfere with main questions related to the jurisdictional function. However, he/she may intervene to control the material functioning of the Administration of Justice as a public service (for instance, the behaviour of the judicial civil servants.) Nevertheless, it seems that the LODP is inclined to put the Ombudsman to one side regarding the direct investigation of cases of ill-functioning of the Administration of Justice. Indeed, Article 13 establishes that in those cases the Ombudsman must address his/her complaints to the Public Prosecutor so that the latter adopts the relevant decisions or transmits them to the governing body of the Judiciary. It has to be pointed out that in the last years the Spanish Ombudsman has received a great number of complaints concerning the Administration of Justice and in the transaction of some of them the Ombudsman has acted straightaway and without the intermediates that the LODP imposes on him/her.

(b) Military Administration

Article 14 of the LODP establishes a specific limit for the action of the Spanish Ombudsman in the sphere of the Military Administration: the prohibition to interfere in the command of National Defence. This limit aside, the Ombudsman may carry out his/her functions in this field in the same way as he/she may in the Civil Administration.

(c) Administration of the Autonomous Communities

Spain is a State composed of seventeen Autonomous Communities which have political autonomy. These Autonomous Communities are credited with authority over several material fields and have political institutions (Parliament, Government) and an Administration of their own to implement this authority. Likewise, although the Spanish Constitution does not state this explicitly, in the exercise of the self-government recognized by the constitutional text, the Autonomous Communities may establish Ombudsmen of autonomic scope. That way, some Autonomous Communities already have the institution of the autonomous Ombudsman. These autonomous Ombudsmen have, in general, a juridical form similar to that of the State Ombudsman, although with a scope of action logically reduced to that of the Autonomous Administration. That forces one to explain the issue of the relationship between the State Ombudsman and the autonomous Ombudsmen.

Article 12 of the LODP establishes that the State Ombudsman has universal jurisdiction over all Administrations. Consequently, the State Ombudsman has no juridical limit as to the supervision of the Administration of an Autonomous Community, even if it has an autonomous Ombudsman. Nevertheless, the LODP states that the autonomous Ombudsmen shall coordinate their functions with the ones of the State Ombudsman and that the latter can ask for their cooperation. The law 36/1985 regulates the relationships between the State Ombudsman and the autonomous Ombudsmen, taking as a basis the principles of coordination, collaboration and cooperation and the establishment of agreements between these institutions.

In practice, in spite of the legal framework already described, the conclusion of agreements and the periodic meetings between the State Ombudsman and the autonomous Ombudsmen, there have been many cases of overlap. However, it has to be pointed out that in the field of supervision of the Local Administration there has been, through an informal agreement, a clear division of jurisdiction that goes beyond the strict legal provisions. In that way the autonomous Ombudsmen control the actions of the Local Administration without restrictions and this is one of the most relevant fields of intervention.

Facing the future, the most autonomist doctrinal orientations suggest a reform of Article 12 of the LODP so that the actions of the State Ombudsman and of the autonomous Ombudsmen are distributed according to the division of jurisdiction between the Central State and the Autonomous Communities. That is, the State Ombudsman ought to control the central Administration and the autonomous Ombudsmen the autonomous Administrations.

(d) Parliamentary Administration

The LODP does not provide for the possibility that the Spanish Ombudsman may control the Parliament's administrative activity. Nevertheless, the functional independence of the Ombudsman in relation to Parliament and the aforementioned wide sense of the term Administration provide support for that possibility (for instance, in the administrative acts of the bodies of the Houses as regards personnel.)

7. *Proceedings*

A. *Ex officio Action*

The LODP (Article 9) allows the Spanish Ombudsman to exercise his/her functions without being asked to. It is enough for him/her to learn of some administrative irregularity to act. This ex officio action of the Spanish Ombudsman underlines the intention of the Spanish legislation to provide this institution with autonomy in the exercise of its functions.

B. *Intervention at the Petition of a Party*

(a) The complaints brought by citizens or legal entities

Most actions of the Spanish Ombudsman begin with the filing of a complaint. A complaint is any claim before the Ombudsman brought by a person in relation to an administrative action which is allegedly irregular or which violates constitutional rights (Article 9 LODP).

Through complaints, one guarantees direct access to the Ombudsman, without intermediaries of any kind. The LODP (Articles 10.1 and 15) regulates the capacity and the formal requirements of the filing of complaints in very open and simple terms. In this sense, the complaints can be filed by any person or legal entity that invokes a genuine interest. The fact of being a foreigner, minor, resident or not, legal incapacity, internment in a penitentiary or a detention centre and the relation of dependence to a public power are no obstacle to the filing of a complaint. As to the formal requirements, the complaint has to be signed with the name of the interested person and his/her address, has to enclose a reasoned brief and has to be filed within the period of a year from the time when knowledge of the facts was acquired. There is no need for a lawyer and the proceedings before the Ombudsman are free of charge for the interested person. Also to guarantee direct access to the Ombudsman, all previous censure and interference with any communication between this institution and the people who are in detention, internment or custody centres are forbidden (art 16 LODP).

(b) Petitions of Members of Parliament or of parliamentary committees

Article 10.2 of the LODP takes into account the possibility that the Members of Parliament, senators and parliamentary committees of investigation or those related to the defence of constitutional rights may forward petitions to the Ombudsman in the field of jurisdiction of the said institution. Usually this precept applies when the citizens address a petition regarding the protection of rights or administrative disfunctions to a Member of Parliament, to the Committee of Petitions of each House or to the Joint Committee in charge of the relationships with the Ombudsman. Insofar as neither Members of Parliament nor the said committees can develop tasks of investigation on the petitions, it is logical to forward them to the Ombudsman. Nevertheless, the fact that the petition comes from Parliament does not mandatorily force the Ombudsman to intervene, as this will go against the functional independence of this institution as established in Article 6 of the LODP. This is established in Article 31.2 of the LODP which allows for the possibility that the Ombudsman may decide not to investigate the facts stated in a parliamentary petition.

C. *Admissibility of the Complaints*

(a) Acknowledgment of receipt and admission of the transaction

When the Ombudsman receives a complaint, he/she has to inform the interested person (Article 17 LODP). In accordance with this very same precept, he/she has to decide immediately afterwards whether he/she proceeds with the complaint. If the Ombudsman decides not to admit the complaint because it is a matter foreign to his/her jurisdiction or is pending judicial resolution, he/she has to communicate this to the affected person by means of a reasoned brief.

When examining the data of the filed complaints which appear in the Annual Reports of the Spanish Ombudsman, we notice that they are high in number, more than that of other countries when balanced with the population figures. In 1983, for instance, there were more than thirty thousand complaints and in 1996 they exceeded twenty five thousand, even though in some years this was reduced to thirteen thousand, as in 1995. The increasing knowledge of the citizens of the scope of intervention of the Ombudsman partly accounts for the decrease in the number of complaints. Nevertheless, the lack of information in 1994 concerning the mission of the Ombudsman is obvious, for of the total of filed complaints only 52% were admitted.

(b) Investigation and resolution

Once a complaint is declared admissible, the Ombudsman carries out the appropriate investigation in order to clarify the facts and be able to adopt a decision. The interested person and the affected Administration must be informed of the final resolution. The scope of the investigation and of the resolutions shall be examined in the next section of the present report, on the powers of the Spanish Ombudsman.

(c) Time limit

The LODP does not establish a time limit for dealing with the complaints. Logically, it depends on the greater or lesser complexity of a particular matter and of the Administration's attitude. The Spanish Ombudsman has progressively reduced the time for deciding on the complaints, which is a positive fact for the credibility of the institution and for the efficient protection of rights.

D. *Permanent Functioning*

As stated in Article 11 of the LODP the Ombudsman is an institution that functions without interruption. Therefore its activities are altered neither by the dissolution of Parliament nor by the declaration of a state of emergency or of a state of siege.

8. *Powers*

A. *Investigation*

In relation to the complaints and matters transacted *ex officio*, the Spanish Ombudsman has several powers of investigation. In this sense, the LODP (Articles 18 to 22) confers on the Ombudsman the power to request all kinds of information and documentation from the Administration, to visit any administrative department and to have interviews with the civil servants and authorities that he/she thinks necessary. He/she even can ask for legally classified documents that may only be denied to him/her by the Cabinet. Article 19 of the LODP, on the other hand, compels all public powers to preferentially and urgently assist the Ombudsman in all his/her investigations.

B. *Powers to Ensure the Collaboration of the Administration during the Investigations*

(a) The public statement of lack of collaboration

All the procedure of the investigations carried out by the Ombudsman must be conducted in strict confidence and with special measures if secret documents are involved. Nevertheless, if the Ombudsman considers that the attitude of the Administration or of any of its civil servants prevents or hinders his/her investigation, the LODP (Articles 18.2 and 24.1) authorizes him/her to make a public statement classifying such an attitude as "hostile and hindering". This classification will appear in the Annual Report that the Ombudsman sends to Parliament and, if deemed suitable, in a special report on the subject.

(b) Transfer of Record to the Public Prosecutor for the institution of criminal proceedings for the offence of disobedience

Article 24.2 of the LODP and Article 502.2 of the Penal Code establish that a civil servant who hampers an investigation by the Ombudsman by denying or hindering the supply of information or documentation, commits an offence of disobedience. The penalty[1] for such an offence is a fine that ranges from three

[1] Monetary penalty imposed by monthly shares. The amount of each share is settled by the judge according to the financial status of the convicted person taking into account a minimum and a

to twelve months and incapacitation to hold a public post for a period that ranges between six months and two years. Starting from this penal classification, the Spanish Ombudsman has an important pressure mechanism at his/her disposal in cases in which the personnel in the service of the Administration is especially reluctant to collaborate. In such a case, the Ombudsman is authorized to transfer the record to the Public Prosecutor so that he/she may undertake criminal proceedings.

C. *Resolutions on the Investigations*

All investigations carried out by the Ombudsman have to end with a decision. The decision may be that the investigation be shelved or it may contain a pronouncement on the complaint or on the action started ex officio. In both cases the Ombudsman must inform the interested person and the affected Administration of the adopted resolution (Article 31 LODP). If he/she learns of presumably criminal behaviour or facts, he/she has to inform the Public Prosecutor so that the latter may institute the appropriate criminal proceedings (Article 25 LODP). Leaving aside this exceptional case, we shall next examine the character and contents of the ordinary resolutions of the Spanish Ombudsman.

(a) Lack of coercive power

The Spanish Ombudsman does not have the coercive and compelling power characteristic of judicial bodies. Therefore, the Ombudsman can neither cancel nor revoke administrative acts. The LODP (Article 28.1) is clear about the matter and shapes the Ombudsman in the form of an institution authorized only to express opinions and to suggest modifications.

(b) Power of direction: warnings, recommendations, reminders and suggestions

As we have just pointed out, the Spanish Ombudsman is an institution of a simply persuasive nature. Articles 28 and 30 of the LODP set out a series of instruments by means of which the Ombudsman may let the Administration know his/her opinion: warnings, recommendations, reminders and suggestions. The difference in meaning between these terms is a slight one and one does not find all of them in each of the resolutions of the Ombudsman. In any case, they allow the description of the diverse contents of the Ombudsman's resolutions.

A warning is a remark on behaviour, an organizational defect or the obsolete nature of a rule. It may contain some kind of admonition so as to stop particular behaviour, for instance.

The aim of the reminders of the legal duties of the authorities and civil servants of the Administration is to underline the cases in which the Administration transgresses a norm. They have a certain recriminatory burden.

Recommendations and suggestions hardly differ and, in the publications of the Spanish Ombudsman, are treated together. By means of recommendations and suggestions the Ombudsman may issue out the following directions: urge the modification of a particular act; propose a change of judgement in the

---

maximum for share fixed by the Penal Code.

adoption of certain administrative decisions; propose to the Administration and the Parliament the desirability of enacting new norms or of modifying the existing ones.

In practice, the areas of the Administration to which the recommendations and suggestions of the Ombudsman are usually addressed, are work and social security, public health, justice and social affairs. In general, the response of the Administration is a positive one. It is worth pointing out that several modifications of legislative norms and administrative regulations had their origin in the Ombudsman's recommendations.

D. *Dissemination of the Actions and Resolutions: Identification and Publicity of the Non-compliance of the Administration*

The authorities and civil servants of the Administration affected by the Ombudsman's resolutions have a month to answer the directions made and in a reasonable period of time they have to comply with the recommendations or else sufficiently justify their nonobservance (Article 30 LODP). Logically, the authority and prestige that the institution of the Ombudsman has earned with the rigorousness and the sense of responsibility of its actions, are the first guarantee for the fulfilment of the directions addressed to the Administration.

However, this is not enough to ensure that the Administration will follow the opinions expressed by the Ombudsman. For that reason, a persuasive institution like the Ombudsman needs to disseminate and publicize its activities. A basic instrument for this is the Annual Report that the Ombudsman has to submit to Parliament. In this Report the investigations of the Ombudsman and his/her resolutions must appear, together with the cases in which the Administration has not answered the directions of the Ombudsman or has not sufficiently justified the noncompliance with his/her suggestions (Article 30.2 and 33 LODP). To reinforce the dissemination of his/her recommendations, the Spanish Ombudsman publishes them separately, over and above the Annual Report.

E. *Legitimation in Judicial Procedures*

As we have already stated, the investigation and the formulation of suggestions are the two main powers of the Spanish Ombudsman. In addition to these, he/she has authority to take part in certain judicial procedures. These are powers that are not part of his/her ordinary or daily activity but, because of their relevance, deserve specific commentary. Through them the Ombudsman somehow moves away from the framework of a persuasive institution to enter into the dynamics of potential confrontation with other institutions.

(a) Habeas corpus

In cases of illegal arrest of a citizen, the Spanish Ombudsman can institute proceedings so that the judge decides on the matter. This provision is not in the Constitution; it was introduced by the Spanish organic law 6/1984. The literature has criticized the granting of this power to the Ombudsman because the aforementioned law has a long list of individuals with authority to lodge the habeas corpus. Therefore, this function does not have much sense. The practice seems to corroborate this since the Ombudsman has hardly made use of it.

b) Appeal of unconstitutionality

The Spanish Constitution (Articles 161 and 162) grants the Ombudsman the power to lodge before the Constitutional Court an appeal of unconstitutionality against laws and norms with the rank of law, both of the central State and of the Autonomous Communities. The Ombudsman may adopt this decision on behalf of a citizen or on its own initiative only within the three months following the official publication of the norm. In that way, the Ombudsman may interfere in the normative activity of the legislative power and executive power, even if the simple lodging of the appeal does not imply the suspension of the challenged norm. It has to be noted that the norms challengeable in this way are only parliamentary laws and norms with rank of Government decrees, not decrees of the executive power which are inferior to acts of parliament and Government decrees.

One might wonder wether the Ombudsman has any kind of material limit to the lodging of this appeal, i.e., if he/she may only do it in the face of possible violations within his functional sphere (rights, the Administration's action). In juridical terms the answer has to be "no" although in practice he/she tends to be more sensitive to the questions that directly affect his/her jurisdiction.

Doctrinal opinion on the desirability of recognizing this power of the Spanish Ombudsman is not unanimous. For some authors it is positive that the Ombudsman can lodge the appeal of unconstitutionally because this clearly proves its independence from Parliament. At the same time -and this is a suitable argument of indubitable weight- the legitimacy of the Ombudsman opens a more neutral channel to urge the control of the constitutionality of laws outside the more directly political attitudes of other legitimate individuals like the Members of Parliament and public institutions (central Cabinet, legislative power and Cabinet of the Autonomous Communities). Thanks to this legitimacy the Ombudsman may act as the spokesperson of citizens and communities who do not have such a legitimacy.

Nevertheless there have also been voices against this power of the Spanish Ombudsman. There is no doubt that to challenge a law has a great political significance, and therefore the use of this power implies the risk of politicization of the institution. To prevent such a risk the Ombudsman must act with caution and not make systematic use of this power. The practice followed by the Spanish Ombudsman follows this line and it is thus sustained in his/her Reports. Sometimes there has perhaps been excessive caution and the non-lodging of the appeal against laws regarding terrorism and public safety has been an object of criticism. There have been few appeals but they have concerned laws in matters as relevant as conscientious objection to military service, alien citizens, trade-union freedom, automated data processing and the right of asylum, among others. Most resolutions are estimative and that shows again the caution and the rigour of the Spanish Ombudsman in this field.

c) Appeal for protection

The Spanish Constitution (Articles 161 and 162) and the legislation allow the Ombudsman to lodge an appeal for protection before the Constitutional Court when faced with acts of the public powers that violate the fundamental rights of citizens. Since any citizen affected by a violation of a fundamental right is entitled to lodge an appeal for protection, it seems that the exercise of this power by the Ombudsman must be saved for unusual cases. Up to now the scant use of this faculty by the Ombudsman proves its unusual nature.

9. *Relationships with the Parliament*

A. *The Parliamentary Joint Committee*

Article 2.2 of the LODP establishes the creation of a Joint Committee of both Houses of the Spanish Parliament in charge of the relationships with the Ombudsman. In previous pages we have referred to the authority of this Committee in the process of appointing the Ombudsman and his/her Deputy Ombudsmen and in the possible stimulation of the powers of this institution. Leaving that aside, the most relevant activity of the said Committee is the initial learning of the Annual Report of the Ombudsman. Other cases of relationship between the Ombudsman and the Joint Committee that will contribute to a greater closeness between Parliament and Ombudsman remain to be explored and specified.

B. *The Annual Report*

Once a year the Spanish Ombudsman must send a Report to Parliament in accordance with the constitutional mandate of Article 54, developed by the LODP (Articles 32 and 33). The submission and debate of this Report is the basis of the ordinary relationship between the Ombudsman and Parliament. The Report may be understood as an account of the Ombudsman's actions before the body that elected him/her and it was thus viewed in all the countries in which the Ombudsman is appointed by Parliament. On the other hand, the Annual Report is nowadays the basic element through which the Ombudsman publicizes his/her activities: investigations, directions to the Administration, identification of the civil servants and authorities that hinder or do not respect his/her actions.

The LODP does not state when to submit the Report but practice has placed it in the first quarter of the following year. According to a Resolution of April 21, 1992 of the Presiding Boards of the Houses, the Report is to be learned of initially by the Joint Committee according to the following procedure: the statement of the Ombudsman followed by the intervention of the parliamentary groups to ask questions or request explanations. It has to be pointed out that the Joint Committee does not pronounce on the Report.

After the examination of the Joint Committee, the Report goes to the Plenary Assembly of each House. There it is processed in accordance with the provisions of the parliamentary Rules of Procedure and some Resolutions of the respective Presidents of 1992. In each plenary sitting, the Ombudsman makes a summary of the Report and leaves the sitting. Next, each parliamentary group states its position, but they cannot vote resolutions on the matter. Note, thus, that the Houses can declare themselves neither in favour nor against the Report of the Ombudsman. This is justified so as to ensure respect for the autonomy of the Ombudsman and to prevent politicization in the transaction of the Report. What is less justified is the fact that the transaction of the Report only allows Parliament to have a very general knowledge thereof. For this reason the literature has suggested the desirability of a more detailed and sectorialized Report by the Joint Committee.

The Parliamentary Committees on Human Rights

In Spain there is no Committee on Human Rights like the one provided for in Article 55.14 of the Constitution of Ethiopia, which is very open and allows for a parliamentary, extra-parliamentary or mixed composition Committee.

In the Spanish Parliament there are parliamentary committees that deal with human rights. On the one hand, there is the Joint Committee in charge of the relationships with the Ombudsman, whose functions have already been examined. On the other, each House has a Committee on petitions. These committees receive letters from citizens in which they address issues related to the respect of constitutional rights. In practice, these committees do not carry out investigations on these issues, they limit themselves to sending the issues to the Ombudsman and to informing the Administration.

In those Autonomous Communities which have an Ombudsman, the situation described in the previous paragraph is reproduced.

Different is the situation that has taken place in some Autonomous Communities before the creation of the Ombudsman or in those that decided not to endow themselves with this institution. In this way, in the Autonomous Community of Catalonia and in that of the Basque Country, parliamentary committees on human rights were established with the mission to investigate possible violations of the said rights in their respective territories and to put forward proposals. These committees tried to carry out a similar task to that of the Ombudsman, although without the juridical and material instruments of this institution. At present, the Committees on Petitions of the Parliaments of the Autonomous Communities which have no Ombudsman carry out actions similar to those that developed in the Committees on Human Rights in Catalonia and the Basque Country before the creation of the Ombudsman.

In the case of Catalonia, once the Ombudsman was created, the Committee on Human Rights disappeared. However, this is not the case in the Basque Country. At present, in the Basque Country, there is a Committee on Human Rights with three main features: one, its activity does not overlap with that of the Basque Ombudsman, since its duty is not the investigation and resolution of citizens' specific complaints; two, it is in charge of the relationships with the Ombudsman; and three, it devotes itself to the study and debate of political proposals which have repercussions for human rights. This latter aspect of its activity causes the Committee on Human Rights of the Basque Parliament to meet very often and its debates and resolutions to make news.

As an example, we may mention the influence of this Committee in causing Basque prisoners for crimes of terrorism to be taken to prisons in the Basque Country.

Bibliography

Pérez-Ugena, María. *El Defensor del Pueblo y las Cortes Generales.* Madrid. Publicaciones del Congreso de los Diputados. 1996.

Díez, Laura. *Los Ombudsmen de las Comunidades Autónomas.* Ph.D. Dissertation. Universitat de Barcelona. 1997.

Díez, Laura. *Los defensores del pueblo (Ombudsmen) de las CC.AA.* Madrid. Senado. 1999 Annual Reports of the Defensor del Pueblo.

LEGISLATION

Constitution of Spain

Article 54
An organic law shall regulate the institution of the Defender of the People as the High Commissioner of the Parliament, appointed for the protection of the rights contained in this Title, for which purpose he may supervise the activity of the administration, informing the Parliament of it.

Organic Act Regarding the Ombudsman

Organic Act 3/1981, April 6th Regarding the Ombudsman
Boletín Official del Estado [Official State Bulletin] nr.109, May 1981 [as amended]

Part One
Appointment, Functions and Term of Office

Chapter One
Nature and Appointment

Article 1
The Ombudsman[2] is the High Commissioner of Parliament[3] appointed by it to defend the rights established in Part I of the Constitution, for which purpose he may supervise the activities of the Administration and report thereon to Parliament. He shall exercise the functions entrusted to him by the Constitution and this Act.

Article 2
1. The Ombudsman shall be elected by Parliament for a term of five years, and shall address it through the Speakers of the Congress and the Senate, respectively.
2. A Joint Congress-Senate Committee shall be appointed by Parliament, to be responsible for liaison with the Ombudsman and for reporting thereon to their respective Plenums whenever necessary.[4]
3. This Committee shall meet whenever so jointly decided by the Speakers of the Congress and the Senate and, in all cases, in order to propose to the Plenums the candidate or

[2] The name of the Ombudsman in Spanish is "El Defensor del Pueblo" (The Defender of the People).
[3] The name of the Spanish Parliament is "Las Cortes Generales" (the General Assembly); it comprises a Lower House, the Congress, and an Upper House, the Senate.
[4] Organic Act 2/1992, March 5th, amending Organic Act 3/1981 Regarding the Ombudsman, for the purpose of establishing a Joint Congress-Senate Committee for liaison with the Ombudsman, the Preamble of which is a follows: "Organic Act 3/1981, April 8th, which establishes the legal framework for the Ombudsman, provides in Article Two, section 2, for the creation of two Committees responsible for liaison with the Ombudsman, in the Congress and Senate respectively.

Although it is true that on certain occasions both Committees may, and under some circumstances must, hold joint meetings, the fact that the usual form of procedure is independent often hinders the relationship between the Parliament as an institutional whole comprising two Houses, and the Ombudsman of which is the High Commissioner.

With a view to correcting this deficiency and seeking to establish a more efficient relationship with the irreplaceable institution of the Ombudsman, it would seem advisable, as long as it does not contravene the Constitution, to establish a single Committee in Parliament, responsible for liaison with the Ombudsman and comprising members of both the Congress and the Senate.

candidates for the Ombudsman. The Committee's decisions shall be adopted by simple majority.[5]

4. Once the candidate or candidates have been proposed, a Congressional Plenum shall be held once no less than ten days have elapsed in order to elect him. The candidate who obtains the favourable vote of three-fifths of the Members of Congress, and is subsequently ratified by the Senate within a maximum of twenty days and by this same majority, shall be appointed.
5. Should the aforementioned majorities not be obtained, a further meeting of the Committee shall be held within a maximum of one month in order to make further proposals. In such cases, once a three-fifths majority has been obtained in Congress, the appointment shall be made when an absolute majority is obtained in the Senate.
6. Following the appointment of the Ombudsman, the Joint Congress-Senate Committee shall meet again in order to give its prior consent to the appointment of the Deputy Ombudsmen proposed by him.

Article 3

Any Spanish citizen who has attained legal majority and enjoys full civil and political rights may be elected Ombudsman.

Article 4

1. The Speakers of the Congress and the Senate shall jointly authorize with their signatures the appointment of the Ombudsman, which shall be published in the "Official State Bulletin".
2. The Ombudsman shall take office in the presence of the Procedures Committees of both Houses meeting jointly, and shall take oath or promise to perform his duties faithfully.

Chapter II
Dismissal, Resignation and Replacement

Article 5

1. The Ombudsman shall be relieved of this duties in any of the following cases:
   (1) Resignation;
   (2) Expiry of this term of office;
   (3) Death or unexpected incapacity;
   (4) Flagrant negligence in fulfilling the obligations and duties of his office;
   (5) Non-appealable criminal conviction.
2. The post shall be declared vacant by the Speaker of Congress in the event of death, resignation or expiry of the term of office. In all other cases it shall be decided by a three-fifths majority of the Members of each House, following debate and the granting of an audience to the person concerned.
3. Upon the post becoming vacant, the procedure for appointing a new Ombudsman shall be commenced within one month.
4. In the event of the death, dismissal or temporary or permanent incapacity of the Ombudsman, and until Parliament makes a subsequent appointment, the Deputy Ombudsmen, in order of seniority, shall fulfil his duties.

Chapter III
Prerogatives, Immunities and Incompatibilities

Article 6

1. The Ombudsman shall not be subject to any binding terms of reference whatsoever. He shall not receive instructions from any authority. He shall perform his duties independently and according to his own criteria.

---

[5] Drafted according to Organic Act 2/1992, March 5th.

2. The Ombudsman shall enjoy immunity. He may not be arrested, subjected to disciplinary proceeding, fined, prosecuted or judged on account of opinions he may express or acts he may commit in performing the duties of his office.
3. In all other cases, and while he continues to perform his duties, the Ombudsman may not be arrested or held in custody except in the event of in flagrante delicto; in decisions regarding his accusation, imprisonment, prosecution and trial the Criminal Division of the High Court has exclusive jurisdiction.
4. The aforementioned rules shall be applicable to the Deputy Ombudsmen in the performance of their duties.

Article 7

1. The post of Ombudsman is incompatible with any elected office; with any political position or activities involving political propaganda; with remaining in active service in any Public Administration; with belonging to a political party or performing management duties in a political party or in a trade union, association or foundation, or employment in the service thereof; with practising the professions of judge or prosecutor; and with any liberal profession, or business or working activity.
2. Within ten days of his appointment and before taking office, the Ombudsman must terminate any situation of incompatibility that may affect him, it being understood that in failing to do so he thereby rejects his appointment.
3. If the incompatibility should arise after taking office, it is understood that he shall resign therefrom on the date that the incompatibility occurs.

Chapter IV
The Deputy Ombudsmen

Article 8

1. The Ombudsman shall be assisted by a First Deputy Ombudsman and a Second Deputy Ombudsman to whom he may delegate his duties and who shall replace him, in hierarchical order, in their fulfilment, in the event of his temporary incapacity or his dismissal.
2. The Ombudsman shall appoint and dismiss his Deputy Ombudsmen, following approval by both Houses, in accordance with their Regulations.
3. The appointments of the Deputies shall be published in the "Official State Bulletin".
4. The provisions contained in Articles 3, 6 and 7 of this Act regarding the Ombudsman shall be applicable to his Deputies.

Part II
Procedure

Chapter I
Initiation and Scope of Investigations

Article 9

1. The Ombudsman may instigate and pursue, ex officio or in response to a request from the party concerned, any investigation conducive to clarifying the actions or decisions of the Public Administration and its agents regarding citizens, as established in the provisions of Article 103 (1) of the Constitution and the respectful observance it requires of the rights proclaimed in Part I thereof.
2. The Ombudsman has authority to investigate the activities of Ministers, administrative authorities, civil servants and any person acting in the service of the Public Administration.

Article 10

1. Any individual or legal entity who invokes a legitimate interest may address the Ombudsman, without any restrictions whatsoever. There shall be no legal impediments

on the grounds of nationality, residence, gender, legal minority, legal incapacity, confinement in a penitential institution or, in general, any special relationship of subordination to or dependence on a Public Administration or authority.

2. Individual Deputies and Senators, investigatory Committees or those connected with the general or partial defence of public rights and liberties and, especially, those established in Parliament to liaise with the Ombudsman, may, in writing and stating their grounds, request the intervention of the Ombudsman to investigate or clarify the actions, decisions or specific conduct of the Public Administration which may affect an individual citizen or group of citizens and which fall within his competence.[6]
3. No administrative authority may submit complaints to the Ombudsman regarding affairs within its own competence.

Article 11

1. The activities of the Ombudsman shall not be interrupted in the event that Parliament is not in session, has been dissolved, or its mandate has expired.
2. In the circumstances described in the previous paragraph, the Ombudsman shall address the Standing Committees of the Houses of Parliament.
3. The declaration of a state of emergency or siege shall not interrupt the activities of the Ombudsman, nor the right of citizens to have access to him, without prejudice to the provisions o£ Article 55 of the Constitution.

Chapter II
Scope of Competence

Article 12

1. The Ombudsman may in all cases, whether ex officio or at the request of a party concerned, supervise the activities of the Autonomous Communities, within the scope of competence defined by this Act.
2. For the purposes of the previous paragraph, Autonomous Community bodies similar to the Ombudsman shall coordinate their functions with the latter, who may request their co-operation.

Article 13

Whenever the Ombudsman – receives complaints regarding the functioning of the Administration of Justice, he must refer them to the Public Prosecutor to allow the latter to investigate their foundation and take appropriate legal action, or else refer them to the General Council of the Judiciary, according. to the type of complaint involved, independently of any reference that he may make to the matter in his annual report to Parliament.

Article 14

The Ombudsman shall protect the rights proclaimed in Part I of the Constitution in the field of Military Administration, without however causing any interference in the command of National Defence.

Chapter III
Complaints procedure

Article 15

1. All complaints submitted must be signed by the party concerned, giving his name and address in a document stating the ground for the complaint, on ordinary paper and within a maximum of one year from the time of becoming acquainted with the matters giving rise to it.
2. All action by the Ombudsman shall be free of charge for the party concerned, and

---

[6]Organic Act 2/1992, March 5th.

attendance by a lawyer or solicitor shall not be compulsory. Receipt of all complaints shall be acknowledged.

Article 16

1. Correspondence addressed to the Ombudsman from any institution of detention, confinement or custody may not be subjected to any form of censorship whatsoever
2. Nor may the conversations which take place between the Ombudsman or his delegates and any other person enumerated in the previous paragraph be listened to or interfered with.

Article 17

1. The Ombudsman shall record and acknowledge receipt of the complaints made, which he shall either proceed with or reject. In the latter case, he shall do so in writing, stating his reasons. He may inform the party concerned about the most appropriate channels for taking action if, in his opinion, these exist, independently of the fact that the party concerned may adopt those it considers to be most pertinent.
2. The Ombudsman shall not investigate individually any complaints that are pending judicial decision, and he shall suspend any investigation already commenced if a claim or appeal is lodged by the person concerned before the ordinary courts or the Constitutional Court. However, this shall not prevent the investigation of general problems raised in the complaints submitted. In all cases, he shall ensure that the Administration, in due time and manner, resolves the requests and appeals that have been submitted to it.
3. The Ombudsman shall reject anonymous complaints and may reject those in which he perceives bad faith, lack of grounds or an unfounded claim, and in addition those whose investigation might infringe the legitimate rights of a third party. His decisions may not be appealed against.

Article 18

1. Once a complaint has been accepted, the Ombudsman shall begin appropriate summary informal investigations to clarify the allegations contained therein. In all cases he shall report the substance of the complaint to the pertinent administrative agency or office for the purpose of ensuring that a written report be submitted within fifteen days by its director. This period may be extended if, in the opinion of the Ombudsman, circumstances so warrant.
2. Refusal or failure on the part of the civil servant or his superiors responsible for sending the initial report requested may be considered by the Ombudsman as a hostile act which obstructs his functions. He shall immediately make such an act public and draw attention to it in his annual or special report, as the case may be, to Parliament.

Chapter IV
Obligatory Co-operation of Bodies Requested to do so

Article 19

1. All public authorities are obliged to give preferential and urgent assistance to the Ombudsman in his investigations and inspections.
2. During the stage of verifying and investigating a complaint or in the case or proceedings initiated ex officio, the Ombudsman, his Deputy, or the person delegated by him may present himself at in any establishment of the Public Administration or attached thereto or responsible for a public service, in order to verify any necessary information, hold relevant personal interviews or examine pertinent records and documents.
3. In the pursuit of this objective he may not be denied access to any administrative record or document related to the activity or service under investigation, without prejudice to the provisions of Article 22 of this Act.

Article 20

1. Should the complaint to be investigated concern the conduct of persons in the service

of the Administration in connection with the duties they perform, the Ombudsman shall so inform them and the immediate superior or body to which the former are attached.

2. The persons concerned shall reply in writing, supplying whatever documents and supporting evidence they may consider appropriate, within the period established, which in no case may be less than ten days and which may be extended at their request by half the period originally granted.
3. The Ombudsman may verify the veracity of such documents and propose to the civil servant concerned that he be interviewed, in order to furnish further details. Civil servants who refuse to comply may be required by the Ombudsman to submit to him in writing the reasons justifying their decision.
4. The information a civil servant may furnish through personal testimony in the course of an investigation shall be treated as confidential, subject to the provisions of the Criminal Procedure Act regarding the reporting of acts which may constitute criminal offences.

Article 21
Should a hierarchical superior or entity forbid a civil servant under his orders or in its service from replying to a demand from the Ombudsman or from holding an interview with him, he or it must state such prohibition in writing, justifying such action, both to the civil servant and to the Ombudsman himself. The Ombudsman shall thereafter direct whatever investigatory procedures may be necessary to the aforesaid hierarchical superior.

Chapter V
Confidential Documents

Article 22
1. The Ombudsman may request the public authorities to furnish all the documents he considers necessary to the performance of this duties, including those classified as confidential. In the latter case, the failure to furnish said documents must be approved by the Council of Ministers and accompanied by a document attesting to their approval of such refusal.
2. The investigations and relevant procedures conducted by the Ombudsman and his staff shall be performed in absolute secrecy, with respect to both private individuals and offices and other public bodies, without prejudice to the considerations that the Ombudsman may consider appropriate for inclusion in his reports to Parliament. Special measures of protection shall be taken concerning documents classified as confidential.
3. Should he be of the opinion that a document declared to be confidential and not made available by the Administration could decisively affect the progress of his investigation, he shall notify the Joint Congress-Senate Committee referred to in Article 2 of this Act.[7]

Chapter VI
Responsibilities of Authorities and Civil Servants

Article 23
Should the investigations conducted reveal that the complaint was presumably the result of abuse, arbitrariness, discrimination, error, negligence or omission on the part of a civil servant, the Ombudsman may request the person concerned to state his views on the matter. On the same date he shall send a copy of this letter to the civil servant's hierarchical superior, accompanied by any suggestions that he may consider appropriate.

Article 24
1. Persistence in a hostile attitude or the hindering of the work of the Ombudsman by

---

[7] Organic Act 2/1992, March 5th.

any body, civil servants, officials or persons in the service of the Public Administration may be the subject of a special report, in addition to being stressed in the appropriate section of his annual report.
2. A civil servant who obstructs an investigation by the Ombudsman by refusing to send the reports he requests or facilitating his access to the administrative records or documents necessary for the investigation, or is negligent in so doing, shall be guilty of an offence of contempt. The Ombudsman shall provide the Public Prosecutor with the records necessary for taking appropriate action.

Article 25
1. If, in the performance he duties of his office, the Ombudsman should obtain knowledge of presumably criminal acts or behaviour, he must immediately notify the Attorney-General.
2. The above notwithstanding, the Attorney-General shall inform the Ombudsman periodically, or whenever so requested by the latter, of the proceedings instituted at his request.
3. The Attorney-General shall notify the Ombudsman of all possible administrative irregularities with which the Public Prosecutor becomes aware in the performance of his duties.

Article 26
The Ombudsman may, ex officio, bring actions for liability against all authorities, civil servants and governmental or administrative agents, including local agents, without needing under any circumstances previously to submit a written claim.

Chapter VII
Reimbursement of Expenses to Individuals

Article 27
Expenses incurred or material losses sustained by individuals who have not themselves lodged a complaint but are called upon by the Ombudsman to provide information shall be reimbursed; such expenses will be met from the latter's budget once duly justified.

Part III
Decisions

Chapter I
Content of Decisions

Article 28
1. Although not empowered to modify or overrule the acts and decisions of the Public Administration, the Ombudsman may nevertheless suggest modifications in the criteria employed in their production.
2. If as a result of this investigations he should reach the conclusion that rigorous compliance with a regulation may lead to situations that are unfair or harmful to those persons thereby affected, he may suggest to the competent legislative body or the Administration that it be modified.
3. If action has been taken in connection with services rendered by private individuals with due administrative authorization, the Ombudsman may urge the competent administrative authorities to exercise their powers of inspection and sanction.

Article 29
The Ombudsman is entitled to lodge appeals alleging unconstitutionality and individual appeals for relief, as provided by the Constitution and the Organic Act Regarding the Constitutional Court.[8]

---

[8] See the Organic Act Regarding the Constitutional Court, § 2.1, Articles 31.1b, 46.1 and 46.2.

Article 30

1. The Ombudsman may, in the course of this investigations, give advice and make recommendations to authorities and officials in the Public Administration, remind them of their legal duties and make suggestions regarding the adoption of new measures. In all cases such authorities and officials shall be obliged to reply in writing within a maximum period of one month.
2. If within a reasonable period of time after such recommendations appropriate steps are not taken to implement them by the administrative authority concerned, or if the latter fails to inform the Ombudsman of its reasons for non-compliance, the Ombudsman may inform the Minister of the Department concerned, or the highest authority of the Administration concerned, of the particulars of the case and the recommendations made. If adequate justification is not forthcoming, he shall mention the matter in his annual or special report, together with the names of the authorities or civil servants responsible for this situation, as a case in which although the Ombudsman thought that positive solution was possible, it was not however achieved.

Chapter II
Notifications and Communications

Article 31

1. The Ombudsman shall inform the party concerned of the results of his investigations and operations, and similarly of the reply from the Administration or civil servants involved, except in the event that on account of their subject matter they should be considered confidential or declared secret.
2. Should his intervention have been initiated under the provisions of Article 102, the Ombudsman shall inform the Member of Parliament or competent committee that requested investigation of the matter and, upon its completion, of the results obtained. Equally, should he decide not to intervene he shall communicate his decision, giving his reasons.
3. The Ombudsman shall communicate the results of his investigations, whether positive or negative, to the authority, civil servant or administrative office in respect of which they were initiated.

Chapter III
Reports to Parliament

Article 32

1. The Ombudsman shall inform Parliament annually of the action that he has taken in an annual report submitted to it when meeting in ordinary session.
2. When the seriousness or urgency of the situation makes it advisable to do so, he may submit a special report that he shall present to the Standing Committees of the Houses of Parliament, if these latter are not in session.
3. The annual reports and, when applicable, the special reports, shall be published.

Article 33

1. The Ombudsman shall give an account in his annual report of the number and type of complaints filed, of those rejected and the reasons for their rejection, and of those investigated, together with the results of the investigations, specifying the suggestions or recommendations accepted by the Public Administration.
2. No personal data that enables public identification of the parties involved in investigation proceedings shall appear in the report, without prejudice to the provisions of Article 24(1).
3. The report shall include and appendix, directed to Parliament, detailing the settlement of the budget of the institution during the corresponding period.
4. An oral summary of the report shall be presented by the Ombudsman to the Plenums

of both Houses. It shall be open to debate by the parliamentary groups in order that they may state their positions.

PART IV
Human and Financial Resources

Chapter I
Staff

Article 34
The Ombudsman may freely appoint the advisers necessary for the execution of his duties, in accordance with the Regulations and within budgetary limits.[9]

Article 35
1. Persons in the service of the Ombudsman shall, while so remaining, be deemed as being in the service of Parliament.
2. In the case of civil servants from the Public Administration, the position held by them prior to joining the office of the Ombudsman shall be reserved for them, and the time served with the latter shall be taken into consideration for all purposes.

Article 36
Deputy Ombudsmen and advisers shall automatically be relieved of their duties when a new Ombudsman, appointed by Parliament, takes office.

Chapter II
Financial Resources

Article 37
The financial resources necessary for the operation of the institution shall constitute an item of the Parliamentary Budget.

Transitional Provision

Five years after the coming into force of this Act, the Ombudsman may submit to Parliament a detailed report containing the amendments that he considers should be made thereto.

---

[9]See the Regulations on the Organization and Functioning of the Ombudsman, adopted by the Congress and Senate Standing Committees at their joint meeting on April 6, 1983, and amended at the joint meeting o£ the Congress and Senate Standing Committees on April 21, 1992.

The Swedish Parliamentary Ombudsman System

Claes Eklundh*

Introduction

If one wants to understand the role and the impact of the Swedish Parliamentary Ombudsmen it is of great use to have some knowledge of the Swedish administrative system and of the historical background of the Ombudsman institution. There are especially two factors that should be emphasized. The first is the historical importance of the principle of the rule of law in the Swedish administration and the second is the comparative independence of the Swedish administrative authorities combined with the principle of accountability under criminal law of every official for his actions when exercising public power.

Historical Background

The office of the Parliamentary Ombudsman was created in 1809 as a part of the new constitution that was adopted that year. It had, however, a prototype in the office of the King's Ombudsman, which was created in 1713 by King Charles XII, who ruled as an absolute monarch. The King at that time was staying in Turkey after having been abroad for 13 years and as a result of the his absence from Sweden disorder had arisen in the Swedish administration. In order to stop this, the King ordained that a new office should be created in Sweden to be headed by a person with the title of The Highest Ombudsman, i.e. the King's foremost representative. His duty was to ensure that the officials obeyed the law and otherwise fulfilled their obligations. The weapon of the Ombudsman was the right to prosecute those officials that were found at fault. This office, later known as the office of the Chancellor of Justice (Justitiekansler), still exists.

After the death of King Charles in 1718 Sweden had some decades of Parliamentary rule, and between 1766 and 1772 the Swedish Parliament, the Riksdag, exercised the right to appoint the Chancellor of Justice. The year 1766 is important in Swedish constitutional history also for another reason. In that year Sweden was given its first Freedom of the Press Act which *inter alia* contained provisions laying down the principle of public access to official documents which still is an important part of the Swedish constitution.

The royal prerogative of appointing the Chancellor of Justice was restored in

*Chief Parliamentary Ombudsman.

K. Hossain et al. (eds), Human Rights Commissions and Ombudsman Offices, 423–436.

1772. After a new period of royal absolutism, King Gustavus Adolphus was dethroned in 1809 and the Riksdag adopted a new constitution based on the principle of balance of power between King and Riksdag. The constitution provided for the appointment by the King of the Chancellor of Justice and for the election by the Riksdag of a *Justitieombudsman.* This Ombudsman should be "a man of known legal ability and outstanding integrity". His duty was to supervise, in his capacity as a representative of the Riksdag, the observance of laws and decrees by all judges and other officials. Like the Chancellor of Justice, he was a prosecutor.

One reason for the creation of the new office was that the Riksdag wanted to have a supervisory institution of its own that was entirely independent of the King. Another important difference between the King's Ombudsman and the Parliamentary Ombudsman was that the former acted in the King's interest, whereas the supervisory activities of the latter should have as their aim the protection of the rights of the individual citizen.

In 1915 the Riksdag created a separate office for the supervision of the armed forces – the *Militieombudsman* – and thus, from 1915, Sweden had two Parliamentary Ombudsmen. In 1968 the two offices were amalgamated into one institution consisting of three Ombudsmen. In 1976 the office was reorganized and the number of Ombudsmen increased to the present number of four.

The Parliamentary Ombudsmen and the Constitution

The most important provisions concerning the Parliamentary Ombudsmen are laid down in the Constitution of 1974. The activities of the Ombudsmen are a part of the parliamentary control of government. This control is divided between the Riksdag and the Ombudsmen in such a way that the Riksdag supervises the Cabinet and the Cabinet ministers, whereas the Ombudsmen, on behalf of the Riksdag, supervise the way in which the laws are applied by the courts of law and by the administrative authorities of the state and the local government.

The reason for this division is to be found in the special constitutional relation between the Cabinet on one side and the administration on the other. A Swedish Cabinet Minister is not head of a ministry in the usual sense; he has at his disposal only a rather small staff – usually between 100 and 200 persons – who prepare bills, governmental decrees and other cabinet decisions. The administrative work is instead carried out by semi-independent agencies headed by civil servants. This means *inter alia* that a Cabinet Minister is not allowed to give orders to the authorities within his area of responsibility; this can be done only by the Cabinet as such and is usually done in general terms, e.g. by issuing decrees or guidelines for the use of the funds appropriated for the activities of the authorities.

Consequently a Minister is not personally responsible – legally or politically – for the single actions of an administrative authority or an official. That a Minister can never be held responsible for a decision of a Court of Law goes without saying.

The division of supervisory powers between the Riksdag and the Ombudsmen means *inter alia* that the activities of the Ombudsmen can be regulated by the Riksdag only in general terms, i.e. by an act of law. Thus the Riksdag cannot give an Ombudsman instructions as to which individual cases he should investigate or dismiss, nor can the Ombudsmen accept such instructions.

The Duties of the Ombudsmen

The main object of the Ombudsmen's activities is the safeguarding of the principle of the rule of law and the protection of the rights and freedoms of the individual as laid down in the Constitution and Swedish law.

It is said in the Ombudsman Act that it is the particular duty of the Ombudsmen to ensure that the courts of law and the administrative authorities observe the provision of the constitution concerning objectivity and impartiality and that the fundamental rights and freedoms of the citizens are not encroached upon in the process of public administration.

The last mentioned provision alludes to the detailed Bill of Rights in the Swedish constitution which lays down *inter alia* the freedom of speech, the freedom of assembly, the right to demonstration, the freedom of association and the freedom of religion, which are prerequisites of a democratic society. The Bill of Rights also protects different aspects of the integrity of the individual, e.g. his right to communicate privately with others, his right to privacy in his home and his freedom of movement. These rights and freedoms can be limited only by means of statutory law decided by the Riksdag. The public authorities thus cannot interfere with the rights and freedoms of an individual except when this is expressly allowed by an act of law. In addition, the European Convention on Human Rights has recently been incorporated into Swedish domestic law.

The Jurisdiction of the Ombudsmen

The Ombudsmen's supervision covers virtually all governmental agencies and the local government as well as the individual members of their staff. They thus supervise *inter alia* the police – even the security police – the military and the prison administration.

The Ombudsmen also supervise all other persons who exercise public power. When e.g. an employee of the state owned company responsible for the safety controls of cars prohibits the use of a faulty car, he is subject to the Ombudsmen's supervision.

Also the courts are supervised by the Ombudsmen. It is essential, however, that the Ombudsmen do not interfere in the judicial decisions of the courts, since this would be in direct conflict with the fundamental principle that the courts shall carry out their duties in an independent way subject only to the contents of the law. For this reason, the Ombudsmen as a rule do not make pronouncements concerning the way in which the courts apply the law or assess the evidence in a case. The Ombudsmen's main concern in supervising the courts of law and the administrative courts is, instead, to ensure that the cases are tried according to the rules on court procedure, and that judgement is rendered within a reasonable time.

Judgements are not entirely exempt from supervision, however. Sometimes a judgement is manifestly wrong; a person might for instance have been sentenced to a more severe penalty than the law allows. In such cases the Ombudsmen will take action.

The Investigative Powers of the Ombudsmen

The Ombudsmen have vast powers of investigation which are laid down in the constitution. Thus they have access to all official documents. Even though the work of the Swedish administration is based on the principle of transparency, i.e. the right of every individual to have access to the documents of the authorities, some information must be kept secret in order to protect e.g. the safety of the Realm or the personal integrity of an individual. The Ombudsmen have access also to classified documents, however. This is obviously a prerequisite for an effective supervision of the security police. Furthermore, every official supervised by the Ombudsmen is obliged to give them all the information they might ask for and to assist them with investigations and to cooperate in other ways.

The Weapons of the Ombudsmen

The Ombudsmen·s office is usually described as an extraordinary institution. This means *inter alia* that they do not supplant the regular supervisory institutions within the public administration. They are entirely independent of the Government and do not in any way take part in the ordinary decision-making activities of the authorities. They do not function as an instance of appeal and they cannot change a decision made by a court or an administrative agency, nor can they order a court or an authority to act in a certain way.

The role of the Ombudsmen is, instead, based on the principle of personal accountability of every official for his decisions. When the Ombudsman·s Office started its activities nearly 190 years ago, its main character was that of a prosecutor's office. Whenever an official was found at fault, the Ombudsman instituted legal proceedings against him or – in minor cases – requested disciplinary measures.

The Ombudsmen have kept this prosecuting role, but today prosecutions are not very frequent due to the fact that very few of the errors discovered by the Ombudsmen are serious enough to deserve punishment under criminal law. The right to prosecute negligent officials is still an important basis for the authority of the Ombudsmen·s Office, however, and it gives a special weight to the critical pronouncements made by the Ombudsmen. They can prosecute any official under their supervision before an ordinary court of law for any crime committed in his job and they also have the right to initiate disciplinary proceedings.

Even though the Ombudsmen have this right – and duty – to prosecute officials who are guilty of e.g. misuse or negligent use of public power, the Ombudsmen·s office cannot be described as a crime-fighting organization. The main task of the Ombudsmen is instead to try to prevent mistakes from occurring. Their most important weapon for this purpose is the power to admonish officials found at fault. If an Ombudsman finds a measure to be inadequate, improper or unwise but not punishable under criminal law, he will point out how, in his opinion, the matter should have been handled. The Ombudsmen also have the right to make pronouncements laying down guidelines for proper judicial and administrative behaviour. This has proved to be a very effective way of improving the quality of the Swedish administration. One reason for this is that it is considered to be very embarrassing for an official to be publicly criticized by the Ombudsman.

The Ombudsmen may also address the Cabinet or the Riksdag asking for amendments of the law.

The Organization

There are at present four Parliamentary Ombudsmen, all of whom are elected by the Riksdag at a plenary sitting for a period of four years. The elections are prepared by the Riksdag's Committee on the Constitution. The Ombudsman Office is strictly apolitical, and it has been a tradition that an Ombudsman should be acceptable to all the political parties represented in the Riksdag. Re-elections are possible and indeed frequent.

The Ombudsmen usually come from the judiciary and are recruited from among persons who are or would be suitable as Justices of the Supreme Court or the Supreme Administrative Court.

One of the Ombudsmen is head of the Ombudsmen·s office. He cannot, however, interfere in the supervisory activities of the other Ombudsmen. Each Ombudsman is responsible for his actions only to the Riksdag. It is obvious that an Ombudsman cannot fulfil his role if he does not enjoy the confidence of the Riksdag. The activities of the Ombudsmen are scrutinized by the Riksdag's Committee on the Constitution on the basis of their annual report. If an Ombudsman does not have the confidence of the Riksdag, he can be dismissed immediately by a majority vote.

The Ombudsmen are assisted by a staff of about 50 (at present about 30 lawyers as well as registrars, secretaries and administrative staff). Only an Ombudsman, however, is authorized to sign a final decision even if it is only a question of dismissing a complaint without further investigation. The legally trained staff are usually recruited from the judicial authorities and most of the are junior judges in the judicial career.

The Ombudsmen·s office receives its funds directly from the Riksdag without any intervention of the Ministry of Finance.

The Handling of Complaint Cases

When the Ombudsman·s Office started its activities, all the cases were taken up on the Ombudsman·s own initiative. After some time, however, people began to send in complaints to the Ombudsman, and the handling of complaint cases now constitutes the main part of the Ombudsmen's activities. The annual number of complaints recently is approximately 5,000.

The Riksdag considers the handling of complaint cases to be the central part of the work of the Ombudsmen. There are several reasons for this. The most important aspect is that in a democratic society based on the principle of the rule of law every individual should have the right to have the dealings of the authorities scrutinized from a legal point of view by a competent agency that is quite independent of the Government. It is also considered to be of great importance that every official is aware that his actions can be scrutinized by the Ombudsman and that action may be taken against him if he has acted in an incorrect way.

Everyone – even citizens of other countries or people not living in Sweden – can complain to the Ombudsmen. There is no rule saying that the complainant must be personally concerned in the matter. No absolute time limit is set, but it is prescribed that the Ombudsmen should not, except on special grounds, start an investigation if the matter complained of took place more than two years prior to the receipt of the complaint.

Complaints should be presented in writing. When necessary, however, a member of the staff will help the complainant to word his letter. No fee is charged. Anonymous complaints are not admissible but they sometimes give an Ombudsman cause to start an investigation on his own initiative.

In most cases a decision by an administrative authority can be appealed against to an administrative court that has the right to review the matter in its entirety. So if a person wants to have a decision changed he should lodge an appeal. But he might also want to have the responsible official punished or admonished because of the way in which he has handled the matter. If this is the case he can complain to the Ombudsman.

There is no rule saying that existing judicial or administrative remedies should be exhausted before a complaint is lodged. Normally, however, an Ombudsmen does not intervene while the matter is pending in a court or an appeal is still possible. An intervention will usually be made at this stage only when it is alleged that the case does not advance or that judgement is not delivered within a reasonable time after the hearing.

The largest categories of complaints relate to social welfare, prison administration, the police and the courts of law. Together these areas account for almost half the total number of complaints in a year. Another important field of activity is to see to it that the authorities obey the rules concerning the public access to official documents and the right of public officials to give information to the media.

Only 12–14% of all complaint cases give rise to some kind of criticism by the Ombudsmen. No less than 40% are even dismissed without any investigation. In many cases the complaints are based on a misunderstanding; the action complained of is in fact in accordance with the law. People also often complain about having been sentenced by a court for a crime that they say that they did not commit. As has already been said, this as a rule is not a matter for the ombudsmen; the correct course is, instead, to appeal against the judgment to the competent court of law.

It should be added that the Ombudsmen are authorized to refer to other agencies, e.g. the public prosecutors, such complaint cases as cannot be dismissed, but can be more efficiently handled by e.g. the police or a public prosecutor. The complaint cases that are not dismissed or referred to another agency are investigated by the Ombudsmen. Often the first step is to request the relevant documents from the authority concerned. In many cases it is possible to deduce from these documents alone that there is not sufficient cause for the complaint. This will then be dismissed at this stage. In the rest of the complaint cases the

Ombudsman will ask the authority or official concerned for an explanation in writing. If the complainant is personally concerned in the matter, he will be given an opportunity to comment on the explanation given by the authority. Sometimes further correspondence may take place, and the opinions of experts or competent bodies may be requested. Oral hearings are sometimes held in order to obtain more or better evidence.

If, in the course of his investigation, the Ombudsman finds that there is reason to believe that an official has committed a crime in his job, he has the same obligation to start a criminal investigation as a public prosecutor. In such cases the investigation is carried out according to the provisions of the Code of Judicial Procedure, and the Ombudsmen then often make use of their constitutional right to request the assistance of a public prosecutor. If an official is suspected of a crime his duty to give the Ombudsman full and truthful information comes to an end. Instead he has the same right as every person suspected of a crime to remain silent.

If an Ombudsman finds that there is sufficient ground for a prosecution he is obliged to prosecute in the same way as an ordinary public prosecutor. The Ombudsmen in such cases are usually represented by a public prosecutor or a member of the Ombudsmen's staff.

When the investigation has been completed the Ombudsman pronounces his decision, which – like most other documents in the Ombudsmen·s office, including complaints – is open to the public. It is of great importance for the efficiency of the Ombudsman institution that the principle of transparency is applied as widely as possible to its activities. The Swedish national news agency has a room of its own in the Ombudsmen's office where representatives of the agency read the Ombudsmen's incoming and outgoing mail.

The Ombudsmen's decisions are often very detailed and they are in many respects written in the same way as the judgements of the courts of law. They are often reported in the mass media, and such decisions as are of interest to the members of the Riksdag, to judges, civil servants etc. are afterwards published in the Ombudsmen's Annual Report. The decisions are also often distributed by the concerned central agency to its subordinate authorities.

Cases Initiated by the Ombudsmen

In order to make the best possible use of the resources of the Ombudsmen's office the Ombudsmen are not only allowed to choose which complaints should be dismissed and which should be investigated but they are also entitled to start investigations on their own initiative. The majority of these are based on observations made during inspections. Sometimes reports in the newspapers or in the radio or TV give the Ombudsmen cause to open investigations.

Furthermore, when investigating a complaint case, an Ombudsman sometimes discovers errors or unsatisfactory conditions which are not covered by the complaint. He will then act on his own initiative and open a new investigation.

The methods of investigation used in cases initiated by the Ombudsmen themselves are the same as those used in the complaint cases. As an Ombudsman does not open an investigation without good reason, it is understandable that a much higher percentage of these cases result in criticism by the Ombudsmen than the complaint cases. On average the percentage of criticism in the cases initiated by the Ombudsmen is 80%.

Inspections

Ever since the Ombudsman Institution was established, the Ombudsmen have made inspections from time to time of public authorities all over the country. The Ombudsmen together spend 50–70 days each year inspecting authorities of different kinds. Inspections are also carried out by members of the Ombudsmen·s staff on their behalf.

During an inspection, much time is spent in perusing files and other documents. The Ombudsman will meet with the head of the authority and other senior members of its staff. When a prison, mental hospital or a similar establishment is inspected, the inmates will be given the opportunity to meet the Ombudsman and express their grievances if they have any.

The inspections are of great value in several ways. They give the Ombudsmen and their staff the opportunity to meet the people who are serving in the authorities in their proper surroundings and to get to know their working conditions. It is also much easier to find errors of a systematic nature in the work of an authority at an inspection than from dealing with complaint cases.

Also, the knowledge that any authority can be inspected by an ombudsman at any time contributes to keeping the officials on their toes.

Annual Reports

Under the Ombudsman Act, the Ombudsmen shall submit a printed report to the Riksdag every year. This report usually consists of about 500 pages and gives a full account of all those cases handled by the Ombudsmen that are considered to be of a general interest. A summary in English is appended to the report. The report is studied by the Riksdag·s Committee on the Constitution. The Committee then reports to the Riksdag. The Committee's report might be discussed at a plenary session of the Riksdag. The Annual Report is also read by judges, civil servants, law professors etc.

The Impact of the Ombudsmen

It is of course difficult to assess the impact of the Ombudsman institution in Swedish society. But it may safely be stated that it is hardly possible to imagine the Swedish constitution without the Parliamentary Ombudsmen.

One important reason for the success of the office is that it functions as a stabilizing factor in Swedish society by offering the ordinary citizen a cheap and simple way of having the actions of an authority impartially scrutinized as to their legality and fairness. By exercising an effective supervision of the public authorities, the Ombudsman institution strengthens the confidence of the general public in the authorities.

The Ombudsman institution also is of great help to the authorities by offering advice and clarifying the contents of the law concerning e.g. administrative and judicial procedure.

The task of preserving the rule of law and protecting the rights and freedoms of the individual cannot of course be left exclusively to the Ombudsmen. They cannot replace such law preserving agencies as the courts of law or the public prosecutors. In Sweden the Ombudsman institution has, however, proved to be an indispensable complement to them. The specific qualities of the Ombudsman institution give it a practical and psychological effect that cannot be taken over by any other agency. Among other things it has an important preventive effect; a lot of errors probably never occur because of the existence of the Parliamentary Ombudsmen.

LEGISLATION

Act with Instructions for the Parliamentary Ombudsmen

issued 13 November 1986
consolidated 1 April 1999

In accordance with the decision of the Riksdag the following has been determined.

Tasks

1. In accordance with 8.10 of the Riksdag Act, there are four Ombudsmen, a Chief Parliamentary Ombudsman and three Parliamentary Ombudsmen.

The Chief Parliamentary Ombudsman and the Parliamentary Ombudsmen are to supervise, to the extent laid down in Article 2, that those who exercise public authority are to obey the laws and other statutes and fulfil their obligations in other respects. Act (1995:404).

2. Those supervised by the Ombudsmen are
   (1) state and municipal authorities,
   (2) officials and other employees of these authorities,
   (3) other individuals whose employment or assignment involves the exercise of public authority, insofar as this aspect of such activity is concerned,
   (4) officials and those employed by public enterprises, while carrying out, on behalf of such an enterprise, activities in which through the agency of the enterprise the Government exercises decisive influence,
   Where officers in the armed forces are concerned, however, this supervision extends only to commissioned officers with the rank of second-lieutenant or above, and to those of corresponding rank.
   The supervision of the Ombudsmen does not extend to
   (1) Members of the Riksdag,
   (2) The Riksdag Board of Administration, the Riksdag's Election Review Board, the Riksdag's Complaints Board or the Clerk of the Chamber.
   (3) Members of the Governing Board of the Riksbank, members of the Executive Board of the Riksbank, except to the extent of their involvement in exercise of the powers of the Riksbank to make decisions in accordance with the Act on the Regulation of Currency and Credit (1992:1602),
   (4) the Government or Ministers,
   (5) the Chancellor of Justice, and
   (6) members of policy-making municipal bodies.
   An Ombudsman is not subject to the supervision of any other Ombudsman.
   The term official is used in this act, unless otherwise indicated by the context, to refer to those who are subject to the supervision of the Ombudsmen.

3. The Ombudsmen are to ensure in particular that the courts and public authorities in the course of their activities obey the injunction of the Instrument of Government about objectivity and impartiality and that the fundamental rights and freedoms of citizens are not encroached upon in public administration.

   In supervision of municipal authorities the Ombudsmen are to take into consideration the forms taken by municipal self-determination.
4. The Ombudsmen are to contribute to remedying deficiencies in legislation. If, during the course of their supervisory activities, reason is given to raise the question of amending legislation or of some other measure by the state, the Ombudsmen may then make such representations to the Riksdag or the Government.

   The Parliamentary Ombudsmen are to consult the Chief Parliamentary Ombudsman before making the representations referred to in the above paragraph.
5. Supervision is exercised by the Ombudsmen in assessing complaints made by the public and by means of inspections and such other inquiries as the Ombudsmen may find necessary.

   The Ombudsmen are to consult the Chief Parliamentary Ombudsman on the inspections and other inquiries they intend to carry out.
6. The Ombudsmen conclude cases with a decision, which states an opinion as to whether a measure taken by an authority or an official is in breach of the law or some other statute, or is otherwise erroneous or inappropriate. The Ombudsmen may also make statements intended to promote uniform and appropriate application of the law.

   In the role of extra-ordinary prosecutor, an Ombudsman may initiate legal proceedings against an official who, in disregarding the obligations of his office or his commission, has committed a criminal offence other than an offence against the Freedom of the Press Act or right to freedom of expression. If an inquiry into a case gives an Ombudsman reason to believe that such a criminal offence has been committed, the stipulations in the law concerning preliminary inquiries, prosecution and waiver of prosecution are to apply, together with those regarding the powers otherwise afforded to prosecutors in criminal cases subject to public prosecution. Cases brought before a district court are to be pursued to the Supreme Court only if there are exceptional grounds for doing so.

   If proceedings can be taken by means of disciplinary measures against an official who, in disregarding the obligations of his office or his commission, has committed an error, the Ombudsmen may report the matter to those empowered to decide on such measures. In the case of an individual with professional certification or some other authorization entitling him to practise within the medical profession, as a dentist, or in retail trade in pharmaceutical products, or as a veterinary surgeon, who has displayed gross incompetence in his professional activities or shown himself in some other way to be obviously unsuitable to practise, the Ombudsmen may submit a report to those who have the authority to decide on the revocation of the qualification or the authorization. A similar request for limitation of the scope of the qualification may be made when somebody with such qualifications has abused his powers in some other way. If an individual with professional certification or some other authorization entitling him to practise within the medical profession, as a dentist, or in retail trade in pharmaceutical products, has displayed incompetence in his professional activities or shown himself in some other way unsuitable to practise his profession, the Ombudsman may request the imposition of a probationary period of those who have the authority to make such a decision.

   Should the Ombudsmen consider it necessary that the official be dismissed or temporarily deprived of his office because of criminal acts or gross or repeated misconduct, the Ombudsman may report the matter to those empowered to decide on such a measure.

   When an Ombudsman has made a report of the kind referred to in the two preceding paragraphs, he is to be given the opportunity to supplement his own inquiry into the case, and to submit an opinion on any inquiry into the case carried out by some other person, as well as the right to be present if oral questioning occurs. This is not to apply, however, if the case concerns temporary deprival of office. Act (1998:540)

7. If an authority has decided against an official in a case involving application of special regulations in the law or other statutes concerning officials and matters of discipline, or dismissal or temporary deprival of office because of criminal acts or misconduct, an Ombudsman may refer the case to a court of law for amendment of the decision. This is also to apply to the decision of an authority in a case concerning disciplinary measures against medical or hospital staff, veterinary surgeons, those serving in the armed forces or subject to discipline according to the Act on Discipline within Total Defence etc. (1994:1811) as well as the decision of an authority in cases concerning probationary periods or issues concerning certification of the kind referred to in the third paragraph of Article 6. More detailed regulations about such referral are issued in the form of law or some other statute.

   If an official, in accordance with the stipulations in force, has applied to a court for amendment of a decision of the kind referred to in the above paragraph, and if the decision was made as a result of a report from an Ombudsman, the Ombudsman is to act on behalf of the public against the official during the dispute. This is also to apply if the Ombudsman has sought amendment of the decision.

   The stipulations of laws or other statutes applying to employers are, where disputes referred to in this paragraph are concerned, to apply correspondingly to the Ombudsmen. The stipulations in 4.7 and 5.1 of the Act on Litigation in Labour Disputes (1974:371) are not, however, to apply in cases where the action is being brought by an Ombudsman. Act (1998:540).
8. The Ombudsmen should not intervene against a subordinate official with no independent powers, unless there are exceptional reasons for doing so.
9. The powers of the Ombudsmen to initiate legal proceedings against a member of the Supreme Court or the Supreme Administrative Court or to press for the dismissal or deprival of office of such an official, or for the requirement that the official submit to medical examination are laid down in the Instrument of Government.
10. The Ombudsmen are obliged to initiate and prosecute those legal proceedings which the Committee on the Constitution has decided to institute against a Minister, in accordance with 12.3 of the Instrument of Government, and also legal proceedings against officials within the Riksdag or its agencies decided by committees of the Riksdag, in accordance with the regulations, but not, however, legal proceedings against an Ombudsman.

    The Ombudsmen are also obliged to assist committees of the Riksdag in preliminary inquiries concerning those officials cited in the previous paragraph.
11. The Ombudsmen are to submit, by 15 November at the latest, each year a printed report on the discharge of their office covering the period from 1 July of the preceding year until the following 30 June. This report is to contain an account of the actions which have been taken by virtue of paragraph 1 of Article 4, paragraphs 2 – 4 of Article 6, and Article 7, together with other significant decisions published by the Ombudsmen. The report is also to contain a survey of their activities in other respects.

Organization

12. In accordance with 8.10 of the Riksdag Act, the Chief Parliamentary Ombudsman is the administrative head and decides on the overall direction activities are to take. In his administrative directives he is to issue regulations about the organization of these activities and the allocation of cases among the Ombudsmen.
13. The activities of the Ombudsmen are to be administered by an Ombudsmen's secretariat (Ombudsmannaexpedition), which is to employ an Administrative Director, Heads

of Division and other administrative staff as laid down by the Riksdag. To the extent needed, and insofar as funds are available, the Chief Parliamentary Ombudsman may appoint other staff, experts and referees. The Chief Parliamentary Ombudsman is to decide on the duties assigned to the staff.

The Administrative Director is to direct the work of the secretariat, as subordinate to the Chief Parliamentary Ombudsman, and is otherwise to afford the Ombudsmen such assistance as they may require.

14. In addition to these instructions and those laid down in his administrative directives, the Chief Parliamentary Ombudsman is to issue the rules and regulations needed for the work of the secretariat.

    The Chief Parliamentary Ombudsman is to consult the Committee on the Constitution on organizational issues of importance.

    Before consultation with the Committee on the Constitution, an Ombudsman is to consult the Chief Parliamentary Ombudsman.

15. Irrespective of the import of the administrative directives, the Chief Parliamentary Ombudsman may make a specific decision allocating a particular case or group of cases to himself or one of the other Ombudsmen.

    In addition, the Chief Parliamentary Ombudsman may in the administrative directives or through some other decision authorize:

    - officials within the Ombudsmen's secretariat to take measures in preparing a case,
    - officials to carry out inspections, without, however, the right while doing so to make comments or other pronouncements on behalf of the Ombudsman, and also
    - the administrative director to make administrative decisions, but not however concerning the appointment of heads of division.

    The Chief Parliamentary Ombudsman is to decide whether a Deputy Ombudsman is to serve as an Ombudsman. A Deputy Ombudsmen may be appointed to serve if an Ombudsman is prevented by a considerable period of illness or on some other special grounds from performing his duties, or if a need arises for the services of a Deputy Ombudsman for some other reason. Act (1995:404).

16. When the Chief Parliamentary Ombudsman is on holiday or is prevented from discharging his duties, of the other Ombudsman the one with the longest period of service is to act as his deputy. If two or more of the Ombudsmen have served for the same length of time, the oldest is to take precedence. Act (1995:404).

Complaints

17. Complaints should be made in writing. The written complaint should indicate which authority the complaint is made about, the action which the complainant is referring to, the date of the action, together with the name and address of the complainant. If the complainant possesses a document which is of significance in dealing with and assessing the case, this should be appended.

    A person who has been deprived of his liberty may write to the Ombudsmen, without being prevented by the restrictions on sending letters and other documents which may apply to him.

    At the complainant's request, confirmation is to be issued by the secretariat of receipt of the complaint.

General regulations about the treatment of cases

18. If an issue arising from a complaint is of such a nature that it can appropriately be investigated and appraised by an authority other than the Ombudsman, and if that authority has not previously reviewed the matter, the Ombudsman may refer the complaint to the authority for action. Complaints may, however, only be referred to the Chancellor of Justice after prior agreement.

    If a complaint concerns an official who is a member of the Swedish Bar Association, and if the issue raised by the complaint is such that it can, in accordance with the fourth paragraph of 8.7 of the Code of Judicial Procedure, be appraised by a body within the Bar Association, the Ombudsman may refer the complaint to the Association for action.

19. The Ombudsmen shall inform a complainant without delay as to whether his complaint has been rejected, filed, referred to some other agency, in accordance with Article 18, or has been made the subject of an inquiry.
20. The Ombudsmen should not initiate inquiries into circumstances which date back two or more years, unless there are exceptional grounds for doing so.
21. The Ombudsmen are to carry out the investigative measures required in appraising complaints and other cases.

    When the Ombudsmen, in accordance with the stipulations of the Instrument of Government, request information and statements in cases other than those in which it has been decided to institute a preliminary inquiry, they may do so on penalty of fine not exceeding 10,000 Swedish Crowns. The Ombudsmen may impose such a penalty, if incurred.

    If there are ground for suspecting that an official subject to the regulations about disciplinary measures in the Act on Official Employment (1994:260), is guilty of misconduct for which disciplinary measures should be invoked, and there is reason to fear that a written caution, as laid down in the article 17 of that Act, cannot be issued to him within two years of the misconduct, the Ombudsmen may issue a corresponding caution. This provision is also to apply to those who, by virtue of other statutes, are also subject to regulations on disciplinary measures and to cautions and corresponding notification.

    When an Ombudsman is present at the deliberations of a court or other public authority, he does not have the right to express an opinion. Act (1997:561).
22. An Ombudsman may authorize some other person to administer an inquiry which he has decided to initiate and to institute and prosecute legal proceedings he has decided on, unless these measures concern a member of the Supreme Court or the Supreme Administrative Court.

    A decision to appeal a judgement or a decision to a superior court may only be made by an Ombudsman.

    In cases referred to in Article 7, the Ombudsman may appoint an official on the Ombudsmen's staff to prosecute the legal proceedings on behalf of the Ombudsman.

    In cases referred to in the third and fourth paragraphs of Article 6, the Ombudsmen may authorize officials on the Ombudsmen's staff to undertake action required.
23. Cases are concluded after oral presentation, for which an official on the staff of the ombudsmen's secretariat or specially appointed for the task is responsible. Decisions to reject a case or file it, can, however, be made without such presentation. The Ombudsman may also conclude other cases without oral presentation if there are exceptional grounds for doing so.

    Documents that have been submitted to the Parliamentary Ombudsman in connection with a case may not be returned until the case has been concluded. If in such a case an authority is deprived of the original document, this may be returned subject to the submission of a certified copy of the document. Act (1994:1649)
24. A journal is to be kept for all cases and for the actions taken in connection with them.

    Documentary records for every decision are to be kept at the Ombudsmen's secretariat showing who made the decision, who was responsible for the oral presentation and the date and content of the decision. A register is to be kept of specially designated decisions.

    Written records are to be kept during inspections and when needed for other reasons.

Miscellaneous regulations

25. When the annual report is submitted to the Riksdag, journals, written records and registers covering the same period are to be presented at the same time to the Committee on the Constitution.
26. The Ombudsmen's secretariat is to be open to the public during the hours decided on by the Chief Parliamentary Ombudsman.
27. Documents are to be issued free of charge, unless otherwise justified for special reasons.

    If a charge is to be made, it should be fixed according to the regulations in force for public authorities in general.

    A decision to impose a charge cannot be appealed against.
28. The Chief Parliamentary Ombudsman appoints officials within the Ombudsmen's secretariat and other staff, insofar as he has not delegated these tasks, as laid down in Article 15, to the Administrative Director.
29. Regulations concerning appeal against decisions in matters of appointment to posts or otherwise affecting staff within the Ombudsmen's secretariat, are laid down in the Regulations for Appeal for the Riksdag and its Agencies.

The Investigator-General (Ombudsman) of Zambia

J.K. Kampekete*

Introduction

This paper will concentrate on the Ombudsman institution. This is so because the Human Rights Commission is now an independent Constitutional body. It is now fully functional.

In Zambia the idea of creating an office of Ombudsman was established in 1969. This office was to be known as the Commission for Investigations (Zambia's version of the Office of the Ombudsman). This was the result of the recommendation made to the Zambian Government by the Chona Commission of Inquiry which gathered information on the establishment of a One Party State in Zambia. This Commission enumerated the reasons for the desirability of establishing the institution. The head of this office was to be known as the Investigator-General whose responsibility would be, inter alia, to investigate any matter of individual injustice or administrative abuse of power and authority involving corruption, tribalism, nepotism, intimidation and other administrative wrongs.

Constitutional and Legal Basis

The concept of the Ombudsman system was to be based on certain legal instruments, namely Part IX of the Constitution of Zambia of the second Republic (Art. 117 of the Constitution of Zambia, 1973). This provided for the establishment of this office, known as the Commission for Investigations, and spelt out its jurisdiction and powers. Under this Constitution an Act of Parliament to be known as the Commission for Investigations Act Cap 183 was enacted in 1974. Both these legal instruments were amended in 1991, when the country introduced a multi-party democratic form of government and later in 1996. They are now known as "The Constitution of Zambia of 1996" and the "Commission for Investigations Act No. 20 of 1991".

In view of the aforesaid, the provisions which define the tasks and organizational structure of the Institution of Ombudsman are contained in the Act of Parliament especially sections 4 to 6 thereof (Commission for Investigations Act

*Advocate of the High Court and Senior Legal Officer in the Commission for Investigations.

K. Hossain et al. (eds), Human Rights Commissions and Ombudsman Offices, 437–448.

No. 20 of 1991). The Constitution merely creates the office of the Investigator-General in Article 90. This arrangement in Zambia is not perceived as a disadvantage with respect to the independence of this institution.

Details

Our experience has shown that the Act of Parliament is the best instrument to provide for the details of the functions, procedures, powers etc. of this office. This is supplemented by the Regulations thereto. This is spelt out in the Constitution at Article 90 (13) which provides:

> "The functions, powers and procedures of the Investigator-General shall be as provided by an Act of Parliament".

Power of Appointment in the Office of Ombudsman

Power to appoint the Ombudsman and the Commissioners in Zambia is vested in the President as follows. The Investigator-General is appointed by the President under Article 90(1) and (2) of the Constitution while the three Commissioners are appointed under Section 4 and 5 of the said Act. Here, the procedure for appointment of the Ombudsman by the President is followed. Both of the appointments are required by law to be ratified by the National Assembly (see Section 5 (3)(b) of the Amendment thereof).

The fact that the appointment is not made by Parliament is not considered a disadvantage in Zambia because:

(a) Our form of government is an Executive one and not a Parliamentary one. In view of this fact, it is only fair that the President makes the appointment.
(b) In fact, Parliament now participates in the appointment by way of ratifying such appointments (Section 5(3)(b) of the Act). In the Zambian situation the obligation to report to the President is not regarded as a disadvantage or as a weakness in the system as there is a report submitted to Parliament in Zambia. In fact, under the enabling Act, the institution submits reports to both the President and the National Assembly. To the President, a report is submitted of every investigation conducted, (Section 20 of the Act) and to Parliament, an annual report is submitted (Section 22(1) and (2) of the Act). This appraises the Parliamentarians of the activities of the Institution.

Independence and Impartiality

In Zambia, the Constitution appears not to provide specifically for the independence of the institution, as is the case with the Namibian Constitution which expressly provides as follows: "The Ombudsman shall be independent and subject only to this Constitution and the Law".

But in the Zambian Constitution the independence of this institution is assured in the following manner:

(a) The person appointed is a Judge of the High Court (Article 90(2)(b)). This appears to be deliberate because a Judge is renowned to be of an independent frame of mind and he/she is only influenced in his decisions by the legal and constitutional provisions.

(b) Removal from office of the Ombudsman who is a Judge is also provided for in the Constitution by Article 90.

Firstly, the age of vacation of the office by the Investigator-General is fixed at 65 years by Article 90 (3) and Article 90(5) provides that "A person appointed as Investigator-General may be removed from office ... but shall not be so removed except in accordance with the provisions of this Article". In Article 90(6) the National Assembly has to make a resolution supported by not less than two-thirds of all members of Parliament to support the decision to investigate the Investigator-General. The Speaker then sends a copy thereof to Chief Justice who appoints a tribunal to inquire into the matter and thereafter report to the President, who upon the tribunal's advice could remove the Investigator-General.

The foregoing procedure ensures the independence of Investigator-General's office. He cannot be removed by unconstitutional procedures.

Furthermore, our experience in Zambia is that, since the Ombudsman institution was established in 1974, the Executive has never interfered with the operations or existence of the Ombudsman. Secondly the President has since that time *never rejected* any recommendation made to him by the Ombudsman. This does not in any way mean he is a mere rubber stamp. He has the freedom and discretion to vary or reject any recommendation made to him.

Impartiality

The minimum requirements to guarantee impartiality are the following. The Ombudsman should observe persuasion and effectiveness to maintain impartiality by being neither the advocate of a complainant nor counsel to the administrator or management. In terms of finance the Ombudsman is responsible for working out his own budget. It should not be unnecessarily controlled. The office of the Ombudsman must be financed adequately.

Independent Staff: These should have adequate facilities such as adequate transport, accommodation and salaries. They should not be left to be influenced by either the aggrieved or the administrator being investigated, through, the receipt of favours, monetary or otherwise. This Commission is yet to achieve these goals. Efforts continue to be made, though under difficult conditions.

Appointments: Staff should be selected by the Ombudsman's office itself, who should determine their conditions of service, salaries and qualifications. Under the current restructuring exercise of the civil Service, this Commission has made proposals to enable it be vested with legal powers to do this.

Separation of His Field of Competence from the Courts and Human Rights Commission

The Ombudsman's competence in Zambia is appropriately formulated under the current provisions contained in the Commission for Investigations Act referred to (ante). Similarly the Courts and the Human Rights Commission are also covered by their respective Acts of Parliament and constitutional provisions.

Separation

- Matters before the courts of law cannot be handled by the Office of the Ombudsman and vice versa. The Courts can only review the Ombudsman's action if he acts outside his jurisdiction.
- The Ombudsman merely investigates cases of maladministration and then makes recommendations to the Executive arm of the Government (it does not make final decisions or judgements). This applies also to the Human Rights Commission but courts try cases and pass judgements.
- The Ombudsman has restricted jurisdiction whilst the courts have a wider one. This applies also to Human rights Commission etc.

Complaints Regarding Acts of Government

If complaints concern acts of government this also includes inaction of government organs and acts/actions of government officials (Permanent Secretaries, Ministers, Managing directors, General Managers in para-statal companies). Complainable government acts are all cases of maladministration perpetrated by police, para-statal companies, the Ministry of Defence etc.

Exceptions are the cases outside the jurisdiction of this office such as private companies, acts of an international nature (say affecting foreign governments); matters before the Courts of Law and those between private persons.

Complaint Handling

- Complaints can be lodged directly with the Ombudsman or under the directive of the President, as provided by law.
- The Ombudsman can decide independently to entertain a complaint. Formal requirements for lodging complaints are spelt out under the enabling Act.

These are as follows:

- A complaint or allegation may be made by an individual or any body of persons whether incorporate or not.
- Such complaints may be made orally or in writing and still be addressed to the Secretary. Oral complaints are reduced to writing by the Secretary.
- Every complaint or allegation must be signed or thumb printed by the person making it.
- No complaint or allegation shall be received by the Ombudsman unless it is made within a period of two years from the date on which the facts giving rise to such complaint became known to the person making the complaint or allegation. But the Ombudsman can use his/her discretion and receive the complaint not made within two years.
- Letters containing complaints or allegation can be transmitted to the Commission through the Post office or could be faxed.

Investigation, Report and Recommendation

The Ombudsman's office is not restricted as to the grounds on which Government action is to be judged except that such grounds must fall within its legal jurisdiction and such matters must be based on maladministration. They could be legal, administrative or grounds of effective or good governance. As to the grounds of legality, questions asked are – did the government official act according to law or regulations when he acted against the complainant? In fact elsewhere it is stated that in the work of most Ombudsmen legality is indeed a central criterion for judging administrative actions of government or its officials. For instance the Act of Instruction of the Parliamentary Ombudsman of Sweden is quoted as beginning as follows: "The Parliamentary Ombudsman shall .... supervise the observance of laws and other statutes by those exercising public activity". Thus it is not surprising that many Ombudsmen have a legal background and lawyers constitute an important part of the staff of Ombudsman offices.

This is by no means the only weapon the Ombudsman can apply. The most lengthy formulation is the consideration based on *maladministration* leading to injustice. Good governance entails observance of the principles of natural justice and the Rule of Law even when dealing with administrative matters.

A complaint is considered as well founded if:

(a) Such complaint falls within the Ombudsman's jurisdiction as provided by the enabling Act of Parliament.
(b) If it is made by individual aggrieved or any body of persons whether incorporate or not and is signed or thumb printed.

Other types of complaints are rejected for falling outside the jurisdiction of this office, for delayed lodging of the complaint (over 2 years); for such complaint being before a Court of Law or tribunal etc.

Reporting and Recommendation

This process is clearly provided for in the Act of Parliament. The Ombudsman submits a report to the President after concluding his investigation of a complaint. This report contains a summary of the evidence taken with the conclusions and recommendations of the Ombudsman. It states what action is taken by the person or entity investigated to ameliorate or correct the situation.

A recommendation could state the compensation to be paid to the injured person. If the recommendation is adopted by the President the Ombudsman attends to the enforcement of the same (section 21).

Every year a report on the activities is submitted to parliament.

LEGISLATION

Constitution of Zambia

Part V

[...]

90. [The Investigator-General]

(1) There shall be an Investigator-General of the Republic who shall be appointed by the President in consultation with the Judicial Service Commission and shall be the Chairman of the Commission for Investigations.

(2) A person shall not be qualified for appointment as Investigator-General:

(a) unless he is qualified to be appointed a judge of the High Court; or
(b) if he holds the office of President, Vice-President, Minister or Deputy Minister, is a member of the National Assembly or is a public officer.

(3) Subject to the provisions of this section, a person appointed Investigator-General shall vacate his office on attaining the age of sixty-five years:

Provided that the President may permit a person who has attained that age to continue in office for such period as may be necessary to complete and submit any report on, or do any other thing in relation to, any investigation that was commenced by him before the attained age.

(4) A person appointed as Investigator-General shall forthwith vacate any office prescribed by an Act of Parliament.

(5) A person appointed as Investigator-General may be removed from office for incompetence or inability to perform the functions of his office (whether arising from infirmity of body or mind or from any other cause) or from misbehaviour, but shall not be so removed except in accordance with the provisions of this Article.

(6) If the National Assembly by resolution supported by the votes of not less than two-thirds of all the members of that House, resolves that the question of removing the Investigator-General ought to be investigated, the Speaker of the National Assembly shall send a copy to the Chief Justice who shall appoint a tribunal consisting of a Chairman and two other persons to inquire into the matter.

(7) The Chairman and one other member of the tribunal shall be persons who hold or have held high judicial office.

(8) The tribunal shall inquire into the matter and report thereon to the President.

(9) Where such a tribunal advises the President that the Investigator-General ought to be removed from office for incompetence or inability or for misbehaviour, the President shall remove the Investigator-General from office.

(10) If the question of removing the Investigator-General from office has been referred to a tribunal under this Article, the President may suspend him from performing any functions of his office, and any such suspension may at any time be revoked by the President and shall in any case cease to have effect if the tribunal shall advise the President that the Investigator-General ought not to be removed.

(11) If there is a vacancy in the office of the Investigator-General, or if the Investigator-General is temporarily absent from Zambia or otherwise unable to exercise the functions of his office, the President may appoint a person qualified to be a Judge of the High Court to exercise the functions of the office of the Investigator-General under this Article.

(12) A person appointed to the office of Investigator-General may resign upon giving three months' notice to the President.

(13) The functions, powers and procedures of the Investigator-General shall be as provided by an Act of Parliament.
(As amended by Act No. 18 of 1996)

Part XII
Human Rights Commission
(As amended by Act No. 18 of 1996)

Article

125. [Establishment of Human Rights Commission and its independence]
(1) There is hereby established a Human Rights Commission.
(2) The Human Rights Commission shall be autonomous.

126. [Functions, powers, composition, procedure, etc. of Human Rights Commission]

The functions, powers, composition, funding and administrative procedures, including the employment of staff, of the Human Rights Commission shall be prescribed by or under an Act of Parliament.

Commission for Investigations Act 1991

Act No. 20 of 1991

Date of Assent: 28th August, 1991

An Act to establish a Commission for Investigations, to provide for its powers, privileges and immunities and to provide for matters connected with os incidental to the forgoing.

[6th September; 1991

ENACTED by the Parliament of Zambia

Part I
Preliminary

1. This Act may be cited as the Commission for Investigations Act, 1991.
2. In this Act, unless the context otherwise requires
   "chairman" in relation to the Commission means the Investigator-General; or any Commissioner elected as such at any meeting of the Commission;
   "Commission" means the Commission for Investigations established by this Act;
   "Commissioner" means a member of the Commission other than the Investigator-General;
   "the Court" means the High Court;
   "high judicial office" means the office of a judge of a court of unlimited jurisdiction in civil and criminal matters in some part of the Commonwealth or in the Republic of Ireland or the office of a judge of a court having jurisdiction in appeals from such a court;
   "Investigator-General" means the Investigator-General appointed under Article 90 of the Constitution.
   "local authority" means a council established under the Local Government Act and any other authority declared by Act of Parliament to be a local authority;
   "Member" in relation to the Commission means Commissioner or the Investigator-General;
   "Secretary" means the person appointed under section six to be the secretary of the Commission;
3. (1) This Act shall apply to
      (a) any person in the service of the Republic;
      (b) the members and persons in the service of local authority;
      (c) the members and persons in the service of any institution or organization, whether established by or under an Act of Parliament or otherwise, in which the Government holds a majority of shares or exercises financial or administrative control;
      (d) the members and persons in the service of any Commission established by or under the Constitution or any Act of Parliament;
      but shall not apply to the President.
   (2) Notwithstanding subsection (1), the Commission shall have no power to question or receive any decision of any court or of any judicial officer in the exercise of his judicial functions, or any decision of a tribunal established by law for the performance of judicial functions in the exercise of such functions, or any matter relating to the exercise of the prerogative of mercy.

Part II
Establishment of Commission and Appointments

4. (1) There is hereby established a Commission for Investigations which shall consist of an Investigator-General and three Commissioners who shall be appointed by the President.
   (2) The Commission may act notwithstanding any vacancy or the absence of any member.
5. (1) A person shall not be qualified for appointment as a Commissioner if he holds the office of President, Vice President, Minister or Deputy Minister or if he is a member of the National Assembly (or a public officer).
   (2) Subject to the provisions of this section, a person appointed a Commissioner shall vacate office at the expiration of three years from the date of his appointment, and shall not be qualified to be reappointed as such within three years of his last ceasing to hold such office.
   (3) A person appointed a Commissioner may be removed from office by the President for inability to discharge the functions of his office (whether arising from infirmity of mind or body or for any other reason) or for misbehaviour.
6. The Commission shall employ a secretary and such other members of the staff of the Commission as the Commission may determine who shall be public officers.
7. (1) Every Member shall, on appointment, take an oath in the form set out in Part I of the First Schedule.
   (2) The Secretary and such other members of the staff of the Commission as the Chairman may require so to do shall, on appointment, take an oath in the form set out in Part II of the First Schedule.
   (3) Where any person is required to take an oath under the provisions of this section and-
   (a) he has no religious belief; or
   (b) the taking of an oath is contrary to his religious belief;
   he may take a solemn affirmation in the form of an oath on appointment substituting the words "solemnly and sincerely declare and affirm" for word "swear" and omitting the words "So Help Me God".
   (4) Every oath or affirmation taken by a Member shall be administered by the President and every oath or affirmation taken by the secretary or any other member of the staff of the Commission shall be administered by a Judge.

Part III
Power and Procedure

8. The Commission shall have jurisdiction to inquire into the conduct of any person to whom this Act applies in the exercise of his office or authority, or in abuse thereof-
   (a) whenever so directed by the President; and
   (b) unless the President otherwise directs, in any case in which it considers that an allegation of maladministration or abuse of office or authority by any such person ought to be investigated.
9. (1) A complaint or allegation under this Act may be made by any individual, or by any body of persons whether incorporate or not.
   (2) Any such complaint or allegations may be made orally or in writing and shall be addressed to the secretary who shall, in the case of an oral complaint or allegation, reduce the same to writing.
   (3) Every complaint or allegation shall be signed or thumb printed by the person making it.
   (4) No complaint or allegation shall be received by the Commission unless it is made within a period of two years from the date on which the facts giving rise to any such complaint or allegation became known to the person making the complaint

or allegation:

Provided that the Commission may in its absolute discretion receive complaints or allegations not made within the said period.

10. (1) No investigations under this Act shall be conducted concerning any allegation or grievances where the complainant or the person aggrieved has, or has had at any material time, the right or opportunity of obtaining relief or seeking redress by means of,

(a) an application or representation to any executive authority; or

(b) an application, appeal. reference or review to or before a tribunal established by or under any law; or

(c) proceedings in a court of law.

Provided that the Commission may conduct an investigation where it is satisfied that, in the particular circumstances of the case, it would be unreasonable to expect the complaint or the person aggrieved to resort or to have resorted to any of the foregoing means without fear, or undue hardships, expense or delay.

(2) The Commission may refuse to conduct, or may decide to discontinue, an investigation where it is satisfied that-

(a) the complaint is trivial, frivolous, vexatious or not made in good faith; or

(b) the inquiry would be unnecessary, improper or fruitless.

(3) The Commission shall, in any case in which it decides not to conduct an investigation, or decides to discontinue, an investigation, inform the complainant in writing accordingly but shall not be bound to give any reasons therefor.

11. Subject to the provisions of this Act, the jurisdiction and powers conferred on the Commission may be exercised notwithstanding any provision in any written law to the effect that an act or omission shall be final, or that no appeal shall lie in respect thereof, or that no proceeding or decision shall be challenged, reviewed, quashed or called in question.

12. Where it appears to the Commission that any inquiry under this Act is likely to be frustrated or prejudiced by an action taken or about to be taken by any person to whom this Act applies, the Commission may make such orders issue such writs and give such directions as it may consider appropriate for the purpose of conducting any investigation, and any such order, writ or direction shall have the same force as an order, writ or direction of the Court.

13. (1) The Commission shall have the power to summon witnesses and to examine witnesses under oath and for such purposes all the Members are hereby authorized to administer oaths.

(2) A summons for the attendance of a witness or the production of documents shall be in 1-G Form 3 set out in the Second Schedule and shall be served in the same manner as if it were a subpoena for the attendance of a witness at a civil trial in the Court.

(3) The Commission may by warrant order the arrest of any person who, having reasonable notice of the time and place at which he is required to attend before the Commission, fails to do so and any such warrant shall be in 1-G Form 4 set out in the Second Schedule and shall be served as if it were a warrant issued by the Court.

14. Subject as hereinafter provided, the Commission may, for the purposes of an inquiry under this Act, require any person who in its opinion is able to furnish information or produce documents relevant to the investigation to furnish any such information or produce any such document, and no obligation to maintain secrecy or other restriction upon the disclosure of information, whether imposed by law or otherwise, shall apply to the disclosure of information for the purposes of an investigation under this Act; and the Republic shall not be entitled in relation to any such investigation

to any such privilege in respect of the production of documents or the giving of evidence as is allowed by law in legal proceedings:

Provided that where the President certified that the giving of any information, or the production of any document:

(i) might prejudice the security, defence or international relations of the Republic, or the investigation or detection of offences; or

(ii) might involve the disclosure of the deliberations of the Cabinet or any sub-committee of the Cabinet relating to matters of a secret or confidential nature and would be injurious to the public interest;

the Commission shall not require the information to be given or, as the case may be, the document to be produced.

15. For the purposes of this Act, the Commission may by warrant in 1-G Form 7 set out in the Second Schedule enter upon any premises and thereon carry out any inspection for the purposes of an investigation:

Provided that where the President certifies that entry upon or inspection of any premises:

(i) might prejudice the security, defence or international relations of the Republic, or the investigation or detection of offences; or

(ii) might involve the disclosure of the deliberations of the Cabinet or any sub-committee of the Cabinet relating to matters of a secret or confidential nature, and would be injurious to the public interest;

the Commission shall not enter upon or inspect any such premises.

16. Every investigation shall be conducted in camera.

17. (1) The procedure for conducting an investigation shall be such as the Investigator-General considers appropriate in the circumstances of the case, and without prejudice to the generality of the foregoing provisions:

(a) the Investigator-General may authorize any member of the Commission to exercise any of the powers of the Commission for the purposes of an investigation, and

(b) the Commission may obtain information from such persons in such manner, and make such investigations, as it thinks fit.

(2) No person shall as of right be entitled to be represented by a legal practitioner or to be heard:

Provided that where the Commission proposes to conduct an investigation pursuant to a complaint or allegation under this Act, it shall afford to the principal Officer of any department or authority concerned, and to any other person who is alleged to have taken or authorized the action complained of, an opportunity to comment on any allegations made to the Commission, and no comment that is adverse to any person, department or authority shall be contained in a report to the President unless such person, department or authority has been afforded the opportunity aforesaid.

18. A person summoned as a witness under this Act may, on the order of the Commission, be paid from moneys appropriated by Parliament for the purpose of such allowances as may be prescribed by the Commission.

19. (1) If any person:

(a) being a witness before the Commission, without lawful excuse refuses to be sworn or affirmed, or having been sworn or affirmed refuses to answer fully and satisfactorily any question lawfully put to him; or

(b) having been sworn or affirmed knowingly gives false testimony touching any matter which is material to any question under investigation;

(c) wilfully insults, interrupts or otherwise obstructs any member or any member of the Staff of the Commission in the performance of his functions under this Act;

(d) wilfully disobeys any order made under section thirteen;
he shall be guilty of an offence and the Commission may certify such offence to the Court and may by warrant in 1-G Form 10 set out in the Second Schedule order the arrest of any such person.

(2) Where any person is arrested pursuant to an order of the Commission or an offences certified under this section, the Court may inquire into the matter and deal with the person charged in any manner in which the Court could deal with him if he had committed the like offence in relation to the Court.

Part IV
Reports and Enforcement
Submission of reports to the President

20. The Commission shall submit to the President a report of every investigation it has conducted which shall contain-
(a) a summary of the evidence taken together with the conclusions and recommendations of the Commission
(b) a statement of any action that has been taken by any person whose conduct is under investigation or by the department or authority of which such person is a member or in which he is employed, to correct or ameliorate any conduct, procedure, act or omission that is adversely commented on in the report;
(c) where any person has suffered loss or injury as a result of any alleged misconduct, maladministration or abuse of office or authority by any person whose conduct is under investigations, and the Commission, has found allegations to be true, the Commission may in its recommendations state that compensation should be paid to the person who has suffered such loss of inquiry or to any dependant of such person, and shall determine the sum which it recommends as compensation.

21. (1) The President may, on receipt of the report of the Commission on any investigation conducted by it, or during the continuance of any such investigation, take such decision in respect of the matter investigated or being investigated into by the Commission as he thinks fit.
(2) When the commission receives such decision, it shall, as soon as may be-
(a) notify the complaint in I-G Form 8 set out in the Second Schedule of the result of the investigation into his complaint or allegation;
(b) inform in I-G Form 9 set out in the Second Schedule the person against whom the complaint or allegation was made of the effect of the President's decision, in so far as the same may be known to the Commission.
(3) A report required to be submitted to the National Assembly shall not disclose the identity or contain any statement which may point to the identity of any person into whose conduct an investigation has been or is about to be made.
(4) Failure on the part of any person, body or authority to comply with any order given by the Commission under subsection (2) may be investigated by the Commission and reported to the President, as if it were an investigation conducted under the provisions of this Act.
(5) Any sum of money directed by the President to be paid as compensation following a recommendation made in accordance with paragraph (c) of section twenty shall be a charge on the general revenues of the Republic.

22. (1) The Commission shall, as soon as may be after the 31st December in each year submit a report on its operations to the National Assembly.
(2) A report under this section shall not disclose the identity or contain any statement which may point to the identity of any person into whose conduct an investigation has been or is about to be made.

Part V
Immunities of the Commission

23. No investigation, proceeding, process or report of the Commission shall be held bad for any error or irregularity of form or be challenged, reviewed, quashed or called in question in any court save on the ground of lack of jurisdiction.
24. (1) No proceedings, civil, or criminal, shall lie against any member or member of the staff of the
Commission, for anything done in good faith in the course of the exercise of his functions under this Act.
(2) Subject to the provisions of this Act, no member or any such person as aforesaid shall be called to give evidence before any court or tribunal in respect of anything coming to his knowledge in the exercise of his functions under this Act.
25. The Commission may, by statutory instrument, make rules prescribing anything which under this Act may be prescribed.
26. (1) Notwithstanding the repeal of the Constitution in the Schedule to the Constitution of Zambia Act, 1973, the members of the Commission established by Article one hundred and seventeen of that Constitution shall continue to hold office as members of the commission established by this Act, subject to the same terms and conditions as apply to the holders of office referred to in section nine of the Constitution of Zambia Act, 1991.
(2) Any person who is holding or acting in any office in the Commission shall continue in office as if the appointment was made under this Act.
(3) The Commission for Investigations Act, 1974, is hereby repealed.

Chapter IV
Dual Systems

Canada

Canadian Human Rights Commission

Michelle Falardeau Ramsay

Tasks and Competences

The mandate, role and structure of the Canadian Human Rights Commission [CHRC] are outlined in the *Canadian Human Rights Act*, and its role with regard to employment equity is contained in the *Employment Equity Act* (see legislation below).

The Canadian Human Rights Commission administers the *Canadian Human Rights Act* and ensures that the principles of equal opportunity and non-discrimination are followed in all areas of federal jurisdiction. The Commission's mandate includes:

- investigating complaints of discrimination in employment and in provision of services based on the grounds enumerated in the Act;
- investigating complaints alleging inequities in pay between men and women who are performing work of equal value;
- developing and conducting information programs to promote public understanding of the Act and of the role and activities of the Commission.

Under the federal *Employment Equity Act*, the Commission is also authorized to conduct audits of employers under federal jurisdiction to determine their compliance with the Act, negotiate undertakings when an employer is found not in compliance and issue a direction in cases where it fails to negotiate written undertakings.

The sphere of competence of the Human Rights Commission is determined by the fundamental right to equal opportunity in employment or the provision of services without being hindered by discriminatory practices based on eleven prohibited grounds: race, national or ethnic origin, colour, religion, age, sex, sexual orientation, marital status, family status, disability and conviction for which a pardon was granted.

When a complaint is based on actions that occurred more than one year prior to the contact with the CHRC, the Commission can exercise its discretion to refuse to deal with the complaint.

The Commission is authorized to investigate on site and to obtain and review any documents relevant to the investigation. Where necessary, the Commission may seek a warrant "to enter and search any premises in order to carry out such enquiries as are reasonably necessary for the investigation" (S. 43(2.1))

The *Canadian Human Rights Act* applies to all areas of federal jurisdiction. This includes: federal departments and agencies, Crown corporations, private

K. Hossain et al. (eds), Human Rights Commissions and Ombudsman Offices, 453–457.

companies which regularly transport goods or people across provincial or national borders, chartered banks, companies which handle radioactive materials, interprovincial or international pipelines, broadcasting companies and telephone companies. Other employers and organizations fall under the jurisdiction of provincial human rights commissions.

Complaints against members of the legislature are rare, but the Commission has successfully investigated a small number. Judges are office holders and are therefore not subject to the Commission's jurisdiction. They are, however, subject to investigation by the Canadian Judicial Council.

The Commission has jurisdiction over private sector (non-state) employers, providing they are within federal jurisdiction.

The Commission may be asked to comment on draft legislation by the Minister of Justice; it can and often does provide comments on draft legislation even when such advice has not been solicited, sometimes by writing the responsible Minister, sometimes by appearing before Standing Legislative Committee reviewing the draft legislation, sometimes by way of comment in its Annual Report.

Any individual or group of individuals having reasonable grounds for believing that a person is engaging or has engaged in a discriminatory practice may file a complaint with the Commission. Complainants normally contact the offices of the Commission directly. They may also be represented by legal counsel, a union representative, or other third party of their choice.

Organizations can file complaints as long as they are based in Canada. Groups and organizations, including NGOs, can file complaints, provided that the respondent falls under federal jurisdiction and there are reasonable grounds for believing that the respondent is engaging or has engaged in a discriminatory practice.

Organization

The Commission is composed of two full-time and up to six part-time commissioners. The Chief Commissioner and other Commissioners are appointed by Governor-in-Council, that is the Governor General on the advice of the Prime Minister/Cabinet. The Chief Commissioner is appointed for a term not to exceed seven years, and part-time Commissioners for a term not exceeding three years. The appointee may be reappointed to the same position, but renewal is not automatic.

Commission members hold office "during good behaviour" and only the Governor-in-Council can remove Commissioners. Removal requires the consent of both Houses of Parliament: the Senate and the House of Commons.

The Canadian Human Rights Commission meets all the requirements of an independent body. It has a secure mandate, set out in law, which cannot be unilaterally revoked; it reports directly to Parliament; it is headed by a person who cannot be fired without just cause; it has a secure financial base which it controls and which cannot be significantly altered without public discussion; it has the authority to obtain information necessary to come to informed decisions; it has the authority to meet and review issues within its competence in private and without interference, and to set its own rules of procedure; it has the authority to make its findings and views public without prior authorization or approval of the government.

The Governor in Council is accountable for its appointments. Commissioners can only be removed from office by the Governor in Council for failing to hold office "during good behaviour".

Salary, benefits and other terms and conditions of employment for the Chief Commissioner are established by the Privy Council Office. Part-time Commissioners are paid from the CHRC's budget for attendance at meetings of the Commission or other work for the Commission at the Chief Commissioner's request.

The CHRC's annual budget is allocated by the Treasury Board of Canada on the same basis as government departments and other government agencies. The Commission itself controls its spending within that budget.

The Canadian Human Rights Commission is the national commission, which deals with matters under federal jurisdiction (see above). Each province also has a human rights code and a commission which deals with matters under provincial jurisdiction.

In addition to the Chief Commissioner, Deputy Chief Commissioner, and part-time Commissioners, the CHRC has a permanent Secretary General who is appointed under the terms of the *Public Service Employment Act*, i.e. normally by competition. It also has approximately 180 staff.

The Secretary General is appointed by the Public Service Commission of Canada through a selection process in which the Chief Commissioner plays an active role. Authority for appointments to positions at the executive level in the public service rests with the Public Service Commission. Payment of salary is fixed by the Treasury Board according to the level of the job. The Secretary-General position is considered equivalent to an Assistant Deputy Minister, a very senior rank within the Public Service.

The Commission's staff are selected by the Secretary General and senior managers of the Commission and are appointed under the terms of the *Public Service Employment Act*. The Commission can increase the number of staff, depending on its financial resources.

Procedure

It must be established that the complaint falls within federal jurisdiction, and that the allegations are related to one of the eleven grounds of discrimination under the CHRA. Complainants should exhaust other available remedies. There is no cost to individuals who file a complaint. As long as a potential complainant's initial contact with the Commission occurs within one year of the alleged incident of discrimination, the complaint would not be considered to be out of time, even if they then pursue other available remedies.

Commission staff communicate with complainants and respondents in their preferred official language (English or French). Information regarding complaints is available in many other languages.

Information, including witness statements, is gathered by the investigator assigned to a complaint. At the completion of an investigation, the investigator prepares a written report, which is disclosed to the parties. The parties may submit written comments on the investigation report. The report and comments, if any, are then submitted to the Commissioners at one of their regular meetings, and the Commissioners decide on the complaint's disposition. The parties are then informed in writing of the Commission's decision.

The Commission may decide to send a case to conciliation, a process aimed at settling the issue to the satisfaction of both parties and to the Commission. Settlements arrived at in conciliation are legally binding. If conciliation fails, the Commission would consider referring the matter to be heard by a Tribunal. Approximately 5% of cases reviewed by the Commission are referred to the Tribunal.

Rulings

The Commission is charged with investigating complaints and carrying forth those which it deems worthy of a full hearing by a Human Rights Tribunal, which can then inquire into complaints brought before it and determine whether or not a breach of the *Act* has been established and what is an appropriate remedy. Besides referring a complaint to a Tribunal, the Commission can make several other types of determinations, including appointing a conciliator to help the parties try and settle the complaint, or deciding that no further proceedings are warranted. It can also approve a settlement agreement between the parties.

The Canadian Human Rights Tribunal is a quasi-judicial body which was created by Parliament under the *Canadian Human Rights Act* to inquire into complaints of discrimination and to decide if particular cases have contravened that Act. Complaints are referred to the Tribunal by the Canadian Human Rights Commission.

The Tribunal inquires into complaints of discrimination through public hearings. The parties present their arguments, much as they would in a court of law, by calling witnesses and experts to testify, and by entering documents as evidence. Based on the evidence and guided by the principles of natural justice, the Tribunal determines whether discrimination has occurred under the *Canadian Human Rights Act*. The cases referred to the Tribunal generally involve complicated legal issues, new human rights issues, unexplored areas of discrimination, or multifaceted evidentiary complaints that must be heard under oath. Decisions of the Tribunal are reviewable by the Federal Court of Canada.

Decisions by the Commission are final, although the parties can apply to the Courts to have them reviewed. The Commission itself decides which cases to publicize. Decisions by the Tribunal are binding in the same way as court decisions.

Only the Human Rights Tribunal can award compensation to a victim of discrimination, for loss of wages or expenses incurred as a result of the discriminatory practice. It may also order the respondent to pay up to $20,000 for the victim's suffering. However, the Commission does conciliate settlement agreements which do contain clauses concerning compensation when this is warranted.

The decisions of the Commission are not all published, however the Commission makes a point of publicizing significant cases through press releases. Decisions of the Tribunal, however, are published.

Parties to a complaint may request that the Federal Court of Canada conduct a judicial review of a decision by the Commission.

In 1997, the CHRC received 1,527 complaints. That same year, 725 cases were dealt with by the Commission by sending them to Tribunal or to conciliation, by approving settlements, or by deciding to dismiss them, not to deal with them, or take no further proceedings. About 1,500 other cases were resolved through other processes, including early resolution, referrals to alternate mechanisms, or because the complainants did not wish to pursue the matter.

Review of the Experience of Existing Human Rights Commissions

A difficulty we experience is that the process has become increasingly litigious. The complaints process is also slower than we would like it to be. In the legislative area, there are weaknesses which should be addressed, for example, the ability to deal with systemic discrimination not easily attachable through individual complaints, and equal pay provisions that have not been effective. Our public education campaigns are also limited by a lack of sufficient resources.

Complaint Handling at the Canadian Human Rights Commission

Gerald Savard*

It goes without saying, that no one system of human rights protection is perfect or necessarily applicable to all countries and contexts. Historical, demographic and constitutional differences make this a given. In Canada, we have developed a model that is clearly the product of our own set of characteristics, including the fact that we are a federal state, with provinces that have clear and distinct areas of jurisdiction separate and apart from that of the central government. As a result, Canada does not have a single institution or a single piece of legislation that deals with the broad range of human rights which are elaborated in international covenants and conventions. Other countries have and may take a different approach which reflects their particular characteristics. I think you will find it useful, however, to learn how the Canadian approach has worked and to get a sense of our institutional framework for protecting human rights.

In Canada, basic political and civil rights – like the right to freedom of association or freedom of expression – are well-established in our political culture in 1982, these rights were entrenched in our new constitution as part of our charter of rights and freedoms. The charter was inspired by the universal declaration and the international conventions which followed, of particular significance is the importance it places on equality rights, which the courts have interpreted very broadly, and reinforced through a number of significant decisions. The charter does, however, have its limitations in the sense that it covers only acts of government, and has no direct impact on activities in the private sector. Moreover, in order to challenge a government action under the chapter, an individual or group must go through the courts, a process which can, of course, be lengthy and costly.

Human rights legislation in Canada is intended to provide a more prompt and inexpensive remedy for victims of discrimination, along with relatively informal procedures. In fact, long before we had our Charter of Rights and Freedoms, human rights laws began to be adopted at the provincial level, which would provide Canadians with protection in the area of equality rights. It is interesting to note that, in the Canadian context, the right to be treated equally without regard to such factors as sex, race, age, religion and so on is what many people think of when they hear the expression "Human Rights".

*Director General, Canadian Human Rights Commission.

K. Hossain et al. (eds), Human Rights Commissions and Ombudsman Offices, 459–510.

The Canadian Human Rights Act

Since Canada is a federal state, with ten provinces and two territories that have their own powers under the constitution, it is not surprising that the first human rights laws were adopted at the provincial level, the first Human Rights Commission was established by the province of Ontario in 1962. The remaining provinces set up commissions in the years that followed, and all now provide similar protection in matters under their respective jurisdictions.

In 1977, the federal parliament adopted the Canadian Human Rights Act. The Act prohibits discrimination in employment and services in federal jurisdiction: that is, the federal government, government-owned corporations, and such federally regulated industries as banking, transportation, and telecommunications. The Act has been amended several times since its adoption, and it now deals with eleven prohibited grounds of discrimination: sex, race, colour, national origin, religion, age, disability, marital status, family status, conviction for a crime for which one has been pardoned, and sexual orientation.

The Canadian Human Rights Act established the mandate of the Canadian Human Rights Commission, which began operating in 1978. The Commission, it should be noted, is independent from the government: we report to the Canadian Parliament, not to a government Minister. And although we are financed by government and the Commissioners are government appointees, the government in no way interferes with our operations. In fact, we often find ourselves on the opposite side of the government in court cases; and regularly criticize the government of the day in our annual reports.

Broadly speaking, the Commission has four functions:

- to investigate and attempt to resolve complaints of discrimination;
- to monitor and report on the Human Rights situation in Canada;
- to engage in public education, research, and other activities designed to promote compliance with the Act; and
- to ensure that federal employers comply with another piece of legislation: the Employment Equity Act. This last function is one I discuss briefly a little later on.

The commission consists of a chief commissioner, who serves on a full-time basis, and can include a deputy chief commissioner and up to six part-time commissioners. Currently, there are five part-time commissioners representing different parts of Canada, and with very diverse backgrounds: for example, one of our part-time commissioners is a Holocaust survivor, one is originally from India, one is a person with a disability, and another is an aboriginal Canadian.

In addition to the Commissioners, we have approximately 180 staff at our headquarters in Ottawa and in six regional offices across the country. Our annual budget is about 15 million Canadian dollars a year that is a relatively small budget for an agency that covers a large country like Canada, and we spend a great deal of time trying to figure out how we can use our meagre resources as efficiently as possible.

Dealing with Complaints

Handling discrimination complaints from members of the public is the Canadian Human Rights Commission's primary function. It is certainly the function which takes up most of our financial and human resources, since it is non-discretionary: that is, if someone comes to us with a complaint, we cannot just turn that person away because of a lack of time or staff.

We receive something in the area of 50,000 inquiries form the public each year, and approximately 2,000 of these deal with matters that come under the Commission's jurisdiction. These complaints range from allegations of sexual or racial harassment; to discrimination in hiring of promotion; to allegations of pay inequities between male and female employees; to differential treatment in the provision of Government services, or private sector services such as air transportation.

After establishing that a complaint falls within the Commission's jurisdiction and is based on one of the grounds of discrimination cited in Human Rights Act, we frequently try to resolve the matter informally by discussing the situation with the parties involved. If the parties can come to an agreement right away we consider the matter closed and the complaints goes no further.

If an early resolution is not possible, the complaint is investigated by Commission staff, and a report of the investigation goes to the Commissioners at one of their regular meetings. The Commissioners consider approximately 100 of these complaints each time they meet. At that stage, the Commissioners have the option of either dismissing the complaint due to lack of evidence of discrimination; or trying to negotiate a formal settlement through a procedure we call conciliation; or sending the complaint to a Human Rights Tribunal.

A Human Rights Tribunal is a quasi-judicial body with the specific mandate to adjudicate human rights complaints. It is not part of the Commission and is independently appointed. A tribunal has the power to determine whether or not a particular action or policy was discriminatory under the Canadian Human Rights Act; and if so, order a remedy. A tribunal can order an employer, for example, to pay a complainant financial compensation for lost wages and damages, but perhaps more importantly, it can order a respondent to change a policy or practice that it finds to be discriminatory. Tribunal decisions are filed with the federal court of Canada and have the weight of federal court decisions: a respondent who fails to comply with a tribunal decision can be charged with contempt of court.

It is important to note that the Human Rights Commissions and Tribunals in Canada deal with legally enforceable rights and are not Ombudsmen in the traditional sense. Human rights laws have been recognized by our courts as having quasi-constitutional status. It is this that give Commissions their strength, and makes them potentially powerful agents of social change.

Systemic Discrimination

Much of our work, and the work of the other Commissions in Canada, has to do with individual complaints of discrimination. In recent years, however, Commissions have been putting greater emphasis on what we call "systemic" discrimination. Here the situations the law confronts are not aberrational in the sense of being a departure form the norm, but are continuing features of everyday life. The focus is not on the circumstances of a particular individual; for example, the job applicant who does not get hired because of his ethnic origin, or the woman who is sexually harassed by her supervisor. Instead, the focus is on discriminatory aspects of the broader social context, aspects which have developed, usually, for complex historical reasons, and which persist because they have become such a part of our lives. In Canada, these include realities such as the continued underemployment of aboriginal people and people with disabilities; continuing pay inequities between men and women in the workforce, and the glass ceiling encountered by members of visible minorities trying to rise to management positions.

It is in the area of systemic discrimination, in fact, that Human Rights Commissions may be most effective. Commissions can, by referring and arguing key complaints at tribunals and in the courts, bring about changes in common practices, procedures, government policy, and legislation which have far-reaching effects on society as a whole. While only about two per cent of all complaints are referred to a Human Rights Tribunal, the Tribunal's decisions have had a significant impact on Canadian human rights law and practice. For example, one human rights tribunal ordered that all combat-related positions in the Canadian armed forces be opened to women, another ordered the federal agency responsible for elections to make all polling places accessible to people with disabilities, another ordered the Government to provide spousal benefits to its homosexual employees in established same-sex relationships. Similarly, the courts have clarified the nature of sexual harassment in employment and the extent to which employers can be held accountable for the actions of their employees who harass colleagues or subordinates; they have also, over the years, clarified the concept of "reasonable accommodation", which places a positive onus on employers and service providers to modify their places of work or methods of service delivery to take into account the special needs of individuals with disabilities, family responsibilities, or religious obligations.

This is also where another of the Commission's functions comes in, which I mentioned earlier. We are charged with ensuring that federal employers comply with a piece of legislation called the Employment Equity Act. This Law requires federal employers, including the federal public services and private companies under federal jurisdiction, to file annual reports on the representation levels in their workforces of four traditionally disadvantaged groups in Canadian society: women, aboriginal people, persons with disabilities, and members of visible minorities.

When their workforces do not reflect the availability of these groups in the general labour market, employers are required to prepare plans which establish hiring and promotion goals for workers in the under-represented groups, provide for the elimination of barriers, such as employment policies, which limit the employment opportunities of target group members, and identify positive steps that can be taken to attract and promote them. The law gives the Canadian Human Rights Commission the authority to audit employers to ensure that they are in compliance with their obligations. Employers who have not met the requirements are expected to negotiate undertakings with the Commission to bring them into compliance, and can be referred to an Employment Equity Tribunal in cases where they disagree with the commission as to what kind of remedial action is required.

The employment equity regime is still very new – the first audits were only undertaken last November – but we are hopeful that, as the process gets into full swing, more and more employers will build employment equity into their human resource processes as a matter of course, and that the result will be workplaces that are more equitable in every sense of the word.

Challenges

We are, of course, proud of the work our Commission had done over its nearly 20-year history, and there is no question that we can point to important accomplishments during that time. I also think it is fair to say that Canada's Human Rights Commissions enjoy broad public support. However, there is no denying that the Commissions have at times been subject to criticism. Some complainants and advocacy groups, for example, feel that our procedures are too bureaucratic and legalistic, that respondents in human rights complaints get off too easily with a meagre pay-out or a slap on the wrist, and that we are not forceful enough in our condemnation of governments or employers whose human rights practices are less than ideal.

On the respondents' side, we are often told that we are too "intrusive", too concerned with "trivial" or "frivolous" allegations, and unfairly biassed in favour of complainants. This is probably in part the result of the Commission's dual role as human rights advocate and, at the same time, objective voice when dealing with complaints, both of which our Act requires of us. While advocacy and objectivity are not necessarily mutually-exclusive, one can understand concerns about how this can work in practice. One of our provincial governments has dealt with this issue by creating separate agencies, one to deal with complaints and another to promote human rights.

Another criticism that has been levelled at Human Rights Commissions over the years is that it takes them too long to deal with complaints. On the one hand, Human Rights Commissions were created to provide relatively informal and accessible procedures. On the other hand, growing workloads, together with funding which had failed to keep pace with this growth, have made it difficult for Human Rights Commissions consistently to meet these expectations.

Our challenge, given increased workload and resource constraints, is to be more creative in finding ways to improve the effectiveness of our procedures. One approach we have taken to the problem of delays and backlogs at the Canadian Human Rights Commission is to streamline our complaints procedure so that more straightforward complaints are processed in less than 9 months. This procedure has been in place for about three years and has proven to be effective in reducing complaints-processing time. Another relatively recent measure was the establishment of a special unit to group and deal with similar complaints in a co-ordinated manner.

We know there is room for improvement at the Canadian Human Rights Commission, and we are always re-evaluating our procedures to make them more effective. Even a well-established institution like ours needs to adapt to changing conditions and changing demands. This is especially true because it seems that, the stronger and more effective we are, the higher the public expectations of our performance. It bears repeating that no single human rights protection system is necessarily perfect for every country. But I believe the Canadian model has been a successful one, overall, and I hope that other delegates are looking at ways of promoting human rights in their own countries will find that certain elements of our approach and past experience can serve as a useful guide.

LEGISLATION

Canadian Human Rights Act

CHAPTER H-6

An Act to extend the laws in Canada that proscribe discrimination

Short title
1. This Act may be cited as the Canadian Human Rights Act.
1976–77, c. 33, s. 1.

Purpose of Act
2. The purpose of this Act is to extend the laws in Canada to give effect, within the purview of matters coming within the legislative authority of Parliament, to the principle that all individuals should have an opportunity equal with other individuals to make for themselves the lives that they are able and wish to have and to have their needs accommodated, consistent with their duties and obligations as members of society, without being hindered in or prevented from doing so by discriminatory practices based on race, national or ethnic origin, colour, religion, age, sex, sexual orientation, marital status, family status, disability or conviction for an offence for which a pardon has been granted.
R.S., 1985, c. H-6, s. 2; 1996, c. 14, s. 1; 1998, c. 9, s. 9.

PART I
Proscribed Discrimination
General
Prohibited grounds of discrimination

3. (1) For all purposes of this Act, the prohibited grounds of discrimination are race, national or ethnic origin, colour, religion, age, sex, sexual orientation, marital status, family status, disability and conviction for which a pardon has been granted.

Idem
(2) Where the ground of discrimination is pregnancy or child-birth, the discrimination shall be deemed to be on the ground of sex.
R.S., 1985, c. H-6, s. 3; 1996, c. 14, s. 2.

Multiple grounds of discrimination
3.1 For greater certainty, a discriminatory practice includes a practice based on one or more prohibited grounds of discrimination or on the effect of a combination of prohibited grounds.
1998, c. 9, s. 11.

Orders regarding discriminatory practices
4. A discriminatory practice, as described in sections 5 to 14.1, may be the subject of a complaint under Part III and anyone found to be engaging or to have engaged in a discriminatory practice may be made subject to an order as provided in sections 53 and 54.
R.S., 1985, c. H-6, s. 4; 1998, c. 9, s. 11.

Discriminatory Practices
Denial of good, service, facility or accommodation
5. It is a discriminatory practice in the provision of goods, services, facilities or accommodation customarily available to the general public

(a) to deny, or to deny access to, any such good, service, facility or accommodation to any individual, or

(b) to differentiate adversely in relation to any individual, on a prohibited ground of discrimination.
1976–77, c. 33, s. 5.

Denial of commercial premises or residential accommodation
6. It is a discriminatory practice in the provision of commercial premises or residential accommodation
(a) to deny occupancy of such premises or accommodation to any individual, or
(b) to differentiate adversely in relation to any individual,
on a prohibited ground of discrimination.
1976–77, c. 33, s. 6.

Employment
7. It is a discriminatory practice, directly or indirectly,
(a) to refuse to employ or continue to employ any individual, or
(b) in the course of employment, to differentiate adversely in relation to an employee,
on a prohibited ground of discrimination.
1976–77, c. 33, s. 7.

Employment applications, advertisements
8. It is a discriminatory practice
(a) to use or circulate any form of application for employment, or
(b) in connection with employment or prospective employment, to publish any advertisement or to make any written or oral inquiry that expresses or implies any limitation, specification or preference based on a prohibited ground of discrimination.
1976–77, c. 33, s. 8.

Employee organizations
9. (1) It is a discriminatory practice for an employee organization on a prohibited ground of discrimination
(a) to exclude an individual from full membership in the organization;
(b) to expel or suspend a member of the organization; or
(c) to limit, segregate, classify or otherwise act in relation to an individual in a way that would deprive the individual of employment opportunities, or limit employment opportunities or otherwise adversely affect the status of the individual, where the individual is a member of the organization or where any of the obligations of the organization pursuant to a collective agreement relate to the individual.

Exception
(2) Notwithstanding subsection (1), it is not a discriminatory practice for an employee organization to exclude, expel or suspend an individual from membership in the organization because that individual has reached the normal age of retirement for individuals working in positions similar to the position of that individual.

(3) [Repealed, 1998, c. 9, s. 12]
R.S., 1985, c. H-6, s. 9; 1998, c. 9, s. 12.
Discriminatory policy or practice
10. It is a discriminatory practice for an employer, employee organization or employer organization
(a) to establish or pursue a policy or practice, or
(b) to enter into an agreement affecting recruitment, referral, hiring, promotion, training, apprenticeship, transfer or any other matter relating to employment or prospective employment,
that deprives or tends to deprive an individual or class of individuals of any employment opportunities on a prohibited ground of discrimination.
R.S., 1985, c. H-6, s. 10; 1998, c. 9, s. 13(E).

Equal wages
11. (1) It is a discriminatory practice for an employer to establish or maintain differences in wages between male and female employees employed in the same establishment who are performing work of equal value.

Assessment of value of work
(2) In assessing the value of work performed by employees employed in the same establishment, the criterion to be applied is the composite of the skill, effort and responsibility required in the performance of the work and the conditions under which the work is performed.

Separate establishments
(3) Separate establishments established or maintained by an employer solely or principally for the purpose of establishing or maintaining differences in wages between male and female employees shall be deemed for the purposes of this section to be the same establishment.

Different wages based on prescribed reasonable factors
(4) Notwithstanding subsection (1), it is not a discriminatory practice to pay to male and female employees different wages if the difference is based on a factor prescribed by guidelines, issued by the Canadian Human Rights Commission pursuant to subsection 27(2), to be a reasonable factor that justifies the difference.

Idem
(5) For greater certainty, sex does not constitute a reasonable factor justifying a difference in wages.

No reduction of wages
(6) An employer shall not reduce wages in order to eliminate a discriminatory practice described in this section.

Definition of "wages"
(7) For the purposes of this section, "wages" means any form of remuneration payable for work performed by an individual and includes
(a) salaries, commissions, vacation pay, dismissal wages and bonuses;
(b) reasonable value for board, rent, housing and lodging;
(c) payments in kind;
(d) employer contributions to pension funds or plans, long-term disability plans and all forms of health insurance plans; and
(e) any other advantage received directly or indirectly from the individual's employer.
1976–77, c. 33, s. 11.

Publication of discriminatory notices, etc.
12. It is a discriminatory practice to publish or display before the public or to cause to be published or displayed before the public any notice, sign, symbol, emblem or other representation that
(a) expresses or implies discrimination or an intention to discriminate, or
(b) incites or is calculated to incite others to discriminate
if the discrimination expressed or implied, intended to be expressed or implied or incited or calculated to be incited would otherwise, if engaged in, be a discriminatory practice described in any of sections 5 to 11 or in section 14.
1976–77, c. 33, s. 12; 1980–81–82–83, c. 143, s. 6.

Hate messages
13. (1) It is a discriminatory practice for a person or a group of persons acting in concert to communicate telephonically or to cause to be so communicated, repeatedly, in whole or in part by means of the facilities of a telecommunication undertaking within the legislative authority of Parliament, any matter that is likely to expose a person or persons

to hatred or contempt by reason of the fact that that person or those persons are identifiable on the basis of a prohibited ground of discrimination.

Exception
(2) Subsection (1) does not apply in respect of any matter that is communicated in whole or in part by means of the facilities of a broadcasting undertaking.

Interpretation
(3) For the purposes of this section, no owner or operator of a telecommunication undertaking communicates or causes to be communicated any matter described in subsection (1) by reason only that the facilities of a telecommunication undertaking owned or operated by that person are used by other persons for the transmission of that matter.
1976–77, c. 33, s. 13.

Harassment
14. (1) It is a discriminatory practice,
(a) in the provision of goods, services, facilities or accommodation customarily available to the general public,
(b) in the provision of commercial premises or residential accommodation, or
(c) in matters related to employment,
to harass an individual on a prohibited ground of discrimination.

Sexual harassment
(2) Without limiting the generality of subsection (1), sexual harassment shall, for the purposes of that subsection, be deemed to be harassment on a prohibited ground of discrimination.
1980–81–82–83, c. 143, s. 7.

Retaliation
14.1 It is a discriminatory practice for a person against whom a complaint has been filed under Part III, or any person acting on their behalf, to retaliate or threaten retaliation against the individual who filed the complaint or the alleged victim.
1998, c. 9, s. 14.

Exceptions
15. (1) It is not a discriminatory practice if
(a) any refusal, exclusion, expulsion, suspension, limitation, specification or preference in relation to any employment is established by an employer to be based on a bona fide occupational requirement;
(b) employment of an individual is refused or terminated because that individual has not reached the minimum age, or has reached the maximum age, that applies to that employment by law or under regulations, which may be made by the Governor in Council for the purposes of this paragraph;
(c) an individual's employment is terminated because that individual has reached the normal age of retirement for employees working in positions similar to the position of that individual;
(d) the terms and conditions of any pension fund or plan established by an employer, employee organization or employer organization provide for the compulsory vesting or locking-in of pension contributions at a fixed or determinable age in accordance with sections 17 and 18 of the Pension Benefits Standards Act, 1985;
(e) an individual is discriminated against on a prohibited ground of discrimination in a manner that is prescribed by guidelines, issued by the Canadian Human Rights Commission pursuant to subsection 27(2), to be reasonable;
(f) an employer, employee organization or employer organization grants a female employee special leave or benefits in connection with pregnancy or child-birth or grants employees special leave or benefits to assist them in the care of their children; or
(g) in the circumstances described in section 5 or 6, an individual is denied any goods,

services, facilities or accommodation or access thereto or occupancy of any commercial premises or residential accommodation or is a victim of any adverse differentiation and there is bona fide justification for that denial or differentiation.

Accommodation of needs
(2) For any practice mentioned in paragraph (1)(a) to be considered to be based on a bona fide occupational requirement and for any practice mentioned in paragraph (1)(g) to be considered to have a bona fide justification, it must be established that accommodation of the needs of an individual or a class of individuals affected would impose undue hardship on the person who would have to accommodate those needs, considering health, safety and cost.

Regulations
(3) The Governor in Council may make regulations prescribing standards for assessing undue hardship.

Publication of proposed regulations
(4) Each regulation that the Governor in Council proposes to make under subsection (3) shall be published in the Canada Gazette and a reasonable opportunity shall be given to interested persons to make representations in respect of it.

Consultations
(5) The Canadian Human Rights Commission shall conduct public consultations concerning any regulation proposed to be made by the Governor in Council under subsection (3) and shall file a report of the results of the consultations with the Minister within a reasonable time after the publication of the proposed regulation in the Canada Gazette.

Exception
(6) A proposed regulation need not be published more than once, whether or not it has been amended as a result of any representations.

Making of regulations
(7) The Governor in Council may proceed to make regulations under subsection (3) after six months have elapsed since the publication of the proposed regulations in the Canada Gazette, whether or not a report described in subsection (5) is filed.

Application
(8) This section applies in respect of a practice regardless of whether it results in direct discrimination or adverse effect discrimination.

Universality of service for Canadian Forces
(9) Subsection (2) is subject to the principle of universality of service under which members of the Canadian Forces must at all times and under any circumstances perform any functions that they may be required to perform.
R.S., 1985, c. H-6, s. 15; R.S., 1985, c. 32 (2nd Supp.), s. 41; 1998, c. 9, ss. 10, 15.

Special programs
16. (1) It is not a discriminatory practice for a person to adopt or carry out a special program, plan or arrangement designed to prevent disadvantages that are likely to be suffered by, or to eliminate or reduce disadvantages that are suffered by, any group of individuals when those disadvantages would be based on or related to the prohibited grounds of discrimination, by improving opportunities respecting goods, services, facilities, accommodation or employment in relation to that group.

Advice and assistance
(2) The Canadian Human Rights Commission, may
(a) make general recommendations concerning desirable objectives for special programs, plans or arrangements referred to in subsection (1); and
(b) on application, give such advice and assistance with respect to the adoption or

carrying out of a special program, plan or arrangement referred to in subsection (1) as will serve to aid in the achievement of the objectives the program, plan or arrangement was designed to achieve.

Collection of information relating to prohibited grounds
(3) It is not a discriminatory practice to collect information relating to a prohibited ground of discrimination if the information is intended to be used in adopting or carrying out a special program, plan or arrangement under subsection (1).
R.S., 1985, c. H-6, s. 16; 1998, c. 9, s. 16.

Plans to meet the needs of disabled persons
17. (1) A person who proposes to implement a plan for adapting any services, facilities, premises, equipment or operations to meet the needs of persons arising from a disability may apply to the Canadian Human Rights Commission for approval of the plan.

Approval of plan
(2) The Commission may, by written notice to a person making an application pursuant to subsection (1), approve the plan if the Commission is satisfied that the plan is appropriate for meeting the needs of persons arising from a disability.

Effect of approval of accommodation plan
(3) Where any services, facilities, premises, equipment or operations are adapted in accordance with a plan approved under subsection (2), matters for which the plan provides do not constitute any basis for a complaint under Part III regarding discrimination based on any disability in respect of which the plan was approved.

Notice when application not granted
(4) When the Commission decides not to grant an application made pursuant to subsection (1), it shall send a written notice of its decision to the applicant setting out the reasons for its decision.
1980–81–82–83, c. 143, s. 9.

Rescinding approval of plan
18. (1) If the Canadian Human Rights Commission is satisfied that, by reason of any change in circumstances, a plan approved under subsection 17(2) has ceased to be appropriate for meeting the needs of persons arising from a disability, the Commission may, by written notice to the person who proposes to carry out or maintains the adaptation contemplated by the plan or any part thereof, rescind its approval of the plan to the extent required by the change in circumstances.

Effect where approval rescinded
(2) To the extent to which approval of a plan is rescinded under subsection (1), subsection 17(3) does not apply to the plan if the discriminatory practice to which the complaint relates is subsequent to the rescission of the approval.

Statement of reasons for rescinding approval
(3) Where the Commission rescinds approval of a plan pursuant to subsection (1), it shall include in the notice referred to therein a statement of its reasons therefor.
1980–81–82–83, c. 143, s. 9.

Opportunity to make representations
19. (1) Before making its decision on an application or rescinding approval of a plan pursuant to section 17 or 18, the Canadian Human Rights Commission shall afford each person directly concerned with the matter an opportunity to make representations with respect thereto.

Restriction on deeming plan inappropriate
(2) For the purposes of sections 17 and 18, a plan shall not, by reason only that it does

not conform to any standards prescribed pursuant to section 24, be deemed to be inappropriate for meeting the needs of persons arising from disability.
1980–81–82–83, c. 143, s. 9.

Certain provisions not discriminatory
20. A provision of a pension or insurance fund or plan that preserves rights acquired before March 1, 1978 or that preserves pension or other benefits accrued before that day does not constitute the basis for a complaint under Part III that an employer, employee organization or employer organization is engaging or has engaged in a discriminatory practice.
R.S., 1985, c. H-6, s. 20; 1998, c. 9, s. 17.

Funds and plans
21. The establishment of separate pension funds or plans for different groups of employees does not constitute the basis for a complaint under Part III that an employer, employee organization or employer organization is engaging or has engaged in a discriminatory practice if the employees are not grouped in those funds or plans according to a prohibited ground of discrimination.
R.S., 1985, c. H-6, s. 21; 1998, c. 9, s. 17.

Regulations
22. The Governor in Council may, by regulation, prescribe the provisions of any pension or insurance fund or plan, in addition to the provisions described in sections 20 and 21, that do not constitute the basis for a complaint under Part III that an employer, employee organization or employer organization is engaging or has engaged in a discriminatory practice.
R.S., 1985, c. H-6, s. 22; 1998, c. 9, s. 17.

Regulations
23. The Governor in Council may make regulations respecting the terms and conditions to be included in or applicable to any contract, licence or grant made or granted by Her Majesty in right of Canada providing for
(a) the prohibition of discriminatory practices described in sections 5 to 14.1; and
(b) the resolution, by the procedure set out in Part III, of complaints of discriminatory practices contrary to such terms and conditions.
R.S., 1985, c. H-6, s. 23; 1998, c. 9, s. 18.

Accessibility standards
24. (1) The Governor in Council may, for the benefit of persons having any disability, make regulations prescribing standards of accessibility to services, facilities or premises.

Effect of meeting accessibility standards
(2) Where standards prescribed pursuant to subsection (1) are met in providing access to any services, facilities or premises, a matter of access thereto does not constitute any basis for a complaint under Part III regarding discrimination based on any disability in respect of which the standards are prescribed.

Publication of proposed regulations
(3) Subject to subsection (4), a copy of each regulation that the Governor in Council proposes to make pursuant to this section shall be published in the Canada Gazette and a reasonable opportunity shall be afforded to interested persons to make representations with respect thereto.

Exception
(4) Subsection (3) does not apply in respect of a proposed regulation that has been published pursuant to that subsection, whether or not it has been amended as a result of representations made pursuant to that subsection.

Discriminatory practice not constituted by variance from standards
(5) Nothing shall, by virtue only of its being at variance with any standards prescribed pursuant to subsection (1), be deemed to constitute a discriminatory practice.
1980–81–82–83, c. 143, s. 11.

Definitions
25. In this Act,
"conviction for which a pardon has been granted" means a conviction of an individual for an offence in respect of which a pardon has been granted by any authority under law and, if granted or issued under the Criminal Records Act, has not been revoked or ceased to have effect;
"disability" means any previous or existing mental or physical disability and includes disfigurement and previous or existing dependence on alcohol or a drug.
"employee organization" includes a trade union or other organization of employees or a local, the purposes of which include the negotiation of terms and conditions of employment on behalf of employees;
"employer organization" means an organization of employers the purposes of which include the regulation of relations between employers and employees;
"employment" includes a contractual relationship with an individual for the provision of services personally by the individual;
"Tribunal" means the Canadian Human Rights Tribunal established by section 48.1.
R.S., 1985, c. H-6, s. 25; 1992, c. 22, s. 13; 1998, c. 9, s. 19.

PART II
Canadian Human Rights Commission

Commission established
26. (1) A commission is hereby established to be known as the Canadian Human Rights Commission, in this Part and Part III referred to as the "Commission", consisting of a Chief Commissioner, a Deputy Chief Commissioner and not less than three or more than six other members, to be appointed by the Governor in Council.

Members
(2) The Chief Commissioner and Deputy Chief Commissioner are full-time members of the Commission and the other members may be appointed as full-time or part-time members of the Commission.

Term of appointment
(3) Each full-time member of the Commission may be appointed for a term not exceeding seven years and each part-time member may be appointed for a term not exceeding three years.

Tenure
(4) Each member of the Commission holds office during good behaviour but may be removed by the Governor in Council on address of the Senate and House of Commons.

Re-appointment
(5) A member of the Commission is eligible to be re-appointed in the same or another capacity.
1976–77, c. 33, s. 21.

Powers, Duties and Functions
27. (1) In addition to its duties under Part III with respect to complaints regarding discriminatory practices, the Commission is generally responsible for the administration of this Part and Parts I and III and
(a) shall develop and conduct information programs to foster public understanding of this Act and of the role and activities of the Commission thereunder and to foster

public recognition of the principle described in section 2;
(b) shall undertake or sponsor research programs relating to its duties and functions under this Act and respecting the principle described in section 2;
(c) shall maintain close liaison with similar bodies or authorities in the provinces in order to foster common policies and practices and to avoid conflicts respecting the handling of complaints in cases of overlapping jurisdiction;
(d) shall perform duties and functions to be performed by it pursuant to any agreement entered into under subsection 28(2);
(e) may consider such recommendations, suggestions and requests concerning human rights and freedoms as it receives from any source and, where deemed by the Commission to be appropriate, include in a report referred to in section 61 reference to and comment on any such recommendation, suggestion or request;
(f) shall carry out or cause to be carried out such studies concerning human rights and freedoms as may be referred to it by the Minister of Justice and include in a report referred to in section 61 a report setting out the results of each such study together with such recommendations in relation thereto as it considers appropriate;
(g) may review any regulations, rules, orders, by-laws and other instruments made pursuant to an Act of Parliament and, where deemed by the Commission to be appropriate, include in a report referred to in section 61 reference to and comment on any provision thereof that in its opinion is inconsistent with the principle described in section 2; and
(h) shall, so far as is practical and consistent with the application of Part III, try by persuasion, publicity or any other means that it considers appropriate to discourage and reduce discriminatory practices referred to in sections 5 to 14.1.

Guidelines
(2) The Commission may, on application or on its own initiative, by order, issue a guideline setting out the extent to which and the manner in which, in the opinion of the Commission, any provision of this Act applies in a class of cases described in the guideline.

Guideline binding
(3) A guideline issued under subsection (2) is, until it is revoked or modified, binding on the Commission and any member or panel assigned under subsection 49(2) with respect to the resolution of a complaint under Part III regarding a case falling within the description contained in the guideline.

Publication
(4) Each guideline issued under subsection (2) shall be published in Part II of the Canada Gazette.
R.S., 1985, c. H-6, s. 27; 1998, c. 9, s. 20.

Assignment of duties
28. (1) On the recommendation of the Commission, the Governor in Council may, by order, assign to persons or classes of persons specified in the order who are engaged in the performance of the duties and functions of the Department of Human Resources Development such of the duties and functions of the Commission in relation to discriminatory practices in employment outside the public service of Canada as are specified in the order.

Interdelegation
(2) Subject to the approval of the Governor in Council, the Commission may enter into agreements with similar bodies or authorities in the provinces providing for the performance by the Commission on behalf of those bodies or authorities of duties or functions specified in the agreements or for the performance by those bodies or authorities on behalf of the Commission of duties or functions so specified.
R.S., 1985, c. H-6, s. 28; 1996, c. 11, s. 61.

Regulations
29. The Governor in Council, on the recommendation of the Commission, may make

regulations authorizing the Commission to exercise such powers and perform such duties and functions, in addition to those prescribed by this Act, as are necessary to carry out the provisions of this Part and Parts I and III.
1976–77, c. 33, s. 23.

Remuneration
Salaries and remuneration
30. (1) Each full-time member of the Commission shall be paid a salary to be fixed by the Governor in Council and each part-time member of the Commission may be paid such remuneration, as is prescribed by by-law of the Commission, for attendance at meetings of the Commission, or of any division or committee of the Commission, that the member is requested by the Chief Commissioner to attend.

Additional remuneration
(2) A part-time member of the Commission may, for any period during which that member, with the approval of the Chief Commissioner, performs any duties and functions additional to the normal duties and functions of that member on behalf of the Commission, be paid such additional remuneration as is prescribed by by-law of the Commission.

Travel expenses
(3) Each member of the Commission is entitled to be paid such travel and living expenses incurred by the member in the performance of duties and functions under this Act as are prescribed by by-law of the Commission.
1976–77, c. 33, s. 24.

Officers and Staff
Chief Commissioner
31. (1) The Chief Commissioner is the chief executive officer of the Commission and has supervision over and direction of the Commission and its staff and shall preside at meetings of the Commission.

Absence or incapacity
(2) In the event of the absence or incapacity of the Chief Commissioner, or if that office is vacant, the Deputy Chief Commissioner has all the powers and may perform all the duties and functions of the Chief Commissioner.

Idem
(3) In the event of the absence or incapacity of the Chief Commissioner and the Deputy Chief Commissioner, or if those offices are vacant, the full-time member with the most seniority has all the powers and may perform all the duties and functions of the Chief Commissioner.
1976–77, c. 33, s. 25.

Staff
32. (1) Such officers and employees as are necessary for the proper conduct of the work of the Commission shall be appointed in accordance with the Public Service Employment Act.

Contractual assistance
(2) The Commission may, for specific projects, enter into contracts for the services of persons having technical or specialized knowledge of any matter relating to the work of the Commission to advise and assist the Commission in the exercise of its powers or the performance of its duties and functions under this Act, and those persons may be paid such remuneration and expenses as may be prescribed by by-law of the Commission.
1976–77, c. 33, s. 26.

Compliance with security requirements
33. (1) Every member of the Commission and every person employed by the Commission

who is required to receive or obtain information relating to any investigation under this Act shall, with respect to access to and the use of such information, comply with any security requirements applicable to, and take any oath of secrecy required to be taken by, individuals who normally have access to and use of such information.

Disclosure

(2) Every member of the Commission and every person employed by the Commission shall take every reasonable precaution to avoid disclosing any matter the disclosure of which

(a) might be injurious to international relations, national defence or security or federal-provincial relations;

(b) would disclose a confidence of the Queen's Privy Council for Canada;

(c) would be likely to disclose information obtained or prepared by any investigative body of the Government of Canada

  (i) in relation to national security,

  (ii) in the course of investigations pertaining to the detection or suppression of crime generally, or

  (iii) in the course of investigations pertaining to particular offences against any Act of Parliament;

(d) might, in respect of any individual under sentence for an offence against any Act of Parliament,

  (i) lead to a serious disruption of that individual's institutional, parole or mandatory supervision program,

  (ii) reveal information originally obtained on a promise of confidentiality, express or implied, or

  (iii) result in physical or other harm to that individual or any other person;

(e) might impede the functioning of a court of law, or a quasi-judicial board, commission or other tribunal or any inquiry established under the Inquiries Act; or

(f) might disclose legal opinions or advice provided to a government department or body or privileged communications between lawyer and client in a matter of government business.

1976–77, c. 33, s. 27.

Head office

34. (1) The head office of the Commission shall be in the National Capital Region described in the schedule to the National Capital Act.

Other offices

(2) The Commission may establish such regional or branch offices, not exceeding twelve, as it considers necessary to carry out its powers, duties and functions under this Act.

Meetings

(3) The Commission may meet for the conduct of its affairs at such times and in such places as the Chief Commissioner considers necessary or desirable.

1976–77, c. 33, s. 28.

Majority is a decision of the Commission

35. A decision of the majority of the members present at a meeting of the Commission, if the members present constitute a quorum, is a decision of the Commission.

1976–77, c. 33, s. 28.

Establishment of divisions

36. (1) For the purposes of the affairs of the Commission, the Chief Commissioner may establish divisions of the Commission and all or any of the powers, duties and functions of the Commission, except the making of by-laws, may, as directed by the Commission, be exercised or performed by all or any of those divisions.

Designation of presiding officer
(2) Where a division of the Commission has been established pursuant to subsection (1), the Chief Commissioner may designate one of the members of the division to act as the presiding officer of the division.
1976–77, c. 33, s. 28.

By-laws
37. (1) The Commission may make by-laws for the conduct of its affairs and, without limiting the generality of the foregoing, may make by-laws

(a) respecting the calling of meetings of the Commission or any division thereof and the fixing of quorums for the purposes of those meetings;
(b) respecting the conduct of business at meetings of the Commission or any division thereof;
(c) respecting the establishment of committees of the Commission, the delegation of powers, duties and functions to those committees and the fixing of quorums for meetings thereof;
(d) respecting the procedure to be followed in dealing with complaints under Part III that have arisen in the Yukon Territory, the Northwest Territories or Nunavut;
(e) prescribing the rates of remuneration to be paid to part-time members of the Commission and any person engaged under subsection 32(2); and
(f) prescribing reasonable rates of travel and living expenses to be paid to members of the Commission and any person engaged under subsection 32(2).

Treasury Board approval
(2) No by-law made under paragraph (1)(e) or (f) has effect unless it is approved by the Treasury Board.
R.S., 1985, c. H-6, s. 37; 1993, c. 28, s. 78; 1998, c. 9, s. 21.

Superannuation, etc.

38. The full-time members of the Commission are deemed to be persons employed in the Public Service for the purposes of the Public Service Superannuation Act and to be employed in the public service of Canada for the purposes of the Government Employees Compensation Act and any regulations made under section 9 of the Aeronautics Act.
1976–77, c. 33, s. 30.

PART III

DISCRIMINATORY PRACTICES AND GENERAL PROVISIONS

Definition of "discriminatory practice"
39. For the purposes of this Part, a "discriminatory practice" means any practice that is a discriminatory practice within the meaning of sections 5 to 14.1.
R.S., 1985, c. H-6, s. 39; 1998, c. 9, s. 22.

Complaints
40. (1) Subject to subsections (5) and (7), any individual or group of individuals having reasonable grounds for believing that a person is engaging or has engaged in a discriminatory practice may file with the Commission a complaint in a form acceptable to the Commission.

Consent of victim
(2) If a complaint is made by someone other than the individual who is alleged to be the victim of the discriminatory practice to which the complaint relates, the Commission may refuse to deal with the complaint unless the alleged victim consents thereto.

Investigation commenced by Commission
(3) Where the Commission has reasonable grounds for believing that a person is engaging or has engaged in a discriminatory practice, the Commission may initiate a complaint.

Limitation
(3.1) No complaint may be initiated under subsection (3) as a result of information obtained by the Commission in the course of the administration of the Employment Equity Act.

Complaints may be dealt with together
(4) If complaints are filed jointly or separately by more than one individual or group alleging that a particular person is engaging or has engaged in a discriminatory practice or a series of similar discriminatory practices and the Commission is satisfied that the complaints involve substantially the same issues of fact and law, it may deal with the complaints together under this Part and may request the Chairperson of the Tribunal to institute a single inquiry into the complaints under section 49.

No complaints to be considered in certain cases
(5) No complaint in relation to a discriminatory practice may be dealt with by the Commission under this Part unless the act or omission that constitutes the practice
(a) occurred in Canada and the victim of the practice was at the time of the act or omission either lawfully present in Canada or, if temporarily absent from Canada, entitled to return to Canada;
(b) occurred in Canada and was a discriminatory practice within the meaning of section 5, 8, 10, 12 or 13 in respect of which no particular individual is identifiable as the victim; or
(c) occurred outside Canada and the victim of the practice was at the time of the act or omission a Canadian citizen or an individual lawfully admitted to Canada for permanent residence.

Determination of status
(6) Where a question arises under subsection (5) as to the status of an individual in relation to a complaint, the Commission shall refer the question of status to the appropriate Minister and shall not proceed with the complaint unless the question of status is resolved thereby in favour of the complainant.

No complaints to be dealt with in certain cases
(7) No complaint may be dealt with by the Commission pursuant to subsection (1) that relates to the terms and conditions of a superannuation or pension fund or plan, if the relief sought would require action to be taken that would deprive any contributor to, participant in or member of, the fund or plan of any rights acquired under the fund or plan before March 1, 1978 or of any pension or other benefits accrued under the fund or plan to that date, including
(a) any rights and benefits based on a particular age of retirement; and
(b) any accrued survivor's benefits.
R.S., 1985, c. H-6, s. 40; R.S., 1985, c. 31 (1st Supp.), s. 62; 1995, c. 44, s. 47; 1998, c. 9, s. 23.

Definitions
40.1 (1) In this section,
"designated groups" has the meaning assigned in section 3 of the Employment Equity Act;
"employer" means a person who or organization that discharges the obligations of an employer under the Employment Equity Act.

Employment equity complaints
(2) No complaint may be dealt with by the Commission pursuant to section 40 where
(a) the complaint is made against an employer alleging that the employer has engaged in a discriminatory practice set out in section 7 or paragraph 10(a); and
(b) the complaint is based solely on statistical information that purports to show that members of one or more designated groups are underrepresented in the employer's workforce.

1995, c. 44, s. 48.

Commission to deal with complaint
41. (1) Subject to section 40, the Commission shall deal with any complaint filed with it unless in respect of that complaint it appears to the Commission that
(a) the alleged victim of the discriminatory practice to which the complaint relates ought to exhaust grievance or review procedures otherwise reasonably available;
(b) the complaint is one that could more appropriately be dealt with, initially or completely, according to a procedure provided for under an Act of Parliament other than this Act;
(c) the complaint is beyond the jurisdiction of the Commission;
(d) the complaint is trivial, frivolous, vexatious or made in bad faith; or
(e) the complaint is based on acts or omissions the last of which occurred more than one year, or such longer period of time as the Commission considers appropriate in the circumstances, before receipt of the complaint.

Commission may decline to deal with complaint
(2) The Commission may decline to deal with a complaint referred to in paragraph (a) in respect of an employer where it is of the opinion that the matter has been adequately dealt with in the employer's employment equity plan prepared pursuant to section 10 of the Employment Equity Act.

Meaning of "employer"
(3) In this section, "employer" means a person who or organization that discharges the obligations of an employer under the Employment Equity Act.
R.S., 1985, c. H-6, s. 41; 1994, c. 26, s. 34(F); 1995, c. 44, s. 49.

Notice
42. (1) Subject to subsection (2), when the Commission decides not to deal with a complaint, it shall send a written notice of its decision to the complainant setting out the reason for its decision.

Attributing fault for delay
(2) Before deciding that a complaint will not be dealt with because a procedure referred to in paragraph 41(a) has not been exhausted, the Commission shall satisfy itself that the failure to exhaust the procedure was attributable to the complainant and not to another.
1976–77, c. 33, s. 34.

Investigation
Designation of investigator
43. (1) The Commission may designate a person, in this Part referred to as an "investigator", to investigate a complaint.

Manner of investigation
(2) An investigator shall investigate a complaint in a manner authorized by regulations made pursuant to subsection (4).

Power to enter
(2.1) Subject to such limitations as the Governor in Council may prescribe in the interests of national defence or security, an investigator with a warrant issued under subsection (2.2) may, at any reasonable time, enter and search any premises in order to carry out such inquiries as are reasonably necessary for the investigation of a complaint.

Authority to issue warrant
(2.2) Where on ex parte application a judge of the Federal Court is satisfied by information on oath that there are reasonable grounds to believe that there is in any premises any evidence relevant to the investigation of a complaint, the judge may issue a warrant under the judge's hand authorizing the investigator named therein to enter and search those

premises for any such evidence subject to such conditions as may be specified in the warrant.

Use of force
(2.3) In executing a warrant issued under subsection (2.2), the investigator named therein shall not use force unless the investigator is accompanied by a peace officer and the use of force has been specifically authorized in the warrant.

Production of books
(2.4) An investigator may require any individual found in any premises entered pursuant to this section to produce for inspection or for the purpose of obtaining copies thereof or extracts therefrom any books or other documents containing any matter relevant to the investigation being conducted by the investigator.

Obstruction
(3) No person shall obstruct an investigator in the investigation of a complaint.

Regulations
(4) The Governor in Council may make regulations
(a) prescribing procedures to be followed by investigators;
(b) authorizing the manner in which complaints are to be investigated pursuant to this Part; and
(c) prescribing limitations for the purpose of subsection (2.1).
R.S., 1985, c. H-6, s. 43; R.S., 1985, c. 31 (1st Supp.), s. 63.

Report
44. (1) An investigator shall, as soon as possible after the conclusion of an investigation, submit to the Commission a report of the findings of the investigation.

Action on receipt of report
(2) If, on receipt of a report referred to in subsection (1), the Commission is satisfied
(a) that the complainant ought to exhaust grievance or review procedures otherwise reasonably available, or
(b) that the complaint could more appropriately be dealt with, initially or completely, by means of a procedure provided for under an Act of Parliament other than this Act, it shall refer the complainant to the appropriate authority.

Idem
(3) On receipt of a report referred to in subsection (1), the Commission
(a) may request the Chairperson of the Tribunal to institute an inquiry under section 49 into the complaint to which the report relates if the Commission is satisfied
  (i) that, having regard to all the circumstances of the complaint, an inquiry into the complaint is warranted, and
  (ii) that the complaint to which the report relates should not be referred pursuant to subsection (2) or dismissed on any ground mentioned in paragraphs 41(c) to (e); or
(b) shall dismiss the complaint to which the report relates if it is satisfied
  (i) that, having regard to all the circumstances of the complaint, an inquiry into the complaint is not warranted, or
  (ii) that the complaint should be dismissed on any ground mentioned in paragraphs 41(c) to (e).

Notice
(4) After receipt of a report referred to in subsection (1), the Commission
(a) shall notify in writing the complainant and the person against whom the complaint was made of its action under subsection (2) or (3); and
(b) may, in such manner as it sees fit, notify any other person whom it considers necessary to notify of its action under subsection (2) or (3).
R.S., 1985, c. H-6, s. 44; R.S., 1985, c. 31 (1st Supp.), s. 64; 1998, c. 9, s. 24.

Definition of "Review Committee"
45. (1) In this section and section 46, "Review Committee" has the meaning assigned to that expression by the Canadian Security Intelligence Service Act.

Complaint involving security considerations
(2) When, at any stage after the filing of a complaint and before the commencement of a hearing before a member or panel in respect of the complaint, the Commission receives written notice from a minister of the Crown that the practice to which the complaint relates was based on considerations relating to the security of Canada, the Commission may
(a) dismiss the complaint; or
(b) refer the matter to the Review Committee.

Notice
(3) After receipt of a notice mentioned in subsection (2), the Commission
(a) shall notify in writing the complainant and the person against whom the complaint was made of its action under paragraph (2)(a) or (b); and
(b) may, in such manner as it sees fit, notify any other person whom it considers necessary to notify of its action under paragraph 2(a) or (b).

Stay of procedures
(4) Where the Commission has referred the matter to the Review Committee pursuant to paragraph (2)(b), it shall not deal with the complaint until the Review Committee has, pursuant to subsection 46(1), provided it with a report in relation to the matter.

Application of the Canadian Security Intelligence Service Act
(5) Where a matter is referred to the Review Committee pursuant to paragraph (2)(b), subsections 39(2) and (3) and sections 43, 44 and 47 to 51 of the Canadian Security Intelligence Service Act apply, with such modifications as the circumstances require, to the matter as if the referral were a complaint made pursuant to section 42 of that Act except that a reference in any of those provisions to "deputy head" shall be read as a reference to the minister referred to in subsection (2).

Statement to be sent to person affected
(6) The Review Committee shall, as soon as practicable after a matter in relation to a complaint is referred to it pursuant to paragraph (2)(b), send to the complainant a statement summarizing such information available to it as will enable the complainant to be as fully informed as possible of the circumstances giving rise to the referral.
R.S., 1985, c. H-6, s. 45; 1998, c. 9, s. 25.

Report
46. (1) On completion of its investigation under section 45, the Review Committee shall, not later than forty-five days after the matter is referred to it pursuant to paragraph 45(2)(b), provide the Commission, the minister referred to in subsection 45(2) and the complainant with a report containing the findings of the Committee.

Action on receipt of report
(2) After considering a report provided pursuant to subsection (1), the Commission
(a) may dismiss the complaint or, where it does not do so, shall proceed to deal with the complaint pursuant to this Part; and
(b) shall notify, in writing, the complainant and the person against whom the complaint was made of its action under paragraph (a) and may, in such manner as it sees fit, notify any other person whom it considers necessary to notify of that action.
1984, c. 21, s. 73.

Conciliator
Appointment of conciliator
47. (1) Subject to subsection (2), the Commission may, on the filing of a complaint, or if the complaint has not been

(a) settled in the course of investigation by an investigator,
(b) referred or dismissed under subsection 44(2) or (3) or paragraph 45(2)(a) or 46(2)(a), or
(c) settled after receipt by the parties of the notice referred to in subsection 44(4),
appoint a person, in this Part referred to as a "conciliator", for the purpose of attempting to bring about a settlement of the complaint.

Eligibility
(2) A person is not eligible to act as a conciliator in respect of a complaint if that person has already acted as an investigator in respect of that complaint.

Confidentiality
(3) Any information received by a conciliator in the course of attempting to reach a settlement of a complaint is confidential and may not be disclosed except with the consent of the person who gave the information.
1976–77, c. 33, s. 37; 1984, c. 21, s. 74.

Settlement
Referral of a settlement to Commission
48. (1) When, at any stage after the filing of a complaint and before the commencement of a hearing before a Human Rights Tribunal in respect thereof, a settlement is agreed on by the parties, the terms of the settlement shall be referred to the Commission for approval or rejection.

Certificate
(2) If the Commission approves or rejects the terms of a settlement referred to in subsection (1), it shall so certify and notify the parties.

Enforcement of settlement
(3) A settlement approved under this section may, for the purpose of enforcement, be made an order of the Federal Court on application to that Court by the Commission or a party to the settlement.
R.S., 1985, c. H-6, s. 48; 1998, c. 9, s. 26.

CANADIAN HUMAN RIGHTS TRIBUNAL

Establishment of Tribunal
48.1 (1) There is hereby established a tribunal to be known as the Canadian Human Rights Tribunal consisting, subject to subsection (6), of a maximum of fifteen members, including a Chairperson and a Vice-chairperson, as may be appointed by the Governor in Council.

Qualifications for appointment of members
(2) Persons appointed as members of the Tribunal must have experience, expertise and interest in, and sensitivity to, human rights.

Legal qualifications
(3) The Chairperson and Vice-chairperson must be members in good standing of the bar of a province or the Chambre des notaires du Québec for at least ten years and at least two of the other members of the Tribunal must be members in good standing of the bar of a province or the Chambre des notaires du Québec.

Regional representation
(4) Appointments are to be made having regard to the need for regional representation in the membership of the Tribunal.

Appointment of temporary members – incapacity
(5) If a member is absent or incapacitated, the Governor in Council may, despite subsection (1), appoint a temporary substitute member to act during the absence or incapacity.

Appointment of temporary members – workload
(6) The Governor in Council may appoint temporary members to the Tribunal for a term of not more than three years whenever, in the opinion of the Governor in Council, the workload of the Tribunal so requires.
R.S., 1985, c. 31 (1st Supp.), s. 65; 1998, c. 9, s. 27.

Terms of office
48.2 (1) The Chairperson and Vice-chairperson are to be appointed to hold office during good behaviour for terms of not more than seven years, and the other members are to be appointed to hold office during good behaviour for terms of not more than five years, but the Chairperson may be removed from office by the Governor in Council for cause and the Vice-chairperson and the other members may be subject to remedial or disciplinary measures in accordance with section 48.3.

Acting after expiration of appointment
(2) A member whose appointment expires may, with the approval of the Chairperson, conclude any inquiry that the member has begun, and a person performing duties under this subsection is deemed to be a part-time member for the purposes of sections 48.3, 48.6, 50 and 52 to 58.

Reappointment
(3) The Chairperson, Vice-chairperson or any other member whose term has expired is eligible for reappointment in the same or any other capacity.
R.S., 1985, c. 31 (1st Supp.), s. 65; 1998, c. 9, s. 27.

Remedial and disciplinary measures
48.3 (1) The Chairperson of the Tribunal may request the Minister of Justice to decide whether a member should be subject to remedial or disciplinary measures for any reason set out in paragraphs (13)(a) to (d).

Measures
(2) On receipt of the request, the Minister may take one or more of the following measures:
(a) obtain, in an informal and expeditious manner, any information that the Minister considers necessary;
(b) refer the matter for mediation, if the Minister is satisfied that the issues in relation to the request may be appropriately resolved by mediation;
(c) request of the Governor in Council that an inquiry be held under subsection (3); or
(d) advise the Chairperson that the Minister considers that it is not necessary to take further measures under this Act.

Appointment of inquirer
(3) On receipt of a request referred to in paragraph (2)(c), the Governor in Council may, on the recommendation of the Minister, appoint a judge of a superior court to conduct the inquiry.

Powers
(4) The judge has all the powers, rights and privileges that are vested in a superior court, including the power to
(a) issue a summons requiring any person to appear at the time and place specified in the summons in order to testify about all matters within the person's knowledge relative to the inquiry and to produce any document or thing relative to the inquiry that the person has or controls; and
(b) administer oaths and examine any person on oath.

Staff

(5) The judge may engage the services of counsel and other persons having technical or specialized knowledge to assist the judge in conducting the inquiry, and may establish the terms and conditions of their engagement and, with the approval of the Treasury Board, fix and pay their remuneration and expenses.

Inquiry in public

(6) Subject to subsections (7) and (8), an inquiry shall be conducted in public.

Confidentiality of inquiry

(7) The judge may, on application, take any appropriate measures and make any order that the judge considers necessary to ensure the confidentiality of the inquiry if, after having considered all available alternative measures, the judge is satisfied that

(a) there is a real and substantial risk that matters involving public security will be disclosed;

(b) there is a real and substantial risk to the fairness of the inquiry such that the need to prevent disclosure outweighs the societal interest that the inquiry be conducted in public; or

(c) there is a serious possibility that the life, liberty or security of a person will be endangered.

Confidentiality of application

(8) If the judge considers it appropriate, the judge may take any measures and make any order that the judge considers necessary to ensure the confidentiality of a hearing held in respect of an application under subsection (7).

Rules of evidence

(9) In conducting an inquiry, the judge is not bound by any legal or technical rules of evidence and may receive, and base a decision on, evidence presented in the proceedings that the judge considers credible or trustworthy in the circumstances of the case.

Intervenors

(10) An interested party may, with leave of the judge, intervene in an inquiry on any terms and conditions that the judge considers appropriate.

Right to be heard

(11) The member who is the subject of the inquiry shall be given reasonable notice of the subject-matter of the inquiry and of the time and place of any hearing and shall be given an opportunity, in person or by counsel, to be heard at the hearing, to cross-examine witnesses and to present evidence.

Report to Minister

(12) After an inquiry has been completed, the judge shall submit a report containing the judge's findings and recommendations, if any, to the Minister.

Recommendations

(13) The judge may, in the report, recommend that the member be suspended without pay or removed from office or that any other disciplinary measure or any remedial measure be taken if, in the judge's opinion, the member

(a) has become incapacitated from the proper execution of that office by reason of infirmity;

(b) has been guilty of misconduct;

(c) has failed in the proper execution of that office; or

(d) has been placed, by conduct or otherwise, in a position that is incompatible with the due execution of that office.

Transmission of report to Governor in Council

(14) When the Minister receives the report, the Minister shall send it to the Governor

in Council who may, if the Governor in Council considers it appropriate, suspend the member without pay, remove the member from office or impose any other disciplinary measure or any remedial measure.
R.S., 1985, c. 31 (1st Supp.), s. 65; 1998, c. 9, s. 27.

Status of members
48.4 (1) The Chairperson and Vice-chairperson are to be appointed as full-time members of the Tribunal, and the other members are to be appointed as either full-time or part-time members.

Functions of Chairperson
(2) The Chairperson is the chief executive officer of the Tribunal and has supervision over and direction of its work, including the allocation of work among the members and the management of the Tribunal's internal affairs.

Functions of Vice-chairperson
(3) The Vice-chairperson shall assist the Chairperson and shall perform the functions of the Chairperson if the Chairperson is absent or unable to act or the office of Chairperson is vacant.

Acting Chairperson
(4) The Governor in Council may authorize a member of the Tribunal to perform the functions of the Chairperson on a temporary basis if the Chairperson and Vice-chairperson are absent or unable to act or if both of those offices are vacant.
R.S., 1985, c. 31 (1st Supp.), s. 65; 1998, c. 9, s. 27.

Residence
48.5 The full-time members of the Tribunal shall reside in the National Capital Region, as described in the schedule to the National Capital Act, or within forty kilometres of that Region.
R.S., 1985, c. 31 (1st Supp.), s. 65; 1998, c. 9, s. 27.

Remuneration
48.6 (1) The members of the Tribunal shall be paid such remuneration as may be fixed by the Governor in Council.

Travel expenses
(2) Members are entitled to be paid travel and living expenses incurred in carrying out duties as members of the Tribunal while absent from their place of residence, but the expenses must not exceed the maximum limits authorized by the Treasury Board directives for employees of the Government of Canada.

Deemed employment in public service of Canada
(3) Members are deemed to be employed in the public service of Canada for the purposes of the Government Employees Compensation Act and any regulations made under section 9 of the Aeronautics Act.
1998, c. 9, s. 27.

Head office
48.7 The head office of the Tribunal shall be in the National Capital Region, as described in the schedule to the National Capital Act.
1998, c. 9, s. 27.

Registrar and other staff
48.8 (1) The registrar and the other officers and employees necessary for the proper conduct of the work of the Tribunal shall be appointed in accordance with the Public Service Employment Act.

Technical experts
(2) The Chairperson may engage persons having technical or special knowledge to assist

or advise members of the Tribunal in any matter and may, with the approval of the Treasury Board, fix their remuneration and reimburse their expenses in the same manner as the expenses of members of the Tribunal are reimbursed.
1998, c. 9, s. 27.

Conduct of proceedings
48.9 (1) Proceedings before the Tribunal shall be conducted as informally and expeditiously as the requirements of natural justice and the rules of procedure allow.

Tribunal rules of procedure
(2) The Chairperson may make rules of procedure governing the practice and procedure before the Tribunal, including, but not limited to, rules governing
(a) the giving of notices to parties;
(b) the addition of parties and interested persons to the proceedings;
(c) the summoning of witnesses;
(d) the production and service of documents;
(e) discovery proceedings;
(f) pre-hearing conferences;
(g) the introduction of evidence;
(h) time limits within which hearings must be held and decisions must be made; and
(i) awards of interest.

Publication of proposed rules
(3) Subject to subsection (4), a copy of each rule that the Tribunal proposes to make shall be published in the Canada Gazette and a reasonable opportunity shall be given to interested persons to make representations with respect to it.

Exception
(4) A proposed rule need not be published more than once, whether or not it has been amended as a result of any representations.
1998, c. 9, s. 27.

Inquiries into Complaints
Request for inquiry
49. (1) At any stage after the filing of a complaint, the Commission may request the Chairperson of the Tribunal to institute an inquiry into the complaint if the Commission is satisfied that, having regard to all the circumstances of the complaint, an inquiry is warranted.

Chairperson to institute inquiry
(2) On receipt of a request, the Chairperson shall institute an inquiry by assigning a member of the Tribunal to inquire into the complaint, but the Chairperson may assign a panel of three members if he or she considers that the complexity of the complaint requires the inquiry to be conducted by three members.

Chair of panel
(3) If a panel of three members has been assigned to inquire into the complaint, the Chairperson shall designate one of them to chair the inquiry, but the Chairperson shall chair the inquiry if he or she is a member of the panel.

Copy of rules to parties
(4) The Chairperson shall make a copy of the rules of procedure available to each party to the complaint.

Qualification of member
(5) If the complaint involves a question about whether another Act or a regulation made under another Act is inconsistent with this Act or a regulation made under it, the member assigned to inquire into the complaint or, if three members have been assigned, the

member chairing the inquiry, must be a member of the bar of a province or the Chambre des notaires du Québec.

Question raised subsequently
(6) If a question as described in subsection (5) arises after a member or panel has been assigned and the requirements of that subsection are not met, the inquiry shall nevertheless proceed with the member or panel as designated.
R.S., 1985, c. H-6, s. 49; R.S., 1985, c. 31 (1st Supp.), s. 66; 1998, c. 9, s. 27.

Conduct of inquiry
50. (1) After due notice to the Commission, the complainant, the person against whom the complaint was made and, at the discretion of the member or panel conducting the inquiry, any other interested party, the member or panel shall inquire into the complaint and shall give all parties to whom notice has been given a full and ample opportunity, in person or through counsel, to appear at the inquiry, present evidence and make representations.

Power to determine questions of law or fact
(2) In the course of hearing and determining any matter under inquiry, the member or panel may decide all questions of law or fact necessary to determining the matter.

Additional powers
(3) In relation to a hearing of the inquiry, the member or panel may
(a) in the same manner and to the same extent as a superior court of record, summon and enforce the attendance of witnesses and compel them to give oral or written evidence on oath and to produce any documents and things that the member or panel considers necessary for the full hearing and consideration of the complaint;
(b) administer oaths;
(c) subject to subsections (4) and (5), receive and accept any evidence and other information, whether on oath or by affidavit or otherwise, that the member or panel sees fit, whether or not that evidence or information is or would be admissible in a court of law;
(d) lengthen or shorten any time limit established by the rules of procedure; and
(e) decide any procedural or evidentiary question arising during the hearing.

Limitation in relation to evidence
(4) The member or panel may not admit or accept as evidence anything that would be inadmissible in a court by reason of any privilege under the law of evidence.

Conciliators as witnesses
(5) A conciliator appointed to settle the complaint is not a competent or compellable witness at the hearing.

Witness fees
(6) Any person summoned to attend the hearing is entitled in the discretion of the member or panel to receive the same fees and allowances as those paid to persons summoned to attend before the Federal Court.
R.S., 1985, c. H-6, s. 50; 1998, c. 9, s. 27.

Duty of Commission on appearing
51. In appearing at a hearing, presenting evidence and making representations, the Commission shall adopt such position as, in its opinion, is in the public interest having regard to the nature of the complaint.
R.S., 1985, c. H-6, s. 51; 1998, c. 9, s. 27.

Hearing in public subject to confidentiality order
52. (1) An inquiry shall be conducted in public, but the member or panel conducting the inquiry may, on application, take any measures and make any order that the member or panel considers necessary to ensure the confidentiality of the inquiry if the member or

panel is satisfied, during the inquiry or as a result of the inquiry being conducted in public, that

(a) there is a real and substantial risk that matters involving public security will be disclosed;
(b) there is a real and substantial risk to the fairness of the inquiry such that the need to prevent disclosure outweighs the societal interest that the inquiry be conducted in public;
(c) there is a real and substantial risk that the disclosure of personal or other matters will cause undue hardship to the persons involved such that the need to prevent disclosure outweighs the societal interest that the inquiry be conducted in public; or
(d) there is a serious possibility that the life, liberty or security of a person will be endangered.

Confidentiality of application

(2) If the member or panel considers it appropriate, the member or panel may take any measures and make any order that the member or panel considers necessary to ensure the confidentiality of a hearing held in respect of an application under subsection (1). R.S., 1985, c. H-6, s. 52; 1998, c. 9, s. 27.

Complaint dismissed

53. (1) At the conclusion of an inquiry, the member or panel conducting the inquiry shall dismiss the complaint if the member or panel finds that the complaint is not substantiated.

Complaint substantiated

(2) If at the conclusion of the inquiry the member or panel finds that the complaint is substantiated, the member or panel may, subject to section 54, make an order against the person found to be engaging or to have engaged in the discriminatory practice and include in the order any of the following terms that the member or panel considers appropriate:

(a) that the person cease the discriminatory practice and take measures, in consultation with the Commission on the general purposes of the measures, to redress the practice or to prevent the same or a similar practice from occurring in future, including
    (i) the adoption of a special program, plan or arrangement referred to in subsection 16(1), or
    (ii) making an application for approval and implementing a plan under section 17;
(b) that the person make available to the victim of the discriminatory practice, on the first reasonable occasion, the rights, opportunities or privileges that are being or were denied the victim as a result of the practice;
(c) that the person compensate the victim for any or all of the wages that the victim was deprived of and for any expenses incurred by the victim as a result of the discriminatory practice;
(d) that the person compensate the victim for any or all additional costs of obtaining alternative goods, services, facilities or accommodation and for any expenses incurred by the victim as a result of the discriminatory practice; and
(e) that the person compensate the victim, by an amount not exceeding twenty thousand dollars, for any pain and suffering that the victim experienced as a result of the discriminatory practice.

Special compensation

(3) In addition to any order under subsection (2), the member or panel may order the person to pay such compensation not exceeding twenty thousand dollars to the victim as the member or panel may determine if the member or panel finds that the person is engaging or has engaged in the discriminatory practice wilfully or recklessly.

Interest

(4) Subject to the rules made under section 48.9, an order to pay compensation under

this section may include an award of interest at a rate and for a period that the member or panel considers appropriate.
R.S., 1985, c. H-6, s. 53; 1998, c. 9, s. 27.

Orders relating to hate messages
54. (1) If a member or panel finds that a complaint related to a discriminatory practice described in section 13 is substantiated, the member or panel may make only one or more of the following orders:
(a) an order containing terms referred to in paragraph 53(2)(a);
(b) an order under subsection 53(3) to compensate a victim specifically identified in the communication that constituted the discriminatory practice; and
(c) an order to pay a penalty of not more than ten thousand dollars.

Factors
(1.1) In deciding whether to order the person to pay the penalty, the member or panel shall take into account the following factors:
(a) the nature, circumstances, extent and gravity of the discriminatory practice; and
(b) the wilfulness or intent of the person who engaged in the discriminatory practice, any prior discriminatory practices that the person has engaged in and the person's ability to pay the penalty.

Idem
(2) No order under subsection 53(2) may contain a term
(a) requiring the removal of an individual from a position if that individual accepted employment in that position in good faith; or
(b) requiring the expulsion of an occupant from any premises or accommodation, if that occupant obtained such premises or accommodation in good faith.
R.S., 1985, c. H-6, s. 54; 1998, c. 9, s. 28.

Definitions
54.1 (1) In this section,
"designated groups" has the meaning assigned in section 3 of the Employment Equity Act; and
"employer" means a person who or organization that discharges the obligations of an employer under the Employment Equity Act.

Limitation of order re employment equity
(2) Where a Tribunal finds that a complaint against an employer is substantiated, it may not make an order pursuant to subparagraph 53(2)(a)(i) requiring the employer to adopt a special program, plan or arrangement containing
(a) positive policies and practices designed to ensure that members of designated groups achieve increased representation in the employer's workforce; or
(b) goals and timetables for achieving that increased representation.

Interpretation
(3) For greater certainty, subsection (2) shall not be construed as limiting the power of a Tribunal, under paragraph 53(2)(a), to make an order requiring an employer to cease or otherwise correct a discriminatory practice.
1995, c. 44, s. 50.

55. and 56. [Repealed, 1998, c. 9, s. 29]
Enforcement of order
57. An order under section 53 or 54 may, for the purpose of enforcement, be made an order of the Federal Court by following the usual practice and procedure or by the Commission filing in the Registry of the Court a copy of the order certified to be a true copy.
R.S., 1985, c. H-6, s. 57; 1998, c. 9, s. 29.

Application respecting disclosure of information

58. (1) If an investigator or a member or panel of the Tribunal requires the disclosure of any information and a minister of the Crown or any other interested person objects to its disclosure, the Commission may apply to the Federal Court for a determination of the matter.

Certificate

(2) Where the Commission applies to the Federal Court pursuant to subsection (1) and the minister of the Crown or other person interested objects to the disclosure in accordance with sections 37 to 39 of the Canada Evidence Act, the matter shall be determined in accordance with the terms of those sections.

No certificate

(3) Where the Commission applies to the Federal Court pursuant to subsection (1) but the minister of the Crown or other person interested does not within ninety days thereafter object to the disclosure in accordance with sections 37 to 39 of the Canada Evidence Act, the Court may take such action as it deems appropriate.
R.S., 1985, c. H-6, s. 58; 1998, c. 9, s. 30.

Intimidation or discrimination

59. No person shall threaten, intimidate or discriminate against an individual because that individual has made a complaint or given evidence or assisted in any way in respect of the initiation or prosecution of a complaint or other proceeding under this Part, or because that individual proposes to do so.
1976–77, c. 33, s. 45.

Offences and Punishment

Offence

60. (1) Every person is guilty of an offence who
(a) [Repealed, 1998, c. 9, s. 31]
(b) obstructs a member or panel in carrying out its functions under this Part; or
(c) contravenes subsection 11(6) or 43(3) or section 59.

Punishment

(2) A person who is guilty of an offence under subsection (1) is liable on summary conviction to a fine not exceeding $50,000.

Prosecution of employer or employee organization

(3) A prosecution for an offence under this section may be brought against an employer organization or employee organization and in the name of the organization and, for the purpose of the prosecution, the organization is deemed to be a person and any act or thing done or omitted by an officer or agent of the organization within the scope of their authority to act on behalf of the organization is deemed to be an act or thing done or omitted by the organization.

Consent of Attorney General

(4) A prosecution for an offence under this section may not be instituted except by or with the consent of the Attorney General of Canada.

Limitation period

(5) A prosecution for an offence under this section may not be instituted more than one year after the subject-matter of the proceedings arose.
R.S., 1985, c. H-6, s. 60; 1998, c. 9, s. 31.

Reports

Annual report of Commission

61. (1) The Commission shall, within three months after December 31 in each year, prepare and submit to Parliament a report on the activities of the Commission under

this Part and Part II for that year, including references to and comments on any matter referred to in paragraph 27(1)(e) or (g) that it considers appropriate.

Special reports
(2) The Commission may, at any time, prepare and submit to Parliament a special report referring to and commenting on any matter within the scope of its powers, duties and functions if, in its opinion, the matter is of such urgency or importance that a report on it should not be deferred until the time provided for submission of its next annual report under subsection (1).

Annual report of Tribunal
(3) The Tribunal shall, within three months after December 31 in each year, prepare and submit to Parliament a report on its activities under this Act for that year.

Transmission of report
(4) Every report under this section shall be submitted by being transmitted to the Speaker of the Senate and to the Speaker of the House of Commons for tabling in those Houses.
R.S., 1985, c. H-6, s. 61; 1998, c. 9, s. 32.

Minister Responsible
Minister of Justice
61.1 The Minister of Justice is responsible for this Act, and the powers of the Governor in Council to make regulations under this Act, with the exception of section 29, are exercisable on the recommendation of that Minister.
1998, c. 9, s. 32.

Application
Limitation
62. (1) This Part and Parts I and II do not apply to or in respect of any superannuation or pension fund or plan established by an Act of Parliament enacted before March 1, 1978.

Review of Acts referred to in subsection (1)
(2) The Commission shall keep under review those Acts of Parliament enacted before March 1, 1978 by which any superannuation or pension fund or plan is established and, where the Commission deems it to be appropriate, it may include in a report mentioned in section 61 reference to and comment on any provision of any of those Acts that in its opinion is inconsistent with the principle described in section 2.
1976–77, c. 33, s. 48.

Application in the territories
63. Where a complaint under this Part relates to an act or omission that occurred in the Yukon Territory, the Northwest Territories or Nunavut, it may not be dealt with under this Part unless the act or omission could be the subject of a complaint under this Part had it occurred in a province.
R.S., 1985, c. H-6, s. 63; 1993, c. 28, s. 78.

Canadian Forces and Royal Canadian Mounted Police
64. For the purposes of this Part and Parts I and II, members of the Canadian Forces and the Royal Canadian Mounted Police are deemed to be employed by the Crown.
1976–77, c. 33, s. 48.

Acts of employees, etc.
65. (1) Subject to subsection (2), any act or omission committed by an officer, a director, an employee or an agent of any person, association or organization in the course of the employment of the officer, director, employee or agent shall, for the purposes of this Act, be deemed to be an act or omission committed by that person, association or organization.

Exculpation
(2) An act or omission shall not, by virtue of subsection (1), be deemed to be an act or

omission committed by a person, association or organization if it is established that the person, association or organization did not consent to the commission of the act or omission and exercised all due diligence to prevent the act or omission from being committed and, subsequently, to mitigate or avoid the effect thereof.
1980–81–82–83, c. 143, s. 23.

PART IV
APPLICATION

Binding on Her Majesty
66. (1) This Act is binding on Her Majesty in right of Canada, except in matters respecting the Government of the Yukon Territory, the Northwest Territories or Nunavut.

Commencement
(2) The exception referred to in subsection (1) shall come into operation in respect of the Government of the Yukon Territory on a day to be fixed by proclamation.

Idem
(3) The exception referred to in subsection (1) shall come into operation in respect of the Government of the Northwest Territories on a day to be fixed by proclamation.

Idem
(4) The exception referred to in subsection (1) shall come into operation in respect of the Government of Nunavut on a day to be fixed by order of the Governor in Council.
R.S., 1985, c. H-6, s. 66; 1993, c. 28, s. 78.

Saving
67. Nothing in this Act affects any provision of the Indian Act or any provision made under or pursuant to that Act.
1976–77, c. 33, s. 63.

RELATED PROVISIONS
– R.S., 1985, c. 31 (1st Supp.), s. 68:

Transitional
"68. Every Tribunal appointed prior to the coming into force of this Act shall continue to act as though this Part had not come into force."
– 1998, c. 9, ss. 33, 34:

Definition of "commencement day"
33. (1) In this section, "commencement day" means the day on which this section comes into force.

Members cease to hold office
(2) Subject to subsections (3), (4) and (5), the members of the Human Rights Tribunal Panel cease to hold office on the commencement day.

Continuing jurisdiction of Human Rights Tribunal
(3) The members of any Human Rights Tribunal appointed under the Canadian Human Rights Act before the commencement day have jurisdiction with respect to any inquiry into the complaint in respect of which the Human Rights Tribunal was appointed.

Continuing jurisdiction of Review Tribunal
(4) The members of any Review Tribunal constituted under the Canadian Human Rights Act before the commencement day have jurisdiction with respect to any appeal against a decision or order of a Human Rights Tribunal.

Continuing jurisdiction of Employment Equity Review Tribunal
(5) The members of any Employment Equity Review Tribunal established under section 28 or 39 of the Employment Equity Act before the commencement day have jurisdiction over any matter in respect of which the Tribunal was established.

Supervision by Chairperson of Canadian Human Rights Tribunal
(6) The Chairperson of the Canadian Human Rights Tribunal has supervision over and direction of the work of any Human Rights Tribunal, Review Tribunal or Employment Equity Review Tribunal referred to in subsection (3), (4) or (5).

Remuneration
(7) Each member of a Human Rights Tribunal, Review Tribunal or Employment Equity Review Tribunal referred to in subsection (3), (4) or (5), other than such a member who is appointed as a full-time member of the Canadian Human Rights Tribunal, shall be paid such remuneration as may be fixed by the Governor in Council.

Travel expenses
(8) Each member of a Human Rights Tribunal, Review Tribunal or Employment Equity Review Tribunal referred to in subsection (3), (4) or (5) is entitled to be paid travel and living expenses incurred in carrying out duties as a member of that Tribunal while absent from their place of residence, but the expenses must not exceed the maximum limits authorized by Treasury Board directive for employees of the Government of Canada.

Commission employees serving the Human Rights Tribunal Panel
34. (1) This Act does not affect the status of an employee who, immediately before the coming into force of this subsection, occupied a position in the Canadian Human Rights Commission and performed services on a full-time basis for the Human Rights Tribunal Panel, except that the employee shall, on the coming into force of this subsection, occupy that position in the Canadian Human Rights Tribunal.

Definition of "employee"
(2) In this section, "employee" has the same meaning as in subsection 2(1) of the Public Service Employment Act.

Employment Equity Act

Chapter E-5.4 (1995, c. 44) [E-5.401]

An Act respecting employment equity
[Assented to 15th December, 1995]

Her Majesty, by and with the advice and consent of the Senate and House of Commons of Canada, enacts as follows:

Short title
1. This Act may be cited as the Employment Equity Act.

Purpose of Act
2. The purpose of this Act is to achieve equality in the workplace so that no person shall be denied employment opportunities or benefits for reasons unrelated to ability and, in the fulfilment of that goal, to correct the conditions of disadvantage in employment experienced by women, aboriginal peoples, persons with disabilities and members of visible minorities by giving effect to the principle that employment equity means more than treating persons in the same way but also requires special measures and the accommodation of differences.

Interpretation
Definitions
3. In this Act,
"aboriginal peoples" means persons who are Indians, Inuit or Métis;
"Canadian workforce" means all persons in Canada of working age who are willing and able to work;
"Chairperson" means the chairperson of the Canadian Human Rights Tribunal;

"Commission" means the Canadian Human Rights Commission established under section 26 of the Canadian Human Rights Act;
"compliance officer" means a person designated as an employment equity compliance review officer pursuant to subsection 22(3);
"designated groups" means women, aboriginal peoples, persons with disabilities and members of visible minorities;
"members of visible minorities" means persons, other than aboriginal peoples, who are non-Caucasian in race or non-white in colour;
"Minister" means such member of the Queen's Privy Council for Canada as is designated by the Governor in Council as the Minister for the purposes of this Act;
"Panel" [Repealed, 1998, c. 9, s. 37]
"persons with disabilities" means persons who have a long-term or recurring physical, mental, sensory, psychiatric or learning impairment and who
(a) consider themselves to be disadvantaged in employment by reason of that impairment, or
(b) believe that a employer or potential employer is likely to consider them to be disadvantaged in employment by reason of that impairment, and includes persons whose functional limitations owing to their impairment have been accommodated in their current job or workplace;
["prescribed" Version anglaise seulement]
"prescribed" means prescribed by the regulations;
"private sector employer" means any person who employs one hundred or more employees on or in connection with a federal work, undertaking or business as defined in section 2 of the Canada Labour Code and includes any corporation established to perform any function or duty on behalf of the Government of Canada that employs one hundred or more employees, but does not include
(a) a person who employs employees on or in connection with a work, undertaking or business of a local or private nature in the Yukon Territory, the Northwest Territories or Nunavut, or
(b) a departmental corporation as defined in section 2 of the Financial Administration Act;
"representatives" means
(a) those persons who have been designated by employees to act as their representatives, or
(b) bargaining agents, where bargaining agents represent the employees;
"Tribunal" means an Employment Equity Review Tribunal established by subsection 28(1).
1993, c. 28, s. 78; 1995, c. 44, s. 3; 1998, c. 9, s. 37, c. 15, s. 25.

Application
4. (1) This Act applies to
(a) private sector employers;
(b) the portions of the public service of Canada set out in Part I of Schedule I to the Public Service Staff Relations Act;
(c) the portions of the public service of Canada set out in Part II of ScheduleI to the Public Service Staff Relations Act that employ one hundred or more employees; and
(d) such other portion of the public sector employing one hundred or more employees, including the Canadian Forces and the Royal Canadian Mounted Police, as may be specified by order of the Governor in Council on the recommendation of the Treasury Board, in consultation with the minister responsible for the specified portion.

Royal Canadian Mounted Police
(2) For the purposes of this Act,
(a) the Royal Canadian Mounted Police is deemed to consist only of its members within the meaning of subsection 2(1) of the Royal Canadian Mounted Police Act;

(b) the Royal Canadian Mounted Police is deemed not to be included in Part I of Schedule I to the Public Service Staff Relations Act; and
(c) civilian employees appointed or employed in accordance with section 10 of the Royal Canadian Mounted Police Act are deemed to be included in Part I of Schedule I to the Public Service Staff Relations Act.

Canadian Forces and Royal Canadian Mounted Police
(3) Members of the Canadian Forces and the Royal Canadian Mounted Police are deemed to be employees for the purposes of this Act.

Responsibilities of Treasury Board and Public Service Commission
(4) The Treasury Board and the Public Service Commission, each acting within the scope of its powers, duties and functions under the Financial Administration Act and the Public Service Employment Act, are responsible for carrying out the obligations of an employer under this Act in relation to employees employed in those portions of the public service referred to in paragraph (1)(b).

Deemed employer
(5) Every portion of the public sector referred to in paragraphs (1)(c) and (d) is deemed to be an employer for the purposes of this Act in relation to employees employed in that portion except that, with respect to any of those portions for which the Public Service Commission exercises any power or performs any duty or function under the Public Service Employment Act, the Public Service Commission and that portion are responsible for carrying out the obligations of an employer under this Act.

References to employer
(6) In this Act, a reference to an employer is deemed, in relation to those portions of the public sector referred to in
(a) paragraph (1)(b), to be a reference to the Treasury Board and the Public Service Commission, each acting within the scope of its powers, duties and functions under the Financial Administration Act and the Public Service Employment Act; and
(b) paragraphs (1)(c) and (d) for which the Public Service Commission exercises any power or performs any duty or function under the Public Service Employment Act, to be a reference to the employer and the Public Service Commission.

Delegation by Treasury Board and Public Service Commission
(7) The Treasury Board and the Public Service Commission may, for the purpose of carrying out their obligations under this Act in relation to a portion of the public service or other portion of the public sector referred to in subsection (1), authorize the chief executive officer or deputy head concerned to exercise, in relation to that portion, any of the powers and perform any of the duties and functions of the Treasury Board or the Public Service Commission, as the case may be, referred to in this section.

Delegation by chief executive officer or deputy head
(8) Any chief executive officer or deputy head authorized under subsection (7) to exercise any of the powers and perform any of the duties and functions of the Treasury Board or Public Service Commission may, subject to and in accordance with the authorization given to that officer or deputy head, authorize one or more persons to exercise any of those powers and perform any of those duties and functions.

PART I
EMPLOYMENT EQUITY

Employer Obligations

Employer's duty
5. Every employer shall implement employment equity by

(a) identifying and eliminating employment barriers against persons in designated groups that result from the employer's employment systems, policies and practices that are not authorized by law; and
(b) instituting such positive policies and practices and making such reasonable accommodations as will ensure that persons in designated groups achieve a degree of representation in each occupational group in the employer's workforce that reflects their representation in
  (i) the Canadian workforce, or
  (ii) those segments of the Canadian workforce that are identifiable by qualification, eligibility or geography and from which the employer may reasonably be expected to draw employees.

Employer not required to take certain measures
6. The obligation to implement employment equity does not require an employer
(a) to take a particular measure to implement employment equity where the taking of that measure would cause undue hardship to the employer;
(b) to hire or promote unqualified persons;
(c) with respect to the public sector, to hire or promote persons without basing the hiring or promotion on selection according to merit in cases where the Public Service Employment Act requires that hiring or promotion be based on selection according to merit; or
(d) to create new positions in its workforce.

Employment of aboriginal peoples
7. Notwithstanding any other provision of this Act, where a private sector employer is engaged primarily in promoting or serving the interests of aboriginal peoples, the employer may give preference in employment to aboriginal peoples or employ only aboriginal peoples, unless that preference or employment would constitute a discriminatory practice under the Canadian Human Rights Act.

Certain rights not employment barriers
8. (1) Employee seniority rights with respect to a layoff or recall under a collective agreement or pursuant to the established practices of an employer are deemed not to be employment barriers within the meaning of this Act.

Other seniority rights
(2) Unless they are found to constitute a discriminatory practice under the Canadian Human Rights Act, employee seniority rights other than those referred to in subsection (1), including rights acquired under workforce adjustment policies implemented when an employer is downsizing or restructuring, under a collective agreement or pursuant to an established practice, are deemed not to be employment barriers within the meaning of this Act.

Adverse impact on employment opportunities
(3) Notwithstanding subsections (1) and (2), where, after a review under paragraph 9(1)(b), it appears that a right referred to in either of those subsections that is provided for under a collective agreement may have an adverse impact on the employment opportunities of persons in designated groups, the employer and its employees' representatives shall consult with each other concerning measures that may be taken to minimize the adverse impact.

Public sector
(4) The following are not, in relation to the public sector, employment barriers within the meaning of the Act, namely,
(a) priorities for appointment under the Public Service Employment Act or regulations made by the Public Service Commission; and

(b) workforce adjustment measures established by the Treasury Board, including measures set out in the Workforce Adjustment Directive, or by the Public Service Commission or any other portion of the public sector referred to in paragraphs 4(1)(c) and (d).

Analysis and review

9. (1) For the purpose of implementing employment equity, every employer shall

(a) collect information and conduct an analysis of the employer's workforce, in accordance with the regulations, in order to determine the degree of the underrepresentation of persons in designated groups in each occupational group in that workforce; and

(b) conduct a review of the employer's employment systems, policies and practices, in accordance with the regulations, in order to identify employment barriers against persons in designated groups that result from those systems, policies and practices.

Self-identification

(2) Only those employees who identify themselves to an employer, or agree to be identified by an employer, as aboriginal peoples, members of visible minorities or persons with disabilities are to be counted as members of those designated groups for the purposes of implementing employment equity.

Confidentiality of information

(3) Information collected by an employer under paragraph (1)(a) is confidential and shall be used only for the purpose of implementing the employer's obligations under this Act.

Employment equity plan

10. (1) The employer shall prepare an employment equity plan that

(a) specifies the positive policies and practices that are to be instituted by the employer in the short term for the hiring, training, promotion and retention of persons in designated groups and for the making of reasonable accommodations for those persons, to correct the underrepresentation of those persons identified by the analysis under paragraph 9(1)(a);

(b) specifies the measures to be taken by the employer in the short term for the elimination of any employment barriers identified by the review under paragraph 9(1)(b);

(c) establishes a timetable for the implementation of the matters referred to in paragraphs (a) and (b);

(d) where underrepresentation has been identified by the analysis, establishes short term numerical goals for the hiring and promotion of persons in designated groups in order to increase their representation in each occupational group in the workforce in which underrepresentation has been identified and sets out measures to be taken in each year to meet those goals;

(e) sets out the employer's longer term goals for increasing the representation of persons in designated groups in the employer's workforce and the employer's strategy for achieving those goals; and

(f) provides for any other matter that may be prescribed.

Establishment of numerical goals

(2) In establishing the short term numerical goals referred to in paragraph (1)(d), every employer shall consider

(a) the degree of underrepresentation of persons in each designated group in each occupational group within the employer's workforce;

(b) the availability of qualified persons in designated groups within the employer's workforce and in the Canadian workforce;

(c) the anticipated growth or reduction of the employer's workforce during the period in respect of which the numerical goals apply;

(d) the anticipated turnover of employees within the employer's workforce during the period in respect of which the numerical goals apply; and

(e) any other factor that may be prescribed.

Definitions
(3) In this section, "short term" means a period of not less than one year and not more than three years, and "longer term" means a period of more than three years.

Reasonable progress
11. Every employer shall ensure that its employment equity plan would, if implemented, constitute reasonable progress toward implementing employment equity as required by this Act.

Implementation and monitoring of plan
12. Every employer shall
(a) make all reasonable efforts to implement its employment equity plan; and
(b) monitor implementation of its plan on a regular basis to assess whether reasonable progress toward implementing employment equity is being made.

Periodic review and revision of plan
13. Every employer shall, at least once during the period in respect of which the short term numerical goals referred to in paragraph 10(1)(d) are established, review its employment equity plan and revise it by
(a) updating the numerical goals, taking into account the factors referred to in subsection 10(2); and
(b) making any other changes that are necessary as a result of an assessment made pursuant to paragraph 12(b) or as a result of changing circumstances.

Information about employment equity
14. Every employer shall provide information to its employees explaining the purpose of employment equity and shall keep its employees informed about measures the employer has undertaken or is planning to undertake to implement employment equity and the progress the employer has made in implementing employment equity.

Consultation with employee representatives
15. (1) Every employer shall consult with its employees' representatives by inviting the representatives to provide their views concerning
(a) the assistance that the representatives could provide to the employer to facilitate the implementation of employment equity in its workplace and the communication to its employees of matters relating to employment equity; and
(b) the preparation, implementation and revision of the employer's employment equity plan.

Where employees represented by bargaining agents
(2) Where employees are represented by a bargaining agent, the bargaining agent shall participate in a consultation under subsection (1).

Collaboration
(3) Every employer and its employees' representatives shall collaborate in the preparation, implementation and revision of the employer's employment equity plan.

Rule of interpretation
(4) Consultation under subsection (1) and collaboration under subsection (3) are not forms of co-management.

New employers
16. (1) A person who becomes an employer after the day on which this section comes into force shall, within eighteen months after becoming an employer, comply with sections 9 and 10.

Compliance audit

(2) The Commission may not conduct a compliance audit of the discharge of the obligations of a person referred to in subsection (1) within two years after the day on which that person becomes an employer.

Records and Reports

Employment equity records

17. Every employer shall, in accordance with the regulations, establish and maintain employment equity records in respect of the employer's workforce, the employer's employment equity plan and the implementation of employment equity by the employer.

Reports of private sector employers

18. (1) Every private sector employer shall, on or before June 1 in each year, file with the Minister a report in respect of the immediately preceding calendar year containing information in accordance with prescribed instructions, indicating, in the prescribed manner and form,

(a) the industrial sector in which its employees are employed, the location of the employer and its employees, the number of its employees and the number of those employees who are members of designated groups;

(b) the occupational groups in which its employees are employed and the degree of representation of persons who are members of designated groups in each occupational group;

(c) the salary ranges of its employees and the degree of representation of persons who are members of designated groups in each range and in each prescribed subdivision of the range; and

(d) the number of its employees hired, promoted and terminated and the degree of representation in those numbers of persons who are members of designated groups.

Interpretation

(2) For the purposes of subsection (1), an employer is the person who or organization that was the employer on December 31 in the immediately preceding year.

Electronic filing

(3) An employer may file a report using electronic media in a manner specified in writing by the Minister and, in such a case, the report is deemed to have been filed on the day that the Minister acknowledges receipt of it.

Self-identification

(4) Only those employees who identify themselves to their employer, or agree to be identified by their employer, as aboriginal peoples, members of visible minorities and persons with disabilities are to be counted as members of those designated groups for the purposes of the report.

Certificate required

(5) A report shall be certified, in the prescribed manner, as to the accuracy of the information contained in it and shall be signed by the employer or, where the employer is a corporation, by a prescribed person on behalf of the corporation.

Additional information

(6) An employer shall include in a report a description of

(a) the measures taken by the employer during the reporting period to implement employment equity and the results achieved; and

(b) the consultations between the employer and its employees' representatives during the reporting period concerning the implementation of employment equity.

Consolidated reports

(7) Where, in the opinion of the Minister, associated or related federal works, undertakings or businesses are operated by two or more employers having common control

or direction, the Minister may, on the application of the employers, authorize them to file a consolidated report with respect to employees employed by them on or in connection with those works, undertakings or businesses.

Exemption for private sector employers
(8) The Minister may, on the application of an employer, exempt the employer from any or all of the requirements of this section for a period not exceeding one year if, in the opinion of the Minister, special circumstances warrant the exemption.

Copy to employees' representatives
(9) An employer shall, on filing a report with the Minister under this section, provide its employees' representatives with a copy of the report.

Copy to Commission
(10) The Minister shall, on receipt of a report, send a copy of it to the Commission.

Availability of reports of private sector employers
19. (1) Subject to subsection (2), every report filed under subsection 18(1) shall be available for public inspection at such places as may be designated, and in such form as may be determined, by the Minister, and any person may, on payment of a prescribed fee, not to exceed the costs of furnishing a copy, obtain from the Minister a copy of any of the reports.

Withholding of report
(2) The Minister may, on the application of an employer, withhold the employer's report from public inspection for a period not exceeding one year if, in the opinion of the Minister, special circumstances warrant the withholding.

Consolidation to be tabled
20. The Minister shall in each year prepare a report consisting of a consolidation of the reports filed under subsection 18(1) together with an analysis of those reports and shall cause the report to be laid before each House of Parliament not later than the fifteenth sitting day that that House of Parliament is sitting after the report is completed.

Report of Treasury Board
21. (1) The President of the Treasury Board shall, in each fiscal year, cause to be laid before each House of Parliament a report in respect of the state of employment equity in the portions of the public service referred to in paragraph 4(1)(b) during the immediately preceding fiscal year.

Contents of report
(2) The report referred to in subsection (1) shall consist of
(a) a consolidation and analysis of
- (i) the number of employees employed in each portion of the public service referred to in paragraph 4(1)(b) and the number of persons who are members of each designated group so employed,
- (ii) the total number of employees employed in all portions of the public service referred to in paragraph 4(1)(b) in each province and in the National Capital Region and the number of persons who are members of each designated group so employed,
- (iii) the occupational groups of employees and the degree of representation of persons who are members of each designated group in each occupational group,
- (iv) the salary ranges of employees and the degree of representation of persons who are members of each designated group in each range and in any subdivision of the range, and
- (v) the numbers of employees hired, promoted and terminated and the degree of representation, in those numbers, of persons who are members of each designated group;

(b) a description of the principal measures taken by the Treasury Board during the reporting period to implement employment equity and the results achieved;
(c) a description of the consultations between the Treasury Board and its employees' representatives during the reporting period concerning the implementation of employment equity; and
(d) any other information that the President of the Treasury Board considers relevant.

Requirement to provide information
(3) Each portion of the public sector referred to in paragraphs 4(1)(c) and (d), other than the Canadian Security Intelligence Service, shall, within six months after the end of each fiscal year, provide to the President of the Treasury Board a report containing the information referred to in subsection (4) in relation to that portion during that fiscal year and the President shall cause the reports, together with the report referred to in subsection (1), to be laid
before each House of Parliament.

Contents of report
(4) A report referred to in subsection (3) shall consist of
(a) the information referred to in subparagraphs (2)(a)(i) to (v) in relation to that portion;
(b) an analysis of the information referred to in paragraph (a); and
(c) the information referred to in paragraphs (2)(b) to (d) in relation to that portion.

Requirement to provide information
(5) The Canadian Security Intelligence Service shall, within six months after the end of each fiscal year, provide to the President of the Treasury Board a report containing the information referred to in subsection (6) in relation to that portion during that fiscal year and the President shall cause the report, together with the report referred to in subsection (1), to be laid before each House of Parliament.

Contents of report
(6) A report referred to in subsection (5) shall consist of
(a) the percentage of employees employed in that portion who are members of each designated group;
(b) the occupational groups of employees in that portion and the percentage of persons who are members of each designated group in each occupational group;
(c) the salary ranges of employees in that portion and the percentage of persons who are members of each designated group in each range and in any subdivision of the range;
(d) the percentage of employees hired, promoted and terminated in that portion who are members of each designated group;
(e) an analysis of the information referred to in paragraphs (a) to (d); and
(f) the information referred to in paragraphs (2)(b) to (d) in relation to that portion.

Copy to Commission
(7) The President of the Treasury Board shall, as soon as possible after a report referred to in any of subsections (1), (3) and (5) is laid before each House of Parliament, send a copy of the report to the Commission.

Copies to employees' representatives
(8) As soon as possible after a report referred to in this section is laid before each House of Parliament,
(a) in the case of a report referred to in subsection (1), the President of the Treasury Board,
(b) in the case of a report referred to in subsection (3), each portion of the public sector referred to in that subsection, and
(c) in the case of a report referred to in subsection (5), the Canadian Security Intelligence Service,
shall send a copy of the report to its employees' representatives.

PART II
COMPLIANCE

Compliance audits
22. (1) The Commission is responsible for the enforcement of the obligations imposed on employers by sections 5, 9 to 15 and 17.

Guiding policy
(2) The Commission shall, in discharging its responsibility under subsection (1), be guided by the policy that, wherever possible, cases of non-compliance be resolved through persuasion and the negotiation of written undertakings pursuant to subsection 25(1) and that directions be issued under subsection 25(2) or (3) and applications for orders be made under subsection 27(2) only as a last resort.

Compliance officers designated
(3) The Commission may designate any person or category of persons as employment equity compliance review officers for the purposes of conducting compliance audits of employers.

Where compliance officer may not act
(4) No person who has been designated as an investigator under section 43 of the Canadian Human Rights Act to investigate a complaint under that Act in respect of an employer may, during the investigation, conduct a compliance audit of that employer.

Delegation by Commission
(5) The Commission may authorize any officer or employee of the Commission whom the Commission considers appropriate to exercise any power and perform any duty or function of the Commission under this Act and any power so exercised and any duty or function so performed shall be deemed to have been exercised or performed by the Commission.

Powers of compliance officers
23. (1) For the purposes of ensuring compliance with the provisions referred to in subsection 22(1), a compliance officer may conduct a compliance audit of an employer and, for that purpose, may
(a) at any reasonable time, enter any place in which the officer believes on reasonable grounds there is any thing relevant to the enforcement of any of those provisions; and
(b) require any person to produce for examination or copying any record, book of account or other document that the officer believes on reasonable grounds contains information that is relevant to the enforcement of any of those provisions.

Data processing systems and copying equipment
(2) In conducting a compliance audit, a compliance officer may
(a) reproduce or cause to be reproduced any record from a data processing system in the form of a print-out or other intelligible output and remove the print-out or other output for examination and copying; and
(b) use or cause to be used any copying equipment at the place to make copies of any record, book of account or other document.

Certificate to be produced
(3) Compliance officers shall be furnished with certificates in a form established by the Commission certifying their designation as compliance officers and, on entering a place under paragraph (1)(a), a compliance officer shall show the certificate to the person in charge of the place if the person requests proof of the officer's designation.

Assistance to compliance officers
(4) The person in charge of a place entered pursuant to paragraph (1)(a) and every person found in the place shall

(a) give the compliance officer all reasonable assistance to enable the officer to exercise the powers conferred on compliance officers by this section; and
(b) provide the officer with any information relevant to the enforcement of this Act that the officer may reasonably require.

Security requirements
24. Every compliance officer or any other person acting on behalf of or under the direction of the Commission who receives or obtains information relating to a compliance audit under this Act shall, with respect to access to and use of that information by that compliance officer or person, satisfy any security requirements applicable to, and take any oath of secrecy required to be taken by, persons who normally have access to and use of that information.

Undertakings and Directions
Employer undertaking
25. (1) Where a compliance officer is of the opinion that an employer
(a) has not collected information or conducted an analysis referred to in paragraph 9(1)(a) or conducted a review referred to in paragraph 9(1)(b),
(b) has not prepared an employment equity plan referred to in section 10,
(c) has prepared an employment equity plan that does not meet the requirements of sections 10 and 11,
(d) has not made all reasonable efforts to implement its employment equity plan in accordance with section 12,
(e) has failed to review and revise its employment equity plan in accordance with section 13,
(f) has failed to provide information to its employees in accordance with section 14,
(g) has failed to consult with its employees' representatives in accordance with section 15, or
(h) has failed to establish and maintain employment equity records as required by section 17,
the compliance officer shall inform the employer of the non-compliance and shall attempt to negotiate a written undertaking from the employer to take specified measures to remedy the non-compliance.

Information re underrepresentation
(1.1) Where
(a) an employer has been informed of a non-compliance by a compliance officer under subsection (1) and the finding of non-compliance is based, in whole or in part, on the apparent underrepresentation of aboriginal peoples, members of visible minorities or persons with disabilities in the employer's work force, as reflected in the employer's work force analysis conducted pursuant to paragraph 9(1)(a), and
(b) the employer believes that the apparent underrepresentation is attributable to the decision of employees who may be members of the designated groups concerned not to identify themselves as such or not to agree to be identified by the employer as such under subsection 9(2),
the employer may inform the compliance officer of such belief.

Reason for underrepresentation to be considered
(1.2) Where the employer satisfies the compliance officer that the finding of non-compliance is attributable, in whole or in part, to the reason described in paragraph (1.1)(b) and that the employer has made all reasonable efforts to implement employment equity, the compliance officer shall take the reason into account in exercising any powers under this section.

No employer identification of individual employees
(1.3) In satisfying the compliance officer under subsection (1.2) that the finding of non-compliance is attributable, in whole or in part, to the reason mentioned in paragraph

(1.1)(b), the employer must do so by means other than the identification of individual employees in its work force that the employer believes are members of designated groups who have not identified themselves as such, or agreed to be identified by the employer as such, under subsection 9(2).

Direction

(2) Where a compliance officer fails to obtain a written undertaking that, in the opinion of the compliance officer, would be sufficient to remedy the non-compliance, the compliance officer shall notify the Commission of the non-compliance and the Commission may issue and send, by registered mail, a direction to the employer

(a) setting out the facts on which the officer's finding of non-compliance is based; and
(b) requiring the employer to take such actions as are specified in the direction to remedy the non-compliance.

Breach of undertaking

(3) Where a compliance officer obtains a written undertaking and the compliance officer is of the opinion that the employer has breached the undertaking, the compliance officer shall notify the Commission of the non-compliance and the Commission may issue and send, by registered mail, a direction to the employer requiring the employer to take such actions as are specified in the direction to remedy the non-compliance.

Amendment of direction

(4) The Commission may rescind or amend a direction issued by the Commission pursuant to subsection (2) or (3) on the presentation of new facts or on being satisfied that the direction was issued without knowledge of, or was based on a mistake as to, a material fact.

Direction of Commission

26. (1) Where a compliance officer is of the opinion that an employer has failed to give reasonable assistance or to provide information as required by subsection 23(4), the compliance officer shall notify the Commission of the non-compliance and the Commission may issue and send, by registered mail, a direction to the employer

(a) setting out the facts on which the officer's finding of non-compliance is based; and
(b) requiring the employer to take such actions as are specified in the direction to remedy the non-compliance.

Amendment of direction

(2) The Commission may rescind or amend a direction issued pursuant to subsection (1) on the presentation of new facts or on being satisfied that the direction was issued without knowledge of, or was based on a mistake as to, a material fact.

Requests for Review or Order

Employer's request for review

27. (1) An employer to whom a direction is issued under subsection 25(2) or (3) or 26(1) may make a request to the Chairperson for a review of the direction

(a) in the case of a direction issued under subsection 25(2) or (3), within sixty days after the day on which it is issued; and
(b) in the case of a direction issued under subsection 26(1), within thirty days after the day on which it is issued.

Commission may apply

(2) If the Commission is of the opinion that an employer has failed to comply with a direction issued by the Commission, the Commission may apply to the Chairperson for an order confirming the direction.

Limitation

(3) No application may be made pursuant to subsection (2) where the employer has requested a review in accordance with subsection (1).
1995, c. 44, s. 27; 1998, c. 9, s. 38.

Employment Equity Review Tribunals

Establishment of Tribunals
28. (1) If an employer makes a request under subsection 27(1) or the Commission makes an application under subsection 27(2), the Chairperson shall establish an Employment Equity Review Tribunal to consider the request or application.

Composition
(2) The Chairperson shall appoint a Tribunal consisting of one member of the Canadian Human Rights Tribunal, but the Chairperson may appoint a Tribunal of three members if the Chairperson considers that the complexity or precedential significance of the request or application requires a Tribunal of three members.

Qualifications of members
(3) The Chairperson shall, in appointing members of the Tribunal, take into consideration their knowledge and experience in employment equity matters.

Presiding
(4) If a Tribunal consists of more than one member, the Chairperson shall designate one of the members to preside over the hearings of the Tribunal.

Acting after expiration of appointment
(4.1) A member whose appointment expires may, with the approval of the Chairperson, conclude any hearing that the member has begun, and a person performing duties under this section is deemed to be a part-time member for the purposes of section 48.3 of the Canadian Human Rights Act.

Remuneration
(5) The members of a Tribunal shall be paid such remuneration as may be provided for under subsection 48.6(1) of the Canadian Human Rights Act.

Travel expenses
(6) Members are entitled to be paid any travel and living expenses incurred in carrying out duties as members of the Tribunal while absent from their ordinary place of residence that may be provided for under subsection 48.6(2) of the Canadian Human Rights Act.

Technical experts
(7) The Chairperson may engage and, subject to the approval of the Treasury Board, fix the remuneration of persons having technical or special knowledge to assist or advise a Tribunal in any matter.

Government services and facilities
(8) In performing its duties and functions, a Tribunal shall, where available, make use of the services and facilities of departments, boards and agencies of the Government of Canada.

Rules
(9) The Chairperson may make rules governing the practice and procedure of Tribunals.

Security requirements
(10) Every member or other person acting on behalf of or under the direction of a Tribunal who receives or obtains information relating to a request or application referred to in subsection (1) shall, with respect to access to and use of that information by that member or other person, satisfy any security requirements applicable to, and take any oath of secrecy required to be taken by, persons who normally have access to and use of that information.
1995, c. 44, s. 28; 1998, c. 9, s. 39.

Powers of Tribunal
29. (1) A Tribunal may
(a) in the same manner and to the same extent as a superior court of record, summon and enforce the attendance of witnesses and compel them to give oral and written evidence on oath and to produce such documents and things as the Tribunal considers necessary for a full review;
(b) administer oaths; and
(c) receive and accept such evidence and other information, whether on oath or by affidavit or otherwise, as the Tribunal sees fit, whether or not that evidence or information would be admissible in a court of law.

How matters to be dealt with
(2) A Tribunal shall conduct any matter that comes before it as informally and expeditiously as the circumstances and considerations of fairness and natural justice permit.

Hearings to be public
(3) Subject to subsection (4), a hearing before a Tribunal shall be conducted in public.

Hearings may be in camera
(4) A hearing before a Tribunal may, on the request of an employer, be held in camera if the employer establishes to the satisfaction of the Tribunal that the circumstances of the case so require.

Reasons for decision
(5) A Tribunal shall provide the parties to a proceeding before the Tribunal with written reasons for its decision.

Reasons for decision
(6) A Tribunal shall, on request by any person, provide the person with a copy of any decision of the Tribunal, including a decision under subsection (4) to hold a hearing in camera, together with the written reasons for the decision.

Decision of Tribunal
30. (1) A Tribunal may, after hearing a request made under subsection 27(1) or an application made under subsection 27(2),
(a) by order, confirm, vary or rescind the Commission's direction; and
(b) make any other order it considers appropriate and reasonable in the circumstances to remedy the non-compliance.

Board may vary or rescind
(2) A Tribunal may vary or rescind any order made by it.

Orders are final
(3) An order of a Tribunal is final and, except for judicial review under the Federal Court Act, is not subject to appeal or review by any court.

Enforcement of orders
31. (1) Any order of a Tribunal made under section 30 may, for the purposes of its enforcement, be made an order of the Federal Court and is enforceable in the same manner as an order of that Court.

Procedure
(2) To make an order of a Tribunal an order of the Federal Court, the usual practice and procedure of the Court may be followed or a certified copy of the order may be filed with the registrar of the Court, and from the time of filing the order becomes an order of the Court.

Report of activities of Human Rights Commission
32. The Commission shall include in its annual report referred to in section 61 of the

Canadian Human Rights Act a report of its activities, including an assessment of their effectiveness, under this Act during the year.

Limitations respecting Directions and Orders

Limitation

33. (1) The Commission may not give a direction under section 25 or 26 and no Tribunal may make an order under section 30 where that direction or order would

(a) cause undue hardship on an employer;
(b) require an employer to hire or promote unqualified persons;
(c) with respect to the public sector, require an employer to hire or promote persons without basing the hiring or promotion on selection according to merit in cases where the Public Service Employment Act requires that hiring or promotion be based on selection according to merit, or impose on the Public Service Commission an obligation to exercise its discretion regarding exclusion orders or regulations;
(d) require an employer to create new positions in its workforce;
(e) impose a quota on an employer; or
(f) in the case of a direction or order respecting the establishment of short term numerical goals, fail to take into account the factors set out in subsection 10(2).

Meaning of "quota"

(2) In paragraph (1)(e), "quota" means a requirement to hire or promote a fixed and arbitrary number of persons during a given period.

Public sector

(3) In making a direction or order that applies to the public sector, the Commission, in the case of a direction, and a Tribunal, in the case of an order, shall take into account the respective roles and responsibilities of

(a) the Public Service Commission and the Treasury Board under the Public Service Employment Act and the Financial Administration Act; or
(b) a portion of the public sector referred to in paragraph 4(1)(c) or (d) under any other Act of Parliament.

Privileged Information

Privileged information

34. (1) Information obtained by the Commission under this Act is privileged and shall not knowingly be, or be permitted to be, communicated, disclosed or made available without the written consent of the person from whom it was obtained.

Evidence and production of documents

(2) No member of the Commission or person employed by it who obtains information that is privileged under subsection (1) shall be required, in connection with any legal proceedings, other than proceedings relating to the administration or enforcement of this Act, to give evidence relating to that information or to produce any statement or other writing containing that information.

Communication or disclosure of information

(3) Information that is privileged under subsection (1) may, on any terms and conditions that the Commission considers appropriate, be communicated or disclosed to a minister of the Crown in right of Canada or to any officer or employee of Her Majesty in right of Canada for any purpose relating to the administration or enforcement of this Act.

Exception

(4) Nothing in this section prohibits the communication or disclosure of information for the purposes of legal proceedings relating to the administration or enforcement of this Act.

Employer's consent required

(5) No information obtained by the Commission or a Tribunal under this Act may be

used in any proceedings under any other Act without the consent of the employer concerned.

PART III
ASSESSMENT OF MONETARY PENALTIES

Violations

35. (1) Every private sector employer commits a violation of this Act who
(a) without reasonable excuse, fails to file an employment equity report as required by section 18;
(b) without reasonable excuse, fails to include in the employment equity report any information that is required, by section 18 and the regulations, to be included; or
(c) provides any information in the employment equity report that the employer knows to be false or misleading.

Continuing violations

(2) A violation that is committed or continued on more than one day constitutes a separate violation for each day on which it is committed or continued.

Violations not offences

(3) A violation is not an offence and accordingly the Criminal Code does not apply in respect of a violation.

Assessment of monetary penalty

36. (1) The Minister may, within two years after the day on which the Minister becomes aware of a violation, issue a notice of assessment of a monetary penalty in respect of the violation and send it by registered mail to the private sector employer.

Limit

(2) The amount of a monetary penalty shall not exceed
(a) $10,000 for a single violation; and
(b) $50,000 for repeated or continued violations.

Factors to be considered

(3) In assessing the amount of a monetary penalty, the Minister shall take into account
(a) the nature, circumstances, extent and gravity of the violation; and
(b) the wilfulness or intent of the private sector employer and the employer's history of prior violations.

Notice of assessment of monetary penalty

37. A notice of the assessment of a monetary penalty shall
(a) identify the alleged violation;
(b) specify the amount of the monetary penalty; and
(c) specify the place where the employer may pay the monetary penalty.

Options

Employer's options

38. (1) An employer may, not later than thirty days after receiving a notice of assessment of a monetary penalty,
(a) comply with the notice; or
(b) contest the assessment of the monetary penalty by making a written application to the Minister for a review, by a Tribunal, of that assessment.

Copy of application

(2) If the Minister receives a written application, the Minister shall send a copy of it to the Chairperson.

Copy of notice of assessment

(3) If an employer who is issued a notice of assessment of a monetary penalty fails to

exercise one of the options set out in subsection (1) within the period referred to in that subsection, the Minister shall send a copy of the notice to
the Chairperson.
1995, c. 44, s. 38; 1998, c. 9, s. 40.

Review by Tribunal
39. (1) On receipt of a copy of a written application or a copy of a notice of assessment, the Chairperson shall establish a Tribunal consisting of one member selected from the Canadian Human Rights Tribunal to review the assessment and shall
(a) send, by registered mail, a request that the employer appear before the Tribunal at the time and place set out in the request to hear the allegations against the employer in respect of the alleged violation; and
(b) in writing, advise the Minister who issued the notice of assessment of the time and place set out in the request.

Failure to appear before Tribunal
(2) Where an employer to whom a request is sent fails to appear before a Tribunal at the time and place set out in the request, the Tribunal shall consider all the information that is presented to it by the Minister in relation to the alleged violation.

Opportunity to make representations
(3) In conducting its review, a Tribunal shall provide the Minister and the employer with a full opportunity consistent with procedural fairness and natural justice to present evidence and make representations to it with respect to the alleged violation.

Determination of Tribunal
(4) Where at the conclusion of its proceedings a Tribunal determines that the employer
(a) has not committed the alleged violation, the Tribunal shall immediately inform the employer and the Minister of its determination and no further proceedings shall be taken against the employer in respect of the alleged violation; or
(b) has committed the alleged violation, the Tribunal shall immediately
(i) issue to the Minister a certificate, in the prescribed form, of its determination that sets out an amount, not exceeding the applicable amount set out in subsection 36(2), determined by the Tribunal to be payable by the employer in respect of the violation, and
(ii) send a copy of the certificate to the employer by registered mail.

Factors to be considered
(5) In determining an amount under subparagraph (4)(b)(i), a Tribunal shall take into account the factors set out in subsection 36(3).

Burden of proof
(6) In proceedings under this section, the Minister has the burden of proving, on a balance of probabilities, that an employer has committed the alleged violation.

Certificate
(7) A certificate that purports to have been issued by a Tribunal under subparagraph (4)(b)(i) is evidence of the facts stated in the certificate, without proof of the signature or official character of the person appearing to have signed the certificate.

Determinations are final
(8) A determination of a Tribunal under this section is final and, except for judicial review under the Federal Court Act, is not subject to appeal or review by any court.
1995, c. 44, s. 39; 1998, c. 9, s. 41.

Enforcement of Monetary Penalties
Registration of certificate
40. (1) A certificate issued under subparagraph 39(4)(b)(i) may be registered in the

Federal Court and when registered has the same force and effect, and all proceedings may be taken on the certificate, as if the certificate were a judgment in that Court obtained by Her Majesty in right of Canada against the employer named in the certificate for a debt in the amount set out in the certificate.

Recovery of costs and charges
(2) All reasonable costs and charges associated with registration of the certificate are recoverable in like manner as if they were part of the amount determined by the Tribunal under subparagraph 39(4)(b)(i).

PART IV
GENERAL

Regulations
41. (1) The Governor in Council may make regulations
(a) defining, for the purposes of the Act, the expressions "employee", "hired", "occupational group", "promoted", "salary" and "terminated";
(b) prescribing the manner of calculating the number of employees employed by an employer for the purpose of determining when an employer is considered to employ one hundred or more employees;
(c) governing the collection of information and the conduct of analyses referred to in paragraph 9(1)(a) and the conduct of reviews referred to in paragraph 9(1)(b);
(d) governing the establishment and maintenance of employment equity records referred to in section 17;
(e) prescribing anything that is to be prescribed by this Act; and
(f) generally, for carrying out the purposes and provisions of this Act.

Application
(2) A regulation made pursuant to subsection (1) may be of general application or may apply to a particular employer or group of employers.

Where regulations apply to public sector
(3) No regulation may be made under subsection (1) that applies to the public sector without prior consultation with the Treasury Board.

Inconsistent meanings
(4) No expression defined pursuant to paragraph (1)(a) that applies to the public sector shall be given a meaning that is inconsistent with the meaning that that expression or any similar expression is given under the Public Service Employment Act.

Adaptation of Act to certain portions
(5) The Governor in Council may, taking into account the operational effectiveness of the appropriate portion of the public sector referred to in paragraph (a) or (b), make any regulation that the Governor in Council considers necessary to adapt this Act or the regulations or any provision of this Act or the regulations to accommodate
(a) the Canadian Security Intelligence Service; or
(b) where an order is made under paragraph 4(1)(d) in relation to the Canadian Forces or the Royal Canadian Mounted Police, the Canadian Forces or the Royal Canadian Mounted Police.

Requirements
(6) A regulation made under subsection (5) shall be made on the recommendation of the Treasury Board after consultation with
(a) in the case of a regulation respecting the Canadian Security Intelligence Service, or the Royal Canadian Mounted Police, the Solicitor General; and
(b) in the case of a regulation respecting the Canadian Forces, the Minister of National Defence.

Requirements may differ
(7) The effect of a regulation made under subsection (5) with respect to any matter may differ from the effect of the Act or the regulations or of any provision of the Act or the regulations with respect to that matter.

Powers, duties and functions of Minister
42. (1) The Minister is responsible for
(a) developing and conducting information programs to foster public understanding of this Act and to foster public recognition of the purpose of this Act;
(b) undertaking research related to the purpose of this Act;
(c) promoting, by any means that the Minister considers appropriate, the purpose of this Act;
(d) publishing and disseminating information, issuing guidelines and providing advice to private sector employers and employee representatives regarding the implementation of employment equity; and
(e) developing and conducting programs to recognize private sector employers for outstanding achievement in implementing employment equity.

Federal Contractors Program
(2) The Minister is responsible for the administration of the Federal Contractors Program for Employment Equity and shall, in discharging that responsibility, ensure that the requirements of that Program with respect to the implementation of employment equity by contractors to whom the Program applies are equivalent to the requirements with respect to the implementation of employment equity by an employer under this Act.

Labour market information
(3) The Minister shall make available to employers any relevant labour market information that the Minister has respecting designated groups in the Canadian workforce in order to assist employers in fulfilling their obligations under this Act.

Delegation
43. The Minister may authorize those persons employed in the public service of Canada whom the Minister considers to be appropriate to exercise any of the powers and perform any of the duties and functions that may be or are required to be exercised or performed by the Minister under this Act or the regulations, and any power exercised or duty or function performed by any person so authorized shall be deemed to have been exercised or performed by the Minister.

Review of operation of Act
44. (1) Five years after the coming into force of this Act, and at the end of every five year period thereafter, a comprehensive review of the provisions and operation of this Act including the effect of those provisions shall be undertaken by such committee of the House of Commons as may be designated or established by the House for that purpose.

Tabling of report
(2) A committee shall, within six months after the completion of a review referred to in subsection (1), submit a report on its review to the House of Commons including a statement of any changes the committee would recommend.

TRANSITIONAL PROVISION

Compliance with certain provisions
45. The Treasury Board, the Public Service Commission and any person who is an employer to whom the Employment Equity Act, R.S., c. 23 (2nd Supp.), applied shall, within one year after the coming into force of this section, comply with sections 9 and 10 of this Act.

CONSEQUENTIAL AMENDMENTS

46. to 53. [Amendments]

REPEAL

54. [Repeal]

COMING INTO FORCE

Coming into force
*55. This Act or any provision of this Act comes into force on a day or days to be fixed by order of the Governor in Council.

RELATED PROVISIONS

– 1998, c. 9, s. 33:

Definition of "commencement day"
33. (1) In this section, "commencement day" means the day on which this section comes into force.

Members cease to hold office
(2) Subject to subsections (3), (4) and (5), the members of the Human Rights Tribunal Panel cease to hold office on the commencement day.

Continuing jurisdiction of Human Rights Tribunal
(3) The members of any Human Rights Tribunal appointed under the Canadian Human Rights Act before the commencement day have jurisdiction with respect to any inquiry into the complaint in respect of which the Human Rights Tribunal was appointed.

Continuing jurisdiction of Review Tribunal
(4) The members of any Review Tribunal constituted under the Canadian Human Rights Act before the commencement day have jurisdiction with respect to any appeal against a decision or order of a Human Rights Tribunal.

Continuing jurisdiction of Employment Equity Review Tribunal
(5) The members of any Employment Equity Review Tribunal established under section 28 or 39 of the Employment Equity Act before the commencement day have jurisdiction over any matter in respect of which the Tribunal was established.

Supervision by Chairperson of Canadian Human Rights Tribunal
(6) The Chairperson of the Canadian Human Rights Tribunal has supervision over and direction of the work of any Human Rights Tribunal, Review Tribunal or Employment Equity Review Tribunal referred to in subsection (3), (4) or (5).

Remuneration
(7) Each member of a Human Rights Tribunal, Review Tribunal or Employment Equity Review Tribunal referred to in subsection (3), (4) or (5), other than such a member who is appointed as a full-time member of the Canadian Human Rights Tribunal, shall be paid such remuneration as may be fixed by the Governor in Council.

Travel expenses
(8) Each member of a Human Rights Tribunal, Review Tribunal or Employment Equity Review Tribunal referred to in subsection (3), (4) or (5) is entitled to be paid travel and living expenses incurred in carrying out duties as a member of that Tribunal while absent from their place of residence, but the expenses must not exceed the maximum limits authorized by Treasury Board directive for employees of the Government of Canada.

---

*[Note: Act in force October 24, 1996, see SI/96–93.]

The Ombudsman of Ontario, Canada

Roberta L. Jamieson*

The Legal Foundation for the Ombudsman

The Ombudsman in Ontario is one of eight provincial Ombudsman institutions which have been created in Canada. In addition, one of our two northern territories has created an Ombudsman. At the federal level, Canada has not yet created an Ombudsman with broad jurisdiction and the Constitution does not make provisions for this institution. It has however created specialised Ombudsman in the fields of Connection's, Official Languages and Information and Privacy. (Canada is also the site of the International Ombudsman Institute.)

The Ombudsman of Ontario is established by provincial legislation, the Ombudsman Act R.S.O. 1990 c. 0.6.

Selection of the Ombudsman

The Act prescribes that the appointment of the Ombudsman shall be by the Lieutenant Governor in Council on the address of the Assembly. In practical terms, and because of the nature of the Ombudsman's role with respect to government, there is a tradition that the appointment of the Ombudsman is done by consensus of all political parties.

It is presumed that in a Parliamentary system, the Legislature is the overseer of the government. The Ombudsman is an Officer of the Legislature which assists the Legislature in fulfilling this responsibility. The theory is that the Parliament holds the government accountable to be fair and just. If a member of the public believes the government has failed to meet that standard in its day to day administrative dealings, the Ombudsman is mandated to investigate the allegation of unfairness and resolve the issue. If the government is found to be unfair or unjust, the Ombudsman may make recommendations regarding corrective and remedial action. If the government fails to implement the recommendations, the Ombudsman then may report the unfairness or injustice to Parliament so it may take appropriate action.

It is only as a result of the Ombudsman being an Officer of the Parliament with the power to raise issues publicly that the traditional role of Parliament is enhanced. The Ombudsman cannot be ignored by government with impunity.

*Ombudsman of Ontario.

K. Hossain et al. (eds), Human Rights Commissions and Ombudsman Offices, 511–524.

Independence and Impartiality

The independence of the Ombudsman is secured in a number of ways. On an administrative basis, the Ombudsman has the power to hire staff and set terms of employment, to locate and operate her offices. Her staff are not members of the public service. The Ombudsman has -must have – broad autonomy to organize internally, to administer affairs, to determine her own procedures. Since the Ombudsman is not a part of the government and is at arm's length from the Legislature, the Ombudsman is not obliged to follow government procedures.

The independence of the Ombudsman is also enhanced by providing for a long term of office with removal only for cause. Almost by definition, the Ombudsman's role invites controversy. Governments do not enjoy being criticized. The Ombudsman must be free to act without fear of retribution. A term of office which goes well beyond the life of any particular government is required. In Ontario, the term of office is ten years. The Ombudsman is not permitted to hold any other office or other employment.

The Ombudsman's files are private and confidential, even from the Legislature itself. The Ombudsman and her staff may not be called upon to testify in court regarding information obtained in the performance of their duties.

The Impartiality of the Ombudsman

The impartiality of the Ombudsman is sought at the time of appointment by having all political parties within the Legislature reach consensus on the person to be appointed. Once appointed, it is the Ombudsman herself who must protect her credibility by ensuring she is scrupulously impartial. There may be no involvement in political activity by the Ombudsman. If the Ombudsman should be perceived to be favouring any political party, her credibility could be seriously damaged.

Complaints Regarding Acts of Government

In Ontario, which has a population of approximately 11 million, the Ombudsman deals with about 30,000 complaints and inquiries annually. The Ombudsman's jurisdiction is broad and includes the ability to investigate complaints about the actions or omissions of all provincial governmental organizations, including Ministries, commissions, boards and agencies. In Ontario, for example, the Ombudsman may investigate complaints about the administration of the Human Rights Commission and quasi-judicial administrative tribunals. The Ombudsman also deals with complaints from inmates in correctional facilities.

It is important to note that the Ombudsman is the place of last resort to deal with a complaint. The Ombudsman cannot investigate a complaint where a person has recourse to a statutory right of appeal or review. In addition, the public is encouraged to first use existing internal complaint-handling mechanisms so that the governmental organization itself has the opportunity to remedy the matter. It is generally only after these efforts have failed that the Ombudsman will consider an investigation. An Ombudsman usually can investigate complaints of both acts and omissions of governmental organizations.

Any person affected by a decision of government, or any affected group, may bring a complaint to the Ombudsman. In addition, complaints can be brought by a Member of the Provincial Parliament on behalf of one or more of his/her constituents.

In addition, it is very important that an Ombudsman be able to investigate on his/her own initiative. There may be situations in which a member of the public may be fearful of coming forward or whose identity must be protected. There may be other situations where, in conducting one investigation, the Ombudsman might come across other issues which are deserving of an investigation. Increasingly the ability to review systemic and system-wide issues throughout an agency or across government is providing an important means of not only addressing existing problems in the administration of government but also preventing problems for the future.

Investigations, Reports and Recommendations

In the case of Ontario, the Ombudsman Act sets out the grounds on which the Ombudsman may find that a complaint may be supported. The Ombudsman may in any case where there is evidence to support a complaint, conclude that a decision, recommendation, act or omission, which was investigated:

- appears to have been contrary to law;
- was unreasonable, unjust, oppressive, or improperly discriminatory, or was in accordance with a rule of law or a provision of any Act or a practice that is or may be unreasonable, unjust, oppressive, or improperly discriminatory;
- was based wholly or partly on a mistake of law or fact; or
- was wrong.

A complaint may be supported if a discretionary power has been exercised for an improper purpose or on irrelevant grounds or if irrelevant considerations were taken into account, or where reasons should have been given for the exercise of discretionary power and they were not given.

This expresses the full formal set of grounds. However, it is only a small percentage of cases which reaches this point. Very often, complaints are resolved early on in contacts with the government. If that can be done, it is not necessary for the Ombudsman to conclude a formal investigation. As well, even after an investigation begins, resolution might be achieved.

As part of the Ontario Ombudsman process, a summary which outlines the Ombudsman's tentative conclusions and recommendations is sent to the governmental organization before the Ombudsman's views are finalised. Then being fully aware of the Ombudsman's position, a governmental organization may decide to make further representations or to implement the Ombudsman's recommendations at this stage. If the organization's response is not adequate, the Ombudsman may forward a report to the minister and the Premier.

Finally, the Ombudsman has the power to present a report to the Legislature, and such a report becomes a public document. The Legislature may deal with the report by debate and/or by referring consideration of the report to its Standing Committee on the Ombudsman.

Investigative Powers

In Ontario, the Ombudsman has considerable investigative powers to assist her in the exercise of her mandate. However, experience has shown that once a culture has been established in the public service that promotes co-operation in resolving complaints with the Ombudsman, it is rare that the powers have to be exercised in any forceful manner. The Ombudsman has the power to enter upon any premises occupied by any governmental organization and inspect the premises and carry out any investigation. For example, Ombudsman staff often inspect jails and correctional centres during the course of investigations.

The Ombudsman may hear or obtain information from such persons as she thinks fit, and make such inquiries as she deems necessary. In particular, the Ombudsman may require any officer or employee of a government organization to furnish any information useful to an investigation, and to produce any documents or things which relate to a particular matter under investigation.

The Ombudsman may summon before her any person – including a complainant or an officer or employee of a governmental organization – for an examination under oath. Any person who obstructs or hinders the Ombudsman in the performance of her role or fails to comply with any lawful requirement of the Ombudsman, or who makes any false statements is guilty of an offense and subject to fine and/or imprisonment.

Where the Ombudsman during or after an investigation is of the opinion that there is evidence of a breach of duty or of misconduct on the part of a government officer or employee, she may refer the matter to the appropriate authority.

Access and Equity

It is important that the Ombudsman be accessible to the people who are most likely to have greater involvement with government, most likely to be the subject of unfair treatment, and least able to defend their interests. "Accessibility" goes far beyond having an office which is open to anyone who wishes to attend at those premises. All members of the public, all groups, should be able to see themselves represented in the Ombudsman's staff. They should be treated in accordance with their circumstances and needs, along with respect for their particular culture. They should also be able to discuss their complaint in their own language with a member of the Ombudsman's staff.

The Ombudsman as Advocate

The Ombudsman may also be active in promoting a culture of fairness within government, and in educating the public about its right to complain and in this manner improve the quality of government service. It is of little benefit to the public to have an Ombudsman if the public does not know the office exists, or how to make a complaint, or lacks the confidence that complaints will be treated with respect. This is particularly important when dealing with complaints from the most vulnerable members of the public.

The Ombudsman is not, however, an advocate of any particular interest other than that of fairness and justice in the administration of government. The Ombudsman does not take the side of the complainant, but rather conducts an impartial investigation. Members of the public will see the Ombudsman not as a champion of their cause, but rather as someone who understands their respective needs and who will be vigorous in promoting the principles of fairness and justice in the public service.

The Ombudsman is not obliged, however, to wait for an unfair situation to produce a complaint. The Ombudsman may appear before Legislative Committees to point out provisions of legislation which do not provide the public with the right to have independent resolution of their complaints against government.

Accountability

Often the question, "To whom does the Ombudsman report?" is asked. Perhaps the question might better be phrased, "How is the independence of the Ombudsman balanced with accountability?", and the reverse of that question, "How is the Ombudsman to be held accountable without interfering with independence?"

The Ombudsman is held accountable in a variety of ways. The financial transactions of the Ombudsman are examined annually by an auditor who is also an Officer of the Legislature. The Ombudsman is required to make an annual report to the Legislature, which sets out the manner in which her mandate has been exercised over the course of the year and provides a sampling of cases which illustrate her work. The Legislative Assembly may inquire into a matter which the Ombudsman has brought to its attention. At last resort, the Ombudsman may be removed from office for cause on the address of the Legislature.

Perhaps the most effective, and yet most subtle, way in which the Ombudsman is held accountable is that her credibility and ability to have her recommendations implemented depends upon having the support of the public and the legislature. If she does not remain non-partisan, if she cannot back up her recommendations with competent investigation, if she does not fiercely defend her independence from government, she cannot be effective as an Ombudsman. This is the true measure of accountability.

The manner in which the Ombudsman operates is as important as the powers which are provided. The Ombudsman must provide easy access to complainants. The process must permit great agility and flexibility in finding means of resolving complaints, and yet be fair both to government and complainant. The goal is to achieve resolution rather than to determine who is right and wrong. This is why the Ombudsman calls for few formalities in the process of investigation and resolution and is often able to provide quick solutions.

LEGISLATION

Ontario Ombudsman Act

Revised Statutes of Ontario, 1990, Chapter O.6

Definitions
1. In this Act,

"governmental organization" means a Ministry, commission, board or other administrative unit of the Government of Ontario, and includes any agency thereof; ("organization gouvernementale")
"minister" means a member of the Executive Council. ("ministre") R.S.O. 1990, c. O.6, s. 1.

Ombudsman
2. There shall be appointed, as an officer of the Legislature, an Ombudsman to exercise the powers and perform the duties prescribed by this Act. R.S.O. 1990, c. O.6, s. 2.

Appointment
3. The Ombudsman shall be appointed by the Lieutenant Governor in Council on the address of the Assembly. R.S.O. 1990, c. O.6, s. 3.

Term of office and removal
4. (1) Subject to subsection (2), the Ombudsman shall hold office for a term of ten years and may be reappointed for a further term or terms, but is removable at any time for cause by the Lieutenant Governor in Council on the address of the Assembly.

Retirement
4. (2) The Ombudsman shall retire upon attaining the age of sixty-five years but, where the Ombudsman attains the age of sixty-five years before having served five years in office, he or she shall retire upon serving five years in office. R.S.O. 1990, c. O.6, s. 4.

Nature of employment
5. (1) The Ombudsman shall devote himself or herself exclusively to the duties of the Ombudsman's office and shall not hold any other office under the Crown or engage in any other employment. R.S.O. 1990, c. O.6, s. 5 (1).

Non-application
5. (2) The Public Service Act does not apply to the Ombudsman. 1996, c. 6, s. 4.

Salary
6. (1) The Ombudsman shall be paid a salary to be fixed by the Lieutenant Governor in Council.
6. (2) The salary of the Ombudsman shall not be reduced except on address of the Assembly.

Expenses
6. (3) The Ombudsman is entitled to be paid reasonable travelling and living expenses while absent from his or her ordinary place of residence in the exercise of the Ombudsman's functions under this Act. R.S.O. 1990, c. O.6, s. 6 (1–3).

Pension
6. (4) The Ombudsman is a member of the Public Service Pension Plan. 1996, c. 6, s. 5.

Temporary Ombudsman
7. In the event of the death or resignation of the Ombudsman while the Legislature is not in session or if the Ombudsman is unable or neglects to perform the functions of his or her office, the Lieutenant Governor in Council may appoint a temporary Ombudsman, to hold office for a term of not more than six months, who shall, while in such office, have the powers and duties and perform the functions of the Ombudsman and shall be paid such salary or other remuneration and expenses as the Lieutenant Governor in Council may fix. R.S.O. 1990, c. O.6, s. 7.

Employees
8. (1) Subject to the approval of the Lieutenant Governor in Council, the Ombudsman may employ such employees as the Ombudsman considers necessary for the efficient operation of his or her office and may determine their salary and remuneration and terms and conditions of employment.

Benefits
8. (2) The employee benefits applicable from time to time to the public servants of Ontario with respect to,
(a) cumulative vacation and sick leave credits for regular attendance and payments in respect of such credits;
(b) plans for group life insurance, medical-surgical insurance or long-term income protection; and
(c) the granting of leave of absence,
apply to the permanent and full-time employees of the Ombudsman and where such benefits are provided for in regulations made under the Public Service Act, the Ombudsman, or any person authorized in writing by him or her, may exercise the powers and duties of a Minister or Deputy Minister or of the Civil Service Commission under such regulations.

Employees' pension benefits
8. (3) The Ombudsman shall be deemed to have been designated by the Lieutenant Governor in Council under the Public Service Pension Act as an organization whose permanent and full-time probationary staff are required to be members of the Public Service Pension Plan. R.S.O. 1990, c. O.6, s. 8.

Premises and supplies
9. The Ombudsman may lease such premises and acquire such equipment and supplies as are necessary for the efficient operation of his or her office. R.S.O. 1990, c. O.6, s. 9.

Audit
10. The accounts and financial transactions of the office of the Ombudsman shall be audited annually by the Provincial Auditor. R.S.O. 1990, c. O.6, s. 10.

Annual report
11. The Ombudsman shall report annually upon the affairs of the Ombudsman's office to the Speaker of the Assembly who shall cause the report to be laid before the Assembly if it is in session or, if not, at the next session. R.S.O. 1990, c. O.6, s. 11.

Oath of office and secrecy
12. (1) Before commencing the duties of his or her office, the Ombudsman shall take an oath, to be administered by the Speaker of the Assembly, that he or she will faithfully and impartially exercise the functions of his or her office and that he or she will not, except in accordance with subsection (2), disclose any information received by him or her as Ombudsman.

Disclosure
12. (2) The Ombudsman may disclose in any report made by him or her under this Act such matters as in the Ombudsman's opinion ought to be disclosed in order to establish grounds for his or her conclusions and recommendations. R.S.O. 1990, c. O.6, s. 12.

Application of Act
13. This Act does not apply,
(a) to judges or to the functions of any court; or
(b) to deliberations and proceedings of the Executive Council or any committee thereof. R.S.O. 1990, c. O.6, s. 13.

Function of Ombudsman
14. (1) The function of the Ombudsman is to investigate any decision or recommendation made or any act done or omitted in the course of the administration of a governmental organization and affecting any person or body of persons in his, her or its personal capacity.

Investigation on complaint
14. (2) The Ombudsman may make any such investigation on a complaint made to him

or her by any person affected or by any member of the Assembly to whom a complaint is made by any person affected, or of the Ombudsman's own motion.

Powers paramount
14. (3) The powers conferred on the Ombudsman by this Act may be exercised despite any provision in any Act to the effect that any such decision, recommendation, act or omission is final, or that no appeal lies in respect thereof, or that no proceeding or decision of the person or organization whose decision, recommendation, act or omission it is shall be challenged, reviewed, quashed or called in question.

Decisions not reviewable
14. (4) Nothing in this Act empowers the Ombudsman to investigate any decision, recommendation, act or omission,
(a) in respect of which there is, under any Act, a right of appeal or objection, or a right to apply for a hearing or review, on the merits of the case to any court, or to any tribunal constituted by or under any Act, until that right of appeal or objection or application has been exercised in the particular case, or until after any time for the exercise of that right has expired;
(b) of any person acting as legal adviser to the Crown or acting as counsel to the Crown in relation to any proceedings.

Application to Divisional Court to determine jurisdiction
14. (5) If any question arises whether the Ombudsman has jurisdiction to investigate any case or class of cases under this Act, the Ombudsman may, if he or she thinks fit, apply to the Divisional Court for a declaratory order determining the question. R.S.O. 1990, c. O.6, s. 14.

Guidance rules
15. (1) The Assembly may make general rules for the guidance of the Ombudsman in the exercise of his or her functions under this Act.
(2) All rules made under this section shall be deemed to be regulations within the meaning of the Regulations Act.
(3) Subject to this Act and any rules made under this section, the Ombudsman may determine his or her procedures. R.S.O. 1990, c. O.6, s. 15.

Mode of complaint
16. (1) Every complaint to the Ombudsman shall be made in writing.

To be forwarded
(2) Despite any provision in any Act, where any letter written by,
(a) an inmate of any provincial correctional institution;
(b) a person held in a place of secure or open custody designated under subsection 24 (1) of the Young Offenders Act (Canada); or
(c) a patient in a provincial psychiatric facility,
is addressed to the Ombudsman it shall be immediately forwarded, unopened, to the Ombudsman by the person for the time being in charge of the institution, place of secure or open custody or facility. R.S.O. 1990, c. O.6, s. 16.

Ombudsman may refuse to investigate complaint
17. (1) If, in the course of the investigation of any complaint within his or her jurisdiction, it appears to the Ombudsman,
(a) that under the law or existing administrative practice there is an adequate remedy for the complainant, whether or not the complainant has availed himself, herself or itself of it; or
(b) that, having regard to all the circumstances of the case, any further investigation is unnecessary,
the Ombudsman may in his or her discretion refuse to investigate the matter further.

(2) Without limiting the generality of the powers conferred on the Ombudsman by this Act, the Ombudsman may in his or her discretion decide not to investigate, or, as the case may require, not to further investigate, any complaint if it relates to any decision, recommendation, act or omission of which the complainant has had knowledge for more than twelve months before the complaint is received by the Ombudsman, or, if in his or her opinion,

(a) the subject-matter of the complaint is trivial;
(b) the complaint is frivolous or vexatious or is not made in good faith; or
(c) the complainant has not a sufficient personal interest in the subject-matter of the complaint.

Complainant to be informed
(3) In any case where the Ombudsman decides not to investigate or further investigate a complaint, the Ombudsman shall inform the complainant in writing of that decision, and may if he or she thinks fit state the reasons therefor. R.S.O. 1990, c. O.6, s. 17.

Proceedings of Ombudsman
18. (1) Before investigating any matter, the Ombudsman shall inform the head of the governmental organization affected of his or her intention to make the investigation.

Investigation to be in private
(2) Every investigation by the Ombudsman under this Act shall be conducted in private.

Where hearing necessary
(3) The Ombudsman may hear or obtain information from such persons as he or she thinks fit, and may make such inquiries as he or she thinks fit and it is not necessary for the Ombudsman to hold any hearing and no person is entitled as of right to be heard by the Ombudsman, but, if at any time during the course of an investigation, it appears to the Ombudsman that there may be sufficient grounds for him or her to make any report or recommendation that may adversely affect any governmental or person, the Ombudsman shall give to that organization or person an opportunity to make representations respecting the adverse report or recommendation, either personally or by counsel.

May consult minister
(4) The Ombudsman may in his or her discretion, at any time during or after any investigation, consult any minister who is concerned in the matter of the investigation.

Must consult minister
(5) On the request of any minister in relation to any investigation, or in any case where any investigation relates to any recommendation made to a minister, the Ombudsman shall consult that minister after making the investigation and before forming a final opinion on any of the matters referred to in subsection 21 (1) or (2).

Breach of duty or misconduct
(6) If, during or after an investigation, the Ombudsman is of opinion that there is evidence of a breach of duty or of misconduct on the part of any officer or employee of any governmental organization, the Ombudsman may refer the matter to the appropriate authority. R.S.O. 1990, c. O.6, s. 18.

Evidence
19. (1) The Ombudsman may from time to time require any officer, employee or member of any governmental organization who in his or her opinion is able to give any information relating to any matter that is being investigated by the Ombudsman to furnish to him or her any such information, and to produce any documents or things which in the Ombudsman's opinion relate to any such matter and which may be in the possession or under the control of that person.

Examination under oath
(2) The Ombudsman may summon before him or her and examine on oath,

(a) any complainant;
(b) any person who is an officer or employee or member of any governmental organization and who, in the Ombudsman's opinion, is able to give any information mentioned in subsection (1); or
(c) any other person who, in the Ombudsman's opinion, is able to give any information mentioned in subsection (1),

and for that purpose may administer an oath.

Secrecy
(3) Subject to subsection (4), no person who is bound by the provisions of any Act, other than the Public Service Act, to maintain secrecy in relation to, or not to disclose, any matter shall be required to supply any information to or answer any question put by the Ombudsman in relation to that matter, or to produce to the Ombudsman any document or thing relating to it, if compliance with that requirement would be in breach of the obligation of secrecy or non-disclosure.
(4) With the previous consent in writing of any complainant, any person to whom subsection (3) applies may be required by the Ombudsman to supply information or answer any question or produce any document or thing relating only to the complainant, and it is the duty of the person to comply with that requirement.

Privileges
(5) Every person has the same privileges in relation to the giving of information, the answering of questions, and the production of documents and things as witnesses have in any court.

Protection
(6) Except on the trial of any person for perjury in respect of the person's sworn testimony, no statement made or answer given by that or any other person in the course of any inquiry by or any proceedings before the Ombudsman is admissible in evidence against any person in any court or at any inquiry or in any other proceedings, and no evidence in respect of proceedings before the Ombudsman shall be given against any person.

Right to object to answer
(7) A person giving a statement or answer in the course of any inquiry or proceeding before the Ombudsman shall be informed by the Ombudsman of the right to object to answer any question under section 5 of the Canada Evidence Act.

Prosecution
(8) No person is liable to prosecution for an offence against any Act, other than this Act, by reason of his or her compliance with any requirement of the Ombudsman under this section.

Fees
(9) Where any person is required by the Ombudsman to attend before him or her for the purposes of this section, the person is entitled to the same fees, allowances, and expenses as if he or she were a witness in the Ontario Court (General Division), and the provisions of any Act, regulation or rule in that behalf apply accordingly. R.S.O. 1990, c. O.6, s. 19.

Disclosure of certain matters not to be required
20. (1) Where the Attorney General certifies that the giving of any information or the answering of any question or the production of any document or thing,
(a) might interfere with or impede investigation or detection of offences;
(b) might involve the disclosure of the deliberations of the Executive Council; or
(c) might involve the disclosure of proceedings of the Executive Council or of any committee of the Executive Council, relating to matters of a secret or confidential nature, and would be injurious to the public interest,

the Ombudsman shall not require the information or answer to be given or, as the case may be, the document or thing to be produced.

(2) Subject to subsection (1), the rule of law which authorizes or requires the withholding of any document, or the refusal to answer any question, on the ground that the disclosure of the document or the answering of the question would be injurious to the public interest does not apply in respect of any investigation by or proceedings before the Ombudsman. R.S.O. 1990, c. O.6, s. 20.

Procedure after investigation

21. (1) This section applies in every case where, after making an investigation under this Act, the Ombudsman is of opinion that the decision, recommendation, act or omission which was the subject-matter of the investigation,

(a) appears to have been contrary to law;
(b) was unreasonable, unjust, oppressive, or improperly discriminatory, or was in accordance with a rule of law or a provision of any Act or a practice that is or may be unreasonable, unjust, oppressive, or improperly discriminatory;
(c) was based wholly or partly on a mistake of law or fact; or
(d) was wrong.

(2) This section also applies in any case where the Ombudsman is of opinion that in the making of the decision or recommendation, or in the doing or omission of the act, a discretionary power has been exercised for an improper purpose or on irrelevant grounds or on the taking into account of irrelevant considerations, or that, in the case of a decision made in the exercise of any discretionary power, reasons should have been given for the decision.

Ombudsman's report and recommendations

(3) If in any case to which this section applies the Ombudsman is of opinion,

(a) that the matter should be referred to the appropriate authority for further consideration;
(b) that the omission should be rectified;
(c) that the decision or recommendation should be cancelled or varied;
(d) that any practice on which the decision, recommendation, act or omission was based should be altered;
(e) that any law on which the decision, recommendation, act or omission was based should be reconsidered;
(f) that reasons should have been given for the decision or recommendation; or
(g) that any other steps should be taken,

the Ombudsman shall report his or her opinion, and the reasons therefor, to the appropriate governmental organization, and may make such recommendations as he or she thinks fit and the Ombudsman may request the governmental organization to notify him or her, within a specified time, of the steps, if any, that it proposes to take to give effect to his or her recommendations and the Ombudsman shall also send a copy of his or her report and recommendations to the minister concerned.

Where no appropriate action taken

(4) If within a reasonable time after the report is made no action is taken which seems to the Ombudsman to be adequate and appropriate, the Ombudsman, in his or her discretion, after considering the comments, if any, made by or on behalf of any governmental organization affected, may send a copy of the report and recommendations to the Premier, and may thereafter make such report to the Assembly on the matter as he or she thinks fit.

(5) The Ombudsman shall attach to every report sent or made under subsection (4) a copy of any comments made by or on behalf of the governmental organization affected. R.S.O. 1990, c. O.6, s. 21.

Complainant to be informed of result of investigation

22. (1) Where, on any investigation following a complaint, the Ombudsman makes a recommendation under subsection 21 (3), and no action which seems to the Ombudsman to be adequate and appropriate is taken thereon within a reasonable time, the Ombudsman shall inform the complainant of his or her recommendation, and may make such comments on the matter as he or she thinks fit.

(2) The Ombudsman shall in any case inform the complainant, in such manner and at such time as he or she thinks proper, of the result of the investigation. R.S.O. 1990, c. O.6, s. 22.

Proceedings not to be questioned or to be subject to review

23. No proceeding of the Ombudsman shall be held bad for want of form, and, except on the ground of lack of jurisdiction, no proceeding or decision of the Ombudsman is liable to be challenged, reviewed, quashed or called in question in any court. R.S.O. 1990, c. O.6, s. 23.

Proceedings privileged

24. (1) No proceedings lie against the Ombudsman, or against any person holding any office or appointment under the Ombudsman, for anything he or she may do or report or say in the course of the exercise or intended exercise of his or her functions under this Act, unless it is shown that he or she acted in bad faith.

(2) The Ombudsman, and any such person as aforesaid, shall not be called to give evidence in any court, or in any proceedings of a judicial nature, in respect of anything coming to his or her knowledge in the exercise of his or her functions under this Act.

(3) Anything said or any information supplied or any document or thing produced by any person in the course of any inquiry by or proceedings before the Ombudsman under this Act is privileged in the same manner as if the inquiry or proceedings were proceedings in a court. R.S.O. 1990, c. O.6, s. 24.

Power of entry of premises

25. (1) For the purposes of this Act, the Ombudsman may at any time enter upon any premises occupied by any governmental organization and inspect the premises and carry out therein any investigation within his or her jurisdiction.

Notice of entry

(2) Before entering any premises under subsection (1), the Ombudsman shall notify the head of the governmental organization occupying the premises of his or her purpose.

Notice to desist

(3) The Attorney General may by notice to the Ombudsman exclude the application of subsection (1) to any specified premises or class of premises if he or she is satisfied that the exercise of the powers mentioned in subsection (1) might be prejudicial to the public interest.

Order of judge

(4) Where a notice is given under subsection (3) and in the opinion of the Ombudsman it is necessary to take an action apparently prevented by the notice, the Ombudsman may apply to a judge of the Ontario Court (General Division) for an order setting aside the notice in respect of such action and, where the judge is satisfied that such action would not be prejudicial to the public interest, he or she may make the order. R.S.O. 1990, c. O.6, s. 25.

Delegation of powers

26. (1) The Ombudsman may in writing delegate to any person holding any office under him or her any of the Ombudsman's powers under this Act except the power of delegation under this section and the power to make a report under this Act.

Delegation is revocable
(2) Every delegation under this section is revocable at will and no such delegation prevents the exercise by the Ombudsman of any power so delegated.

Restrictions and conditions
(3) Every such delegation may be made subject to such restrictions and conditions as the Ombudsman thinks fit.

Continuing effect of delegation
(4) In the event that the Ombudsman by whom any such delegation is made ceases to hold office, the delegation continues in effect so long as the delegate continues in office or until revoked by a succeeding Ombudsman.

Evidence of obligation
(5) Any person purporting to exercise any power of the Ombudsman by virtue of a delegation under this section shall, when required so to do, produce evidence of his or her authority to exercise the power. R.S.O. 1990, c. O.6, s. 26.

Offences and penalties
27. Every person who,
(a) without lawful justification or excuse, wilfully obstructs, hinders or resists the Ombudsman or any other person in the performance of his or her functions under this Act; or
(b) without lawful justification or excuse, refuses or wilfully fails to comply with any lawful requirement of the Ombudsman or any other person under this Act; or
(c) wilfully makes any false statement to or misleads or attempts to mislead the Ombudsman or any other person in the exercise of his or her functions under this Act,
is guilty of an offence and liable on conviction to a fine of not more than $500 or to imprisonment for a term of not more than three months, or to both. R.S.O. 1990, c. O.6, s. 27.

Rights under Act do not affect other rights, etc.
28. The provisions of this Act are in addition to the provisions of any other Act or rule of law under which any remedy or right of appeal or objection is provided for any person, or any procedure is provided for the inquiry into or investigation of any matter, and nothing in this Act limits or affects any such remedy or right of appeal or objection or procedure. R.S.O. 1990, c. O.6, s. 28.

Regulation Under Ombudsman Act

General Rules R.R.O. 1990, Reg. 865

Revised Regulations of Ontario, 1990, Regulation 865
No Amendments
This Regulation is made in English only

1. The Ombudsman shall, no later than three months after the end of the Ombudsman's reporting period, table his or her Annual or Semi-Annual Report, as the case may be, with the Speaker of the Legislative Assembly. R.R.O. 1990, Reg. 865, s. 1.

2. The Ombudsman and his or her staff shall not, except where permitted by the Act in carrying out functions thereunder, disclose to any third party any information received by the Ombudsman or his or her staff while carrying out any of the functions of the Ombudsman under the Act. R.R.O. 1990, Reg. 865, s. 2.

3. A member of the Ombudsman's staff carrying out Ombudsman functions under the Act, shall not express to anyone, other than to the Ombudsman or to his or her authorized

delegate, his or her opinion, recommendation or other similar comments respecting the decision, recommendation, act or omission purported to have been committed by or on behalf of the governmental organization in question or respecting anything else arising out of the investigation of the complaint by the Ombudsman and the Ombudsman's staff. R.R.O. 1990, Reg. 865, s. 3.

4. (1) Preliminary investigations by the Ombudsman's office shall be limited to cases wherein further information is required by the Ombudsman or any member of his or her staff either to confirm a complaint or wherein immediate assistance of a complainant is required and the circumstances of the complaint make the immediate implementation of the procedural requirements of the Act impossible.
(2) Once the substance of the complaint has been confirmed by the Ombudsman or his or her staff or where the immediate disposition of the complaint is neither possible nor advisable, the requirements of the Act must be followed. R.R.O. 1990, Reg. 865, s. 4.

5. Where at any time during the course of an investigation it appears to the Ombudsman that there may be sufficient grounds for formulating opinions under subsections 21 (1) and (2) of the Act or of making any recommendations under subsection 21 (3) of the Act, which has the effect of altering, opposing or causing the original decision, recommendation, act or omission to be changed in any way, the Ombudsman shall give the governmental organization and any person who is identified or is capable of being identified as having made or committed or caused to be made or committed, as the case may be, the decision, recommendation, act or omission, an opportunity to make representations respecting the adverse report or recommendations either personally or by counsel. R.R.O. 1990, Reg. 865, s. 5.

6. All reports of the Ombudsman made to governmental organizations in accordance with section 21 of the Act shall contain opinions in the wording of subsection 21 (1) and recommendations within the wording of subsection 21 (3). R.R.O. 1990, Reg. 865, s. 6.

7. In all cases where the Ombudsman has concluded that a response by a governmental organization to a report made by the Ombudsman under subsection 21 (3) of the Act is neither adequate nor appropriate, and where the Ombudsman wishes ultimately, if the matter cannot be resolved, to seek support for his or her recommendation in the Legislature, the report under subsection 21 (3) shall be referred to the Premier before it is referred to the Legislature. R.R.O. 1990, Reg. 865, s. 7.

(Note: See Votes and Proceedings of the Legislative Assembly No. 99, dated Thursday, November 22nd, 1979, received and adopted by the House on that date for the source of this Regulation.)

Malawi

Malawi's Human Rights Commission

E.M. Singini*

Tasks, Competencies and Organizational Structure

1. Parliament determines the tasks, the competencies (functions and powers) and the organizational structure of the Human Rights Commission and these are to be found in the Constitution (which established the Human Rights Commission) and the Human Rights Commission Act, 1998, which lays down provisions for the operational functioning of the Human Rights Commission.

2. The tasks of the Human Rights Commission are

(a) to be competent in every respect to protect and promote human rights in the broadest sense possible and to investigate violations of human rights on its own motion op upon complaints received from any person, class of persons or body.;
(b) to act as a source of human rights information for the Government and people of Malawi;
(c) to assist in educating the public on, and promoting awareness of, and respect for, human rights;
(d) to promote more particularly the human rights of vulnerable groups, such as children, illiterate persons, persons with disabilities and elderly;
(e) to consider, deliberate upon, and make recommendations regarding any human rights issues, on its own volition or as may be referred to it by the Government;
(f) to study the status and effect of legislation, judicial decisions and administrative provisions for the protection and promotion of human rights and to prepare reports on such matters and submit the reports, with such recommendations or observations as the Commission considers appropriate, to the authorities concerned or to any other appropriate authorities;
(g) to perform any other function which the Government may assign to the Commission in connection with the duties of Malawi under those international agreements in the field of human rights to which Malawi is a party, without derogation from the fact that the Government shall remain primarily responsible for performing such functions;
(h) to submit to the President, Parliament or any other competent authority, on an advisory basis, either at the request of the President, Parliament or such other authority or on its own volition, its opinions, recommendations,

*Law Commissioner.

K. Hossain et al. (eds), Human Rights Commissions and Ombudsman Offices, 527–532.

proposals or reports on any matter concerning the protection and promotion of the human rights;

(i) to examine any legislation, judicial decisions or administrative provisions in force as well as Bills and administrative proposals and make such recommendations as it considers appropriate in order to ensure that such legislation, judicial decisions, administrative provisions, Bills and administrative proposals conform to the fundamental principles of human rights;

(j) where necessary, to recommend the adoption of new legislation or administrative provisions, or the repeal, replacement or amendment of legislation or administrative provisions in force and relating to human rights;

(k) to comment publicly or as it sees fit on any general or specific situation of violation of human rights and recommend initiatives or measures to put an end to such situation;

(l) to promote ratification by Malawi of any international human rights instruments;

(m) to promote the harmonization of national legislation and practices with international human rights instruments to which Malawi is a party and to promote and monitor their effective implementation;

(n) to contribute to the reports which Malawi is required to submit pursuant to treaty obligations and, where necessity, express its opinions on the subject matter but always with due regard to its status as an independent national institution;

(o) to co-operate with agencies of the United Nations, the Organizations of African Unity, the Commonwealth and other multilateral or regional institutions and national institutions of other countries which are competent in the area of protection and promotion of human rights;

(p) to assist in the formulation of programs for the teaching of, and research in, human rights and, where appropriate to take part in their execution in institutions and other bodies, including in schools, universities and professional circles;

(q) to publicize human rights with the aim of increasing public awareness;

(r) freely and without any hindrance whatsoever to consider any questions falling within its competence;

(s) to hear any person and obtain any information or any other evidence necessary for assessing situations falling within its competence;

(t) to carry out investigations and conduct searches in connection with its powers, duties and function;

(u) exercise unhindered authority to visit prisons or any place of detention of persons including police cells, with or without notice;

(v) develop work relationships with non-governmental organizations devoted to protecting and promoting human rights including those organizations which promote economic and social development or which protect and promote the interest of vulnerable groups such as children, illiterate persons, persons with disabilities and the elderly;

(w) maintain consultation with other independent national institutions or bodies, such as the Law Commission, the Ombudsman and the Inspectorate of Prisons, in order to foster common policies, practices and approaches and to promote co-operation in relation to the handling of matters in cases of overlapping jurisdiction;

(x) progressively operate at the national, regional, district and other levels so as to enhance its outreach in the Republic;

(y) to do or perform such other acts or things as are reasonably required for the exercise of its powers and the performance of its duties and functions.

3. The sphere of competence of the Human Rights Commission covers all human rights enshrined in the Bill of Rights incorporated in the Constitution or accorded by any other law, including international treaties to which Malawi is a party.

4. There is no limitation on bringing a claim with regard to the time lapsed since the alleged violations were committed.

5. The Human Rights Commission has power to investigate on the spot any alleged violations of human rights, except that in the case of search of any premises a warrant of a magistrate is required and in the case of seizure of property an order of the Registrar of the High Court in required to authorize the entry or the seizure.

6. Legislature, judiciary and all organs of the Government and its agencies, and all natural and legal persons in Malawi are obliged to respect and uphold the human rights guaranteed by the Constitution or any other applicable law. The sphere of competence of the Human Rights Commission extends therefore to all organs of the State at national, regional local and district level.

7. As stated in paragraph 6 above, in addition to acts of the executive the Human Rights Commission can also judge the acts of members of the legislature and acts of the judiciary and can also entertain complaints by non-state actors.

8. The Human Rights Commission can comment on acts of the legislature before or after such acts have come into force.

9. The Human Rights Commission may hear and consider complaints and petitions within its competence brought before it by individuals or groups of individuals. Complaints may be brought before the Human Rights Commission on behalf of individuals or groups of individuals by the individuals or groups themselves, third parties, non-governmental organizations having an appropriate interest in the matter. Thus, family members are competent to bring up complaints before the Human Rights Commission.

10. There is nothing to restrict the Human Rights Commission from entertaining general complaints or comments or concerns by international organizations regarding specific legislation or administrative procedures. The Human Rights Commission has power to make recommendations to the competent authority, proposing amendments or reforms of the laws, regulations or administrative provisions or practices identified to be the source of difficulties or hardships complained about.

11. As stated in paragraph 9 above, a NGO is competent to bring complaints to the Human Rights Commission and there is no restriction as to where the NGO is established as long as the complaint concerns issues within the jurisdiction of the Human Rights Commission.

Organization

12. The Human Rights Commission is to consist of seven members as follows:

(a) two *ex-officio* members, namely the Law Commissioner and the Ombudsman;
(b) five other members formally appointed by the President but selected jointly by the two *ex-officio* members from nominations submitted by reputable human rights NGOs's following a public invitation for such nominations issued jointly by the two *ex-officio* members. The five are to serve in office for three years and are eligible for reappointment. They can be removed from office only on grounds of incompetence or incapacity or in case of the members becoming compromised to the extent that their ability impartially to exercise the duties of office is seriously in question, and they can be so removed by the President on the joints recommendation of the two *ex-officio* members.

13. The Human Rights Commission is accountable largely to Parliament, the body to which it submits reports, but it is also required to keep the President fully informed on matters concerning the general conduct of the affairs of the Human Rights Commission.

The independence of the Human Rights Commission is guaranteed by the Constitution which does not subject the Human Rights Commission to any other authority; by international practice regarding the status and functioning of national institutions for the protection and promotion of human rights; and by the Human Rights Commission Act which provides that all authorities (including all organs of the Government), bodies and persons shall recognize the status of the Human Rights Commission as a national institution independent of the authority or direction of any other body or person.

The Act further provides that every member of the Human Rights Commission or of a committee of the Human Rights Commission or of the staff of the Human Rights Commission shall serve independently and impartially and exercise his or her powers or perform his or her duties and functions in good faith and without fear or favour. The Act also makes it and offence for any person or body to interfere with, hinder or obstruct the Human Rights Commission, any of its members or any of its committees or any of its staff in exercising their powers or performing their duties.

14. Members of the Human Rights Commission are remunerated for their work out of the funds of the Human Rights Commission which are appropriated by Parliament.

15. Human Rights Commission funds are allocated by the Treasury through Appropriation Acts and under a separate vote which is not part of the vote of another Government ministry or department. The annual allocation is determined in discussion between the Human Rights Commission and Treasury, then endorsed by Cabinet before being appropriated by Parliament. The allocation may be spent as the Human Rights Commission sees fit.

16. There is one Human Rights Commission for the whole country. The Act requires that the Commission shall progressively establish offices at the regional. District and local area levels in addition to its principal office. Malawi has three administrative regions and twenty-six districts.

17. The Human Rights Commission is to have a permanent secretariat to be headed by an Executive Secretary to be appointed by the Human Rights Commission itself on such terms and conditions as the Human Rights Commission shall itself determine. Eligibility for appointment to the office of the Executive Secretary is that *the person has had experience and shown capacity in a profession or in activities devoted or relevant to the protection and promotion of human rights.* Staff salaries are to be paid out of the funds of the Human Rights Commission as appropriated by Parliament.

18. The Human Rights Commission has power to appoint its own staff directly on terms and conditions determined by the Human Rights Commission and can increase the number of its staff as it sees fit on account of need.

Procedure

19. There are no prior requirements before a complaint can be heard as to costs, deadlines or exhaustion of other remedies. There is free legal aid available generally in the country and this could be applied for in cases before the Human Rights Commission. The question of compensation for costs involved could always be considered as part of the remedies which the Human Rights Commission has powers to grant.

20. There are no requirements or restrictions as to the language to be used in proceedings before the Human Rights Commission. The official language in Malawi is English and it is expected that proceedings and rulings will, wherever possible, be recorded in the English language.

21. On procedure for hearings, the Act states that the Human Rights Commission shall have the power to determine its own procedure for the conduct of hearings of matters brought before it, but may otherwise be guided by such procedures as may be prescribed by regulations made under the Act. Such regulations are yet to be made.

Rulings

22. The Constitution categorically prohibits the Human Rights Commission from exercising, or being granted, powers of a legislative or judicial nature.

23. In view of the prohibition as stated in paragraph 22 above, it has come to be understood that Human Rights Commission's rulings only have the status of opinion or advice but have compelling or persuasive force given that the rulings are to be published and reported to Parliament annually or at more frequent intervals. The Human Rights Commission decides on publication of its rulings.

24. Under its general powers of granting remedies, the Human Rights Commission can recommend an award of compensation to complainants by the Government or by whoever has been complained against.

25. Rulings of the Human Rights Commission are to be published as part of its reports to Parliament.

26. Rulings of the Human Rights Commission are not necessarily in last resort. They are administrative rulings and as such they could be subjected to judicial review by superior courts.

27. Approximately *thirty* complaints are received per annum and a few have resulted in rulings by the Human Rights Commission.

Review of Experience of Malawi's Human Rights Commission

28. The main problem for Malawi has been the very inordinate delay in promulgating the Human Rights Commission Act which was before Cabinet and Parliament since March 1997. The Bill was finally passed by Parliament during the sitting in June 1998. It was published and became law on 11th August 1998.

Lack of this operational legislation has meant a delay in appointing the additional five members of the Human Rights Commission and thus delaying the constitution of its full membership. It has also meant lack of operational procedures for the effective functioning of the Human Rights Commission.

It also recommended that provisions in the operational statute should go further than is the case under the Bill in Malawi by guaranteeing that funds appropriated by Parliament should not, during the currency of the financial year be reduced by the executive organ of the Government under any circumstances. Such a financial guarantee would greatly enhance the independence of the Human Rights Commission.

A General Overview of the Set up of the Malawi Office of the Ombudsman

James Makoza Chirwa*

Background

For well over three decades, Malawi's governance has been characterized by a single party administration. This scenario was a product of previous Republican Constitutional provisions which did not allow the formation and existence of political pluralism. The single party administration was coated with gross violations of human rights, and specifically, citizens were denied fundamental freedoms among others, of expression, association and or assembly and were subjected to torture in and outside prisons occasioned by government machinery. Notwithstanding their conscience, Malawians were engulfed with fear and a vicious circle redounding to the perpetuation of gross injustices and rights violations.

As there is a limit to everything, 'monsoon' winds of political change started blowing across the Central African country Malawi. Things started changing in early 1992 when the Church openly spoke against the type and or quality of governance. This was followed and backed by the formation of pressure groups (now political parties).

Pressure on the former administration intensified and subsequently, on 18th May 1993, Malawians went to the polls in a referendum to choose between one party system of governance and political pluralism, and came out as victors – having opted for the latter. As a result, political pluralism became legitimate.

In their efforts to help change things during the political transition, the pressure groups of the United Democratic Front (now a ruling party) and the Alliance for Democracy (now a minor opposition party represented in the National Assembly) mentioned in their respective manifestos the need to create the institution of the Ombudsman and during the constitutional hearing, helped amend the Constitution. Malawians supported the idea and indeed the concept was provided for in the Transitional Republican Constitution.

Duties, Functions and Powers of the Malawi Office of the Ombudsman

The functions, duties and powers of the Ombudsman Institution in Malawi are provided for by Section 123(1) of the new Republic Constitution which came into effect on 18th May, 1994 and Section 5 of the Ombudsman Act, 1996. The

*Ombudsman.

K. Hossain et al. (eds), Human Rights Commissions and Ombudsman Offices, 533–550.

Republican Constitution was created by Malawians during the political transition from a one party system of government to political pluralism while the Ombudsman act was passed by the National Assembly and was assented to by the President of the Republic of Malawi on 26th June, 1996.

Under Section 123(1) of the Republican Constitution functions and powers of the Ombudsman are provided for as follows:

> "The Office of the Ombudsman may investigate any and all cases where it is alleged that a person has suffered injustice and it does not appear that there is any remedy reasonably available by way of proceedings in court or by way of appeal from a court or where there is no other practicable remedy."

This entails that the Office of the Ombudsman receives and investigates complaints that have exhausted locally available mechanisms of redress.

And Section 5 of the Ombudsman Act, 1996 places the duties, functions and powers of the Ombudsman into a broader and explicit perspective. This Section provides as follows:

> "5(1). Subject to the Constitution, the Ombudsman shall inquire and investigate and take such action or steps on any request or complaint in any instance or matter laid before the Ombudsman and concerning any alleged instance or matter of abuse of power or unfair treatment of any person by an official in the employ of any organ of Government, or manifest injustice or conduct by such official which would properly be regarded as oppressive or unfair in an open and democratic society."

In this perspective, functions and powers of the Ombudsman comprise the promotion of administrative justice and respect for human rights through the process of sound and impartial investigations. And Section 5 (2) of the Ombudsman Act streamlines the functions and powers of the Ombudsman to embrace unreasonable, unjust or unfair decisions or recommendations taken or made by or under authority of any organ of government or any act of omission of such organ or any practice.

As if this is not enough, the Ombudsman is also bestowed with constitutional obligations as a member of the Prisons Inspectorate (Chapter XVII – of the Constitution), a co-chairperson of the Human Rights Commission, a member of the Police Service Commission (under Chapter XII of the Constitution), and indeed, a member of the two-man Senate (with the Speaker) yet to be established (Chapter VI of the Constitution). Allied to this, the Ombudsman sits on the Inter-ministerial Committee on Human Rights.

All those obligations relate to the promotion of the respect for and protection of human rights and furtherance of administrative justice. While the central tenet of the Ombudsman is administrative justice, the following fundamental freedoms enjoy the protection of the Ombudsman:

(a) a right to personal liberty
(b) a right to human dignity and personal freedoms
(c) a right to equal and effective protection against any discrimination on grounds of race, colour, sex, language, religion, political or other opinion, nationality, ethnic or social origin, disability, property, birth or other status
(d) rights of women
(e) right to fair and safe labour practices and to fair remuneration

(f) right to freely engage m economic activity, to work or to pursue a livelihood anywhere in Malawi
(g) right to freedom of association
(h) right to freedom of conscience, religion, belief or thought, and to academic freedom
(i) right to freedom of opinion
(j) freedom of expression
(k) freedom of movement and residence
(l) access to justice and legal remedies
(m) arrest, detention and fair trial

The Ombudsman promotes these rights through the aforementioned functions and powers including networking with other national institutions and NGOs.

As an alternative to the formal court system, the Ombudsman's receipt of complaints entails reasonable flexibility and disregards times lapsed between the commitment of the alleged violations rights or injustices.

The Ombudsman's flexibility extends to the conduct of investigations. He/she could undertake on the spot investigations and better still own motion investigation depending upon the nature of the alleged complaint and situation. Sometimes the ombudsman could refer (or refers) complaints to other competent institutions including NGO's and religious institutions for redress.

Section (5) of the Ombudsman Act, 1996, limits the Ombudsman's competency to cases that involve organs of government – be it a ministry, a Statutory Corporation etc. Private entities are exempted. The Ombudsman, cannot under Section 123(2) of the Republican Constitution oust decisions of the court of competent jurisdiction. And although the law is silent on the matter, the Ombudsman cannot review the decisions of the Legislature nor the Cabinet. And all legislative complaints fall within the jurisdiction of the Law commission, another constitutional Office.

Independence and Privileges of the Ombudsman

Under Section 122 of the Republican Constitution, the ombudsman is bestowed with complete independence in the exercise of his/her functions. Hence the Ombudsman is far from the interference of whomsoever. This is to promote impartiality and activity in the exercise of the aforementioned Ombudsman functions.

In an effort to promote or magnify this independence and resultant impartiality, Section 4 of the Ombudsman Act, 1996, empowers the ombudsman to appoint his own staff. This Section provides as follows:

> "The Ombudsman shall in the performance of his functions be assisted by staff appointed by him for that purpose on terms and conditions to be determined by agreement with such staff."

Allied to this, the Ombudsman is under Section 122(1) of the Republican Constitution and Section 3 of the Ombudsman Act, 1996, appointed by the Public Appointments Committee of the National Assembly. The law requires that the announcement of the vacancy be publicly made by the Clerk of the National Assembly. In the case of Malawi, the vacancy was announced for thirty days in several local papers to attract a wide range of candidates. The selection process took three months. This vigorous search ensures fairness on the part of the competing candidates. Since the ombudsman is not expected to report to an individual person of authority, his independence is ensured.

Furthermore, in the case of Malawi, the constitutional provision (Section 125(a) requires that a person holding the Office of the Ombudsman shall be provided with necessary resources to discharge the functions of that Office.

Adding on this, Section 183(3) ensures a continued salary of the Ombudsman as is the case with the salary of the President and Chief Justice; and the expenditure incurred to convene Parliament. The Section provides as follows:

"(3) No money shall be withdrawn from the consolidated fund save in respect of the following classes of expenditure [...] (b) the salary of the Ombudsman."

The Ombudsman is also, under Section 125 (1) of the Republican Constitution conferred a right to enjoy, with respect to his or her official functions, similar protection and privileges in so far as they are enjoyed by members of Parliament. Immunity, under the Ombudsman's Act 1996, extends to the Ombudsman staff provided their functions are carried out in good faith.

Better still, the removal from Office of a person holding the Office of the Ombudsman is not easy. The removal can only arise:

(a) when the one holding the Office reaches the age of sixty five years; or
(b) for gross misconduct by the one holding Office.

In this regard, only the Public Appointment Committee (PAC) of the National Assembly can decide. However, both the Ombudsman and his staff are required by law to exercise secrecy with regard to information connected to the Ombudsman investigations. This is not at the expense of transparency and accountability, though.

The practice so far has been has been in conformity with the law. The Institution of Ombudsman is adequately funded by government. Allied to this, the Office has so far received remarkable financial assistance from donor agencies such as the European Union and the Danish Centre for Human Rights, a Danish NGO. In this regard, it could be said that the independence of the institution shall not be sabotaged by deliberately inadequate financial provisions to the Office.

Investigations, Report and Recommendation.

The Ombudsman investigations ideally are confined to the application of administrative procedures, to regulations, policies, and actions or decisions by the organs of government. They encompass grounds of efficiency, effectivity, and good governance. Under Section 124 of the Republican Constitution, the Ombudsman is provided with full powers of investigations as follows:

(a) subpoena the attendance of any person who the Ombudsman reasonably believes to be connected with any investigation being undertaken by that Office;
(b) require the immediate disclosure of information and production of documents of any kind, from any public body;

(c) question any person who the Ombudsman reasonably believes to be connected with an investigation that is being undertaken by that Office; and
(d) initiate contempt proceedings before the High Court against any person or authority in connection with the non-compliance with the powers conferred in this Section.

Further to this, Section 125(b) of the Republican Constitution entitles a person holding the Office of the Ombudsman to the fullest cooperation of any person or authority of whom he or she requests assistance in connection with the duties of that Office.

In the initial stages, the cooperation from most responding organs in respect of a matter was much lacking. The reason was initially considered to be the lack of knowledge and/or awareness by the public regarding the powers and functions of the Ombudsman. Now that a number of civic awareness campaigns have been administered, there is a speedy change.

In respect of Investigations, the Ombudsman makes a detailed report of the findings on a particular case to the responding organ. When need arises, a complainant is also furnished with a copy. In the same investigation report, the Ombudsman details his recommendations. However, Section 127 of the Republican Constitution requires the Ombudsman to "lay, each year, before the National Assembly a report which shall include a record of all complaints and applications to the Office of the Ombudsman, a record of the exercise of powers in relation to applications of the remedies afforded to applicants in respect of grievances and shall also include a record of general recommendations of the Ombudsman in respect of grievances".

Conclusion

The Office of the Ombudsman is created Under Chapter X of the Republican Constitution and the enabling law, the Ombudsman Act 1996 bestowed it with complete independence. The Ombudsman is appointed by an independent Public Appointments Committee (PAC) of the National Assembly, who in turn appoints his own staff. In the process, independence and impartiality in the performance of the Ombudsman functions are ensured. While the Ombudsman may investigate any and all cases of alleged injustice, his investigations are by the Ombudsman Act 1996 confined to the organs of government. However, the Ombudsman has full constitutional powers of investigation and enjoys full cooperation from any person connected with the case(s) under investigations.

LEGISLATION

Constitution of the Republic of Malawi

[Protection of human rights and freedoms]

15.

1. The human rights and freedoms enshrined in this Chapter shall be respected and upheld by the executive, legislature and judiciary and all organs of the Government

and its agencies and, where applicable to them, by all natural and legal persons in Malawi and shall be enforceable in the manner prescribed in this Chapter.
2. Any person or group of persons with sufficient interest in the protection and enforcement of rights under this Chapter shall be entitled to the assistance of the courts, the Ombudsman, the Human Rights Commission and other organs of Government to ensure the promotion, protection and redress of grievance in respect of those rights.

Chapter X

The Ombudsman
120. There shall be a public office known as the office of the Ombudsman which shall have such powers, functions and responsibilities as are conferred upon that office by this Constitution and any other law.

121. In the exercise of his or her powers, functions and duties the Ombudsman shall be completely independent of the interference or direction of any other person or authority.

122.
1. Nominations for appointment to the office of Ombudsman shall be received from the public by way of a public advertisement placed by the Clerk to the National Assembly and the successful candidate shall be appointed by the Public Appointments Committee in accordance with the requirements of this section.
2. The person appointed to the office of Ombudsman shall:
1. have sufficient knowledge of the law;
2. be publicly regarded as a person who can make impartial judgements;
3. have sufficient knowledge of the workings of Government;
4. not have had any criminal convictions and not have been a bankrupt;
5. be otherwise competent and capable of performing the duties of his or her office;
6. not be the President, Vice-President, a Minister or Deputy Minister, a serving public officer or a member of Parliament; and
7. not hold any other public office unless otherwise provided for in this Constitution.

123.
1. The office of the Ombudsman may investigate any and all cases where it is alleged that a person has suffered injustice and it does not appear that there is any remedy reasonably available by way of proceedings in a court or by way of appeal from a court or where there is no other practicable remedy.
2. Notwithstanding subsection (1), the powers of the office of the Ombudsman under this section shall not oust the jurisdiction of the courts and the decisions and exercise of powers by the Ombudsman shall be reviewable by the High Court on the application of any person with sufficient interest in a case the Ombudsman has determined.

124. The Ombudsman shall have full powers to:
1. subpoena the attendance of any person who the Ombudsman reasonably believes to be connected with any investigation being undertaken by that office;
2. require the immediate disclosure of information and the production of documents of any kind, from any public body;
3. question any person who the Ombudsman reasonably believes to be connected with an investigation that is being undertaken by that office; and
4. initiate contempt proceedings before the High Court against any person or authority in connexion with non-compliance with the powers conferred in this section.

125. A person holding the office of Ombudsman shall:
1. be provided with the necessary resources to discharge the functions of that office;
2. be entitled to the fullest co-operation of any person or authority of whom he or she requests assistance in connexion with the duties of that office;

3. enjoy, with respect to his or her official functions, similar protection and privileges in so far as they are appropriate as are enjoyed by members of Parliament; and
4. be paid a salary to be charged to the Consolidated Fund and which shall not be reduced without the consent of the office holder.

126. Where the investigations of the Ombudsman reveal sufficient evidence to satisfy him or her that an injustice has been done, the Ombudsman shall:
1. direct that appropriate administrative action be taken to redress the grievance;
2. cause the appropriate authority to ensure that there are, in future, reasonably practicable remedies to redress a grievance; and
3. refer a case to the Director of Public Prosecutions with a recommendation for prosecution, and, in the event of a refusal by the Director of Public Prosecutions to proceed with the case, the Ombudsman shall have the power to require reasons for the refusal.

127. The Ombudsman shall lay, each year, before the Nation Assembly a report which shall include a record of all complaints and applications to the office of Ombudsman, a record of the exercise of powers in relation to applications, of the remedies afforded to applicants in respect of grievances and shall also include a record of the general recommendations of the Ombudsman in respect of grievances.

128.
1. A person appointed to the office of Ombudsman shall serve a term of not more than five years, provided that the Public Appointments Committee may appoint that person for such further terms of five years as it considers appropriate unless that Committee sooner terminates that appointment in accordance with this section.
2. A person appointed to the office of Ombudsman shall not be removed by the Public Appointments Committee, except
   1. in such circumstances where had that person not been Ombudsman, that person would have been disqualified from being appointed;
   2. for gross misconduct; or
   3. on reaching the age of sixty-five years.

Chapter Xl
Human Rights Commission

129. There shall be a Human Rights Commission the primary function of which shall be the protection and investigation of violations of the rights accorded by this Constitution or any other law.

130. The Human Rights Commission shall, with respect to the applications of an individual or class of persons, or on its own motion, have such powers of investigation and recommendation as are reasonably necessary for the effective promotion of the rights conferred by or under this Constitution, but shall not exercise a judicial or legislative function and shall not be given powers so to do.

131. (1) The Human Rights Commission shall consist of
(a) the person for the time holding the office of Law Commissioner;
(b) the person for the time being holding the position of Ombudsman:
Provided that, save as prescribed by this section, no other member of the Human Rights Commission shall be a person in any public office or the President or Vice-President, a Minister or Deputy Minister or a member of Parliament.
(c) such persons as shall be nominated from time to time in that behalf by those organizations that are considered in the absolute discretion of both the Law Commissioner and the Ombudsman to be reputable organizations representative of Malawian Society and that are wholly or largely concerned with the promotion of the rights and freedoms guaranteed by this Constitution.
(2) The Law Commissioner and the Ombudsman shall jointly refer the name of persons

nominated under paragraph (c) of subsection (1) to the President who shall formally appoint such persons as members of the Human Rights Commission.

[...]

Article 155. [The Police Service Commission]

1. There shall be a Police Service Commission with such powers and functions as are conferred upon it by this Constitution or an Act of Parliament.
2. Subject to this Constitution, power to appoint persons to hold or act in offices in the Malawi Police Force other than that of Inspector General of Police, including the power to confirm appointments, and to remove such persons from office shall vest in the Police Service Commission.
3. The Police Service Commission shall, subject to this Constitution and any general directions of an Act of Parliament, exercise disciplinary control over persons holding or acting in any office to which this section applies.

157. [Composition]

1. The Police Service Commission shall consist of the following members:

(a) such Justice of Appeal or Judge as may for the time being be nominated in that behalf by the Judicial Service Commission and who shall be the Chairman of the Police Service Commission;
(b) such member of the Civil Service Commission as may for the time being be nominated in that behalf by the Civil Service Commission;
(c) the Inspector General of Police or such senior officer in the Malawi Police Force as the Inspector General may for the time being nominate in that behalf;
(d) the Ombudsman; and
(e) such legal practitioner as may for the time being be nominated in that behalf by the President and confirmed by the Public Appointments Committee.

[...]

Human Rights Commission Act 1998

The Malawi Gazette Supplement, dated 11th August, 1998 containing an Act (No. 5C)

(Published 11th August, 1998)
Act No. 27 of 1998

I assent
Bakili Mululzi
President
27th June, 1998

An Act to make provision relating to the status and functioning of the Human Rights Commission established under Chapter XI of the Constitution and to provide for matters ancillary thereto or connected therewith

Enacted by the Parliament of Malawi as follows-

1. This Act may be cited as the Human Rights Commission Act, 1998

2. In this Act, unless the context otherwise requires
"appointed members" means members of the Commission appointed under section 131 (1) (c) of the Constitution, being those other than the Law Commissioner and the Ombudsman;
"Commission" means the Human Rights Commission established under Chapter XI of the Constitution;

"Executive Secretary" means the officer of the Commission appointed under section 28;
"human rights" means human rights guaranteed by or under the Constitution or any other law in force in Malawi, including international law;
"premises" includes land, any building or structure, any vehicle, conveyance, ship, boat. vessel, aircraft or container;

Part II – Membership of the Commission

3. The number of other members of the commission appointed under section 131 (1) (c) of the Constitution (in this Act referred to as appointed members") shall not exceed five at any one time unless the President, on the recommendation of the Commission, by Order published in the Gazette, prescribes a greater number of appointed members.

4. (1) The procedure for nominating appointed members shall involve first the issuing of a public advertisement, signed jointly by the law Commissioner and the Ombudsman, directed to the organizations described in section 131 (1) (c)of the constitution, being those which both the Law Commissioner and the Ombudsman, in their absolute discretion, consider to be reputable organizations representative of Malawian society and that are wholly or largely concerned with the promotion of rights and fundamental freedoms guaranteed by the Constitution.
(2) The advertisement under subsection (1) shall invite all appropriate organizations to nominate up to two persons who are independent, non-partisan and of high integrity and standing from within or outside the organization for appointment as member or members of the Commission, and to do so within thirty days of the date of the publication of the advertisement and in writing addressed to the Commission, giving the full name and address of any person so nominated and his curriculum vitae.
(3) The Law Commissioner and the Ombudsman shall-
(a) jointly assess the reputation of the nominating organizations and may, for that purpose, seek other or further information pertaining to any nominated person from the person himself or any other person or source before recommending who among the nominated persons shall be formally appointed by the President as members of the Commission;
(b) according to their assessment under paragraph (a), keep a lists of reserved names of nominated persons to be appointed to fill any casual vacancy for the reminder of the term of a member who vacates office before the expiry of the term prescribed in section 5 (1).
(4) A list of the names of nominating organizations, the names of the persons nominated and the names of the persons formally appointed by the President and the resultant membership of the Commission shall be published in the Gazette.

5. (1) Appointed members of the Commission shall hold office for a term of three years, and shall be eligible for reappointment.
(2) when making recommendations for appointment after the expiry of the three-year term, the Law Commissioner and the Ombudsman shall have regard to the need to maintain a reasonable degree of continuity on the membership of the Commission, so that at least half of the appointed members shall be re-appointed for the next term of office.
(3) A casual vacancy in the office of an appointed member shall occur if the member-
(a) is removed from office under section 131 (30 of the Constitution;
(b) dies; or
(c) resigns his office in accordance with subsection (4).
(4) An appointed member may at any time resign his office by giving one month notice addressed to the Law Commissioner and the Ombudsman who shall jointly transmit such notice to the President.
(5) A casual vacancy on the membership of the Commission shall be filled by the appointment of a person on the list of reserved names of nominated persons kept pursuant to section 4 (4).

(6) A person appointed to fill a casual vacancy shall serve for the reminder of the term of office but no person shall be so appointed where the remainder of the term of office is a period of less than six months.

6. (1) There shall be a Chairman of the Commission who shall be elected by the Commission from
among the appointed members at a meeting of the Commission attended by all members.
(2) Subject to subsection (3), the Chairman shall hold office as such until the expiry of his term of office as member of the Commission.
(3) The Chairman may be removed from office as such by the Commission for good cause and upon the unanimous decision of the rest of the members of the Commission.

7. Members of the Commission shall be paid such honorarium for membership and such allowances when discharging their duties as the Commission shall reasonably determine, subject to the approval of the Public Appointments Committee of Parliament.

8. (1) The Commission may establish such number of its own committees as it considers necessary for the performance of its functions and may assign to such committees any of its functions without prejudice to the power of the Commission itself to perform the function.
(2) The composition of every committee of the Commission shall include one or more members of the Commission and may include persons who are not members of the Commission but shall not include members of staff of the Commission.
(3) Subject to any general or special directions of the Commission, every committee shall have power to determine its own procedure.

9. (1) The Commission may invite or engage any person or persons to assist with the conduct of any inquiry or investigation before the Commission.
(2) The Commission or a committee of the Commission may invite any person, on account of his special knowledge or expertise, for any duration of time to take part in its deliberations at any meeting but such person shall not be entitled to vote at such meetings.

Part III – Competence and Responsibilities of the Commission

10. The provisions of this Part are in furtherance of, and without prejudice to, the generality of the mandate, powers and functions of the Commission conferred by the Constitution.

11. All authorities (including all organs of the Government) bodies and persons shall recognize the status of the Commission as a national institution independent of the authority or direction of any other body or person.

12. The Commission shall be competent in every respect to protect and promote human rights in Malawi in the broadest sense possible and to investigate violations of human rights on its own motion.

13. (1) The duties and functions of the Commission shall be
(a) to act as a source of human rights information for the Government and the people of Malawi;
(b) to assist in educating the public on, and promoting awareness and respect for, human rights;
(c) to promote more particularly the human rights of vulnerable groups, such as children, illiterate persons, persons with disabilities and the elderly;
(d) to consider, deliberate upon, and make recommendations regarding any human rights issues, on its own volition or as may be referred to it by the Government;
(e) to study the status and effect of legislation, judicial decisions and administrative provisions for the protection and promotion of human rights and to prepare reports on such matters and submit the reports, with such recommendations or observations

as the Commission considers appropriate, to the authorities concerned or to any other appropriate authorities;

(f) to perform any other function which the Government may assign to the commission in connection with the duties of Malawi under those international agreements in the field of human rights to which Malawi is a party, without derogation from the fact that the Government shall remain primarily responsible for performing such functions.

(2) The Commission shall keep the President fully informed on matters concerning the general conduct of the affairs of the Commission.

14. The Commission shall have the following responsibilities:

(a) to submit to the President, Parliament or any other competent authority, on an advisory basis, either at the request of the President, Parliament or such other authority or on its own volition, its opinions, recommendations, proposals or reports on any matters concerning the protection and promotion of human rights;

(b) To examine any legislation, judicial decisions or administrative provisions in force as well as Bills and administrative proposals and make recommendations as it considers appropriate in order to ensure that such legislation, judicial decisions, administrative provisions, Bills and administrative proposals conform to the fundamental principles of human rights;

(c) where necessary, to recommend the adoption of new legislation administrative provisions, or the repeal, replacement or amendment legislation or administrative provisions in force and relating to human rights;

(d) to comment publicly or as it sees fit on any general or specific situation of violation of human rights and to recommend initiatives or measures to put an end to such situation;

(e) to promote ratification by Malawi of any international human rights instruments;

(f) to promote the harmonisation of national legislation and practices with international human rights instruments to which Malawi is a party and to promote and monitor their effective implementation;

(g) to contribute to the reports which Malawi is required to submit pursuant to treaty obligations and, where necessary, express its opinions on the subject matter but always with due regard to its status as an independent national institution;

(h) to co-operate with agencies of the United Nations, the Organization of African Unity, the Commonwealth and other countries which are competent in the area of protection and promotion of human rights;

(i) to assist in the formulation of programs for the teaching of, and research in, human rights and where appropriate, toe take part in their execution in institution and other bodies, including in schools, universities and professional circles; and

(j) to publicise human rights with the aim of increasing public awareness.

15. The Commission shall:

(a) freely and without any hindrance whatsoever consider any questions falling within its competence;

(b) hear any person and obtain any information or any other evidence necessary for assessing situations falling within its competence;

(c) subject to the provisions of Part VI, carry out investigations and conduct searches in connection with matters that are before it or generally in connection with its powers, duties and functions;

(d) exercise unhindered authority to visit prisons or any place of detention of persons including police cells, with or without notice;

(e) develop work relationships with non-governmental organizations devoted to protecting and promoting human rights, including those organizations which promote economics and social development or which protect and promote the interest of vulnerable groups such as children, illiterate persons, persons with disabilities and the elderly;

(f) Maintain consultation with other independent national institutions or bodies, such as the Law Commission, the Ombudsman and the Inspectorate of Prisons, in order to foster common policies, practices and approaches and to promote co-operation in relation to the handling of matters in cases of overlapping jurisdiction;
(g) progressively operate at the national, regional, district and other levels so as to enhance its outreach in the Republic; and
(h) to do or perform such other acts or things as are reasonably required for the exercise of its powers and the performance of its duties and functions.

Part IV – Hearings, Investigations and Remedies

16. (1) The Commission may hear and consider complaints and petitions within its competence brought before it by individuals or groups of individuals.
(2) Complaints may be brought before the Commission on behalf of individuals or groups of individuals by the individuals themselves, legal practitioners, their representatives, third parties, non-governmental organizations, professional associations or any other representative organizations having an appropriate interest in the matter.

17. The Commission shall have power to determine its own procedure for the conduct of hearings of matters brought before it but may otherwise e guided by such procedures as may be prescribed by regulations made under this Act.

18. (1) For the purposes of conducting investigations necessary for the exercise of its powers and performance of its duties and functions, the Commission shall have powers:
(a) through a member of the Commission or any member of its staff designated in writing by a member of the Commission or by the Commission either generally or specially to require from any person such particulars and information as may be reasonably necessary in connection with any investigation;
(b) to require any person by notice in writing under the hand of a member of the Commission to appear before it at a time and place specified in such notice and to produce to it all articles or documents in the possession or custody or under the control of any such person and which may be necessary in connection with that investigation:
Provided that
I. Such notice shall contain the reasons why the presence of such person is required and why any such article or document should be produced;
II. When appearing and being examined before the Commission, such person may be assisted by a legal practitioner and shall be entitled to peruse or examine the articles and documents to refresh his memory;
(c) through a member of the Commission, to administer an oath to, or take an affirmation from, any person referred to in paragraph (b), or any person present at the place referred to in paragraph (b), irrespective of whether or not such person has been required under that paragraph to appear before it, and question him under such oath or affirmation in connection with any matter which may be necessary in connection with that investigation.
(2) A notice under subsection (1) shall not be effectively served unless it is delivered by
(a) a member of the Commission
(b) a member of the staff of the Commission
(c) a police officer or any other person,
authorized in that behalf by the Commission in relation to an investigation.
(3) Any person questioned under subsection (1) shall -
(a) be competent and compellable to answer all questions put to him regarding any fact or matter connected with the investigation;
(b) be competent and compellable to produce to the Commission any article or document in his possession or custody or under his control which may be necessary in connection

with that investigation.
(4) The Law regarding privilege as applicable to a witness summoned to give evidence in a criminal case in a court of law shall apply in relation to the questioning of a person under subsection (1).
(5) If it appears to the Commission during the course of an investigation that any person is being implicated in the matter being investigated, the Commission shall afford such person an opportunity to be heard in connection therewith by way of the giving of evidence or the making of submissions and such person or his legal representative shall be entitled, through the Commission, to question other witnesses, determined by the Commission, who have appeared before the Commission pursuant to this section.
(6) The Commission may direct that any person or category of persons or all persons the presence of whom, in the opinion of the Commission, is not desirable shall not be present at the proceedings or any part thereof during, or in the course of, an investigation.
(7) The Commission may in its sole discretion conduct open or closed hearings during its investigation of any matter.

19. (1) Any
(a) member of the Commission;
(b) member of the staff of the Commission
(c) police officer or other person,
authorized in that behalf by the Commission may subject to the provisions of this section, for the purposes an of an investigation, enter any premises on or in which any thing connected with that investigation is or is reasonably suspected to be.
(2) The entry and search of any premises under this section shall be conducted with strict regard to decency and order, which shall include regard to
(a) a person's right to respect for and protection of his dignity;
(b) the right to freedom and security of the person; and
(c) the right to his personal privacy.
(3) A person authorized under subsection (1) may, subject to the provisions of this section
(a) inspect and search the premises and there make such enquiry's as he may deem necessary;
(b) examine any article or document found on or in the premises;
(c) request from the owner or person in control of the premises or from any person in whose possession or control an article or document is information regarding the article or document;
(d) make copies of or take extracts from any book or document found on or in the premises;
(e) request from any person who has, or whom he has reason to believe has, the necessary information, an explanation regarding that article or document;
(f) attach any thing on or in the premises which in his opinion has a bearing on the investigation concerned;
(g) remove from the premises, against issue of a receipt, the article or document for further examination or for safe custody, but any article or document so removed, shall be returned as soon as possible after the purpose for such removal has been accomplished.

20. (1) Entry and search of any premises under this Act shall only be upon a warrant issued by a magistrate if it appears to the magistrate from information on oath that there are reasonable grounds for believing that any article or document, which has a bearing on the investigation concerned, is on such premises
(2) A warrant issued under this section may be issued on any day and shall be of force until
(a) it is executed; or
(b) it is cancelled by the person who issued it or, if such person is not available, by any person with like authority; or
(c) the expiry of one month from the day of its issue; or

(d) the purpose for the issuing of the warrant has lapsed, whichever occurs first.
(3) A person executing a warrant under this section shall, at the commencement of such execution, hand the person referred to in the warrant or the person who is the owner or in control of the premises a copy of the warrant and identify himself, if such person is present or, if such person is not present, affix a copy of the warrant to the premises at a prominent visible place.

21. If during the execution of a warrant under this Part a person claims that an article or document found on or in the premises concerned contains privileged information and refuses the inspection or removal of such article or document, the person executing the warrant shall, if he is of the opinion that the article or document contains information that has a bearing on the investigation and that such information is necessary for the investigation, request the Registrar or an Assistant Registrar of the High Court to issue an order to attach and remove that article or document for safe custody until a court has made a ruling on the question whether the information concerned is privileged or not, but such an order shall lapse if after thirty days from the date of its issue no court has made such ruling.

22. Upon hearing complaints brought before it or based upon any investigation sit has carried out or at any stage, the Commission
(a) shall seek an amicable settlement through conciliation and, where appropriate, on the basis of confidentiality;
(b) shall inform the complainant and the respondent of their respective right, remedies or obligations and the Commission shall promote a party's access to the remedies;
(c) may, as provided by sections 15 (2) and 46 (2) (b) of the Constitution, render such assistance or advice as the party that brought the complaint or petition may reasonable require;
(d) may transmit a complaint, petition or any other matter to any other competent authority as prescribed by the law or as otherwise the Commission thinks fit; or
(e) make recommendations to the competent authority, proposing amendments or reforms of the laws, regulations or administrative provisions or practices if the Commission has identified such laws, regulations or administrative provisions to have created the difficulties or hardships encountered by the persons who brought the complaints or petitions; and
(f) may recommend to the relevant authority the prosecution of any person found to have violated human rights or the taking of any other action and any such authority shall consider the recommendation and take such action as it deems appropriate.

Part V – Meetings

23. (1) The Commission shall meet as often as its business requires and in any event not less than once every two months.
(2) Meetings of the Commission shall be held at such places and times as the Commission shall determine:
Provided that the first meeting and any meeting at which the Chairman of the Commission is to be elected shall be convened by the Law Commissioner in consultations with the Ombudsman and shall be presided over by the Law Commissioner until the Chairman is elected.
(3) A meeting of the Commission shall be convened at the direction of the Chairman by written notice of not less than seven days, but such period of notice may be suspended with if in the opinion of the Chairman the urgency of any business or matter to be brought before the meeting so requires.
(4) The quorum for any meeting of the Commission or a committee of the Commission shall be formed by the presence of more than half of the members of the Commission or committee.

(5) Save as otherwise provided in subsection (2), meetings of the Commission shall be presided over by the Chairman of the Commission and, in the absence of the Chairman, members present may elect one of their number from among appointed members to preside.

24. (1) The chairman of every committee of the Commission shall be such member of the committee who is also a member of the Commission as the Commission shall designate.
(2) The chairman of a committee of the Commission shall preside over meetings of the committee and in his absence the members present may elect one of their number to preside.

25. The Commission, and every committee of the Commission, shall cause minutes of its meetings to be recorded and kept.

26. Save as provided in section 6 (3) in relation to the removal from office of the Chairman of the Commission, the decision of the Commission or of a committee of the Commission at any meeting shall be that of the majority of the members present and voting and in the event of a tie the person presiding shall have a casting vote in addition to his deliberative vote.

Part VI – Administration

27. The Commission shall exercise regular supervision of the work of the Commission and over the members of staff of the Commission in the performance of their duties.

28. (1) There shall be the office of Executive Secretary of the Commission which shall be a public office.
(2) The Executive Secretary shall be appointed by the Commission on such terms and conditions as the Commission shall determine.
(3) The office of the Executive Secretary shall be held by a person who has had experience and shown capacity in a profession or in activities devoted or relevant to the protection and promotion of human rights.

29. Subject to the general and special directions of the Commission, the Executive Secretary shall be responsible for the day to day management of the Commission and the administrative control of the other members of staff of the Commission and, in that regard shall be answerable and accountable to the Commission.

30. (1) There shall be employed in the service of the Commission, subordinate to the Executive Secretary, such other management professional, research, technical, administrative and other support staff as the Commission shall consider necessary for the exercise of its powers and the performance of its duties and functions and who shall be officers in the public service.
(2) The staff of the commission under subsection (1) shall be appointed by the Commission on such terms and conditions as the Commission shall determine:
Provided that the Commission may by directions in writing delegate to the Executive Secretary the appointment of its staff in such junior rank as it shall specify and the Executive Secretary shall report to the Commission every appointment he has made pursuant to this subsection.

31. (1) The Executive Secretary, or any other officer of the Commission as the Executive Secretary shall designate with the approval of the Commission, shall attend meetings of the Commission or any committee of the Commission to record the minutes of the meetings and to take part in the deliberations thereof subject to the directions of the Commissions or committee but shall not be entitled to vote.
(2) Where in any meeting the deliberations of the Commission or of a committee of the Commission concerns the Executive Secretary or any officer of the Commission designated

to attend the meeting, the Commission or the committee, as the case may be, may exclude the Executive Secretary or such officer from the meeting.

Part VII – Finance

32. (1) The Government shall adequately fund the Commission to enable it to exercise its powers and perform its duties and functions and so as to ensure its independence and impartiality.
(2) The Commission may receive any donations of funds, materials and any other form of assistance for the purposes of tits duties and functions;
Provided that no such donation shall jeopardise or compromise the independence and impartiality of the Commission.

33. The Commission shall be liable to account to Parliament for its funds in the manner applicable to Government departments and the accounts of the Commission shall be liable to audit by the Auditor General.

Part VIII – Miscellaneous

34. (1) Every member of the Commission of a committee of the Commission or of the staff of the Commission shall serve independently and impartially and exercise his powers or perform his duties and functions in good faith and without fear or favour.
(2) No organ of the Government and no member or employee of an organ of the Government nor any other person or body of persons, shall interfere with, hinder or obstruct the Commission, any committee of the Commission, any member of the Commission or of such committee or of the staff of the Commission or any person duly authorized to act in the service of the Commission in the exercise of its or his or her powers or the performance of its or his duties and functions.
(3) Any person who contravenes subsection (2) shall be guilty of an offence and liable to a fine of K20,000 and to imprisonment for five years.
(4) All organs of the Government shall accord the Commission such assistance and co-operation as may be reasonably required for the exercise of its powers and performance of its duties and functions and for the protection of the independence, impartiality and the due dignity of the Commission.

35. No person shall conduct an investigation on behalf of the Commission or render assistance
with regard to such investigation in respect of a matter in which he has any material or other interest which might preclude him from exercising his powers or performing his duties or functions a fair, unbiased and proper manner; and where any person fails to disclose such interest or conducts an investigation or renders assistance whit regard thereto in contravention of his section, the Commission may take such steps as it considers necessary to ensure a fair, unbiased and proper investigation.

36. Every member of the Commission (including the Law Commissioner and the Ombudsman) shall as such member, as soon as practicable-
(a) after the commencements of this Act, in case of a member holding office at the commencement of this Act;
(b) after his appointment, in the case of a member holding office subsequent to the commencement of this Act,
take an oath or make an affirmation for the due execution of his office before the president in the form set out in the Schedule to this Act;
Provided that in the case of an affirmation the form shall be modified so as to substitute the word "affirm" for the word "swear" and by omitting the last sentence in the form.

37. In addition to any specific report which the Commission may at any other time submit to any authority under this Act, the Commission shall within three months after

the end of every calendar year submit a report to Parliament on the activities it has carried out during that calendar year.

38. The Minister may, on the advice of the Commission, make regulations for the better carrying out of the provisions of the is Act.

SCHEDULE s. 36
Oath of Office of Member of the Commission

I ____________, being a member of the Human Rights Commission, do swear that I will well and truly perform the functions of that office according to the Constitution and the laws of the Republic of Malawi without fear, favour, affection or ill will. So help me God.

Passed in Parliament this seventeenth day of June, one thousand, nine hundred and ninety-eight.

R.L. Grondwe
Clerk of Parliament

Organizations

1. Public Affairs Committee (PAC)
2. Centre for Advice, Research and Education on Rights (CARER)
3. Centre for Human Rights and Rehabilitation (CHRR)
4. Civil Liberties Committee (CILIC)
5. Council for Non Governmental Organizations (CONGOMA)
6. Disabled Persons Association in Malawi (DIPAM)
7. Human Rights Forum for the Disabled and other Disadvantaged
8. Malawi Institute of Democratic and Economic Affairs (MIDEA)
9. Permanent Committee on Women and Children Affairs
10. Society for the Advancement of Women
11. Women's Voice
12. Women Lawyers Association
13. National Women's Rights and Lobby Group
14. Association of Progressive Women
15. Malawi Professional Women Associations
16. Youth Arm Organization
17. Youth Care Services
18. Centre for Youth and Children Affairs
19. Youth Watch Mzuzu
20. Eye of the Child
21. The Elderly People Association
22. The Malawi Red Cross
23. The Episcopal Conference of Malawi
24. The Catholic Commission for Justice and Peace in Malawi
25. Synod of Blantyre, Church of Central African Presbytery
26. Synod of Nkhoma, Church of Central African Presbytery
27. Synod of Livingstonia, Church of Central African Presbytery
28. The Anglican Council in Malawi
29. The Seventh Day Adventist Church South East African Union
30. The Baptist Mission in Malawi
31. Church of the Nazarene
32. The Evangelical Lutheran in Malawi
33. The Bible Society of Malawi
34. The Muslim Association of Malawi

35. The Law Society
36. The Medical Council of Malawi
37. The Society for the Advancement of Science in Malawi
38. The University of Malawi
39. Malawi Congress of Trade Union
40. Civil Service Trade Union
41. Teachers Union of Malawi
42. Media Council of Malawi

Nigeria

National Human Rights Commission of Nigeria

Muhammed Tabiu*

Introduction

The Law establishing the National Human Rights Commission, Decree 22, of 1995, was signed into law on 27th September, 1995. It makes provision for the functions, powers and basic structure of the Commission.

Mandate and Competence of the Commission

Section 5 of the enabling law empowers the Commission to perform the following functions:

(a) deal with all matters relating to the protection of human rights as guaranteed by the Constitution of the Federal Republic of Nigeria 1979, as amended, the African Charter on Human and Peoples' Rights and the Universal Declaration of Human Rights and other International Treaties on Human Rights to which Nigeria is a signatory;
(b) monitor and investigate all alleged cases of human rights violations in Nigeria and make appropriate recommendations to the Federal Military Government for the prosecution and such other actions as it may deem expedient in each circumstance;
(c) assist victims of human rights violations and seek appropriate redress and remedies on their behalf;
(d) undertake studies on all matters pertaining to human rights and assist the Federal Government in the formulation of appropriate polices on the guarantee of human rights;
(e) publish from time to time reports on the state of human rights protection in Nigeria;
(f) organize local and international seminars, workshops and conferences on human rights issues for public enlightenment;
(g) liaise and co-operate with local and international organizations on human rights with the purpose of advancing the promotion and protection of human rights;
(h) participate in all international activities relating to the promotion and protection of human rights;

*Executive Secretary of the National Human Rights Commission of Nigeria.

K. Hossain et al. (eds), Human Rights Commissions and Ombudsman Offices, 553–559.

(i) maintain a library, collect data and disseminate information and materials on human rights generally; and
(j) carry out such other functions as are necessary or expedient for the performance of its functions.

Scope of Competence

The mandate of the Commission is extensive in scope, covering all fundamental rights enshrined in the constitution, as well as the rights protected by international instruments. Nigeria is a signatory to the International Covenant on Civil and Political Rights, the International Covenant on Economic, Social and Cultural Rights, the Convention on the Rights of the Child, and the Convention on the Elimination of all Forms of Discrimination Against Women, among others. It has also had a bill of rights in its constitution since 1960, covering the whole range of civil and political rights.

In discharging this mandate the Commission takes into account the existence of other bodies performing related jobs such as the Public Complaints Commission, the Code of Conduct Bureau and Tribunal, the Committee on the Prerogative of Mercy, and the Federal Character Commission.

Broadly categorized the Commission's mandate consists of:

(1) treatment of complaints of human rights violations;
(2) human rights promotion and education and
(3) advising government on human rights policy including legislation affecting human rights.

The Commission's competence in these matters covers all persons and institutions in Nigeria, including the Executive, Legislature, Judiciary and non-state actors. It however does not sit on appeal over judicial decisions. In fact complaints on matters that are pending before courts of law are not normally accepted by the Commission. Nonetheless in numerous cases the Commission has intervened to urge for speedy disposal of cases on trial before courts of law. Examples are the well-known case of Chief Moshood Abiola who was accused of treason and the case of so-called 'Ogoni 19' accused of murder. In both cases the accused persons had spent years in detention without the cases making appreciable progress. The Commission intervened with very strong recommendations for expeditious disposal of the cases or release. The Commission has also accepted complaints from condemned prisoners in various prisons whose appeals were not making progress. It investigated these complaints and discovered that the problem lied in the prisoners' lack of resources to pay the required fees, file the relevant documents and prosecute their appeals. The Commission intervened in these cases by securing a waiver of the fees and seeking legal assistance for the appellants. Finally the Commission also accepts complaints regarding cases in courts of law where there is an allegation against judges of misconduct or high-handedness which has occasioned human rights violation.

In short although the Commission does not accept complaints challenging the merits of judicial decisions, it does accept complaints of human rights violations occasioned by protracted delays or alleged misconduct by judicial officers. The Commission has also in may cases intervened to demand respect by the Executive for court judgments.

The Commission is competent to receive complaints from any part of the country and investigate the complaints, including on-site investigation of alleged violations of human rights..

Role of NGOs

NGOs play a vital role in the Commission's work. In particular the Commission recognizes the competence of NGOs to submit complaints either for themselves or on behalf of other victims. In practice the Commission has received and treated complaints form NGOs like Constitutional Rights Project and Civil Liberties Organization. An example is the case of 110 inmates awaiting trials in Kirikiri Maximum Security Prison, Lagos, accused of various offense some of whom had been in detention for eight to ten years without being arraigned before courts of competent jurisdiction. Constitutional Rights Project (CRP), an NGO based in Lagos, brought the matter to the attention of the Commission. The Commission's intervention led to the immediate release of over half of the detainees and the arraignment of the others for trial before competent courts. The participation of the NGOs has brought the Commission's complaint mechanism much closer to the public.

In addition the Commission has carried out many collaborative programmes with NGOs for the training of target groups such as the police, judges and prison officers. It also solicits contributions from NGOs when formulating recommendations to be submitted to the Government on important human rights issues. For instance the Commission embarked on a Prisons Inspection Project in 1997. In September of that year it organized a seminar on the administration of criminal justice in Abuja in which relevant NGOs as well as state institutions like the Judiciary, the Police, the Prisons Service and the Directors of Public Prosecution participated. The resolutions of the seminar were incorporated into the Commission's recommendations for Prison and panel reforms, which were submitted to the Government.

Organizational Structure

Governing Council

The Governing Council of the Commission consists of sixteen Members, including the Chairman and the Executive Secretary. They are appointed by the Head of State to represent various interests including the legal profession, non-governmental organizations working in the field of human rights, the media, and the Ministries of Justice, Foreign Affairs and Internal Affairs. A member may be removed from office by the Head of State if he is satisfied that it is not in the interest of the public that the member should remain in office.

The Head of State, General Sani Abacha, inaugurated the Governing Council of the Commission on 17th June 1996, with Hon. Justice P.K. Nwokedi, a retired Justice of the Supreme Court, as Chairman.

Responsibility for discharging the functions of the Commission rests with the Governing Council, which meets at least once every month. The Chairman and Members of the Council, except the Executive Secretary, hold office for a term of 4 years on a part-time basis. The Executive Secretary holds office for a term of 5 years.

The Secretariat

The Secretariat of the Commission is headed by the Executive Secretary, who is the Chief Executive Officer of the Commission and responsible for its day to day operation. The Executive Secretary, like other members is appointed and may be removed. He occupies the status of a Permanent Secretary for the duration of his appointment and his remuneration is paid by the Federal Government. Currently the Commission has four (4) Departments, that is (i) Legal and Investigation, (ii) Public Affairs and Information, (iii) Research, Planning and Statistics, and (iv) Administration and Finance. At the moment 50 senior staff are employed in the Secretariat. The Governing Council appoints the staff of the Commission.

Zonal Offices

To reach out to the grass roots level, in a country of about 1 million square kilometres and a population of over 110 million, the Commission recognizes the necessity of establishing its offices at the State and Local Government levels. This is a long-term plan. In the meantime the country has been divided into 6 zones for the purpose of establishing zonal offices, each to take care of a group of states. The zonal offices facilitate the Commission's promotional and protective work in each zone.

Complaint Procedure

Manner of Lodging Complaints

Complaints may be lodged with the Commission by the following:

(i) Any person acting in his or her own interest;
(ii) Any person acting on behalf of another person who cannot act in his or her own name;
(iii) Any person acting as a member of or in the interest of a group or a class of persons; iv) An association acting in the interest of its members.

Complaints may be made in writing or orally to the national office of the Commission or to a representative of the Commission at the zonal or other office. The complaint must be signed or thumb-printed by the complainant or his agent. A complaint made orally must be reduced to writing by the officer or representative of the Commission to whom the complaint is made and signed or thumb-printed by the complainant or his agent.

A complaint must contain the full name and contact address of the Complainant and the body or person against whom the complaint is made. Full particulars of the complaint and the facts in its support must also be stated, as well as the relief sought. A complaint should not be made in abusive language.

A complaint is normally submitted in English, the official language. A complaint submitted in another language has to be translated into English.

Treatment of Complaints

On receiving a complaint the Commission decides if the complaint falls within its jurisdiction. If it does, then the Commission forwards it to the person, or the head of the body or organization alleged to have committed the violation for comment. The latter has 21 days from receipt of the complaint within which to respond, unless the Commission specifies a longer period.

If it deems fit, the Commission may assign an investigator or officer of the Commission to carry out a preliminary investigation into any complaint lodged with it. If following the preliminary investigation the Governing Council of the Commission decides that the complaint cannot be mediated upon or settled, it may decide to institute a full investigation. Such a decision will be conveyed in writing to the Complainant and the respondent, who will also be informed of the date, time and place of the hearing. Persons appearing before the Council for investigation may appear in person or be represented by counsel of their choice.

At the conclusion of the investigation the Council will inform the complainant and respondent of its findings, and may thereafter forward its comments and recommendations to the Federal Government.

Redress

In respect of any complaint lodged with it, and which if finds admissible, the Commission makes recommendations with a view to resolving the issue, and forwards the recommendation to the Federal Government of Nigeria, or the agencies responsible for the alleged violation.

A recommendation may include:

(i) recourse to a court of law at the instance of the Commission or of the person directly involved; or
(ii) appropriate sanctions against the offending officer.

The Commission's recommendations aim at reconciliation, redress, reparation, compensation, restoration, or any other remedy or redress for a right infringed or deprived.

Representation

The meetings of the Governing Council of the Commission and of its committees are private. The council may however, if it deems it necessary, permit a person making a complaint or against whom a complaints is made to be represented during consideration of the complaint.

Provisional Measures

Before or after making recommendations in respect of a complaint, the council may ask that provisional measures be taken in order to avoid irreparable harm to a person.

Funding

The Commission is funded by the Federal Government. Each year it submits its budget estimates to the Government covering personnel costs, other overhead expenses and its capital projects. The approved funds are released by the Ministry of Finance directly to the Commission.

In practice the funds made available have been insufficient to enable the Commission finance the various projects that it considers necessary. The law establishing the Commission allows it to accept gifts, endowments and other contributions. This opportunity has not been much used, but it does not provide an opening that is likely to be helpful in the future, without relenting in the efforts to secure better funding from the Government.

Conclusion: Review of Experience

The Commission started operating when the Governing Council was inaugurated in June 1996. It has operated fully, however, for only about a year now. The following are some points noted through this experience that may be found useful in setting up an Ethiopian Human Rights Commission.

Prioritising its Works

The Commission has been granted a wide mandate. It found it necessary to prioritise its work. The objective of prioritisation is to apply the usually limited resources to attend to the most pressing and productive of the many demands. In a country where other institutions exists with functions similar or closely related to those of the Human Rights Commission, prioritisation also includes avoiding duplication and conflict.

Power to Obtain Information

A Commission with investigative function should have the power of access to relevant information. The law establishing the Nigerian Commission grants it powers in general terms (s.6). We discovered that it is better to state these powers in specific terms, as is the case with our Public Complaints Commission. Recommendations have been made for amendment of the Decree to this effect.

Assertion of Independence

It is generally recognized that a national human rights institution must assert its independence from the government. In theory this is achieved through legal provisions regarding the appointment and removal of members, operational powers, etc. In practice however a lot of it has do with the personal integrity of the members. In addition, the effectiveness of a national institution also depends on its ability to demonstrate autonomy from other existing partisan political forces.

Effective Working Relations

Human Rights institutions usually have only advisory powers. How effectively they can discharge this function depends on the confidence that is reposed in their advise. The requisite expertise is of course necessary; but in addition a national institution must reach out to the various government departments, agencies and functionaries, and sensitize them to the importance and relevance of its advice. We have therefore found it useful to cultivate an effective working relationship with various government departments and functionaries.

An effective working relationship with the civil society, and non governmental organizations in particular, has also been found to be important, especially for operational and educational functions.

Delegation of Functions and Powers

Both the law establishing a national institution and the procedures for its operation should be flexible enough to allow sufficient devolution of functions and powers. Over-centralization may cripple a national institution, depriving it of the ability to respond effectively and in time. Of course proper safeguards should be put in place to prevent misuse or abuse of delegated powers.

Accessibility

One of the difficulties of running a new national institution is that of ensuring its accessibility. A lot of resources are needed to reach the nooks and corners of the country for promotional and investigation work. The answer is of course to provide the resources. The approach of the National Human Rights Commission of Nigeria is to take the task in phases by first establishing the head office, and gradually going to the level of zonal offices, state offices and perhaps even lower. In the meantime, however, all effort is being made to achieve accessibility (within the available resources and constraints) through publications, radio and TV, public lectures and human rights training programme.

It is to be added here that it is also necessary to raise public awareness of the nature and function of a national institution. This is not only for the purpose of accessibility of the services it offers, which is very important, but also because a public ignorant of the nature of a national institution may entertain expectations which the institution is incapable of satisfying because of the nature of its mandate. That may bring about a gap between its capabilities and public expectation, which could be detrimental to its credibility.

The Ombudsman Institution – The Nigerian Experience

Chief J. I. Edokpa*

Introduction

Speaking in general terms, one has to acknowledge the fact that in every civilised society, there exist a whole gamut of instruments which may be subtle or insidious, statutory or non-statutory by which society achieves conformity and sustains orderliness. Examples of non-statutory instruments include the sermon on the pulpit, the pressures of trade unions, non-governmental organizations, or the press amongst others. All over the world, ways are constantly being sought to discharge the official responsibilities of large complex organizations without treading on individual rights, needs and wishes. What would look like desperate moves by several nations for additional safeguards and protection, outside the judiciary, for the poor and underprivileged. poignantly underscores the necessity and relevance of the Ombudsman Institution.

This paper examines the brief historical antecedents; the structure; the laws as well as the limitations of the Nigerian Ombudsman within the socio-geopolitical and economic setting of the Nigerian polity, and makes a brief statement on the impact of the Ombudsman institution on good governance in Nigeria.

Historical Background

The immediate post-colonial Nigeria witnessed a burgeoning growth in the size of the public service. This was partly due to the inchoate nature of the emerging business class. The private sector was unable to take advantage of the vacuum left by the colonialist. The ultimate aim of the average Nigerian elite, then, was to take up appointment in the Civil Service. The resultant effect was the tremendous growth in the public service coupled with the preponderance of so-called bureaucrats and technocrats alike.

The growth of the public sector was further enhanced by the oil boom and the strengthening of so-called "state welfarism".

Post-colonial instability characterized by coups and counter-coups further enhanced the myth of indispensability woven around the bureaucrats. The inexperience of the military in matters of politics, its absolute dependence on the bureaucrats, coupled with its attempt to shield the bureaucrats from undue litigation (through Decrees and Edicts) facilitated the ascendance of bureaucracy

*Honourable Chief Commissioner, Public Complaints Commission, Abuja – Nigeria.

K. Hossain et al. (eds), Human Rights Commissions and Ombudsman Offices, 561–575.

and the attendant bureau pathologies such as maladministration, injustice arising from negligence, inefficiency, ineffectiveness and abuse of office.

The military regime of late General Murtala Mohamed, which took over power in 1975, indicted the civil service for lack of discipline, favouritism, misuse of public funds, arrogance, ostentatious living, flagrant abuse of office, deprivation of people's rights and liberties; perversion of time honoured procedures and norms, red-tapism, etc. It was against the backdrop of these administrative vices that the Udoji Public Service Review Panel recommended the establishment of the Public Complaints Commission. Thus, in October 1975, Decree No. 31 establishing the Public Complaints Commission as an independent, impartial, extra-judicial statutory body, was promulgated.

The main reasons given for the establishment of the Public Complaints Commission were:

(i) As a method of promoting accountability and administrative reforms and liberty;
(ii) As an effective control mechanism against public officers who were believed to be too powerful, arrogant, inefficient and tardy. That is, to remind them that an administrative error or abuse would not pass unnoticed;
(iii) As a result of the inadequacies of existing judicial control of administrative actions. For instance, apart from the exorbitant fees charged by legal practitioners, they lack the statutory or official powers or means to probe into administrative complaints.

Again, apart from the delays and long adjournments that became the hallmark of the Nigerian Law Courts – the courts were not equipped to try non-justiciable issues or trivial, day to day, administrative problems e.g. promotion supersession, witch hunting, etc.

Organizational Structure

In terms of organization structure, it is instructive to note that unlike what obtains in some countries where a single Ombudsman could be appointed to investigate administrative grievances, the Nigerian Ombudsman system is based on the appointment of Public Complaints Commissioners (Regional/State Ombudsman) for each State of the Federation but whose activities are coordinated by the Chief Public Complaints Commissioner at the Headquarters. In other words, Nigeria operates a (Regional) States and National Ombudsman system.

All staff of the Commission, apart from the State Commissioners, are employed by the Chief Commissioner. There are three major Departments i.e. Investigation, Personnel Management and Accounts Departments as well as other Units such as Public Enlightenment, Legal, Research and Statistics Units. The Nigerian Ombudsman recruits his staff from the main-stream labour market. Graduates in Law or Social Sciences are recruited to occupy the post of Investigation Officers, while non-graduates are recruited as Investigation Assistants. Other Departments and Units play supportive roles to the Investigation Department. Although the staff of the Nigerian Ombudsman are independent of the Civil

Service, they enjoy the same salary structure and retirement or pension benefits as their colleagues in the Civil Service.

One of the major problems facing the Nigerian Ombudsman Institution today is in the area of training. Incidentally this is the pivot around which the developments of the future must be tied. At the moment there are limited training facilities for the Nigerian Ombudsman staff. On assumption of duty, I directed the Investigation Officers to join their colleagues in the Personnel Management Department in writing competitive civil Service Confirmation or Promotion examinations in Civil Service Rules, Law or Local Legislation and Financial Instructions. In addition, we organize in-house training workshops for Investigation Officers to sharpen their investigating skills or techniques.

It is relevant to state here that the Nigerian Ombudsman's office is a self-accounting institution, entitled to make its own budget proposals and defend these. Funds are disbursed by the Chief Public Complaints Commissioner to the State Commissioners (Ombudsmen) in accordance with their needs and the funds available. An annual meeting of the Chief Commissioner and all other State Commissioners is held to discuss the budget, plans and performance appraisal, etc. As for location, it is important to add here that the office of the Nigerian Ombudsman is situated outside the building or premises of the main Civil Service or Ministries. This is to enable the Ombudsman effectively to play its watchdog role within the parameter set for it by the governing laws or regulations and to avoid interference's from the regular civil service.

Activities of the Public Complaints Commission

The Decree (31 of 1975) establishing the Public Complaints Commission – now an Act (specifically Cap. 377 of the Laws of Nigeria 1990 edition) – stipulates that "a Commissioner shall have power to investigate either on his own initiative or following complaints lodged before him by any other person, any administrative action taken by:

(a) any Department or Ministry of the Federal or any State Government;
(b) any Department of any Local Government authority (howsoever designated) set up in any State of the Federation;
(c) any Statutory Corporation or public institution set up by any Government in Nigeria;
(d) any Company incorporated under or pursuant to the Companies and Allied Matters Act whether owned by any Government aforesaid or by private individuals in Nigeria or otherwise howsoever; or
(e) any officer or servant of any of the afore-mentioned bodies."

The Decree also enjoins every Commissioner to ensure that administrative action by any person or body mentioned above would not result in the commitment of any act of injustice against any citizen of Nigeria or any other person resident in Nigeria.

In this connection, the Commissioner is empowered to investigate with care, administrative acts which are or appear to be:

"(i) contrary to any law or regulation;
(ii) mistaken in law or arbitrary in the ascertainment of facts;

(iii) unreasonable, unfair, oppressive or inconsistent with the general functions or administrative organs;
(iv) improper in motivation or based on irrelevant considerations;
(v) unclear or inadequately explained, or
(vi) otherwise objectionable"

The Decree also empowers a Commissioner to investigate administrative procedures of any Court of Law in Nigeria. In this regard, the Commissioner shall have access to all information necessary for the efficient performance of his duties under the Act and for this purpose may visit and inspect any premises belonging to any person or body aforesaid.

Operational Procedure

Normally, complaints are lodged in writing and signed by the complainants. If the complainant is illiterate, his verbal complaint is reduced to written form by an official of the Commission. His complaint is then read to him in the language he understands. This is done in the presence of a witness. All three then attach their signatures or append their right thumb impressions. Complaints are usually submitted to the Commission or sent by post. Alternatively, they could be slotted into the Complaint boxes located in the Local Government Headquarters in the case of complainants in rural locations. There are also five Area Offices in each State manned by Area Officers. These could be approached with complaints.

It is also a requirement that relevant documents should be attached to the petition to facilitate, ease and speed the investigation. Once a complaint is registered, investigation processes are put into operation. If the complaint is such that another body would handle it better, the complainant is often directed to this body, e.g. many complaints on rent are lodged with the Commission and are directed to the Rent Tribunal. This is done by our staff to lend assistance to the complainant. If the complaint falls within the jurisdiction of the Commission, the organization complained against is given a chance to comment on the petition in accordance with the principle of audi alteram partem. If the comment is not forthcoming, a follow-up action is taken. In some cases, corrective action is taken by the organization at this stage and the case is closed. When there is a clear conflict, further investigation is carried out which may take the form of a visit to the organization and examination of records or an invitation to the top officials of the organization to bring to the Commission relevant documents for examination.

To sustain confidence in the Commission, the law stipulates that a complaint lodged before the Commissioner shall not be made public by any person except a commissioner; and any person who contravenes this provision shall be guilty of an offence and shall be liable on conviction to a fine of N 500.00 or imprisonment for six months or to both such fine and imprisonment.

To ensure that the Commission is not obstructed in the performance of its duties, the law stipulates that if any person required to furnish information under this Decree (now Act) fails to do so or in purported compliance with such requirement, knowingly or recklessly makes any statement which is false, he shall be guilty of an offence and liable on conviction to a fine of N 500.00 or imprisonment for six months or to both such fine and imprisonment.

Similarly, any person who wilfully obstructs, interferes with, assaults or resists any Commissioner or any other officer or servant of the Commission in the execution of his duty under this Decree or who aids, invites, induces or abets any other person to obstruct, interfere with, assault or resist any such Commissioner, officer or servant shall be guilty of an offence and liable on conviction to a fine of N 500.00 or imprisonment for six months or to both such fine and imprisonment.

To avoid frivolity, the law stipulates that any person who in respect of any complaint lodged by him knowingly makes to a Commissioner any statement, whether or not in writing, which is false, shall be guilty of an offence and shall on conviction be sentenced to imprisonment for one year without the option of a fine.

Most noteworthy of all is the stipulation that a Commissioner shall not be subject to the direction or control of any other person or authority in the discharge of his duties. When a case has been fully investigated and all the facts fully documented, the Commissioner then approaches the final stage in either of two ways:

(i) he may appeal to the organization concerned to effect a corrective measure or reconsider an earlier decision; or to effect an alteration of a regulation or ruling or

(ii) he may take some semi-aggressive posture e.g. report erring companies to the Presidency.

In addition to the foregoing, a Commissioner is obliged, where he discovers in the course of investigation of a case that a crime may have been committed by a person, to report such to the appropriate authority or recommend that that person be prosecuted. Where he also feels that the conduct of a person is such that disciplinary action should be taken against him, he shall make a report to the appropriate authority who shall take such action as may be necessary in the circumstances.

No fees are charged for the Commission's services. After the receipt of a complaint, an acknowledgement is made to the complainant. At the conclusion of the investigation, the complainant is also informed of its outcome.

Publicity

It is a fact that for the Ombudsman to be effective the general public must know of its existence and functions. Again, media report remains the ultimate weapon in the armoury of the Nigerian Ombudsman as obtains in many other countries.

Consequently, an organic relationship exists between the Nigerian Ombudsman and the press on the one hand and the complainant or the oppressed on the other. Notwithstanding this relationship, it is sad to note that 22 years after the establishment of the Ombudsman Institution in Nigeria a significant percentage of the country's population are yet to become acquainted with its functions, due largely to the increasing rate of privatisation and commercialisation of the print and electronic media in Nigeria.

As a way out, both the Nigerian National and Regional Ombudsmen periodically participate in radio and TV programmes such as interviews, etc. We also undertake enlightenment tours during which the Ombudsman usually addresses members of the public about its functions and activities.

An information and Public Enlightenment Unit exists at the offices of the Ombudsman. The Unit is charged with the responsibility of publicising the activities of the Commission.

Limitations of Commissioners' Powers

As is usual with any organization, the law provides some limitations in the exercise of a Commissioner's powers. Consequently, the law stipulates that a Commissioner shall not investigate any matter:

(a) that is clearly outside its terms of reference;
(b) that is pending before the National Council of States, or the Executive Council;
(c) that is before the Armed Forces Ruling Council (National Assembly);
(d) that is before the House Committee on Public Petitions;
(e) that is pending before any Court of Law in Nigeria;
(f) relating to anything done or purported to be done in respect of any member of the Armed Forces in Nigeria under the Army Act 1960, the Navy Act 1964, the Air Force Act 1964 or the Police Act, as the case may be;
(g) in which the complainant has not, in the opinion of the Commissioner, exhausted all available legal or administrative procedures;
(h) relating to any act or thing done before 29th July, 1975, or in respect of which the complaint is lodged later than twelve months after the date of the act or thing done from which the complaint arose; and
(i) in which the complainant has no personal interest.

It is necessary to note that once a decision is taken on a complaint by any of the Commissioners, that decision is final and it cannot be reviewed by another Commissioner.

Impact of the Public Complaints Commission on Good Governance in Nigeria

The Nigerian Public Complaints Commission has been playing the crucial role of an administrative watchdog – having handled numerous complaints made against public servants in Federal and State Ministries, Local Governments, Statutory Corporations and the Private Sector. A few examples of such complaints include: non-payment of compensation for lands acquired, wrongful termination of appointments, refusal or delays in payment to contractors after successful completion of jobs, missing parcels or postal orders, police brutalities, non-payment of death or retirement benefits, etc.

In spite of the pervasive apathy of some people to government service oriented programmes, the Nigerian Ombudsman has continued to enjoy the patronage of all classes of Nigerians not only the poor, and the underprivileged but this time around some well to do individuals who want to save money and time involved in litigation in courts. The phenomenal increase in the number of cases received and treated by the Commission over the years is not unconnected with the perceived or imagined state of the socio-political economy, job security, pervasive labour unrest and its multiple effects on work and workplace.

A close study of the Commission's modus operandi shows that the Commission always endeavours to get to the root of any complaint lodged with it in order properly to provide redress for the aggrieved and thus eliminate the ground of discontent capable of brewing ill-feelings and dissatisfaction.

It is relevant to state here that the achievements of the Nigerian Ombudsman over the years derives to a large extent from the cautionary effects its existence has on decision makers as well as the tremendous respect that bureaucrats accorded the Ombudsman which is a result of the latter's reasoned judgements and decisions based on principle rather than expediency. Since its inception the Nigerian Ombudsman has been saddled with the responsibility of providing a viable option that is not only free and less cumbersome but a more peaceful and conciliatory way of seeking redress for the proverbial common man and certainly not as an instrument of harassment or demonstration of naked power.

I boldly say with every sense of modesty that the efforts of the Public Complaints Commission (Nigeria's Ombudsman) for the past 22 years, to supplement government's desire for a noble and just society has achieved some appreciable fruitful results evidenced and attested to by numerous unsolicited letters of commendation that pour into the Commission's offices everywhere in the country from complainants who have had cause to drink from its unpolluted stream of justice.

In conclusion, since the powers of Government pervade the day to day life of its citizens, there is need to ensure non-abuse in the exercise of these powers. This is the role the Nigerian Ombudsman has successfully performed these 22 years.

LEGISLATION

National Human Rights Commission Decree 1995

Supplement to Official Gazette Extraordinary No. 28, Vol. 82, 6th October 1995
Part A

Decree No. 22

[27th September, 1995)

Whereas considering that the United Nations Charter and several provisions of the Constitution of the Federal Republic of Nigeria 1979, as amended, are based on the principles of the dignity, and equality of all human beings and seek, among other basic objectives the promotion and respect for human rights and fundamental freedoms for all without distinction as to race, sex, language or religion;

And whereas to facilitate Nigeria's implementation of its Various treaty obligations, including, but not limited to, the Universal Declaration on Human Rights, the International Convention on the Elimination of all forms of Racial Discrimination, and the African Charter on Human and People's Rights;

And Whereas in furtherance of the above objectives and in its determination to provide a forum for Public enlightenment and dialogue on and to limit controversy and confrontation over allegations of human rights violation by public officers and agencies and to reaffirm the sacred and inviolable nature of human and other Fundamental rights;

Now therefore the Federal Military Government hereby decrees as follows:

Part I – Establishment of the National Human Rights Commission, etc.

1. (1) There is hereby established a body to be known as the National Human Rights Commission (in this Decree referred to as the "Commission").
(2) The Commission shall be a body corporate with perpetual succession and a common seal and may sue and be sued in it corporate name.
2. (1) There shall be for the Commission a Governing Council (in this Decree referred to as "the Council") which shall be responsible for the discharge of the functions of the Commission.
(2) The Council shall consist of
(a) Chairman who shall be a retired Justice of the Supreme Court of Nigeria or the Court of Appeal or a retired Judge of the High Court of a State;
(b) a representative each of the following Federal Ministries, that is
(i) Justice,
(ii) Foreign Affairs,
(iii) Internal Affairs
(c) three representatives of registered human rights organizations in Nigeria;
(d) two legal practitioners who shall not have less than ten years post qualification experience;
(e) the representatives of the media, at least, two of whom shall be from the private sector;
(f) three other persons to represent a variety of interests; and
(g) the Executive Secretary of the Commission.
(3) The Chairman and members of the Commission shall be
(a) persons of proven integrity; and
(b) appointed by the Head of State, Commander-in-Chief of the Armed Forces, on the recommendation of the Attorney-General of the Federation.
(4) The supplementary provisions set out in the Schedule to this Decree shall have effect with respect to the proceedings of the Council and the other matters contained therein.

3. (1) A member of the Council, other than the Executive Secretary, shall hold office for a term of four years and may be re-appointed for one further term of four years and no more.
(2) A member of the Council may at any time resign his office in writing addressed to the Head of State, Commander-in-Chief of the armed Forces and which resignation shall become effective, on acceptance by the Head of State, Commander-in-Chief of the Armed Forces.
(3) Members of the Council shall be paid such allowances, as may be determined by the Federal Government.

4. (1) A member of the council shall cease to hold office if-
(a) he becomes of unsound mind: or
(b) he becomes bankrupt or makes a compromise with his creditors; or
(c) he is convicted of a felony or of any offence involving dishonesty; or
(d) he is guilty of serious misconduct in relation to his duties.
(2) A member of the Council may be removed from office by the Head of State, Commander-in-Chief of the Armed Forces if he is satisfied that it is not in the interest of the public that the member should remain in office.
(3) Where a vacancy occurs in the in membership of the Council; it shall be filled by the appointment of a success or to hold office for the remainder of the term of office of his predecessor, so however that the successor shall represent the same interest and shall be appointed by the Head of State, Commander-in-Chief of the Armed Forces.

Part II – Functions and Powers

5. The Commission shall-
(a) deal with all matters relating to the protection of human rights as, guaranteed by the

Constitution of the Federal Republic of Nigeria 1979, as amended, the African Charter on Human and Peoples' Rights, the United Nations Charter and the Universal Declaration on Human Rights and other International Treaties on human rights to which Nigeria is a signatory;

(b) monitor and investigate all alleged cases of human rights violation in Nigeria and make appropriate recommendation to the Federal Military Government for the prosecution and such other
actions as it may deem expedient in each circumstance;

(c) assist victims of human rights violation and seek appropriate redress and remedies on their behalf;

(d) undertake studies on all matters pertaining to human rights and assist the Federal Government in the formulation of appropriate policies on the guarantee of human rights.

(e) publish, from time to time, reports on the state of human rights Protection in Nigeria;

(f) organize local and international seminars, workshops and conferences on human rights issues for public enlightenment;

(g) liaise and co-operate with local and international organizations on human rights with the purpose of advancing the promotion and protection of human rights;

(h) participate in all international activities relating to the promotion and protection of human rights;

(i) maintain a library, collect data and disseminate information and materials on human rights generally; and

(j) carry out all such other functions as are necessary or expedient for the performance of its functions under this Decree.

6. The Commission shall have power to-

(a) do all things which by this Decree or any other enactment are required or permitted to be done by the Commission; and

(b) do such other things as are necessary or expedient for the performance of its functions tinder this Decree.

Part III – Staff

7. (1) There shall be for the Commission an Executive Secretary, who shall be the chief executive of the Commission and be appointed by the Head of State, Commander-in-Chief of the Armed Forces, on the recommendation of the Attorney-General of the Federation.

(2) The Executive Secretary shall hold office for a term of five years in the first instance on such terms and conditions as the Head of State, Commander-in-Chief of the Armed Forces, may, on the recommendation of the Attorney-General of the Federation determine, and may be reappointed for one further term of five years and no more.

(3) Subject to such general directions as the Council may give, the Executive Secretary shall be responsible for the day-to-day administration of the Commission and the implementation of the decisions of the Council.

(4) The Executive Secretary shall perform the functions of keeping the record of proceedings and decisions of the Council and such other functions as the Council may, from time to time, direct.

8. (1) The Council shall have power to appoint directly, and either on transfer or on secondment from any public service in the Federation, such number of employees as may, in the opinion of the Council, be required to assist the Commission in the discharge of any of its functions under this Decree, and shall have power to pay to persons so employed such remuneration (including allowances) as the Council may, determine.

(2) The terms and conditions of service (including terms and conditions as to remuneration, allowances, pensions, gratuities and other benefits) of the persons employed by the Commission shall be as determined by the Council from time to time.

(3) The Council may engage such consultants and advisers as it may require for the proper and efficient discharge of the functions of the Commission.

9. The Commission may, subject to the provisions of this Decree, make staff regulations relating generally to the conditions of service of the employees of the Commission and without prejudice to the generality of the foregoing, such regulations may provide for
(a) the appointment, promotion and disciplinary control (including dismissal) of employees of the Commission; and
(b) appeals by such employees against dismissal or other disciplinary measures.

10. The Commission shall, with the approval of the Attorney-General of the Federation, determine its conditions of service, including pensions and gratuities, as are appropriate for its employees.

11. (1) It is hereby declared that service in the Commission is a scheduled service and shall be deemed to be pensionable under the Pensions Act and, accordingly, employees of the Commission shall in respect of their service in the Commission, be entitled to pensions, gratuities and other retirement benefits as are prescribed thereunder.
(2) Notwithstanding the provisions of subsection (1) of this section, nothing in this Decree shall prevent the appointment of a person to any office on terms which preclude the grant of a pension or gratuity in respect of that office.

Part IV – Financial Provisions

12. (1) The Commission shall establish and maintain a fund which shall be applied towards the discharge of its functions under this Decree.
(2) There shall be paid and credited to the fund established pursuant to subsection (1) of this section-
(a) such sums as may be provided by the Government of the Federation for the Commission;
(b) any fees charged for services rendered by the Commission; and
(c) all other sums accruing to the Commission by way of gifts, testamentary depositions, endowments and contributions from philanthropic persons and organizations or otherwise however.

13. (1) The Commission may accept gifts of land, money or other property on such terms and conditions, if any, as may be specified by the person or organization making the gift.
(2) The Commission shall not accept any gift if the conditions attached by the person or organization making the gift are inconsistent with the functions of the Commission.

14. (1) The Council may, with the consent or in accordance with any specific authority given by the Attorney-General of the Federation, borrow by way of loan or overdraft from any source approved by the Attorney-General of the Federation, such specified amount of money as may be required by the Commission for meeting its obligations and discharging its functions under this Decree.
(2) The Council may, subject to the provisions of this Decree and the conditions of any trust created in respect of any property, invest all or any of its funds with the like consent or general authority of the Attorney General of the Federation.
(3) The council may invest any surplus funds of the Commission in securities prescribed by the Trustee Investments Act or such other securities as may, from time to time, be approved by the Attorney-General of the Federation.
(4) Subject to the provisions of the Land Use Act, and any special or general direction which the Attorney-General of the Federation may give in that behalf, the Council may acquire or lease any land required for its purpose under this Decree.

15. (1) The Council shall cause to be prepared, not later than 30th September in each year, an estimate of the expenditure and income of the Commission during the next

succeeding year and when prepared they shall be submitted, through the Attorney-General of the Federation, to the Federal Executive Council for approval.
(2) The Council shall cause to be kept proper accounts and proper records in relation thereto and when certified by the Council such accounts shall be audited as provided in subsection (3) of this section.
(3) The accounts of the Commission shall be audited by auditors appointed from the list of auditors and in accordance with the guidelines issued by the Auditor-General of the Federation and the fees of the auditors and the expenses for the audit generally shall be paid from the funds of the
Commission.

16. The Council shall, not later than six months after the end of each year, submit, through the Attorney-General of the Federation, to the Federal Executive Council a report on the activities of the Commission and its administration during the immediately proceeding year and shall include in the report the audited accounts of the Commission and the auditors comments thereon.

Part V – Miscellaneous Provisions

17. Subject to the provisions of this Decree, the Attorney-General of the Federation may give to the Council such directives of a general nature with regard to the exercise by the Council of its functions under this Decree.

18. The Attorney-General of the Federation may make such regulations as he deems to be necessary or expedient for giving full effect to the provisions of this Decree.

19. In this Decree, unless the context otherwise requires
"Commission" means the National Human Rights Commission established under section 1(1) of this Decree;
"Council" means the Governing Council established for the Commission under section 2(1) of this Decree.
20. This Decree may be cited as the National Human Rights Commission Decree 1995.

SCHEDULE Section 2(4)
Supplementary Provisions Relating to the Council, etc.

Proceedings of the Council

1. (1) Subject to this Decree and section 27 of the Interpretation Act, the Council may make standing orders regulating its proceedings or those of any of its committees.
(2) The quorum of the Council shall be nine members, including the Chairman or, in his absence, the person elected under paragraph 2(2) of this Schedule to preside, and seven other members and the quorum of any committee of the Council shall be determined by the Council.
2. (1) The Council shall meet at least once a month in each calendar year and subject thereto, the Council shall meet whenever it is summoned by the Chairman, and if the Chairman is required to do so, by notice given to him by not less than four other members, he shall summon a meeting of the Council to be held within fourteen days from the date on which the notice is given.
(2) At any meeting of the Council, the Chairman shall preside but if he is absent, the members present at the meeting shall elect one of their number to preside at that meeting.
(3) Where the Council desires to obtain the advice of any person on a particular matter, the Council may co-opt him to the Council for such period as it thinks fit, but a person who is in attendance by virtue of this sub-paragraph shall not be entitled to vote at any meeting of the Council and shall not count towards a quorum.
(4) The decision of the Council shall be by simple majority.

Committees
3. (1) The Council may appoint one or more committees to carry out, on behalf of the Council, such of its functions as the Council may determine.
(2) A committee appointed under sub-paragraph (1) of this paragraph shall consist of such number of persons (not necessarily members of the Council) as may be determined by the Council, and a person other than a member of the Council, shall hold office on the committee in accordance with the
terms of his appointment.
(3) A decision of a committee of the Council shall be of no effect until it is confirmed by the Council.

Miscellaneous
[...]

Public Complaints Commission Act

Laws of Nigeria 1990, Chapter 377

An Act to establish the Public Complaints Commission with wide powers to inquire into complaints by members of the public concerning the administrative action of any public authority and companies or their officials, and other matters ancillary thereto.
[16th.October, 1975]

1. (1) There shall be established a commission to be known as the Public Complaints Commission (hereinafter in this Act referred to as "the Commission") which shall consist of a Chief Commissioner and such number of other Commissioners as the National Assembly may, from time to time, determine.
(2) The Commission may establish such number of branches of the Commission in the States of the Federation as the National Assembly may from time to time determine.

2. (1) The Chief Commissioner and other Commissioners shall be appointed by the National Assembly and shall be persons of proven integrity and shall possess such other qualifications as the National Assembly may determine.
(2) Subject to subsection (3) of this section, a Commissioner shall hold office for a term of three years in the first instance and shall be eligible for re-appointment for a second term of three years and shall vacate his office at the expiration of a period of six years.
(3) A Commissioner may at any time be removed from his office or appointment by the National Assembly.
(4) There shall be paid to the Chief Commissioner or other Commissioners such salaries and allowances as the President may from time to time direct.
(5) There shall also be paid to every Commissioner upon completion of his period of service a gratuity calculated in such manner as the President may direct.
(6) The amounts payable under this section shall be charged upon and paid out of the Consolidated Revenue Fund of the Federation.
(7) A Commissioner shall not while holding office hold any other office of emolument whether in the public service or elsewhere.

3. (1) The Chief Commissioner shall appointment additional officers and servants (not being Commissioners) as he may determine to assist him and other Commissioners in the discharge of their functions under this Act.
(2) The remuneration and tenure of office of other officers and servants of the Commission shall be determined by the Chief Commissioner after consultation with the federal Civil Service Commission.

4.(1) The Federal Civil Service Commission may by order published in the Federal Gazette declare the office of any person employed in the Commission to be a pensionable

office for the purposes of the Pensions Act; and any order so made may be given retrospective effect but shall not be made to take effect on a date earlier than 16th October 1975.
(2) Subject to subsections (3) and (4) of this section, the Pensions Act shall, in its application by virtue of subsection (1) of this section to any office, have effect as if the office were in the public service of the Federation within the meaning of the Constitution of the Federal Republic of Nigeria.
(3) For the purposes of the application of the provisions of the Pensions Act in accordance with subsection(2) of this section any power exercisable thereunder by a Minister or other authority of the Government of the Federation, other than the power to make regulations under section 23 thereof,
is hereby vested in and shall be exercisable by the Commission and not by any other person or authority.
(4) Nothing in the foregoing provisions of this section shall prevent the appointment by a person to any office in the Commission on terms which preclude the grant of a pension or gratuity in respect of service in that office.
(5) It is hereby declared for the avoidance of doubt, that references in this section to persons employed in the Commission do not include references to Commissioners.

5. (1) All Commissioners shall be responsible to the National Assembly but the Chief Commissioner shall be responsible for coordinating the work of all other Commissioners.
(2) A Commissioner shall have power to investigate either on his own initiative or following complaints lodged before him by any other person, any administrative action taken by-
(a) any Department or Ministry of the Federal or any State Government;
(b) any Department of any local government authority (howsoever designates)set up in any State in the Federation;
(c) any statutory corporation or public institution set up by any Government in Nigeria;
(d) any company incorporated under or pursuant to the Companies and Allied Matters Act whether owned by any Government aforesaid or by private individuals in Nigeria or otherwise howsoever; or
(e) any officer or servant of any of the afore-mentioned bodies.
(3) For the purpose of this Act-
(a) the Chief Commissioner may determine the manner by which complaints are to be lodged;
(b) any Commissioner may decide in his absolute discretion whether, and if so, in what manner he should notify the public of his action or intended action in any particular case;
(c) any Commissioner shall have access to all information necessary for the efficient performance of his duties under this Act and for this purpose may visit and inspect any premises belonging to any person or body mentioned in subsection (2) of this section;
(d) every Commissioner shall ensure that administrative action by any person or body mentioned in subsection (2) will not result in the commitment of any act of injustice against any citizen of Nigeria or any other person resident in Nigeria and for that purpose he shall investigate with special care administrative acts which are or appear to be:
   (i) contrary to any law or regulation,
   (ii) mistaken in law or arbitrary in the ascertainment of fact,
   (iii) unreasonable, unfair, oppressive or inconsistent with the general functions of administrative organs,
   (iv) improper in motivation or based on irrelevant considerations,
   (v) unclear or inadequately explained, or
   (vi) otherwise objectionable; and

(e) a Commissioner shall be competent to investigate administrative procedures of any court of law in Nigeria.

(4) Where concurrent complaints are lodged with more than one Commissioner, the Chief Commissioner shall decide which Commissioner shall deal with the matter and his decision thereon shall be final.

(5) All Commissioners and all the staff of the Commission shall maintain secrecy in respect of matters so designated by reason of source or content, so however that a Commissioner may, in any report made by him, disclose such matters as in his opinion ought to be disclosed in order to establish grounds for his conclusions and recommendations.

(6) In the exercise of the powers conferred upon a Commissioner by this section, the Commissioner shall not be subject to the direction or control of any other person or authority.

(7) It shall be the duty of any body or person required by a Commissioner to furnish information pursuant to subsection (3)(c) of this section to comply with such requirement not later than thirty days from receipt thereof.

6. (1) A Commissioner shall not investigate any matter-

(a) that is clearly outside his terms of reference;

(b) that is pending before the National Assembly, the National Council of State or the National Council of Ministers;

(c) that is pending before any court of law in Nigeria;

(d) relating to anything done or purported to be done in respect of any member of the Armed Forces in Nigeria or the Nigeria Police Force under the Nigerian Army Act, the Navy Act, the Air Force Act or the Police Act, as the case may be;

(e) in which the complainant has not, in the opinion of the Commissioner, exhausted all available legal or administrative procedures;

(f) relating to any act or thing done before 29th July 1975 or in respect of which the complaint is lodged later than twelve months after the date of the act or thing done from which the complaint arose;

(g) in which the complainant has no personal interest.

(2) For the purposes of paragraph (b) of subsection (1) of this section, a notice signed by the Secretary to the Federal Government and addressed to the Commissioner certifying that any matter is pending before any of the bodies mentioned in that paragraph shall be conclusive as to the tendency of the matter.

(3) In every case where a Commissioner decides not to investigate a complaint he shall state the reason therefor.

7. (1) A commissioner may recommend to the appropriate person or responsible administrative agency after due investigation of any complaint any of the following steps, that is-

(a) that a further consideration of the matter be made;

(b) that a modification or cancellation of the offending administrative or other act be effected;

(c) that an alteration of a regulation or ruling be effected;

(d) that full reasons behind a particular administrative or other act be given.

(2) Where appropriate, a Commissioner may refer cases where he feels that existing laws or administrative regulations or procedures are inadequate to the National Assembly or the appropriate Governor or to an other appropriate person or body.

(3) In every case where a Commissioner discovers that a crime may have been committed by any person, he shall report his findings to the appropriate authority or recommend that that person be prosecuted.

(4) In every case where a Commissioner is of the opinion that the conduct of any person is such that disciplinary action against such a person be taken, he shall make a report in that regard to the appropriate authority which shall take such further action as may be necessary in the circumstances.

8. (1) Any complaint lodged before the Commission shall not be made public by any person except a Commissioner and any person who contravenes the provisions of this subsection shall be guilty of an offence and shall be liable on conviction to a fine of N5OO or imprisonment for six months or to both such fine and imprisonment.
(2) If any person required to furnish information under this Act fails to do so or in purported compliance with such requirement to furnish information knowingly or recklessly makes any statement which is false in a material particular, he shall be guilty of an offence and liable on conviction to a fine of N5OO or imprisonment for 6 months or to both such fine and imprisonment.
(3) Any person who wilful obstructs, interferes with, assaults or resists any Commissioner or any other officer or servant of the Commission in the execution of his duty under this Act or who aids, invites, induces or abets any other person to obstruct, interfere with, assault or resist any such Commissioner, officer or servant shall be guilty of an offence and liable on conviction to a fine of N500 or imprisonment for six months or to both such fine and imprisonment.
(4) Any person who in respect of any complaint lodged by him knowingly makes to a Commissioner any statement, whether or not in writing, which is false in any material particular shall be guilty of an offence and shall on conviction be sentenced to imprisonment for one year without the option of a fine.

9. (1) In the discharge of his functions under this Act Commissioner shall have power to summon in writing any person who in the opinion of the Commissioner is in the position to testify on any matter before him, to give evidence in the matter and any person who fails to appear when required to do so shall be guilty of an offence under this Act.
(2) Any person guilty of an offence under this section shall on conviction be liable to a fine of N5OO or imprisonment for six months or to both such fine and imprisonment.

10. (1) No Commissioner shall be liable to be sued in any court of law for any act done or omitted to be done in the due exercise of his duties under or pursuant to this Act.
(2) Any report, statement or other communication or record of any meeting, investigation or proceedings which a Commissioner, officer or servant of the Commission may make in the due exercise of his functions under this Act shall be privileged in that its production may not be compelled in any legal proceedings if the Attorney-General of the Federation certifies that such production is not in the public interest.

9. [sic] In this Act, unless the context otherwise requires-
"Commission" means the Public Complaints Commission established under section 1 of this Act;
"law" means any Act, Law, Decree or Edict and includes any subsidiary legislation made under any of them;
"Commissioner" means any person appointed as such pursuant to section 2 of this Act and references to Com- missioner or Commissioners include, where appropriate, references to the Chief Commissioner.

11. (1) This Act may be cited as the Public Complaints Commission Act.
(2) The provisions of this Act are in addition to and do not in any manner derogate from the provisions of any other laws guaranteeing liberty of access to courts of law for redress.
(3) For the avoidance of doubt the powers granted to a Commissioner under this Act may be exercised by him notwithstanding the provisions of other laws which declare the finality of any administrative act.

Uganda

The Uganda Human Rights Commission, Including the Office of the Inspectorate of Government (Ombudsman)

Edmond R.B. Nkalubo*

The Uganda Human Rights Commission

The Uganda Human Rights Commission (UHRC) is a constitutionally independent and self-accounting commission of the government of the Republic of Uganda set up by law to safeguard the human rights of the people of Uganda. The UHRC is a legal entity enshrined in the Uganda Constitution of 1995 under Article 51–58 and created by the Uganda Human Rights Commission Act (Act No. 4) of 1997.

Historically the UHRC is a direct descendant of the Commission of Inquiry into Human Rights violations. This commission, chaired by Justice Arthur Oder, investigated and heard testimony about the massive human rights violations that occurred from Independence on 9th October 1962 to 26th January 1986, the date that the National Resistance Movement/Army (NRM/A) seized state power. It played a key role in impartially laying bare the history of those painful decades, healing the wounds and strengthening the resolve of the population that such human rights abuses, most of them state-inspired, never again occur.

During the constitution-making process (1989–1995), numerous Ugandans who made submissions to the Constitutional Commission expressed the need for a permanent human rights body to protect human rights. The delegates to the Constitutional Assembly in 1994 – 95 unanimously agreed to the enshrining of a permanent human rights commission within the Constitution to act as a watchdog, an educator, a mediator and investigator in the area of human rights.

Background to the UHRC

Uganda's history, especially since independence in 1962, has been characterized by gross violation of human rights. These violations had many causes, including undemocratic regimes, disrespect for Uganda's Constitution and laws, internal conflicts and wars, undisciplined security organs, and the inability of the people to stand up and defend their human rights and freedoms. Human rights violations caused dangerous divisions among the people, which in turn caused other human rights violations.

*Foundation for Human Rights Initiative.

K. Hossain et al. (eds), Human Rights Commissions and Ombudsman Offices, 579–611.

A great number of innocent people perished. Many were illegally detained, tortured or forced into exile. Personal liberty was infringed upon and the right to privacy violated. The freedoms of thought, belief, religion, conscience, association, assembly and movement were restricted. Many people lived under fear; suspects and prisoners were subjected to terrible torture and often died in detention. Violations caused Ugandans to lose faith in their justice system.

The Commission of Inquiry into Violation of Human Rights or Oder Commission clearly established that government organs were leading violators of human rights. These included the army, police, prisons and the numerous intelligence organizations which successive regimes illegally set up to sow terror. Some politicians and their functionaries became deeply involved in violations, giving credence to the general belief that most human rights violations were state-inspired and supported. Police cells, prisons, barracks, offices run by the intelligence organizations and even private residential houses became widely known and feared as places of torture and murder.

On assumption of state power in January 1986, the NRM/A promised to address this situation of human rights abuse through its Ten-Point Programme and "the fundamental change". One of its first decisions was to appoint the Commission of Inquiry, chaired by Justice Arthur Oder, to investigate human rights violations since 1962 and recommend how to prevent future violations. One of its key recommendations was the establishment of a permanent institution of human rights to act as the 'watchdog' of human rights in Uganda. Similarly, the general public recommended to the Uganda Constitutional Commission, chaired by Justice Benjamin Odoki, that a permanent and independent human rights body be enshrined in the Constitution. This was acted upon by the Constitutional Commission and the Constituent Assembly: the 1995 Constitution provides for a permanent Human Rights Commission.

The UHRC is established under Article 51(1) of the Constitution. Article 51(3) and (4) prescribes that the Chairperson of the Commission shall be a Judge of the High Court or a person qualified to hold that office and that members of the Commission shall be persons of high moral character and proven integrity who would serve for a period of six years and be eligible for re-appointment.

Article 52(1) of the Constitution and Section 8 of the UHR Commission Act (Act No. 4) of 1997 specify the functions of the UHRC as follows:

- to investigate at its own initiative or on a complaint made by any person or group of persons against the violation of any human rights;
- to visit jails, prisons, and places of detention or related facilities with a view to assessing and inspecting conditions of the inmates and make recommendations;
- to establish a continuing programme of research, education and information to enhance respect of human rights;
- to recommend to Parliament effective measures to promote human rights, including provision of compensation to victims of violations of human rights, or their families;
- to create and sustain within society the awareness of the provisions of the Constitution as the fundamental law of the people of Uganda;
- to educate and encourage the public to defend this Constitution at all times against all forms of abuse and violation;

- to formulate, implement and oversee programmes intended to inculcate in the citizens of Uganda awareness of their civic responsibilities and an appreciation of their rights and obligations as free people;
- to monitor the government's compliance with international treaty and convention obligations on human rights; and
- to perform such other functions as may be provided by law.

Article 48(1) of the Constitution also states that:

"The Uganda Human Rights Commission shall review the case of a person who is restricted or detained and to whom Article 47 of the Constitution applies, not later than twenty one days after the commencement of the restriction or detention, and after that, at intervals of not more than thirty days."

Under Section 8(1)(c) of the Act, the UHRC has an additional function of visiting any place or building where a person is suspected to be illegally detained.

The powers of the UHRC are spelt out in Article 53 of the Constitution and from section 18 to 26 of the Commission Act. These powers are the following:

- to issue summons or other orders requiring the attendance of any person before the Commission and the production of any document or record relevant to any investigation by the Commission;
- to question any person in respect of any subject matter under investigation before the Commission;
- to require any person to disclose any information within his or her knowledge relevant to any investigation by the Commission; and
- to commit persons for contempt of its orders.

The UHRC may, if satisfied that there has been an infringement of a human right or freedom, order:

- the release of a detained or restricted person;
- payment of compensation; or
- any other legal remedy or redress.

In the performance of its functions, the UHRC shall not investigate:

- any matter which is pending before a court or judicial tribunal; or
- a matter involving the relations or dealings between the Government and the Government of any foreign state or international organization; or
- a matter relating to the exercise of the prerogative of mercy.

The UHRC started work in November 1996 after the Chairperson and members were appointed. Its immediate objective was to conceptualise and concretize the notion of a human rights commission so as to create an effective national institution. The UHRC needed to find a 'home' to operate from and to publicise its existence and functions to the Ugandan citizenry, international community and human rights organizations. Until the end of March 1997, the Commission operated from the premises of the Oder Commission.

It then moved to its present rented offices on plot 22/24 Buganda Road. Media publicity and courtesy calls brought a swift response that indicated that the UHRC would be well utilized.

After an initial needs assessment, the UHRC began a detailed study of its mandate and a comparative study of other national commissions for human rights. This allowed it to determine its short and long-term activities and the staff, funds and organization it needs to be effective.

The UHRC set up four departments, each with its own committee. The Legal and Complaints Department:

- receives complaints and carries out preliminary investigations;
- analyses complaints and advises the UHRC on the action to take;
- handles all legal aspects and matters of the UHRC's operations;
- offers counsel services to the UHRC to sit as a court;
- executes the UHRC's orders.

The Investigations Department:

- carries out investigations on cases submitted to it by the Legal and complaints Department and by the UHRC as a whole;
- undertakes investigations on the initiative of the UHRC on any aspect of human rights violations which has come to the attention of the UHRC or which the UHRC has decided to investigate;
- regularly reports to the UHRC on cases of human rights violations which demand urgent action;
- guides the UHRC when it sits as a court to hear investigated cases, examine witnesses and reach decisions.

The Education, Training and Research Department:

- conducts needs assessments and develops civic education materials and methods for the education of citizens;
- works with the Ministry of Education and National Curriculum Development Centre (NCDC) to design and publish civic education syllabi for all institutions of learning, from primary to tertiary institutions;
- designs education programmes on the Constitution and organizes workshops, seminars and conferences as approved by the UHRC;
- carries out research studies on priority areas of human rights;
- arranges sessions for training trainers of human rights throughout the districts;
- organizes for publication the UHRC's educational material;
- devises ways in which the UHRC collaborates with the relevant constitutional and governmental institutions and non-governmental institutions and non-governmental organizations (NGO's) which deal with human rights and related issues.

The Finance and Administration Department

- carries out the general administration of the UHRC;
- manages the finances;
- caters for personnel welfare and recruitment of staff;
- provides logistical support to the UHRC;
- formulates and costs the UHRC's programmes and projects;
- seeks funding;
- keeps documents and records;
- liases with the Ministry of Justice and Constitutional Affairs, Ministry of Public Service and the Ministry of Finance.

Each department is supervised by a Commissioner-in-charge and has a head of department and a skeleton staff. On the committee of each department there are at least two Commissioners and a number of senior staff. All departments work with a common purpose, in close collaboration, and under the effective direction of the Chairperson. All activities of each department are carried out by the UHRC as a team, which approves the programme, engages in the activities and regularly evaluates them.

The Prisons Committee:

- draws up the programme for regular visits and investigation of prisons, police cells, remand homes, barracks and approved schools for young people;
- alerts the UHRC on any matters related to the conditions of prisoners and suspects which demand an immediate action;
- assists in designing educational programmes on human rights for police and prisons officers and suspects and prisoners;
- reports regularly to the UHRC on findings made and actions recommended.

The Treaties Committee:

- keeps the UHRC up-to-date on all international treaties on human rights ratified by the state and the obligations contained in each;
- monitors on a regular basis government's compliance with the obligations of each treaty;
- liases with the relevant government departments and ministries to find out how government is fulfilling its reporting obligations on each treaty;
- monitors the successes, failures and problems of programmes and policies designed to implement those obligations;
- scrutinizes every relevant Bill proposed by government to see whether it respects the principles and obligations of the international human rights treaties or conventions which Uganda has ratified.

The Editorial Committee:

- edits the UHRC periodical reports and the annual report to Parliament;
- edits the proceedings of seminars and conclusions of research projects; and
- edits the UHRC's civic educational material,

The Publicity Committee:

- endeavours to make the UHRC and its services known by all people in all areas of Uganda;
- organizes the use of radio, television and print media to promote awareness of human rights;
- devises ways of using popular means to promote a human rights culture among the people;
- follows-up on a daily basis any item on human rights published in the print media or voiced on the electronic media and keeps the UHRC fully informed.

The Library Committee:

- supervises the creation of a human rights library and documentation centre;
- relates with human rights libraries, centres and commissions to receive publications, visual aids and video films; and

– sensitizes and guides the public in utilizing the library and documentation centre.

Staff and Activities

The UHRC did not find it easy to find people who were prepared and qualified to do the kind of work that the UHRC must do. It began work with only one senior administrative officer and a few junior staff; it took until August and November 1997 to assemble the necessary initial senior staff, including heads of departments. A priority for 1998 is to give the staff the opportunity to acquire additional technical knowledge and skills. More senior staff are still needed but cannot be recruited due to lack of funds.

Despite these constraints, the UHRC achieved many first year goals. Its publicity and awareness programme made it widely known. It received and dealt with numerous complaints. It visited prisons and police stations countrywide, offering civic education to staff and inmates. It held workshops and seminars, designed educational materials, and drew up operational guidelines and rules of procedure. Indeed, the only function that the UHRC has failed to perform to date is to sit as a court. The reason for this is the technical steps through which the rules for such a sitting have to pass.

Inadequate Funds for the Programmes

By the time the UHRC commenced its work in November 1997, the 1996–97 financial year was already half over. The government budget provided little for the UHRC. The 1997–8 budget also failed to meet the UHRC's essential requirements.

Article 155(2) and (3) of the Constitution stipulates as follows:

"The head of any self-accounting department, commission or organization set up under this Constitution shall cause to be submitted to the President, at least two months before the end of each financial year, estimates of administrative and development expenditure and estimates of revenues of the respective department, commission or organization for the following year.

The estimates prepared under clause (2) of this article shall be laid before Parliament by the President under clause (1) of this article without revision but with any recommendations that the Government may have on them."

Investigations Carried Out

Under Article 52(1)(a) of the Constitution, the UHRC is charged with the responsibility and task of investigating violations of human rights. Investigations are conducted when complaints of violations are brought before the UHRC. The UHRC can also initiate investigations. The UHRC has an Investigations Department, which works closely with the Legal and Complaints Department and the Prisons Committee. Visits to prisons or reports by former detainees often reveal violations that need investigation.

Under Article 52(1)(b) of the Constitution, the UHRC has the function of "visiting jails, prisons and places of detention or related facilities with a view to assessing and inspecting conditions of inmates and make recommendations". To carry out these functions effectively, the UHRC set up a Prisons Committee. This Committee draws up programmes of visits to prisons and all places where people are detained. The visits involve all Commissioners and senior staff who go in groups to different areas of the country. Upon their return, each group submits a report that is discussed by the UHRC. Actions are taken on findings, including drawing the attention of the authorities concerned.

Through the Department of Education, Training and Research, the UHRC carries out four of its constitutional functions as stipulated in Article 52(1)(c),(e),(f) and (g). These are:

- to establish a continuing programme of research, education and information to enhance respect for human rights;
- to create and sustain within society awareness of the provisions of the Constitution as the fundamental law of the people of Uganda;
- to educate and encourage the general public to defend this Constitution at all times against all forms of abuse and violation;
- to formulate, implement and oversee programmes intended to inculcate in the citizens of Uganda awareness of their civic responsibilities and an appreciation of their rights and obligations as free people.

Civic Education, Training and Research in Human Rights and the Constitution

The UHRC set up six programmes for the public on human rights and the Constitution:

(a) civic education for the general public
(b) research on human rights and freedoms
(c) publication of educational material
(d) civic education for schools
(e) education on the Constitution
(f) co-ordination and overseeing of civic education programmes in the country.

Civic Education for the Public

These human rights education programmes are designed to help people to understand their human rights, to recognize when their rights are being violated, and to know the legal and other proper means to defend them. The target groups for this civic education include rural and urban local communities; local council leaders; political, religious, cultural and other opinion leaders; civil society, and government, particularly the civil service, police, prisons, army and intelligence. They also include vulnerable groups, such as women, children, persons with disability, workers, minorities, refugees and displaced people; organizations working for the empowerment of these vulnerable groups, and professionals, such as lawyers and doctors, whose work relates to human rights.

Research on Human Rights and Freedoms

The main purpose is to research priority areas of human rights to discover the underlying causes of their constant and widespread violation. From this UHRC will be able to suggest remedies to improve respect of those rights. The following are of vital concern: cultural practices, customs and traditions which violate human rights; domestic violence; the phenomenon of street children, and society's attitudes to people with disabilities.

Publication of Civic Educational Material

The UHRC regularly prepares civic education material, usually after feedback from seminars and workshops. Publishing material is a key way to create and sustain a human rights culture in Uganda. There are four types of publications. The first are those that arise from the various functions of the UHRC: its findings; proceedings of its workshops and seminars; and the papers it develops on specific topics. The second is a monthly human rights newsletter. The third are educational materials designed specifically for each of the major sections of society. And the fourth are simplified reports on the UHRC research projects to remove common obstacles to human rights violations.

Civic Education for Schools

Schools have the potential to play an immense role in creating and advancing a culture of human rights awareness and respect. UHRC and other stakeholders have as a goal the development of school syllabi on human rights. These syllabi would cover from primary one to university. This task involves numerous actors, including: the UHRC; several other constitutional bodies, the Ministries of Education, Justice, Local Government, Gender and Community Development, the National Curriculum Development Centre; and NGOS.

Education on the Constitution

The UHRC involved in availing copies of the Constitution to people in all parts of the country for purchase and study. In addition, it is supporting translation of the Constitution into local languages and the production of a simplified version of the Constitution. Finally, it is designing study programmes on the Constitution and utilizing all possible ways to make the Constitution wide known and respected so as to inculcate a culture of constitutionalism and rule of law.

Co-ordination and Overseeing of Civic Education Programmes

In 1997 the UHRC set itself an overall goal to sensitise people on the existence and functions of the UHRC and on the human rights laid down in the Constitution and other international instruments. As 1997 was its maiden year, it was not possible to realise all it had hoped. Nevertheless much was still achieved.

Planned activities included:

- conducting a civic education needs assessment and drawing up a comprehensive five year civic education programme;
- publishing a UHRC brochure and operational guidelines for the public about how the UHRC works and how to use it effectively;
- organizing national seminars on burning human rights issues;
- preparing speeches and papers on human rights for various categories of people, conducting civic education in districts and among security organs,
- weekly radio programmes in six languages;
- occasional television programmes;
- use of print media;
- courses to train trainers of human rights.

Monitoring Government's Compliance with International Instruments on Human Rights

Since the creation of the United Nations (UN), a variety of committees have examined in great detail questions of human rights. As a result, a number of human rights instruments have been adopted by the UN. All UN members are encouraged to subscribe to these standards by signing and ratifying them. Once this is done, states are required to translate these standards into domestic laws and to take steps to implement the obligations. These instruments confer legal obligations on consenting states; the Constitution therefore imposes the requirement that government compliance should be monitored.

The UHRC is mandated by the Constitution under Article 52(1)(h) to monitor Government compliance with international treaty and convention obligations on human rights. The UHRC's understanding of this mandate is that it should study and identify all obligations created by the human right instruments to which Uganda is a party and monitor whether or not the government is complying with those obligations. For example, Article 14 of the Convention on the Elimination of Discrimination against Women calls upon the contracting states to take certain measures to improve the conditions of living for rural women. The UHRC's view is that it is mandated to monitor what steps the government has taken to realise this right. It will then report to Parliament with recommendations.

Some instruments require the government to make periodic reports to the UN about what it is doing to meet its obligations under the instruments. The UHRC also monitors whether reporting is being done and the content of such reports.

This chapter identifies to Parliament the major human rights instruments signed and ratified by Uganda. It briefly describes the most important obligations of the instruments and comments as to whether steps have been taken to meet them and if those steps are sufficient. As can be seen from the list of instruments, Uganda has done very well in acceding to international human rights instruments.

THE INSPECTORATE OF THE GOVERNMENT

Background

The Inspectorate of Government was established in 1986 when the National Resistance Movement NRM Government came into power. This was done in fulfilment of the seventh point of the Ten Points Political Programme which states that: "Africa being a continent that is never in shortage of problems, has also the problem of corruption – particularly bribery and misuse of office to serve personal interests."

Corruption is indeed a problem that ranks with problems of structural distortions in development, planning or trade. A cheaper option can be ignored in preference to a less efficient one, because of the officials concerned who see a chance of making illegal commissions by adopting the useful options.

These types of decisions can cause distortions of great magnitude. Therefore, to enable the tackling of our backwardness, corruption must be eliminated once and for all.

At the time the office came to be known as the office of the Inspector General of Government (IGG) and was officially established by the Inspector General of Government statute No. 2 of 1988 as a Public office to oversee the functioning of other public offices in Uganda.

The IGG Statute provided for the functions of office under section 7 as follows:

(a) To inquire into allegations of violations in human rights committed against any person in Uganda by a person in a public office;
(b) To inquire into the methods by which law enforcing agents and the state security agencies perform their functions and the extent to which practices and procedures employed in the performance of such functions uphold, encourage or interfere with law in Uganda.
(c) To take necessary measures for detection and prevention of corruption in public offices.
(d) To investigate the conduct of any public officer which may be connected with or conducive to
    (i) the abuse of office or authority
    (ii) the neglect of his official duties
    (iii) economic malpractice by the officer.
(e) To perform any other functions that the president may prescribe.

The Statute empowered the IGG to investigate into the violations of human rights, breach of the rule of law, corruption, abuse of office occasioning injustice and neglect of duty and any other aspects his power permit.

Thus the IGG previously used to visit prisons and other detention centres to check on the treatment of detainee and make recommendations on improvement of their conditions. To fulfill the above function, the IGG has powers to obtain evidence deemed necessary from any public office or private office that has transacted business with a public office including searching and seeing such evidence. The IGG may in writing authorize any other person to execute his instructions and may even use force as may be necessary in the circumstance and may be accompanied or assisted by law enforcement officers as he deems necessary. The IGG is also given special powers under the statute of inspection into Bank accounts and other accounts, safes or deposit boxes in a Bank.

Any person who willfully or who unlawfully refuses to comply with an order of the IGG commits an offence and on conviction is liable to a term of imprisonment.

Exceptions to these powers include:

(a) Matters to which might prejudice the security, defence or international relations of Uganda
(b) Situations where the investigations involves disclosure of cabinet proceedings, and
(c) Matters which are sub judice or cases which are in the process of being heard in court of law.

The Inspectorate of Government is Uganda's ombudsman office. The term ombudsman was defined in a 1974 Resolution of the International Bar Association as:

> "An office provided for by the constitution or by action of the legislature or Parliament and headed by an independent high level public official who is responsible to the legislature or parliament, who receives complaints from aggrieved persons against government agencies, officials and employees or who acts on his own motion and has powers to investigate, recommend corrective measures and issue reports."

An Ombudsman office such as the IGG has two primary functions:
(a) the protection of the individual
(b) the monitoring of certain activities of government.

The protection of the citizen is the primary function and the office ensures that government observes the rule of law and remains within the limits of proper conducts.

The Current Status of the Inspectorate of Government

The promulgation of the 1995 Constitution brought about some changes and for this reason the Statute is soon to be amended to bring it in line with the constitutional provisions. First and foremost the name of the office was changed from the office of the Inspector General of Government to the Inspectorate of Government.

Functions
The office is a constitutional body and its functions are as follows:

(Article 225(1) of the 1995 Constitution)

(i) To promote and foster strict adherence to the rule of law and Principles of Natural Justice in administration;
(ii) To eliminate and foster the elimination of corruption abuse of authority and of public office;
(iii) To promote fair, efficient and good governance in public offices;
(iv) Subject to the provisions of the constitution to supervise the enforcement

of the Leadership Code of Conduct.

(v) To investigate any act, omission, advice, decision or recommendation by a public officer or any other authority to which article 225 of the Constitution applies, taken, made, given or done in the exercise of administrative functions and

(vi) To stimulate public awareness about the values of constitutionalism in general and the activities of its office, in particular, through any media and other means it considers appropriate.

It should be noted that this office is still an ombudsman office and performs the functions of an ombudsman office as outlined above. Although the office shed some of its human rights functions to the Uganda Human Rights Commission, implicit in its current mandate are elements of human rights that I will not labour to explain.

Structure

The constitution provides for an Inspector General of Government and two deputies to be appointed by the president on approval of parliament, currently however, there is only one Deputy Inspector General of Government.

There are three (3) directories each headed by the director. These are:

(i) The Directorate of legal affairs which is responsible for all legal affairs in the inspectorate including prosecutions;

(ii) The Directorate of operation which is responsible for investigations and the implementation of the leadership code of conduct;

(iii) The Directorate of Education and Prevention which is responsible for all matters on public awareness and education.

The Inspector General of Government may investigate any matter on its initiative or upon complaint made to it by any member of the public, whether or not that person has personally suffered any injustice by reason of that matter.

Jurisdiction of Inspectorate

The Jurisdiction of the Inspector of Government cover officers or leaders whether employed in public service or not, and also such institutions, organizations, or enterprise as parliament may prescribe by law.

Independence of the Inspector General of Government

The Inspector General of Government is independent in the performance of his functions and not subjected to any direction or control of any person or authority but only responsible to the Parliament.

Financial Resources

The Inspector General of Government has an independent budget appropriated by Parliament and controlled by the Inspectorate.

Special Powers of Inspectorate

The Inspectorate of government have power to investigate, cause investigation, arrest, cause arrest, prosecute or cause prosecution in respect of cases involving corruption, abuse of authority of public office.

Reports of Inspectorate

The Inspectorate of Government submit to Parliament at least once in every six months a report on the performance of its functions making such recommendations as it considers necessary and containing information parliament may require.

Methodology

In carrying out its investigations the office may act on its own initiative or upon a complaint made to it by members of the public or referred to it from other public offices and NGOS.

For instance the office follows up the queries made by the Auditor General on the various government agencies. Complaints to the office may be in writing or reduced into writing if oral. The Inspector General may also have a hotline to enable people to report cases without having to come physically to the office. Therefore in carrying out its functions the Inspectorate compliments rather than duplicate the work of agencies.

All investigations and complaints are handled with strict confidentiality. Previously the IGG was only limited to reporting and making recommendations on findings and relying on the goodwill of those involved to implement the recommendations. However, under the new 1995 Constitution the IGG has powers to prosecute cases it has handled.

Recommendations

The following recommendations are deemed by this author as greatly paramount in setting up the National Commission for the Protection of Human Rights and Ombudsman in the Federal Democratic Republic of Ethiopia.

1. The Commission should be free from any state inspired rulings and to be manned by impartial officers of proven integrity who will protect the rights of all people of Ethiopia regardless of
   (a) nationality, race, colour and ethnicity
   (b) political affiliation and views
   (c) education, Age and Gender
   (d) religious background and fundamentalism.
2. To hold powers of a court to be able to summon or order any person to attend before it and produce any record or documents relevant to any investigations by the commission.

3. To interrogate and introspect any person of interest and in respect of any subject matter under its investigations e.g.
   (i) complaints of mal-administration
   (ii) complaints based on international human rights norms
   (iii) complaints regarding corrupt practices by officials
   (iv) complaints for systematic improvements in administration.
4. To act as an advocacy agency.
5. Giving assistance to complaints in court and those who fail to support themselves in the courts of low.
6. Recommending fresh amendments to existing legislation and to undertake research and encourage systematic improvements in the executive.
7. To research, educate, monitor and bring about national compliance of the executive and international human rights instruments.
8. It should provide awareness and education programmes on human rights across the border.
9. To be imbued with public inquiry powers and mandate.
10. To research, compile and educate information through visitation to jails, prisons and detention centres or related facilities with an objective of assessing and inspecting conditions of the inmates and make recommendations.
11. For the Commission totally to refrain from investigating any matter which is pending before a court of law involving the relations of dealings between the Federal Democratic Republic of Ethiopia and the Government of any other foreign state or international organization or a matter relating to the exercise of the prerogative of mercy.
12. The Commission should direct any person to disclose any information within his or her knowledge relevant to any instigation by the Commission and Ombudsman.
13. The Commission should educate the masses as to its limitations in case any person or authority is dissatisfied with an order made by the commission has the right to appeal to the High Court of appeal.
14. For the commission to commit persons for contempt of its orders.
15. In case the commission through its investigations network becomes satisfied that there has been a violation of human rights or freedom, it may order for the release of a detained or restricted person, payment of compensation or order any other legal remedy, redress or alternative.
16. To establish various departments within its internal organizations and to recruit qualitative calibre of staff in this structures, namely:
    (i) Legal and Complaints
    (ii) Investigation and threats
    (iii) Education and Research
    (iv) Finance and Administration.
17. Publicly to condemn any repugnant cultures that do abuse human rights including religious laws that infringe the rights of their adherents like cultural norms and initiations that are forcibly administered on members against their will.

LEGISLATION

The Constitution of the Republic of Uganda 1995

Chapter 4.

[...]

Uganda Human Rights Commission.

51. (1) There shall be a Commission called the Uganda Human Rights Commission.
(2) The Commission shall be composed of a Chairperson and not less than three other persons appointed by the President with the approval of Parliament.
(3) The Chairperson of the Commission shall be a Judge of the High Court or a person qualified to hold that office.
(4) The Chairperson and members of the commission shall be persons of high moral character and proven integrity and shall serve for a period of six years and be eligible for re-appointment.

Functions of Human Rights Commission.
52. (1) The Commission shall have the following functions of Human
(a) to investigate, at its own initiative or on a complaint made by any person or group of persons against the violation of any human right;
(b) to visit jails, prisons, and places of detention or related facilities with a view to assessing and inspecting conditions of the inmates and make recommendations;
(c) to establish a continuing programme of research, education and information to enhance respect of human rights;
(d) to recommend to Parliament effective measures to promote human rights. including provision of compensation to victims of violations of human rights, or their families;
(e) to create and sustain within society the awareness of the provisions of this Constitution as the fundamental law of the people of Uganda;
(f) to educate and encourage the public to defend this Constitution at all times against all forms of abuse and violation.
(g) to formulate, implement and oversee programmes intended to inculcate in the citizens of Uganda awareness of their civic responsibilities and an appreciation of their rights and obligations as free people;
(h) to monitor the Government's compliance with international treaty and convention obligations on human rights; and
(1) to perform such other functions as may be provided by law.
(2) The Uganda Human Rights Commission shall publish periodical reports on its findings and submit annual reports to Parliament on the state of human rights and freedoms in the country.
(3) In the performance of its functions, the Uganda Human Rights Commission shall:
(a) establish its operational guidelines and rules of procedure;
(b) request the assistance of any department, bureau, office, agency or person in the performance of its functions; and
(c) observe the rules of natural justice.

Powers of the Commission.
53. (1) In the performance of its functions, the Commission shall have the powers of a court:
(a) to issue summons or other orders requiring the attendance of any person before the Commission and the production of any document or record relevant to any investigation by the Commission;
(b) to question any person in respect of any subject matter under investigation before the commission;

(c) to require any person to disclose any information within his or her knowledge relevant to any investigation by the Commission
(d) to commit persons for contempt of its orders
(2) The Commission may, if satisfied that there has been an infringement of a human right or freedom. order:
(a) the release of a detained or restricted person;
(b) payment of compensation; or
(c) any other legal remedy or redress.
(3) A person or authority dissatisfied with an order made by the Commission under clause (1) of this article, has a right to appeal to the High Court.
(4) The Commission shall not investigate:
(a) any matter which is pending before a court or judicial tribunal; or
(b) a matter involving the relations or dealings between the Government and the Government of any foreign State or international organisation; or
(c) a matter relating to the exercise of the prerogative of mercy.

Independence of the Commission
54. Subject to this Constitution, the Commission shall be independent and shall not, in the performance of its duties, be subject to the direction or control of any person or control authority.

55. (1) The Commission shall be self-accounting and all the administrative expenses including salaries, allowances and pensions payable to persons serving with the Commission shall be charged on the Consolidated Fund.
(2) The Chairperson and other members of the Commission shall be paid such salaries and allowances as Parliament may prescribe.

Removal of Commissioners
56. The provisions of this Constitution relating to the removal of a Judge of the High Removal of Court from office shall, with the necessary modifications, apply to the removal from office of a member of the Commission.

Staff of Commission
57. The appointment of the officers and other employees of the Commission shall be Staff of made by the Commission in consultation with the Public Service Commission.

Parliament to make laws regarding functions of Commission
58. Parliament may make laws to regulate and facilitate the performance of the functions of the Uganda Human Rights Commission.

[...]

Chapter 13
Inspectorate of Government

223. (1) There shall be an Inspectorate of Government
(2) The Inspectorate of Government shall consist of:
(a) the Inspector-General of Government; and
(b) such number of Deputy Inspectors-General as Parliament may prescribe.
(3) At least one of the persons referred to in clause (2) of this article shall be a person qualified to be appointed a Judge of the High Court.
(4) The Inspector-General of Government and a Deputy Inspector-General shall be appointed by the President with the approval of Parliament and shall not, while holding office, hold any other office of emolument in the public service.
(5) A person shall not be eligible for appointment as Inspector-General of Government or Deputy Inspector-General of Government unless that person:
(a) is a citizen of Uganda; and

(b) is a person of high moral character and proven integrity; and
(c) possesses considerable experience and demonstrated competence and is of high caliber in the conduct of public affairs.

(6) A person shall resign his or her office on appointment an Inspector-General or a Deputy Inspector-General, if that person is:
(a) a member of Parliament
(b) a member of a local government council; or
(c) a member of the executive of a political party

(7) The Inspector-General of Government and Deputy Inspectors-General shall hold office for a term of four years but shall be eligible for re-appointment only once.

(8) The remuneration and other conditions of service of members of the Inspectorate of Government shall be prescribed by Parliament and the salaries and allowances of members of the Inspectorate shall be charged on the Consolidated Fund.

Removal of Inspector-General and Deputy Inspector-General

224. The Inspector-General or a Deputy Inspector-General and may be removed from office by the President on the recommendation of a special tribunal constituted by Parliament only for:
(a) inability to perform the functions of his or her office arising from infirmity of body or mind; or
(b) misconduct, misbehaviour or conduct unbecoming of the holder of the office; or
(c) incompetence.

Functions of Inspectorate

225. (1) The functions of the Inspectorate of Government shall be prescribed by Parliament and shall include the following:
(a) to promote and foster strict adherence to the rule of law and principles of natural justice in administration;
(b) to eliminate and foster the elimination of corruption, abuse of authority and of public office;
(c) to promote fair, efficient and good governance in public offices;
(d) subject to the provisions of this Constitution, to supervise the enforcement of the Leadership Code of Conduct;
(e) to investigate any act, omission, advice, decision or recommendation by a public officer or any other authority to which this article applies, taken, made, given or done in exercise of administrative functions; and
(f) to stimulate public awareness about the values of constitutionalism in general and the activities of its office, in particular, through any media and other means it considers appropriate.

(2) The Inspectorate of Government may investigate any matter referred to in paragraph (e) of clause (1) of this article, on its own initiative or upon complaint made to it by any member of the public, whether or not that person has personally suffered any injustice by reason of that matter.

Jurisdiction of Inspectorate

226. The jurisdiction of the Inspectorate of Government shall cover officers or leaders whether employed in the public service or not, and also such institutions, organisations or enterprises as Parliament may prescribe by law.

Independence of Inspectorate

227. The Inspectorate of Government shall be independent in performance of its functions and shall not be subject to the of direction or control of any person or authority and shall only be responsible to Parliament.

Branches of Inspectorate

228. The Inspectorate of Government may establish branches of at district and other administrative levels as it considers fit for the better performance of its functions.

Resources of Inspectorate

229. (1) The Inspectorate of Government shall have an independent budget appropriated by Parliament, and controlled by the Inspectorate.

(2) It shall be the duty of the State to facilitate the employment by the Inspectorate of such adequate and qualified staff as are needed to enable the Inspectorate to perform its functions effectively and efficiently.

Special Powers to the Inspectorate

230. (1) The Inspectorate of Government shall have power to investigate, cause investigation, arrest, cause arrest, prosecute cause prosecution in respect of cases involving corruption, abuse of authority or of public office.

(2) The Inspector-General of Government may, during the course of his or her duties or as a consequence of his or her findings, make such orders and give such directions as are necessary and appropriate in the circumstances.

(3) Subject to the provisions of any law, the Inspectorate of Government shall have power to enter and inspect the premises or property of any department of Government, person or any authority, to call for, examine and where necessary, retain any document or item in connection with the case being investigated, found on the premises; and may, in those premises, carry out any investigation for the
purpose of its functions.

(4) The Inspectorate of Government shall, when enforcing the Leadership Code of Conduct, have all the powers conferred on it by this Chapter in addition to any other powers conferred by law.

(5) Subject to this Constitution, Parliament shall enact any law necessary for enabling the Inspectorate of Government to discharge its functions effectively and efficiently and in particular, to ensure that the discharge of those functions is not frustrated by any person or authority.

Reports of Inspectorate

231. (1) The Inspectorate of Government shall submit to Parliament at least once in every six months, a report on the performance of its functions, making such recommendations as it considers necessary and containing such information as Parliament may require.

(2) A copy of the report referred to in clause (1) of this article shall be forwarded by the inspectorate of Government to the President; and where any matter contained in the report relates to the administration of any local authority, an extract of the portion of the report on the matter shall be forwarded to that local authority.

(3) The Speaker shall lay before Parliament the report submitted under clause (1) of this article within thirty days after it has been submitted, if Parliament is then in session, or, if Parliament is not in session, within thirty days after the commencement of its next session.

Powers of Parliament regarding Inspectorate

232. (1) Parliament shall, subject to the provisions of this Constitution, make laws to give effect to the provisions of this Chapter.

(2) Laws made for the purpose of this Chapter may, in particular, provide:

(a) for regulating the procedure for the making of complaints and requests to the Inspectorate of Government and for the exercise of its functions;

(b) for conferring such powers on it and imposing such duties on persons concerned as are necessary to facilitate it in the performance of its functions;

(c) for ensuring accessibility to the services of the Inspectorate by the general public and decentralising the exercise of those functions and where necessary, for enabling the delegation by the Inspectorate of any of those functions to other authorities or persons at district or lower local government levels; and

(d) for regulating the functioning of the Inspectorate of Government in relation to other institutions or bodies established under this Constitution or any other law.

The Uganda Human Rights Commission Act 1997

An Act to make provision in relation to the Uganda Human Rights Commission in pursuance of paragraph (i) of clause (1) of article 52 and article 58 of the Constitution.

Date of Assent: 10th April, 1997
Date of Commencement: 2nd May, 1997.

Be it enacted by Parliament as follows:
1. This Act may be cited as the Uganda Human Rights Commission Act, 1997.

2. In this Act, unless the context otherwise requires
"Chairperson" means the Chairperson of the Commission;
"Commission" means the Uganda Human Rights Commission established by article 51 of the Constitution;
"Commissioner" means a member of the Commission;
"currency point" means the value specified in the First Schedule to this Act in relation to a currency point;
"Minister" means the Minister responsible for justice;
"Secretary" means the Secretary to the Commission appointed under section 10 of this Act.

3. (1) The Chairperson and other members of the Uganda Human Rights Commission shall be appointed by the President with the approval of Parliament.
(2) The members of the Commission other than the Chairperson, shall not be less than three.

4. (1) Every member of the Commission shall, before assuming his or her duties as Commissioner, take and subscribe the oath specified in Part I of the Second Schedule to this Act.
(2) The Secretary shall, before assuming the performance of his or her functions under this Act, take and subscribe the Oath specified in Part II of the Second Schedule to this Act.
(3) Any other officer or employee of the Commission may be directed by the Commission to take and subscribe the oath specified in Part II of the Second Schedule to this Act.
(4) Where before the commencement of this Act any person has been appointed a member or Secretary of the Commission, that person shall take and subscribe the appropriate oath under this section as soon as possible after the commencement of this Act.

5. The Chairperson shall
(a) be the head of the Commission;
(b) be responsible for the direction of the affairs and for the administration of the Commission; and
(c) monitor and supervise the work of the Secretary.

6. A person holding any of the following offices shall C relinquish that office on appointment as a member of the Commission
(a) a member of Parliament;
(b) a member of a local government council;
(c) a member of the executive of a political party or political organization;
(d) a public officer.

7. The members of the Commission shall hold office on a full time basis.

8. (1) The Commission shall have the following functions:
(a) to investigate, at its own initiative or on complaint made by any person or group of persons against the violation of any human right;
(b) to visit jails, prisons, and places of detention or related facilities with a view to assessing and inspecting conditions of the inmates and make, recommendations;
(c) to visit any place or building where a person is suspected to be illegally detained;

(d) to establish a continuing programme of research. education and information to enhance respect of human rights;
(e) to recommend to Parliament effective measures to promote human rights, including provision of compensation to victims of violations of human rights, or their families;
(f) to create and sustain within society the awareness of the provisions of the Constitution as the fundamental law of the people of Uganda;
(g) to educate and encourage the public to defend the Constitution at all times against all forms of abuse and violation.
(h) to formulate, implement and oversee programmes intended to inculcate in the citizens of Uganda awareness of their civic responsibilities and an appreciation of their rights and obligations as free people;
(i) to monitor the Government's compliance with international treaty and convention obligations on human rights;
(j) to carry out the functions of the Commission under article 48 of the Constitution; and
(k) to perform such other functions as may be provided by law.

(2) Decisions of the Commission under clause (2) of article 53 of the Constitution shall have effect as those of a court and shall be enforced in the same manner.

(3) For the avoidance of doubt, the Commission shall, in the carrying out of its functions, deal only with violations of human rights alleged to have taken place on or after the coming into force of the Constitution.

(4) The recommendations required to be made by the Commission under paragraph (b) of subsection (l) shall be to the appropriate Ministry, department or other authority whose functions relate to the matter on which the recommendations are made.

(5) Recommendations made to Parliament by the Commission under paragraph (e) of subsection (1) of this section, shall be addressed to the Speaker of Parliament and signed by the Chairperson of the Commission; and a copy of the recommendations shall be forwarded to the President.

(6) The annual report required by clause (1) of article 52 of the Constitution to be submitted to Parliament shall be addressed to the Speaker of Parliament and signed by the Chairperson of the Commission; and a copy of it shall be forwarded to the President.

9. The Commission may establish offices at district and other administrative levels as it considers fit for the better performance of its functions.

10. (1) The Commission shall have a Secretary who shall be appointed by the commission in consultation with the Public Service Commission upon such terms and conditions as may be determined by the Commission in consultation wit the Public Service Commission and specified in his or her instrument of appointment; but the terms and conditions shall not be less favourable than those of a Permanent Secretary.

(2) The Secretary shall be a person qualified to be appointed to the office of Permanent Secretary.

(3) Subject to the powers of the Chairperson under section 5 and to the general control of the Commission, the Secretary shall
(a) be responsible for the carrying out of the policy decision of the Commission and the day to day administration and management of the affairs of the commission and the control of the other staff of the commission.
(b) be responsible for arranging the business for and the recording and keeping of the minutes of all decisions and
(c) perform any other functions assigned to him or her by the Commission.

(4) The Secretary is, unless in any particular case the Commission otherwise directs in writing, entitled to attend all meetings of the Commission but shall have no vote on any matter falling to be decided by the Commission at any such meeting.

(5) The Secretary may be removed by the Commission only for
(a) inability to perform the functions of his or her office arising, out of physical or mental incapacity; or

(b) misbehaviour or misconduct; or
(c) incompetence.
(6) Before the Secretary is removed under subsection (5) he or she shall be informed of the case against him or her and be given adequate opportunity to defend himself or herself against any allegations made against him or her.

11. (1) The Commission shall also have such other officers and employees as may be necessary for the discharge of its functions.
(2) The officers and employees referred to in subsection (1) shall be appointed by the Commission in consultation with the Public Service Commission, and shall hold office upon such terms and conditions as may be determined by the Commission in consultation with the Public Service Commission.
(3) Public officers may at the request of the Commission be seconded to the service of the Commission.
(4) The Commission may, in consultation with the Public Service Commission, engage the services of consultants, experts and advisers to assist it in the discharge of its functions and may pay to them remuneration at such rates as may be determined by the Commission after similar consultation.

12. (1) Meetings of the Commission shall be presided over by the Chairperson, and in the absence of the Chairperson the members of the Commission present may appoint a member from among their number to preside over the meeting.
(2) Every decision of the Commission shall, so far as possible, be by consensus.
(3) In any vote at any meeting of the Commission, each Commissioner shall have one vote and none shall have a casting vote.
(4) The Commission shall otherwise have power to prescribe its own procedure.

13. (1) Parliament shall ensure that adequate, resources and facilities are provided to the Commission to enable it to perform its functions effectively.
(2) The administrative expenses of the Commission shall be charged on the Consolidated Fund.
(3) The Fund of the Commission may, with approval of the Minister acting in consultation with the Minister responsible for finance, include grants and donations from sources within or outside Uganda to enable the Commission to discharge its functions.
(4) All funds provided to the Commission under article 55 of the Constitution or under this Act shall be administered and controlled by the Secretary who shall be the accounting officer in accordance with the Public Finance Act.

14. A member of the Commission or any employee or other person performing any function of the Commission under direction of the Commission, shall not be personally liable to any civil proceedings for any act done in good faith in the performance of those functions.

15. The Commission shall have a seal which shall be in such form as the Commission may determine and, subject to the provisions of any law, be applied in such circumstances as the Commission may determine.

16. (1) The Attorney-General may attend upon the Commission and give such assistance to it as the Commission may from time to time request.
(2) A witness before the Commission may also be represented by counsel.

17. The Commission shall have power to cause a witness to be examined on oath or affirmation.

18. (1) The evidence of every witness shall be taken down and the witness may, if he or she requests it, be given a copy of it.
(2) The Commission shall have power to commit persons for contempt of its orders.

(3) A person alleged to be in contempt may be represented by counsel in proceedings for the alleged contempt.

19. (1) Any person summoned by and appearing before the Commission as a witness is entitled to be paid by way of reimbursement of his or her expenses, such allowances as are payable to a witness appearing before the High Court in criminal proceedings.
(2) Any other person invited by the Commission to attend any meeting of the Commission to assist the Commission may be paid by the Commission such allowances as the Commission may consider reasonable.

20. A witness appearing before the Commission shall have the same immunities and privileges as if he or she were a witness before the High Court.

21. Any rules of court applicable to civil or criminal proceedings in the High Court may be applied by the commission for the purposes of the exercise of its powers under article 53 of the Constitution or any other of its functions subject to such modifications as may be made by the Chief Justice by statutory instrument in consultation with the Commission.

22. (1)The Chief Justice shall make rules of court for regulating appeals to the High Court from orders of the commission made under clause (2) of article 53 of the Constitution.
(2) Rules made under subsection (1) of this section may without prejudice to the general effect of subsection (1), make provision for
(a) the period within which an appeal may be lodged;
(b) forms and fees in relation to such appeals;
(c) the procedure generally for hearing such appeals; and
(d) the application to such appeals with or without modifications of any rules of court applicable to the High Court.

23. Without prejudice to the Commission's power to commit for contempt, any person who wilfully obstructs or interferes with the exercise of its functions, commits an offence and is liable, on conviction to a fine not exceeding sixty currency points or imprisonment not exceeding two years or both.

24. No person who in good faith gives any information to the Commission or assist the Commission in the exercise of its functions, shall be punished in any way for doing so.

25. No complaint shall be brought before the Commission after the expiration of five years from the date on which the alleged violation of a human right to which the complaint relates, occurred.

26. Where a person entitled to bring a complaint before the Commission against any violation of a human right is incapacitated from doing so by reason of age, infirmity of body or mind, detention or other just cause, whether similar to the foregoing or not, then the complaint may be brought at any time within five years after the incapacity ceases or the person entitled to bring the complaint dies, whichever event first occurs.

27. The Commission may, in consultation with the Minister, make regulations for the carrying into effect of the provisions of this Act and in particular for facilitating the work of the Commission.
28. The Minister may, with the approval of the Cabinet by statutory instrument, amend the First Schedule to this Act.

FIRST SCHEDULE

Currency Point

A currency point represents twenty thousand Uganda shillings.

SECOND SCHEDULE

Part 1
Oath of Members of Uganda Human Rights Commission

I ___________ being appointed Chairperson/Member of the Uganda Human Rights Commission, swear in the name of the Almighty God/solemnly affirm that I will well and truly exercise the functions Of Chairperson/ member of the Uganda Human Rights Commission and do the right to all manner of people in accordance with the laws of the Republic of Uganda without fear of favour, affection or ill-will. (So help me God).

Part II
Oath of Secretary/officer of Commission.

I ___________ being appointed Secretary to/officer of/ the Commission/ being called upon to perform the functions of Secretary to/ officer of/ the Commission swear in the name of the Almighty God/ solemnly affirm/ that I will not directly or indirectly reveal to any unauthorized person or otherwise than in the course of duty, the contents or any part of the contents of any documents, communication or information which may come to my knowledge in the course of my duties as such. (So help me God).

The Inspector-General of Government Statute 1987

A Statute to provide for the establishment, functions and power of the office of the Inspector-General of Government and for matters connected therewith or incidental thereto

Date of Assent: 19th March, 1988
Date of Commencement: (see section 27.)

Be it enacted by the President and the National Resistance Council as follows::

Part I – Preliminary Provisions

1. In this Statute, unless the context otherwise requires,
"Appointments Board" means the Appointments Board established under the provisions of section 4 of this Statute;
"Deputy Inspector-General" means the Deputy Inspector-General" of Government appointed under the provisions of section 3 of this Statute;
"Inspector-General" means the Inspector-General of Government appointed under section 3 of this Statute;
"Legislature" means that body which for the time being is responsible for performing the functions of the National Assembly;
"Public office" includes,
(a) a Government department, undertaking or service;
(b) a company in which the Government has shares;
(c) a public corporation;
(d) the Cabinet;
(e) the National Assembly;
(f) a court of law;
(g) the Uganda Police Force;
(h) the Uganda Prisons Service;
(i) a school, college or other public institution of learning;
(j) the Uganda Armed Forces or the National Resistance Army;
(k) a District Administration;
(l) a Resistance Council or Committee thereof;
(m) an urban authority;
(n) a municipal council, town board or committee thereof;
(o) a trade union;

(p) a co-operative society;
(q) a political party;
(r) a council, board, society or committee established by law for the control and regulation of any profession;
(s) a commission, association or similar body whether corporate or not, established by law, for the purposes of administering public funds in any form, or for the purpose of promoting,
   (i) public health;
   (ii) public undertakings or public utility;
   (iii) education;
   (iv) sports;
   (v) culture;
   (vi) literature;
   (vii) science;
   (viii) arts; and
(t) any other office that offers service to the public or that administers funds on behalf of the public or a part thereof;

"public officer" means a person serving in a public office; and
"Secretary" means the Secretary in the office of the Inspector-General of Government, appointed under section 3 of this Statute.

Part II – Establishment of Office and Appointments

2. (1) There is established the office of the Inspector- General of Government, which shall be a public office.
(2) Notwithstanding the provisions of subsection (l) hereof, the office of the Inspector-General of Government shall not be subject to the direction or control of any other authority, but shall be directly responsible to the President.

3. (1) The office of the Inspector-General of Government shall consist of the following, namely,
(a) the Inspector-General, to be appointed by the President;
(b) the Deputy Inspector-General, to be appointed by the President;
(c) a Secretary, to be appointed by the President, and who shall head the administrative structure of the office;
(d) Counsel, to be appointed by the Appointments Board, and who shall be legal advisor to the office; and
(e) such other officers and supporting staff as the Inspector-General may, from time to time, deem necessary, to be appointed by the Appointments Board, for the implementation, execution and Promotion of the objectives, functions and duties of the office.

(2) A person shall not qualify for appointment as Inspector-General or Deputy Inspector-General unless he has served in a field or discipline relevant to the work of the office of Inspector-General of Government, for not less than seven years.
(3) Notwithstanding the provisions of subsection (1) of this section, the Inspector-General may in the performance of his duties under this Statute, engage the services of, or work in consultation with any other public office.
(4) A person who, at the commencement of this Statute, is serving in an office specified in this section, shall continue so serving, after the said commencement and shall be deemed to have been duly appointed to that office under the provisions of this Statute, and any duties or functions performed or powers exercised by such person by virtue of his said office before the said commencement, shall be deemed to have been validly performed or exercised under the provisions of this Statute.

4. (1) There is established an Appointments Board consisting of the following, namely,

(a) the Inspector-General who shall be the Chairman of the Board;
(b) the Deputy Inspector-General;
(c) the Secretary in the office of the Inspector-General of Government who shall be the Secretary to the Board;
(d) the Chairman of the Public Service Commission or any other Commissioner authorized by him in that behalf;
(e) the Permanent Secretary responsible for the Public Service and Cabinet Affairs; and
(f) two other members to be appointed by the President.
(2) The functions of the Appointments Board shall include,
(a) the establishment of posts with the office of the Inspector-General;
(b) the appointment of officers and staff of the office of the inspector-General in accordance with section 3 of this Statute;
(c) the making of regulations for the discipline of officers and staff of the Office of the Inspector-General; and
(d) the performance of any other functions that the President may assign to the Board.

5. (1) Every person appointed to an office under the provisions of this Statute shall, before entering upon the duties of his office, take the appropriate oath set out in Part A of the First Schedule to this Statute.
(2) A person appointed to an office set out in the first column of Part A of the First Schedule shall take the oath specified in the second column thereof, which shall be administered by the authority specified in the third column thereof.

6. (1) The salaries and allowances of the Inspector-General and the Deputy Inspector-General shall be charged on and issued out of the Consolidated Fund.
(2) The officers and staff of the office of the Inspector- General shall be paid such salaries and allowances as The Inspector-General, with the approval of the legislature, shall determine,

Part III – Functions and Powers

7. (1) The Inspector-General is charged with the duty of protecting and promoting the protection of human rights and the rule of law in Uganda, and eliminating and fostering the elimination of corruption and abuse of public offices, and without prejudice to the generality of the foregoing, he shall perform the following functions,
(a) to inquire into allegations of violation of human rights committed against any person in Uganda by a person in a public office, and in particular,
  (i) the arbitrary deprivation of human life;
  (ii) the arbitrary arrest and consequent detention without trial;
  (iii) the denial of a fair and public trial before an impartial and independent court of law;
  (iv) the subjection of any person to torture, inhuman and degrading treatment; and
  (v) the unlawful acquisition, possession, damage or destruction or private property;
(b) to inquire into the methods by which law enforcing agents and the state security agencies execute their functions, and the extent to which the practices and procedures employed in the execution of such functions uphold, encourage or interfere with the rule of law in Uganda;
(c) to take necessary measures for the detection and prevention of corruption in public offices and in particular,
  (i) to examine the practices and procedures of the said offices in order to facilitate the discovery of corrupt practices and to secure the revision of methods of work or procedure which, in the opinion of the Inspector-General may be con- decide to corrupt practices;
  (ii) to advise the said offices on ways and means of preventing corrupt practices and

on methods of work or procedure conducive to the effective performance of their duties and which, in the opinion of the Inspector-General, would reduce the incidences of corruption;

(iii) to disseminate information on the evil and dangerous effects of corruption on society;

(iv) to enlist and foster public support against corrupt practices; and

(v) to receive and investigate complaints of alleged or suspected corrupt practices and injustices and make recommendations for appropriate action thereon;

(d) to investigate the conduct of any public officer which may be connected with or conducive to,

(i) the abuse of his office or authority;

(ii) the neglect of his official duties;

(iii) economic malpractice's by the officer; and

(e) to perform any other functions that the President may prescribe.

(2) In the performance of his functions under this Statute, the Inspector-General may in addition to receiving complaints from the public, initiate investigations.

(3) The Inspector-General may in the performance of his duties under this section, investigate into the actions of any person, that may have been done while that person was serving in a public office, notwithstanding that at the time of the investigation, such person may have ceased serving in that office.

8. For the purposes of performing his functions under this Statute, the Inspector-General shall have the following powers,

(a) to authorize in writing, any officer under his charge to conduct an inquiry or investigation into an allegation of violation of human rights, breach of the rule of law, corruption, abuse of office occasioning injustice, and neglect of duty, and any other aspect that the Inspector-General is empowered to investigate into;

(b) to require a public officer or any other person to answer questions concerning his duties or those of another person, and to order the production for inspection of any standing orders, directives or office instructions relating to the duties of each public officer or person;

(c) to require any person in charge of a public office to produce or furnish within a specified time, any document or certified true copy thereof which is in his possession or under his charge; and

(d) to do any other thing necessary for the performance of the functions of the Inspector-General under this Statute.

9. (1) In addition to the powers specified in section 8 of this Statute, the Inspector-General, the Deputy Inspector-General or any other officer authorized by the Inspector-General in that behalf, shall in the performance of their duties and functions under this Statute,

(a) have access to all books, returns, reports and other documents relating to the work in any public office;

(b) at any time have access to and be able to search the premises of any public office, or of any vessel, aircraft or other vehicle, if there is reason to suspect that property corruptly or otherwise unlawfully acquired has been placed, deposited or concealed therein.

(2) An officer conducting a search under subsection (1) of this section shall only do so on the express instruction of the Inspector-General or the Deputy Inspector-General who shall issue a search warrant to this effect, in the form specified in the Second Schedule to this Statute.

(3) For the purposes of exercising his powers of access and search under subsection (1) of this section, the Inspector-General or other officer authorized in that behalf may use such reasonable force as may be necessary in the circumstances and may be accompanied

or assisted by such other law enforcement officers as he deems necessary to assist him to enter into or upon the premises, vessel, aircraft or vehicle, as the case may be.
(4) Notwithstanding the provisions of subsections (1), (2) and (3) of this section, where the President certifies that the entry upon or inspection of any premises, vessel, aircraft or vehicle.
(a) might prejudice the security, defence or international relations of Uganda or the investigation or detection of offences; or
(b) might involve the disclosure of the deliberations of the Cabinet or a committee thereof relating to matters of a secret or confidential nature and would be injurious to the public interest,
the Inspector-General shall not exercise his powers of access and search with respect to such premises, vessel, aircraft or vehicle.

10. (1) The Inspector-General may, by order under his hand, authorize an officer under his charge to investigate any bank account, share account, purchase account, expense account or any other account, or any safe or deposit box in a bank.
(2) An order made under subsection (1) of this section shall be sufficient authority for the disclosure or production by any person of information, accounts, documents or articles as may be required by the officer so authorized.
(3) Any person who wilfully and unlawfully refuses to comply with the order of the Inspector-General issued under this section commits an offence and shall be liable on conviction to a term of imprisonment not exceeding three years or to a fine not exceeding seven thousand shillings, or to both such fine and imprisonment.

Part IV – Procedure for Investigations.

11. The Inspector-General may, by Statutory Instrument under his hand, prescribe rules of procedure generally for the conduct of investigations and for any matter that is necessary for the efficient performance of the functions under this Statute.

12. (1) The Inspector-General shall have jurisdiction to investigate and inquire into,
(a) any of the acts mentioned in subsection (1) of section 7 of this Statute, committed by a public officer in the exercise of his official duties; and
(b) any other matter that may, from time to time, be specified or directed by the President, for investigation.
(2) Notwithstanding the provisions of subsection (1) hereof, the Inspector-General shall not have power to question or review any of the following matters,
(a) the decision of any court of law or of any judicial officer in the exercise of his judicial functions; or
(b) the decision of any tribunal established by law in the exercise of its functions; or
(c) any matter which is sub-judice; or
(d) any matter relating to the exercise of the prerogative of mercy; or
(e) any matter the review or investigation of which has been certified by the President as likely to,
   (i) be prejudicial to the security, defence or international relations of Uganda, or to the investigation or detection of offences; or
   (ii) involve the disclosure of proceedings and deliberations of the Cabinet or a Committee thereof, relating, to matters of a secret or confidential nature and would be injurious to the public interest.
(3) Where the Inspector-General is satisfied that,
(a) the complainant has at any material time had the right or opportunity of obtaining relief or redress by means of,
   (i) an application or representation to any executive authority; or
   (ii) an application, appeal, reference or review to or before a tribunal established by law; or

(iii) proceedings in a court of law; or
(b) the complaint is trivial, frivolous, vexatious or not made in good faith; or
(c) the investigation would be unnecessary, improper or futile,
he may decline to conduct an investigation and accordingly inform the complainant in writing, but be shall not be bound to give any reasons therefor.

13. (1) The procedure for conducting an investigation shall be such the Inspector-General considers appropriate in the circumstances of each case, and without prejudice to the generality of the fore-going, the Inspector-General may obtain information from such person and in such manner, and make such inquiries as he deems necessary.
(2) All proceedings, investigations and inquiries by the Inspector-General shall be conducted in strict confidence and an official of the office of the Inspector-General shall not communicate or divulge any information which has come to his knowledge in the course of his duties, to any person, otherwise than in the performance of his said duties under this Statute.
(3) A person who contravenes the provisions of sub-section (2) of this section commits an offence and shall on conviction be liable to a term of imprisonment not exceeding eighteen months or to a fine not exceeding three thousand shillings.

14. No proceedings, investigations or inquiries by the office of the Inspector-General shall be held null and void by reason only of an informality or irregularity in the procedure, and except on the ground of lack of jurisdiction, no such proceedings, investigations or inquiries shall be liable to be challenged, reviewed, quashed called in question in any court of law.

15. (1) No proceedings, whether civil or criminal, shall lie against the Inspector-General, the Deputy Inspector- General, an officer or any other person employed to execute the orders or warrants of the Inspector-General, for anything done in good faith and in the course of the performance of his duties under this Statute.
(2) Subject to the provisions of this Statute, no officer or person serving in the office of the Inspector-General, shall be compelled to give evidence before any court or tribunal in respect of anything coming to his knowledge by virtue of his said service.

16. Subject to any other law which enjoins the disclosure of classified information, anything said, information supplied, document, paper or thing produced in the course of an inquiry, under this Statute shall be privileged in the same manner as if the inquiry were a proceeding in a court of law, and a report of the Inspector-General shall be privileged in the same manner as if it were a record and judgement of a proceeding in court.

Part V – Investigations.

17. (1) A complaint or allegation under the provisions of this Statute may be made by an individual or by any body of persons whether corporate or not, and shall be strictly confidential and addressed directly to the Inspector-General.
(2) Notwithstanding the provisions of any written law, where a prisoner, or an employee in a public office, makes an allegation or complaint to the Inspector-General under the provisions of this Statute, such allegation or complaint shall not be made through, or subject to the scrutiny of, the prison officials or the immediate supervisor or employer, as the case may be.
(3) A complaint or allegation made under this Statute shall be,
(a) made by the complainant or his legal representative;
(b) in writing and addressed to the Inspector-General, except where the complainant cannot write in which case the Inspector-General shall translate the oral complaint into a written one; and
(c) signed or thumbprinted by the complainant.
(4) No complaint or allegation shall be received by the Inspector-General unless it is

made within a period of two years from the date on which the facts giving rise to such complaint or allegation arose:
Provided that in exceptional circumstances and in his absolute discretion the Inspector-General may receive a complaint or allegation lodged after the specified period.
(5) The provisions of subsections (3) and (4) of this section shall not apply to a complaint or allegation relating to a criminal offence.

18. No person shall as of right be entitled to be heard before the Inspector-General but where the Inspector- General proposes to conduct an investigation pursuant to a complaint or allegation under this Statute, he shall give the head of the public office concerned and any other person who is the subject of the complaint or allegation, an opportunity to reply to the complaint or allegation made against him, and no matter that is adverse to any person, or public office shall be included in a report of the Inspector-General unless such person or head of such office has been given a prior hearing.

19. (1) Subject to the provisions of this Statute, the Inspector-General may summon any person who in his opinion is able to give information relating to any matter relevant to the inquiry being conducted by him, to appear before him and to furnish such information and produce any documents, papers or things that may be in the possession or under the control of that person and may, by order under his hand, summon that person to attend before the Inspector-General at a specified time and place and to be examined on oath, which oath shall be in Form 2 of the Second Schedule.
(2) The summons issued under subsection (1) of this section shall be in Form 3 of the Second Schedule to this Statute.
(3) Where a person is to be examined on oath pursuant to this section, any officer duly authorized by the Inspector-General or the Deputy Inspector-General, in that behalf, may administer that oath.
(4) A summons issued under this section shall be served on the person to whom it is directed, by an officer from the Inspector-General office or by a police officer, in the manner prescribed for the service of a witness summons in civil proceedings before a court of law.

20. (1) Where a person on whom a summons under section 19 of this Statute has been duly served, does not attend at the specified time and place, and the Inspector-General is satisfied that,
(a) the summons was properly and duly served; and
(b) the person to whom the summons was directed, wilfully and without lawful justification avoided service, the Inspector-General may issue a warrant of arrest in Form 4 of the Second Schedule to this Statute, to be executed by a police officer, to apprehend such person and bring him before the Inspector-General at a specified time and place.
(2) A person, apprehended under the provisions of subsection (1) of this section shall within twenty-four hours of his arrest or as soon thereafter is Practicable, be brought before the Inspector-General.

21. The Inspector-General may pay to any person summoned before him under the provisions of this Statute, such allowances or sums in respect of expenses properly incurred by that person as the Inspector-General may deem appropriate.

22. A person who,
(a) wilfully and without lawful justification or excuse disobeys an order of the Inspector-General for his attendance or for the production of a document, paper or thing; or
(b) without lawful justification or excuse refuses to be examined before or to answer questions relating to an inquiry put to him by the Inspector-General; or;
(c) knowingly presents to the Inspector-General a false or fabricated document or makes a false statement with intent to deceive or mislead the investigation officers; or
(d) publishes any scandalous libel on the office of the Inspector-General; or

(e) creates or joins in any disturbance which interrupts or is to likely to interrupt the proceedings of the Inspector-General; or
(f) without lawful justification or excuse, wilfully obstructs or hinders a person acting in the exercise of the powers conferred by this Statute, commits an offence and shall, on conviction, be liable to imprisonment for a term not exceeding three years or to a fine not exceeding seven thousand shillings.

Part VI – Reports.

23. (1) The inspector-General shall,
(a) from time to time, submit to he President a full report on the proceedings of every inquiry together with his conclusions and recommendations; and
(b) submit to the legislature a summary of such report, twice every year, within three months after the 30th day of June and 31st day of December, respectively.
(2) In addition to any other matter required to be contained in a report made to the president on a inquiry, the report shall contain a statement of any action taken by a person whose conduct has been under inquiry or by the public office or authority employing such a person, to correct or ameliorate and conduct, procedure, act or commission that is adversely commented upon in the report.
(3) The report submitted to the president under the provision of this section shall be strictly confidential, and any summary report submitted to the legislature shall not disclose the identity or contain any statement which may point to the identity of any person into whose conduct an investigation has been or is about to be made, unless the legislature by resolution requires the Inspector-General to provide more details or information in respect thereof.

24. On receipt of a report the President may take or cause to be taken against the public officer in respect of whom such report is made, such action as may be taken under, or in accordance with the provisions of any written law.

Part VII – General Provisions

25. The Inspector-General may, by Statutory Instrument, make regulations in respect of any of the things required to be done by him under this Statute, and generally for the better carrying out of his duties and functions thereunder.

26. Sub-article (3) of Article 97 of the Constitution is amended by,
(a) deleting the word "and" occurring therein and substituting a comma therefor;
(b) substituting for the full-stop at the end thereof a command
(c) inserting immediately after the comma at the end thereof the phrase, "Inspector-General of Government and Deputy Inspector-General of Government".

27. This Statute shall come into force on such date as the President may, by Statutory Instrument, appoint.

Schedules

FIRST SCHEDULE

Part A

A. Oath of the Inspector-General of Government

I, ______________, having been appointed Inspector-General of Government/Deputy Inspector-General of Government, do swear that I will at all times well and truly serve the sovereign State of Uganda in that office, that I will support and uphold the Constitution as by lay established, that I will, without fear or favour, affection or ill-will, discharge the functions of the Office of Inspector-General of Government/Deputy Inspector-General of Government, and that I will not directly or indirectly reveal to any unauthorized person, any matters as shall come to my knowledge in the discharge of my duties, and committed to my secrecy. So help me God.

B. Official Oath

I, ____________, been appointed to exercise the functions of Secretary/ Counsel/Officer/member of staff in the Office of the Inspector- General of Government, swear that I will at all times well and truly serve the sovereign State of Uganda, that I will support and uphold the Constitution as by law established, and that I will not directly or indirectly reveal to any unauthorized person any matter, document, communication or information whatsoever as shall come to my knowledge in the discharge of my duties and committed to my secrecy. So help me God.

PART B

COLUMN 1
Person to take Oath

1. The Inspector-General of Government
2. The Deputy Inspector-General of Government
3. The Secretary
4. Counsel
5. Officers
6. Other staff

COLUMN 2
Nature of Oath
[omitted]

COLUMN 3
Authority to Administer Oath
[omitted]

SECOND SCHEDULE

Search Warrant. Form 1

The Republic of Uganda.

The Inspector-general of Government
Statute, 1987.
(Section 9(2)).

Warrant of Entry and Search.

Inquiry No ____________, 19 ________

To ____________________
(Officer designated by the Inspector-General.)

WHEREAS a complaint has been lodged with the Inspector-General of Government:

AND WHEREAS the Inspector-General has decided to conduct an investigation into the alleged complaint:

NOW, THEREFORE you are hereby authorized and ordered to enter the premises of ____________ (name of person)

at ____________ (description of premises)

in the day time, and there diligently, carry out an inspection and collect any oral and documentary evidence concerning the said inquiry from the said premises and bring it before the Inspector- general of Government to be used for the purpose of the said investigation.

ISSUED at ____________ this ________ day of ____________, 19 ________
Inspector-General of Government.

Witness Oath. Form 2.

I, ____________ swear by Almighty God that the evidence I shall give shall be the truth, the whole truth and nothing but the truth.

Witness Summons. Form 3.

The Republic of Uganda.

The Inspector-general of Government
Statute, 1987.
(Section 19 (2)).

Witness Summons.

Inquiry No ____________, 19 ________

To ____________________ (full name).

Of ____________________ (full address)

You are ordered to attend before the Inspector-General of Government at ____________
on the ________ day of 19 ________ at ________ hours, and so from day to day until your attendance is dispensed with, to give evidence in the said inquiry:

AND ALSO to bring with you and to produce at the said time and place the following documents:

____

DATED at ____________ this ________ day of ____________, 19 ________

Inspector-General of Government.

Warrant of Arrest Form 4

The Republic of Uganda.
The Inspector-general of Government
Statute, 1987.
(Section 20 (1)).

Warrant of Arrest
Inquire No ____________, 19 ________

To: ____________ (Police Officer and other authorized Officers)

WHEREAS ____________________ (full) name,

of ____________________ (full address,
was ordered to appear before the Inspector-General of government at ____________,
on the ________ day of ____________, 19 ________, and subsequent days to testify what he/she knew and /or to produce specified documents in relation to the above stated inquiry, and the said ____________ (name), has not appeared according to the summons issued in that regard and has not excused hi/her failure to:

NOW, THEREFORE, you are hereby ordered to apprehend, bring and have the said ____________ before the Inspector-General at ____________ (place), on the ________ day of ________, 19 ________.

ISSUED at ____________ this ________ day of ____________, 19 ________

Inspector-General of Government

Chapter V

Multi Organ Systems

South Africa

The Role of Human Rights Institutions in South Africa

David McQuoid-Mason*

Introduction

In this paper it is intended briefly to discuss the role, achievements and cost of state-funded human rights institutions in South Africa. The following will be considered:

(a) The Public Protector.
(b) The Human Rights Commission.
(c) The Commission for Gender Equality.
(d) The Youth Commission.
(e) The Commission for Restitution of Land Rights.
(f) The Truth and Reconciliation Commission.

Thereafter brief reference will be made to several other institutions which also support human rights and democracy.

The Public Protector[1]

The office of the Public Protector was created by Section 110 of the interim Constitution[2] and Section 182 of the final Constitution.[3] The first Public Protector, Advocate Selby Baqwa, was appointed in June 1995[4] and began operating in October 1995.[5]

Role

The role of the Public Protector is to investigate complaints from people who feel that they have been treated unfairly by a government agency or official. Political parties may also ask the Public Protector to investigate allegations of misconduct within the state bureaucracy. An example of this is the investigation

---

* Professor of Law, University of Natal.
[1] See also the paper S.A.M. Baqwa, *South Africa's Ombudsman*, below.
[2] Constitution of the Republic of South Africa Act 200 of 1993.
[3] Constitution of the Republic of South Africa Act 108 of 1996.
[4] Human Rights Committee, *Human Rights Review* (1996) 28.
[5] Human Rights Committee, *Human Rights Review* (1996) 26. The contact person at the Public Protector's Office is Ms Elsabe de Waal (telephone: +27 12 322 2916). The address is Private Bag 677, Pretoria 0001.

K. Hossain et al. (eds), Human Rights Commissions and Ombudsman Offices, 617–625.

by the Public Protector, at the request of the Democratic Party, of the use by the Department of Health of R14 million (US$3 million) of donor's money to promote AIDS awareness through the controversial musical, Sarafina 2. The Public Protector's report on the incident was widely praised for its balanced approach to what was a highly sensitive political issue.

Only decisions of the courts are beyond the jurisdiction of the Public Protector. The Public Protector serves for a non-renewable term of seven years.

Achievements

The Public Protector's office received 2351 new cases in 1996 and finalised 769 despite severe capacity limitations.[6] By 17 October 1997 the office had received about 2000 complaints and settled 590 of them. Many of these were from former public servants who were complaining about late retrenchment and pension pay-outs. Other complaints were about conditions in prison.[7]

Budget

The budget in 1997 was R5.8 million (US$1.3 million), and the Public Protector earns R367 650 (US$79,783). There are 23 permanent members of staff.[8]

The Human Rights Commission[9]

The Human Rights Commission was established in terms of Section 115 of the interim Constitution and Section 184 of the final Constitution. Mr Barney Pityana was appointed as Chairperson of the Commission in September 1995,[10] and the Commission commenced operations in March 1996.[11]

Role

The role of the Human Rights Commission is to build and promote a culture of human rights and to monitor the extension of rights to all citizens in line with the Bill of Rights in the Constitution. It has the power to demand annual reports from government departments on their progress in implementing socio-economic rights. It may also investigate specific instances in which public or private institutions are alleged to have violated the human rights of citizens. Thus, for instance, complaints about racism in public schools would be sent to the Human Rights Commission's Office for investigation. After such investigation it would make a recommendation to the appropriate authority.[12]

---

[6] Human Rights Committee, *Human Rights Review* (1996) 28.
[7] *The Mercury* 17 October 1997.
[8] Ibid.
[9] See also the paper, N. Barney Pityana, *The South African Human Rights Commission*, below.
[10] Ibid.
[11] Human Rights Committee *Human Rights Review* (1996) 26. The contact person is John Majapelo (telephone: + 27 11 484 8300), and the address is Private Bag 2700, Houghton 2041.
[12] *The Mercury* 17 October 1997.

Achievements

Between 1 January and 30 September 1997 the Commission received 1439 complaints. Of these 588 were either rejected or referred, 95 were being investigated, 203 telephonic complaints were settled by offering advice, 371 were being assessed, and 182 were awaiting attention. Three of the 11 original Commissioners have resigned, citing tensions arising from bureaucratic inefficiency and problems between staff and their managers.

Budget

The Human Rights Commission is a permanent body with an annual budget of R6.8 million (US$1.5 million). The Chairperson earns R400,000 (US$86,957). There are 10 Commissioners and 34 members of staff.[13] The Commission does not believe that it can carry out its mandate on its existing budget. It has thus prepared a business plan requesting R32 million (US$7 million) for the current year.[14]

The Commission for Gender Equality

The Commission for Gender Equality was established in terms of Section 119 of the interim and Section 187 of the final Constitution. Ms Thenjiwe Mtintso was appointed Chairperson of the Commission, and it began operations in June 1997. It has a five year lifespan which can be renewed once.[15]

Role

The role of the Commission on Gender Equality is to ensure equality among men and women by promoting respect for the ideals of gender equality and by ensuring people are not discriminated against because of their gender. It also advises and educates on issues relating to gender equality. It has wide powers of search and entry.

Achievements

The Commission has only been operating since June 1997. It has produced a report on gender equality, made submissions to Parliament, addressed meetings and consulted widely with 80 government and civil society bodies. The Commission's 300 page report and report-backs to about 250 meetings around the country are acclaimed as successes.[16]

Budget

The annual budget is R2 million (US$434,783), which has been swallowed up by salaries alone. The Commission needs more money to do its work properly and claims that it should receive four times the amount allocated.

---

[13] Ibid.
[14] Human Rights Committee, *Human Rights Review* (1996) 28.
[15] *The Mercury*, 17 October 1997. The contact person at the Commission's Offices is Mr Faried Esack (telephone: +27 12 322 4482), and the address is Private Bag 91, Pretoria 0001.
[16] *The Mercury*, 17 October 1997.

The Chairperson's salary package is R252,273 (US$54,842) and the 11 Commissioners earn R203,133 (US$44,159) each.

The Youth Commission

The Youth Commission has no constitutional status, but was established by the National Youth Commission Act.[17] It has been located at the office of the Deputy President, Thabo Mbeki. The Chairperson of the Youth Commission, Mahlengi Bhengu, was appointed in 1996.[18]

Role

The role of the Youth Commission is to be the Government's chief advisory body on youth affairs. To this end it was created to ensure that the rights of the youth are upheld and that their needs are met. Its main task is to devise a national youth policy for presentation to the government. It may also monitor public and private bodies, and is required to conduct information and education programmes for the youth.[19]

Achievements

In July 1997 the Commission presented its first annual 'activity report' to President Mandela informing him about its work. The Commission does not have the legal or infrastructural resources to receive and deal with complaints, although it may 'facilitate assistance', and possibly provide funding.[20]

Budget

The Youth Commission receives a budget of R6.9 million (US$1.5 million), and the Chairperson is paid R320,000 (US$69,565) per annum. The five Commissioners have been appointed for a five year term which may be renewed. The Commission employs 15 permanent members of staff.[21]

Commission for the Restitution of Land Rights

The Commission for the Restitution of Land Rights was established in terms of the Restitution of Land Rights Act[22] as required by Section 122 of the interim Constitution. The Commission was appointed in January 1995 and began operating in March 1995.[23] Its five year lifespan may be extended by 10 years. The Chairperson of the Commission is Joe Seramane.[24]

---

[17] Act 19 of 1996 s 2(1).
[18] The contact person for the Commission is Paul Johnson (telephone: +27 12 328 4708), and the address is Private Bag X911, Pretoria 0001.
[19] Section 3; cf *The Mercury*, 17 October 1997.
[20] Ibid.
[21] Ibid.
[22] Act 22 of 1994 s 4(1).
[23] Human Rights Committee, *Human Rights Review* (1996) 26.
[24] The contact person is Thys Human (telephone: +27 12 341 7900), and the address is PO Box 56720, Pretoria 0001.

Role

The role of the Commission is to assist individuals, communities and descendants of individuals who have unfairly lost their land since 1913. They may lodge claims for the return of the land or for reparation in the form of alternative land, money or other relief. The Commission's job is to investigate claims and to try and settle disputes without recourse to the courts. It may also prepare claims on behalf of aggrieved parties. The claims may then be forwarded the Land Claims Court for a ruling.[25]

Achievements

The Land Commission has successfully finalised two claims: one by the Elandskloof community which received state purchased farms at Citrusdale in the Western Cape, and the other at District Six also in the Western Cape. The claims in respect of Cato Manor in Durban are still in the balance. By 31 July 1997, 16,670 individual claims had been lodged: 3086 in rural areas and 13,584 in cities. Some claims have been grouped, which may help overcome the case backlog.[26]

Budget

In 1997 the budget of the Land Commission was cut by 60% to R6.9 million (US$1.5 million). The Commission has 65 permanent and 74 contract workers. The Chairperson earns R349,735 (US$76,029) per annum.

The Truth and Reconciliation Commission[27]

The Truth and Reconciliation Commission was established in terms of the post-amble to the interim Constitution,[28] and the Promotion of National Unity and Reconciliation Act of 1995.[29] The Commission was appointed in December 1995 and began operations in March 1996. The Chairperson of the Commission is Archbishop Desmond Tutu.[30]

Role

The role of the Truth and Reconciliation Committee is threefold:

(a) to compile a picture of human rights abuses during the apartheid era;
(b) to restore to victims their human dignity by having them tell their stories and to recommend how they can be helped; and
(c) to consider granting civil and criminal amnesty to people who committed

[25] *The Mercury*, 17 October 1997.
[26] Ibid.
[27] See also the paper Alex Boraine, *The Truth and Reconciliation Commission in South Africa*, above, part I.
[28] Entitled 'National Unity and Reconciliation'.
[29] Act 34 of 1995 s 2(1).
[30] The contact person is Sello Rabothata (telephone: +27 11 333 6330), and the address is 10th Floor Sanlam Centre, Corner Jeppe and von Wielligh Streets, Johannesburg 2001.

atrocities for what they now claim were political reasons, providing that they give full details of the acts for which they are seeking amnesty.

The Commission had until 30 April 1998 to finish its investigations, and until 31 July 1998 to finish hearing amnesty applications.[31]

Achievements

The Truth and Reconciliation Commission has received 12,000 statements from victims. About 2000 of these have given evidence in public. The Commission has had about 7000 amnesty applications, of which some 1700 have been dealt with so far. Fifty amnesty applications were granted after hearings and 23 dealt with in chambers. Seventeen people were denied amnesty and 1648 have been refused amnesties on their papers. About another 600 applications need to be considered in chambers and 1635 dealt with in hearings.[32]

Budget

The budget for the Truth and Reconciliation Commission in 1997 was R50 million (US$10.8 million), and it employs 300 people on contract. Most of the contracts expire on 30 April 1998. The Chairperson earns R292,000 (US$63,478) per annum.

Other Commissions Supporting Human Rights and Democracy

In addition to the above there are a number of other Commissions and bodies that support democracy and human rights in South Africa. These are the following:

(i) The Commission for the Promotion and Protection of Rights of Cultural, Religious and Linguistic Communities;
(ii) The Auditor-General;
(iii) The Electoral Commission;
(iv) The Independent Broadcasting Authority; and
(v) The Pan South African Language Board.

It is intended to deal briefly with each of these.

Commission for the Promotion and Protection of the Rights of Cultural, Religious and Linguistic Communities

The Commission was established in terms of Section 185 of the final Constitution[33] and its role is the following:

(i) to promote respect for the rights of cultural, religious and linguistic communities;

[31] *The Mercury*, 17 October 1997. [These dates were subsequently extended to 31 July 1998 for TRC investigations and to 1999 for Amnesty hearings – editorial note].
[32] Ibid.
[33] Constitution of the Republic of South Africa Act 108 of 1996.

(ii) to promote and develop peace, friendship, humanity, tolerance and national unity among cultural, religious and linguistic communities, on the basis of equality, non-discrimination and free association; and
(iii) to recommend the establishment or recognition, in accordance with national legislation, of a cultural or other council or councils for a community or communities in South Africa.[34]

The Commission has the power to monitor, investigate, research, educate, lobby, advise and report on issues concerning the rights of cultural, religious and linguistic communities,[35] and may report any matter to the Human Rights Commission.[36]

The Auditor-General

In terms of the final Constitution the Auditor-General is appointed for a fixed, non-renewable term of between five and ten years.[37]

The Auditor-General must audit and report on the accounts, financial statements and financial management of:

(i) all national and provincial state departments and administrations;
(ii) all municipalities; and
(iii) any other institution or accounting entity required by national or provincial legislation to be audited by the Auditor-General.[38]

In addition to the above, and any other duties imposed by legislation, the Auditor-General may audit and report on the accounts, financial statements and financial management of:

(i) any institution funded from the National Revenue Fund or a Provincial Revenue Fund or by a municipality; or
(ii) any institution that is authorized in terms of any law to receive money for a public purpose.[39]

The Auditor-General must submit audit reports to any legislature that has a direct interest in the audit, and to any other authority prescribed by national legislation. All reports must be made public.[40]

The Electoral Commission

The Electoral Commission is referred to in the final Constitution as being required to be composed of at least three persons.[41] The Electoral Commission Act[42] provides for the establishment of the Commission[43] which consists of five

---

[34] Section 185(1).
[35] Section 185(2).
[36] Section 185(3).
[37] Section 189.
[38] Section 188(1).
[39] Section 188(2).
[40] Section 188(3).
[41] Section 191.
[42] Act 51 of 1996.
[43] Section 3.

persons.[44] The Chairperson of the Electoral Commission is Justice Johan Kriegler of the Constitutional Court.

The role of the Electoral Commission is:

(i) to manage elections of national, provincial and municipal legislative bodies in accordance with national legislation;
(ii) to ensure that those elections are free and fair; and
(iii) to declare the results of those elections within a period that must be prescribed by national legislation and that is as short as is reasonably possible.[45]

Independent Broadcasting Authority

The final Constitution provides that national legislation must be introduced to establish an independent authority to regulate broadcasting in the public interest, and to ensure fairness and a diversity of views broadly representing South African society.[46] This has been done by the Independent Broadcasting Authority Act[47] which provided for the setting up of the authority prior to the implementation of the final Constitution.[48]

The Pan South African Language Board

The Board was established under the Pan South African Language Board Act[49] in 1996 to promote the 11 official languages in South Africa, as well as other languages. The 13 members of the Board were appointed in April 1996, and consist of the following: four practising language workers, three language planners, five members with special knowledge of language matters in South Africa, and a legal expert with special knowledge of language legislation.[50]

Conclusion

The South African Constitution has established a number of Commissions to protect the new democracy in the country. Permanent Commissions have been established to ensure that the provisions in the Bill of Rights are complied with. Temporary Commissions have been set up to deal with transitional issues consequent upon the change from apartheid to democracy, and their life spans will depend upon how soon they can achieve their goals. The cost of establishing so many Commissions has been considerable, and it may be necessary to undertake some form of rationalisation of their operations without detracting from their individual watchdog roles.

Since March 1995 the government has spent more than R287 million (US$62.4

[44] Section 6(1).
[45] Section 190(1).
[46] Section 192.
[47] Act 153 of 1993.
[48] Section 2(1).
[49] Act 59 of 1995 s 2(1).
[50] Human Rights Committee, *Human Rights Review* (1996) 29.

million) on the six main Commissions that were established to support democracy in South Africa. The Chairperson of the Human Rights Commission has suggested that there needs to be a 'consultative forum' of all the Commissions to work out new ground rules to avoid duplication of their work. He also suggested that they begin sharing offices with other facilities in the provinces, and that they should share information concerning their goals, achievements and cost.[51]

---

[51] *The Mercury*, 17 October 1997.

National Institutions at Work: The Case of the South African Human Rights Commission

N. Barney Pityana*

The South African Human Rights Commission was established in 1995 according to the provisions of the 1993 interim Constitution and the Human Rights Commission Act 1994. The Constitutional Principles negotiated by all political formations in the country and on which the present constitution of the country is based entrenches certain fundamental principles like "universally accepted fundamental rights, freedoms and civil liberties which shall be provided for and protected by entrenched and justiciable provisions in the Constitution ...". The Principles also affirm the principles of equality and an independent and impartial judiciary. The Principles also make special reference to the need to guarantee the independence and impartiality of certain state institutions among them the Public Protector. The Bill of Rights is incorporated in both South African Constitutions.

It is very important to pause and to take note of the significance of these moves for South Africa. South Africa had been considered a democracy since the Statute of Westminster in 1931. During that time the country was ruled according to the Westminster model, with its peculiar sovereignty of parliament doctrine, by successive white minority regimes. The last of these under the National Party, had been in power since 1948 and imposed a system of apartheid. Under apartheid, violations of human rights, principally a systematic state policy of racial discrimination, political repression and a wholesale contravention of civil and political rights, became the norm. It was to capture this sentiment for advancement and transformation, for a qualitative difference for the people of South Africa from a past where discrimination and violation of human rights was the norm to a rights-based society that the Postamble to the 1993 Constitution was adopted:

> "This Constitution provides a historic bridge between the past of a deeply divided society characterized by strife, conflict, untold suffering and injustice, and a future founded on the recognition of human rights, democracy and peaceful co-existence and development opportunities for all South Africans, irrespective of colour, race, class, belief or sex."

The new dispensation in South Africa sought to assure South Africans of their life, liberty and fundamental rights as a means of building national unity and reconciliation. The final Constitution (1996) affirms the principles first enshrined

*Chairperson, South African Human Rights Commission.

K. Hossain et al. (eds), Human Rights Commissions and Ombudsman Offices, 627–638.

in the interim Constitution but does so not just by restating basic principles but defines the identity of the new South Africa and affirms its fundamental values:

"The Republic of South Africa is one sovereign democratic state founded on the following values:

Human Dignity, the achievement of equality and the advancement of human rights and freedoms,

Non-racialism and non-sexism,

Supremacy of the Constitution and the rule of law."

The Constitution gives added weight to these universal norms and principles by giving them the authority of high moral or ethical imperatives.

These values, however, should never be simply high-sounding statements devoid of content or the force of action. To affirm them the Constitution has a justiciable Bill of Rights. The Bill of Rights satisfies the requirements of the Constitutional Principles and has set provisions for amendment. Sections of the Bill of Rights are also considered non-derogable during states of emergency. The Bill of Rights is considered to be "the cornerstone of democracy in South Africa." The state is required to "respect, protect, promote and fulfill the rights in the Bill of Rights". That means that there is a positive duty on the state to take steps to protect and promote fundamental rights. In other words the primary responsibility for promoting and protecting human rights devolves on the state. For that reason we have been emphatic about this responsibility and we have been going further to say that the observance of human rights is an essential and integral component of governance. Therefore there cannot be an aspect of government that is not informed by considerations of human rights.

The Constitution does not, however, take the view that the task of promoting and protecting human rights is the sole responsibility of government. Besides asserting that all citizens have certain responsibilities and duties as citizens, it has gone further and established state institutions supporting democracy among whom is the Public Protector, the Human Rights Commission and the Commission for Gender Equality. The Constitution states that these institutions are "independent and subject only to the Constitution and the law, and they must be impartial and must exercise their powers and perform their functions without fear, favour or prejudice ..." The Constitution then defines the functions of the institutions and sets out procedures for appointments. The powers of the Commission are regulated by separate legislation.

Establishment and Operation

Upon assuming office, the Commissioners adopted a structure for the Commission and allocated responsibilities to each commissioner. The way in which that was done was by way of defining the roles and responsibilities of the Commission and of individual members. We examined the nature of our independence and how, in the light of that, we were to establish our relationships especially with government. We deliberated on the requirement of impartiality and decided that members should desist from active participation in party politics and we opened a register of members' interests.

What we did was to allocate at least one full-time commissioner to a province and we set up committees on specific issues as proposed by Section 5 of the Act. This system of committees opened a window of opportunity for the Commission to cooperate with NGOs and to bring into the policy formation aspect of our work other experts from outside the Commission. In this way the groundwork was laid of co-operation between the Commission and NGOs as well as with human rights experts and advocates from outside the Commission.

The Secretariat of the Commission was to carry out the policy of the Commission in programmes or projects that entailed application and implementation of policy. The Commission elected the Chief Executive Officer (CEO). Her tasks are to appoint staff, to manage and administer control over the staff, she is the accounting officer for state resources and is accountable for all her functions to the Commission. With the CEO the Commission organized the secretariat into four units or departments: Finance & Administration; Legal Services; Education, Training & Information as well as Research & Documentation. It was also decided that the Commission would operate offices in all nine provinces but that all provincial operations would largely be focussed on education, training and information, receiving and documenting complaints. The Commission was insistent that there was only one commission and that no federal institution was intended by these arrangements. The Commission negotiated with the Public Service Commission a staff complement which was later signed by the President and published in the Government Gazette.

The powers of the Commission were introduced gradually in order to allow the Commission to establish itself. By May 1996, the staff regulations were gazetted and all the powers of the Commission came into effect. Once that was achieved, the recruitment of staff began in earnest.

Relations with the Executive

The government is very supportive of the Commission. It was necessary, however, for the Commission to set out from the very beginning its relationships with the government on a clear footing. The Commission recognized that it had to deal with government on the basis of partnership. It had to negotiate, for example, adequate funding for the operations of the Commission, it also had to have access to information held by government. The Act obliges government officers to give the Commission "such assistance as may be reasonably required for the protection of the independence, impartiality and dignity of the Commission" (Section 4(3)). In addition organs of state are debarred from "interfering with, hindering or obstructing the Commission ... in the exercise of or performance of its, his or her powers, duties and functions" (Section 4(2)). There are penalties attached to anyone found guilty of the above breaches. In addition, proceedings of the Commission are public and the rules of contempt of court apply in relation to the maintenance of orderly behaviour, the authority of the Commission, defamation and protection for acts done by commissioners in the course of duty. At the same time the Commission has power to subpoena witnesses, take out search warrants and to hear evidence in the course of its investigations into human rights violations. In all of these activities the Commission must rely on the co-operation and assistance of organs of state including police, officers of the court, civil servants and cabinet ministers.

We have had reason to be concerned at times as to whether there was understanding of the obligations of government and civil service about the extent of the powers and reliance of the Commission on co-operation and partnership with government. There were variations of understanding of the nature and meaning of "independence" depending on who one spoke to among cabinet ministers. Politicians seemed to be resentful about the extent of the "independence" of the state institutions. In order to address these and other issues, the Commission arranged briefing sessions with as many cabinet ministers as we could manage. We asked them to brief us about steps they were taking as the Executive to ensure compliance in their portfolios with the Bill of Rights and how they could assist with the establishment of a culture of human rights. Those ministers we met with valued the exercise and, I suppose, those who did not see the value of it just did not give us an appointment! We also held meetings with all the political parties represented in parliament. We shared with them the work and vision of the Commission and we discussed ways in which they could enhance the observance of human rights in the course of their parliamentary duties. We have met in this way with all but one political party.

We still felt that there needed to be a deeper understanding of our complementary responsibilities in order to ensure better cooperation. We proposed to government a draft Memorandum of Understanding. The memo set out the duties, rights and responsibilities of the Commission and government. The memo was submitted to government for its comment. To date no official reply has been forthcoming. We have heard from sources in the office of the Deputy President that there was reluctance on the part of government to sign a document like this with a state institution. What this suggests to us, once again, is a lack of understanding of the nature of independence which is granted to us by law. We are pursuing the matter.

Independence of the Commission

One of the ways in which the 'independence' of the Commission was severely tested has been in the administrative arrangements for the funding of the Commission. Upon assuming office we were informed that a sum of R6.1 million had been allocated for the work of the Commission; that this money was being channelled through the Department of Justice. We queried the amount and asked how the budget was arrived at and we questioned the arrangement whereby the funding of the Commission was being channelled through a government ministry. We did so because we feared that these arrangements would compromise the independence of the Commission. First, we did not believe that state officials could determine without our participation how we were to go about doing our work. Secondly, we believed that it was inappropriate for an independent national institution to be dependent upon and supervised by a government department to undertake its work. The ideal situation, we argued, was that the Commission be based in the Office of the President. It was argued that the Ministry of Justice was simply a convenient channel for administrative purposes and that there was no intention of interfering with the independence of the Commission. We believed that. In fact the Minister of Justice has been most insistent on this issue. However, we had to admit that public perceptions of questionable status would be hard to counter with such arrangements. One of the ways in which the Commission established its independence was by the physical arrangement of ensuring that the offices of the Commission were not government premises or buildings shared with government departments. Government had no problems with that.

Where we struggled most, however, was on the issue of the budget of the Commission as well as the salaries of members of the Commission. We argued that the salaries and terms and conditions of employment of members of the Commission should give effect to the status and esteem which their positions allowed and that the budget should be adequate for the Commission to carry out its tasks. Our arguments were strongly backed by the desire to conform to the Paris Principles, the basic standard adopted by the General Assembly for the status of national institutions. Government never adequately countered our arguments, but we were told that all institutions which depended on the public fiscus had to be subjected to the budgetary stringency shared by all, that independent institutions also had to be accountable and the executive in a democracy had the ultimate power to decide spending priorities. We objected to the fact that we were not directly participating in the decisions which determined our budget.

We wrote two substantial Memos to the Deputy President. One dealt with the arrangements for meeting the financial needs of the Commission (16 August 1996). We noted that Section 181(3) of the Constitution not only obliged state organs to give assistance to the Commission but that they must do so as "to ensure the independence impartiality, dignity and effectiveness" of the institution. We argued that the present arrangements were in conflict with the provisions of the Act which required that the Commission participate in the budget process not through another state department, but as if it was a fully-fledged department of state (Section 16(3) of the Act). The other was a legal opinion of what "independence" for a national institution meant and how accountability functioned in the light of that independence (30 May 1997). The Opinion compared the meaning of independence with that of the judiciary but distinguished it. It also drew from comparative case law from commonwealth countries and the United States. We believe firmly that we could mount a legal challenge against the government in the Constitutional Court as a last resort.

We discussed the matter fully with the Speaker of the National Assembly to whom we are required to report annually. We can say that there was much understanding of our position. We are now in the process of submitting a report to the National Assembly setting out the difficulties with present arrangements and proposing alternatives. We are co-operating with other independent state institutions established in terms of Chapter 9 of the Constitution. We hope that a mechanism could be found for the administrative arrangements to be supervised by parliament, as the Constitution appears to have intended all along. The battle for independence is, I believe, almost over.

Programmes

The mandate of the Commission is very broad and comprehensive and yet the resources are and will always be finite. We, therefore, took responsibility to undertake a comprehensive strategic planning exercise. Through this process we agreed a Mission Statement, a Vision as well Objectives of the Commission. We also set out six strategic goals and means of achieving them. This was set in the context of a multiple year programme: 1997–2000. The Mission Statement is simple and yet conveys the full meaning and intent of the Constitution and the Act:

"The South African Human Rights Commission is the national institution established to entrench constitutional democracy. It is committed to promote respect for observance of and the protection of human rights for everyone without fear or favour."

The goals define the programmes we are to undertake to fulfill our mandate. The Commission organized a national Human Rights Conference in May 1997. That conference brought together civil servants, NGOs, academics and human rights experts as well as the legal profession to map out a comprehensive agenda for human rights in South Africa. About 300 participants attended the conference. It served to bond the Commission with the various publics it serves and developed a vital partnership and cooperation between the Commission and its partners. We believe that the conference helped to bring about a better understanding of the work of the Commission. More seriously, the conference set out an agenda which the Commission is seeking to implement – and by which the Commission seeks to be judged. The Statement produced by the conference has become an important source of policy for the Commission. No sooner had we done that, however, did we realise that none of our vision could be fulfilled without a substantial improvement in our budget. These exercises, however, helped shape the scope and extent of human rights work in South Africa. I believe that government took careful note of this situation.

At the beginning of this financial year, the budget of the Commission was considerably improved. In order to take account of the expectations that had been created as a result of our public exposure in the period since our establishment and for the purpose of planning our programmes, this year the Commission undertook a planning exercise as a result of which work plans were developed which would advance the goals previously established, address the agenda set by Conference and utilize prudently the available resources. The Work Plan of the Commission for the year 1998/99 sets out only a few focal areas of operation: Equality; Social and Economic Rights; Administration of Justice. In addition to these there is ongoing work of the Commission in terms of complaints handling, education and information and a number of time-limited projects. What we wanted to do was to resist the temptation to be over-committed to the extent that we can hardly be effective in the things we do and others would be unable to detect the priorities we have set ourselves.

Complaints Handling

The handling and management of complaints can be said to be the heart of the Commission. We receive about 200 complaints a week. The processing of the complaints has taken some time to streamline. The position of the Commission to complaints can be said to be rather ambiguous. At one level, the Commission has no desire to be 'complaints-driven'. By this we mean getting to a situation where the whole of the work of the Commission is determined by the avalanche of complaints we believe we shall always receive. The reason we do not wish to find ourselves in such a situation is because we fear that individual complaints in themselves do not necessarily indicate areas of greatest need or address the concerns of the most vulnerable members of our communities many of whom may find the requirements of written statements forbidding and generally the milieu of the Commission rendering assistance inaccessible. Yet we have a very strong belief that the value of a national institution in a democracy is that it affords many ordinary people an opportunity to be heard sympathetically. People need to have the assurance that without cost to themselves and at minimal inconvenience, they can approach an institution of ordinary people to come to their assistance. We believe that a national institution can ensure justice to ordinary people speedily, with minimal fuss and, hopefully, in a less adversarial environment. This requires an attitude of openness and availability. It is this latter conviction that outweighs our first concern.

And yet we have taken the view that individual complaints may have value insofar as they give indicators of trends of violations prevalent in society. That is why our Act allows the Commission an opportunity to alert Parliament to prison conditions, we developed a programme on racism in schools and, likewise, we are about to undertake an inquiry into conditions in selected farms in the Northern Province. Public inquiries are very important because they are the only public mechanisms whereby the Commission can be seen at work. When it does, it gives confidence to people who have been victims of human rights violations and it sends messages to violators that in this new dispensation, human rights violations will not be tolerated.

Finally, through this process of considering complaints, the Commission may make a decision about matters that should be taken to litigation. This is a step the Commission has been very reluctant to indulge in. The main reason is that it is expensive to do so but also that it is time consuming. And yet, we see the courts as an important element in the development of human rights jurisprudence and in this the Commission has an important role to play. For that reason we are very selective about matters we would be prepared to argue before the Constitutional Court. Generally, it should be a matter that cannot otherwise be settled and which will establish a legal precedent. The Commission, of course, is not a judicial body and, as such, its findings and recommendations may need to be placed before a court for enforcement. We take the view, though, that until the findings in terms of Section 15 of the Act are challenged in court, they are binding on all parties.

We have appreciated the assistance of partners like the Australian Commission, the Canadian Commission, Finland and the Office of the United Nations High Commissioner for Human Rights who have all in different ways encouraged us and provided much needed expertise and computer software to improve our complaints handling and management.

Human Rights Education and Public Awareness

This is another aspect of the work of the Commission that requires an enormous resource outlay and skills. Not only must there be skills in articulating human rights principles but that one must have the ability to communicate them effectively to a wide range of people. Effective human rights education, training and information is also important for the image of the organization.

In our Commission we have a sense that human rights education must take pride of place. The reason is simply that after years of repression and a culture of insensitivity and lack of meaningful dialogue among South Africa's races, diverse language and cultural groups, among the young and the old, rural and urban people, religious groups and the diversities of political opinions, South Africans needed to be educated about the meaning of their rights at all levels. The development of a rights-based culture has many pitfalls. Certainly the prevalence of crime and unwarranted violence in society militates against the development and extension of rights. Government is under tremendous pressure to curtail rights, as human rights are perceived to be soft on crime.

Public education and conscientisation is an important tool of human rights education. But because of the extent of the task, strategic decisions had to be taken. For example tenders for a public information and awareness campaign showed that a basic campaign would cost about R6 million a year. There were better quotations we received for about R12 million. In the end, we cut our campaign considerably to R1 million. This year (1998) we intend to run another campaign which will cost more than the R1 million we budgeted for last year.

At the informal level, the Commission has been engaged in partnership with selected government departments especially those in the law and order cluster: police, prisons and the civil service, especially immigration officers, and has been running human rights training seminars and workshops. For the general public we are planning seminars around the equality legislation drafting we are undertaking with the Ministry of Justice. At the formal level, the Commission is assisting the Department of Education develop curricula in human rights education for use in schools as part of the new syllabus. We have joined with the department in a wide range of issues of human rights in education from corporal punishment and alternative ways of discipline to the development of a culture of teaching, learning and service. In terms of output, we have produced manuals, simple English versions of the Bill of Rights, posters and information brochures. All of these, in the context of the new South Africa, have to be produced in 11 official languages – count the cost!

Other Programmes

I have made reference above to three project foci the Commission has adopted for this year. A brief word on these. What I believe is worth emphasising about some of these, at least, is the importance of those programmes we undertake in partnership with government. Among these I would highlight the process which will lead to the drafting of legislation on equality. The Ministry of Justice and us have embarked on this project which is required by the Constitution to be done within three years of the adoption of the Constitution. The Minister of Justice felt that it would be important for the Commission to be involved in this because the drafting of the law should be within a framework that is arrived at after wide consultations. The Commission, which already has special emphasis on racism and on the rights of people with disability, has been engaged in shaping, with the department, a framework for the law that must be passed in two years time.

The second level of cooperation is in the drafting of the National Action Plan for Human Rights. The NAP has been inspired and motivated by the Commission. We managed to persuade government about the importance of this in the development of a culture of human rights in our country. Cabinet has approved cooperation on this issue and, in the context of the 50th Anniversary of the Universal Declaration of Human Rights, South Africa hopes to adopt a National Plan of Action on Human Rights this year. At the same time, the Commission persuaded government to have a National Committee to organize events to commemorate the 50th Anniversary and 1998 the International Human Rights Year. These two events are convened by the Deputy Minister of Justice and show a remarkable degree of cooperation between the government and the Commission.

Finally, I wish to make reference to the Social and Economic Rights. The South African Bill of Rights makes provision for a number of selected rights under the Covenant on Economic, Social and Cultural Rights (1966). These are the rights to food, housing, health care, water, social welfare, a clean and healthy environment and education. There is no reference to the right to development nor to a right to work. In keeping with international practice, the Constitution, while intending these rights to be as applicable, enforceable and justiciable as any, nonetheless has utilized language, universally accepted, which renders direct enforceability difficult. The drafters of the Constitution wanted to ensure that the rights enshrined in the Bill of Rights were understood holistically as universal, interrelated and interdependent. Yet the language of "access to ..." and the duty of the state to "take reasonable legislative and other measures within its available resources to achieve the progressive realisation of each of these rights" is bound to elude enforceability. In fact there have already been several key judgments in South Africa which indicate that the courts will be reluctant to assume the role they believe rightly belongs to the executive of determining the distribution of resources. We believe that this trend needs to be challenged.

The Constitution, however, has not left the matter entirely to the discretion of the executive. In Section 184(3) it places a duty on the Human Rights Commission to require state organs to report to us on "measures that they have taken towards the realisation of the rights ... concerning housing, health care, food, water, social security, education and the environment ..." This obligation seems to suggest that the information we receive should be the basis of a report, although the Constitution is not explicit in this regard. The need for a report, though, is widely accepted because the intention of this provision is to render state departments and organs accountable. They are to account so that government can be seen to be taking these rights seriously. In tackling this task, the Commission joined in partnership with some research institutions that have provided invaluable expertise and assisted us to popularise social and economic rights.

In order to give effect to this constitutional provision, workshops were arranged for the staff of the Commission in order to elaborate the responsibility, with other role players including the relevant government departments in order to ensure informed assistance. We then drafted letters of inquiry or protocols which were distributed to the departments according to each of the rights stated in the Constitution. Although it has taken some time and that there is some unevenness in the responses, we are pleased with the cooperation we received from state departments all round. The analysis of the information has been assigned to one of the research centres. In addition we have commissioned a reputable research agency to undertake a survey on the popular perceptions on delivery of social and economic rights. We are planning to submit the report to parliament in July 1998.

Because of the importance we attach to social and economic rights for a country like South Africa, we have teamed up with SANGOCO (South African National NGO Coalition) to do national hearings on poverty. The hearings have been taking place since March 1998. The hearings have been important because they underline the significance of social and economic rights for our human rights culture, they provide a forum for ordinary people to speak with dignity about their experiences of struggling against poverty and to share their ideas with others. In a sense peoples' participation enables the development of a policy framework that is both relevant to the needs of the people and informative. The hearings on poverty have been consuming much time and resources. Clearly, it is not an exercise that can be done on an annual basis. Being the first year of reporting on our monitoring of social and economic rights, we have felt that a rounded approach was important.

Accountability

As a Commission we have taken the issue of accountability seriously. We do so because we believe that a national institution is a public agency funded through taxpayers money to give effect to the Constitution. Somehow, therefore, people must have a sense of understanding how it operates, how it must participate and shape its programmes, how it must be relevant and can be questioned about its effectiveness. One statutory mechanism of accountability is through the annual report. It needs to be stated that the Commission is neither accountable to the government nor answerable to it for the use to which its resources are spent. The Commission is required to submit a report on its activities and performance to the National Assembly at least once a year (Section 181(5) of the Constitution). The Speaker of the National Assembly then takes the responsibility for tabling the report in parliament. Members of parliament often ask questions about the work of the Commission and the Minister of Justice as the line function minister responsible for human rights gives the answers which we would have drafted for him.

Because we were not satisfied that there was no real debate on our report in the National Assembly, this year we asked the Portfolio Committee on Justice to hold public hearings on our report which they did on 17 March 1998. The hearings were open to the press and members of the public. They allowed parliamentarians to ask the Commission probing questions about our activities, our budget, our strategies for the development of a culture of human rights. By so doing we believe that we increased the level of understanding of the work of the Commission in parliament. Members of the Commission also found the exercise very valuable. As referred to above, another way in which we have sought to increase the understanding of the work of the Commission in parliament has been through our briefings of political parties.

Besides the efforts we have made through parliament, the Auditor General is also required to submit a report to the National Assembly on the extent to which the Commission manages the money entrusted to it according to treasury regulations. Although it is not necessary to do so, we usually publish this report with our annual report.

Challenges

Our Commission has been in operation for only a brief two years. Throughout we have recognized that the Commission needed to earn credibility and respect of all the people of South Africa. We have had to make sure that we undertake our activities with integrity especially in a climate like that of South Africa which is very highly charged politically. As a Commission we have struggled among ourselves about constructing a common vision and acting together on it. Partly because members of the Commission are drawn from across the political spectrum, it has been necessary to debate issues and approaches among ourselves exhaustively. There have been times where the point of difference has not been about our political allegiances but about strategies to be adopted. In that case different personalities come to the fore. We have struggled with that not always in a satisfactory manner. It has been important, nonetheless, for us to be drawn from a wide spectrum of South African society but that has its frustrations although the end result is always satisfying.

The second challenge we face is how we can increase appreciation of human rights, especially the avenues available through the Commission for bringing redress for human rights violations. As commissioners we have invested a lot of effort at public information campaigns. During our first year we did road shows up and down the country, we use radio and printed media to raise the profile of the Commission. We have had invaluable discussions with judges in various divisions and we value the cooperation we receive from our Constitutional Court judges. What has emerged from these consultations is the role that a national institution like ours can play in the administration of justice. This is particularly so in a situation like South Africa's where there are considerable delays in the processing of cases because of long court rolls, ineffective and inefficient management of the criminal justice system and incompetence in the investigation of crime. The Commission has a role to play in monitoring, training and making proposals about how the system can be improved. In addition many judges have considered that the Commission can develop its alternative resolution of disputes system provided for in Section 8 of the Act.

Our greatest and most unhappy challenge though has been to work with an unresponsive media. There is a level in which human rights in general and the Commission in particular, are not seen to be serving the interests of the media. Partly this has to do with the need to sensationalise news reporting. More fundamentally, the issue is that the media in South Africa, especially the printed media, operates from an ideological position at variance with what we seek to achieve. The media operates as a mouthpiece of the white opposition parties in parliament. That means that it reflects the policy positions of the opposition parties. This position issues from a great deal of scrutiny of public expenditure. In such a perspective, a Commission like ours is considered wasteful. There have been efforts to suggest that the mandate of the Commission is too wide, that we should concentrate only on human rights education; others suggest we should monitor the violation of civil and political rights on the part of state agencies. It was considered that a streamlined institution like that would be cost effective. These debates are very fundamental and go to the heart of what the role and contribution of a national institution can be in the development of our constitutional democracy. We have held regular meetings with the editors of our largest newspapers and with the SABC, the public broadcaster. Generally, we continue to debate these matters but to no avail. We have also improved our public relations. Many of the activities of the Commission are now widely reported in the media. We recognize that what we need most urgently is to publish our own newsletter as well as a journal. The costs of this, however, are beyond our means. We hope to start this year by publishing a regular newsletter.

We have also considered it important to position the Commission at the cutting edge of debate about human rights. We believe that we must be taking an advanced position on many issues on human rights. We are beginning a process of weekly reflection and analysis of stories that are reported in the media. This helps sharpen the approach of colleagues, commissioners and staff, on the latest issues in human rights. We also manage to share ideas and we agree on common action. The other programme we intend to initiate this year is a monthly seminar on critical human rights issues. We shall invite speakers and have a roundtable discussion on human rights issues like a critical analysis of the judgments of the Constitutional Court or any other reflection on human rights issues. There is interest in the proposal from judges in the Constitutional Court and in the high court, from human rights legal practitioners, from academics and NGOs. We believe that the Commission should provide a forum for some of the most advanced ideas on human rights to emerge. This will be another means whereby we give effect to our vision that the Commission should be the focal point of human rights discourse and practice in South Africa.

South Africa's Ombudsman

S.A.M. Baqwa*

Let me begin by stating that the Public Protector should be seen as a referee, not for, nor against, either side, whether it be the individual or the administration, and I would like to quote from a speech delivered by the honourable President Mandela to underline this statement.

At the International Workshop for Ombudsmen office investigators in Africa, organized by my Office and held in Pretoria on the 26th August 1996, the Honourable President made this statement which rang strange, but true, and I quote:

"I can imagine the role of being the Public Protector or an Ombudsman..., at some point or another, being a lonesome one. Naturally you are sometimes faced with opposition from the State Administration's side, because you have to pry into their work. Fortunately, I think it is not long before it is realised that the Ombudsman, or whatever the institution is called in each of your countries, is as much there for the private individual as it is for the administration."

He then goes on to explain this as follows:

"You may wonder why I, as Head of State, and being one of the persons against whom the might of this institution might be brought to bear, sound optimistic and ecstatic at the establishment of this office. It is because, as the Ombudsman of Alaska once put it: 'Ombudsman are men and women who act as neutral, non-partisan investigators of government decision or actions. In this role, Ombudsman act as a 'Public Watchdog', but can also protect Public Officials from unfair criticism by a co-worker or citizen. The mission of Ombudsman is to help make government more efficient, ethical responsive and fair.' In this context it becomes quite clear that this concept not only implies the protection of the citizen, but also embraces my protection as well as the protection of the State I represent."

Against this background then, I would like to say the following. Governments in all countries are perceived to be the guardians of the people and the interests of the people over whom they govern. It is a truism however, that the governments which are managed or operated by human beings are as fallible as the human beings who constitute them.

Who watches over and controls the actions of these governors? This question has exercised the minds of scholars, politicians and ordinary people from time immemorial. The institution of the Public Protector is an attempt to address

*The Public Protector.

K. Hossain et al. (eds), Human Rights Commissions and Ombudsman Offices, 639–663.

this question. In order to get an adequate answer to this question, the institution as such, and how it operates, will have to be examined.

The Ombudsman

The debate about the Ombudsman began in South Africa as early as 1945 and continued intermittently through to 1973. It was however only in 1979 when the Government of the day was forced to establish an institution akin to that of the Ombudsman by what became known as the Information Scandal. Officials of the Department of Information expended colossal sums of money in unauthorized projects both inside and outside South Africa, and failed to account properly for their expenditure. The impact was so huge that it ultimately resulted in the dramatic political demise of both the Minister responsible and the then Prime Minister.

Subsequently the Government established the Office of the Advocate-General which, though similar to that of the Ombudsman, had several limitations of power.

This Office was followed up by the establishment of the Office of the Ombudsman in 1991. This was the very first time that the Institution was established in the form in which it is generally understood internationally. This Office operated until 1995.

The Public Protector

The Office of the Public Protector is established by Chapter 9 of the Constitution of South Africa, Act 108 of 1996. This is South Africa's version of the Ombudsman. Thereby, South Africa contributes to the many different names of titles given to persons who hold such an office. Some of these titles are: Avocado de Populo (Roumania), the Parliamentary Commissioner for Administration (United Kingdom), the Public Complaints Commissioner (Nigeria) Defensor del Pueblo (Spain and Argentina) and the Investigator-General (Zambia). The different names or titles are not of much importance though. What is important is the power and ability of the particular official to obtain redress for aggrieved members of the public.

It is section 182 of the Constitution which established the office of the Public Protector as a Constitutional Institution whose role it is to protect citizens against administrative excesses and wrongdoing.

Given the Interim Constitution's underlying principles of accountability, openness, freedom and quality, the Office of the Public Protector was instituted to achieve the following objectives:

1. to ensure that public sector institutions do not, in their functions, abuse their powers;
2. to guarantee that public servants observe and uphold the constitutional principles and directives; and
3. to build and sustain, in the public sector, a sense and culture of service, responsibility, discipline and honesty.

The Public Protector is appointed by Parliament and the letter of appointment is written and signed by the President. The procedure is to be found the Constitution (Section 193). It is as follows.

A committee of the House of Assembly composed of one member of each party represented in parliament nominates a person after interviewing all applicants. If the name nominated is approved of by the National Assembly by resolution adopted by a majority of at least 60 percent of the members present and voting, the nominee gets appointed as Public Protector.

If the appointment were not to be made by Parliament, this would be viewed as a disadvantage because the independence of the Institution of the Ombudsman may be effected. If he/she is for example appointed by the president alone, he/she may become or be perceived to be beholden to the President. If the Institution of the Ombudsman does not report to Parliament this could also be a weakness that could taint his/her independence. For example, reporting to the executive could subordinate his/her authority and independence.

The jurisdiction of the Public Protector is in the main concentrated on the investigation of maladministration and making of recommendations regarding complaints of aggrieved persons against state institutions, administrative bodies, officials and employees, about unreasonable, unfair and discourteous administrative action. Through investigation, mediation, conciliation and even negotiation, the Public Protector is enabled to bring about a settlement between the complainant and the administration; the revocation of an officials decision; or even a change in policy.

The office of the Public Protector can be approached informally without involving any complicated procedures and processes. His/her services are available at no cost to the individual complainant. If an illiterate person should wish to present a complaint to the Public Protector's office, he will be assisted to do so. The sense of utter powerlessness and frustration which the individual experiences when his rights have been infringed and he/she is forced to face the might of administrative bureaucracy is eliminated.

The Public Protector can execute his functions both formally and informally. She/he has extensive powers to take formal evidence and issue subpoenas. He can investigate maladministration at any level of government. He also possesses extensive powers of search and seizure. The Public Protector may not investigate court decisions (Section 182(3) Constitution).

In respect of every investigation of a serious nature carried out by him or her, the Public Protector must submit half-yearly reports concerning his findings relating to maladministration to Parliament, and recommend administrative action or the steps to be taken. Such reports must also be published for general information.

Further, the hallmark of the Public Protector's office is his/her independence. This must not only be perceived, but must be seen to exist. The Public Protector must always be seen as an objective and impartial official, who does not take sides with one or the other. The concept of independence is important in order to lend credibility to the Public Protector's Office. His independence is entrenched, he appoints his own staff (at the moment about 30) and runs his own budget.

In 1974 the office of the Public Protector was defined by the International Bar Association as follows:

"An office provided for by the constitution or by action of the legislature or parliament and headed by an independent, high level public official who is responsible to the legislature or parliament, who receives complaints from aggrieved persons against government agencies, officials and employees or who acts on his own motion and who has the power to investigate, recommend corrective action, and issue reports."

This is an accurate description of the role of the Public Protector in South Africa.

The establishment of the office of the Public Protector arises out of the realisation that any Government in the modern day industrial state must be concerned with good order in the society it governs. The Government should constantly be asking itself whether there is any official impropriety or insensitivity in its administration.

If this question is answered in the affirmative, it must ask itself how such impropriety or insensitivity can be speedily resolved. Needless to say, the yardstick that the Government uses to test the property of administrative actions in South Africa is the Bill of (Human) Rights.

The traditional safeguards that have been used by the constitutional governments, as has been the case in South Africa, have been Internal Review of Administrative Actions, Judicial Review, and Fiscal Superintendency, in order to address the concerns mentioned above. Whilst, undoubtedly, these standard controls play an important role as a bulwark against administrative excesses, it is a fact that they in themselves do not effectively provide for a remedy against all, or many, forms of maladministration.

A State is not genuinely constitutional by virtue of the fact that it possesses a Constitution. It only achieves that quality or status when the Constitution acquires a practical significance, in other words, when the principles and rights enshrined in it can be translated effectively into practice.

The Constitution of South Africa, No 108 of 1996 has established a number of institutions as important additions to the armoury of mechanisms that are employed to create an image of fair and stable government as in Chapter 9 thereof. Institutions which support constitutional democracy – such as the Constitutional Court, the Human Rights Commission, The Commission for Gender Equality, The Auditor-General and the Public Protector – can function individually or in tandem with each other. Each of these institutions are regulated by the Constitution which must be read together with the national legislation applicable to each institution. When supplementing and/or complementing each other they form an effective catch-net for any slip in the exercise of the administrative power.

The Public Protector is however the one institution amongst these various watchdog institutions mentioned, with the most general mandate and as such the widest scope of control over executive power.

Because of this, to some extent it can operate as a clearing house, referring appropriate cases to the other so-called constitutional "watchdogs".

Since the present incumbent took office (October 1995), some 7000 complaints have been received. So the institution has proved to be quite popular.

Conclusion

Although there are appropriate cases where the Public Protector might be considered to be the panacea to all ills, when it comes to the protection of the individual and prevention of shortcomings in the public administration, his office is but one of the constitutional mechanisms for the control of the executive power. It must, therefore, be borne in mind that the effective functioning of the Office of the Public Protector can, and should in many instances, be enhanced by the complementary and supplementary working of one or more of the other Watchdogs. This has been proven in the past and is sure to happen again in future.

The importance of the Office of the Public Protector however, in working in tandem with these other constitutional institutions for the control of executive power, lies in the fact that he had the wider and more general mandate, so that the sphere of investigation becomes wider, and in view of the fact that this office is more ready accessible, it is possible for members of the public to approach this office, no matter how humble or sophisticated, literate or illiterate, formal or informal they may be.

The establishment of the office if a positive sign for in the words of Caiden, Macdermot & Sander (International Handbook – Evolution):

> "The existence of an independent ombudsman office denotes a clear indication by the rulers that they recognize obligations and duties to the ruled, that the ruled should be treated justly, promptly, and courteously, that they should be granted their due according to the law, and that public business should be conducted honestly and efficaciously."

LEGISLATION

Constitution of South Africa 1996

Chapter 9 State Institutions Supporting Constitutional Democracy

[Title 0 General Provision]

Section 181 Establishment and governing principles
(1) The following state institutions strengthen constitutional democracy in the Republic:
(a) The Public Protector.
(b) The Human Rights Commission.
(c) The Commission for the Promotion and Protection of the Rights of Cultural, Religious and Linguistic Communities.
(d) The Commission for Gender Equality.
(e) The Auditor-General.
(f) The Electoral Commission.
(2) These institutions are independent, and subject only to the Constitution and the law, and they must be impartial and must exercise their powers and perform their functions without fear, favour or prejudice.
(3) Other organs of state, through legislative and other measures, must assist and protect these institutions to ensure the independence, impartiality, dignity and effectiveness of these institutions.
(4) No person or organ of state may interfere with the functioning of these institutions.
(5) These institutions are accountable to the National Assembly, and must report on their activities and the performance of their functions to the Assembly at least once a year.

[Title 1] Public Protector

Section 182 Functions of Public Protector
(1) The Public Protector has the power, as regulated by national legislation:
(a) to investigate any conduct in state affairs, or in the public administration in any sphere of government, that is alleged or suspected to be improper or to result in any impropriety or prejudice;

(b) to report on that conduct; and
(c) to take appropriate remedial action.

(2) The Public Protector has the additional powers and functions prescribed by national legislation.
(3) The Public Protector may not investigate court decisions.
(4) The Public Protector must be accessible to all persons and communities.
(5) Any report issued by the Public Protector must be open to the public unless exceptional circumstances, to be determined in terms of national legislation, require that a report be kept confidential.

Section 183 Tenure
The Public Protector is appointed for a non-renewable period of seven years.

[Title 2] Human Rights Commission
Section 184 Functions of Human Rights Commission
(1) The Human Rights Commission must:
(a) promote respect for human rights and a culture of human rights;
(b) promote the protection, development and attainment of human rights; and
(c) monitor and assess the observance of human rights in the Republic.
(2) The Human Rights Commission has the powers, as regulated by national legislation, necessary to perform its functions, including the power:
(a) to investigate and to report on the observance of human rights;
(b) to take steps to secure appropriate redress where human rights have been violated;
(c) to carry out research; and
(d) to educate.
(3) Each year, the Human Rights Commission must require relevant organs of state to provide the Commission with information on the measures that they have taken towards the realisation of the rights in the Bill of Rights concerning housing, health care, food, water, social security, education and the environment.
(4) The Human Rights Commission has the additional powers and functions prescribed by national legislation.

[Title 3] Commission for the Promotion and Protection of the Rights of Cultural, Religious and Linguistic Communities

Section 185 Functions of Commission
(1) The primary objects of the Commission for the Promotion and Protection of the Rights of Cultural, Religious and Linguistic Communities are:
(a) to promote respect for the rights of cultural, religious and linguistic communities;
(b) to promote and develop peace, friendship, humanity, tolerance and national unity among cultural, religious and linguistic communities, on the basis of equality, non-discrimination and free association; and
(c) to recommend the establishment or recognition, in accordance with national legislation, of a cultural or other council or councils for a community or communities in South Africa.
(2) The Commission has the power, as regulated by national legislation, necessary to achieve its primary objects, including the power to monitor, investigate, research, educate, lobby, advise and report on issues concerning the rights of cultural, religious and linguistic communities.
(3) The Commission may report any matter which falls within its powers and functions to the Human Rights Commission for investigation.
(4) The Commission has the additional powers and functions prescribed by national legislation.

Section 186 Composition of Commission
(1) The number of members of the Commission for the Promotion and Protection of the

Rights of Cultural, Religious and Linguistic Communities and their appointment and terms of office must be prescribed by national legislation.
(2) The composition of the Commission must:
(a) be broadly representative of the main cultural, religious and linguistic communities in South Africa; and
(b) broadly reflect the gender composition of South Africa.

[Title 4] Commission for Gender Equality

Section 187 Functions of Commission for Gender Equality
(1) The Commission for Gender Equality must promote respect for gender equality and the protection, development and attainment of gender equality.
(2) The Commission for Gender Equality has the power, as regulated by national legislation, necessary to perform its functions, including the power to monitor, investigate, research, educate, lobby, advise and report on issues concerning gender equality.
(3) The Commission for Gender Equality has the additional powers and functions prescribed by national legislation.

[Title 5] Auditor-General

Section 188 Functions of Auditor-General
(1) The Auditor-General must audit and report on the accounts, financial statements and financial management of:
(a) all national and provincial state departments and administrations;
(b) all municipalities; and
(c) any other institution or accounting entity required by national or provincial legislation to be audited by the Auditor-General.
(2) In addition to the duties prescribed in subsection (1), and subject to any legislation, the Auditor-General may audit and report on the accounts, financial statements and financial management of:
(a) any institution funded from the National Revenue Fund or a Provincial Revenue Fund or by a municipality; or
(b) any institution that is authorized in terms of any law to receive money for a public purpose. (3) The Auditor-General must submit audit reports to any legislature that has a direct interest in the audit, and to any other authority prescribed by national legislation. All reports must be made public.
(4) The Auditor-General has the additional powers and functions prescribed by national legislation.

Section 189 Tenure
The Auditor-General must be appointed for a fixed, non-renewable term of between five and ten years.

[Title 6] Electoral Commission

Section 190 Functions of Electoral Commission
(1) The Electoral Commission must:
(a) manage elections of national, provincial and municipal legislative bodies in accordance with national legislation;
(b) ensure that those elections are free and fair; and
(c) declare the results of those elections within a period that must be prescribed by national legislation and that is as short as reasonably possible.
(2) The Electoral Commission has the additional powers and functions prescribed by national legislation.

Section 191 Composition of Electoral Commission
The Electoral Commission must be composed of at least three persons. The number of members and their terms of office must be prescribed by national legislation.

[Title 7] Independent Authority to Regulate Broadcasting

Section 192 Broadcasting Authority
National legislation must establish an independent authority to regulate broadcasting in the public interest, and to ensure fairness and a diversity of views broadly representing South African society.

[Title 8] General Provisions

Section 193 Appointments
(1) The Public Protector and members of any Commission established by this Chapter must be women or men who:
(a) are South African citizens;
(b) are fit and proper persons to hold the particular office; and
(c) comply with any other requirements prescribed by national legislation.
(2) The need for a Commission established by this Chapter to reflect broadly the race and gender composition of South Africa must be considered when members are appointed.
(3) The Auditor-General must be a woman or a man who is a South African citizen and a fit and proper person to hold that office. Specialised knowledge of, or experience in, auditing, state finances and public administration must be given due regard in appointing the Auditor-General.
(4) The President, on the recommendation of the National Assembly, must appoint the Public Protector, the Auditor-General and members of:
(a) the Human Rights Commission;
(b) the Commission for Gender Equality; and
(c) the Electoral Commission.
(5) The National Assembly must recommend persons:
(a) nominated by a committee of the Assembly proportionally composed of members of all parties represented in the Assembly; and
(b) approved by the Assembly by a resolution adopted with a supporting vote:
  (i) of at least 60 per cent of the members of the Assembly, if the recommendation concerns the appointment of the Public Protector or the Auditor-General; or
  (ii) of a majority of the members of the Assembly, if the recommendation concerns the appointment of a member of a Commission.
(6) The involvement of civil society in the recommendation process may be provided for as envisaged in section 59(1)(a).

Section 194 Removal from office
(1) The Public Protector, the Auditor-General or a member of a Commission established by this Chapter may be removed from office only on:
(a) the ground of misconduct, incapacity or incompetence;
(b) a finding to that effect by a committee of the National Assembly; and
(c) the adoption by the Assembly of a resolution calling for that person's removal from office.
(2) A resolution of the National Assembly concerning the removal from office of:
(a) the Public Protector or the Auditor-General must be adopted with a supporting vote of at least two thirds of the members of the Assembly; or
(b) a member of a commission must be adopted with a supporting vote of a majority of the members of the Assembly.
(2) The President:
(a) may suspend a person from office at any time after the start of the proceedings of a committee of the National Assembly for the removal of that person; and
(b) must remove a person from office upon adoption by the Assembly of the resolution calling for that person's removal.

Public Protector Act, 1994

No. 23 of 1994

OFFICE OF THE PRESIDENT
No. 2012
25 November 1994

It is hereby notified that the President has assented to the following Act, which is hereby published for general information:

ACT

To provide for matters incidental to the office of the Public Protector as contemplated in the Constitution of the Republic of South Africa, 1993; and to provide for matters connected therewith. (English text signed by the President.) (Assented to 16 November 1994.)

PREAMBLE

WHEREAS sections 110 to 114 of the Constitution of the Republic of South Africa, 1993 (Act No. 200 of 1993), provide for the establishment of the office of Public Protector in order to investigate matters and to protect the public against matters such as maladministration in connection with the affairs of government, improper conduct by a person performing a public function, improper acts with respect to public money, improper or unlawful enrichment of a person performing a public function and an act or omission by a person performing a public function resulting in improper prejudice to another person;

AND WHEREAS the Constitution envisages further legislation to provide for certain ancillary matters pertaining to the office of Public Protector, including the remuneration and conditions of employment, immunities and privileges, powers and functions and staff of the Public Protector;

BE IT THEREFORE ENACTED by the Parliament of the Republic of South Africa, as follows:

Definitions

1. In this Act, unless the context otherwise indicates:

(i) "committee" means a committee established under section 2(1);
(ii) "Deputy Public Protector" means any person appointed in terms of section 3(2);
(iii) "investigation" means an investigation referred to in section 7;
(iv) "joint committee" means a committee referred to in section 110(2)(a) of the Constitution;
(v) "member of the office of the Public Protector" includes the Public Protector, a Deputy Public Protector, a member of the staff of the Public Protector and any person contemplated in sections 3(12) and 7(3)(b);
(vi) "new Constitution" means the new Constitution contemplated in Chapter 5 of the Constitution;
(vii) "Provincial Public Protector" means any person appointed as such in terms of a law contemplated in section 114(1) of the Constitution;
(viii) "Public Protector" means any person appointed as such in terms of section 110(2) of the Constitution;
(ix) "Public Service Commission" means the Commission established by section 209(1) of the Constitution.

Appointment of committee, remuneration, vacancies in office and other terms and conditions of employment of Public Protector

2. (1) Parliament shall, in accordance with the rules and orders of Parliament, appoint a committee for the purpose of considering matters referred to it in terms of this Act.

(2) The remuneration and other terms and conditions of employment of the Public Protector shall, subject to section 110(6) of the Constitution, from time to time be determined by Parliament upon the advice of the committee: Provided that such remuneration shall not be less than that of a judge of the Supreme Court of South Africa.

(3) Parliament or, if Parliament is not in session, the joint committee may allow a Public Protector to vacate his or her office:

(a) on account of continued ill-health; or

(b) at his or her request: Provided that such request shall be addressed to Parliament or the joint committee, as the case may be, at least three calender months prior to the date on which he or she wishes to vacate such office, unless Parliament or the joint committee, as the case may be, allows a shorter period in a specific case.

(4) If the joint committee allows a Public Protector to vacate his or her office in terms of subsection (3), the chairperson of the joint committee shall communicate the vacation of office by message to Parliament.

(5) The Public Protector may, at any time, approach the committee with regard to any matter in respect of which Parliament has functions pertaining to the office of the Public Protector.

Deputy Public Protector and staff of Public Protector

3. (1) The Public Protector shall, subject to his or her directions and control, in the performance of his or her functions under this Act and the Constitution, be assisted by:

(a) one or more Deputy Public Protectors;

(b) a suitably qualified and experienced person as Chief Administrative Officer, appointed by the Public Protector or seconded in terms of subsection (12), for the purpose of assisting the Public Protector in the performance of all financial, administrative and clerical functions pertaining to the office of the Public Protector; and

(c) such staff, seconded in terms of subsection (12) or appointed by the Public Protector, as may be necessary to enable the Public Protector to perform his or her functions.

(2) (a)
The President shall, subject to the provisions of paragraph (b), appoint one or more persons, qualified to be appointed as a Public Protector in terms of the Constitution, as Deputy Public Protectors.

(b) An appointment in terms of paragraph (a) shall only be made from persons:

(i) nominated by the joint committee after consultation with the Public Protector; and

(ii) approved by the National Assembly and the Senate by a resolution adopted by at least 75 per cent of the members present and voting at a joint meeting.

(c) If any nomination is not approved as contemplated in paragraph (b)(ii), the joint committee shall nominate another person in accordance with paragraph (b) (i).

(d) If the Public Protector has not yet been appointed or if the office of Public Protector is vacant or if, on account of his or her incapacity, the Public Protector cannot be consulted at the time when it is necessary to nominate a person in terms of paragraph (b)(i), the joint committee may nominate persons without undertaking the consultation contemplated in the said paragraph (b)(i). (e) Unless the new Constitution provides otherwise, a Deputy Public Protector shall hold office for a period of seven years. (f) The provisions of section 2(3) and (4) shall apply mutatis mutandis in respect of a Deputy Public Protector.

(3) A Deputy Public Protector shall have such powers as the Public Protector may delegate to him or her.

(4) Whenever the Public Protector is, for any reason, unable to perform the functions of

his or her office, or while the appointment of a person to the office of Public Protector is pending, the most senior Deputy Public Protector available shall perform such functions.
(5) If a vacancy occurs in the office of Deputy Public Protector the President may, subject to the provisions of this section, appoint another person to that office.
(6) The President may, on the grounds of misbehaviour, incapacity or incompetence, determined by the joint committee after consultation with the Public Protector, and upon receipt of an address from both the National Assembly and the Senate requesting the removal of a Deputy Public Protector, remove such Deputy Public Protector from office.
(7) The President may, in consultation with the Public Protector, suspend a Deputy Public Protector pending a decision in terms of subsection (6).
(8) The remuneration and other terms and conditions of employment of a Deputy Public Protector shall from time to time be determined by Parliament upon the advice of the committee.
(9) The persons appointed by the Public Protector in terms of subsection (1)(b) or (c) shall receive such remuneration, allowances and other employment benefits and shall be appointed on such terms and conditions and for such periods, as the Public Protector may determine.
(10) In exercising his or her powers in terms of subsections (1) and (9), the Public Protector shall consult with the Minister of Finance and the Public Service Commission.
(11) (a)
A document setting out the remuneration, allowances and other conditions of employment determined by the Public Protector in terms of subsection (9), shall be Tabled in Parliament within 14 days after such determination.
(b) If Parliament disapproves of any determination such determination shall cease to be of force to the extent to which it is so disapproved.
(c) If a determination ceases to be of force as contemplated in paragraph (b):
(i) anything done in terms of such determination up to the date on which such determination ceases to be of force shall be deemed to have been done validly; and
(ii) any right, privilege, obligation or liability acquired, accrued or incurred up to the said date under and by virtue of such determination, shall lapse upon the said date.
(12) The Public Protector may, in the performance of the functions contemplated in subsection (1)(b), at his or her request after consultation with the Public Service Commission, be assisted by officers in the Public Service seconded to the service of the Public Protector in terms of any law regulating such secondment.
(13) A member of the office of the Public Protector shall:
(a) serve impartially and independently and perform his or her functions in good faith and without fear, favour, bias or prejudice;
(b) serve in a full-time capacity to the exclusion of any other duty or obligation arising out of any other employment or occupation or the holding of any other office: Provided that the committee may exempt a Deputy Public Protector and a person contemplated in section 7(3)(b) shall be exempted from the provisions of this paragraph.
(14) No person, other than a person contemplated in section 7(3), shall conduct an investigation contemplated in section 7 or render assistance with regard thereto in respect of a matter in which he or she has any pecuniary interest or any other interest which might preclude him or her from performing his or her functions in a fair, unbiased and proper manner.
(15) If any person fails to disclose an interest contemplated in subsection (14) and conducts or renders assistance with regard to an investigation contemplated in section 7, while having an interest in the matter being investigated, the Public Protector may take such steps as he or she deems necessary to ensure a fair, unbiased and proper investigation.

Finances and accountability

4. (1) The Chief Administrative Officer referred to in section 3(1)(b):

(a) shall, subject to the Exchequer Act, 1975 (Act No. 66 of 1975):

 (i) be charged with the responsibility of accounting for money received or paid out for or on account of the office of the Public Protector;

 (ii) cause the necessary accounting and other related records to be kept; and

(b) may exercise such powers and shall perform such duties as the Public Protector may from time to time confer upon or assign to him or her, and shall in respect thereof be accountable to the Public Protector.

(2) The records referred to in subsection (1)(a)(ii) shall be audited by the Auditor-General. Liability of Public Protector

5. (1) The office of the Public Protector shall be a juristic person.

(2) The State Liability Act, 1957 (Act No. 20 of 1957), shall apply mutatis mutandis in respect of the office of the Public Protector, and in such application a reference in that Act to "the Minister of the department concerned" shall be construed as a reference to the Public Protector in his or her official capacity.

(3) Neither a member of the office of the Public Protector nor the office of the Public Protector shall be liable in respect of anything reflected in any report, finding, point of view or recommendation made or expressed in good faith and submitted to Parliament or made known in terms of this Act or the Constitution.

Reporting matters to and additional powers of Public Protector

6. (1) Any matter in respect of which the Public Protector has jurisdiction may be reported to the Public Protector by any person:

(a) by means of a written or oral declaration under oath or after having made an affirmation, specifying:

 (i) the nature of the matter in question;

 (ii) the grounds on which he or she feels that an investigation is necessary;

 (iii) all other relevant information known to him or her; or

(b) by such other means as the Public Protector may allow with a view to making his or her office accessible to all persons.

(2) A member of the office of the Public Protector shall render the necessary assistance, free of charge, to enable any person to comply with subsection (1).

(3) The Public Protector may refuse to investigate a matter reported to him or her, if the person ostensibly prejudiced in the matter is:

(a) an officer or employee in the service of the State or is a person to whom the provisions of the Public Service Act, 1994 (Proclamation No. 103 of 1994), are applicable and has, in connection with such matter, not taken all reasonable steps to exhaust the remedies conferred upon him or her in terms of the said Public Service Act, 1994; or

(b) prejudiced by an act or omission referred to in subsection (4)(d) or section 112(1)(a)(v) of the Constitution and has not taken all reasonable steps to exhaust his or her legal remedies in connection with such matter.

(4) In addition to the powers and functions assigned to the Public Protector by section 112 of the Constitution, he or she shall be competent to investigate, on his or her own initiative or on receipt of a complaint, any alleged:

(a) maladministration in connection with the affairs of any institution in which the State is the majority or controlling shareholder or of any public entity as defined in section 1 of the Reporting by Public Entities Act, 1992 (Act No. 93 of 1992);

(b) abuse or unjustifiable exercise of power or unfair, capricious, discourteous or other improper conduct or undue delay by a person performing a function connected with his or her employment by an institution or entity contemplated in paragraph (a);

(c) improper or unlawful enrichment or receipt of any improper advantage, or promise of such enrichment or advantage, by a person as a result of an act or omission in connection with the affairs of an institution or entity contemplated in paragraph (a); or

(d) act or omission by a person in the employ of an institution or entity contemplated in paragraph (a), which results in unlawful or improper prejudice to any other person.

(5) The Public Protector shall be competent to investigate, on his or her own initiative or on receipt of a complaint, any alleged attempt to do anything which he or she may investigate under section 112 of the Constitution or subsection (4).

Investigation by Public Protector

7. (1) The procedure to be followed in conducting an investigation shall be determined by the Public Protector with due regard to the circumstances of each case, and the Public Protector may direct that any category of persons or all persons whose presence is not desirable, shall not be present at the proceedings during the investigation or any part thereof.

(2) Notwithstanding anything to the contrary contained in any law no person shall disclose to any other person the contents of any document in the possession of a member of the office of the Public Protector or the record of any evidence given before the Public Protector, a Deputy Public Protector or a person contemplated in subsection (3)(b) during an investigation, unless the Public Protector determines otherwise.

(3) (a) The Public Protector may, at any time prior to or during an investigation, request any person:

- (i) at any level of government, subject to any law governing the terms and conditions of employment of such person;
- (ii) performing a public function, subject to any law governing the terms and conditions of the appointment of such person; or
- (iii) otherwise subject to the jurisdiction of the Public Protector, to assist him or her, under his or her supervision and control, in the performance of his or her functions with regard to a particular investigation or investigations in general.

(b) The Public Protector may designate any person to conduct an investigation or any part thereof on his or her behalf and to report to him or her and for that purpose such a person shall have such powers as the Public Protector may assign to him or her, and the provisions of section 9 and the instructions issued by the Treasury under section 39 of the Exchequer Act, 1975 (Act No. 66 of 1975), in respect of Commissions of Inquiry, shall apply mutatis mutandis in respect of that person.

(4) (a)

For the purposes of conducting an investigation the Public Protector may direct any person to submit an affidavit or affirmed declaration or to appear before him or her to give evidence or to produce any document in his or her possession or under his or her control which has a bearing on the matter being investigated, and may examine such person.

(b) The Public Protector or any person duly authorized thereto by him or her may request an explanation from any person whom he or she reasonably suspects of having information which has a bearing on a matter being or to be investigated.

(5) A direction referred to in subsection (4)(a) shall be by way of a subpoena containing particulars of the matter in connection with which the person subpoenaed is required to appear before the Public Protector and shall be signed by the Public Protector and served on the person subpoenaed either by a registered letter sent through the post or by delivery by a person authorized thereto by the Public Protector.

(6) The Public Protector may require any person appearing as a witness before him or her under subsection (4) to give evidence on oath or after having made an affirmation.

(7) The Public Protector may administer an oath to or accept an affirmation from any such person.

(8) Any person appearing before the Public Protector by virtue of the provisions of subsection (4) may be assisted at such examination by an advocate or an attorney and shall be entitled to peruse such of the documents or records referred to in subsection (2) as are reasonably necessary to refresh his or her memory.

(9) If it appears to the Public Protector during the course of an investigation that any person is being implicated in the matter being investigated, the Public Protector shall afford such person an opportunity to be heard in connection therewith by way of the giving of evidence, and such person or his or her legal representative shall be entitled, through the Public Protector, to question other witnesses, determined by the Public Protector, who have appeared before the Public Protector in terms of this section.
(10) The provisions of this section shall be applicable to any person referred to in subsection (9).

Publication of findings
8. (1) The Public Protector may, subject to the provisions of subsection (3), in the manner he or she deems fit, make known to any person any finding, point of view or recommendation in respect of a matter investigated by him or her.
(2) The Public Protector shall submit to Parliament half-yearly reports on the findings in respect of investigations of a serious nature, which were conducted during the half-year concerned: Provided that the Public Protector shall, at any time, submit a report to Parliament on the findings of a particular investigation if:
(a) he or she deems it necessary;
(b) he or she deems it in the public interest;
(c) it requires the urgent attention of, or an intervention by Parliament;
(d) he or she is requested to do so by the Speaker of the National Assembly; or
(e) he or she is requested to do so by the President of the Senate.
(3) The findings of an investigation by the Public Protector shall, when he or she deems it fit but as soon as possible, be made available to the complainant and to any person implicated thereby.

Contempt of Public Protector
9. (1) No person shall:
(a) insult the Public Protector or a Deputy Public Protector;
(b) in connection with an investigation do anything which, if the said investigation had been proceedings in a court of law, would have constituted contempt of court.
(2) Nothing contained in this Act shall prohibit the discussion in Parliament of a matter being investigated or which has been investigated in terms of this Act by the Public Protector.

Compensation for expenses
10. The Public Protector may, with the specific or general approval of the Minister of Finance or any person authorized by the said Minister to so approve, order that the expenses or a portion of the expenses incurred by any person in the course of or in connection with an investigation by the Public Protector, be paid from State funds to that person.

Offences and penalties
11. (1) Any person who contravenes the provisions of sections 3(14), 7(2) and 9 of this Act, or section 111(3) of the Constitution, shall be guilty of an offence.
(2) Any person who fails to disclose an interest contemplated in section 3(14), shall be guilty of an offence.
(3) Any person who, without just cause, refuses or fails to comply with a direction under section 112(3)(a) of the Constitution or section 7(4)(a) of this Act or refuses to answer any question put to him or her under those paragraphs or gives to such question an answer which to his or her knowledge is false, or refuses to take the oath or to make an affirmation at the request of the Public Protector in terms of section 7(6), shall be guilty of an offence.
(4) Any person convicted of an offence in terms of this Act shall be liable to a fine not exceeding R40 000 or to imprisonment for a period not exceeding 12 months or to both such fine and such imprisonment.

Guidelines for provincial public protectors
12. (1) The Public Protector shall as soon as possible after a provincial public protector has been appointed under a law contemplated in section 114(1) of the Constitution, and after consultation with the provincial public protectors, publish in the Gazette a notice setting out general guidelines in accordance with which a provincial public protector shall exercise and perform his or her powers and functions as contemplated in section 114(4) of the Constitution:
Provided that this subsection shall not be construed as prohibiting a provincial public protector from departing from such guidelines in a particular case in consultation with the Public Protector.
(2) Unless provided otherwise in a law of a provincial legislature contemplated in section 114(1) of the Constitution, the provisions of sections 5 up to and including section 11 shall mutatis mutandis apply to a provincial public protector in respect of an investigation into a matter by him or her: Provided that a reference to "Public Protector" shall be construed as a reference to a provincial public protector, a reference to "Parliament" shall be construed as a reference to a provincial legislature and a reference to "Minister of Finance" shall be construed as a reference to the member of the Executive Council responsible for finance.

Application of Act
13. The provisions of this Act shall not affect any investigation under, or the performance or exercise of any duty or power imposed or conferred by or under, any law.

Repeal of laws
14. The Ombudsman Act, 1979 (Act No. 118 of 1979), the Advocate-General Amendment Act, 1983 (Act No. 55 of 1983), and the Advocate-General Amendment Act, 1991 (Act No. 104 of 1991), are hereby repealed.

Short title
15. This Act shall be called the Public Protector Act, 1994.

Human Rights Commission Act 1994

No. 54 of 1994

Office of the President
No. 2095 7 December 1994

It is hereby notified that the President has assented to the following Act, which is hereby published for general information:

ACT

To regulate matters incidental to the establishment of the Human Rights Commission by the Constitution of the Republic of South Africa, 1993; and to provide for matters connected therewith.
(Afrikaans text signed by the President.) (Assented to 23 November 1994.)

PREAMBLE

WHEREAS sections 115 up to and including 118 of the Constitution of the Republic of South Africa, 1993 (Act No. 200 of 1993), provide for the establishment of a Human Rights Commission; the appointment of the members of the Commission; the conferring of certain powers on and assignment of certain duties and functions to the Commission; the appointment of a chief executive officer of the Commission; and the tabling by the President in the National Assembly and the Senate of reports by the Commission;

AND WHEREAS the Constitution provides that the Human Rights Commission shall, inter alia, be competent and obliged to promote the observance of, respect for and the protection of fundamental rights; to develop an awareness of fundamental rights among all people of the Republic; to make recommendations to organs of state at all levels of government where it considers such action advisable for the adoption of progressive measures for the promotion of fundamental rights within the framework of the law and the Constitution; to undertake such studies for report on or relating to fundamental rights as it considers advisable in the performance of its functions; to request any organ of state to supply it with information on any legislative or executive measures adopted by it relating to fundamental rights; and to investigate any alleged violation of fundamental rights and to assist any person adversely affected thereby to secure redress;

AND WHEREAS the Constitution envisages further powers, duties and functions to be conferred on or assigned to the Human Rights Commission by law, and that staff of the Commission be appointed on such terms and conditions of service as may be determined by or under an Act of Parliament;

BE IT THEREFORE ENACTED by the Parliament of the Republic of South Africa, as follows:

Definitions
1. In this Act unless the context otherwise indicates:
(i) "Chairperson" means the chairperson of the Commission referred to in section 115(1) and (5) of the Constitution;
(ii) "Commission" means the Human Rights Commission established by section 115(1) of the Constitution;
(iii) "committee" means a committee established under section 5;
(iv) "fundamental rights" includes the fundamental rights contained in Chapter 3 of the Constitution; (i)
(v) "investigation" means an investigation under section 9;
(vi) "organ of state" includes any statutory body or functionary;
(vii) "premises" includes land, any building or structure, or any vehicle, conveyance, ship, boat, vessel, aircraft or container; and
(viii) "private dwelling" means any part of any building or structure which is occupied as a residence or any part of any building or structure or outdoor living area which is accessory to, and used wholly or principally for, the purposes of residence.

Seat of Commission
2. (1) The seat of the Commission shall be determined by the President.
(2) The Commission may establish such offices as it may consider necessary to enable it to exercise its powers and to perform its duties and functions conferred on or assigned to it by the Constitution, this Act or any other law.

Term of office of members of Commission
3. (1) The members of the Commission referred to in section 115(1) of the Constitution may be appointed as full-time or part-time members and shall hold office for such fixed term as the President may determine at the time of such appointment, but not exceeding seven years: Provided that not less than five members are appointed on a full-time basis: Provided further that the President shall remove any member from office if:
(a) such removal is requested by a joint committee composed as contemplated in section 115(3)(a) of the Constitution; and
(b) such request is approved by the National Assembly and the Senate by a resolution adopted by a majority of at least 75 per cent of the members present and voting at a joint meeting.
(2) The President may, in consultation with the Commission, appoint a part-time member as a full-time member for the unexpired portion of the part-time member's term of office.

(3) Any person whose term of office as a member of the Commission has expired, may be reappointed for one additional term.
(4) A member of the Commission may resign from office by submitting at least three months' written notice thereof to Parliament, unless Parliament by resolution allows a shorter period in a specific case.

Independence and impartiality
4. (1) A member of the Commission or a member of the staff of the Commission shall serve impartially and independently and exercise or perform his or her powers, duties and functions in good faith and without fear, favour, bias or prejudice and subject only to the Constitution and the law.
(2) No organ of state and no member or employee of an organ of state nor any other person shall interfere with, hinder or obstruct the Commission, any member thereof or a person appointed under section 5(1) or 16(1) or (6) in the exercise or performance of its, his or her powers, duties and functions.
(3) All organs of state shall afford the Commission such assistance as may be reasonably required for the protection of the independence, impartiality and dignity of the Commission.
(4) No person shall conduct an investigation or render assistance with regard thereto in respect of a matter in which he or she has any pecuniary or any other interest which might preclude him or her from exercising or performing his or her powers, duties and functions in a fair, unbiased and proper manner.
(5) If any person fails to disclose an interest contemplated in subsection (4) and conducts or renders assistance with regard to an investigation, while having an interest so contemplated in the matter being investigated, the Commission may take such steps as it deems necessary to ensure a fair, unbiased and proper investigation.

Committees of Commission
5. (1) The Commission may establish one or more committees consisting of one or more members of the Commission designated by the Commission and one or more other persons, if any, whom the Commission may appoint for that purpose and for the period determined by it.
(2) The Commission may extend the period of an appointment made by it under subsection (1) or withdraw such appointment during the period referred to in that subsection.
(3) The Commission shall designate a chairperson for every committee and, if it deems it necessary, a vice-chairperson.
(4) A committee shall, subject to the directions of the Commission, exercise such powers and perform such duties and functions of the Commission as the Commission may confer on or assign to it and follow such procedure during such exercising of powers and performance of duties and functions as the Commission may direct.
(5) On completion of the duties and functions assigned to it in terms of subsection (4), a committee shall submit a report thereon to the Commission.
(6) The Commission may at any time dissolve any committee.

Commission may approach President or Parliament
6. The Commission may, at any time, approach either the President or Parliament with regard to any matter relating to the exercising of its powers or the performance of its duties and functions.

Powers, duties and functions of Commission
7. (1) In addition to any other powers, duties and functions conferred on or assigned to it by section 116 of the Constitution, this Act or any other law, the Commission:
(a) shall develop and conduct information programmes to foster public understanding of this Act, Chapter 3 of the Constitution and the role and activities of the Commission;
(b) shall maintain close liaison with institutions, bodies or authorities similar to the

Commission in order to foster common policies and practices and to promote cooperation in relation to the handling of complaints in cases of overlapping jurisdiction;
(c) may consider such recommendations, suggestions and requests concerning fundamental rights as it may receive from any source;
(d) shall carry out or cause to be carried out such studies concerning fundamental rights as may be referred to it by the President and the Commission shall include in a report referred to in section 118 of the Constitution a report setting out the results of each study together with such recommendations in relation thereto as it considers appropriate;
(e) may bring proceedings in a competent court or tribunal in its own name, or on behalf of a person or a group or class of persons.

(2) All organs of state shall afford the Commission such assistance as may be reasonably required for the effective exercising of its powers and performance of its duties and functions.

Mediation, conciliation or negotiation by Commission

8. The Commission may, by mediation, conciliation or negotiation endeavour:
(a) to resolve any dispute; or
(b) to rectify any act or omission, emanating from or constituting a violation of or threat to any fundamental right.

Investigations by Commission

9. (1) Pursuant to the provisions of section 116(3) of the Constitution the Commission may, in order to enable it to exercise its powers and perform its duties and functions:
(a) conduct or cause to be conducted any investigation that is necessary for that purpose;
(b) through a member of the Commission, or any member of its staff designated in writing by a member of the Commission, require from any person such particulars and information as may be reasonably necessary in connection with any investigation;
(c) require any person by notice in writing under the hand of a member of the Commission, addressed and delivered by a member of its staff or a sheriff, in relation to an investigation, to appear before it at a time and place specified in such notice and to produce to it all articles or documents in the possession or custody or under the control of any such person and which may be necessary in connection with that investigation: Provided that such notice shall contain the reasons why such person's presence is needed and why any such article or document should be produced;
(d) through a member of the Commission, administer an oath to or take an affirmation from any person referred to in paragraph (c), or any person present at the place referred to in paragraph (c), irrespective of whether or, not such person has been required under the said paragraph (c) to appear before it, and question him or her under oath or affirmation in connection with any matter which may be necessary in connection with that investigation.

(2) (a)
Any person questioned under subsection (1) shall, subject to the provisions of paragraph (b) and subsections (3) and (4):
(i) be competent and compelled to answer all questions put to him or her regarding any fact or matter connected with the investigation of the Commission notwithstanding that the answer may incriminate him or her;
(ii) be compelled to produce to the Commission any article or document in his or her possession or custody or under his or her control which may be necessary in connection with that investigation.

(b) A person referred to in paragraph (a) shall only be competent and compelled to answer a question or be compelled to produce any article or document contemplated in that paragraph if:
(i) the Commission, after consultation with the attorney-general who has jurisdiction, issues an order to that effect; and

(ii) the Commission is satisfied that to require such information from such person is reasonable, necessary and justifiable in an open and democratic society based on freedom and equality; and

(iii) in the Commission's judgement, such person has refused or is likely to refuse to answer a question or to produce any article or document on the basis of his or her privilege against self-incrimination.

(3) (a)

Any incriminating answer or information obtained or incriminating evidence directly or indirectly derived from a questioning in terms of subsection (1) shall not be admissible as evidence against the person concerned in criminal proceedings in a court of law or before any body or institution established by or under any law: Provided that incriminating evidence arising from such questioning shall be admissible in criminal proceedings where the person stands trial on a charge of perjury or a charge contemplated in section 18(b) of this Act or in section 319(3) of the Criminal Procedure Act, 1955 (Act No. 56 of 1955).

(b) Subject to the provisions of subsection (2)(a)(i), the law regarding privilege as applicable to a witness summoned to give evidence in a criminal case in a court of law shall apply in relation to the questioning of a person in terms of subsection (1).

(4) Any person appearing before the Commission by virtue of the provisions of subsection (1)(c) and (d) may be assisted at such examination by an advocate or an attorney, or both, and shall be entitled to peruse such of the documents referred to in subsection (1)(c) or minutes as are reasonably necessary to refresh his or her memory.

(5) If it appears to the Commission during the course of an investigation that any person is being implicated in the matter being investigated, the Commission shall afford such person an opportunity to be heard in connection therewith by way of the giving of evidence or the making of submissions and such person or his or her legal representative shall be entitled, through the Commission, to question other witnesses, determined by the Commission, who have appeared before the Commission in terms of this section.

(6) Subject to the provisions of this Act, the procedure to be followed in conducting an investigation shall be determined by the Commission with due regard to the circumstances of each case.

(7) The Commission shall from time to time by notice in the Gazette make known the particulars of the procedure which it has determined in terms of subsection (6).

(8) The Commission may direct that any person or category of persons or all persons the presence of whom is not desirable, shall not be present at the proceedings during the investigation or any part thereof.

Entering and search of premises and attachment and removal of articles

10. (1) Any member of the Commission, or any member of the staff of the Commission or a police officer authorized thereto by a member of the Commission, may, subject to the provisions of this section, for the purposes of an investigation, enter any premises on or in which anything connected with that investigation is or is suspected to be.

(2) The entry and search of any premises under this section shall be conducted with strict regard to decency and order, which shall include regard to:

(a) a person's right to respect for and protection of his or her dignity;

(b) the right to freedom and security of the person; and

(c) the right to his or her personal privacy.

(3) A member or police officer contemplated in subsection (1) may, subject to the provisions of this section:

(a) inspect and search the premises referred to in that subsection, and there make such enquiries as he or she may deem necessary;

(b) examine any article or document found on or in the premises;

(c) request from the owner or person in control of the premises or from any person in whose possession or control that article or document is, information regarding that

article or document;
(d) make copies of or take extracts from any book or document found on or in the premises;
(e) request from any person whom he or she suspects of having the necessary information, an explanation regarding that article or document; attach anything on or in the premises which in his or her opinion has a bearing on the investigation concerned;
(g) if he or she wishes to retain anything on or in the premises contemplated in paragraph (f) for further examination or for safe custody, against the issue of a receipt, remove it from the premises: Provided that any article that has been so removed, shall be returned as soon as possible after the purpose for such removal has been accomplished.

(4) Any person from whom information is required in terms of subsection (3)(a), (c) and (e) may be assisted at such enquiry by an advocate or an attorney, or both, and shall at the commencement of such enquiry be so informed.

(5)(a) Subject to the provisions of subsection (6), the premises referred to in subsection (1) shall only be entered by virtue of an entry warrant issued by a magistrate, or judge of the Supreme Court, if it appears to such magistrate or judge from information on oath that there are reasonable grounds for believing that any article or document, which has a bearing on the investigation concerned, is in the possession or under the control of any person or on or in any premises within such magistrate's or judge's area of jurisdiction.
(b) Subject to the provisions of subsection (6), the functions referred to in subsection (3) shall only be performed by virtue of a search warrant issued by a magistrate, or judge of the Supreme Court, if it appears to such magistrate or judge from information on oath that there are reasonable grounds for believing that an article or document referred to in paragraph (a) is in the possession or under the control of any person or on or in any premises within such magistrate's or judge's area of jurisdiction.
(c) A warrant issued in terms of this subsection shall authorize any member of the Commission or any member of the staff of the Commission or a police officer to perform the functions referred to in subsection (3) and shall to that end authorize such person to enter and search any premises identified in the warrant.
(d) A warrant issued in terms of this subsection shall be executed by day, unless the person issuing the warrant in writing authorizes the execution thereof by night at times which are reasonable in the circumstances.
(e) A warrant issued in terms of this subsection may be issued on any day and shall be of force, until:
   (i) it is executed; or
   (ii) it is cancelled by the person who issued it or, if such person is not available, by any person with like authority; or
   (iii) the expiry of one month from the day of its issue; or
   (iv) the purpose for the issuing of the warrant has lapsed, whichever may occur first.
(f) A person executing a warrant under this section shall, at the commencement of such execution, hand the person referred to in the warrant or the owner or the person in control of the premises, if such a person is present, a copy of the warrant: Provided that if such person is not present, he or she shall affix a copy of the warrant to the premises at a prominent and visible place.
(g) A person executing a warrant under this subsection or an entry or search under subsection (6) shall, at the commencement of such execution, identify himself or herself and if that person requires authorization to execute a warrant under this section, the particulars of such authorization shall also be furnished.

(6) Subject to the provisions of subsections (2), (3), (4), (5)(g), (7) and (8), any member of the Commission, or any member of the staff of the Commission or a police officer upon request by a member of the Commission, may, without an entry and search warrant, enter and search any premises, other than a private dwelling, for the purposes of attaching and removing, if necessary, any article or document:
(a) if the person or persons who may consent to the entering and search for and

attachment and removal of an article or document consents or consent to such entering, search, attachment and removal of the article or document concerned; or

(b) if he or she, on reasonable grounds, believes:
   (i) that a warrant will be issued to him or her under subsection (5) if he or she applies for such warrant; and
   (ii) that the delay in obtaining such a warrant would defeat the object of the entry and search.

(7) An entry and search in terms of subsection (6) shall be executed by day unless the execution thereof by night is justifiable and necessary.

(8)(a) A person who may lawfully under this section enter and search any premises may use such force as may be reasonably necessary to overcome any resistance against such entry and search of the premises, including the breaking of any door or window of such premises: Provided that such person shall first audibly demand admission to the premises and notify the purpose for which he or she seeks to enter and search such premises.

(b) The proviso to paragraph (a) shall not apply where the person concerned is on reasonable grounds of the opinion that any article or document which is the subject of the search may be destroyed or disposed of if the provisions of the said proviso are first complied with.

(9) If during the execution of a warrant in terms of section 10(5)(b) or a search in terms of section 10(6), a person claims that an article or document found on or in the premises concerned contains privileged information and refuses the inspection or removal of such article or document, the person executing the warrant or search shall, if he or she is of the opinion that the article or document contains information that has a bearing on the investigation and that such information is necessary for the investigation, request the registrar of the Supreme Court which has jurisdiction or his or her delegate, to attach and remove that article or document for safe custody until a court of law has made a ruling on the question whether the information concerned is privileged or not.

Vacancies in Commission

11. (1) A vacancy in the Commission shall occur:

(a) when a member's term of office expires;

(b) when a member dies;

(c) when a member is removed from office in terms of the second proviso to section 3(1); or

(d) when a member's resignation, submitted in accordance with section 3(4), takes effect.

(2) A vacancy in the Commission shall:

(a) not affect the validity of the proceedings or decisions of the Commission; and

(b) be filled as soon as practicable in accordance with section 115(3) of the Constitution.

Meetings of Commission

12. (1) The meetings of the Commission shall be held at the times and places determined by the Commission: Provided that the first meeting shall be held at the time and place determined by the Minister of Justice.

(2) If the Chairperson is absent from a meeting of the Commission, the Deputy Chairperson referred to in section 115(5) of the Constitution shall act as chairperson, and if both the Chairperson and Deputy Chairperson are absent from a meeting of the Commission, the members present shall elect one from among their number to preside at that meeting.

(3) The quorum for any meeting of the Commission shall be a majority of the total number of members.

(4) The decision of the majority of the members of the Commission present at a meeting thereof shall be the decision of the Commission, and in the event of an equality of votes concerning any matter, the member presiding shall have a casting vote in addition to his or her deliberative vote.

(5) The Commission shall determine its own procedure and shall cause minutes to be kept of the proceedings.
(6) The Commission shall from time to time by notice in the Gazette make known the particulars of the procedure which it has determined in terms of subsection (5).

Remuneration and allowances of members of Commission
13. (1) The remuneration, allowances and other terms and conditions of office and service benefits of the full-time and part-time members of the Commission shall be determined by the President in consultation with the Cabinet and the Minister of Finance.
(2) The remuneration of the members of the Commission shall not be reduced during their continuation in office.
(3) A part-time member of the Commission may, for any period during which that member, with the approval of the Commission, performs additional duties and functions, be paid such additional remuneration as may be determined by the President in consultation with the Cabinet and the Minister of Finance.

Compensation for certain expenses and damage
14. (1) Subject to the provisions of subsection (2), the Commission may, with the specific or general concurrence of the Minister of Finance, order that the expenses or a portion of the expenses incurred by any person in the course of or in connection with an investigation by the Commission, be paid from State funds.
(2) Any person appearing before the Commission in terms of section 9(1)(c) who is not in the public service, shall be entitled to receive from moneys appropriated by law for such purpose, as witness fees, an amount equal to the amount which he or she would have received as witness fees had he or she been summoned to attend criminal proceedings in the Supreme Court held at the place mentioned in the written notice in question.
(3) If a person has suffered damage in the course of the execution of an entry or search warrant in terms of section 10(5) (a) or (b) or an entry or search contemplated in section 10(6), under circumstances where no person responsible for the premises was present at the time of the causing of the damage and the damage was caused by force used to gain entry as contemplated in section 10(8)(a), the Commission may order that such damage be made good from State funds.

Reports by Commission
15. (1) The Commission may, subject to the provisions of subsection (3), in the manner it deems fit, make known to any person any finding, point of view or recommendation in respect of a matter investigated by it.
(2) In addition to the report contemplated in section 118 of the Constitution, the Commission shall submit to the President and Parliament quarterly reports on the findings in respect of functions and investigations of a serious nature which were performed or conducted by it during that quarter: Provided that the Commission may, at any time, submit a report to the President and Parliament if it deems it necessary.
(3) The findings of an investigation by the Commission shall, when it deems it fit but as soon as possible, be made available to the complainant and any person implicated thereby.

Staff, finances and accountability
16. (1) The Commission shall at its first meeting or as soon as practicable thereafter appoint a director as chief executive officer of the Commission in accordance with section 117(1) of the Constitution, who:
(a) shall, in consultation with the Public Service Commission and the Minister of Finance and subject to subsection (5), appoint such staff in accordance with section 117(1) of the Constitution as may be reasonably necessary to assist him or her with the work incidental to the performance by the Commission of its functions;
(b) shall be responsible for the management of and administrative control over the staff appointed in terms of paragraph (a), and shall for those purposes be accountable to the Commission;

(c) shall, subject to the Exchequer Act, 1975 (Act No. 66 of 1975):
   (i) be charged with the responsibility of accounting for State money received or paid out for or on account of the Commission;
   (ii) cause the necessary accounting and other related records to be kept;
(d) may exercise the powers and shall perform the duties and functions which the Commission may from time to time confer upon or assign to him or her in order to achieve the objects of the Commission, and shall for those purposes be accountable to the Commission.

(2) The records referred to in subsection (1)(c)(ii) shall be audited by the Auditor-General.

(3) The defrayal of expenditure in connection with matters provided for in this Act or in sections 115 up to and including 118 of the Constitution shall be subject to:
(a) requests being received mutatis mutandis in the form as prescribed for the budgetary processes of departments of State; and
(b) the provisions of the Exchequer Act, 1975, and the regulations and instructions issued in terms thereof, as well as the Auditor-General Act, 1989 (Act No. 52 of 1989).

(4) The chief executive officer of the Commission shall be appointed on such terms and conditions and shall receive such remuneration, allowances and other service benefits as the Commission may determine in accordance with the regulations under section 19.

(5) The other staff of the Commission shall be appointed on such terms and conditions and shall receive such remuneration, allowances and other service benefits as the chief executive officer may determine in accordance with the regulations under section 19.

(6) The Commission may, in consultation with the Public Service Commission, in the exercise of its powers or the performance of its duties and functions by or under this Act, the Constitution or any other law, for specific projects, enter into contracts for the services of persons having technical or specialised knowledge of any matter relating to the work of the Commission, and with the concurrence of the Minister of Finance, determine the remuneration, including reimbursement for travelling, subsistence and other expenses, of such persons.

Legal proceedings against Commission

17. (1) The Commission shall be a juristic person.

(2) The State Liability Act, 1957 (Act No. 20 of 1957), shall apply mutatis mutandis in respect of the Commission, and in such application a reference in that Act to "the Minister of the department concerned" shall be construed as a reference to the Chairperson.

(3) No:
(a) member of the Commission;
(b) member of the staff of the Commission;
(c) person contemplated in section 16(6); or
(d) member of any committee, not being a member of the Commission, shall be liable in respect of anything reflected in any report, finding, point of view or recommendation made or expressed in good faith and submitted to Parliament or made known in terms of this Act or the Constitution.

Offences and penalties

18. A person who:
(a) without just cause refuses or fails to comply with a notice under section 9(1)(c) or refuses to take the oath or to make an affirmation at the request of the Commission in terms of section 9(1)(d) or refuses to answer any question put to him or her under section 9(1)(d) or refuses or fails to furnish particulars or information required from him or her under that section;
(b) after having been sworn or having made an affirmation contemplated in section 9(1)(d), gives false evidence before the Commission on any matter, knowing such evidence to be false or not knowing or believing it to be true;
(c) wilfully interrupts the proceedings at an investigation or misbehaves himself or herself in any manner in the place where such investigation is being held;

(d) defames the Commission or a member of the Commission in his or her official capacity;
(e) in connection with any investigation does anything which, if such investigation were proceedings in a court of law, would have constituted contempt of court; anticipates any findings of the Commission regarding an investigation in a manner calculated to influence its proceedings or such findings;
(g) does anything calculated improperly to influence the Commission in respect of any matter being or to be considered by the Commission in connection with an investigation;
(h) contravenes any provision of section 4(2);
(i) fails to afford the Commission the necessary assistance referred to in section 4(3) or 7(2);
(j) acts contrary to the authority of an entry warrant issued under section 10(5)(a) or a search warrant issued under section 10(5)(b) or, without being authorized thereto under section 10, enters or searches any premises or attaches any article or document or performs any act contemplated in section 10(3), shall be guilty of an offence and liable on conviction to a fine or to imprisonment for a period not exceeding six months.

Regulations
19. (1) The President may, after the Commission has made a recommendation and after consultation with the Public Service Commission, make regulations regarding the following matters in relation to the staff of the Commission:
(a) (i) The different categories of salaries and scales of salaries which shall be applicable to the different categories of members of staff;
(ii) the requirements for appointment and the appointment, promotion, discharge and disciplinary steps;
(iii) the recognition of appropriate qualifications and experience for the purposes of the determination of salaries;
(iv) the procedure and manner of and criteria for evaluation, and the conditions or requirements for the purposes of promotion;
(b) the powers, duties, conduct, discipline, hours of attendance and leave of absence, including leave gratuity, and any other condition of service;
(c) the creation of posts on the establishment of the Commission;
(d) the training of staff, including financial assistance for such training;
(e) a code of conduct to be complied with by staff;
(f) the provision of official transport;
(g) the conditions on which and the circumstances under which remuneration for over-time duty, and travel, subsistence, climatic, local and other allowances, may be paid;
(h) subject to section 17, the legal liability of any member of staff in respect of any act done in terms of this Act or any other law and the legal liability emanating from the use of official transport;
(i) the circumstances under which and the conditions and manner in which a member of staff may be found to be guilty of misconduct, or to be suffering from continued ill-health, or of incapacity to carry out his or her duties of office efficiently;
(j) the procedure for dealing with complaints and grievances of members of staff and the manner in which and time when or period wherein and person to whom documents in connection with requests and communications of such members of staff shall be submitted;
(k) the membership or conditions of membership of a particular pension fund and the contributions to and the rights, privileges and obligations of members of staff or their dependants with regard to such a pension fund;
(l) the membership or conditions of membership of a particular medical aid scheme or medical aid society and the manner in and the conditions on which membership fees and other moneys which are payable or owing by or in respect of members of staff or their dependants, to a medical aid scheme or medical aid society, may be recovered

from the salaries of such members of staff and paid to such medical aid scheme or medical aid society;

(m) the contributions to and the rights, privileges and obligations of members of staff or their dependants with regard to such a medical aid scheme or medical aid society;

(n) in general, any matter which is not in conflict with this Act or the Constitution and which is reasonably necessary for the regulation of the terms and conditions of service of members of staff.

(2) Any regulation under this section relating to State expenditure, shall be made in consultation with the Minister of Finance.

Short title and commencement

20. This Act shall be called the *Human Rights Commission Act, 1994*, and shall come into operation on a date fixed by the President by proclamation in the Gazette.

United Kingdom

Human Rights Mechanisms in the United Kingdom

Stephen C. Neff* and Eric Avebury**

Introduction: The UK Legal System

Several basic features of the United Kingdom (UK) legal system should be borne in mind. One is that British law rests on a fundamental presumption of liberty, i.e., the principle that individuals have a standing right to do anything, unless there is a rule of law – either statutory or common law – forbidding the act in question.

The British legal system is the fruit of historical evolution far more than of conscious planning. There is no written constitution for the country and therefore no constitutionally entrenched bill of rights. Consequently, human rights statutory provisions or institutions cannot possess an entrenched constitutional status. Nor do the courts have the power to overturn legislation on the ground of incompatibility with a constitution. The UK also does not have comprehensive codes of civil or criminal law or procedure. Instead, it has an underlying system of unwritten common law, supplemented and altered over many centuries by statutory enactments.

Traditionally, individual rights in the UK have been protected primarily by individuals themselves resorting to the regular courts for the upholding of the rule of law. (For the principal mechanisms by which this is done, see below.) The UK traditionally has not relied, to any significant extent, on "dedicated" guardian agencies such as ombudsmen or human-rights commissions.

This tradition of leaving individual citizens to rely on the general rule of law to safeguard their human rights has, however, been shown over the years to have many shortcomings. (The UK's experience with the European Convention on Human Rights has been highly instructive in this regard.) The tendency has been to deal with these shortcomings on a piecemeal basis. This has been particularly evident in the manner in which ombudsmen and human-rights commissions have been created since the mid 1960s. These have been created in particular areas, with limited remits. Instead of a single all-purpose ombudsman or human-rights commission, there has been instead a rather untidy proliferation of limited-function bodies, without a coherent over-all design.

The UK is a party to all of the major international human rights conventions and therefore has a legal obligation under international law to ensure that the rights set out in these conventions are effectively protected. None of these

*University of Edinburgh.
**Vice-chair, Parliamentary Human Rights Group.

K. Hossain et al. (eds), Human Rights Commissions and Ombudsman Offices, 667–689.

conventions, however, has been incorporated into the UK's national law. This means that persons cannot invoke these conventions in litigation in British courts. (For current plans to allow the enforcement of the norms of the European Convention on Human Rights in British law, see below.)

Finally, it may be noted that, within the UK, Scotland has a separate legal system. Northern Ireland also has a number of distinctive legal features. With regard to the human rights norms and processes discussed here, the differences between Scotland and the rest of the UK are minor. Differences between Northern Ireland and the rest of the UK are, in some respects, rather greater. The discussion below will indicate, where appropriate, the areas in which the component parts of the UK are treated differently.

Ombudsmen And Similar Entities

As noted above, there is no general, all-purpose ombudsman for the UK. Since 1967, however, there has been a proliferation of ombudsmen in specific areas, with limited remits. Many of these are largely unconnected with human rights (dealing with matters such as banking, insurance, investment, pensions, funerals and the building industry). A number of them, however, do have important human rights duties, as described below. Sometimes these ombudsman functions are performed by single persons, and sometimes by collective bodies.

There is a UK Ombudsman Association, which sets out criteria which should be satisfied before the term "ombudsman" should be applicable. According to these standards ombudsmen should be independent of the persons or bodies which they investigate or oversee. They should also not require consent for their investigations by the very entities concerned. They should have fixed and secure appointments. They should be independent in their decisions as to whether they have jurisdiction over a given complaint. There should be direct access to them by the public, and their existence should be publicised to the general public. They should have access to information which they need to assess the merits of complaints. There should be a "reasonable expectation" of implementation of their recommendations – together with the power to publicise cases in which recommendations are not adopted. They should also publish annual reports. It will be noted from the descriptions below that not all UK ombudsmen meet all of these standards.

The principal areas in which there are ombudsmen who perform human rights functions are the following.

Central Government

The principal ombudsman – and the first to be appointed – is known technically as the Parliamentary Commissioner for Administration (PCA) or less formally as the Parliamentary Ombudsman. This post was established by the Parliamentary Commissioner Act 1967. The Parliamentary Ombudsman is not a civil servant but is an independent officer of the House of Commons, nominally appointed by the Queen for an indefinite term and reporting to the Parliament.

The Parliamentary Ombudsman deals with the actions of designated departments of the central government. This list of departments within the PCA's remit was significantly expanded by the Parliamentary and Health Service Commissioners Act 1987 (from less than fifty to more than one hundred), with further expansions possible by order in council. The decisions of government ministers of the designated departments are within the PCA's jurisdiction.

The Parliamentary Ombudsman is principally concerned with such matters as maladministration, the giving of wrong advice and unjustifiable delays by the relevant government departments. Also within his remit are complaints about the refusal of access to information (arising from the Code of Practice on Access to Government Information). A notable, and controversial, matter which is expressly excluded from the PCA's remit is the matter of personnel administration in the civil service. (Attempts to bring this subject into the PCA's jurisdiction have been made but have not succeeded.)

The public does not have direct access to the Parliamentary Ombudsman. Complaints must be submitted first to a member of parliament (MP), normally within twelve months of the act complained of. (When complaints are wrongly sent by members of the public directly to the PCA, his practice is to forward suitable cases to the appropriate MP for action in the normal way.) MPs are not required to bring the matters to the PCA's attention. When they do so, the PCA has a complete discretion as to whether to investigate the matter. In gathering information, he has the same compulsory powers as the High Court; and he can apply to the courts for punitive action in cases of obstruction or contempt. He cannot be denied access to any information, however secret – but he is limited as to his right to disclose information, since he is subject to the Official Secrets Act 1989.

Reports from investigations are normally not made public, but are made to the MP who forwarded the complaint and to the government department concerned. In general, the departments comply with the PCA's recommendations. In cases where departments fail to remedy shortcomings, however, the PCA can make special reports for general publication. This has happened very rarely.

Local Government

For dealing with complaints against local government authorities, there are Commissions for Local Administration (CLAs) for England and Wales, created by the Local Government Act 1974. The Parliamentary Ombudsman is an ex officio member of these bodies. In the case of England, there is a territorial subdividing of the Commission's duties. For Scotland, there is a single Commissioner for Local Administration in Scotland, established by the Local Government (Scotland) Act 1975. All of these officials are appointed for indefinite terms by the relevant Secretary of State.

The remit of these CLAs is rather limited. The principal subject of complaints to them is allocation of government-owned housing. (For analogous provisions regarding privately-provided housing, see "Private-sector housing" below.) The internal running of schools, most notably, is not within their remit (even though education is, by far, the major function of local governments). Initially, the jurisdiction of the CLAs of England and Wales was slightly greater than for Scotland, in that the CLA for Scotland was not empowered to investigate complaints of maladministration by individual members of local government.

This limitation, however, was removed by the Scottish Legal Services Ombudsman and Commissioner for Local Administration in Scotland Act 1997.

During the early period of their operation, complaints could not be made directly by the public to the CLAs. They had to be made to local authority members first. The local authority members were, however, required to forward all complaints to the relevant CLA. (In the exceptional case where local authority members refused to forward complaints, the CLAs could accept the complaints directly from the public.)

Since then, the procedures have altered. The current procedure (provided for by the Local Government Act 1988) allows complaints to be made directly to the CLAs – although the CLAs nonetheless are still required to be satisfied that the authority complained against had a reasonable opportunity to resolve the matter on its own. After this relaxation of the "local remedies" principle, there was a dramatic rise in the caseload of the CLAs.

The CLAs have no enforcement powers. Their principal means of action is publicity. They issue reports on their investigations, which the local authorities concerned are required to advertise and to make available to the general public for inspection (and copying) for three weeks. The local authority concerned must notify the CLA within three months of what action it intends to take pursuant to a report. If the CLA is not satisfied with this response, it can make a further report, which must be advertised and made available in the same manner as the first one. If the CLA believes the response is still not adequate, he can require the local authority to publish in a local newspaper (at its own expense) an explanation of its non-compliance.

Legal Services

For England and Wales, a Legal Services Ombudsman was established by the Courts and Legal Services Act 1990. He is appointed by the Lord Chancellor. Unusually for ombudsmen, this appointment is for a three-year term. The analogous position for Scotland is the Scottish Legal Services Ombudsman, established by the Law Reform (Miscellaneous Provisions) (Scotland) Act 1990. This person is appointed by the Secretary of State for an indefinite term. These Ombudsmen may not be members of the professions in question. All legal services are within the remit of these Ombudsmen, including the licensed conveyancing of property.

The purpose of these Ombudsmen is not to deal with complaint from the public at first instance, but rather to review the adequacy with which the relevant professional disciplinary bodies deal with complaints about the quality of professional services. Consequently, complaints must go in first instance to the relevant professional bodies. Only if a complainant is dissatisfied with the way in which the matter was dealt with at that stage can the complainant be taken to the Ombudsman. In Scotland, the Ombudsman has been empowered by the Scottish Legal Services Ombudsman and Commissioner for Local Administration in Scotland Act 1997 to recommend (but not to compel) the relevant professional bodies to award compensation for losses of up to £1000.

Data Protection

The Data Protection Registrar, although not officially called an ombudsman, has nevertheless been described by the government as "an Ombudsman for data subjects". The position was established by the Data Protection Act 1984. The Registrar is appointed nominally by the Queen for an indefinite term.

Anybody who stores personal data on computer has to register with the Data Protection Registrar and, in so doing, to state the purposes for which the data is being held and to identify persons to whom it can be disclosed. The Data Protection Registrar is empowered to investigate complaints from individuals who believe that data relating to them is being held on computer and used incompatibly with the information given upon registration. Persons dissatisfied with a decision of the Registrar can appeal to a Data Protection Tribunal, which is comprised of both lawyers and lay members. (The chair and deputy chairs of this tribunal are appointed by the Lord Chancellor. They must be lawyers of at least seven years' standing. Lay members are appointed by the Secretary of State. The tribunal is intended to contain representatives of both data users and data subjects.)

There are currently plans to extend data-protection laws in several respects, mandated by a 1995 directive from the European Communities. Individuals will have a right to prevent personal data from being used for certain commercial purposes such as marketing. Conditions are to be placed on the processing of sensitive data (such as information about health and ethnic origin). Individuals will have access to a wider range of personal data (most notably, to some data held by non-computer methods); and there are to be wider arrangements for legal action and compensation for unlawful uses of data. The Data Protection Registrar will also be re-designated as the "Data Protection Commissioner".

Health Services

The positions of Health Service Commissioner for England and for Wales were created by the National Health Service Reorganization Act 1973. The corresponding position for Scotland was created by the National Health Service (Scotland) Act 1972. These Health Services Ombudsmen (as they are known) are appointed nominally by the Queen for indefinite terms.

These Ombudsmen can investigate complaints by the general public about failures of service or maladministration which result in personal hardship or injustice. The Health Service Commissioners (Amendment) Act 1996 extended their remit to the investigation of complaints about family physicians, including complaints about clinical decisions. Refusals to provide information are also covered. The remit does not extend to privately provided health services (unless they are paid for by the National Health Service).

Complaints by members of the public must go first to the body which is being complained about (e.g., the particular hospital, clinic or surgery which is allegedly at fault). If the complainant believes that the complaint has not been satisfactorily dealt with, he can ask for a review by an independent panel, usually consisting of three members and chaired by an independent person.

Prisons

The Prisons Ombudsman differs from the others in not having a statutory basis (or even an Internet web-site). The position was established in 1993, pursuant to the Woolf Report on prison disturbances submitted to the government in

1991. The Prisons Ombudsman is appointed by the Home Secretary. The terms of reference of the post are found in the Proposal for Ministerial Consideration (of 1992), together with a Note of Arrangements of 1994, although these do not constitute a comprehensive public statement of the remit of the position.

The Prisons Ombudsman's functions extend to all areas of activity of the Prison Service, both procedural and substantive, which affect individual prisoners (although prisoners must exhaust internal grievance procedures before the Ombudsman can act). His sphere of activities extends to privatised prisons as well as to government-operated ones. Forms of detention under authorities other than the Prison Service are not within his remit (for example, detentions by the police or the Immigration Service).

Even within the sphere of the Prison Service, several important matters are clearly outside of the Prisons Ombudsman's remit. He does not have the power to re-hear disciplinary cases brought by the prison administrations against prisoners. Complaints about the Parole Board and the Probation Service are outside of his remit. Finally, the Ombudsman may not deal with the exercise by the Secretary of State of his discretionary power to determine the release dates of mandatory life sentence prisoners. In 1996, the remit of the Ombudsman was curtailed further, in that he was deprived of the right to investigate ministerial decisions of any nature.

The Prisons Ombudsman's only power is to make recommendations to the Home Secretary on individual cases, although the secretary is not legally obligated to follow the advice. The Prisons Ombudsman is therefore, in effect, an adviser to the Home Secretary on matters relating to the treatment of prisoners. Human rights groups interested in prisoners' rights have been deeply disappointed at the limited scope of the Ombudsman's powers.

The work of the Prisons Ombudsman has not proceeded altogether smoothly. Part of the reason is the lack of precision as to the terms of his remit, which has resulted in a number of jurisdictional disputes between the Ombudsman and the Prison Service. There have also been disagreements between the Ombudsman and the Prison Service over access to documentation.

It should be noted that, in addition to the Prisons Ombudsman, there is a Board of Visitors for each prison, charged with overseeing the administration of that prison. These Boards consist largely of part-time lay persons from the local area. They are formally independent; but, like the Prisons Ombudsman, they report to the Home Secretary rather than to the Parliament. One of the functions of the Boards of Visitors is to hear and adjudicate on grievances voiced by prisoners. They have no power, however, to inquire into the death of a prisoner in the prison, even though the number of non-natural deaths occurring in the prisons, including self-inflicted deaths, has increased sharply in recent years. There is also an Inspector of Prisons, an office established by the Criminal Justice Act 1982.

Private-sector Housing

When substantial stocks of government-owned housing were privatised in the 1980s, much of the housing was taken over by private associations for rental purposes. To provide protection for tenants, the government created, in the Housing Act 1996, the legal category of "social landlords" (meaning landlords who provide direct services to their tenants). Social landlords are required to enter into government-approved schemes, one requirement of which is that there must be, for each scheme, a housing ombudsman.

This ombudsman must have the power to order compensation for losses or to suspend contractual rights and duties of landlords and tenants. In essence, this arrangement is the private-sector counterpart of the ombudsman service performed for public-sector housing by the Local Government Ombudsmen (see above).

Press and Broadcasting Standards

There is a Broadcasting Standards Commission, which consists of up to fifteen persons appointed by the Secretary of State for National Heritage. It was originally established as the Broadcasting Complaints Commission by the Broadcasting Act 1980. In 1997, pursuant to the Broadcasting Act 1996, this body was merged with the Broadcasting Standards Council to form the present Broadcasting Standards Commission. The remit of this body is rather wider than its name would indicate, since it covers not only the whole of radio and television broadcasting but also cable, satellite, text and digital services.

The Broadcasting Standards Commission has three principal functions. First, it monitors, researches on and reports on standards and fairness in broadcasting (covering such matters as political bias in the media). Second, it produces codes of practice on standards and fairness. Finally, it has a committee which receives and adjudicates two categories of complaints: fairness complaints and standards complaints. Fairness complaints deal with such matters as the accuracy of coverage by the media. Standards complaints deal with matters such as intrusions into privacy. (The procedures differ somewhat for these two categories.)

When complaints of either kind are held by the Commission to be well-founded, only a very limited form of relief can be granted: the publisher of the offending material can be required to publicise the Commission's own finding. The Commission cannot compel the publisher to apologise to the complainant, or to issue a correction of inaccurate material, or to give financial compensation.

In addition, there is a privately-established body known as the Press Complaints Commission, set up in 1991. It is a self-regulation mechanism for the newspaper industry, although there have also been indications that, because it performs a public function, its actions may be subject to judicial review by the courts (see below). The Commission has published a code of practice covering such issues as inaccuracy of press stories, invasions of privacy, misrepresentation and harassment. It deals with individual complaints in these areas and also issues general guidance to newspaper editors.

Police

A Police Complaints Authority covers England and Wales (but not Scotland or Northern Ireland). The original institution in this area was the Police Complaints Board, which was established by the Police Act 1976. Dissatisfaction with the system, dramatically illustrated by a serious outbreak of urban rioting in 1981, led to a revamping of the system, in the Police and Criminal Evidence Act 1984, which replaced the Police Complaints Board by the present Police Complaints

Authority. The powers and procedures are now set out in the Police Act 1996. The Authority consists of a chairman appointed nominally by the Queen, plus at least eight additional members (none of whom may be a former police constable) appointed by the Secretary of State.

The principal task of the Authority is to investigate serious complaints about the conduct of police officers. The authority also, however, can in certain circumstances deal with non-complaint issues voluntarily referred by the police services themselves. The principal remedy is to order the taking of disciplinary proceedings against a police officer.

The Authority does not have jurisdiction over the newly-established National Criminal Intelligence Service or the National Crime Squad. Instead, the legislation establishing these bodies (the Police Act 1997) simply requires the government to "make provision" for complaints. The legislation allows – but does not require – the government to establish arrangements "corresponding or similar" to those described above.

For Scotland, there is no parallel independent authority. Instead, the chief constable of each police force deals with complaints against persons under his jurisdiction, as provided by the Police (Discipline)(Scotland) Regulations 1967. This process has been criticized for affording insufficient oversight of police activities. It may be noted, however, that, if a complaint alleges criminal conduct by police officers, the matter is referred to the prosecution service (known in Scotland as procurator fiscal service), which is independent of the police.

For Northern Ireland, there is an Independent Commission for Police Complaints for Northern Ireland, created by the Police (Northern Ireland) Order 1987. This supervises the investigation of complaints by the public against members of the Royal Ulster Constabulary and also reviews disciplinary action and monitors the operation of an informal dispute resolution procedure. In addition, an Independent Commissioner for Holding Centres has existed since 1992. He is specifically concerned with monitoring the treatment of terrorist suspects detained in holding centres, to ensure that the various stipulated procedures are complied with. This official is not, however, empowered to investigate complaints against the police. Any complaints which he receives must be forwarded to the Chief Constable for investigation (where it may then be overseen, in due course, by the Independent Commission).

Trade Unions

In the trade union area, there are two ombudsmen, who have essentially a legal-aid function. The Commissioner for the Rights of Trade Union Members was established by the Employment Act 1988. He is appointed by the Secretary of State for an indefinite term.

His primary function is to protect individual trade-union members from mistreatment by their unions and to assist such members in taking action against their trade unions for mistreatment. The concerns of the legislation include safeguarding the rights of workers in disciplinary proceedings against them by their trade unions, cases of removal from trade-union office, safeguarding the fairness of balloting (when that is required) and preventing the misuse of trade-union funds or property. The Ombudsman is empowered to assist the union member in legal proceedings that arise in such matters.

The other ombudsman is the Commissioner for Protection Against Unlawful Industrial Action, established by the Trade Union Reform and Employment Rights Act 1993. He is also appointed by the Secretary of State for an indefinite term. His chief function is to assist members of the general public in taking legal action for injury resulting from unlawful industrial action.

Northern Ireland (general)

When Northern Ireland had its own parliament (i.e., before 1972), there was an Ombudsman for Northern Ireland corresponding to the PCA, established in 1969. That same year, a second official, known as the Commissioner for Complaints was established. When the Northern Ireland Assembly was suspended in 1972, these offices continued to exist, except that their monitoring was now, perforce, directed towards activities of the UK central government departments as they affect Northern Ireland. Since 1973, the two posts have been held by the same person, although the functions of the two offices remain distinct.

In his capacity as Ombudsman for Northern Ireland, the Ombudsman carries out, for Northern Ireland, approximately the combined functions of the PCA, plus the Local Government and the Health Services Ombudsmen. In addition (and unlike the PCA), he is authorized to deal with personnel complaints. Like the PCA, the Ombudsman, in his capacity as Ombudsman for Northern Ireland, can only receive complaints from members of parliament, not directly from the general public.

In his capacity as Commissioner for Complaints, however, the Ombudsman has rather more latitude. He can receive complaints directly from the public. His jurisdiction extends to personnel matters (as it does in his other capacity). Also, as Commissioner for Complaints, he is allowed to deal with commercial and contractual matters. Another notable point about this Ombudsman is that, in his capacity as Commissioner for Complaints, he is allowed to seek court orders enforcing his findings. This includes seeking injunctive relief in situations in which persistent maladministration seems likely. (This power appears, however, to be used comparatively infrequently.)

Human Rights Commissions and Related Bodies

As noted above, the UK does not have a general, all-purpose human rights commission, just as it does not have a general, all-purpose ombudsman. Forceful arguments have been advanced by human rights activists and scholars that there is a need for such a body. But these urgings have not been acted upon.

As in the case of ombudsmen (although not to the same extent), a number of human rights commission-style bodies with limited remits have been created. They are the following.

Commission for Racial Equality

The Race Relations Board was established by the Race Relations Act 1965. It was succeeded by the Commission for Racial Equality (CRE), established by the Race Relations Act 1976. It is comprised of eight to fifteen members, appointed by the Secretary of State.

The CRE works in the fields of employment, housing and the provision of goods, facilities and services to the public. It has a promotional function: assisting research and educational activities, assisting organizations (even providing financial assistance) and generally promoting harmonious race relations, equality of opportunity and the elimination of racial discrimination.

In addition, the CRE can assist individuals in the bringing of legal actions in the regular courts if an important point of principle is at stake in the action or if it is deemed unreasonable to expect the individual to pursue the legal claim without assistance.

Most notably, the CRE has investigative and enforcement powers in its own right. It can undertake formal investigations, which can take either of two forms. One is a "named person" investigation, directed at a particular party (although this can only be undertaken if the CRE suspects that a discriminatory act actually had taken place in the past). If a "named person" investigation leads the CRE to conclude, that a discriminatory practice is in effect, it can issue a "non-discrimination notice" ordering that the practice be discontinued. It can also order the providing of information to the CRE or to other parties as to steps taken to change the practice. The other type is a general investigation, which does not require a prior belief that discrimination had actually occurred. Failure by persons to co-operate with either type of investigation is a criminal offence.

Much dissatisfaction has been expressed with the way in the CRE operates – much of it to the effect that its freedom of action is too severely restricted. The CRE itself proposed an amendment to its enabling legislation in 1985, removing the prior-belief requirement for "named person" investigations; but this proposed change was not made.

There is a separate CRE for Northern Ireland, which is soon to be merged into the Fair Employment Commission for Northern Ireland (see below).

Equal Opportunities Commission

The Equal Opportunities Commission (EOC), established by the Sex Discrimination Act 1975, is a counterpart of the CRE in the area of sex discrimination. Like the CRE, it is composed of eight to fifteen members, appointed by the Secretary of State. It has a promotional role like that of the CRE.

Also like the CRE, it can assist individuals in bringing legal actions in the courts. The limitations on its investigative powers are also similar to those of the CRE.

There is a separate EOC for Northern Ireland, which, along with the Northern Ireland CRE, is to be merged into the Fair Employment Commission for Northern Ireland (see below).

Criminal Cases Review Commissions

The establishment of these bodies resulted from public concern in recent years over a number of highly publicised cases of miscarriage of justice. In response to this concern, the Criminal Appeals Act 1995 created, for England, Wales and Northern Ireland, the Criminal Cases Review Commission. Its members are appointed by the Queen on the recommendation of the Prime Minister. It must have at least eleven members, at least one-third of whom must be legally qualified of ten years standing.

The Commission is not a judicial body. It accordingly has no power to reverse convictions or to revise sentences. Instead, it has the power to investigate past cases and to refer them back to the appellate courts for an additional appeal of either convictions or sentences. The exercise of this power, however, is subject to some important constraints. There must be a "real possibility" that prior convictions will be reversed on a further appeal, and there must also be legal points or evidence that had not been brought to the courts' attention in the earlier, regular proceedings. (In "exceptional circumstances", however, these restrictions can be waived by the commission.) The commission has the power to conduct investigations, including calling for documents from public authorities.

For Scotland, an analogous body, the Scottish Criminal Cases Review Commission, was created by the Crime and Punishment (Scotland) Act 1997. Its members are appointed by the Queen on the recommendation of the Secretary of State. It consists of at least three members (one-third of whom must be legally qualified of ten years standing). The jurisdiction and functions of this body are similar (though not identical) to those of the commission for England, Wales and Northern Ireland.

Fair Employment Commission for Northern Ireland

Established (under a slightly different name) in 1969, this body is designed to promote non-discrimination on the basis of religion in Northern Ireland. It consists of a chairman plus five to eleven members. It publishes a non-legally-binding code of practice for employers. It keeps a register of employers, who are required to file annual reports with the commission providing information on the composition of their workforces and of applicants for jobs.

The Commission has the power to undertake investigations of employment practices. It can seek undertakings and serve notices on firms regarding policies for the promotion of equal opportunity or the supplying of information to the Commission. If these undertakings or notices are not complied with, the Commission can seek enforcement through the courts. The Commission can also hear complaints of discrimination by individuals and can apply to the courts to stop discriminatory advertising for jobs. Appeals are available from the Commission's decisions and actions to a Fair Employment Tribunal and, from there, to the regular courts.

As noted above, it is envisaged that the Commission on Racial Equality and the Equal Opportunities Commission for Northern Ireland will be merged into this Fair Employment Commission.

Standing Advisory Commission on Human Rights (for Northern Ireland)

In Northern Ireland, there is a Standing Advisory Commission on Human Rights, created by the Northern Ireland (Constitution) Act 1973. It is a purely advisory body. Its role is to advise the Secretary of State as to the adequacy or inadequacy of the substantive law on discrimination on the basis of religion or political belief, as well as on the procedures for the redress of grievances.

The Northern Ireland agreement of April 1998 envisages the establishment of a Northern Ireland Human Rights Commission by UK legislation, which will be independent of the government. This agreement is, however, subject to approval by referendum.

Other Human Rights Safeguards in UK Law

As noted above, despite the proliferation of ombudsmen and commissions, it remains the case that, in the British legal tradition, human rights abuses are often remedied through individual legal action in the regular courts. A picture of human rights in British law would therefore not be balanced if it did not point out the principal legal mechanisms available, as well as certain other important means of safeguarding human rights. The most important of these are the following.

Civil Actions Against Public Officials for Violations of Law

In UK law, the general principle is that individual public officials are not exempt, by virtue of their offices, from the duty to adhere to the general law. Consequently, civil actions are available to persons who are injured by ordinary torts (delicts) committed by public officials in the course of their duties, such as acts of trespass or battery. The standard remedy is money damages, although injunctions are available as well. Under the Crown Proceedings Act 1947, civil actions in tort (delict) may also be maintained against the Crown as such in a wide variety of circumstances.

Judicial Review of Official Acts

Even though (as noted above) the UK does not possess a written constitution against which the lawfulness of statutes can be assessed, the British courts can, nevertheless, review the legality of decisions made by persons performing any public function. That is to say, the courts can determine whether persons performing public functions have acted outside the scope of the discretion given to them by the relevant laws governing their actions. This type of proceeding is known as judicial review.

Judicial review differs from an ordinary civil action in that it is not designed to act as a challenge to the merits of decisions. Nor is it designed to compensate the claimant for damage incurred. Judicial review is designed to stop persons exercising public powers from exceeding the scope of those powers. The standard remedy is the vacating of the official action in question.

The ombudsmen themselves are subject to judicial review, as are the Boards of Visitors of prisons, the Commission on Racial Equality and the Equal Opportunities Commission. There have been indications that acts of the Press Complaints Commission are also subject to judicial review, although this has not yet been definitively determined.

Challenges to Forms of Detention

The oldest form of challenge to the legality of any form of detention is an application to a court for a writ of habeas corpus. (This process has essentially entered into international human rights law, most notably in Article 9 of the

International Covenant on Civil and Political Rights.) Under this process, a court determines whether a person who is in detention is being lawfully held. If not, the immediate release of the person is ordered.

In the specific area of compulsory hospitalisation on mental-health grounds, there is an analogous process, which is based on the medical merits of the case. The Mental Health Act 1983 provides for the compulsory admission to a hospital in certain prescribed circumstances (basically, if the person's own health or safety or that of others is at risk). Within the first fourteen days following admission, the patient can apply to a Medical Health Review Tribunal for a review of his case. If the tribunal disagrees with the medical assessment on which the admission was based, the tribunal can order the patient's release.

Unlawfully Obtained Evidence in Criminal Trials

There is not a blanket rule forbidding the prosecution from making use of evidence which was procured unlawfully. Section 78 of the Police and Criminal Evidence Act 1984, however, grants to judges the discretion to exclude such evidence in particular cases, if the demands of fairness so require.

Recourse to the European Commission and Court of Human Rights

Since 1966, it has been possible for individual applicants in the UK to apply to the European Commission on Human Rights for a determination of the legality of British government actions under the European Convention on Human Rights. There have been a huge number of such applications since then, many of which have been successful before the Commission or the European Court of Human Rights. A number of important changes in British law have been made as a result. This experience demonstrates the importance that an international mechanism can have in safeguarding the human rights of persons. Even a legal system as well developed as the British one has been found to be deficient in a substantial number of areas.

There is currently legislation before Parliament to make enforcement of European Convention rights more effective in British law by several means. Most notably, the legislation provides that: (i) all public officials, in the exercise of any discretion, will be required to act consistently with the Convention; (ii) the courts will be enabled to invalidate secondary (but not primary) legislation on the ground of incompatibility with the Convention; (iii) courts will be required to interpret legislation, wherever possible, compatibly with the European Convention; and (iv) a "fast-track" mechanism will be established, for changing any statutes which are declared by the courts to be incompatible with the Convention.

The devolution of governmental powers to assemblies in Scotland and Wales does not include the power to enact laws incompatible with the European Convention. Therefore, any acts of these assemblies that are incompatible with the European Convention will be subject to being struck down by the courts as being ultra vires the powers of the assemblies.

Actions of Members of Parliament

An important function of members of Parliament (MPs) is the performing of services for their constituents. Sometimes, these services consist in obtaining redress for infringements of human rights. Action can be taken by MPs either privately or publicly, on the floor of the legislature.

Activities of Human Rights NGOs

One of the most essential guarantees of human rights in Britain is the vigilance of non-governmental organizations (NGOs) in the human rights sphere. They engage in a large range of activities, including giving advice to individuals, assisting in litigation, monitoring government actions, pressing for changes in the law and publicising abuses. Some groups specialise in certain areas, while others deal with the whole range of international human rights. In terms of alerting the general public to human rights issues, the mass media – protected by the fundamental principle of freedom of the press – also perform an invaluable service. In addition, NGOs have standing, under certain circumstances, to pursue actions for judicial review (as described above) in the areas of their concern.

LEGISLATION

Parliamentary Commissioner Act 1967

(1967 c 13)

The Parliamentary Commissioner for Administration
1. Appointment and tenure of office
(1) For the purpose of conducting investigations in accordance with the following provisions of this Act there shall be appointed a Commissioner, to be known as the Parliamentary Commissioner for Administration.
(2) Her Majesty may by Letters Patent from time to time appoint a person to be the Commissioner, and any person so appointed shall (subject to [(subsections (3) and (3A)] of this section) hold office during good behaviour.
(3) A person appointed to be the Commissioner may be relieved of office by Her Majesty at his own request, or may be removed from office by Her Majesty in consequence of Addresses from both Houses of Parliament, and shall in any case vacate office on completing the year of service in which he attains the age of sixty-five years.
[(3A) Her Majesty may declare the office of Commissioner to have been vacated if satisfied that the person appointed to be the Commissioner is incapable for medical reasons:
(a) of performing duties of his office; and
(b) of requesting to be relieved of it.]
(4), (5) ...

2. Salary and pension
(1) There shall be paid to the holder of the office of Commissioner a salary at the rate (subject to subsection (2) of this section) of £ 8,600 a year.
(2) The House of Commons may from time to time by resolution increase the rate of the salary payable under this section, and any such resolution may take effect from the date on which it is passed or such other date as may be specified therein.
(3) The provisions of Schedule 1 to this Act shall have effect with respect to the pensions

and other benefits to be paid to or in respect of persons who have held office as Commissioner.
(4) The salary payable to a holder of the office of Commissioner shall be abated by the amount of any pension payable to him in respect of any public office in the United Kingdom or elsewhere to which he had previously been appointed or elected; ...
(4A) In computing the salary of a former holder of the office of Commissioner for the purposes of the said Schedule 1
(a) any abatement of that salary under subsection (4) above
(b) any temporary abatement of that salary in the national interest, and
(c) any voluntary surrender of that salary in whole or in part,
shall be disregarded.
(5) Any salary, pension or other benefit payable by virtue of this section shall be charged on and issued out of the Consolidated Fund.

3. Administrative provisions
(1) The Commissioner may appoint such officers as he may determine with the approval of the Treasury as to numbers and conditions of service.
(2) Any function of the Commissioner under this Act may be performed by any officer of the Commissioner authorized for that purpose by the Commissioner (or may be performed by any officer so authorized
(a) of the Health Service Commissioner for England;
(b) (applies to Scotland only); or
(c) of the Health Service Commissioner for Wales).
(3) The expenses of the Commissioner under this Act, to such amount as may be sanctioned by the Treasury, shall be defrayed out of moneys provided by Parliament.

3A. Appointment of acting Commissioner
(1) Where the office of Commissioner becomes vacant, Her Majesty may, pending the appointment of a new Commissioner, appoint a person under this section to act as the Commissioner at any time during the period of twelve months beginning with the date on which the vacancy arose.
(2) A person appointed under this section shall hold office during Her Majesty's pleasure and, subject to that, shall hold office
(a) until the appointment of a new Commissioner or the expiry of the period of twelve months beginning with the date on which the vacancy arose, whichever occurs first; and
(b) in other respects, in accordance with the terms and conditions of his appointment which shall be such as the Treasury may determine.
(3) A person appointed under this section shall, while he holds office, be treated for all purposes, except those of section 2 of this Act, as the Commissioner.
(4) Any salary, pension or other benefit payable by virtue of this section shall be charged on and issued out of the Consolidated Fund.

Investigation by the Commissioner
4. Departments etc. subject to investigation
(1) Subject to the provisions of this section and to the notes contained in Schedule 2 to this Act, this Act applies to the government departments, corporations and unincorporated bodies listed in that Schedule; and references in this Act to an authority to which this Act applies are references to any such corporation or body.
(2) Her Majesty may by Order in Council amend Schedule 2 to this Act by the alteration of any entry or note, the removal of any entry or note or the insertion of any additional entry or note.
(3) An Order in Council may only insert an entry if
(a) it relates
(i) to a government department; or

(ii) to a corporation or body whose functions are exercised on behalf of the Crown; or

(b) it relates to a corporation or body

(i) which is established by virtue of Her Majesty's prerogative or by an Act of Parliament or on Order in Council or order made under an Act of Parliament or which is established in any other way by a Minister of the Crown in his capacity as a Minister or by z government department;

(ii) at least half of whose revenues derive directly from money provided by Parliament, a levy authorized by an enactment, a fee or charge of any other description so authorized or more than one of those sources; and

(iii) which is wholly or partly constituted by appointment made by Her Majesty or a Minister of the Crown or government department.

(4) No entry shall be made in respect of a corporation or body whose sole activity is, or whose main activities are, included among the activities specified in subsection (5) below.

(5) The activities mentioned in subsection (4) above are:

(a) the provision of education, or the provision of training otherwise than under the Industrial Training Act 1982;

(b) the development of curricula, the conduct of examinations or the validation of educational courses;

(c) the control of entry to any profession or the regulation of the conduct of members of any profession;

(d) the investigation of complaints by members of the public regarding the actions of any person or body, or the supervision or review of such investigations or of steps taken following them.

(6) No entry shall be made in respect of a corporation or body operating in an exclusively or predominantly commercial manner or a corporation carrying on under national ownership an industry or undertaking or part of an industry or undertaking.

(7) Any statutory instrument made by virtue of this section shall be subject to annulment in pursuance of a resolution of either House of Parliament.

(8) In this Act

(a) any reference to a government department to which this Act applies includes a reference to any of the Ministers or officers of such a department; and

(b) any reference to an authority to which this Act applies includes a reference to any members or officers of such an authority.

5. Matters subject to investigation

(1) Subject to the provisions of this section, the Commissioner may investigate any action taken by or on behalf of a government department or other authority to which this Act applies, being action taken in the exercise of administrative functions of that department or authority, in any case where

(a) a written complaint is duly made to a member of the House of Commons by a member of the public who claims to have sustained injustice in consequence of maladministration in connection with the action so taken; and

(b) the complaint is referred to the Commissioner, with the consent of the person who made it, by a member of that House with a request to conduct an investigation thereon.

(2) Except as hereinafter provided, the Commissioner shall not conduct an investigation under this Act in respect of any of the following matters, that is to say

(a) any action in respect of which the person aggrieved has or had a right of appeal, reference or review to or before a tribunal constituted by or under any enactment or by virtue of Her Majesty's prerogative;

(b) any action in respect of which the person aggrieved has or had a remedy by way of proceedings in any court of law:

Provided that the Commissioner may conduct an investigation notwithstanding that the person aggrieved has or had such a right or remedy if satisfied that in the particular circumstances it is not reasonable to expect him to resort or have resorted to it.

(3) Without prejudice to subsection (2) of this section, the Commissioner shall not conduct an investigation under this Act in respect of any such action or matter as is described in Schedule 3 to this Act.

(4) Her Majesty may by Order in Council amend the said Schedule 3 so as to exclude from the provisions of that Schedule such actions or matters as may be described in the Order; and any statutory instrument made by virtue of this subsection shall be subject to annulment in pursuance of a resolution of either House of Parliament.

(5) In determining whether to initiate, continue or discontinue an investigation under this Act, the Commissioner shall, subject to the foregoing provisions of this section, act in accordance with his own discretion; and any question whether a complaint is duly made under this Act shall be determined by the Commissioner.

[(6) For the purposes of this section, administrative functions exercisable by any person appointed by the Lord Chancellor as a member of the administrative staff of any court or tribunal shall be taken to be administrative functions of the Lord Chancellor's Department or, in Northern Ireland, of the Northern Ireland Court Service.]

(7) For the purposes of this section, administrative functions exercisable by any person appointed as a member of the administrative staff of a relevant tribunal (a) by a government department or authority to which this Act applies; or (b) with the consent (whether as to remuneration and other terms and conditions of service or otherwise) of such a department or authority, shall be taken to be administrative functions of that department or authority.

(8) In subsection (7) of this section, "relevant tribunal" means a tribunal listed in Schedule 4 to this Act.

(9) Her Majesty may by Order in Council amend the said Schedule 4 by the alteration or removal of any entry or the insertion of any additional entry; and any statutory instrument made by virtue of this subsection shall be subject to annulment in pursuance of a resolution of either House of Parliament.

6. Provisions relating to complaints

(1) A complaint under this Act may be made by any individual, or by any body of persons whether incorporated or not, not being-:

(a) a local authority or other authority or body constituted for purposes of the public service or of Local government or for the purposes of carrying on under national ownership any industry or undertaking or part of an industry or undertaking;
(b) any other authority or body whose members are appointed by Her Majesty or any Minister of the Crown or government department, or whose revenues consist wholly or mainly of moneys provided by Parliament.

(2) Where the person by whom a complaint might have been made under the foregoing provisions of this Act has died or is for any reason unable to act for himself, the complaint may be made by his personal representative or by a member of his family or other individual suitable to represent him; but except as aforesaid a complaint shall not be entertained under this Act unless made by the person aggrieved himself.

(3) A complaint shall not be entertained under this Act unless it is made to a member of the House of Commons not later than twelve months from the day on which the person aggrieved first had notice of the matters alleged in the complaint; but the Commissioner may conduct an investigation pursuant to a complaint not made within that period if he considers that there are special circumstances which make it proper to do so.

(4) [Except as provided in subsection (5) below] a complaint shall not be entertained under this Act unless the person aggrieved is resident in the United Kingdom (or, if he is dead, was so resident at the time of his death) or the complaint relates to action taken in relation to him while he was present in the United Kingdom or on an installation in a designated area within the meaning of the Continental Shelf Act 1964 or on a ship

registered in the United Kingdom or an aircraft so registered, or in relation to rights or obligations which accrued or arose in the United Kingdom or on such an installation, ship or aircraft.

[(5) A complaint may be entertained under this Act in circumstances not falling within subsection (4) above where

(a) the complaint relates to action taken in any country or territory outside the United Kingdom by an officer (not being an honorary consular officer) in the exercise of a consular function on behalf of the Government of the United Kingdom; and

(b) the person aggrieved is a citizen of the United Kingdom and Colonies who, under section 2 of the Immigration Act 1971, has the right of abode in the United Kingdom.]

7. Procedure in respect of investigations

(1) Where the Commissioner proposes to conduct an investigation pursuant to a complaint under this Act, he shall afford to the principal officer of the department or authority concerned, and to any person who is alleged in the complaint to have taken or authorized the action complained of, an opportunity to comment on any allegations contained in the complaint.

(2) Every such investigation shall be conducted in private, but except as aforesaid the procedure for conducting an investigation shall be such as the Commissioner considers appropriate in the circumstances of the case; and without prejudice to the generality of the foregoing provision the Commissioner may obtain information from such persons and in such manner, and make such inquiries, as he thinks fit, and may determine whether any person may be represented, by counsel or solicitor or otherwise, in the investigation.

(3) The Commissioner may, if he thinks fit, pay to the person by whom the complaint was made and to any other person who attends or furnishes information for the purposes of an investigation under this Act

(a) sums in respect of expenses properly incurred by them;

(b) allowances by way of compensation for the loss of their time,

in accordance with such scales and subject to such conditions as may be determined by the Treasury.

(4) The conduct of an investigation under this Act shall not affect any action taken by the department or authority concerned, or any power or duty of that department or authority to take further action with respect to any matters subject to the investigation; but where the person aggrieved has been removed from the United Kingdom under any Order in force under the Aliens Restriction Acts 1914 and 1919 or under the Commonwealth Immigrants Act 1962, he shall, if the Commissioner so directs, be permitted to re-enter and remain in the United Kingdom, subject to such conditions as the Secretary of State may direct, for the purposes of the investigation.

8. Evidence

(1) For the purposes of an investigation under this Act the Commissioner may require any Minister, officer or member of the department or authority concerned or any other person who in his opinion is able to furnish information or produce documents relevant to the investigation to furnish any such information or produce any such document.

(2) For the purposes of any such investigation the Commissioner shall have the same powers as the Court in respect of the attendance and examination of witnesses (including the administration of oaths or affirmations and the examination of witnesses abroad) and in respect of the production of documents.

(3) No obligation to maintain secrecy or other restriction upon the disclosure of information obtained by or furnished to persons in Her Majesty's service, whether imposed by any enactment or by any rule of law, shall apply to the disclosure of information for the purposes of an investigation under this Act; and the Crown shall not be entitled in relation to any such investigation to any such privilege in respect of the production of documents or the giving of evidence as is allowed by law in legal proceedings.

(4) No person shall be required or authorized by virtue of this Act to furnish any

information or answer any question relating to proceedings of the Cabinet or of any committee of the Cabinet or to produce so much of any document as relates to such proceedings; and for the purposes of this subsection a certificate issued by the Secretary of the Cabinet with the approval of the Prime Minister and certifying that any information, question, document or part of a document so relates shall be conclusive.
(5) Subject to subsection (3) of this section, no person shall be compelled for the purposes of an investigation under this Act to give any evidence or produce any document which he could not be compelled to give or produce in (civil] proceedings before the Court.

9. Obstruction and contempt
(1) If any person without lawful excuse obstructs the Commissioner or any officer of the Commissioner in the performance of his functions under this Act, or is guilty of any act or omission in relation to any investigation under this Act which, if that investigation were a proceeding in the Court, would constitute contempt of court, the Commissioner may certify the offence to the Court.
(2) Where an offence is certified under this section, the Court may inquire into the matter and, after hearing any witnesses who may be produced against or on behalf of the person charged with the offence, and after hearing any statement that may be offered in defence, deal with him in any manner in which the Court could deal with him if he had committed the like offence in relation to the Court.
(3) Nothing in this section shall be construed as applying to the taking of any such action as is mentioned in subsection (4) of section 7 of this Act.

10. Reports by Commissioner
(1) In any case where the Commissioner conducts an investigation under this Act or decides not to conduct such an investigation, he shall send to the member of the House of Commons by whom the request for investigation was made (or if he is no longer a member of that House, to such member of that House as the Commissioner thinks appropriate) a report of the results of the investigation or, as the case may be, a statement of his reasons for not conducting an investigation.
(2) In any case where the Commissioner conducts an investigation under this Act, he shall also send a report of the results of the investigation to the principal officer of the department or authority concerned and to any other person who is alleged in the relevant complaint to have taken or authorized the action complained of.
(3) If, after conducting an investigation under this Act, it appears to the Commissioner that injustice has been caused to the person aggrieved in consequence of maladministration and that the injustice has not been, or will not be, remedied, he may, if he thinks fit, lay before each House of Parliament a special report upon the case.
(4) The Commissioner shall annually lay before each House of Parliament a general report on the performance of his functions under this Act and may from rime to rime lay before each House of parliament such other reports with respect to those functions as he thinks fit.
(5) For the purposes of the law of defamation, any such publication as is hereinafter mentioned shall be absolutely privileged, that is to say
(a) the publication of any matter by the Commissioner in making a report to either House of Parliament for the purposes of this Act;
(b) the publication of any matter by a member of the House of Commons in communicating with the Commissioner or his officers for those purposes or by the Commissioner or his officers in communicating with such a member for those purposes;
(c) the publication by such a member to the person by whom a complaint was made under this Act of a report or statement sent to the member in respect of the complaint in pursuance of section (1) of this section;
(d) the publication by the Commissioner to such a person as is mentioned in subsection (2) of this section of a report to that person in pursuance of that subsection.

11. Provision for secrecy of information

(1) ...

(2) Information obtained by the Commissioner or his officers in the course of or for the purposes of an investigation under this Act shall not be disclosed except

(a) for the purposes of the investigation and of any report to be made thereon under this Act;

(b) for the purposes of any proceedings for an offence under [the Official Secrets Act 1911 to 1989] alleged to have been committed in respect of information obtained by the Commissioner or any of his officers by virtue of this Act or for an offence of perjury alleged to have been committed in the course of an investigation under this Act or for the purposes of an inquiry with a view to the taking of such proceedings; or

(c) for the purposes of any proceedings under section 9 of this Act;

and the Commissioner and his officers shall not be called upon to give evidence in any proceedings (other than such proceedings as aforesaid) of matters coming to his or their knowledge in the course of an investigation under this Act.

[(2A) Where the Commissioner also holds office as a Health Service Commissioner and a person initiates a complaint to him in his capacity as such a Commissioner which relates partly to a matter with respect to which that person has previously initiated a complaint under this Act, or subsequently initiates such a complaint, information obtained by the Commissioner or his officers in the course of or for the purposes of investigating the complaint under this Act may be disclosed for the purposes of his carrying out his functions in relation to the other complaint.]

(3) A Minister of the Crown may give notice in writing to the Commissioner with respect to any document or information specified in the notice, or any class of documents or information so specified, that in the opinion of the Minister the disclosure of that document or information, or of documents or information of that class, would be prejudicial to the safety of the State or otherwise contrary to the public interest; and where such a notice is given nothing in this Act shall be construed as authorizing or requiring the Commissioner or any officer of the Commissioner to communicate to any person or for any purpose any document or information specified in the notice, or any document or information of a class so specified.

(4) The references in this section to a Minister of the Crown include references to the Commissioners of Customs and Excise and the Commissioners of Inland Revenue.

11A. Consultations between Parliamentary Commissioner and Health Service Commissioners

(1) Where, at any stage in the course of conducting an investigation under this Act, the Commissioner forms the opinion that the complaint relates partly to a by a government department or other authority in the exercise of a discretion vested in that department or authority.

Supplemental

12. Interpretation

(1) In this Act the following expressions have the meanings hereby respectively assigned to them, that is to say

"action" includes failure to act, and other expressions connoting action shall be construed accordingly;

"the Commissioner" means the Parliamentary Commissioner for Administration;

"the Court" means, in relation to England and Wales the High Court, in relation to Scotland the Court of Session, and in relation to Northern Ireland the High Court of Northern Ireland;

"enactment" includes an enactment of the Parliament of Northern Ireland and any instrument made by virtue of an enactment;

"officer" includes employee;

"person aggrieved" means the person who claims or is alleged to have sustained such injustice as is mentioned in section 5 (1) (a) of this Act;
"tribunal" includes the person constituting a tribunal consisting of one person.
(2) References in this Act to any enactment are references to that enactment as amended or extended by or under any other enactment.
(3) It is hereby declared that nothing in this Act authorizes or requires the Commissioner to question the merits of a decision taken without maladministration by a government department or other authority in the exercise of a discretion vested in that department or authority.

13. Application to Northern Ireland
(1) Subject to the provisions of this section, this Act extends to Northern Ireland.
(2) Nothing in this section shall be construed as authorizing the inclusion among the departments and authorities to which this Act applies of any department of the Government of Northern Ireland, or any authority [or body] established by or with the authority of the Parliament of Northern Ireland; but this Act shall apply to any such department [authority or body], in relation to any action taken by them as agent for a department or authority to which this Act applies, as it applies to the last-mentioned department or authority.
(3) In section 6 of this Act the references to a Minister of the Crown or government department and to Parliament shall include references to a Minister or department of the Government of Northern Ireland and to the Parliament of Northern Ireland.
(4) In section 8 of this Act the references to the Cabinet shall include references to the (Northern Ireland Executive], and in relation to (that Executive) for the reference to the Prime Minister there shall be substituted a reference to the Prime Minister of Northern Ireland.

14. Short title and commencement
(1) This Act may be cited as the Parliamentary Commissioner Act 1967.
(2) This Act shall come into force on such date as Her Majesty may by Order in Council appoint.
(3) A complaint under this Act may be made in respect of matters (whenever arising]; and for the purposes of subsection (3) of section 6 of this Act any time elapsing between the date of the passing and the date of the commencement of this Act (but not any time before the first of those dates) shall be disregarded.

Schedule 1
Pensions and other benefits
[...]

Schedule 2
Departments etc. subject to investigation
[...]

Schedule 3

Section 5
Matters Not Subject to Investigation
1. Action taken in matters certified by a Secretary of State or other Minister of the Crown to affect relations or dealings between the Government of the United Kingdom and any other Government or any international organization of States or Governments.

2. Action taken, in any country or territory outside the United Kingdom, by or on behalf of any officer representing or acting under the authority of Her Majesty in respect of the United Kingdom, or any other officer of the Government of the United Kingdom [other

than action which is taken by an officer (not being an honorary consular officer) in the exercise of a consular function on behalf of the Government of the United Kingdom ...]

3. Action taken in connection with the administration of the government of any country or territory outside the United Kingdom which forms part of Her Majesty's dominions or in which Her Majesty has jurisdiction.

4. Action taken by the Secretary of State under the Extradition Act 1870(, the Fugitive Offenders Act 1967 or the Extradition Act 1989].

5. Action taken by or with the authority of the Secretary of State for the purposes of investigating crime or of protecting the security of the State, including action so taken with respect to passports.

6. The commencement or conduct of civil or criminal proceedings before any court of law in the United Kingdom, of proceedings at any place under the Naval Discipline Act 1957, the Army Act 1955 or the Air Force Act 1955, or of proceedings before any intentional court or tribunal.

[6A. Action taken by any person appointed by the Lord Chancellor as a member of the administrative staff of any court or tribunal, so far as that action is taken at the direction, or on the authority (whether express or implied), of any person acting in a judicial capacity or in his capacity as a member of the tribunal.]

[6B. (1) Action taken by any member of the administrative staff of a relevant tribunal, so far as that action is taken at the direction, or on the authority (whether express or implied), of any person acting in his capacity as a member of the tribunal. (2) In this paragraph, "relevant tribunal" has the meaning given by section 5(8) of this.

7. Any exercise of the prerogative of mercy or of the power of a Secretary of State to make a reference in respect of any person to the Court of Appeal, the High Court of Justiciary or the Courts-Martial Appeal Court.

8. Action taken on behalf of the Minister of Health or the Secretary of State by a [(Health Authority, a Special Health Authority] (except the Rampton Hospital Review Board] [... the Rampton Hospital Board,] [the Broadmoor Hospital Board or the Moss Side and Park Lane Hospitals Board,] ... a Health Board or the Common Services Agency for the Scottish Health Service [by the Dental Practice Board or the Scottish Dental Practice Board]], or by the Public Health Laboratory Service Board.

9. Action taken in matters relating to contractual or other commercial transactions, whether within the United Kingdom or elsewhere, being transactions of a government department or authority to which this Act applies or of any such authority or body as is mentioned in paragraph (a) or (b) of subsection (1) of section 6 of this Act and not being transactions for or relating to- (a) the acquisition of land compulsorily or in circumstances in which it could be acquired compulsorily; (b) the disposal as surplus of land acquired compulsorily or in such circumstances as aforesaid.

10. [(1)] Action taken in respect of appointments or removals, pay, discipline, superannuation or other personnel matters, in relation to

(a) service in any of the armed forces of the Crown, including reserve and auxiliary and cadet forces;
(b) service in any office or employment under the Crown or under any authority [to which this Act applies]; or
(c) service in any office or employment, or under any contract for services, in respect of which power to take action, or to determine or approve the action to be taken, in such matters is vested in Her Majesty, any Minister of the Crown or any such authority as aforesaid.

[(2) Sub-paragraph (1)(c) above shall not apply to any action (not otherwise excluded from investigation by this Schedule) which is taken by the Secretary of State in connection with:

(a) the provision of information relating to the terms and conditions of any employment covered by an agreement entered into by him under section 12(1) of the Overseas Development and Co-operation Act 1980 or
(b) the provision of any allowance, grant or supplement or any benefit (other than those relating to superannuation) arising from the designation of any person in accordance with such an agreement.

11. The grant of honours, awards or privileges within the gift of the Crown, including the grant of Royal Charters.

SCHEDULE 4

Section 5(8)
Relevant Tribunals For Purposes of Section 5(7)
Tribunals constituted in Great Britain under regulations made under section 4 of the Vaccine Damage Payments Act 1979.

Child support appeal tribunals constituted under section 21 of the Child Support Act 1991.

Social security appeal tribunals constituted under section 41 of the Social Security Administration Act 1992.

Disability appeal tribunals constituted under section 43 of that Act. Medical appeal tribunals constituted under section 50 of that Act.]

The Commission for Racial Equality

Christopher Boothman*

Tasks and Competencies

The commission for Racial Equality (CRE) is a statutory body created by Act of Parliament: the Race Relations Act 1976 [RRA]. It replaced earlier arrangements under the Race Relations acts of 1965 and 1968. The CRE's mission is to work for a just society which gives everyone an equal chance to work learn and live free from discrimination and prejudice and from the fear of racial harassment and violence.

The three central duties which inform all the CRE's work, are:

(a) to work towards the elimination of discrimination on grounds of colour, race, nationality or ethnic or national origins;
(b) to promote equality of opportunity and good relations between persons of different racial groups;
(c) to keep the working of the Race Relations Act under review and when required to draw up proposals for its amendment.

Other important statutory duties include:

- discharging its functions in accordance with arrangements approved by the Home Secretary;
- reporting annually to the Home Secretary on the work of the CRE;
- keeping proper accounts and preparing a statement each accounting year for the Home Secretary and Auditor General;
- considering every application for assistance submitted by any individual who believes they are victim of racial discrimination;
- keeping a register of non-discrimination notices.

The central duties inform all the CRE's work. The duty to work towards the elimination of discrimination sets the context for the CRE's law enforcement powers. In order to fulfil its duties the CRE has the following competencies:

- to appoint staff;
- to give advice or other assistance to individual victims of discrimination in connection with legal action under the RRA
- to give financial or other assistance to organizations which appear to be

*Commissioner for Racial Equality.

K. Hossain et al. (eds), Human Rights Commissions and Ombudsman Offices, 691–730.

concerned with the promotion of equality of opportunity and good relations between persons of different racial groups;
- to bring certain kinds of legal action in its own name against alleged discriminators;
- to conduct formal investigations;
- to demand information in connection with formal investigations;
- to issue non-discrimination notices in connection with formal investigations;
- to issue Codes of Practice.

Codes of Practice

In practice there is a detailed procedure which involves the publication of a draft code, extensive consultation, modification of the draft code after taking account of representations followed by approval by the relevant Minister. The Minister is required to approve the draft code or publish details of his reasons for withholding approval. Upon approval the draft code is required to be laid before both Houses of Parliament and subject to the negative resolution procedure. If no such resolution is passed within 40 days the Commission can issue the code in the form of the draft and it will come into force at such time as determined by the Minister. The Commission may modify existing codes of practice but is required to follow the same procedure as for the issue of a new code.

A failure to observe a code does not itself render a person liable to legal or administrative proceedings. However in any court or tribunal proceedings any breach of a code is admissible as evidence which can be taken into account in determining whether or nor an act of discrimination has occurred.

Rights

The RRA creates no general rights for the individual as such. However, it does render certain specified acts or types of behaviour as unlawful in specified fields of activity. The main types of unlawful act/behaviour that an individual can challenge are:

- direct racial discrimination
- indirect racial discrimination and
- victimisation
- aiding unlawful facts.

Direct Discrimination

This occurs when a person is treated less favourably on "racial grounds" than others in the same or similar circumstances. "Racial grounds" include not only race but also colour, nationality (including citizenship) and ethnic or national origin.

Examples: A person is denied a job or service because they are Black. A person is denied a job or service because they are American. A person is denied a job or service because of their partner's race.

Indirect Discrimination

There are four elements to indirect racial discrimination:

- the application of a rule or requirement which is essential and is applied to all
- a far smaller proportion of people of your racial group can comply with the rule or requirement than the proportion of people of other racial groups;
- there is no reasonable justification for the rule or requirement;
- you are disadvantaged by the rule;

Example: A stated requirement that all job applicants must be 6 ft. tall will adversely affect many racial groups who are generally much shorter. This height requirement will be unlawful if there is no reasonable explanation for it. An organization operating a practice of not providing services to a part of a town where there is a high proportion of people from a certain racial group.

Victimisation

Unlawful victimisation occurs where a person is treated less favourable as a result of making a complaint of racial discrimination or helping someone else make a complaint.

Example: Where a white doorman refuses to follow an instruction to bar black people from entering a club and is dismissed as a consequence.

Aiding Unlawful Acts

Anyone who knowingly aids another to act unlawfully under the RRA is treated as if they had committed the act themselves. In a related provision employers are vicariously liable for the acts of employees.

Commission Named Proceedings

As well as assisting cases brought by individuals, the Commission has the power to bring certain types of proceedings which relate to following types of unlawful act or behaviour:

- discriminatory advertisements;
- discriminatory instructions;
- pressure to discriminate;
- discriminatory practices
- persistent discrimination.

Discriminatory Advertisements

It is unlawful to publish or cause to be published an advertisement which indicates or might reasonably be taken to indicate an intention to discriminate on the grounds of race. The term "advertisement" includes every form of advertisement, whether to the public or not, and whether in a newspaper or other publication, by television or radio, by display of notices, signs, labels, show cards or goods, by distribution of samples, circulars, catalogues, price lists or other material, by exhibition of pictures, models or films, or in any other way. It is a criminal offence knowingly or recklessly to make such a statement which is found to be materially false or misleading. The offence carries a fine of £400 upon summary conviction.

Instructions to Discriminate

It is unlawful for a person in authority to instruct or influence another to do an act of unlawful discrimination. It is also unlawful to procure or attempt to procure the doing of such an act. These phrases have a wide meaning and cover the use of words which bring about or attempt to bring about a certain course of action.

Pressure to Discriminate

It is unlawful for any person to induce, or attempt to induce, a person to do any act of unlawful racial discrimination. The term "induce" means to persuade or prevail upon or to bring about. A mere request to discriminate is caught. The Act also prohibits attempted inducement and indirect pressure to discriminate.

Discriminatory Practices

The CRE is empowered to take advance action against practices or arrangements which would be discriminatory (requirements or conditions) if they were to be applied to members of particular racial groups.

Persistent Discrimination

If a person has been subject to a finding of unlawful discrimination by a tribunal or is the subject of a current non-discrimination notice the Commission may apply to a county court for an injunction if it appears that unless restrained that person will repeat discriminatory acts. If the court is satisfied that the application is well founded it may grant an injunction or order on the terms applied or more limited terms.

Judicial Review

The Commission has the power to apply to the High Court for judicial review of any racially discriminatory decisions made by public bodies (generally local or central government). It can assist individuals to seek judicial review where there is no other appropriate remedy.

Specified Fields

The Race Relations Act applies to certain specified fields only:

- job application and employment, including police, armed forces
- contract workers, including barristers

- partnership
- membership or benefits of trade unions, employers organizations, trades or professional organizations;
- bodies who confer authorization or qualifications for professions
- persons who provide vocational training
- employment agencies
- education
- housing
- planning decisions
- the provision of goods, facilities and services to the public
- membership of clubs.

Limitation Period

In relation to employment related discrimination individuals are generally required to submit a notice of complaint to an Industrial Tribunal within 3 months of knowledge of the act. In relation to service related discrimination individuals are generally required to issue proceedings within 6 months of knowledge of the act. With regard to the types of legal action the CRE can take itself the limitation is generally 6 months but it can be 3 months. There is no stated limitation period in respect of the power of formal investigation.

Organization

The CRE is a body corporate consisting of at least 8 but not more than 15 Commissioners who are appointed by the Government Minister with responsibility for Home Affairs – the Home Secretary. Commissioners can only be removed by the Home Secretary on specified grounds.

Commissioners may be appointed either full time or part time. The Home Secretary is required to appoint a Chairman and at least one Deputy Chairman from among the Commissioners. By convention a full time Chairman is appointed for 5 years and two part time Deputy Chairmen are appointed for 2 years. The other Commissioners are appointed for two years periods which can be extended. They are remunerated for attendance at specified meetings or for specified work.

Although the CRE is Government appointed and Government funded it is regarded as independent because it has a legal identity, duties and powers in its own right. Although it has a special relationship with the Government, the CRE does not shirk from taking or supporting law enforcement action against Government Departments and Government officials.

The CRE is funded by a direct grant of approximately £14 Million from the Government (Home Office). The budget is determined by the Treasury in consultation with the Home Office as part of the Public Expenditure Budget exercise. The CRE generally agrees a breakdown of its budget with the Home Office, in advance, in terms of salaries for Commissioners and staff, overheads, legal budget and grants to external organizations. However, once the funds are received there is considerable flexibility in how the money can be spent limited only to duties and powers.

Geographical Remit

The CRE covers the whole of England, Wales and Scotland. There is a separate CRE for Northern Ireland which the Government proposes to merge with the Equal Opportunities Commission for Northern Ireland, the Fair Employment Commission for Northern Ireland and the Northern Ireland Disability Council, to form a single Equality Commission.

Organizational Structure

The staff structure is headed by an Executive Director who is appointed by Chairman and Deputy Chairmen. The Executive Director leads the Corporate Management Team and is Accounting Officer for the organization. The CRE mainly employs its own staff, currently approximately 200. The majority of staff in the CRE are organized in three geographical teams London & South, Midlands & Wales, North & Scotland. It has offices in London, Birmingham, Leicester, Cardiff, Leeds, Manchester and Edinburgh. There are also a number of staff in central teams including Legal, Communications & Campaigns and Equality Policy Consultancy and Central Services.

Procedures

Applications for Assistance

The CRE has discretion to provide advice or other assistance to individual victims of racial discrimination upon application on the ground that:

(a) the case raises a question of principle;
(b) it is unreasonable to expect the applicant to deal with the case unaided, having regard to the complexity of the case or any other matter; or
(c) some other special consideration applies.

Other factors that are relevant to the decision making exercise are:

(a) whether or not the case has a reasonable prospect of success;
(b) the cost implications of the case.

In practice the Commission has a wide discretion as to whether or not to provide assistance and also as to how much assistance to provide if any. The assistance may include the giving of advice, attempting to procure a settlement, arranging advice by a lawyer, arranging representation or other assistance.

One of the CRE's main priorities is to ensure that all victims of discrimination have access to advice, assistance and where necessary representation.

The Commission is required to process every written application for assistance, in connection with an actual or prospective complaint under the Act, within a period of two months of receipt. The Commission is required to:

(a) consider the application after making such inquires as it thinks fit;
(b) decide whether or not to grant it; and
(c) inform the applicant of the decision in writing stating whether or not the Commission will provide assistance and what form it will take.

Every six weeks a Committee of CRE Commissioners considers and makes decisions on applications for assistance.

Such Inquiries as it Thinks Fit

In order to comply with the duty to conduct an inquiry, the Commission will assist individuals to prepare a Race Relations Act section 65 questionnaire to serve on the respondent. The questionnaire serves a dual purpose. If it is issued promptly and answered fully it can dissuade an applicant from pursuing a case in the tribunal. It also assists the Commission to make a judgement on the merits of the case. The CRE expects questionnaires to be completed and returned within 21 days of service because of the strict statutory time limits on decision making. Failure to complete and return a questionnaire may result in the Commission in representation being provided to an applicant. The statutory procedure by way of questionnaire is the way in which parliament has made provision for an applicant to advance his or her case of discrimination. Tribunals are encouraged to take a serious view of any unsatisfactory answers and have ample power to draw adverse inferences (Carrington v Helix Lighting Ltd (1990) IRLR 6 EAT). In relation to disputes about job appointments, information as to the qualifications of successful candidates and other relevant information should generally be disclosed. However employers are not obliged to disclose names and addresses (Oxford v Department of Health and Social Security (1977) IRLR 225 EAT).

Remedies

Prior to 1994 there was a limit on how much an individual could be awarded in an employment related matter of £ 11,000. The Government removed the limit by enacting new legislation as a consequence of a ruling of the European Court that held that a ceiling for sex discrimination cases was contrary to the Treaty of Rome. Recent awards have been made in De Souza v London Borough of Lambeth; Chan v London Borough of Hackney. Settlements have been reached in Curry v Goldman Sachs.

Formal Investigation

The CRE has the power to initiate formal investigations and must conduct a formal investigation if required to do so by the Home Secretary. There are two types of formal investigation that can be conducted by the Commission, "general" and "named person" (or belief). A general investigation can be conducted for any purpose connected to the Commission's general section 43 duties i.e. the Commission has the power to mount a general investigation into any matter which impacts on race relations in its widest sense even if the matter does not concern unlawful racial discrimination. (Home Office v CRE). A named person investigation can only be proposed when the Commission has grounds to believe that an act of unlawful racial discrimination has occurred (in Re Prestige plc (1984) IRLR 166 HL). To enable the Commission to embark upon a named person investigation, it is enough that there is mere reasonable suspicion i.e. material before the Commission sufficient to raise in the minds of reasonable men possessed of the experience of covert racial discrimination that has been acquired by the Commission, a suspicion that the person named may have carried out acts of racial discrimination of a kind which it is proposed to investigate. It is not necessary for the Commission to believe that an act of discrimination has occurred on a balance of probability (London Borough of Hillingdon v CRE (1982) IRLR 424 HL). The Commission must draw up terms of reference before mounting any investigation and give the required notice. In relation to general investigations there is a duty to give general notice to all persons who are likely to be affected by it. A general notice appearing in relevant national or local newspapers or journals is sufficient. However a more detailed procedure must be followed to embark upon a named person or belief investigation. Prior to embarking upon a named person investigation the Commission is obliged to draw up and serve terms of reference specifying the type of acts of discrimination which the Commission believes have occurred. The terms of reference then define the scope of the investigation. However the Commission may draw the terms of the investigation quite wide if there is justification to infer a general policy of racial discrimination based on individual acts.

In connection with named person investigations the Commission is also required to:

(a) draw up and serve grounds for belief;
(b) offer the named person an opportunity to make oral or written representations, or both;
(c) inform the named person of the right of representation by counsel, solicitor or any other person who is not unsuitable.

Power to Obtain Information

During the course of a named person investigation the Commission can require anyone to produce information or attend an investigation, by serving a notice in the prescribed form, so long as the information or evidence could be required by the High Court. If a person fails to comply with a notice or the commission has reasonable cause to suspect that he will not comply with it, a county court order can be sought requiring compliance. Further it is a criminal offence to:

(a) wilfully alter, suppress, conceal or destroy a document which has been requested by a notice or order to produce; or
(b) knowingly or recklessly make a statement which is materially false in complying with a notice or order.

On summary conviction a person will be liable to a fine. The power to obtain information can only be exercised with the authority of the Home Secretary in the case of general investigations.

Disclosure of Information

It is unlawful for the Commission to disclose any information it obtains in connection with a formal investigation unless:

(a) it has the consent of those who have provided the information;
(b) it has a court order;

(c) the information is in the form of a summary or general statement that does not identify individuals; or
(d) the information constitutes a report of the Commission's findings.

Non-discrimination Notices

If during a named person investigation the Commission becomes satisfied that a contravention of the Act has occurred, it is empowered to issue a non-discrimination notice. However before a notice can be served the Commission must first:

(a) give notice that it is minded to issue a non-discrimination notice, specifying the grounds on which it is based;
(b) offer an opportunity of making oral or written representations or both within a period of not less than 21 days; and
(c) take account of any representations made

At the representations stage the CRE is not obliged to permit the witnesses upon whose evidence it has relied to be cross examined (CRE ex parte Cottrell & Rothon (1980) IRLR 279 HC).

Following the representations stage the Commission may serve a non-discrimination notice if it is satisfied on a balance of probabilities that the person is committing or has committed discriminatory acts. Such a notice may require a person:

(a) not to commit such acts; and
(b) where compliance involves changing practices or other arrangements:
    (i) to inform the Commission that changes have been effected and what those changes are; and
    (ii) to take such steps as may be reasonably required by the notice for the purpose of affording that information to others concerned.

In addition, a non-discrimination notice may also require such other information reasonably required in order to prove the notice has been complied with. It may specify the manner and form in which any information is to be furnished.

There is a right of appeal against the service of a notice which must be made within six weeks after the service of the notice to an industrial tribunal. Since an appeal can be made to an industrial tribunal, courts will not ordinarily intervene by way of judicial review (CRE ex parte Westminster City Council (1984) IRLR 230 HC). If the tribunal feels that the appeal is well founded, it may quash any requirement in the notice or substitute different requirements. The tribunal may examine not only the reasonableness of the requirements in the notice but also the facts that gave rise to the finding of discrimination, including evidence from witnesses (CRE v Amari Plastics Ltd (1982) IRLR 252 CA). A non-discrimination notice only becomes final after the right of appeal period has expired or the industrial tribunal has ratified or altered the notice or the appeal has been withdrawn or abandoned. Once it becomes final it remains in force for five years and failure to observe it's requirements can lead to enforcement proceedings. A notice becomes final after the lapse of five years.

Recommendations and Public Reports of Investigations

During or after an investigation the Commission may make recommendations:
(a) to any person whose policies or practices should be changed with a view to promoting equality of opportunity; or
(b) to the Home Secretary for changes to the law or otherwise.

The Commission has a duty to draw up a report of its findings in formal investigations and to make the report available to the public. The respondents named in the report are given an opportunity to comment on a draft and the Commission will take representations into account.

Investigations reports will either be published or made available for inspection at the Commission's offices.

There is no power to order financial remedy.

LEGISLATION

The Race Relations Act 1976

(1976 c. 74)

Part I
Discrimination to Which Act Applies

1. Racial discrimination
(1) A person discriminates against another in any circumstances relevant for the purposes of any provision of this Act if
(a) on racial grounds he treats that other less favourably than he treats or would treat other persons; or
(b) he applies to that other a requirement or condition which he applies or would apply equally to persons not of the same racial group as that other but
(i) which is such that the proportion of persons of the same racial group as that other who can comply with it is considerably smaller than the proportion of persons not of that racial group who can comply with it; and
(ii) which he cannot show to be justifiable irrespective of the colour, race, nationality or ethnic or national origins of the person to whom it is applied; and
(iii) which is to the detriment of that other because he cannot comply with it.
(2) It is hereby declared that, for the purposes of this Act, segregating a person from other persons on racial grounds is treating him less favourably than they are treated.

2. Discrimination by way of victimisation
(1) A person ("the discriminator") discriminates against another person ("the person victimised") in any circumstances relevant for the purposes of any provision of this Act if he treats the person victimised less favourably than in those circumstances he treats or would treat other persons, and does so by reason that the person victimised has
(a) brought proceedings against the discriminator or any other person under this Act; or
(b) given evidence or information in connection with proceedings brought by any person against the discriminator or any other person under this Act; or
(c) otherwise done anything under or by reference to this Act in relation to the discriminator or any other person; or
(d) alleged that the discriminator or any other person has committed an act which (whether or not the allegation so states) would amount to a contravention of this Act,
or by reason that the discriminator knows that the person victimised intends to do any

of those things, or suspects that the person victimised has done, or intends to do, any of them.
(2) Subsection (1) does not apply to treatment of a person by reason of any allegation made by him if the allegation was false and not made in good faith.

3. Meaning of "racial grounds"; "racial group" etc.
(1) In this Act, unless the context otherwise requires
"racial grounds" means any of the following grounds, namely colour, race nationality or ethnic or national origins
"racial group" means a group of persons defined by reference to colour, race, nationality or ethnic or national origins, and references to a person's racial group refer to any racial group into which he falls.
(2) The fact that a racial group comprises two or more distinct racial groups does not prevent it from constituting a particular racial group for the purposes of this Act.
(3) In this Act
(a) references to discrimination refer to any discrimination falling within section 1 or 2; and
(b) references to racial discrimination refer to any discrimination falling within section 1 and related expressions shall be construed accordingly.
(4) A comparison of the case of a person of a particular racial group with that of a person not of that group under section 1 (1) must be such that the relevant circumstances in the one case are the same, or not materially different, in the other.

Part II
Discrimination in The Employment Field

Discrimination by employers
4. Discrimination against applicants and employees
(1) It is unlawful for a person in relation to employment by him at an establishment in Great Britain, to discriminate against another
(a) in the arrangements he makes for the purpose of determining who should be offered that employment; or
(b) in the terms on which he offers him that employment; or
(c) by refusing or deliberately omitting to offer him that employment.
(2) It is unlawful for a person, in the case of a person employed by him at an establishment in Great Britain, to discriminate against that employee
(a) in the terms of employment which he affords him; or
(b) in the way he affords him access to opportunities for promotion, transfer or training, or to any other benefits, facilities or services, or by refusing or deliberately omitting to afford him access to them; or
(c) by dismissing him, or subjecting him to any other detriment.
(3)Except in relation to discrimination falling within section 2, subsections (1) and (2) do not apply to employment for the purposes of a private household.
(4) Subsection (2) does not apply to benefits, facilities or services of any description if the employer is concerned with the provision (for payment or not) of benefits, facilities or services of that description to the public, or to a section of the public comprising the employee in question, unless
(a) that provision differs in a material respect from the provision of the benefits, facilities or services by the employer to his employees; or
(b) the provision of the benefits, facilities or services to the employee in question is regulated by his contract of employment; or
(c) the benefits, facilities or services relate to training.

5. Exceptions for genuine occupational qualifications
(1) In relation to racial discrimination

(a) section,4 (I) (a) or (c) does not apply to any employment where being of a particular racial group is a genuine occupational qualification for the job; and
(b) section 4 (z) (b) does not apply to opportunities for promotion or transfer to, or training for, such employment.
(2) Being of a particular racial group is a genuine occupational qualification for a job only where
(a) the job involves participation in a dramatic performance or other entertainment in a capacity for which a person of that racial group is required for reasons of authenticity; or
(b) the j ob involves participation as an artist's or photographic model in the production of a work of art, visual image or sequence of visual images for which a person of that racial group is required for reasons of authenticity; or
(c) the job involves working in a place where food or drink is (for payment or not) provided to and consumed by members of the public or a section of the public in a particular setting for which, in that job, a person of that racial group is required for reasons of authenticity; or
(d) the holder of the job provides persons of that racial group with personal services promoting their welfare, and those services can most effectively be provided by a person of that racial group.
(3) Subsection (2) applies where some only of the duties of the job fall within paragraph (a), (b), (c) or (d) as well as where all of them do.
(4) Paragraph (a), (b), (c) or (d) of subsection (2) does not apply in relation to the filling of a vacancy at a time when the employer already has employees of the racial group in question
(a) who are capable of carrying out the duties falling within that paragraph; and
(b) whom it would be reasonable to employ on those duties; and
(c) whose numbers are sufficient to meet the employer's likely requirements in respect of those duties without undue inconvenience.

6. Exception for employment intended to provide training in skills to be exercised outside Great Britain
Nothing in section 4 shall render unlawful any act done by an employer for the benefit of a person not ordinarily resident in Great Britain in or in connection with employing him at an establishment in Great Britain, where the purpose of that employment is to provide him with training in skills which he appears to the employer to intend to exercise wholly outside Great Britain.

7. Discrimination against contract workers
(1) This section applies to any work for a person ("the principal") which is available for doing by individuals ("contract workers") who are employed not by the principal himself but by another person, who supplies them under a contract made with the principal.
(2) It is unlawful for the principal, in relation to work to which this section applies, to discriminate against a contract worker
(a) in the terms on which he allows him to do that work; or
(b) by not allowing him to do it or continue to do it; or
(c) in the way he affords him access to any benefits, facilities or services or by refusing or deliberately omitting to afford him access to them; or
(d) by subjecting him to any other detriment.
(3) The principal does not contravene subsection (2) (U) by doing any act in relation to a person not of a particular racial group at a time when, if the work were to be done by a person taken into the principal's employment, being of that racial group would be a genuine occupational qualification for the job.
(4) Nothing in this section shall render unlawful any act done by the principal for the benefit of a contract worker not ordinarily resident in Great Britain in or in connection with allowing him to do work to which this section applies, where the purpose of his

being allowed to do that work is to provide him with training skills which he appears to the principal to intend to exercise wholly outside Great Britain.
(5) Subsection (2) (c) does not apply to benefits, facilities or services of any description if the principal is concerned with the provision (for payment or not) of benefits facilities or services of that description to the public, or to a section of the public to which the contract worker in question belongs, unless that provision differs in a material respect from the provision of the benefits, facilities or services by the principal to his contract workers.

8. Meaning of employment at establishment in Great Britain
(1) For the purposes of this Part ("the relevant purposes"), employment is to be regarded as being at an establishment in Great Britain unless the employee does his work wholly or mainly outside Great Britain.
(2) In relation to
(a) employment on board a ship registered at a port of registry in Great Britain; or.
(b) employment on an aircraft or hovercraft registered in the United Kingdom and operated by a person who has his principal place of business, or is ordinarily resident in Great Britain, other than an aircraft or hovercraft while so operated in pursuance of a contract with a person who has his principal place of business, or is ordinarily resident, outside the United Kingdom,
subsection (1) shall have effect as if the words "or mainly" were omitted.
(3) In the case of employment on board a ship registered at a port of registry in Great Britain (except where the employee does his work wholly outside Great Britain) the ship shall for the relevant purposes be deemed to be the establishment.
(4) Where work is not done at an establishment it shall be treated for the relevant purposes as done at the establishment from which it is done or (where it is not done from any establishment) at the establishment with which it has the closest connection.
(5) In relation to employment concerned with exploration of the sea bed or subsoil or the exploitation of their natural resources Her Majesty may by Order in Council provide that subsections (1) to (3) shall have 'effect as if in both subsection (1) and subsection (3) the last reference to Great Britain included any area for the time being designated under section I (7) of the Continental Shelf Act 1964, except an area or part of an area in which the law of Northern Ireland applies.
(6) An Order in Council under subsection (5) may provide that, in relation to the employment to which the Order applies, this Part is to have effect with such modifications as are specified in the Order.
(7) An Order in Council under subsection (5) shall be of no effect unless a draft of the Order has been laid before and approved by resolution of each House of Parliament.

9. Exception for seamen recruited abroad
(1) Nothing in section 4 shall render unlawful any act done by an employer in or in connection with employment by him on any ship in the case of a person who applied or was engaged for that employment outside Great Britain.
(2) Nothing in section 7 shall, as regards work to which that section applies, render unlawful any act done by the principal in or in connection with such work on any ship in the case of a contract worker who was engaged outside Great Britain by the person by whom he is supplied.
(3) Subsections (2) and (2) do not apply to employment or work concerned with exploration of the sea bed or subsoil or the exploitation of their natural resources in any area for the time being designated under section 1 (7) of the Continental Shelf Act 1964, not being an area or part of an area in which the law of Northern Ireland applies.
(4) For the purposes of subsection (1) a person brought to Great Britain with a view to his entering into an agreement in Great Britain to be employed on any ship shall be treated and having applied for the employment outside Great Britain.

10. Partnerships
It is unlawful for a firm consisting of six or more partners, in relation to a position as partner in the firm, to discriminate against a person
(a) in the arrangements they make for the purpose of determining who should be offered that position; or
(b) in the terms on which they offer him that position; or
(c) by refusing or deliberately omitting to offer him that position; or
(d) in a case where the person already holds that position
 (i) in the way they afford him success to any benefits, facilities or services, or by refusing or deliberately omitting to afford him access to them; or
 (ii) by expelling him from that position, or subjecting him to any other detriment.
(2) Subsection (1) shall apply in relation to persons proposing to form themselves into a partnership as it applies in relation to a firm.
(3) Subsection (1) (a) and (c) do not apply to a position as partner where, if it were employment, being of a particular racial group would he a genuine occupational qualification for the job.
(4) In the case of a limited partnership references in this section to a partner shall be construed as references to a general partner as defined in section g or the Limited Partnerships Act 1997.

11. Trade unions etc.
(1) This section applies to an organization of workers, an organization of employers, or any other organization whose members carry on a particular provision or trade for the purposes of which the organization exists.
(2) It is unlawful for an organization to which this section applies, in the case of a person who is not a member of the organization, to discriminate against him
(a) in the terms on which it is prepared to admit him to membership; or
(b) by refusing, or deliberately omitting to accept, his application for membership.
(3) It is unlawful for an organization to which this section applies, in the case of a person who is a member of the organization, to discriminate against him
(a) in the way it affords him access to any benefits, facilities or services, or by refusing or deliberately omitting to afford him access to them; or
(b) by depriving him of membership, or varying the terms on which he is a member; or
(c) by subjecting him to any other deterrent.

12. Qualifying bodies
It is unlawful for an authority or body which can confer an authorization or qualification which is needed for, or facilitates, engagement in a particular profession or trade to discriminate against a person
(a) in the terms on which it is prepared to confer on him that authorization or qualification; or
(b) by refusing, or deliberately omitting to grant, his application for it; or (c) by withdrawing it from him or varying the terms on which he holds it.
(2) In this section
(a) "authorization or qualification" includes recognition, registration, enrolment, approval and certification;
(b) "confer" includes renew or extend.
(3) Subsection (1) does not apply to discrimination which is rendered unlawful by section 17 or 18.

13. Vocational training bodies
It is unlawful for a person to whom this subsection applies, in the case of an individual seeking or undergoing training which would help to fit him for any employment, to discriminate against him
(a) in terms on which that person affords him access to any training courses or other facilities; or

(b) by refusing or deliberately omitting to afford him such access; or
(c) by terminating his training.
(2) Subsection (1) applies to:
(a) industrial training; boards established under section i of the Industrial Training Act 1964;
(b) the Manpower Services Commission, the Employment Service Agency, and the Training Services Agency;
(c) any association which comprises employers and has as its principal object, or one of its principal objects, affording their employees access to training facilities;
(d) any other person providing facilities for training for employment, being a person designated for the purposes of this paragraph in an order made by the Secretary of State.
(3) Subsection (1) does not apply to discrimination which is rendered unlawful by section 17 or 18.

14. Employment agencies
(1) It is unlawful for an employment agency to discriminate against a person
(a) in the terms on which the agency offers to provide any of its services; or
(b) by refusing or deliberately omitting to provide any of its services; or
(c) in the way it provides any of its services.
(2) It is unlawful for a local education authority or an education authority to do any act in the performance of its functions under section 8 of the Employment and Training Act 1973 which constitutes discrimination.
(3) References in subsection (1) to the services of an employment agency include guidance on careers and any other services related to employment.
(4) This section does not apply if the discrimination only concerns employment which the employer could lawfully refuse to offer the person in question.
(5) An employment agency or local education authority or an education authority shall not be subject to any liability under this section if it proves
(a) that it acted in reliance on a statement made to it by the employer to the effect that, by reason of the operation of subsection (4), its action would not be unlawful; and
(b) that it was reasonable for it to rely on the statement.
(6) A person who knowingly or recklessly makes a statement such as is referred to in subsection (5) (a) which in a material respect is false or misleading commits an offence, and shall be liable on summary conviction to a fine not exceeding £400.

15. Manpower Services Commission etc.
(1) It is unlawful for any of the following bodies to discriminate in the provision of facilities or services under section 2 of the Employment and Training Act 1973–
(a) the Manpower Service Commission
(b) the Employment Service Agency;
(c) the Training Services Agency.
(2)This section does not apply in a case where :
(a) section 13 applies; or
(b) the body is acting as an employment agency.

16. Police
(1) For the purposes of this Part, the holding of the office of constable shall be treated as employment
(a) by the chief officer of police as respects any act done by him in relation to a constable or that office;
(b) by the police authority as respects any act done by them in relation to a constable or that office.
(2) There shall be paid out of the police fund

(a) any compensation, costs or expenses awarded against a chief officer of police in any proceedings brought against him under this Act, and any costs or expenses incurred by him in any such proceedings so far as not recovered by him in the proceedings; and
(b) any sum required by a chief officer of police for the settlement of any claim made against him under this Act if the settlement is approved by the police authority.

(3) Any proceedings under this Act which, by virtue of subsection (1) would be against a chief officer of police shall be brought against the chief office: of police for the time being or, m the case of a vacancy in that office, against the person for the time being performing the functions of that office; and references in subsection (2) to the chief officer of police shall be construed accordingly.

(4) Subsection (1) applies to a police cadet and appointment as a police cadet as it applies to a constable and the office of constable.

(5) In this section"chief of police"
(a) in relation to a person appointed, or an appointment failing to be made, under a specified Act, has the same meaning as in the Police Act,
(b) in relation to any other person or appointment, means the officer who has the direction and control of the body of constables or cadets in question;

"the Police Act" means, for England and Wales, the Police Act 1964 or, for Scotland, the Police (Scotland) Act 1967;

"police authority":
(a) in relation to a person appointed, or an appointment falling to be made, under a specified Act, has the same meaning as in the Police Act,
(b) in relation to any other person or appointment, means the authority by whom the person in question is or on appointment would be paid;

"police cadet" means any Person appointed to undergo training with a view to becoming a constable;

"police fund" in relation to a chief officer of police within paragraph (a) of the above definition of that term has the same meaning as in the Police Act, and in any other case means money provided by the police authority;

"specified Act" means the Metropolitan Police Act 1829, the City of London Police Act 1839 or the Police Act.

Part III Discrimination in Other Fields

Education

17. Discrimination by bodies in charge of educational establishments
It is unlawful, in relation to an educational establishment falling within column 1 of the following table, for a person indicated in relation to the establishment in column 2 (the "responsible body") to discriminate against a person
(a) in the terms on which it offers to admit him to the establishment as a pupil; or
(b) by refusing or deliberately omitting to accept an application for his admission to the establishment as a pupil; or
(c) where he is a pupil of the establishment:
   (i) in the way it affords him access to any benefits, facilities or services, or by refusing or deliberately omitting to afford him access to them; or
   (ii) by excluding him from the establishment or subjecting him to any other detriment.

Table England And Wales
[omitted]

18. Other discrimination by local education authorities
It is unlawful for a local education authority, in carrying out such of its functions under the Education Acts 1944 to 1975 as do not fall under section 17, to do any act which constitutes racial discrimination.
(2) (Applies to Scotland.)

19. General duty in public sector of education
(1) Without prejudice to its obligation to comply with any other provision of this Act, a body to which this subsection applies shall be under a general duty to secure that facilities for education provided by it, and any ancillary benefits or services, are provided without racial discrimination.
(2) The following provisions of the Education Act 1944, namely
(a) section 68 (power of Secretary of State to require duties under that Act to be exercised reasonably); and
(b) section 99 (powers of Secretary of State where local education authorities etc. are in default),
shall apply to the performance by a body to which subsection (1) applies of the duties imposed by sections y and 18, and shall also apply to the performance of the general duty imposed by subsection (1), as they apply to the performance by a local education authority of a duty imposed by that Act.
(3) (Applies to Scotland.)
(4) The sanctions in subsections (2) and (3) shall be the only sanctions for breach of the general duty in subsection (1), but without prejudice to the enforcement of sections 17 and 18 under section 57 or otherwise (where the breach is also a contravention of either of those sections).
(5)(Applies to Scotland.)
(6) Subsection (1) applies to
(a) local education authorities in England and Wales;
(b) (applies to Scotland);
(c) any other body which is a responsible body in relation to
(i) an establishment falling within paragraph I, 3 or 7 of the table in section y;
(ii) an establishment designated under section 24 (1) of the Sex Discrimination Act 1975 as falling within paragraph (ct) or (c) of section 24 (2) of that Act;
(iii) an establishment designated under the said section 24 (1) as falling within paragraph (b) of the said section 24 (2) where the grants in question are payable under section 100 of the Education Act 1944.

Goods, facilities, services and premises
20. Discrimination in provision of goods, facilities or services
(1) It is unlawful for any person concerned with the provision (for payment or not) of goods, facilities or services to the public or a section of the public to discriminate against a person who seeks to obtain or use those goods, facilities or services
(a) by refusing or deliberately omitting to provide him with any of them; or
(b) by refusing or deliberately omitting to provide him with goods, facilities or services of the like quality, in the like manner and on the like terms as are normal in the first-mentioned person's case in relation to other members of the public or (where the person so seeking belongs to a section of the public) to other members of that section.
(2) The following are examples of the facilities and services mentioned in subsection (1):
(a) access to and use of any place which members of the public are permitted to enter;
(b) accommodation in a hotel, boarding house or other similar establishment;
(c) facilities by way of banking or insurance or for grants, loans, credit or finance;
(d) facilities for education;
(e) facilities for entertainment, recreation or refreshment;
(f) facilities for transport or travel;
(g) the services of any profession or trade, or any local or other public authority.

21. Discrimination in disposal or management of premises
(1) It is unlawful for a person, in relation to premises in Great Britain of which he has power to dispose, to discriminate against another
(a) in the terms on which he offers him those premises; or
(b) by refusing his application for those premises; or

(c) in his treatment of him in relation to any list of persons in need of premises of that description.

(2) It is unlawful for a person, in relation to premises managed by him, to discriminate against a person occupying the premises

(a) in the way he affords him access to any benefits or facilities, or by refusing or deliberately omitting to afford him access to them; or

(b) by evicting him, or subjecting him to any other detriment.

(3) Subsection (1) does not apply to a person who owns an estate or interest in the premises and wholly occupies them unless he uses the services of an estate agent for the purposes of the disposal of the premises, or publishes or causes to be published an advertisement m connection with the disposal.

22. Exception from ss. 20 (1) and 21: small dwellings

(1) Sections 20 (1) and 21 do not apply to the provision by a person of accommodation in any premises, or the disposal of premises by him, if:

(a) that person or a near relative of his ("the relevant occupier") resides, and intends to continue to reside, on the premises; and

(b) there is on the premises, in addition to the accommodation occupied by the relevant occupier, accommodation (not being storage accommodation or means of access) shared by the relevant occupier with other persons residing on the premises who are not members of his household; and

(c) the premises are small premises.

(2) Premises shall be treated for the purposes of this section as small premises if

(a) in the case of premises comprising residential accommodation for one or more households (under separate letting or similar agreements) in addition to the accommodation occupied by the relevant occupier, there is not normally residential accommodation for more than two such households and only the relevant occupier and any member of his household reside in the accommodation occupied by him;

(b) in the case of premises not falling within paragraph (a), there is not normally residential accommodation on the premises for more than six persons in addition to the relevant occupier and any members of his household.

23. Further exceptions from ss. 20 (1) and 21 (1) Sections 20 (r) and 21 do not apply

(a) to discrimination which is rendered unlawful by any provision of Part II or section 17 or 18; or

(b) to discrimination which would be rendered unlawful by any provision of Part II but for any of the following provisions, namely sections 4 (3), 5 (1) (b), 6, 7 (4), 9 and 14 (4).

(2) Section 20 (1) does not apply to anything done by a person as a participant in arrangements under which he (for reward or not) takes into his home, and treats as if they were members of his family, children, elderly persons, or persons requiring a special degree of care and attention.

24. Discrimination: consent for assignment or sub-letting

(1) Where the licence or consent of the landlord or of any other person is required for the disposal to any person of premises in Great Britain comprised in a tenancy it is unlawful for the landlord or other person to discriminate against a person by withholding the licence or consent for disposal of the premises to him.

(2) Subsection (1) does not apply if

(a) the person withholding a licence or consent, or a near relative of his ("the relevant occupier") resides, and intends to continue to reside on the premises; and

(b) there is on the premises, in addition to the accommodation occupied by the relevant occupier, accommodation (not being storage accommodation or means of access) shared by the relevant occupier with other persons residing on the premises who are not members of his household; and

(c) the premises are small premises.

(3) Section 22 (2) (meaning of "small premises") shall apply for the purposes of this as well as of that section.

(4) In this section "tenancy" means a tenancy created by a lease or sublease, by an agreement for a lease or sub-lease or by a tenancy agreement or in pursuance of any enactment; and "disposal" in relation to premises comprised in a tenancy, includes assignment or assignation of the tenancy and sub-letting or parting with possession of the premises or any part of the premises.

(5) This section applies to tenancies created before the passing of this Act, as well as to others.

25. Discrimination: associations not within s. 11

(1) This section applies to any association of persons (however described, whether corporate or unincorporated and whether or not its activities are carried on for profit) if

(a) it has twenty-five or more members and

(b) admission to membership is regulated by its constitution and is so conducted that the members do not constitute a section of the public within the meaning of section 20 (1); and

(c) it is not an organization to which section m applies.

(2) It is unlawful for an association to which this section applies, in the case of a person who is not a member of the association, to discriminate against him:

(a) in the terms on which it is prepared to admit him to membership; or

(b) by refusing or deliberately omitting to accept his application for membership.

(3) It is unlawful for an association to which this section applies in the case of a person who is a member or associate of the association, to discriminate against him:

(a) in the way it affords him access to any benefits, facilities or services, or by refusing or deliberately omitting to afford him access to them; or

(b) in the case of a member, by depriving him of membership, or varying the terms on which he is a member; or

(c) in the case of an associate, by depriving him of his rights as an associate, or varying those rights; or

(d) in either case, by subjecting him to any other detriment.

(4) For the purposes of this section

(a) a person is a member of an association if he belongs to it by virtue of his admission to any sort of membership provided for by its constitution (and is not merely a person with certain rights under its constitution by virtue of his membership of some other association) and references to membership of an association shall be construed accordingly;

(b) a person is an associate of an association to which this section applies if, not being a member of it, he has under its constitution some or all of the rights enjoyed by members (or would have apart from any provision in its constitution authorizing the refusal of those rights in particular cases).

26. Exception from s. 25 for certain associations

(1) An association to which section 25 applies is within this subsection if the main object of the association is to enable the benefits of membership (whatever they may be) to be enjoyed by persons of a particular racial group defined otherwise than by reference to colour; and in determining whether that is the main object of an association regard shall be had to the essential character of the association and to all relevant circumstances including, in particular, the extent to which the affairs of the association are so conducted that the persons primarily enjoying the benefits of membership are of the racial group in question.

(2) In the case of an association within subsection (1) nothing in section 25 shall render unlawful any act not involving discrimination on the ground of colour.

Extent

27. Extent of Part III

(1) Sections 17 to 19 do not apply to benefits, facilities or services outside Great Britain except

(a) travel on a ship registered at a port of registry in Great Britain; and
(b) benefits, facilities or services provided on a ship so registered.

(2) Section 20 (1):

(a) does not apply to goods facilities or services outside Great Britain except as provided in subsections (3) and (4) and
(b) does not apply to facilities by way of banking or insurance or for grants, loans, credit or finance, where the facilities are for a purpose to be carried out, or in connection with risks wholly or mainly arising, outside Great Britain.

(3) Section 20 (1) applies to the provision of facilities for travel outside Great Britain where the refusal or omission occurs in Great Britain or on a ship, aircraft or hovercraft within subsection (4).

(4) Section 20 (r) applies on and in relation to

(a) any ship registered at a port of registry in Great Britain; and
(b) any aircraft or hovercraft registered in the United Kingdom and operated by a person who has his principal place of business, or is ordinarily resident, in Great Britain,

even if the ship, aircraft or hovercraft is outside Great Britain.

(5) This section shall not render unlawful an act done in or over a country outside the United Kingdom, or in or over that country's territorial waters, for the purpose of complying with the laws of that country.

Part IV Other Unlawful Acts

28. Discriminatory practices

(1) In this section "discriminatory practice" means the application of a requirement or condition which results in an act of discrimination which is unlawful by virtue of any provision of Part II or III taken with section 1 (1) (b), or which would be likely to result in such an act of discrimination if the persons to whom it is applied included persons of any particular racial group as regards which there has been no occasion for applying it.

(2) A person acts in contravention of this section if and so long as

(a) he applies a discriminatory practice; or
(b) he operates practices or other arrangements which in any circumstances would call for the application by him of a discriminatory practice.

(3) Proceedings in respect of a contravention of this section shall be brought only by the Commission in accordance with sections 58 to 62.

29. Discriminatory advertisements

It is unlawful to publish or to cause to be published an advertisement which indicates, or might reasonably be understood as indicating, an intention by a person to do an act of discrimination, whether the doing of that act by him would be lawful or, by virtue of Part II or III, unlawful.

(2) Subsection (1) does not apply to an advertisement

(a) if the intended act would be lawful by virtue of any of sections 5, 6, 7 (3) and (4), 10 (3), 26, 34 (2), 35 to 39 and 41; or
(b) if the advertisement relates to the services of an employment agency (within the meaning of section 14 (1)) and the intended act only concerns employment which the employer could by virtue of section 5, 6 or 7 (3) or (4) lawfully refuse to offer to persons against whom the advertisement indicates an intention to discriminate.

(3) Subsection (1) does not apply to an advertisement which indicates that persons of any class defined otherwise than by reference to colour, race or ethnic or national origins are required for employment outside Great Britain.

(4) The publisher of an advertisement made unlawful by subsection (1) shall not be

subject to any liability under that subsection in respect of the publication of the advertisement if he proves

(a) that the advertisement was published in reliance on a statement made to him by the person who caused it to be published to the effect that, by reason of the operation of subsection (2) or (3), the publication would not be lawful; and
(b) that it was reasonable for him to rely on the statement.

(5) A person who knowingly or recklessly makes a statement such as is mentioned in subsection (4) (a) which in a material respect is false or misleading commits an offence, and shall be liable on summary conviction to a fine not exceeding £400.

30. Instructions to discriminate

It is unlawful for a person

(a) who has authority over another person; or
(b) in accordance with whose wishes that other person is accustomed to act,

to instruct him to do any act which is unlawful by virtue of Part II or III, or procure or attempt to procure the doing by him of any such act.

31. Pressure to discriminate

(1) It is unlawful to induce, or attempt to induce, a person to do any act which contravenes Part II or III.

(2) An attempted inducement is not prevented from falling within subsection (1) because it is not made directly to the person in question, if it is made in such a way that he is likely to hear of it.

32. Liability of employers and principals

(1) Anything done by a person in the course of his employment shall be treated for the purposes of this Act (except as regards offences thereunder) as done by his employer as well as by him, whether or not it was done with the employer's knowledge or approval.

(2) Anything done by a person as agent for another person with the authority (whether express or implied, and whether precedent or subsequent) of that other person shall be treated for the purposes of this Act (except as regards offences thereunder) as done by that other person as well as by him.

(3) In proceedings brought under this Act against any person in respect of an act alleged to have been done by an employee of his it shall be a defence for that person to prove that he took such steps as were reasonably practicable to prevent the employee from doing that act, or from doing in the course of his employment acts of that description.

33. Aiding unlawful acts

(1) A person who knowingly aids another person to do an act made unlawful by this Act shall be treated for the purposes of this Act as himself doing an unlawful act of the like description.

(2) For the purposes of subsection (1) an employee or agent for whose act the employer or principal is liable under section 32 (or would be so liable but for section 32 (3)) shall be deemed to aid the doing of the act by the employer or principal.

(3) A person does not under this section knowingly aid another to do an unlawful act if

(a) he acts in reliance on a statement made to him by that other person that, by reason of any provision of this Act, the act which he aids would not be unlawful; and
(b) it is reasonable for him to rely on the statement.

(4) A person who knowingly or recklessly makes a statement such as is mentioned in subsection (3) (a) which in a material respect is false or misleading commits an offence, and shall be liable on summary conviction to a fine not exceeding £400.

Part V – Charities

34. Charities

(1) A provision which is contained in a charitable instrument (whenever that instrument

took or takes effect) and which provides for conferring benefits or persons of a class defined by reference to colour shall have effect for all purpose: as if it provided for conferring the like benefits

(a) on persons of the class which results if the restriction by reference to colour is disregarded, or
(b) where the original class is defined by reference to colour only, of persons generally; but nothing in this subsection shall be taken to alter the effect of any provision as regards any time before the coming into operation of this subsection.

(2) Nothing in Parts II to IV shall
(a) be construed as affecting a provision to which this subsection applies or
(b) render unlawful an act which is done in order to give effect to such provision.

(3) Subsection (2) applies to any provision which is contained in a charitable instrument (whenever that instrument took or takes effect) and which provides for conferring benefits on persons of a class defined otherwise than by reference to colour (including a class resulting from the operation of subsection (1)).

In this section "charitable instrument" means an enactment or other instrument passed or made for charitable purposes, or an enactment or other instrument so far as it relates to charitable purposes.

In the application of this section to England and Wales, "charitable purposes" means purposes which are exclusively charitable according to the law of England and Wales.

Part VI – General Exceptions From Parts II to IV

35. Special needs of racial groups in regard to education, training or welfare

Nothing in Parts II to IV shall render unlawful any act done in affording persons of a particular racial group access to facilities or services to meet the special needs of persons of that group in regard to their education, training or welfare, or any ancillary benefits.

36. Provision of education or training for persons not ordinarily resident in Great Britain

Nothing in Parts II to IV shall render unlawful any act done by a person for the benefit of persons not ordinarily resident in Great Britain in affording them access to facilities for education or training or any ancillary benefits, where it appears to him that the persons in question do not intend to remain in Great Britain after their period of education or training there.

37. Discriminatory training by certain bodies

(1) Nothing in Parts II to IV shall render unlawful any act done in relation to particular work by a training body in or in connection with

(a) affording only persons of a particular racial group access to facilities for training which would help to fit them for that work; or
(b) encouraging only persons of a particular racial group to take advantage of opportunities for doing that work,

   where it appears to the training body that at any time within the twelve months immediately preceding the doing of the act

   (i) there were no persons of that group among those doing that work in Great Britain; or
   (ii) the proportion of persons of that group among those doing that work in Great Britain was small in comparison with the proportion of persons of that group among the population of Great Britain.

(2) Where in relation to particular work it appears to a training body that although the condition for the operation of subsection (1) is not met for the whole of Great Britain it is met for an area within Great Britain, nothing in Parts II to IV shall render unlawful any act done by the training body in or in connection with

(a) affording persons who are of the racial group in question, and who appear likely to take up that world in that area, access to facilities for training which would help to fit them for that work; or

(b) encouraging persons of that group to take advantage of opportunities in the area for doing that work.

(3) In this section "training body" means

(a) a person mentioned in section 23 (2) (a) or (b); or

(b) any other person being a person designated for the purposes of this section in an order made by the Secretary of State.

38. Other discriminatory training etc.

(1) Nothing in Parts II to IV shall render unlawful any act done by an employer in relation to particular work in his employment at a particular establishment in Great Britain, being an act done in or in connection with

(a) affording only those of his employees working at that establishment who are of a particular racial group access to facilities for training which would help to fit them for that work; or

(b) encouraging only persons of a particular racial group to take advantage of opportunities for doing that work at that establishment, where any of the conditions in subsection (2) was satisfied at any time within the twelve months immediately preceding the doing of the act.

(2) Those conditions are

(a) that there are no persons of the racial group in question among those doing that work at that establishment; or

(b) that the proportion of persons of that group among those doing that work at that establishment is small in comparison with the proportion of persons of that group

(i) among all those employed by that employer there; or

(ii) among the population of the area from which that employer normally recruits persons for work in his employment at that establishment.

(3) Nothing in section II shall render unlawful any act done by an organization to which that section applies in or in connection with

(a) affording only members of the organization who are of a particular racial group access to facilities for training which would help to fit them for holding a post of any kind in the organization; or

(b) encouraging only members of the organization who are of a particular racial group to take advantage of opportunities for holding such posts in the organization,

where either of the conditions in subsection (4) was satisfied at any time within the twelve months immediately preceding the doing of the act.

(4) Those conditions are

(a) that there are no persons of the racial group in question among persons holding such posts in that organization; or

(b) that the proportion of persons of that group among those holding such posts in that organization is small in comparison with the proportion of persons of that group among the members of the organization.

(5) Nothing in Parts II to IV shall render unlawful any act done by an organization to which section II applies in or in connection with encouraging only persons of a particular racial group to become members of the organization where at any time within the twelve months immediately preceding the doing of the act

(a) no persons of that group were members of the organization; or

(b) the proportion of persons of that group among members of the organization was small in comparison with the proportion of persons of that group among those eligible for membership of the organization.

(6) Section 8 (meaning of employment at establishment in Great Britain) shall apply for the purposes of this section as if this section were contained in Part II.

39. Sports and competitions

Nothing in Parts II to IV shall render unlawful any act whereby a person discriminates

against another on the basis of that other's nationality or place of birth or the length of time for which he has been resident in a particular area or place, if the act is done
(a) in selecting one or more persons to represent a country, place or area, or any related association, in any sport or game; or
(b) in pursuance of the rules of any competition so far as they relate to eligibility to compete in any sport or game.

40. Indirect access to benefits, etc.
(1) References in this Act to the affording by any person of access to benefits, facilities or services are not limited to benefits, facilities or services provided by that person himself, but include any means by which it is in that person's power to facilitate access to benefits, facilities or services provided by any other person (the "actual provider").
(2) Where by any provision of this Act the affording by any person of access to benefits, facilities or services in a discriminatory way is in certain circumstances prevented from being unlawful, the effect of the provision shall extend also to the liability under this Act of any actual provider.

41. Acts done under statutory authority etc.
(1) Nothing in Parts II to IV shall render unlawful any act of discrimination done
(a) in pursuance of any enactment or Order in Council; or
(b) in pursuance of any instrument made under any enactment by a Minister of the Crown; or
(c) in order to comply with any condition or requirement imposed by a Minister of the Crown (whether before or after the passing of this Act) by virtue of any enactment.

References in this subsection to an enactment, Order in Council or instrument include an enactment, Order in Council or instrument passed or made after the passing of this Act.
(2) Nothing in Parts II to IV shall render unlawful any act whereby a person discriminates against another on the basis of that other's nationality or place of ordinary residence or the length of time for which he has been present or resident in or outside the United Kingdom or an area within the United Kingdom, if that act is done
(a) in pursuance of any arrangements made (whether before or after the passing of this Act) by or with the approval of, or for the time being approved by, a Minister of the Crown; or
(b) in order to comply with any condition imposed (whether before or after the passing of this Act) by a Minister of the Crown.

42. Acts safeguarding national security
Nothing in Parts II to IV shall render unlawful an act done for the purpose of safeguarding national security.

Part VII – The Commission For Racial Equality

General

43. Establishment and duties of Commission
(1) There shall be a body of Commissioners named the Commission for Racial Equality consisting of at least eight but not more than fifteen individuals each appointed by the Secretary of State on a full-time or part-time basis, which shall have the following duties
(a) to work towards the elimination of discrimination;
(b) to promote equality of opportunity, and good relations, between persons of different racial groups generally; and
(c) to keep under review the working of this Act and, when they are so required by the Secretary of State or otherwise think it necessary, draw up and submit to the Secretary of State proposals for amending it.
(2) The Secretary of State shall appoint
(a) one of the Commissioners to be chairman of the Commission; and

(b) either one or more of the Commissioners (as the Secretary of State thinks fit) to be deputy chairman or deputy chairmen of the Commission.

(3) The Secretary of State may by order amend subsection (1) so far as it regulates the number of Commissioners.

(4) Schedule I shall have effect with respect to the Commission.

(5) The Race Relations Board and the Community Relations Commission are hereby abolished.

44. Assistance to organizations

(1) The Commission may give financial or other assistance to any organization appearing to the Commission to be concerned with the promotion of equality of opportunity, and good relations, between persons of different racial groups but shall not give any such financial assistance out of money provided (through the Secretary of State) by Parliament except with the approval of the Secretary of State given with the consent of the Treasury.

(2) Except in so far as other arrangements for their discharge are made and approved under paragraph 12 of Schedule I

(a) the Commission's functions under subsection (2); and

(b) other functions of the Commission in relation to matters connected with the giving of such financial or other assistance as is mentioned in that subsection,

shall be discharged under the general direction of the Commission by a committee of the Commission consisting of at least three but not more than five Commissioners, of whom one shall be the deputy chairman or one of the deputy chairmen of the Commission.

45. Research and education

(1) The Commission may undertake or assist (financially or otherwise) the undertaking by other persons of any research, and any educational activities which appear to the Commission necessary or expedient for the purposes of section 43 (1).

(2) The Commission may make charges for educational or other facilities or services made available by them.

46. Annual reports

(1) As soon as practicable after the end of each calendar year the Commission shall make to the Secretary of State a report on their activities during the year (an "annual report").

(2) Each annual report shall include a general survey of developments, during the period to which it relates, in respect of matters falling within the scope of the Commission's functions.

(3) The Secretary of State shall lay a copy of every annual report before each House of Parliament, and shall cause the report to be published.

47. Codes of practice

(1) The Commission may issue codes of practice containing such practical guidance as the Commission think fit for either or both of the following purposes, namely

(a) the elimination of discrimination in the field of employment;

(b) the promotion of equality of opportunity in that field between persons of different racial groups.

(2) When the Commission propose to issue a code of practice, they shall prepare and publish a draft of that code, shall consider any representations made to them about the draft and may modify the draft accordingly.

(3) In the course of preparing any draft code of practice for eventual publication under subsection (2) the Commission shall consult with

(a) such organizations or associations of organizations representative of employers or of workers; and

(b) such other organizations, or bodies,

as appear to the Commission to be appropriate.

(4) If the Commission determine to proceed with the draft, they shall transmit the draft to the Secretary of State who shall :
(a) if he approves of it, lay it before both Houses of Parliament and
(b) if he does not approve of it, publish details of his reasons for withholding approval.
(5) If, within the period of forty days beginning with the day on which a copy of a draft code of practice is laid before each House of Parliament, or if such copies are laid on different days, with the later of the two days, either House so resolves, no further proceedings shall be taken thereon, but without prejudice to the laying before Parliament of a new draft.
(6) In reckoning the period of forty days referred to in subsection (5) no account shall be taken of any period during which Parliament is dissolved or prorogued or during which both Houses are adjourned for more than four days.
(7) If no such resolution is passed as is referred to in subsection (5), the Commission shall issue the code in the form of the draft and the code shall come into effect on such day as the Secretary of State may by order appoint.
(8) Without prejudice to section 74 (3), an order under subsection (5) may contain such transitional provisions or savings as appear to the Secretary of State to be necessary or expedient in connection with the code of Practice thereby brought into operation.
(9) The Commission may from time to time revise the whole or any part of a code of practice issued under this section and issue that revised code, and subsections (2) to (8) shall apply (with appropriate modifications) to such a revised code as they apply to the first issue of a code.
(10) A failure on the part of any person to observe any provision of a code of practice shall not of itself render him liable to any proceedings; but in any proceedings under this Act before an industrial tribunal any code of practice issued under this section shall be admissible in evidence, and if any provision of such a code appears to the tribunal to be relevant to any question arising in the proceedings it shall be taken into account in determining that question.

Without prejudice to subsection (1), a code of practice issued under this section may include such practical guidance as the Commission think fit as to what steps it is reasonably practicable for employers to take for the purpose of preventing their employees from doing in the course of their employment acts made unlawful by this Act.
(11) Without prejudice to subsection (1), a code of practice issued under this section may include such practical guidance as the Commission think fit as to what steps it is reasonably practicable for employers to take for the purpose of preventing their employees from doing in the course of their employment acts made unlawful by this Act.

Investigations
48. Power to conduct formal investigations
(1) Without prejudice to their general power to do anything requisite for the performance of their duties under section 43 (1) the Commission may if they think fit, and shall if required by the Secretary of State, conduct a formal investigation for any purpose connected with the carrying out of those duties.
(2) The Commission may, with the approval of the Secretary of State appoint, on a full-time or part-time basis, one or more individuals as additional Commissioners for the purposes of a formal investigation.
((3)) The Commission may nominate one or more Commissioners, with or without one or more additional Commissioners, to conduct a formal investigation on their behalf, and may delegate any of their functions in relation to the investigation to the persons so nominated.

49. Terms of reference
(1) The Commission shall not embark on a formal investigation unless the requirements of this section have been complied with.
(2) Terms of reference for the investigation shall be drawn up by the Commission or, if

the Commission were required by the Secretary of State to conduct the investigation, by the Secretary of State after consulting the Commission.
(3) It shall be the duty of the Commission to give general notice of the holding of the investigation unless the terms of reference confine it to activities of persons named in them, but in such a case the Commission shall in the prescribed manner give those persons notice of the holding of the investigation.
(4) Where the terms of reference of the investigation confine it to activities of persons named in them and the Commission in the course of it propose to investigate any act made unlawful by this Act which they believe that a person so named may have done, the Commission shall
(a) inform that person of their belief and of their Proposal to investigate the act in question; and
(b) offer him an opportunity of making oral or written representations with regard to it (or both oral and written representations if he thinks fit);
and a person so named who avails himself of an opportunity under this subsection of making oral representations may be represented
(i) by counsel or a solicitor; or
(ii) by some other person of his choice, not being a person to whom the Commission object on the ground that he is unsuitable.
(5) The Commission or, if the Commission were required by the Secretary of State to conduct the investigation, the Secretary of State after consulting the Commission may from time to time revise the terms of reference; and subsections (1), (3) and (4) shall apply to the revised investigation and terms of reference as they applied to the original.

50. Power to obtain information
(1) For the purposes of a formal investigation the Commission, by a notice in the prescribed form served on him in the prescribed manner
(a) may require any person to furnish such written information as may be described in the notice, and may specify the time at which, and the manner and form in which, the information is to be furnished;
(b) may require any person to attend at such time and place as is specified in the notice and give oral information about, and produce all documents in his possession or control relating to, any matter specified in the notice.
(2) Except as provided by section 60, a notice shall be served under subsection (1) only where
(a) service of the notice was authorized by an order made by the Secretary of State; or
(b) the terms of reference of the investigation state that the Commission believe that a person named in them may have done or may be doing acts of all or any of the following descriptions
(i) unlawful discriminatory acts;
(ii) contraventions of section 28; and
(iii) contraventions of sections 29, 30 or 31, and confine the investigation to those acts.
(3) A notice under subsection (1) shall not require a person
(a) to give information, or produce any documents, which he could not be compelled to give in evidence, or produce, in civil proceedings before the High Court or the Court of Session; or
(b) to attend at any place unless the necessary expenses of his journey to and from that place are paid or tendered to him.
(4) If a person fails to comply with a notice served on him under subsection (1) or the Commission have reasonable cause to believe that he intends not to comply with it, the Commission may apply to a county court or, in Scotland, a sheriff court for an order requiring him to comply with it or with such directions for the like purpose as may be contained in the order.
(5) Section 84 of the County Courts Act 1959(penalty for neglecting witness summons)

shall apply to failure without reasonable excuse to comply with an order of a county court under subsection (4) as it applies in the cases provided in the said section 84.

(6) A person commits an offence if he

(a) wilfully alters, suppresses, conceals or destroys a document which he has been required by a notice or order under this section to produce; or

(b) in complying with such a notice or order, knowingly or recklessly makes any statement which is false in a material particular,

and shall be liable on summary conviction to a fine not exceeding £400.

(7) Proceedings for an offence under subsection (6) may (without prejudice to any jurisdiction exercisable apart from this subsection) be instituted

(a) against any person at any place at which he has an office or other place of business:

(b) against an individual at any place where he resides, or at which he is for the time being.

51. Recommendations and reports on formal investigations

If in the light of any of their findings in a formal investigation it appears to the Commission necessary or expedient, whether during the course of the investigation or after its conclusion

(a) to make to any person, with a view to promoting equality of opportunity between persons of different racial groups who are affected by any of his activities, recommendations for changes in his policies or procedures, or as to any other matters; or

(b) to make to the Secretary of State any recommendations, whether for changes in the law or otherwise,

the Commission shall make those recommendations accordingly.

(2) The Commission shall prepare a report of their findings in any formal investigation conducted by them.

(3) If the formal investigation is one required by the Secretary of State(a) the Commission shall deliver the report to the Secretary of State; and (b) the Secretary of State shall cause the report to be published,

and, unless required by the Secretary of State, the Commission shall not publish the report.

(4) If the formal investigation is not one required by the Secretary of State, the Commission shall either publish the report, or make it available for inspection in accordance with subsection (5).

(5) Where under subsection (4) a report is to be made available for inspection, any person shall be entitled, on payment of such fee (if any) as may be determined by the Commission :

(a) to inspect the report during ordinary office hours and take copies of all or any part of the report; or

(b) to obtain from the Commission a copy, certified by the Commission to be correct, of the report.

(6) The Commission may, if they think fit, determine that the right conferred by subsection (5) (a) shall be exercisable in relation to a copy of the report instead of, or in addition to, the original.

(7)The Commission shall give general notice of the place or places where, and the times when, reports may be inspected under subsection (5).

52. Restriction on disclosure of information

(1) No information given to the Commission by any person ("the informant") in connection with a formal investigation shall be disclosed by the Commission, or by any person who is or has been a Commissioner, additional Commissioner or employee of the Commission, except

(a) on the order of any court; or

(b) with the informant s consent; or

(c) in the form of a summary or other general statement published by the Commission which does not identify the informant or any other person to whom the information relates, or

(d) in a report of the investigation published by the Commission or made available for inspection under section 51 (5); or
(e) to the Commissioners, additional Commissioners or employees of the Commission, or, so far as may be necessary for the proper performance of the functions of the Commission, to other persons; or
(f) for the purpose of any civil proceedings under this Act to which the Commission are a party, or any criminal proceedings.
(2) Any person who discloses information in contravention of subsection (1) commits an offence and shall be liable on summary conviction to a fine not exceeding £400.
(3) In preparing any report for publication or for inspection the Commission shall exclude, so far as is consistent with their duties and the object of the report, any matter which relates to the private affairs of any individual or the business interests of any person where the publication of that matter might, in the opinion of the Commission, prejudicially affect that individual or person.

Part VIII – Enforcement

General
53. Restriction of proceedings for breach of Act
(1) Except as provided by this Act no proceedings, whether civil or criminal shall be against any person in respect of an act by reason that the act is unlawful by virtue of a provision of this Act.
(2) Subsection (1) does not preclude the making of an order of certiorari, mandamus or prohibition.
(3) (applies to Scotland)

54. Jurisdiction of industrial tribunals
(1) complaint by any person ("the complainant") that another person ("the respondent")
(a) has committed an act of discrimination against the complainant which is unlawful by virtue of Part II; or
(b) is by virtue of section 32 or 33 to be treated as having committed such an act of discrimination against the complainant,
may be presented to an industrial tribunal.
(c) Subsection (1) does not apply to a complaint under section 12 (1) of an act in respect of which an appeal, or proceedings in the nature of an appeal may be brought under any enactment, or to a complaint to which section 75 (8) applies.

55. Conciliation in employment cases
(1) Where a complaint has been presented to an industrial tribunal under section 54 and a copy of the complaint has been sent to a conciliation officer, it shall be the duty of the conciliation officer
(a) if he is requested to do so both by the complainant and by the respondent; or
(b) if, in the absence of requests by the complainant and the respondent, he considers that he could act under this subsection with a reasonable prospect of success,
to endeavour to promote a settlement of the complaint without its being determined by an in
(2) Where, before a complaint such as is mentioned in subsection (2) has been presented to an industrial tribunal a request is made to a conciliation officer to make his services available in the matter by a person who, if the complaint were so presented, would be the complainant or respondent, subsection (1) shall apply as if the complaint had been so presented and a copy of it had been sent to the conciliation officer.
(3) In proceeding under subsection (1) or (2), a conciliation officer shall where appropriate have regard to the desirability of encouraging the use of other procedures available for the settlement of grievances.
(4) Anything communicated to a conciliation officer in connection with the performance

of his functions under this section shall not be admissible in evidence in any proceedings before an industrial tribunal except with the consent of the person who communicated it to that officer.

56. Remedies on complaint under s 54

(1) Where an [employment tribunal] finds that a complaint presented to it under section 54 is well-founded, the tribunal shall make such of the following as it considers just and equitable

(a) an order declaring the rights of the complainant and the respondent in relation to the act to which the complaint relates;

(b) an order requiring the respondent to pay to the complainant compensation of an amount corresponding to any damages he could have been ordered by a county court or by a sheriff court to pay to the complainant if the complaint had fallen to be dealt with under section 57;

(c) a recommendation that the respondent take within a specified period action appearing to the tribunal to be practicable for the purpose of obviating or reducing the adverse effect on the complainant of any act of discrimination to which the complaint relates.

(2),(3) [rescinded]

(4) If without reasonable justification the respondent to a complaint fails to comply with a recommendation made by an [employment tribunal] under subsection (1)(c), then, if it thinks it just and equitable to do so

(a) the tribunal may ... increase the amount of compensation required to be paid to the complainant in respect of the complaint by an order made under subsection (1)(b); or

(b) if an order under subsection (1)(b) could have been made but was not, the tribunal may make such an order.

[(5) The Secretary of State may by regulations make provision:

(a) for enabling a tribunal, where an amount of compensation falls to be awarded under subsection (1)(b), to include in the award interest on that amount; and

(b) specifying, for cases where a tribunal decides that an award is to include an amount in respect of interest, the manner in which and the periods and rate by reference to which the interest is to be determined;

and the regulations may contain such incidental and supplementary provisions as the Secretary of State considers appropriate.

(6) The Secretary of State may by regulations modify the operation of any order made under [section 14 of [the Employment Tribunals Act 1996]](power to make provision as to interest on sums payable in pursuance of [employment tribunal] decisions) to the extent that it relates to an award of compensation under subsection (1)(b).]

Part IX – Enforcement of Part III

57. Claims under Part III

(1) A claim by any person ("the claimant") that another person ("the respondent"):

(a) has committed an act of discrimination against the claimant which is unlawful by virtue of Part III; or

(b) is by virtue of section 32 or 33 to be treated as having committed such an act of discrimination against the claimant, may be made the subject of civil proceedings in like manner as any other claim in tort or (in Scotland) in reparation for breach of statutory duty.

(2) Proceedings under subsection (1) :

(a) shall, in England and Wales, be brought only in a designated county court; and

(b) ... but all such remedies shall be obtainable in such proceedings as, apart from this subsection and section 53(1) would be obtainable in the High Court or the Court of Session, as the case may be.

(3) As respects an unlawful act of discrimination falling within section 1(1)(b), no award of damages shall be made if the respondent proves that the requirement or condition in

question was not applied with the intention of treating the claimant unfavourably on racial grounds.
(4) For the avoidance of doubt it is hereby declared that damages in respect of an unlawful act of discrimination may include compensation for injury to feelings whether or not they include compensation under any other head.
(5) Civil proceedings in respect of a claim by any person that he has been discriminated against in contravention of section 17 or 18 by a body to which section 19(1) applies shall not be instituted unless the claimant has given notice of the claim to the Secretary of State and either the Secretary of State has by notice informed the claimant that the Secretary of State does not require further time to consider the matter, or the period of two months has elapsed since the claimant gave notice to the Secretary of State; but nothing in this subsection applies to a counterclaim.
(6) [applies to Scotland only]

Non-discrimination notices
58. Issue of non-discrimination notice
(1) This section applies to
(a) an unlawful discriminatory act; and
(b) an act contravening section 28; and
(c) an act contravening section 29, 30 or 31,
and so applies whether or not proceedings have been brought in respect of the act.
(2) If in the course of a formal investigation the Commission become satisfied that a person is committing, or has committed, any such acts, the Commission may in the prescribed manner serve on him a notice in the prescribed form ("a non-discrimination notice") requiring him
(a) not to commit any such acts; and
(b) where compliance with paragraph (a) involves changes in any of his practices or other arrangements
(i) to inform the Commission that he has effected those changes and what those changes are; and
(ii) to take such steps as may be reasonably required by the notice for the purpose of affording that information to other persons concerned.
(3) A non-discrimination notice may also require the person on whom it is served to furnish the Commission with such other information as may be reasonably required by the notice in order to verify that the notice has been complied with..
(4) The notice may specify the time at which, and the manner and form in which, any information is to be furnished to the Commission, but the time at which any information is to be furnished in compliance with the notice shall not be later than five years after the notice has become final.
(5) The Commission shall not serve a non-discrimination notice in respect of any person unless they have first
(a) given him notice that they are minded to issue a non-discrimination notice in his case, specifying the grounds on which they contemplate doing so, and
(b) offered him an opportunity of making oral or written representations in the matter (or both oral and written representations if he thinks fit) within a period of not less than 28 days specified in the notice; and
(c) taken account of any representations so made by him.
(6) Subsection (2) does not apply to any acts in respect of which the Secretary of State could exercise the powers conferred on him by section 19 (2) and (3), but if the Commission become aware of any such acts they shall give notice of them to the Secretary of State.
(7) Section 50 (4) shall apply to requirements under subsection (2) (b), (3) and (q.) contained in a non-discrimination notice which has become final as it applies to requirements in a notice served under section 50 (1).

59. Appeal against non-discrimination notice
Not later than sis weeks after a non-discrimination notice is served on any person he may appeal against any requirement of the notice
(a) to an industrial tribunal, so far as the requirement relates to acts which are within the jurisdiction of the tribunal;
(b) to a designated county court or a sheriff court, so far as the requirement relates to acts which are within the jurisdiction of the court and are not within the jurisdiction of an industrial tribunal.
(2) Where the tribunal or court considers a requirement in respect of which an appeal is brought under subsection (1) to be unreasonable because it is based on an incorrect finding of fact or for any other reason, the tribunal or court shall quash the requirement.
(3) On quashing a requirement under subsection (2) the tribunal or court may direct that the non-discrimination notice shall be treated as if, in place of the requirement quashed, it had contained a requirement in terms specified in the direction.
(4) Subsection (1) does not apply to a requirement treated as included in a non-discrimination notice by virtue of a direction under subsection (3).

60. Investigation as to compliance with non-discrimination notice
(1) If:
(a) the terms of reference of a formal investigation state that its purpose is to determine whether any requirements of a non-discrimination notice are being or have been carried out, but section 50 (2) (b) does not apply; and
(b) section 49 (3) is complied with in relation to the investigation on a date ("the commencement date") not later than the expiration of the period of five 5 years beginning when the non-discrimination notice became final,
the Commission may within the period referred to in subsection (2) serve notices under section 50 (1) for the purposes of the investigation without needing to obtain the consent of the Secretary of State.
(2) The said period begins on the commencement date and ends on the later of the following dates
(a) the date on which the period of five years mentioned in subsection (1) (b) expires;
(b) the date two years after the commencement date.

61. Register of non-discrimination notices
(1) The Commission shall establish and maintain a register ("the register") of non-discrimination notices which have become final.
(2) Any person shall be entitled, on payment of such fee (if any) as may be determined by the Commission
(a) to inspect the register during ordinary office hours and take copies of any entry; or
(b) to obtain from the Commission a copy, certified by the Commission to be correct, of any entry in the register.
(3) The Commission may, if they think fit, determine that the right conferred by subsection (2) (a) shall be exercisable in relation to a copy of the register instead of, or in addition to, the original.
(4) The Commission shall give general notice of the place or places where, and the times when, the register or a copy of it may be inspected.

Other enforcement by Commission
62. Persistent discrimination
If, during the period of five years beginning on the date on which any of the following became final in the case of any person, namely
(a) a non-discrimination notice served on him; or
(b) a finding by a tribunal or court under section 54 or 57; that he has done an unlawful discriminatory act; or
(c) a finding by a court in proceedings under section y or 20 of the Race Relations Act

1968 that he has done an act which was unlawful by virtue of any provision of Part I of that Act,

it appears to the Commission that unless restrained he is likely to do one or more acts falling within paragraph (b), or contravening section 28, the Commission may apply to a designated county court for an injunction, or to a sheriff court for an order, restraining him from doing so; and the court, if satisfied that the application is well-founded, may grant the injunction or order in the terms applied for or in more limited terms.

(2) In proceedings under this section the Commission shall not allege that the person to whom the proceedings relate has done an act falling within sub section (1) (b) or contravening section 28 which is within the jurisdiction of an industrial tribunal unless a finding by an industrial tribunal that he did that act has become final.

63. Enforcement of ss. 29 to 31

(1) Proceedings in respect of a contravention of section 29, 30 and 31 shall be brought only by the Commission in accordance with the following provisions of this section.

(2) The proceedings shall be

(a) an application for a decision whether the alleged contravention occurred; or

(b) an application under subsection (4), or both.

(3) An application under subsection (2) (a) shall be made

(a) in a case based on any provision of Part II, to an industrial tribunal; and

(b) in any other case, to a designated county court or a sheriff court.

(4) If it appears to the Commission

(a) that a person has done an act which by virtue of section 29, 30 or 31 was unlawful; and

(b) that unless restrained he is likely to any further acts which by virtue of that section are unlawful,

the Commission may apply to a designated county court for an injunction, or to a sheriff court for an order, restraining him from doing such acts; and the court, if satisfied that the application is well-founded, may grant the injunction or order in the terms applied for or more limited terms.

(5) In proceedings under subsection (4) the Commission shall not allege that the person to whom the proceedings relate has done an act which is unlawful under this Act and within the jurisdiction of an industrial tribunal unless a finding by an industrial tribunal that he did that act has become final.

64. Preliminary action in employment cases

(1) With a view to making an application under section 62 (1) or 63 (4) in relation to a person the Commission may present to an industrial tribunal a complaint that he has done an act within the jurisdiction of an industrial tribunal, and if the tribunal considers that the complaint is well-founded it shall make a finding to that effect and, if it thinks it just and equitable to do so in the case of an act contravening any provision of Part II may also (as if the complaint had been presented by the person discriminated against) make an order such as is referred to in section 56 (2) (a), or a recommendation such as is referred to in section 56 (1) (c), or both.

(2) Subsection (1) is without prejudice to the jurisdiction conferred by section 63 (2).

(3) In sections 62 and 63 and this section, the acts "within the jurisdiction of an industrial tribunal" are those in respect of which such jurisdiction is conferred by sections 54 and 63.

65. Help for aggrieved persons in obtaining information etc.

(1) With a view to helping a person ("the person aggrieved") who considers he may have been discriminated against in contravention of this Act to decide whether to institute proceedings and, if he does so, to formulate and present his case in the most effective manner, the Secretary of State shall by order prescribe

(a) forms by which the person aggrieved may question the respondent on his reasons for doing any relevant act, or on any other matter which is or may be relevant; and

(b) forms by which the respondent may if he so wishes reply to any questions.

(2) Where the person aggrieved questions the respondent (whether in accordance with an order under subsection (1) or not)

(a) the question, and any reply by the respondent (whether in accordance with such an order or not) shall, subject to the following provisions of this section, be admissible as evidence in the proceedings;

(b) if it appears to the court or tribunal that the respondent deliberately, and without reasonable excuse, omitted to reply within a reasonable period or that his reply is evasive or equivocal, the court or tribunal may draw any inference from that fact that it considers it just and equitable to draw, including an inference that he committed an unlawful act.

(3) The Secretary of State may by order

(a) prescribe the period within which questions must be duly served in order to be admissible under subsection (2) (a); and

(b) prescribe the manner in which a question, and any reply by the respondent, may be duly served.

(4) Rules may enable the court entertaining a claim under section 57 to determine, before the date fixed for the hearing of the claim, whether a question or reply is admissible under this section or not.

(5) This section is without prejudice to any other enactment or rule of law regulating interlocutory and preliminary matters in proceedings before a county court, sheriff court or industrial tribunal, and has effect subject to any enactment or rule of law regulating the admissibility of evidence in such proceedings.

(6) In this section "respondent" includes a prospective respondent and "rules"

(a) in relation to county court proceedings, means county court rules;

(b) (applies to Scotland).

66. Assistance by Commission

(1) Where, in relation to proceedings or prospective proceedings under this Act, an individual who is an actual or prospective complainant or claimant applies to the Commission for assistance under this section, the Commission shall consider the application and may grant it if they think fit to do so

(a) on the ground that the case raises a question of principle; or

(b) on the ground that it is unreasonable having regard to the complexity of the case, or to the applicant's position in relation to the respondent or another person involved, or to any other matter, to expect the applicant to deal with the case unaided; or

(c) by reason of any other special consideration.

(2) Assistance by the Commission under this section may include:

(a) giving advice;

(b) procuring or attempting to procure the settlement of any matter in dispute;

(c) arranging for the giving of advice or assistance by a solicitor or counsel;

(d) arranging for representation by any person, including all such assistance as is usually given by a solicitor or counsel in the steps preliminary or incidental to any proceedings or in arriving at or giving effect to a compromise to avoid or bring to an end any proceedings;

(e) any other form of assistance which the Commission may consider appropriate,

but paragraph (d) shall not affect the law and practice regulating the descriptions of persons who may appear in, conduct, defend, and address the court in, any proceedings.

(3) Where under subsection (1) an application for assistance under this section is made in writing, the Commission shall, within the period of two months beginning when the application is received

(a) consider the application after making such enquiries as they think fit; and

(b) decide whether or not to grant it; and

(c) inform the applicant of their decision stating whether or not assistance under this section is to be provided by the Commission and, if so, what form it will take.

(4) If, in a case where subsection (3) applies, the Commission within the period of two months there mentioned give notice to the applicant that, in relation to his application

(a) the period of two months allowed them by that subsection is by virtue of the notice extended to three months; and

(b) the reference to two months in section 68 (3) is by virtue of the notice to be read as a reference to three months,

subsection (3) and section 68 (3) shall have effect accordingly.

(5) In so far as expenses are incurred by the Commission in providing the applicant with assistance under this section, the recovery of those expenses (as taxed or assessed in such manner as may be prescribed by rules or regulations) shall constitute a first charge for the benefit of the Commission

(a) on any costs or expenses which (whether by virtue of a judgment or order of a court or tribunal or an agreement or otherwise) are payable to the applicant by any other person in respect of the matter in connection with which the assistance is given; and

(b) so far as relates to any costs or expenses, on his rights under any compromise or settlement arrived at in connection with that matter to avoid or bring to an end any proceedings.

(6) The charge conferred by subsection (5) is subject to any charge under the Legal Aid Act 1974, or any charge or obligation for payment in priority to other debts under the Legal Aid and Advice (Scotland) Acts 1967 and 1972, and is subject to any provision in any of those Acts for payment of any sum into the legal aid fund.

(7) In this section "respondent" includes a prospective respondent and "rules or regulations":

(a) in relation to county court proceedings, means county court rules;

(b) (applies to Scotland);

(c) in relation to industrial tribunal proceedings, means regulations made under paragraph 21 of Schedule I to the Trade Union and Labour Relations Act 1974.

67. Sheriff courts and designated county courts

(1) For the purposes of this Act a "designated" county court is one designated for the time being for those purposes by an order made by the Lord Chancellor.

(2) An order under subsection (1) designating any county court for the purposes of this Act shall assign to that court as its district for those purposes any county court district or two or more county court districts.

(3) A designated county court or a sheriff court shall have jurisdiction to entertain proceedings under this Act with respect to an act done on a ship, aircraft or hovercraft outside its district, including such an act done outside Great Britain.

(4) In any proceedings under this Act in a designated county court or a sheriff court the judge oi sheriff shall, unless with the consent of the parties he sits without assessors be assisted by two assessors appointed from a list of persons prepared and maintained by the Secretary of State, being persons appearing to the Secretary of State to have special knowledge and experience of problems connected with relations between persons of different racial groups.

(5) The remuneration of assessors appointed under subsection (4) shall be at such rate as may with the approval of the Minister for the Civil Service be determined by the Lord Chancellor (for proceedings in England and Wales) or the Lord President of the Court of Session (for proceedings in Scotland).

(6) Without prejudice to section 74 (3) an order for the discontinuance of the jurisdiction of any county court under this Act, whether wholly or within a part of the district assigned to it for the purposes of this Act, may include provision with respect to any proceedings under this Act commenced in that court before the order comes into operation.

Period within which proceedings to be brought

68. Period within which proceedings to be brought

(1) An industrial tribunal shall not consider a complaint under section 54, unless it is presented to the tribunal before the end of the period of three months beginning when the act complained of was done.
(2) A county court or a sheriff court shall not consider a claim under section 57 unless proceedings in respect of the claim are instituted before the end of
(a) the period of six months beginning when the act complained of w·as done; or
(b) in a case to which section 57 (5) applies, the period of eight months so beginning.
(3) Where, in relation to proceedings or prospective proceedings by way of a claim under section 57, an application for assistance under section 66 is made to the Commission before the end of the period of six or, as the case may be, eight months mentioned in paragraph (a) or (b) of subsection (2), the period allowed by that paragraph for instituting proceedings in respect of the claim shall be extended by two months.
(4) An industrial tribunal, county court or sheriff court shall not consider an application under section 63 (2) (a) unless it is made before the end of the period of six months beginning when the act to which it relates was done; and a county court or sheriff court shall not consider an application under section 63 (4) unless it is made before the end of the period of five years so beginning.
(5) An industrial tribunal shall not consider a complaint under section 69. (1) unless it is presented to the tribunal before the end of the period of six months beginning when the act complained of was done.
(6) A court or tribunal may nevertheless consider any such complaint, claim or application which is out of time if in all the circumstances of the case, it considers that it is just and equitable to do so.
(7) For the purposes of this section :
(a) when the inclusion of any term in a contract renders the malting of the contract an unlawful act that act shall be treated as extending throughout the duration of the contract; and
(b) any act extending over a period shall be treated as done at the end of that period; and
(c) a deliberate omission shall be treated as done when the person in question decided upon it;

and in the absence of evidence establishing the contrary a person shall be taken for the purposes of this section to decide upon an omission when he does an act inconsistent with doing the omitted act or if he has done no such inconsistent act, when the period expires within which he might reasonably have been expected to do the omitted act if it was to be done.

Evidence

69. Evidence

(1) Any finding by a court under section 19 or 20 of the Race Relations Act 1968, or by a court or industrial tribunal under this Act, in respect of any act shall, if it has become final, be treated as conclusive in any proceedings under this Act.
(2) In any proceedings under this Act a certificate signed by or on behalf of a Minister of the Crown and certifying
(a) that any arrangements or conditions specified in the certificate were made, approved or imposed by a Minister of the Crown and were in operation at a time or throughout a period so specified for
(b) that an act specified in the certificate was done for the purpose of safeguarding national security,

shall be conclusive evidence of the matters certified.
(3) A document purporting to be a certificate such as is mentioned in subsection (2) shall be received in evidence and, unless the contrary is proved, shall be deemed to be such a certificate.

70. Incitement to racial hatred

(1) The Public Order Act 1936 shall be amended in accordance with the following provisions of this section. [...]

Part X
Supplemental
[...]

Schedules
Section 43

Schedule I
The Commission For Racial Equality

Incorporation and status
1. On the appointment by the Secretary of State of the first Commissioners, the Commission shall come into existence as a body corporate.
2. (1) The Commission are not an emanation of the Crown, and shall not act or be treated as the servant or agent of the Crown.
(2) Accordingly
(a) neither the Commission nor a Commissioner or member of its staff as such is entitled to any status, immunity, privilege or exemption enjoyed by the Crown;
(b) the Commissioners and members of the staff of the Commission as such are not civil servants; and
(c) the Commission's property is not property of, or held on behalf of, the Crown.

Tenure of office of Commissioners
3. (1) A Commissioner shall hold and vacate his office in accordance with the terms of his appointment.
(2) A person shall not be appointed a Commissioner for more than five years. (3) With the consent of the Commissioner concerned, the Secretary of State may alter the terms of an appointment so as to make a full-time Commissioner into a part-time Commissioner or vice versa, or for any other purpose.
(4) A Commissioner may resign by notice to the Secretary of State.
(5) The Secretary of State may terminate the appointment of a Commissioner if satisfied that
(a) without the consent of the Commission, he failed to attend the meetings of the Commission during a continuous period of six months beginning not earlier than nine months before the termination; or
(b) he is an undischarged bankrupt, or has made an arrangement with his creditors, or is insolvent within the meaning of paragraph g (2) of Schedule 3 to the Conveyancing and Feudal Reform (Scotland) Act 1970; or
(c) he is by reason of physical or mental illness, or for any other reason, incapable of carrying out his duties.
(6) Past service as a Commissioner is no bar to re-appointment.

Tenure of office of chairman and deputy chairmen
4. (1) The chairman and each deputy chairman shall hold and vacate his office in accordance with the terms of his appointment, and may resign by notice to the Secretary of State.
(2) The office of the chairman or a deputy chairman is vacated if he ceases to be a Commissioner.
(3) Past service as chairman or a deputy chairman is no bar to re-appointment.

Remuneration of Commissioners
5. The Secretary of State may pay, or make such payments towards the provision of, such remuneration, pensions, allowances or gratuities to or in respect of the Commissioners or any of them as, with the consent of the Minister for the Civil Service, he may determine.

6. Where a person ceases to be a Commissioner otherwise than on the expiry of his term of office, and it appears to the Secretary of State that there are special circumstances which make it right for that person to receive compensation, the Secretary of State may, with the consent of the Minister for the Civil Service, direct the Commission to make to that person a payment of such amount as, with the consent of that Minister, the Secretary of State may determine.

Additional Commissioners

7. (1) Paragraphs 2 (2), 3 (s) and (6), and 6 shall apply to additional Commissioners appointed under section 98 (2) as they apply to Commissioners.

(2) The Commission may pay, or make such payments towards the provision of, such remuneration, pensions, allowances or gratuities to or in respect of an additional Commissioner as the Secretary of State, with the consent of the Minister for the Civil Service, may determine.

(3) With the approval of the Secretary of State and the consent of the additional Commissioner concerned, the Commission may alter the terms of an appointment of an additional Commissioner so as to make a full-time additional Commissioner into a part-time additional Commissioner or vice versa, or for any other purpose.

(4) An additional Commissioner may resign by notice to the Commission.

(5) The Secretary of State, or the Commission acting with the approval of the Secretary of State, may terminate the appointment of an additional Commissioner if satisfied that

(a) without reasonable excuse he failed to carry out the duties for which he was appointed during a continuous period of three months beginning not earlier than six months before the termination; or
(b) he is a person such as is mentioned in paragraph 3 (g) (b); or
(c) he is by reason of physical or mental illness, or for any other reason, incapable of carrying out his duties.

(6) The appointment of an additional Commissioner shall terminate at the conclusion of the investigation for which he was appointed, if not sooner.

Staff

8. The Commission may, after consultation with the Secretary of State, appoint such officers and servants as they think fit, subject to the approval of the Minister for the Civil Service as to numbers and as to remuneration and other terms and conditions of service.

9. (1) Employment with the Commission shall be included among the kinds of employment to which a superannuation scheme under section I of the Superannuation Act 1972 can apply, and accordingly in Schedule I to that Act (in which those kinds of employment are listed) the words "Commission for Racial Equality" shall be inserted after the words "Commission on Industrial Relations."

(2) Where a person who is employed by the Commission and is by reference to that employment a participant in a scheme under section I of the Superannuation Act 1972 becomes a Commissioner or an additional Commissioner, the Minister for the Civil Service may determine that his service as a Commissioner or additional Commissioner shall be treated for the purposes of the scheme as service as an employee of the Commission.

10. (1) In this paragraph

"the new Commission" means the Commission for Racial Equality;

"present Commission employee" means a person who immediately before the repeal date is employed by the Community Relations Commission; "private pension scheme" means a scheme for the payment of pensions, allowances or gratuities other than one made under section I of the Superannuation Act 1972;

"the repeal date" means the date on which the repeal of the Race Relations Act 1968 by this Act takes effect.

(2) If a present Commission employee enters the employment of the new Commission

on the repeal date and on so doing elects to be covered for his service in that employment by a private pension scheme in which tie was a participant in respect of his service in the employment of the Community Relations Commission the new Commission may make such payments towards the provision of benefits to or in respect of him under that scheme (or any other private pension scheme replacing it) as may be determined by the new Commission with the consent of the Secretary of State given with the approval of the Minister for the Civil Service; and it shall be the duty of the new Commission and those Ministers in the exercise of their functions under this sub-paragraph to ensure that his rights under the scheme do not become less advantageous than they were when he entered the employment of the new Commission.

(3) Where a person who is employed by the new Commission and is in respect of that employment a participant in a private pension scheme becomes a Commissioner or an additional Commissioner, his service as a Commissioner or additional Commissioner may be treated for the purposes of the scheme as service as an employee of the new Commission.

11. The Employers' Liability (Compulsory Insurance) Act 1969 shall not require insurance to be effected by the Commission.

Advisory committees

12. The Commission may, with the approval of the Secretary of State, appoint advisory committees for the purpose of such of their functions as they think fit.

Proceedings and business

13. (1) Subject to the provisions of this Act

(a) the Commission shall discharge their functions in accordance with arrangements made by the Commission and approved by the Secretary of State; and

(b) arrangements so made and approved may provide for the discharge under the general direction of the Commission of any of the Commission's functions by a committee of the Commission, or by two or more Commissioners.

(2) Anything done by or in relation to a committee of the Commission or Commissioners, in the discharge of the Commission's functions shall have the same effect as if done by or in relation to the Commission.

14. The validity of any proceedings of the Commission shall not be affected by any vacancy among the members of the Commission or by any defect in the appointment of any Commissioner or additional Commissioner.

15. The quorum for meetings of the Commission shall in the first instance be determined by a meeting of the Commission attended by not less than five Commissioners.

Finance

16. The Secretary of State shall pay to the Commission expenses incurred or to be incurred by them under paragraph 6, 7, 8 or so of this Schedule or paragraph of Schedule z, and, with the consent of the Minister for the Civil Service and the Treasury, shall pay to the Commission such sums as the Secretary of State thinks fit for enabling the Commission to meet other expenses.

17. (1) The accounting year of the Commission shall be the twelve months ending on 31st March.

(2) It shall be the duty of the Commission

(a) to keep proper accounts and proper records in relation to the accounts;

(b) to prepare in respect of each accounting year a statement of accounts in such form as the Secretary of State may direct with the approval of the Treasury; and

(c) to send copies of the statement of the Secretary of State and the Comptroller and Auditor General before the end of the month of November next following the accounting year to which the statement relates.

(3) The Comptroller and Auditor General shall examine, certify and report on each statement received by him in pursuance of this Schedule and shall lay copies of each statement and of his report before each House of Parliament.

Disqualification Acts

18. (1) In Part II of Schedule I to the House of Commons Disqualification Act 1975 and Part II of Schedule I to the Northern Ireland Assembly Disqualification Act 1975 (bodies of which all members are disqualified under those Acts), there shall (at the appropriate place in alphabetical order) be inserted the following entry:

"The Commission for Racial Equality".

(2) In Part III of Schedule I to each of those Acts of 1975 (other disqualifying offices) there shall (at the appropriate place in alphabetical order) be inserted the following entry:

"Additional Commissioner of the Commission for Racial Equality".

Chapter VI

National Human Rights Institutions in Africa

National Human Rights Institutions in Africa[1]

Richard Carver* and Paul Hunt**

Introduction

Many people are sceptical about government-sponsored human rights institutions regulating the behaviour of governments. Yet in principle it is no different from the executive being subject to the legal supervision of the judiciary. As United Nation studies have shown, national human rights institutions are found in many countries and some have become effective instruments for the protection and promotion of fundamental freedoms.[2]

The last decade has seen a proliferation of these institutions in Africa. In that period, official bodies charged with promoting or protecting human rights have been established in Zimbabwe, Swaziland, Uganda, Togo, Zaire, Benin, The Gambia, Namibia, Equatorial Guinea, Cameroon and Gabon.[3] They have in common their recent origin, but the differences between them are striking. The Zimbabwean Ombudsman cannot investigate alleged human rights violations by the security forces, whereas the Ugandan Inspector-General of Government can. The Ugandan official can also investigate corruption and the Namibian Ombudsman can look at the dangers of environmental degradation. The African Centre for Democracy and Human Rights Studies in The Gambia does not investigate specific human rights violations – it is concerned with research and promotion – whereas the Commission Nationale des Droits de l'Homme in Togo does both. It is not a coincidence that all these bodies have emerged in the last ten years; rather, it reflects increased awareness of human rights issues on the part of governments. In particular, this is embodied in the African Charter of Human and Peoples' Rights, the human rights instrument drafted by the Organization of African Unity (OAU) after the fall of three African leaders with egregious human rights records: Idi Amin of Uganda, Jean-Bedel Bokassa of the Central African Republic and Macias Nguema of Equatorial Guinea. The

[1]Acknowledgement: This report was originally written for the African Centre for Democracy and Human Rights Studies, The Gambia, 1991.

*Author on Africa and Human Rights.

**Solicitor, Associate Director of the African Center for Democracy and Human Rights Studies, Fellow of the Human Rights Centre, University of Essex, England.

[2]See, for example, UN doc,. E/CN. 4/4/1989/47, National Institutions for the Protection and Promotion of Human Rights – Updated Report of the Secretary-General.

[3]Since this paper was completed we have learned of the creation in late 1990 of a further Ombudsman-type institution in Senegal: Le Médiateur de la République.

K. Hossain et al. (eds), Human Rights Commissions and Ombudsman Offices, 733–758.

Charter entered into force in 1986, after ratification by a majority of OAU member states. Article 26 stipulates that:

> States parties to the present Charter shall have the duty to guarantee the independence of the Courts and shall allow the establishment and improvement of appropriate national institutions entrusted with the promotion and protection of the rights and freedoms guaranteed by the present Charter.

There are exceptions, but in practice the formation of national institutions has tended to take place in one of two circumstances. In Zimbabwe, Uganda and Namibia, it followed the removal of a government with a poor human rights record; the creation of a human rights body was a symbolic statement of intent that things would be better under the new regime. Alternatively, human rights institutions have been set up after a government has come under criticism for its human rights record, as in Zaire, Togo, Benin, Cameroon and Equatorial Guinea. It is intended to signal a will to improve. The Togolese Commission was set up as a direct successor to a commission of inquiry investigating allegations of torture published by Amnesty International. The announcement of the formation of a commission in Equatorial Guinea came only days after publication of a critical Amnesty International report in September 1990.

Experience suggests, however, that the effectiveness of a human rights institution can be quite autonomous from the intentions of the government which set it up. Given suitable constitutional guarantees, good procedures and adequate resources, a human rights institution may succeed even if it was launched to improve the government's international image. The eleven institutions already listed, along with a number of earlier ones still surviving, generally follow one of three different models:

Ombudsman. The model of the Swedish Ombudsman has been the one most widely used in Commonwealth Africa. However, African Ombudsmen differ in important respects from the Swedish original; for example, most are answerable to the head of state rather than to the legislature. There are also significant differences between them. Tanzania, Nigeria and Zambia have multi-member institutions, while Ghana, Mauritius and Zimbabwe have individuals; the institutions in Uganda and Namibia have broader mandates and investigative powers than many of their counterparts. The function of Ombudsmen is almost exclusively investigative, they have little or no role in human rights promotion.

National Commission. Togo, Benin and Cameroon have all adopted a similar model of a multi-member national commission with a mandate to investigate allegations of human rights abuse, advise the government on human rights matters (for example, relations with UN bodies) and promote awareness of human rights in the country at large. They comprise representatives of different professional groups, although the method of selecting members varies.

Government Department. The Département des Droits et des Libertés du Citoyen in Zaire provides the model for this. Gabon appears to be following a similar path. The role of the Zairian Department, headed by a State Commissioner (Minister), has been to investigate allegations of abuse, but also to represent the government at international human rights forums.

Not all the national human rights institutions under review correspond neatly with one of these models. The African Centre, in The Gambia, for example, is closer to an international institute for human rights promotion, training and research, than it is to any of the three models. Nonetheless, as a general guide the models are helpful and are frequently used in this paper. The first section of the paper provides a brief historical review of permanent national human rights institutions in Africa. The second, drawing on African experience, considers three key features of official human rights bodies: mandate, appointment and accountability, and investigations. By way of short case studies, the third section looks more closely at the institutions in Tanzania, Togo, Uganda, Zaire and The Gambia. The paper concludes with observations and suggestions about African national human rights institutions. The appendix is a directory of official human rights bodies in Africa.

Historical Review

The first national human rights institution to established in Africa was the Tanzanian Permanent Commission of Enquiry (PCE), which began operations in 1966. The PCE was set up as part of a new framework for protecting the rights of citizens to replace the institutions of the western-style, pluralist state. The Commission was granted a broad mandate to investigate different types of human rights abuse and maladministration.

The Mauritian Ombudsman was first envisaged in the Constitutions of 1967 and 1968, although the first one was appointed in 1970. Mauritius, unlike Tanzania, retained the institutions of Westminster-style government. The Ombudsman is appointed on the recommendation of parliamentary leaders.

The 1973 Zambian Constitution provided for the creation or a Commission for Investigations, which began operating in 1974. Like the Tanzanian institution, it is a multi-member body with broad powers, although its mandate does not include investigating corruption, which comes under a separate Anti-Corruption Commission.

The Sudanese People's Assembly Committee for Administrative Control, established in 1973, was one of the few African Ombudsmen to be answerable to the legislature, on the Swedish model, rather than the executive. It has also been one of the least effective, largely because of material and logistic problems. It was handling only 200 cases a year – the same number as Mauritius, which has one twentieth of its population.[4] The Committee was abolished, almost by accident, in 1985. It owed its existence to the 1973 Constitution, which was repealed after a coup d'état in April 1985.[5]

The Nigerian Public Complaints Commission, established in 1975 after the coup d'état led by General Murtala Mohammed, mirrors the country's federal structure, with a central headquarters and branches in each state capital. The Ghanaian Ombudsman, first envisaged in the 1969 Constitution, was not established until 1980 after delays caused by successive changes of government.

The Zimbabwean Ombudsman, anticipated in the 1979 Zimbabwe Rhodesia Constitution, was established by law in 1982 and began work the following year.

[4] John Hatchard, "The institution of the Ombudsman in Africa with special reference to Zimbabwe", International and Comparative Law Quarterly 35, (1986), at p. 255.

[5] John Hatchard, "The Ombudsman in Africa Revisited" ICLQ.

Like the Nigerian Commission, but unlike the Tanzanian and Zambian institutions, Zimbabwe's Ombudsman has narrow terms of reference, with no powers to investigate the police, army or other security forces.

The Swaziland Ombudsman, established in 1983, only operated until 1987. After the coronation of King Mswati in 1986 the office was abolished by King's Decree. However, the Ombudsman had not been particularly effective, probably because he was also the secretary to the Liqoqo, the supreme council of state, and thus lacked credibility as an impartial arbiter on human rights issues.[6]

The Département des Droits et Libertés du Citoyen, established in Zaire in 1986, differed from previous institutions in that it was a government ministry, although it had a specific mandate to investigate the abuse of human rights. By 1991 it appeared to be non-operational.

The Ugandan Inspector-General of Government (IGG) was established by statute in 1987, although he had begun to operate informally the previous year. The office was created after careful study of existing laws governing Ombudsmen, but represents a considerable departure. The Inspector-General's terms of reference are broad, covering not only maladministration and abuse of power, but also human rights violations – most previous offices do not use this term – and corruption. This expansion of mandate undoubtedly reflects the fact that the government which established the office had recently come to power after more than 15 years of gross human rights abuse and corruption. The IGG also has the power, which he frequently uses, to undertake investigations on his own initiative, without waiting for complaints from a citizen.

The Commission Nationale des Droits de l'Homme in Togo, established in 1987, was also an attempt to overcome a long history of human rights complaints, but this time without a change in government. Two years later Benin, which had also come under sharp criticism from Amnesty International, set up the Commission Béninoise des Droits de L'Homme. The constitutions of the two commissions are similar, with memberships composed of representatives of professional bodies such as the Bar Association and mandates covering both protection and promotion of human rights. However, the Togolese body seems to have been more active and has had a significant impact on respect for human rights.

The Gambian Parliament established the African Centre for Democracy and Human Rights Studies in June 1989; its first Director was appointed the following year. The Centre has only a promotional role, but in relation to Africa as a whole and not just The Gambia. It has an international staff and is governed by an international council of human rights experts.

In November 1990 the Cameroonian National Assembly passed a law creating a National Commission on Human Rights and Freedoms, along similar lines to those in Togo and Benin. Cameroon has also come under renewed criticism in 1991 for legal measures against journalists and political critics, as well as the killing of anti-government protestors.

As already mentioned, the announcement of the formation of a human rights commission in Equatorial Guinea in September 1990 was also apparently prompted by criticism from Amnesty International. We do not have details of the commission's constitution, but according to press reports an interesting

---

[6] Hatchard, "The Ombudsman in Africa Revisited". Also id. "The Ombudsman in the Commonwealth", Commonwealth Human Rights Initiative (forthcoming).

feature is that it is answerable to the legislature rather than the executive. Given the absence of free elections, however, the distinction may be purely formal.

The Ombudsman established under the independence constitution in Namibia represents a considerable refinement of the office. As in Uganda, the office-holder is specifically empowered both to investigate human rights accuses and to review pre-independence legislation to assess whether it conforms with the rights guaranteed in the constitution. The Ombudsman's powers to enforce decisions are also greater, since s/he may apply to a court for an interdict, or injunction, to prevent an abuse of power or human rights violation.

Most recently, Gabon established a Ministère des Droits de l'Homme chargé des Relations avec le Parliament, in November 1990. The first incumbent is André Mba Obame. His office appears to be analogous to Zaire' s human rights Department.

Africa's first national human rights institution, Tanzania, was seen as part of a more democratic relationship between citizens and the one-party state. Ironically, recent institutions have been seen as part of a general trend towards multi-party political systems. In Togo the human rights commission is part of the process of democratisation of the country. It is the agency which, by dispelling fear on the part of the citizens, must contribute to a new type of relationship between, citizens and the Administration.[7]

Key Features

Mandate

For the purposes of this study, 17 bodies have been put together as "national human rights institutions", but their terms of reference or mandates vary greatly and often do not even include the term 'human rights'.

Generally, the function of an Ombudsman includes the investigation of maladministration and abuse of office. This can certainly entail abuse of human rights, for example, if individuals. are subject to discrimination or the arbitrary seizure of their property. A typical definition is contained in the Mauritius Constitution of 1968. The Ombudsman was mandated to investigate any case "in which a member of the public claims, or appears to the Ombudsman, to have sustained injustice in consequence of maladministration".[8]

The Zimbabwe Constitution of 1980 refines this further:

> "The Ombudsman may investigate action taken by any officer or authority referred to in subsection (2) in the exercise of the administrative functions of that officer or authority in any case where it is alleged that. a person has suffered injustice in consequence of that action and it does not appear that there is any remedy reasonably available by way of proceedings in a court of appeal from a court."[9]

More recently, the Ugandan and Namibian institutions have the investigation of alleged human rights abuse as an explicit part of their mandate. Both institutions are also interesting for extending the function of an Ombudsman into new

[7] Annual Report of the Activities of the National Commission on Human Rights, October 21, 1988, p. 22.

[8] Mauritius Constitution 1968, Chapter IX.

[9] Zimbabwe Constitution 1980, s. 108(1).

areas. The Ugandan Inspector-General is required to investigate corruption, a bane of Ugandan society.[10] The Namibian Ombudsman is empowered to investigate complaints of environmental degradation, which have been a particular problem because of overfishing of its territorial waters and extensive exploitation of finite mineral resources.[11]

Like the new Ombudsmen in Uganda and Namibia, the Commissions in Togo, Benin and Cameroon and the ministries in Zaire and Gabon are explicitly human rights bodies. The mandate of the National Commission on Human Rights and Freedoms in Cameroon is similar to, although more extensive than, those of the Togolese and Béninoise Commissions. The Commission is empowered to:

- receive all denunciations relating to violations of human rights an freedoms;
- conduct all enquiries and carry out all the necessary investigations on violations or human rights and freedoms and report thereon to the President of the Republic;
- refer cases of violations of human rights and freedoms to the competent authorities;
- as and when necessary, inspect all types of penitentiaries, police stations and gendarmerie brigades in the presence of the State Counsel with jurisdiction or his representative. Such inspections may lead to the drafting of a report submitted to the competent authorities;
- study all matters relating to the defence and promotion of human rights and freedoms;
- propose to public authorities measures to be taken in the area of human rights and freedoms;
- collect and disseminate international documentation relating to human rights and freedoms;
- co-ordinate, where necessary, the activities of non-governmental organizations wishing to participate in its tasks and whose stated objective is to work in Cameroon for the defence and promotion of human rights and freedoms;
- maintain, where necessary, relations with the United Nations Organization, international organizations, and foreign committees or associations pursuing humanitarian objectives, and inform the Minister in charge of external relations thereon.[12]

In every mandate, however, there are areas that cannot be investigated. The Ugandan President, for example, can intervene to certify that a particular investigation would jeopardise national security or government secrecy. Other heads of state have similar powers. In most countries – Zaire is an exception – the institution cannot review the decision of a court or other legally constituted tribunal. There is an important distinction between institutions which are empowered to investigate abuses involving the police and security forces, and others, such as in Zimbabwe and Nigeria, which cannot. When the Ombudsman Act was debated in the Zimbabwe Parliament in 1982, this omission was criticized. The Minister of Justice replied that there were two reasons for excluding

[10] Inspector-General of Government Statute, 1987, s. 7.
[11] Namibian Constitution, Article 91 (c).
[12] Decree No. 90–1459 of 8 November 1990, Article 2 (English version).

investigation of the security forces, except when the complaint is lodged by serving personnel. First, such investigation "might have the result of inhibiting the activities of (these forces) much to the detriment of the State". Secondly, there would be too many complaints, since any prisoner would "rush to the Ombudsman and complain."[13] In practice this has not been a problem in other countries with similar institutions like Tanzania, Zambia and Uganda, which enjoy jurisdiction over the security forces. The human rights commissions in Togo, Benin and Cameroon, as well as the ministry in Zaire, are all empowered to investigate abuses involving the security forces. In Nigeria, it has been argued that the Public Complaints Commission has in practice been investigating the armed forces and police, even though this is not formally within its mandate.[14]

Another important distinction is between those institutions which only investigate allegations of human rights abuse and those which are also engaged in promotion. Generally, the Ombudsman model involves no promotional role. Namibia is an exception in that the Ombudsman is empowered to recommend legal reforms to safeguard constitutional rights; another is Tanzania, where commissioners sometimes engage in promotional work when visiting villages. By contrast, the Francophone human rights commissions all have a clearly defined role in promoting human rights, both through public education and by advising the government on appropriate measures. The African Centre for Democracy and Human Rights Studies, based in The Gambia, is unusual because its mandate is confined to the promotion of human and peoples' rights through training and research.

Appointment and Accountability

In the original Swedish institution the Ombudsman was appointed by and answerable to Parliament. Indeed, when first established almost 200 years ago the institution was seen as a counterbalance against absolute monarchy. In Africa, however, most Ombudsmen and other human rights bodies are appointed by and answerable to the head of state. The extreme cases are those of Zaire and Gabon where the official concerned is a government minister. Institutions in Nigeria, Uganda, Tanzania and Benin, which are dissimilar in many other respects, are all composed of direct presidential nominees, although some are appointed by virtue of their position in professional organizations. It is only in Togo that a majority of the commission's 13 members are nominated representatives of professional bodies and institutions such as the trade unions an the Red Cross. Presidential power of appointment is also moderated in Zimbabwe, Zambia and Namibia by the fact that it must be exercised on the recommendation of the Judicial Service Commission, so the institution concerned should be at least as independent as the judiciary. Until its abolition, Sudan's Committee for Administrative Control provided a rare example of an African institution, based on the Ombudsman model, answerable to the legislature. Formally, at least, Equatorial Guinea follows that model. Mauritius provides an unusual surviving example of the role of the legislature, with an Ombudsman who is appointed by

[13] Hatchard, "The institution of the Ombudsman".

[14] P.A. Oluyede, Nigerian Administrative Law, Ibadan, 1988, pp. 393–410.

the Governor-General – effectively the head of state – on the recommendation of the Prime Minister and the leader of the parliamentary opposition.[15]

Although in most cases the institution is answerable to the President, it is common for a summary report to be issued to legislature and published. The annual report of the African Centre is laid before the Gambian Parliament. Again, the Togolese Commission is unusual in that it reports to the President of the Supreme Court.

The size of the membership of human rights institutions varies from the single-member institutions to the 45-member Béninoise commission. Namibia has a single Ombudsman, Zimbabwe has an Ombudsman and deputy, Uganda has an Inspector-General and deputy, Tanzania has a chairman and two commissioners, Zambia an Investigator-General and three commissioners, Togo 13 commissioners, Nigeria a chief commissioner and 12 others and Cameroon 21 commissioners.

The qualification for membership vary. A number, like Ghana and Namibia, require that an Ombudsman be a qualified lawyer, although multi-member organizations allow for a greater variety of experience. Zimbabwe requires that an Ombudsman be a senior lawyer or civil servant or "a person of ability and experience and distinguished in the public life of Zimbabwe".[16] In fact the Ombudsman who has held office since 1983 is a High Court judge from Zambia, reflecting the importance attached to him being someone of clear independence. Uganda does not require a legal qualification, but an appointee must have "served in a field or discipline relevant to the work of the office of Inspector-General of Government, for not less than seven years".[17] The present Inspector-General is an economist and his deputy a banker. Like other commissions, Cameroon's institution provides for a variety of experience by including representatives of the churches, press and legal profession – although all are presidential nominees.

The personal characteristics required are more difficult to define. Generally it is required that individuals surrender any position in the public service since this could create a conflict of interest. Clearly this does not apply to those commissions where individuals are nominated as professional representatives. Generally the Francophone commissions have gone into greater detail in defining the character of a commission member. The law establishing the Béninoise Commission, for example stipulates:

> "No one may be a member of the Commission if his life is tainted by any act which damages his honour, probity, dignity or credibility."[18]

Generally, as Hatchard points out, these high standards appear to have been observed. He knows of only one instance of an Ombudsman being removed, a Public Complaints Commissioner in Oyo State, Nigeria in 1988.[19] Since then the Deputy Ombudsman in Zimbabwe has been suspended pending investigation, but these are rare exceptions. Most members of national human rights

---

[15] Mauritius Constitution 1968. The Governor-General may also consult leaders of other parliamentary parties, at his discretion.

[16] Ombudsman Act, 1982, s. 3(1).

[17] Inspector-General of Government Statute, 1987, s. 3(2).

[18] Loi No 89-004 du 12 mai 1989, Article 5.

[19] Hatchard, "The Ombudsman in the Commonwealth".

institutions hold office for a fixed period. The Zimbabwean Ombudsman originally held office for three years, renewable once for a further three years.[20] This was later amended to allow the incumbent to remain in office.[21] Members of the Nigerian Public Complaints Commission also have a maximum of two three-year terms, but they may be removed by the government at any time.[22] Exceptions include Uganda, where the Inspector-General has no fixed period of office, and Namibia, where the Ombudsman holds office until the age of 65. In Namibia the Ombudsman may only be removed on grounds of mental infirmity or gross misconduct, on the recommendation of the Judicial Service Commission.[23] In Ghana the grounds for removal are similar and have to be adjudicated by a tribunal composed of Judges of Appeal.[24] In Uganda, there is no provision for the Inspector-General's removal. It is common to find a provision giving immunity to the members – and sometimes staff – of a human rights institution for acts carried out in good faith in the course of their duties. This is the case in Uganda and Tanzania, for example, where there is an additional provision protecting officials of the institution from testifying in court on information gathered in the course of their investigations.[25] In Togo and Benin the immunity is granted for all offences, except on the authorization of the Supreme Court, and extends for one year after a person ceases to be a commission member.[26] The Gambian authorities have granted diplomatic privileges and immunities to the African Centre and its staff, akin to those usually accorded to embassies and diplomats.[27]

Investigations

Except for the African Centre in The Gambia, all the institutions under review have the power to investigate allegations that a citizen's human rights have been violated by state authorities. No institution has unfettered authority to launch an investigation. Usually there will be no investigation unless a complaint has been received and often, as in Nigeria, the complainant must have a personal interest in the case. Increasingly, however, as in Uganda, Togo, Benin, Zaire and Namibia, human rights institutions will investigate complaints submitted by national or international non-governmental organizations. This trend recognizes that potential complainants may be too intimidated to make a formal submission or unable to complain because they are in incommunicado detention. A few institutions, like Uganda's Inspector-General, may themselves initiate an investigation, either on the basis of information gathered informally or because they

[20] Ombudsman Act,.1982.
[21] Ombudsman (Amendment) Act, 1989.
[22] Public Complaints Commission Decree, 3l, 1975.
[23] Namibia Constitution, Article 94.
[24] Ombudsman Act 1980, s. 4; Ghana Constitution 1979. Article 128.
[25] Permanent Commission of Enquiry Act, 1966, s. 19; Inspector-General of Government Statute, 1987, s. 15.
[26] Loi No 87–09 du 9 juin 1987, Article 22; Loi No 89–004 du 12 mai 1989, Article 14.
[27] Agreement dated 4 April 1991, between the Government of The Gambia and the African Centre for Democracy and Human Rights' Studies under the Diplomatic Privileges (International Organizations) Act1968.

have noted a particular pattern of abuse. The Zambian institution can initiate are investigation "unless directed otherwise" by the President.[28]

Often, particularly in Ombudsman-type bodies, there is a specific requirement that a complainant must have exhausted all other domestic remedies. This is the case in Ghana and Nigeria, for example, as well as Zaire. Zimbabwe, Zambia and Mauritius all require that a complainant has exhausted other domestic remedies but allows the Ombudsman some discretion "if satisfied that in the particular circumstances it is not reasonable to expect him to resort or to have resorted to it".[29] Again Uganda is an exception, although the Inspector-General has the discretion to refuse to investigate such a case.[30] The commissions in Togo, Benin and Cameroon do not specify whether other remedies should have been exhausted, but the practice in Togo appears to have been flexible on this point.

The conduct of the investigation can vary enormously. The Ombudsman-style of institution stresses the informality and confidentiality of the investigation, with the emphasis on resolving complaints by conciliation. The Ugandan Inspector-General, who deals with a high proportion of politically sensitive corruption and human rights cases, is less likely to achieve results by conciliation and has broadly defined powers:

> "The procedure for conducting an investigation shall be such as the Inspector-General considers appropriate in the circumstances of each case, and without prejudice to the generality of the foregoing, the Inspector-General may obtain information from such person and in such manner, and make such inquiries as he deems necessary."[31]

By contrast the human rights commissions all have a procedure for formal examination of witnesses, although they also tend to stress their preference for conciliation. The commissions in Togo and Benin have an elaborately defined procedure for investigation, although it is often unnecessary to embark upon it. Most human rights institutions, whether Ombudsmen or commissions, are vested with quasi-judicial powers to subpoena witnesses or documentation and to conduct on-site visits to the scene of alleged human rights abuse. Investigative institutions have other quasi-judicial features. The immunity conferred upon members and officials of the institutions are similar to those enjoyed by the judiciary. In some cases, such as in Tanzania, all information gathered by the investigating body is privileged.[32]

In other respects, however, investigations conducted by national human rights institutions do not resemble civil or criminal proceedings before a court of law. The Ghanaian Special Investigation Board investigating the murder in 1982 of three judges and a retired army officer, apparently by government agents, was clear about the distinction between its role and that of a criminal investigation:

> "In an investigation of this nature, there is no issue between parties for us to resolve, as in a litigation; and no one appears before us to defend himself, as in a criminal trial. Indeed we have no adjudicating powers. We do not think that the Board is bound to act judicially in the sense that it is bound to hear evidence from both sides and to come to

---

[28] Commission for Investigations Act, 1974, s. 7.
[29] Commission for Investigations Act, 1974, s. 9.
[30] Inspector-General of Government Statute 1987, s. 12 (3) (a).
[31] Inspector-General of Government Statute, 1987, s. 13(1).
[32] Permanent Commission of Enquiry Act, 1966, s. 19(2).

a judicial decision approximately in the same way that a Court must do. We are appointed solely to find the facts, establish the kidnapping and murder of the four persons, as well as the surrounding circumstances, and to submit our findings to the Attorney-General ..."[33]

Most cases are decided by conciliation so the question of rules of evidence seldom arises. Where rules of evidence are needed, a national institution rarely adopts those used in court. As a Ugandan commission of inquiry investigating "disappearances" in 1974 observed:

"If the rules of evidence as laid down in the evidence Act ... were to govern such inquiries, it would be virtually impossible, in view of the numerous restrictions concerning admissibility and relevancy of evidence, etc., to make any headway at all. It is for this reason that hearsay evidence has always been admitted and, as will be seen from the manner in which we approached and tackled such evidence, we were fully alive to the dangers of relying upon it wholesale and, wherever possible, we endeavoured to subject such evidence to close scrutiny and also, wherever possible, looked for corroboration for the same.[34]

Courts employ two different standards of proof: 'beyond a reasonable doubt' (criminal cases) and 'a balance of probabilities' (civil cases). If used at all, the proof usually adopted by national institutions investigating human rights abuses will be closer to the civil than the criminal standard. In most instances the proceedings of the human rights institutions are confidential, even if there are formal hearings. In Uganda: "All proceedings, investigations and inquiries by the Inspector-General shall be conducted in strict confidence."[35] Nevertheless, details of his inquiries, particularly in corruption cases, have had a habit of finding their way into the Ugandan press.

The Nigerian and Togolese institutions allow for an interesting exception, whereby details of an investigation may be made public at the commission's discretion. There is usually no automatic right for a person to be heard before a human rights investigation. In Tanzania, Zambia and Uganda, this is made explicit in the relevant Acts, but there is also a guarantee that there will be no adverse reference to an individual in a report unless that person has had the opportunity to be heard.[36]

The Béninoise Commission, like its counterpart in Togo, has the power to initiate action in the courts.[37] Usually, Ombudsman-style institutions cannot institute court proceedings, but Ghana and Namibia are exceptional. In Ghana:

"For the purposes of performing his functions under the Constitution and any other law the Ombudsman may bring actions before any Court in Ghana and seek any and all remedies which may be available. from such Court."[38]

The Namibian Ombudsman may apply to the courts for:

"... an interdict or other suitable remedy to secure the termination of the offending action or conduct, or the abandonment or alteration of the offending procedures.[39]

---

[33] Report of the Special investigation Board (Kidnapping and Killing of Specified Persons), pp. 7–8.

[34] Report of the Commission of Inquiry into the Disappearance of People in Uganda since the 25th January 1971, p. 783.

[35] Inspector-General of Government Statute, 1987, s. 13(2).

[36] Permanent Commission of Enquiry Act, 1966, s. 10 (2); Commission for Investigations Act, 1974, s. 17; Inspector-General of Government Statute, 1987, s. 18.

[37] Loi No 89-004 du 12 mai 1989, Article 12.

[38] Ombudsman Act 1980, s. 4(7).

[39] Namibia Constitution, Article 91(e)(dd).

This would include an injunction or a writ of habeas corpus. The Ombudsman can also bring proceedings:

"... to interdict enforcement of legislation or regulation if the offending action or conduct is sought to be justified by subordinate legislation or regulation which is grossly unreasonable or otherwise ultra vires.[40]

He also has the important power to refer cases directly to the Prosecutor-General, without the prior approval of the President or other government official.

Case Studies

Tanzania

The Permanent Commission of Enquiry, the first national human rights institution in Africa, was also one of the earliest Commonwealth Ombudsmen, predating the creation of the Parliamentary Commissioner for the Administration in the United Kingdom. It continues to do effective work, handling some 3000 cases a year, yet it is little known outside the country. The better known Inspector-General of Government in Uganda was modelled on the Tanzanian Commission in several important respects.

The PCE was set up in 1966 on the recommendation of the Presidential Commission on the Establishment of a Democratic One-Party State. It was an attempt to establish a mechanism of accountability as an alternative to the Westminster-style institutions which Tanzania had inherited from Britain. This was the period of the Arusha Declaration and the policy of socialism and self-reliance. The Commission has always functioned as an arm of presidential government, although it has been suggested that this was not the initial conception:

"It appears that the Commission as now constituted is different from that originally conceived – it was perhaps intended to be an independent, quasi-judicial tribunal, even though its responsibility in the case of a complaint was to end with its recommendations to the President. Under the present rules, it becomes more of a presidential instrument."[41]

The institution's mandate is broad. It can inquire into any case of alleged "misconduct or abuse of office,[42] with the usual limitations restricting investigation of court decisions. "Unless otherwise directed" by the President, it can initiate investigations.[43] The Commission's first chairman wrote that it could investigate:

"arbitrary decisions or arrests, omissions, improper use of discretionary powers, decisions made with bad or malicious motive or decisions that have been influenced by irrelevant considerations, unnecessary or unexplained delays, obvious wrong decisions, misapplication or misinterpretation of Laws, By-Laws or Regulations."[44]

---

[40] Namibia Constitution, Article 91(e)(ee).

[41] J.P.W.B. McAuslan and Y.P. Ghai, "Constitutional Innovation and Political Stability in Tanzania", Journal of Modern African Studies, Cambridge, Vol IV, No. 4, 1966, p. 506.

[42] Interim Constitution of Tanzania, 1965, s. 67.

[43] Ibid, s. 67 (2).

[44] R. Martin, Personal Freedom and the Law in Tanzania: A study of Socialist State Administration, Nairobi, 1974, p. 213.

Interestingly, the Commission also scrutinizes decisions of officials of the ruling single party. Its first chairman also suggested that it could investigate workings of the Preventive Detention Act, including recommendations of the Advisor Committee which reviews detention orders.[45]

The PCE's jurisdiction and powers:

"... may be exercised notwithstanding any provision in written law to the effect that an act or omission shall be final, or that no appeal shall lie in respect thereof, or that no proceeding or decision shall be challenged, reviewed quashed or called into question."[46]

The Commission also has powers to subpoena witnesses and documents and search premises. Commissioners are immune from prosecution and may not give evidence in court on proceedings of the PCE or evidence which it has gathered. The PCE' s work cannot be challenged in court except on grounds of lack of jurisdiction. In the early years the PCE made a concerted effort to travel in the rural areas of Tanzania to explain their rights to people. The first annual report points out that the commissioners preferred to stay in hotels and guest-houses, not in the homes of the Regional Administration, noting sensibly:

"There is a general tendency among members of the public to think that it is impossible to arrive objectively at an impartial decision against an official who gives you hospitality."[47]

There appears to have been informality in these early years which later disappeared. Ghai observed in the 1960s that the PCE "acted as a 'poor man's lawyer or adviser' in cases outside its own jurisdiction."[48] By contrast, the annual report for 1980–1 notes drily:

"... among the complaints it receives, most of them have not exhausted existing appellant authorities laid down by law or regulations. Hence they are not investigated but referred to the appropriate authorities."[49]

Togo

The formation of the Commission Nationale des Droits de l'Homme (CNDH) in 1987 was foreshadowed by international reports that political prisoners had been tortured. A commission of inquiry was set up to investigate the allegations, concluding that they were true. However, the commission was forced to delete this crucial finding.[50]

The CNDH, which was subsequently established as a permanent institution, has a considerable degree of formal independence. Its membership of thirteen consists of two judges, two lawyers, a deputy in the legislature, a representative of youth, a workers' representative, a women's representative, a traditional chief, a member of the medical association, a law lecturer, and a representative of Togolese Red Cross.[51]

[45] Ibid, p. 194.

[46] Permanent Commission of Enquiry Act, 1966, s. 8.

[47] The Annual Report of the Permanent Commission of Enquiry 1966–7,. Government Printer. Dar es Salaam, 1968.

[48] Y.P. Ghai, "Ombudsman and Others", EAJ, VI, 8, 1969.

[49] Annual Report of the Permanent Commission of Enquiry July 1980 – June 1981, Government Printer, Dar es Salaam, p. 5.

[50] Amnesty International, Rapport 1987, p. 85.

[51] Loi No 87-09 du 9 juin 1987, Article 5.

Members hold office for four years, which is renewable (presumably indefinitely).[52] The Commission is described as not falling "under any form of administrative bureaucratic supervision".[53]

The Commission is unusual among bodies investigating human rights abuses in that it has also played an important role in human rights promotion and education. It has organized, for example, training courses for magistrates, lawyers, police officers and civil servants, as well as information tours in all prefectures in the country. The meetings on these tours are generally conducted in local languages and are aimed at giving people a basic conception of their internationally guaranteed rights.

The Commission is empowered to receive complaints from any Togolese citizen, foreign resident or private group (this has allowed it to receive and investigate complaints from Amnesty International). Sometimes its intervention enables the complainant to withdraw the accusation.[54] But if this does not happen, the following procedure is set in motion:

"Within three days of receiving a petition, the Executive Committee of the Commission, which is composed of five members, must meet to consider the petition and, if it is admissible, to appoint a member of the Commission as special rapporteur to conduct an inquiry in connection with it. To this end the special rapporteur is empowered, inter alia, to have, access to any reports, records and other documents and to any objects and remises connected with the inquiry; he may be compared to an ombudsman in that, if necessary, he works together with the Government department concerned to find ways and means of remedying the violation referred to in the petition. He has 15 days from the time of his appointment in which to submit a report on his investigation and, as appropriate, to express his views and make recommendations to the Commission. If the violation continues, the Commission meets immediately to consider the report and to take measures to put an end to the violation, in particular by applying for a remedy to the courts, the parliament or the Head of State."[55]

Details of an investigation are confidential, but may be made public at the Commission's discretion. The Commission lacks formal powers to enforce its decisions. It cannot impose damages or other sanctions. One course of action available to the Commission is the institution of proceedings in the courts. In no circumstances may the Commission "in any way serve as a substitute for the courts nor call into question their decisions"; on the other hand, it is empowered to intervene if legal proceedings are unreasonably protracted.[56] According to its annual report, the Commission's function is to make the existing administrative machinery function properly.[57]

In 1987, its first year of operation, the Commission reported that it investigated 187 petitions that it found to be valid. The largest category, 64 cases, related to arbitrary detention. About half of these were reported to have been resolved by

---

[52] Loi No 87-09 du 9 juin 1987, Article 5.

[53] Annual Report of the Activities of the National Commission on Human Rights October 21 1987–October 21, 1988, p. 2.

[54] Annual Report, 1987–8, p. 13.

[55] Addendum to Togo's report to the Human Rights Committee under Article 40 of the International Covenant on Civil and Political Rights, CCPR/C/36/Add.5, 11 November 1988, p. 4.

[56] Annual Report of the Activities of the National Commission on Human Rights, 1987–1988, p. 20.However, the Commission does not have the power to intervene "en cas de deni manifeste de justice". (Loi No. 87-09 du 9 juin 1987, Article 12).

[57] Ibid, p. 12.

either the release or prosecution of the prisoner concerned. Initially it appeared that the Commission's progress in dealing with arbitrary detention was not matched by its work on torture. It investigated only two out of five torture cases presented to it by Amnesty International and appeared to have been over-ready to take denials of police and military officials at face value. However, in September 1990 the chief of police was dismissed after the Commission had verified allegations that detained students had been tortured.

Also in 1990, the Commission intervened effectively to prevent the banning of an independent newspaper, Forum Hebdo, which had published an article critical of President Mobutu of Zaire.

In April 1991, the Commission was charged with investigating the deaths of at least 26 people whose bodies where discovered in a lagoon at the time of anti-government demonstrations in Lomé. Its report, completed in July 1991, unequivocally holds the army responsible for killing the protesters and demands the President identifies the specific personnel responsible with a view to bringing them to justice.[58] The forthrightness of the report signals the Commission's confidence in its own independence and stature.

Uganda

The office of Inspector-General of Government was conceived in parallel with another human rights institution: the Commission of Inquiry into Human Rights Violations. The latter, chaired by a High Court judge, was a judicial commission mandated to investigate human rights violations in Uganda from independence in 1962 until 26 January 1986 – the date when the National Resistance Army (NRA) seized power in Kampala. Investigating human rights violations from that date onwards was to be the responsibility of the Inspector-General.

The Inspector-General's twin mandate of investigating corruption and human rights abuse reflects the NRA's pre-occupations in its 10-point programme, effectively the manifesto on which it came to power. The appointment of Augustine Ruzindana, a personal friend and student colleague of President Museveni, as Inspector-General clearly reflected the importance attached to the office, but also raised doubts about his impartiality. Ruzindana's conduct of the post has dispelled those doubts, although it might still be wondered whether there is sufficient institutional independence, had the Inspector-General not been such a strong character. Ruzindana himself argues that it has been a strength of the Inspectorate that it was closely identified with the presidency:

> "The fact that we are responsible to the President is actually designed to enhance this independence because then we do not fall under the jurisdiction of any other office we are likely to investigate. You would recall that when I started the office, Parliament was virtually non-existent, in which case reporting to Parliament would have emasculated the office from its inception. The good-will of Government was emphasised by the President lending his prestige to the office. In our context, this is an advantage, not a liability."[59]

The office has four functions:

– to inquire into allegations of human rights violations, particularly arbitrary

[58] Commission Nationale des Droits de l'Homme, Procès-verbal d'enquete, d'avis et de recommandations, Lomé, July 1991.

[59] Letter From Augustine Ruzindana to Richard Carver, November 1989.

killings, arbitrary arrest and detention, denial of fair trial, torture and unlawful acquisition of or damage to property;
- to investigate how far law enforcement agencies respect the rule of law;
- to detect and prevent corruption;
- to investigate maladministration and abuse of office.[60]

The Inspector-General enjoys extensive inquisitorial powers and immunity. He can seize documents, conduct a search and subpoena witnesses, with the power to issue an arrest warrant for failure to comply. Before the Inspector-General takes on a case, the complainant need not have exhausted all other remedies.[61] He has the power to initiate his own investigations: "The Inspectorate does not just wait for complaints to be brought to it, but it also goes out to unearth corruption and maladministration whether the public complains or not."[62]

The services of the Inspectorate are provided for the public "free of charge in a congenial and informal atmosphere."[63] It has neither an administrative nor judicial role; its job is only to investigate "malfunctioning of the Government system and ... maladministration by public officers".[64] Investigations into corruption have formed the bulk of the Inspector-General's work. The Inspector-General's mandate excludes examination of court decisions, matters which are subjudice or the President's exercise of his prerogative of mercy. In addition the President can order him not to investigate matters which he regards as endangering national security or Cabinet secrecy.

Ruzindana argues persuasively that his popular anti-corruption work has the effect of strengthening his hand in dealing with human rights abuse:

> "There is a natural scepticism about a Government institution investigating Government malpractices. Once we have established in one area that we could actually effectively investigate Government malpractices the chances of establishing some credibility while investigating human rights are very high."[65]

However, a contrary argument is that the Inspector-General has responsibility for more than he can realistically handle – at least without a major expansion of staff and resources. He has been effective in a number of cases when he has intervened over arbitrary detentions in the capital, but has had little or no impact on the worst human rights abuses, which have taken place away from Kampala in northern and eastern Uganda. In May 1991, the Inspector-General was assigned responsibility for investigating the torture of members of parliament arrested by the army. In previous high-profile cases investigations have been conducted either by a judicial commission or by the army itself. In the latter cases the investigations appear to have been ineffective.[66]

---

[60] Inspector-General of Government Statute, Statute 2, 1987, s. 7.
[61] Inspector-General; of Government Statute, 1987, s. 12(3) (a).
[62] General information on the Office of Inspector-General of Government, p. 7. See also Inspector-General of Government Statute, 1987, s. 7 (2).
[63] General Information about the office of Inspector-General, p. 3
[64] General Information on the Office of Inspector-General of Government, p.7.
[65] Letter from Augustine Ruzindana to Richard Carver, November 1989.
[66] The judicial commission was established to investigate the police killing of protesting students at Makerere University in December 1990. At the time of writing it had not reported, although unlike the army investigations it had held public hearings of evidence.

Zaire

The creation of the Department des Droits et des Libertés du Citoyen in 1966 was a response by the Zairian Government to repeated international criticism of its human rights record. In practice, however, the department has lacked the credibility of, say, the Togolese Commission Nationale des Droits de l'Homme, and in many quarters it has not been seen as an effective mechanism for human rights protection. In 1991 the Department appears to have been disbanded or at least downgraded in status.

Unlike most of the human rights institutions reviewed, the Department was not an autonomous official body but a government ministry. This clearly had an effect on its credibility as an impartial mechanism for investigating complaints against government bodies. The State Commissioner in charge of the Department at its inception was a former chef du cabinet to President Mobutu, Maitre Nimy Mayidika Ngimi. While this indicated that some importance was attached to the Department it also suggested that there was little distance between it and the presidency. This impression was confirmed by the fact that it was the Department; usually in the person of Maitre Nimy, who appeared before the UN's Human Rights Committee in Geneva to defend the government's human rights record, as well as fulfilling the same functions in more public forums, for example on the White House lawn in Washington.[67] This, combined with its unusual practice of publishing the names of its complainants, made it probably the least popular of the institutions under review. In 1987 it received only 123 complaints, of which only a handful related to alleged abuses by the security agencies. Most dealt with grievances within the civil service.[68]

The Lawyers' Committee for Human Rights has studied the workings of the Department closely and has itself submitted cases for investigation. In a recent report the Lawyers' Committee diagnosed the Department's weaknesses as coming from three sources: "structural constraints; incapacity to sanction violators; and inadequate public reporting."[69] The structural problem is the Department's status as a ministry and its lack of formal independence.

Its reluctance to take effective action is exemplified by the case of Kamunga Mwimpe, a 24-year-old woman suspected of having an affair with the husband of a member of the Central Committee of the ruling party, Mayuma Kala. Kamunga "disappeared" on 23 June 1988, reportedly at Mayuma's behest. The Department has been investigating the case since 14 September 1988 without result. Kamunga's family has been told by security officers that she was held in a security cell and later reports suggest that she died in detention. Apparently no one has raised the matter with Mayuma.

The ineffectiveness of its public reporting is shown by the fact that, although the Department reports the names of its complainants, it has failed to publish its promised *fichier de moralité*, listing egregious human rights violators. The Lawyers' Committee reports that staff the Department have submitted names for inclusion on such a list, but that the central leadership has failed to do so.

[67] Richard Carver, "Called to account: How African governments investigate human rights violations", African Affairs 89, 356; pp. 391–415.
[68] Droits et Libertés du Citoyen, Receuil des Decisions, no date.
[69] Lawyers' Committee for Human Rights, Zaire: Repression as Policy, New York, 1990, p. 138.

The Lawyers' Committee adds a fourth reason for the Department's weakness, namely its public defence of the government's human rights record in international forums. As well as discouraging potential complainants, this has led to situations where the Department has publicly defended the government over cases which it was supposedly investigating. Thus in 1989, Maitre Nimy was quoted in the foreign press as stating that an opposition leader, Tshisekedi wa Mulumba was free, when he was in fact under house arrest and the department was supposed to be investigating a complaint to that effect. The Lawyers' Committee concluded:

"The (Department) cannot with equal vigour promote the reputation of Zaire in all forums and, at the same time, defend the rights of its own citizens. By failing to reconcile its conflicting missions, the (Department) is unable to effectively serve its advocacy function."[70]

The Gambia

The African Centre for Democracy and Human Rights Studies has some of the features usually associated with national human rights institutions. It is established under the national laws of The Gambia, for example, and is partly financed from government funds.[71] In addition, its Patron is the President of The Gambia.[72]

In some other respects, however, the African Centre has the features of an international human rights organization. As its name suggests, the African Centre' s mandate includes, but is not confined to, The Gambia.[73] The two training courses organized by the African Centre in May 1991, for example, were for magistrates from Benin, Cameroon, Gabon, Guinea, and Togo, and for senior public officials from Ghana, Sierra Leone and the Gambia. Although the African Centre's first Director is a Gambian, his staff is international. The organization's governing Council includes African nationals from outside The Gambia, as well as human rights experts from Europe and Canada. The African Centre's international character was further reinforced when it was granted diplomatic privileges and immunities in April 1991.[74]

The organization's mandate is not investigative, but exclusively promotional. Indeed, there is no investigative human rights institution in The Gambia. The Centre is enjoined, "in cooperation with other African and international institutions, (to) encourage the promotion of human and peoples' rights through training and research."[75] Accordingly, it may organize meetings:

"... involving people from all over the Continent for the purpose of exchanging ideas on common problems,.., sponsor public lectures in different parts of Africa; indicate and assist in the implementation of human rights related projects in Africa; and ... publish periodicals and journals."[76]

The African Centre has begun to implement its mandate by publishing its

---

[70] Ibid, p. 152.
[71] African Centre for Democracy and Human Rights Studies Act, 1989.
[72] Ibid, s. 5 (1).
[73] Ibid, s. 4(1).
[74] See endnote 25.
[75] African Centre for Democracy and Human Rights Studies Act, 1989, s. 4(1).
[76] African Centre for Democracy and Human Rights Studies Act, s. 4(2) (a–d).

bilingual 'African Human Rights Newsletter' and a series of human rights occasional Papers, organizing training workshops and developing a documentation unit which specialises in democracy and human rights in Africa. In 1992 or 1993, it plans to launch a short, annual human rights course for non-governmental organizations and public officials.

Unlike any other national institution under review, the African Centre has observer status with the African Commission on Human and Peoples' Rights. The Chair of the African Commission is ex-officio a member of the African Centre's governing Council. At present, the African Centre and the African Commission's secretariat are located on different floors in the same building. Predictably, both the African Charter on Human and Peoples' Rights, and the work of the African Commission, receive considerable attention in the African Centre's programmes. Nonetheless, the African Centre and African Commission are completely separate organizations. The African Commission has both a promotional and protective role: it may hear complaints from individuals that a state party has violated the African Charter. Unlike the African Centre, the African Commission enjoys the status of an inter-governmental organization established by the OAU.

Even for organizations like the African Centre which have no investigative function, independence remains an important issue. In the case of the African Centre, its independence is enhanced by a diversified funding base, diplomatic status and the international character of its governing Council and staff. Although The Gambia's Attorney General is ex-officio Chair of the governing Council, Presidential nominees comprise a minority of Council members.

The UN has played a key role in the formation of the African Centre. The UN centre for Human Rights, Geneva, has encouraged The Gambian initiative and continues to contribute advice, practical support and multilateral financial assistance. The UN's Under-Secretary-General for Human Rights, Mr. Jan Martenson, is a member of the African Centre's governing Council.

The African Centre is difficult to categorise. Probably, the organizations most similar to it are the Inter-American Institute for Human Rights, in San José, Costa Rica, and the International Institute of Human Rights in Strasbourg, France.

Observations and Suggestions

In this final section we discuss some of the more important issues raised earlier about the law and practice of international human rights institutions. Some general points and principles are identified which might be kept in mind as states formulate appropriate and effective human rights institutions in their jurisdictions. Among the observations and suggestions there are no prescriptions: national institutions will vary with national circumstances.

Independence and Impartiality

It is essential that human rights investigations are impartial: they must not display bias and should be prepared to reach truthful conclusions, however awkward these may be. The independence of a human rights institution is the most effective guarantee of its impartiality.

Independence is a relative term. All the institutions reviewed in this paper are official ones by definition. The crucial point is that those doing the investigating should be independent of those who are the subject of the investigation. This has been clearly argued by Amnesty International, for example, in a submission to the new Ugandan Government in 1986 arguing for the formation of a permanent human rights institution:

"The investigating body, however constituted, should be able to demonstrate its independence from the detaining and interrogating authorities as well as from governmental pressure and influence. In order that its findings prove credible, the government might include among its members people nominated by independent non-governmental bodies such as the Uganda Law Society and the Uganda Medical Association."[77]

This argument is far from being universally accepted. Hatchard considers: "The perceived need for an 'independent' body to investigate such matters is perhaps overstated."[78] McAuslan and Ghai, discussing the Tanzanian institution, consider that its lack of formal independence from the state machinery is a strength. They describe it as:

"... a new institution which could be within the reach of the ordinary citizen, would provide a possibility of redress, and would not at the same time antagonise too greatly the government and party bureaucracy. This last is an important point, for plans to increase surveillance and control of the bureaucracies must take into account their views, otherwise such institutions as are created will be stifled at birth."[79]

This sees the issue from the point of view of those under scrutiny, rather than the public who are seeking protection for their rights. In practice, most of the institutions under review have maintained a degree of formal independence from the bodies they are called upon to investigate, except Zaire's government department. More information is needed about the mandate, powers and practice of Gabon's new Minister of human rights, before assessing whether or not he has more formal independence than his Zairian counterpart. However, most of the institutions have been closely associated with the office of the president. The historical reasons for this are clear, given the weakness of the legislature in most African countries. Hatchard argues pragmatically:

"... unless the ombudsman is seen to have the blessing of the head of state it may well be very difficult for him to operate effectively."[80]

In the worst case, the problem is that a President can intervene to stop an investigation or can tell the institution what it should be looking at. In a number of countries, the head of state has either or both of these powers in the law establishing the human rights institution. More commonly the role of the President as protector of the human rights institution creates unwritten limits

---

[77] Amnesty International, Memorandum to the Government of the Republic of Uganda, September 1986, p. 13. One of the present authors has argued elsewhere: "The impartiality, and thus the effectiveness, of inquiry hinges upon its independence. Unless the investigators are formally independent of those under investigation there is no guarantee of impartiality. This is the difference between the Togolese and Zairian examples, where each human rights investigation was set up in a similar political context. One has exhibited a degree of independence and effectiveness; the other has not", Carver, p. 411.

[78] Hatchard, "The Ombudsman in Africa Revisited".

[79] McAuslan and Ghai, p. 501.

[80] Hatchard, "The Institution of the Ombudsman in Africa".

to what can be investigated. The experience of human rights bodies accountable to the legislature has not so far been a positive one in Africa, but this may change with the emergence of popularly elected and representative national assemblies in a number of countries. There are a number of formal guarantees of independence which deserve particular attention:

- Appointment:
  In most instances, the appointment of the members of a human rights institution is the sole prerogative of the head of state. Exceptions include countries where the appointment is made on the recommendation of the Judicial Service Commission – Zimbabwe, Zambia and Namibia – or where members are nominated by non-governmental bodies, as in Togo. The public credibility of an institution is enhanced if appointments are not exclusively in presidential hands.
- Security of tenure:
  This is regarded as an important protection of the independence of the judiciary, yet few of the human rights institutions studied have guaranteed long-term security of tenure. Generally, members are appointed for three or four year terms renewable once. It does not reinforce the impartiality of the institution if its members are concerned about whether their contracts will be renewed. Members should be given long-term contracts, with a guarantee that they can only be removed for gross misconduct or mental incapacity. This should be determined by an impartial, autonomous body such as a Judicial Service Commission, as in Namibia, or a tribunal of Appeal Court judges, as in Ghana.
- Immunity:
  In most cases members – and sometimes staff – of human rights institutions have immunity from prosecution for any act carried out in the course of their duty. Sometimes, as in Tanzania, the entire proceedings of the institution privileged in a manner that is analogous to court proceedings. In some countries, such as Togo and Benin, specific penalties are prescribed for interference in the work of the human rights institution. Immunity is an important attribute affording protection against unwelcome governmental interference.
- Publicity:
  Non-governmental human rights organizations have generally argued that; investigations should be conducted publicly as a safeguard of impartiality. The Amnesty International document on Uganda, already quoted, continues:

"The methods an findings should be public. At a minimum the results and reasoning of any particular investigation should be made public ... It would serve to reassure the general public if a full record of the hearings and its findings were published."[81]

A British Royal Commission set up to review procedure for tribunals of inquiry reached a similar conclusion:

"It is said that sometimes witnesses are willing to give evidence only if they are allowed to give it in private or in confidence. This is no doubt true. But such evidence in matters of this kind is treated as suspect by the general public and, in our view, rightly so. Secrecy increases the quantity of evidence but tends to debase its quality."[82]

---

[81] Amnesty International, Memorandum, p.14.
[82] Report of Royal Commission on Tribunals of Inquiry, 1966 p. 20.

If the findings of an investigation are public, it is much more likely that a government can be held accountable for its actions, and much less likely that abuses will recur. This has certainly been the case with ad hoc commissions of inquiry. The Ghanian Special Investigation Board, which has already been mentioned, took this view:

> "If it is the truth that we speak, does it matter whether we speak it in public or in private? ... No one has a right to be heard in camera however exalted his position in the Republic of Ghana."[83]

The Board's report resulted in the trial and conviction of government members and officials on charges of murdering three judges and a retired army officer. By contrast the findings of a commission of inquiry into army killings in the Matabeleland region of Zimbabwe in 1983 were never made public. The army unit alleged to be responsible was reassigned to Matabeleland the following year and the pattern of killings recurred.[84]

It is striking, however, that none of the investigative institutions under review operates publicly. The partial exception is the Zairian human rights department which published the names of all its complainants. This may explain why it used to receive relatively few complaints. Without exception, the institutions regard the confidentiality of their investigative procedures as a strength. Clearly this view is shared by complainants who fear reprisals from those they are petitioning against.

Nigeria and Togo each have useful provisions although for publicity at the discretion of the commission. This might be adopted elsewhere, with the additional possibility of publicity at the request of a complainant. It is also important that the substance of any findings against government officials is made public after investigations are concluded: the purpose of confidentiality should be to protect the citizen not to shield the government from criticism.

- Budget:
  An institution's funding has a bearing on both its effectiveness and independence. In practice, lack of resources is the greatest problem faced by most human rights institutions. The Public Complaints Commission in Rivers State, Nigeria, laments:

> "The pathetic transport situation has greatly affected the Commission's activities adversely, particularly investigation of complaints as will be seen in the statistics presently."[85]

The annual report goes into great detail about the poor state of the commission's vehicles, which seems to be regarded as the most crucial factor determining the effectiveness of its work. The problem is a common one, although in some respects the Nigerian Commission is well-endowed, employing 199 investigators.[86] In 1988, the Togolese Commission reported that it had only five full-time employees, all administrative staff.[87]

---

[83] Report of the Special Investigation Board (Kidnapping and Killing of Specified Persons), pp. 7–8.
[84] Amnesty International Report, 1985, p. 115
[85] Annual Report of the Public Complaints Commission, Rivers State, 1989.
[86] Hatchard, "The Ombudsman in the Commonwealth".
[87] Annual Report of the Activities of the National Commission on Human Rights, 1987–1988, p. 29.

All the talk about independence and impartiality is irrelevant if the institution does not have the basic resources to do its job. It is common to find, as in Uganda and Zambia, that the institution is reasonably effective in the capital city, but largely irrelevant elsewhere in the country. Problems of transport, in particular, are common to most institutions in Africa. However, the security forces, which are often responsible for human right violations, generally do not have problems getting around the country. If governments attach importance to human rights, then they must ensure that institutions charged with their protection are equally mobile.

Often the human rights institution is allocated resources by central government. It may end up, as in Togo, also seeking funds from elsewhere. The Togolese Commission is subsidised for about a quarter of its budget from the United States Government and a private German foundation. There are dangers in over-reliance on one or two outside funders. It can lead to charges of political partiality. Diversified funding base, on the other hand, helps to ensure independence. The African Centre in Banjul, for example, receives funds from a variety of governmental, non-governmental and multilateral sources, although the Gambian Government pays the bulk of the institution's overheads.

The amount of multilateral funding available for human rights work in developing countries is increasing, not only though the UN Voluntary Fund for Technical Co-operation in the Field of Human Rights, but also under the Lome Convention IV.[88] This trend recognizes human rights protection is not cost-free and that developing countries may need help to finance it. One advantage of multilateral, rather than bilateral, support is that it reduces the risk of political interference by funders.

In conclusion, diversified funding, with a multilateral component, deserves consideration by national human rights institutions. The institution's own government, however, must not escape altogether its obligation to pay for human rights promotion and protection.[89]

Human Rights Institutions and the Judiciary

When the first human rights institution was set up in Tanzania, it was clearly intended as an alternative to judicial protection of human rights. In the 1960s, Tanzania did not have a Bill of Rights. This was partly because of hostility on

[88] For details of UNCOHR contact the Un Centre for Human Rights, Palais des Nations, 1211 Geneva 10, Switzerland. Lome IV, the fourth ACP-EEC Convention, was signed on 15 December 1989 but has not yet entered into force. In relation to the promotion of human rights Article 5(3) or the Convention is of special interest: "... financial resources may be allocated ... to the promotion of human rights ... through specific schemes, public or private, ... particularly in the legal sphere ... Resources may also be given to support the establishment of structures to promote human rights. Priority shall be given to schemes of regional scope."

[89] As the Togolese Commission noted: "Actually, the mistake would be to distrust State financing; since, as we have said, the commission is a State institution and not a private organization whose resources should be provided by its members ... The State must, therefore, give high priority to ensuring its continued existence ...", Annual Report of the Activities of the National Commission on Human Rights, 1987–88, p. 24.

the part of government to the judiciary, but also because of a feeling that the courts were too remote from most ordinary people.

In the 1990s, the situation has changed considerably. Tanzania is one of a number of countries with a justiciable Bill of Rights. In many instances, as in Zimbabwe, the narrow mandate of the human rights institution is based on the assumption that the judiciary will take the lead in protecting human rights. The Zimbabwean ombudsman looks at narrower matters of maladministration. However, the fact that the Zimbabwean judiciary has been vigorous in its defence of constitutional rights cannot hide the fact that most citizens are too poor to hire a lawyer and take their case to court. This was recognized in the early years of the Tanzanian Commission:

Equally to the point is the fact that a Bill of Rights can only be adjudicated upon effectively in the High Court, and this means that such protection as it offers will rarely be invoked by the majority of citizens in a poor country.[90]

Many people find the judicial system too remote and intimidating, as the Tanzanian institution found: "The Commission of course advises the complainants to take legal action. In some cases our clients refuse, saying that if it involved going to court, they would rather sacrifice their rights than jeopardise their future and that in some cases to do so, would mean inviting troubles."[91]

The difficulties associated with legal proceedings partly explain why some national institutions are granted two important powers. In Uganda, the Inspector-General can take a case even if the complainant has not exhausted all other remedies. Secondly, in Tanzania, Zambia and Uganda, the institutions are authorized to launch an investigation on their own initiative; they do not depend on individuals who, through ignorance, fear or because they are imprisoned, do not lodge a complaint.

However, if the judiciary is to maintain its independence and have an effective role in protecting human rights, it is essential that national human rights institutions do not have the power to review court decisions or matters which are subjudice. Most are explicitly prohibited from investigating such matters. The Togolese Commission provides a limited and useful exception: it may intervene in legal proceedings if there is a delay in dealing with a case, but not to deal with the substance.

By way of summary, in practice an individual's right legal advice and access to the courts is restricted. Provided they are granted the necessary powers, national institutions can help to make up for these shortcomings of the legal system. It is unhelpful, however, if they review legal proceedings which remain subjudice. More valuable is a power enabling national institutions to intervene where there is unacceptable delay in the legal process.

Compulsory Powers and Enforcement

Some of the national institutions under review have compulsory powers, such as to order the production of documents and the appearance of witnesses. But none of them have formal powers of enforcement, such as the imposition of

[90] McAuslan and Ghai, p. 501
[91] Annual Report of the Permanent Commission of Enquiry 1967– 8, p. 6.

damages or other sanctions. Instead, they rely upon informal and indirect means of enforcement.

In practice, an intervention by a national institution may cause the human rights violation to stop, for example, through the release of someone who is arbitrarily detained. Informal enforcement may also occur in cases where the institution resolves a dispute, by bringing the parties together and mediating.

Indirect enforcement may arise from a national institution's recommendation to the executive. If adopted, a recommendation may result in a victim receiving compensation; a wrong-doer may be prosecuted or subjected to disciplinary proceedings. The power to initiate court proceedings on behalf of a complainant is another means of indirect enforcement available to some institutions, in particular commissions (Togo, Benin, Cameroon) and more rarely, Ombudsmen (Ghana, Namibia).

In Namibia, the Ombudsman is empowered to apply to the courts for an interdict, or injunction, to stop a human rights violation. He or she can also recommend directly to the Prosecutor-General that criminal proceedings should be taken against an official. In other words, although the Ombudsman is a presidential appointee, it is not the head of state who decides what action should be taken as a result of investigations. This is a significant step away from the human rights institution being an arm of presidential government.

A free press and influential legislature is likely enhance an institution's powers of enforcement. Tabling reports in Parliament brings them to the attention of legislators and the press. If an institution is empowered to make reports to a Minister or the President, "it is desirable ... that (they are) required to table the report in Parliament within a stated period"."[92]

Compulsory powers and means of enforcement available to investigative national institutions are among their most impotent features. Without effective powers, the institution will be virtually impotent and its procedures are likely to fall into disrepute.[93]

Governmental and Non-governmental Human Rights Bodies

The Togolese Commission was set up at a time when there was limited freedom of association and no non-governmental human rights groups. In the last year, two such groups have been established and the commission's chairman has resigned in order to pursue a career in opposition politics. The conclusion of many human rights activists in Togo was that the commission was simply a phase of their work which can now be superseded by non-governmental activity.

In our opinion this view is misguided. There are two important reasons why official human rights bodies complement non-governmental groups. The first is a matter of principle: governments should be obliged to investigate allegations of human rights abuse because they are accountable for the behaviour of their own officers. The second is a pragmatic reason: an official body can be granted formal powers which could never be given to a non-government group. It would be impossible for a private human rights organization to issue a subpoena or apply for a search warrant.

---

[92] P.H. Bailey, "On Establishing National Human Rights Bodies", January 1986, 222–231 at p.229.

[93] See endnote 1, paras. 71–72.

It is argued by many both inside and outside government that non-governmental groups, as well as churches, the press and opposition parties, will do the job of investigating more effectively because they have no bias in favour of the government. But that is not an argument against official human rights institutions: it simply means that their independence should be safeguarded.

Official and unofficial human rights bodies have different strengths and weaknesses. Institutions are likely to have good access to senior figures in the government; non-government groups will probably have closer links with the grassroots. In some situations, collaboration may increase the effectiveness of both organizations.[94]

The Importance of Promotion

One area where there can be particularly fruitful collaboration is in human rights promotion. This is seriously neglected. Of the institutions studied, the one most effectively engaged in both promotional and protective work is the Togolese Commission.

There are three areas where promotional work is particularly important:

- Recommending legal changes in order to increase respect for human rights. A number of institutions have this power, although it does not appear to have been widely used. The obvious first step is to examine domestic law to see whether it conforms to international human rights standards.
- Training of law enforcement officers and others in domestic and international human rights standards.
  The Togolese Commission and African Centre in The Gambia have begun this work. Although much abuse of human rights is wilful, some also results from ignorance on the part of officials. Education and training can make a significant difference.
- Public information about human rights.

Again, in Togo and The Gambia this has begun in a systematic way, although some institutions, like the Tanzanian Commission, have also engaged in a form of promotional work. The Togolese Commission has noted an increase in the number of petitions of complaint after it has carried out promotional tours. Elsewhere, non-governmental groups have published excellent public information material in local languages.[95] Perhaps human rights groups can integrate radio programmes into their public information activities.

Human rights promotion and protection are closely connected: effective promotion will lead to improved protection. Whenever resources permit, national institutions should devise promotional programmes of training, education, public information, research, documentation and legal reform. No doubt they will find a willing collaborator in the African Commission on Human and Peoples' Rights which, unlike any other regional inter-governmental organization, has no explicit promotional mandate.[96]

---

[94]In Uganda, for example, contact between the Inspector-General of Government and the non-governmental Uganda Human Rights Activists has probably increased the effectiveness of both bodies.

[95]See for example, the publications of the Legal Resources Foundation, P.O. Box 918, Harare.

[96]African Charter on Human and People's Rights, Article 45(1). The African Commission's Secretariat can be contacted at P.O. Box 673, Banjul, The Gambia.

Human Rights in Africa: Values, Institutions, Opportunities

Alex de Waal*

Overview

It is frequently embarrassing to be a known as a 'human rights activist' in Africa today. Using the label 'human rights' in countries across the continent regularly invites derision. Many ordinary African citizens see that human rights organizations prosper while human rights are routinely violated. Many human rights organizations held out high hopes, but have failed to deliver. There is a sense of betrayal, felt most acutely in the countries where human rights have been most outrageously violated.

Few would disagree that there is a human rights crisis in Africa. It is hard to think of a country in which the promises of the Universal Declaration of Human Rights, now half a century old, are being fulfilled. There is plenty of work for those concerned with human rights. The need for human rights organizations appears greater than ever. But I am going to argue in this paper that the crisis in human rights is also located within the institutions that are supposed to protect human rights, including United Nations institutions, western governments with human rights components in their foreign policies and aid programmes, and the non-governmental human rights organizations (shortly: human rights organizations or HROs), which have played a key role in setting the international human rights agenda for the 1990s. The methods which these institutions have deployed to promote the values of universal human rights have not always been appropriate to the realities of Africa. But they rarely if ever recognize this problem, and make the error of conflating their own institutional practices with the rights that they, usually sincerely, endeavour to uphold.

In this paper I emphasise that it is essential to distinguish between the universal values of human rights and the specific institutions that can be used to further them in particular social and political circumstances. The formulae for "human rights" that are advanced by most international human rights organizations are in fact a political illusion. In Africa today, political illusions are dangerous luxuries, and when they explode, as they inevitably do, the damage can be considerable.

---

*Inter Africa Group, Addis Ababa. This paper has been written in a personal capacity and the views expressed are those of the author alone and should not be taken to represent the position of any organization.

K. Hossain et al. (eds), Human Rights Commissions and Ombudsman Offices, 759–781.

I am sure that many of my colleagues in international human rights organizations will be somewhat baffled. Some will interpret my critique as an assault on human rights values themselves. I believe that should they do so, they will be making a mistake – perhaps a rather dangerous mistake. International human rights organizations and human rights policies run a serious risk of discrediting the idea of human rights in Africa.

Human Rights Traditions in Western Europe and North America

Every culture and society has a concept of human rights. But it is western human rights traditions originating in Enlightenment Europe that have come to dominate the world. In the first section of this paper I attempt a very brief overview of four traditions of rights activism in the West. The widespread usage of "human rights" is extremely recent, although philosophers have used comparable terms for many centuries. Until the last few decades, people did not struggle for abstract conceptions of rights but for changes that would directly bring benefits to their lives. This we may call the "first generation" of human rights struggle. There were few rights organizations as such and the aims and methods used in these struggles were extremely varied, sometimes making little or no reference to the concept of "rights" at all.

Primary Mobilization

Historically, the struggle for civil and political liberties was a struggle against religious intolerance, monarchical absolutism and heavy taxation. It began in Europe and its north American colonies. People were mobilized to struggle for freedom of religion and freedom of conscience, and social and economic progress. These were highly political struggles. Asserting freedom of conscience in England required a civil war and the execution of a monarch, while establishing the sovereignty of parliament required the deposition of another king. The American Constitution required a successful rebellion, and the French assertion of the "Rights of Man" needed a revolution. More recently, struggles for rights have often been non-violent, using the freedoms established by revolution or granted by rulers who recognized that autocracy could best be preserved by providing space for civil liberties.

The nineteenth century campaigns in Britain against the trans-Atlantic slave trade and against child labour in factories ("Yorkshire Slavery" as the campaigners called it) combined a measure of religiously inspired philanthropy with liberal plutocratic self interest. In India at the turn of the century, the British Raj recognized that containing the pressures of Indian nationalism required implementing effective policies for preventing famine, because recurrent epidemic starvation was discrediting British rule abroad, and, even more seriously, stirring up unrest in the sub-continent itself. The British policy of making minor concessions worked for almost half a century, until the failure to prevent the eminently preventable 1943 Bengal famine brought shame on British rule. It was a gross violation of basic economic rights and it stimulated popular pressure for the basic political right of independence, which was duly achieved a few years later.

Similarly, throughout this century in Europe and America, popular mobilization for civil and political rights has been inseparable from pursuit of social, economic and cultural rights. To put it more strongly, people have mobilized in pursuit of protecting their own interests, to remove restrictions on their personal lives, and to oppose threats to their personal welfare, aspirations and dignity. This is the core of human rights, and it is a very hard core indeed. Examples include the women's movement: the campaign first for the right to vote and then for equality under the law. Trade union rights and legislation on employment – and indeed for national economic policies to promote employment – is another case. Campaigns for nuclear disarmament and the withdrawal of troops from Vietnam and Northern Ireland are another instance. The recent environmental movements in the developed world have been stimulated by very immediate concerns for preserving people's surroundings. Perhaps the defining instance is the American civil liberties movement in the 1960s: a non-violent movement by citizens to claim their right to send their children to schools, to obtain jobs, to vote for their representatives. Legitimate self interest set in a universal moral idiom is extremely powerful.

This is politics. This is the slow and often painful struggle for people to establish what is rightfully theirs. This is the practical negotiation of a social contract.

Any attempt to create a definition of these diverse social and political movements would be doomed to failure. But there are some key ingredients that have contributed to success.

One essential element is mass mobilization. The physical fact of so many people demanding their rights was instrumental in these movements. A second element is nonviolence. Most (not all) have used non-violent methods, or used symbolic violence only. This has given them the moral high ground over their oppressors. The discipline of non-violence has also been very importance in keeping the moral vision of the movements intact. On the governmental side, these movements have required a certain degree of tolerance to survive. Mahatma Gandhi's independence movement could have been violently crushed by the British, but in what was arguably its most enlightened step ever, it chose not to try.

Where a government is ready to be utterly ruthless in suppressing its citizens, non-violent resistance may not be an option. The African National Congress was a non-violent movement for the first half of this century, but this achieved nothing and it was pushed to armed struggle.

Primary activism is a complicated process. It is not simply a matter of making people come out by whipping up their passions. On the contrary, it requires a moral vision, and a patient commitment to public education and community assistance. Many of the elements that were to become prominent in "secondary activism" such as research, documentation, publishing and using the law, were also widely used in primary mobilization.

It is important to note that in no sense was this primary mobilization "neutral" or "impartial" – and still less was it "non-political". Quite the reverse: these men and women were pursuing highly controversial political goals that challenged the supremacy of a government or of one section of society.

Legal Aid and Public Interest Litigation

The foundation of protection for human rights is the rule of law. Rights commonly exist in law (provided for by constitutions or common law) that may not be upheld in practice, either through custom and neglect, or through abrogation of rights by governmental institutions. Laws often also need clarification which can only be obtained through test cases.

Actually using the courts is a classic area in which respect for civil and political rights is dependent on exercise of social and economic rights. In most countries access to the courts is expensive, sometimes prohibitively so. In many countries, women, members of ethnic or social minorities, and people living in remote rural areas, face enormous obstacles in pursuing their rights through the judicial system. On the other hand, wealthy and powerful people are often able to use the courts in a way that selectively benefits them. The British libel laws are a notorious example in which wealth enables certain individuals to use the courts to intimidate newspapers and individuals, and in practice to suppress free speech. In many countries, property and land law, or divorce and inheritance laws, are often cases in which the practice of law favours wealthy and powerful sections of society.

Legal aid and public interest litigation are an important tradition of western legal practice. They have been essential in providing a counter-balance to the use of the judicial system in favour of the privileged. To work, they require some important preconditions, in particular a strong political tradition of the rule of law. In some of the most authoritarian or autocratic societies, this formal legalism has been present (e.g. 19th century Britain and Apartheid South Africa), while in some ostensibly more democratic ones, the courts have been much less independent or their judgements have simply been ignored by the executive.

The tradition of legal aid and public interest litigation is bound up, sometimes very closely, with primary mobilization. The law has been one means used by disadvantaged groups to challenge discrimination and systemic violations of rights. Meanwhile, legal aid clinics have been an important means of educating people about their rights and in turn prompting them to form associations to protect them.

Philanthropy

Philanthropy has played a subsidiary role in rights activism. There is no doubt that in cases such as the campaigns against slavery and child labour or in Henri Dunant's creation of the ICRC and the first Geneva Convention, the moral activism of individuals who had no direct material interest in the cause for which they struggled, was important. A sense of philanthropy among radicals also proved significant in support for some progressive causes such as Indian decolonisation and the struggle against Apartheid. Their work of documentation, publishing, arousing public concern and outrage, and lobbying parliamentarians, is in some respects the direct ancestor of today's "second generation" activism. Many of their methods also made an important contribution to primary movements.

However, while important cross-currents in the western tradition of philanthropy may support rights activism, the trend as a whole is against it. Charity strongly supports the status quo: it is a privilege for the "deserving poor" to receive the benefactions of the rich. Under British law, human rights activities are defined as non-charitable, and organizations such as Amnesty International are denied the tax benefits of being a registered charity.

The Laws of War

The laws of war (in recent decades known as international humanitarian law) is arguably the oldest "human rights" tradition of all. The concept of "the warrior's honour" and constraints on warfare in the name of humanity are found in all societies. In modern times, international humanitarian law has been different and complementary to human rights law, in that the latter is concerned with the relationship between a sovereign state and its citizens, while international humanitarian law, is applicable where this relationship does not exist or has broken down entirely through armed conflict. International humanitarian law is not human rights law: it recognizes and legitimises the right of a combatant to kill and commit other acts that in other circumstances would be considered human rights violations. International humanitarian law, does of course contain human rights provisions (such as the right to a trial) and reflects concepts of individual rights (notably in Common Article 3 of the Geneva Conventions), but its philosophy is markedly different from human rights law. Also, save in exceptional circumstances such as the international criminal tribunals of the late 1940s and late 1990s, there have been no mechanisms for penal sanctions except those voluntarily imposed by belligerent forces on their own soldiers. International humanitarian law is not international law either: it is founded on the distinction between jus ad bellum (the right to wage war) and jus in bello (the conduct of war), and preserves the latter by refusing to judge the former.

One of the main philosophical and practical reasons for the separation of international humanitarian law from human rights law is that, if human rights law were applied in conflict, it would instantly be violated and brought into disrepute.

The laws of war are highly significant to this discussion because, among other things, they embody a formal recognition that respect for human rights is specific to the context. In the circumstances of armed conflict a different set of rules is called for. Moreover, the essence of international humanitarian law is practicability, not aspiration. They are an attempt to achieve a workable balance between legitimate military necessity and basic humanity. The concept of "proportionality" is fundamental to international humanitarian law,: the infliction of death, suffering and damage should be proportional to the military threat to be faced or advantage to be gained. In addition, each army's adoption of the Geneva Conventions is usually subject to their interpretation of justifiable exceptions to the rules.

Second Generation Human Rights Organizations

The "second generation" of human rights organizations have come into existence since the late 1970s. Although there have been predecessors as far back as the Anti-Slavery Society (founded in the 1840s) and Amnesty International (established in 1961), it was only at this time that the wider phenomenon of non-governmental "human rights organizations" became significant. These organizations depend not on mass mobilization, but on the "short cut" of "mobilizing shame." They use research, documentation and publication, combined with skilful use of the media and lobbying politicians, to make their concerns known.

Their basic premise is that if people know about an abuse, they will be moved to want to stop it.

The origins of second-generation activism lie in the success of many primary movements in the west, particularly the American civil rights movement. Rights, which had previously been marginal concerns, became legitimate subjects for professional work. Politicians were ready to listen. Some of the veterans of these struggles decided to put their efforts into deepening and broadening human rights work, notably in trying to influence US foreign policy and assist citizens in other countries – notably Latin America and Eastern Europe – replicate their own successes.

Primary mobilization is very time consuming and difficult. Social changes in the west have made it more so. The generations that came of age in the 1970s and afterwards have been noticeably less activist than their parents. This may be a function of greater peace and prosperity, of geographical and social mobility leading to a decline in sense of "community", the rise of television, or other factors. For whatever reason, it became both more attractive and more possible to undertake "secondary activism".

A particular event was instrumental in creating a rich seam to be mined by the second generation activists. This was the signing of the Helsinki Accords in 1975, which included a "final basket" concerned with human rights. One historian of the Cold War has written:

> "In retrospect, the Helsinki treaties of 1975 appear as the West's secret weapon, a time bomb planted in the heart of the Soviet Empire. Throughout Eastern Europe and the Soviet Union itself, a handful of brave and determined campaigners used the human rights provisions of the Helsinki "Final Basket' to insist that their governments live up to the commitments they had signed."[1]

Ultimately, and to the total surprise of both super-powers, citizens' mobilization in Eastern Europe to defend the rights enshrined in these Accords became the lever that brought down the Berlin Wall and brought the Cold War to an end. The peaceful end of Central European Communism was one of the great victories of primary rights mobilization led by Solidarity in Poland, and the churches and organizations such as Helsinki Citizens' Assemblies in various countries. Charter 77 in Czechoslovakia was more a movement of intellectuals and artists, and less a popular mobilization, but at the key moment in 1989, its leaders were ready to take to the streets themselves: not only did they help organize the demonstrations that brought down Communist rule but they put themselves at the forefront of those protests.

In much of the former Soviet Union, particularly the trans-Caucasus, the story is rather different, with the opportunities for successful peaceful opposition being much smaller.

In Western Europe and North America, the most significant response to the human rights provisions of the Helsinki Accords was markedly different. The seminal institution was Helsinki Watch, soon to team up with Americas Watch to become Human Rights Watch. This has become the model for innumerable other human rights organizations.

In the 1980s these second generation human rights organizations seemed to

---

[1] Martin Walker, The Cold War, London, Vintage, 1994, p. 237.

have discovered a short cut to the respect for human rights. It was no longer necessary to bring the people on to the streets, or to tramp around small towns speaking to audiences in church halls. Instead, journalists could expose human rights atrocities in the media, professional lobbyists could get Congressmen and women to ask awkward questions and even pass legislation tying US assistance to human rights guarantees, and occasionally lawyers could bring cases to national or international courts. Aryeh Neier, founding director of Human Rights Watch, called it "mobilizing shame." This form of activism constrained the US government – a bit – and heartened the anti-Communist activists in the eastern bloc. And although the primary mobilization was fading – the local roots of the human rights movement were being neglected – the legacy of the civil rights movement left enough of a domestic constituency to legitimise and constrain the "second generation" activists.

Along with choosing to focus on research, publishing and lobbying, the new human rights organizations made a critical decision on their mandates. They decided to confine themselves to violations of fundamental rights such as torture, arbitrary detention and execution, along with restrictions on civil and political liberties. Overwhelmingly, they are not concerned with social, economic and cultural rights nor with the social and economic obstacles to establishing the rule of law. Some are even opposed to recognising social and economic rights as true rights at all. The decision was partly philosophical and partly practical (initially, the human rights organizations resources and influence were severely limited). But it has had profound consequences particularly in the post-Cold War era.

What are Second Generation Human Rights Organizations?

The main characteristics of second generation or secondary activism include the following. First, human rights activism has become professionalised. A profession has arisen, dominated by lawyers, journalists and publishers, but without the formal accoutrements of a profession such as certification or registration. There is a strong sense of a "human rights community", particularly in New York and Washington DC. Peer pressures within this community are very important: there is a strong internal conformism. Some of the new human rights professionals have first hand experience of primary mobilization (especially the founders of organizations such as Human Rights Watch) and others are themselves former victims of human rights abuses. But an increasing number are college graduates who are drawn to the profession from a combination of seeing it as an attractive career, along with personal moral concerns. There is a simple generational phenomenon at work: most human rights organizations are now staffed by people who did not grow up during the domestic struggle for civil rights and for whom human rights is less a vocation than a profession. Their peer group is in government, academia, law and commerce and they do not have the moral reference group of protest marchers that so strongly influenced their predecessors.

Second, a new kind of specialist institution has emerged. human rights organizations typically have mandates framed by lawyers referring to articles in the Universal Declaration of Human Rights or something similar. They take their funding from philanthropic foundations and corporations (especially in the US), sometimes from governments or quasi-governmental foundations (especially in

Europe). A few, like Amnesty International, have mass membership, but this is growing uncommon. They have career structures and administrative hierarchies. Like any institutions, after a while, they give more and more emphasis to preserving their institutional viability. This contrasts with primary movements, whose mandates arise from very specific issues, and for whom institutionalization is developed only as an instrumental strategy for helping to achieve these goals.

Third, arising from the legally defined mandates, there is a universalisation or internationalisation of concern. Second generation organizations may work with issue specific or case specific organizations, but they do not aim at mobilizing a mass constituency. Rather, they tend to focus on influencing a liberal and educated elite on behalf of people in faraway countries.

Fourth, these organizations focus on documentation, publishing and using the media. Their essential rationale is that if an abuse is publicised, public opinion and the conscience (and sense of dignity) of policy makers will ensure that action is taken against it. Some human rights organizations have been little more than specialist publishing houses. As other forms of media develop, they have also adapted marketing techniques from commercial companies and relief agencies. For example, they may try to "humanise" their "product" by presenting individual victims whom their "consumers" can identify with, using these as representatives of a much wider problem.

This relates to the focus on high profile individuals. Some organizations, like Amnesty International, deal almost entirely with individual cases. Others prefer to highlight prominent people – if you are a prisoner it is very helpful to be writer, lawyer, Olympic athlete, princess or of course a human rights activist. It's unfortunate if you are a peasant: some western human rights activists may take up your case, but not many, and not with much vigour.

A particular brand of this approach is the sanctification of prominent individual human rights activists. There are some very brave and determined individuals around the world who have stood up, sometimes almost alone, against tyranny. And these people deserve our support. But it is questionable if the western human rights organizations' cult of the human rights hero is actually supporting their cause. It worked in the 1980s, but it has arguably become overblown now. The generous and sometimes indiscriminate award of human rights prizes can create more problems than it solves. To elevate one individual from a broader movement risks creating vanities and jealousies amongst the leaders of the movement, apart from the way in which it can misrepresent the nature of the struggle. Sometimes the search for the appropriate individual can become absurd: I have been rung up many times by mainly American human rights organizations looking for a character reference for some supposedly prominent human rights activist in north east Africa, whose name I have never heard before. And of course there is the problem that the definition of "human rights activist" has an element of subjectivity, compounded by the danger that these people may not always follow the approved "human rights" career after getting their awards. The Roman Catholic Church prefers to elevate people to the sainthood only after they have died: it might be prudent for human rights organizations to follow this model.

The award of human rights prizes actually has more to do with publicising the human rights organizations back home – and providing a focus for fund-raising events – than in promoting human rights in other countries. When the two aims harmonise it is fortunate.

Fifth, many of these organizations focus much effort on influencing the policies of their national governments, particularly the US government. The lobbyists' charm, pragmatism, and inside knowledge are indispensable tools in this work. Some have become so adept at this that it appears to be their prime justification, almost an end in itself. The "influence trap", whereby principles are incrementally abandoned in order to maintain a "in" with government, is an ever-present danger.

Secondary activism in the United States began in the early 1980s in an adversarial confrontation with government. That decade was an ideal opportunity for pioneering secondary activism. It was a Republican decade; most human rights organizations were staffed by Democrats. The US had a global reach and with the globalization of anti-Communist containment, there was no part of the world, however small or faraway, that did not have some US "angle" to it. The American government was either propping up a pro-western regime or trying to undermine a pro-Soviet one, or at the very least had a significant influence on policy. At the same time, the ideology of freedom meant that there was moral leverage on US foreign policy. The gap between rhetoric and reality was relentlessly and brilliantly exploited.

In the 1990s, this has changed. Years have passed and staff have changed. There is a Democrat administration. Along with the institutionalization of human rights organizations as lobbying organizations, a revolving door has emerged between human rights organizations, legal firms, academia, think tanks, UN, and above all the US Administration. This happens at various levels, from human rights organization board members who take senior government posts to interns who work for members of Congress and then switch to human rights organizations, or vice versa. It follows that this elite governmental stratum is the peer group for these "international" human rights organizations. They share the same world views.

Sixth, their relationship with foreign (formerly Eastern Bloc, now predominantly third world) governments responsible for abuses has, by contrast, remained largely adversarial. In the 1980s, Communist countries were remarkably vulnerable to the moral challenge based on human rights. Under pressure, they released political prisoners, let Jews emigrate, allowed dissidents to organize. Most of the time, they played by the rules. Meanwhile, pro-American governments (notably in Latin America where the human rights movement focussed much of its energies) had to respond to pressure from the US administration. They could not embarrass their patron overly much, and had to show that "authoritarian" pro-Western regimes were more law abiding than "totalitarian" Communists.

In the 1990s, the adversarial stance has not changed. In dealing with governments in Africa, Asia and Latin America, principle counts more than influence, to the extent that some human rights organizations appear to be dogmatic, insisting on operating in their standard manner even when it is obviously not the best strategy for producing practical results. Thus, for a western human rights organization to become engaged in helping an African government set up its legal system, or collaborating with a legal aid scheme, might be rejected on the grounds that it would compromise the "independence" (or by implication the ethical purity) of the human rights organization. Similarly, they will be ready to recommend cutting aid or trade links to an abusive government, but will be reluctant to press for expanding aid to a government committed to human rights.

Many western human rights organizations also criticize their national governments. HRW criticizes the US administration and Amnesty International criticizes the British government. But the power relations here are markedly different, and these organizations are part of democratic national political processes.

Lastly, and especially in the post-Cold War era, many of the human rights organizations' concerns have converged with international humanitarian organizations, such as UNICEF, CARE, Oxfam and others. Many of the places where human rights violations are most acute are no longer authoritarian states, but so-called "complex emergencies", otherwise known as civil wars which have unleashed mass human displacement and hunger. In such cases, human rights organizations have begun to tread on uncertain ground. Where there are no effective governments (such as Somalia) conventional human rights activism cannot work. Monitoring the laws of war remains a valid exercise, but the 1990s have seen strong pressures to revise these laws. Along with international humanitarian agencies, human rights organizations have participated in the attempts to develop novel legal doctrines such as humanitarian intervention and the privileging of humanitarian agencies under international humanitarian law and its offspring: "humanitarian principles". A critique of these initiatives falls outside the scope of this paper.

Successes of Second Generation Human Rights Organizations

Following the triumph of Eastern Europe in 1989, these organizations have really succeeded in setting the human rights agenda for the 1990s. They are the model for how to do it. They deserve our congratulations: theirs was a tremendous success.

But their success was also a product of historical circumstance. As argued above, Human Rights Watch was a child of the last decade of the Cold War. The zenith of the second generation organization's power was, ironically, the moment at which their project began to unravel. When the Cold War ended, realities became much more complicated.

It is notoriously difficult for human rights organizations to measure their successes and failures. But there are two unquestionable successes.

First, massive abuses cannot occur in secret any more. It is extremely unlikely that large scale abuses, such as the massacres perpetrated by the Khmer Rouge in Cambodia, the Government of Burundi in 1972, or the USSR's Gulag, would occur again without being widely known around the world.

Secondly, human rights concerns have become an internationally legitimate subject. No dictator can refuse to acknowledge the legitimacy of international concern over his treatment of his own citizens. This is reflected in the passing of much human rights legislation at the UN and European Parliament, etc. In turn, it also legitimises the international search to uncover human rights abuses in faraway places. There has been enough determination among human rights organizations and journalists to expose, for example, the Sudan Government's secret attempts to destroy the Nuba people or the Indonesian Government's wars in East Timor and Irian Jaya.

But these successes are not without their problems. Human rights activism is not a science in which one can predict cause and effect with total confidence. There is some evidence that the tools have become blunted.

Possible Failures of Second Generation Human Rights Organizations

Perhaps the most serious challenge to the work that human rights organizations do is the question of whether exposure of abuses actually leads to genuine pressure to stop them. The entire second generation human rights organization project is premised on this assumption. Two very experienced human rights activists have posed this question.

The assumption, since the UN signed its historic declaration half a century ago, has been that if people knew enough, if the quality of research and reporting was good enough, if the information reached the right people, then action was bound to follow. That is turning out to be false. In any other field of human endeavour, such meagre results as are being seen today for such an enormous quantum of effort would not be tolerated.[2]

The context of this criticism was Rwanda: the first unmistakable case of genocide since the adoption of the Genocide Convention in 1948. The killings were televised. And the world did nothing. The challenge posed by Rwanda will be a major theme of the last part of this paper.

One of the reasons for the decline in effectiveness is "overkill". There is simply so much human rights information around, and so little attempt to calibrate and prioritise, that it is difficult for the public or policymakers to discern a case of genocide amid all the "noise" of detentions and extra judicial executions. The way in which humanitarian relief agencies have also entered the picture, presenting wars, massacres and genocides as crises needing charitable relief, has also complicated the picture.

It is likely that the professional standards of human rights investigations have also slipped. The expansion in numbers of human rights organizations and their reliance on American and European staff members, some of whom have little or no experience of the countries they are "covering", and the use of interns who are wholly new to the business, has led to an increasing number of cases of poor research and unsubstantiated allegations. The human rights organizations rarely admit to this but it is becoming a serious problem of credibility. Serious though these cases are, it would be a mistake to see them as the disease: rather they are the symptom of a deeper problem.

A second and related failing has been that much new human rights legislation has been adopted, but to uncertain effect. The numerous new instruments of human rights have been ignored more often than they have been followed. As I shall argue below, this is only partly a problem of governments cynically abusing rights. Partly it is a problem of human rights organizations being unrealistic, and therefore not in practice serving their aims.

A third failing has been that many abusers have found creative new ways of circumventing the system. Human rights activism works according to certain well-known formulae. For example, there are Amnesty International's "prisoners of conscience." To avoid the difficulties of holding known prisoners of conscience, governments have adopted various tactics. One, used for a while by the Sudan Government, was to arrest political opponents for a very brief time in non-regular detention centres, and then – just as word was reaching the London

---

[2]Caroline Moorhead and Ursula Owen, "Time to think again." Index on Censorship, January 1996, p. 55.

offices of AI – release them. But ask them to report on a daily basis to a security office. And then perhaps re-arrest them, but rapidly release them. The effect was basically the same on the political opponent, but the Sudan Government could claim that it held no political prisoners. Another, more disturbing response, appears to be the way in which some Latin American dictatorships simply made their opponents "disappear", partly as a way of circumventing the problems the governments would encounter with AI. Even discussing this possibility has caused very severe consternation at AI.

There are many other ways for abusive governments to achieve their goals while avoiding censure by human rights organizations. Another example is to create ethnic unrest and use ethnic militias to carry out the government's will.

A fourth failing is that while it has proved possible for second generation human rights organizations to influence western government policy, this has rarely been so when there are vested interests at work in the opposite direction. One example is the Clinton Administration's award of Most Favoured Nation status to China, giving the priority to commercial interests over the pressures of human rights organizations. A second example is the failure of the land mines campaign in the US to get support from the Administration to ban anti-personnel mines. By contrast, the European, east Asian and Southern African mines campaigns, which involved mobilizing numerous citizens' groups in a form of primary mobilization, did successfully change governments' policies, overriding the vested interests of mines manufacturers. The neglect of the roots of the human rights movement has paid a price.

Perhaps the most important failing, however, has been political hubris. "International" human rights organizations based in western capitals have assumed that, because human rights are universal, their model of work is universal. This has led to a cultural and political insensitivity that is at times almost funny. Human Rights Watch's headquarters recently moved to the Empire State Building in New York City. If they were aware of the message that this move would send to the rest of the world – particularly those countries with direct experience of being part of other countries' empires – it was a sign of insensitivity, not to say arrogance. If they were not aware of this, it is perhaps even more revealing.

Human Rights Organizations as an Exportable Commodity

The historical reality is that respect for human rights has developed in countries through popular mobilization and the use of a legal system by citizens themselves. Where these political and institutional preconditions do not exist, human rights work is more akin to trying to protect civilians using international humanitarian law,: exhortation, persuasion and pressure are required from an external source. In short, negotiation not preaching. However, what has happened is that the model of second generation human rights organizations has been uncritically exported from the liberal democracies to other countries with very different historical experiences. In some places this has worked, and in others it has not. In addition, the model has even been applied to conflicts, merging the formerly distinct traditions of human rights law and international humanitarian law.

The second generation human rights organization arose from particular historical circumstances which made it effective in that context (the last decade of the

Cold War). The times have changed. But the institutional context for preserving these institutions has persisted. The institutional donors are still there, the media are still interested and western governments are still highly receptive to the information and analysis (though the returns to activism in terms of policy changes have been in sharp decline). Above all, this model of human rights organization has become institutionalized, and those within the system can see no other. It is self perpetuating and self legitimising.

The same institutional context that has maintained the western human rights organization in its current form has also encouraged the creation of African, Asian and Latin American human rights organizations on the same model. In countries where there is a strong tradition of popular mobilization, liberal government and the rule of law, this can work reasonably well. Where there is not, it is deeply problematic.

There are a number of characteristic syndromes that rights-watching human rights organizations tend to be vulnerable to, especially in Africa. This is not a universal rule, and in fact many of the organizations are well aware of these problems and strive to avoid them.

One is "donorism": the African human rights organization's institutional survival depends upon getting funding from foreign donors who work according to a standard bureaucratic format. Much of the energy of the organization is devoted to writing project proposals, negotiating with donors, and preparing the right kinds of reports. Along with financial dependence on donors this creates accountability oriented towards external interests. These interests may be institutional rather than overtly political, but the tendency is there. It also means that the organization is obliged to adopt a certain model of activities: a professionalisation rather than a democratisation.

A second problem is commercial opportunism: running a human rights organization can become a means of earning a living. With the decline in state provided professional employment, many capable professionals need to find niches for themselves, and this is one.

The third and perhaps the most serious problem is that involvement in a local human rights organization can become a means of political opportunism. It is common to have a revolving door between political office and human rights monitoring and activism. Criticising the human rights record of a government is perhaps the most legitimate means of criticising it, and can become a cover for smuggling in many other non-human rights criticisms as well. Involvement in a human rights organization can give a politician profile and publicity as well as moral protection and an income. A number of presidential hopefuls in Kenya have human rights prizes on their office walls.

The current attempts to formulate a UN Declaration on Human Rights Defenders, while an intrinsically laudable exercise, may run into the danger of over-privileging the second generation human rights organization. It is questionable whether human rights law is the best mechanism for protecting human rights defenders, on the grounds that where human rights defenders are most needed, states are unlikely to be respectful of the more arcane pieces of human rights legislation. There is also a problem that if one tries to define human rights activities, one may end up restricting them – for example a universalistic definition of human rights might exclude or marginalise groups campaigning for minority rights or those promoting social and economic rights. But failing to define what is a "human rights defender" might also open the door to an abuse of the Declaration – any opposition political activist could claim to be a "human rights defender" – with the risk of jeopardising all human rights work. Even worse, by singling out human rights organizations for privileged treatment, it runs the risk of focussing human rights concern on human rights organizations rather than ordinary people. This is not the legislators' intention, but might be the result. In short, the process is coloured by the concerns of second generation human rights organizations and the lawyers who tend to dominate them.

Many human rights activists in Africa are unhappy with the way in which the second generation model is open to abuse and has discredited their profession in the eyes of citizens and governments – and even some donors. Some are making strenuous efforts to avoid these pitfalls. But the constraints and dangers remain.

The organizations that work best tend to be those that are organically linked to the material interests of a community or profession. Their concern is commonly using civil and political liberties to advance their material well-being: the practical integration of civil and political rights with social and economic ones. These groups include self help groups such as revolving credit organizations or marketing co-operatives, professional associations and legal aid organizations.

One of the reasons why human rights institutions do not export very well from America and Europe is the sole focus on civil and political rights, excluding social and economic ones. In the West, this has enabled "human rights" to be adopted into governments' aid and economic policy in a deeply problematic way.

Human Rights as a Foreign Policy Tool for Western Governments

One of the successes of western human rights organizations has been the adoption of "human rights" and "ethics" into the foreign policies of their governments. But this has proved to be a double-edged sword. Governments have been ready to use human rights rhetoric in foreign policy statements and (less often) to act in ways consonant with those policies. They have also been more amenable to pressure from human rights organizations. But they have also appropriated the concept of "human rights" and bent it to serve other ends.

Aid Conditionalities

The imposition of conditionalities on aid provision has been one of the most common elements of western governments' human rights policies. This began when domestic human rights organizations objected to their aid being sullied by being used for human rights violations, for example when US supplied weaponry or US-trained military personnel were implicated in atrocities in El Salvador. It broadened to a much wider range of conditions on any form of aid, sometimes to an absurd degree. For example, US aid for UN population control programmes in Kenya was held up because according to US law, the US (where abortion is legal) cannot support population control in Kenya (where abortion is illegal) through an organization that does not oppose abortion.

Such cases aside, there are fundamental problems with aid conditionalities on human rights. To start with, there are double standards. Strategically or commercially important aid recipients are routinely exempted from this conditionality, for the simple and good reason that they would just reject the aid and not change their behaviour. Hence Israel, China and Indonesia, to name but three examples, have almost entirely escaped any effective conditioning of aid to human rights. By contrast, poor and aid dependent countries tend not to have much strategic or commercial significance for aid donors, so aid conditionality is both domestically possible and could, in theory, actually work. So poorer countries face tougher conditions.

Because the leading western human rights organizations have deliberately blinded themselves to social and economic rights – insisting that poverty is no excuse for rights violations – they do not see this systematic double standard. Rather, they are just upset that countries like China and Indonesia escape the "proper" sanctions.

A second problem is the regular shifting of the goalposts. In the last decade, the focus of donor conditionality has, broadly speaking, changed from tying aid to basic human rights, to tying it to multi-party electoral systems, and more recently to tying it to fighting corruption. None of these conditionalities has been implemented consistently enough across donors and across different kinds of aid provision, or for long enough, for there to be any real incentive for recipients to change their behaviour. Concerted action – for example in the case of the Paris Club towards Kenya in 1991 – has occasionally produced dramatic changes in a recipient's political strategies, but these have tended to be superficial or short-lived. And meanwhile, economic conditionalities imposed by the IMF have proved much more enduring and powerful, with the result that determined governments, however poor, have been able to attract foreign aid by agreeing to structural adjustment programmes while ignoring the then current human rights or democracy conditionalities of aid. Uganda is a case in point.

A third problem with human rights conditions is that they are almost entirely negative. Aid is cut off when there is a perceived violation, but those who conform to the requirements rarely get a positive reward. Punitive sanctions are by far the most popular instrument that donors use to link aid and human rights. It is easy to see why: they are a powerful gesture to the domestic human rights lobbies that are so influential, and they are not only cheap, they actually save the donor money. By contrast, programmes to support police forces or prisons are expensive, long term and unlikely to gain much domestic approval – on the contrary, as all police forces and prison services have a tendency to commit abuses sooner or later, they are virtually a guaranteed way of getting criticized by human rights organizations.

The fourth problem is conditionality overload. Many western governments-particularly the US – have proliferated the number of human rights preconditions on assistance. If all these preconditions were enforced it would be all-but-impossible for the US to have a foreign assistance programme at all, so complicated and far-reaching are they. So they are not enforced except in an ad hoc manner when a particularly persistent NGO demands it or when a desk officer wants to make a point to a recipient country. And the recipient country treats the exercise in a pragmatic or even cynical manner.

A fifth problem with human rights conditionality is that the most common instrument, punitive conditionality, is an arbitrary measure without due process. The entire aid process is notoriously lacking in transparency and democratic accountability, but the sudden withdrawal of aid is perhaps the most arbitrary and opaque of all measures. In response to an alleged abuse, the donor makes a diplomatic representation and immediately suspends aid. The recipient has no right of appeal. There is no independent means of either assessing whether the allegation was justified, whether the abuse has been rectified, or whether the sanctions have had the desired effect. The whole exercise is in fact likely to generate cynicism among the sanctioned recipient. It is a simple but valid truism that democracy and human rights cannot be promoted by methods that are themselves arbitrary and lack due process.

This points to the final and fundamental problem with aid and human rights. While the aid process itself is not democratised or transparent, it will be incapable of making a systematic contribution to human rights and democracy in the recipient country. This is a complex subject, but it is remarkable how most donor and NGO assistance is not open to any form of public scrutiny. Ironically, it is the World Bank, the most regularly demonised of all aid institutions, that has led the way in opening itself up for public scrutiny and consultation.

While aid negotiations remain secretive, a very large part of the governmental apparatus in poor and aid dependent countries will remain undemocratic. It is only by making the aid encounter more open and more democratic than the other aspects of domestic politics in the recipient country that there will be a real chance of aid sustaining democratic processes and structures.

It is extraordinary how resistant donor governments are to acknowledging this elementary point. The UK's Department for International Development recently commissioned a paper on human rights and development assistance. This was passed around the different sections of the Department, and major British NGOs and human rights organizations, and some academics as well. Only one commentator – myself – made the point that there was no mention of democratising the aid process itself.

Free Enterprise as a Fundamental Right

One of the most significant elements in western donor policy on human rights in the 1980s and 1990s has been the systematic de-linking of civil and political rights from social and economic rights. Western human rights organizations have, for the most part, gone along with this or even encouraged it. This has allowed western donors to follow policies that on the one hand promote democratisation, and on the other to enforce economic policies on poor countries that mean that the electorate is forbidden from having any say at all in economic policy.

The ideological rationale for this belief is that any form of state intrusion into economic life is a violation of liberty. Political liberty must be coterminous with economic liberty. This is a doctrine that no western government would dare enforce at home, where elections are most often contested over governments' economic policies, and special-interest pressure groups ensure that subsidies are granted to agriculture and industry. No western electorate would consider democracy worthwhile if the next government's economic policies had been completely determined in advance by the IMF.

Structural adjustment programmes have another profound effect on human rights. Governments' public spending is squeezed so hard that they cannot train and pay enough policemen and judges, or provide enough prisons. Lawyers command high salaries, as the accounts of any American human rights organization will demonstrate. It is simply not true to say that human rights are free, unless one is prepared to tolerate "people's justice", such as some liberation fronts have developed while in the field, for all levels of justice including enforcing the commercial code.

In the early 1990s, it was fashionable for international financial institutions (and some others) to predict and welcome the near-total demise of the state in Africa and the former Communist countries. More recently, the role of the state has been acknowledged as a prerequisite for a market economy. The following statement, referring to the former Eastern Bloc, is equally valid for Africa.

The post-Communist challenge is to restore the authority of states without re-collectivizing societies. State repair is the main condition of market-based prosperity, on which, in turn, depends our ability to tame, if not solve, the "post-Communist" problems of nations, races and borders.[3]

The strongest and most legitimate states in Eastern Europe have been those best able to manage the transition to a market economy, surviving the "shock therapy" of instant economic liberalisation. Only the fact that the market economy has in fact delivery a modicum of prosperity has averted a major crisis of legitimacy in these countries. But it is notable that a number of ex-Communist parties have been voted back into power.

As argued above, historically the protection of civil and political liberties has been intimately tied with the promotion of social and economic rights. If the latter are de-legitimised by externally-enforced economic polices, then the former are in danger of losing their credibility too.

Have Human Rights Instruments become "Over-Inflated"?

In important respects, international second-generation human rights activism is more akin to the ICRC's attempts to gain belligerents' compliance with the laws of war than citizens' attempts to guarantee their rights vis-a-vis their governments under the law. The human rights organizations can exhort and embarrass and occasionally enforce punitive sanctions, but their ability to mobilize the people or develop the law is very limited. This is an illuminating parallel because a number of scholars believe that in recent years, international humanitarian law has become too complex and demanding, and thus impractical.

This process can be dated from the Additional Protocols to the Geneva Conventions, agreed in 1977. The Additional Protocols filled some important gaps in their predecessors, but also blurred some important distinctions and were written in a legalistic manner that made them more remote from the realities of war. One authoritative commentator has concluded that their impact was to make international humanitarian law "overinflated."[4] His argument was that the introduction of some external political considerations into the drafting of the laws, in particular the characterization of wars of national liberation as "international", undermined the clarity and practicability of the Geneva

---

[3]Robert Skidelsky, The World After Communism: A polemic for our times, London, Macmillan, 1995, p. 164.

[4]Geoffrey Best, War and Law since 1945, Oxford, Clarendon Press, 1994, p. 419.

Conventions. In addition the insistence on giving all civilians the same degree of protection – irrespective of whether they were small children or guerrillas out of uniform or munitions workers – challenges the law's foundation in a military commander's sense of a legitimate military objective. The fear is that if the law is too demanding, commanders will simply ignore it, and thus bring the entire edifice of international humanitarian law into disrepute.

If "overinflation" was a problem in 1977, it has become a crisis since then. In the last two decades, human rights law and international humanitarian law, have become increasingly overlapping and even fused together. There has been an elaboration of international humanitarian law along several paths. One of these paths is the refinement of the concept of "customary international humanitarian law", which usually takes the strongest restrictions on the conduct of war to be found in any document and then applies this across the board.

A second path is the development of "humanitarian principles" by discussion among aid agencies. These are statements of high principle which have the effect of further restraining belligerents while lifting the hitherto strict conditions imposed on relief agencies in conflict, instead giving them what amounts to blanket protection come what may. For example, the Red Cross's ten-point "Code of Conduct", drawn up in 1994 and "approved" by governments and NGOs in 1995, consists principally of abstract statements about the aims of humanitarian relief, counterposed by far-reaching concrete demands from host governments and belligerents to respect and privilege relief agencies. A professor of international relations commented:

> "Not one of the ten points addressed in any way the critical issue of how to protect vulnerable populations and aid activities, nor how impartial relief work could be combined with human-rights advocacy, sanctions or other coercive measures. [Donor] governments and NGOs appeared to be addressing humanitarian issues in a pious and abstract manner far removed from the harsh dilemmas resulting from wars."[5]

A third path has been the activism of the UN Security Council in developing, in an ad hoc way, doctrines of humanitarian intervention and the privileges of humanitarian organizations and the widening mandate of agencies such as UNHCR.

In these processes of attempted lawmaking, soldiers – particularly those actually fighting the wars in question – are notable by their absence. The foundation of international humanitarian law, in practicability and acceptance by soldiers, has been abandoned in favour of the law-making privileges of lawyers and humanitarian officials.

The "over-inflation" of international humanitarian law reached a crisis point in the Great Lakes region of central Africa during and after the Genocide of the Rwandese Tutsis. This point will be returned to later.

Arguably, a similar process of inflating human rights standards and demands has taken place in international human rights law and practice. The case of the proposed UN declaration on human rights defenders is one case among others. High standards are to be welcomed. Sovereign states should respect their citizens, and their citizens should demand and enforce that respect through the law. But

---

[5]Adam Roberts, "Humanitarian Action in War: Aid, protection and impartiality in a policy vacuum," London, IISS, Adelphi Paper no 305, 1996, pp. 60–1.

the object of any international exercise in promoting human rights should be more pragmatic.

The multiplication of human rights organizations and their activities has both contributed to and been partly driven by a plethora of new human rights instruments. United Nations bureaucracies produce these because it is their job to do so, and governments sign them because it is unbecoming not to. All these human rights instruments, on the rights of children, and women, and minorities, displaced people, relief workers, etc, are all laudable. But they are all "soft" law: aspirations rather than justiciable instruments.

This proliferation of laws is a problem. Many are impractical. Some cannot realistically be implemented. Others have been signed by governments that do not have the capacity or the will to implement them. This is actually a sign of disrespect for the rule of law. In many cases the signatory governments do not take them seriously because they know they are not justiciable. Thus the Sudan Government has signed the Convention on the Rights of the Child but continues to violate it flagrantly. In other cases they are signed by countries that have functioning legal systems, but in some cases they are so over justiciable that the court procedures will be so elaborate, protracted and open to innumerable appeals that it is likely they will not be taken seriously. In the US for example, there are few professions held in such public contempt as lawyers.

In addition the proliferation of human rights law, reflecting the proliferation of institutions developing it, coincides with the weakening of states' sovereign power to enforce these laws, because of economic globalization and the dominance of neo-liberal economic doctrine that reduces the state's economic reach.

The rather indiscriminate proliferation of human rights instruments opens the door to challenges to the core of liberal human rights based on "Asian values" or the prioritisation of economic rights. In their more legitimate forms, these challenges identify the social and economic preconditions for effective institutions to protect human rights (i.e. national security, the rule of law, a measure of economic prosperity) and seek to prioritise these alongside liberal human rights. In a less legitimate manner, these challenges can also be a means of distracting attention from inexcusable abuses.

It is important to reclaim human rights from over-control by the lawyers and lawyerly institutions.

The Genocide in Rwanda and the Routinisation of Human Rights

The most insidious effect of the growth of human rights organizations has been to make the protection of human rights into a business, removed from the basic material and political struggles of ordinary citizens. If it becomes the responsibility of a special brand of professionals to promote human rights, then citizens can be subtly disqualified from engaging in rights work. Similarly, if human rights organizations are responsible for preventing or protesting against abuses, then other citizens can rest content that the work is being done and they need not worry.

The way in which human rights work has become a routine and a concern for a professional elite has, arguably, contributed to the worst ever crisis for the human rights movement. That is Rwanda.

In 1993–4, Rwanda was a model for second generation human rights activism. There were seven local organizations active, supported by a range of vigorous western organizations who were unusually collaborative. Western donors were deeply concerned. Even the UN force in the country (UNAMIR) had a mandate for promoting human rights. Thus there was an illusion that Rwandan human rights activists had international protection, and could work with bravery in the face of an authoritarian state and its agents, apparently safe in the knowledge that the "international community" had undertaken to protect them.

When the Rwandese human rights community was wiped out there was nothing that the international human rights organizations could do, and the UN chose to do nothing. Under extreme pressure, some former human rights activists, along with a disturbing number of priests, journalists and aid workers, themselves joined in the killings. Among the others, some went to great lengths to conceal the culpability of some of their friends and relations. These were of course exceptional circumstances and human rights activists are no more nor less human than anyone else. But the cult of celebrating the human rights hero did not stand Rwanda, nor the cause of human rights, in good stead. Neither did the institutionalized, routine cataloguing of human rights abuses on a day-to-day basis.

International human rights organizations have proved extremely defensive when the facts have come out that some former human rights activists in Rwanda submitted to the 'genocidaires' demands and became killers. Some even seem to have killed with relish. This discomfort reflects the way in which the second generation human rights organizations have fetishized themselves: they cannot distinguish between human rights values and the actually existing human rights institutions, which are inevitably flawed like all human institutions. This is going to prove a profound crisis for this form of activism: it will be a major test of its maturity whether it is able to acknowledge this crisis, apologise for its errors, and learn from them.

Even before the crisis of human rights activists who became involved in genocide emerged, another profound problem had arisen. Let me illustrate with the case of Amnesty International though there are other organizations in broadly the same situation. The genocide of the Rwandese Tutsis lasted something less than one hundred days. Up to one million people were murdered. This was a short, confusing and dangerous period to do human rights research. It was possible, as proved by my colleague Rakiya Omaar, who produced a 750 page document during this period and the following month,[6] but she is an exceptional individual. Amnesty International succeeded in putting out a fourteen page statement on the genocide. In the aftermath, which was also a confused period in which some survivors and some Tutsi soldiers distraught with grief and anger took revenge on suspected killers – some of them guilty, some of them probably not guilty – Amnesty International did succeed in sending a mission to Rwanda. It produced a report of fourteen pages, concerned with some hundred or so revenge killings. Some of these allegations were refuted by a delegation from Physicians for Human Rights that also happened to be in Rwanda at the time and was in the places at the times when incidents were supposed to have happened, but what they saw was very different. Over the

[6]African Rights, Rwanda: Death, Despair and Defiance, London, September 1994.

subsequent months and years, numerous human rights organizations including a UN human rights monitoring programme have meticulously documented many abuses by the new government. Some have been substantiated, others not. By contrast, their efforts to investigate the Genocide have been rather meagre. Their efforts to document the murder of survivors and witnesses – in fact the renewed attempt at committing genocide by the same extremist forces – were also belated and minor, at best.

It is striking that the UN Special Rapporteur also issued a report warning of genocide in eastern Zaire in early 1996. He was speaking of the Interahamwe, now in exile in Zaire and some Zairean forces killing local Zairean Tutsis. The human rights community did not take this up. But the alleged mass killings of Hutu civilians and militia by the Rwandese Patriotic Army and Zairean rebel forces became a *cause celebre* of the human rights movement.

These mass killings, if substantiated, are grave violations of international humanitarian law. Relief agencies and human rights organizations have been vociferous in condemning these alleged violations of the Geneva Conventions. But there is a very important sense in which the relief agencies and human rights organizations themselves brought international humanitarian law into disrepute, by both over-inflating it and by violating its requirements by their own actions.

This is a complex story and a summary will have to suffice. The humanitarians' violations of international humanitarian law fall into three categories. One, they insisted on awarding refugee status to people who were fugitives from justice, namely the Interahamwe and the former Rwandese army, and their hostage civilian population. They also violated refugee law by not demilitarising the "refugee" camps. UNHCR's presence in these camps was probably unlawful. Two, international humanitarian law has rigorous preconditions on humanitarian assistance if it is to be considered neutral and impartial. These include not allowing aid to be diverted or to support a war effort. These conditions were not met, yet the relief agencies who did not meet them still claimed protected status under international humanitarian law.. Third, the agencies interpreted international humanitarian law – and their own elaboration of it, called "humanitarian principles" – to mean that it was not legitimate for one belligerent (the Rwandese Patriotic Army and its allied Zairean rebel forces) to attack another (the Interahamwe and former Rwandese army) simply because the former were based in a populated area receiving relief aid. This is absurd. They compounded this error by calling for an international military intervention to protect their aid programmes and by extension not only the civilian population but the Interahamwe too. Thus some humanitarian agencies tried to abolish the foundations of international humanitarian law, namely the concepts of proportionality in use of military force and the legitimate military objective, and to immunise themselves from any obligations under international humanitarian law. The entire structure of international humanitarian law, is jeopardised by these actions, which turn international humanitarian law from a practicable reality into a naive and unrealisable aim.

The issue is partly one of political bias and double standards. But there is also a question of the apparent incapacity of the human rights organizations to grapple with the enormity of genocide and the challenge it poses. Genocide cannot simply be dealt with by means of routine human rights reporting, and then, when it is over, by regarding it as a "past abuse" requiring straightforward judicial action, albeit by a special international criminal tribunal. Genocide is more than just a multiple killing. It is a crime that destroys the capacity of a society in incalculable ways. It is so profoundly demoralising – in the sense of creating despair among survivors and a moral crisis and vacuity among killers and accomplices – that far more far reaching measures are required. The men and women who wrote the 1948 Genocide Convention, who had seen the death camps of Nazi Germany, knew this, which is why they drafted the simplest and most ambitious of all international treaties.

This is not to excuse the new Government of Rwanda for its mistakes and abuses. But it is to begin understanding something of what has happened, and to begin appreciating that it is completely inappropriate for the UN or human rights organizations to continue with "business as usual" in Rwanda. Still less have the human rights organizations and relief agencies the moral authority to dictate the actions of the survivors of the genocide and those who are trying to rebuild the country. Human rights are founded upon justice, and justice is a much more powerful and deeply rooted concept than any of the practices of the foreign human rights organizations and relief agencies.

It is as though human rights organizations were astronomers who have developed powerful telescopes for watching the stars. When the sun comes out, astronomers can still see the stars through their telescopes. But these astronomers have become blind to the sun: they are still following their tiny little stars.

A Human Rights Agenda for Africa

Rwanda is, thank goodness, exceptional, though there are parallels with the Ethiopian experience that will be instantly recognisable. There are also compelling parallels with Europe in the 1940s, when the foundations of the modern human rights order were laid.

Probably the greatest human rights outrages of the century were those of Nazi Germany, and arguably the greatest citizens' mobilization of all time was the Allied effort of the Second World War. Though not a human rights movement as such, this did result in the historic watershed of the post-war human rights and humanitarian legislation of the United Nations. The Universal Declaration of Human Rights reflects not only the victorious governments' horror at what the world had just undergone, but the popular democratic pressures on them. The Universal Declaration, alongside the other great pieces of humanitarian law such as the 1948 Genocide Convention, the 1949 Geneva Conventions and the 1951 UN Refugee Convention, are both a product of their times and documents of enduring, universal validity. Among other things, the Universal Declaration clearly asserts that civil and political rights are indistinguishable from social, economic and cultural rights, while the Charter of the United Nations links respect for human rights to peace between nations.

These basic instruments speak particularly strongly to Africa today: a continent emerging from genocide, total war, and economic disaster, in which political extremism and continuing economic problems such as unemployment and painfully slow reconstruction pose a threat to democratic aspirations.

For the international context in Africa today, I believe that a return to these fundamentals is very important. They can be seen as a triangle of three sets of balancing principles.

The first are twins of realism and idealism. In the Geneva Conventions we see realistic practicability. There is nothing in there that a humane but professional military commander will disagree with. Yet when we turn to the Genocide Convention we have the simplest and starkest of all international treaties. It lays an absolute and non-negotiable obligation on states to prevent and punish genocide. Let us recall that the men and women who drafted these two Conventions, within a year of each other, had seen both war and genocide. They saw the first as a regrettable reality, the second as absolutely unacceptable.

The second principles are statehood and citizenship. The UN is an association of sovereign states. The prerequisite of being an accepted member is agreeing to respect the rights of citizens. Citizenship is itself a right and carries with it rights. But states remain the foundation of both the international system and the system of human rights. Many of the states were of course new: the process of decolonisation, beginning in India, was one important legacy of the war.

The third pairing is civil and political liberties, on the one side, and social and economic rights on the other. While the shattered states of western Europe and Japan were painfully and slowly reconstructing their civil and political institutions, they were also rebuilding their economies. The United States' Marshall Plan provided much of the finance for ambitious state-centred reconstruction programmes.

This is the sort of international legal, political and economic framework that would be extremely positive in enabling the pursuit and protection of human rights in African countries. Internally within African states, I believe that there are lessons that follow from the general analysis of this paper. There is the importance of primary mobilization. This is up to citizens. It is also up to governments to allow it to happen and to succeed. But if primary mobilization is to be focussed on social and economic rights, as historically much of it has been in Europe and America, then there must be some capacity for citizens to decide over the basics of economic and social policy.

The rule of law is of course paramount. This is far more than the formalities of having an independent judiciary and judges with security of tenure – though those are important. It is also a question of having a judicial system that has the confidence of the people, and is accessible to the people. This cannot be decreed. It is a long struggle, for government institutions such as the office of an Ombudsman or Human Rights Commissioner, for lawyers and legal aid programmes, and for the citizens themselves.

Lastly, for all their problems, second generation human rights organizations are here to stay. There is a role for private human rights organizations monitoring human rights abuses. National human rights organizations can do it well in their own countries, indeed it is their right to do so. But theirs is a heavy responsibility too, to avoid some of the dangers to which I have alluded. Rather than springing from rooted primary organizations, human rights organizations in Africa should develop popular constituencies. One of the means that they can use for this is focussing on social and economic rights and using civil and political liberties to press for them.

Part Three

Principles and Guidelines for Establishing Human Rights Institutions

Ombudsman – Essential Elements

Harley Johnson*

The concept of ombudsmanship is a phenomenon with traces of similar institutions being found in ancient history. Yet the modern role of government oversight through an institution such as this is relatively very young. When one reviews the past few years and begins to list the countries, provinces or states, cities and municipalities, the rapid spread of the institution is nothing short of miraculous. Also, the forms offices of Ombudsman around the world have taken, indicate very strongly that it is malleable, can be moulded into different cultures with relative ease without losing its competency to address properly complaints from citizens and systemic issues involved in supplying government services. It appears to be capable of widespread variations to suit specific political or cultural requirements. Before one thinks, however, that it is a panacea for all the ills or alleged ills of government let me warn you that it is not. It is strong, resilient, it is malleable, but it is only proven effective under certain circumstances.

A first question which should be addressed however, when setting up such an institution as an Ombudsman is: why? Why do we need one and what do we want and expect it to accomplish? Only then can the criteria for establishing one be fully explored and fleshed out. Too often though, a concept can fire up an image in one's mind which may support the development of that concept without first understanding the base question as to "why". This question must be addressed at a local level and not be suggested nor imposed by some other jurisdiction. We are talking here of Ethiopia. You have indicated that there are some problems and you have heard in the past from very capable people including Stephen Owen from Canada. You have dealt with the philosophies of Ombudsmanship and now it is time to look next at the specific criteria in establishing an Office of Ombudsman – in this fashion, a deeper understanding of the task ahead will evolve.

The stability of an office greatly depends on how the appointment of the office came about in the first place. Many offices around the world are established through a legislative act or law and this appears to be sufficient in most of those jurisdictions. However, when an office is established by a Constitutional Amendment or as a part of a Constitution, then supported by a legislative enactment, it is much more difficult for changes to occur to that office based on shifting political winds. Placing it in the Constitution has the effect of ensuring continuity of an investigative process with concurrent stabilisation of the systems of the delivery of competent government services.

*International Ombudsman Institute.

K. Hossain et al. (eds), Human Rights Commissions and Ombudsman Offices, 785–790.

In addition, the supporting legislative enactment should lay out the answers to the first question above: why such an office as well as outlining the exact role and functions that a Parliament wishes the Ombudsman to be responsible for whatever it is made responsible for. For example: for general administrative complaints or systemic reviews of administrative procedures, or directed or requested investigations on administrative process. These are the roles of what might be termed the Classical model of an Ombudsman as first established by Sweden and other Scandinavian countries, picked up by New Zealand and copied by the Canadian provinces and Australia as well as around the world.

Some jurisdictions have established an Ombudsman with a specific or a single purpose to suit a specific need within that jurisdiction, for example, an Ombudsman for Human Rights, for discriminatory practices, for military, police, corrections, workers compensation issues etc. Some of these models do not have the independence from government supervision as does the classical model but they have been very effective within the scope of their responsibilities.

Other offices have been established on the basis of a "Commission", for example Tanzania (called the Permanent Commission of Inquiry) and Papua New Guinea (called the Ombudsman Commission). Austria has established a three person Ombudsman structure with the positions being filled by elected officials representing different political parties. Some of these models closely resemble the classical Human Rights Model with expanded jurisdiction to include administrative or corruption issues. All these models work *if* they are capable of operating independent of actual or perceived influence from government. In other words, there is no one best way. What works best in one jurisdiction may be inappropriate in another. What must be right for Ethiopia is a structure that works in the political culture of Ethiopia.

When establishing a structure, review the question why before getting into setting out legislation or deciding *how* such a structure will work. Once decided as to why, review the criteria used in establishing successful Ombudsman offices around the world. As you will see, the criteria are not mutually exclusive, in fact they are inextricably linked in so many ways.

Essential Elements

Independence

I have already touched on this issue but the issue is one of the most important criteria for success. Independence means the ability to investigate, review, and decide on the issues being reviewed without interference, actual or perceived. One method to accomplish this is to have the Ombudsman report directly to a parliament rather than through a cabinet minister, prime minister or president.

Impartiality

The more arms length an ombudsman is from the political structure, the more independent that person is seen to be by both the public and public servants. In addition, the selection of a person who is well respected and competent in the areas within jurisdiction is absolutely necessary. Failure to adhere to this principle supports the suspicion that many have of government. Trust has to be established in order for an Ombudsman to be effective. The selection of a 'wrong' person for the role, will undermine any good that such an office can accomplish.

Investigator

The Ombudsman is primarily an investigator. A keen understanding of evidence, what constitutes evidence and the meaning of the evidence uncovered is a skill but it also is a skill that is not exclusive to one profession. In most jurisdictions, the Ombudsman is a supervisor of investigations who at times must look above the individual issue under review with the intent to recommend a remedy to correct a system that caused the issue in the first place.

Powers of Recommendation

Most Ombudsmen have the power to recommend corrective action if error is found rather than making absolute decisions. To get concurrence with a recommendation, the Ombudsman uses the power of the office (its independence and impartiality), the evidence collected and what is felt to be moral suasion (persuasion as to the correctness of rectifying a wrong) in achieving resolution to the issues under investigation. Normally, an Ombudsman investigation is restricted to 'government' and does not extend to the private sector except where that private sector is implementing government policy (but not in all jurisdictions).

Jurisdiction

The jurisdiction of the Ombudsman should be clearly set out in the founding documents of the office. Should a dispute evolve as to the jurisdiction of the Ombudsman, then a competent authority who can decide whether the issue is inside or outside the jurisdiction should be listed in the enacting legislation.

Confidentiality

Information that comes into an Ombudsman's hands is in general, private. This includes personal information about a complainant *and* information supplied by a government agency to the Ombudsman. The Ombudsman should not become a discovery mechanism for legal action and therefore it should be the Ombudsman who decides what information is for public consumption and what is not. A general rule is if the information is of a personal nature, then it should not be shared but if it is information about a system of service delivery, then it may be made public in order for that system to be corrected.

Delegation

The Ombudsman needs to have the freedom to choose staff and to delegate staff responsibilities including the 'acting' Ombudsman role. Some jurisdictions have parliament chosen a deputy Ombudsman.

Communications

The Ombudsman must have the skill to communicate with others, regardless of the level of education or language skills. Not only does an Ombudsman communicate with the public and government on a constant basis, but also with the media.

Referrals

The ability to accept referrals from other agencies and government departments is appropriate. However one jurisdiction (Britain) requires the Parliamentary Commissioner for Administration and Health Service Commissioner to have a case referred through a member of parliament. This policy is currently under review. In addition, an Ombudsman usually has the authority to refer criminal matters to a competent authority for investigation. Some Ombudsman models specify that an Ombudsman may institute criminal proceedings in certain cases, specifically government officials in the case of corruption issues.

Discretion

The Ombudsman should have the ability to exclude frivolous or vexatious complaints, and most jurisdictions require any appeals to be completed before an Ombudsman can investigate. This is however, not an absolute requirement and would depend on the issue. Take for example a complaint of dealing with an issue in an untimely manner. It would be absurd to have that type of complaint go through all available appeals as that would only add to the time to resolve issues.

Fees

There should be no fees associated with having an Ombudsman review a complaint or issue. Should this criteria not be followed, it becomes only a service which involves those who can afford it – usually not the segment that may need the service most and it may imply other concerns such as the potential corrupting influence.

Prisons and Mental Hospitals

The Ombudsman needs to have access to any state run facility without being required to specify why to some official. In addition, occupants of a state run facility require the ability to contact an Ombudsman without the facility officials' authority. This is even more important if human rights are within jurisdiction.

Government Files

No restrictions should be built into the system for limiting access to government files. Trust and confidentiality are a necessary component of an Ombudsman structure in any system of government and to restrict access to information makes no sense at all.

Public Reporting

Reporting only to a government does not fulfill the mandate of an Ombudsman, but a public report following an investigation does. If the investigation supports a government action, the public has the right to know that no wrongdoing has occurred. On the other hand, if an investigation supports a complaint and nothing is being done to correct that complaint or the system which caused the concern, the public also, has the right to know.

Review

There should be no review of the Ombudsman investigation except in the general sense when renewal of a term of office is at issue. Any review at this stage should be based on whether or not the role of Ombudsman has been fulfilled properly, not based on a specific investigation or issue.

Concrete Models

Where do we go from here? There are a number of models to follow in establishing an office such as the Office of an Ombudsman, some more effective than others.

Malta

One of the most successful establishments of an Ombudsman's office was accomplished through the Commonwealth Secretariat in London. The former Chief Ombudsman from New Zealand, Sir John Robertson, was hired as a consultant and supervised the establishment process from its conception, the development of the legislation, the hiring of the first Ombudsman and the establishment of operational procedures.

USSR

Many of the breakaway states are in the process of establishing offices with the assistance of a former President of the United States Ombudsman Association (Dean Gottehrer) through the USAID program and the United Nations Development program.

Thailand, Cambodia, Vietnam

Discussions are being conducted now through the Institute for Dispute Resolution, University of Victoria (Stephen Owen) sponsored by the Parliamentary Centre and the Canadian International Development Agency.

Yukon Territory

As a serving Ombudsman, I also set up the office in the Yukon, a territory in northern Canada; as such I was responsible for two different jurisdictions at the same time.

There are other examples of assistance which can be discussed further. There are many people interested in assisting a country as Ethiopia in developing an Office of the Ombudsman. This symposium is an example where delegates from such diverse areas as Norway, the Netherlands, Nigeria, Slovenia, Sweden, Columbia, Mexico and Argentina are all there to assist and discuss – many of whom have assisted the development of this concept in countries other than their own through visits, symposiums, reviewing legislation and supplying whatever assistance they could.

It matters not what you call the institution of ombudsman, it does matter why you establish such an office, how you establish that office, what you want that office to accomplish, who you choose to accomplish the tasks at hand, and the support you give to that office.

The bottom line is that you have the opportunity to do something. We can assist in keeping the development of that concept from getting off the rails, but it is up to the country establishing an ombudsman institution to ensure that the railbed is properly founded.

The Role of a National Commission in the Protection of Human Rights

Tom Hadden*

Introduction

The opportunity to make a contribution to the deliberations of parliamentarians and human rights activists in Ethiopia is particularly welcome during a period in which we in Northern Ireland are working on a new political settlement of a thirty year conflict, a settlement which is based on the recognition of individual and communal rights and equality.

The package on which the people in Northern Ireland are voting is quite complex since it is designed to reflect the political rights and interests of two communities with different national allegiances and aspirations. But it is firmly based on the recognition and protection of human rights, including not only the rights of individuals and of the members of both major communities but also of those who belong to neither. As in Ethiopia, many of the details both in the formulation of individual and communal rights and in the mechanisms for monitoring and enforcement remain to be worked out. But some aspects of the process in which politicians and human rights activists in Northern Ireland are engaged may be relevant in Ethiopia.

The first is that the human rights and equality agendas have been an integral part of the settlement process in the sense that all the parties agreed that it would not be possible to adopt new structures for the protection of human rights in advance of a general political settlement. In that sense the constitutional protections for minorities in the proposed political structures and the human rights provisions of the settlement merge into each other and cannot be disentangled.

The second is that all the parties have accepted that the new bill of rights for Northern Ireland which is provided for in the Agreement as a means of protecting individual and communal rights in Northern Ireland must be firmly based on the principles and formulations in the wide range of international human rights covenants, though there will obviously be scope for argument and debate on which particular rights are to be incorporated into national constitutional law in Northern Ireland.

The third is that all the parties have agreed that it will not be sufficient to

*Centre for International and Comparative Human Rights Law, Queen's University of Belfast, Northern Ireland.

K. Hossain et al. (eds), Human Rights Commissions and Ombudsman Offices, 791–799.

adopt a new bill of rights, but that new administrative structures will be required to help ensure that the rights are effectively protected. The Agreement therefore provides for the establishment of a new Northern Ireland Human Rights Commission and a new Equality Commission.

National and International Protection of Human Rights

A creative interplay between national and international law is essential to the effective protection of human rights. The historic bills of rights, such as the French Declaration of the Rights of Man and the Citizen and the American Bill of Rights incorporated in the United States Constitution, were drafted to meet the particular circumstances of the late eighteenth century, and were enforceable only in national courts. But they provided a lasting model for the fundamental rights included in the constitutions of many European, American and African states as they emerged from royal or colonial rule. They also provided the model for the initial international documents, the Universal Declaration of Human Rights in 1948 and the European Convention on Fundamental Rights and Freedoms in 1951. These and the increasing number of subsequent international human rights declarations and covenants now set an international standard for the protection of individual and communal rights throughout the world. But the primary means of protection and enforcement of these rights is still a matter for national law.

The formal means of reflecting this interplay of national and internal law in most European states has been the incorporation of the provisions of the European Convention into national law so that the rights are directly enforceable in national courts. The United Kingdom and the Irish Republic are now the only members of the European Union not to have done so, though the process has recently been started in the United Kingdom.[1]

The incorporation of these basic human rights into national law, however is unlikely to be sufficient. In almost every state there are particular circumstances, not least the existence of different ethnic or national groups with the state, which may require the adoption of additional individual or group rights. One means of achieving this may be to adopt in a national bill of rights particularly appropriate provisions of the various more detailed international covenants such as the Convention on the Elimination of All Forms of Racial Discrimination or in a European context the new European Framework Convention for the Protection of National Minorities. This approach was recommended in a report which members of the Queen's University Human Rights Centre prepared for the Irish Government in 1996 entitled The Protection of Human Rights in the context of Peace and Reconciliation in Ireland, and seems likely to be followed in the preparation of a specific Bill of Individual and Communal Rights in Northern Ireland.

The standards of international human rights law which are not incorporated directly or indirectly into national law, however, cannot be ignored. Most international human rights conventions now contain a reporting system which

---

[1]The British Human Rights Act 1999, which incorporates the European Convention on Human Rights, has entered into force in October 2000.

requires signatory states to submit reports and discuss progress with an international committee of experts. Even if a state has not ratified a convention it will be expected in the political and diplomatic sphere to adhere to widely accepted human rights norms. There is an important role for national human rights commissions and non-governmental organizations in all these aspects of both national and international law.

Monitoring and Enforcement

It will already be clear that the effective protection of human rights, whether in Northern Ireland or in an emerging democracy like Ethiopia requires more than the acceptance of international standards and their incorporation into national law. Experience in many jurisdictions has been that the formal acceptance of a bill of rights or constitutional guarantees of human rights may have little immediate impact, whether as a result of a lack of experience in the legal profession or the judiciary or a lack of commitment to change by governmental agencies. In the United Kingdom and some other common law jurisdictions there is a particularly strong tradition of respect for the doctrine of parliamentary sovereignty and of judicial deference to governmental decisions, especially where issues of national security or public order are involved. There is a corresponding tradition of judicial deference to state officials in many emerging democracies. Consequently there may be little direct judicial and legal experience of the implementation of fundamental rights in national law.

The creation of effective structures for monitoring and enforcement of any new fundamental rights at national level may therefore be as important as the enactment of the rights themselves. This is likely to involve three distinct elements:

1. one or more human rights commissions to monitor and assist in the enforcement of the full range of fundamental rights;
2. judicial institutions and procedures for the selection of judges which will command public confidence;
3. the development through education and training of a general human rights culture in all governmental agencies and in society as a whole.

Human Rights Commissions

International Standards for National Commissions

The idea that all states should create official human rights commissions with powers to act independently of government has been given further support by the Paris Principles relating to the Status of National Institutions discussed within the United Nations in the context of the Vienna Conference on Human Rights in 1994. These principles leave a good deal of discretion to states on the precise competence and powers of human rights commissions, but emphasise that they should have as broad a mandate as possible "to promote and protect human rights", including the power to make recommendations to government, and to investigate and report on both general and specific violations. They also emphasise that any such commission should be completely independent of government, should be pluralist and representative of society as a whole, and should have adequate funding so as not to be subject to any governmental or financial control which might affect its independence.

Human Rights and Anti-discrimination Commissions in Common Law Jurisdictions

The idea that state-funded commissions should be established to monitor and assist in the prevention of discrimination and the promotion and protection of human rights was well established long before the adoption of the Paris Principles. But there is considerable variation in their constitution and powers.

In Britain the practice has been to establish single purpose agencies to monitor and assist in enforcing the law on discrimination: currently these are the Commission for Racial Equality in respect of racial discrimination and the Equal Opportunities Commission in respect of sex discrimination. In Northern Ireland similar agencies have been established in respect of religious and political discrimination, currently the Fair Employment Commission, and sex discrimination, the Equal Opportunities Commission for Northern Ireland. There is also a specific agency, the Community Relations Council, with the broader task of promoting mutual tolerance in all spheres throughout Northern Ireland. Finally there is a general purpose agency, the Standing Advisory Commission on Human Rights established in 1973 under the Northern Ireland Constitution Act, though it differs from the standard British model in being purely advisory without power to make findings or pursue legal action in respect of individual cases. In Canada and Australia the tendency has been to establish general purpose human rights commissions, both at a federal and state or provincial level, with similar powers and duties in respect of the full range of human rights and discrimination.

There has also been some variation in the precise powers granted to these human rights and discrimination agencies. Initially, both in Britain and elsewhere, it was usual to give powers to the agencies to investigate complaints and make findings of discrimination or breaches of rights. But this gave rise to some conflict over their proper role. In so far as they were established to promote human rights or to prevent discrimination they were expected to encourage individual complainants to come forward, to give them assistance in pursuing their claims and to carry out research on patterns of violation or discrimination. But this often made it difficult for the agency to act as an impartial adjudication body since it was likely to be perceived, especially by defendants, as being inherently biassed in favour of the complainant. The tendency in recent years has been to remove powers of adjudication from the agencies to independent tribunals or courts, thus leaving the agency free to pursue a positive policy in promoting the interests of victims of human rights violations or discrimination both in general terms and also in assisting individual complainants to pursue actions for compensation or redress in the courts. This is the current position in respect of all the discrimination agencies in Britain.

The exception to both these models is the Standing Advisory Commission on Human Rights in Northern Ireland. While it does have a broad mandate to promote and protect human rights it fails to meet a number of the Paris Principles, notably in that it has no power to investigate specific cases, in that its secretary is a civil servant within its sponsoring department, the Northern

Ireland Office, and in that it requires governmental approval for all major items of expenditure. Nor has it any powers to take action on behalf of complainants or even to assist them in doing so. Its only active engagement to date, though it was initially resisted by the government, has been in making submissions as amicus curiae in respect of relevant cases before the European Court of Human Rights and in providing material for international committees dealing with British Government reports. Its record in promoting and protecting human rights during the height of the conflict in Northern Ireland has been correspondingly limited and many of its members have found their position intensely frustrating. As a former member I would argue strongly against the creation of a purely advisory body of this kind.

There is a continuing debate throughout the United Kingdom on the future mandates and powers of these various commissions. And as might be expected it is a matter on which there are strong vested interests. There has been strong resistance from the established anti-discrimination commissions to the creation of an all-purpose human rights commission for the United Kingdom as a whole on the ground that the issues involved in race and sex and other forms of discrimination were different and that separate single purpose agencies were required to deal effectively with each of them. In Northern Ireland there was also strong initial opposition on similar grounds to a proposal to create a single human rights commission. The recent multi-party Agreement, however, has renewed the proposal for the amalgamation of the existing anti-discrimination agencies into a single Equality Commission and has also proposed the creation of a new Human Rights Commission with stronger powers than the Standing Advisory Commission. Ultimately this is a matter that can be resolved only through the political process rather than by technical legal arguments. But there is no theoretical reason to oppose and some practical and financial arguments to support the creation of a single human rights commission with responsibility for all aspects of human rights, which might then establish specialised units to deal with each major area of activity. There are examples of effective all-purpose human rights agencies in Canada and Australia (and elsewhere).

A Human Rights Commission for Ethiopia

Any new human rights commission or commissions which may be established in Ethiopia should clearly comply both with these general internationally agreed principles and also build on the experience of anti-discrimination agencies in other jurisdictions. The essential requirements may perhaps be summarised as follows:

1. It should be independent of government and its members should be broadly representative of the society within which it works.
2. It should have power to investigate and report on both general and individual violations of human rights.
3. It should have power to scrutinize and report on the human rights implications of proposed legislation.
4. It should have power both to initiate legal proceedings either in its own right or on behalf of individuals or groups and to assist individuals and groups to initiate proceedings.

5. It should have power to make reports and submissions to international monitoring bodies on all aspects of human rights in Ethiopia.
6. It should have power to engage in general promotional and educational activities.
7. It should have sufficient resources free from detailed governmental control to carry out its functions effectively.

Human Rights and Constitutional Courts

Some form of independent judicial adjudication on alleged human rights violations is essential for the effective protection of the rights guaranteed under any bill or charter of rights. Without it the expectations raised by the adoption of the bill or charter can become a source of further division and conflict. This is particularly so in a divided society in which activists on all sides can assert the denial of fundamental rights on their own interpretation of the relevant provisions as a ground for continuing rejection of any political accommodation. It follows that the adjudicating body must be constituted and operate in such a way that its decisions will be generally accepted on all sides and that they will actually be implemented. The authority of the European Court of Human Rights to make final decisions on the compatibility of national laws or practices with the European Convention, for example, lies in the fact that its judges are drawn from all member states of the Council of Europe. The fact that it has no power to invalidate national legislation or national governmental decisions, though it can order that compensation be paid to individual victims, is less important since Article 13 of the Convention imposes a binding obligation on states to provide an effective remedy for breaches of its terms. In a national context compliance with this requirement means that a constitutional or human rights court must have the same powers as other courts to invalidate legislation and overrule governmental decisions as well as to award compensation.

The effective protection of fundamental rights in any jurisdiction is therefore likely to require the establishment of a human rights or constitutional court which meets the following criteria:

1. independence from government;
2. general acceptance of the legitimacy of its decisions by all sections of the population;
3. authority to make binding rulings;
4. appropriate provision for the implementation of its decisions and the compensation of victims.

Some ways in which these criteria might be met under various possible structures will be discussed in turn.

The minimum requirement in respect of independence is that members of a human rights or constitutional court should have the same independence from government as ordinary judges. In Britain this has traditionally been guaranteed by providing that judges once appointed cannot be removed before retirement otherwise than by a vote of both Houses of Parliament. But this provides no protection against governmental bias in the initial selection of judges. In the United States some further protection is provided by the practice of holding

Senate and Congressional hearings on all Presidential nominations for the Supreme Court. These hearings, however, have not prevented the tendency on the part of most Presidents to make nominations on the basis of the known political preferences of candidates with a view to influencing the balance of power on the Supreme Court. In countries like Britain, where governmental control of parliamentary proceedings is considerably greater than in the United States, some further safeguards in respect of the balance of appointments may be desirable to ensure effective as well as formal independence.

General public acceptance of the legitimacy of decisions by a human rights or constitutional court is affected as much by the perceived balance of representation on the court as by its perceived independence. Even in relatively homogeneous societies concern is often expressed about the privileged background and conservative attitudes of most senior judges and the absence of representation from women and minority communities. In divided societies the balance of representation from each major community is likely to have an even greater effect on public perceptions of the legitimacy of particular decisions. On international human rights courts this problem can be avoided by the selection of judges from a wide range of different jurisdictions. The European Commission and Court of Human Rights, for example, are composed of representatives from each member country and significant decisions are made by panels of as many as 20 to 30 judges. On national human rights or constitutional courts other means must be sought to ensure appropriate balance and thus to enhance the authority and legitimacy of their decisions. In homogeneous states the usual approach is to provide for larger panels of judges. But this may not be sufficient in divided societies. In some cases balanced representation may be achieved by informal conventions in the selection of panels for sensitive cases. But more formal provisions may be preferred. In South Africa, for example, the Constitution of 1996 provides for nominations for appointment to the new constitutional court to be made by a Judicial Service Commission having regard "to the need to constitute a court which is independent and competent and representative in respect of race and gender". It also permits the appointment of competent persons other than judges to two of the eleven positions.

The effectiveness of a constitutional or human rights court depends ultimately on the way in which its judges approach their task. American judges have shown their ability to adopt positive and flexible interpretations of the fundamental rights in the United States Constitution. British judges have little experience in dealing with rights of this kind and have shown little appetite for moving beyond the essentially procedural principles of judicial review. This in itself may be an additional ground for broadening the range of those eligible for appointment to such a court, for example by extending the range of those eligible for appointment to legal academics and others with expertise in human rights law and practice. But it may also be possible to assist and encourage existing judges in their new task by a programme of seminars and discussions with judges in other jurisdictions.

The Creation of a Human Rights Culture

Respect for human rights is an attitude of mind. The enactment of a bill of rights and the provision of enforcement procedures will not in themselves ensure that ordinary people's rights are actually respected. Impressive bills of rights and legal enforcement systems are often to be found in countries with the most oppressive regimes or where intercommunal conflict is rampant. If those in control of state power or the police or soldiers who act on their behalf are unconcerned about the violation of the fundamental rights of those who challenge or threaten them in any way, there is often little that lawyers or courts can do to protect them. Legal challenges in national or international courts, even if they are successful, will achieve little unless there is some basic commitment to human rights values at all levels of government and throughout the community. This is particularly important in countries where paramilitary or insurgent groups – or those who merely express their support for the activities of others on their behalf – have had scant regard for the fundamental rights of others if that stood in the way of the pursuit of their own communal interests. If human rights are to be effectively protected positive action is needed to create a culture of human rights which pervades all the institutions of government and of civil society.

The training of governmental officials in the obligations imposed on them by human rights conventions is an essential part of this task. There is a temptation for some government officials, particular those in the security forces and the police, to regard those who allege that any of their activities are in breach of human rights as natural enemies. That is a misconception. All international human rights conventions have been drawn up by or on behalf of governments which are naturally interested in the maintenance of stability. Consequently there is nothing in international human rights standards which poses any threat to resolute action by state officials acting on behalf of a legitimate government for the prevention and control of criminal activity or the suppression of paramilitary or politically motivated violence. And there are strong arguments for the position that law enforcement carried out in compliance with international standards is likely to be more effective than methods which involve breaches of human rights. But there is clearly a substantial job to be done to persuade many of those involved, not least members of security forces involved in dealing with paramilitary violence, that this is so and to train them effectively in the use of legitimate techniques. The effective implementation of human rights must therefore include an active programme for training all government officials in the importance of human rights values and in the particular standards for each area of government activity which have been drawn up by relevant international agencies.

A commitment of this kind is particularly important in respect of members of the police and other security forces. It is common in all areas of conflict to find that there is a widespread belief that members of the army or the police have been guilty of systematic abuses in the operation of emergency laws. Whatever new structures for policing and security are agreed in an attempt to remedy this problem, there will be a need to demonstrate the commitment of all involved not only to the rule of law but also to the implementation of current international standards. A series of international agreed principles and codes of conduct for many aspects of policing and security have been drawn up within the United Nations in recent years. The most important are the Code of Conduct for Law Enforcement Officials of 1979, the Basic Principles for the use of Force and Firearms by Law Enforcement Officials of 1990, and the Principles on the Effective Prevention and Investigation of Arbitrary and Summary Executions of 1989. A formal commitment by the relevant authorities that all members of the police and security forces would be trained in and effectively bound by these principles would go some way to build confidence in all sections of the community that basic human rights would be respected under any new policing and security arrangements.

There is an equally pressing need to promote underlying human rights values throughout the community. This is not simply a matter of ensuring that the list of basic human rights is widely understood at all levels of society. An equally essential element is an understanding of the relationship between asserting individual and communal rights and respecting the corresponding rights of others. An obvious starting point is in education. There is clearly scope for greater emphasis on all aspects of human rights and mutual tolerance in all parts of the school curriculum and for a positive programme for the development of suitable educational materials and training programmes for teachers.

Experience in other jurisdictions has demonstrated that respect for the human rights of all and tolerance for different identities cannot be achieved merely by changing attitudes at the level of governmental agencies, however crucial that may be. The whole population and all communities must be engaged through a wide range of organizations and networks. Many of these, including women's and anti-poverty groups as well as religious and professional bodies and human rights pressure groups, can do vital voluntary work within and between the main communities. All should be encouraged to contribute to the shaping and delivery of any human rights programme and adequate resources should be provided to enable them to do so. Statutory agencies could play a major role in this process by encouraging voluntary bodies to become involved in the promotion of human rights and tolerance. One possibility would be to provide for nominations for places on any new human rights commission by non-government organizations and other voluntary sector bodies. The media also have a vital part to play in publicising and explaining the ideas behind any such programme. This too may require the training of journalists in the essentials of human rights principles and their sources in national and international law. This might be sponsored by a human rights commission without in any way infringing the proper independence of the media or their freedom to criticize.

Human Rights Commissions

Brian Burdekin*

Introduction and Definition[1]

In considering ways of strengthening national institutions on human rights it is first necessary to define which institutions we are examining. All organs of state and indeed all sectors of society have important roles and responsibilities in relation to human rights – reflecting the fact that the law of human rights is now relevant to almost every aspect of government activity and many other areas of life. However, I take our topic as addressing institutions whose functions are specifically defined in terms of the protection and promotion of human rights. These institutions generally bear a title such as "Human Rights Commission" although, as will be seen, some are concerned more specifically with discrimination on a particular basis (such as race or sex) or the rights of a specific group (such as children).

This paper does not, therefore, deal directly with the fundamentally important role of an independent judiciary in protecting human rights, nor (except as it relates to the institutions under discussion) with the judicial application of human rights through a constitutional or statutory Bill of Rights, such as have now been adopted by a significant number of countries.

The Office of Ombudsman and Human Rights Commissions

The office of ombudsman is now well established in many Commonwealth jurisdictions. In a number of countries an ombudsman is maintained together with a Human Rights Commission or similar body. In some cases (such as Canada and New Zealand) there is also a judicially enforceable Bill of Rights. Clearly, in these countries at least, the different institutions are regarded as performing basically distinct functions. The main distinctions may be defined as follows:

(a) In most cases the jurisdiction of the Ombudsman is to ensure general fairness and legality in pubic administration. The jurisdiction of a human rights commission is more specifically focussed on human rights and non discrimination, and, at least so far as non-discrimination is concerned, frequently extends beyond actions of government to include other areas of public life

*Office of the High Commissioner for Human Rights, Geneva; formerly Federal Human Rights Commissioner of Australia.

[1] I am indebted to Mr. David Mason at our Commission for preparing a first draft of this chapter.

K. Hossain et al. (eds), Human Rights Commissions and Ombudsman Offices, 801–834.

– such as discrimination by private employers. 'The Swedish model constitutes an exception from the general model, and is discussed further below.'(In Sweden, in addition to the Parliamentary Ombudsmen with general jurisdiction, there are Ombudsmen for Ethnic Discrimination, Equal Opportunities and other matters).[2]

(b) In general, the principal focus of activity for an Ombudsman is dealing with individual complaints. Human Rights commissions generally also have this function, but tend to embody a broader range of powers – including educational and promotional activities, and review of legislation.

(c) A number of human rights commissions have international standards on human rights as the explicit or implicit basis of their work – whereas for an Ombudsman the principal basis is generally domestic legislation, with international standards being, at most, of indirect relevance.[3] In a number of common law countries, the Ombudsman is seen as approaching issues of "justice" from precepts of administrative law and good administrative practice – rather than on the basis of international human rights law.

In principle, however, there need be no fundamental inconsistency between the functions of an Ombudsman and of a human rights commission. In some countries it might be considered economical to combine the functions by conferring on the Ombudsman the specific human rights jurisdiction, and wider promotional and policy functions (in addition to complaint handling) which a separate human rights commission would generally have. Sufficient resources and sufficiently clear human rights responsibilities would, however, have to be provided for to ensure that the effective focus on human rights issues was not lost by this strategy.

The office of the Procurator, which exists principally in republics and states of the former Soviet Union and in Eastern Europe, also has some similarities with the office of the Ombudsman, being concerned with legality and propriety in administration. However, the Procurator also has direct responsibilities for instituting criminal prosecutions, which may well conflict with this institution being entrusted with the tasks of a national human rights commission.[4]

Scope of the Paper

This paper does not purport to provide a comprehensive account of every national institution which falls within its scope. Apart from limits of space and time, the increasing awareness of the importance of national institutions has recently been accompanied by rapid developments – so that it is entirely possible that important institutions have developed of which I remain unaware. This only emphasises the importance of having a continuing exchange of ideas and information.

---

[2]There are (in addition to those specified above) Ombudsmen to deal with consumer complaints; to oversee fair competitive practices in the market; and to deal with complaints against the press. These last three institutions are outside the scope of this paper.

[3]In Finland, however, the Parliamentary Ombudsman is reported to have referred to the International Covenant on Civil and Political Rights in a number of recommendations UN Doc. E/CN.4/1991/23.

[4]Others more familiar with civil law and socialist legal traditions might have different perceptions on this issue.

In my view it is obvious that no single model of national institution or institutions can, or should be recommended as the appropriate mechanism for all countries to fulfil their international human rights obligations. Although each nation can benefit from the experience of others, national institutions must be developed taking into account national conditions and existing institutional frameworks.

An important part of the framework for discussion in this area are the regional arrangements and institutions, if any, which exist – and the extent to which they can, or should, perform some of the same functions as national institutions. In my view, however, they clearly cannot supplant the need for effective national machinery.

Much depends on the nature of the national constitution in particular whether it contains a bill of rights and, if so, the content and range of rights covered and the mechanisms for enforcement provided. It is also important whether the constitutional structure is that of a unitary State, a federation or confederation, or other variations.

Recent momentous developments in international affairs must also be taken into account. Existing national structures are re-forming or dissolving rapidly in several areas. This will present important opportunities for developments relating to national human rights machinery.

Domestic and International Scope

At the same time as acknowledging differing national conditions it is necessary to re-emphasise the universality of human rights and the obligations of all governments to their peoples.

At a legal level this is clear: by the act of joining the United Nations, States subscribe to the basic purposes of the organization enumerated in the Charter – including the promotion and protection of human rights – and undertake to cooperate for these purposes. But it is also relevant in considering national institutions to recall that human rights have deep roots in the traditions of all peoples – even if this is not reflected in the practices of their governments.

The Universal Declaration of Human Rights did not spring fully formed from the minds of delegates to the United Nations. It derived largely from a common reflection on national constitutional and legal provisions and traditions. Nor was it the work of people from any particular tradition. Although the General Assembly, at the time of the drafting of the Declaration, was clearly less representative than it now is, careful study of the drafting history indicates the range and significance of contributions from many different traditions. The Declaration, as is often noted, bears the influence of common law systems, in their various terms; of civil law; and of socialist systems and legal thinking.

Less often noted are the contributions of Latin and South American, Arabic and Asian nations, despite the smaller numbers then represented. Least well represented, of course, were African nations since for most the realisation of the right to self-determination – now recognized in positive law at the head of the human rights covenants – was still in the future. In this context, therefore, it is particularly notable that as many of those nations gained their independence the provisions of the Universal Declaration were incorporated, more or less directly, in their national Constitutions. (This degree of reflection in national law is indeed, one of the bases for the view of many commentators that at least major elements of the Universal Declaration have achieved the status of customary international law.)[5]

The Universal Declaration and later human rights instruments to which it gave birth, call for measures of implementation at the national level. International commitments and standards, and international machinery, however sophisticated, are a very long way from the direct realisation of human rights for most individuals. It is primarily at the national level, including through national institutions, that human rights must be made a reality in the lives of men, women and children throughout the world. Each of the principal human rights instruments developed by the United Nations recognizes this, in requiring nations not merely to "respect" human rights, but to take appropriate measures to "ensure" these rights, or "to take steps by all appropriate means" for their realisation.[6]

Clearly, there are a variety of national measures which may be adopted to achieve these goals – in addition to such essential prerequisites as the effective rule of law, independence of the judiciary, freedom of information and expression and, importantly, the protection provided by freely chosen democratic representative institutions. In particular, a number of States have incorporated specified human rights instruments (particularly the International Covenant on Civil and Political Rights) directly into national law. This is necessary in most common law countries, for example, to give human rights instruments legal effect – since the general position of the courts in these countries is that treaty obligations are not effective in domestic law without specific statutory incorporation. A number of common law countries and others, as already noted, have reproduced provisions of these instruments in national constitutions. In other cases, by constitutional provisions, or as a matter of legal doctrine, treaty obligations in general take precedence over domestic law.[7]

Equally clearly, however, as the last 40 years have graphically demonstrated, legal provisions simply referring to or incorporating international instruments are not enough. (René Cassin noted this in the drafting of the International Covenant on Economic, Social and Cultural Rights when be said "it would be deceiving the peoples of the world to let them think that a legal provision was

---

[5] On the basis of human rights in African traditions see for example K. M'Baye, Background Paper, UN Seminar on Establishment of Regional Commissions on Human Rights, with Special Reference to Africa, UN Doc. HR/Liberia/1979/Bp.2.

[6] The obligation to "respect" human rights may be said to impose a "negative" obligation not to violate human rights. But the obligation to "ensure" is of critical importance and goes much further. It clearly imposes an obligation to act positively to guarantee such rights. On the nature of these obligations see for example P. Alston and F. Quinn, "The Nature and Scope of States Parties' Obligations under the International Covenant on Economic, Social and Cultural Rights", (1987) 9 Human Rights Quarterly 156.

[7] Note for example the provision of Article 43 of the Constitution of Togo: "From the date of their publication duly ratified treaties and agreements shall take precedence over the laws, provided that all such treaties and agreements are applied by the other party": see UN Doc CCPR/C/36/Add. 5. par. 37. Note however that in the United States of America – where treaties are similarly declared by the Constitution to be the "supreme law of the land" – doubts have been raised as to whether the human rights treaties are "self executing" so as to be legally effective without a further process of incorporation by national law. The basis of this doubt is that in their terms the human rights treaties oblige States Parties to take measures, rather than directly conferring legally enforceable rights on individuals.

all that was required ... when in fact an entire social structure had had to be transformed by a series of legislative and other measures".[8]

The protection and promotion of human rights is not a fixed state to be achieved prior to or immediately after the ratification of international instruments, but a continuing, challenging enterprise.[9] It is the central thesis of this paper that appropriate national human rights institutions are essential to the realisation of the rights recognized in United Nations human rights instruments.

Such institutions can be roughly divided into several categories – based on the criterion of "domestic or international scope":

(1) Those which are concerned solely with human rights in the international arena, but which appear to lack any significant direct domestic jurisdiction (such as the sections on human rights maintained by many Ministries of Foreign Affairs), are outside the scope of this paper.

(2) A number of institutions are primarily national in focus, but also have the function of conducting public information in relation to international human rights law. An example of such an institution is the Finnish Committee on International Human Rights Issues (comprising representatives from each of the political parties, as well as representatives nominated by the national sections of the Red Cross and Amnesty International), the role of which is described in Finland's third Periodic Report to the Human Rights Committee[10] as to assist the Ministry of Foreign Affairs on human rights issues and to conduct public education. The membership of this Committee includes the Deputy Parliamentary Ombudsman (which may serve to some extent to facilitate coordination between international policy on human rights and domestic implementation).

(3) Some national institutions have a fully mixed jurisdiction, with principal or major responsibilities relating both to domestic and international policies on human rights. In France, for example,[11] the National Advisory Commission for Human Rights (composed of representatives of relevant associations, a number of prominent individuals in the field of human rights, four members of parliament and a number of non-voting representatives of government) has both national and international responsibilities – being concerned with human rights violations both in France and abroad.[12] In Ecuador, the Ad Hoc Commission on Human

---

[8] UN Doc. E/CN.4/SR.232 (1951); and see P. Alston and G. Quinn, op.cit.

[9] The view has also been expressed in the Australian High Court that even at the level of legal implementation, in some cases simply reciting the terms of international instruments may be insufficient to give them legal effect in national law without further process of translation into more specific rights and obligations: see Dawson, J. in Gerhardy v Brown (1985) 159 Commonwealth Law Reports 70 at p.157. Note also the comments of the Hon. Justice P.N. Bhagwati: " It is obvious that a certain degree of positivisation or particularisation is required if specific human rights are going to have practical force ...", Inaugural Address, in Developing Human Rights Jurisprudence: the Domestic application of International Human Rights Norms (Report of the Judicial Colloquium, Bangalore 1988, Commonwealth Secretariat, p.xx.)

[10] UN Doc. CCPR/C/58/Add.5.

[11] UN Doc. E/CN.4/1991/23.

[12] In Turkey, the Human Rights Inquiry Commission (whose membership is determined by the National Assembly according to a formula of party representation) also has a mixed jurisdiction. This institution proposes legislative amendments and investigates complaints within Turkey by reference to international human rights treaties to which Turkey is party. It also has the function of examining violations of human rights in other countries when necessary and transmitting views on these to the parliamentarians of the country concerned. (UN Doc. E/CN.4/1991/23/Add. 1)

Rights of the National Congress has, together with a range of domestic human rights responsibilities, the functions of following up human rights complaints against Ecuador in international bodies, and monitoring respect for human rights internationally, with particular reference to Latin America.[13]

This model offers the advantage of relating domestic and international policy. In particular, in some countries, it may be one means of ensuring that the limited number of available personnel with expertise in the international law of human rights have some responsibilities for, or influence on, domestic law, policy and administration. That is, it may assist in avoiding the current tendency (which is widespread) for bureaucratic familiarity with international human rights instruments to be confined to Ministries of Foreign Affairs – while major responsibilities relevant to national implementation of human rights rest with domestic departments or agencies.

Disadvantages of such a model may include the imposition of an excessive workload on one institution – compared to its resources.[14] There may also be the possibility of conflict of responsibilities in some cases (depending on the way the institution's charter is framed). To the extent that an institution is responsible not simply for providing; advice, but for contributing to the formulation of foreign policy on human rights, it could be placed in the position of defending the nation's record internationally while criticising it at home.

(4) A further model is that typified by the Australian national Commission, the Human Rights and Equal Opportunity Commission. This Commission administers legislation directly based on, and incorporating, United Nations human rights instruments. The functions of the Commission are principally domestic, but it also has a degree of international competence – to the extent that this is ancillary to its domestic functions.

The instruments currently within the jurisdiction of the Australian Commission are:

- the International Covenant on Civil and Political Rights (ICCPR);
- the Convention on the Elimination of all forms of Racial Discrimination (CERD);
- the Convention on the Elimination of all forms of Discrimination against Women (CEDAW)
- the Declaration of the Rights of the Child;
- the Declaration on the Rights of Disabled Persons;
- the Declaration on the Rights of Mentally Retarded Persons; and
- the International Labour Organization's Discrimination (Employment and Occupation) Convention.[15]

---

[13] UN Doc. CCPR/C/58/Add.9.

[14] This is suggested, for example. by the Second Periodic Report of Zaire to the Human Rights Committee, UN. Doc. CCPR/Cl57/Add. l, which states: "The Department of Citizens' Rights and Civil Freedoms, operating within a rather modest budget, is required to do virtually everything."

[15] Within the Commission, the Sex Discrimination Commissioner has particular responsibilities for promotion and implementation of CEDAW. The Race Discrimination Commissioner has similar responsibilities regarding CERD, and the Human Rights Commissioner has primary responsibility for the remaining instruments listed, and any others which may be added to the Commission's jurisdiction. Details of the structure of the Australian Commission are given a Appendix A.

This extensive jurisdiction enables the Commission to promote human rights in an integrated way. Federal law also provides for further instruments to be added to the Commission's responsibilities. The Commission has recommended, for example, that this be done in relation to the Convention on the Rights of the Child.[16]

There are a number of advantages in giving national institutions a charter directly based on international human rights instruments. First, it serves as a convenient point of reference by which the degree of domestic implementation of human rights may be assessed – both internally and externally.

Second, it facilitates the development of experience and jurisprudence in applying international standards which, though framed by reference to national conditions, may be applicable by others.

Third, it is increasingly clear that international machinery for the protection of human rights, both Charter based (such as the Commission on Human Rights and mechanisms created under its mandate), and the treaty based Committees (such in their function of receiving individual complaints and in consideration of reports) are limited in the number of problems, situations and cases which they can handle. This is not to denigrate the importance of these bodies or the need to provide them with adequate resources and pursue means of making their operation more effective.[17] However, with growing international acceptance of these mechanisms, and in particular of the treaty based provisions for individual complaints, there is a need squarely to face the danger of overloading the machinery which should form the peak of the international system for protection and promotion of human rights by placing excessive reliance on it to perform tasks which, in the first instance, should be more appropriately and effectively addressed at the national level.

Fourth, as far as the international system is concerned, national machinery has important preventive functions – either in preventing human rights violations from occurring, or in achieving resolution of cases, and redress for violations of rights, before the international level is reached.

One particular benefit of national institutions having a specific basis in international human rights instruments is that it addresses the problem of cases falling through gaps in domestic legal categories. It is clear, for example, that common law systems, although containing important human rights elements, by themselves offer very inadequate protection of human rights particularly concerning

---

[16] The jurisdiction of the National Human Rights Commission of Togo, while emphasising civil and political rights in particular, also clearly extends to human rights more generally: see Initial Report of Togo to the Human Rights Committee, UN Doc. ICCPR/C/36/Add.5. The New Zealand Human Rights Commission Act, s.6(a), specifies that the functions of the Commission include reporting to the Prime Minister from time to time on "the desirability of legislative, administrative or other action to give better protection to human rights and to ensure better compliance with standards laid down in international instruments on human rights". In Guatemala, the Attorney for Human Rights is appointed by Congress for defence of human rights, both as recognized under The Constitution and in the Universal Declaration of Human Rights and international treaties.

[17] Discussed in the important report to the General Assembly by Professor Philip Alston, UN Doc A/44/668.

discrimination[18] and the rights of especially disadvantaged groups (such as the mentally ill).[19]

Fifth, where an individual complaint is not resolved at the national level and comes before a body such as the Human Rights Committee, the Committee on the Elimination of Racial Discrimination or the Committee Against Torture (where the nation concerned has taken the requisite steps to make those procedures available), prior consideration of the matter based on the same international standards by a national body is likely to be of considerable assistance to the international Committee concerned.

Sixth, with respect to the reporting systems instituted under United Nations instruments, a national institution dealing directly with the human rights instrument in question may be of great assistance both to the monitoring body in gaining accurate and authoritative information, and to the Government concerned in compiling information to fulfil its reporting obligation. Given the proliferation of reporting requirements, the extent of overlap between requirements under different treaties, and the difficulties experienced by many governments in collecting information to fulfil their obligations, the model of an integrated national commission to deal with all or many of the international human rights instruments to which the nation is party, has particular advantages. In some cases, depending on the extent of the national commission's jurisdiction, the annual report of such a body could effectively serve as the basis for substantial parts of the nation's report under the relevant instruments.

A number of national commissions whose principal functions are domestic also have responsibility for providing advice to government on a range of international actions relating to human rights, particularly in relation to the negotiation and ratification of international instruments. This is the case, for example, in relation to the New Zealand Human Rights Commission. The legislation establishing that Commission[20] expressly gives it the function of reporting on "the desirability of the acceptance by New Zealand of any international instrument on human rights". The more general responsibility of the Australian Commission, to recommend action by Australia in relation to human rights, also includes advising the government on negotiation and ratification of international instruments.

---

[18] W. Tarnopolsky, "Race relations commissions in Canada, Australia, New Zealand, the United Kingdom and the United States", (1985) 6 Human Rights Law Journal 145, at pp.151–154, gives a concise summary of the narrow coverage and pathetically inadequate remedies provided by the common law in relation to racial discrimination. For example, when, on the basis of racial discrimination, the West Indian international cricketer Leary Constantine and his family were refused admission (in insulting and degrading terms) to a London hotel where they had booked to stay, the common law courts could only award five pounds damages, Constantine v. Imperial Hotels Ltd. (1944) 1 K.B. 693. Had the hotel refused him service rather than accommodation, no remedy at all would apparently have been available.

[19] With respect to the rights of the mentally ill, the Principles for the Protection of Persons with Mental Illness and for the Improvement of Mental health Care (UN Doc. E/CN.4/1991/39, Annex 1), which were adopted by the Commission on Human Rights at its 1991 session and will be adopted by the General Assembly later this year, provide some much needed standards for the proper protection of this particularly disadvantaged and stigmatised group of people.

[20] New Zealand, Human Rights Commission Act 1977 s.6(b), and see Mr Justice Wallace, "The New Zealand Human Rights Commission" (1989) 58 Nordic Journal of International Law 155.

Participation in International Meetings

Clearly, governments have the power to determine both how they wish to be officially represented internationally and what, if any, international functions they confer on national human rights commissions. There are, however, a number of roles which national commissions may useful play in international meetings, in addition to providing advice or information to their government beforehand:

(a) In general it is possible for governments to request that members of national commissions serve as expert members of government delegations to United Nations treaty monitoring bodies. Australia has done this, for example, in presenting reports to the Human Rights Committee and the Committee on the Elimination of Racial Discrimination. In each case the Committee expressed appreciation for being able to receive information from people directly responsible for administering legislation implementing the international instrument in question. Where the national Commission is independent from direction by Government,[21] it is of course necessary to ensure that this independence is not compromised when participating in a Government delegation. In our experience this is quite possible if Commissions act as advisers to the delegation, rather than as members of it.

(b) Members of national commissions may, in some cases, also usefully serve on government delegations in the negotiation of international instruments. Members of the Australia Commission have recently been included in the Australian delegation involved in drafting the Convention on the Rights of the Child and the Principles on the Protection of the Human Rights of Mentally Ill Persons. They have also participated in working groups of the Commission on Human Rights, in drafting the Declaration on the Rights of Indigenous Peoples, and in negotiating draft Standard Rules for the Equalisation of Opportunities for Disabled Persons (presently before a Working Group of the Social Development Commission). The contribution of national commissions has generally been recognized as valuable in this area. The authority of the substantial body of international instruments already adopted depends, in part, on the efforts which have been made to ensure that these instruments reflect national experience.[22] Participation by members of national commissions is likely to contribute to this purpose.

(c) Several national commissions have also recently made significant contributions to international discussions on human rights matters, as experts in their own right rather than on government delegations. It may soon be appropriate, therefore, for the United Nations to acknowledge the role of national commissions in an appropriate form, without trespassing on the right of governments to determine the form of their own representation in

---

[21] As is the case with the Australian Commission.

[22] Note the related comments by Justice Rajsoomer Lallah, Member of the Human Rights Committee: "Far too often in the past, the question of human rights at the international level has tended to be dealt with solely by Foreign Ministries, admittedly with the assistance of Home Office legal advisers. It is to be wondered whether that is enough. It is the courts which normally deal with the implementation of human rights or their violations at grassroots level. The time has perhaps come to ensure that the thinking of the judiciary is tapped in a systematic way, and that it should be involved at the international level", Rajsoomer Lallah, International Human Rights Norms, in: Developing Human Rights Jurisprudence, Commonwealth Secretariat, p. 21.

international political bodies. (It appears, for example, rather anomalous that provision is made for formal recognition only of non-government organizations, some of whose focus on human rights is considerably less direct than national human rights commissions.)

(d) Some national human rights institutions have their responsibilities defined by reference to purely domestic legislation rather than by reference to international instruments. However, a number of these institutions have expressed recognition of the relevance of international instruments and the importance of international experience. The Canadian Commission, for example, although administering legislation which does not explicitly refer to international instruments, describes its role[23] as "to put institutional flesh on the bare bones of (Canada's) international commitments on human rights". There are numerous similarities between the domestic legislation of many countries on human rights and non-discrimination and the relevant international instruments – even where such instruments are not referred to in the legislation itself. Where national legislation has particular shortcomings (for example in adequately defining discrimination to be combatted) legislation elsewhere may have effectively addressed these.

This highlights the importance of comparing experience. The annual reports of a number of national commissions afford valuable material for comparative study,[24] as do various commercially produced law reports which deal with particular national institutions and legislation.[25] There are also several journals which include materials on national institutions within a more general regional or international focus[26] and the Commonwealth Secretariat's Human Rights Unit makes comparative information available. Further, there are the relatively brief but useful reports on national institutions prepared for the General Assembly[27] and the Commission on Human Rights,[28] shortly to be consolidated in a manual on national institutions by the Centre for Human Rights.[29]

Where they exist, regional arrangements offer valuable opportunities for sharing national experience. However, such arrangements remain absent in the Asian-Pacific region, so that institutions in this region are particularly in need of active strategies to ensure that they benefit from experience elsewhere. In recognition of this, the Australian and New Zealand commissions have a continuing program of staff exchanges. The Australian Commission also has a program of staff exchanges with the Danish Centre of Human Rights and has placed staff with the United Nations Centre for Human Rights.

---

[23] Canadian Human Rights Commission, Annual Report 1990, p. 11.

[24] The annual Report of the Canadian Commission should be mentioned in this context. It has the advantage, in terms of accessibility, of French and English text in one volume.

[25] The Australian and New Zealand Equal Opportunity Reporter is interesting in this respect, since it is inherently international and comparative, dealing with both the Federal and State (provincial) human rights legislation and institutions of Australia and New Zealand.

[26] The Nordic Journal of International Law, for example, has included articles on the Australian and New Zealand national commissions.

[27] UN Docs. A/36/440; A/38/416.

[28] UN Docs. E/CN.4/1987/37; E/CN.4/1989/47 and Add. 1; E/CN.4/1991/23 and Add. 1.

[29] There is more that could be, and needs to be, done in making comparative information available in published form: not only by the United Nations – which has recently made national institutions and human rights in general a much higher priority in is public information activity, but by each of our own national institutions. There are, however, limits to the extent to which written reports can

Participation in the Drafting of Legislation

Most national commissions have the power to make recommendations for the introduction of new legislation, or amendment of existing legislation, to protect human rights. In the case of several institutions which include members of the legislature, or appointed by the legislature,[30] this may be one way in which the legislature ensures human rights receive their proper place on the legislative agenda.

Institutions which are distinct from the legislature, either as independent statutory commissions or within an executive department, also have functions relating to the drafting of legislation. There are a number of reasons for conferring these functions on national commissions.

Review of Human Rights Legislation

National commissions which are responsible for administration of human rights legislation will often be in the best position to identify areas where this legislation requires improvement, either because of technical defects or because experience has indicated human rights problems which existing legislation does not adequately address. National institutions responsible for dealing with complaints in individual cases have concrete knowledge (which the legislature may not have in the same detail) concerning human rights problems in society. Where the national commission has power to conduct wide-ranging national inquiries, and is directed to work with non government organizations, as is the case in Australia, this provides a further basis for legislative recommendations.[31]

Drafting or Review of Other Legislation (existing or proposed)

National commissions on human rights generally have the power to review legislation in any area affecting human rights, rather than being confined to review of, or recommendations concerning, specific human rights legislation. The Australian Commission, for example, has functions of reporting on the consistency with human rights of all existing enactments and proposed enactments,[32] as well as the more specifically expressed functions of reporting on laws that should be made or actions taken in relation to human rights.[33] The New Zealand Commission also has the function of reporting on human rights implications of proposed legislation.[34] Clearly, such a function should supplement, rather than

reflect the particularities of national conditions and the work of national commissions. Direct contacts are therefore particularly useful.

[30] For example, the Human Rights Commission of the Congress of the Republic in Guatemala, see UN Doc. E/CN.4/1991/3; the National Congress Ad Hoc Commission on Human Rights in Ecuador – see UN Doc. CCPR/C/58/Add.9; and the Human Rights Inquiry Commission of Turkey, see UN Doc. E/CN.4/1991/23/Add. 1.

[31] The Australian Commission has recommended new legislation, or improvements to existing human rights legislation, in a range of areas including the rights of people with disabilities, protection against age discrimination and discrimination relating to HIV or AIDS, measures against incitement to racial hatred, varius aspects of sex discrimination, and the enforcement of the Commission's determinations.

[32] Human Rights and Equal Opportunities [furthermore: HREOC] Act s.11(1)(e).

[33] HREOC Act s.11(1)(k).

[34] New Zealand Human Rights Commission Act s.6(2).

displace, the responsibility of all other agencies of government (particularly ministries of justice) and the legislature itself to ensure all legislation is consistent with human rights.

The Chairperson of the New Zealand Human Rights Commission has noted that this function is the one particularly likely to bring the Commission into conflict with the Government.[35] In 1991 an instance of such conflict occurred in Australia in relation to legislation introduced by the Federal Government to ban all advertising containing "political matter" (political matter being very widely defined, and "advertising" not being defined at all) from radio and television. As Federal Human Rights Commissioner I advised the government that such a ban would (a) be inconsistent with the rights to receive and impart information and ideas recognized in Article 17 of the ICCPR; (b) had the potential to interfere with the political rights recognized in Article 25 of the same Covenant; and (c) would have a discriminatory impact on people with disabilities in respect of each of these rights. This advice was released publicly, (pursuant to a request under freedom of information legislation). The Government has now amended the legislation and a Parliamentary Committee is currently considering the matter.

Recommending Legislative Action

An important factor is whether the national commission can initiate a recommendation for legislative action itself, or only on reference from the government or Parliament. In some instances government authorities may not be aware of relevant human rights issues. The Canadian Human Rights Commission has noted[36] the danger that once human rights laws are in place, the legislature may neglect the need for continuing improvements to the legislation. In some cases, governments may regard it as politically inconvenient to receive recommendations from human rights commissions. Particularly where the commission is part of the Parliament, legislation or parliamentary procedure may require that matters having human rights implications be referred to the national commission. In other cases, however there may be no legal compulsion on the Government to refer proposed legislation to the commission. (For example in Australia the Human Rights and Equal Opportunity Commission Act allows the Attorney-General to refer proposed legislation to the Commission, but does not require him to do so.) For these reasons, the power to initiate legislative recommendations is important.

Quasi Judicial Powers

The question of whether national human rights institutions have quasi judicial powers raises a number of important issues.

---

[35] See Wallace (above), at p. 157.

[36] Annual Report, 1990.

Power to Compel Production of Documents and Giving of Evidence and Powers to Prevent Interference with Activities

Offices of Ombudsmen appear to be invariably invested with these powers to assist them in their investigations. Specific human rights commissions clearly also require these powers in order to be effective, particularly in investigating actions of government agencies. In the case of bodies formed within the legislature, these powers are generally inherent in the Parliament itself. In cases where the national commission is a separate body, these powers need to be specifically conferred.[37]

In Canada, powers to enter and search premises, and require production of evidence etcetera, are vested in investigators and tribunals instituted under the Human Rights Act rather than in the Human Rights Commission itself.[38] In Australia, the national Commission itself has power to require production of documents and to compel the giving of evidence.[39]

At the time of the creation of Australia's national commission, these powers were the object of much misconceived criticism to the effect that the new Commission constituted a "star chamber" which itself would be a threat to human rights. This criticism overlooked a number of provisions which ensure that the Commission operates consistently with human rights. For example, there is specific provision for refusal to give evidence on the grounds of self incrimination.[40] The Commission also has a firm policy that its compulsory powers should only be used where absolutely necessary, in keeping with the emphasis of the legislation on settlement by conciliation.

The Australian Attorney-General is able to order that evidence should not be produced if it would prejudice the fair trial or safety of any person or national security.[41] The Commission itself is able to order that evidence given to it should not be published, in order to protect the human rights of any person. The Commission is specifically required to observe the principles of natural justice.[42] It is also subject to administrative appeal machinery and to judicial review. These safeguards are important in ensuring that a national human rights commission operates in accordance with the law.

---

[37] In Togo, the national commission has juridical powers, see UN Doc. CCPR/C/36/Add.5. In Guatemala, a similar position applies to the Attorney for Human Rights appointed by the Congress to work in association with the Human Rights Commission of the Congress of the Republic, see UN Doc. E/CN.4/1991/23. In Mexico, the National Commission on Human Rights has authority to demand all appropriate information for the purposes of its functions, similarly to an Ombudsman: see UN Doc. E/CN.4/1991/23/Add. 1.

[38] The Canadian Human Rights Act s.5 provides that a tribunal established under the Act "may, in the same manner and to the same extent as a superior court of record summon and enforce the attendance of witnesses and compel them to give oral or written evidence on oath and to produce such documents or things as the Tribunal deems requisite to the full hearing and consideration of the complaint".

[39] HREOC Act ss. 21, 22.

[40] HREOC Act s.23(3).

[41] HREOC Act s.24.

[42] Where the Commission proposes to report that a person has engaged in an act which is inconsistent with human rights or constitutes discrimination, that person must be given the opportunity to make oral or written submissions: HREOC Act s.27.

Power to Make Determinations

A number of human rights institutions, in particular those directly associated with the legislature, deal with complaints (after preliminary analysis and. verification) principally by referring them to other appropriate authorities for investigation or institution of legal proceedings.[43]

It is common for the charters of national human rights commissions to emphasise settlement of complaints by conciliation wherever possible (particularly complaints of discrimination). At the international level, conciliation as an effective means of resolving disputes has been emphasised in the practice of the International Labour Organization and in a number of instruments adopted by that organization. At the national level, conciliation has frequently been found highly effective in resolving complaints by a settlement agreed to by the parties, thus avoiding the need for the law to impose a settlement. In Australia, for example, the vast majority of complaints brought in the Commission are either successfully conciliated or withdrawn voluntarily, rather than requiring formal determination.

However, where a solution cannot be agreed by conciliation, the issue arises of what determinative powers are available. Experience in dealing with discrimination cases in Australia has been that where legally enforceable remedies are ultimately available, this contributes to the effectiveness of conciliation. The desire to avoid more formal legal proceedings gives parties an additional incentive to conciliate their disputes if possible.

In a number of countries, the human rights commission itself has no determinative powers, but may refer matters to the courts or to a specialised human rights or equal opportunity tribunal. This is the position, for example, under the New Zealand Human Rights Commission Act, which provides for an Equal Opportunities Tribunal.

In Sweden, if the Equal Opportunities Ombudsman is unable to negotiate a settlement in a case of sex discrimination, the case may be referred to the Labour Court.[44] In cases where the Equal Opportunities Ombudsman has unsuccessfully sought to persuade employers to take positive measures to promote equality, an injunction may be requested from a separate body, the Equal Opportunities Commission.[45]

In the United Kingdom, the Equal Opportunity Commission (which deals with sex discrimination) and the Commission for Racial Equality do not themselves have determinative powers.[46] If a complaint of discrimination cannot be settled by conciliation, it may be referred to a court or, in employment related cases, to an industrial tribunal.

---

[43] The Attorney for Human Rights in Guatemala im empowered to institute legal proceedings after investigation of a complaint: see UN Doc E/CN.4/1991/23. The Human Rights Inquiry Commission in Turkey examines complaints and refers them to relevant authorities; see UN Doc. E/CN.4/1991/23/Add. In Ecuador the National Congress Ad Hoc Commission on Human Rights has the function of analysis and verification of complaints of human rights violations and the institution of proceedings against officials responsible: see UN Doc. CCPR/C/58/Add.9.

[44] UN Doc. E/CN.4/1991/23 par.31.

[45] See Fact Sheet on Sweden: The Swedish Ombudsmen, published by the Swedish Institute; and the country report on Sweden, above Part Two, III, by Claes Eklundh.

[46] On these bodies, see e.g. the third periodic report of the UK to the Human Rights Committee, UN Doc. CCPR/C/58/Add.6 paras.39–42, 51–53; and the country reports above, Part V.

The various pieces of legislation administered by the Australian national Commission offer a range of models in relation to determinative powers. Under the Sex Discrimination Act and the Racial Discrimination Act, if complaints cannot be settled by conciliation, they may be referred for determination to a tribunal hearing. The tribunal consists of the Human Rights and Equal Opportunity Commission itself, rather than a separate body. However, the interests of natural justice are protected by legislative provisions specifying that the Commissioner responsible for conciliation in a case (for example the Sex Discrimination Commissioner in the case of sex discrimination complaints) is not permitted to sit as part of the tribunal or to take part in any Commission decisions relating to the case.

Because of the strict separation of powers which the courts have held to exist under the Australian federal Constitution, commission determinations in these cases are not directly legally binding. However a complainant, or the commission itself, may take enforcement proceedings in the Federal Court. The Commission has recommended, and the Australian Parliament is presently considering, measures to reduce the need in the enforcement proceedings for the rehearing of evidence already presented to the Commission.[47]

Under the Human Rights and Equal Opportunity Commission Act (which deals with employment discrimination, and complaints against Federal government departments and agencies in relation to civil and political rights and the rights of children and people with disabilities) the Commission may make findings, but these are contained in a report which must be tabled in Parliament, rather than in the form of an enforceable or binding determination.

Experience has indicated a number of advantages in having a specialist tribunal with binding or enforceable jurisdiction.

(a) Such a tribunal will develop expertise in human rights and discrimination law (which in some cases is less well developed in the general court system). As well as leading to more effective handling of individual cases, this is expertise on which the judiciary and other institutions with relevant responsibilities may draw.

(b) It is possible to design hearings by a human rights tribunal to be less expensive, less formal and more accessible than court proceedings. This is particularly important for human rights and anti-discrimination legislation to be effective in protecting the rights of people who are, in many cases, both economically disadvantaged and also disadvantaged by sophisticated systems of advocacy and pleadings.

(c) In a number of countries, including Australia, it has been found advantageous to provide for more flexible remedies to deal with human rights violations than have traditionally been available through the courts.

(d) In many cases the composition of the judiciary is not highly representative of the social composition of the population, and, in particular, contains few representatives of the classes of people most likely to suffer discrimination. The very fact of discrimination means that women, people with disabilities, indigenous people and others experiencing discrimination on the basis of

[47] Under the Privacy Act, the Privacy Commissioner has power in some circumstances to make determinations which are more directly legally binding on Federal government agencies.

race, religion or other characteristics may be less likely to rise through professional training and experience to the point where they are considered for judicial appointment, particularly at higher levels (apart from any more direct discrimination in the process of judicial appointment itself). It is possible to make a specialist tribunal more representative, also by specifying that it should include members with particular responsibilities regarding specified groups.[48] Legislation may also specify that the tribunal should include members drawn directly from particular disadvantaged groups, either on a permanent basis or for particular cases

It has generally been recognized that where a specialist tribunal is created, its decisions should be reviewable by the judiciary. This role obviously provides an important reason for ensuring that judges are adequately trained in the principles of human rights law.

Activities For Promotion And Protection of Human Rights

As already noted, both national experience and the terms of international human rights instruments indicate that legislative measures alone are not adequate to guarantee the effective enjoyment of human rights. Other active measures of promotion and protection are also needed. In particular, it is necessary to ensure that effective and accessible remedies are available to translate the theoretical protection of the law into practice, and that human rights and the legislative machinery are made widely known to victims and potential victims of violations of rights, to government agencies, employers and others exercising significant power in society, and to the community generally. It is also important to promote consideration of human rights on a wider basis than simply that of individual violations and complaints: in legislation, in the administration and interpretation of the law, and in the formation of social policy. National commissions have extremely important functions in each of these respects. The very fact that a body such as a Human Rights Commission exists to promote human rights indicates a recognition that simply passing legislation is not, by itself, sufficient.

Effective and Accessible Remedies

Different provisions for receipt of individual complaints are discussed in a later section of this paper. A major reason for vesting this jurisdiction in a national commission (rather than relying on civil, administrative and criminal law remedies through the courts) is to increase the accessibility of remedies to members of disadvantaged groups. There are a number of examples in national experience of the ineffectiveness of anti-discrimination legislation relying only on remedies through the courts.

Considerable shortcomings of early legislation in this area (particularly that

[48] As for example by the inclusion of the Race Discrimination Commissioner and Sex Discrimination Commissioner within Australia's national human rights Commission. Proposals for addition of commissioners with specific responsibilities regarding Aboriginal people and for a Children's Commissioner are presently being considered by the national government. The concept of a Disability Commissioner has also been raised by members of the community in the context of proposed further national legislation on the rights of people with disabilities.

of the United States and Canada) have been pointed out, both with respect to models which rely on penal or criminal law and with respect to models which rely on civil court remedies.[49]

With respect to models relying on penal or criminal law the following shortcomings have been mentioned:

- frequently the police and prosecution authorities did not act to enforce these laws;
- victims of discrimination were frequently reluctant to institute a private prosecution;
- there were difficulties arising from the rules of evidence, particularly where proof beyond reasonable doubt of discriminatory action and discriminatory purpose was required;
- the judiciary in some cases were reluctant to convict, regarding anti-discrimination law as an interference with traditional notions of freedom of contract;
- without any agency responsible for public education and promotion of the legislation, most people were unaware of its existence;
- criminal law penalties for perpetrators of discriminatory actions did not, in themselves, provide the person discriminated against with any effective remedy or compensation.

To this list may be added the fact that not all discrimination results from a conscious and deliberate discriminatory intention so as to be culpable in the usual criminal law sense. Discrimination may be equally damaging when it results, as is frequently the case, from stereotyped attitudes or from failure to be aware of the needs of a particular group.

With respect to laws providing for civil remedies through the courts shortcomings mentioned have included the following:

- Litigation, and fees for lawyers, are expensive in many countries. Many victims of discrimination cannot afford these costs.
- The compensation received (even if the action is successful) may be less than the legal costs incurred. This is particularly the case where only individual complaints are provided for. A great and damaging social wrong, such as racial discrimination in access to public places, might result in relatively small financial compensation to each individual (so that it might not be financially feasible for any one person to take legal action).
- Individual legal actions, even where successfully undertaken, might be insufficient to change widespread discriminatory practices. It might be economical for the discriminator to simply pay damages to those victims sufficiently determined, well informed and well resourced to sue, rather than change the discriminatory practice.
- Civil proceedings, though less restricted in procedure than criminal cases, may nonetheless involve technical problems of proof.
- Some discrimination cases in particular those where indirect or systemic

[49] See e.g. Tarnopolsky, pp.167–69, who also cites Maslow and Robinson, Civil rights legislation and the fight for equality, 1862–1952, (1953) 20 University of Chicago Law Review 363. Similar problems were encountered with the first Australian anti-discrimination legislation, the South Australian prohibition of Discrimination Act 1966.

discrimination is sought to be shown by analysis of patterns of disadvantage, require specialised skills which many lawyers and courts may not have.

- Particularly in countries where the judicial system is primarily based on adversarial procedures, court proceedings may often result in confrontation rather than negotiation and settlement of disputes. Court proceedings may not, therefore, be the best approach where the critical need is a change in attitudes, or where discrimination or interference with rights was unintentional.

Human rights commissions and similar bodies therefore have an important role in making remedies effective and accessible Dealing with complaints by conciliation is relatively informal and inexpensive.[50] In many cases it can lead to the parties agreeing on a solution much more suited to the individual circumstances of the case than any remedy which a court could order, including redesigning policies and practices which have a discriminatory effect. The settlement agreed need not be confined in its application to the individual case, whereas for courts in many countries there are difficulties in making an order which applies to persons other than the immediate parties to the action. Conciliated settlements may also have important effects in changing attitudes.

Involvement in Legal Proceedings

Several human rights institutions which lack determinative powers but which refer complaints to courts or tribunals may appear in the courts and tribunals in support of a complainant's case. The Canadian Human Rights Commission, for example, has such a function.

The Australian Commission is able to appear in court to support orders for the enforcement of Commission determinations. It also has a more general power to intervene in legal proceedings, not confined to those brought under human rights legislation, in order to bring relevant principles of human rights law to the attention of the court. Exercise of this power is conditional on the leave of the court, and (in a practical sense) on there being a basis in domestic law for the application of international human rights instruments. Where such instruments are effectively incorporated into domestic law, a similar function to this would appear to be of considerable relevance, in its direct effects in individual case:.s and in educating the judiciary and the legal profession generally.

Community Education, Awareness of Human Rights and Participation

National commissions are of major importance in promoting awareness of human rights, and generally have public education and information as an important function.[51] Part of this function is directly related to complaint handling.[52]

[50] The court system, in many countries, is now effectively beyond the reach of those except the well-to-do or those of the poor who can arrange to get legal aid. For example, in Australia an action in the County or District Court now costs at least A$40,000 on average, and a Supreme Court action at least A$60,000 on average. The Australian Commission does not, of course, charge complainants but the average cost per complaint is A$500.

[51] This function is expressly provided for in the responsibilities of the Australian national Commission under each of the Acts it administers. Similarly, the New Zealand Human Rights Commission has the function "to promote by education and publicity respect for and observance of human rights" listed first among its statutory functions, New Zealand Human Rights Commission Act s.5(1)(a).

[52] In Australia, for example, the national commission has conducted a major awareness campaign for young women on the protection provided by the Sex Discrimination Act against sexual harassment, particularly in employment and education. This arose from an analysis of individual complaints

A number of national institutions also place particular emphasis on human rights training for government officials – including the police and the military. (The Philippines commission, for example, has done important work in this area.) This education seeks to build a culture of human rights wherein human rights violations are less likely to occur.

But there is also in most countries an urgent need to educate the general community concerning human rights. The comment that legal measures alone are insufficient for realisation of human rights applies to all categories of human rights, whether designated as "civil and political", "economic. social and cultural", or according to other classifications. While it is clear from experience that different methods may be needed for the realisation of different rights, it is also clear that simple divisions cannot be drawn along the lines of civil and political rights on the one hand and economic social and cultural rights on the other. The realisation of civil and political rights often requires considerable resource commitments, including assistance to disadvantaged groups to enable them to assert their rights. Conversely, the idea that the realisation of economic social and cultural rights is simply a matter of provision of adequate resources is a caricature of these rights as human rights, as well as being contradicted by experience.

Despite the clear position in international law that the different categories of rights are indivisible,[53] arguments continue to be advanced that one or the other has priority: in simple terms, that civil and political rights are irrelevant until basic economic needs are met; or, conversely, that if certain political rights are respected that satisfaction of economic needs will follow.

Human rights must involve opportunities for people to shape their own lives individually and collectively. A major challenge for national institutions, including specific human rights institutions, is to ensure that rather than being bureaucratically remote, they promote participation and the empowerment of disadvantaged groups in society.[54]

Public Inquiry Powers

A problem in giving effect to economic and social rights, in particular (but also in systemic discrimination affecting other rights), is that the issues may often be too wide to be addressed by an individual complaint. One of the most significant and innovative powers given to the Australian Commission is the power to conduct public inquiries. This power enables the commission to investigate and report on human rights problems of a more general nature. Typically, public

---

which showed that few young women were aware of their rights and how to exercise those rights. As well as indicating how to seek a remedy for discrimination, this campaign had a preventive purpose – to assist young women in preventing this form of discrimination from occurring.

[53]Note for example the comment of the Justice Bhagwati: " ... each category of human rights is indispensable for the enjoyment of the other. Hence, it is axiomatic that the promotion, respect for and enjoyment of one category of human rights cannot justify the denial of the other category of human rights", Inaugural Address, in: Developing Human Rights Jurisprudence: the Domestic Application of International Human Rights Norms (Report of the Judicial Colloquium, Bangalore 1988), Commonwealth Secretariat, p. xxii.

[54]In Australia this is particularly the case with respect to our indigenous peoples Aborigines and Torres Strait Islanders. However, it is also, an urgent need with respect to the mentally ill and other groups which have long suffered gross discrimination and stigmatisation.

inquiries by the Commission have involved taking oral evidence in public hearings (and confidentially where necessary), receiving written submissions from interested individuals, NGOs and government agencies, further research and analysis of the evidence in the light of relevant international human rights standards, and publication of a report with findings and recommendations which is presented to Parliament.

Public inquiries on human rights issues have an important educational function in addition to identifying human rights problems or abuses and recommending solutions. This power is particularly effective in dealing with situations which involve people who do not have the financial or social resources to lodge individual complaints.

Major inquiries recently conducted in Australia have included:

(i) a national inquiry into homeless children;
(ii) a localised inquiry concerning lack of services to particular Aboriginal communities;
(iii) a national inquiry on racist violence;
(iv) a localised inquiry on health services to an Aboriginal community.
(v) a national inquiry on the human rights of people with mental illness (which is not yet completed.)

(Details of these inquiries are provided as Appendix B to this paper.)

Relations with Non-government Organizations (NGOs)

Relations with non-government organizations also need to be emphasised. These are of critical importance to the promotion and protection of human rights by any national commission.

A number of national institutions include representatives trom community organizations within their membership.[55] Several national commissions have associated with them a formally constituted advisory body including representatives of the community or of community organizations. In Mexico, for example, the National Commission on Human Rights has a Council composed of persons prominent in human rights, which conducts studies and issues recommendations to the Commission.[56] In Australia, the legislation which created the national commission permits establishment of a number of such committees to advise the Commission. Moreover, it specifically requires the establishment by the Government of a Committee to advise on matters of discrimination and equality in employment.[57]

---

[55] For example the National Human Rights Commission of Togo set up in 1987 included an elected representative of the Togolese Red Cross, and two lawyers elected by the Bar Association, in addition to elected representatives of women, youth, workers, and the traditional chiefs, together with a number of other members: Initial Report of Togo to the Human Rights Committee, UN Doc. CCPR/C/36/Add.5.

[56] UN Doc. E/CN.4/1991/23/Add. 1. In addition, there are bodies which facilitate consultation directly between the community and the government. In Morocco the Human Rights Consultative Council serves as a forum for consultation on human rights between non-governmental organizations and the government, see UN Doc. E/CN.4/ 1991 /23.

[57] When the Government completes the steps to establish this Committee, it will comprise in addition to representatives of employer organizations, government and unions, representatives of relevant groups including women, Australia's indigenous peoples and People with disabilities. This Committee will advise the Commission on policy issues in this area, and is also expected to be of great assistance

In addition to formal links through advisory bodies, or community representation in the membership of national Commissions, cooperation with community organizations more generally is important. In many countries the number of non-government organizations concerned with issues which include human rights aspects is very large, making it impossible that they all be included directly in advisory bodies or in Commission membership.

The Australian national commission's charter specifically mandates us to work with non-government organizations, which we do with a large number, both on long term policy, through regular consultations, and on a day to day basis. Several examples of specific types of cooperation are:

(1) The Australian Commission conducts a regular formal consultation, generally on an annual basis, to which non-government organizations interested in human rights are invited. More frequent informal consultations are conducted on specific issues. This consultation gives NGOs information which they can use in their various fields of human rights activity, as well as assisting to coordinate their efforts. It also assists the Commission to ensure that its work program and methods of work are of continuing; relevance to the community.

(2) The Convention on the Rights of the Child provides a recent example of close cooperative work between the Australian Commission ad NGOs in relation to an international instrument.

First, in providing advice to the Government on its position in the drafting of the Convention, the Commission took account of views expressed by NGOs in its regular consultations.

Second, the Commission coordinated a group of NGOs which, together with the Commission itself, engaged in public education and promotion concerning the Convention: through the national media, through publications, and through community networks. This work was crucial in achieving relatively early ratification of the Convention in view of misunderstandings regarding human rights law and the role of the United Nations which continue to exist in some sections of the community. The third stage is that the Commission, jointly with a major national NGO, is currently conducting a review of Australian law and practice relating to children, based on the Convention, which will result in recommendations to Government on further necessary measures for implementation of the Convention. This review includes a survey both of non-government organizations and of government agencies. The information gathered should be of assistance in ensuring that Australia's first report to the Committee for the Rights of the Child is as comprehensive and accurate as possible.

(3) In the area of the rights of people with physical, intellectual, sensory and psychiatric disabilities, the Australian Commission has worked closely with non-government organizations to promote the translation of international standards into national legislative protection.

The Commission engaged a major NGO representing people with disabilities, in cooperation with other NGOs in the field, to produce a report on areas of

---

in community education and promotion of non-discriminatory practices. Its advice will be of particular value in dealing with the practical implementation of non-discrimination in various employment settings. There is also a specific Privacy Advisory Committee comprising representatives of interested organizations to provide advice to the Privacy Commissioner on issues in relation to the protection of the right to privacy.

need for increased protection. After two years of consultation and research, the Commission put proposals to the national government for legislation against discrimination in this area. The Commission is now participating in a government committee preparing that legislation, and in continuing to consult with NGOs as legislative proposals develop.

(4) NGOs can also play a crucial role in what may be termed the "empowerment" of members of disadvantaged groups to bring their concerns to the attention of national commissions.

A specific example may be found in the conduct of the Australian Commission's public inquiry on the human rights of people affected by mental illness. Because of experience of discrimination and denial of rights, and in some cases more directly because of their medical condition, many people with mental illness are reluctant te approach any official body directly. Community organizations have played an important role in facilitating evidence by many individuals to this inquiry, either by serving as an intermediary or by providing them with encouragement personally to make submissions. The advice of such organizations has also been valuable to the Commission in designing its procedures to be as accessible as possible.

Specific Issues or General Human Rights Jurisdiction

A structural feature which has important implications for the work of national institutions in promoting and protecting human rights is whether there are several institutions with jurisdiction to deal with specific categories of rights and/or discrimination, or only one national commission with more general human rights jurisdiction.

A number of national institutions have jurisdiction defined by reference to any human rights treaties to which the nation is a party.[58] The Australian Commission has jurisdiction only in relation to the international instruments included in its legislation but, as already noted, these cover a very wide range of rights and there is provision for further instruments to be added.[59]

In Canada, the Human Rights Commission has jurisdiction to deal with discrimination on a wide range of grounds, including sex, race, religion. marital or family status, disability or age. The Commission does not have direct jurisdiction regarding civil and political or economic, social and cultural rights per se, but only so far as these are affected by discrimination. However, in democratic and economically developed societies such as Canada or Australia, many violations of civil and political or economic social and cultural rights are likely to

[58] For example the Turkish Human Rights Inquiry Commission, see UN Doc. E/CN.4/ 1991/23/Add.1: the Philippines Commission on Human Rights and the Guatemala Attorney for Human Rights: see UN Doc. E/CN.4/1991/23.

[59] The Australian Commission's jurisdiction covers discrimination on grounds of sex or race in a wide range of areas, and on other grounds including; religion, national origin or nationality, social origin, political opinion, sexual preference, marital status, criminal or medical record, trade union action, age, impairment, or disability of any kind in relation to employment, as well as jurisdiction in relation to civil and political rights, the rights of children and the rights of people with disabilities. The Privacy Commissioner is also a member of the Commission and is assisted by Commission staff in his functions.

include an element of discrimination against disadvantaged and relatively politically powerless groups.[60] In practice, therefore, the Canadian Commission may be seen as exercising a fairly broad human rights jurisdiction, despite the fact that the direct enforcement of civil and political rights as such (and of some economic, social and cultural rights, in particular Aboriginal rights and language rights) is allocated separately to the courts under the Canadian Charter of Rights. and Freedoms.

In New Zealand, the Human Rights Commission has jurisdiction in relation to human rights generally, and specific jurisdiction in relation to discrimination on grounds of sex, marital status and religious or ethical belief. Jurisdiction over racial discrimination is exercised by the Race Relations Conciliator, who is a member of the Human Rights Commission but has separate statutory responsibilities and maintains a distinct staff. There is also a separate Children's Ombudsman in New Zealand and in a number of other jurisdictions.

In the United Kingdom, the Equal Opportunities Commission has jurisdiction in relation to sex discrimination while the Commission for Racial Equality has jurisdiction regarding racial discrimination, but there is no national commission with general human rights jurisdiction.[61]

In Sweden, as noted earlier, there are a number of Ombudsmen. The Ombudsman Against Ethnic Discrimination deals with racial discrimination in the labour market and in other aspects of public life. The Equal Opportunities Ombudsman deals with sex discrimination. The jurisdiction of the Parliamentary Ombudsman is not specifically defined by reference to human rights but includes some human rights issues within the more general jurisdiction to supervise actions of government authorities.[62] In Finland there is also a separate Equality Ombudsman who deals with issues of sex discrimination.[63]

In our experience, there are a number of advantages in having an integrated human rights body rather than separate bodies to deal with different grounds of discrimination and other aspects of human rights.[64] Where the different grounds of discrimination are combined under the jurisdiction of an integrated Commission, connections and similarities between different discrimination issues can be more clearly seen. This has several consequences:

(a) It promotes cooperation between members of different disadvantaged groups and gives each an interest in the protection of the others.
(b) Consequently, the political position of a human rights commission is made more secure. This can be of considerable importance since it is inevitable that from time to time effective advocacy of human rights will involve disagreement with significant political forces in society.

---

[60] Thus in Australia, although civil and political rights are generally well respected, equality of civil and political right is not in fact enjoyed by Aboriginal people, by people with disabilities, by many children, or in some cases by people of non-English-speaking backgrounds. In most cases, though not always, the human rights of the majority and the politically powerful are likely to be reasonably well protected by the democratic political process.

[61] There my be some relationship between this fact and the relatively high number of cases before the European Commission on Human Rights which have concerned the United Kingdom.

[62] UN Doc. CCPR/C/58/Add.7.

[63] UN Doc. E/CN.4/1991/23.

[64] A number of these points are noted by Tarnopolsky, (above), at p.169.

(c) Expertise and experience in one area of discrimination, both in legal interpretation and in practical measures, will frequently be relevant in other areas.
(d) An integrated body makes possible more effective use of resources and specialised expertise, including in human rights law.

Another very important feature of an integrated human rights body is that it helps to counteract the impression that anti-discrimination law unfairly gives special rights to particular groups.[65] A more helpful and less divisive approach is that human rights law exists to ensure the equal right of all persons to enjoyment of human rights, including members of minorities who are in particular need of protection. It also reinforces the fact that equality and non-discrimination are an integral part of human rights in international law rather than being something distinct.[66] This approach is emphasised particularly in those countries (Australia and New Zealand for example) where the same body has responsibility for anti-discrimination law and in relation to civil and political rights more directly.

Particular bodies for particular areas of discrimination and human rights have the advantage of ensuring that the issues within their jurisdiction (for example sex discrimination or the rights of indigenous peoples) receive appropriate priority, and may assist in ensuring that the issues in each area are dealt with by persons of appropriate expertise and sensitivity. These concerns, however, would appear to be equally capable of being addressed by instituting an integrated collegiate body with designated officers having specific responsibilities. Clearly, in an integrated body, it is necessary to ensure that each area receives proper priority and a share of resources relative to the needs which exist. The degree of integration achievable in practice is, of course, dependent to some extent on national conditions, including the views in this respect of the disadvantaged groups principally concerned.

Relations With Individuals

Individual Complaints

Although in some countries the main function of specific human rights institutions is to provide advice to government on issues of policy and legislation, it is generally recognized that an important function of a human rights commission is to accept complaints from individuals.[67] Of course, dealing with individual complaints is also a principal function of an Ombudsman.

---

[65] Much ill-informed comment to this effect was made in Australia, for example, in the early period of operation of race and sex discrimination laws.

[66] See similarly Wallace, (above), at p. 159. This is particularly important to emphasise in common law countries where there has been a tendency to think of human rights only in terms of civil liberties. In the same paper Wallace noted that the New Zealand Commission has advised that its jurisdiction regarding discrimination is too narrow, see p.160.

[67] This is the case with independent commissions with specific statutory functions regarding human rights and/or discrimination, such as those of Australia, Canada, New Zealand, the Philippines, Togo, and the United Kingdom; with a number of bodies established within government departments, such as the Mexican National Commission on Human Rights, established within the Department of the Interior; and with a number of bodies associated directly with national Parliaments, such as in Ecuador, Guatemala and Turkey.

"Class Actions" and Representative Complaints

In several jurisdictions there is provision for an individual affected by discrimination or other human rights violation to complain not only on his or her own behalf but on behalf of others similarly affected.[68] In Australia, the Sex Discrimination Act[69] lists a number of factors which will allow a matter to be considered as a representative complaint: that the complainant is a member of the class affected or likely to be affected; that the complainant has personally been affected by the conduct in question; that the class of persons is so numerous that it is impractical to deal with the matter simply by joining a number of specified individuals to the complaint; that there are questions of law or fact common to the members of the class; that the claims of the complainant are typical of the claims of the class; that multiple complaints would be likely to produce inconsistent results; and that the grounds for the action complained of appear to apply to the whole class, making it appropriate to grant remedies to the class as a whole. The same section also provides, however, that a matter may be dealt with as a representative complaint wherever this is demanded by the justice of the case.

Provision for representative complaints helps to ensure that more general social problems are not treated only on an individual basis in the complaint process. Problems of a purely individual complaint based approach have already been noted. In particular, a successful individual complaint may not always be enough to secure a change in a more widespread discriminatory practice, and the damage to any one person (and therefore the likely amount of compensation) may not be sufficient to make it worthwhile even to take action. A representative complaint may also help to reduce the disparity in resources between individual complainants on one side and a large institution, such as a corporation or government agency, on the other. Representative complaints appear particularly appropriate in cases of indirect discrimination, where an apparently non-discriminatory requirement in fact has a disproportionate and unjustifiable adverse impact on disadvantaged group.

Complaints by Third parties or NGOs

The most vulnerable members of society may not be in a position to lodge a complaint or to authorize others to do so on their behalf, because of the very circumstances which render them vulnerable: for example, persons detained incommunicado, or people with severe physical, intellectual or psychiatric disabilities, or whose legal capacity is limited for other reasons. This last group includes, importantly, children.

This is addressed to some extent by provisions allowing a number of national commissions to receive complaints from third parties or from non-governmental

---

[68] Examples of such provisions may be found in the Canadian Human Rights Act s.40(4) and the Australian Sex Discrimination Act ss.50, 70, 71 and 72. The Australian Sex Discrimination Act s.61 also allows the Commission itself to decide that a number of individual complaints should be heard together.

[69] Section 70(2).

organizations.[70] More specific provision is made in some cases for complaints by trade unions.[71]

Specific provisions allowing third parties and non-governmental organizations to bring complaints are desirable, to avoid technical arguments regarding who has "standing" to complain. Where such complaints are possible, it would also appear desirable to specify that the complaint should proceed if the person on whose behalf the complaint is made does not wish it to proceed.[72]

Can the Commission Initiate Investigations Itself?

A number of national human rights institutions have jurisdiction to initiate an investigation of possible cases of discrimination or other human rights abuses without needing to receive a formal complaint.[73]

This power is important, given that many sections of society remain at best inadequately aware of their rights and how to exercise them; that vulnerable groups or individuals suffering violations of human rights (for example, prisoners or persons affected by mental illness) do not always have effective representative organizations or advocates to act on their behalf; and that people or groups who are the victims of violations of human rights may be reluctant to approach any official agency with a complaint.

Relations with the State

A variety of institutional types have been noted in this paper:

- institutions created by decision of the Parliament and including members of the legislature;
- institutions constituted within a government department such as the Ministry of the Interior or the Ministry of Foreign Affairs;
- institutions created by legislation.

The first two of these types may be seen as having some advantage in more direct involvement in the process of legislation and policy making. However, an important feature of a separate commission set up by statute is its greater

---

[70] This is the case, for example, with the National Human Right Commission of Togo, see UN Doc. CCPR/C/36/Add.5; and the Canadian Human Rights Commission, Canadian Human Rights Commission Act s.40(1).

[71] Such provision is made in Australia under the Discrimination Act s.50, and the Racial Discrimination Act s.22. The Human Rights and Equal Opportunity Commission Act does not specify any restrictions on which may complain and therefore implicitly permits complaints by third parties, NGOs and trade unions.

[72] Such provision is made in Canada (Canadian Human Rights Act s.41), and in Australia under the Human Rights and Equal Opportunity Commission Act s.20(2).

[73] For example, the Philippines Commission on human rights may investigate cases on its own motion, see UN Doc. E/CN.4/1991/23. The Canadian Human Rights Commission Act, s.40(3), provides that the Commission may initiate an investigation itself where it has "reasonable grounds" to believe that a person is engaging in a discriminatory practice. The Australian Commission has power to initiate an investigation in any case "where it appears to the Commission to be desirable to do so", Human Right and Equal Opportunity Commission Act s.20(1); or in the case of race and sex discrimination "where it appears to the Commission that a person has done an act which is unlawful" under the legislation, Racial Discrimination Act s.24, Sex Discrimination Act s.52.

independence from government. In Australia for example, although the functions of the national commission include giving advice to government, the Commission is independent by law and is not subject to direction by government in the performance of its functions, including in handling complaints and in initiation of national or local inquiries. This independence has been a crucial part of the effectiveness of the Commission's operations.[74]

Advisory Or Binding Jurisdiction

The Ombudsman and similar institutions do not generally make binding determinations, but either refer cases to the courts or other bodies with power to take binding decisions, or else make non-binding recommendations addressed to the government agency which is the subject of the complaint or to the legislature.

A number of more specific human rights institutions also appear to have a purely advisory jurisdiction. The principal force of the recommendations of such institutions is the force of public opinion.[75] For such institutions to be effective, therefore, it is important that their reports and recommendations be made public and that this function should be independent of government control.[76]

In several instances, national human rights institutions have binding jurisdiction in some areas (or have associated with them specialist tribunals which have binding jurisdiction) but advisory jurisdiction only in other respects. Commonly there is a distinction between certain grounds of discrimination which are declared unlawful, and regarding which binding determinations may be made, and other human rights matters, regarding which advisory jurisdiction only is created. This is the position, for example, in New Zealand. In Australia, determinations under the Sex Discrimination Act, the Racial Discrimination Act and under aspects of the Privacy Act are enforceable.[77] In cases of discrimination on other grounds such as disability, sexual preference and age (these being additional grounds of discrimination declared pursuant to Article 1 of the Discrimination (Employment and Occupation) Convention) and in cases regarding rights under the International Covenant on Civil and Political Rights, the Declaration of the Rights of the Child and the UN Declarations on the rights of people with disabilities, the Commission has power only to report and make recommendations.[78]

---

[74]The New Zealand Commission regards its own independence as similarly vital, see Wallace, (above), at p.157.

[75]This has been noted, for example, by Mexico regarding its National Commission on Human Rights: "The strength of its recommendations is of a moral nature, in accordance with the Commission's credibility in society, and is enhanced by the fact that failure to comply with its recommendations will be commented on in its periodic public reports, which would imply a high political cost for the authority involved", UN Doc. E/CN.4/1991/23/Add.1 par. 2.

[76]In Australia, the Human Rights and Equal Opportunity Commission reports to the Attorney-General, who is required to lay the reports of the Commission before Parliament: Human Rights and Equal Opportunity Commission Act s.46. In addition, the Commission's functions of promoting public awareness and discussion of human rights permit it to publish papers itself.

[77]As noted earlier this requires enforcement action through the courts in the case of sex and race discrimination since Commission determinations are not immediately binding.

[78]The Commission has recently recommended legislation to enable binding; determinations to be made regarding discrimination on an number co further grounds including age and disability.

Power to make non-binding recommendations and experience gained in the operation of legislation on this basis may in some instances be useful as a transitional measure before the introduction of legislation providing for enforceable remedies. This model allows for a period of community education before legislation is introduced imposing binding obligations, and affords government agencies, employers and other interested parties a period to adjust their practices. It may also be a means of ensuring that problems in the operation of legislation are discovered before enforceable legislation is introduced. In particular, it may be important to give judges some guidance in the interpretation of human rights law in cases where the judiciary is not familiar with interpreting and applying statements of rights to give international law domestic application.

Conflicts of Jurisdiction

National Commissions and the Courts

As noted earlier, in several countries there is both a national human rights commission or similar body with jurisdiction to receive complaints, and a judicially enforceable Bill of Rights. Where these jurisdictions overlap, complainants may be expected to approach whichever institution appears more likely to give the remedy desired although, as discussed above, problems in effective access to the courts for members of disadvantaged groups (and indeed, in many countries, for all but a minority of the population) mean the national commission may remain the only remedy effectively available.

As administrative bodies, national commissions established under human rights legislation are generally subject to the supervision of the courts, including in their interpretation of this legislation. However, in specific cases where commissions are not directly bound by a court decision they may tend to take a broad approach, had more on the purposes of the legislation – whereas courts (at least in common law countries) may adhere more closely to stricter domestic rules of legal interpretation.

One area where conflicts may arise is in approaches to positive measures designed to promote equality for disadvantaged groups. In some cases courts taking; a formalist approach to discrimination law may regard these as constituting "reverse discrimination".[79]

One interesting mechanism for ensuring that measures which are not in fact discriminatory are not struck down by a formalist approach to anti-discrimination law by the court (without providing for excessively wide legislative exceptions) is the provision in the Australian Sex Discrimination Act for the Human Rights and Equal Opportunity Commission to grant exemptions from provisions of the Act. This power is required to be exercised consistently with the purposes of the legislation and is subject to judicial review, so that it is not used to undermine the protection of the law against discrimination. The power to grant

---

Legislation on disability is currently being prepared by the Federal Government, in consultation with the Commission, as noted earlier in this paper.

[79] For discussion of problems in this area see e.g. W. Sadurski, "Gerhardy v. Brown v. the concept of discrimination" (1985) 11 Sydney Law Review 5.

exemptions has also been relevant in avoiding misinterpretations of anti-discrimination law in industrial tribunals. In other jurisdictions, a simitar purpose is served by provisions which allow the human rights or anti-discrimination commission to certify that a measure or program for the benefit of a disadvantaged group, or measures conforming to certain guidelines, are permissible.

Human Rights Commissions, Ombudsmen and Other Agencies

In many cases where a human rights complaint is made against a government agency, it may be possible for the matter to be dealt with either by the human rights commission or by the Ombudsman – where both exist. In such cases it is necessary for one agency to be able to refer complaints to another, and for both agencies to maintain good communications. In Australia, areas where both the human rights commission and the Ombudsman have been involved have not caused conflicts of jurisdiction to any significant extent.

Federal – State Conflicts

A detailed examination of the operation of human rights institutions in federal systems is beyond the scope of this paper. It is important, however, that where both federal and state or provincial human rights mechanisms and legislation exist, these should be effectively coordinated – so that individuals are not deprived of a remedy by jurisdictional conflicts and so that more effective or appropriate provisions or procedures in one jurisdiction are not displaced by less suitable measures in the other.

In Australia, federal legislation displaces any inconsistent state legislation by virtue of the Australian Constitution.[80] Both the Sex Discrimination Act and the Racial Discrimination Act contain provisions indicating to the courts that the federal legislation does not displace any state legislation which is capable of operating together with the federal legislation and which furthers the objects of the relevant international Convention in each case.[81]

Conclusion and Recommendations

1. The jurisdiction of a human rights commission should be defined as broadly as possible.
2. This jurisdiction should include monitoring and reporting on the nation's compliance with international instruments on human rights. National commissions should be involved in the preparation and presentation of country reports under human rights treaties.
3. Preferably, the charter of the commission should be established by law or by the Constitution.
4. The independence of the commission should be specified in its charter, including by providing for fixed terms of appointment for its members.

[80] Section 109.

[81] The Convention on the Elimination of Discrimination Against Women and the Convention on the Elimination of Racial Discrimination.

5. Where a number of human rights institutions exist in a country, their functioning should be closely coordinated.
6. A desirable model incorporates the greatest possible degree of integration of responsibility for different types of human rights and discrimination, together with specific legislative and institutional provisions to protect and promote the rights of particularly disadvantaged or vulnerable groups.
7. A national commission on human rights should be mandated to consult and work with non-government organizations. It is desirable for human rights commissions to be accompanied by formal advisory bodies or other structures to ensure close contact with NGOs.
8. National commissions should be authorized to work with and consult international organizations and other national commissions.
9. National commissions should have broadly defined promotional and educational functions in relation to human rights.
10. National commissions should have power to review existing and proposed legislation for consistency with human rights, and recommend legislative and other measures to protect human rights.
11. National commissions have an essential role in providing effective and accessible remedies in cases of discrimination and human rights violations. National commissions should, therefore, be authorized to receive complaints from individuals on their own behalf; from individuals representing themselves and others similarly affected ("class actions"); from third parties; and from NGOs, including trade unions and other representative organizations.
12. National commissions should also be empowered to undertake broader investigations, including by conducting public inquiries involving taking of evidence and making a public report.
13. National commissions should be authorized to initiate investigations on their own initiative.
14. Procedures for making a complaint and for the handling of complaints should be as simple, accessible and inexpensive as possible. Provision should be made for the commission to attempt to resolve complaints by conciliation. Confidentiality of the conciliation process is an important part of its effectiveness.
15. Provision should be made for referral of complaints by the human rights commission to other agencies including the courts and the Ombudsman (where a separate office of the Ombudsman exists) in appropriate cases.
16. The Commission should have power to gather evidence and require production of documents and other evidence for the purposes of its investigations.
17. Where a complaint cannot be resolved by conciliation, provision should be made for a determination to be made. Preferably, such determination should in the first instance be made by the human rights commission or by a specialist human rights tribunal.
18. Effective and accessible means of enforcement of the determinations of the commission or tribunal should be provided.
19. In some cases, depending on national conditions including other institutions which exist, it may be appropriate to give recommendations of the human rights commission advisory rather than binding status.
20. In cases where determinations or recommendations of the human rights

commission are advisory rather than binding, these should be made publicly available. Provision should be made, in particular, for the tabling of the reports of national commissions before the legislature.

APPENDIX A

Structure And Functions of Australian Human Rights and Equal Opportunity Commission

Human Rights and Equal Opportunities Act

Functions of Commission

11. (1) The functions of the Commission are

(a) such functions as are conferred on the Commission by the Racial Discrimination Act 1975, the Sex Discrimination Act 1984 or any other enactment;

(b) such functions as are to be performed by the Commission pursuant to an arrangement in force under section 16;

(c) such functions as are expressed to be conferred on the Commission by any State enactment being functions in reaction to which the Minister has made a declaration under section 18;

(d) the functions conferred on the Commission by section 31;

(e) to examine enactments and (when requested to do so by the Minister) proposed enactments, for the purpose of ascertaining whether the enactments or proposed enactments, as the case may be, are, or would be, inconsistent with or contrary to any human right, and to report to the Minister the results of any such examination;

(f) to inquire into any act or practice that may be inconsistent with or contrary to any human right, and

  (i) where the Commission considers it appropriate to do so – to endeavour, by conciliation, to effect a settlement of the matters that gave rise to the inquiry; and

  (ii) where the Commission is of the opinion that the act or practice is inconsistent with or contrary to any human right, and the Commission has not considered it appropriate to endeavour to effect a settlement of the matters that gave rise to the inquiry or has endeavoured without success to effect such a settlement – to report to the Minister in relation to the inquiry;

(g) to promote an understanding and acceptance, and the public discussion, of human rights in Australia;

(h) to undertake research and educational programs and other programs, on behalf of the Commonwealth, for the purpose of promoting human rights, and to coordinate any such programs undertaken by any other persons or authorities on behalf of the Commonwealth;

(j) on its own initiative or when requested by the Minister, to report to the Minister as to the laws that should be made by the Parliament, or action that should be taken by the Commonwealth, on matters relating to human rights;

(k) on its own initiative or when requested by the Minister, to report to the Minister as to the action (if any) that, in the opinion of the Commission, needs to be taken by Australia in order to comply with the provisions of the Covenant, of the Declarations or of any relevant international instrument;

(m) on its own initiative or when requested by the Minister, to examine any relevant international instrument for the purpose of ascertaining whether there are any inconsistencies between that instrument and the Covenant, the Declaration or any other relevant international instrument, and to report to the Minister the results of any such examination;

(n) to prepare, and to publish in such manner as the Commission considers appropriate, guidelines for the avoidance of acts or practices of a kind in respect of which the Commission has a function under paragraph (t);

(o) where the Commission considers it appropriate to do so, with the leave of the court hearing the proceedings and subject to any conditions imposed by the court to intervene in proceedings that involve human rights issues; and

(p) to do anything incidental or conducive to the performance of any of the preceding functions.

(2) The Commission shall not

(a) regard an enactment or proposed enactment as being inconsistent with or contrary to any human right for the purposes of paragraph (1) (e) by reason of a provision of the enactment or proposed enactment that is included solely for the purpose of securing adequate advancement of particular persons or groups of persons in order to enable them to enjoy or exercise human rights equally with other persons; or

(b) regard an act or practice as being inconsistent with or contrary to any human right for the purposes of paragraph (1) (f) where the act or practice is done or engaged in solely for the purpose referred to in paragraph (a) of this sub-section."

Note. Paragraph 11 (b) and (c) refer to functions pursuant to cooperative arrangements with State governments. Section 31 confers on the Commission similar functions regarding discrimination in employment as section 11 confers regarding human rights.

APPENDIX B

Public Inquiries on Human Rights in Australia

The Toomelah Inquiry

The first public inquiry conducted by the Australian Human Rights and Equal Opportunity Commission was a local inquiry into the economic and social rights of the Toomelah Aboriginal community, having regard to the standards laid down in the Convention on the Elimination of All Forms of Racial Discrimination. The inquiry conducted hearings in the area itself (near the New South Wales / Queensland border) and received evidence from individual members of the Aboriginal and non-Aboriginal communities, from local community organizations and leaders, and from federal, state and local government authorities. The community had experienced a long history of dislocation, discrimination and inadequate servicing. The standard of housing, health, education, water and other basic services was totally inadequate, (as in many other Aboriginal communities) and well below that enjoyed by neighbouring towns with a white population.

The inquiry identified fundamental problem in coordination, allocation and acceptance of responsibilities between different government departments and different levels of government. (These problems have adverse effects on Aboriginal communities in many other parts of Australia.)

The inquiry has resulted in significant improvements in the services provided to the local community involved. The Commission was concerned, however, that similar problems in other communities might not be addressed. We are therefore conducting a follow up project on the adequacy of water supplies to remote Aboriginal communities generally. The Commission is approaching the issue not as an abstract engineering issue but on the basis of consultations with the affected communities. As with the Toomelah inquiry itself, however, the announcement of this project by the Commission has resulted in several positive responses from government even before the Commission has reported its findings.

The Homeless Children Inquiry

The Homeless Children Inquiry was a national inquiry conducted by the Commission with reference to the principles of the Declaration of the Rights of the Child (stipulating that children are entitled to special protection, adequate housing and protection against neglect, cruelty and exploitation). The report of this inquiry was presented to the federal government and parliament in February 1989 and then made public. The inquiry did more than just describe the problem, affecting tens of thousands of children. It identified the inadequacies of government responses, and made recommendations to correct them. Some of these recommendations went into some detail on the design of social programs. (This level of involvement with the details of policy was found necessary to give definite content to the economic and social rights involved.)

Giving practical effect to rights with significant public resource implications involves political processes. The level of responses to the homeless children inquiry – in public and political discussion, and in program responses (the federal government has provided $100 Million over four years) already implemented or proposed – has resulted, in large part, from the human rights basis of the inquiry. That is, to have a situation identified as a major breach of fundamental international standards on human rights is not just a legal point – it is, in itself, a major political argument.

The inquiry heard evidence in every State and Territory from a wide range of people and organizations. That extensive process of consultation assisted in framing a comprehensive set of recommendations on a wide range of issues dealt with by applicable human rights principles.

A government inquiry conducted without reference to human rights principles might look at homelessness purely as a problem in the supply of housing. Human right instruments dictate a broader approach. First, the right to housing requires that shelter be accessible to young people – not just physically available. It also requires that a range of appropriate accommodation options be available, particularly for those groups who are the subject of particular disadvantage and/or discrimination (such as Aboriginal young people – and young people with disabilities).

Other relevant rights – including the right to special protection and, specifically, protection against neglect or abuse – led the inquiry to conclude that accommodation services should be integrated with other support services where these are necessary, (including services to promote family reconciliation wherever possible and appropriate). Increased assistance and support services for families were also emphasised by the inquiry as a means of preventing homelessness, (partly arising from the references in the international human rights instruments to the central role of the family).

Human rights principles also led the inquiry to reject simplistic solutions, like forcing young people to return home if they are mature enough to make their own decision not to, or locking homeless children up in institutions.

The inquiry was also concerned by the vulnerability of homeless young people in their contact with the legal system. It made recommendations for improving the availability, accessibility and quality of advocacy and information services in dealing with the criminal justice system, child welfare systems and social security and accommodation authorities. These recommendations, although directly related to the needs of homeless children, are also relevant to the protection of the rights of all children and young people, both regarding civil and political rights and economic and social rights.

The commission is continuing to actively monitor government responses to the Inquiry's report, including by reconvening the formal hearings of the Inquiry to receive evidence from governments and community organizations on the implementation of its recommendations. The Federal government and most State governments have implemented a number of major changes to programs in response to the report of this inquiry.

The Racist Violence Inquiry

This national inquiry was conducted by reference to the Convention on the Elimination of All Forms of Racial Discrimination. It examined racist violence and intimidation as forms of racial discrimination, and assessed their impact on the equal enjoyment of human rights in the civil, political, economic, social and cultural spheres.

The Report of the Inquiry, released in March 1991 analysed the adequacy of government and community responses, in particular by reference to the right to the equal protection of the law. It also examined preventive measures. The Inquiry found that racist violence against Aboriginal people was widespread and included officially perpetrated violence. It found that although the number of incidents of racist violence against other groups was relatively low, there was a need for improved measures and procedures.

The Report recommended legislative measures in a number of areas, including that Australia should introduce national legislation against incitement to racial hatred, in order to fulfil its obligations under Article 4(a) of the Convention on the Elimination of All Forms of Racial Discrimination. The Federal Government is presently considering implementation of this recommendation. The Inquiry also made major recommendations in the areas of community education, and human rights training for public officials including police. The Commission is now working with both State and Federal authorities to put these recommendations into effect.

The Cooktown Inquiry

This inquiry concerned the provision of medical and health services to three Aboriginal communities in North Queensland. It was prompted by a number of incidents where it was alleged that racial discrimination had led directly to inadequate medical care for Aboriginal people. Again, the Inquiry took evidence from the local community, from government agencies and community organizations. The Report of the Inquiry was released in August 1991.

The Report does not fix responsibility on individuals for individual acts of racial discrimination. It is concerned, rather, to improve enjoyment of social rights in this area by dealing with inadequacies and inequalities in health care available, and in the need for increased Aboriginal community participation in the planning and operation of health services.

The Mental Illness Inquiry

The Commission is presently conducting a national inquiry on the human rights of people affected by mental illness – principally by reference to the International Covenant on Civil and Political Rights, the declaration on the Rights of Disabled Persons and the Principles for the Protection of Mentally Ill Persons and for the improvement of Mental Health Care (adopted early this year by the Commission on Human Rights). The inquiry has already received hundreds of written submissions and taken oral evidence from several hundred people affected by mental illness and organizations representing them, families and carers, experts and government authorities.

The major human rights issues concerning mental illness which have received attention as human rights issues in Australia prior to this inquiry have been civil and political rights issues concerning involuntary treatment and detention, and protection against abuse. Clearly there are serious issues to be considered concerning the legal protection required in this respect.

The international instruments, however, also recognize a much wider range of rights which are extremely important and which the Inquiry will address – including rights to treatment, rehabilitation, education, counselling and other services the right to economic and social security and a decent living standard and the right to protection from discrimination, including in employment and in other areas of social life.

Appendix

Ethiopian Legislation Establishing the Institution of the Ombudsman and the Human Rights Commission

Introductory Note

Article 55, sub-articles 14 and 15 respectively, of the Constitution of the Federal and Democratic Republic of Ethiopia, provides for the establishment of a Human Rights Commission and an Ombudsman Institution by the House of Peoples' Representatives. The Constitution further mandates the House to determine by law the powers, functions and the membership of the two institutions.

The International Conference of 1998, of which the papers are collected in this volume, was one step in the process towards establishing these institutions. It was preceded by a national conference, the purpose of which was to introduce Members of Parliament and others involved with drafting and upholding the proposed laws, to the concepts, functions and roles of the Human Rights Commission and Ombudsman in various socio-cultural and political contexts.

The International Conference of 1998 was followed up by a series of activities under the aegis of the House of Peoples' Representatives, especially its Legal Affairs Standing Committee. A working document was prepared by Judge Mesfin Gebre Hiwot, which was the basis for a document outlining a full series of issues and alternatives concerning the choices to be made in setting up the two institutions. This in its turn, was the basis for a round of consultations of the public. It involved a series of public hearings and discussions held at twelve towns around the country from 1st to the 5th of May 1999. This consultation of civil society resulted in a bill being introced in the course of 1999. After careful consideration by the House of the Peoples' Representatives, legislation was passed and proclaimed on the 4 July 2000. The Ethiopian Human Rights Commission Establishment Proclamation was published as Proclamation No. 210/2000 in the Negarit Gazeta, 6th year No. 40, pp. 1356–1366; the Institution of the Ombudsman Establishment Proclamation was published as Proclamation No. 211/2000 in the Negarit Gazeta, 6th year, No. 41, pp. 1367–1376.

K. Hossain et al. (eds), Human Rights Commissions and Ombudsman Offices, 837.

APPENDIX

PROCLAMATION NO. 210 /2000

A Proclamation to Provide for the Establishment of the Human Rights Commission

WHEREAS, the goal to jointly build one political community founded on the rule of law, as one of the basic objectives of the nations/ nationalities and peoples of Ethiopia., is to be achieved by guaranteeing respect for the fundamental rights and freedoms of the individual and of nations/ nationalities and peoples;

WHEREAS, the immense sacrifice paid by the people of Ethiopia, in the protracted struggle they waged with a view to bringing about a democratic order and to enhancing their socio-economic development, calls for paving the way for the unfettered protection of human rights;

WHEREAS, the Constitution of the Federal Democratic Republic of Ethiopia guarantees respect for peoples' rights and freedoms and provides that Federal and Regional government organs, at all levels, and their respective officials shall have the responsibility and duty to respect and enforce said rights and freedoms;

WHEREAS, it is found necessary to establish a Human Rights Commission, as one of the organs that play a major role in enforcing such rights and freedoms, and to determine its powers and functions, by law, in conformity with the provisions of the Constitution;

NOW, THEREFORE, in accordance with sub-Articl[e]s (1) and (14) of Article 55 of the Constitution, of the Federal Democratic Republic of Ethiopia, it is hereby proclaimed as follows:

Part One

General Provisions

1. *Short Title*
   This Proclamation may be cited as the "Ethiopian Human Rights Commission Establishment Proclamation No. 210 /2000."
2. *Definitions*
   Unless the context requires otherwise, in this Proclamation:
   (1) "Appointee" means the Chief Commissioner for Human Rights, the Deputy Chief Commissioner or Commissioners heading the children and women affairs [department], and commissioners at the level of branch offices, appointed by the House, in accordance with this Proclamation;
   (2) "Staff" includes department heads, professionals and other support staff of the Commission;
   (3) "Family Member" means a person of relation by consanguinity or affinity, in accordance with the Civil Code of Ethiopia;

K. Hossain et al. (eds), Human Rights Commissions and Ombudsman Offices, 839–847.

(4) "House" means the House of Peoples' Representatives of the Federal Democratic Republic of Ethiopia;
(5) "Human Right" includes fundamental rights and freedoms recognized under the Constitution of the Federal Democratic Republic of Ethiopia and those enshrined in the international agreement[s] ratified by the country;
(6) "Person" means any natural or juridical person;
(7) "Region" means any of those specified under Article 47 (1) of the Constitution of the Federal Democratic Republic of Ethiopia and, for the purposes of this Proclamation, includes the Addis Ababa City Administration and the Dire Dawa Administration;
(8) "Government" means the Federal, or a Regional Government;
(9) "Third Party" means a deputy, an association or a non-governmental organization representing an individual or a group;
(10) "Investigator" means a staff [member] assigned, by the Chief Commissioner, to conduct investigation.

3. *Establishment*
(1) The Human Rights Commission of Ethiopia (hereinafter referred to as "the Commission") is hereby established as an autonomous organ of the Federal Government having its own juridical personality.
(2) The Commission shall be accountable to the House.

4. *Scope*
(1) This Proclamation shall also apply to violation of human rights committed in any Region.
(2) Provisions of this Proclamation set out in the masculine gender shall also apply to the feminine gender.

5. *Objective*
The objective of the Commission shall be to educate the public [to] be aware of human rights[,] see to it that human rights are protected, respected and fully enforced as well as to have the necessary measure[s] taken where they are found to have been violated.

6. *Powers and Duties*
The Commission shall have the powers and duties to:
(1) ensure that the human rights and freedoms provided for under the Constitution of the Federal Democratic Republic of Ethiopia are respected by all citizens, organs of state, political organizations and other associations as well as by their respective officials;
(2) ensure that laws, regulations and directives as well as government decisions and orders do not contravene the human and democratic rights of citizens guaranteed by the Constitution;
(3) educate the public, using the mass media and other means, with a view to enhancing its tradition of respect for, and demand for enforcement of, rights upon acquiring sufficient awareness regarding human rights;
(4) undertake investigation, upon complaint or its own initiation, in respect of human rights violations;
(5) make recommendations for the revision of existing laws, enactment of new laws and formulation of policies.
(6) provide consultancy services on matters of human rights;
(7) forward its opinion on human rights reports to be submitted to international organs;
(8) to translate into local vernaculars, international human rights instruments adopted by Ethiopia and disperse the same;
(9) participate in international human rights meetings, conferences or symposia;

(10) own property, enter into contracts, sue and be sued in its own name;
(11) perform such other activities as may be necessary to attain its objective.

7. *Limitation of Power*
The Commission shall have full powers to receive and investigate all complaints on human rights violations made against any person, save cases brought before the House, the House of the Federation, Regional Councils or before the courts of law, at any level.

8. *Organization of the Commission*
The Commission shall have:
(1) a Council of Commissioners;
(2) (a) a Chief Commissioner;
(b) a Deputy Chief Commissioner;
(c) a Commissioner heading the Children and Women affairs [department],
(d) [o]ther[] Commissioners and
(e) the necessary staff.

9. *Head Office*
The Commission shall have its Head Office in Addis Ababa and it may have branch offices at any place as may be determined by House.

10. *Appointment*
(1) The Chief Commissioner, the Deputy Chief Commissioner and other Commissioners shall be appointed by the House.
(2) The appointment of the Chief Commissioner, the Deputy Chief Commissioner and of other Commissioners shall be made as under the following selection procedure:
(a) the appointees shall be recruited by a Nomination Committee to be formed pursuant to Article 11 hereunder;
(b) the nominees shall have to receive the support of a two-thirds vote of the members of the Committee;
(c) the list of nominees shall be presented to the House, by the Speaker, for it to vote upon;
(d) the nominees shall be appointed upon receipt of the support of a two-thirds vote of the House.

11. *Composition of the Nomination Committee*
The Nomination Committee shall have the following members:
(1) the Speaker of the House .... Chairperson
(2) the Speaker of the House of the Federation .... Member(s)
(3) seven members to be elected from among members of the House Member(s)
(4) two members of the House to be elected by joint agreement of opposition parties having seats in the House .... Member
(5) the President of the Federal Supreme Court .... Member
(6) a representative of the Ethiopian Orthodox Church .... Member
(7) a representative of the Ethiopian Islamic Council .... Member
(8) a representative of the Ethiopian Evangelical Church .... Member
(9) a representative of the Ethiopian Catholic Church .... Member

12. *Criteria for Appointment*
Any person who:
(1) is loyal to the Constitution of the Federal Democratic Republic of Ethiopia;
(2) upholds respect for human rights;
(3) is trained in law or other relevant discipline or has acquired extensive knowledge through experience;
(4) is reputed for his diligence, honesty and good conduct;

(5) has not been convicted for a criminal offence;
(6) is an Ethiopian national;
(7) is of enough good health to assume the post;
(8) is above thirty-five years of age
may be an appointee.

13. *Accountability*
(1) The Chief Commissioner shall be accountable to the House.
(2) The Deputy Chief Commissioner and other Commissioners shall be accountable to the Chief Commissioner.

14. *Term of Office*
(1) The term of office of an appointee shall be five years.
(2) Upon expiry of the term of office specified under sub-Article (1) of this Article, the appointee may be re-appointed.
(3) [A] person discharged from responsibility or removed from office, as under Article 15, shall not, unless re-appointed, assume a post in legislative, executive and judicial organs for about six months thereafter.

15. *Grounds for Removal of an Appointee*
(1) An appointee may be removed from office or discharged from responsibility upon the following circumstances:
(a) upon resignation, subject to a three-month prior written notice;
(b) where it is ascertained that he is incapable of properly discharging his duties due to illness;
(c) where he is found to have committed an act of human rights violation;
(d) where he is found to be corrupt or to have committed other unlawful act;
(e) where it is ascertained that he is of manifest incompetence;
(f) upon termination of his term of office.
(2) Within six months of the removal or discharge of an appointee, as under sub-Article (1) of this Article, another appointee shall be made to replace him.

16. *Procedure for Removal of an Appointee*
(1) An appointee shall be removed from office, upon the grounds specified under Article 15 (1) (b – (e) hereof, subsequent to investigation of the matter by a Special Inquiry Tribunal to be formed pursuant to Article 17.
(2) [A]n appointee shall be removed from office, where the House finds that the recommendation submitted to it, as supported by the majority vote of the Special Inquiry Tribunal, is correct and where it upholds same by a two-thirds majority vote.

17. *Composition of the Special Inquiry Tribunal*
The Special Inquiry Tribunal shall have the following members:
(1) the Deputy Speaker of the House .... Chairperson
(2) the Deputy Speaker of the House of the Federation .... Member(s)
(3) three members to be elected by the House .... Member(s)
(4) a member of the House to be elected by joint agreement of opposition parties having seats in the House .... Member(s)
(5) the Vice-President of the Federal Supreme Court .... Member(s)

18. *Prohibition to Engage in Other Employment*
(1) An appointee shall not be allowed to engage in other gainful, public or private employment during his term of office.
(2) Notwithstanding the provisions of sub-Article (1) of this Article, the House may allow otherwise in consideration of the particular profession in which the appointee is required to make contribution.

Part Two

Powers and Duties of Appointees

19. *Powers and Duties of the Chief Commissioner*
    (1) The Chief Commissioner shall be the top executive of the Commission and, as such, shall exercise the powers and duties of the Commission provided for herein.
    (2) Without prejudice to the generality stated under sub-Article (1) of this Article, the Chief Commissioner shall:
        (a) employ and administer the staff, in accordance with directive to be adopted by the Council of the Commissioners.
        (b) prepare and submit to the House, the budget of the Commission dealt upon by the Council of Commissioners and implement same upon approval;
        (c) transfer a case where he has sufficient grounds, from one investigation section or investigator to another; or investigate, himself, a case of human right violation committed anywhere;
        (d) undertake study of recurrent human right violations and forward together with remedial proposals to the House;
        (e) give his opinion on reports prepared by the Federal Government in respect of human rights protection;
        (f) prepare, and submit to the House, draft legislation on human rights; give his opinion on those prepared otherwise;
        (g) submit a report, to the House, on matters of human rights and on the activities of the Commission;
        (h) take part in meetings by way of representing the Commission, establish working relations with Federal and Regional government organs as well as with non-governmental organizations;
        (i) [o]rganize, [c]oordinate and follow up branch offices;
        (j) perform such other activities as may be assigned to him by the House.
    (3) The Chief Commissioner may, to the extent necessary for the efficient performance of the Commission, delegate part of his powers and duties, other than those specified under sub-Article 2 (b), (f) and (g) of this Article and Article 35 (2), to Commissioners or other officials of the Commission.

20. *Powers and Duties of the Deputy Chief Commissioner*
    The Deputy Chief Commissioner shall:
    (1) assist the Chief Commissioner in planning, organizing, directing and coordinating the activities of the head office of the Commission;
    (2) undertake the activities of the Chief Commissioner, in the absence of the latter;
    (3) carry out such other activities as may be assigned to him by the Chief Commissioner.

21. *Powers and Duties of Commissioners of Branch Offices*
    In addition to exercising, within the local jurisdiction of a branch office, the powers and duties vested in the Commission, other than those specified under Sub-Articles (7) and (9) of Article 6 of this Proclamation; the Commissioner shall, as the superior head of a branch office, have the following powers and duties:
    (1) to transfer a case from one investigation section or investigator to another or to conduct investigation himself, where he has a good cause.
    (2) to submit, to the Chief Commissioner, a detailed report on matters of human rights;
    (3) to direct and organize the branch office as well as to administer its professionals and support staff, in accordance with directives issued by the Commission;
    (4) to effect payments in accordance with the budget allocated to the branch office;
    (5) to establish working relations, as a representative of the branch office, with

Regional government organs and non-governmental organizations operating within the Region;

(6) to perform such other activities as may be assigned to him by the Chief Commissioner.

Part Three

Rules of Procedure of the Commission

22. *The Right to Lodge Complaints*
   (1) A complaint may be lodged by a person claiming that his rights are violated or, by his Spouse, family member, representative or by a third party.
   (2) The Commission may, in consideration of the gravity of the human right violation committed, receive anonymous complaints.
   (3) Without prejudice to the provisions of Article 7 hereof, the right to lodge complaints, as under this Proclamation, shall be no bar to the institution of criminal or civil proceedings over the same case.
   (4) The Commission shall receive and investigate complaints, free of any charge.

23. *Lodging Complaints*
   (1) A complaint may be lodged, with the Commission, orally, in writing or in any other manner.
   (2) Complaints shall, to the extent possible, be submitted together with supporting evidence.
   (3) Complaints may be made in Amharic or in the working language of a Region.

24. *Investigation*
   (1) The Commission may conduct investigation on the basis of complaints submitted to it.
   (2) The Commission shall have the power to conduct investigation, on its own initiation, where it so finds necessary.

25. *Ordering the Production of Evidence*
   In order to undertake necessary examination, within a reasonable time, the Commission may order that:
   (1) those complained against appear, at a specific time, for questioning or that they submit their defence;
   (2) witnesses appear, at a specific time, and give their testimony;
   (3) any person in possession of evidence, relevant to the case, produce same.

26. *Remedies*
   (1) The Commission shall make all the effort it can summon to settle, amicably, a complaint brought before it.
   (2) It shall notify, in writing, the findings of its investigation, and its opinion thereon, to the superior head of the concerned organ and to the complainant.
   (3) The remedy proposed by the Commission, pursuant to this Article, shall expressly state that the act having caused the grievance be discontinued, that the directive having caused the grievance be rendered inapplicable and that the injustice committed be redressed or that any other appropriate measure be taken.
   (4) Complaints submitted to the Commission shall be accorded with due response, within a short period of time.

27. *The Right to Object*
   (1) Any complainant or accused shall have the right to object to the official, next in hierarchy, where he is aggrieved by a remedy proposed by a subordinate appointee

or official of the Commission, within one month from the time he came to know of such proposed remedy.

(2) An appointee or official who receives an objection, pursuant to sub-Article (1) of this Article, may modify, stay the execution of, reverse or confirm the remedy having been proposed.

(3) The decision to be rendered by the Chief Commissioner shall be final.

28. *Duty to Notify of Fault*
Where the Commission, in the process of conducting investigations, believes that a crime or an administrative fault is committed, it shall have the duty to, forthwith, notify same to the concerned organ or official.

29. *Overlap of Jurisdiction*

(1) Where cases falling both under the jurisdiction of the Commission and of the Institution of the Ombudsman materialize, the question of which of them would investigate shall be determined upon their mutual consultation.

(2) Failing determination of the matter, as under Sub-Article (1) of this Article, the organ before which the case is lodged shall undertake the investigation.

Part Four

Administration of the Council of Commissioners and Staff of the Commission

30. *Council of the Commissioners*

(1) Council of the Commissioners (hereinafter referred to as "the Council") is hereby established.

(2) The Council shall have the following members:

(a) the Chief Commissioner .... Chairperson

(b) the Deputy Chief Commissioner .... Deputy Chairperson

(c) other Commissioners .... Members

(3) The Council shall elect its secretary from among its members.

(4) The Council may draw-up its own rules of procedure.

31. *Powers and Duties of the Council*
The Council shall have the following powers and duties:

(1) to adopt directives and by-laws necessary for the implementation of this Proclamation;

(2) to discuss on the draft budget of the Commission;

(3) to adopt staff regulations in conformity with the basic principles of federal civil service laws;

(4) to appoint department heads of the Commission and branch offices of same;

(5) to examine, and decide on, cases, petitions or complaints submitted to it in relation to staff administration, within short period of time;

(6) to appoint heads, at the level of branch offices, of the children and women affairs department;

(7) to hear disciplinary cases, relating to department heads.

32. *The Right to Appeal*

(1) Any department head of the commission aggrieved by administrative decisions rendered by the Council may appeal to the Speaker of the House within one month from the date such decision has been made.

(2) Decision rendered pursuant to Sub-Article (1) of this Article shall be final.

33. *Utilization of Outside Professionals*
The Commission may utilize, for a specific task and for a definite duration, outside professionals necessary for its functions, subject to making appropriate remunerations.

34. *Observance of Secrecy*
Unless ordered by a court or otherwise permitted by the Chief Commissioner, any appointee or staff of the Commission or any professional employed pursuant to Article 33 of this Proclamation, shall have the obligation not to disclose, at all times, any secret known to him in connection with his duty.

35. *Immunity*
No:
(1) appointee, or
(2) investigator
of the Commission may be arrested or detained without the permission of the House or the Chief Commissioner, respectively, except when caught in flagrante delicto, for a serious offence.

Part Five

Miscellaneous Provisions

36. *Budget*
(1) The budget of the Commission shall be drawn from the following sources:
(a) budgetary subsidy to be allocated by the government;
(b) assistance, grant and any other source.
(2) Of the monies obtained from the sources mentioned under sub-Article (1) of this Article, an amount equivalent to a quarterly portion, shall, in advance, be deposited at the National Bank of Ethiopia, or at another bank designated by the Bank, and shall be utilized, in acc[or]dance with financial regulations of the government, for purposes of implementing the objectives of the Commission.

37. *Books of Accounts*
(1) The Commission shall keep complete and accurate books of accounts.
(2) The accounts of the Commission shall be audited, annually, by an organ to be designated by the House.

38. *Duty to Cooperate*
Any person shall provide the necessary assistance, with a view to helping the Commission exercise its powers and duties.

39. *Reporting*
(1) The Commission shall issue an official report, as may be necessary.
(2) The Commission shall exercise transparency in respect of its mode of operation, including issuance of regular reports.
(3) Notwithstanding the provisions of sub-Article (2) of this Article, the Commission shall have the duty to exercise caution in respect of matters to be kept secret, with a view to not endangering national security and well-being or to protecting individual lives.

40. *Non-Answerability for Defamation*
(1) No complaint lodged pursuant to this Proclamation, shall, entail liability for defamation.
(2) No report of the Commission submitted to the House, on the findings of an investigation undertaken, nor any other correspondence of the Commission, relating to its activities, shall entail liability for defamation.

41. *Penalty*
(1) Any person who, having received summons from the Commission, or been called upon by it, does not appear or respond, without good cause, within the time

fixed or is not willing to produce a document or to have same examined, shall be punishable with imprisonment from one month to six months or with a fine from two hundred to one thousand Birr or with both.

(2) Any person who causes harm to witnesses before the Commission or to persons having produced a document before it or who, without good cause, fails to take measures within three months from receipt of reports, recommendations and suggestions of the Commission or does not state the reasons for such failure shall be punishable with imprisonment from three to five years or with a fine from six thousand to ten thousand Birr or with both; unless punishable with more severe penalty under the penal law.

42. *Transitory Provision*
Complaints on violation of human rights that are under investigation by the House, prior to the enactment of this Proclamation, shall be investigated by the Commission.

43. *Inapplicable Laws*
No law or practice, inconsistent with this Proclamation, shall be applicable in respect of matters provided for in this Proclamation.

44. *Effective Date*
This Proclamation shall enter into force as of the 4th day of July, 2000.

Done at Addis Ababa, this 4th day of July, 2000.

NEGASO GIDADA (DR.)
PRESIDENT OF THE FEDERAL DEMOCRATIC
REPUBLIC OF ETHIOPIA

PROCLAMATION NO. 211/2000

A Proclamation to Provide for the Establishment of the Institution of the Ombudsman

WHEREAS, the immense sacrifice paid by the people of Ethiopia, in the protracted struggle they waged with a view to securing political power and to realizing the rule of law, calls for taking the due measure of laying the foundation for good governance, by way of setting up an easily accessible means for the prevention or rectification of administrative abuses arbitrarily committed against citizens;

WHEREAS, the interlinkage of the activities, and of the decision-making power, of executive organs of government with the daily lives and the rights of citizens is an ever-increasing and widening circumstance;

WHEREAS, it is necessary to duly rectify or prevent the unjust decisions and orders of executive organs and officials thereof, given under said circumstance;

WHEREAS, in order that citizens, having suffered from maladministration, are not left without redress, their want for an institution before which they may complain and seek remedies, with easy access, needs to be fulfilled;

WHEREAS, the legislature, as a representative of the people, has the responsibility to ensure that the executive organ carries out its functions in accordance with the law and that its administrative decisions are not rendered in violation of citizens' rights;

WHEREAS, with a view to enhancing the principle thereof, !t is found necessary to establish, and to determine the powers and duties of, the Office of Ombudsman, as one of the parliamentary institutions instrumental in the control of the occurrence of maladministration;

NOW, THEREFORE, in accordance with Article 55 (1) and (15) of the Constitution, it is hereby proclaimed as follows:

Part One

General Provisions

1. *Short Title*
   This Proclamation may be cited as the "Institution of the Ombudsman Establishment Proclamation No. 211 /2000.11

2. *Definitions*
   Unless the context requires otherwise, in this Proclamation:
   (1) "Appointee" means the Chief Ombudsman, the Deputy Chief Ombudsman or an Ombudsman, at the level of a branch office, or who follows up the affairs of children and women appointed in accordance with this Proclamation;

K. Hossain et al. (eds), Human Rights Commissions and Ombudsman Offices, 849–857.

(2) "Staff" includes department heads, professionals and support staff of the Institution;
(3) "Family Member" means a person of relation by consanguinity or affinity, in accordance with the Civil Code of Ethiopia;
(4) "House" means the House of Peoples' Representatives of the Federal Democratic Republic of Ethiopia;
(5) "Maladministration" includes acts committed, or decisions given, by executive government organs, in contravention of administrative laws, the labour law or other laws relating to administration;
(6) "Official" means an elected representative or an appointee or official of an executive government organ;
(7) "Person" means any natural or juridical person;
(8) "Region" means any of those specified under Article 47 (1) of the Constitution of the Federal Democratic Republic of Ethiopia and, for the purposes of this Proclamation, includes the Addis Ababa City Administration and the Dire Dawa Administration;
(9) "Government" means the Federal, or a Regional Government;
(10) "Public Enterprise" means a production, distribution, service rendering or other enterprise, under the ownership of the Federal or a Regional Government;
(11) "Government Office" means a Ministry, a Commission, an Authority, an Agency, an Institute or any other government office;
(12) "Investigator" means a staff assigned, by the Chief Ombudsman, to conduct an investigation;
(13) "Executive Organ" includes a government office or a public enterprise as well as organs rendering administrative or related services within the judiciary or the legislature;.
(14) "Law" includes the Constitution of the Federal Democratic Republic of Ethiopia, the Constitution of a Region as well as federal or regional laws and regulations.

3. *Establishment*
(1) The Institution of the Ombudsman (hereinafter referred to as "the Institution") is hereby established as an autonomous organ of the Federal Government having its own juridical personality.
(2) The Institution shall be accountable to the House.

4. *Scope*
(1) The provisions of this Proclamation set out in the masculine gender shall also apply to the feminine gender.
(2) This Proclamation shall also apply to maladministration committed by the executive organs, and officials thereof, of a Regional Government.

5. *Objective*
The objective of the Institution shall be to see to bringing about good governance that is of high quality, efficient and transparent, and [is] based on the rule of law, by way of ensuring that citizens' rights and benefits, provided for by law are respected by organs of the executive.

6. *Powers and Duties*
The Institution shall have the powers and duties to:
(1) supervise that administrative directives issued, and decisions given, by executive organs and the practices thereof do not contravene the constitutional rights of citizens and the law as well;
(2) receive, and investigate, complaints in respect of maladministration;
(3) conduct supervision, with a view to ensuring that the executive carries out its functions in accordance with the law and to preventing maladministration;
(4) seek remedies in case[s] where it believes maladministration has occurred;

(5) undertake studies and research on ways and means of curbing maladministration;
(6) make recommendations for the revision of existing laws, practices or directives and for the enactment of new laws and formulation of policies, with a view to bringing about better governance;
(7) perform such other functions as are related to its objective.

7. *Limitation of Power*
The Institution shall have no power to investigate:
(1) decisions given by Councils, established by election, in their legislative capacity;
(2) cases pending in courts of Law, at any level;
(3) matters under investigation by the Office of the Auditor-General; or
(4) decisions given by Security Forces and units of the Defence Forces, in respect of matters of national security or defence.

8. *Organization of the Institution*
The institution shall have:
(1) a Council of [..] Ombudsm[e]n
(2) (a) a Chief Ombudsman;
(b) a Deputy Chief Ombudsman;
(c) an Ombudsman heading the children and women affairs [department];
(d) Ombudsmen heading branch offices; and
(e) the necessary staff.

9. *Head office*
The Institution shall have its Head office in Addis Ababa and it may have branch offices in other places to be determined by the House.

10. *Appointment*
(1) The Chief Ombudsman, the Deputy Chief Ombudsman and other Ombudsmen shall be appointed by the House.
(2) The appointment of the Chief Ombudsman, the Deputy Chief Ombudsman and of other Ombudsmen shall be made as under the following procedure:
(a) the appointees shall be recruited by a Nomination Committee to be formed pursuant to Article 11 hereunder;
(b) the nominees shall have to receive the support of a two-thirds vote of the members of the Committee;
(c) the list of nominees shall be presented to the House, by the Speaker, to be voted upon;
(d) the nominees shall be appointed upon receipt of a two-thirds vote of the House.

11. *Composition of the Nomination Committee*
The Nomination Committee shall have the following members:
(1) the Speaker of the House .... Chairperson
(2) the Speaker of the House of the Federation .... Member(s)
(3) five members to be elected from among members, by the House Member(s)
(4) two members of the House to be elected by joint agreement of opposition parties having seats in the House .... Member(s)
(5) the President of the Federal Supreme Court .... Member(s)

12. *Criteria for Appointment*
Any person who:
(1) is loyal to the Constitution of the Federal Democratic Republic of Ethiopia;
(2) is trained in law, administration or other relevant discipline or has acquired adequate knowledge through experience;
(3) is reputed for his diligence, honesty and good conduct;
(4) has not been convicted for a criminal offence;

(5) is an Ethiopian national;
(6) is of enough good health to assume the post; and
(7) is above thirty-five years of age;
may be appointed as an Ombudsman.

13. *Accountability*
(1) The Chief Ombudsman shall be accountable to the House.
(2) The Deputy Chief Ombudsman and other Ombudsmen shall be accountable to the Chief Ombudsman.

14. *Term of Office*
(1) The term of office of an appointee shall be five years.
(2) Upon expiry of the term of office specified under sub-Article (1) of this Article, an appointee may be re-appointed.
(3) An appointee discharged from responsibility or removed from office' as under Article 15 (1) hereunder, shall not unless re-appointed, assume a post in legislative, executive and judicial organs for about six months thereafter.

15. *Grounds for Removal of an Appointee*
(1) An appointee may be removed from office or discharged from responsibility upon the following circumstances:
(a) upon resignation, subject to a three-month prior written notice;
(b) where it is ascertained that he is incapable of properly discharging his duties, due to illness;
(c) where he is found to be corrupt or to have committed other unlawful act;
(d) where it is ascertained that he is of manifest incompetence;
(e) upon termination of his term of office.
(2) Within six months of the removal or discharge of an appointee, as under sub-Article (1) of this Article, another appointee shall be made to replace him.

16. *Procedure for Removal of an Appointee*
(1) An appointee shall be removed from office, upon the grounds specified under Article 15 (1) (b–(d) herein, subsequent to investigation of the matter by a Special Inquiry Tribunal to be formed under Article 17 hereof.
(2) An appointee shall be removed from office, where the House finds that the recommendation submitted to it, as supported by the majority vote of the Special Inquiry Tribunal, is correct and where it upholds same by a two-thirds majority vote.

17. *Composition of the Special Inquiry Tribunal*
The Special Inquiry Tribunal shall have the following members:
(1) the Deputy Speaker of the House .... Chairperson
(2) the Deputy Speaker of the House of the Federation .... Member(s)
(3) three members to be elected by the House .... Member(s)
(4) a member of the House to be elected by joint agreement of opposition parties having seats in the House .... Member(s)
(5) the Vice-President of the Federal Supreme Court .... Member(s)

18. *Prohibition to Engage in Other Employment*
(1) An appointee shall not be allowed to engage in other gainful, public or private employment during his term of office.
(2) Notwithstanding the provisions of sub-Article (1) of this Article, the House may allow otherwise in consideration of the particular profession in which the appointee is required to make contribution.

Part Two

Powers and Duties of Appointees

19. *Powers and Duties of the Chief Ombudsman*
    (1) The Chief Ombudsman shall be the superior head of the Institution and, as such, shall exercise the powers and duties of the Institution provided for under this Proclamation.
    (2) Without prejudice to the generality stated under sub-Article (1) of this Article, the Chief Ombudsman shall:
        (a) employ and administer the staff, in accordance with the directive to be adopted by the Council of the Ombudsmen.
        (b) prepare and directly submit, to the House, the budget of the Institution and implement same upon approval;
        (c) transfer a case, where he has sufficient grounds, from one investigation section or investigator to another or, himself, investigate a case of maladministration occurring anywhere;
        (d) undertake study of recurrent cases of maladministration and forward together with remedial proposals to the House;
        (e) prepare and submit draft administrative legislation, give his opinion on those prepared otherwise;
        (f) submit a report, to the House, on matters of maladministration and on the activities of the Institution;
        (g) take part in meetings by way of representing the Institution, establish working relations with Federal and Regional government organs as well as with non-governmental organizations;
        (h) organize, as well as coordinate and follow up the activities of, branch offices;
        (i) undertake such other activities as are assigned to him by the House.
    (3) The Chief Ombudsman may, to the extent necessary for the efficient performance of the Institution, delegate part of his powers and duties, other than those specified under sub-Article (2) (b), (e) and (f) of this Article and under Article 35(2), to Ombudsmen or to other officials of the Institution.

20. *Powers and Duties of the Deputy Chief Ombudsman*
    Pursuant to directives from the Chief Ombudsman, the Deputy Chief Ombudsman shall:
    (1) assist the Chief Ombudsman in planning, organizing, directing and coordinating the activities of the head office of the Institution;
    (2) undertake the activities of the Chief Ombudsman in the absence of the latter;
    (3) carry out such other activities as may be assigned to him by the Chief Ombudsman.

21. *Powers and Duties of Ombudsmen of Branch Offices*
    In addition to exercising, within the local jurisdiction of a branch office, the powers and duties of the Institution specified under Article 6 of this Proclamation; an Ombudsman shall, as the superior head of a branch office, have the following powers and duties:
    (1) to ensure that administrative and other laws, regulations and directives are observed;
    (2) to transfer an administrative case from one investigation section or investigator to another or to conduct the investigation himself, where it has a good cause;
    (3) to submit, to the Chief Ombudsman and to the government of the Region wherein it is situate[d], a detailed report on matters of maladministration;
    (4) to forward proposals for the revision of laws and practices inconsistent with principles of good governance;

(5) to direct the branch office, in accordance with directives from the Institution;
(6) to effect payments in accordance with the budget allocated to the branch office;
(7) to establish working relations, as a representative of the branch office, with Regional government organs and non-governmental organizations operating within its local jurisdiction;
(8) to perform such other functions as are assigned to him by the Chief Ombudsman.

Part Three

Rules of Procedure of the Institution

22. *The Right to Lodge Complaints*
   (1) A complaint may be lodged by a person, claiming to have suffered from maladministration or, by his spouse, family member, his representative or by a third party.
   (2) The Institution may in consideration of the gravity of the maladministration committed, receive anonymous complaints.
   (3) Prior to lodging a complaint with the Institution, in respect of an act of maladministration from which he suffered, any person shall bring the complaint before the relevant organs.
   (4) Without prejudice to the provisions of Article 7 hereof, the right to lodge complaints, as under this Proclamation, shall be no bar to the institution of criminal or civil proceedings over the same case.
   (5) The Institution shall receive and investigate complaints, free of any charge.

23. *Lodging Complaints*
   (1) A complaint may be lodged with the Institution orally, in writing or in any other manner.
   (2) Complaints shall, to the extent possible, be submitted together with supporting evidence.
   (3) Complaints may be made in Amharic or in the working language of a Region.

24. *Investigation*
   (1) The Institution may conduct investigation on the basis of complaints submitted to it.
   (2) The Institution shall have the power to conduct investigation on its own initiation, where it so finds necessary.

25. *Ordering the Production of Evidence*
   In order to undertake necessary examination within a reasonable time, the Institution may order that:
   (1) those complained against appear, at a specific time and place, for questioning or that they submit their defence;
   (2) witnesses appear, at a specific time and place, and give their testimony;
   (3) any person in possession of evidence relevant to the case, produce same.

26. *Remedies*
   (1) The Institution shall make all the effort it can summon to settle a complaint brought before it amicably.
   (2) It shall notify, in writing, the findings of its investigation, and its opinion thereon, to the superior head of the concerned organ and to the complainant.
   (3) The remedy proposed by the Institution, pursuant to sub-Article (2) of this Article, shall expressly state that the act or practice having caused the maladministration be discontinued, or that the directive having caused same be rendered inapplicable, and that the maladministration committed be rectified, or that any

other appropriate measure be taken.

(4) Complaints submitted to the Institution shall be accorded due response, within a short period of time.

27. *The Right to Object*

(1) Any complainant or accused shall have the right to object to the appointee or official next in hierarchy where he is aggrieved by a remedy proposed by a subordinate appointee, or official of the Institution, within one month from the time he is notified, in writing, of such proposed remedy.

(2) An official who receives an objection, pursuant to sub-Article (1) of this Article, may modify, stay the execution of, reverse or confirm the remedy having been proposed.

(3) A decision rendered by the chief ombudsman shall be final.

28. *Duty to Notify of Fault*

Where the Institution, in the process of conducting investigations, believes that a crime or an administrative fault is committed, it shall have the duty to, forthwith, notify in writing, immediately to the concerned organ or official.

29. *Overlap of Jurisdiction*

(1) Where cases falling both under the jurisdiction of the Institution and of the Ethiopian Human Right Commission materialize, the question of which of them would investigate same shall be determined upon their mutual consultation.

(2) Failing determination of the matter, as under sub-Article (1) of this Article, the organ before wich the case is lodged shall undertake the investigation.

Part Four

The Council of Ombudsmen and Administration of the Staff of the Institution

30. *Council of Ombudsmen of the Institution*

(1) Council of Ombudsmen of the Institution (hereinafter referred to as "the Council") is hereby established.

(2) The Council shall have the following members:

(a) the Chief Ombudsman .... Chairperson

(b) the Deputy Chief Ombudsman .... Deputy Chairperson

(c) other Ombudsmen .... Members

(3) The Council shall elect its secretary from among its members.

(4) The Council may draw-up its own rules of procedure.

31. *Powers and Duties of the Council*

The Council shall have the following powers and duties:

(1) to adopt directives and by-laws necessary for the implementation of this Proclamation;

(2) to discuss on draft budget of the Institution;

(3) to adopt staff regulations in conformity with the basic principles of Federal Civil Service laws;

(4) to appoint department heads;

(5) to examine, and render a final decision, within a short period of time, on cases, petitions or complaints submitted to it in relation to staff administration;

(6) to hear disciplinary cases relating to department heads.

32. *The Right to Appeal*

(1) Any department head of the Institution aggrieved by administrative decisions rendered by the Council may appeal to the Speaker of the House within one month from the date such decision has been made.

(2) Decisions rendered pursuant sub-Article (1) of this Article shall be final.

33. *Utilization of Outside Professionals*
The Institution may utilize, for a specific task and for a definite duration, outside professionals necessary for its functions, subject to making appropriate remunerations.

34. *Observance of Secrecy*
Unless ordered by a court or otherwise permitted by the Chief Ombudsman, any appointee, or staff, or Professional employed pursuant to Article 33 of this Proclamation or staff or any other person shall have the obligation not to disclose, at all times, any secret known to him in connection with his duty.

35. *Immunity*
No:
(1) appointee, or
(2) investigator
of the Institution may be arrested or detained without the permission of the House or the Chief Ombudsman, respectively, except when caught in flagrante delicto, for a serious offence.

Part Five

Miscellaneous Provisions

36. *Budget*
(1) The budget of the Institution shall be drawn from the following sources:
(a) budgetary subsidy to be allocated by the government;
(b) assistance, grant and any other source.
(2) From the budget allocated to the Institution, an amount equivalent to a quarterly portion of its recurrent budget shall, in advance, be deposited at the National Bank of Ethiopia, or at another bank designated by the Bank, and shall be utilized, in accordance with financial regulations of the government, for purposes of implementing the objective of the Institution.

37. *Books of Accounts*
(1) The Institution shall keep complete and accurate books of accounts.
(2) The accounts of the Institution shall be audited, annually, by an organ to be designated by the House.

38. *Duty to Cooperate*
Any person shall provide the necessary assistance, with a view to helping the Institution exercise its powers and duties.

39. *Reporting*
(1) The Institution shall issue an official report, as may be necessary.
(2) The Institution shall exercise transparency in respect of its mode of operation, including issuance of regular reports.
(3) Notwithstanding the provisions of sub-Article (2) of this Article, the Institution shall have the duty to exercise caution in respect of matters to be kept secret, with a view to not endangering national security and well-being or to protecting individual lives.

40. *Non-Answerability for Defamation*
(1) No complaint lodged pursuant to this Proclamation shall, entail liability for defamation.
(2) No report of the Institution submitted to the House, on the findings of an

investigation undertaken, nor any other correspondence of the Institution, relating to its activities shall entail liability for defamation.

41. *Penalty*
(1) Any person who, having received summons from the Institution, or been called upon by it otherwise, does not appear or respond without good cause, within the time fixed, or is not willing to produce a document or to have same examined shall he punishable with imprisonment from one month to six months or with a fine from two hundred to one thousand Birr or with both.
(2) Unless punishable with more severe penalty under the penal law, any person who causes harm to persons who have witnessed before the Institution, or to persons having produced a document before it or who, without good cause, fails to take measures within three months from receipt of reports, recommendations and suggestions of the Institution or does not state the reasons for such failure, shall be punishable with imprisonment from three to five years or with a fine from six thousand to ten thousand Birr or with both.

42. *Transitory Provision*
Complaints on maladministration that are under investigation by the House, prior to the enactment of this Proclamation, shall be investigated by the Institution.

43. *Inapplicable Laws*
No law or practice, inconsistent with this Proclamation, shall be applicable in respect of matters provided for in this Proclamation.

44. *Effective Date*
This Proclamation shall enter into force as of the 4th day of July, 2000

Done at Addis Ababa, this 4th day of July, 2000.

NEGASO GIDADA (DR.)
PRESIDENT OF THE FEDERAL DEMOCRATIC
REPUBLIC OF ETHIOPIA

Index

Note to the reader:

This index in the main contains cross references to the various country reports. For details on the relevant legislation, the reader is referred to the detailed list of contents at the beginning of the book.

African Centre for Democracy and Human Rights Studies 750–751
Auditor-General 623
Australia 806, 819–820, 821, 831 ff.
Benin 734
Broadcasting Standards Commission 673
Cambodia 115 ff.
Child Rights 133 ff.
Children's Commissioner and Ombudsman 142–143, 149–151
Commission for Gender Equality 619–620
Commission for the Promotion and Protection of Rights of Cultural, Religious and Linguistic Communities 622
Commission for Racial Equality 675, 691–730
Commission for Restitution of Land Rights 620–621
Commissioner for Protection Against Unlawful Industrial Action 675
Commissioner for the Rights of Trade Union Members 674
corruption 197–198
Criminal Cases Review Commission 676

Data Protection Registrar 670
Defensor del Pueblo 233 ff., 414
Dual systems 157–158

Electoral Commission 623
Ethiopia 7–35, 97–99, 795–796, 835 ff.
Equal Opportunities Commission 676

Fair Employment Commission for Northern Ireland 677
federalism 44–48
France 805

harmful traditions 196
Health Service Commissioner 671
human rights commissions
- access
  - Cameroon 178–179
  - Canada 454
  - Ghana 190
  - India 214
  - Nigeria 556, 559
  - South Africa 632–633
- access by IO's/NGO's 825
  - Cameroon 179
  - Ghana 190
  - India 214
  - Malawi 529
- admissibility of complaints
  - Canada 455
  - Ghana 192–193
  - India 217
  - Malawi 531
  - Nigeria 556
  - time limits
    - Canada 453
    - Ghana 193
    - India 213
    - Malawi 529
    - UK (race) 695

appointment 739–741
Canada 454
India 214–215
budget
Cameroon 173–174, 182
Canada 455
Ghana 190, 199
India 216
Malawi 530
Nigeria 558
South Africa 630
Uganda 584
UK (race) 695
case load
Cameroon 179
Canada 457, 461
Ghana 194, 199
India 218, 219
Malawi 531
competence 159–160, 737–739, 741–744
Cameroon 173
Canada 453, 460
Ghana 191
India 212
Malawi 527–529
Nigeria 553
Uganda 580
UK (race) 691–692, 694–695, 697
federal/territorial scope
India 213, 216
Canada 453–454, 455
Malawi 530
Nigeria 555, 556
UK (race) 696
complaints
Cameroon 178
Canada 455
Ghana 194–195
India 213–214, 217
UK (race) 696–697
composition
Cameroon 171, 181
Canada 460
Ghana 189
India 211, 214
Malawi 530
Nigeria 555
UK (race) 695
decentralized authorities
India 213
excluded authorities
Malawi 529
Nigeria 554
human rights education
Uganda 585–586
independence 161–162, 752–755
Canada 454
Ghana 188
India 215
Malawi 530
Nigeria 558
South Africa 629–631
UK (race) 695
investigative powers 160–161, 756–757, 813–814
Cameroon 180
Canada 453, 461–462
Ghana 192
India 213, 217
Malawi 529
Nigeria 558
Uganda 581, 584–585
UK (race) 697
judiciary 755–756, 796–797, 818, 828
Cameroon 179
Canada 456, 461
India 213, 219
Malawi 529, 531
Nigeria 554, 557
South Africa 633, 637
UK (race) 699
language
Cameroon 179
Canada 455
India 217
Malawi 531
Nigeria 556
legal basis
Cameroon 170–171
Canada 453, 460
Ghana 188
India 211
Malawi 527
Nigeria 553
South Africa 627
Uganda 579
UK (race) 691
legislature 811–812
Cameroon 173
Canada 454
India 213
Malawi 529
NGO's 757, 765 ff., 820–822
Cameroon 173, 176
Canada 454
Ghana 198–199
India 214
Malawi 529

Nigeria 555
South Africa 636
organization
Cameroon 171–172
Canada 455, 460
Ghana 190
India 216–217
Malawi 531
Nigeria 556, 558, 559
South Africa 628–629
Uganda 582–584
UK (race) 695, 696
private actors
Canada 454
India 213
prisoners 788
Cameroon 180
Ghana 196
Uganda 583, 585
UK 671–672
procedure
Canada 455–456
India 217
Malawi 531
Nigeria 557
UK (race) 692, 693 ff.
protected rights
Canada 453
Ghana 194
India 212–213
Malawi 529
Nigeria 554
UK (race) 692
promotional role 758
Cameroon 174 ff.
Ghana 196
South Africa 633–634
Uganda 582,583
publicity
Canada 456
India 218
Malawi 531
Nigeria 559
South Africa 636, 637
relation to IO's 803–810
Cameroon 176, 177
India 214
Uganda 587
relation to ombudsman 159
remedies 162–163, 816–818
Nigeria 557
Uganda 581
UK (race) 694, 699
compensation
India 218
Uganda 581
UK (race) 697
remuneration
Cameroon 182
Canada 455
Ghana 199
India 216
Malawi 530
South Africa 631
reports
Cameroon 173, 179
UK (race) 700
rulings
Canada 456
Ghana 192
Malawi 531
appeal
Canada 457
India 218
enforcement
Ghana 193–194
India 214, 218
status of 827
Cameroon 181
Ghana 189,193
India 218
Malawi 531
staff
Cameroon 172, 182
India 217

Independent Broadcasting Authority 624
Inspectorate General (*see also* Uganda) 747–748
Investigator General 437 ff.

Legal Services Ombudsman 669

Malta 789
Mauritius 320, 325–329
Multi-organ systems 157–158
Médiateur 271
minorities 48–50

NGO's 63–79
Northern Ireland 675
Norway's Children's Ombudsman 143–146

Ombudsman institutions
access
Austria 251
Belgium 272
Costa Rica 305

Netherlands 347
Nigeria 564
Ontario 513, 514
Slovenia 375
Spain 406
Sweden 428
Uganda 591
UK 669, 670
access by IO's/NGO's 825
Costa Rica 305
Namibia 334–335
admissibility of complaints
Argentina 235
Austria 251
Belgium 274–275
Colombia 291
Costa Rica 310
Mauritius 317, 318
Namibia 335
Netherlands 348
Nigeria 566
Spain 407
Sweden 428
Zambia 440, 441
time limits
Costa Rica 301
Spain 408
Zambia 441
appointment 739–741
Argentina 234
Austria 249, 256–257
Belgium 281
Colombia 289
Costa Rica 306
Malawi 535–536
Mauritius 316
Namibia 332–333
Netherlands 344
Nigeria 562
Norway 365
Ontario 511
Slovenia 374
South Africa 64‘
Spain 396–398
Sweden 427
Zambia 438
budget
Austria 249
Belgium 280
Colombia 290
Costa Rica 308
Malawi 536
Namibia 332
Netherlands 344
Nigeria 563
Spain 403
Sweden 427
Uganda 591
case load
Austria 257–258
Costa Rica 314
South Africa 642
Sweden 427
competence 159–160, 737–739
Argentina 235
Austria 249
Belgium 273
Costa Rica 300–301
Malawi 534
Mauritius 317
Namibia 333–334
Netherlands 345 ff.
Nigeria 563
Norway 366
Ontario 512–513
Slovenia 375
South Africa 640, 641
Spain 404
Sweden 425, 430
Uganda 588, 589–590
UK 668–669, 670
federal scope
Austria 237
Belgium 272–273
Nigeria 562
Spain 405
territorial scope
Costa Rica 309
decentralized authorities
Belgium 272
Costa Rica 302
Netherlands 347
Norway 366
Spain 405–406
excluded authorities
Argentina 236
Colombia 291
Malawi 535
Mauritius 317–318
Namibia 334
Netherlands 347
Norway 366
Spain 405
Uganda 589
impartiality
Colombia 290
Namibia 331
Norway 366

Ontario 512
Spain 398–399
Zambia 439
independence 161–162, 752–755
Argentina 234
Belgium 280–282
Colombia 289–290
Costa Rica 307
Malawi 535, 536
Mauritius 316–317
Namibia 331–332
Nigeria 565
Norway 365
Ontario 512
Slovenia 374
South Africa 641–642
Spain 394–396, 401
Uganda 590
Zambia 438 ff.
investigative powers 160–162, 756–757, 813–814
Argentina 236
Austria 255–256
Belgium 278
Colombia 291–292
Costa Rica 301
Malawi 535, 536–357
Mauritius 318–319
Namibia 335–336
Netherlands 350
Norway 366
Ontario 514
Slovenia 375, 376
South Africa 641
Spain 408
Sweden 426
Uganda 588–589, 591
judiciary 158–159, 755–756, 818, 828
Argentina 235
Austria 249, 258–259
Belgium 271, 273–274
Colombia 291, 292
Costa Rica 302
Mauritius 318
Namibia 337
Netherlands 345
Nigeria 564
Slovenia 375, 376
Spain 404–405, 408, 410–412
Sweden 428
Uganda 589
language
Costa Rica 310
legal basis
Argentina 233
Austria 247, 248
Belgium 279
Colombia 289
Costa Rica 300
Malawi 533–534
Mauritius 315
Namibia 331
Netherlands 343
Norway 365
Ontario 511
Slovenia 373
South Africa 640
Spain 393
Sweden 424
Uganda 589
UK 668, 669
Zambia 437
legislature 811–812
Argentina 235
Belgium 277
Colombia 292
Costa Rica 302, 304
Malawi 535
Mauritius 317, 318
Netherlands 345
Ontario 515
Slovenia 375–376
Spain 411
Sweden 425
NGO's 757–758, 765 ff., 820–822
organization
Austria 256
Belgium 282
Costa Rica 309
Malawi 535
Mauritius 316–317
Nigeria 562–563
Netherlands 344–345
Slovenia 373
Spain 401–403
Sweden 427
Uganda 590
Zambia 439
private actors
Costa Rica 303–304
Spain 404
Sweden 425
procedure
Austria 253–254, 255
Costa Rica 310–311
Mauritius 318
Netherlands 349
Sweden 428

protected rights
- Belgium 270, 274, 275
- Colombia 291
- Costa Rica 301
- Malawi 534–535
- Netherlands 352
- Nigeria 563–564
- Ontario 513
- Slovenia 376
- Spain 403–404
- Sweden 425
- Uganda 588
- UK 668
- Zambia 440–441

publicity
- Argentina 234,236
- Austria 254, 259
- Belgium 278
- Costa Rica 313
- Mauritius 317
- Netherlands 353–354
- Nigeria 565–566
- Slovenia 377
- Spain 410
- Sweden 429
- UK 670

relation to human rights commission 159
- Malawi 534

relation to IO's 803–810

remedies 162–163, 816–818
- compensation
- Slovenia 376

remuneration
- Costa Rica 308
- Malawi 536
- Mauritius 316

reports
- Colombia 292
- Malawi 537
- Namibia 337–338
- Netherlands 350 ff.
- Norway 367
- Ontario 515
- Slovenia 376
- South Africa 641
- Spain 412
- Sweden 430
- Uganda 591
- UK 669
- Zambia 441

rulings
- Austria 252 ff.
- Belgium 278–279
- Costa Rica 312
- Mauritius 319–320
- Namibia 335–336
- Netherlands 350
- Norway 367
- Spain 409
- Sweden 429
- Uganda 591
- UK 670
- appeal
  - Austria 255
  - Costa Rica 313–314
- compensation
  - Costa Rica 312–313
  - Zambia 441
- enforcement
  - Belgium 278
  - Netherlands 352
  - Spain 410–412
  - Sweden 426
- status of 827
  - Austria 255
  - Colombia 290
  - Mauritius 320
  - Namibia 337
  - Netherlands 351
  - Slovenia 377
  - Spain 409
  - Sweden 426

Pan South African Language Board 624
Paris principles 4, 26, 62, 171, 181, 182, 793
Parliamentary Ombudsman 669
Police Complaints Authority 673
Prisons Ombudsman 671
Public Protector 617–618, 639 ff.

refugees 180, 305
relationship between human rights commissions and ombudsman 801–802
Rwanda 777 ff.
Rwanda, International Criminal Tribunal for 101 ff.

Single Systems 157–158
Social Landlords 672
Standing Advisory Commission on Human Rights (Northern Ireland) 677

Tanzania 744–745
Togo 734, 745–747, 758
Truth and Reconciliation Commission 89–95, 621–622

Youth Commission 620

Zaire 749–750